Personnel/Human Resource Management

Fifth Edition

Personnel/Human Resource Management

Gary Dessler
Professor of Business
Florida International University

PRENTICE HALL
Englewood Cliffs, New Jersey 07632

Library of Congress Cataloging-in-Publication Data

Dessler, Gary
    Personnel/human resource management / Gary Dessler. — 5th ed.
      p. cm.
    Rev. ed. of: Personnel management. 4th ed. Englewood Cliffs, N.J.
    Prentice Hall, c1988.
    Includes indexes.
    ISBN 0-13-445966-0
    1. Personnel management. I. Dessler, Gary Personnel
management. II. Title.
HF5549.D4379 1991
658.3—dc20   90-45734
                                 CIP

Acquisitions editor: Alison Reeves
Editorial/production supervision: Alison D. Gnerre
Interior and cover design: Butler/Udell
Cover art: Max Weber (American, 1881–1961), *Rush Hour, N.Y.,* National
Gallery of Art
Prepress buyer: Trudy Pisciotti
Manufacturing buyer: Robert Anderson

Dedicated to my son, Derek

 ©1991, 1988, 1984, 1981, 1978 by Prentice-Hall, Inc.
A Division of Simon & Schuster
Englewood Cliffs, New Jersey 07632

Printed in the United States of America
10 9 8 7 6 5 4 3 2 1

ISBN 0-13-445966-0

Prentice-Hall International (UK) Limited, *London*
Prentice-Hall of Australia Pty. Limited, *Sydney*
Prentice-Hall Canada Inc., *Toronto*
Prentice-Hall Hispanoamericana, S.A., *Mexico*
Prentice-Hall of India Private Limited, *New Delhi*
Prentice-Hall of Japan, Inc., *Tokyo*
Simon & Schuster Asia Pte. Ltd., *Singapore*
Editora Prentice-Hall do Brasil, Ltda., *Rio de Janeiro*

Contents

Preface

Personnel/Human Resource Management provides students in human resource management/personnel management courses and practicing managers with a complete, comprehensive review of essential personnel management concepts and techniques in a highly readable and understandable form.

This fifth edition has several distinguishing characteristics. While it focuses almost entirely on essential personnel management topics like job analysis, testing, compensation, and appraisal, *motivating employees* and developing a *personnel management philosophy* are used as integrating themes. Practical applications—such as how to appraise performance, how to establish pay plans, and how to handle grievances—are used throughout to provide students with important personnel management skills. All managers have personnel-related responsibilities, and so *Personnel/Human Resource Management* is aimed at all students of management, not just those who will someday carry the title of Human Resource Manager. The legal environment of personnel management—equal employment, labor relations, and occupational safety—is covered fully. Experiential exercises and/or cases are provided at the end of each chapter; these give students an opportunity to meet in small groups and apply the concepts and techniques found in each chapter. A complete instructors' manual and test bank are available, as is a new computer package and several other supplements described below. A continuing case provides vignettes for each chapter that illustrate the front line supervisor's role in personnel management. Adopters of the last edition will find Chapter 9 ("Fundamentals of Motivation") has been completely rewritten and revised. The link between motivation and personnel management has been strengthened, and several new, applied topics—including behavior modification, job design, and job enrichment—have been added. Material on employee discipline has been strengthened and consolidated in Chapter 17, and now covers both positive and negative discipline as well as avoiding wrongful dismissal charges. There is a new chapter on strategic issues in personnel, and much new material on international HRM. An all-new computerized test bank has been carefully written and tested.

Many other important changes have been made in this fifth edition. Every chapter has been updated so as to include the latest material on topics such as the possible impact of equal employment court decisions (including Wards Cove, *Patterson* vs. *McLean, Price Waterhouse* vs. *Hopkins*), controlling benefit costs due to AIDS, wrongful discharge, substance abuse, and health insurance costs containment. As this fifth edition goes to press I feel even more strongly than I did when the first was published that all managers—not just human resource/personnel managers—need a strong foundation in personnel management concepts and techniques to do their jobs. I have therefore tried to increase the practical techniques contained in this book by adding many new "how-to" topics such as how to deal with substance abusers and how to avoid wrongful dismissal charges. And, there have also been several other major changes to this new edition, which are described here.

COMPUTER APPLICATIONS IN PERSONNEL

Many illustrations of how computers are used in personnel management have been added. Specifically, three changes were made here: First, new applications were added to many chapters; for example, describing how computers are used to link performance appraisal with merit pay. Second, to underscore the computers' use in personnel, you'll find new "computer boxes" in most chapters. These highlight computer applications appropriate to each chapter's material, such as utilization analysis in the equal employment chapter, computerized interactive performance tests in the testing chapter, computer-aided interviews in the interviewing chapter, and computerized grievance management in the labor relations chapter. An all new computer exercises supplement has also been produced.

INTERNATIONAL ASPECTS OF PERSONNEL

In addition to adding international applications illustrations to many chapters, there is a new comprehensive appendix on "International Issues in Human Resource Management." This covers topics such as international aspects of human resource selection, training, and compensation management, as well as managing intercountry differences in personnel-related laws and requirements.

SMALL BUSINESS APPLICATIONS

At least two-thirds of the jobs opening up in any year are in small businesses and, in addition, many students will end up in businesses of their own. A new feature of this edition is therefore the inclusion of a number of concrete, practical small business applications, which show how smaller businesses with limited resources and limited time can implement improved human resource management procedures. In Chapter 3, for instance, you'll find an example of how to use the widely available *Dictionary of Occupational Titles* to do a job analysis, complete with special client-tested forms. Other examples include procedures for setting up a training program in small business, incentive hints for smaller employers, and developing a workable pay plan for a smaller business.

Adopters of the last edition will find Chapter 13 ("Nonfinancial Motivation Techniques) completely revised, with an all-new emphasis on the Human Resource Manager's roll in setting up and running quality improvement programs, particularly in service enterprises. Included is an example of the program used by Florida Power and Light Company, the first employer outside of Japan to win the Deming Prize for quality.

ABC NEWS/PH VIDEOS

Underscoring the practical, real-world orientation of this book, it now includes a customized video library available for class use. Based on ABC News shows such as *World News Tonight,* and *Business World,* you will have available pre-taped, contemporary shows dealing with relevant topics such as age discrimination, child-care systems, balancing work and family, and test validity (in particular, an ABC News *Nightline* discussion of SAT's: "Are They Valid?"). About 12 special tapes are available.

STRATEGIC ISSUES IN PERSONNEL MANAGEMENT

An all-new chapter (19) has been added, "Strategic Issues in Personnel Management." This covers in detail topics such as: the effects of environmental trends (economic, political, social, and so on) on human resource management; the evolving labor shortage and the effects of other demographic trends; the evolving role of human resource management; strategic management; strategic planning and human resource management; and how to develop personnel policies and manuals.

While I am solely responsible for the contents in *Personnel/Human Resource Management,* I want to thank several people for their professional assistance. This includes the following reviewers: Professor Floyd Patrick, Eastern Michigan University; Professor Roger Weikle, Winthrop College, South Carolina; Professor Joseph McCune, Rutgers University, New Brunswick, NJ; Professor Daniel Gallagher, James Madison University, Virginia; Professor Paul Champagne, Old Dominion University, Virginia; Professor Michael H. Korzeniowski, La Salle University, Pennsylvania; Professor Dennis Dossett, University of Missouri, St. Louis; and Professor Gerald Ferris, Texas A & M University. The assistance of all the reviewers was extremely useful, but I want to single out Professor Weikle, who was asked to provide several more comprehensive reviews, and Averill Marcus, Esq., who reviewed certain portions of the employment law-related chapters for me. Dr. Nancy Kauffman, University of North Carolina at Asheville wrote many of the new computer boxes for this new edition. She has practical experience as both a professor who uses computer applications in her personnel management courses, as well as a consultant and former personnel manager. Professor Hrach Bedrosian of New York University's Stern School shared his impressions of the fourth edition and its supplements with me. Dr. Elias Awad of the McIntire School of Business at the University of Virginia provided the basic data for one of the computer boxes. Professor Casey Ichniowski of the Graduate School of Business Administration, Columbia University, provided me with certain background information for Chapter 19, and was kind enough to share with me a copy of the *Competitive Edge* (Scott, Foresman and Company, 1989), a book of excellent personnel computer simulations he coauthored. At Prentice-Hall the dedicated efforts of Alison Reeves, executive editor, and Alison Gnerre, production editor, helped make this book better than it would otherwise have been.

My son, Derek, was always a source of encouragement and useful advice, and my wife, Claudia, assisted me with the index and reviewed portions of the manuscript.

Gary Dessler

Personnel/Human Resource Management

Chapter 1

Introduction to Personnel/Human Resource Management: Philosophy and Plan

When you finish studying this chapter, you should be able to:

1. Explain what personnel management is and the role it plays in the management process.
2. Give several examples of how personnel management concepts and techniques can be of use to all managers.
3. Compare and contrast line and staff authority.
4. Cite the personnel management responsibilities of line managers and staff (personnel) managers.
5. Discuss the factors that influence one's personnel management philosophy.
6. Compare and contrast Theory X and Theory Y management assumptions.
7. Present and explain the rationale for our Motivation Model.

OVERVIEW

The purpose of this chapter is to explain what personnel management is and the plan of this book. We will see that Personnel/Human Resource Management—activities like recruiting, hiring, training, appraising, and paying employees—is both a part of every manager's job and a separate staff function, one through which the personnel director assists all managers in important ways. We also explain some factors that affect your philosophy of personnel management and explain how personnel activities can affect productivity and performance at work. Finally, we end by outlining the Motivation Model that is used to tie together the chapters in this book and to relate each chapter to the theme of motivating employees.

♦ **WHAT IS PERSONNEL MANAGEMENT?**

To understand what personnel management is, we have to first ask what managers do. Most experts agree that there are five basic functions all managers perform: planning, organizing, staffing, leading, and controlling. In total, these functions represent what is often called the **management process.**[1] Some of the specific activities involved in each function include:

> **management process** The five basic functions of planning, organizing, staffing, leading, and controlling.

Planning: Establishing goals and standards; developing rules and procedures; developing plans and forecasting—predicting or projecting some future occurrence.

Organizing: Giving each subordinate a specific task; establishing departments; delegating authority to subordinates; establishing channels of authority and communication; coordinating the work of subordinates.

Staffing: Deciding what type of people should be hired; recruiting prospective employees; selecting employees; setting performance standards; compensating employees; evaluating performance; counseling employees; training and developing employees.

Leading: Getting others to get the job done; maintaining morale, motivating subordinates.

Controlling: Setting standards such as sales quotas, quality standards, or production levels; checking to see how actual performance compares with these standards; taking corrective action as needed.

In this book, we are going to focus on one of these functions, the *staffing* or **personnel management function. Personnel management** (frequently known today as Human Resource Management, or as Personnel, Human Resource, or simply HR management in this text) refers to the concepts and techniques you need to carry out the *people* or *personnel* aspects of your management job. These include:

> **personnel management** The concepts and techniques one needs to carry out the "people" or human resource aspects of a management position, including recruiting, screening, training, rewarding, and appraising.

Job analysis (determining the nature of each employee's job)

Planning labor needs and *recruiting* job candidates

Selecting job candidates

Orienting and *training* new employees

Wage and salary management (how to *compensate* employees)

Providing *incentives* and *benefits*

Appraising performance

Face-to-face *communicating* (interviewing, counseling, disciplining)

Developing managers

And what a manager should know about:

Equal opportunity and affirmative action

Employee health and safety

Handling grievances and labor relations

♦ **WHY IS PERSONNEL/HR MANAGEMENT IMPORTANT TO ALL MANAGERS?**

Why are these concepts and techniques important to all managers? Perhaps it's easier to answer this by listing some of the personnel mistakes you *don't* want to make while managing. For example, *you don't want:*

To hire the wrong person for the job

High turnover

Your people not doing their best

To waste time with useless interviews

To have your company taken to court because of your discriminatory actions

To have your company cited under federal occupational safety laws for unsafe practices.

To have some of your employees think their salaries are unfair and inequitable relative to others in the organization

A lack of training undermining your department's effectiveness

To commit any unfair labor practices

Carefully studying this book can help you avoid mistakes like these. And more important, it can help ensure that you get results—through others. Remember that you could do everything else right as a manager—like lay brilliant plans, draw clear organization charts, set up modern assembly lines, and use sophisticated accounting controls—and yet still fail as a manager (by hiring the wrong people or by not motivating subordinates, for instance). On the other hand, many managers—whether presidents, generals, governors, or supervisors—have been successful even with inadequate plans, organization, or controls. They were successful because they had the knack for hiring the right people for the right jobs and motivating, appraising, and developing them. Remember as you read this book that *getting results* is the bottom line of managing and that, as a manager, you will have to get these results through people. As one company president summed up:

> For many years it has been said that capital is the bottleneck for a developing industry. I don't think this any longer holds true. I think it's the work force and the company's inability to recruit and maintain a good work force that does constitute the bottleneck for production. I don't know of any major project backed by good ideas, vigor, and enthusiasm that has been stopped by a shortage of cash. I do know of industries whose growth has been partly stopped or hampered because they can't maintain an efficient and enthusiastic labor force, and I think this will hold true even more in the future. . . .[2]

♦ THE CHANGING ENVIRONMENT OF PERSONNEL MANAGEMENT

As important as Personnel has been in the past, its importance will grow in the future. This is because changes are occurring today in the environment of personnel management, changes that are requiring personnel to play an evermore crucial role in organizations. For example, more service-type jobs will demand more care in selecting and training courteous employees, while a diminishing supply of employees will make recruiting more difficult than ever. While trends like these are explained more fully in later chapters, a brief review at this point can help explain the important role today of personnel management.

Service Economy Trends Impacting Personnel

An enormous shift from manufacturing to services has taken place in North America and Western Europe. Today, for example, nearly two-thirds of the U.S. work force is employed in producing and delivering services: in fact, the manufacturing work force declined over 12% during the 1980s. And of all the 21 million or so new jobs added by the U.S. economy in the 1990s, virtually all will be in services, in industries like fast foods, retailing, consulting, teaching, and legal work.

To see why this change is important for personnel, you needn't look further than your local fast-food, clothing, or dry cleaning store. In their book *Service America!*, Karl Albrecht and Ron Zemke point out that in service businesses "critical incidents can make you or break you" and that what they call "the last four feet" can mean success or failure for your firm. In discussing a retail furniture chain, for instance, they relate how "much of the enormous advertising investment evaporated at the moment when a customer walked into the store and encountered a non-supportive psychological environment."[3] All of those thousands of dollars they spent on advertising were effective, in terms of getting the customers to walk in the front door. But once they're in the door, "it's up to the people in the store to take over at the last four feet." And here, if your customer is confronted by a salesperson who is tactless, or unprepared to discuss the pros and cons of your different products, or (even worse) downright discourteous, all your other efforts will have been for naught. Service organizations have little to sell but their service, and that makes them uniquely dependent on their employees' aptitudes and motivation.

Personnel management therefore plays a crucial role in service companies. Specific examples include:

Service and quality of work life. To get the best from your employees requires that the culture, morale, and psychological environment of the company be positive, and one barometer of this is the overall *quality of work life* of the workplace itself. Quality of work life can be defined as the degree to which employees can satisfy their important personal needs at work. It involves, according to one expert, at least the following factors:[4]

1. A job worth doing
2. Safe and secure working conditions
3. Adequate pay and benefits
4. Job security
5. Competent supervision
6. Feedback on job performance
7. Opportunities to learn and grow in the job
8. A chance to get ahead on merit
9. Positive social climate
10. Justice and fair play

As explained in later chapters, the Human Resource Manager is normally charged with designing and implementing the systems to improve many of these factors. For example, job design (explained in Chapters 4 and 13) helps insure that the job is worth doing, and employee safety and health programs (Chapter 18) are aimed at ensuring safe and secure working conditions. Similarly, pay and benefits (Chapters 10 through 12), promotions based on merit (Chapter 15), and feedback on job performance (performance appraisal, Chapter 14) are all essentially personnel/HR responsibilities. An effective Human Resource Management department thus helps to create the overall fabric—the quality of work life—within which service employees can be motivated to do their jobs.

Service and selection. In many respects effective selection is the first line of defense for service companies. It has been noted, for instance, that there are "quite a few who lack the temperament, maturity, social skills, and tolerance for frequent human contact" and that the first step in avoiding this problem is screening and selection.[5] Yet, ironically, many of the front-line jobs in service firms are often minimum wage positions with relatively little career potential. As a result, the selection job is complicated by the fact that there is often a relatively limited work history to go by when hiring into these entry-level positions. The sorts of personnel screening and testing techniques discussed in Chapter 3 thus take on a critical importance in service firms.

Service and training. Poorly trained or untrained front-line service people usually have no choice but to improvise whatever methods they can to help them do their jobs; this can in turn have a corrosive effect on service performance.[6] Many of the most important employees in service companies are front-line employees who are dealing with customers every day. Unlike errors made by some "back office" or production workers, errors made on the front line normally can't be easily detected by inspectors. As a result, the sorts of training and development techniques explained in Chapters 7 and 8 are important ones for service companies.

Service and performance measurement and feedback. The fact that front-line service employees often fill positions that aren't subject to traditional types of "inspection" demands an effective way to measure and evaluate their performance. Techniques like those explained in Chapter 14 (performance appraisal) are therefore important here.

While other examples could be cited, the basic point is that in today's economy, personnel is more important than ever. The vast majority of employees today are in service jobs, working for service organizations that range from colleges to florists to zoos. (Even among manufacturing firms, companies find that their competitive advantage lies not just in their products but in the quality of the accompanying service that they provide.) And in an economy like this one, which relies so heavily on motivated front-line people, the concepts and techniques of personnel take on a new significance.

Demographic Trends Impacting Personnel

Just when it is becoming more important than ever to hire and train an effective front-line work force, the rate of growth of the nation's work force is projected to drop over the next few years. For example, the labor force will expand by about 21 million people (or 18%) in the 1990s. This marks a dramatic slowdown in labor-force growth, which between 1972 and 1986 grew by almost 31 million people, or 35%. This will make the HR manager's job more difficult in terms of recruiting, screening, and training employees.

At the same time, the nature of the work force will change dramatically, too. For one thing, its composition will change to include greater numbers of minorities and women. For example, between now and the year 2000, the white labor force is projected to increase less than 15%, while the black labor force will grow by nearly 29%, and the hispanic labor force by more than 74%. Also, women are projected to account for about 64% of the net increase in the labor force in the 1990s. Related to this, about two-thirds of all single mothers (separated, divorced, widowed, or never married) are in the labor force today, as are almost 45% of mothers with children under three. The Human Resource Department will increasingly be called upon to help companies accommodate these new employees, with new child care and maternity leave provisions, for example, and with basic skills training where such training is required.

Technological Trends Impacting Personnel

At the same time, technological advances will continue to shift employment from some occupations to others while contributing to gradual increases in productivity. Technological improvements (in telecommunications, computerization, and automation, for instance) are increasingly shifting work from blue collar and clerical functions to technical, managerial, and professional ones. Jobs and organizations' structures will have to be redesigned, new incentive and compensation plans instituted, new job descriptions written, and new employee selection, evaluation, and training programs instituted. These trends, too, will therefore influence personnel management.

Competitive and Managerial Trends Impacting Personnel

Increasing international and domestic pressures will also continue to shape organizations. The increasing internationalization of business and intensification of competition mean that downsizing today has become a continuing corporate activity. At the same time, increased competition and shorter product life cycles are creating the need for more flexible, adaptable companies, ones that are more decentralized and participative and that rely on cooperative project teams to "intrapreneur" new products and ensure customers' needs are fulfilled. HR management will be in the vanguard helping companies like these make the required changes, in activities ranging from writing new job descriptions to hiring new international managers to instituting more effective incentive plans.

Other Factors Impacting Personnel

There are numerous other social, economic, and political trends shaping personnel management. For example, only a fraction of the jobs in the United States require more than a high school education, yet an increasing number of workers have college degrees. As the supply of college graduates slowly outstrips demand, more graduates will find themselves in jobs for which they are over-qualified. Dealing with the resultant dissatisfaction and learning how to motivate a better-educated work force will therefore become critical personnel issues in the future.

Some also feel that basic work values are changing. Years ago, it was assumed that a "work ethic" motivated workers to work hard and do their best. Today, some feel this commitment to work is on the decline; if so, motivating employees may become a more difficult task.

Related to this, men and women of all ages (but particularly the young) often seem more interested in choosing a life-style and career than just a job. Therefore, career development and adapting work to the flexible life-styles and changing interests of workers will become increasingly important.

Also, as we will see in this book, a variety of laws continue to be passed, laws which constrain the actions managers can take. For example, equal employment opportunity laws bar discrimination on the basis of race, age, religion, sex, or national origin. As a result, all managers are now legally bound to uncover and correct instances of discrimination. Mandated health benefits represent another example of legal challenges with which HR management will have to cope. In some states employers are already legally bound to provide health benefits to employees. And other laws—for example, covering occupational safety and health or labor relations—are among the other personnel-related constraints that all managers will have to deal with now and in the years ahead.

In summary, several trends—including the emergence of a service economy, demographic trends, technological trends, competitive/managerial trends, and political–legal trends—are all contributing to the way that organizations do business, and (more particularly) to the role played in companies by personnel. Personnel activities and good personnel skills should thus become even more crucial in the years ahead because of these trends and one other factor: The need to improve performance at work.

There are many ways to improve performance at work. For example, many legislative factors may inhibit productivity (such as required pollution control equipment and occupational safety equipment). Yet many believe that reducing or eliminating legislative controls would actually have an adverse effect on society. In any case, this is not a factor that any individual manager usually has much control over. Worker productivity could also be increased by investing more heavily in more modern equipment—whether robots on an assembly line or word processors for secretaries. While useful, though, this is only part of the solution since, ultimately, virtually all service and manufacturing activities (no matter how automated) rely heavily on human beings. Even in the most highly automated auto assembly plants, for example, poor employee attendance, a resistant attitude on the part of workers, and worker sabotage can drastically curtail productivity. And, in relatively nonautomated industries, this is especially the case.

Another way to improve productivity and performance (and the one focused on in this book) is to improve human behavior at work through the application of modern human resource management concepts and techniques. There are, in other words, human resource management concepts and techniques that are being used today in organizations that have been shown to be effective for improving the productivity and performance of employees, and explaining how to use these techniques is one purpose of this book. We explain, for example, how to use interviewing and other selection techniques to hire high-performers; how to train and motivate employees; and how to use incentives, benefits, and positive reinforcement to improve performance at work. In summary, the need to improve productivity and performance at work will have an important influence on managers over the next few years, and explaining how to improve motivation and performance through modern personnel management techniques is thus a basic theme of this book.

Productivity and Human Resource Management

Can human resource management techniques really impact a company's bottom line? Here the answer is a definite "yes."[7] As one writer says, "productivity is the problem—and personnel is definitely part of the solution."[8] He says that personnel management techniques as applied both by personnel/HR management departments and by line managers have already had a big impact on productivity and performance. In the U.S. government, for example, researchers found that using a personnel screening test to choose high-potential computer programmers could result in savings of millions of dollars per year. As another example, R. J. Reynolds invested $2.5 million in a company-sponsored health maintenance organization (HMO). (An HMO is an alternative to a traditional health care insurance plan. With an HMO the company contracts with a group of doctors and other health professionals to service all the firm's employees, usually at company expense.) Reynolds found that under the HMO, employee hospitalization declined 52%. Savings for 30,000 employees, as compared with their conventional plan, permitted payback of the investment in 24 months, plus the gains enjoyed from increased productivity.[9]

Savings like these should multiply in the years ahead. According to a Hay Group survey, about half of the 927 human resources professionals they surveyed cited *productivity* as their top priority over the next few years, while compensation ranked second in importance, with 41% calling it a priority.[10]

The dominant trend in personnel management over the next few years will therefore be to keep labor costs down, and companies will do this in three main ways. According to a study by Hewitt Associates, "The first line of attack on this problem in most businesses is to institute tough headcount controls that go beyond temporary expedients like hiring freezes." To do this, companies are finding ways to operate permanently with fewer employees per unit output, and this is particularly affecting salaried professionals: Companies are forcing a decrease in the number of staff jobs compared to line and a decrease in the number of line managers per production worker. In fact, massive layoffs are already taking place, as evidenced by the widely publicized release by companies like AT&T and Eastman Kodak of tens of thousands of employees.

After headcount control, the next step in controlling labor costs is limiting gains in compensation, both cash pay and employee benefits. By the early 1990s, for instance, salary increases had dropped to about 5% from a peak of 10% in 1981, in part due to reduced inflation rates. Beyond this, though, companies are finding ways to give pay increases without adding to their salary bases. For example, lump-sum bonus payments are being used for both salaried and hourly workers, and individual incentives and group profit sharing are spreading. The main reason for this is to reinforce the concept of "pay for performance" and thus relate compensation costs to the companies' well-being. An added and important advantage is that by making periodic lump-sum awards, employers avoid building up their base pay rate, as would occur if raises were awarded as salary increases each year.

Third, employers are controlling labor costs by controlling medical benefits costs. They are doing this by changing the content of their medical plans, specifically by forcing employees to pay some part of their medical expenses. There is a growing use of front-end deductibles for hospital benefits (such deductibles grew from 14% in 1980 to over 50% in 1989) and a trend toward more medical premium sharing by employees, for instance.[11]

Many other examples could be cited. Productivity incentives like *Scanlon plans* can have a marked effect on performance, for instance. *Occupational safety and health programs* can reduce costs for lost-time accidents and illnesses. *Methods-improvement training* can improve the efficiency of employees. Even in relatively "hard-nosed" industries like steel, managers are beginning to find that human resource techniques can boost performance—techniques like *quality circles*, in which employees are asked to identify performance bottlenecks and suggest solutions.[12] The fact is that virtually every topic discussed in this book—job analysis, interviewing, testing, training, incentives, and appraisal, for instance—can and will have a measurable impact on productivity and performance. As a result, the subject of human resource management has taken on a new and more crucial importance in the performance-oriented 1990s. This is because the human resources function is at the very center of the cost containment efforts of industry today.

LINE AND STAFF ASPECTS OF PERSONNEL/ HUMAN RESOURCE MANAGEMENT

All managers are, in a sense, personnel managers, since they all get involved in activities like recruiting, interviewing, selecting, and training. Yet most firms also have a Human Resource Department with its own human resource manager. How do the duties of this human resource manager and his or her staff relate to the human resource management duties of the other "line" managers in the firm? Before proceeding, let's answer this question, starting with a short definition of "line" versus "staff" authority.

♦ LINE VERSUS STAFF AUTHORITY

authority The right to make decisions, direct others' work, and give orders.

Authority is the right to make decisions, to direct the work of others, and to give orders. In management, it is convenient to distinguish between two types of authority: line authority and staff authority.

Line managers are authorized to direct the work of subordinates—they're always someone's boss. In addition, line managers are in charge of accomplishing the basic goals of the organization. (Production managers and sales managers are almost always line managers, for example.) **Staff managers,** on the other hand, are authorized to *assist and advise* line managers in accomplishing these basic goals. These ideas are illustrated in Figure 1.1. Here (as is usually the case) the human resource manager is a *staff manager.* He or she is responsible for advising line managers (like those for production and marketing) in areas like recruiting, hiring, and compensation. The managers for production and marketing are *line managers.* They have direct responsibility for accomplishing the basic goals of the organization. They also have the authority to direct the work of various subordinates.

◆ LINE MANAGERS' HUMAN RESOURCE MANAGEMENT RESPONSIBILITIES

According to one expert, "The direct handling of people is, and always has been, an integral part of every line manager's responsibility, from president down to the lowest level supervisor."[13]

For example, one major company outlines their line supervisor's responsibilities for effective human resource management under the following general headings:

1. *Placing* the right person on the right job
2. Starting new employees in the organization (orientation)
3. *Training* employees for jobs that are new to them
4. *Improving job performance* of each person
5. *Gaining creative cooperation* and developing smooth working relationships
6. *Interpreting* the company policies and procedures

FIGURE 1.1
Line and Staff Authority

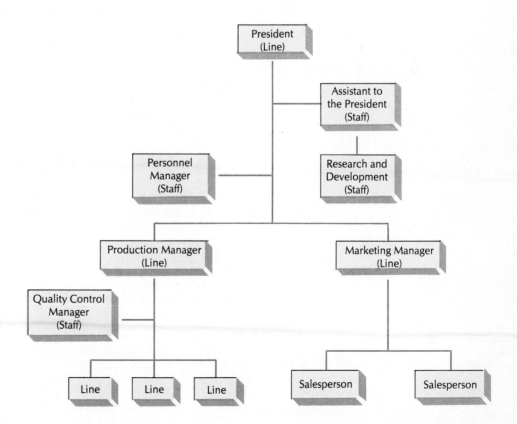

7. *Controlling* labor costs
8. *Developing* potential abilities of each person
9. Creating and maintaining a high level of departmental *morale*
10. *Protecting* health and physical condition of employees

In small organizations, line managers may carry out all these personnel management duties unassisted. But as the organization grows, they need the assistance, specialized knowledge, and advice of a separate human resource staff.[14]

♦ PERSONNEL DEPARTMENT STAFF'S PERSONNEL MANAGEMENT RESPONSIBILITIES

The personnel (or human resource) department provides this specialized assistance.[15] In doing so, the personnel manager carries out three distinct functions, as follows:

1. *A line function.* First, the personnel manager performs a *line* function by directing the activities of the people in his or her own department and in service areas (like the plant cafeteria). In other words, he or she exerts *line authority* within the personnel department. Personnel managers are also likely to exert **implied authority.** This is because line managers know the personnel director often has access to top management in personnel areas like testing and affirmative action. As a result, personnel directors' "suggestions" are often viewed as "orders from topside." And this implied authority often carries even more weight with supervisors troubled with human resource/personnel problems.

2. *A coordinative function.* Personnel managers also function as coordinators of personnel activities, a duty often referred to as **functional control.** Here the personnel director and department act as "the right arm of the top executive to assure him that personnel objectives, policies, and procedures (concerning, for example, occupational safety and health) which have been approved and adopted are being consistently carried out by line managers."[16]

3. *Staff (service) functions.* **Staff (service) functions** or service to line management is the "bread and butter" of the personnel manager's job. For example, Personnel *assists* in the hiring, training, evaluating, rewarding, counseling, promoting, and firing of employees at all levels. It also *administers* the various benefit programs (health and accident insurance, retirement, vacation, etc.). It *assists* line managers in their attempts to comply with equal employment and occupational safety laws. And it has an important role with respect to grievances and labor relations.[17] As part of these service activities, the personnel manager (and department) also carry out an "innovator" role. They do this by providing "up to date information on current trends and new methods of solving problems."[18] For example, there is today much interest in instituting quality improvement teams and in providing career planning for employees. Personnel managers stay on top of such trends and help their organizations implement the necessary programs.

A summary of the positions you might find in a large company's human resource department is presented in the organization chart in Figure 1.2. As you can see, positions normally found within the large personnel department include compensation and benefits manager, employment and recruiting supervisor, training specialist, employee relations executive, safety supervisor, and industrial nurse. Examples of job duties here include:

Recruiters: Maintain contact within the community and may travel extensively to search for qualified job applicants.

implied authority The authority exerted by a personnel manager by virtue of others' knowledge that he or she has access to top management (in areas like testing and affirmative action).

functional control The control exerted by a personnel manager as coordinator of personnel activities.

staff (service) function The function of a personnel manager in assisting and advising line management.

FIGURE 1.2
Positions Often Found Within a Large Personnel Department

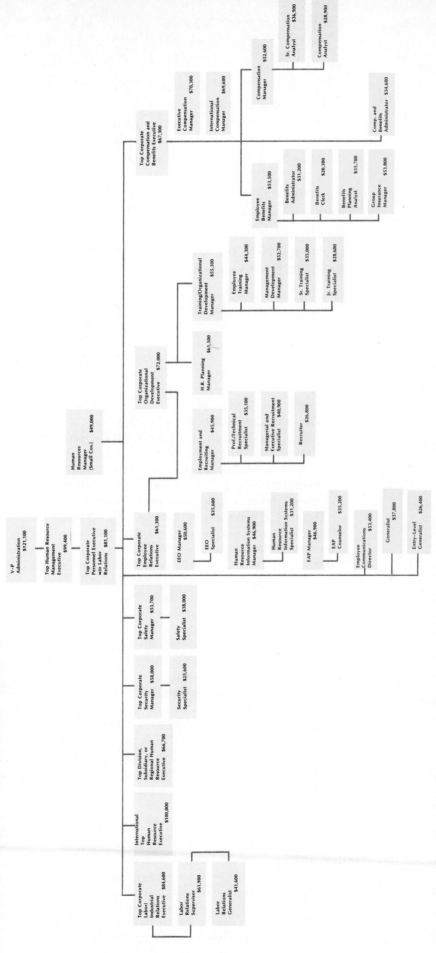

Source: Bureau of National Affairs, *Datagraph*, October 6, 1988, pp. 316–317.

Equal Employment Opportunity (EEO) Representatives or Affirmative Action Coordinators: Investigate and resolve EEO grievances, examine organizational practices for potential violations, and compile and submit EEO reports.

Job Analysts: Collect and examine detailed information about job duties to prepare job descriptions.

Compensation Managers: Handle the organization's employee benefits program, primarily health insurance and pension plans.

Training Specialists: Responsible for planning, organizing, and directing a wide range of training activities.

Labor Relations Specialists: Advise management on all aspects of union-management relations.[19]

♦ **COOPERATIVE LINE AND STAFF HUMAN RESOURCE MANAGEMENT: AN EXAMPLE**

Exactly what personnel management activities are carried out by line managers and staff managers? There's no single division of line and staff responsibility that could be applied across the board in all organizations. But to show you what such a division might look like, we've presented an example in Figure 1.3.[20] This shows some possible manager-related responsibilities of line managers and staff managers in four areas: *recruiting and hiring, safety, training,* and *labor relations.*

For example, in the area of *recruiting and hiring* it's the line manager's responsibility to specify the qualifications of employees needed to fill specific positions. Then the personnel/HR department takes over. They develop sources of qualified applicants and conduct initial screening interviews. They administer the appropriate tests. Then they refer the best applicants to the supervisor (line manager) who interviews and selects the ones he or she wants. A similar division of duties between line and staff is presented (in Figure 1.3) for the *safety, training,* and *labor relations* areas.

In summary, you should see that personnel management is an integral part of *every* manager's job. Whether you're a first-line supervisor, middle manager, or president, whether you're a production manager, sales manager, office manager, hospital administrator, county manager (or personnel manager!), getting results through people is the name of the game. And to do this, a good working knowledge of the personnel management concepts and techniques discussed in this book is vital.

In practice, such line-staff divisions of work are in fact quite common, as shown in Table 1.1. As you can see from this recent sample of personnel/HR managers, most "personnel" duties are actually accomplished jointly, using both line and staff. In some areas (such as administering unemployment compensation and flexible benefits plans) it is Human Resources that plays the major role. In others (such as interviewing and disciplinary actions), the actual personnel duties are split more evenly between Personnel/HR and the line department. In any event it is obvious that in practice good Personnel/HR is a joint, cooperative effort, with both personnel staff and line managers working together.

HOW THIS BOOK WILL HELP YOU

As we explained previously, all managers will need good human resource management skills to deal with an increasingly sophisticated work force and changing job demands. In light of this, how exactly can studying this book help you? In five ways. First, this book will increase your *knowledge*

A. RECRUITING AND HIRING

Personnel: Employment Specialists (Staff)

1. *Develop* sources of qualified applicants from local labor market. This requires carefully planned community relations, speeches, and advertisements, and active high school, college, and technical school recruiting. (**Step 2**)
2. Conduct *skilled* interviews, give *scientific* tests, and make thorough reference checks, using requisition and job description as guides. Screening must meet company standards and conform with *employment laws*. (**Step 3**)
3. Refer best candidates to supervisor after physical examinations and qualifications for the positions available have been carefully *evaluated*. (**Step 4**)
4. Give new employees preliminary *indoctrination* about the company, benefit plans, general safety, first aid, shift hours, etc. (**Step 6**)
5. Keep *complete record* of current performance and future potential of each employee. (**Step 10**)
6. *Diagnose* information given in separation interviews, determine cause, and take positive steps to correct. (**Step 12**)

Department Supervision (Line)

1. Prepare *requisition* outlining specific qualifications of employees needed to fill specific positions. Help create reputation that will attract applicants. (**Step 1**)
2. *Interview* and *select* from candidates screened by Personnel. Make specific *job assignments* that will utilize new employees' highest skills to promote maximum production. (**Step 5**)
3. *Indoctrinate* employees with specific details regarding the sections and jobs where they are to be assigned—safety rules, pay, hours, "our customs." (**Step 7**)
4. *Instruct* and *train* on the job according to planned training program already worked out with Personnel. (**Step 8**)
5. *Follow up, develop,* and *rate* employee job performance; *decide on* promotion, transfer, layoff, or discharge. (**Step 9**)
6. Hold *separation* interview when employees leave; determine causes. Make internal department *adjustments* to minimize turnover. (**Step 11**)

B. SAFETY

Personnel: Safety Specialist (Staff)

1. Arrange periodic *inspections* by trained engineer in order to *promote* safe working conditions, use of protective equipment, etc. Make *recommendations* for accident prevention.
2. *Analyze* jobs to develop safe practice rules. Utilize communications skills to get rules understood and accepted. Promote safety education.
3. Function as engineering *consultant* regarding the *design* of new machinery, guards, and safety devices; proper floor maintenance; and procedures for safe operation of machinery.
4. *Investigate* accidents; analyze causes, safety reports; *interpret* statistics; submit *recommendations* for accident prevention based on broad know-how.
5. Work with insurance carrier on workers' compensation cases through courts; should have *technical knowledge of law.*
6. *Prepare* material for safety meetings: statistics on accident causes, progress reports, educational material.

Department Supervision (Line)

1. Assist in *working out* practical safety applications; *decide on* appropriations to cover costs of installations (guards, lighting, materials handling, etc.) consistent with production and budget standards.
2. *Direct employees* in the consistent application of safe work habits; give *recognition* to careful workers and to safety suggestions submitted.
3. Set up adequate *controls* to assure that guards and devices are used; *develop* employee sense of responsibility and supervisory follow-up.
4. *Enforce* good housekeeping standards; set a good *example* in safety; maintain consistent *discipline* in administration of safety rules.
5. Prepare *reports of accidents* promptly and accurately; *consistently apply* practical preventive measures recommended by safety specialists.
6. *Work with* the safety committee to *apply* safety measures developed with it. Demonstrate interest in daily behavior.

(continued)

FIGURE 1.3
(continued)

C. TRAINING

Personnel: Training Specialist (Staff)

1. *Research* to develop overall plans, objectives, responsibility, and needs; develop outside contacts and information.
2. *Help* president develop overall *approach* and *plan* for supervisory and executive development to meet organization needs. Administer and coordinate program.
3. Give *advice* and *assistance* to *sparkplug* company units in planning, organizing, conducting employee and supervisory training and educational programs.
4. *Prepare* training outlines and visual aids in accordance with latest research in education in order to accelerate learning.
5. *Train* department supervisors to develop teaching skills in order to conduct their own training most effectively.
6. Provide conference leadership in certain types of training; *evaluate* results.

Department Supervision (Line)

1. Recognize and *decide on* department training *needs;* advise Personnel on focus needed and specific application.
2. Sincerely and *actively implement* executive development according to overall plans. Share *information,* provide challenging assignments, and coach.
3. *Utilize* Personnel training specialists to help decide on tailor-made programs to meet department needs for job, apprentice, and supervisory training.
4. Give daily *coaching* and individual *training* to subordinates to meet job standards; judge their progress and suggest areas for improvement.
5. *Assume* responsibility, in some areas, for running department training to develop potentials of people.
6. *Decide on* future training as result of evaluations of past training activities.

D. LABOR RELATIONS

Personnel: Labor Relations Specialist (Staff)

1. *Diagnose underlying causes* of labor difficulties, *anticipate* disruptions, work with line management on preventive measures to *stabilize* and *build trust in* relationships.
2. Carry on skilled *research* in preparation of labor contract: objectives, terms wordings. *Integrate* external data and internal needs.
3. Act as management *spokesperson* or *advisor* to company negotiators in bargaining with unions or as *liaison* with company lawyer on technical matters.
4. *Train* all levels of management in *contract interpretation* and administration; handle legal and nonlegal interpretation questions; maintain and administer seniority lists accurately.
5. *Advise* supervisors and *find out the facts* on grievances; interpret contracts, policies, precedents, when request; be company *adviser* or *spokesperson* on third-stage grievances and in arbitration.
6. Maintain continued direct contacts with top union officials, local, national and international; keep an open *channel of communication* on major issues.

Department Supervision (Line)

1. *Establish day-to-day relationship* of mutual respect and trust with union officials; apply labor laws and labor contracts consistently, firmly, fairly.
2. *Advise* company negotiators of contract changes needed to *promote* smooth, efficient department production.
3. *Assist* in bargaining sessions where department issues are involved; explain special problems and give technical advice.
4. *Consistently* apply labor contract terms, after training or advice by Personnel staff; apply seniority principles in promotion, transfer, layoff, etc.
5. Make final *decisions* on grievances after careful investigations and consideration of advice from Human Resources. Gather background data requested by Personnel.
6. Maintain on-the-job *direct contacts* with department union stewards and employees in order to build sound relationships.

TABLE 1.1 Human Resource Activities: Line–Staff Assignments

Activity	Company Has Activity	(No. of Cos.)	RESPONSIBILITY FOR THE ACTIVITY IS ASSIGNED TO:[1]		
			HR Dept. Only	HR and Other Dept(s).	Other Dept(s). Only
Interviewing	99%	(681)	37%	61%	2%
Personnel recordkeeping/ information systems	99	(680)	77	22	1
Vacation/leave processing	99	(680)	51	35	14
Insurance benefits administration	99	(677)	87	8	5
Orientation/induction	99	(675)	61	37	2
Wage/salary adjustment processing	99	(674)	77	22	1
Workers' compensation administration	98	(672)	73	15	12
Promotion/transfer/ separation processing	98	(672)	71	28	1
Disciplinary procedures	98	(671)	43	55	2
Payroll administration	98	(669)	25	25	50
Recruiting	98	(668)	73	25	2
Job descriptions	97	(666)	62	35	2
Unemployment compensation	97	(666)	82	11	7
Wage/salary policy development	97	(665)	80	18	2
Performance appraisal, management	97	(665)	47	44	8
Performance appraisal, nonmanagement	97	(663)	47	45	8
EEO/affirmative action	97	(662)	87	11	2
Administrative services	97	(662)	15	16	69
Purchasing	95	(654)	3	7	90
Maintenance/janitorial services	95	(653)	10	5	85
Safety programs/OSHA compliance	95	(650)	46	33	20
Job evaluation	94	(647)	70	28	2
Security measures	94	(646)	22	22	57
Training, nonmanagement	94	(641)	21	51	28
Supervisory training	94	(641)	48	44	8
Exit interviews	93	(639)	86	13	1
Complaint procedures	92	(633)	54	44	2
Job analysis	91	(626)	75	23	3
Employee communications/ publications	91	(624)	43	37	21
Award/recognition programs	91	(624)	66	29	5
Pension/retirement plan administration	90	(618)	'3	18	8
Public/media relations	89	(612)	17	17	66
Travel/transportation services	89%	(608)	9%	14%	77%
Management development	88	(604)	49	44	6
Community service	88	(601)	30	31	39
Business insurance/risk management	88	(600)	12	17	72
Recreation/social programs	86	(590)	61	30	9

(continued)

TABLE 1.1 (continued)

Activity	Company Has Activity	(No. of Cos.)	RESPONSIBILITY FOR THE ACTIVITY IS ASSIGNED TO:[1]		
			HR Dept. Only	HR and Other Dept(s).	Other Dept(s). Only
Tuition aid/scholarships	86	(590)	83	12	4
Human resource forecasting/planning	85	(580)	58	37	5
Preemployment testing	80	(551)	85	12	3
Executive compensation	80	(548)	55	26	19
Relocation	75	(512)	75	20	5
Office/clerical services	73	(502)	16	22	62
Organization development	73	(498)	46	44	10
Career planning/ development	72	(489)	51	45	5
Food service/cafeteria	70	(478)	36	6	58
Employee assistance plan/ counseling	69	(472)	83	14	4
Incentive pay plans	69	(472)	50	38	12
College recruiting	67	(462)	79	17	4
Productivity/motivation programs	67	(461)	26	61	13
Medical services	61	(414)	73	12	15
Suggestion systems	60	(408)	46	35	19
Health/wellness program	58	(400)	78	14	8
Outplacement	58	(396)	91	8	1
Attitude surveys	55	(374)	81	16	3
Thrift/savings plan administration	53	(364)	71	21	8
Preretirement counseling	52	(356)	90	4	5
Union/labor relations	50	(344)	71	27	2
Library	44	(301)	21	9	70
Profit sharing plan administration	39	(273)	59	23	18
Flexible benefits plan administration	36	(245)	87	11	3
Stock plan administration	33	(227)	57	20	23
Flexible spending account administration	29	(197)	83	11	6
Child care center	10	(67)	36	9	55

[1]Percentages are based on companies providing data on where responsiblity for the activity is assigned. Percentages may not add to 100 due to rounding.

Source: "Personnel Activities: Line–Staff Assignments," Bureau of National Affairs, *Bulletin to Management*, September 1, 1988, p. 2.

of human resource management concepts and techniques and will provide you with the human resource management vocabulary most supervisors find they need on the job. In today's modern workplace, supervisors must at least understand the meaning of personnel terms like *unfair labor practices, job evaluation,* and *adverse impact* and, at a minimum, studying this book will familiarize you with these terms—as a brief review of the Glossary will illustrate.

More important, though, carefully studying this book can provide you with the basis of many important human resource *management skills.* By carefully studying this book, in other words, you should not only learn the meaning of human resource management terms like *performance appraisal, interviewing,* and *job analysis,* you should be well on your way to understanding how to use and apply these techniques on the job. This should not only help you and your subordinates perform better, but should also help you avoid the sorts of errors that we alluded to earlier.

Third, even if you don't have plans to go into personnel management yourself, companies are increasingly promoting their best people up *through* personnel. Delta Airlines, Eli Lilly, and IBM are among the firms that do this. The moral is that even if you have no current plans for going into personnel, the "people" aspects of the business have become so important today that you have to assume that you may do a stint in personnel on your way to the top; carefully studying this book should give you a big jump on preparing for that job.

Fourth, if you *are* interested in personnel management as a career, you'll get the basic foundation that you'll need here to begin your work—or update your knowledge and skills—in this exciting and fast-moving field: You'll learn the latest fair employment laws, for instance, and the most modern appraisal and compensation techniques as well.

Should you consider human resource management as a career? The answer, of course, depends on your aptitudes, interests, and skills; after all, you want to spend your career doing something that you like and that you're good at. But your decision regarding a career will also depend in part on how attractive personnel management is as a career, and here the prospects seem to be good indeed. The change from a production- to a service-centered (and, thus, more people-oriented) society, the increased education of workers, new laws, and the emerging interest in quality improvement at work all seem to indicate that human resource management will be a vital and growing career in the years ahead.

Finally, studying this book could also sensitize you to employees' needs and perhaps *change your attitudes and assumptions,* and thereby your behavior toward the people you deal with at work. Studying what this book has to say about activities like appraising, interviewing, disciplining, and compensating employees can, in other words, help to shape your *philosophy of human resource management* at work, a subject to which we turn now.

♦ DEVELOPING YOUR HUMAN RESOURCE MANAGEMENT PHILOSOPHY

People's actions are always based in part on the basic assumptions they make, and this is especially true with regard to human resource management. The basic assumptions you make about people, such as whether they can be trusted, whether they dislike work, whether they can be creative, why they act as they do, and how they should be treated, comprise your philosophy of human resource management. And every personnel decision you make—the people you hire, the training you provide, the benefits you offer—reflects (for better or worse) this basic philosophy.

How do you go about developing such a philosophy? To some extent, it is preordained. There is no doubt that a person brings to a job an initial philosophy based on his or her experiences, education, and background. But this philosophy doesn't have to be set in stone. It should and will continually evolve as the person accumulates new knowledge and experiences. Let's therefore discuss some of the factors that will influence your own evolving philosophy.

Influence of Top Management's Philosophy

One of the things molding your personnel philosophy will be that of your employer's top management. While top management's philosophy may or may not be stated, it will usually be communicated by their actions and permeate every level and department in the organization. For example, here is part of the personnel philosophy of Edwin Land, founder and former chief executive officer of the Polaroid Corporation:

> to give everyone working for the company a personal opportunity within the company for full exercise of his talents—to express his opinions, to share in the progress in the company as far as his capacity permits, and to earn enough money so that the need for earning more will not always be the first thing on his mind. The opportunity, in short, to make his work here a fully rewarding and important part of his life.[21]

What sort of impact does a philosophy like this have? For one thing, all personnel policies and actions at Polaroid flow directly or indirectly from Land's basic aims. For example, there is a top-level human resource policy committee. This consists of top corporate officers and is chaired by a senior vice-president, and members of the human resource department serve as staff, providing advice to the committee. The existence of this high-powered committee reflects the company's commitment to Land's personnel philosophy. And its existence helps ensure that all Polaroid human resource policies and practices—such as in the areas of training, promotions, and layoffs—also reflect this basic philosophy.

Influence of Your Own Basic Assumptions About People

Your personnel management philosophy will also be influenced by the basic assumptions you make about people. For example, Douglas McGregor distinguishes between two sets of assumptions that he classified as **Theory X** and **Theory Y**. He says that the Theory X assumptions hold that:

Theory X The set of assumptions which holds that workers cannot be trusted and must be coerced into doing their jobs.

Theory Y McGregor's alternative theory that people do *not* have an aversion to work and are capable of self-control in the work situation.

1. The average human being has an inherent dislike of work and will avoid it if he can.
2. Because of this human characteristic of dislike of work, most people must be coerced, controlled, directed, and threatened with punishment to get them to put forth adequate effort.
3. The average human being prefers to be directed and wishes to avoid responsibility.

At the other extreme, some managers' actions reflect a set of Theory Y assumptions. These hold that:

1. The average human being does not inherently dislike work.
2. External control and the threat of punishment are not the only means for bringing about effort toward organizational objectives.
3. People are motivated best by satisfying their higher-order needs for achievement, esteem, and self-actualization.
4. The average human being learns, under proper conditions, not only to accept but also to seek responsibilities.
5. The capacity to exercise a relatively high degree of imagination, ingenuity, and creativity in the solution of organizational problems is widely, not narrowly, distributed in the population.[22]

System I The organizational system, described by Rensis Likert, in which managers mistrust subordinates and thus feel compelled to coerce them to work. (Corresponds to Theory X.)

System IV Likert's alternative system in which managers have confidence in workers and purposely involve them in decision-making processes. (Corresponds to Theory Y.)

Rensis Likert says that assumptions like these manifest themselves in two basic types or systems of organizations, which he calls **System I** and **System IV**. In System I organizations, he says:

1. Management is seen as having no confidence or trust in subordinates.
2. The bulk of decisions and the goal setting of the organization are made at the top.
3. Subordinates are forced to work with fear, threats, and punishment.
4. Control is highly concentrated in top management.

In their place, Likert proposes System IV, an organization built on Theory Y-type assumptions. In System IV organizations:

1. Management is seen as having complete confidence and trust in subordinates.
2. Decision making is widely dispersed and decentralized.
3. Workers are motivated by participation and involvement in decision making.
4. There is extensive, friendly superior-subordinate interaction.
5. There is widespread responsibility for control, with the lower echelon fully involved.[23]

In addition to factors like top management's philosophy and your assumptions, there is another—*the need to motivate employees*—that will affect your personnel philosophy, and this factor is so important that it is a central theme of this book.

♦ MOTIVATION: A CENTRAL ISSUE

Motivating employees has always been a major concern of managers, and it's easy to see why. Managers get things done through others, and if you can't motivate your employees to get their jobs done, you are destined to fail as a manager.

This ability to motivate employees will be even more important in the future, since fundamental changes are taking place in the nature of work and the work force. Productivity is down. Workers are becoming better educated and more concerned with their life-styles. There is a shift from blue-collar to white-collar workers. And a multitude of new laws alter the techniques through which managers can ensure high production. It seems apparent that the days of the purely Theory X manager are numbered; managers will need new tools for tapping employees' higher-level needs—for motivating them.

The question of how to motivate someone is a complex one, and one for which there are no quick answers. Yet one "law" of motivation seems to apply quite consistently: *People are usually motivated or driven to behave in a way that they feel leads to rewards.* So as a rough-and-ready rule, motivating someone requires two things: first, find out what the person wants and hold it out as a possible reward; and second, see to it that he feels that effort on his part will probably lead to obtaining that reward. One without the other won't suffice: telling someone you'll make her sales manager if her monthly sales hit $1 million won't motivate her (even if she *wants* to be sales manager) unless she *also* thinks there's a reasonable chance she can in fact make sales of $1 million; both *desire* and *ability* are required.

Personnel Management Motivation Model

People are motivated to accomplish those tasks that they feel (1) will lead to (2) rewards. (Motivation, in other words, requires both *ability* and *desire*.) This is the essence of motivation. And it's an idea that has important implications for all your personnel management activities. Let's see how this **motivation model** operates by working through Figure 1.4.

As you can see, each personnel management activity contributes to your workers' motivation. For example (see Figure 1.4), your first task is to answer the question, "Could my employee do the job if he or she wanted to?" And there are several personnel management things you can do to help ensure that the answer is yes. First, analyze the job: Here, you carefully determine the skill requirements of the job and develop job descriptions. Next is

motivation model The model of human behavior emphasizing that people are motivated to accomplish those tasks that they feel (1) will lead to (2) rewards. It stresses that both ability and desire are required for motivation.

FIGURE 1.4
Motivation Model

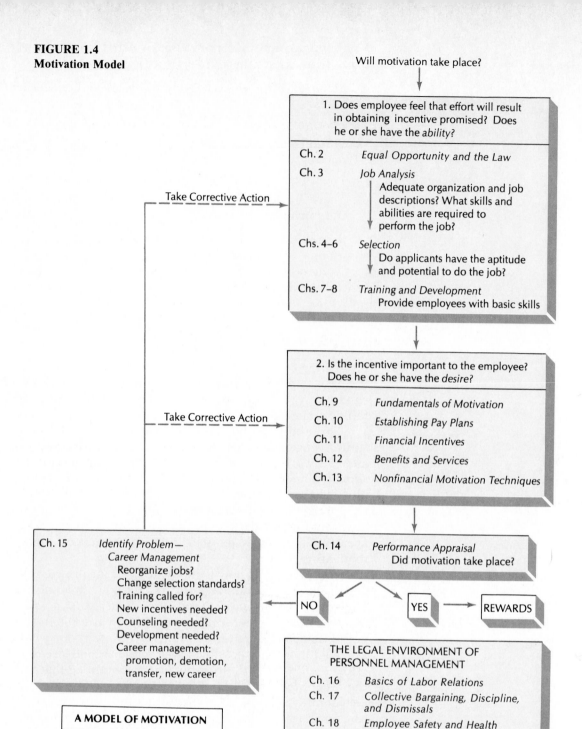

Will motivation take place?

1. Does employee feel that effort will result in obtaining incentive promised? Does he or she have the *ability*?

Ch. 2	*Equal Opportunity and the Law*
Ch. 3	*Job Analysis*
	Adequate organization and job descriptions? What skills and abilities are required to perform the job?
Chs. 4–6	*Selection*
	Do applicants have the aptitude and potential to do the job?
Chs. 7–8	*Training and Development*
	Provide employees with basic skills

Take Corrective Action

2. Is the incentive important to the employee? Does he or she have the *desire*?

Ch. 9	*Fundamentals of Motivation*
Ch. 10	*Establishing Pay Plans*
Ch. 11	*Financial Incentives*
Ch. 12	*Benefits and Services*
Ch. 13	*Nonfinancial Motivation Techniques*

Take Corrective Action

Ch. 15 *Identify Problem—*
Career Management
Reorganize jobs?
Change selection standards?
Training called for?
New incentives needed?
Counseling needed?
Development needed?
Career management: promotion, demotion, transfer, new career

Ch. 14 *Performance Appraisal*
Did motivation take place?

NO   YES   REWARDS

A MODEL OF MOTIVATION

THE LEGAL ENVIRONMENT OF PERSONNEL MANAGEMENT

Ch. 16	*Basics of Labor Relations*
Ch. 17	*Collective Bargaining, Discipline, and Dismissals*
Ch. 18	*Employee Safety and Health*
Ch. 19	*Strategic Issues in Personnel Management*

selection: Here you ensure that you hire persons with the aptitude and potential to do the job. Third, you orient and train these people: Here you provide them with the basic skills they need to carry out their jobs. Thus, if you've done everything right to this point, you can at least be fairly sure that subordinates *will feel they are capable of accomplishing their tasks—* that they have the *ability* to do so.

Next (again, see Figure 1.4), you ask, "Is the reward important to the employees—do they have the *desire* to do the job?" This, you recall, is our second requirement for motivating someone, and it involves some of your

PERSONNEL MANAGEMENT:

ON THE FRONT LINE

The main theme of this book is that personnel management—activities like recruiting, selecting, training, and rewarding employees—is not just the job of some central personnel group but rather a job in which every manager must engage. Perhaps nowhere is this more apparent than in the typical small service business. Here the owner/manager usually has no personnel staff to rely on although the success of his or her enterprise (not to mention his or her family's peace of mind) often depends largely on the effectiveness through which workers are recruited, hired, trained, evaluated, and rewarded. Therefore, to help illustrate and emphasize the front-line manager's personnel role we will use, throughout this book, a continuing case based on an actual small business in the southeastern United States. Each chapter's segment of the case will illustrate how the case's main player—owner/manager Jennifer Carter—confronts and solves personnel problems each day at work by applying the concepts and techniques of that particular chapter. Here is some background information you will need to answer questions that arise in subsequent chapters.

Carter Cleaning Centers

Jennifer Carter graduated from State University in June 1984, and after considering several job offers decided to do what she really always planned to do—go into business with her father Jack Carter.

Jack Carter opened his first laundromat in 1970 and his second in 1972. The main attraction to him of these coin laundry businesses was that they were capital rather than labor intensive; thus, once the investment in machinery was made, the stores could be run with just one unskilled attendant and none of the labor problems one normally expects from being in the retail service business.

The attractiveness of operating with virtually no skilled labor notwithstanding, Jack had decided by 1974 to expand the services in each of his stores to include the dry cleaning and pressing of clothes. He embarked, in other words, on a strategy of related diversification in that he added new services that were related to and consistent with his existing coin laundry activities. He added these new services in part because he wanted to better utilize the unused space in the rather large stores he currently had under lease and partly because he was, as he put it, "tired of sending out the dry cleaning and pressing work that came in from our coin laundry clients to a dry cleaner five miles away who then took most of what should have been our profits." To reflect their new expanded line of services he renamed each of his two stores "Carter Cleaning Centers" and was sufficiently satisfied with their performance to open four more of the same type of stores over the next five years. Each store had its own on-site manager and, on average, about seven employees and annual revenues of about $300,000. It was this six-store chain of cleaning centers that Jennifer joined upon graduating from State University.

Her understanding with her father was that she would serve as a trouble-shooter/consultant to the elder Carter with the aim of both learning the business and bringing to it modern management concepts and techniques for solving the business's problems and facilitating its growth.

most important personnel management activities. For example, it helps determine the *wages* and *salaries* you pay employees, their *financial incentives,* and the *nonfinancial incentives* they'll need to get their jobs done.

Now (if you've done an effective job in your personnel management activities) your employees should be motivated and performance should be high. Your next step (again, see Figure 1.4) is to *appraise performance.* Here you ask, "Did motivation take place?" and "If not, why not?" If the answer is no, you have to identify the problem. Should you reorganize? Change your selection standards? Provide more training? Develop new incentives? Provide counseling? In other words, you *identify the problem* (if any) and *take corrective action.*

We will use our personnel management motivation model (Figure 1.4) throughout this book. It helps show how the chapters relate to one another. And *it helps show how each personnel management activity contributes directly to your employees' motivation.*

Personnel Management: A Systems View

You can also use our model to help you take a systems "tying it all together" view of your personnel management responsibilities. As you can see in Figure 1.4, each of your personnel actions has an influence on all the others. For example, the people you hire will help determine the training that's necessary, the appropriate incentive system, and so forth.

Or take another example. Many managers are surprised when they can't motivate their subordinates, even after applying the sorts of "motivation" techniques we discuss in our motivation chapters. The reason, of course, is that *all* your personnel actions—the people you hire, the training you provide, how you appraise performance, and so on—affect motivation. Thus, motivation really begins with your hiring decisions—with finding the right person for the right job. And it's further affected by the training you provide, your incentive plan, and how you appraise performance. It is this *interrelatedness* among the personnel activities that our model also helps to emphasize.

THE PLAN OF THIS BOOK

This book is built around two basic themes. First, we assume that personnel management is the responsibility of *every* manager—not just of those in the personnel department. So throughout this book, you'll find an emphasis on practical material that you as a manager will need in carrying out your day-to-day management responsibilities. The second theme is that motivating employees is a basic cornerstone of a sound personnel management philosophy. We've therefore used our motivation model to structure the presentation of topics in this book. Here is our plan:

Part One—Recruitment and Placement

This part is aimed at ensuring that you are able to staff your unit with people who are capable—who have the *ability* to get their jobs done. In terms of motivation (as you can see from our model), it's aimed at ensuring that the first big requirement for motivation—*that each employee knows he or she can "do the job" successfully and obtain the reward*—is met. This first part contains the following chapters:

Chapter 2   *Equal Opportunity and the Law* (what you'll need to know about equal opportunity laws as they relate to human resource management activities like interviewing, selecting employees, and performance appraisal)

Chapter 3   *Job Analysis* (how to analyze a job; how to determine the "human" requirements of the job, as well as its specific duties and responsibilities)

Chapter 4   *Personnel Planning and Recruiting* (determining what sorts of people need to be hired; recruiting them)

Chapter 5 *Employee Testing and Selection* (techniques—like testing—you can use to ensure that you're hiring the right people)

Chapter 6 *Interviewing Job Candidates* (how to interview candidates to help ensure that you hire the right person for the right job)

Part Two—Training and Development

In addition to having the right traits and backgrounds, employees must also be *trained and developed* if they are to do their jobs. In this part we therefore cover:

Chapter 7 *Orientation and Technical Training* (providing the training necessary to ensure that your employees have the knowledge and skills necessary to accomplish their tasks)

Chapter 8 *Management Development Today* (concepts and techniques for developing more capable employees, managers, and organizations)

Part Three—Compensation and Motivation

This part is aimed at giving you the knowledge you will need to meet the second big requirement of motivating employees—*seeing to it that the rewards are important ones to your employees*—that they have the *desire* to do their jobs. Here we will cover:

Chapter 9 *Fundamentals of Motivation* (a more detailed look at what motivation is and how to motivate employees)

Chapter 10 *Establishing Pay Plans* (how to develop equitable, practical pay plans for your employees)

Chapters 11 and 12 *Financial Incentives* and *Benefits and Services* (how to provide special financial incentives and benefits to assist you in motivating your employees)

Chapter 13 *Nonfinancial Motivation Techniques* (how to use techniques like quality circles to motivate your employees)

Part Four—Appraisal and Career Management

In Part Four we turn to the concepts and techniques you will need for appraising your employees' performance and making any necessary changes. We will discuss:

Chapter 14 *Performance Appraisal* (techniques for appraising performance)

Chapter 15 *Career Management: From First Assignment to Retirement* (managing career decisions like career planning, promotions, and transfers)

Part Five—The Legal Environment of Personnel Management

Finally we will discuss some critical personnel-related legislation. Here, we focus on providing you with the practical knowledge you'll need in carrying out your day-to-day responsibilities. We will cover:

Chapters 16 and 17 *Basics of Labor Relations* and *Collective Bargaining, Discipline, and Dissmissals* (a review of what you need to know about labor laws and avoiding "unfair labor practices" and how to handle grievances)

Chapter 18 *Employee Safety and Health* (the causes of accidents, how to make the workplace safe, and laws governing your responsibilities in regard to employee safety and health)

Chapter 19 *Strategic Issues in Personnel Management* (the role that personnel plays in employer's strategic planning process and personnel policies used to implement that plan; a summary and tying together of the materials in this book and a further definition of a "Personnel philosophy")

SUMMARY

1. There are certain basic functions all managers perform: planning, organizing, staffing, leading, and controlling. These represent what is often called the *management process.*

2. Staffing—or personnel management—is the function focused on in this book. It includes activities like recruiting, selecting, training, compensating, appraising, and developing.

3. Several trends—including the emergence of a service economy, demographic trends, technological trends, competitive/managerial trends, and political–legal trends—are all contributing to the way that organizations do business, and (more particularly) to the role played in companies by personnel.

4. All managers are authorized to direct the work of subordinates—they are always someone's boss. Line managers also have direct responsibility for accomplishing the basic goals of the organization. Staff managers are authorized to assist and advise line managers in accomplishing these basic goals.

5. Personnel management is very much a part of *every* line manager's responsibility. These personnel management responsibilities include placing the right person on the right job, orienting, training, and working to improve his or her job performance.

6. The human resource manager (and his or her department) carry out three main functions. First, he or she exerts *line authority* in his or her own unit and implied authority elsewhere in the organization. He or she exerts a *coordinative function* to ensure that the personnel objectives and policies of the organization are coordinated and carried out. And he or she provides various *staff services* to line management; for example, the personnel manager or department assists in the hiring, training, evaluation, rewarding, promotion, and disciplining of employees at all levels.

7. Peoples' actions are always based in part on the basic assumptions they make, and this is why it is important to develop an overall guiding philosophy of personnel management. Factors that will influence your own personnel management philosophy include prior experiences, education, and background; top management's philosophy; your basic assumptions about people; and the need to motivate subordinates and improve performance and productivity at work.

8. Because motivation is so important, this book is organized around the motivation model as a framework. The material in Parts One and Two is aimed at ensuring that the first major requirement for motivation—that each employee is capable of accomplishing the task and obtaining the reward—is met. Part Three is aimed at explaining how to develop

an attractive reward system. Part Four turns to the concepts and techniques needed for appraising employee's performance and making any necessary changes. Finally, in Part Five some crucial personnel–related laws and skills are discussed.

9. The remainder of this book is aimed at providing *all* managers (not just future human resource managers) with the practical concepts and techniques needed to carry out the personnel management aspects of their jobs. But, while studying these chapters, also make sure to understand (by following our framework) how each chapter's material relates to motivating employees.

KEY TERMS

management process	staff manager	Theory Y
personnel (or human resource) management	implied authority	System I
	functional control	System IV
authority	staff (service) functions	motivation model
line manager	Theory X	

DISCUSSION QUESTIONS

1. Explain what personnel management is and how it relates to the management process.
2. Give several examples of how personnel management concepts and techniques can be of use to all managers.
3. Compare and contrast the work of line and staff managers; give examples of each.
4. What do we mean by a "personnel management philosophy"? What factors influence it? Why is it important?
5. Compare and contrast Theory X and Theory Y management assumptions.
6. Present and explain the rationale for our motivation model.

♦ APPLICATION EXERCISES

♦ CASE INCIDENT   Jack Nelson's Problem

As a new member of the board of directors for a local savings and loan association, Jack Nelson was being introduced to all the employees in the home office. When he was introduced to Ruth, he was curious about her work and asked her what her machine did. Ruth replied that she really did not know what the machine was called or what it did. She explained that she had only been working there for two months. She did, however, know precisely how to operate the machine and, according to her supervisor, she was an excellent employee.

At one of the branch offices, the supervisor in charge spoke to Mr. Nelson quite confidentially, telling him that "something was wrong" but she didn't know what. For one thing, she explained, employee turnover was too high and no sooner had one employee been put on a job, when another one resigned. With customers to see and loans to be made, she explained that she had little time to work with the new employees as they came and went.

All branch supervisors hired their own employees with no communications with the home office or other branches. When an opening developed, the supervisor tried to find a suitable employee to replace the worker who quit.

After touring the 22 branches and finding similar problems in many of them, Mr. Nelson wondered what the home office should do or what action he should take. The savings and loan firm was generally regarded as a well-run institution that had grown from 27 to 191 employees during the past eight years. The more he thought about the matter, the more puzzled Mr. Nelson became. He couldn't quite put his finger on the problem, and he didn't know whether or not to report his findings to the president.

Questions

1. What do you think was causing some of the problems in the savings and loan home office and branches?

2. Do you think setting up a personnel unit in the main office would help?

3. What functions should it carry out, specifically? What personnel functions would then be carried out by supervisors and other line managers?

Source: Claude S. George, Jr., *Supervision in Action*, pp. 126–127. © 1977. Reprinted by permission of Prentice-Hall, Englewood Cliffs, New Jersey.

NOTES

1. This discussion is based on Gary Dessler, *Management Fundamentals* (Reston, Va.: Reston, 1977), p. 2; William Berliner and William McClarney, *Management Practice and Training* (Homewood, Ill.: Irwin, 1974), p. 11.

2. Quoted in Fred K. Foulkes, "The Expanding Role of the Personnel Function," *Harvard Business Review* (March–April 1975), pp. 71–84.

3. Karl Albrecht and Ron Zemke, *Service America!* (Homewood, Ill.: Dow Jones-Irwin, 1985), pp. 96–117.

4. Karl Albrecht, *At America's Service* (Homewood, Ill.: Dow Jones-Irwin, 1988), p. 169.

5. Albrecht and Zemke, *Service America!*, p. 101.

6. Based on Albrecht and Zemke, *Service America!*, p. 99.

7. See, for example, Wayne F. Cascio, *Costing Human Resources: The Financial Impact of Behavior in Organizations* (Boston: Kent, 1982).

8. Lawrence Baytos, "Nine Strategies for Productivity Improvement," *Personnel Journal*, Vol. 58 (July 1979), pp. 446–449.

9. Ibid., p. 454.

10. *The Hay Group News*, December 1985.

11. Thomas Paine, "Outlook for Compensation and Benefits: 1986 and Beyond," Hewitt Associates, October 30, 1985.

12. "Steel Seeks Higher Output via Workplace Reform," *Business Week*, August 18, 1980, p. 98.

13. The remainder of this section is based largely on Robert Saltonstall, "Who's Who in Personnel Administration," *Harvard Business Review*, Vol. 33 (July–August 1955), pp. 75–83, reprinted in Paul Pigors, Charles Meyers, and F. P. Malm, *Management of Human Resources* (New York: McGraw-Hill, 1969), pp. 61–73.

14. Saltonstall, "Who's Who," p. 63.

15. For a detailed discussion of the responsibilities and duties of the human resource department, see Mary Zippo, "Personal Activities: Where the Dollars Went in 1979," *Personnel*, Vol. 57 (March–April 1980), pp. 61–67; and "ASPA-BNA Survey No. 49, Personnel Activities, Budgets, and Staffs: 1985–1986," *BNA Bulletin to Management*, June 5, 1986.

16. Saltonstall, "Who's Who," p. 65.

17. Fred K. Foulkes and Henry Morgan, "Organizing and Staffing the Personnel Function," *Harvard Business Review*, Vol. 56 (May–June 1977), p. 146.

18. Ibid., p. 149.

19. U.S. Department of Labor, Bureau of Labor Statistics, *Occupational Outlook Handbook*, Bulletin 2250, 1986–1987 Edition, pp. 45–47.

20. Saltonstall, "Who's Who," pp. 68–69.

21. Quoted in Foulkes and Morgan, "Organizing and Staffing the Personnel Function," p. 144.

22. Douglas McGregor, *The Human Side of Enterprise* (New York: McGraw-Hill, 1960), pp. 16–18, quoted in Daniel Wren, *The Evolution of Management Thought* (New York: Ronald Press, 1972), pp. 449–450.

23. Based on Paul Hersey and Kenneth Blanchard, *Management of Organizational Behavior* (Englewood Cliffs, N.J.: Prentice-Hall, 1969), pp. 52–56.

PART ONE

RECRUITMENT AND PLACEMENT

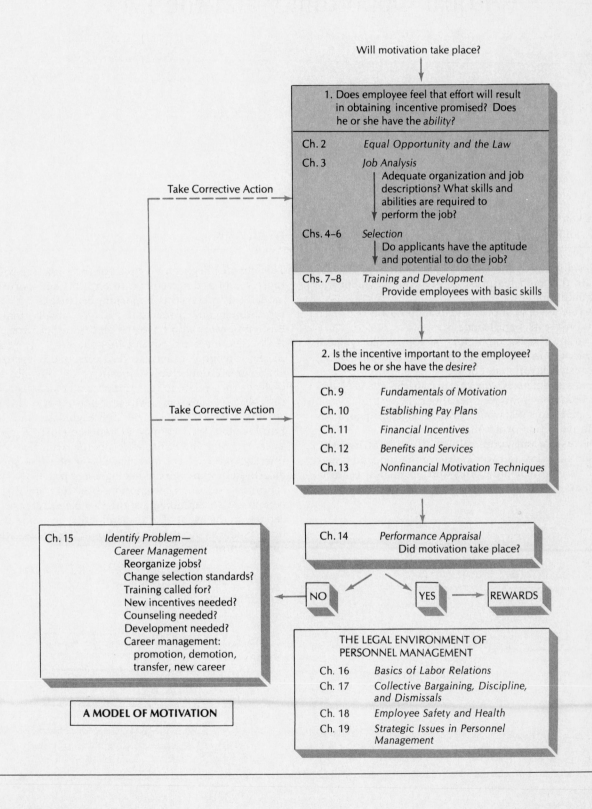

Will motivation take place?

1. Does employee feel that effort will result in obtaining incentive promised? Does he or she have the *ability?*

Ch. 2	Equal Opportunity and the Law
Ch. 3	Job Analysis
	Adequate organization and job descriptions? What skills and abilities are required to perform the job?
Chs. 4–6	Selection
	Do applicants have the aptitude and potential to do the job?
Chs. 7–8	Training and Development
	Provide employees with basic skills

Take Corrective Action

2. Is the incentive important to the employee? Does he or she have the *desire?*

Ch. 9	Fundamentals of Motivation
Ch. 10	Establishing Pay Plans
Ch. 11	Financial Incentives
Ch. 12	Benefits and Services
Ch. 13	Nonfinancial Motivation Techniques

Take Corrective Action

Ch. 15	Identify Problem—
	Career Management
	Reorganize jobs?
	Change selection standards?
	Training called for?
	New incentives needed?
	Counseling needed?
	Development needed?
	Career management: promotion, demotion, transfer, new career

| Ch. 14 | Performance Appraisal |
| | Did motivation take place? |

NO   YES → REWARDS

A MODEL OF MOTIVATION

THE LEGAL ENVIRONMENT OF PERSONNEL MANAGEMENT

Ch. 16	Basics of Labor Relations
Ch. 17	Collective Bargaining, Discipline, and Dismissals
Ch. 18	Employee Safety and Health
Ch. 19	Strategic Issues in Personnel Management

Chapter 2

Equal Opportunity and the Law

When you finish studying this chapter, you should be able to:

1. Avoid many employment discrimination problems.
2. Cite the main features of recent employment discrimination laws.
3. Define adverse impact and explain how it is proved and what its significance is.
4. Cite specific discriminatory personnel management practices in recruitment, selection and promotion, transfer, layoffs, and benefits.
5. Explain defenses you can use in the event of discriminatory practice allegations.
6. Explain how you would go about setting up an affirmative action program.
7. Discuss recent court rulings affecting affirmative action, claims of reverse discrimination, and issues of women and minorities and promotion requirements.

OVERVIEW

This chapter begins a new part of the book, the part on recruitment and placement. In terms of our motivation model, this material is important because it is through recruitment and placement that you ensure that you hire employees who have the ability to perform effectively. The main purpose of this chapter is to provide the knowledge you need to deal effectively with equal employment opportunity questions on the job, especially as they relate to recruitment and placement. First reviewed are some employment discrimination laws, including Title VII of the 1964 Civil Rights Act and Equal Employment Opportunity Commission (EEOC) guidelines. We describe in broad terms the main features of this legislation. Next is a discussion of some specific discriminatory personnel management practices—in recruitment, selection, promotion, transfers, layoffs, and benefits. Also explained are the two basic defenses you can use in the event of a discriminatory practice allegation: business necessity and bona fide occupational qualification.

♦ SOME BACKGROUND

Legislation barring discrimination against members of minority groups in the United States is certainly nothing new. For example, the Fifth Amendment to the U.S. Constitution (ratified in 1791) states that "no person shall . . . be deprived of life, liberty, or property, without due process of the law." The Thirteenth Amendment (ratified in 1865) outlawed slavery and has been held by the courts to bar racial discrimination. The Fourteenth Amendment (ratified in 1868) makes it illegal for any state to "make or enforce any law which shall abridge the privileges and immunities of citizens of the United States," and the courts have generally viewed this law as barring discrimination on the basis of sex or national origin, as well as race. Section 1981 of Title 42 of the U.S. Code, passed into law over 100 years ago as the Civil Rights Act of 1866, gives all persons within the jurisdiction of the United States the same right to make and enforce contracts and benefit from the laws of the land; as we'll see, this has in recent years become an important legal basis for attacking discrimination.[1] Other laws as well as various court decisions indicate that discrimination against minorities was illegal as early as the turn of the century—at least in theory.[2]

As a practical matter, though, Congress and various presidents were reluctant to initiate dramatic action on equal employment issues until the early 1960s. At that point, "they were finally prompted to act primarily as a result of civil unrest among the minorities and women," who eventually became protected by the new equal rights legislation and the agencies created to implement and enforce it.[3] More recently, a series of Supreme Court rulings in the late 1980s then had the effect of slowing and perhaps rolling back some of the gains made by minorities and women. Equal Employment legislation and its enforcement are discussed in the rest of this chapter.

But before proceeding it is important to emphasize how crucial a complete understanding of these laws is. Today no manager from first-line supervisor to president can get through a workday without facing discrimination-related problems. Today, every time you advertise a job opening or recruit, interview, test, or select a candidate or appraise an employee, it is necessary to take into account these equal rights laws. And that is only the beginning—a variety of other personnel management-related activities, including disciplinary actions, promotion, transfer, layoffs, and benefits, are also affected by this legislation. And, as a manager, a complete understanding of these new laws is necessary, not only for your own protection, but to protect the interests of your organization as well.

♦ TITLE VII OF THE 1964 CIVIL RIGHTS ACT

What the Law Says

Title VII of the 1964 Civil Rights Act The section of the act that says you cannot discriminate on the basis of race, color, religion, sex, or national origin with respect to employment.

One of the first of these new laws was **Title VII of the 1964 Civil Rights Act.** Title VII (as amended by the 1972 Equal Employment Opportunity Act) states that an employer cannot discriminate on the basis of race, color, religion, sex, or national origin. Specifically, it states that it shall be an unlawful employment practice for an employer:[4]

1. *To fail or refuse to hire or to discharge an individual* or otherwise to discriminate against any individual with respect to his compensation, terms, conditions, or privileges of employment, because of such individual's race, color, religion, sex, or national origin.

2. *To limit, segregate, or classify his employees or applicants for employment* in any way that would deprive or tend to deprive any individual

of employment opportunities or otherwise adversely affect his status as an employee, because of such individual's race, color, religion, sex, or national origin.[5]

Who Does Title VII Cover?

Title VII of the Civil Rights Act bars discrimination on the part of all public or private employers of 15 or more persons. In addition, it covers all private and public educational institutions, the federal government, and state and local governments. Public and private employment agencies are similarly barred from failing or refusing to refer for employment any individual because of race, color, religion, sex, or national origin. Labor unions with 15 or more members are barred from excluding, expelling, or classifying their membership because of race, color, religion, sex, or national origin. Joint labor-management committees established for selecting workers for apprenticeships and training similarly cannot discriminate against individuals.

The EEOC

Equal Employment Opportunity Commission (EEOC) The commission, created by Title VII, empowered to investigate job discrimination complaints and sue on behalf of complainants.

EEOC stands for **Equal Employment Opportunity Commission,** which was instituted by Title VII. The EEOC consists of five members who are appointed by the president with the advice and consent of the Senate; each member serves a term of five years.

The establishment of the EEOC greatly enhanced the federal government's ability to enforce equal employment opportunity laws. Its basic procedure is as follows: The EEOC receives and investigates job discrimination complaints from aggrieved individuals. When it finds reasonable cause that the charges are justified, it attempts (through conciliation) to reach an agreement eliminating all aspects of the discrimination. If this conciliation fails, the EEOC has the power to go directly to court to enforce the law. Under the Equal Employment Opportunity Act of 1972, discrimination charges may be filed by EEOC *on behalf of* an aggrieved individual, as well as by the individuals themselves. This procedure is explained in more detail later in this chapter.

◆ EXECUTIVE ORDERS

executive orders Orders issued by President Johnson that imposed requirements even stricter than those in Title VII upon federal contractors.

Under **executive orders** issued by former President Johnson, employers who do business with the U.S. government have an obligation beyond that imposed by Title VII to refrain from employment discrimination.

These orders prohibit employment discrimination by employers with federal contracts of more than $10,000 (and by their subcontractors), and by contractors and subcontractors in federally assisted construction projects. In addition, Executive Order 11246 (as amended by Executive Order 11375) imposes three other obligations on federal contractors. First, unlike Title VII, the executive orders require that contractors take **affirmative action** to ensure equal employment opportunity (we will explain affirmative action later). All firms with contracts over $50,000 and 50 or more employees must develop and implement such programs. Second, the orders state a policy against employment discrimination based on *age or physical handicap,* in addition to race, color, religion, sex, or national origin. Finally, these orders also established the **Office of Federal Contract Compliance Programs (OFCCP).** It is responsible for implementing the executive orders and ensuring the compliance of federal contractors.

affirmative action Steps in recruitment, hiring, upgrading jobs, and so on that are designed and taken for the purpose of eliminating the present effects of past discrimination.

Office of Federal Contract Compliance Programs (OFCCP) This office is responsible for implementing the executive orders and ensuring compliance of federal contractors.

◆ EQUAL PAY ACT OF 1963

Equal Pay Act The act requiring equal pay for equal work, regardless of sex.

The **Equal Pay Act of 1963** (amended in 1972) made it unlawful to discriminate in pay on the basis of sex when jobs require equal work—equivalent skills, effort, and responsibility—and are performed under similar working conditions. However, differences in pay do not violate the act if the difference is based on a seniority system, a merit system, a system that measures earnings by quantity or quality of production, or a differential based on any factor other than sex.

◆ AGE DISCRIMINATION IN EMPLOYMENT ACT OF 1967

Age Discrimination in Employment Act of 1967 The act prohibiting arbitrary age discrimination and specifically protecting individuals over 40 years old.

The **Age Discrimination in Employment Act of 1967** made it unlawful to discriminate against employees or applicants for employment who are between 40 and 65 years of age. As amended by Congress in 1978 the act extended protection to age 70 for most workers and without upper limit for employees of the federal government. While originally administered by the Department of Labor, responsibility for the act was transferred to the EEOC in 1979.

A 1973 Supreme Court ruling held that most states and local agencies when acting in the role of employer must also adhere to provisions of the act that protect workers from age discrimination. Subsequent actions by Congress have eliminated the age cap of 70, effectively ending most mandatory retirement.

One-fourth of the court actions filed by the EEOC one recent year were ADEA cases. This act is a "favored statute" among employees and lawyers because it allows jury trials and double damages to those proving "willful" discrimination.[6]

◆ VOCATIONAL REHABILITATION ACT OF 1973

Vocational Rehabilitation Act of 1973 The act requiring certain federal contractors to take affirmative action for disabled persons.

This act required employers with federal contracts over $2,500 to take affirmative action for the employment of handicapped persons, persons "who have a physical or mental impairment which substantially limits one or more of such person's major life activities." Of course, the act does not require that an unqualified person be hired, but does require that an employer take steps to accommodate a handicapped worker unless doing so imposes an undue hardship on the employer.[7]

Americans with Disabilities Act The act requiring employers to make reasonable accommodations for disabled employees, and prohibits discrimination against disabled persons.

The **Americans with Disabilities Act** became law in 1990. Among other things it extends to most employers' the need to make reasonable accommodations for disabled employees at work. It also prohibits discrimination against disabled persons qualified for a job, in hiring, firing or promotion

Legal Aspects of AIDS at Work

Arline v. *School Board of Nassau County* U.S. Supreme Court ruling that persons with contagious diseases are covered by the Vocational Rehabilitation Act of 1973.

The Vocational Rehabilitation Act has recently taken on added prominence because of the likelihood it can be used to prohibit discrimination against people with AIDS. In **School Board of Nassau County v. Arline,** the Supreme Court ruled in 1987 that persons with contagious diseases are covered by the act. In this particular case a school teacher (Arline) was dismissed because she had tuberculosis, an infectious respiratory disease.[8] To that point it was often assumed that merely having a contagious disease meant the person was left unprotected under the Rehabilitation Act. In *Arline,* however, the Supreme Court held that the opposite was true: that the fact a disease is contagious can by itself place an employee under the protection of the act since the mere fear of the disease (rather than its actual likelihood of being transmitted) might cause employers to discriminate against the ailing persons. While the point hasn't been tested yet in the Supreme Court, it therefore seems likely that a person with AIDS would be protected by the Rehabilitation Act, at least as long as he or she is otherwise qualified to continue working, and can be reasonably accommodated by the employer.[9] In any case numerous state laws now protect people with AIDS from discrimination. Furthermore, the guidelines issued by the Labor Department's Office of Federal Contract Compliance Programs also require that AIDS-type diseases be treated as covered by the Rehabilitation Act.[10] The bottom line seems to be that for many or most employers discriminating against people with AIDS would be viewed by the courts and enforcement agencies as unlawful.[11]

♦ VIETNAM ERA VETERANS' READJUSTMENT ASSISTANCE ACT OF 1974

Vietnam Era Veterans's Readjustment Assistance Act of 1974 Requires that employers with government contracts of $10,000 or more take affirmative action to employ and advance disabled veterans and qualified veterans of the Vietnam era.

The provisions of the **Vietnam Era Veterans' Readjustment Act of 1974** require that employers with government contracts of $10,000 or more take affirmative action to employ and advance disabled veterans and qualified veterans of the Vietnam era. The act is administered by the OFCCP.[12] As of March 1988, federal contractors who have contracts worth $10,000 or more must file a new form with the Department of Labor. The form lists the number of "special disabled" veterans and Vietnam era veterans they employ and related information.[13]

♦ PREGNANCY DISCRIMINATION ACT OF 1978

Pregnancy Discrimination Act (PDA) An amendment to Title VII of the Civil Rights Act that prohibits sex discrimination based on "pregnancy, childbirth, or related medical conditions." It requires employers to provide benefits—including sick leave and disability benefits and health and medical insurance—the same as for any employee not able to work because of disability.

California Federal Savings and Loan Association v. *Guerra* U.S. Supreme Court ruling that employers must provide pregnant employees unpaid pregnancy leave for the period during which the employee is disabled because of the pregnancy, childbirth, or related medical conditions.

In 1978, Congress passed the **Pregnancy Discrimination Act** as an amendment to the Civil Rights Act of 1964, Title VII. The act broadened the definition of sex discrimination to encompass pregnancy, childbirth, or related medical conditions. It prohibits using these factors for discrimination in hiring, promotion, suspension or discharge, or any other term or condition of employment.[14] Basically, what the act says is that if an employer offers its employees disability coverage, pregnancy and childbirth must be treated like any other disability and must be included in the plan as a covered condition.[15] In January 1987, the U.S. Supreme Court ruled in *California Federal Savings and Loan Association* v. *Guerra* that if an employer offers no disability leave to any of its employees it *can* (but need not necessarily) grant pregnancy leave to a woman who requests it when disabled for pregnancy, childbirth, or a related medical condition, although men get no comparable benefits.[16]

♦ FEDERAL AGENCY GUIDELINES

federal agency guidelines Guidelines issued by federal agencies charged with ensuring compliance with equal employment federal legislation, that explain recommended employer procedures in detail.

The federal agencies charged with ensuring compliance with the aforementioned laws and executive orders have also issued their own guidelines on these matters. The overall purpose of these **federal agency guidelines** is to explain in detail the procedures these agencies recommend that employers follow in complying with the equal opportunity laws.

Uniform Guidelines on Employee Selection Procedures

For example, detailed guidelines to be used by employers were approved in 1978 by the EEOC, Civil Service Commission, Department of Labor, and Department of Justice.[17] These uniform guidelines supersede earlier guidelines developed by the EEOC alone in 1970 and set forth "highly recommended" procedures regarding such matters as employee selection, recordkeeping, preemployment inquiries, and affirmative action programs. As an example, the guidelines specify that any employment selection devices (including but not limited to written tests) that screen out disproportionate numbers of women or minorities must be *validated*. The guidelines also explain in detail *how* an employer can validate a selection device. (This procedure will be explained in Chapter 5.) For its part, the OFCCP has its own *Manual of Guidelines*. It covers federal contractors on the antibias and affirmative action provisions of Executive Order 11246, the 1973 Rehabilitation Act, and the Vietnam Era Veterans Readjustment Assistance Act.[18]

Recently, the American Psychological Association published the latest *Standards for Educational Psychological Testing,* and many experts expect that this document, which represents a consensus among testing experts, "will be used in court to help judges resolve disagreements about the quality of . . . validity studies that arise during litigation."[19]

EEOC Guidelines

The EEOC has also issued updated guidelines clarifying and revising its position regarding matters like *national origin discrimination, age,* and *sexual harassment.*[20]

For example, these guidelines define national origin very broadly as a *place* of origin rather than as country of origin, thus extending coverage beyond that of sovereign nations. Thus, a Bostonian in southern California would be protected under these antidiscrimination guidelines, as would the spouse of someone with a foreign-sounding name.

The EEOC also published guidelines in 1981 that further explained and revised the agency's position on age discrimination.[21] Recall that the Age Discrimination in Employment Act of 1967 (as amended) prohibited employers from discrimination against persons 40 to 70 years of age merely because of age. Subsequent EEOC guidelines stated that it was unlawful to discriminate in hiring (or in any way) by giving preference because of age to individuals *within* the 40 to 70 age bracket. Thus, if two people apply for the same job, and one is 45 and the other is 55, you may not lawfully turn down the 55-year-old candidate because of his or her age and expect to defend yourself by saying that you hired someone over 40—in this case someone 45 years of age.[22] Similarly, you could not promote a 41-year-old worker rather than a 51-year-old person on the basis of age alone. In help-wanted notices or advertisements you cannot use terms like "age 25 to 35," "young," or "college student," since these terms may deter applications from older persons. Similarly, you cannot use phrases like "age 40 to 50," "retired person," or "supplement your pension," since to do so might discriminate against others within the protected (40–70) group.

♦ SEXUAL HARASSMENT

sexual harassment Harassment, on the basis of sex, that has the purpose or effect of substantially interfering with a person's work performance or creating an intimidating, hostile, or offensive work environment.

The EEOC has also issued interpretive guidelines on **sexual harassment.** These guidelines state that employers have an affirmative duty to maintain a workplace free of sexual harassment and intimidation.[23] These and related guidelines state that harassment on the basis of sex is a violation of Title VII when such conduct has the purpose or effect of substantially interfering with a person's work performance or creating an intimidating, hostile, or offensive work environment.

The guidelines define sexual harassment as "unwelcome sexual advances, requests for sexual favors, and other verbal or physical conduct of a sexual nature that takes place under any of the following conditions":[24]

1. Submission to such conduct is made either explicitly or implicitly a term or condition of an individual's employment.

2. Submission to or rejection of such conduct by an individual is used as the basis for employment decisions affecting such individual.
3. Such conduct has the purpose or effect of unreasonably interfering with an individual's work performance or creating an intimidating, hostile, or offensive work environment. In determining whether the alleged conduct constitutes sexual harassment, the Commission will look at the record as a whole and the totality of the circumstances, such as the nature of the sexual advances and the context in which the alleged incidents occurred. The determination of the legality of a particular action will be made from the facts, on a case-by-case basis.

There are several ways an employee can prove sexual harassment. The most direct is to prove that rejecting a supervisor's advances adversely affected the employee's tangible benefits, like raises or promotions. For example, in one case the employee was able to show that continued job success and advancement were dependent on her agreeing to the sexual demands of her supervisors. And she showed that after an initial complaint to her employer she was subjected to adverse performance evaluations, disciplinary layoffs, and other adverse actions.[25]

However, it's not always necessary to show that the harassment had tangible consequences such as a demotion or termination. For example, in one case the court found that a male supervisor's sexual harassment had substantially affected a female employee's emotional and psychological ability to the point where she felt she had to quit her job. Therefore, even though no direct threats or promises were made in exchange for sexual advances, the fact that the advances interfered with the woman's performance and created an offensive work environment were enough to prove that sexual harassment had occurred. On the other hand, the courts will not interpret as sexual harassment any sexual relationships that arise during the course of employment but that do not have substantial effect on that employment.[26]

To qualify as sexual harassment, the advances do not have to be made by the person's supervisor: an employee's coworkers (or even the employer's customers) can cause the employer to be held responsible for sexual harassment. In one case, for instance, the court held that a sexually provocative uniform that the employer required resulted in lewd comments and innuendos by customers toward the employee; when she complained that she would no longer wear the uniform, she was fired. Since the employer could not show that there was a job-related necessity for requiring such a uniform (and because the uniform was required only for female employees), the court ruled that the employer, in effect, was responsible for the sexually harassing behavior. The EEOC guidelines also state that an employer is liable for the sexually harassing acts of its nonsupervisory employees, too, if the employer knew or should have known of the harassing conduct.

The U.S. Supreme Court's first decision on sexual harassment was **Meritor Savings Bank, FSB v. Vinson**, decided in June 1986. In this case there were three sexual harassment issues before the court:

(1) Whether a hostile work environment (where hostility is due to the victim's sex) in which the victim does not suffer any economic injury violates Title VII, (2) whether an employee's voluntary participation in sexual acts with a manager constitutes a valid defense for an employer to a Title VII complaint, and (3) whether an employer is liable for the conduct of supervisors or coworkers when the employer is unaware of that conduct.[27]

The court's ruling broadly endorsed the EEOC guidelines (issues 1 and 2), but the majority on a 5-to-4 split vote declined to issue a definitive ruling

Meritor Savings Bank, FSB v. Vinson U.S. Supreme Court's first decision on sexual harassment. Held that existence of a hostile environment even without economic hardship is sufficient to prove harassment, even if participation was voluntary.

on employers' automatic liability (issue 3). However, the clear message of the decision is that employers should establish accessible and meaningful complaint procedures for employee claims of sexual harassment.

What the Employer Should Do

In light of the recent Supreme Court ruling on sexual harassment, employers can take a number of steps to minimize liability if a sexual harassment claim is filed against the organization and to prevent such claims arising in the first place:

1. Issue a strong policy statement condemning such behavior. The policy should include a workable definition of sexual harassment, spell out possible actions against those who harass others, and make it clear that retaliatory action against an employee who makes charges will not be tolerated. An example, presented in Figure 2.1, states, for example, that "The policy *prohibits* behavior that is *not* welcomed . . .".

2. Inform all employees about the policy prohibiting sexual harassment and of their rights under the policy.

3. Develop a complaint procedure.

4. Establish a management response system that includes an immediate reaction and investigation by senior management.

5. Begin management training sessions with supervisors and managers to increase their own awareness of the issues.

6. Discipline managers and employees involved in sexual harassment.

7. Keep thorough records of complaints, investigations, and actions taken.

8. Conduct exit interviews that uncover any complaints and that acknowledge by signature the reasons for leaving.

9. Republish the sexual harassment policy periodically.

FIGURE 2.1
A Sample Company Policy Statement on Sexual Harassment
Source: Reprinted, by permission of the publisher, from Frederick L. Sullivan, "Sexual Harassment: The Supreme Court's Ruling," *Personnel*, December 1986, p. 4, copyright 1986, American Management Association, New York. All rights reserved.

I. *Policy Statement*

It is the policy of _____ that no employee be harassed by another employee or supervisor on the basis of sex and that no personnel action be taken affecting an employee (either favorably or unfavorably) on the basis of conduct that is not related to work performance. Such conduct may include submitting to sexual advances, refusing to submit to sexual advances, protesting sexual overtures, or raising a complaint concerning the alleged violation of this policy.

II. *The Reason For This Policy*

The purpose of this policy is not to regulate our employees' personal lives or morality. The policy was formulated to protect our employees—both males and females—against unsolicited and unwelcomed sexual overtures or conduct, either physical or verbal. It prohibits employee misconduct that may upset employee morale and interfere with employees' work and efficiency. Some forms of misconduct may even constitute a violation of equal employment opportunity law.

III. *The Type of Conduct Covered by this Policy*

A. Sexual harassment does not refer to occasional compliments of a socially acceptable nature or welcome social relationships.

B. The policy *prohibits* any demand for sexual favors that is accompanied by a promise of favorable job treatment or a threat concerning the employee's employment.

C. The policy *prohibits* subtle pressure for sexual favors, including implying or threatening that an applicant's or employee's cooperation of a sexual nature (or refusal thereof) will have any effect on the person's employment, job assignment, wages, promotion, or on any other conditions of employment or future job opportunities.

D. The policy *prohibits* behavior that is *not* welcomed by the employee and is personally *offensive.*

1. Repeated sexual flirtations, advances, or propositions.
2. Continued or repeated verbal abuse of a sexual nature, sexually related comments and joking, graphic, or degrading comments about an employee's appearance, or the display of sexually suggestive objects or pictures.
3. Any uninvited physical contact or touching, such as patting, pinching, or constant brushing against another's body.

IV. *Violations of this Policy*

Violations of this policy will not be permitted. Any employee or supervisor who violates this policy will be subject to discipline up to and including discharge.

V. *Complaints or Questions*

A. Any employee who feels that he or she is a victim of sexual harassment should immediately report the matter to _____ (an EEO officer; *someone other than the employee's immediate supervisor*). The matter will be thoroughly investigated.

B. Any questions regarding this policy or a specific fact situation should be brought to the appropriate supervisor, a higher-level supervisor, or to _____ (*EEO Officer*).

C. The confidentiality and privacy of our employees and those involved will be respected during the investigation.

D. If an employee brings the matter to _____ (*EEO Officer*) and does not believe the situation has been satisfactorily resolved, the employee should then bring her/his complaint to _____ (a vice-president or other high-ranking management official).

10. Encourage upward communication through periodic written attitude surveys, hot lines, suggestion boxes, and other feedback procedures to discover employees' feelings concerning any evidence of sexual harassment and to keep management informed.[28]

While sexual harassment can take many forms, ranging from physical assault to suggestive gestures, it is interesting that one study concludes that it is not necessarily the most "serious" forms of sexual harassment that are most likely to lead to the filing of formal charges. In fact, the most frequently reported behaviors involved not assault but unwanted physical contact, offensive language, and the sexual propositions unlinked to employment conditions. What, then, triggered the filing of formal charges?

According to this study, "The most compelling finding is that over 65% of the sexual harassment cases involved job discharge. The second most frequently reported consequence was a voluntary quit (16%). Based on this, these researchers conclude:

> These findings suggest that the outcomes or consequences of sexual harassment may have more of an influence on the filing of formal sexual harassment charges than the behaviors themselves or the offensive working conditions created by such behaviors. Job discharge, for example, could quite likely fire one's sense of injustice to the degree necessary to initiate formal action. Additionally, the desire to reclaim a desired job and/or the feeling of "nothing left to lose" may prompt the filing of formal sexual harassment "charges."[29]

What the Individual Can Do

An employee—either male or female—who believes he or she has been sexually harassed can also take several steps to eliminate the problem. The first step should be a verbal request to the harasser and his or her boss that the unwanted overtures cease because the conduct is unwelcome. The next step is for the offended person to write a letter to the accused. This should be a polite, low-key letter written in three parts. The first part should be a detailed statement of facts as the writer sees them: "This is what I think happened . . ." (include all facts and relevant dates). In the second part of the letter, the writer should describe his or her feelings and what damage the writer thinks has been done (e.g., "Your action made me feel terrible"; "I'm deeply embarrassed . . ."). Here mention any perceived or actual cost and damages along with feelings of dismay, distrust, and so on. Next, the accuser should state what he or she would like to have happen next. For example, "I ask that our relationship from now on be on a purely professional basis." The accuser should, according to one expert, deliver the letter in person if possible, to ensure that it arrived and know when it arrived; if necessary, a witness should accompany the writer to be present when the letter is delivered. Finally, the individual should report the unwelcome conduct and unsuccessful efforts to get it to stop to the harasser's manager or to the Human Resource Director (or both) verbally and in writing. This will leave no doubt that the employer has notice of the unwelcome nature of the conduct and create an obligation on the part of the employer to investigate and take warranted corrective action. If the letter and appeals to the employer do not suffice, the accuser should turn to the local office of the EEOC to file the necessary claim.[30] The individual can also consult an attorney about suing the harasser for assault and battery, intentional infliction of emotional distress, and injunctive relief and to recover compensatory and punitive damages if the harassment is of a serious nature.

♦ SELECTED EARLY COURT DECISIONS REGARDING EQUAL EMPLOYMENT OPPORTUNITY

While Congress and the executive branch have enacted fair employment laws and issued orders and guidelines, the courts have had to interpret them. For example, when exactly is an employer's selection test unfairly discriminatory? To what extent can an employer practice "reverse discrimination" in an attempt to rectify past unfair practices against minorities or women? Some of the most important early court decisions regarding questions like these can be summarized as follows. (Recent court decisions reflecting among other things a shifting balance in the Supreme Court are discussed in the following section.)

Griggs v. *The Duke Power Company*

Griggs v. *The Duke Power Company* Case heard by the Supreme Court in which the plaintiff argued that his employer's requirement that coalhandlers be high school graduates was unfairly discriminatory. In finding for the plaintiff, the Court ruled that discrimination need not be overt to be illegal, that employment practices must be related to job performance, and that the burden of proof is on the employer to show that hiring standards are job related.

The *Griggs* case is a landmark one, since the Supreme Court used it to define what was meant by unfair discrimination. In this case, a suit was brought against the Duke Power Company on behalf of Willie Griggs, an applicant for a job as a coal handler. The company required its coal handlers to be high school graduates. Griggs claimed this requirement was illegally discriminatory because it wasn't related to success on the job (wasn't *valid*) and because it resulted in more blacks than whites being rejected for these jobs.

The company lost the case. The decision of the court was unanimous, and in his written opinion Chief Justice Burger laid out three crucial rulings affecting equal employment legislation. First, the court ruled that discrimination on the part of the employer *need not be overt;* in other words, the employer does not have to be shown to have intentionally discriminated against the employee or applicant—it need only be shown that discrimination did take place. Second, the court held that an employment practice (in this case requiring the high school degree) must be shown to be *job related* if it has an unequal (disparate) impact on members of a protected class. In the words of Justice Burger,

> The act proscribes not only overt discrimination but also practices that are fair in form, but discriminatory in operation. The touchstone is business necessity. If an employment practice which operates to exclude Negroes cannot be shown to be related to job performance the practice is prohibited.[31]

Chief Justice Burger's opinion also *clearly placed the burden of proof on the employer to show that the hiring practice is job related.* Thus, the *employer* must show that the employment practice (in this case, requiring a high school degree) is needed to perform the job satisfactorily if it has disparate impact on members of a protected class.

In summary, the Court's opinion in this case can be reduced to two principles:

1. Title VII prohibits practices having disproportionate adverse impact on different race, color, sex, religion, or national origin groups.
2. Business necessity or job relatedness is a defense for using such practices.

Albemarle Paper Company v. *Moody*

Albermarle Paper Company v. *Moody* Supreme Court case in which it was ruled that the validity of job tests must be documented and that employee performance standards must be unambiguous.

In the *Albemarle* case,[32] the Supreme Court addressed the issue of how to validate an employment practice like a selection test. In the *Griggs* case, the Supreme Court had decided a screening tool (like a test) had to be job related or *valid,* in that performance on the test must be related to performance on the job. The *Albemarle* case is important because here the court provided more details regarding how an employer should validate its screening tools—in other words, how it should prove that the test or other screening tools are related to or *predict* performance on the job. In the *Albemarle* case, for instance, the Court emphasized that if a test is to be used to screen candidates for a job, then the nature of that job—its specific duties and responsibilities—must first be carefully analyzed and documented. Similarly, the Court rules that the performance standards for employees on the job in question should be clear and unambiguous, so the employer could intelligently identify which employees were performing better than others.

In arriving at its decision, the Court also cited the EEOC guidelines concerning acceptable selection procedures and made these guidelines the "law of the land."[33] Specifically, the court's ruling had the effect of establishing the detailed EEOC (now federal) guidelines on validation as the procedures for validating employment practices.[34]

◆ RECENT EQUAL EMPLOYMENT OPPORTUNITY DECISIONS: A SHIFTING SUPREME COURT

Introduction

After more or less championing the cause of minorities and women in the workplace for three decades, a series of decisions by the Supreme Court in 1989 signaled a shift toward narrowing the scope of civil rights protection. Several factors (including the addition of several legal conservatives to the Supreme Court) helped to explain the change. However, whatever the factors were, the results, unless countered by new legislation by Congress (some of which is already pending), are quite dramatic. For example, in one case (*Wards Cove* v. *Atonio*) the court ruled, 5 to 4, that an employer does *not* have to prove that it has a legitimate reason for its employment practices, even if those practices are apparently discriminatory based on statistics. Instead the *plaintiff* (the applicant or employee claiming discrimination) has to prove that only illegal discrimination could have caused the disparity. The decisions in these cases are so fundamental to equal employment opportunity practice that we should review them in some detail.

Price Waterhouse v. *Hopkins*

The background of this case was as follows:[35] In 1982, the plaintiff, a woman, was proposed for partnership in the accounting firm she worked for. At the time, the firm had 662 partners, of whom 7 were women. In 1982, 88 candidates were proposed for partnership, but only 1—the employee who sued—was a woman. Of the 88, 47 became partners, 21 were rejected, and 20 were "held" for further consideration the following year. The employee who sued had brought $25 million in business with the State Department into the firm—but her promotion was held for further consideration. She responded by resigning and bringing suit under Title VII.

At the trial, it was found that both unlawful and lawful factors had contributed to her being passed over. She showed that her sex had been an unlawful factor in her denial of promotion, while the employer showed that "abrasiveness" had been a lawful factor, the trial court found. She won her case and won on appeal, but the U.S. Supreme Court eventually (on May 1, 1989) reversed the U.S. Court of Appeals for the District of Columbia Circuit. Said the Supreme Court: "we hold that when a plaintiff in a Title VII case proves that her gender played a motivating part in an employment decision, the defendant may avoid a finding of liability only by providing a preponderance of the evidence that it would have made the same decision even if it had not taken the plaintiff's gender into account."[36]

What does this mean in practice? It will probably make it easier for employers to defend their decisions, especially in cases like this one where there is direct evidence of discrimination or a "smoking gun" with respect to the challenged practice. It has been argued, for example, that in a case like this one of the strongest defenses employers can offer is consistency with past practice. For example, an employer can defend itself by showing that abrasiveness was an important motive in not promoting this woman, and further that the company's practice has been to also reject the candidacies of other, male, employees based on their abrasiveness. In other words, showing that "abrasive" people are routinely denied promotion regardless of race or sex might be a sufficient defense given the Supreme Court's decision in this case. Further showing that other members of the protected group—in this case women—were in fact promoted in the past would also help in a defense. In any event, the employer's hand is strengthened.

Wards Cove Packing Company v. *Atonio*

Wards Cove v. *Atonio* U.S. Supreme Court decision that makes it difficult to prove a case of unlawful discrimination against an employer.

The *Wards Cove* case is an extremely important one for the field of employment law. It is important because the Supreme Court's decision makes it much more difficult to prove a case of unlawful (disparate impact) discrimination against an employer. (**Disparate impact** means there is an unintentional disparity between the proportion of a protected group applying for a position and the proportion getting the job. In **disparate treatment** the disparity is allegedly intentional.)

disparate impact Means there is an unintentional disparity between the proportion of a protected group applying for a position and the proportion getting the job.

The Supreme Court acted in a 15-year-old case of alleged racial discrimination in Alaskan salmon canneries.[37] The facts of the case were as follows. Unskilled jobs in the canneries are held mostly by nonwhite Alaskans of Japanese, Filipino, Chinese, and Alaskan native descent while higher-paid noncannery jobs (carpenters, accountants, etc.) are mostly held by white employees who are recruited in the Seattle area. Cannery and noncannery workers at Wards Cove Packing Company are housed and fed separately, with the predominantly white noncannery workers assigned to more desirable, better insulated bunkhouses. The racial minorities at the canneries sued, claiming that the employment practices at the canneries discriminated and also had the effect of blocking them from getting the higher-paying jobs. Decisions at the lower courts were mixed; the U.S. Supreme Court's ruling came down rather clearly on the side of the employer.

disparate treatment Means there is an intentional disparity between the proportion of a protected group and the proportion getting the job.

To understand the importance of the Supreme Court's *Ward Cove* decision it is necessary to step back several years. In the Civil Rights Act of 1964 (as explained earlier) Congress stated that an employer cannot discriminate on the basis of race, color, religion, sex, or national origin. In *Griggs* v. *Duke Power Company* (also discussed earlier), the Supreme Court defined what was meant by unfair discrimination and *clearly* placed the burden of proof on the employer to show that the hiring practice in question is job related *when it has disparate impact on members of a protected class*. In the *Griggs* case the court also defined disparate impact, holding that it occurs when an employer has a policy or practice that appears to be neutral (such as the requirement in *Griggs* that all employees have a high school diploma), but that is, in practice, discriminatory.[38] After the *Griggs* case, proving that you were illegally discriminated against often just involved showing statistically that a biased situation existed. For example, the applicant or employee might simply have to show that one classification of jobs was primarily held by whites while a second less attractive classification of jobs was held by blacks. Having made his or her statistical case, the burden of proof then shifted to the employer to prove that its employment practices served a necessary business purpose—a defense which became known as the *business necessity defense*. Mounting a defense in such a case was often so expensive that many employers just didn't try.

Wards Cove basically changed all that. After *Wards Cove*, statistics alone no longer show unlawful discrimination under Title VII. Rather, there must also be a showing by the employee that any statistical imbalance that exists was *caused* by a particular challenged policy or practice of the employer *and the burden of proof is on the applicant/employee to prove that.* Under *Griggs*, once bias was shown by the employee, it was up to the employer to demonstrate that its practices were justified by reasonable business necessity.[39] Under *Wards Cove*, statistical imbalances themselves no longer demonstrate disparate impact: Instead the employee/applicant has to prove that the statistical imbalances were caused by an employment policy or practice of the employer.[40]

Patterson v. McLean Credit Union

The Supreme Court's decision in *Patterson* further weakens the rights of minorities and women under the country's civil rights legislation. According to the court's opinion the basic facts of the case were as follows. The employee testified that her supervisor periodically stared at her for several minutes at a time, gave her too many tasks, caused her to complain that she was under too much pressure, and gave her tasks that included sweeping and dusting which were not jobs given to white employees. On one occasion, she testified that her supervisor told her that blacks are known to work slower than whites. She also alleged that her supervisor criticized her in staff meetings while not similarly criticizing white employees.

The main issue in *Patterson* revolved around Section 1981 of the Civil Rights Act of 1866, which we discussed earlier in this chapter. Section 1981 (rather than the more recent Title VII) was used increasingly in the late 1970s and early 1980s to attack racial discrimination in employment. This was because the section permits the plaintiff to seek compensatory and punitive damages (in addition to back pay), covers all employers irrespective of the number of employees they have, and provides for a jury trial which is not available under Title VII. On the other hand, Title VII can produce an order stopping the discriminatory conduct and providing for back pay, but can't produce the other monetary damages that may have resulted from the claimed discrimination. Furthermore, Title VII applies only to employers with 15 or more employees. The Civil Rights Act of 1866 therefore gave employees who were discriminated against more clout in their suits against employers than would Title VII.

Patterson changed all that. In it the justices concluded that as reprehensible as was the treatment of the employee (if her allegations were true) she could not bring her action under Section 1981.

In this case, the Supreme Court restricted the use of Section 1981. It basically held that Section 1981 of the Civil Rights Act of 1866 could be used by minorities and women if their complaint involved either a refusal to make a contract or the impairment of the person's ability to enforce her established contract rights, neither of which, said the Court, applied in this case.[41]

Martin v. Wilks

The *Wilks* case began in 1974 and was decided by the U.S. Supreme Court on June 12, 1989. Briefly, the case began when the NAACP and seven black firefighters sued the city of Birmingham, Alabama, for practicing racial discrimination. A settlement was worked out in which the city agreed to promote one black for every white it promoted. This resulted in a consent decree in which the courts allowed both parties to the suit to settle their disagreement as they had agreed. A group of white firefighters subsequently sued the city to try and stop the decree from being implemented, basically saying that the decree would have the effect of discriminating against white firefighters. This case involves the issue of affirmative action, which, as we'll see later in this chapter, means efforts made by employers that are designed to eliminate the present effects of past discrimination.

Settlements like the one reached between the NAACP and the black firefighters under the supervision of the court meant, up until *Wilks*, that the employer was protected (under a court consent decree) from lawsuits by disgruntled white males. White males, for instance, couldn't sue employers who, when operating under such consent decrees, agreed to promote a certain proportion of blacks. One could reasonably assume that if employers no longer believed they were protected from such suits by white males, they might be much more reluctant to enter into such affirmative action settlements; it is exactly this type of protection that the *Wilks* decision strips from employers.

In this case the court, on a 5-to-4 vote, agreed with the Eleventh Circuit Court that one who is not a party to the original court proceedings that led to a consent decree, or who did not agree to the original decree, is not bound by the decree, and can sue on a claim of reverse discrimination. The *Wilks* decision is therefore a change in the prevailing law; up until the *Wilks* decision most federal appeals courts had held that consent decrees cannot be attacked after they take affect. It may have a chilling affect on the formation of such agreements in the future.[42]

◆ STATE AND LOCAL EQUAL EMPLOYMENT OPPORTUNITY LAWS

In addition to the federal laws, virtually all states and many local governments also prohibit employment discrimination.

In most cases the effect of the state and local laws is to further restrict employers regarding their treatment of job applicants and employees. In many cases, state equal employment opportunity laws cover employers (like those with fewer than 15 employees) who are not covered by federal legislation.[43] Similarly, some local governments extend the protection of age discrimination laws to young people as well, barring discrimination not only of those over 40, but those over 17 as well; here, for instance, it would be illegal to advertise for "mature" applicants since that might discourage some teenagers from applying. The point is that a wide range of actions by many employers that might be legal under federal laws are illegal under state and local laws.[44]

State and local equal employment opportunity agencies (often called Human Resources Commissions, Commissions on Human Relations, or Fair Employment Commissions) also play a role in the equal employment compliance process. When the EEOC receives a discrimination charge, it usually defers it for a limited time to the state and local agencies that have comparable jurisdiction. Then, if satisfactory remedies are not achieved, the charges are referred back to the EEOC for resolution.

◆ SUMMARY

Selected equal employment opportunity legislation, executive orders, and agency guidelines are summarized in Table 2.1.

TABLE 2.1 Summary of Important Equal Employment Opportunity Actions

ACTION	WHAT IT DOES
Title VII of 1964 Civil Rights Act, as amended	Bars discrimination because of race, color, religion, sex, or national origin; instituted EEOC
Executive orders	Prohibit employment discrimination by employers with federal contracts of more than $10,000 (and their subcontractors); establish office of federal compliance; require affirmative action programs
Federal agency guidelines	Indicate policy covering discrimination based on sex, national origin, and religion, as well as employee selection procedures; for example, require validation of tests
Supreme Court decisions: *Griggs* v. *Duke Power Co.*, *Albermarle* v. *Moody*	Ruled that job requirements must be related to job success; that discrimination need not be overt to be proved; that the burden of proof is on the employer to prove the qualification is valid
Equal Pay Act of 1963	Requires equal pay for men and women for performing similar work
Age Discrimination in Employment Act of 1967	Prohibits discriminating against a person 40–65 in any area of employment because of age
State and local laws	Often cover organizations too small to be covered by federal laws
Vocational Rehibilitation Act of 1973	Requires affirmative action to employ and promote qualified handicapped persons and prohibits discrimination against handicapped persons
Pregnancy Discrimination Act of 1978	Prohibits discrimination in employment against pregnant women, or related conditions
Vietnam Era Veterans' Readjustment Assistance Act of 1974	Requires affirmative action in employment for veterans of the Vietnam war era
Wards Cove v. *Atonio*, *Patterson* v. *McLean Credit Union*	These Supreme Court decisions made it more difficult to prove a case of unlawful discrimination against an employer
Martin v. *Wilks*	This case allows consent degrees to be attacked and may thus have a chilling affect on certain affirmative action programs
Americans with Disabilities Act of 1990	Strengthens the need for most employers to make reasonable accommodations for disabled employees at work; prohibits discrimination

♦ WHAT IS ADVERSE IMPACT?

adverse impact The overall impact of employer practices that result in significantly higher percentages of members of minorities and other protected groups being rejected for employment, placement, or promotion.

Up until the *Wards Cove* decision, a person who felt he or she was unintentionally discriminated against needed only to establish a prima facie case of discrimination: This meant showing that the employer's selection procedures had an **adverse impact** on a protected minority group. Adverse impact "refers to the total employment process that results in a significantly higher percentage of a protected group in the candidate population being rejected for employment, placement, or promotion."[45]

What did this mean? If a minority (protected group) applicant for the job feels he's been discriminated against, he needed only show that your selection procedures resulted in an adverse impact on his minority group. (For example, if 80% of the white applicants passed the test, but only 20% of the black applicants passed, a black applicant had a prima facie case proving adverse impact.) *Then, once the employee had proved his point, the burden of proof shifted to you, the employer.* It became *your* task to prove that your test, application blank, interview, or the like, was a valid predictor of performance on the job (and that it was applied fairly and equitably to both minorities and nonminorities).

Wards Cove changed all that. Before *Wards* a plaintiff might just show that all clerical jobs were filled by women, and all higher level jobs by men; then the employer had to prove its hiring practice (such as a test) was job-related. After *Wards* the plaintiff must also show that there were qualified women in the labor pool and that the specific employer practice caused these women not to be hired; the burden of proof has switched to the plaintiff.[46] As of 1990, Congress was considering the Civil Rights Bill of 1990, which would again shift the burden of proof to the employer. (It might also allow jury trials and compensatory and punitive damages.) It thus seems quite possible that employers may again soon have the burden of proof, and will need the tools to defend their positions; these are explained next.

♦ HOW CAN ADVERSE IMPACT BE PROVED?

Shifting as it does the burden of proof from the employer to employee makes it much harder for the plaintiff to make his or her case. Previously it was actually not too difficult for an applicant to show that one of your personnel procedures (such as a selection test) had an adverse impact on a protected group. Four basic approaches can be used.

disparate rejection rates One test for adverse impact, in which it can be demonstrated that there is a discrepancy between rates of rejection of members of a protected group and of others.

1. *Disparate Rejection Rates.* This involves comparing the rejection rates between a minority group and another group (usually the remaining nonminority applicants). For example, ask, "Is there a disparity between the percentage of blacks among those *applying* for a particular position and the percentage of blacks among those *hired* for the position?" Or, "Do proportionately more blacks than whites fail the written examination you give to all applicants?" If the answer to either question is yes, you and your firm could be faced with a lawsuit.

Federal agencies adopted a formula to determine when disparate rejection rates actually exist. Their guidelines state that "a selection rate for any racial, ethnic or sex group which is less than 4/5 or 80% of the rate for the group with the highest rate will generally be regarded as evidence of adverse impact, while a greater than 4/5 rate will generally not be regarded as evidence of adverse impact." For example, suppose 90% of male applicants are hired, but only 60% of female applicants are hired. Then, since 60% is less than four-fifths of 90%, adverse impact exists as far as these federal agencies are concerned.[47]

restricted policy Another test for adverse impact, involving demonstration that an employer's hiring practices exclude a protected group, whether intentionally or not.

2. *Restricted Policy.* The **restricted policy** approach means demonstrating that the employer has (intentionally *or* unintentionally) been using a hiring policy to exclude members of a protected group. Here the problem is usually obvious. For example, policies have been unearthed against hiring bartenders under six feet tall. Evidence of restricted policies like these (against women) is enough to prove adverse impact and open you to litigation.

3. *Population Comparisons.* This approach involves comparing the percentage of a firm's minority group employees and the percentage of that minority in the general population in the surrounding community.[48] This approach can be complicated to use in practice. For some jobs (such as manual laborer or secretary), it makes sense to compare the percentage of minority employees with the percentage of minorities in the surrounding community, since these employees will in fact be drawn from the surrounding community. However, for some jobs—like engineers—the surrounding community may not be the relevant labor market, since these people may have to be recruited nationwide. Determining whether an employer has enough black engineers might thus involve determining the number of black engineers available nationwide rather than just in the surrounding community. Defining the *relevant labor market* is thus a crucial task here.

4. *McDonnell-Douglas Test.* This approach involves showing that the applicant was qualified, but was rejected by the employer who continued seeking applicants for the position. It is used in situations of (intentional) disparate *treatment* rather than (unintentional) disparate *impact* (for which approaches 1–3 above are used). Here the rejected protected class candidate uses the following guidelines as set forth by the U.S. Supreme Court: (a) that he or she belongs to a protected class; (b) that he or she applied and was qualified for a job in which the employer was seeking applicants; (c) that, despite this qualification, he or she was rejected; and (d) that, after his or her rejection, the position remained open and the employer continued to seek applications from persons of complainant's qualifications. If all these conditions are met, then a *prima facie* case of disparate treatment is established. At that point the employer is required to articulate a legitimate non-discriminatory reason for its action and produce evidence but not prove that it acted on the basis of such a reason. If it meets this relatively easy standard, the plaintiff then has the burden of proving that the employer's articulated reason is merely a pretext for engaging in unlawful discrimination.

Bringing a Case of Discrimination: Summary

Assume that you turn down a member of a protected group for a job based on a test score (although it could have been some other employment practice like interview questions or application blank responses). Further assume that the person believes that he or she was discriminated against due to being in a protected class and decides to sue your company.

Before *Wards Cove*, all he or she basically had to do was show that your test had an *adverse impact* on members of his or her minority group, and there are four approaches that could be used to show that such adverse impact exists: disparate rejection rates, restricted policy, population comparison, and the McDonnell-Douglas test. Once the person had shown the existence of adverse impact to the satisfaction of the court, the burden of proof shifted to you, the employer, who then had to defend yourself against the charges of discrimination.

After *Wards Cove*, that is no longer the case. Now, to prove a prima facie case in a disparate-impact suit under Title VII, the plaintiff has to both prove adverse impact and also demonstrate that it is the application of a specific or particular employment practice in your company that has created the disparate impact under attack. However, note that even after both requirements are met by the plaintiff there is nothing in the law that says that your employment practice (like a test) is unusable.

In this regard, there are basically two defenses that the employer can use: the *bona fide occupational qualification* (*BFOQ*) defense and the *business necessity* defense. Either can be used to *justify* an employment practice that has been shown to have an adverse impact on the members of some minority group.[49]

♦ BONA FIDE OCCUPATIONAL QUALIFICATION

Bona fide occupational qualification (BFOQ) Requirement that an employee be of a certain religion, sex, or national origin where that is reasonably necessary to the organization's normal operation. Specified by the 1964 Civil Rights Act.

One approach your employer can use to defend itself against charges of discrimination is to claim that the employment practice is a **bona fide occupational qualification** for performing the job. Specifically, Title VII provides that "it should not be an unlawful employment practice for an employer to hire an employee . . . on the basis of religion, sex, or national origin *in those certain instances where religion, sex, or national origin is a bona fide occupational qualification* reasonably necessary to the normal operation of that particular business or enterprise." BFOQ is not so much a defense as a statutory exception to the equal employment opportunity laws. It is an exception that is written into the laws and that allows employers to discriminate in certain very specific instances. The BFOQ exception is usually interpreted narrowly by the courts. As a practical matter, it is used primarily (but not exclusively) as a defense against charges of intentional discrimination based on age. BFOQ is essentially a defense to a disparate treatment case based upon direct evidence of intentional discrimination and not to disparate (unintentional) impact discrimination.

Age as a BFOQ

The Age Discrimination in Employment Act (ADEA) does permit disparate treatment in those instances where age is a BFOQ. For example, age is a BFOQ where federal requirements impose a compulsory age limit, such as where the Federal Aviation Agency sets a ceiling of age 64 for pilots. Actors required for youthful or elderly roles or persons used to advertise or promote the sales of products designed for youthful or elderly consumers are other instances where age may be a BFOQ. As another example, a bus line's maximum-age hiring policy for bus drivers has been held to be a BFOQ by the courts. The court said that the essence of the business was safe transportation of passengers and that as such the employer could strive to employ the most qualified persons available.[50] Yet recent Supreme Court decisions such as *Western Airlines, Inc.* v. *Criswell* seem to be narrowing BFOQ exceptions under ADEA. In this case the Court held that the airline could not impose a mandatory retirement age (of 60) for flight engineers, even though they could for pilots. Similarly, in *Johnson* v. *Mayor and City Council of Baltimore*, the Court held that the city of Baltimore could not require its firefighters to retire at age 55.

In fact, you must keep in mind that there has been a dramatic increase in the number of employment-related age discrimination complaints filed with state and federal agencies over the past few years: The number of complaints rose from about 5,000 in 1979 to over 27,000 in 1987.[51] There are several reasons for this, including increasing numbers of older workers, increasingly militant older workers, corporate downsizings, and the prospect of collecting double damages (as plaintiffs can under the Age Discrimination in Employment Act).[52]

Employer defenses against such ADEA claims usually fall into one of two categories: BFOQ or FOA (Factors Other than Age). Employers using the BFOQ defense admit their personnel decisions were based on age but seek to justify them by showing that the decisions were reasonably necessary to normal business operations. (Here, for example, an airline might insist that a pilot maximum-age requirement is necessary for the safe transportation of its passengers.) An employer who raises the FOA defense generally argues that its actions were "reasonable" based on some business factor other than age, such as the terminated person's poor performance.

Handicap as a BFOQ

Under the Vocational Rehabilitation Act of 1973, most federal contractors (and their subcontractors) must take affirmative action to employ and promote qualified handicapped persons. However, this does not mean that the employer must endanger others by placing a handicapped employee in a position where the handicap would pose a threat. Therefore, in certain situations, a handicap may be a bona fide occupational qualification on a job.[53]

Religion as a BFOQ

Religion may be a BFOQ in the case of religious organizations or societies that require employees to share their particular religion. For example, religion may be a BFOQ when hiring persons to teach in a denominational school. Similarly, practices such as Saturday work rules that adversely affect certain religious groups are excusable if the employer "is unable to reasonably accommodate . . . without undue hardship."[54] In this and in all cases, however, the BFOQ defense is construed very narrowly by the courts.

Sex as a BFOQ

It is difficult today to claim that sex is a BFOQ for most jobs for which you are recruiting. For example, sex is not accepted as a BFOQ for positions just because they require overtime or the lifting of heavy objects. Sex is not a BFOQ for parole and probation officers, nor, of course, is sex a BFOQ for flight attendants.[55] Courts have said that it is illegal to apply a "no marriage" rule to stewardesses (and not to male employees) even though one airline claimed the rule was justified as a BFOQ due to customer preference. On the other hand, sex may be a BFOQ for positions requiring specific physical characteristics necessarily possessed by one sex. These include positions like actor, model, and restroom attendant.

National Origin as a BFOQ

In some cases a person's country of national origin may be a BFOQ. For example, in certain instances an employer who is running the Chinese pavilion at a fair might claim that Chinese heritage is a BFOQ for persons to be selected as pavilion employees to deal with the public.

♦ BUSINESS NECESSITY

business necessity Justification for an otherwise discriminatory employment practice, provided there is an overriding legitimate business purpose.

The **business necessity** defense basically involves showing that there is an overriding business purpose for the discriminatory practice and that the practice is therefore acceptable.

It's not easy proving that a practice is required for "business necessity."[56] The Supreme Court has made it clear that business necessity does not encompass such matters as inconvenience, annoyance, or expense to the employer. The Second Circuit Court of Appeals held that business necessity means an "irresistible demand" and that to be retained the practice "must not only directly foster safety and efficiency" but also be essential to these goals.[57] Similarly, another court held that

> the test is whether there exists an overriding legitimate business purpose such that the practice is necessary to the safe and efficient operation of a business; thus, the business purpose must be sufficiently compelling to override any racial impact; and the challenged practice must effectively carry out the business purpose it is alleged to serve.[58]

Thus, to repeat, it is not easy to prove that a practice is required for business necessity. For example, an employer cannot generally discharge employees whose wages have been garnished merely because garnishment creates an inconvenience for the employer. On the other hand, the business necessity defense has been used successfully by many employers. Thus, in *Spurlock* v. *United Airlines*, a minority candidate sued United Airlines, stating that its requirements that pilot candidates have 500 flight hours and college degrees were unfairly discriminatory. The court agreed that these requirements did have an adverse impact on members of the person's minority group. However, the court held that in light of the cost of the training program and the tremendous human and economic risks involved in hiring unqualified candidates, the selection standards were required by business necessity and were job related.[59] In general, when a job requires a small amount of skill and training, the courts scrutinize closely any preemployment standards or criteria that discriminate against minorities. The employer in such instances has a heavy burden to demonstrate that the practices are job related. However, there is a correspondingly lighter burden where the job requires a high degree of skill and where the economic and human risks in hiring an unqualified applicant are great.[60]

validity A test's validity is the accuracy with which a test, interview, or other hiring procedure measures what it is supposed to measure, or otherwise fulfills its stated function.

Attempts by employers to show that their selection tests (or other employment practices) are valid represent one example of the business-necessity defense. Here the employer is required to show that the test or other practice is job related—in other words, that it is a valid predictor of performance on the job. Where such **validity** can be established, the courts have often supported the use of the test or other employment practice as a business necessity. Used in this context, the word validity basically means the degree to which the test or other employment practice is related to or predicts performance on the job; validation will be explained in more detail in Chapter 5.

♦ OTHER CONSIDERATIONS IN DISCRIMINATORY PRACTICE DEFENSES

There are three other things to stress in regard to defending yourself against charges of discrimination. First, *good intentions* on your part are no excuse. As the Supreme Court held in the *Griggs* case,

> Good intent or absence of discriminatory intent does not redeem procedures or testing mechanisms that operate as built-in headwinds for minority groups and are unrelated to measuring job capability.[61]

Second, employers cannot count on hiding behind collective bargaining agreements (for instance, by claiming that the discriminatory practice is required by a union agreement). Courts have often held that equal employment opportunity laws take precedence over the rights embodied in a labor contract. However, in a related matter, the U.S. Supreme Court, in its *Stotts* decision, did recently hold that a court cannot require retention of black employees hired under a consent decree in preference to white employees with greater seniority who were protected by a bona fide seniority system. As of now, there is disagreement regarding whether this decision also extends to hiring, recruitment, promotions, transfers, and layoffs not governed by seniority systems.[62]

Finally, remember that while a defense is often the most sensible response to charges of discrimination, it is not the only response. When confronted with the fact that one or more of your personnel practices is discriminatory, you can react by agreeing to eliminate the illegal practice and (where required) by compensating the people you discriminated against.

ILLUSTRATIVE DISCRIMINATORY EMPLOYMENT PRACTICES

♦ A NOTE ON WHAT YOU CAN AND CANNOT DO

Before proceeding it is important to clarify what federal fair employment laws allow (and do not allow) you to say and do. Federal laws like Title VII usually do *not* expressly ban preemployment questions about an applicant's race, color, religion, sex, or national origin. In other words, "with the exception of personnel policies calling for outright discrimination against the members of some protected group, it is not really the intrinsic nature of an employer's personnel policies or practices that the courts object to. Instead, it is the *result* of applying a policy or practice in a particular way or in a particular context that leads to an *adverse impact* on some protected group."[63] For example, it is not illegal to ask a job candidate about her marital status (although at first glance such a question might seem discriminatory). In reality, you can *ask* such a question as long as you can show either that you do not discriminate or that the practice can be defended as a BFOQ or business necessity.

But, in practice, there are two good reasons why most employers try to avoid using such questionable practices. First, while federal law may not bar asking such questions, recall that many state and local laws do. Second, the EEOC has said that it will *disapprove* of such practices (as asking women their marital status or applicants their age). Therefore, just asking such questions may raise a red flag that draws the attention of the EEOC and other regulatory agencies. Employers who use such practices will thus increase their chances of having to defend themselves against charges of discriminatory employment practices.

In summary, inquiries and practices like those summarized on the next few pages are not illegal per se. They are "problem questions" that *may* be potentially illegal. They are problem questions because they tend to identify an applicant as a member of a protected group or to adversely affect members of a protected group. However, they become *illegal* questions *if it can be shown that the questions as used do screen out a greater proportion of a protected group's applicants and that the employer cannot prove the practice is required as a BFOQ or a business necessity.* Thus, if you are sure that your hiring practices do not adversely affect the members of a protected group— that, for example, you hire the same proportion of female applicants as male—then you may choose to continue asking such problem questions. Similarly, if you are convinced that an employment practice (like a question about age) is required as a BFOQ or business necessity, you may choose to continue using it. However, these questions will draw the attention of regulatory agencies. Therefore, most employers do attempt to eliminate them, or at least to delay asking them until after the applicant has been hired, when the questions might be useful for, say, insurance purposes.

We can now turn to a listing of some of the specific discriminatory personnel management practices you should avoid.[64]

PERSONNEL MANAGEMENT:
ON THE FRONT LINE

One of the first problems Jennifer faced at Carter Cleaning Centers concerned the inadequacies of the firm's current personnel management practices and procedures.

One thing that particularly concerned her was the lack of attention that had been given to equal employment matters. Virtually all hiring was handled independently by each store manager, and the managers themselves had received no training regarding such fundamental matters as the types of questions that should not be asked of job applicants. It was therefore not unusual—in fact was even routine—for female applicants to be asked questions such as "Who's going to take care of your children while you are at work?" and for minority applicants to be asked questions about arrest records and credit histories. Nonminority applicants—three store managers were white males, by the way, and three were white females—were not asked questions such as these, Jennifer discerned from her interviews with the managers.

Based on discussions with her father, Jennifer deduced that part of the reason for the laid-back attitude toward equal employment stemmed from (1) her father's lack of sophistication regarding the legal requirements and (2) the practical fact that, as Jack put it, "Virtually all our workers are women or minority members anyway, so no one can really come in here and accuse us of being discriminatory, can they?"

Jennifer decided to mull that question over, but before she could, she was faced with two serious equal rights problems. Two women in one of her stores privately confided to her that their manager was making unwelcome sexual advances toward them, and one claimed he had threatened to fire her unless she "socialized" with him after hours. And on a fact-finding trip to another store, an elderly gentleman—he was 73 years old—complained of the fact that although he had almost 50 years' experience in the business, he was being paid less than people half his age who were doing the very same job. Her review of the stores resulted in the following questions:

1. Is it true, as Jack Carter claims, that "we can't be accused of being discriminatory because we hire mostly women and minorities anyway?"

2. How should Jennifer and her company address the sexual harassment charges and problems?

3. How should she and her company address the possible problems of age discrimination?

4. Given the fact that each of their stores has only a handful of employees, is her company in fact covered by equal rights legislation?

5. And finally, aside from the specific problems, what other personnel management matters (application forms, training, etc.) have to be reviewed given the need to bring them into compliance with equal rights laws?

♦ RECRUITMENT

Word of Mouth

You cannot rely upon word-of-mouth dissemination of information about work opportunities where your work force is all or substantially all white or all members of some other class such as all female, all Hispanic, etc.

Misleading Information

It is unlawful to give false or misleading information to members of any group or to fail or refuse to advise them of work opportunities and the procedures for obtaining them.

Help Wanted Ads

"Help wanted—male" and "Help wanted—female" advertising classifications are violations of laws forbidding sex discrimination in employment unless sex is a bona fide occupational qualification for the job advertised.[65] Also, you cannot advertise in any way that suggests that applicants are being discriminated against because of their age. For example, you cannot advertise for a "young" man or woman.

◆ SELECTION STANDARDS

Educational Requirements

An educational requirement may be held illegal where (1) it can be shown that minority groups are less likely to possess the educational qualifications (such as a high school degree), and (2) such qualifications are also not job related. For example, in the *Griggs* v. *Duke Power* case, a high school diploma was found *both* unnecessary for job performance *and* discriminatory against blacks. In other cases, a public school board was found to have unlawfully discriminated against blacks by requiring a master's degree (and specific scores on Graduate Record Examinations) *that had not been validated* as predictors of job performance. A requirement for a college degree for management trainee positions was found to be unfairly discriminatory against blacks in another case.

Tests

According to former Chief Justice Burger,

> Nothing in the [Title VII] act precludes the use of testing or measuring procedures; obviously they are useful. What Congress has forbidden is giving these devices and mechanisms controlling force *unless they are demonstrating a reasonable measure of job performance.*

Tests which disproportionately screen out minorities or women *and* which are not job related are deemed unlawful by the courts. But remember that the fact that a test (or other selection standard) that screens out a disproportionate number of minorities or women is not *by itself* sufficient to prove that the test *unfairly* discriminates. To do this, it must also be shown that the tests (or other screening devices) are not job related.

Preference to Relatives

You cannot give preference to relatives of your current employees with respect to employment opportunities if your current employees are substantially nonminority.

Height, Weight, and Physical Characteristics

Physical characteristics (such as height and weight) that can have an adverse impact upon certain ethnic groups or women are unlawful unless they can be shown to be job related. For example, one company required that a person weigh a minimum of 150 pounds for positions on its assembly lines. This requirement was held to discriminate unfairly against women.

Arrest Records

You cannot ask about or use a person's arrest record to disqualify him or her automatically for a position since there is always a presumption of innocence until proven guilty. In addition, (1) arrest records in general have not been shown valid for predicting job performance and (2) a higher proportion of blacks than whites have been arrested. Thus, disqualifying applicants based on arrest records automatically has an adverse impact on blacks. Therefore, unless security clearance is necessary, you cannot ask an applicant whether he or she has ever been arrested or spent time in jail. However, you can ask about *conviction* records and then determine on a case-by-case basis if the facts concerning any conviction justify refusal to employ an applicant in a particular position.

Discharge Due to Garnishment

A disproportionately higher number of minorities are subjected to garnishment procedures. (Here creditors make a claim to a portion of the person's wages.) Therefore, firing a minority whose salary has been garnished is illegal, unless you can show some overriding "business necessity."

Other Hiring Standards

A number of other selection standards or tools have been held unlawful because some or all of their elements adversely affect minorities *and* were not shown to be job related. These include personal history interviews, background investigations, medical exams, psychological exams, and polygraph tests. Again, you *can* use these devices, but you *must* prove that what they test is job related.

♦ SAMPLE DISCRIMINATORY PROMOTION, TRANSFER, AND LAYOFF PRACTICES

Fair employment laws protect not just job *applicants* but an employer's *currente employees* as well.[66] The equal pay act requires that equal wages be paid for substantially similar work performed by men and women. Similarly, Title VII prohibits discrimination in compensation regardless of race, national origin, religion, or sex. With respect to promotions, terminations, and disciplinary actions, standards for determining when a person will be promoted, terminated, or disciplined should also be the same for all employees. Therefore, any employment practices regarding pay, promotion, termination, discipline, or benefits which (1) are applied differently to different classes of persons, (2) have the effect of adversely affecting members of a protected group, and (3) cannot be shown to be required as a BFOQ or business necessity may be held to be illegally discriminatory.

Personal Appearance Regulations and Title VII

Employees have filed suits against employers' dress and appearance codes under Title VII, usually claiming sex discrimination but sometimes claiming racial discrimination as well. A sampling of what has been ruled to be acceptable or unacceptable personal appearance codes would thus be worthwhile.[67]

Dress. In general, employers do not violate Title VII's ban on sex bias by requiring all employees to dress conservatively. For example, a supervisor's suggestion that a female attorney tone down her attire was permissible where the firm consistently sought to maintain a conservative dress style and where men were also counseled on the conservativeness of their dress.

Grooming. Minor gender-related differences in personal appearance are also usually deemed lawful where they reflect customary codes of grooming. For example, short hair requirements for men but not for women probably wouldn't constitute sex bias under Title VII, nor would letting women but not men wear earrings.

Hair. Hair styles, beards, sideburns, and mustaches have also come in for scrutiny by the courts: Here again the courts usually rule in favor of the employers. For example, employer rules against facial hair do not constitute sex discrimination because they discriminate only between clean-shaven and bearded men, a type of discrimination not qualified as sex bias under Title VII. In many cases courts have also rejected arguments that grooming regulations such as prohibitions against cornrow hair styles are racially biased in that they infringe on black employees' expression of cultural identification. In one case involving American Airlines, for example, the court decided that an all-braided hair style is a characteristic easily changed and not worn exclusively or even predominently by black people.

Uniforms. When it comes to discriminatory uniforms and suggestive attire, however, courts have frequently sided with the employee. For example, a bank's dress policy requiring female employees to wear prescribed uniforms consisting of five basic color coordinated items but requiring male employees only to wear "appropriate business attire" is an example of a discriminatory uniform. Similarly, requiring female salesclerks to wear smocks, while male clerks were allowed to wear business attire, or hospitals requiring female technologists to wear white or pastel colored uniforms while male technologists could wear white lab coats over street clothing was ruled discriminatory. And requiring female employees (such as waitresses) to wear sexually suggestive attire as a condition of employment also has been ruled as violating Title VII in many cases.[68]

THE EEOC ENFORCEMENT PROCESS

♦ PROCESSING A CHARGE

There are several factors involved in filing and processing an employment discrimination charge with the EEOC.[69] The charge itself must generally be filed within 180 days after the alleged unlawful practice took place. This charge must be filed in writing and under oath (or on behalf of) either the person claiming to be aggrieved or by a member of the EEOC who has reasonable cause to believe that a violation occurred. In practice, the Supreme Court has approved the EEOC's practice of accepting a charge, orally referring it to the state or local agency on behalf of the charging party, and then, if the matter has not been cleared up, beginning to process it upon the expiration of a deferral period without requiring the filing of a new charge.[70] In practice, then, a person's charge to the EEOC is often first deferred to the relevant state or local regulatory agency; if the latter waives jurisdiction or cannot obtain a satisfactory solution to the charge, it is referred back to the EEOC. (Note that if the EEOC does not sue on behalf of the charging party it must issue that person a Notice of Right to Sue irrespective of whether it finds "cause" or "no cause" to believe that unlawful discrimination occurred. The charging party must file a lawsuit in federal district court within 90 days of receipt of that Notice of Right to Sue.)

After a charge is filed (or the state or local deferral period is ended), the EEOC must serve notice of the charge on the employer within 10 days. The EEOC then investigates the charge to determine if there is reasonable cause to believe it is true; it is expected to make this determination within 120 days. If no reasonable cause is found, the EEOC must dismiss the charge, in which case the person who filed the charge has 90 days to file a suit on his or her own behalf. If reasonable cause for the charge *is* found, the EEOC must attempt to conciliate. If this conciliation is not satisfactory, it may bring a civil suit in a federal district court, or issue a Notice of Right to Sue to the person who filed the charge. In Figure 2.2 are summarized some important questions an employer should ask once receiving notice from the EEOC that a bias complaint has been filed. Note that the questions include, for example, "To what protected group does the worker belong?" and "Is the employee protected by more than one statute?"[71]

◆ CONCILIATION PROCEEDINGS

Under Title VII, the EEOC is allowed 30 days to work out a conciliation agreement between the parties before a suit is brought. The EEOC conciliator first meets with the employee to determine what remedy would be satisfactory and then tries to persuade the employer to accept the remedy. If accepted by both parties, a conciliation agreement is reached, signed, and submitted to the EEOC for approval. Finally (if the EEOC is unable to obtain an acceptable conciliation agreement within 30 days after a finding of reasonable cause to believe that discrimination occurred), it may sue the employer in a federal district court.

◆ HOW TO RESPOND TO EMPLOYMENT DISCRIMINATION CHARGES

There are several things to keep in mind when confronted by a charge of illegal employment discrimination; some of the more important can be summarized as follows:[72]

Investigating the Charge

First, remember that the EEOC investigators are not judges and are not empowered to act as courts; they cannot make findings of discrimination on their own, but can merely make recommendations. If the EEOC eventually

FIGURE 2.2
Questions to Ask When an Employer Receives Notice That a Bias Complaint Has Been Filed
Source: Gail J. Wright, assistant counsel for the NAACP's Legal Defense and Education Fund, quoted in Bureau of National Affairs, *Fair Employment Practices*, January 7, 1988, p. 3.

1. To what protected group does the worker belong? Is the employee protected by more than one statute?

2. Would the action complained of have been taken if the worker were not a member of a protected group? Is the action having an adverse impact on other members of a protected group?

3. Is the employee's charge of discrimination subject to attack because it was not filed on time, according to the applicable law?

4. In the case of a sexual harassment claim, are there offensive posters or calendars on display in the workplace?

5. Do the employees' personnel records demonstrate discriminatory treatment in the form of unjustified warnings and reprimands?

6. In reviewing the nature of the action complained of, can it be characterized as disparate impact or disparate treatment? Can it be characterized as an individual complaint or a class action?

7. What are the company's probable defenses and rebuttal?

8. Who are the decision makers involved in the employment action, and what would be their effectiveness as potential witnesses?

9. What are the prospects for a settlement of the case that would be satisfactory to all involved?

determines that an employer may be in violation of a law, its only recourse is to file a suit or issue a Notice of Right to Sue to the person who filed the charge.

As far as documents are concerned, it may often be in your employer's best interests to cooperate (or appear cooperative), but remember that the EEOC can only ask for, not demand, the submission of documents.[73] The EEOC can *ask* employers to submit documents and *ask* for the appearance and testimony of witnesses under oath. However, it cannot compel employers to do so. If your employer feels that the EEOC has overstepped its authority and refuses to cooperate, the commission's only recourse is to obtain a court subpoena.

It may also be in your employer's best interest to submit to the EEOC a position statement based on your own investigation of the matter. A recent congressional investigation found, at least in the Chicago office of the EEOC, that EEOC investigators were writing up cases based solely on the position statement filed by the employer because the EEOC is under such internal pressure to resolve cases. In other words, at least in Chicago, Congress found that EEOC investigators were resolving cases based only on the employer's position paper. According to one management attorney, your position statements should contain words to the effect that "We understand that a charge of discrimination has been filed against this establishment and this statement is to inform the agency that the company has a policy against discrimination and would not discriminate in the manner charged in the complaint." The statement should be supported by some statistical analysis of the work force, copies of any documents that support your employer's position, or an explanation of any legitimate business justification for the employment decision that is the subject of the complaint.[74]

If a predetermination settlement isn't reached, the EEOC will make a complete investigation of the charge, and here there are three major principles your employer should follow. First, your employer should ensure that there is information in the EEOC's file demonstrating *lack of merit* of the charge; often, the best way to do that is by *not* answering the EEOC's questionnaire, but by providing a detailed statement describing your defense in its best and most persuasive light.

Second, your employer *should* limit the information supplied as narrowly as possible to only those issues raised in the charge itself. For example, if the charge only alleges sex discrimination, do not respond unwittingly to the EEOC's request for a breakdown of your employees by age and sex. Finally, seek *as much information* as you can about the charging party's claim in order to ensure you understand it and its ramifications.

The Fact-Finding Conference

You should also be aware of the problems that can arise in the EEOC's "fact-finding conferences." According to the Commission, these conferences are supposed to be informal meetings held early in the investigatory process aimed at defining issues and determining if there's a basis for negotiation. According to one expert, though, the EEOC's emphasis here is often on settlement. Its investigators therefore use the conferences to find weak spots in each party's respective position so that they can use this information as leverage to push for a settlement.

If your employer wants a settlement, the fact-finding conference can be a good forum at which to negotiate, but there are three big problems to watch out for. First, the only official record maintained is the notes taken by the EEOC investigator, and the parties cannot have access to them to rectify mistakes or clarify facts. Second, while your employer can bring an attorney, the EEOC often "seems to go out of its way to tell employers that an attorney's presence is unnecessary."[75] Finally, these conferences are

COMPUTER APPLICATION IN EQUAL

EMPLOYMENT: UTILIZATION ANALYSIS

Companies and universities that have grants or contracts with the federal government periodically are required to complete utilization analyses, which are then submitted to the Department of Labor's Office of Contract Compliance Programs (OFCCP). The basis of comparison may be the most recently completed census or a valid industry survey. The comparison is made between (1) company employees in various EEO categories or subgroups (women, blacks, etc.) and (2) the number of people in the recruitment area who state that they have comparable skills in response to census or employment service requests for information.

A report format, called the Availability Analysis, accepted by OFCCP allows the employer to assign appropriate weights to the following eight factors which are incorporated into the report: (1) general population, but including only those subgroups who are seeking employment; (2) % unemployment; (3) % workforce; (4) requisite skills available in the immediate area; (5) requisite skills available in the recruitment area; (6) feeder jobs from which internal employees may be promoted or transferred; (7) training institutions in recruitment area; and (8) internal training available. In other words, this is the employer's opportunity to show the effect on hiring of certain ingredients in the internal and external environments for that specific company. Thus, if there is no adequate training facility for crafts in the area, that factor may have no value (zero) in addressing recruitment needs for Category 5: Skilled Crafts. On the other hand, the company might hire plumbers' helpers and, over a period of three years, train those helpers both on-the-job and in the classroom so that the employees can sit for the licensing exam. In this case, internal training would account for a significant portion of individuals placed into the position of plumber. The company could examine the percentage hired versus the percentage promoted over the last few years to appropriately balance the weights. The usual goal for any given category is for the labor force of the company to approximate the general population's availability of that skill level.

Spreadsheets can easily accommodate these comparisons through user-friendly formulas which calculate weights, percentages, sums, and complicated "if–then" statements. Employees are roughly divided into approximately seven categories which differentiate between sales, clerical, crafts, technical, supervisors, professionals, and executives. These main groups are then subdivided by salary ranges. Within each group, the employees are counted according to race and sex. When a spreadsheet has been established, the count in each category (black male, black female, etc.) may be manually entered along with the number of vacancies that were filled the previous year. All of the other data are then completed by the spreadsheet as your formulas pull from the few entries you have made.

The population of the labor area usually changes only with the census. The percentage of unemployment, which is calculated by the state employment service, changes monthly. The weight that you assign each factor should change infrequently, unless there has been a significant change in one of the factors, such as the unemployment rate. After the formulas have been established and the raw data entered, the spreadsheet will compare availability with actual current utilization. If underutilization exists, the spreadsheet is able to calculate the percentage of underutilization, how many hires/transfers are needed to overcome the underutilization, and how many need to be hired in the current year. The OFCCP report must be calculated for the major minorities (such as black and Hispanic, or whatever protected groups represent more than 10%–12% of the labor force in your immediate geographical area) and females.

The reason that this information should be built into a spreadsheet is so that goals for the given year may be available to recruiters and hiring supervisors at the beginning of the measured year. While affirmative action does not require the company to favor protected groups (assuming there is no court order to require partiality), significant underutilization in a particular group strongly suggests that the recruitment techniques need to be examined.

often arranged soon after a charge is filed, before your employer has been fully informed of the charges and facts of the case.

An employer should thoroughly prepare witnesses who are going to testify at a fact-finding conference, especially supervisors and managers, because their statements can be considered admissions against the employer's interest. Therefore, before appearing, they need to be aware of the legal significance of the facts they will present and the possible claims that may be made by the charging party and other witnesses.

◆ THE EEOC'S DETERMINATION AND THE ATTEMPTED CONCILIATION

If the fact-finding conference does not solve the matter, the EEOC's investigator will determine whether there is reason to believe ("cause") or not to believe ("no cause") that discrimination may have taken place, and there are several things to keep in mind here. First, the investigator's recommendation is often the determining factor in whether the EEOC finds cause, so it is usually best to be courteous and cooperative (within limits). Second, if there is a finding of "cause," review the finding very carefully and make certain that any inaccuracies are pointed out in a letter to the EEOC. Use this letter to again try to convince the EEOC, the charging party, and the charging party's attorney that the charge is without merit, in spite of the finding. Finally, keep in mind that even with a "no cause" finding, the charging party will still be issued a "right to sue letter" by the EEOC and will then be allowed 90 days (from receipt of the letter) to bring a private lawsuit.

If the EEOC issues a "cause" finding, it will ask you to "conciliate." However, some experts argue against conciliating at this point, for several reasons. First, the EEOC often views conciliation not as a compromise but as complete relief to the charging party. Second, "if you have properly investigated and evaluated the case previously, there may be no real advantage in settling at this stage. It is more than likely (based on the statistics) that no suit will be filed by the EEOC."[76] Furthermore, even if a lawsuit is later filed by either the EEOC or the charging party, the employer can consider settling after receiving the complaint.

◆ AVOIDING DISCRIMINATION LAWSUITS

Employment discrimination claims constitute the largest number of civil suits filed annually in federal courts, with about 112,000 job bias charges filed with the EEOC alone recently. As a result, some companies are setting up internal dispute resolution procedures similar to the following one at Aetna Life and Casualty Company:

Step 1.

First the employee discusses the problem with a supervisor, who may consult other members of the management team who might have handled similar problems.

Step 2.

Here the employee may contact a divisional personnel consultant for a case review if he or she is dissatisfied with the results of the first step. The employee is then informed and advised on plausible alternatives.

Step 3.

If the employee believes that company policy is not being followed, he or she may then request a corporate level review of the case and a corporate consultant will review the case with management. The employee is then notified of the decision in writing.

Step 4.

Finally, a senior management review committee may be asked to review the case. The committee itself is comprised of the senior vice-president of the Employees' Division as well as the vice-presidents of corporate personnel and corporate public involvement.[77]

◆ INTERNATIONAL: FOREIGN ENFORCEMENT OF CIVIL RIGHTS

The question of whether American employers operating overseas have to conform with equal employment laws with regard to their overseas American work force is currently a matter of some debate.[79] In at least one instance, the U.S. Court of Appeals of New Orleans rejected extra territorial application of Title VII. However, the EEOC is seeking to overturn that ruling and has adopted a policy statement on the application of Title VII to American firms overseas, their overseas subsidiaries, and foreign firms in September 1988. In March 1989 the EEOC also outlined its interpretation of the application of the Age Discrimination in Employment Act and the Equal Pay Act to overseas employers. The basic position of the EEOC is that it will closely examine charges of job bias against U.S. companies operating abroad and that "If an American owned or controlled business expects to find any comfort for its human resources decisions in dealing with American employees abroad, it is on safer ground by starting with the assumption that compliance with U.S. Civil Rights laws remains mandatory even off the shore of this country."

All Canadian jurisdictions have also enacted human rights legislation.[78] All the statutes prohibit discrimination on the basis of race, national origin, color, religion or creed, sex, marital status, and age. The age groups protected vary among jurisdictions, with the most common being between the ages of 40 or 45 and 65. Discrimination due to physical disability is proscribed in seven jurisdictions. Similarly, all Canadian jurisdictions have laws that require equal pay for equal work within the same establishment. These provisions have been incorporated either in human rights legislation (federal jurisdiction, Alberta, British Columbia, New Brunswick, Newfoundland, Northwest Territories, Prince Edward Island, and Quebec) or in labor standards legislation (Manitoba, Nova Scotia, Ontario, Saskatchewan, and Yukon Territory). These statutes apply to employers, employment agencies, and trade unions. Discrimination is prohibited with respect to advertising and terms and conditions of employment including promotion, transfer, and training. As in the United States and Britain, legal discrimination under the Canadian Human Rights Act (as well as numerous decisions by boards of inquiry in several provinces) is determined not by the employer's intentions but by the results of the employer's actions.

Enforcement of equal employment legislation in all Canadian jurisdictions involves investigation based on employee complaints (although Human Rights Commissions may sometimes file a complaint or commence an investigation themselves). All the acts provide for the settlement of complaints, if possible, by conciliation and persuasion and for an initial, informal investigation into a complaint by an officer who is directed to effect the settlement. If conciliation fails, a board of inquiry is usually appointed; it may issue orders for compliance, compensation, and so on. This order may be appealed to the Supreme Court of the province on questions of law, fact, or both. The federal jurisdiction allows an appeal by either the complainant or defendant to a review tribunal, if the original tribunal has fewer than three members. In practice, the emphasis has been on obtaining a satisfactory settlement rather than determining legal guilt.

AFFIRMATIVE ACTION PROGRAMS

◆ EQUAL EMPLOYMENT OPPORTUNITY VERSUS AFFIRMATIVE ACTION

Equal employment opportunity aims to ensure that anyone regardless of race, color, sex, religion, national origin, or age has an equal chance for a job based on his or her qualifications.

extra effort Employment practices, beyond the ordinary, designed to implement affirmative action.

Affirmative action goes beyond equal employment opportunity. It requires the employer to make an **extra effort** to hire and promote those in the protected group. Affirmative action thus includes those specific actions (in recruitment, hiring, promotions, and compensation) that are designed to eliminate the present effects of past discrimination. According to the EEOC, the most important measure of an affirmative action program is its results. The program should result in "measurable, yearly improvements in hiring, training, and promotion of minorities and females" in all parts of your organization. And, says the EEOC, all company officials, managers, and supervisors should clearly understand their own responsibilities for carrying out equal employment opportunity and affirmative action as a basic part of their jobs.

◆ STEPS IN AN AFFIRMATIVE ACTION PROGRAM

According to the EEOC, in an affirmative action program the employer ideally takes eight steps, as follows:

1. Issues a written equal employment policy indicating that it is an equal employment opportunity employer, as well as a statement indicating the employer's commitment to affirmative action.

2. Appoints a top official with responsibility and authority to direct and implement the program.

3. Publicizes the equal employment policy and affirmative action commitment.

4. Surveys present minority and female employment by department and job classification to determine locations where affirmative action programs are especially desirable. (See Figure 2.3.)

5. Develops goals and timetables to improve utilization of minorities, males, and females in each area where utilization has been identified.

6. Develops and implements specific programs to achieve these goals. According to the EEOC, this is the heart of the affirmative action program. Here the employer has to review its entire personnel management system (including recruitment, selection, promotion, compensation, and disciplining) to identify barriers to equal employment opportunity and to make needed changes.

7. Establishes an internal audit and reporting system to monitor and evaluate progress in each aspect of the program.

FIGURE 2.3
Affirmative Action Program/Quarterly Statistical Report
Source: "Affirmative Action and Equal Employment," U.S. Equal Employment Opportunity Commission, January 1974.

Organizational Unit _____

Location _____

Time Period _____

Form T

Job Categories	All Employees			Male				Female			
	Total	Male	Female	Negro	Oriental	American Indian	Spanish Surnamed American	Negro	Oriental	American Indian	Spanish Surnamed American
Officials & Managers	(1)	(2)	(3)	(4)	(5)	(6)	(7)	(8)	(9)	(10)	(11)
Professionals											
Technicians											
Sales Workers											
Office & Clerical											
TOTAL Lines 1-5											
Craftsmen (Skilled)											
Operatives (Semi-Skilled)											
Laborers (Unskilled)											
Service											
Total Lines 7-10											
TOTAL All Lines											

In columns 1, 2, and 3, include all employees in the establishment including those in min. groups. (The data below shall be included in the figures for the appropriate occupation categories above.)

On-the-job trainees											
Apprentices											
Production											
White Collar											

(Report only employees enrolled in formal on-the-job training programs.)

Date of Survey _____

Person Preparing Report _____

Name (Typed) _____   Signature _____

8. Develops support for the affirmative action program, both inside the company (among supervisors, for instance) and outside the company, in the community.[80]

♦ AFFIRMATIVE ACTION: TWO BASIC STRATEGIES

When designing an affirmative action plan, your employer can choose either of two basic strategies to pursue—the **good faith effort strategy** or the **quota strategy**—each with its own risks.[81] The first emphasizes identifying and eliminating the obstacles to hiring and promoting women and minorities, on the assumption that eliminating these obstacles will result in increased utilization of women and minorities. The quota strategy, on the other hand, mandates bottom-line results by instituting hiring and promotion restrictions.

Good Faith Effort Strategy

This strategy is aimed at changing the practices that have contributed to the exclusion or underutilization of minority groups or females. Specific actions here might include placing advertisements where they can reach target groups, supporting day care services and flexible working hours for

good faith effort strategy Employment strategy aimed at changing practices that have contributed in the past to excluding or underutilizing protected groups.

quota strategy Employment strategy aimed at mandating the same results as the good faith effort strategy through specific hiring and promotion restrictions.

women with small children, and establishing a training program to enable minority group members to better compete for entry-level jobs. The basic assumption here is that if existing obstacles are identified and eliminated, the desired results (improved utilization of minority members and women) will follow.

The basic risk here is that if the desired results are *not* achieved (in terms of hiring or promoting more minorities or women), your employer must then convince the EEO compliance officer that (1) a reasonable effort to hire or promote more protected individuals has taken place and (2) that failure to do so resulted from factors outside the employer's control. Should management fail to convince the EEOC, it may then find itself in an unenviable negotiating position. The EEOC compliance officer has considerable leverage in the form of economic sanctions (through possible federal contract termination) and through legal action. In the absence of results, the employer may find it has little power to resist any recommendations the compliance officer might make with respect to the employer's taking additional steps to eliminate the effects of past discriminatory actions.

Quota Strategy

Whereas the good faith strategy attempts to get results by eliminating obstacles, the quota strategy aims at mandating results through hiring and promotion restrictions. With the quota strategy, "desirable" hiring goals are operationally treated as required employment quotas.

During the last ten years, the courts have been grappling with the role of quotas in hiring, and particularly with claims of **reverse discrimination** by white males. A series of cases has addressed these issues without a uniform answer emerging. In *Bakke* v. *The Regents of the University of California* (1978), white student Allen Bakke had been denied admission to the University of California at Davis Medical School, allegedly because of the school's affirmative action quota system that required that a specific number of openings go to minority applicants. In a 5-to-4 vote, the Court struck down the school's policy that made race the only factor in considering applications for a certain number of class openings and thus allowed Bakke to be admitted.

In **United Steelworkers of America** v. **Weber** (1979) involving Kaiser Aluminum and Chemical Company, the Supreme Court found for the company. By a 5-to-2 vote, the Court rejected the complaint of Brian Weber, a white employee of the company. Weber, a 32-year-old lab technician, had claimed that a union-management plan that reserved 50% of certain training positions for minority workers violated the antidiscrimination provisions of the Civil Rights Act of 1964 by discriminating against white males. In its opinion, the Court specifically avoided detailing "the line of demarcation between permissible and impermissible affirmative action plans." The justices avoided, in other words, clarifying the elements of an acceptable or unacceptable affirmative action plan, focusing instead on the unique characteristics of the Kaiser situation. In its majority opinion, however, the Court did state that Title VII was not intended to forbid all race-related affirmative action. The effect of the Court decision was to permit Kaiser to continue letting minorities and women with less seniority than Weber (and other white males) to be admitted to the training program. Again, however, the Court's decision is a narrow one, stating only that Kaiser's plan at that specific plant was permissible. The questions of (1) when preferential treatment becomes discrimination and (2) under what circumstances discrimination will be temporarily permitted were not fully clarified in *Bakke* or *Weber*.

However, subsequent U.S. Supreme Court cases have continued to ad-

reverse discrimination Claim that due to affirmative action quota systems, white males are discriminated against.

United Steel Workers of America v. *Weber* Supreme Court case in which the plaintiff claimed being a victim of reverse discrimination.

dress those issues and clarify more specifically the scope and intent of affirmative action:

Firefighters Local No. 1784 v. *Stotts* (1984): The Court ruled that Title VII prohibits courts from requiring racial preferences as a remedy for prior discrimination unless the preference benefits only those individuals who were the actual victims of discrimination.[82]

Wygant v. *Jackson Board of Education* (1986): The Court struck down a mechanism in a collective bargaining agreement that gave preferential treatment to minority teachers in the event of a layoff.[83]

Local 28 Sheet Metal Workers v. *EEOC* (1986): The Court ruled that Title VII empowers a court to order a union to use quotas to overcome "egregious discrimination" and that the quota may benefit individuals who are not themselves victims of past unlawful union discrimination.[84]

International Association of Firefighters v. *The City of Cleveland* (1986): The Court upheld a consent decree that reserved a specific number of promotions for minority firemen and established percentage goals for minority promotions.[85]

U.S. v. *Paradise* (1987): The Court ruled that the courts can impose racial quotas to address the most serious cases of racial discrimination.[86]

Johnson v. *Transportation Agency, Santa Clara County* (1987): Public and private employers may voluntarily adopt hiring and promotion goals to benefit minorities and women. This ruling will limit claims of reverse discrimination by white males.[87]

Martin v. *Wilks* (1989): An employer who has signed a consent decree requiring affirmative action under court supervision can be sued for reverse discrimination provided the person (or persons) bringing suit was not a party to the original consent decree.

At the present time there is no clear agreement on how far firms can go with their affirmative action programs as indicated by these court rulings. While the *Johnson* case appeared to be a fairly clear endorsement for affirmative action, the *Martin* case may well have a chilling effect on employers' intentions to enter into affirmative action consent decrees.

A Practical Approach

According to one writer, these legal uncertainties suggest that the good faith effort strategy is often preferable to the quota strategy.[88] However, using the good faith strategy depends on your ability to engage in activities that convince the compliance officer that a good faith effort to improve the status of minorities and women in your company was in fact made. An employer might reasonably ask, therefore, "What specific actions should I take to be able to show that I have in fact made a good faith effort?"

One recent study helps answer this question. Questionnaires were sent to EEOC compliance officers who were asked to rate about 30 possible actions on their importance in evaluating the compliance effort of a hypothetical company. This company was described as having determined that minorities were underutilized in several blue-collar and white-collar jobs. The compliance officers were asked to indicate the possible tactics or actions they thought the employer could take in order to show evidence of an acceptable good faith effort affirmative action program.

As summarized in Table 2.2, the results of this study showed that there were six main areas for action:

1. Increasing the minority female applicant flow.
2. Demonstrating top management support for the equal employment policy.

TABLE 2.2 Specific Actions in a "Good Faith Effort" Strategy

AREAS FOR ACTION	OVERALL OBJECTIVES	POSSIBLE TACTICS
1. Increasing minority female applicant flow	To ensure that minorities and females are not systematically excluded and to encourage those individuals to apply	1. Include minority colleges and universities in campus recruitment programs 2. Place employment advertising in minority-oriented print and broadcast media 3. Retain applications of unhired minority female applicants to be reviewed as vacancies occur
2. Demonstrating top-management support for EEO policy	To indicate to all employees that top management considers affirmative action and equal employment opportunity important	1. Prepare written reports evaluating progress toward affirmative action goals as frequently as other management control reports are prepared 2. Involve the line supervisors in the establishment of the affirmative action hiring goals 3. Appoint an EEO coordinator who is both highly visible within the facility and from a department other than personnel
3. Demonstrating EEO commitment to the local community	To indicate to the public and local labor market management's concern for equal employment opportunity	1. Appoint key management personnel to serve on community relations board or similar organizations 2. Establish a formal EEO complaint procedure within the facility 3. Establish an on-the-job training program at the facility 4. Establish or support existing child-care facilities
4. Keeping employees informed	To communicate to employees the specifics of the affirmative action programs, including their rights, benefits, and opportunities	1. Discuss EEO matters, such as program success and new program efforts, in internal newsletter 2. Display EEO policy statement in work areas 3. Explain the EEO policy, job posting procedures, tuition refund programs, and so on, during the new employee orientation procedure
5. Broadening skills of incumbent employees	To increase the advancement opportunities and potential of employees	1. Provide tuition refund benefits to all employees 2. Institute a job rotation program within work groups
6. Internalizing the EEO policy	To encourage adherence to the EEO policy through modification of the organization's control, communication, and reward systems	1. Incorporate affirmative action progress into the performance evaluations of line supervisors 2. Directly notify eligible employees of advancement and training opportunities as vacancies occur 3. Formalize and communicate sanctions for violations of EEO policy

3. Demonstrating equal employment commitment to the community.
4. Keeping employees informed.
5. Broadening the work skills of incumbent employees.
6. Internalizing the equal employment policy to encourage supervisors' support of it.

Some of the possible tactics or actions that the compliance officers felt would reflect a good faith effort on the part of the employer are also summarized in Table 2.2. For example, a good faith effort aimed at increasing the minority female applicant flow might involve actions like "include minority colleges and universities in campus recruitment programs" and "retain applications of unhired minority female applicants to be reviewed as vacancies occur." Actions like these, this writer concludes, can help to ensure that the employer's good faith effort is an effective one, both in improving the employer's utilization of minorities and women and in convincing the EEOC that a good faith effort to do so was made.

SUMMARY

1. Legislation barring discrimination is nothing new. For example, the Fifth Amendment to the U.S. Constitution (ratified in 1791) states that no person shall be deprived of life, liberty, or property without due process of law.

2. As a reaction to changing values in America, new legislation barring employment discrimination has been passed in the last three decades. This includes Title VII of the 1964 Civil Rights Act (as amended) (which bars discrimination because of race, color, religion, sex, or national origin), various executive orders, federal guidelines (covering procedures for validating employee selection tools, etc.), the Equal Pay Act of 1963, and the Age Discrimination in Employment Act of 1967. In addition, various court decisions (such as *Griggs* v. *Duke Power Company*) and state and local laws bar various aspects of discrimination.

3. The EEOC was created by Title VII of the Civil Rights Act. It is empowered to try conciliating discrimination complaints, but if this fails, the EEOC has the power to go directly to court to enforce the law.

4. A person who feels he or she has been discriminated against by a personnel procedure or decision must prove either that he or she was subjected to unlawful disparate treatment (intentional discrimination) or that the procedure in question has a disparate impact upon members of his or her protected class. Disparate treatment can be proven under the *McDonnell-Douglas* standards, while disparate impact proof can involve disparate rejection rates, restrictive policies, or population comparisons. Once a prima facie case of disparate *treatment* is established, an employer must produce evidence that its decision was based upon legitimate nondiscriminatory reasons. If the employer does that, the person claiming discrimination must prove the employer's reasons are pretextual. Once a prima facie case of disparate *impact* is established, the employer must produce evidence that the allegedly discriminatory practice or procedure is job related and is based upon a not insubstantial business reason. If it does so, the employee must prove a less discriminatory alternative existed that would have been equally effective in achieving the employer's legitimate objectives or disprove the employer's justification for disparate impact.

5. Various specific discriminatory human resource management practices that an employer should probably avoid were discussed:

a. *In recruitment.* An employer usually should not rely on word-of-mouth advertising or give false or misleading information to minority group members. Also (usually), do not specify the desired sex in advertising or in any way suggest that applicants might be discriminated against.

b. *In selection.* Avoid using any educational or other requirements where (1) it can be shown that minority group members are less likely to possess the qualification and (2) such requirement is also not job related. Tests that disproportionately screen out minorities and women *and that are not job related* are deemed unlawful by the courts. Do not give preference to relatives of current employees (when most are nonminority) or specify physical characteristics unless it can be proved they are needed for job performance. Similarly, a person's arrest record should not be used to disqualify him or her automatically for a position, nor should a person be fired whose salary has been garnished. Remember that you *can* use various tests and standards, but must prove that they are job related or show that they are not used to discriminate against protected groups.

6. In practice, a person's charge to the EEOC is often first referred to a local agency. When it does proceed, and if it finds reasonable cause to believe that discrimination occurred, EEOC has 30 days to try to work out a conciliation. Important points for the employer to remember include (a) EEOC investigators can only make recommendations, (b) you can't be compelled to submit documents without a court order, and (c) limit the information you do submit. Also, make sure you clearly document your position (as the employer).

7. There are two basic defenses an employer can use in the event of a discriminatory practice allegation. One is *business necessity.* Attempts to show that tests (or other selection standards) are valid is one example of this defense. *Bona fide occupational qualification* is the second defense. This is applied where, for example, religion, national origin, or sex is a bona fide requirement of the job (such as for actors or actresses). An employer's "good intentions" or a collective bargaining agreement are not defenses. (A third defense is that the decision was made on the basis of legitimate nondiscriminatory reasons (like poor performance) having nothing to do with the prohibited discrimination alleged.)

8. Eight steps in an affirmative action program (based on suggestions from the EEOC) are (a) issue a written equal employment *policy*, (b) *appoint* a top official, (c) *publicize* policy, (d) *survey* present minority and female employment, (e) *develop* goals and timetables, (f) develop and implement *specific programs* to achieve goals, (g) establish an *internal audit* and reporting system, and (h) *develop support* of in-house and community programs.

KEY TERMS

Title VII of the 1964 Civil Rights Act

Equal Employment Opportunity Commission (EEOC)

Executive orders

Affirmative action

Office of Federal Contract Compliance Programs (OFCCP)

Equal Pay Act of 1963

Age Discrimination in Employment Act of 1967

Vocational Rehabilitation Act of 1973

School Board of Nassau County v. *Arline*

Americans with Disabilities Act

Vietnam Era Veterans' Readjustment Assistance Act of 1974

Pregnancy Discrimination Act of 1978

California Federal Savings and Loan Association v. *Guerra*

Federal agency guidelines

Sexual harassment

Meritor Savings Bank, FSB v. *Vinson*

Griggs v. *The Duke Power Company*

Albemarle Paper Company v. *Moody*

Wards Cove v. *Atonio*

Disparate Impact

Disparate Treatment

Adverse impact

Disparate rejection rates

Restricted policy

Bona Fide Occupational Qualification (BFOQ)

Business necessity

Validity

Extra effort

Good faith effort strategy

Quota strategy

Reverse discrimination

United Steelworkers of America v. *Weber*

DISCUSSION QUESTIONS

1. What is Title VII? What does it say?

2. What important precedents were set by the *Griggs* v. *Duke Power Company* case? The *Albemarle* v. *Moody* case?

3. What is adverse impact? How can it be proven?

4. Assume you are a supervisor on an assembly line; you are responsible for hiring subordinates, supervising them, and recommending them for promotion. Compile a list of discriminatory management practices you should avoid.

5. Explain the defenses and exceptions to discriminatory practice allegations.

6. What is the difference between affirmative action and equal employment opportunity? Explain how you would set up an affirmative action program.

7. Compare and contrast the issues presented in *Bakke* and *Weber* with new court rulings on affirmative action. What is the current direction of affirmative action as a policy in light of the *Johnson* ruling?

◆ APPLICATION EXERCISES

◆ CASE INCIDENT 1   Eliminating the Effects of Past Discrimination

The Swormsville Company has a job career ladder which starts at job class 1, the lowest paid, and ends at job class 24, the highest. Normally one moves up the ladder, from job class to job class, with the worker who has had the job longest in any one job class being given preference whenever there is a vacancy in the next higher job class. In the past, however, there was one major exception: no black could be promoted above job class 5.

Assuming this discriminatory provision is eliminated, what should the rights be of Mr. X, a black with 24 years' departmental seniority, who is still in job class 5 while whites with equal seniority are now in job class 15? Three possibilities have been suggested:

1. Mr. X moves immediately to job 15, even though this means displacing someone currently on the job and even though he does not have the training and experience to handle the job.

2. Mr. X will be given special training and he will be moved upward from job to job as fast as his abilities permit him, in each case having first priority for any vacancy, but not displacing anyone from a job.

3. As the longest-service man in job class 5, Mr. X can move to job class 6 when there is a vacancy, but he can't move to job class 7 until all those currently in job class 6 are promoted.

Questions

1. Which of these alternatives seems most fair? Can you devise a fairer one?

2. Would the nature of the jobs make any difference to your answer?

♦ CASE INCIDENT 2

"Friendly Visits" from the EEOC

In general, four main categories of jobs were present in Synco Company's plant operation: operators, laboratory technicians, maintenance technicians, and laborers. Shortly after a change in ownership, several local unions were organized by employees in the various job categories and these unions were readily accepted by Synco's management as an example of good faith in their workers. Each union represented a craft or occupation, and each union entered into collective bargaining on its own resources.

The first three job categories, that is, operators, laboratory technicians, and maintenance technicians, had been traditionally filed with white job applicants. The laborer jobs had always been filed with black job applicants due to these same demands and pressures. Over an earlier period of government ownership, this practice of having "racial job categories" had inadvertently become an implicitly accepted fact of life by management and workers alike.

Early in 1986, Bob Kiligan was promoted from labor relations manager to industrial relations director. Bob had joined Synco's management team in 1981 at the age of 28 after working for the Teamster's Union as an organizer while he worked on his master's degree in industrial relations at one of the better universities in the East. During one of his frequent visits to one of the owner companies, Felbs & Dobbs Company, Inc., the subject of Synco's hiring procedures was discussed and Bob decided that a complete employment test battery should be developed for Synco. Shortly thereafter, Felbs & Dobbs sent in a test specialist to develop the battery. The specialist set up the battery during a period of one week based upon his objective observations and his intuitive but well trained feelings concerning the various job categories present in Synco's rubber plant operation. Both Bob Kiligan and Al Royens, Synco's training and employment manager, were pleased with their "more professional looking" test battery.

About a year later, Bob Kiligan received a visit from a representative of the U.S. Equal Employment Opportunities Commission (EEOC). The representative was a black lawyer in his late twenties, and he seemed quite friendly and open in his manner. He informed Bob that complaints had been filed in his office by two of Synco's laborers charging racial discrimination in Synco's promotion policies. Both of the employees, Sy Washington and Willie Nord, claimed that they had applied for different job categories when the job openings were advertised on the company bulletin board, a practice initiated by Al Royens to implement the policy of "promotion from within." They felt that they had been consistently passed over for these promotions in favor of white workers with the same qualifications as their own. Bob Kiligan assured the EEOC representative that he would look into the matter immediately and inform him in writing of the results of his investigation.

After the government representative had left his office, Bob decided to handle the investigation personally. He had the reputation of doing things "himself," and he put all of his "lone wolf" experience into putting together the facts available. The company records showed that Sy Washington had been employed as a laborer by Synco since 1976, and that he had indeed applied for several promotion opportunities over the last two years. Although the employment tests were one of the main criteria used in promotion decisions, Washington had never received any tests due to the fact that there were no tests when he was hired in 1976. Washington had been turned down for promotion each time he applied due to "just satisfactory" work ratings and the fact that his superior did not consider him to be "too bright."

Willie Nord, who was several years younger than Washington, had been employed as a laborer in 1981 and had received the hiring test in use at that time. Nord's applications for promotion opportunities over the last two years had been turned down due to his low test scores and his supervisor's evaluation that Nord was also not "too bright" and had to be supervised constantly.

Kiligan then checked the personnel folders of the men who had been accepted for promotion. He noted that all of these men had done well on the original test or the new test battery and that each had received many excellent ratings from their supervisors before they had been promoted.

In meeting with the supervisors of the two laborers, Kiligan inquired if they had been approached by the men themselves or their union representative concerning the fact that they had not received any promotions. Both of the supervisors remembered comments by the men that they were upset due to being consistently passed over for promotion, but neither supervisor had been approached by the laborers' union questioning this consistency. Neither supervisor had felt that the discontent shown by the men was serious enough to warrant an "upward" communication. The supervisors reiterated their positions that neither Washington nor Nord was "bright" enough to deserve a promotion into another job category.

When Bob Kiligan arrived back at his office, he called Al Royens into his office and told him that he wanted all the present employees to have a chance to take the new employment test battery. Al immediately set about accomplishing his task and completed it sooner than expected due to the fact that many of the old employees who had not been tested did not want to take the test battery regardless of its importance as a promotion criterion.

Bob Kiligan wrote the EEOC office concerning the results of his investigation and the actions he had taken to test all of the plant workers that were interested in being tested. He also informed the EEOC that the concerned laborers had taken the test battery and that their scores on the battery when combined with their supervisor's ratings still showed them to be unsuitable for promotion to a better paying job category. He assured the EEOC that all the employees who had been promoted had received much higher scores on the test battery and much better work ratings by their supervisors before they had received promotions. Kiligan ended the letter by expressing his feelings that the introduction of standard testing and ratings for all employees had corrected all possible deficits in Synco's promotion policies and that the present system was fair and nondiscriminatory.

A year and a few months went by without a reply from the EEOC. Neither the laborers' union nor the concerned employees themselves were heard from concerning the promotion matter. Both Sy Washington and Willie Nord, however, had tried again, unsuccessfully, to be promoted. Bob Kiligan left Synco to accept the position of industrial relations director in another company and he was replaced by Glenn Doyle.

Doyle was an "old hand" at industrial relations as he had consistently worked in one area or another concerned with industrial relations ever since he had received his law degree late in the thirties. He had the reputation of being tough, but fair, in all of his dealings with both individual employees and their unions.

One morning Glenn Doyle was studying the facts of an arbitration outcome when the lawyer from the EEOC called for an appointment. Doyle granted the appointment for an afternoon later in the week, and after he hung up the phone, he called in Al Royens to see what he knew about the matter. Al gave him the facts of the case that he had been involved with, and Doyle obtained the rest of his information from the reports and letter written by Bob Kiligan. Glenn then phoned some of his friends in industrial relations positions in other companies to obtain information about the lawyer who was to "visit." With all of this information at his disposal, Glenn formulated his strategy for dealing with the matter.

Later that week, Glenn Doyle and Al Royens both greeted the lawyer from EEOC when he arrived and all three men went into Glenn's office. Again the young lawyer was as congenial as could be expected under the circumstances and he quickly got down to business.

"Mr. Doyle, our office has investigated the discrimination complaints filed by two of your employees, Mr. Nord and Mr. Washington, and we have also taken into account the comments and actions described in a letter to our office from Mr. Kiligan, your predecessor. In the EEOC's opinion, three separate and indisputable facts stand out in this case. First, the segregation apparent in your dressing rooms, washrooms, and eating and drinking facilities tend to support an atmosphere of discrimination at Synco. Second, there are no Negroes employed by Synco in anything other than menial type jobs, and this also supports contentions of discrimination in your corporation. Third, we have noticed that the tests used as promotion criteria have not been shown to be relevant to job performance at Synco."

The young lawyer sat forward in his chair a little, looking directly into Glenn Doyle's eyes, and smiled in a friendly manner before he said, "When all of these facts are combined, we feel the evidence weighs heavily that our clients have been discriminated against at Synco in terms of promotion opportunities, if not in other areas also. Now what the EEOC wants to know is this: what does Synco plan to do to assure fair opportunities for our clients, to repay these two men for the personal injury and economic loss they have suffered, and to assure that the same situation does not occur again with other minority employees?"

Questions
See the questions in step 2 of the Experiential Exercise that follows.

Source: Adapted from a case prepared by Lee D. Stokes of Louisiana State University, Baton Rouge, under the supervision of Leon C. Megginson, as a basis for class discussion. Cases are not designed to present illustrations of either correct or incorrect handling of administrative situations. All names have been disguised. Reprinted by permission from Robert D. Hay, Edmund R. Gray, and James E. Gates, *Business and Society* (Cincinnati: South-Western, 1976), pp. 236–239. Case Incident 1 from George Strauss and Leonard Sayles, *Personnel* (Englewood Cliffs, N.J.: Prentice-Hall, 1972), p. 483.

EXPERIENTIAL EXERCISE

Purpose. The purpose of this exercise is to provide practice in analyzing and applying knowledge of equal opportunity legislation to a realistic problem.

Required Understanding. Be thoroughly familiar with the material presented in this chapter. In addition read "'Friendly Visits' from the EEOC," the case on which this experiential exercise is based.

How to Set Up the Exercise/Instructions:
1. Divide the class into groups of four or five students.
2. Each group should develop answers to the following questions:
   a. What was wrong about the way Bob Kiligan and Al Royens handled the first visit from the EEOC?
   b. How did the EEOC lawyer prove "adverse impact"?
   c. Cite specific discriminatory personnel practices at Synco Rubber Company in various personnel management areas (recruitment, selection, etc.).
   d. How could the Synco Company defend themselves against the allegations of discriminatory practice?
3. Develop the outline of an affirmative action program for Synco Rubber Company.
4. If time permits, a spokesperson from each group can present his or her group's findings. Would it make sense for this company to try to defend itself against the discrimination allegations?

NOTES
1. "Section 1981 Covers Racial Discrimination in Hiring and Promotions—But No Other Situations," Commerce Clearing House, *Human Resources Management*, June 28, 1989, p. 116. It should be noted that as a result of court decisions interpreting the Supreme Court's decision in *Patterson* v. *McLean Credit Union*, it is debatable whether §1981 will apply to all promotion decisions unless the promotion in issue is deemed to constitute the making of a new contract.
2. Portions of this chapter are based on or quoted from *Principles of Employment Discrimination Law*, International Association of Official Human Rights Agencies, Washington, D.C. In addition, see W. Clay Hamner and Frank Schmidt, *Contemporary Problems in Personnel*, rev. ed. (Chicago: St. Clair Press, 1977), Chapter 3. Employment discrimination law is a changing field, and the appropriateness of the rules, guidelines, and conclusions in this book may also be affected by factors unique to an employer's operation. They should, therefore, be reviewed by the employer's attorney before implementation.
3. James Higgins, "A Manager's Guide to the Equal Employment Opportunity Laws," *Personnel Journal*, Vol. 55, no. 8 (August 1976), p. 406.
4. The Equal Employment Opportunity Act of 1972, Sub-Committee on Labor or the Committee of Labor and Public Welfare, United States Senate (March 1972), p. 3. In general, it is not discrimination, but *unfair* discrimination against a person merely because of that person's race, age, sex, national origin, or religion, that is forbidden by federal statutes. In the federal government's *Uniform Employee Selection Guidelines*, "unfair" discrimination is defined as follows: "unfairness is demonstrated through a showing that members of a particular interest group perform better or poorer on the job than their scores on the selection procedure (test, etc.) would indicate through comparison with how members of the other groups performed. . . ." For a discussion of the meaning of fairness, see James Ledvinka, "The Statistical Definition of Fairness in the Federal Selection Guidelines and Its Implications for Minority Employment," *Personnel Psychology*, Vol. 32 (August 1979), pp. 551–562. In summary, a selection device (like a test) *may* discriminate—say between low and high performers. However, it is *unfair* discrimination that is illegal, discrimination that is based solely on the person's race, age, sex, national origin, or religion.
5. A growing issue today is whether homosexuals are due equal protection from discrimination. Initially attempts to assert that discrimination based on sexual orientation was illegal were unsuccessful, and even the EEOC was unsympathetic. However, a recent case (*Watkins* v. *U.S. Army*, F.2d 1428, 1429, 9th Cir. 1988) involving an Army sergeant forced to resign after 14 years, notable service may possibly open the door to successful suits by identifying homosexuals as a "suspect class that deserve special protection against discrimination." Sabrina Wrenn, "Gay Rights and Workplace Discrimination," *Personnel Journal*, Vol. 67, no. 10 (October 1988), p. 94.

6. Bureau of National Affairs, "Age Discrimination Claims: Overview and Update," *Fair Employment Practices,* December 10, 1987, p. 152.

7. Note that under the Rehabilitation Act, the law strictly speaking applied only to a particular "program" of the employer. In March 1988 Congress passed the Civil Rights Restoration Act of 1987, overturning this interpretation. Now, with few exceptions, any institution, organization, corporation, state agency, or municipality using federal funding in any of its programs must abide by the section of the act prohibiting discriminating against handicapped individuals. See Bureau of National Affairs, "Federal Law Mandates Affirmative Action for Handicapped," *Fair Employment Practices,* March 30, 1989, p. 42.

8. Steven Fox, "Employment Provisions of the Rehabilitation Act," *Personnel Journal,* Vol. 66, no. 10 (October 1987), p. 140.

9. Commerce Clearing House, "Is AIDS a Protected Handicap?" *Human Resource Management Ideas and Trends,* March 20, 1987, p. 46.

10. Bureau of National Affairs, "Guidelines on AIDS," *Fair Employment Practices,* March 30, 1989, p. 39.

11. David B. Ritter and Ronald Turner, "AIDS: Employer Concerns and Options," *Labor Law Journal,* Vol. 38, no. 2 (February 1987), pp. 67–83.

12. Howard J. Anderson and Michael D. Levin-Epstein, *Primer of Equal Employment Opportunity,* 2nd ed. (Washington, D.C.: Bureau of National Affairs, 1982), pp. 5–7.

13. Commerce Clearing House, "Federal Contractors Must File VETS–100 by March 31," *Ideas and Trends,* February 23, 1988, p. 32.

14. Ann Harriman, *Women/Men Management* (New York: Praeger, 1985), pp. 66–68.

15. Commerce Clearing House, "Pregnancy Leave," *Ideas and Trends,* January 23, 1987, p. 10.

16. Bureau of National Affairs, "High Court Upholds Pregnancy Law," *Fair Employment Practices,* January 22, 1987, p. 7; Betty Sonthard Murphy, Wayne E. Barlow, and D. Diane Hatch, "Manager's Newsfront: U.S. Supreme Court Approves Preferential Treatment for Pregnancy," *Personnel Journal,* Vol. 66, no. 3 (March 1987), p. 18.

17. Thomas Dhanens, "Implications of the New EEOC Guidelines," *Personnel,* Vol. 56 (September–October 1979), pp. 32–39.

18. Bureau of National Affairs, "First Two Chapters of Long-Awaited Manual Released by OFCCP," *Fair Employment Practices,* January 5, 1989, p. 6.

19. Lawrence S. Kleiman and Robert Faley, "The Applications of Professional and Legal Guidelines for Court Decisions Involving Criterion-Related Validity: A Review and Analysis," *Personnel Psychology,* Vol. 38, no. 4 (Winter 1985), pp. 803–833.

20. Oscar A. Ornati and Margaret J. Eisen, "Are You Complying with EEOC's New Rules on National Origin Discrimination?" *Personnel,* Vol. 58 (March–April 1981), pp. 12–20; Paul S. Greenlaw and John P. Kohl, "National Origin Discrimination and the New EEOC Guidelines," *Personnel Journal,* Vol. 60, no. 8 (August 1981), pp. 634–636.

21. Paul S. Greenlaw and John P. Kohl, "Age Discrimination and Employment Guidelines," *Personnel Journal,* Vol. 61, no. 3 (March 1982), pp. 224–228.

22. 29 CFR 1625.2(a) quoted in Greenlaw and Kohl, "Age Discrimination."

23. Patricia Linenberger and Timothy Keaveny, "Sexual Harassment: The Employer's Legal Obligations," *Personnel,* Vol. 58 (November–December 1981), pp. 60–68.

24. Mary Rowe, "Dealing with Sexual Harassment," *Harvard Business Review,* Vol. 61 (May–June 1981), pp. 42–46.

25. Robert H. Faley, "Sexual Harassment: Critical Review of Legal Cases with General Principles and Preventive Measures," *Personnel Psychology,* Vol. 35, no. 3 (Autumn 1982), pp. 590–591; Bureau of National Affairs, "In Terms of Sexual Harassment, What Makes an Environment 'Hostile'?" *Fair Employment Practices,* June 1988, p. 78.

26. Linenberger and Keaveny, "Sexual Harassment."

27. Michael W. Sculnick, "The Supreme Court 1985–86 EEO Decisions: A Review," *Employment Relations Today*, Vol. 13, no. 3 (Fall 1986), pp. 197–206; *Brown* v. *City of Guthrie*, 22FET Cases 1627, 1980.

28. Frederick L. Sullivan, "Sexual Harassment: The Supreme Court Ruling," *Personnel*, Vol. 65, no. 12 (December 1986), pp. 42–44. Also see the following for additional information on sexual harassment: Jonathan S. Monat and Angel Gomez, "Decisional Standards Used by Arbitrators in Sexual Harassment Cases," *Labor Law Journal*, Vol. 37, no. 10 (October 1986), pp. 712–718; George M. Sullivan and William H. Nowlin, "Critical New Aspects of Sexual Harassment Law," *Labor Law Journal*, Vol. 37, no. 9 (September 1986), pp. 617–623.

29. Quoted in David Terpstra and Susan Cook, "Complainant Characteristics and Reported Behaviors as Consequences Associated with Formal Sexual Harassment Charges," *Personnel Psychology*, Vol. 38, no. 2 (Autumn 1985), pp. 559–574.

30. Rowe, "Dealing with Sexual Harassment."

31. *Griggs* v. *Duke Power Company*, 3FEP Cases 175.

32. James Ledvinka, *Federal Regulation of Personnel and Human Resource Management* (Boston: Kent, 1982), p. 41.

33. 10FEP cases 1181.

34. James Ledvinka and Lyle Schoenfeldt, "Legal Development in Employment Testing: Albemarle and Beyond," *Personnel Psychology*, Vol. 31, no. 1 (Spring 1978), pp. 1–13. It should be noted that the court, in its *Albemarle* opinion, made one important modification regarding the EEOC guidelines. The guidelines required that employers using tests that screened out disproportionate numbers of minorities or women had to validate those tests—prove that they did in fact predict performance on the job—*and further had to prove that there was no other alternative screening device the employer could use that did not screen out disproportionate numbers of minorities and women.* This second requirement proved a virtually impossible burden for employers. Up through the *Griggs* decision, it was not enough to just validate the test; instead, the employer also had to show that some other tests or screening tools were not available that were (1) also valid but that (2) did not screen out a disproportionate number of minorities or women. In the *Albemarle* case the court held that the burden of proof was no longer on the employer to show that there was no suitable alternative screening device available. Instead, the burden for that is now on the charging party (the person allegedly discriminated against) to show that a suitable alternative is available. Ledvinka and Schoenfeldt, "Legal Development," p. 4; Gary Lubben, Dwayne Thompson, and Charles Klasson, "Performance Appraisal: The Legal Implications of Title VII," *Personnel* (May–June 1980), pp. 11–21. Note, however, that the *new* uniform guidelines (Section 3B) still seem to insist that employers find and use the selection procedure that has the least adverse impact on minorities and women. This point, therefore, is still a matter of debate.

35. This was quoted from Commerce Clearing House, "Supreme Court Releases First 'Mixed Motives' Decision Under Title VII," *Ideas and Trends*, May 17, 1989, p. 82.

36. Ibid., p. 82.

37. "High Court Makes Race, Sex Bias in Work Place Tougher to Prove," *The Miami Herald*, June 6, 1989, p. 4A.

38. Commerce Clearing House, "The Supreme Court Explains How Statistics Are to Be Used in Fair Employment Suits," *Ideas and Trends*, June 14, 1989, p. 109.

39. These are based on "The Supreme Court Explains How Statistics Are to Be Used in Fair Employment Suits," p. 101.

40. Based on Ibid., p. 101.

41. *Patterson* v. *McLean Credit Union*, Docket no. 87–107, June 15, 1989, p. 11.

42. Commerce Clearing House, "Those Who Played No Role in Original Consent Decree Can Sue for Reverse Discrimination," *Ideas and Trends*, June 28, 1989, p. 115.

43. James Ledvinka and Robert Gatewood, "EEO Issues with Preemployment Inquiries," *Personnel Administrator*, Vol. 22, no. 2 (February 1977), pp. 22–26.

44. These are based on Bureau of National Affairs, "A Wrap-up of State Legislation:

1988 Anti-bias Laws Focus on AIDS," *Fair Employment Practices*, January 5, 1989, pp. 3–4.

45. John Klinfelter and James Thompkins, "Adverse Impact in Employment Selection," *Public Personnel Management* (May–June 1976), pp. 199–204.

46. *Wards Cove Packing Company, Inc.* v. *Atonio*, U.S. Supreme Court Docket no. 87–1387, June 5, 1989, pp. 12–13.

47. H. John Bernardin, Richard Beatty, and Walter Jensin, "The New Uniform Guidelines on Employee Selection Procedures in the Context of University Personnel Decisions," *Personnel Psychology*, Vol. 33 (Summer 1980), pp. 301–316.

48. See Howard Bloch and Robert Pennington, "Labor Market Analysis as a Test of Discrimination," *Personnel Journal*, Vol. 59, no. 8 (August 1980), pp. 649–652.

49. International Association of Official Human Rights Agencies, *Principles of Employment Discrimination Law*, James M. Higgins, "A Manager's Guide to the Equal Opportunity Laws," *Personnel*, Vol. 55 (August 1976); James Ledvinka, *Federal Regulation of Personnel*.

50. *Usery* v. *Tamiami Trail Tours*, 12FEP cases 1233; see also Howard Anderson, *Primer of Equal Employment Opportunity*, p. 57.

51. Robert H. Faley, Lawrence Kleiman, and Mark Lengnick-Hall, "Age Discrimination and Personnel Psychology: A Review and Synthesis of the Legal Literature with Implications for Future Research," *Personnel Psychology*, Vol. 37, no. 2 (Summer 1984), pp. 327–350; Bureau of National Affairs, *Fair Employment Practices*, December 10, 1987, p. 152.

52. *Benjamin* v. *United Merchants and Manufacturers*, CA2, 1989, 49FEP cases 1020, discussed in Bureau of National Affairs, *Fair Employment Practices*, May 25, 1989, p. 61; Bureau of National Affairs, *Fair Employment Practices*, February 18, 1988, p. 19.

53. Ledvinka, *Federal Regulation*, p. 81.

54. Ledvinka, *Federal Regulation*, p. 82. For a further discussion of religious and other types of accommodation and what they involve see, for example, Bureau of National Affairs, *Fair Employment Practices*, January 21, 1988, pp. 9–10; Bureau of National Affairs, *Fair Employment Practices*, April 14, 1988, pp. 45–46; and James G. Frierson, "Religion in the Work Place," *Personnel Journal*, Vol. 67, no. 7 (July 1988), pp. 60–67.

55. Ledvinka, *Federal Regulation*.

56. Anderson, *Primer of Equal Employment Opportunity*, pp. 13–14.

57. *U.S.* v. *Bethlehem Steel Company*, 3FEP cases 589.

58. *Robinson* v. *Lorillard Corporation*, 3FEP cases 653.

59. *Spurlock* v. *United Airlines*, 5FEP cases 17.

60. Anderson, *Primer of Equal Employment Opportunity*, p. 14.

61. Quoted in Wayne Cascio, *Applied Psychology in Personnel Management* (Reston, Va.: Reston, 1978), p. 25.

62. *Firefighters Local 1784* v. *Stotts* (BNA, April 14, 1985).

63. Ledvinka and Gatewood, "EEO Issues with Preemployment Inquiries," pp. 22–26.

64. Ibid.

65. Howard J. Anderson and Michael D. Levin-Epstein, *Primer of Equal Opportunity*, 2nd ed. (Washington, D.C.: Bureau of National Affairs, 1982), p. 28.

66. This is based on Anderson, *Primer of Equal Employment Opportunity*, pp. 93–97.

67. This is based on Bureau of National Affairs, *Fair Employment Practices*, April 13, 1989, pp. 45–47.

68. Eric Matusewitch, "Tailor Your Dress Codes," *Personnel Journal*, Vol. 68, no. 2 (February 1989), pp. 86–91.

69. It is not clear what the fallout of *Wards Cove* will be for the Equal Employment Opportunity Commission, but it is unlikely that the members of the Commission will reduce their enforcement activities substantially over the next few years.

Even during President Reagan's administration—often viewed as a not particularly supportive period for equal rights enforcement in the United States—an EEOC press release dated June 13, 1988 says it filed 527 court actions during fiscal year 1987, "setting an agency record for legal activity and maintaining its high level of enforcement on behalf of persons discriminated against in the work place." The release continues: "A record high 430 lawsuits were filed on the merits of discrimination charges in fiscal 1987, topping the previous record of 427 direct suits and interventions filed in fiscal 1986. Cases filed under Title VII of the 1964 Civil Rights Act totaled 320. Age Discrimination in Employment Act and Equal Pay Act cases totaled 69 and 12 filings, respectively. Twenty-nine cases were filed concurrently under Title VII and ADEA or Title VII and EPA. Agency investigative subpoena enforcement actions totaled 97, slightly below the 99 filed in fiscal 1986." Furthermore, in fiscal 1987, "The commission resolved more cases of discrimination through litigation than ever before: 460 as compared to 386 in fiscal 1986, the previous record number of resolutions. Direct suits and interventions accounted for 357 of the resolutions and there were 103 subpoena enforcement actions." EEOC news release dated June 13, 1988, and titled "EEOC Continues Record Enforcement Pace in Fiscal Year 1987." Quoted in Commerce Clearing House, *Ideas and Trends*, June 28, 1988, pp. 101–102.

70. If the charge was filed initially with a state or local agency within 180 days after the alleged unlawful practice occurred, the charge may then be filed with the EEOC within 30 days after the practice occurred or within 30 days after the person received notice that the state or local agency has ended its proceedings.

71. Paul S. Greenlaw, "Reverse Discrimination: The Supreme Court's Dilemma, *Personnel Journal*, Vol. 67, no. 1 (January 1988), pp. 84–89.

72. Robert H. Sheahan, "Responding to Employment Discrimination Charges," *Personnel Journal*, Vol. 60, no. 3 (March 1981), pp. 217–220; Wayne Baham, "Learn to Deal with Agency Investigations," *Personnel Journal*, Vol. 67, no. 9 (September 1988), pp. 104–107.

73. Note, however, that there are certain general guidelines regarding the archival data your firm must periodically compile. See E. Bryan Kennedy, "Archival Data Must Be Accurate," *Personnel Journal*, Vol. 6, no. 11 (November 1988), pp. 108–111.

74. Based on Commerce Clearing House, *Ideas and Trends*, January 23, 1987, pp. 14–15.

75. Ibid., p. 219.

76. Ibid., p. 220.

77. Quoted from BNA *Fair Employment Practices*, February 9, 1984, p. 4.

78. This discussion is based on and in part quoted from Harish C. Jain, "Canadian Legal Approaches to Sex Equality in the Workplace," *Monthly Labor Review*, October 1982, pp. 38–42.

79. Bureau of Naitonal Affairs, *Fair Employment Practices*, March 30, 1989, p. 37.

80. *Affirmative Action and Equal Employment*, U.S. Equal Employment Opportunity Commission, Washington, D.C. (January 1974); Antonio Handler Chayes, "Make Your Equal Opportunity Program Court Proof," *Harvard Business Review* (September 1974), pp. 81–89.

81. This discussion is based on Kenneth Marino, "Conducting an Internal Compliance Review of Affirmative Action," *Personnel*, Vol. 59 (March–April 1980), pp. 24–34.

82. See James R. Redeker, "The Supreme Court on Affirmative Action: Conflicting Opinions," *Personnel*, Vol. 65, no. 10 (October 1986).

83. See Michael W. Sculnick, "The Supreme Court 1985–86 EEO Decisions: A Review," *Employment Relations Today*, Vol. 13, no. 3 (Fall 1986).

84. Ibid.

85. Ibid.

86. Ibid.

87. Aric Press and Ann McDaniel, "A Woman's Day in Court," *Newsweek,* April 6, 1987, pp. 58–59.

88. Marino, "Conducting an Internal Compliance Review of Affirmative Action"; Lawrence Kleiman and Robert Faley, "Voluntary Affirmative Action and Preferential Treatment: Legal and Research Implications," *Personnel Psychology,* Vol. 42, no. 3, (Autumn 1988), pp. 481–496.

Chapter 3

Job Analysis

When you finish studying this chapter, you should be able to:

1. Explain how to perform a job analysis.
2. Explain how to prepare job descriptions and job specifications.
3. Compare and contrast six methods of collecting job analysis data.

OVERVIEW

The main purpose of this chapter is to explain how to analyze—determine the specific duties and responsibilities of—a job. First, we discuss some basics of organizing, including organization charts. Next, we explain job analysis. Here you determine in detail what the job entails and what kind of people should be hired for the job. We discuss several techniques for analyzing jobs and for writing job descriptions. Job analysis is in many ways the first personnel activity that affects motivation. Most people aren't motivated to perform a job when they find they haven't the skills and ability to do the job, and it's through job analysis that you determine what the job entails and what skills and abilities to look for in candidates for the job.

♦ THE PURPOSE OF ORGANIZATION

The purpose of organization is to give each person a separate, distinct job and to ensure that these jobs are coordinated in such a way that the organization accomplishes its goals. Organizations are never ends in themselves, but are means to an end—that "end" being the accomplishment of the organization's goals. Thus,

> An organization consists of people who carry out differentiated jobs that are coordinated to contribute to the organization's goals.

The way in which your company is organized derives or should derive from the plans you have for your firm. If your plan is to double sales in the next two years, then you might find that new managers for marketing, human resources, and manufacturing are required. Provision for these new positions will have to be made in your organization. Similarly, plans to expand into new geographic areas, to enter new businesses, or to consolidate operations always have consequences for how your enterprise will be organized.

♦ ORGANIZATION CHARTS

organization chart A chart showing the titles of managers' positions and connecting them by lines indicating accountability and responsibility.

The usual way of depicting an organization is with an organization chart, as shown in Figure 3.1. An **organization chart** is a "snapshot" of the organization at a particular point in time and shows the skeleton of the organization structure in chart form. It provides the title of each manager's position

FIGURE 3.1
Organization Chart
Source: Gary Dessler, *Management Fundamentals,* 4th ed. (Englewood Cliffs, N.J.: Prentice-Hall, 1985), p. 106.

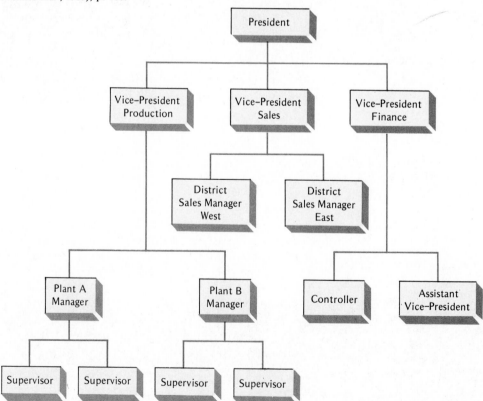

and, by means of connecting lines, shows who is accountable to whom and who is in charge of what department.

The organization chart does not tell you everything about the organization, any more than a road map tells you everything about the towns along its routes. Organization charts do *not* provide *job descriptions*. These describe the specifics of each job in terms of the actual day-to-day activities and responsibilities the person is expected to perform. (*Job analysis*, which we'll also discuss in this chapter, provides these job descriptions.) Nor does the organization chart show the actual patterns of communication in the organization. It also does not show how closely employees are supervised or the actual level of authority and power that each position holder in the organization has. What it *does* show are the position titles and the "chain of command" from the top of the organization to the bottom.

Most organizations have, or should have, organization charts because they are helpful in informing employees of what their jobs are and how these jobs relate to others in the organization. On the other hand, many organizations have been quite successful without organization charts, while others have failed in spite of them.

Several computerized systems are available for producing and modifying organization charts with the aid of a personal computer. Such systems facilitate the production of charts and reduce considerably the time and effort involved in evaluating alternative organizational arrangements and visualizing what those alternatives would look like.[1]

In summary, organization charts are useful because they:

1. Show titles of each manager's job.
2. Show who is accountable to whom.
3. Show who is in charge of what department.
4. Show what sorts of departments have been established.
5. Show the "chain of command."
6. Let each employee know his or her job title and "place" in the organization.

But organization charts do *not* show you:

1. Job descriptions of specific day-to-day duties and responsibilities.
2. Actual patterns of communication in the organization.
3. How closely employees are supervised.
4. The actual level of authority and power each position holder has.

THE NATURE OF JOB ANALYSIS

♦ JOB ANALYSIS DEFINED

job analysis The procedure for determining the duties and skill requirements of a job and the kind of person who should be hired for it.

job description A list of a job's duties, responsibilities, reporting relationships, working conditions, and supervisory responsibilities—one product of a job analysis.

job specification A list of a job's "human requirements," that is, the requisite education, skills, personality, and so on—another product of a job analysis.

Developing an organization structure results in jobs which have to be staffed. **Job analysis** is the procedure through which you determine the duties and nature of the jobs and the kinds of people (in terms of skills and experience) who should be hired for them.[2] It provides you with data on job requirements, which are then used for developing a **job description** (what the job entails) and **job specifications** (what kind of people to hire for the job).

As a supervisor or personnel specialist, you will normally aim to collect one or more of the following types of information by doing the job analysis:[3]

Job activities. First, information is usually collected on the *actual work activities* performed, such as cleaning, sewing, galvanizing, coding, or painting. Sometimes such a list of activities also indicates how, why, and when a worker performs each activity.

Human behaviors. Information on *human behaviors* like sensing, communicating, decision making, and writing may also be compiled. Included here would be information regarding personal job demands in terms of human energy expenditure, walking long distances, and so on.

Machines, tools, equipment, and work aids used. Included here would be information regarding products made, materials processed, knowledge dealt with or applied (such as physics or law), and services rendered (such as counseling or repairing).

Performance standards. Information is also collected regarding the performance standards (in terms of quantity, quality, or time taken for each aspect of the job, for instance), standards by which an employee in this job will be evaluated.

Job context. Here you would include information concerning such matters as physical working conditions, work schedule, and the organizational and social context—for instance, in terms of people with whom the employee would normally be expected to interact. Also included here might be information regarding financial and nonfinancial incentives the job entails.

Human requirements. Finally, information is usually compiled regarding such human requirements of the job as job-related knowledge or skills (education, training, work experience, etc.) and personal attributes (aptitudes, physical characteristics, personality, interests, etc.) required.

◆ USES OF JOB ANALYSIS INFORMATION

As summarized in Figure 3.2, the information produced by the job analysis is used as a basis of several interrelated personnel management activities.

Recruitment and Selection

Job analysis provides you with information on what the job entails and what human requirements are required to carry out these activities. This job description and job specification information is the basis on which you decide what sort of people to recruit and hire.

Compensation

You also need a clear understanding of what each job entails to estimate the value and appropriate compensation for each job. This is because compensation (such as salary and bonus) is usually tied to the job's required skills, education level, safety hazards, and so on—all factors that are identified through job analysis. We'll also see that many employers classify jobs into categories (like Secretary III and IV), and job analysis provides data for determining the relative worth of each job so that each job can be classified.

Performance Appraisal

Performance appraisal involves comparing each employee's actual performance with his or her desired performance. And it is often through job analysis that industrial engineers and other experts determine standards to be achieved and specific activities to be performed.

Training

You will also make use of job analysis information for designing training and development programs. This is because the job analysis and resulting

FIGURE 3.2
Job Analysis Information Flow
Source: Richard J. Henderson, *Compensation Management: Rewarding Performance,* 4th ed., copyright 1985, p. 147. Reprinted by permission of Prentice-Hall, Englewood Cliffs, N.J.

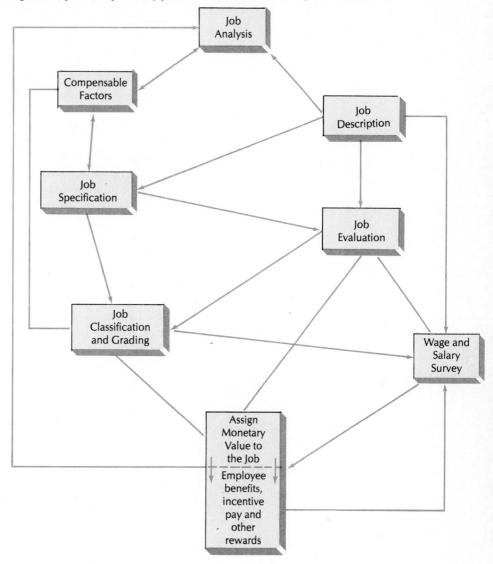

job description show what sorts of skills—and therefore training—are required.

Ensure Complete Assignment of Duties

The job analysis is also useful for ensuring that all the duties that have to be done are in fact assigned to particular positions and that no duties are "lost in the cracks" between positions or employees. For example, in analyzing the current job of your company's production manager, you may find she reports herself as being responsible for two dozen or so specific duties including planning weekly production schedules, purchasing raw materials, and supervising the daily activities of each of her first-line supervisors. Missing, however, is any reference to managing raw material or finished goods inventories, and on further investigation you find that none of the other people in manufacturing are responsible for inventory management either. Your job analysis (based as it is not just on what these employees report as their duties, but on your knowledge of what these jobs should entail) has identified a missing duty that must be assigned. Missing duties like this are often uncovered through job analysis; as a result, job analysis plays a big role in explaining and remedying problems of the sort that would arise if, for example, there was simply no one available to manage inventories.

♦ STEPS IN JOB ANALYSIS

The six steps in doing a job analysis are as follows:

Step 1.

Determine the use of the job analysis information. Start by identifying the use to which the information will be put, since this will determine the types of data you collect and the technique you use to collect them.

As explained in this chapter, there are many methods for collecting job analysis data; they range from qualitative interviews to highly quantified questionnaires. Some techniques—like interviewing the employee and asking the person what the job entails and what his responsibilities are—are uniquely suited for uses like writing job descriptions and selecting employees for the job. Other job analysis techniques (like the position analysis questionnaire briefly mentioned shortly) do not provide descriptive information for job descriptions, but *do* provide numerical ratings for each job; these can then be used to compare jobs to one another for compensation purposes. Your first step should therefore be to determine the use of the job analysis information. Then you can decide how to collect the information.

Step 2.

Collect background information. Next, review available background information such as organization charts, process charts, and job descriptions.[4] *Organization charts* show you how the job in question relates to other jobs and where it fits in the overall organization. The organization chart should identify the title of each position and, by means of its interconnecting lines, show who reports to whom and with whom the job incumbent is expected to communicate.

A *process chart* provides you with a more detailed understanding of the flow of work than you can obtain from the organization chart alone. In its simplest form, a process chart like the one in Figure 3.3 shows the flow of inputs to and outputs from the job under study; in this case, for instance, the inventory control clerk is expected to receive inventory from suppliers, take requests for inventory from the two plant managers, and provide requested inventory to these managers, as well as information to these managers on the status of in-stock inventories. Finally, the existing *job description*, if there is one, can provide a good starting point from which to build your revised job description.

Step 3.

Select representative positions to be analyzed. The next step is to select several representative positions to be analyzed. This is necessary where many similar jobs are to be analyzed and where it is too time consuming to analyze, say, the jobs of all assembly workers.

Step 4.

Collect job analysis information. Your next step is to actually analyze the job by collecting data on job activities, required employee behaviors, working conditions, and human requirements (like the traits and abilities needed

FIGURE 3.3
Process Chart for Analyzing a Job's Work Flow
Source: Richard I. Henderson, *Compensation Management: Rewarding Performance,* 2nd ed., copyright 1979, p. 141. Reprinted by permission of Prentice-Hall, Englewood Cliffs, N.J.

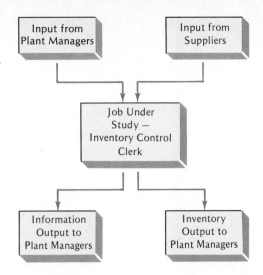

Note: Pinpointing who the employer interacts with can help you determine the nature of his or her responsibilities.

to perform the job). For this, you would use one or more of the job analysis techniques explained in the remainder of this chapter.

Step 5.

Review the information with the participants. The job analysis provides information on the nature and functions of the job, and this information should be verified with the worker performing the job and the person's immediate supervisor. Verifying the information will help to determine if it is factually correct, complete, and easily understood by all concerned. And this "review" step can help gain the person's acceptance of the job analysis data you collected by giving that person a chance to modify your description of the activities he or she performs.

Step 6.

Develop a job description, and job specification. In most cases, a job description and a job specification are two concrete outcomes of the job analysis; these are typically developed next. The *job description* (to repeat) is a written statement that describes the activities and responsibilities of the job, as well as important features of the job such as working conditions and safety hazards. The *job specification* summarizes the personal qualities, traits, skills, and background required for getting the job done, and it may be either a separate document or on the same document as the job description.

METHODS OF COLLECTING JOB ANALYSIS INFORMATION

♦ INTRODUCTION

Once you've collected background information and the job to be analyzed has been identified, your next step is actually to collect information on the duties, responsibilities, and activities of the job. There are various techniques you can use for collecting these data, and we'll discuss the most important ones in this section. In practice, you could use any one of them or combine techniques that best fit your purpose; thus, an interview might be appropriate for developing a job description, whereas the position analysis questionnaire that we'll discuss is more appropriate for determining the worth of a job for compensation purposes.

Who Collects the Job Information?

Collecting job analysis data usually involves a human resource specialist, the worker, and the worker's supervisor. The human resource specialist (like the human resource manager, a job analyst, or a consultant) may be asked to observe and analyze the work being done and then develop a job description and specification. The supervisor and worker will also get involved, perhaps by filling out questionnaires listing the subordinate's activities. Both the supervisor and worker may then be asked to review and verify the job analyst's conclusions regarding the job's activities and duties. Job analysis thus usually involves an integrated effort between the specialist, the supervisor, and the worker.

Job Analysis and Equal Employment Opportunity

Job analysis plays a crucial role in employers' attempts to comply with equal employment opportunity legislation.[5] Federal guidelines and court decisions admonish an employer to do a thorough job analysis before using a screening tool (like a test) for measuring job performance. The main reason is that an employer must be able to show that its screening tools and performance appraisals are actually related to performance on the job in question; to do this, a competent job analysis describing the nature of the job is required.[6] Popular methods for collecting job analysis information are discussed next.

♦ THE INTERVIEW

There are three types of interviews you can use to collect job analysis data: individual interviews with each employee, group interviews with groups of employees having the same job, and supervisor interviews with one or more supervisors who are thoroughly knowledgeable about the job being analyzed. The group interview is used when a large number of employees are performing similar or identical work, since this can be a quick and inexpensive way of learning about the job. As a rule, the worker's immediate supervisor would attend the group session; if not, you should interview the supervisor separately to get that person's perspective on the duties and responsibilities of the job.

Whichever interview you use, it is important that the interviewee fully understand the reason for the interview, since there's a tendency for interviews like these to be misconstrued as "efficiency evaluations." When they are, interviewees may not be willing to describe their jobs or those of their subordinates accurately.

Pros and Cons

The interview is probably the most widely used method for determining the duties and responsibilities of a job, and its wide use reflects its many advantages. Most important, interviewing the worker allows that person to report activities and behavior that might not otherwise come to light. For example, important activities that occur only occasionally or informal communication (between, say, a production supervisor and the sales manager) that would not appear on the organization chart could be unearthed by a skilled interviewer. In addition, an interview can give you an opportunity to explain the need for and functions of the job analysis, as well as allow the interviewee to vent frustrations or views that might otherwise go unnoticed by management. An interview is also a relatively simple and quick way of collecting information.

The major problem with this technique is distortion of information, whether due to outright falsification or an honest misunderstanding.[7] A job analysis is often used as a prelude to changing a job's pay rate. Employees, therefore (to repeat), sometimes view them as efficiency evaluations that may (and often will) affect their pay. Employees thus tend to exaggerate certain responsibilities while minimizing others. Obtaining valid information can thus be a slow and painstaking process.

Typical Questions

Despite their drawbacks, interviews are widely used, with typical interview questions being as follows:

What is the job being performed?

What are the major duties of your position? What exactly do you do?

What different physical locations do you work in?

What are the education, experience, skill, and (where applicable) certification and licensing requirements?

What activities do you participate in?

What are the responsibilities and duties of the job?

What are the basic accountabilities or performance standards that typify your work?

What exactly do the activities you participate in involve?

What are your responsibilities? What are the environmental and working conditions involved?

What are the physical demands of the job? The emotional and mental demands?

What are the health and safety conditions?

Are there any hazards or unusual working conditions you are exposed to?

These questions notwithstanding, it is generally agreed that the most fruitful interviews follow a structured or checklist format. One such *job analysis information format* is presented in the appendix to this chapter; it includes a series of 17 detailed questions regarding such matters as the general purpose of the job; supervisory responsibilities, job duties; and education, experience, and skills required. A form like this can also be used by a job analyst who has opted for collecting information by *observing* the work being done or by administering a *questionnaire*, two methods that will be explained shortly.[8]

Interview Guidelines

There are several things to keep in mind when conducting a job analysis interview. First, if you are doing the job analysis, you and the supervisor should work together to identify the workers who know most about the job as well as workers who might be expected to be the most objective in describing their duties and responsibilities.

Second, you must establish rapport quickly with the interviewee, by knowing the person's name, speaking in easily understood language, briefly reviewing the purpose of the interview, and explaining how the person came to be chosen for the interview.

Third, you should follow a structured guide or checklist, one that lists questions and provides space for answers. This ensures that you'll identify crucial questions ahead of time and that all interviewers (if there are more than one) cover all the required questions. However, make sure to also give the worker some leeway in answering questions, and provide some open-ended questions like "Was there anything we didn't cover with our questions?"

Fourth, when duties are not performed in a regular manner—for instance, when the worker doesn't perform the same job over and over again many times a day—you should ask the worker to list his or her duties *in order of importance* and *frequency* of occurrence. This will ensure that crucial activities that only occur infrequently—like a nurse's occasional emergency room duties—aren't overlooked.

Finally, after completing the interview, review and verify the data. This is normally done by reviewing the information with the worker's immediate supervisor and with the interviewee himself or herself.

♦ QUESTIONNAIRES

Having employees fill out questionnaires in which they describe their job-related duties and responsibilities is another good method for obtaining job analysis information.

The main thing to decide here is how structured the questionnaire should be and what questions to include. At one extreme, some questionnaires are very structured checklists. Each employee is presented with an inventory of perhaps hundreds of specific duties or tasks (like "change and splice wire") and is asked to indicate whether or not he or she performs each task and, if so, how much time is normally spent on each. At the other extreme, the questionnaire can be open ended and simply ask the employee to "describe the major duties of your job." In practice, the best questionnaire often falls between these two extremes. As illustrated in Figure 3.4, a typical job analysis questionnaire might have several open-ended questions (such as "Describe the major duties of your job") as well as structured questions (concerning, for instance, previous experience required).

Whether structured or unstructured, any questionnaire has advantages and disadvantages. A questionnaire is, first, a quick and efficient way of obtaining information from a large number of employees; it's less costly than interviewing hundreds of workers, for instance. On the other hand, developing the questionnaire and testing it (perhaps by making sure the workers understand the questions) can be an expensive and time-consuming process. Therefore, the potentially higher development costs have to be weighed against the time and expense you'll save by not having to interview as many workers.

♦ OBSERVATION

Direct observation is especially useful in jobs that consist mainly of observable physical activity. Jobs like those of janitor, assembly line worker, and accounting clerk are examples. On the other hand, observation is usually not appropriate where the job entails a lot of unmeasurable mental activity (lawyer, design engineer) or if the employee is normally expected to engage in important activities that might occur only occasionally, such as a nurse handling emergencies.

Direct observation is often used in conjunction with interviewing. One approach is to observe the worker on the job during a complete work cycle. (The cycle is the time it takes to complete the job; it could be a minute for an assembly-line worker or an hour, a day, or more for complex jobs.) Here you take notes of all the job activities you observe. Then, after accumulating

Employee Questionnaire

JOB DESCRIPTION QUESTIONNAIRE

Date _____

Company _____ Present Job Title and Grade _____

Dep't _____ Section or Group _____ Supervisor's Name _____

Home Office ☐ Branch or Area Service Office _____

1. Describe major duties of your job: _____

_____

_____

_____

_____

_____

_____

_____

_____

_____

_____

_____

_____

_____

_____

(Attach additional sheets if needed)

2. Other, less important job duties: _____

_____

_____

_____

_____

_____

_____

(Attach additional sheets if needed)

as much information as possible, you interview the worker; the person is encouraged to clarify points not understood and explain what additional activities he or she performs that you didn't observe. Another approach is to observe and interview simultaneously, while the worker performs his or her task. It's often best to withhold questions until after observations are made, however, since this gives you more chance to unobtrusively observe the employee. This in turn helps reduce the chance that the employee will become anxious or in some way distort his or her usual routine.

◆ PARTICIPANT DIARY/LOGS

participant diary/logs Daily listings, made by workers, of every activity in which they engage, along with times—provide comprehensive pictures of various jobs.

Workers can be asked to keep daily **participant diary/logs** or lists of things they do during the day. For every activity he or she engages in, the employee records the activity (along with the time) in a log. This can provide you with

FIGURE 3.4
(continued)

3. List machines or equipment you use:

	Continually	Frequently	Occasionally

4. How much formal education is necessary to do this job (check one):
☐ Less than High School   ☐ High School plus 2-3 yrs of other schooling
☐ High School   ☐ College Degree (4 yrs) Major _____
☐ High School plus 1 yr. of other schooling   ☐ College Degree plus other schooling

List additional specialized courses, subjects or training which are **necessary** but which are **NOT** easily available in High School or College: _____

5. How much previous similar or related work experience is **necessary** for a person starting this job?
☐ None   ☐ 1 to 3 years
☐ Less than 3 months   ☐ 3 to 5 years   ☐ _____
☐ 3 months to 1 year   ☐ 5 to 10 years

6. How long should it take an employee with the **necessary** education and previous experience (as shown above) to become generally familiar with details and to do this job reasonably well?
☐ Two weeks or less   ☐ Six months   ☐ Two years
☐ Three months   ☐ One year   ☐ _____

7. What amount of supervision does this job ordinarily require? Check one:

☐ Frequent; all but minor variations are referred to supervisor.

☐ Several times daily, to report or to get advice and/or assignments. Follow established methods and procedures; refer exceptions.

☐ Occasional, since most duties are repetitive and related, with standard instructions and procedures as guides. Unusual problems are referred, frequently with suggestions for correction.

☐ Limited supervision. The nature of the work is such that it is performed to a large extent on own responsibility after assignment, with some choice of method. Occasionally develop own methods.

☐ Broad objectives are outlined. Work is judged primarily on overall results with much choice of method. Frequently develop methods to achieve desired results.

☐ Little or no direct supervision. Have wide choice in selection, development, and coordination of methods within broad framework of general policies.

8. What are the nature and scope of any **independent** decisions you make? _____

Are your decisions to approve usually reviewed before becoming effective? _____ If so, by whom? _____

Are your decisions to reject usually reviewed before becoming effective? _____ If so, by whom? _____

a very comprehensive picture of the job, especially when it's supplemented with subsequent interviews with the worker and his or her supervisor. The employee might, of course, try to exaggerate some activities and underplay others. However, the detailed, chronological nature of the log tends to mediate against this.

In summary, interviews, questionnaires, observations, and diary/logs are the most popular methods for gathering job analysis data. They all provide realistic information about what job incumbents actually do. They can thus be used for developing job descriptions and job specifications.

♦ U.S. CIVIL SERVICE PROCEDURE

The U.S. Civil Service Commission has developed a job analysis technique that aims to provide a standardized procedure by which different jobs can be compared and classified. With this method the information is compiled

FIGURE 3.4
(continued)

9. In what ways does this job require resourcefulness, originality and/or initiative?
   Examples: _____

10. What kinds of errors are likely to occur on this job? _____

    How are such errors ordinarily checked or discovered? _____

    What would be the effect of such errors, if not caught? _____

11. Check the extent of contacts you have regarding Company business:

	Continually	Frequently	Occasionally	Never	Method (Phone, Letter, In Person)
Employees in other units of the the Company					
Policyholders and/or Agents					
General public; community or trade and professional assns.					
Federal and State Govt Agencies					
Other (specify)					

    Example and purpose of such contacts: _____

12. If the mental and visual alertness required is more than normal: check one in each column:

    ☐ Close
    ☐ Highly concentrated

    ☐ Occasional; periods of short duration
    ☐ Frequent, but with occasional "breaks"
    ☐ Steady and sustained

13. Describe any muscular action, body movement, working positions or posture changes occuring while performing duties which result in unusual fatigue. Estimate percentage of time in each: _____

14. Indicate any disagreeable job conditions to which you are exposed, such as dirt, noise, water, fumes, heat, outside weather, monotony, accident hazards, etc. _____

    If you travel over night on the job, indicate approximate times per month and method: _____

    Approximately how many miles per month do you drive in doing this job? _____

on a "job analysis record sheet." Here, as illustrated in Figure 3.5, identifying information (like job title) and a brief summary of the job are listed first. Next, the specialist lists the job's specific tasks in order of importance. Then, *for each task*, the expert specifies the:

1. Knowledge required (for example, the facts or principles the worker must be acquainted with to do his or her job).
2. Skills required (for example, the skills needed to operate machines or vehicles).
3. Abilities required (for example, mathematical, reasoning, problem solving, or interpersonal abilities).
4. Physical activities involved (for example, pulling, pushing, or carrying).
5. Any special environmental conditions (cramped quarters, vibration, inadequate ventilation, or moving objects).

FIGURE 3.4
(continued)

ANSWER ONLY IF YOU ARE RESPONSIBLE FOR THE WORK OF OTHERS

15. Check below those supervisory responsibilities which are a part of this job:

☐ Instructing   ☐ Allocating personnel

☐ Assigning work   ☐ Acting on employee problems

☐ Reviewing work   ☐ Selecting new employees

☐ Planning work of others   ☐ Transferring/promoting
                                    (Recommend?__ Approve?__)
☐ Maintaining standards   ☐ Disciplining
                                    (Recommend?__ Approve?__)
☐ Coordinating activities   ☐ Discharge
                                    (Recommend?__ Approve?__)

☐ Salary Increases (Recommend?__ Approve?__)

List job titles which are under your _direct_ supervision and the number of employees in each:

_____   _____

_____   _____

_____   _____

_____   _____

_____   _____

Show TOTAL number of employees (including those just above) over which you have supervisory

authority: _____

COMMENTS: (Attach additional sheets if needed):

_____

_____

_____

_____

_____

_____

_____

                              Form completed by: _____

NOTE TO SUPERVISOR: Your signature below indicates that you have reviewed the above job description. If you desire to make revisions, please enter them in RED pencil in the appropriate spaces. If needed, use additional sheets, numbering your comments to match the items in question. These items will be reviewed with you before a final job description is prepared.

How many employees under your supervision   Reviewed by _____

do the job described above?_____   Title _____

6. Typical work incidents (for example, performing under stress in emergencies, working with people beyond giving and receiving instructions, or performing repetitive work).

7. Worker interests areas (the preference the worker should have for activities dealing with "things and objects," or the "communication of data," or "dealing with people," for example).[9]

This is illustrated in Figure 3.5. In this case the first task listed for a "welfare eligibility examiner" is to "decide (determine) eligibility of applicant in order to complete client's application for food stamps using regulatory policies as a guide." Beneath this task are listed the analyst's conclusions concerning the _knowledge_ a welfare eligibility examiner is required to have, any _special skills_ or abilities, types of _physical activities_ involved in this task, special _environmental conditions_, typical _work incidents_, and the sorts of _interests_ that would correspond to this task. An analyst would typically apply his or her own knowledge of the job as well as information ob-

FIGURE 3.5
Portion of a Completed Civil Service Job Analysis Record Sheet

JOB ANALYSIS RECORD SHEET

Identifying Information

Name of Incumbent:	A. Adler
Organization/Unit:	Welfare Services
Title:	Welfare Eligibility Examiner
Date:	11/12/73
Interviewer:	E. Jones

Brief Summary of Job
Conducts interviews, completes applications, determines eligibility, provides information to community sources regarding food stamp program; refers noneligible food stamp applicants to other applicable community resource agencies.

*Tasks**

1. Decides (determines) eligibility of applicant in order to complete client's application for food stamps using regulatory policies as guide.

   Knowledge Required
   —Knowledge of contents and meaning of items on standard application form
   —Knowledge of Social-Health Services food stamp regulatory policies
   —Knowledge of statutes relating to Social-Health Services food stamp program

   Skills Required
   —None

   Abilities Required
   —Ability to read and understand complex instructions such as regulatory policies
   —Ability to read and understand a variety of procedural instructions, written and oral, and convert these to proper actions
   —Ability to use simple arithmetic: addition and subtraction
   —Ability to translate requirements into language appropriate to laymen

   Physical Activities
   —Sedentary

   Environmental Conditions
   —None

   Typical Work Incidents
   —Working with people beyond giving and receiving instructions

   Interest Areas
   —Communication of data
   —Business contact with people
   —Working for the presumed good of people

2. Decides upon, describes, and explains other agencies available for client to contact in order to assist and refer client to appropriate community resource using worker's knowledge of resources available and knowledge of client's needs.

   Knowledge Required
   —Knowledge of functions of various assistance agencies
   —Knowledge of community resources available and their locations
   —Knowledge of referral procedures

   Skills Required
   —None

   Abilities Required
   —Ability to extract (discern) persons' needs from oral discussion
   —Ability to give simple oral and written instructions to persons

   Physical Activities
   —Sedentary

   Environmental Conditions
   —None

   Typical Work Incidents
   —Working with people beyond giving and receiving instructions

   Interest Areas
   —Communication of data
   —Business contact with people
   —Abstract and creative problem solving
   —Working for presumed good of people

---

*This job might typically involve five or six tasks. For *each* task, list the knowledge, skills, abilities, physical activities, environmental conditions, typical work incidents, and interest areas.

tained through interviews, observations, logs, or questionnaires in completing the job analysis record sheet. And, since virtually any job can be broken into its component tasks, each of which is then analyzed in terms of knowledge required, skills required, and so forth, the Civil Service method provides a relatively standardized format by which different jobs can be compared, contrasted, and classified. (In other words, the knowledge, skills, and abilities required to perform, say, an assistant fire chief's job can be contrasted with the knowledge, skills, and abilities required to perform a librarian's job, and if the requirements are similar the jobs can be classified together for pay purposes.)

♦ QUANTITATIVE JOB ANALYSIS TECHNIQUES

While most employers use interviews, questionnaires, observations, or diary/logs for collecting job analysis data, there are many times when these narrative approaches are not entirely appropriate. For example, when your aim is to assign a quantitative value to each job, so the jobs can be compared for pay purposes, a more *quantitative* job analysis approach may be best. Three popular quantitative methods are the *position analysis questionnaire*, the *Department of Labor approach*, and *functional job analysis*.

Position Analysis Questionnaire

position analysis questionnaire (PAQ) A questionnaire used to collect quantifiable data concerning the duties and responsibilities of various jobs.

Researchers at Purdue University have developed what they consider to be a surefire procedure for quantitatively describing jobs.[10] Their **position analysis questionnaire (PAQ)** is a very structured job analysis questionnaire. The PAQ itself is filled in by a job analyst (perhaps yourself), a person who should already be acquainted with the particular job to be analyzed. The PAQ contains 194 items. As in Figure 3.6, each of these 194 items (such as "written materials") *represents a basic item that may or may not play an important role on the job*. The job analyst decides if the item plays a role on the job and, if so, to what extent. In Figure 3.6, for example, "written materials" received a rating of 4, indicating that written materials (like books, reports, office notes, etc.) play a *considerable* role on the job. The advantage of the PAQ is that it provides a quantitative score or profile of any job in terms of how that job rates on five basic dimensions: (1) having decision-making/communications/social responsibilities, (2) performing skilled activities, (3) being physically active, (4) operating vehicles/equipment, and (5) processing information. As a result, the PAQ's real strength is in classifying jobs. In other words, the PAQ allows you to assign a quantitative score to each job based on its decision-making, skilled activities, physical activity, vehicle/equipment operation, and information-processing characteristics. You can therefore use the results of the PAQ to compare jobs to one another and to decide, for instance, which jobs are more challenging;[11] this information can then be used to determine salary or wage levels for each job.[12]

The PAQ has yielded excellent results in the hands of trained job analysts who are familiar with its use, but several limitations have been noted. First, reliability (consistency) has reportedly been a concern when raters other than trained job analysts or related experts complete the PAQ: For example, two untrained raters rating the same job may rate it substantially differently. Second, the PAQ reportedly requires a fairly high level of verbal ability on the part of the rater (possibly postcollege-graduate level). To the extent this is true the PAQ would not be well suited to job analysis situations in which job incumbents or supervisors serve as raters. This underscores the advisability of using trained raters to analyze jobs using the PAQ.[13]

COMPUTER APPLICATION IN JOB ANALYSIS

AND STAFFING: SKILLS INVENTORY

Most managers lack complete, accurate information about their employees' capabilities. Furthermore, when vacancies occur, either due to attrition or to new opportunities, simply posting the opening on a company bulletin board does not guarantee that every employee will see the posting or will interpret the information appropriately. One way to improve the likelihood that qualified internal candidates will be introduced into the selection process is to have a skills inventory completed and updated regularly by employees.

Both the development of the inventory content and the updating of inventories requires significant input from employees. They must believe in the validity of the inventory, and this will happen only if they participate in the development process. If employees have ready access to computers, the inventory can be developed and updated from their workstations. Otherwise, hard copy memos should invite every employee to describe themselves in terms of the range of skills to be listed, the standards which differentiate various skill levels, and how skills should be categorized.

Inventories should be regularly updated, when an employee has completed a course, seminar, workshop, or assignment that is applicable. If computers are not generally available, employees should be allowed time (20 to 30 minutes) each quarter to update the inventory. Time spent on the updating may be minimized by periodically providing each employee with a hard copy of his or her inventory to mark up before the actual data entry. Skills should be reassessed at least annually at the time of performance appraisals. If an employee has questions about interpretations of skill levels or categories, supervisors or HRM personnel should offer assistance. Periodic review of the inventory and the process should occur, and all employees should receive regular training to maintain the validity of the system.

When a vacancy occurs, interviewers (either in HRM or, in small businesses, managers) would specify the parameters of the job in terms of the skill categories and levels. (This would be based on the job analysis.) The computer program would then produce a list of employees who qualify according to these parameters. This list would be modified based on other factors, such as attendance, quality of performance, time in position, or interest of the candidate. Employees otherwise qualified could receive a letter informing them of the opening and inviting them to apply if interested, with a copy to the employee's supervisor.

Expressing interest in a position that offers greater responsibility should be encouraged by a company that is interested in retention. Employees who see company behaviors that encourage growth and development are more likely to stay with the company. Developing a skills inventory system with significant employee input, active encouragement to update, and results that keep employees informed of promotional possibilities will enhance retention.

Another aspect of developing a skills inventory process as described above is straightforward communication with employees. If an employee is otherwise qualified, is invited to apply, does so, and is then found to have either performance or attendance problems, those hindrances to promotion will be addressed because the process encourages informational supervision. Most employees accept constructive criticism if it is offered in a manner designed to help them progress. Further, with employee participation in establishing the content and standards of the inventory, employees should have a better understanding of what is expected of them in order to qualify at specified levels, and should be able to provide valuable job analysis data based on what they actually know about their jobs.

INFORMATION INPUT

1 INFORMATION INPUT

1.1 Sources of Job Information

Rate each of the following items in terms of the extent to which it is used by the worker as a source of information in performing his job.

	Extent of Use (U)
NA	Does not apply
1	Nominal/very infrequent
2	Occasional
3	Moderate
4	Considerable
5	Very substantial

1.1.1 Visual Sources of Job Information

1 |4| Written materials (books, reports, office notes, articles, job instructions, signs, etc.)

2 |2| Quantitative materials (materials which deal with quantities or amounts, such as graphs, accounts, specifications, tables of numbers, etc.)

3 |1| Pictorial materials (pictures or picturelike materials used as *sources* of information, for example, drawings, blueprints, diagrams, maps, tracings, photographic films, x-ray films, TV pictures, etc.)

4 |1| Patterns/related devices (templates, stencils, patterns, etc., used as *sources* of information when *observed* during use; do *not* include here materials described in item 3 above)

5 |2| Visual displays (dials, gauges, signal lights, radarscopes, speedometers, clocks, etc.)

6 |5| Measuring devices (rulers, calipers, tire pressure gauges, scales, thickness gauges, pipettes, thermometers, protractors, etc., used to obtain visual information about physical measurements; do *not* include here devices described in item 5 above)

7 |4| Mechanical devices (tools, equipment, machinery, and other mechanical devices which are *sources* of information when *observed* during use or operation)

8 |3| Materials in process (parts, materials, objects, etc., which are *sources* of information when being modified, worked on, or otherwise processed, such as bread dough being mixed, workpiece being turned in a lathe, fabric being cut, shoe being resoled, etc.)

9 |4| Materials *not* in process (parts, materials, objects, etc., not in the process of being changed or modified, which are *sources* of information when being inspected, handled, packaged, distributed, or selected, etc., such as items or materials in inventory, storage, or distribution channels, items being inspected, etc.)

10 |3| Features of nature (landscapes, fields, geological samples, vegetation, cloud formations, and other features of nature which are observed or inspected to provide information)

11 |2| Man-made features of environment (structures, buildings, dams, highways, bridges, docks, railroads, and other "man-made" or altered aspects of the indoor or outdoor environment which are *observed* or *inspected* to provide job information; do not consider equipment, machines, etc., that an individual uses in his work, as covered by item 7)

Note: This exhibits 11 of the "information input" questions or elements. Other PAQ pages contain questions regarding mental processes, work output, relationships with others, job context, and other job characteristics.

Department of Labor (DOL) Procedure

The U.S. Department of Labor procedure also aims to provide a standardized method by which different jobs can be quantitatively rated, classified, and compared. The heart of this **Department of Labor job analysis** involves rating each job in terms of what an employee does with respect to *data, people,* and *things.*

The basic procedure is as follows. As illustrated in Table 3.1, a set of basic activities or "worker functions" describes what a worker can do with respect to data, people, and things. With respect to *data,* for instance, the basic functions include synthesizing, coordinating, and coping. With respect to *people,* they include mentoring, negotiating, and supervising. With

Department of Labor job analysis Standardized method for rating, classifying, and comparing virtually every kind of job based on data, people, and things.

TABLE 3.1 Basic Department of Labor Worker Functions

	DATA	PEOPLE	THINGS
Basic Activities	0 Synthesizing 1 Coordinating 2 Analyzing 3 Compiling 4 Computing 5 Copying 6 Comparing	0 Mentoring 1 Negotiating 2 Instructing 3 Supervising 4 Diverting 5 Persuading 6 Speaking–signaling 7 Serving 8 Taking instructions–helping	0 Setting up 1 Precision working 2 Operating-controlling 3 Driving-operating 4 Manipulating 5 Tending 6 Feeding–offbearing 7 Handling

Note: Determine employee's job "score" on data, people, and things by observing his or her job and determining, for each of the three categories, which of the basic functions illustrates person's job. "0" is high, "6," "8," and "7" are lows in each column.

Source: U.S. Department of Labor, Manpower Administration, *Handbook for Analyzing Jobs* (Washington, D.C.: U.S. Government Printing Office, 1972), p.73; reprinted in Benjamin Schneider, *Staffing Organizations* (Santa Monica, Calif.: Goodyear, 1976), p. 25.

respect to *things*, the basic functions include manipulating, tending, and handling. Note also that each worker function has been assigned an importance level. Thus, "coordinating" is 1, while copying is 5. If you were analyzing the job of a receptionist/clerk, for example, you might label the job 5, 6, 7, which would represent copying data, speaking-signaling people, and handling things. On the other hand, a psychiatric aide in a hospital might be coded 1, 7, 5 in relation to data, people, and things. In practice, *each task* that the worker performed would be analyzed in terms of data, people, and things. Then the highest combination (say, 4, 6, 5) would be used to identify the job, since this is the highest level that a job incumbent would be expected to attain.

As illustrated in Figure 3.7, the summary sheet produced from the DOL procedure contains several types of information. Listed first is the job title, in this case dough mixer in a bakery. Also listed are the industry in which this job is found and the industry's standard industrial classification code. There is also a brief one- or two-sentence summary of the job and the worker function ratings (in this case 5, 6, 2) for data, people, and things. This indicates that in terms of difficulty level, a dough mixer in a bakery is expected to copy data, speak-signal with people, and operate-control with respect to things. Finally, you would also specify the human requirements of the job in question, for instance, in terms of training time required, aptitudes, and temperaments. As you can see, each job analyzed in this way gets a numerical score (such as 5, 6, 2), and so all jobs with similar scores can be grouped together and paid the same, even though one job might be dough mixer and another mechanics helper.

Functional Job Analysis

This method is based on the DOL approach but provides additional information regarding the job's tasks, objectives, and training requirements.[14]

functional job analysis A method for classifying jobs similar to the Department of Labor job analysis, but additionally taking into account the extent to which instructions, reasoning, judgment, and verbal facility are necessary for performing job tasks.

Functional job analysis differs from the DOL approach in two ways. First, functional job analysis rates the job not only on data, people, and things, but also on the following four dimensions: the extent to which specific *instructions* are necessary to perform the task, the extent to which *reasoning* and *judgment* are required to perform the task, the *mathematical ability* required to perform the task, and the verbal and *language facilities* required to perform the task. Second, functional job analysis also identifies performance standards and training requirements. Performing a job analy-

FIGURE 3.7
Sample Report Based on Department of Labor Job Analysis Technique
Source: Adapted from Benjamin Schneider, *Staffing Organizations* (Pacific Palisades, Calif.: Goodyear, 1976), p. 27.

Sample of the End Result of Using the Department of Labor Job Analysis Technique.

U.S. Department of Labor
Manpower Administration

JOB ANALYSIS SCHEDULE

1. Established Job Title ____ DOUGH MIXER

2. Ind. Assign ____ (bake prod.)

3. SIC Code(s) and Title(s) ____ 2051 Bread and other bakery products

4. JOB SUMMARY:

Operates mixing machine to mix ingredients for straight and sponge (yeast) doughs according to established formulas, directs other workers in fermentation of dough, and curs dough into pieces with hand cutter.

5. WORK PERFORMED RATINGS: (From Exhibit 3.9)

	D	P	(T)
Worker Functions	Data	People	Things
	5	6	2

Work Field ____ Cooking, Food Preparing

6. WORKER TRAITS RATINGS: (To be filled in by analyst)

Training time required

Aptitudes

Temperaments

Interests

Physical Demands

Environment Conditions

sis using functional job analysis therefore allows you to answer the question: To do this task and meet these new standards, what training does the worker require?

An example of a completed functional job analysis summary sheet is presented in Figure 3.8. In this case the job is that of grader (a type of heavy equipment operator used in road building). As illustrated, the functional job analysis provides information on things, data, people, instructions, reasoning, math, and language. All this is quantitatively rated. Also, the summary sheet lists the main tasks involved in the job, performance standards, and training required.

WRITING JOB DESCRIPTIONS

A job description is a written statement of *what* the jobholder actually does, *how* he or she does it, and under *what conditions* the job is performed. This information is in turn used to write a *job specification*. This lists the knowledge, abilities, and skills needed to perform the job satisfactorily.

While there is no standard format you must use in writing a job description, most descriptions contain at least sections on:

PERSONNEL MANAGEMENT:
ON THE FRONT LINE

Based on her review of the stores Jennifer concluded that one of the first matters she had to attend to involved developing job descriptions for her store managers.

As Jennifer tells it, her lessons regarding job descriptions in her basic management and personnel management courses were by themselves insufficient to fully convince her of the pivotal role job descriptions played in the smooth functioning of an enterprise. Many times during her first few weeks on the job Jennifer found herself asking one of her store managers why he was violating what Jennifer knew to be recommended company policies and procedures, and repeatedly the answers were either "Because I didn't know it was my job" or "Because I didn't know that was the way we were supposed to do it." The job description, Jennifer knew, along with a set of standards and procedures which specified what was to be done and how to do it would go a long way toward alleviating this problem.

In general, the store manager is responsible for directing all store activities in such a way that quality work is produced, customer relations and sales are maximized, and profitability is maintained through effective control of labor, supply, and energy costs. In accomplishing that general aim, specific store manager's duties and responsibilities include quality control, store appearance and cleanliness, customer relations, bookkeeping and cash management, cost control and productivity, damage control, pricing, inventory control, spotting and cleaning, machine maintenance, employee's safety and hazardous waste, human resource administration, and pest control.

The questions that Jennifer had to address were these:

1. What should be the format and final form of the store manager's job description?

2. Was it practical to specify standards and procedures in the body of the job description, or should these be kept separate?

3. How should Jennifer go about collecting the information required for the standards, procedures, and job description?

1. Job identification
2. Job summary
3. Relationships, responsibilities, and duties
4. Authority and job standards
5. Working conditions
6. Job specifications

An example of a job description is presented in Figure 3.9.

♦ JOB IDENTIFICATION

The *job identification* section contains, as in Figure 3.9, several types of information.[15] The *job title* specifies the title of the job, such as supervisor of data processing operations, sales manager, or inventory control clerk. (Like the job description itself, you should keep job titles current, and the Department of Labor's *Dictionary of Occupational Titles* can be useful in this regard. It lists titles for thousands of jobs as well as descriptions of typical job duties for each.) The *job status* section of the job description permits quick identification of the exempt or nonexempt status of the job. (Under the Fair Labor Standards Act certain positions, primarily adminis-

FIGURE 3.8

Functional Job Analysis Task Statement

Source: Howard Olson, Sidney A. Fine, David C. Myers, and Margarette C. Jennings, "The Use of Functional Job Analysis in Establishing Performance for Heavy Equipment Operators," *Personnel Psychology,* Summer 1981, p. 354.

TASK CODE: GR-08									
WORKER FUNCTION AND ORIENTATION						WORKER INSTRUCTIONS	GENERAL EDUCATIONAL DEVELOPMENT		
THINGS	%	DATA	%	PEOPLE	%		REASONING	MATH	LANGUAGE
3C	65	3B	25	1A	10	3	2	1	3

GOAL:	OBJECTIVE:
Operates Grader—Output Basic	Backfilling, scarifying, windrowing, cutting firebreak, maintaining haul road, snow removal

TASK: Operates grader manipulating controls to travel forward/back, turn, raise/lower blade, position wheels and blade at correct angles; follows work order, drawing on knowledge and experience, monitoring the performance of the equipment and adapting to the changing situation, constantly alert to the presence and safety of other workers/equipment, in order to perform routine grader tasks such as backfilling, haul road maintenance, snow removal.

(To Perform This Task)

PERFORMANCE STANDARDS	TRAINING CONTENT
DESCRIPTIVE: — Operates equipment properly. — Is alert and attentive. NUMERICAL: — All work meets work order requirements. — No accidents/damage due to improper operating techniques.	FUNCTIONAL: — How to operate grader. — How to do routine grader tasks, such as backfilling, scarifying, windrowing, cutting firebreak, maintaining road, snow removal. SPECIFIC: — Knowledge of specific grader. — Knowledge of work requirements. — Knowledge of specific job site (i.e., layout, soil condition, environment).
(To These Standards)	*(Worker Needs This Training)*

trative and professional, are exempt from the act's overtime and minimum wage provisions.) The *job code* permits easy referencing of all jobs: each job in the organization should be identified with a code; these codes represent important characteristics of the job, such as the wage class to which it belongs. The *date* refers to the date the job description was actually written, and *written by* indicates the person who wrote it. There is also space to indicate who the description was *approved by* and space that indicates the location of the job in terms of its *plant/division* and *department/section.* The *title of the immediate supervisor* is also shown in the identification section.

The job identification section also often contains information regarding the job's salary and/or pay scale. The space *grade/level* indicates the grade or level of the job if there is such a category; for example, a firm may classify secretaries as secretary II, secretary III, and so on. Finally, the *pay range* space provides for the specific pay or pay range of the job.

♦ JOB SUMMARY

The *job summary* should describe the general nature of the job, listing only its major functions or activities. Thus (as in Figure 3.9) the supervisor of data processing "directs the operation of all data processing, data control, and data preparation requirements. Performs other assignments as required." For the job of materials manager, the summary might state that

SAMPLE JOB DESCRIPTION

Supervisor of Data Processing Operations	*Exempt*	*012.168*
Job Title	Status	Job Code
July 3, 1978		*Olympia, Inc. - Main Office*
Date		Plant/Division
		Information
Arthur Allen		*Data Processing - Systems*
Written By		Department/Section
Juanita Montgomery		*12* *736*
Approved By		Grade/Level Points
Manager of Information Systems		*14,800 - Mid 17,760 - 20,720*
Title of Immediate Supervisor		Pay Range

SUMMARY

Directs the operation of all data processing, data control, and data preparation requirements. Performs other assignments as required.

JOB DUTIES*

1. Follows broadly-based directives.
   (a). Operates Independently.
   (b). Informs Manager of Information Systems of activities through weekly, monthly, and/or quarterly schedules.
2. Selects, trains, and develops subordinate personnel.
   (a). Develops spirit of cooperation and understanding among work group members.
   (b). Ensures that work group members receive specialized training as necessary in the proper functioning or execution of machines, equipment, systems, procedures, processes, and/or methods.
   (c). Directs training involving teaching, demonstrating, and/or advising users in productive work methods and effective communications with data processing.
3. Reads and analyzes wide variety of instructional and training information.
   (a). Applies latest concepts and ideas to changing organizational requirements.
   (b). Assists in developing and/or updating manuals, procedures, specifications, etc., relative to organizational requirements and needs.
   (c). Assists in the preparation of specifications and related evaluations of supporting software and hardware.
4. Plans, directs, and controls a wide variety of operational assignments by 5 to 7 subordinates; works closely with other managers, specialists, and technicians within Information Systems as well as with managers in other departments with data needs and with vendors.
   (a). Receives, interprets, develops, and distributes directives ranging from the very simple to the highly complex and technological in nature.
   (b). Establishes and implements annual budget for department.
5. Interacts and communicates with people representing a wide variety of units and organizations.
   (a). Communicates both personally and impersonally, through oral or written directives and memoranda, with all involved parties.
   (b). Attends local meetings of professional organizations in the field of data processing.
*This section should also include description of uncomfortable, dirty, or dangerous assignments.

EMPLOYMENT STANDARDS

In this example, the job specifications section lists employment standards. If there is no job specification section, then the Employment Standards section follows the Job Duties section.

ACCOUNTABILITIES

Successful completion of scheduled activities. Increased use of facility services through expansion of user understanding and satisfaction with delivered product.

"the materials manager purchases economically, regulates deliveries of, stores, and distributes all material necessary on the production line." For the job of mailroom supervisor, "the mailroom supervisor receives, sorts, and delivers all incoming mail properly, and he or she handles all outgoing mail including the accurate and timely posting of such mail."[16]

Try to avoid including a general statement like "performs other assignments as required." Including such a statement can give supervisors more flexibility in assigning duties. However, some experts state unequivocally that "one item frequently found that should *never* be included in a job description is a "cop-out clause" like 'other duties, as assigned,'"[17] since this leaves open the nature of the job—and the people needed to staff it. Remember that the job description should be as specific as possible in order to help you identify the sorts of people you should hire for the job, the job's training requirements, and how the job's incumbent is appraised.

♦ RELATIONSHIPS

The *relationships* statement shows the jobholder's relationships with others inside and outside the organization and might look like this for a human resource manager:[18]

Reports to: vice-president of employee relations.

Supervises: human resource clerk, test administrator, labor relations director, and one secretary.

Works with: all department managers and executive management.

Outside the company: employment agencies, executive recruiting firms, union representatives, state and federal employment offices, and various vendors.[19]

♦ RESPONSIBILITIES AND DUTIES

Another section should be used to present a detailed list of the actual responsibilities and duties of the job. As in Figure 3.9, each of the job's major duties should be listed separately, with one or two sentences then provided for describing each. In the figure, for instance, the duty "selects, trains, and develops subordinate personnel" is further defined as follows: "develops a spirit of cooperation and understanding," "ensures that work group members receive specialized training as necessary," and "directs training involving teaching, demonstrating, and/or advising." Other typical duties for different jobs might include maintaining balanced and controlled inventories, accurate posting of accounts payable, maintaining favorable purchase price variances, and repairing production line tools and equipment.

You can again use the *Dictionary of Occupational Titles* here, this time for itemizing the job's duties and responsibilities. As shown in Figure 3.10, for example, the dictionary lists a human resource manager's specific duties and responsibilities, including "plans and carries out policies relating to all phases of personnel activity," "recruits, interviews, and selects employees to fill vacant positions," and "conducts wage survey within labor market to determine competitive wage rate."

FIGURE 3.10
"Personnel Manager" Description from *Dictionary of Occupational Titles*
Source: *Dictionary of Occupational Titles,* 4th ed. (Washington, D.C.: U.S. Department of Labor, Employment Training Administration, U.S. Employment Service, 1977).

> **166.117-018 MANAGER, PERSONNEL (profess. & kin.)**
> Plans and carries out policies relating to all phases of personnel activity: Recruits, interviews, and selects employees to fill vacant positions. Plans and conducts new employee orientation to foster positive attitude toward company goals. Keeps record of insurance coverage, pension plan, and personnel transactions, such as hires, promotions, transfers, and terminations. Investigates accidents and prepares reports for insurance carrier. Conducts wage survey within labor market to determine competitive wage rate. Prepares budget of personnel operations. Meets with shop stewards and supervisors to resolve grievances. Writes separation notices for employees separating with cause and conducts exist interviews to determine reasons behind separations. Prepares reports and recommends procedures to reduce absenteeism and turnover. Contracts with outside suppliers to provide employee services, such as canteen, transportation, or relocation service. May keep records of hired employee characteristics for government reporting purposes. May negotiate collective bargaining agreement with BUSINESS REPRESENTATIVE, LABOR UNION (profess. & kin.).

♦ AUTHORITY

Another section should define the limits of the jobholder's authority, including his or her decision-making limitations, direct supervision of other personnel, and budgetary limitations. For example, the jobholder might have authority to approve purchase requests up to $500, grant time off or leaves of absence, discipline department personnel, recommend salary increases, and interview and hire new employees.[20]

♦ STANDARDS OF PERFORMANCE

Some job descriptions also contain a *standards of performance* section. This basically states the standards the employee is expected to achieve in each of the job descriptions' main duties and responsibilities.

Setting standards is never an easy matter. However, most managers soon learn that just telling subordinates to "do their best" doesn't provide enough guidance to ensure top performance. One straightforward way of setting standards is to finish the statement: "I will be completely satisfied with your work when . . .". This sentence, if completed for each responsibility listed in the job description, should result in a usable set of performance standards.[21] Some examples would include the following:

DUTY: ACCURATE POSTING OF ACCOUNTS PAYABLE

1. All invoices received are posted within the same working day.
2. All invoices are routed to proper department managers for approval no later than the day following receipt.
3. An average of no more than three posting errors per month occurs.
4. Posting ledger is balanced by the end of the third working day of each month.

DUTY: MEETING DAILY PRODUCTION SCHEDULE

1. Work group produces no less than 426 units per working day.
2. No more than an average of 2% of units is rejected at the next workstation.
3. Work is completed with no more than an average of 5% overtime per week.

♦ WORKING CONDITIONS AND PHYSICAL ENVIRONMENT

The job description will also list any special *working conditions* involved on the job. These might include things like noise level, hazardous conditions, or heat.

♦ JOB DESCRIPTION GUIDELINES

Here are some hints for writing up your job descriptions:[22]

Be clear. The job description should portray the work of the position so well that the duties are clear without reference to other job descriptions.

Indicate scope. In defining the position, be sure to indicate the scope and nature of the work by using phrases such as "for the department" or "as requested by the manager." Include all important relationships.

Be specific. Select the most specific words to show (1) the kind of work, (2) the degree of complexity, (3) the degree of skill required, (4) the extent to which problems are standardized, (5) the extent of the worker's responsibility for each phase of the work, and (6) the degree and type of accountability. Use action words such as *analyze, gather, assemble, plan, devise, infer, deliver, transmit, maintain, supervise,* and *recommend.* Positions at the lower levels of organization generally have the most detailed duties or tasks, while higher-level positions deal with broader aspects.

Be brief. Brief accurate statements usually best accomplish the purpose.

Recheck. Finally, to check whether the description fulfills the basic requirements, ask yourself: Will a new employee understand the job if he or she reads the job description?

♦ SMALL BUSINESS APPLICATIONS: A PRACTICAL APPROACH

Without the benefit of their own job analysts or (in many cases) their own human resource managers, many small business owners face two hurdles when conducting job analyses and writing job descriptions. First (given their need to concentrate on other pressing matters), they often need a more streamlined approach than those provided by questionnaires like the one shown in Figure 3.4. Second, and more important, there is always the reasonable fear that in writing up their own job descriptions they are inadvertently overlooking duties that should be assigned to subordinates or are assigning duties to positions that are usually not associated with such positions: What they need here is a sort of encyclopedia listing all the possible positions they might encounter, including a detailed listing of the duties normally assigned to these positions. Such an "encyclopedia" exists, of course, and is the *Dictionary of Occupational Titles* briefly mentioned earlier. The *Practical Approach to Job Analysis for Small Businesspeople* presented next is built around using this invaluable device and involves the following steps:

Step 1. Decide on a Plan

As explained earlier in this chapter the development of at least the broad guidelines of a plan should precede your writing of an organization chart or job descriptions. What do you expect your sales revenue to be next year and in the next few years? What products do you intend to emphasize? What areas or departments in your company do you think will have to be expanded, reduced, or consolidated given where you plan to go with your firm over the next few years? What kinds of new positions do you think you'll need to be able to accomplish your strategic plans? These are the sorts of questions you should ask before proceeding.

Step 2. Develop an Organization Chart

Your next step should be to develop an organization chart for your firm, and even companies with under 30 employees should do so. Start by drawing up the organization chart as it is now. Then, depending upon how far in advance you're planning, produce a chart showing how you'd like your chart to look in the immediate future (say, in two months) and perhaps two or three other charts showing how you'd like your organization to evolve over the next two or three years.

Step 3. Use Job Analysis/Description Questionnaire

Next, use a job analysis questionnaire to determine what the job entails. You can use one of the more comprehensive job analysis questionnaires (like those in Figure 3.4, or in the appendix to this chapter) to collect job analysis data. A simpler and often satisfactory alternative is to use the job description questionnaire presented in Figure 3.11. You can do this by filling in the information called for on the page (using the procedure outlined below) and by asking your supervisors or the employees themselves to list their job duties (on the bottom of the page), breaking them into daily duties, periodic duties, and duties performed at irregular intervals. A sample of how one of these duties should be described (Figure 3.12) can also be distributed to supervisors and/or employees to illustrate how duties should be described.

FIGURE 3.11
Job Description Questionnaire

Background Data for Job Description

Job Title _____   Department _____

Job Number _____   Written by _____

Today's Date _____   Applicable DOT codes

   I. Applicable DOT Definition(s):

  II. Job Summary:
     (List the more important or regularly performed tasks)

  III. Reports to: _____

  IV. Supervises: _____

   V. Job Duties:
     Briefly describe, for each duty, what employee does and, if possible, how employee does it. Show in parenthesis at end of each duty the approximate percentage of time devoted to duty.)

     A. Daily Duties:

     B. Periodic Duties
       (Indicate whether weekly, monthly, quarterly, etc.)

     C. Duties Performed at Irregular Intervals:

FIGURE 3.12
Background Data For Examples

Example of Job Title: Customer Service Clerk

Example of Job Summary: Answers inquiries and gives directions to customers, authorizes cashing of customers' checks, records and returns lost charge cards, sorts and reviews new credit applications, work at customer service desk in department store.

Example of One Job Duty: Authorizes cashing of checks: Authorizes cashing of personal or payroll checks (up to a specified amount) by customers desiring to make payment by check. Requests identification, such as driver's license, from customers, and examines check to verify date, amount, signature, and endorsement. Initials check, and sends customer to cashier. (10%)

Step 4. Obtain the Dictionary of Occupational Titles

Your next step is to obtain standardized examples of the job descriptions you will need, and for this you will need the *Dictionary of Occupational Titles* (DOT).

The best way to learn how to use the *Dictionary of Occupational Titles* is to buy yourself a copy and begin using it. The *Dictionary* and its one supplement are available for $37.50 from the Superintendent of Documents, Government Printing Office, Washington, D.C. 20402–9325. You can call the order and information desk at 202/783–3238 to verify prices and order your manuals over the phone.

Step 5. Choose Appropriate Definitions and Put on Index Cards

Next, for each department you are writing descriptions for, choose from the DOT job titles and job descriptions that you believe might be appropriate for your own enterprise. For example, suppose you want to develop job descriptions for your employees in the retail sales department of your store. Furthermore, assume that while you've drawn up a tentative organization chart for what you'd like that department to look like, you're not absolutely sure you haven't inadvertently left out one or two positions.

You leaf through occupational code numbers in the DOT starting with 0, 1, or 2 (since these include all professional, technical, and managerial occupations as well as clerical and sales occupations). On page 120 (see Figure 3.13) you find that category 185 refers to "Wholesale and Retail Trade" managers and officials, and you find here "Manager, Department Store" (185.117–010) and "Fashion Coordinator" (185.157–010). Moving on, on page 208 you find that category 261 refers to "Sales Occupations–Apparel" and here you find "Salesperson, Children's Wear," (261.357–046), "Salesperson, Men's Clothing" (261.357–050), and "Salesperson, Women's Wear" (261.357–038). On the off chance that you may have inadvertently left out some titles that might be appropriate, you leaf through the alphabetical index of occupational titles under "Retail Trade Industry" occupations toward the back of the manual and stumble across "Assistant Buyer, Retail Trade" (162.157–022). You decide you should pick up several aspects of this job's duties as well. You now make copies of each of the pertinent descriptions and glue them to index cards. You now have a comprehensive set of the management-related jobs typically found in a retail sales department and can rearrange them on your chart and consolidate positions until you have a division of work that you believe will work for you. Having this array of jobs on cards will help to ensure that you have considered the full range of retail sales-management jobs that might be pertinent for your enterprise. It also helps to ensure that no important retail-management duties are inadvertently left out.

FIGURE 3.13
Page from *Dictionary of Occupational Titles*
Source: *Dictionary of Occupational Titles* (Washington, D.C.: U.S. Department of Labor, 1977), p. 120

184.167-266

message. May chart train movements on graph to estimate arrival times at specified points. May operate teletypewriter to transmit messages to freight offices or other points along line.

184.167-266 TRANSPORTATION-MAINTENANCE SUPERVISOR (any ind.)
Directs and coordinates, through supervisory personnel, activities of workers engaged in maintenance of transportation equipment in an industrial establishment: Confers with department heads to arrange for equipment, such as motor vehicles, railroad rolling stock and equipment, and within-plant trackage systems, to be released from service for inspection, service, or repair. Schedules repairs and follows up on repairs being made.

184.167-270 WATER CONTROL SUPERVISOR (waterworks)
Directs and coordinates, through subordinate supervisory personnel, activities of workers engaged in allocation, regulation, and delivery of government controlled water in irrigation district, and in repair and maintenance of irrigation facilities: Reviews water-rights agreements, irrigation contracts, and departmental policies and regulations to determine equitable distribution of water. Schedules time and amount of water to be delivered to users in accordance with instructions. Inspects channels, siphons, tunnels, weirs, roads, bridges, buildings, and equipment for need of repair and maintenance. Assigns supervisory personnel to sanitation, maintenance and repair activities and inspects work for compliance with prescribed operational procedures and methods. Confers with water users to investigate and resolve complaints and public relations problems. Notifies water users of changes in policies and procedures.

184.167-274 WHARFINGER, CHIEF (water trans.)
Plans and directs activities of persons in wharfinger department to insure that fees assessed shipping companies, using municipal facilities, are in accordance with port tariff: Assigns responsibility to personnel for berthing, compiling dockage, wharfage, demurrage, and storage reports, and enforcing safety regulations. Reviews department reports to verify accuracy of assessments. Assigns berth, dock, and shed space for incoming ships. Prepares recommendations for assignment of facilities to companies on a continuous basis. Analyzes reports to determine efficiency of dock operations and recommends improvements. Contacts representatives of shipping companies to resolve problems pertaining to facilities and to maintain business relationship.

184.167-278 YARD MANAGER (r.r. trans.)
Directs and coordinates activities of workers engaged in makeup and breakup of trains and switching inbound and outbound traffic of railroad yard: Reviews train schedules and switching orders, and observes traffic movement in yard to determine which tracks can be made available to accommodate inbound and outbound traffic. Directs routing of inbound and outbound traffic to specific tracks. Reviews waybills or other shipping records indicating material to be loaded or unloaded, tonnage of cargo, type of carrier, and planned routes. Provides instruction concerning switching of cars, makeup and breakup of trains, and routing of inbound and outbound traffic to insure safe and efficient conduct of yard activities.

184.267-010 FREIGHT-TRAFFIC CONSULTANT (bus. ser.) transportation consultant.
Advises industries, business firms, and individuals concerning methods of preparation of freight for shipment, rates to be applied, and mode of transportation to be used: Consults with client regarding packing procedures and inspects packed or crated goods for conformance to shipping specifications to prevent damage, delay, or penalties. Selects mode of transportation, such as air, water, railroad, or truck without regard to higher rates when speed is necessary. Confers with shipping brokers concerning export and import papers, docking facilities, or packing and marking procedures. Files claims with insurance company for losses, damages, and overcharges of freight shipments.

184.387-010 WHARFINGER (water trans.)
Compiles reports, such as dockage, demurrage, wharfage, and storage, to insure that shipping companies are assessed specified harbor fees: Compares information on statements, records, and reports with ship's manifest to determine that weight, measurement, and classification of commodities are in accordance with tariff. Calculates tariff assessment from ship's manifest to insure that charges are correct. Prepares and submits reports. Inspects sheds and wharves to determine need for repair. Arranges for temporary connection of water and electrical services from wharves. Reads service meters to determine charges to be made.

185 WHOLESALE AND RETAIL TRADE MANAGERS AND OFFICIALS

This group includes managerial occupations concerned with selling merchandise to retailers; to industrial, commercial, institutional or professional users; or to other wholesalers; or acting as agents in buying merchandise for or selling merchandise to such persons or companies.

185.117-010 MANAGER, DEPARTMENT STORE (ret. tr.)
Directs and coordinates, through subordinate managerial personnel, activities of department store selling lines of merchandise in specialized departments: Formulates pricing policies for sale of merchandise, or implements policies set forth by merchandising board. Coordinates activities of non-merchandising departments, as purchasing, credit, accounting, and advertising with merchandising departments to obtain optimum efficiency of operations with minimum costs in order to maximize profits. Develops and implements, through subordinate managerial personnel, policies and procedures for store and departmental operations and customer personnel, and community relations. Negotiates or approves contracts negotiated with suppliers of merchandise, or with other establishments providing security, maintenance, or cleaning services. Reviews operating and financial statements and departmental sales records to determine merchandising activities that require additional sales promotion, clearance sales, or other sales procedures in order to turn over merchandise and achieve profitability of store operations and merchandising objectives.

185.137-010 MANAGER, FAST FOOD SERVICES (ret. tr.; whole. tr.)
Manages franchised or independent fast food or wholesale prepared food establishment: Directs, coordinates, and participates in preparation of, and cooking, wrapping or packing types of food served or prepared by establishment, collecting of monies from in-house or take-out customers, or assembling food orders for wholesale customers. Coordinates activities of workers engaged in keeping business records, collecting and paying accounts, ordering or purchasing supplies, and delivery of foodstuffs to wholesale or retail customers. Interviews, hires, and trains personnel. May contact prospective wholesale customers, such as mobile food vendors, vending machine operators, bar and tavern owners, and institutional personnel, to promote sale of prepared foods, such as doughnuts, sandwiches, and specialty food items. May establish delivery routes and schedules for supplying wholesale customers. Workers are usually classified according to type or name of franchised establishment or type of prepared foodstuff retailed or wholesaled.

185.157-010 FASHION COORDINATOR (ret. tr.) fashion stylist.
Promotes new fashions and coordinates promotional activities, such as fashion shows, to induce consumer acceptance: Studies fashion and trade journals, travels to garment centers, attends fashion shows, and visits manufacturers and merchandise markets to obtain information on fashion trends. Consults with buying personnel to gain advice regarding type of fashions store will purchase and feature for season. Advises publicity and display departments of merchandise to be publicized. Selects garments and accessories to be shown at fashion shows. Provides information on current fashions, style trends, and use of accessories. May contract with models, musicians, caterers, and other personnel to manage staging of shows. May conduct teenage fashion shows and direct activities of store-sponsored club for teenagers.

185.157-014 SUPERVISOR OF SALES (bus. ser.)
Coordinates and publicizes tobacco marketing activities within specified area: Visits tobacco growers, buyers, and auction warehouses to cultivate interest and goodwill. Develops publicity for tobacco industry. Investigates and confirms eligibility of buyers. Collects membership dues for tobacco Board of Trade. Schedules tobacco auction dates. Records quantity and purchase price of tobacco sold daily, and prepares reports specified by board. May prepare report of marketing activities for state and federal agencies. May review and verify reports for individual warehouses. May examine quality and growth of tobacco in fields of individual growers and inform buyers of results.

185.157-018 WHOLESALER (whole. tr.) II
Exports domestic merchandise to foreign merchants and consumers and imports foreign merchandise for sale to domestic merchants or consumers: Arranges for purchase and transportation of imports through company representatives abroad and sells imports to local customers. Sells domestic goods, materials, or products to representatives of foreign companies. May be required to be fluent in language of country in which import or export business is conducted. May specialize in only one phase of foreign trade and be designated as EXPORTER (whole. tr.) or IMPORTER (ret. tr.; whole. tr.).

Step 6. Put Appropriate DOT Summaries on the Top of Your Job Description Form

Next, write a job description for the job you want done in your enterprise. To facilitate this, write the corresponding DOT codes and DOT definitions on the Background Job Description Data Form shown in Figure 3.11. Particularly when (as is usually the case) only one or two DOT definitions apply to the job description you are writing, the DOT definition will give your own definition a firm foundation. It will provide a standardized list of duties and will serve as a constant reminder of the specific duties that should be included in your own definition. Furthermore, including the DOT codes and definitions will facilitate your conversations with the state job services should you use them to help you find employees for your open positions.

Step 7. Complete Your Job Description

Finally, in Figure 3.11, write a job summary that is appropriate for your own job in your enterprise. Then use the job analysis information you obtained in step 3 together with the information you gleaned from the DOT to develop a complete listing of the tasks and duties of each of your jobs.

WRITING JOB SPECIFICATIONS

The job specification takes the job description and answers the question, "What human traits and experience are necessary to do this job well?" It shows you what kind of person to recruit for and for what qualities that person should be tested. The job specification may be a separate section on the job description or a separate document entirely; often it is presented on the back of the job description.[23]

♦ SPECIFICATIONS FOR TRAINED VERSUS UNTRAINED PERSONNEL

Suppose you were looking for a trained bookkeeper (or trained counselor or auto mechanic). In cases like these your job specifications would probably focus on things like length of previous service, quality of any relevant training, and so forth. Thus, it's usually not too difficult to determine the human requirements for placing *already trained* people on a job.

But the problems are more complex when you're seeking *untrained* people for your jobs (probably with the intention of training them on the job). Here you need to specify qualities like physical traits, personality, interests, or sensory skills that imply some potential for performing the job or for having the ability to be trained for the job. For example, if the job requires detailed manipulation on an electronic assembly line, you might want to ensure that the person scores high on a test of finger dexterity. Your goal is thus to identify those personal traits—those human requirements—that validly predict which candidate would do well on the job and which would not. Identifying these human requirements for a job is accomplished either through a subjective, judgmental approach or through statistical analysis.

♦ JOB SPECIFICATIONS BASED ON JUDGMENT

The judgmental approach involves developing the job specifications based on the educated guesses of people like supervisors and human resource managers. The basic procedure here is to ask: "What does it take in terms of education, intelligence, training, and the like to do this job well?"

One of the most extensive judgmental approaches to developing job specifications is contained in the *Dictionary of Occupational Titles*. For jobs in the dictionary, judgments have been made by experts like job analysts and vocational counselors regarding each job's human requirements. Each of these human requirements or traits has been assigned a letter, as follows:

G (intelligence), V (verbal), N (numerical), S (spatial), P (perception), Q (clerical perception), K (motor coordination), F (finger dexterity), M (manual dexterity), E (eye-hand-foot coordination), and C (color dissemination). These ratings reflect the amount of each trait or ability possessed by people with different performance levels currently working on the job.

◆ JOB SPECIFICATIONS BASED ON STATISTICAL ANALYSIS

Basing your job specifications on statistical analysis is the most defensible approach, but it is also the most difficult. Basically, what you do here is (statistically) determine the relationship between (1) some *predictor* or human trait such as height, intelligence, or finger dexterity and (2) some indicator or *criterion* of job effectiveness (such as performance as rated by the supervisor). The basic process involves five steps: (1) analyze the job and decide how to measure job performance, (2) select personal traits like finger dexterity that you believe should predict successful performance, (3) test job candidates for these traits, (4) measure these candidates' subsequent job performance, and (5) statistically analyze the relationship between the human trait (finger dexterity) and job performance. Your objective is to determine whether the former predicts the latter. In this way the human requirements for performing the job can be statistically ascertained.

This method, to repeat, is more defensible than is the judgmental approach. Specifically, equal rights legislation forbids using traits that you can't *prove* distinguish between high and low job performers. Standards that directly or indirectly discriminate on the basis of sex, race, religion, national origin, or age may have to be shown (by you) to be good predictors, and this generally requires a statistical validation study.

SUMMARY

1. The purpose of an organization is to give each person a separate, distinct job and to ensure that these jobs are coordinated in such a way that the organization accomplishes its goals. The usual way of depicting an organization is with an organization chart. These provide the title of each manager's position and, by means of connecting lines, show who is accountable to whom and who is in charge of what department.

2. Developing an organization structure results in jobs that have to be staffed. Job analysis is the procedure through which you find out (1) what the job entails, and (2) what kinds of people should be hired for the job. It involves six steps: (1) Determine the use of the job analysis information, (2) collect background information, (3) select the positions to be analyzed, (4) collect job analysis data, (5) review information with participants, and (6) develop a job description and job specification.

3. There are five *basic techniques* one can use to gather job analysis data: interviews, direct observation, a questionnaire, participant logs, and the U.S. Civil Service Procedure. These are good for developing job descriptions and specifications. The *Department of Labor, functional job analysis,* and *PAQ* approaches result in quantitative ratings of each job and are therefore useful for classifying jobs for pay purposes.

4. The job description should portray the work of the position so well that the duties are clear without reference to other job descriptions. Always ask: "Will the new employee understand the job if he or she reads the job description?"

5. The job specification takes the job description and answers the question: "What human traits and experience are necessary to do this job well?" It tells what kind of person to recruit for and for what qualities that person should be tested. Job specifications are usually based on the educated guesses of managers; however, a more accurate statistical approach to developing job specifications can also be used.

6. Job analysis is in many ways the first personnel activity that affects motivation. Most people can't perform a job when they don't have the ability and skills to do the job. It is through job analysis that you determine what the job entails and what skills and abilities you should look for in job candidates.

7. You can use the *Dictionary of Occupational Titles* to help you write your job descriptions. Find and reproduce the DOT descriptions that relate to the job you're describing. Then use those DOT descriptions to "anchor" your own description and particularly to suggest duties to be included.

KEY TERMS

organization chart

job analysis

job description

job specifications

participant diary/
logs

position analysis
questionnaire (PAQ)

Department of Labor
job analysis

functional job
analysis

DISCUSSION QUESTIONS

1. What items are typically included in the organization chart? What items are not shown on the chart?

2. What is job analysis? How can you make use of the information it provides?

3. We discussed several methods for collecting job analysis data—questionnaires, the position analysis questionnaire, and so on. Compare and contrast these methods, explaining what each is useful for and listing the pros and cons of each.

4. Describe the types of information typically found in a job description.

5. Explain how you would conduct a job analysis.

♦ APPLICATION EXERCISES

♦ CASE INCIDENT — Job Questionnaires

The Arkansas (Little Rock) division of the Pierce Manufacturing Co. has encountered difficulty in its job analysis program. A new human resource director, taking over less than a year ago, began the program by asking employees to fill out a job questionnaire. When answers came in, she asked supervisors to comment. In many cases, employees indicated that they were performing tasks that supervisors questioned. Some supervisors insisted that employees were not actually doing all they claimed. In some cases, supervisors admitted that employees were doing what they claimed but said they should not be doing some of the tasks.

The new human resource director now finds herself faced with a difficult problem. She sought only to find out what each job involved. Now she is being asked to settle arguments as to what should be expected of job holders and, even more difficult, what to do about employees who insist they have long been expected to do more than their supervisors think they are doing.

Questions

1. Should the human resource director ignore these controversies? If so, whose word should she take as to job content? If not, how should she move to resolve the differences?

2. Did she go about the job analysis in the right way? Why? Why not?

---

*Source: Dale Yoder, *Personnel Management and Industrial Relations* (Englewood Cliffs, N.J.: Prentice Hall, 1970), p. 223.

EXPERIENTIAL EXERCISE

Purpose: The purpose of this exercise is to give you experience in developing a job description, by developing one for your instructor.

Required Understanding: You should understand the mechanics of job analysis and be thoroughly familiar with the job analysis questionnaire (Figure 3.5) and the job analysis format (in the appendix to this chapter).

How to Set Up the Exercise/Instructions: Set up groups of four to six students for this exercise. As in all exercises in this book, the groups should be separated and should not converse with each other. Half the groups in the class will develop the job description using the job analysis questionnaire, while the other half of the groups will develop it using the job analysis format. Each student should review the questionnaire or format (as appropriate) before joining his or her group.

1. Each group should do a job analysis of their instructor's job: Half the groups (to repeat) will use the job analysis questionnaire for this purpose, and half will use the job analysis format.

2. Based on this information, each group will develop its own job description and job specification for the instructor.

3. Next, each group should choose a partner group, one that developed the job description and job specification using the alternate method. (A group that used the job analysis questionnaire should be paired with a group that used the job analysis format.)

4. Finally, within each of these new combined groups, compare, contrast, and criticize each of the two sets of job descriptions and job specifications. Did each job analysis method provide different types of information? Which seems superior? Does one seem more advantageous for some types of jobs than others?

Appendix 3.1

Job Analysis Format

JOB ANALYSIS INFORMATION FORMAT

Your Job Title _____ Code _____ Date _____ _____

Class Title _____ Department _____

Your Name _____ Facility _____

Superior's Title _____ Prepared by _____

Superior's Name _____ Hours Worked _____ AM/PM __ to AM/PM __

1. What is the general purpose of your job?

2. What was your last job? If it was in another organization, please name it.

3. To what job would you normally expect to be promoted?

4. If you regularly supervise others, list them by name and job title.

5. If you supervise others, please check those activities that are part of your supervisory duties:

   ___ Hiring   ___ Coaching   ___ Promoting

   ___ Orienting   ___ Counseling   ___ Compensating

   ___ Training   ___ Budgeting   ___ Disciplining

   ___ Scheduling   ___ Directing   ___ Terminating

   ___ Developing   ___ Measuring Performance   ___ Other _____

6. How would you describe the successful completion and results of your work?

7. *Job Duties*—Please briefly describe WHAT you do and, if possible, HOW you do it. Indicate those duties you consider to be most important and/or most difficult.

   (a) *Daily Duties*—

   (b) *Periodic Duties*—(Please indicate whether weekly, monthly, quarterly, etc.)—

   (c) *Duties Performed at Irregular Intervals*—

Signature _____ Date _____

JOB ANALYSIS INFORMATION FORMAT (cont.)

(d)   How long have you been performing these duties?

(e)   Are you now performing unnecessary duties? If yes, please describe.

(f)   Should you be performing duties not now included in your job? If yes, please describe

8. *Education*. Please check the blank that indicates the educational *requirements* for the job, not your *own* educational background.

(a)_____ No formal education required.   (e)_____ 4-Yr. college degree.

(b)_____ Less than high school diploma.   (f)_____ Education beyond under-graduate degree and/or professional license.

(c)_____ High school diploma or equivalent.

(d)_____ 2-Yr. college certificate or equivalent

List advanced degrees or specific professional license or certificate required.

Please indicate the education you had when you were placed on this job.

9. *Experience*. Please check the amount needed to perform your job.

(a)__None   (e)__More than one year to three years

(b)__Less than one month   (f)__Three to five years

(c)__One month to less than six months (g)__Five to ten years

(d)__Six months to one year   (h)__Over ten years

Please indicate the experience you had when you were placed on this job.

10. *Skill*. Please list any skills required in the performance of your job. (For example, amount of accuracy, alertness, precision in working with described tools, methods, systems, etc.)

Please list skills you possessed when you were placed on this job.

11. *Equipment*. Does your work require the use of any equipment? Yes___ No___. If Yes, please list the equipment and check whether you use it rarely, occasionally, or frequently.

Equipment	Rarely	Occasionally	Frequently
(a) _____			
(b) _____			
(c) _____			
(d) _____			

JOB ANALYSIS INFORMATION FORMAT (cont).

12. *Physical Demands.* Please check all undesirable physical demands required on your job and whether you are required to do so rarely, occasionally, or frequently.

		Rarely	Occasionally	Frequently
(a)_____	Handling heavy material			
(b)_____	Awkward or cramped positions			
(c)_____	Excessive working speeds			
(d)_____	Excessive sensory requirements (seeing, hearing, touching, smelling, speaking)			
(e)_____	Vibrating equipment			
(f)_____	Others:_____			

13. *Emotional Demands.* Please check all undesirable emotional demands placed on you by your job and whether it is rarely, occasionally, or frequently.

		Rarely	Occasionally	Frequently
(a)_____	Contacts with general public	_____	_____	_____
(b)_____	Customer contact	_____	_____	_____
(c)_____	Close supervision	_____	_____	_____
(d)_____	Deadlines under pressure	_____	_____	_____
(e)_____	Irregular activity schedules	_____	_____	_____
(f)_____	Working alone	_____	_____	_____
(g)_____	Excessive traveling	_____	_____	_____
(h)_____	Others:	_____	_____	_____

14. *Work Place Location.* Check type of location of your job and if you consider it to be unsatisfactory or satisfactory.

		Unsatisfactory	Satisfactory
(a)_____	Outdoor	_____	_____
(b)_____	Indoor	_____	_____
(c)_____	Underground	_____	_____
(d)_____	Pit	_____	_____
(e)_____	Scaffold	_____	_____

JOB ANALYSIS INFORMATION FORMAT

15. *Physical Surroundings.* Please check whether you consider the following physical conditions of your job to be poor, good, or excellent.

	Poor	Good	Excellent
(a)_____ Lighting	____	____	____
(b)_____ Ventilation	____	____	____
(c)_____ Sudden temperature change	____	____	____
(d)_____ Vibration	____	____	____
(e)_____ Comfort of furnishings	____	____	____

16. *Environmental Conditions.* Please check the objectionable conditions under which you must perform your job and check whether the condition exists rarely, occasionally, or frequently.

	Rarely	Occasionally	Frequently
(a)_____ Dust	____	____	____
(b)_____ Dirt	____	____	____
(c)_____ Heat	____	____	____
(d)_____ Cold	____	____	____
(e)_____ Fumes	____	____	____
(f)_____ Odors	____	____	____
(g)_____ Noise	____	____	____
(h)_____ Wetness	____	____	____
(i)_____ Humidity	____	____	____
(j)_____ Others:	____	____	____

17. *Health and Safety.* Please check all undesirable health and safety factors under which you must perform your job and whether you are required to do so rarely, occasionally, or frequently.

	Rarely	Occasionally	Frequently
(a)_____ Height of elevated workplace	____	____	____
(b)_____ Radiation	____	____	____
(c)_____ Mechanical hazards	____	____	____
(d)_____ Moving objects	____	____	____
(e)_____ Explosives	____	____	____
(f)_____ Electrical hazards	____	____	____
(g)_____ Fire	____	____	____
(h)_____ Others:_____	____	____	____

SUPERVISORY REVIEW

Do the incumbent's responses to the questionnaire accurately describe the work requirements and the work performed in meeting the responsibilities of the job? _____Yes _____ No. If No, please explain and list any significant omissions or additions.

Date _____ Title _____ Signature _____

Source: Richard Henderson, *Compensation Management: Rewarding Performance,* 2nd ed., copyright 1979, pp. 148–152. Reprinted by permission of Prentice-Hall, Englewood Cliffs, N.J.

NOTES

1. For a discussion of alternative uses for job descriptions see Philip C. Grant, "What Use Is a Job Description?" *Personnel Journal* (February 1988), pp. 44–55.

2. Wayne Cascio, *Applied Psychology in Personnel Management* (Reston, Va.: Reston, 1978), p. 132.

3. Ernest J. McCormick, "Job and Task Analysis," in Marvin D. Dunnette, ed., *Handbook of Industrial and Organizational Psychology* (Chicago: Rand McNally, 1976), pp. 651–696.

4. Richard Henderson, *Compensation Management* (Reston, Va.: Reston, 1979), pp. 139–150. See also Patrick W. Wright and Kenneth Wexley, "How to Choose the Kind of Job Analysis You Really Need," *Personnel*, Vol. 62, no. 5 (May 1985), pp. 51–55; C. J. Cranny and Michael E. Doherty, "Importance Ratings in Job Analysis: Note on the Misinterpretation of Factor Analyses," *Journal of Applied Psychology* (May 1988), pp. 320–322. For a discussion of the pros and cons of weighting individual tasks during the job analysis.

5. See, for example, Ernest McCormick, James Shaw, and Angelo DeNisi, "Use of the Position Analysis Questionnaire for Establishing the Job Component Validity of a Test," *Journal of Applied Psychology*, Vol. 64, no. 1 (1979), pp. 51–56; Marvin Tratner, "Task Analysis In the Design of Three Concurrent Validity Studies of the Professional and Administrative Career Examination," *Personnel Psychology*, Vol. 32 (Spring 1979), pp. 109–119.

6. Ibid.

7. Cascio, *Applied Psychology*, p. 140.

8. Appendix from Henderson, *Compensation Management*, pp. 148–152.

9. A complete explanation and definition of each of these seven attributes (knowledge, skills, abilities, etc.) can be found in U.S. Civil Service Commission, *Job Analysis* (Washington, D.C.: U.S. Government Printing Office, December 1976).

10. Note that the PAQ (and other quantitative techniques) can also be used for job evaluation, which is explained in Chapter 10.

11. Again, we will see that *job evaluation* is the process through which jobs are compared to one another and their values determined. While usually viewed as a job analysis technique, the PAQ is, in practice, actually as much or more of a job evaluation technique and could therefore be discussed in either this chapter or in Chapter 10. For a discussion of how to use PAQ for classifying jobs, see Edwin Cornelius III, Theodore Carron, and Marianne Collins, "Job Analysis Models and Job Classifications," *Personnel Psychology*, Vol. 32 (Winter 1979), pp. 693–708. See also Edwin Cornelius III, Frank Schmidt, and Theodore Carron, "Job Classification Approaches and the Implementation of Validity Generalization Results," *Personnel Psychology*, Vol. 37, no. 2 (Summer 1984), pp. 247–260.

12. Jack Smith and Milton Hakel, "Comparisons Among Data Sources, Response Bias, and Reliability and Validity of a Structured Job Analysis Questionnaire," *Personnel Psychology*, Vol. 32 (Winter 1979), pp. 677–692. See also Edwin Cornelius III, Angelo Denisi, and Allyn Blencoe, "Expert and Naive Raters Using the PAQ: Does It Matter?" *Personnel Psychology*, Vol. 37, no. 3 (Autumn 1984), pp. 453–464; Lee Friedman and Robert Harvey, "Can Raters with Reduced Job Description Information Provide Accurate Position Analysis Questionnaire (PAQ) Ratings?" *Personnel Psychology*, Vol. 34 (Winter 1986), pp. 779–789.

13. Robert J. Harvey et al., "Dimensionality of the Job Element Inventory, A Simplified Worker-Oriented Job Analysis Questionnaire," *Journal of Applied Psychology* (November 1988), pp. 639–646; Stephanie Butler and Robert Harvey, "A Comparison of Holistic Versus Decomposed Rating of Position Analysis Questionnaire Work Dimensions," *Personnel Psychology* (Winter 1988), pp. 761–772.

14. This discussion is based on Howard Olson et al., "The Use of Functional Job Analysis in Establishing Performance Standards for Heavy Equipment Operators," *Personnel Psychology*, Vol. 34 (Summer 1981), pp. 351–364.

15. Regarding this discussion, see Henderson, *Compensation Management*, pp. 175–184.

16. James Evered, "How to Write a Good Job Description," *Supervisory Manage-*

ment (April 1981), pp. 14–19; Roger J. Plachy, "Writing Job Descriptions That Get Results," *Personnel* (October 1987), pp. 56–58.

17. Ibid., p. 16.
18. This discussion is based on ibid.
19. Ibid., p. 16.
20. Ibid., p. 17.
21. Ibid., p. 18.
22. Ernest Dale, *Organizations* (New York: American Management Association, 1967).
23. The remainder of this chapter, except as noted, is from Ernest J. McCormick and Joseph Tiffin, *Industrial Psychology* (Englewood Cliffs, N.J.: Prentice-Hall, 1974), pp. 56–61.

Chapter 4

Personnel Planning and Recruiting

**When you finish studying this chapter,
you should be able to:**

1. Cite the steps in recruitment and placement.
2. Discuss the main elements in personnel forecasting.
3. Compare and contrast at least five sources of job candidates.
4. Develop an application blank.
5. Develop and use a weighted application blank.

OVERVIEW

The main purpose of this chapter is to explain how to develop a pool of viable job candidates. A second purpose is to discuss developing and using application blanks and to explain a technique for using application blanks to predict success on the job. Also discussed are personnel planning and forecasting, which involve projecting personnel requirements and supply. Here you develop a pool of qualified candidates for the job, candidates who have the skills and ability to do the job successfully. Application blanks (also discussed in this chapter) are the first step in screening the best candidates for the job.

How do you plan for the openings that inevitably develop in your organization? You could choose to wait for the opening to develop and then try to fill it as best you can. Most managers use this approach and it is probably effective enough for small organizations. But for larger firms (and for managers who want to avoid last-minute scurrying and mistakes), some forecasting and planning are worthwhile.

Remember, though, that to be worthwhile personnel planning has to be *integrated* both internally and externally. This is summarized in Figure 4.1. *Internally,* plans for recruitment, selection, placement, training, and appraisal should be developed in such a way that, for instance, the organization's training plans reflect its plans for recruiting and selecting new employees. *Externally,* your personnel plans should be integrated with the organization's overall planning process, since plans to enter (or not enter) new business, to build (or not build) new plants, or to reduce the level of activities have significant labor implications—in terms of recruiting, and training, for instance.[1]

Personnel plans (like any good plans) are built on premises—basic assumptions about the future—and the purpose of *forecasting* is to develop these basic premises. If it is *personnel* requirements you are planning for, you'll usually need three sets of forecasts: one for your *personnel requirements,* one for the *supply of outside candidates,* and one for your *available internal candidates.*

FORECASTING PERSONNEL REQUIREMENTS

◆ FACTORS IN FORECASTING PERSONNEL REQUIREMENTS

Most managers consider several factors when forecasting personnel requirements.[2] From a practical point of view, *the demand for your product*

FIGURE 4.1
How All Personnel Functions Impact Personnel Planning

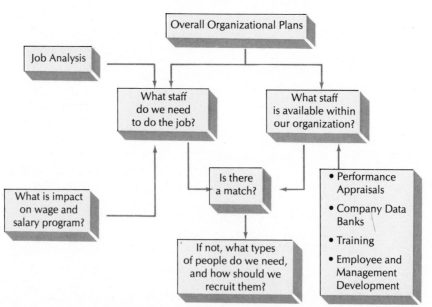

Note: Personnel planning should be integrated externally and internally. Externally it should be integrated with the organization's overall plans, for example, opening new plants, building a new hospital wing, or reducing operations due to an impending recession all have staff implications. Internally, staff planning should be integrated in that planning for all the personnel functions—such as recruiting, training, job analysis, and development—should be integrated or coordinated, for example, hiring 50 new employees means they must be trained, and their wages budgeted for.

or service is paramount.[3] Thus, in a manufacturing firm, sales are projected first. Then the volume of production required to meet these sales requirements is determined. Finally, the staff needed to maintain this volume of output is estimated. But in addition to this "basic requirement" for staff, you will also have to consider several other factors:

1. *Projected turnover* (as a result of resignations or terminations).
2. *Quality and nature* of your employees (in relation to what you see as the changing needs of your organization).
3. *Decisions* to upgrade the quality of products or services or enter into new markets.
4. *Technological and administrative changes* resulting in increased productivity.
5. The *financial resources* available to your department.

Specific techniques for determining human resource requirements include trend analysis, ratio analysis, correlation analysis, and computerized forecasting.[4]

Trend Analysis

A logical way to begin your forecast is by studying your firm's employment trends over the last five years or so. For example, you might compute the number of employees in your firm at the end of each of the last five years, or perhaps the number in each subgroup (like salespeople, production people, secretarial, and administrative) at the end of each of those years. The purpose is to identify employment trends that you think might continue into the future.

trend analysis Study of a firm's past employment needs over a period of years to predict future needs.

Trend analysis is mostly valuable as an initial, exploratory exercise since employment levels rarely depend solely on the passage of time. Instead, other factors (like changes in sales volume and productivity) will also affect your future staffing needs.

Ratio Analysis

ratio analysis A forecasting technique for determining future staff needs by using ratios between sales volume and number of employees needed.

Another approach, **ratio analysis,** determines the *ratio* between (1) some causal factor (like sales volume) and (2) number of employees required (for instance, number of salespeople). For example, suppose you find that a salesperson traditionally generates $500,000 in sales and that in each of the last two years it required ten salespeople to generate $5 million in sales. Also assume that your plans call for increasing your firm's sales to $8 million next year and to $10 million two years hence. Then, if the sales revenue–salespeople ratio remains the same, you would require six new salespeople next year (each of whom produces an extra $500,000 in sales). In the following year you would need an additional four salespeople to generate the extra $2 million in sales (between next year's $8 million and the following year's $10 million in sales).

You can also use ratio analysis to help forecast your other employee requirements. For example, you can compute a salesperson-secretary ratio and thereby determine how many new secretaries will be needed to support the extra sales staff.

As with trend analysis, ratio analysis assumes that productivity remains about the same—for instance that each salesperson can't be motivated to produce much more than $500,000 in sales each. If sales productivity *were* to increase or decrease, then the ratio of sales to salespeople would change, and a forecast based on historical ratios would no longer be as accurate.

An Optional Method: Correlation Analysis

correlation analysis Determination of statistical relationships between two variables, for example, staff levels and a measure of business activity.

Correlation analysis involves finding the statistical relationship between two variables. In the case of forecasting your personnel requirements, correlation analysis would involve determining whether two factors—a measure of business activity and your staffing levels—are related. If they are, then if you can forecast the measure of business activity, you should also be able to forecast your personnel requirements. Correlation analysis can provide a more accurate basis on which to forecast personnel needs than either ratio or trend analysis.

Let's look at an example.[5] A 500-bed hospital in Chicago expects to expand to 1,200 beds over the next five years. The director of nursing and the human resource director want to forecast the requirement for registered nurses. The human resource director therefore decides to determine the relationship between size of hospital (in terms of number of beds) and number of nurses required. She calls five similar hospitals of various sizes and gets the following figures:

SIZE OF HOSPITAL (NUMBER OF BEDS)	NUMBER OF REGISTERED NURSES
200	240
300	260
400	470
500	500
600	620
700	660
800	820
900	860

One way to determine the relationship between size of hospital and nurses would be to draw a scatter plot as illustrated in Figure 4.2. *Hospital size* is shown on the horizontal axis. *Number of nurses* is shown on the vertical axis. If the two factors are correlated, then the points will tend to fall along a straight line, as in Figure 4.2. If you then carefully draw in a line in such a way as to minimize the distances between the line and each one of the plotted points, you will be able to estimate the number of nurses that

FIGURE 4.2

Determining the Relationship Between Hospital Size and Number of Nurses

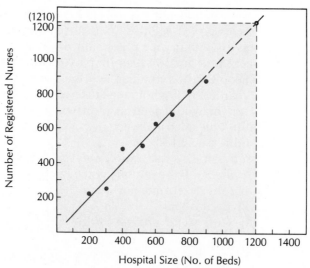

Note: After fitting the line, you can extrapolate—project—how many employees you'll need, given your projected volume.

will be needed for each given hospital size. Thus, for a 1,200-bed hospital, the human resource director would assume she needs about 1,210 nurses.

Using the Computer to Forecast Personnel Requirements

computerized forecasting Determining future staff needs by projecting a firm's sales, volume of production, and personnel required to maintain this volume of output, with computers and software packages.

Some employers use computerized systems for developing personnel requirement forecasts. For example, one expert has developed a **computerized forecasting** package.[6] A personnel specialist, working in conjunction with line managers, compiles the information necessary to develop a computerized forecast of personnel requirements. The data to be supplied include direct labor hours needed to produce one unit of product (a measure of productivity) and three sales projections—minimum, maximum, and probable—for the product line in question. Based on such inputs, the program generates figures on such things as "average staff levels required to meet product demands," as well as separate forecasts for direct labor (such as assembly workers), indirect staff (like secretaries), and exempt staff (like executives).

With a computerized system like this, your employer can quickly translate estimates of projected productivity and sales levels into forecasts of personnel needs and can easily check the effects of *various* levels of productivity and sales on personnel requirements.[7]

Managerial Judgment

Whichever approach you use, *managerial judgment* will play a large role. It is rare that any historical trend, ratio, or relationship will continue unchanged into the future. Judgment is thus needed to modify the forecast based on factors you believe will change in the future. Important factors that may modify your initial forecast of personnel requirements include the following:

1. Decisions to upgrade the quality of products or services or enter into new markets. These have implications for the nature of the employees you'll require. Ask, for instance, whether the skills of current employees are compatible with your organization's new products or services.
2. Technological and administrative changes resulting in increased productivity. Increased efficiency (in terms of output per hour) could reduce personnel needs and might come about through installing new equipment or a new financial incentive plan, for instance.
3. The financial resources available. For example, a larger budget allows you to hire more people and pay higher wages, perhaps with an eye toward increasing the quality of your product or service. Conversely, a projected budget crunch could mean fewer positions to recruit for and lower salary offers.

♦ FORECASTING THE SUPPLY OF INSIDE CANDIDATES

The personnel requirements forecast answers the question: "How many employees will we need?" However, before determining how many new outside candidates to recruit and hire, you must first know how many candidates for your projected job openings will come from within your organization, from the existing ranks; determining this is the purpose of forecasting the supply of inside candidates.

qualifications inventories Systematic records, either manual or computerized, listing employees' education, career and development interests, languages, special skills, etc., to be used in forecasting inside candidates for promotion.

To tap this internal supply of candidates you will first need some way of compiling information on their qualifications. These **qualifications inventories** will contain information on things like each employee's performance record, educational background, and promotability. This information can be compiled either manually or in a computerized system.

Manual Systems and Replacement Charts

There are several types of manual systems you can use to keep track of your employees' qualifications. In the *personnel inventory and development record* shown in Figure 4.3, information is compiled on each employee and then recorded on the inventory. The information includes education, company-sponsored courses taken, career and development interests, languages, and skills. Information like this can then be used to determine which current employees are available for promotion or transfer to projected open positions.

personnel replacement charts Company records showing present performance and promotability of inside candidates for the most important positions.

Some employers use **personnel replacement charts** (see Figure 4.4) to keep track of inside candidates for their most important positions. These show the present performance and promotability for each potential replacement for your employer's important positions. As an alternative, you can

FIGURE 4.3
Personnel Inventory Form Appropriate for Manual Storage and Retrieval

PERSONNEL INVENTORY AND DEVELOPMENT RECORD | Date: month, year

Department	Area or sub-department	Branch or section	Location

Company service date (month, day, year)	Birthdate (month, day, year)	Marital status	Job title

Education — Degree, year obtained, college, and major field of study

Grade school 6 7 8 | High school 9 10 11 12 13

College 1 2 3 4 5

Courses (company sponsored)

Type of course	Subject or course	Year	Type of course	Subject or course	Year

Career and development interests

Are you interested in an alternative type of work? Yes ☐ No ☐ | Would you accept transfer to another division? Yes ☐ No ☐ | Would you accept lateral moves for further development? Yes ☐ No ☐

If yes, specifically what type? | Comment on any qualifying circumstances

Photo

What type of training do you believe you require to:
A) Improve your skills and performance in your present position
B) Improve your experience and abilities for advancement.

Last name

First name

What other assignments do you believe you are qualified to perform now?

Middle name

Languages	Written		Spoken	
	☐	☐	☐	☐
	☐	☐	☐	☐

SS Number

Societies and organizations — Memberships in community organizations, etc., within last five years, indicate name of association and office held, if any

Skills

Type of skill	Certification, if any	Type of skill	Certification, if any

Other significant work experience, and/or military service. (Omit repetitive experiences)

	Location	From yr.	To yr.	

Comments: Other significant experience, recreational activities, hobbies, interests, or personal data.

FIGURE 4.4
Management Personnel Replacement Chart

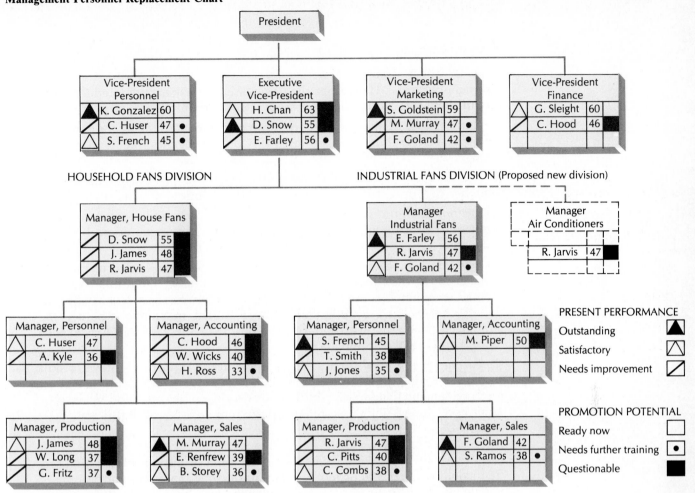

develop a **position replacement card.** Here you make up a card for each position, showing possible replacements as well as present performance, promotion potential, and training required by each possible candidate.

Computerized Information Systems

Particularly for large employers, maintaining qualifications inventories on hundreds or thousands of employees can't be adequately managed manually. Many firms have thus computerized this information, and a number of packaged systems are now available for accomplishing this computerization.[8]

In one such system, employees fill out a 12-page booklet in which they describe their background and experience in a manner that lends itself to computerization. All this information is stored on the computer. When a manager needs a qualified person to fill a position, he or she describes the position (for instance, in terms of the education and skills it entails), and then enters this information into the computer. After scanning its bank of possible candidates, the program presents the manager with a computer printout of qualified candidates.

According to one expert the basic ingredients of such a computerized human resource skills inventory should include the following:

Work experience codes. A list of work experience descriptors, titles, or codes that describe jobs within the company so that the individual's present, previous, and desired jobs can be coded.

Product knowledge. The employee's level of familiarity with each of the employer's product lines or services as an indication of where the person might be transferred or promoted.

Industry experience. The person's industry experiences should be coded, since for certain positions the employee's knowledge of key related industries is very useful.

Formal education. Here enter the name of each postsecondary educational institution attended, the field of study, degree granted, and year granted.

Training courses. Indicate here training courses conducted by the employer and, possibly, training courses taught by outside agents like the American Management Association.

Foreign language skills. Here include a degree of proficiency as well as whether the foreign language is the employee's native tongue.

Relocation limitations. Compile information regarding the employee's willingness to relocate and the locales to which the person would prefer to be relocated.

Career interests. Using the same work experience codes used in the first section above, the employee should indicate what he or she would like to be doing for the employer in the future. Space can be provided for a brief priority of choices, and a code should be included indicating whether the employee's main qualification for the work he or she wants to do is experience, knowledge, or interests.

Performance appraisals. These should be entered into the employee's skill bank and updated periodically to indicate the employee's achievement on each dimension (leadership ability, motivation, communication skills, etc.) appraised, along with a summary of the employee's strengths and deficiencies.[9]

In fact the typical data elements in a human resources information system could number 100 or more. For example, one major vendor of a mainframe personnel/payroll package reportedly used by over 2,000 companies suggests the 140 elements shown in Table 4.1. Notice that these elements range from home address to driver's license number, employee weight, organizational property, salary, sick leave used, skill (type), to veteran status.[10] Note that *skills* are often included in these types of data banks. Including "training courses completed" might only show what the employee is trained to do, not what he or she has actually shown he or she can do. Including skills such as "remove boiler casings and doors" (number of times performed, date last performed, time spent) lets you use your computer to zero in on which employees are competent to accomplish the task that must be done. Here you can even include a skill level in the data bank, perhaps ranging from skill level 1 (can lead or instruct others) down to 2 (can perform the job with minimum supervision), 3 (has some experience: can assist experienced workers), to 4 (has not had opportunity to work on this job.)[11]

The Matter of Privacy

Several recent developments have intensified the human resource manager's need to create better ways to actually control the personnel data that are stored in the organization's data banks. First, there is, as you can see, more information about employees in most employer's data banks. Second, the expansion of end-user computing capabilities offers more opportunities for more people to have access to this data.[12] Third (and related to number 2), the centralized review and approval for each request for information by the department in charge is no longer as practical as it once was. And, finally, under certain legislation (such as the Federal Privacy Act of 1974 and

TABLE 4.1 Typical Data Elements in a Human Resources Information System

Address (work)	Garnishments	Salary change type
Address (home)	Grievance (type)	Salary
Birthdate	Grievance (outcome)	Salary range
Birthplace	Grievance (filing date)	Schools attended
Child support deductions	Handicap status	Service date
Citizenship	Health plan coverage	Service branch
Claim pending (description)	Health plan (no. dependents)	Service discharge type
Claim pending (outcome)	Injury date	Service ending rank
Claim pending (court)	Injury type	Service discharge date
Claim pending (date)	Job location	Sex
Date on current job	Job preference	Sick leave used
Department	Job position number	Sick leave available
Dependent (sex)	Job title	Skill function (type)
Dependent (number of)	Job location	Skill sub-function (type)
Dependent (relationship)	Leave of absence start date	Skill (number of years)
Dependent (birthdate)	Leave of absence end date	Skill (proficiency level)
Dependent (name)	Leave of absence type	Skill (date last used)
Discipline (appeal date)	Life insurance coverage	Skill (location)
Discipline (type of charge)	Marital status	Skill (supervisory)
Discipline (appeal outcome)	Marriage date	Social Security number
Discipline (date of charge)	Medical exam (date)	Spouse's employment
Discipline (outcome)	Medical exam (restrictions)	Spouse's date of death
Discipline (hearing date)	Medical exam (blood type)	Spouse's name
Division	Medical exam (outcome)	Spouse's birthdate
Driver's license (number)	Miscellaneous deductions	Spouse's sex
Driver's license (state)	Name	Spouse's Social Security number
Driver's license (exp. date)	Organizational property	Start date
Education in progress (date)	Pay status	Stock plan membership
Education in progress (type)	Pension plan membership	Supervisor's name
Educational degree (date)	Performance rating	Supervisor's work address
Educational degree (type)	Performance increase ($)	Supervisor's work phone
Educational minor (minor)	Performance increase (%)	Supervisor's title
Educational level attained	Phone number (work)	Termination date
Educational field (major)	Phone number (home)	Termination reason
EEO-1 code	Prior service (term. date)	Training schools attended
Emergency contact (phone)	Prior service (hire date)	Training schools (date)
Emergency contact (name)	Prior service (term. reason)	Training schools (field)
Emergency contact (relation)	Professional license (type)	Training schools completed
Emergency contact (address)	Professional license (date)	Transfer date
Employee weight	Race	Transfer reason
Employee number	Rehire code	Union code
Employee code	Religious preference	Union deductions
Employee status	Salary points	United Way deductions
Employee height	Salary compa ratio	Vacation leave available
Employee date of death	Salary (previous)	Vacation leave used
Federal job code	Salary change date	Veteran status
Full-time/part-time code	Salary change reason	

Source: Donald Harris, "A Matter of Privacy: Managing Personal Data in Company Computers," *Personnel* (February 1987), p. 37.

the New York Personal Privacy Protection Act of 1985), employees may have legal rights regarding who has access to information about their work history and job performance.

Balancing the employer's legitimate right to make this information available to those in the organization who need it with the employees' rights to privacy isn't easy. One approach is to use the *access matrices* incorporated in the software of many data base management systems. Basically, these matrices define the rights of users (specified by name, rank, or functional identification) to have various kinds of access (such as "read only" or "write only") to each data element contained in the data base. Thus the computer programmers that are charged with the job of inputting data regarding employees might be authorized only to "write" information into the data base, while those in accounting are authorized to "read" a limited range of information such as the person's address, phone number, Social Security number, and pension status. The human resource director, on the other hand, might be authorized to both "read and write" all items when interacting with the data base.

♦ FORECASTING THE SUPPLY OF OUTSIDE CANDIDATES

Assuming that there are not enough inside candidates to fill your positions, you will probably next focus on outside candidates—those not currently employed by your organization. Forecasting the supply of outside candidates will involve forecasting *general economic* conditions, *local market* conditions, and *occupational market* conditions.

General Economic Conditions

general economic conditions Forecasting rates of employment based on general business conditions as reported by banks and business publications.

The first step is to forecast **general economic conditions** and the expected prevailing rate of unemployment. Usually, the lower the rate of unemployment, the lower the labor supply and the more difficult it will be to recruit personnel.

There is a wealth of published information you can use to develop economic forecasts. In December of each year, *Business Week* magazine presents its economic forecast for the following year; each week it presents a snapshot of the economy on its *outlook* page. *Fortune* magazine has a monthly forecast of the business outlook that is usually buttressed in its January issue with a forecast for the coming year. *Forbes* magazine has regular articles on business trends both domestic and foreign. Many banks, such as New York's Citibank, Manufacturers Hanover Trust, and Chase Manhattan, publish periodic analyses and forecasts of the economy. Each December the Prudential Insurance Company publishes an economic forecast for the coming year. The University of Michigan publishes a quarterly economic forecast, as noted in Figure 4.5.

Several agencies of the federal government also provide economic forecast information. The U.S. Council of Economic Advisors prepares *Economic Indicators* each month that shows the trend to date of various economic indicators. The regional branches of the Federal Reserve also publish economic reports monthly. The Federal Reserve Bank of St. Louis publishes a monthly summary that reports on various economic indicators.

FIGURE 4.5
Sample Economic Indicators Report
Source: S. H. Hymans, J. P. Crary, and J. C. Wolfe, "The U.S. Economic Outlook for 1987–88," *Economic Outlook USA*, Vol. 13, no. 4 (Fourth Quarter, 1986), p. 9.

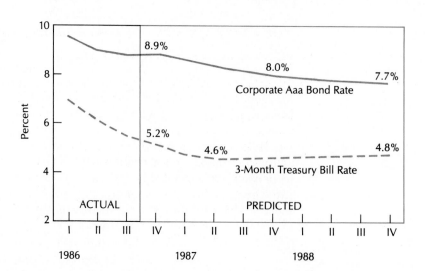

local market conditions Employment may go up or down in a specific city or region, for instance, as a result of factory closing or new industry.

occupational market conditions The Bureau of Labor Statistics of the U.S. Department of Labor publishes projections of labor supply and demand for various occupations, as do other agencies.

Local Market Conditions

Projected **local labor conditions** are also important. For example, the phasing down of the aerospace program some years ago resulted in relatively high unemployment in cities like Seattle, and Cape Canaveral, quite aside from general economic conditions in the country.

Occupational Market Conditions

Finally, you may want to forecast the availability of potential job candidates in specific occupations (engineers, drill press operators, accountants, etc.) for which you will be recruiting. Recently, for instance, there has been an undersupply of accountants, computer programmers, and engineers, while in many cities there has been an oversupply of available grade school and high school teachers.

Forecasts of available labor in different occupations are available from various sources. For example, the Bureau of Labor Statistics of the U.S. Department of Labor periodically publishes projections like those summarized in Table 4.2. This particular forecast shows the growth in demand for the fastest-growing occupations, including aeronautical engineers and computer mechanics. The National Science Foundation regularly forecasts labor market conditions in the science and technology fields. Other agencies providing occupational forecasts include the Public Health Service, the U.S. Employment Service, and the Office of Education.

♦ AN OVERALL PERSONNEL PLANNING SYSTEM

The Commitment Manpower Planning (CMP) System is an approach that can be used for compiling, summarizing, and presenting the results of your overall personnel planning effort. The CMP system consists of three reports: the Supply Report, the Demand Report, and the Manpower Report.[13] The Supply Report shows the expected future status of each key employee over, say, the next five years, and in particular his or her promotability. The Demand Report compiles and summarizes your department's *requirements*, specifically, the number of key positions that will be open due to the creation of new positions, turnover, or promotions.

The Manpower Report

The Manpower Report is the actual personnel plan and combines the Supply Report and Demand Report for each of the years for which you are plan-

TABLE 4.2   Job Forecasts for the Next Decade (Projected Employment Change), 1988–2000

FASTEST GROWING OCCUPATIONS	PERCENTAGE GAIN FORECAST
Paralegals	75.3%
Medical assistants	70
Home health aides	67.9
Radiologic technologists and technicians	66.0
Data processing equipment repairers	61.2
Medical records technicians	59.9
Medical secretaries	58.0
Physical therapists	57.0
Surgical technologists	56.4
Operations research analysts	55.4

Source: "Outlook 2000: Occupational Employment," *Monthly Labor Review*, November 1989, p. 60.

FIGURE 4.6
Overall Manpower Report
Source: Charles F. Russ, Jr., "Manpower Planning Systems: Part II," *Personnel Journal*, Vol. 61, no. 2 (February 1982), p. 122.

	1992	Needs	Var.	1993	Needs	Var.	1994	Needs	Var.	1995	Needs	Var.	1996	Needs	Var.
Plant Superintendent		0	0		0	0		1	0		0	0		0	0
							Robinson, Larry								
Plant Engr. Mgr.		0	0		0	0		1	0		0	0		0	0
							Pressler, Roy								
Plant Controller		0	0		1	1		0	0		0	0		0	0
Supv. Process 1		1	1		0	0		1	1		0	1		0	0
										Rodriguez, Tom		3M			
Supv. Process 2		0	0		1	0		0	0		0	0		0	0
				Powers, John											
Plant Per. Mgr.		0	0		1	0		0	0		0	0		0	0
				White, Judy		2F									
Indust. Engr. Mgr.		0	0		0	0		0	0		1	1		0	0
Safety Mgr.		0	0		1	1		0	0		0	0		0	0
Qual. Cont. Tech.		0	0		0	0		1	1		1	1		1	1

ning. A sample is presented in Figure 4.6. As an example, look at the plant superintendent's position at the top of the report. For two of the years in question there is no need for identifying a new plant superintendent, nor is there a need for an available inside candidate. However, we knew that in 1994 the current plant superintendent would retire. So in that year there was a need to fill one plant superintendent slot. Also in that year we had one available candidate, Larry Robinson, who was already slotted to fill that position. The variance (showing the excess of need over availability for that job) was thus zero for that year. However, the quality-control technician job was a different story. Here, in 1994, 1995, and 1996 we needed one new quality-control technician, but there were no available inside candidates to fill these positions. There was thus a variance of one (1 − 0). We therefore had to plan on going outside the organization to fill these positions or perhaps plan on training as yet unidentified current employees to fill each of these positions.

RECRUITING JOB CANDIDATES

♦ INTRODUCTION

Once you have decided to fill a position (and have received permission to do so), the next step is to develop a pool of applicants using one or more of the recruitment sources described next. Recruiting is an important activity, because the higher the number of applicants the more selective you can be in your hiring. If only two candidates appear for two openings, you may have little choice but to hire them. But if 10 or 20 applicants appear, then you can employ techniques like interviews and tests to screen out all but the best.

Some employers use a *recruiting yield pyramid* to determine the number of applicants they must generate to hire the required number of new employees.[14] As illustrated in Figure 4.7, the pyramid graphically displays the number of new leads you must generate through your recruiting efforts to hire the required number of new employees. In this case, the Ross Accounting Company knows it must hire 50 new entry-level accountants next year. From its experience, it also knows that the ratio of offers made to actual new hires is 2 to 1; about half the people they make offers to accept those offers. Similarly, the firm knows that the ratio of candidates interviewed to offers made is 3 to 2, while the ratio of candidates invited for interviews to candidates actually interviewed has been 4 to 3. Finally, the firm knows that the ratio of new leads generated to candidates actually invited has been 6 to 1; in other words, of six leads that come in from the firm's advertising, college recruiting, and other recruiting efforts, only one lead in six typically gets an invitation to come in for an interview. Given these ratios, the firm knows it must generate 1,200 leads to be able to invite 200 viable candidates to its offices for interviews. It will then get to interview about 150 of those it invites, and from these it will make 100 offers. Of those 100 offers, half (or 50 new CPAs) will be hired.

Recruitment is one area in which line and staff cooperation is essential, for several reasons. The human resource specialist who recruits and does the initial screening for the vacant job is seldom the one responsible for supervising its performance. He or she must therefore have as clear a picture as possible of what the job entails, and this, in turn, means speaking with the supervisor involved. For example, the human resource specialist might want to know something about the behavioral style of the supervisor and the members of the work group. Is it a "tough" group to get along with, for instance? The human resource specialist might also want to visit the work site and review the job description with the supervisor to ensure that the job has not changed since the description was written. Furthermore, the supervisor may be able to supply additional insight into the skills and talents the new worker will need. Personnel planning in general—and recruitment in particular—thus requires close cooperation between line and staff personnel.

♦ INTERNAL SOURCES OF CANDIDATES

While *recruiting* often brings to mind employment agencies and classified ads, *current employees* are often your largest source of recruits. Some surveys even indicated that up to 90% of all management positions are filled internally.[15]

Filling open positions with inside candidates has several benefits. Employees see that competence is rewarded and morale and performance may

FIGURE 4.7
Recruiting Yield Pyramid

thus be enhanced. Inside candidates (having already been with your firm for some time) may be more committed to its goals and less likely to leave. Promotion from within can also boost employee loyalty and provide a longer-term perspective when making managerial decisions. It may also be safer to promote employees from within, since you're more likely to have a more accurate assessment of the person's skills than you would otherwise. Inside candidates may also require less orientation and training than outsiders.

Yet promotion from within can also backfire. Employees who apply for jobs and don't get them may become discontented; informing unsuccessful applicants as to why they were rejected and what remedial actions they might take to be more successful in the future is thus essential.[16] Similarly, many employers require managers to post job openings and interview all inside candidates. Yet the manager often knows ahead of time exactly whom he or she wants to hire, and requiring the person to interview a stream of unsuspecting inside candidates is therefore a waste of time for all concerned. Groups may also not be as satisfied when their new boss is appointed from within their own ranks as when he or she is a newcomer; sometimes, for instance, it is difficult for the newly chosen leader to shake off the reputation of being "one of the gang."[17]

Perhaps the biggest drawback, though, is inbreeding. When an entire management team has been brought up through the ranks, there may be a tendency to make decisions "by the book" and to maintain the status quo, when an innovative and new direction is what's called for. Balancing the benefits of morale and loyalty with the drawback of inbreeding is thus a problem.

Promotion from within, to be effective, requires using job posting, personnel records, and skill banks.[18] **Job posting** means posting the open job and listing its attributes like qualifications, supervisor, working schedule, and pay rate (as in Figure 4.8). Some union contracts require job posting to ensure that union members get first choice of new and better positions. Yet job posting can also be a good practice even in nonunion firms, if it facilitates the transfer and promotion of your qualified inside candidates. Posting is usually not used when promotion to a supervisory position is involved, since management often prefers to select personnel itself for promotion to management levels.[19] Personnel records are also useful here. Examining personnel records (including application blanks) may uncover employees who are working in jobs below their educational or skill levels. It may also reveal persons who have potential for further training or those who already have the right background for the open jobs in question. Computerized systems, discussed previously, can help to ensure that qualified inside candidates are identified and considered for the opening. Some firms also develop *skill banks* that list current employees who have specific skills. For example, under "aerospace engineers," the names of all persons with this experience or training are listed. If you need an engineer in unit A, and the skill bank shows a person with those skills in unit B, that person may be approached about transferring to unit A although he or she is not now using the aerospace skills.

A statement of one firm's job posting policies is presented in Figure 4.9. As you can see, important guiding policies include "All permanent employees . . . are eligible to use the open position listing policy . . . to request consideration for a position," and "A list of open positions will be communicated to all employees in all facilities."

♦ ADVERTISING AS A SOURCE OF CANDIDATES

Advertising is another good source for attracting candidates,[20] but, for help wanted ads to bring results, there are two issues you have to address: the

job posting Posting notices of job openings on company bulletin boards is an effective recruiting method.

FIGURE 4.8
Sample Job Postings
Source: Reprinted, by permission of the publisher, from *Book of Employment Forms*, American Management Association, p. 35. Copyright 1967 by the American Management Association.

35

JOB POSTINGS

JOB CODE NO.	JOB DESCRIPTION	WORKING SCHEDULE	JOB RATE
11-75	OFFICE SUPERVISOR (REQ. NO. 16904) ONE Supervise 10-15 people engaged in clerical activities related to the following: 1. Receiving, scheduling, routing and controlling of orders through the planning, estimating, scheduling and requisitioning cycle. 2. Auditing and processing of documents required for accounting and cost control. 3. Typing of numerical control program tapes, planning and control documents, memoranda, etc. Technical school graduate or equivalent, familiar with mechanical trades, shop processes and shop control procedures from engineering release through shipping. Three to five years' experience in areas of material or production control; shop planning methods or estimating; and supervisor or functional work direction of others. Supervisor: J. Doe Department 981	8:00 a.m. 4:30 p.m.	Open
11-76	METHODS PLANNER/ESTIMATOR (REQ. NO. 16908) ONE 1. Review prints for completeness and add manufacturing instruction. 2. Determine economic methods of fabrication. 3. Prepare operation sheets and program instructions. 4. Estimate labor requirements. 5. Determine material requirements and specify cutting dimension. 6. Estimate costs of all fabrication. 7. Assist in other planning scheduling activities. Background in shop math, including geometry, trigonometry and drafting. Minimum of 4 years' combined experience in machine shop, sheet metal fabrication and assembly, or equivalent. Must be able to read complex blueprints. Supervisor: J. Doe Department 981 FOR THE ABOVE POSTINGS PLEASE CALL EXT. 852	8:00 a.m. 4:30 p.m.	Open

media to be used and the construction of the ad. The selection of the best medium—be it the local paper, *The Wall Street Journal,* or a technical journal—depends on the types of positions for which you're recruiting. Your local newspaper is usually the best source of blue-collar help, clerical employees, and lower-level administrative employees. For specialized employees, you can advertise in trade and professional journals like the *American Psychologist, Sales Management, Chemical Engineering,* and *Electronics News.* And there are publications like *Travel Trade, Women's Wear Daily, American Banker, Hospital Administration,* and the *Chronicle of Higher Education* in which you would most likely place your ads for professionals like bankers, hospital administrators, or educators. One drawback to this type of trade paper advertising is the long lead time that is usually required;

Eligibility

- All permanent employees who have completed their probationary period are eligible to use the open position listing policy in order to request consideration for a position that would constitute a growth opportunity.
- Employees who have been promoted or transferred, or who have changed jobs for any reason, must wait a six-month period before applying for a different position.

Policy

- A list of open positions will be communicated to all employees in all facilities. Notices will include information on job title, salary grade, department, supervisor's name and title, location, brief description of the job content, qualifications, and instructions concerning whether or not candidates will be expected to demonstrate their skills during the interview process.
- Basic job qualifications and experience needed to fill the job will be listed on the sheet. Employees should consult with the human resource department if there are questions concerning the promotional opportunities associated with the job.
- Open position lists will remain on bulletin boards for five working days.
- Forms for use in requesting consideration for an open position may be obtained from the human resource department.
- The human resource department will review requests to substantiate the employee's qualifications for the position.
- The hiring manager will review requests for employees inside the company before going outside the company to fill the position.
- It is the responsibility of the employees to notify their managers of their intent to interview for an open position.
- The hiring manager makes the final decision when filling the position; however, the guidelines for filling any open position are based on the employees' ability, qualifications, experience, background, and the skills they possess that will allow them to carry out the job successfully. It is the responsibility of the hiring manager to notify the previous manager of the intent to hire the employee.
- Employees who are aware of a pending opening, and who will be on vacation when the opening occurs, may leave a request with the human resource department for consideration.
- It is the manager's responsibility to ensure that the human resource department has notified all internal applicants that they did or did not get the job before general announcement by the manager of the person who did get the job.
- "Blanket" applications will not be accepted. Employees should apply each time a position they are interested in becomes available.
- Since preselection often occurs, employees should be planning for their career growth by scheduling time with potential managers before posting, to become acquainted with them, and to secure developmental information to be used in acquiring appropriate skills for future consideration.
- There are occasions when jobs will not be listed. Two such examples might be (1) when a job can be filled best by natural progression or is a logical career path for an employee, and (2) when a job is created to provide a development opportunity for a specific high-performance employee.
- In keeping with this policy, managers are encouraged to work with employees in career development in order to assist them in pursuing upward movement in a particular career path or job ladder.

What the Human Resource Department Does

- Reviews applications for open positions, and checks to see if applicants meet minimum time-on-the-job requirements.
- Reviews background material of applicants with hiring manager. Hiring manager selects the employees qualified for interviews.
- Notifies all applicants who will not be interviewed, and gives them the reasons why.
- Provides counseling to applicants who will not be interviewed.
- Answers questions from interviewed candidates concerning selection, if the interviewing extends beyond the normal three-week period.

What the Manager Does

- Selects employees to be interviewed for the position.
- Contacts employees selected and arranges for interviews.
- Screens interviewed applicants (may contact previous manager for reference).
- Decides who is the best-qualified candidate.
- Informs the human resource department of the selection and provides reasons for rejecting unsuccessful applicants.
- Notifies the successful applicant and his or her current manager.
- Arranges release dates with the current manager (normally two weeks).
- Completes application forms in full, at the bottom of the form, and answers all appropriate question blocks as necessary.
- Notifies the unsuccessful candidates, advising them of reasons for rejection.
- Makes sure that the interview process does not extend more than three weeks beyond the date the notice comes off the bulletin board.

PERSONNEL RECRUITER

Major employer in the Bay Area seeks a seasoned Personnel Recruiter to design, implement & manage a nationwide recruitment program for managerial and selected professional level positions.

Key duties include:
* Reviewing job requisitions;
* Interviewing & evaluating potential candidates & referring the most qualified to the hiring manager;
* Conduct thorough & timely employment reference checks;
* Effectively market the employer to recruitment sources;
* Locate & recruit qualified minority candidates at the managerial & professional level;
* Develop & maintain a wide range of local & national recruitment sources.

Qualifications:
* BA/BS in Business/Personnel Administration or related field; MA in Business or related field preferred;
* Minimum 3 years of increasingly responsible experience in personnel administration coupled with 3-5 years directing a nationwide recruitment program for professional & managerial staff;
* Thorough knowledge and proven ability in up-to-date recruitment techniques, principles & practices;
* Proven abilities to conduct professional interviews, effectively present recommendations;
* Maintain effective working relationships at all levels;
* Possess excellent written, verbal and interpersonal communication skills.

Excellent salary and benefits. For consideration, please send resume with salary history to: Ad #42617, c/o SF Newspapers, P.O. Box 7228, San Francisco, CA 94120. EOE/AA.

there may be a month or more between insertion of the ad and publication of the journal or specialized paper, for instance.

Yet ads remain good sources, and so ads like that in Figure 4.10 continue to appear. Placing help wanted ads in papers like *The Wall Street Journal* can be good sources of middle or senior management personnel. *The Wall Street Journal*, for instance, has several regional editions so that either the entire country or the appropriate geographic area can be targeted for coverage.

Most firms use newspaper ads, but other media are used too. Table 4.3 summarizes when to use each. For example, magazines are best when specialized jobs are involved, such as using a computer engineering magazine to reach computer engineers.

TABLE 4.3   Advantages and Disadvantages of the Major Types of Media

TYPE OF MEDIUM	ADVANTAGES	DISADVANTAGES	WHEN TO USE
Newspapers	Short deadlines. Ad size flexibility. Circulation cencentrated in specific geographic areas. Classified sections well organized for easy access by active job seekers.	Easy for prospects to ignore. Considerable competitive clutter. Circulation not specialized—you must pay for great amount of unwanted readers. Poor printing quality.	When you want to limit recruiting to a specific area. When sufficient numbers of prospects are clustered in a specific area. When enough prospects are reading help wanted ads to fill hiring needs.

(continued)

TABLE 4.3   (continued)

TYPE OF MEDIUM	ADVANTAGES	DISADVANTAGES	WHEN TO USE
Magazines	Specialized magazines reach pinpointed occupation categories. Ad size flexibility. High-quality printing. Prestigious editorial environment. Long life—prospects keep magazines and reread them.	Wide geographic circulation—usually cannot be used to limit recruiting to specific area. Long lead time for ad placement.	When job is specialized. When time and geographic limitations are not of utmost importance. When involved in ongoing recruiting programs.
Directories	Specialized audiences. Long life.	Not timely. Often have competitive clutter.	Only appropriate for ongoing recruiting programs.
Direct mail	Most personal form of advertising. Unlimited number of formats and amount of space. By selecting names by zip code, mailing can be pinpointed to precise geographic area.	Difficult to find mailing list of prospects by occupation at home addresses. Cost for reaching each prospect is high.	If the right mailing list can be found, this is potentially the most effective medium—no other medium gives the prospect as much a feeling of being specially selected. Particularly valuable in competitive situations.
Radio and Television	Difficult to ignore. Can reach prospects who are not actively looking for a job better than newspapers and magazines. Can be limited to specific geographic areas. Creatively flexible. Can dramatize employment story more effectively than printed ads. Little competitive recruitment clutter.	Only brief, uncomplicated messages are possible. Lack of permanence; prospect cannot refer back to it. (Repeated airings necessary to make impression.) Creation and production of commercials—particularly TV—can be time consuming and costly. Lack of special interest selectivity; paying for waste circulation.	In competitive situations when not enough prospects are reading your printed ads. When there are multiple job openings and there are enough prospects in specific geographic area. When a large impact is needed quickly. A "blitz" campaign can saturate an area in two weeks or less. Useful to call attention to printed ads.
Outdoor (roadside billboards) and transit (posters and buses and subways).	Difficult to ignore. Can reach prospects as they are literally traveling to their current jobs. Precise geographic selectivity. Reaches large numbers of people many times at a low cost.	Only very brief message is possible. Requires long lead for preparation and must be in place for long period of time (usually one to three months).	When there is a steady hiring need for large numbers of people that is expected to remain constant over a long period of time.
"Point-of-purchase" (promotional materials at recruiting location).	Calls attention to employment story at time when prospects can take some type of immediate action. Creative flexibility.	Limited usefulness; prospects must visit a recruiting location before it can be effective.	Posters, banners, brochures, audio-visual presentations at special events such as job fairs, open houses, conventions, as part of an employee referral program, at placement offices, or whenever prospects visit at organization facilities.

Source: Bernard S. Hodes, "Planning for Recruitment Advertising: Part II," *Personnel Journal*, Vol. 28, no. 5 (June 1983), p. 499. Reprinted with the permission of *Personnel Journal*, Costa Mesa, Calif. All rights reserved.

Principles of Help Wanted Advertising

In addition to the media to be used, the construction of the ad is also important.

Experienced advertisers use a four-point guide called AIDA to construct their ads. First, you must attract *attention* to the ad. Figure 4.11 shows a page from one paper's classified section. Which ads attract attention? Note that closely printed ads are lost while those using wide borders or a lot of empty space stand out. For the same reason, key positions are often advertised in display ads, where they don't get lost in the columns of classified ads.

Next, develop *interest* in the job. As in Figure 4.12, interest may be created by the nature of the job itself, such as "you'll thrive on challenging work." Sometimes, other aspects of the job, such as its location, can be used to create interest.

Next, create *desire* by amplifying on the interest factors plus the extras of the job in terms of job satisfaction, career development, travel, or similar advantages. Here it is important to write the ad with the target audience in mind. For example, tuition refund and nearby graduate schools appeal to engineers and professional people.

The ad should instigate *action*. Pick up almost any ad, and you'll find some statement like "call today," "write today for more information," or "go to your nearest travel agent and sign up for the trip." The help wanted ad shown in Figure 4.13 is a good example of this.

FIGURE 4.11
A Help Wanted Ad That Draws Attention

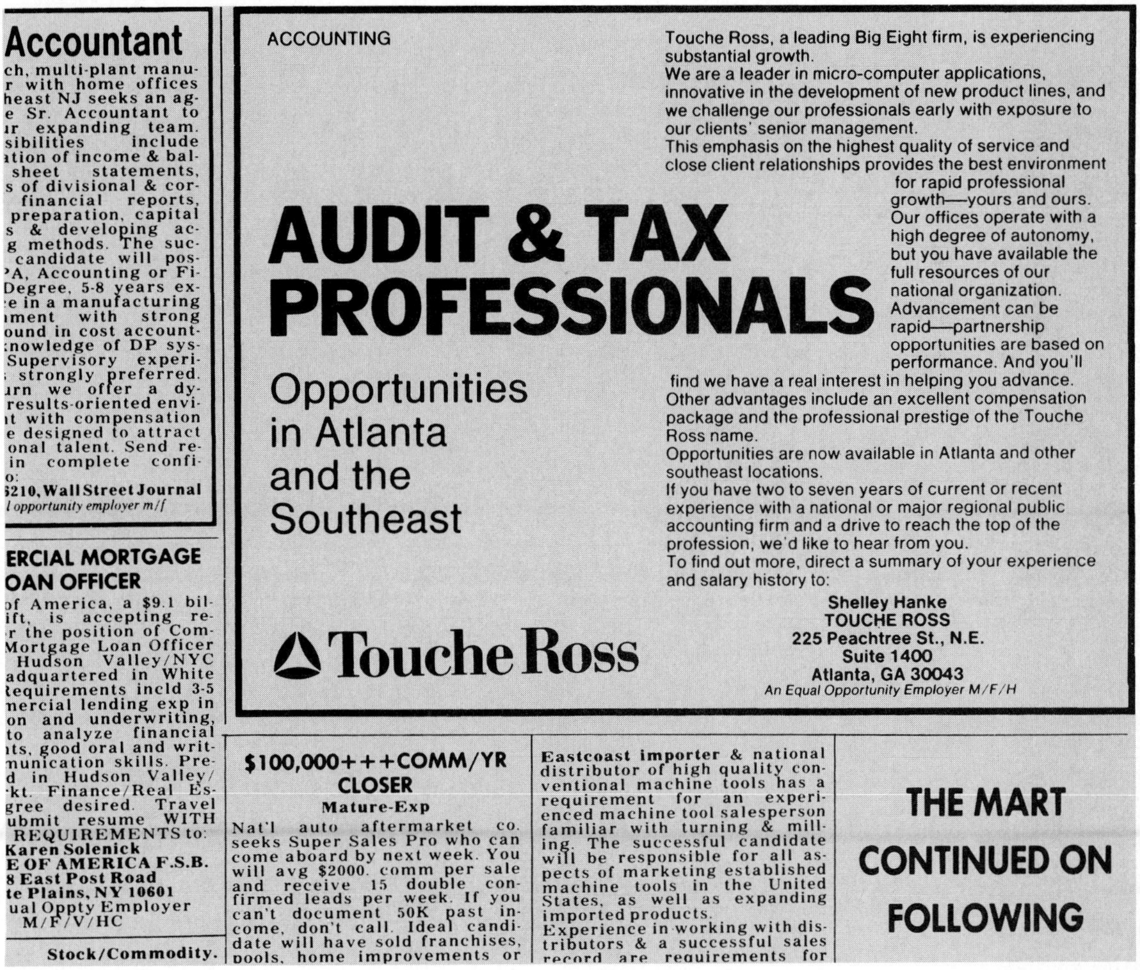

FIGURE 4.12
A Help Wanted Ad That Creates Interest

Group Health Underwriters

WE NEED AN UNDERWRITER WHO'S AN OVERACHIEVER.

To keep pace with our rapidly expanding account base, we're looking for ambitious self starters to join the Employee Benefit Group in our Orinda office. The kind of pro's with proven records and super analytical skills.

If this sounds like you, consider joining The Travelers, a $46 billion insurance and financial services leader.

To qualify, you need at least 3 years of group health underwriting experience where you've gained a solid knowledge of employee benefits coverages. You must also have excellent communications and interpersonal skills.

In return, you'll thrive on challenging work in a dynamic environment. We've recently combined our New Business and Customer Relations Groups, creating a leaner, more aggressive force. As part of this new unit, you'll have broad exposure and career growth opportunities. Plus receive a highly competitive salary and benefits package.

So, if you're an overachiever, join The Travelers. And enjoy a career that's a cut above the rest.

Send your resume, with salary requirements, to: Sonia Mielnik, The Travelers Companies, 30-CR, SF426L1, One Tower Square, Hartford, CT 06183-7060.

TheTravelers
You're better off under the Umbrella.℠

Home Office: The Travelers Companies, Hartford, Connecticut.   An Equal Opportunity Employer.

The increased internationalization of the U.S. economy has created many opportunities for positions with multinational firms. Figure 4.14 gives you an example of the use of ads for these broader opportunities.

Finally, while most employers today know that discriminatory recruitment advertising is generally illegal, one study found that while not blatant, such illegal or questionable advertising still exists.[21] As you know, ads that are sex specific (calling for "man," "woman," "girl Friday," and so forth) are usually discriminatory, as are sex-related gender terms like "yard man," "repair man," or ads implying a certain age (such as "student," "recent grad," or "retiree"). Similarly, terms like "bilingual required," or

FIGURE 4.13
A Help Wanted Ad with a Call to Action
Source: BSA Advertising, San Mateo, Calif.

We Can Take You Places.

Kaiser Permanente Medical Care Program is one of the largest Health Maintenance Organizations in the nation. We offer highly skilled professionals who are committed to those in need of quality medical care to consider these excellent opportunities and experience health care at its best.

We reward our people with competitive salaries, comprehensive benefits, educational programs and the ability to transfer between facilities without losing seniority. Kaiser Permanente is proud to be an equal opportunity employer.

Hayward

For these positions in our Hayward Medical Center please apply Monday-Thursday, 10am-1pm to **Personnel Department, 27400 Hesperian Blvd., Hayward, CA 94545** or call **Ellen Gutstadt at (415) 784-4258.**

Staff Nurses

ER: Nights & On-Call   **ICU/CCU:** Evenings & Nights
L&D: Nights   **Med/Surg:** Nights
ICN: All shifts available   **Float:** All shifts available

Employee Health Service Nurse Practitioner: Requires 5 years of adult practitioner experience and a Master's degree.

Adult Nurse Practitioner: Requires 2 years of experience and a Master's degree.

OB Supervisor: A Bachelors degree, strong clinical and management skills combined with a clinical speciality are necessary to supervise our active tertiary, L&D, Gyn and perinatal units. RN licensure and 3 years of labor and delivery are required. MS degree preferred.

Advice Nurse: Two years of recent Med/Surg experience. Part-time and on-call positions available.

OR Nurses: Day and evening positions available with 6 months experience and a current CA RN license.

Night Shift Supervisor: To work 3 nights per week, Bachelors degree preferred.

We are also accepting applications for:
New Graduate Program: Deadline May 11th, 1987.
Re-entry Program: Deadline May 4th, 1987.

KAISER PERMANENTE
Medical Care Program

"Japanese," are also questionable. As we explained in Chapter 2, employers using ads like these are usually placing themselves in a position of possibly having to defend their rationale for limiting their search to the type of person called for in the ad. Yet despite widespread knowledge of the questionableness of such ads, one national survey of ads found that 2.7 percent of the ads studied were classified as being either questionable or blatantly illegal. Interestingly, questionable ads were not evenly distributed among industries or media: for example, almost 30% of all questionable advertising appeared in trade magazines and another 20% or so of the questionable ads were produced by firms in the hospitality industry.

FIGURE 4.14
A Help Wanted Ad in International Management

INTERNATIONAL OPERATIONS MANAGEMENT TRAINEES

Tokyo, London, Zurich or Frankfurt

Salomon Brothers Inc, a major force in the international investment banking community, has excellent, entry level opportunities for hardworking, energetic individuals to join our International Operations Management Trainee Program. This program is designed to give candidates with little or no previous industry experience both product knowledge and operational management skills.

During this one year training program in our New York City headquarters, you will rotate through various operations areas and participate in a variety of special projects and assignments. The object is to develop a working knowledge of many areas through hands-on experience and participative observation. After your training is complete, you will be assigned to one of our Branch Offices in Japan, London, Zurich or Frankfort.

This position demands an independent thinker who is flexible and capable of demonstrating a high level of initiative. Your ability to develop a management perspective and demonstrate skill in performing many job functions will be important. Excellent communications skills and some fluency in Japanese, French, or German is essential. You must be able to relocate abroad.

We offer an excellent starting salary and a comprehensive benefits program, along with a unique opportunity for career growth. If you have a solid commitment to success and are ready for the challenge, send your resume, including salary history and a cover letter, in complete confidence to: **Management Trainee Recruiter, Salomon Brothers Inc, One New York Plaza, New York, N.Y. 10004.**

We are an Equal Opportunity Employer M/F

Salomon Brothers Inc

♦ EMPLOYMENT AGENCIES
AS A SOURCE OF CANDIDATES

You'll find three basic types of employment agencies: (1) those operated by federal, state, or local governments; (2) those associated with nonprofit organizations; and (3) privately owned agencies.[22]

Public state employment service agencies exist in every state. They are aided and coordinated by the United States Employment Service of the U.S. Department of Labor, which also maintains a nationwide computerized job bank to which all state employment offices are connected. Using the computer-listed job information, an agency interviewer is better able to counsel job applicants concerning available jobs in their own and other geographical areas.

Public agencies are a major source of hourly blue-collar workers, although the experience of many employers with these agencies has been mixed. Applicants for unemployment insurance are required to register with these agencies and to make themselves available for job interviews in order to collect their unemployment payments. Some of these people are not anxious to get back to work, and employers can end up with applicants who have little or no real interest in obtaining immediate employment.

Other employment agencies are associated with nonprofit organizations. For example, most professional and technical societies have units that help their members find jobs. Similarly, many public welfare agencies try to place people who are in special categories, such as those who are physically disabled or are Vietnam veterans.

Private employment agencies are important sources of clerical, white-collar, and managerial personnel. Private agencies charge fees for each applicant they place. These fees are usually set by state law and are posted in their offices. Whether the employer or the candidate pays the fee is mostly determined by market conditions, although the trend in the last few years has been toward "fee-paid jobs" in which the employer and not the candidate pays the fees. The assumption is that the most qualified candidates are presently employed and would not be as willing to switch jobs if they had to pay the fees themselves. Many private agencies now offer (or specialize in) temporary help service and provide secretarial, clerical, or semiskilled labor on a per diem basis. These agencies can be useful in helping you cope with peak loads and fill in for vacationing employees.

There are several reasons to use an employment agency for some or all of your recruiting needs.[23] Employment agencies' ads in *The Wall Street Journal* list advantages like "cut down on your interviews," "interview only the right people," and "have recruiting specialists save you time by finding, interviewing, and selecting only the most qualified candidates for your final hiring process." Some specific situations in which you might want to turn to an agency include the following:

1. Your employer does not have its own human resource department and is therefore not geared up to do the necessary recruiting and screening.
2. Your employer has found it difficult in the past to generate a pool of qualified applicants.
3. Your employer's need for only a few people or an irregular demand for new employees makes it inefficient to maintain an elaborate recruiting office.
4. A particular opening must be filled quickly.
5. There is a perceived need to attract a greater number of minority or female applicants.
6. The recruitment effort is aimed at reaching individuals who are currently employed and who might therefore feel more comfortable answering ads from and dealing with employment agencies rather than competing companies.

One of the main advantages of an employment agency is that it prescreens applicants for your job, but this advantage can also backfire.[24] For example, the employment agency's screening may allow poor applicants to bypass the preliminary stages of your own selection process. Unqualified applicants may thus be sent directly to the supervisors responsible for the hiring, who may in turn naively hire them. Such errors may in turn show up in high turnover and absenteeism rates, morale problems, and low quality and productivity. Similarly, successful applicants may be blocked from entering your applicant pool by improper testing and screening at the employment agency. To help avoid such problems, two experts suggest the following:

1. You should give the agency an accurate and complete job description. The better the employment agency understands the job or jobs to be filled, the greater the likelihood that a reasonable pool of applicants will be generated.
2. You should specify the devices or tools that the employment agency should use in screening potential applicants. Tests, application blanks, and interviews should be a proven part of the employer's selection process. At the very least, you should know which devices the agency uses

and consider their relevance to the selection process. Of particular concern would be any subjective decision-making procedures used by the agency.

3. Where possible, you should periodically review data on accepted or rejected candidates. This will serve as a check on the screening process and provide valuable information if there is a legal challenge to the fairness of the selection process.

4. If feasible, develop a long-term relationship with one or two agencies. It may also be advantageous to designate one person to serve as the liaison between the employer and agency. Similarly, try to have a specific contact on the agency's staff to coordinate your recruiting needs.

There are several things you can do to select the best agency for your needs. Checking with other managers or human resource people will reveal the agencies that have proved to be the most effective at filling the sorts of positions you want to have filled. Another approach is to review seven or eight back issues of the Sunday classified ads in your library to find the agencies that consistently handle the positions you want. This will help narrow the field.

Once you've narrowed the field, there are several questions you should ask to decide which agency is best for your firm: What is the background of the agency's staff? What are the levels of their education and experience and their ages? Do they have the qualifications to understand the sorts of jobs for which you are recruiting? And what is their reputation in the community and with the Better Business Bureau?

Temporary Help Agencies

Temporary help agencies (mentioned earlier) are today an increasingly important type of employment agency. One recent survey reported that over 84% of the questioned employers make use of such agencies and their use seems to be on the increase.[25] Most of the part-time employees hired through these agencies are used for either office/clerical or production/service jobs. The reason most often cited (by 78% of the firms) for calling in agency temporaries was to fill in for absent employees. Other important reasons are to staff short-term projects, to fill vacancies until regular employees are hired, and to fill a need for a specialized skill on a short-term basis. Among firms reporting an increase in agency temporaries, many said that labor shortages had prompted the increase, and this is a need that will probably increase over the next few years. One problem more employers will have to grapple with in the 1990s, as we've seen, is a diminishing supply of labor. Temporary help agencies can help fill the gap by offering employees who are, for one reason or another, not interested in making long-term commitments to single employers.

Maintaining a satisfactory relationship with one of these agencies requires, first, putting time and effort into meeting with several and choosing the one that's best for you. Next, you must ensure that basic policy and procedures questions are answered. Plan on asking about or giving answers to the following:[26]

Invoicing. Get a sample copy of the company's invoice: make sure you understand the invoicing procedure and that it fits your company's needs.

Time Sheets. Also get a sample time sheet. With temps, the time sheet which is signed by the person's supervisor is usually in effect an agreement rather than simply a verification of hours worked. It's therefore important that someone in your company be responsible for reading and understanding each agreement.

Office Hours of Operation. Make sure you understand the temp service's normal office hours and that they coincide with the hours that you or your branches will require their services.

Temp-to-Perm Policy. Specifically, what is the policy if the client wants to hire permanently one of the service's temps? Most services prefer to keep the temp on their payroll for a specific waiting period before moving (at no extra cost) the person to the client's payroll. Make sure you know what the waiting period is and what placement fees, if any, are involved.

Multiple Rates. Some services will provide you with listings of hourly rates charged for each temp category (word processing, secretary, and so forth). Make sure to compare the rates charged by each competing temp service before making your choice.

Recruitment of and Benefits for Temp Employees. Find out how the temp service plans to recruit employees and what sorts of benefits they pay because this should, in turn, determine the quality and quantity of employees they are able to attract.

Inside Staff. Make sure to learn as much as you can about how the temp service's staff, such as the people who interview applicants, match skills to position requirements, and place and dispatch the temp work force. Remember that the people that are sent to you as temp employees will probably only be as good as the temp service's own recruitment and screening processes.

Equipment. Make sure to be clear with the temp agency regarding equipment (computer and otherwise) used by each of your branch offices.

Functions of Your Company. To help the temp service representative better understand your company, make sure to supply him or her with some literature, if available, about your organization.

Dress Code. Make it clear what appropriate attire for the staff at each of your offices or plants is.

Parking. Particularly for temporary employees who may only be working for you for several days, it's important they get information on such matters as whether parking is particularly difficult to find and where parking spaces can usually be found.

Smoking. Whether the company is a no smoking area or (conversely) the particular department to be staffed happens to consist largely of chain smokers, the information has to be passed along to the temp agency.

Lunch Rooms, Nearby Places to Eat. Be ready to provide information on where the temp employees will be able to eat near your organization.

Equal Employment Opportunity Statement. You should get an EEO document from the temp service stating that it is not discriminating when filling temp orders.

Job Description Information. And, of course, make sure to set up a procedure whereby you can be reasonably sure that the temp service understands completely the nature of the job to be filled and the sort of person, in terms of skills and so forth, you want to fill it.

♦ **EXECUTIVE RECRUITERS AS A SOURCE OF CANDIDATES**

Executive recruiters (also known as "head hunters") are retained by employers to seek out top management talent for their clients. They fill jobs in the $40,000 and up category, although $50,000 is often the lower limit. The percentage of your firm's positions filled by these services might be small, but these jobs would include the most crucial executive and technical positions. For your executive positions, "head hunters" may be your *only* source. Their fees are always paid by the employer.

These firms can be very useful. They have many contacts and are especially adept at contacting qualified candidates who are employed and not actively looking to change jobs. They can also keep your firm's name confidential until late into the search process. The recruiter can also save top management time by doing the preliminary work of advertising for the position and screening what could turn out to be hundreds of applicants. The recruiter's fee could actually turn out to be insignificant compared to the cost of the executive time he or she saves.

But there are some pitfalls. As an employer, it is essential to explain completely what sort of candidate is required—and why. Some recruiters are also more salespeople than professionals. They may be more interested in persuading you to hire a candidate than finding one that will really do the job. Recruiters also claim that what their client *says* he or she wants is often not really what is wanted; therefore, be prepared for some in-depth dissecting of your request. In choosing a recruiter, one expert suggests following these guidelines:[27]

1. *Make sure the firm you choose is capable of conducting a thorough search.* Under the code of the Association of Executive Recruiting Consultants, a head hunter cannot approach the executive talent of a former client for a vacancy with a new client for a period of two years after completing a search for the former client. Former clients are thus off limits to the recruiter for a period of two years, and the recruiter must thus make his or her search from a constantly diminishing market. Particularly for the largest executive recruiting firms, it could turn out to be very difficult to deliver a top-notch candidate, since the best potential candidates may already be working for the recruiter's former clients, from which he is barred for two years. One large executive recruiter, for instance, recently confirmed that 2,000 companies were off limits to his firm. As a result, it is important to make sure the recruiting firm you choose is capable of conducting a thorough search, particularly among the competing companies where you believe the best candidate for your position might now be employed.

2. *Ask to meet the individual who will be handling your assignment.* The person handling your search will determine the fate of the search. If this person hasn't the ability to seek out top-notch candidates aggressively and sell them on your firm, it is unlikely you will get to see the best candidates. You therefore have to size up the person who will be handling your assignment to decide whether this is the person you want out there searching for and advocating the top position you seek to fill. Beware of the fact that in wooing a new client the search firm will send along its best "front man," a person with a track record of successfully signing on new clients. However, this is usually not the person who will be doing the actual search, and on whose shoulders the success of the search actually rests. Therefore, make sure to slide past the front man and get to size up the individual who will actually handle your search.

3. *Ask how much the search firm charges.* There are several things to keep in mind here. Search firm fees range from 25% to 35% of the guaranteed annual income attaching to the position being filled. They are often payable one-third as a retainer at the outset, one-third at the end of 30 days, and one-third after 60 days and are not necessarily only paid on a contingency basis. Often, a fee is payable whether or not the search is terminated for any reason. The out-of-pocket expenses are extra and could run up to 10% to 20% of the fee itself, and sometimes more. The front-end retainer is often explained by the fact that there is a lot of front-end

work expended on determining the job specifications, researching the market, and initiating the initial contacts. The search may then take up to six months, but it is commonly completed inside 60 days.

4. *Choose a recruiter you can trust.* This is essential because this person will not only find your firm's strengths, but its weaknesses too. It is therefore important that you find someone that you can trust with what may be privileged information.

5. *Talk to a couple of their clients.* Finally, ask to be given the names of two or three companies for whom the search firm has recently completed assignments. Then, ask such questions as: Did their appraisal of the candidate seem accurate? Did they really conduct a search, or was the job simply filled from their files? And were time and care taken in developing the job specifications?[28]

As a job candidate there are several things to keep in mind when dealing with executive search firms. First, most of these firms pay little heed to unsolicited resumes, preferring instead to ferret out their own candidates. Some firms have also been known to present an unpromising candidate to a client simply to make their other one or two proposed candidates look that much better. Some eager clients may also jump the gun, checking your references and thereby undermining your present position prematurely. Also, keep in mind that executive recruiters and their clients are usually much more impressed with candidates who are obviously "not looking" for a job and that eagerness to take the job has been the downfall of many candidates.[29]

♦ **COLLEGE RECRUITING
AS A SOURCE OF CANDIDATES**

We have already seen that promotion from within is a major source of management candidates. Many of these promotable candidates are originally hired through *college recruiting,* which is therefore an important source of management trainees, as well as of both professional and technical employees.

There are two main problems with on-campus recruiting. First, it is usually both expensive and time consuming from the point of view of the people doing the recruiting. To be done correctly, schedules have to be set well in advance, company brochures printed, records of interviews kept, and much recruiting time spent on campus. A second problem is that recruiters themselves are sometimes ineffective (or worse). Some recruiters are unprepared, show little interest in the candidate, and act superior. Similarly, many recruiters don't effectively screen their student candidates. For example, students' physical attractiveness often outweighs other, more valid traits and skills.[30] Some recruiters also tend to assign females to "female-type" jobs and males to "male-type" jobs.[31] One suggestion is to train recruiters before sending them to the college campus.[32]

You have two main jobs to accomplish as a recruiter on the campus. Your main function is a screening function and is aimed at determining whether a candidate is worthy of further consideration. Exactly which traits you look for will of course be a function of your specific recruiting needs. However, the checklist presented in Figure 4.15 is a typical list of traits sought by college recruiters. Traits to look for include motivation, intellectual ability, and ability to influence and lead others.[33]

While your main function is to find and screen good candidates, your other aim is to *attract* them to your firm. Keeping the student at ease, a sincere and informal attitude, respect for the applicant as an individual, and attention to the other matters addressed in Figure 4.16 can also help you to sell the employer to the interviewee.

FIGURE 4.15
College Applicant Interview Form
Source: Arthur Pell, *Recruiting and Selecting Personnel* (New York: Simon & Schuster, 1969), p. 61.

COLLEGE APPLICANT INTERVIEW REPORT

NAME OF
APPLICANT _____

☐ REGULAR ☐ CO-OP
☐ SUMMER ☐ SUMMER ABROAD

(LAST) (FIRST) (INITIAL) (NICKNAME)

SCHOOL _____ HOME STATE _____

DEGREE(S) HELD AND DATE(S)	MAJOR(S)	SCHOOL(S)	
DEGREE EXPECTED AND DATE	MAJOR	SCHOLASTIC AVG.	RANK IN CLASS

JOBS APPLIED FOR
1. 2. 3.

LOCATION PREFERENCE
1. 2. 3.

APPLICANT'S QUALIFICATIONS FOR OCCUPATIONAL FIELD

SELECTION FACTORS	* RATING
PHYSICAL EQUIPMENT — Are applicant's physical presence, manner, voice and speech patterns assets or liabilities?	
MENTAL EQUIPMENT — Is applicant mentally alert? Does he express himself effectively? Can he think on his feet?	
EMOTIONAL EQUIPMENT — Is applicant emotionally mature? Does he get along with others? Can he influence others?	
INTERESTS, MOTIVATION — Are applicant's expressed and demonstrated interests consistent with the job applied for and his career goals in the Co.? Does he have a high level of aspiration? Is there evidence of adequate motivation to make progress?	
EDUCATION — Were the courses taken by the applicant pertinent to the job? Was the quality such as to reflect real achievement?	
WORK EXPERIENCE — Did previous work experience make a valuable contribution to over-all development?	
PERSONAL, FAMILY HISTORY — Did family relationships and early life circumstances serve to enhance or hinder personal development? Will present personal and family circumstances be a positive or negative factor in applicant's future development?	

COMMENTS —

OVER-ALL RATING: U BA A AA O (CIRCLE ONE)

DISPOSITION
☐ RJ
☐ RV
☐ FU
☐ RF

*	RATING CODE
O	— OUTSTANDING
AA	— ABOVE AVERAGE
A	— AVERAGE
BA	— BELOW AVERAGE
U	— UNSATISFACTORY

DATE _____ INTERVIEWER _____ TITLE _____

As summarized in Table 4.4, employers of course choose their college recruiters largely on the basis of who can do the best job of identifying good applicants and filling all vacancies. Factors in selecting schools in which to recruit include (see Table 4.5) reputation and performance of previous hires from the school.

Applicants who favorably impress the recruiters are generally invited to the employer's office or plant for an on-site visit. To make sure this visit is as fruitful as possible, there are several things that you can do.[34] The letter of invitation to the applicant should be warm and friendly, but businesslike, and the person should be given a choice of dates to visit the com-

FIGURE 4.16
Survey: What College Students Said about College Recruiters
Source: Arthur Pell, *Recruiting and Selecting Personnel* (New York: Simon & Schuster, 1969), p. 58.

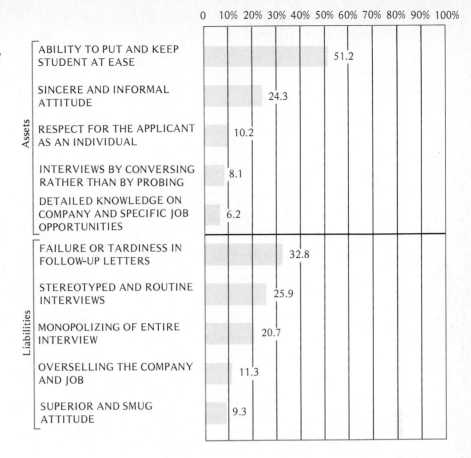

pany. Somebody should be assigned to meet the applicant and act as his or her host, preferably meeting the person at the airport or at his or her hotel. A complete package describing the applicant's schedule as well as other information regarding the employer—such as annual reports and description of benefits—should be waiting for the applicant at the person's hotel. The interviews themselves should be carefully planned and the scheduled adhered to as closely as possible, with interruptions avoided; the candidate should have the undivided attention of each person with whom he or she interviews. Luncheon should be arranged at the plant or at a nearby restaurant or club, preferably hosted by one or more other recently hired gradu-

TABLE 4.4   Factors in Selecting College Recruiters

RECRUITING ASPECT	STRENGTH (1–7)
Identification of high-quality applicants	5.8
Professionalism of recruiters	5.6
Filling all vacancies	5.5
Generating the right number of applicants	5.5
High performance of new recruits	5.4
High retention of new recruits	5.3
High job acceptance rates	5.0
Administrative procedures	4.7
Turn-around times	4.5
Planning and goal setting	4.5
Meeting EEO/AA targets	4.4
Program evaluation	4.3
Cost control	4.2

Source: Reprinted with permission from the March 1987 issue of *Personnel Administrator*. Copyright 1987, The American Society for Personnel Administration, 606 North Washington Street , Alexandria, Va. 22314.

TABLE 4.5 Factors in Selecting Schools in Which to Recruit

TOPIC	IMPORTANCE (1–7)
Reputation in critical skill areas	6.5
General school reputation	5.8
Performance of previous hires from the school	5.7
Location	5.1
Reputation of faculty in critical skill areas	5.1
Previous job offer and acceptance rates	4.6
Past practice	4.5
Number of potential recruits	4.5
Ability to meet EEO targets	4.3
Cost	3.9
Familiarity with faculty members	3.8
SAT or GRE scores	3.0
Alma mater of CEO or other executives	3.0

Source: Reprinted with permission from the March 1987 issue of *Personnel Administrator*. Copyright 1987, The American Society for Personnel Administration, 606 North Washington Street, Alexandria, Va. 22314.

ates with whom the applicant may feel more at ease. An offer, if any, should be made as soon as possible, preferably at the time of visit; if this is not possible, the candidate should be told when he or she can expect a decision. If an offer is made, keep in mind that the applicant may have other offers too and that frequent follow-ups to "find out how the decision process is going" or to "ask if there are any other questions" may help to tilt the applicant in your favor.

◆ REFERRALS AND WALK-INS AS A SOURCE OF CANDIDATES

Particularly for hourly workers, "walk-ins"—direct application at your office—are a major source of applicants.[35] Some organizations encourage such applicants by mounting an "employee referrals" campaign. Announcements of openings and requests for referrals are made in the organization's bulletin and posted on bulletin boards. Prizes are offered for referrals that culminate in hirings. This sort of campaign can cut recruiting costs by eliminating advertising and agency fees. It can also result in higher-quality candidates (since many people are reluctant to refer less qualified candidates). But the success of the campaign depends largely on the morale of your employees.[36] And the campaign can backfire if an employee's referral is rejected and the employee becomes dissatisfied. Using referrals exclusively may also be judged to be discriminatory where most of your current employees are either white or male.

Forty percent of the firms responding to one survey said they use some sort of employee referral system and actually hire about 15% of their people directly through such referrals by current workers. A cash award for referring candidates who are hired is the most common type of referral incentive. Naturally, the total amount a firm spends on its referral program will depend on its size, with large firms reportedly spending about $34,000 on their referral programs (including cash payments for candidates), medium companies spending about $17,000, and small ones with fewer than 500 employees, about $3,600. The cost per hire, though, is the important consideration and was uniformly low, with average per hire expenses of only $388— far below the comparable cost of an employment service.[37]

Particularly for hourly workers, walk-ins are a major source of applicants, and there are also several things to keep in mind here. As a rule, all walk-ins should be treated courteously and diplomatically since the employer's reputation in the community—not to mention the applicant's self-esteem—often rides on such diplomatic treatment. Similarly, many employers ensure that every walk-in gets a brief interview with someone in the human resource office, even if it is only to compile information on the applicant "in case a position should open in the future." Good business practice also requires that all letters of inquiry from applicants be answered promptly and courteously.

♦ EMPLOYEE DATA BASES

Employers are also increasingly turning to computerized resume registries as a way of identifying likely candidates. Several of these computerized registries are now functioning, but the nature of one of the first—Career Placement Registry, Inc. (CPR), of Alexandria, Virginia—provides an illustration of how they work. CPR is not an employment agency, but rather a company that compiles a data base of resumes from people who are looking for jobs. That data base is then available on-line to all businesses, service organizations, and government agencies that subscribe to DIALOG INFORMATION SERVICES, INC., a large computerized information network. (Companies that do not subscribe to DIALOG can have a resume search done by CPR at a cost of about $50 for 12 CPR-registered resumes. Any employer that is aware of CPR can thus have access to its data base of resumes, with or without subscribing to the DIALOG data base.)

CPR compiles resume data bases for both students and recent graduates, and for experienced job seekers. Each fills out data entry forms covering items such as name, address, career objectives (accounting, administration, advertising—52 in all), work experience, type of position desired, and educational background. Along with the "personal summary of qualifications," the form presents a fairly complete picture of each candidate's qualifications, occupational preferences, and desired salary range. The form is then returned to CPR along with a check for the registration fee: students pay $12 to register, while experienced job seekers pay $25 to $45, depending upon desired salary level. Resumes remain in the CPR data base for six months, and are available to employers 24 hours a day, seven days a week. Candidates can also specify their desired geographic areas.

Employers get a manual explaining how to access the data base and can customize their search based on the skills and experience required as well as preferred geographic areas. Employers pay no subscription fee—just the cost of being on-line with DIALOG (about $95 per hour) plus a print charge of $1 per resume. The average cost to search CPR is about $20, according to the company. At the present time this particular system is available to the approximately 50,000 employers that subscribe to DIALOG INFORMATION SERVICES, INC. (which is also available through many university libraries).[38]

♦ OLDER WORKERS AS A SOURCE OF JOB CANDIDATES

As of 1990 there were 44% fewer 18- to 25-year-olds entering the work force than there were in 1979; this has caused many employers to begin looking into alternative sources to help meet their employment needs.[39] For many employers this means "harnessing America's gray power," either by encouraging current retirement-age employees to remain with the company or actively recruiting for employees who are at or near (or beyond) retirement age.[40] Is it practical in terms of productivity to keep older workers on? Here the answer seems to be unequivocably "yes."[41] For example, age-related changes in physical ability, cognitive performance, and personality have little effect on worker's output except in the most physically demanding tasks.[42] Similarly, creative and intellectual achievements do not decline with age, absenteeism drops as age increases, older workers usually display more company loyalty than youthful workers, older workers tend to be more satisfied with their jobs and supervision, and older people can be trained or retrained as effectively as anyone. In summary, with the supply of the usual entry-level age workers shrinking quickly, older workers represent an increasingly important source of employee talent.

Recruiting and attracting older workers involves any or all the sources described earlier (advertising, employment agencies, and so forth), but with one big difference: recruiting and attracting older workers generally requires a concerted effort before the recruiting begins, an effort aimed at making the company an attractive place in which the older worker can work. Specifically,

Examine your personnel policies. Check to make sure your policies and procedures do not discourage recruitment of seniors or encourage valuable older people to leave. For example, employer policies like paying limited or no benefits to part-time workers, promoting early retirement, or offering no flexible work schedules will impede the recruitment and/or retention of valued older workers.

Develop flexible work options. Flexible work patterns including, for example, part-time, less than 30-hour-per-week work weeks, consulting, seasonal work, reduced hours with reduced pay, flextime (building the workday around a core of required hours like 11 to 3, but letting workers otherwise come and go as they please), and similar flexible work patterns are often just what older employees prefer. For example, at Wrigley Company, workers over 65 can progressively shorten their work schedules; another company uses "minishifts" to accommodate those interested in working less than full time.[43]

Create or redesign suitable jobs. At Xerox, for example, unionized hourly workers over 55 with 15 years of service and those over 50 with 20 years of service can bid on jobs at lower stress and lower pay levels if they so desire.

Offer flexible benefit plans. Allowing employees to pick and choose among benefit options can be attractive to older (as well as younger) employees: For example, older employees may put added emphasis on longer vacations or on continued accrual of pension credits than do younger workers.

In summary, your job as a recruiter will obviously be simplified if you can make your company a more attractive place in which to work. This is certainly true of older workers—and increasingly younger workers, too, as competition for a dwindling work force becomes more intense.

◆ PROS AND CONS OF VARIOUS RECRUITING SOURCES

Which sources provide the best candidates? *Employee referrals* are perhaps the best source of employees, while newspaper ads and employment agencies are among the worst.[44] One study compared four recruiting sources (convention/journal ads, newspapers, college placement, and self-initiated walk-ins) in terms of their effectiveness as measured by the following characteristics of the candidates they generated: quality of performance, quantity of performance, dependability, job knowledge, absenteeism, work satisfaction, and job involvement.[45] This study (which focused on research scientists) showed applicants recruited through college placement offices and newspaper ads were inferior in performance (quality and dependability) to those who made contact based on their own initiative or in response to a professional journal/convention advertisement. In terms of absenteeism, those recruited through newspaper ads missed almost twice as many

COMPUTER APPLICATIONS IN PLANNING
AND RECRUITING: RECRUITMENT SOURCES

As companies strive to increase the usefulness of each dollar, it is important for HRM managers to investigate the return earned for recruitment costs. To facilitate this, each employment application should ask how the applicant heard of the company/position. The answers can then be coded for easy data entry. (If a computerized application is used, the applicant would choose from a list of codes.) The usual sources include a relative/friend who is already employed, newspaper, state employment service, employment agency, yellow pages, or radio/TV ad. If more than one newspaper is used, then use a different code for each.

Analysis of the data may show you that different types of positions are filled from different sources. If quality applicants for certain classifications (such as clerical help) come from a particular source, that is where funds should be spent for those vacancies. If few or no quality applicants come from a given source, then review the reasons for using that source. (For example, a commitment to increasing the applicant pool of minorities may be a justification for placing an ad in a paper designed for a given ethnic group, even if most quality applicants from that group are found through traditional newspapers.)

General ads, which use the company logo and an appropriate slogan, may be more cost-effective than ads which list job titles and specifications if the company has a wide variety of positions available. The comparison can be tested by asking applicants which ad brought them in.

It is also possible to retain the dates of the application so that different types of ads may be evaluated. It is expensive to place an ad with a border, for example, but in a city where there is a lot of competition for the same type of employee, the border may be necessary to emphasize the ad. Only an analysis of who responded to which ads combined with an evaluation of the quality of the applicants will determine whether or not that was money well spent. In addition, the comparative costs of the various media should be factored into the analysis. This type of analysis should be reviewed at least quarterly, so that seasonal differences may also be observed.

Research often shows that the best source of quality applicants is current employees. If your analysis agrees, this suggests the importance of keeping your employees informed of vacancies as well as the benefits of working for your company. The effectiveness of your efforts should be evaluated regularly. One way to accomplish this is to computerize a survey listing all vacancies and have it available on a portable computer at various locations. Employees should be able to step up to the screen and complete the survey (listing friends to contact) anonymously within a few minutes. Some surveys include a brief computer game at the end of the survey as a reward. This works well in locations where there are many computer-literate employees.

Whenever a company spends money, it should analyze the return from comparative sources. The computer facilitates this analysis.

---

days as did those referred by any of the other sources. College placement office recruits reported significantly lower levels of job involvement and satisfaction with supervision than did employees recruited in other ways. Taken as a whole, these results indicate that—at least for these research scientists—college placement offices and newspaper ads were poorer sources of employees than were journal/convention advertisements and self-initiated walk-ins.

Recruiting Methods Used

These findings notwithstanding, some sources are more appropriate for recruiting some types of jobs than are others. This is illustrated by a recent study of the recruiting practice of 188 companies. For managerial positions,

80% of the companies used newspaper ads, 75% used private employment agencies, and 65% relied on employee referrals. For professional and technical jobs, 75% used college recruiting, 75% also used ads in newspapers and technical journals, and 70% used private employment agencies. For recruiting sales personnel, 80% of the firms used newspaper ads, 75% used referrals, and 65% also used private employment agencies. For office and plant personnel, on the other hand, referrals and walk-ins were relied on by 90% of the firms, while 80% of the firms used newspaper ads and 70% used public employment agencies.[46]

SMALL BUSINESS RECRUITING APPLICATIONS

♦ USING EXECUTIVE RECRUITERS

There comes a time in the life of most small businesses when it dawns on the owner that the managers he or she has in house are not up to the task of taking the company into the realm of expanded sales: it is at this point that a decision must be made regarding what kinds of people must be hired from outside and how this hiring should take place.

Should the owner decide on the type of person that is required and go out and recruit this person himself or herself? Or should some outside expert be brought in to help with the search?

The heads of most very large companies often won't think twice about retaining executive search firms to conduct a search for them. However, small companies' owners (with their relatively limited funds) will understandably hesitate before committing to a fee that could reach $20,000 to $30,000 (with expenses) for a $60,000 to $70,000 marketing manager. As a small business owner, however, you should keep in mind that this sort of thinking can be very short sighted when you consider what your options actually are.

Engaging in a search like this by yourself is not at all like looking for secretaries, supervisors, or data entry clerks, activities with which you are probably much more familiar. Recruiting lower-level employees can usually be accomplished quite easily by using the techniques described earlier, for instance, by placing ads, using (relatively low cost) employment agencies, or even by placing "help wanted" signs in your front windows. However, executive recruiting, as they say, is a horse of a different color, and if you haven't engaged in a search like this yourself, consider what you're doing carefully before you do it. When you're hiring (or looking to hire) a key executive to help you run your firm chances are you are not going to find the person you want by placing ads or using most of the other traditional approaches. For one thing, the person you want (or should want) is probably already employed and is probably not reading the want ads; if he or she does happen to glance at the ads chances are the person is happy enough where they are now not to take the effort to embark on a job search with you.

In other words, what you'll find you end up with is a drawer full of resumes of people who are, for one reason or another, out of work, or unhappy with their work, or dramatically unsuited for your job (based on the ad that you placed). And it is then going to fall to you to try to find a couple of possible gems in this pile of resumes. You are then going to have to interview and assess these applicants yourself: hardly an attractive proposition in itself, unless you happen to be an expert at interviewing and checking backgrounds (and have nothing else to do).

As you can see, there are two problems with conducting these kinds of executive searches yourself. First, as a nonexpert, you will basically not even know where to begin: You won't know where to place or how to write the ads, you won't know where to search or who to contact, you won't know how to do the sort of job that needs to be done to interview this person in order to screen out the laggards and misfits that may well appear on the surface to be viable candidates, and you won't know enough to really do the kind of background checking that a position at this level calls for. The second big problem is that this entire process is going to be extremely time consuming and is going to deflect your attention from other major duties. Many business owners find that when they consider the opportunity costs involved with doing their own searches, they in fact are not saving any money at all: For example, the money they lose by having to attend to executive recruiting duties cost them X number of sales calls, so that their company actually comes out behind, financially speaking. Instead of being able to assess the chemistry between yourself and 3 carefully screened candidates from an executive recruiter, in other words, you'll find yourself plodding through resumes and interviews with perhaps 20 or 30 possible candidates. Often, in other words, the question is not whether you can afford to use an executive recruiter, but can you afford not to? In any event, if you do decide to do the job yourself, consider retaining the services of an industrial psychologist (ask your friends for some references, or look some up in the Yellow Pages). He or she will be able to spend four or five hours assessing the problem-solving ability, personality, interests, and energy level of the two or three candidates in which you are most interested. While you certainly don't want the psychologist to make the decision for you, the input itself can provide an additional perspective on your candidates.

In summary, as explained earlier in this chapter, executive recruiters bring a lot of specialized skills to their jobs, including the ability to go after likely candidates who are now happily ensconced at other firms, perhaps your competitors. You'll want to check the recruiters out very carefully (as explained earlier), but do consider using one before you decide to do the job yourself.

◆ USING THE STATE JOB SERVICES

One final word about using your local state job service office to help you recruit. You will find that particularly for manual workers, clerical workers, and even (quite often) higher-level employees as well, the job service agencies are a surprisingly helpful source of candidates. If you contact your local office they'll probably send a representative/counselor to discuss your staffing needs and will even draw up short job descriptions that they'll key to the DOT and use in their recruiting efforts. Many of these job service offices are also linked with various governmental agencies that will arrange to subsidize the first three or four months of wages for certain (usually disadvantaged) groups of employees. The job service agencies are also a good source of information on prevailing wages for different classifications of jobs. In any event, if you're thinking of recruiting, it certainly pays to spend an hour or so discussing your needs with one of their counselors.

DEVELOPING AND USING APPLICATION BLANKS

◆ PURPOSE OF APPLICATION BLANKS

application blank Usually, the first step in the screening process for job applicants. The application provides information on education, prior work record, strong and weak points.

Once you have a pool of applicants, you can begin the process of screening and selecting the person you want to hire, and for most employers the **application blank** is the first step in the selection process. (Some firms first require a brief, prescreening interview.) The application blank is a good means of quickly collecting verifiable and therefore fairly accurate historical data from the candidate and usually includes information on such things as education, prior work history, and hobbies.

A filled-in blank or form can give you four types of information.[47] First, you can make judgments on substantive matters, such as "Does the applicant have the education and experience to do the job?" Second, you can draw conclusions about the applicant's previous progress and growth, a trait that is especially important for management candidates. Third, you can also draw some tentative conclusions regarding the applicant's stability based on the person's previous work record. (Here, however, you have to be careful not to assume that an unusual number of job changes necessarily reflects on the applicant's ability; for example, the person's last two employers may have had to lay off large numbers of employees.) Fourth, you may be able to use the data in the application to predict which candidates will succeed on the job and which will not, a point we return to below.

In practice, most organizations use several different application forms. For technical and managerial personnel, for example, the form may require detailed answers to questions concerning the applicant's education and so on. The form for hourly factory workers might focus on the tools and equipment the applicant has used and the like.

Using Job Applications

The applicant blank contains a wealth of information you can use for evaluating candidates. Some practical review guidelines for ferreting out this information include the following:

1. Use applications as a guide to hiring. Job seekers reveal what they think are their strong points on applications and inadvertently reveal their weak ones, too, by playing them down. You can therefore use the application to help identify the candidate's strong and weak points.

2. Study the applicants' employment records. Use the application blank information as a starting point to find out what kinds of jobs they have held, how frequently they have changed jobs, and how ambitious they seem to be.

3. Check the quality of the applicant's writing. For example, an applicant who turns in a hastily scrawled sloppy application may have characteristics you don't want in the particular kind of job you are recruiting for.

4. Study the way applicants reply to questions. Clear, accurate answers probably reflect clear thought processes, while the opposite may be true, too.[48]

♦ EQUAL OPPORTUNITY AND APPLICATION BLANKS

The Fair Employment Laws explained in Chapter 2 have particular relevance when it comes to application blanks. Questions concerning race, religion, age, sex, or national origin are generally not illegal per se under federal laws although they are under some state laws. However, they *are* viewed with disfavor by the EEOC, and the burden of proof will always be on you to prove that the potentially discriminatory items are *both* related to success or failure on the job and not unfairly discriminatory. Thus, you generally can request photographs prior to employment, and even ask such potentially discriminatory questions as, "Have you ever been arrested?" The problem is that an unsuccessful applicant might establish a prima facie case of discrimination by demonstrating that the item produces an adverse impact, say on blacks. Having so demonstrated, the burden of proof could then shift to you to show that the item is a valid predictor of job performance and that it is applied fairly to all applicants—that, for instance, the employer checks arrest records of all applicants, not just minority applicants.

A study of 50 application blanks revealed 17 types of questions that contained possible violations of federal regulations.[49] Many of the items should probably have been left out, because they obviously had the potential for being used in a discriminatory manner. These included questions regarding maiden name or name used previously, height and weight, age, religion, race or color, national origin, and sex. But, in addition, several other more subtle types of potentially discriminatory questions often crept into the forms:

Education. One common violation on many of the applications was a question on the dates of attendance, and graduation from various schools—academic, vocational, or professional. This question may be illegal in that it has an indirect relationship to the applicant's age, since by knowing when the person graduated from high school or college you can usually make a fairly accurate guess about the person's age.

Military background. Questions concerning what branch of the armed forces the applicant served in and type of discharge he or she had are usually considered unlawful.

Arrest records. The courts have usually held that employers violate Title VII by disqualifying applicants from employment because of an arrest record. This item has an adverse impact on minorities and in most cases cannot be shown to be justified by business necessity.

Relatives. While legal for an applicant who is a minor, it is generally not acceptable to ask questions about an applicant's relatives when the applicant is an adult. This is because it can provide a window on the applicant's religion, race, or national origin. However, an employer can ask about any relatives who are currently employed by the employer.

Notify in case of emergency. It is generally legal to require the name, address, and phone number of a person who can be notified in case of emergency. However, asking the relationship of this person could indicate the applicant's marital status or lineage.

Membership in organizations. Many forms ask the applicant to list memberships in clubs, organizations, or societies along with offices held. Most of these employers also carefully add instructions not to include organizations that would reveal race, religion, physical handicaps, marital status, or ancestry—a wise choice of words. Those not adding such a clause may be indirectly asking for the applicant's race or religion, for instance, and thus be guilty of making an unlawful inquiry.

Physical handicaps. It is usually illegal to require the listing of an applicant's physical handicaps, defects, or past illnesses unless the application blank specifically asks only for those that "may interfere with your job performance." Similarly, it is generally illegal to ask whether the applicant has ever received worker's compensation for previous injury or illness.

Marital status. In general, the application should not ask whether an applicant is single, married, divorced, separated, or living with anyone, or the names and ages of the applicant's spouse or children. Similarly, it may be shown to be discriminatory to ask a woman for her husband's occupation and then reject the woman because, say, her husband is in the military and therefore subject to frequent relocation.

Housing. Asking whether an applicant owns, rents, or leases a house may also be discriminatory in that it can adversely impact minority groups and is difficult to explain on grounds of business necessity.

One employer's approach to collecting application blank information is presented in Figure 4.17. This university requires applicants to complete two separate forms. One form contains application blank information that is deemed necessary for evaluating the person's future performance, information regarding, for instance, name and work history. The second form (Figure 4.18) contains information compiled and used solely by the university for its Equal Employment and Affirmative Action Reports. (These reports are required of most employers to monitor and demonstrate compliance with Equal Employment Opportunity law.) This form contains information on age, religion, national origin, and so forth. Note that the form in Figure 4.18 includes a cover letter. This letter makes it clear that while the applicant must complete both forms, the information on the second is used solely for EEO reporting purposes and will not be used for screening applicants.

♦ USING APPLICATION BLANKS TO PREDICT JOB PERFORMANCE

Through a fairly simple procedure (which is explained in the appendix to this chapter), you can find the relationship between (1) responses on the application blank and (2) measures of success on the job. Then you can use each person's application blank to predict which candidates will be successful and which will not, in much the same way that employers use personnel tests for screening. Some examples follow.

Using Application Blanks to Predict Job Tenure

One such study was aimed at reducing turnover at a large insurance company. At the time of the study the company was experiencing a 48% turnover rate among its clerical personnel, meaning that for every two employees hired at the same time, there was about a 50–50 chance that one of the two would not remain with the company 12 months or longer.

This study was done as follows. The researcher obtained the application forms of 160 female clerical employees of the company from the firm's personnel files. The researcher then split the application forms into two categories: long-tenure and short-tenure employees. He then found that some responses on the application blank were highly related to job tenure. He was thereby able to use the company's application forms to predict which of the firm's new applicants would stay on the job and which would not.

The study helped the firm comply with its Equal Employment Opportunity responsibilities. For example, some of the items on the application blank (like marital status) could be viewed as potentially discriminatory. In this case the researcher was able to prove that these items did predict success or failure on the job (long tenure versus short tenure) and that there was a business necessity for asking them.[50]

Using Application Blanks to Predict Employee Theft

Employee theft and pilferage is a serious problem, one that employers find difficult to deal with. Employee shoplifting, pilferage, and theft losses range up to $16 billion per year.[51] Yet special tests aimed at predicting stealing tend to be in-depth tests of personality that are difficult and time consuming to administer and evaluate.

A simple, effective solution is to use the application form to predict which applicants have a higher likelihood of stealing. One researcher carried out studies for both a mass merchandiser and a supermarket in Detroit. He found that responses to some application blank items (like "does not own automobile" and "not living with parents") were highly related to

APPLICATION FOR EMPLOYMENT

IDENTIFICATION
Please Print or Type - USE BLACK OR BLUE INK ONLY

Social Security Number	Last Name	First Name	Middle Initial

Address (Street number and name)	City	County

State	Zip Code	Phone (Home or where you can be reached) ( )	Business Phone ( )

PERSONAL DATA

U.S. Citizen? ☐ Yes ☐ No   If no, do you possess an I-151, an I-551, or an I-94 card stamped "employment authorized"? ☐ Yes ☐ No
If yes, attach or provide a copy of the I-151, I-551, or I-94 card.

Have you ever worked at a university in the State University System of Florida or an agency of the State of Florida? ☐ Yes ☐ No
If yes, when and which university or agency:

Do you have any relative(s) employed by this university? ☐ Yes ☐ No   If yes, provide name(s).

Have you pleaded nolo contendere to, or been convicted of, a first degree misdemeanor or a felony?
☐ Yes ☐ No   If yes, explain fully.*

*A conviction will not necessarily bar you from employment. Each conviction will be judged on its own merit with respect to time, circumstances, seriousness, and the position for which you applied.

WORK PREFERENCES

Are you interested in ☐ full-time or ☐ part-time employment?   I can begin work _____
                                                                                                    (date)
Class titles or positions for which you are applying:

1. _____   3. _____   5. _____

2. _____   4. _____   6. _____

MILITARY

Branch of Service	Date Entered	Date Discharged	Final Rank	Type Discharge

Affirmative Action/Equal Opportunity Employer

FIGURE 4.17
(continued)

EDUCATION

CIRCLE highest grade completed:
1   2   3   4   5   6   7   8   9   10   11   12   GED   College   1   2   3   4   5   Graduate   School   1   2   3   4   5

Schools	Grad?	Name and Location	Dates Attended	Miscellaneous Information		
High School	YES ☐ NO ☐			Major emphasis in high school ☐ Voc. Tech. ☐ Bus. ☐ College Prep.		
Junior/ Community College(s)	YES ☐ NO ☐			S/Q hrs.	Maj./Min.	Degree
College(s) and/or University(s)	YES ☐ NO ☐					
Graduate and/or Professional	YES ☐ NO ☐					
Other Ed. Voc. Tech. School(s)	YES ☐ NO ☐					

EMPLOYMENT HISTORY

Please list all employment starting with present or most recent employer. Account for all periods, including unemployment and service with U.S. Armed Forces. If military experience is to be used as experience, a copy of a completed DD Form 214 must be attached. Also, include relevant voluntary and/or part-time work experience. Use additional sheets, if necessary. May we contact your present employer? ☐ Yes   ☐ No

Current or Last Employer (Name of Firm or Agency)	Mailing Address	

Job Title	Supervisor's Name/Title	Phone Number ( )

Starting Salary $	Ending Salary $	Full-Time	Part-Time	Hrs. Per Week	Dates Employed From_____ To_____

Reason For Leaving:

Duties:

Employer (Name of Firm or Agency)	Mailing Address	

Job Title	Supervisor's Name/Title	Phone Number ( )

Starting Salary $	Ending Salary $	Full-Time	Part-Time	Hrs. Per Week	Dates Employed From_____ To_____

Reason For Leaving:

Duties:

Affirmative Action/Equal Opportunity Employer

FIGURE 4.17
(continued)

Employer (Name of Firm or Agency)			Mailing Address		
Job Title	Supervisor's Name/Title			Phone Number ( )	
Starting Salary $	Ending Salary $	Full-Time	Part-Time	Hrs. Per Week	Dates Employed From_____ To_____
Reason For Leaving:					
Duties:					

Employer (Name of Firm or Agency)			Mailing Address		
Job Title	Supervisor's Name/Title			Phone Number ( )	
Starting Salary $	Ending Salary $	Full-Time	Part-Time	Hrs. Per Week	Dates Employed From_____ To_____
Reason For Leaving:					
Duties:					

Employer (Name of Firm or Agency)			Mailing Address		
Job Title	Supervisor's Name/Title			Phone Number ( )	
Starting Salary $	Ending Salary $	Full-Time	Part-Time	Hrs. Per Week	Dates Employed From_____ To_____
Reason For Leaving:					
Duties:					

SKILLS/LICENSES/CERTIFICATIONS

Use this space to indicate any professional or occupational licensure, registration or certification (e.g., Florida Teaching Certificate, Florida Chauffeur's License, Registered Nurse Certificate, etc.) you currently hold or any special knowledge, skills or abilities (e.g., typing, word processing, shorthand, computer use) you possess. If licensure or certification is required or preferred for a position vacancy, a copy of the licensure or certificate must accompany this application.

AUTHORIZATION AND CERTIFICATION

I hereby authorize the university to verify all information contained in this application and any supplement hereto. I certify that the above statements are true and complete to the best of my knowledge. I further understand that any false statements made by me on this application, or any supplement hereto, may be grounds for immediate discharge or rejection from consideration for further employment.

Signature _____ Date _____

NOTE: Please feel free to supplement this application with additional sheet(s), if necessary.

PERSONNEL MANAGEMENT:

ON THE FRONT LINE

If you were to ask Jennifer and her father what the main problem was in running their firm their answer would be quick and short: hiring good people. Originally begun as a string of coin-operated laundromats requiring virtually no skilled help the chain grew to six stores, each heavily dependent on skilled managers, cleaner-spotters, and pressers. Employees generally have no more than a high school education (often less), and the market for them is very competitive. Over a typical weekend literally dozens of want ads for experienced pressers, or cleaner-spotters generally can be found in area newspapers. All these people are usually paid around $6.00 per hour, and they change jobs frequently. Jennifer and her father are thus faced with the continuing task of recruiting and hiring qualified workers out of a pool of individuals that they feel are almost nomadic in their propensity to move from area to area and job to job. Turnover in their stores (as in the stores of many of their competitors) often approaches 400%. "Don't talk to me about human resources planning and trend analysis," says Jennifer. "We're fighting an economic war and I'm happy just to be able to round up enough live applicants to be able to keep my trenches fully manned."

In light of this problem, Jennifer's father gave her the following assignment:

1. Develop a set of recommendations for me concerning two main issues: First, how would you recommend we go about reducing the turnover in our stores? Next, provide me with a detailed list of recommendations concerning how we should go about increasing our pool of acceptable job applicants so we are no longer faced with the need of hiring almost anyone who walks in the door. Your recommendations regarding the latter should include completely worded advertisements and recommendations regarding any other recruiting strategies you would suggest we use.

FIGURE 4.18
Equal Employment Opportunity Disclaimer Letter for Applicants

EQUAL OPPORTUNITY INFORMATION

The information on the reverse side of this form is requested as part of the affirmative action program and to provide statistical information in compliance with Federal and State regulations. Your response is strictly voluntary and will not result in any adverse treatment.

(reverse side of form)

EQUAL OPPORTUNITY INFORMATION

Date of Birth _____   Social Security Number _____

Racial/Ethnic Data:

☐ Black (Non-Hispanic)   ☐ Native American Indian or Alaskan   ☐ Asian/Pacific Islander

☐ Hispanic   ☐ White (Non-Hispanic)

Sex:

☐ Female   ☐ Male

Do you have any disabling or handicapping conditions: ☐ Yes ☐ No   If yes, please describe: _____
_____

If a handicap has been identified, please describe any accommodations needed to assist you. _____
_____

Position(s) applied for:

_____   _____   _____
_____   _____   _____

Affirmative Action/Equal Opportunity Employer

whether or not the employee was subsequently caught stealing. He was therefore able to identify potential thieves early, before they were hired.

SUMMARY

1. Developing personnel plans requires three forecasts: one for personnel *requirements*, one for the *supply of outside candidates*, and one for the *supply of inside candidates*. To predict the need for personnel, first project the demand for the product or service ("sales"). Next, project the volume of production required to meet these sales estimates; finally, relate personnel needs to these production estimates.

2. Once personnel needs are projected, the next step is to build up a pool of qualified applicants. We discussed several sources of candidates, including internal sources (or promotion from within), advertising, employment agencies, executive recruiters, college recruiting, and referrals and walk-ins. Remember that it is unlawful to discriminate against any individual with respect to employment because of race, color, religion, sex, national origin, or age (unless religion, sex, or origin are bona fide occupational qualifications).

3. The initial selection screening in most organizations begins with an application blank. Most managers just use these to obtain background data. However, you can use application blank data to make *predictions* about the applicant's future performance. For example, application blanks have been used to predict job tenure, job success, and employee theft.

4. Using application blanks to predict success (or some other criteria) assumes you can weight the most important items. In the appendix we present a seven-step method for doing this:

   a. Decide on a measure of success.
   b. Pull the applications of "highs" and "lows."
   c. For each response on the application, determine the percentage of "highs" and the percentage of "lows."
   d. Compute percentage differences for each item.
   e. Convert these percentage differences to weights.
   f. Add up the applicant's total score.
   g. Find the "ideal" total score.

5. Labor planning and recruiting directly affect employee motivation. This is because motivation depends on hiring employees who have the aptitude to do the job well. And the more qualified applicants you have, the higher your selection standards can be. Then, once a pool of qualified applicants is available, you can turn to selecting the best. This process usually begins with effective testing and interviewing, to which we now turn.

KEY TERMS

trend analysis	personnel replacement charts	local market conditions
ratio analysis		
correlation analysis	position replacement cards	occupational market conditions
computerized forecasting	general economic conditions	job posting
qualifications inventories		application blank

1. Compare and contrast at least five sources of job candidates.
2. What types of information can an application blank provide you with?
3. Explain how you would go about weighting an application blank.
4. Discuss some of the ways in which equal rights legislation limits what you can do in recruiting.

♦ APPLICATION EXERCISES

♦ CASE INCIDENT

Only Asians Wanted Here

It was certainly a human resource manager's nightmare. IBM Japan Limited, the firm's Japanese subsidiary, seemed to have been recruiting in Japanese magazines in the U.S. in a discriminatory fashion. While IBM Japan insists they never instructed their employment agency to screen out white people and black people in favor of Asians, it does seem that some discriminatory actions actually might have taken place.

The problem revolves around the employment agencies owned by a Japanese firm called Recruit. According to allegations made by Recruit USA's former staffers, Recruit USA had actually set up a fairly formal system to see to it that only Asians were hired for the IBM Japan jobs. According to one memo submitted by a former staffer to the EEOC, Recruit officials summarized the hiring policy as: "Foreigners, no good—IBM current rule . . . white people, black people—no, but second generation Japanese or others of Asian descent o.k." Another Recruit agency in the U.S. allegedly set up a system of code words to discriminate against people they didn't want to hire. For example, if the job order said "see Adam," it meant the client only wanted a male employee. If the job order said "talk to Haruo," it meant the client only wanted a Japanese worker. The whole story first broke when former Recruit employees described their allegation to the *San Francisco Chronicle*. Then, the EEOC got involved and more allegations were unearthed. Japanese firms and other multinationals are therefore learning the truth of the old saying, "When in Rome, do as the Romans," But in this case it means that when you're doing business in a country, you'd better know and follow the laws of the land.

Questions
1. Do you think a client (in this case IBM Japan) should be held responsible for the actions of an independent employment agency that it hires? Why or why not?
2. Do you think it would be right for a company hiring people in the U.S. for work overseas to discriminate, since it's not hiring people to work in the U.S.? Why or why not?
3. If you were the human resource manager of a company using an employment agency, how would you avoid the sort of discrimination problem described in this case?

EXPERIENTIAL EXERCISE

Purpose: The purpose of this exercise is to give you practice in developing an application blank.

Required Understanding: You will want to be familiar with personnel history items useful to developing an application blank (see Figure 4.20 on page 166), and the job description presented in Figure 3.9 (from Chapter 3). Your objective is to develop an application blank for a data processing supervisor.

How to Set Up the Exercise
1. Set up groups of three or four students.
2. Before joining his or her group, each student should carefully read through the exhibits referred to above. The exercise should take about one hour.

Instructions for the Exercise: Form into assigned groups and compile a list of the application blank items you wish to include in your form. Next, sketch out a rough application blank, showing where each of your items would appear on the page(s).

Each group should then choose a spokesperson to list his or her group's items on the chalkboard. Which items appeared most often? What items seem to be missing? Which items do you think would be most useful if you wanted to develop a weighted application? Which items do you think would be most predictive of the applicant's performance?

Appendix

Weighted Application Blanks

HOW TO WEIGHT APPLICATION BLANKS[52]

Using application blanks to predict success assumes that some responses are more predictive of success than others. For example, suppose you find that most who check the responses "age 21–25" quit within one year, while most who check the box "age 31–35" stay with the company *more* than one year. What you'll need is some method of giving more weight to the latter response, since there will then be more chance of an applicant between 31 and 35 years of age being offered a position. The following is one technique for "weighting" application blank items. (Note: You will have to follow Tables 4.6 and 4.7 and Figure 4.19 carefully.)

TABLE 4.6 Comparison of Responses by Long- and Short-Tenure Employees

APPLICATION BLANK ITEMS (PREDICTORS)	% SHORT TENURE[1]	% LONG TENURE[1]	% DIFFERENCES	WEIGHTS
Local address				
Within city	40%	70%	−30%	−3
Outlying suburbs	60	30	30	3
	100%	100%		
Age				
Under 20	40%	10%	30	3
21–25	20	30	−10	−1
26–30	20	20	0	0
31–35	10	20	−10	−1
35 and over	10	20	−10	−1
	100%	100%		
Previous salary				
Under $15,000	50%	20%	30	3
$15,000–$16,000	20	40	−20	−2
$16,000–$17,000	20	20	0	0
Over $18,000	10	20	−10	−1
	100%	100%		
Age of children				
Preschool	40%	20%	20	2
Public school	20	30	−10	−1
High school or older	40	50	−10	−1
	100%	100%		

[1] *Example:* Forty percent of short-tenure (employees had a "within city" address; 60% of them had a "suburbs" address).

TABLE 4.7 Obtaining a Cutting Score

| | | PERCENTAGE OF SUBJECTS AT OR ABOVE A GIVEN SCORE | | |
| | | A | B | |
	Total Score	Percentage of Long-Tenure Employees	Percentage of Short-Tenure Employees	Index of Differentiation (A minus b)
	21	4	0	4
	20	4	0	4
	19	4	0	4
	18	12	0	12
	17	16	0	16
	16	20	0	20
	15	20	0	20
	14	24	0	24
	13	24	3	21
	12	28	3	25
	11	32	5	27
	10	36	8	28
	9	40	10	30
	8	40	14	26
	7	44	15	29
	6	48	17	31
Cutting Score	5	60	20	40
	4	68	22	46
	3	72	27	45
	2	72	32	40
	1	72	39	33
	0	80	42	38
	−1	80	46	34
	−2	80	54	26
	−3	84	66	18
	−4	92	68	24
	−5	92	76	16
	−6	92	85	7
	−7	96	90	6
	−8	96	94	2
	−9	100	98	2
	−10	100	100	0

Point of Greatest Differentiation (aligned with score 4)

Note: Moving down last column, numbers *rise* till reaching cutting point, and then start *falling,* since it is at this point that there is the *greatest difference* between column A (long tenure) and column B (short tenure).

Source: Edwin A. Fleishman and Alan R. Bass, *Studies in Personnel and Industrial Psychology,* 3rd ed. (Homewood, Ill.: The Dorsey Press, 1974), p. 90.

◆ **STEP 1: DECIDE ON MEASURE OF SUCCESS**

First, decide on what your measure of success will be (this is usually called the *criterion*). It might be tenure on the job, performance, employee theft, et cetera. Then, decide on a *standard*—such as "stayed on the job one year or more," if job tenure is your criterion.

◆ **STEP 2: PICK OUT "HIGH" AND "LOW" PERFORMERS**

Next, for some period (say those hired in 1988) pull out the application blanks for those employees who stayed one year or more (the "long tenures"), and pull out those who stayed less than one year (the "short tenures"). (If there

FIGURE 4.19
Weighted Score of Application

APPLICATION FOR EMPLOYMENT

	Code:* (for use by Personnel Department)
Name: Harvey Hooley	
Address: 108 Elm Street, Springfield	within -3
Age: 23	21-25 -1
Salary on last job: $19,000	over $15,000 -1
Age of children: (if any) 4, and 5	Public -1
Duties on last job:	
Educational history:	
Reason for leaving last job:	
	TOTAL -6

are too many employees involved, some scheme for randomly selecting a sample of employees could be used, although for statistical purposes it is often useful to have as large a sample as practical.)

♦ STEP 3: FOR EACH RESPONSE, DETERMINE THE PERCENTAGE OF "HIGHS" AND THE PERCENTAGE OF "LOWS"

Let's say you decide to focus on 10 application blank items, four of which are presented in Table 4.6. And, again, let's assume that your measure of success (your criterion) is "short tenure" versus "long tenure."

Step 3 would be to indicate for each application blank response (such as "1" for the item "Number of Jobs") the percentage of "short-tenure" applicants that check that response (40% in Table 4.6) and the percentage of "long-tenure" applicants that checked that response (10% in Table 4.6). As an example, we've listed these percentages for the responses for each of the four items in Table 4.6.

♦ STEP 4: COMPUTE PERCENTAGE DIFFERENCES

Next, compute the percentage differences (between the long- and short-tenure percentages) for each response. For the "previous salary" item in Table 4.6, for example, 50% minus 20% is a difference of 30 percentage points; 20% minus 40% equals −20%; 20% minus 20% equals 0%; and 10% minus 20% equals −10%.

♦ STEP 5: CONVERT PERCENTAGE DIFFERENCES TO WEIGHTS

The next step is to convert these percentage differences to integer weights. (This makes them more convenient to use.) Thus the 30% difference would be given a weight of +3. The −10% difference would be given a weight of −1, and so on.

◆ STEP 6: ADD UP EACH "APPLICANT'S" TOTAL SCORE

Your next step is to compute the total score for each of the long- and short-tenure "applicants." You do this for each applicant by finding his or her response to each item and then adding up the weights for these responses. For Harvey Hooley, the applicant shown in Figure 4.21, the total score would be −6.

◆ STEP 7: FIND THE "IDEAL" TOTAL SCORE

Next you find the "ideal" total score. (In our case this is the score *that best differentiates between short- and long-tenure employees.*) One way to do this is illustrated in Table 4.7. Let's say that in our study of long- versus short-tenure employees we found that total scores for applicants ranged from −10 to +21. (There may be several people with each total score.) For each total score, list the percentage of "long"- and "short"-tenure applicants reaching that score. Then in the last column, show the difference between the former and the latter (as in Table 4.7).

In this case our "ideal" score is +4. We arrived at "+4" as follows. Run your finger down the last column in Table 4.7. Halt when the numbers stop climbing and start falling. This is the point at which you draw a horizontal line and find your "ideal" total score.[53] It is the cutoff for the "ideal" score, because at this point there is the *maximum difference* between percentage of long-tenure employees (column A) and percentage of short-tenure employees (column B): Recall you were looking for the score that *best differentiates* between long- and short-tenure employees.

So, would Harvey Hooley be hired? Probably not. On the one hand, Table 4.7 shows that 92% of employees who had scores at least as high as Harvey's (−6 or above) were long-tenure employees (they stayed with your firm for a long time), which is good. On the other hand, 85% of employees who left quickly (the short-tenure employees) also had scores of −6 or higher (from −6 to 21 in Table 4.7). Therefore, −6 is not a very promising score for your firm: there is, after all, almost the same chance that Harvey will leave quickly as that he'll be with you for years to come. You want someone with a score as close to 4 as you can get. Why? Because from your experience there is much more likelihood that such a person will be long- rather than short-tenure.

◆ A LIST OF USEFUL APPLICATION BLANK ITEMS

George England has reviewed a number of studies of weighted application blanks. From his review, he has compiled a list of application blank items that have been found to predict various measures of success on the job. These are presented in Figure 4.20. They include such items as "home town size" and "college grades." A manager can use these as a "menu" for developing a weighted application blank.

◆ SUMMARY

Developing a weighted application blank basically involves determining the relationship between (1) an application blank item (like age) and (2) job performance and then determining the "weight" to be applied to various degrees of that item (such as age 21–30, 31–40, and 41–50). According to two experts, weighted application blanks present an attractive alternative to the use of tests for employment decisions, and this attractiveness stems from several sources:

FIGURE 4.20
Personnel History Items Useful in Developing Weighted Application Blanks
Source: Adapted from George W. England, *Development and Use of Weighted Application Blanks,* rev. ed. (Minneapolis: Industrial Relations Center, University of Minnesota, 1971), pp. 16–19.

PERSONAL
Physical health
Recent illnesses, operations
Time lost from job for certain previous period
    (last two years, etc.)
Living conditions, general
Domicile, whether alone, rooming house, keep
    own house, etc.
Residence, location of
Size of home town
Number of times moved in recent period
Length of time at last address

GENERAL BACKGROUND
Military service and rank
Military discharge record
Early family responsibility

EDUCATION
Education
Educational level of spouse
Educational level of family relatives
Education finances—extent of dependence on
    parents
Type of course studied—grammar school
Major field of study—high school
Specific courses taken in high school or college
Subjects liked, disliked in high school
Type of school attended, private/state
College grades
Scholarship level, grammar school and high school
Graduated at early age compared with classmates

EMPLOYMENT EXPERIENCE
Educational—vocational consistency
Previous occupations (general type of work)
Held job in high school (type of job)
Number of previous jobs
Specific work experience (specific jobs)
Previous (selling) experience
Previous (life insurance sales) experience

Total length of work experience (total years,
    months)
Being in business for self
Previous employee of company now considering
    application
Seniority in present employment
Tenure on previous job
Minimum current living expenses
Salary requests, limits set for accepting job
Earnings expected (in future, 2 years, 5 years,
    etc.)

SOCIAL
Club memberships (social, community, campus,
    high school)
Frequency of attendance at group meetings
Offices held in clubs
Experience as a group leader

INTERESTS
Prefer outside to inside labor
Hobbies
Number of hobbies
Specific type of hobbies, leisure-time activities
    preferred
Sports
Number of sports active in
Most important source of entertainment

PERSONAL CHARACTERISTICS,
ATTITUDES EXPRESSED
Willingness to relocate or transfer
Confidence (as expressed by applicant)
Basic personality needs (five types) as expressed
    by applicant in reply to question on application
    blank
Drive
Stated job preferences

1. Most applicants *expect* to be asked to complete an application form.

2. The weighted application form need have no distinguishable differences from an unscored form.

3. Filling in a blank with verifiable information about one's personal history is less offensive (to most people) than is taking a test in which it is usually presumed that the test score will have something, perhaps everything, to do with whether one is offered employment.

4. Finally, weighted applications are developed on the basis of their statistically proven relationship to performance and should therefore be permissible from a legal (EEOC) standpoint.[54]

LEGAL CONCERNS IN THE USE OF WEIGHTED APPLICATIONS

Although weighted application blanks can be effective screening devices, they can also lead to illegal employment decisions or to decisions that, while not against the equal employment laws in a literal sense, violate the spirit of a law.[55]

The legal pitfalls in the use of weighted application blanks derive largely from two things: (1) the relative ease with which persons other than experienced personnel psychologists can develop weighted application blanks and (2) the fact that many items on the application blank (concerning race or age, for instance) necessarily have an adverse impact on protected groups but are also routinely weighted in the weighting process. Application blank items concerning race, sex, religion, age, or national origin *could* be included, of course, even if they do have an adverse impact, as long as their job relatedness and fairness is provable. Again, however, the problem is that they are "red flags" to the EEOC. Furthermore, the ease with which nonspecialists can develop weighted applications creates the possibility that undesirable items may inadvertently be included by nonexperts who are not fully cognizant of the legal requirements or statistical validation procedures to be used.[56] One implication seems to be that those developing weighted application blanks would do well to steer clear of items (concerning race, and religion, for instance) that clearly have adverse impact. Instead, they should seek out items which, based on a thorough job analysis, seem to be obvious and reasonable prerequisites for success on the job. A second implication is that those who are not experienced personnel psychologists should use this technique (and all testing techniques) with considerable caution.

NOTES

1. Wayne Cascio, *Applied Psychology in Personnel Management* (Reston, Va.: Reston, 1978), p. 158. See also Ernest C. Miller, "Strategic Planning Pays Off," *Personnel Journal* (April 1989), pp. 127–132; Jim Bindl, "Align Plans with Data," *Personnel Journal* (May 1989), pp. 64–71.

2. Herbert G. Heneman, Jr., and George Seitzer, "Manpower Planning and Forecasting in the Firm: An Exploratory Probe," in Elmer Burack and James Walker, *Manpower Planning and Programming* (Boston: Allyn & Bacon, 1972), pp. 102–120; Sheldon Zedeck and Milton Blood, "Selection and Placement," from *Foundations of Behavioral Science Research in Organizations* (Monterey, Calif.: Brooks/Cole, 1974), in J. Richard Hackman, Edward Lawler III, and Lyman Porter, *Perspectives on Behavior in Organizations* (New York: McGraw-Hill, 1977), pp. 103–119. For a discussion of equal employment implications of manpower planning, see James Ledvinka, "Technical Implications of Equal Employment Law for Manpower Planning," *Personnel Psychology*, Vol. 28 (Autumn 1975).

3. Roger Hawk, *The Recruitment Function* (New York: American Management Association, 1967). See also Paul Pakchar, "Effective Manpower Planning," *Personnel Journal*, Vol. 62, no. 10 (October 1983), pp. 826–830.

4. Richard B. Frantzreb, "Human Resource Planning: Forecasting Manpower Needs," *Personnel Journal*, Vol. 60, no. 11 (November 1981), pp. 850–857. See also John Gridley, "Who Will Be Where When? Forecast the Easy Way," *Personnel Journal*, Vol. 65 (May 1986), pp. 50–58.

5. Based on an idea in Elmer H. Burack and Robert D. Smith, *Personnel Management: A Human Resource Systems Approach* (St. Paul, Minn.: West, 1977), pp. 134–135. Reprinted by permission. Copyright 1977 by West Publishing Co. All rights reserved.

6. Glenn Bassett, "Elements of Manpower Forecasting and Scheduling," *Human Resource Management*, Vol. 12, no. 3 (Fall 1973), pp. 35–43, reprinted in Richard Peterson, Lane Tracy, and Allan Cabelly, *Systematic Management of Human Resources* (Reading, Mass.: Addison-Wesley, 1979), pp. 135–146.

7. For an example of a computerized system in use at Citibank, see Paul Sheiber, "A Simple Selection System Called 'Job Match,'" *Personnel Journal*, Vol. 58, no. 1 (January 1979), pp. 26–54.

8. For discussions of skill inventories, see, for example, John Lawrie, "Skill Inventories: Pack for the Future," *Personnel Journal* (March 1987), pp. 127–130; John

Lawrie, "Skill Inventories: A Developmental Process," *Personnel Journal* (October 1987), pp. 108–110.

9. Alfred Walker, "Management Selection Systems That Meet the Challenge of the 80s," *Personnel Journal*, Vol. 60, no. 10 (October 1981), pp. 775–780.

10. Donald Harris, "A Matter of Privacy: Managing Personal Data in Computers," *Personnel* (February 1987), pp. 34–39.

11. Amiel Sharon, "Skills Bank Tracks Talent, Not Training," *Personnel Journal* (June 1988), pp. 44–49.

12. This section is based on Harris, "A Matter of Privacy."

13. Charles F. Russ, Jr., "Manpower Planning Systems: Part II," *Personnel Journal*, Vol. 61, no. 2 (February 1982), pp. 119–123. See also Robert Enderle, "HRIS Models for Staffing," *Personnel Journal* (November 1987), pp. 73–79; Ren Nardoni, "Successful Succession Planning," *Personnel Journal* (May 1989), pp. 106–110.

14. Hawk, *The Recruitment Function*, p. 28; see also J. Scott Lord, "How Recruitment Efforts Can Elevate Credibility," *Personnel Journal* (April 1987), pp. 102–106; Linda Robin, "Troubleshoot Recruitment Problems," *Personnel Journal* (September 1988), pp. 94–99.

15. John Campbell and others, *Managerial Behavior, Performance, and Effectiveness* (New York: McGraw-Hill, 1970), p. 23. See also Allan Halcrow, "Recruitment by Any Other Name Is Turnover," *Personnel Journal*, Vol. 65 (August 1986), pp. 10–15.

16. David Dahl and Patrick Pinto, "Job Posting, an Industry Survey," *Personnel Journal*, Vol. 56, no. 1 (January 1977), pp. 40–41.

17. Jeffrey Daum, "Internal Promotion—Psychological Asset or Debit? A Study of the Effects of Leader Origin," *Organizational Behavior and Human Performance*, Vol. 13 (1975), pp. 404–413.

18. Arthur R. Pell, *Recruiting and Selecting Personnel* (New York: Regents, 1969), pp. 10–12.

19. Ibid., p. 11.

20. Ibid., pp. 16–34. See also Barbara Hunger, "How to Choose a Recruitment Advertising Agency," *Personnel Journal*, Vol. 64, no. 12 (December 1985), pp. 60–62. For an excellent review of ads, see Margaret Magnus, *Personnel Journal*, Vols. 64 and 65, no. 8 (August 1985 and 1986), and Bob Martin, "Recruitment Ad Ventures," *Personnel Journal*, Vol. 66 (August 1987), pp. 46–63.

21. John P. Kohl and David B. Stephens, "Wanted: Recruitment Advertising That Doesn't Discriminate," *Personnel* (February 1989), pp. 18–26.

22. Pell, *Recruiting and Selecting Personnel*, pp. 34–42.

23. Stephen Rubenfeld and Michael Crino, "Are Employment Agencies Jeopardizing Your Selection Process?" *Personnel*, Vol. 58 (September–October 1981), pp. 70–77.

24. Ibid.

25. Bureau of National Affairs, "Part-Time and Other Alternative Staffing Practices," *Bulletin to Management*, June 23, 1988, pp. 1–10.

26. This is based on or quoted from Nancy Howe, "Match Temp Services to Your Needs," *Personnel Journal* (March 1989), pp. 45–51.

27. John Wareham, *Secrets of a Corporate Headhunter* (New York: Playboy Press, 1981), pp. 213–225.

28. Pell, *Recruiting and Selecting Personnel*, pp. 56–63; David L. Chicci and Carl Knapp, "College Recruitment from Start to Finish," *Personnel Journal*, Vol. 59, no. 8 (August 1980), pp. 653–657.

29. Allen J. Cox, *Confessions of a Corporate Headhunter* (New York: Trident Press, 1973).

30. Robert Dipboye, Howard Fronkin, and Ken Wiback, "Relative Importance of Applicant Sex, Attractiveness, and Scholastic Standing in Evaluation of Job Applicant Resumes," *Journal of Applied Psychology*, Vol. 61 (1975), pp. 39–48. See also Laura M. Graves, "College Recruitment: Removing the Personal Bias from Selection Decisions," *Personnel* (March 1989), pp. 48–52.

31. Ibid., pp. 39–48.

32. Ibid. See also, "College Recruiting," in *Personnel* (May–June 1980).

33. See, for example, Richard Becker, "Ten Common Mistakes in College Recruiting—or How to Try Without Really Succeeding," *Personnel*, Vol. 52, no. 2 (March–April 1975), pp. 19–28. See also Sara Rynes and John Boudreau, "College Recruiting in Large Organizations: Practice, Evaluation, and Research Implications," *Personnel Psychology*, Vol. 39 (Winter 1986), pp. 729–757.

34. Pell, *Recruiting and Selecting Personnel*, pp. 62–63.

35. Ibid.

36. Ibid., p. 13.

37. The study on employment referrals was published by Bernard Hodes Advertising, Dept. 100, 555 Madison Avenue, New York, N.Y. 10022. See also Allan Halcrow, "Employees are Your Best Recruiters," *Personnel Journal* (November 1988), pp. 43–49.

38. For further information on this service, you can call CPR at 1–800–368–3093. Their complete address is Career Placement Registry, Inc., 302 Swann Avenue, Alexandria, Va. 23301.

39. Harold E. Johnson, "Older Workers Help Meet Employment Needs," *Personnel Journal* (May 1988), pp. 100–105.

40. This is based on Robert W. Goddard, "How to Harness America's Gray Power," *Personnel Journal* (May 1987), pp. 33–40.

41. Glenn McEvoy and Wayne Cascio, "Cumulative Evidence of the Relationship Between Employee Age and Job Performance," *Journal of Applied Psychology*, Vol. 74, no. 1 (February 1989), pp. 11–17.

42. Goddard, "How to Harness America's Gray Power," p. 33.

43. For this and other examples here, see Goddard, "How to Harness America's Gray Power."

44. P. J. Decker, and E. T. Cornelius, "A Note on Recruiting Sources and Job Survival Rates," *Journal of Applied Psychology*, Vol. 64 (1979), pp. 463–464.

45. James A. Breaugh, "Relations Between Recruiting Sources and Employee Performance, Absenteeism and Work Attitudes," *Academy of Management Journal*, Vol. 24 (March 1981), pp. 142–147; R. Wayne Mondy, Robert Noe, and Robert Edwards, "Successful Recruitment: Matching Sources and Methods," *Personnel* (September 1987), pp. 42–46.

46. *Recruiting Practices*, Personnel Policy Forum, Survey No. 462 (Washington, D.C.: Bureau of National Affairs, August 1979), p. 114; reprinted in Stephen P. Robbins, *Personnel: The Management of Human Resources* (Englewood Cliffs, N.J.: Prentice-Hall, 1982), p. 115. For another view of this see Phillip Swaroff, Alan Bass, and Lizabeth Barclay, "Recruiting Sources: Another Look," *Journal of Applied Psychology*, Vol. 70, no. 4 (1985), pp. 720–728. See also, David Caldwell and W. Austin Stivey, "The Relationship Between Recruiting Source and Employee Success: An Analysis by Race," *Personnel Psychology*, Vol. 36, no. 1 (Spring 1983), pp. 67–72.

47. Pell, *Recruiting and Selecting Personnel*, pp. 96–98. See also Wayne Cascio, "Accuracy of Verifiable Biographical Information Blank Responses," *Journal of Applied Psychology*, Vol. 60 (December 1975), for a discussion of accuracy of biodata.

48. This is based on "Evaluating Employment Applications," in *Personnel Journal*, Vol. 63, no. 1 (January 1984), pp. 22–24, and was reprinted from *Supervisor's Newsletter*, no. 276 (March 1983).

49. Richard Lowell and Jay Deloach, "Equal Employment Opportunity: Are You Overlooking the Application Form?" *Personnel*, Vol. 59 (July–August 1982), pp. 49–55.

50. Wayne Cascio, "Turnover, Biographical Data, and Fair Employment," *Journal of Applied Psychology*, Vol. 61 (October 1976).

51. Quoted in Richard Rosenbaum, "Predictability of Employee Theft Using Weighted Application Blanks," *Journal of Applied Psychology*, Vol. 61 (1976), pp. 94–98.

52. Based on David J. Weiss, "Multivariate Procedures," in Marvin Dunnette, ed., *Handbook of Industrial and Organizational Psychology* (Chicago: Rand McNally, 1967), pp. 345–346. Copyright 1967, John Wiley & Sons, Inc. Reprinted by permission of John Wiley & Sons, Inc.

53. For purposes of proving conformity to equal rights legislation, you'd probably have to use a somewhat more sophisticated statistical technique to find your ideal total score. For a further explanation, see G. W. England, *Development and Use of Weighted Application Blanks*, rev. ed. (Minneapolis: University of Minnesota, Industrial Relations Center, 1971). See also Larry Pace and Lyle Schoenfeldt, "Legal Concerns in the Use of Weighted Applications," *Personnel Psychology*, Vol. 30 (Summer 1977).

54. Paraphrased from Larry Pace and Lyle Schoenfeldt, "Legal Concerns in the Use of Weighted Applications," *Personnel Psychology*, Vol. 30, no. 2 (Summer 1977).

55. Ibid., p. 160.

56. Rosenbaum, "Predictability of Employee Theft," pp. 94–98.

Chapter 5

Employee Testing and Selection

When you finish studying this chapter, you should be able to:

1. Explain what is meant by reliability and validity.
2. Discuss six types of tests.
3. Explain how you would go about validating a test.
4. Give examples of some of the ethical and legal considerations in testing.
5. Cite our testing procedure.
6. Explain the work sampling procedure.
7. Explain what an assessment center is.

OVERVIEW

The purpose of this chapter is to show you how to use several employee selection techniques, including testing, assessment centers, work sampling, and reference checks. First, we discuss testing and the concepts of validity and reliability. We talk about different types of tests, including intelligence tests and achievement tests, and explain a procedure for deciding what tests to use. Work sampling is another selection tool that helps managers formalize a selection criteria they have long used—prior work experience. Finally, we discuss the pros and cons of assessment centers and also present some pointers on background and reference checking, polygraphs, and graphology. Like applications, these selection techniques influence motivation by helping you to select only those candidates who have the skills and abilities to do the job—recall it is the ability to do the job that is one prerequisite to motivation.

One of your most important management jobs involves recruitment and placement—finding the right person for the right job and hiring him or her. This requires screening candidates, and so we have discussed one important screening technique (application blanks). But most managers also use other selection tools for screening (or have them used on them). These include tests, prior work experience, assessment centers, and reference checks; in this chapter we discuss these other selection tools. In the following chapter, we then explain a final selection technique, *interviewing*. (Once you select and hire the person you want, your next step will be to orient and train that person, and we will discuss these subjects in the following chapters.)

THE SELECTION PROCESS

◆ WHY THE SELECTION PROCESS IS IMPORTANT

Employee selection is important for three reasons. First, your own performance will always hinge in part on your subordinates' performance. Employees who haven't the right abilities won't perform effectively, and your performance will therefore suffer.[1] The time to screen out undesirables is thus before they have their foot in the door, not after.

Second, effective screening is important because of what it costs to recruit and hire employees. For example, one expert estimates that the total cost of hiring a manager who earns $60,000 a year is about $47,000, once search fees, interviewing time, reference checking, and travel and moving expenses are taken into consideration.[2]

The cost of hiring nonexecutive employees while not as high proportionally is still high enough to warrant keeping these costs to a minimum. For example, in 1988 companies responding to one survey reported that they spent an average of $5,856 for each exempt (generally, managerial, professional, technical, or administrative employees) hired. The average cost to hire a nonexempt office or clerical worker in 1987 was $961, while the average cost to hire one hourly/production worker in 1987 was $333.[3] The point is that hiring employees at all levels is fairly expensive and you want to keep these expenses to a minimum by not making too many hiring mistakes.

Third, good selection is important because of the legal implications of doing a poor job of selecting employees. For one thing, as we explained in Chapter 2, equal employment legislation, guidelines, and court decisions require that you systematically evaluate the effectiveness of your selection procedures to ensure that you are not unfairly discriminating against minorities or women. Furthermore, a second legal rational for careful selection has emerged in the last few years. Employers increasingly are being held liable for damages stemming from their "negligent hiring" of workers who subsequently commit criminal acts on the job.[4] Specifically, courts are increasingly finding employers liable for damages where employees with criminal records or other prehire problems took advantage of job related access to customer homes or other similar opportunities to commit crimes. Some examples of negligent hiring court cases (concerning, for instance, employees with criminal backgrounds or histories of sexual harrassment) are presented in Figure 5.1.[5] As a result, management attorneys today are warning employers to exercise greater caution in screening in order to avoid liability for such unfortunate incidents. For all these reasons, then, effective selection procedures are essential.

FIGURE 5.1
Negligent Hiring Court Cases
Source: Suzanne H. Cook, "How to Avoid Liability for Negligent Hiring," *Personnel* (November 1988), p. 34.

- *Henley* v. *Prince*, George's County, 305 Md. 320, 503 A. 2d 1333 (1986)
  An employee with a criminal background, which included a conviction for second degree murder, sexually assaulted and murdered a young boy. The management knew of the employee's criminal background before the assault and murder. The parties settled before trial for $440,000.

- *Giles* v. *Shell Oil Corp.*, 487 A. 2d 610 (D.C. 1985)
  A customer was fatally shot by a gas station attendant. The court ruled that Shell Oil Corp. was not liable because the attendant was an employee of the gas station and not of Shell Oil Corp. The court stated that Shell Oil Corp. could have been held liable under negligent hiring if (a) Shell Oil Corp. had employed the gas station attendant and (b) the plaintiff had proved that the employer knew or should have known its employee had behaved dangerously or incompetently, and the employer knew of this behavior and failed to adequately supervise the employee.

- *Ponticas* v. *K.M.S. Investments*, 331 N. W. 2d 907 Minn. (1983)
  An apartment manager with a passkey entered a woman's apartment and raped her. This case points out that an employer has a duty to exercise reasonable care in hiring individuals who, because of the nature of the employment, may pose a threat to members of the public. The employer's duty to exercise reasonable care in hiring includes making a reasonable investigation of the employee's background, the scope of which investigation is directly related to the severity of risk that third parties are subjected to by such an employee. Negligence by the owner and the operator of the apartment complex in hiring the apartment manager was found to be the cause of personal injury to the tenant.

TESTING FOR EMPLOYEE SELECTION

♦ INTRODUCTION: THE USE OF TESTS

testing Testing techniques provide efficient, standardized procedures for screening large numbers of applicants for employment and promotion.

Most employers use tests for hiring or promotion, or both, and so this is one good reason for us to discuss **testing.** But there are other reasons for you to learn about testing. For example, having yourself tested can help you make better career decisions. A knowledge of testing can help you understand how your organization's testing procedures affect you. And a knowledge of testing can help you get the most out of your organization's testing program and help you keep test results in perspective.

The use of tests for hiring, promotion, or both has been increasing in recent years after two decades of decline.[6] In one study, about 90% of companies responding in 1963 said they used tests for screening applicants; by 1975, another survey indicated that only about 42% of responding employers reported doing so.[7] By 1985 about 50% of employers again reported using tests, and by 1988 the figures still seem to be around 50% depending upon the type of test: For instance, about two-thirds of the firms surveyed used skill tests (like typing tests) while only about 17% used personality tests.[8]

In general, testing is more prevalent in larger organizations. For example, only about 30% of employers with fewer than 100 employees reported using tests for hiring, while almost 60% of employers with more than 25,000 employees reported doing so.[9] This reflects several things, including the larger firm's need for efficient, standardized procedures for screening high numbers of applicants and their ability to finance testing programs.

The biggest reason for the relatively diminished use of tests was probably the new, more stringent equal employment laws and regulations instituted in the 1960s.[10] As explained in Chapter 2, these laws had the effect of requiring that more rigorous procedures be used in developing and using tests. Furthermore, the problems of validating and safeguarding tests have probably contributed to their diminished use by increasing the cost to the employer of using them.[11] It is possible that the most recent rulings—including *Wards Cove*—will swing the pendulum back in favor of increased testing. If so, the increased testing will reflect in part the effectiveness of personnel tests as a screening and hiring device. Used properly such tests can improve an employer's ability to hire good employees and reject ones not suited for the jobs being tested for.[12]

BASIC TESTING CONCEPTS

♦ VALIDITY

A test is basically a sample of a person's behavior. However, with some tests, the behavior being sampled is more clearly recognizable than it is with others. Thus, in some cases the behavior you are sampling is obvious from the test itself. A typing test is an example. Here the test clearly corresponds to some on-the-job behavior, in this case, typing. At the other extreme, there may be no apparent relationship between the items on the test and the behavior. This is the case with projective personality tests, for example. Thus, in the *thematic apperception* test illustrated in Figure 5.2, the person is asked to explain how he or she interprets the blurred picture. That interpretation is then used to draw conclusions about the person's personality and behavior.

In summary, some tests are more clearly representative of the behavior they are supposed to be measuring than others. Because of this, it is much harder to "prove" that some tests are measuring what they are purported to measure—that they're *valid*.

A tests's **validity** answers the question: "What does this test measure?"[13] With respect to testing for employee selection, the term "validity"

validity Represents the accuracy with which a test, interview, etc. measures what it purports to measure or fulfills the function it was designed to fill.

FIGURE 5.2
Example of a TAT Card
Source: John Atkinson, ed., *Motives in Fantasy, Action, and Society* (New York: Van Nostrand Reinhold, 1958).

**JUST LOOK AT THE PICTURE BRIEFLY (10 TO 15 SECONDS),
TURN THE PAGE, AND WRITE THE STORY IT SUGGESTS.**

often refers to evidence that the test is job related, in other words, that performance on the test is a *valid predictor* of subsequent performance on the job. A selection test must above all be valid since, without proof of its validity, there is no logical or legally permissible reason to continue using it to screen job applicants. In employment testing, there are two main ways to demonstrate a test's validity, *criterion validity* and *content validity*.[14]

Criterion Validity

criterion validity A type of validity based on showing that scores on the test ("predictors") are related to job performance ("criterion").

Demonstrating **criterion validity** basically involves demonstrating that those who do well on the test also do well on the job, and that those who do poorly on the test do poorly on the job.[15] Thus, the test has validity to the extent that the people with higher test scores perform better on the job. In psychological measurement, a *predictor* is the measurement (in this case, the test score) that you are trying to relate to a *criterion*, like performance on the job. The term *criterion validity* comes from that terminology.

Content Validity

content validity A test that is "content valid" is one in which the test contains a fair sample of the tasks and skills actually needed for the job in question.

You demonstrate the **content validity** of a test by showing that the test constitutes a fair sample of the content of the job.[16] The basic procedure here is to identify the content of the job in terms of job behaviors that are critical to its performance and then randomly select and include a sample of those tasks and behaviors in the tests. A typing test used to hire a typist is an example. If the typing test is a representative sample of the typist's job, then the test is probably content valid.

Demonstrating content validity sounds easier than it is in practice. Demonstrating that the tasks the person performs on the test are in fact a comprehensive and random sample of the tasks performed on the job and demonstrating that the conditions under which the test is taken resemble the work situation is not always easy. For many jobs, other evidence of a test's validity—such as its criterion validity—must therefore be demonstrated as well.

♦ RELIABILITY

A test has two important characteristics, *validity* and *reliability*. Validity is the more important characteristic since, if you cannot ascertain what the test is measuring, it is of little use to you.

reliability If a test is reliable, those who take it will tend to score about the same when retested later or when given an equivalent test.

Reliability is the second important characteristic of a test and refers to its consistency. It is "the consistency of scores obtained by the same person when retested with the identical tests or with an equivalent form of a test."[17] A test's consistency is very important; if a person scores 90 on an intelligence test on a Monday and 130 when retested on Tuesday, you probably wouldn't have much faith in the test.

There are several ways to estimate a test's stability or reliability. You could administer the same test to the same people at two different points in time, comparing their test scores at time 2 with their scores at time 1: This would be a *retest estimate*. Or you could administer a test and then administer what experts believe to be an equivalent test at a later date: This would be an *equivalent-form* estimate.

A test's *internal consistency* is another measure of its reliability. For example, suppose you have 10 items on a test of vocational interests, all of which are supposed to measure, in one way or another, the person's interest in working out of doors. Here, you could administer the test and then statistically analyze the degree to which responses to these 10 items vary together. This would provide a measure of the internal reliability of the test, and is referred to as an *internal comparison* estimate. This is one reason you often find questions that apparently are repetitive on some test questionnaires.

What could cause a test to be unreliable? Imagine for a moment that you are asked to take a test in, say, economics, and then retake an equivalent test, say, one month later. You find that your score changes dramatically.

There are at least four main *sources of error* that might explain this anomaly. First, the items may do a poor job of *sampling* the material; for example, test one focuses more on Chapters 1, 3, 5, and 7, while test two focuses more on Chapters 2, 4, 5, and 8. Furthermore, one or more of the questions (items) may not do a good job of even measuring what it is supposed to measure—such as your knowledge of, say, indifference curves. Second, there may be errors due to *chance response tendencies*. For example, the test itself is so boring or hard or inconsequential that you give up and start answering questions at random. (Highly personal questions on a psychological test might elicit the same response.) Third, there might be errors due to changes in the *testing conditions:* For instance, the room next month may be very noisy. And, finally, there could be *changes in the person* taking the test—in this case, you: You may have studied more, or forgotten more, or your mood may have changed. In any event you can see that many factors can affect a test's stability, its *reliability*.

◆ HOW TO VALIDATE A TEST

What makes a test like the Graduate Record Examination useful for college admissions directors? What makes a mechanical comprehension test useful for a manager trying to hire a machinist?

The answer to both questions is usually that people's scores on these tests have been shown to be *predictive* of how they perform. Thus, other things being equal, students who score high on the graduate admissions tests also do better in graduate school. Applicants who score higher on the mechanical comprehension test perform better as machinists.

In order for any selection test to be useful, an employer has to be fairly sure that scores on the test are related in a predictable way to performance on the job. In other words, it is imperative that you *validate* the test before using it: The employer has to be sure that test scores are a good *predictor* of some *criterion* like job performance. The *validation process* usually requires the expertise of an industrial psychologist and is coordinated by the human resource department. Line management's contribution comes in clearly describing the job and its requirements, so that the human requirements of the job, and the job's standards of performance, are clear to the psychologist. This *validation process* consists of five steps, as follows:

Step 1. Analyze the Job

Your first step is to analyze the job in order to develop job descriptions and job specifications. Here you specify the human traits and skills you believe are required for adequate job performance. For example, must an applicant be aggressive? Is shorthand required? Must the person be able to assemble small, detailed components? These requirements become your *predictors*. They are the human traits and skills you believe to be predictive of success on the job. In this first step, you also have to define what you mean by "success on the job," since it is this success you want predictors for. The standards of success are called *criteria*. You could focus on *production-related criteria* (quantity, quality, etc.), *personnel data* (absenteeism, length of service, etc.), or *judgments* (of persons like supervisors).

Step 2. Choose Your Test

Next you choose tests that you think measure the attributes (predictors) that are important to job success. This choice is usually based on experience, previous research, and "best guesses," and you usually won't start off with just one test. Instead, you choose several tests, combining them into a *battery*. This is aimed at measuring a variety of possible predictors, such as aggressiveness, extroversion, and numerical ability.

Step 3. Administer Test

Next, administer the selected test to your employees. You have two choices at this point. First, you can administer the tests to employees presently on the job. You then would compare their test scores with the *current* performance; this is called con*current* validation. Its main advantage is that data on performance are readily available. The disadvantage is that the current employees *may not be representative of new applicants* (who of course are really the ones you are interested in developing a screening test for). For example, current employees have already received on-the-job training and have been screened by your existing selection techniques.[18]

The most dependable way to validate a test is called *predictive validation*. Here the test is administered to *applicants* before they are hired. Then these applicants are hired using only existing selection techniques, not the results of the new tests you are developing. Then, after these people have been on the job for some time, you measure their performance and compare it to their earlier tests. You can then determine if their performance on the test could have been used to predict their subsequent job performance.

Step 4. Relate Test Scores and Criteria

The next step is to determine if there is a significant relationship between scores (the predictor) and performance (the criterion). The usual way to do this is to determine the statistical relationship between (1) scores on the test and (2) performance through *correlation analysis*, which shows the degree of statistical relationship.

If performance on the test and on the job are correlated, you can develop an **expectancy chart** to present graphically the relationship between the test and job performance. To do this, split the employees into, say, five groups according to their test scores, with those scoring the highest fifth on the test, the second highest fifth, and so on. Then compute the percentage of high job performance *in each of these five test score groups* and present the data in an expectancy chart like in Figure 5.3. As illustrated, this shows the likelihood of an employee being rated a high performer if he or she scores in each of these five test score groups. Thus, a person scoring in the top fifth of the test has a 97% chance of being rated a high performer, while one scoring in the lowest fifth has only a 29% chance of being rated a high performer.[19]

Step 5. Cross-validation and Revalidation

Before putting the test into use, you may want to check it by *cross-validating* it by again performing steps 3 and 4 on a new sample of employees. At a minimum, an expert should revalidate the test periodically to make sure it continues to distinguish accurately between high and low performers.

Note that the procedure you would use to demonstrate *content validity* differs from that used to demonstrate *criterion validity*. Content validity tends to emphasize judgment; a careful job analysis is carried out to identify the work behaviors required, and a sample of those behaviors is then

FIGURE 5.3
Expectancy Chart

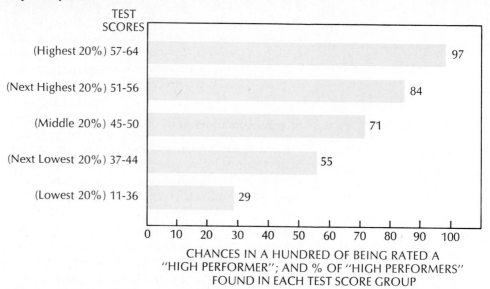

Note: This expectancy chart shows the relation between scores made on the Minnesota Paper Form Board and rated success of junior draftspersons. Example: Those who score between 37 and 44 have a 55% chance of being rated above average; those scoring between 57 and 64 have a 97% chance. Therefore, the higher the score (probably), the higher the person's performance rating on the job. This is because, previously, 55% of those with scores between 37 and 44 were high performers, while 97% of those with scores between 57 and 64 were high performers.

combined into a test that should then be content valid. *The fact that the test is a comprehensive sample of actual, observable, on-the-job behaviors is what lends the test its content validity.* Criterion validity is determined through the five-step procedure described above.

Additional Considerations in the Quest for Validity

Unfortunately, things are not always so simple as they appear, and that is certainly the case when it comes to the matter of validating tests. The five-step process laid out above is a simple and practical one. However, you should also be aware of and consider certain matters that may complicate your quest to arrive at conclusions regarding the validity of the tests you might want to use.

There is, first, the matter of exactly which criterion to use. In brief, the so-called "criterion problem" revolves around ". . . whether different methods of measuring job performance, such as supervisor ratings, production output, and work samples, result in different validity results for the same test."[20] Basically, the problem here is that there are differences in the correlation coefficient when using different criteria. In other words, the same test could have one correlation coefficient when relating scores on a test to one criterion (perhaps using supervisor ratings), and a quite different coefficient when relating scores on a test to a second or other criteria (perhaps using production output). This obviously demands that care be taken in the choice of criteria. Consideration must also be given to analyzing the correlation between predictor and each criterion with the aim of determining why discrepancies (if any) exist.

The second problem has been described in terms of "disenchantment with the usual validity coefficient." This basically refers to the fact that in many cases basing a test's validity on a single correlation coefficient between predictor and criterion (as is often done) may be flawed for at least two reasons.[21] One is "a growing awareness that a single bivariate (two-variable) correlation is virtually uninterpretable."[22] For example, you know a correlation coefficient by itself doesn't show cause and effect: Thus (to use an overworked example), a correlation between smoking and cancer (the tobacco industry would contend) doesn't necessarily *prove* that smoking *leads* to cancer; it may simply reflect the fact that other, unmeasured factors (like emotional stress) lead people to both smoke and get cancer. "Thus," (contend some psychologists) "just how much importance can be lent to a single correlation coefficient—in this case, a validity coefficient that correlates test scores (predictor) and performance (criterion)?"

The other reason for the "disenchantment with the usual validity coefficient" is the possible unreliability of the criterion itself. Specifically, a correlation (validity) coefficient may be deemed questionable because of an unreliable criterion (for instance, haphazard performance appraisal) or the fact that other criteria should have been used, or because of other, related problems. (These problems are studied today under the topics of meta-analysis and validity generalization.) For example, the question can be raised as to how valid a validity coefficient is over the entire range of test scores or criterion. Thus a test may do a good job of predicting performance for very high performers and so (unless the researcher is very careful) thereby produce a high-validity coefficient and an apparently valid test. But the point has been made that this apparent validity may not be generalizable to the lower range of test scores. For example, it may turn out that for some reason test scores correlate very highly for a certain range of performance (or for a certain range of test scores), but not nearly as well in other parts of the range.[23] In any event, the bottom line is that someone embarking on a validity study has to take more care than might be immediately apparent.[24]

♦ SOME USEFUL TESTING GUIDELINES

Here are some basic guidelines[25] for setting up your testing program:[26]

1. *Use tests as supplements.* Do not use tests as your only selection technique; instead, use them to supplement other techniques like interviews and background checks. There are several reasons for this. First, tests are not infallible. Even in the best of cases the test score usually only accounts for about 25% of the variation in the measure of performance. In addition, tests are often better at telling you which candidates will fail than which will succeed.

2. *Validate the tests in your organization.* Both *legal requirements* and *good testing practice* demand that the test be validated in your own organization. The fact that the same tests have been proven valid in similar organizations is *not* sufficient.

3. *Analyze all your current hiring and promotion standards.* Ask questions such as: "What proportion of minority and nonminority applicants are being rejected at each stage of the hiring process?" and "Why am I using this standard—what does it mean in terms of actual behavior on the job?" Remember that the burden of proof is always on you to prove that the predictor (such as intelligence) is related to success or failure on the job.

4. *Keep accurate records.* It is important that you keep accurate records of why each applicant was rejected. For purposes of the Equal Employment Opportunity Commission, a general note such as "not sufficiently well qualified" would not be enough. State, as objectively as possible, why the candidate was rejected. Remember that your reasons for rejecting the candidate may be subject to validation at a later date.

5. *Beware of certain tests.* Certain intelligence tests have been so misused that the EEOC is prejudiced against them. The evidence you provide on

their validity in your organization would have to be overwhelming to permit their use.

6. *Begin your validation program now.* If you don't currently use tests, or if you use tests that haven't been validated, begin your validation study now. Preferably make this a predictive validation study: Administer the tests to applicants, hire the applicants without referring to the test scores, and then (at a later date) correlate their test scores with their performance on the job.

7. *Use a certified psychologist.* The development, validation, and use of selection standards (including tests) generally requires the assistance of a qualified psychologist. Most states require that persons who offer psychological services to the public be certified or licensed. Persons engaged in test validation generally belong to the *American Psychological Association (APA)* and probably to *Division 14 (Division of Industrial and Organizational Psychology)* as well. Most industrial and organizational psychologists hold a Ph.D. degree (the bachelor's degree is never sufficient). A potential consultant should be able to provide evidence of similar work and experience in the area of test validation. He or she should be familiar with the standards for psychological tests and the manual published by the APA. And the consultant should demonstrate familiarity with existing federal and state laws and regulations applicable to equal rights. The names of previous clients should be provided so you can verify references. Competent professionals generally will not make any claims for extraordinary results or guarantee certain, positive outcomes.

8. *Test conditions are important.* Administer your tests in areas that are reasonably private, quiet, well lighted, and ventilated, and all applicants should take the tests under the same test conditions. Once completed, test results should be held in the strictest confidence and only given to individuals who have a legitimate need for the information and also have the ability to understand and interpret the scores.

ETHICAL AND LEGAL QUESTIONS IN TESTING

◆ EQUAL EMPLOYMENT OPPORTUNITY IMPLICATIONS FOR TESTING

Various federal and state laws (including the 1964 Civil Rights Act and 1967 Age Discrimination in Employment Act) bar discrimination with respect to race, color, age, religion, sex, and national origin.[27] These laws were bolstered by the Equal Employment Opportunity Act of 1972, by guidelines published by the EEOC, and by several court decisions and were then modified, as we have seen, rather dramatically in 1989 with decisions such as *Wards Cove*. With respect to testing, these laws (before *Wards Cove*) boiled down to this: (1) You had to be able to *prove* that your tests were related to success or failure on the job (validity), and (2) you had to be able to *prove* that your tests didn't unfairly discriminate against either minority or nonminority subgroups. The burden of proof rested with you; you were presumed "guilty" until proven innocent and had to demonstrate the validity and selection fairness of the allegedly discriminatory item. As of today, as we saw in Chapter 2, unless *Wards Cove* is superseded by new legislation or further Supreme Court decisions, the burden of proof is no longer on the employer but on the employee/plaintiff. Specifically, the U.S. Supreme Court held that the burden of persuading the judge or jury in a lawsuit always lies with the person bringing the complaint. Even when it is the employer's turn to explain why it uses a selection method such as a test that has a discriminatory effect (if such is the case), the employer's burden is only to "produce" an explanation; it does not have the burden of "persuasion." The person bringing the charge—or the person suing—must persuade the judge or jury that the employers explanation is inadequate.[28]

Interestingly, even before *Wards Cove* it appears that a minority of employers were validating their tests. According to one study, fewer than half of those employers with fewer than 10,000 employees had conducted validation studies and less than one-quarter of those with fewer than 1,000 had done so.

The main reason for noncompliance was apparently not that the guidelines were unfeasible but that compliance can be an expensive inconvenience for the employer. For instance, you have to do a validation study, develop a good performance appraisal method, and do a thorough job analysis. In any case, it is too early to tell what effect, if any, *Wards Cove* will have on employers' willingness to validate their tests.

One point that should be made, however, is that you can't avoid the EEO laws just by phasing out your testing program. EEO guidelines and laws apply to any and all screening or selection devices, including interviews, applications, and references. In other words, the same burden of proving job relatedness falls on interviews and other techniques (including performance appraisals) that falls on tests; you could be asked to prove the validity and fairness of *any* screening or selection tool that has been shown to have an adverse impact on a protected group.[29] A detailed explanation of test unfairness is presented in the appendix to this chapter.

Your Alternatives

Let's review where we are at this point. Assume that you've used a test and that a rejected minority candidate has demonstrated adverse impact to the satisfaction of a court. How might the person have done this? One way was to show that the selection rate for, say, his racial group was less than four-fifths of that for the group with the highest selection rate. Thus, if 90% of white applicants passed the test but only 60% of blacks, then (since 60% is less than four-fifths of 90%) adverse impact exists.

You would then have three alternatives. One is to choose an alternative selection procedure that does not have an adverse impact. In other words, you could choose a different test or selection procedure, one that does not adversely impact minorities or women.[30]

The second alternative is to produce an explanation of why the test is valid, in other words, why it is a valid predictor of performance on the job. Ideally, you would do this by conducting your own validation study. Under certain circumstances you may also try to show the validity of the test by using information on the test's validity collected elsewhere.[31] In any event, the plaintiff would then have to prove that your explanation for using the test is inadequate. Based on *Wards Cove*, you wouldn't have to prove the test was valid—the plaintiff, basically, would have to prove it wasn't.[32] Should *Ward's Cove* be superceded by new legislation, employers could again have the burden of proving that their tests (or other selection tools) are valid.

A third alternative—in this case aimed at avoiding adverse impact, rather than reacting to it—is to monitor the selection device to determine if it has disparate impact; if so, then determine if the test is valid. In the absence of disparate impact you can generally use selection devices that may not be valid or otherwise job-related.

Individual Rights of Test Takers and Test Security

Under the American Psychological Association's standard for educational and psychological tests, test takers have certain rights to privacy and information.[33] First, the test taker has the right to the confidentiality of the test results and the right to informed consent regarding the use of these results. Second, the person has the right to expect that only people qualified to interpret the scores will have access to those scores or that sufficient information will accompany the test scores to ensure their appropriate interpretation. Third, he or she has the right to expect that the test is equally fair to all test takers in the sense of being equally familiar or unfamiliar so that the test results reflect the test takers' abilities; the tests, in other words, must be *secure* in that no person taking the tests should have been able to have obtained prior information concerning the questions or answers on the test.[34]

The Issue of Privacy

In addition to the American Psychological Association's standard, imbedded in U.S. law are certain protections regarding an employee's rights to privacy that you should be aware of.

In general (although as we'll see there are several reasons to be quite cautious in using information about employees), there are few restrictions on an employer's right to disseminate information about employees either inside or outside the company. The U.S. Constitution does not expressly provide for the right to privacy, but various U.S. Supreme Court decisions probably protect individuals from intrusive *governmental* action in a variety of contexts.[35] What these laws boil down to is that if you are a federal employee or (in many jurisdictions) a state or local government employee, there are considerable limits on disclosure of personnel information to other individuals or agencies within the agency or outside the agency.[36] The federal privacy act (although not applicable to employees of private firms) provides an indication of the sorts of informational privacy issues that legislatures are concerned about. The act (1) requires that an agency maintain only such information as is relevant and necessary to accomplish its purpose, (2) requires to the greatest extent practical that the information come directly from the individual, (3) establishes safeguards to ensure the security and confidentiality of records, and (4) gives federal employees the right to inspect personnel files and limits the disclosure of personnel information without an employee's consent.[37]

Beyond this the common law of torts does provide some limited protection as far as disclosing information about employees to people outside the company. The most well-known application here involves defamation (either libel or slander). This basically means that if your employer or former employer discloses information that is false and defamatory and that causes you serious injury, you may be able to sue for defamation of character.[38] In general, though, this is easier said than done: Employers (in providing, say a recommendation) generally cannot be sued successfully for defamation unless the employee can show "malice" (that is, ill will, culpable recklessness, or disregard of the employee's rights and this is usually hard to prove).[39] An employer may also be sued for interference with business or prospective business relations if it willfully provides information to another for the purpose of harming a former employee. In addition, you should not disclose to another company that a former employee had filed a charge of discrimination or a lawsuit alleging discrimination or other labor law violation since that has been held to constitute unlawful retaliation.

On the other hand, common law as it applies to invasion of privacy has been recognized in various forms in some states, and here employees have been winning more lawsuits. Such cases usually revolve around "public disclosure of private facts." They involve employees suing employers for disclosing to a large number of people true but embarrassing private facts about the employee. For example, your employee personnel file may (and often will) contain information about private facts regarding your health, job performance, and salary information you may not want disclosed outside the firm. One thing to understand about invasion-of-privacy suits like these is that truth is no defense. One case involved a supervisor in a shouting match with an employee. The supervisor yelled out that the employee's wife had been having sexual relations with certain people. Both the employee and his wife sued the employer for invasion of privacy. The jury found that the employer was liable for invasion of the couple's privacy and awarded damages to both of them. In addition, the jury awarded damages for the couple's additional claim that the supervisor's conduct amounted to an intentional infliction of emotional distress.[40] The point is that in these increasingly litigious times perhaps more discretion is called for then some employers may have shown in the past. Remember, there is now not only a moral but a financial reason for limiting the broadcasting of personal information to the smallest possible radius.

Some guidelines to follow here include:

1. Supervisory training is very important.[41] Employers should meet with everyone from front-line supervisors on up through to middle and upper management to emphasize the importance of confidentiality with regard to information they have or may have about their employees.

2. Next, adopt a strict policy (particularly in areas like drug testing) that only those who "need to know" will share the information. For example, if an employee has been rehabilitated after a period of drug use and that information is not relevant to the employee's functioning in the workplace, then his or her new supervisor may not "need to know."

3. Third, if you know that for some reason the information to be elicited via testing will *not* be kept confidential, you may limit your liability by disclosing that fact prior to testing. For example, if employees who test positive on a drug test are going to be required to use the company's employee assistance program, that should be explained before the tests are given. Similarly, if supervisors are routinely going to be asked to participate in the rehabilitation phase, then employees should understand prior to testing that their supervisors will become involved if they test positive.

TYPES OF TESTS

We can conveniently classify a test according to whether it measures cognitive (mental) abilities, motor and physical abilities, personality and interests, or achievement.[42]

♦ TESTS OF COGNITIVE ABILITIES

Tests in this group include tests of general reasoning ability (intelligence) and tests of specific mental abilities like memory and inductive reasoning.

Intelligence Tests

Intelligence (IQ) tests are tests of general intellectual abilities. They measure not a single trait, but rather several abilities such as memory, vocabulary, verbal fluency, and numerical ability.

As it was originally used, IQ was literally a quotient. The procedure was to divide a child's mental age (as measured by the intelligence test) by his or her chronological age, and then multiply the results by 100. Thus, if an 8-year-old child answered questions as a 10-year-old might, his or her IQ would be 10 divided by 8, times 100, or 125.

For adults, of course, the notion of mental age divided by chronological age wouldn't make much sense, since, for example, we wouldn't necessarily expect a 30-year-old man to be more intelligent than a 25-year-old one. Therefore, an adult's IQ score is actually a *derived* score, one reflecting the extent to which the person is above or below the "average" adult's intelligence score.

Intelligence is often measured with the Stanford-Binet Test or with the Wechsler Test. The picture in Figure 5.4 depicts a man performing one of the tasks that comprise the Wechsler. In this case, he is trying to reconstitute the striped blocks, while his time limit on that task is monitored by a Wechsler Test specialist. Other IQ tests such as the Wonderlic are written and can be administered to groups of people.

Specific Cognitive Abilities

There are also measures of specific mental abilities. These usually include inductive and deductive reasoning, verbal comprehension, memory, and numerical ability.

Tests in this category are often called *aptitude tests,* since they purport to measure the applicant's aptitudes for the job in question. For example, the test of mechanical comprehension illustrated in Figure 5.5 tests the applicant's understanding of basic mechanical principles and, therefore, reflects the person's aptitude for jobs—like that of machinist or engineer— that require mechanical comprehension. Other tests of mechanical aptitude include the *mechanical reasoning test* and the SRA Test of Mechanical Aptitude.

FIGURE 5.4
Material Used in Testing Intelligence with the Wechsler
Source: Courtesy of The Psychological Corporation, New York, N.Y.

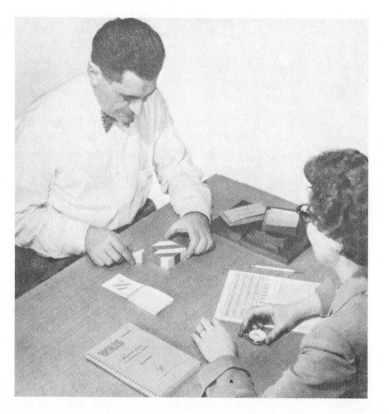

FIGURE 5.5
Two Problems from the Test of Mechanical Comprehension

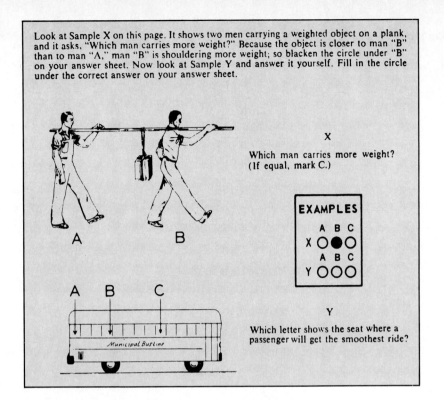

Look at Sample X on this page. It shows two men carrying a weighted object on a plank, and it asks, "Which man carries more weight?" Because the object is closer to man "B" than to man "A," man "B" is shouldering more weight; so blacken the circle under "B" on your answer sheet. Now look at Sample Y and answer it yourself. Fill in the circle under the correct answer on your answer sheet.

X

Which man carries more weight? (If equal, mark C.)

EXAMPLES

A B C
X O ● O
A B C
Y O O O

Y

Which letter shows the seat where a passenger will get the smoothest ride?

◆ TEST OF MOTOR AND PHYSICAL ABILITIES

Motor abilities include tests of coordination and dexterity, while *physical abilities* include strength and stamina. There are many motor abilities that you might be interested in measuring. These include finger dexterity, manual dexterity, speed of arm movement, and reaction time. One example of such a test is the Stromberg Dexterity Test, which is illustrated in Figure 5.6. This test measures the speed and accuracy of simple judgment as well as speed of finger, hand, and arm movements. Other tests include the *Crawford Small Parts Dexterity Test,* the *Minnesota Rate of Manipulation Test,* and the *Purdue Peg Board.*

Tests of *physical* abilities are also sometimes required.[43] Physical abilities include static strength (lifting weights), dynamic strength (like pull-ups), body coordination (as in jumping rope), and stamina.

Tests of motor and physical abilities are often used as indicators of an applicant's trainability for a job.[44] For most jobs, the minimum required physical skills can be developed through technical training. Motor and skills tests provide an indicator of how long it will take the applicant to learn the skills, as well as the accuracy with which he or she will perform them. They can also help to screen out people who for one reason or another might never be able to perform satisfactorily.

◆ MEASURING PERSONALITY AND INTERESTS

A person's mental and physical abilities are seldom enough to explain the person's job performance, since other factors like the person's motivation and interpersonal skills are important as well; personality and interests inventories are sometimes used as possible predictors of such intangibles.

Personality tests are used to measure basic aspects of an applicant's personality, such as introversion, stability, and motivation. Many personality tests are *projective;* an ambiguous stimulus like an ink blot or clouded picture is presented to the person taking the test, who is then asked to inter-

FIGURE 5.6
Minnesota Rate of Manipulation Test (top) and Strongberg Dexterity Test (bottom)
Source: Educational Test Bureau and The Psychological Corporation.

pret or react to it. Since the pictures are ambiguous, the person's interpretation must come from within—be projected. He or she supposedly *projects* into the picture his or her own emotional attitudes and ideas about life; thus, a security-oriented person might describe the man in Figure 5.2 as "worrying about what he'll do if he's fired from his job." Examples of personality tests (which are more properly called personality *inventories*) include the *Thematic Apperception Test, Guilford-Zimmerman Temperament Survey,* and the *Minnesota Multiphasic Personality Inventory*. The Guilford-Zimmerman survey measures personality traits like emotional stability versus moodiness and friendliness versus criticalness. The Minnesota Multiphasic Personality Inventory, on the other hand, taps traits like hypochondria and paranoia.

Personality tests—particularly the projective type—are the most difficult tests to evaluate and use. An expert has to assess the test taker's interpretations and reactions and infer from them the makeup of his or her personality. The usefulness of such tests for selection then assumes that you can find a relationship between some measurable personality trait (like introversion) and success on the job.[45]

Interest inventories compare a person's interests with those of people in various occupations. Thus, if a person takes the Strong-Campbell Inventory, he or she would receive a report showing his or her interests in relation to those of people already in occupations such as accountant, engineer, manager, or medical technician. Interest inventories have many uses. They can be useful in career planning, since a person will likely do better on jobs that involve activities in which he or she is more interested. These tests can also be useful as selection tools. Clearly, if you can select people whose interests are roughly the same as those of successful incumbents in the jobs for which you are recruiting, it is more likely that the applicants will be successful on their new jobs.[46]

♦ ACHIEVEMENT TESTS

An achievement test is basically a measure of what a person has learned. Most of the tests you take in school are thus achievement tests; they measure your "job knowledge" in areas like economics, marketing, or personnel.

Achievement tests are also widely used in employment screening. For example, the *Purdue Test for Machinists and Machine Operators* tests the job knowledge of experienced machinists with questions like "what is meant by 'tolerance'?" Other tests are available for electricians, welders, carpenters, and so forth. In addition to job knowledge, other achievement tests measure the applicant's abilities; a typing test is one example.

WORK SAMPLES AND SIMULATIONS

work samples Choosing several tasks necessary to a job and then testing applicants' performance on these actual tests.

While **work samples** and assessment centers can be considered tests, they differ from most of the tests discussed previously because they focus on measuring job performance directly.[47] Tests of aptitudes and abilities or personality and interests inventories, on the other hand, aim to predict job performance by measuring traits like aptitudes, abilities, or interests.

♦ WORK SAMPLING FOR EMPLOYEE SELECTION

Rationale for Work Sampling

work sampling technique A testing method based on measuring performance on actual, basic job tasks.

The **work sampling technique** is based on the assumption that the best way to determine how a candidate will do on the job is by measuring how that candidate actually performs some of the job's basic tasks:[48] "Why measure traits like intelligence or mechanical aptitude," say some experts, "in the hope that they will predict job performance, when it's simpler to just measure samples of that performance directly?"

There are several advantages to using work sampling. Since you are measuring actual on-the-job tasks, it is harder for the applicant to fake answers. The work sample itself is more clearly relevant to the job you are recruiting for, so in terms of fair employment you may be on safer grounds. The content of the work sample—the actual tasks the person must perform—is not as likely to be unfair to minorities as in a personnel test that inadvertently emphasizes middle-class concepts and values.[49] Work sampling does not delve into the applicant's personality or psyche, so there's almost no chance of it being viewed as an invasion of privacy. And well-designed work samples almost always exhibit better validity than do tests designed to predict performance.

Basic Work Sampling Procedures[50]

The basic procedure involves choosing several tasks that are crucial to performing the job in question and then testing applicants on each of these tasks. Their performance on each task is monitored by an observer who indicates, on a checklist, how well the applicant performs that task. An example of the actual procedure follows:

In developing a work sampling test for maintenance mechanics experts first listed all the possible tasks (like "install pulleys and belts" and "install

COMPUTER APPLICATION IN TESTING:
COMPUTER-INTERACTIVE PERFORMANCE TEST

Microprocessors and minicomputers have opened up new possibilities for measuring various types of performance and we should briefly review some of these.[1] One expert classifies the uses of computers in selection into four kinds of applications. The first simply uses the computer as a way to administer a currently available printed test. Using the computer in this way facilitates scoring and the compilation of cumulative norms.

A second way in which computers are used today in selection testing may be called the *adaptive test*. Adaptive tests automatically tailor a sequence of test items to each examinee, contingent on his or her responses to earlier items in the sequence. In tests like these, correct responses generally trigger more difficult items, for instance. The effect is to reduce substantially the number of test items needed, since those that are either too easy or hard for the examinee are not administered.

Third, computers are being used to enhance the administration of tests where dynamics are involved, as in tests of perceptual speed. Here the computer can be used to present signals rapidly and sequentially to test the person's perceptual speed. Similarly, a test of short-term memory, where the stimulus can be removed from the display and recall required later, is another example of an application here.

Fourth, computers are being used to measure human capabilities not measurable (or easily measurable) by printed tests. For example, measuring capabilities like the ability to function under different time pressures, or under different work load conditions, or, for that matter, the ability to concentrate under stress are not human capabilities easily measured by printed tests. Computers are being used in this area, for instance, by measuring the person's ability to concentrate as various stimuli are projected on the screen.

[1]This is based on Edwin A. Fleishman, "Some New Frontiers in Personnel Selection Research," *Personnel Psychology*, Vol. 41, no. 4 (Winter 1988), pp. 679–701.

and align a motor") that maintenance mechanics would be required to perform. For each task, the experts listed the frequency of performance of the task, and the task's relative importance to the overall job of maintenance mechanic. Thus four crucial tasks here were installing pulleys and belts, disassembling and installing a gear box, installing and aligning a motor, and pressing a bushing into a sprocket.

Next these four tasks were broken down *into the steps needed to complete them*. Each step, of course, could be performed in a slightly different way, and (since some approaches were better than others) the experts gave different weight to different approaches.

This is illustrated in Figure 5.7. Shown at the top is one of the steps required for installing pulleys and belts; that step is "checks key before installing." As listed on the checklist, different possible approaches here include checking the key against (1) the shaft, or (2) the pulley, or (3) against neither. Weights reflecting the worth of each of these approaches are shown on the right of the exhibit.

Next each applicant was required to perform each of the four tasks (such as installing pulleys and belts) and how he or she actually performed each of the steps was monitored by the test administrator. The latter watched the applicant and indicated on a checklist like that in Figure 5.7 the approach the applicant used. Thus, if the applicant checked the key against the pulley before installing it, the test administrator would (as he did here) mark "pulley" for that particular step in the task *installing pulleys and belts*.

FIGURE 5.7
Work Sampling Questions
Source: James E. Campion, "Work Sampling for Personnel Selection," *Journal of Applied Psychology,* Vol. 56 (1972). Copyright 1972 by the American Psychological Association. Reprinted by permission of the author.

"Crucial Tasks" and Sample Questions for Maintenance Mechanics

Scoring Weights

Installing Pulleys and Belts

1. Checks key before installing against:
   _____ shaft — 2
   _____ pulley — 2
   _____ neither — 0

Disassembling and Repairing a Gear Box

10. Removes old bearing with
    _____ press and driver — 3
    _____ bearing puller — 2
    _____ gear puller — 1
    _____ other — 0

Installing and Aligning a Motor

1. Measures radial misalignment with:
   _____ dial indicator — 10
   _____ straight edge — 3
   _____ feel — 1
   _____ visual or other — 0

Pressing a Bushing into Sprocket and Reaming to Fit a Shaft

4. Checks internal diameter of bushing against shaft diameter:
   _____ visually — 1
   _____ hole gauge and micrometers — 3
   _____ Vernier calipers — 2
   _____ scale — 1
   _____ does not check — 0

Finally, the work sampling test was validated, by determining the relationship between the applicant's scores on the work samples and their actual performance on the job. Then, once it was shown that the work sample was a valid predictor of job success, the employer could begin using it for selection.

◆ WHAT ARE MANAGEMENT ASSESSMENT CENTERS?

management assessment centers A situation in which management candidates are asked to make decisions in hypothetical situations and are scored on their performance. It usually also involves testing and the use of management games.

Many organizations use management assessment centers for employee selection, and you may find yourself participating in one as a prerequisite to being hired (or promoted). A **management assessment center** is a two- to three-day experience in which about a dozen management candidates perform realistic management tasks (like making presentations) under the watchful eye of expert appraisers; each candidate's potential for management is thereby *assessed* or appraised.[51] The center itself may be just a conference room, but it is often a special room with a one-way mirror to facilitate the assessors' unobtrusive observations. Examples of the real-life but simulated exercises included in a typical assessment center are as follows:

The in-basket. With this type of exercise, the candidate is faced with an accumulation of reports, memos, notes of incoming phone calls, letters, and other materials collected in the in-basket of the simulated job he or she is to take over. The candidate is asked to take appropriate action on each of these materials by, for example, writing letters, notes, or agendas for meetings. The results of the candidate's actions are then reviewed by the trained evaluators.

The leaderless group discussion. A leaderless group is given a discussion question and told to arrive at a group decision. The raters then evaluate each participant's interpersonal skills, acceptance by the group, leadership, and individual influence.

PERSONNEL MANAGEMENT:

ON THE FRONT LINE

Jennifer and her father have what the latter describes as an easy but hard job when it comes to screening job applicants. It is easy because for two important jobs—the people who actually do the pressing and those who do the cleaning-spotting—the applicants are easily screened with about 20 minutes of on-the-job testing. As with a typist, as Jennifer points out, "a person either knows how to press clothes fast enough or how to use cleaning chemicals and machines, or he or she doesn't, and we find out very quickly by just trying them out on the job."

But, on the other hand, applicant screening for the stores can also be frustratingly *hard* because of the nature of things that Jennifer would like to screen for. Two of the most critical problems facing her company concern employee turnover and employee honesty. As mentioned previously, Jennifer and her father sorely need to implement practices that will reduce the rate of employee turnover. If there is a way to do this through employee testing and screening techniques Jennifer would like to know about it because of the management time and money that is now being wasted by the never-ending need to recruit and hire new employees.

Of even greater concern to Jennifer and her father is the need to institute new practices to screen out those employees who may be predisposed to steal from the company.

Employee theft is an enormous problem for the Carter Cleaning Centers, and one that is not just limited to employees who handle the cash. For example, the cleaner spotter and/or the presser often open the store themselves, without a manager (to get the day's work started), and it is not unusual to have one or more of these people steal supplies or "run a route." Running a route means that an employee canvases his neighborhood to pick up people's clothes for cleaning and then secretly cleans and presses them in the Carter store, using the company's supplies, gas, and power. It would also not be unusual for an unsupervised person (or his or her supervisor, for that matter) to accept a one-hour rush order for cleaning or laundering, quickly clean and press the item, and return it to the customer for payment without making out a proper ticket for the item or posting the sale. The money, of course, goes into the person's pocket instead of into the cash register.

The more serious problem concerns the store manager and the counter people who actually have to handle the cash. According to Jack Carter, "you would not believe the creativity employees use to get around the management controls we set up to cut down on employee theft." As one extreme example of this felonious creativity, Jack tells the following story. "To cut down on the amount of money my employees were stealing, I had a small sign painted and placed in front of all our cash registers. The sign said: Your entire order *free* if we don't give you a cash register receipt when you pay.—Call 962-0734. It was my intention with this sign to force all our cash-handling employees to place their receipts into the cash register where they would be recorded for my accountants. After all, if all the cash that comes in is recorded in the cash register, then we should have a much better handle on stealing in our stores, right? Well, one of our managers found a diabolical way around this. I came into the store one night and noticed that the cash register that this particular manager was using just didn't look right although the sign was dutifully placed in front of it. It turned out that every afternoon at about 5:00 P.M. when the other employees left, this character would pull his own cash register out of a box that he hid underneath all our supplies. Customers coming in would notice the sign and of course the fact that he was meticulous in ringing up every sale. But unbeknownst to them and to us, for about five months the sales that came in for about an hour every day went into his cash register, not mine. It took us that long to figure out where our cash for that store was going."

Given this and similar war stories, Jennifer now has the following questions:

1. What would be the advantages and disadvantages to her company of routinely administering honesty tests to all its employees?

2. Specifically, what other screening techniques could the company use to screen out theft-prone employees, and how exactly could these be used?

3. How should her company terminate employees caught stealing and what kind of procedure should be set up for handling reference calls about these employees when they go to other companies looking for jobs?

Management games. Participants engage in realistic problem solving, usually as members of two or more simulated companies that are competing in the marketplace. Decisions might have to be made about matters like how to advertise and manufacture and how much inventory to keep in stock. Participants thereby exhibit planning and organizational abilities, interpersonal skills, and leadership abilities.

Individual presentations. A participant's communication skills and persuasiveness are evaluated by having the person make an oral presentation of an assigned topic.

Objective tests. All types of paper-and-pencil tests of personality, mental ability, interests, and achievements might also be a part of an assessment center.

The interview. Most centers also require an interview between at least one of the expert assessors and each participant, in which the latter's current interests, background, past performance, and motivation are assessed.

An Example

An assessment center was organized to assess first-line manager's potential for middle management positions.[52] Twelve participants were nominated by their supervisors as having potential, based on their current job performance. For two days, participants took part in exercises aimed at exposing behaviors believed important in this company. For example, participants played a simulated business game, completed an in-basket exercise, and participated in group discussions. In addition, they took several individual tests and exercises and were interviewed.

Six experts observed and assessed each participant's behavior and took notes on special forms. After the two days of exercises, the participants went back to their jobs and the assessors spent two days comparing their observations and making a final evaluation of each participant. A summary report was then developed on each participant; this report outlined his or her potential and defined a development program for each participant that was appropriate for both the company and the participant.

The agenda for a typical two-day assessment center is presented in Figure 5.8. The figure summarizes the nature of each of the exercises in which the candidates participated.

Effectiveness

Assessment centers are used increasingly as a selection tool, with some experts estimating that, since the early 1960s, over 200,000 people worldwide in more than 1,000 organizations have participated in them.[53] Assessment centers were reportedly first used at the American Telephone & Telegraph Company in the 1950s and are still in use there.

Most studies, including those in the Bell System, suggest that assessment centers are useful for predicting success in management positions.[54]

DAY 1

Orientation Meeting

Management Game: "Conglomerate." Forming different types of conglomerates is the goal with four-man teams of participants bartering companies to achieve their planned result. Teams set their own acquisition objectives and must plan and organize to meet them.

Background Interview: A 1½ hour interview conducted by an assessor.

Group Discussion: "Management Problems." Four short cases calling for various forms of management judgment are presented to groups of four participants. In one hour the group, acting as consultants, must resolve the cases and submit its recommendation in writing.

Individual Fact-Finding and Decision-Making Exercise: "The Research Budget." The participant is told that he has just taken over as division manager. He is given a brief description of an incident in which his predecessor has recently turned down a request for funds to continue a research project. The research director is appealing for a reversal of the decision. The participant is given 15 minutes to ask questions to dig out the facts in the case. Following this fact-finding period, he must present his decision orally with supporting reasoning and defend it under challenge.

DAY 2

In-Basket Exercise: "Section Manager's In-Basket." The contents of a section manager's in-basket are simulated. The participant is instructed to go through the contents, solving problems, answering questions, delegating, organizing, scheduling and planning, just as he might do if he were promoted suddenly to the position. An assessor reviews the contents of the completed in-basket and conducts a one-hour interview with the participant to gain further information.

Assigned Role Leaderless Group Discussion: "Compensation Committee." The Compensation Committee is meeting to allocate $8,000 in discretionary salary increases among six supervisory and managerial employees. Each member of the committee (participants) represents a department of the company and is instructed to "do the best he can" for the employee from his department.

Analysis, Presentation, and Group Discussion: "The Pretzel Factory." This financial analysis problem has the participant role-play a consultant called in to advise Carl Flowers of the C. F. Pretzel Company on two problems: what to do about a division of the company that has continually lost money, and whether the corporation should expand. Participants are given data on the company and are asked to recommend appropriate courses of action. They make their recommendation in a seven-minute presentation after which they are formed into a group to come up with a single set of recommendations.

Final Announcements

DAYS 3 and 4

Assessors meet to share their observations on each participant and to arrive at summary evaluations relative to each dimension sought and overall potential.

A recent study of school administrators indicated a significant relationship between the overall assessment center placement recommendation received by the school administrators and supervisory, teacher, and support staff ratings of these administrators on most performance dimensions.[55] Studies also indicate that assessment centers, insofar as they sample actual, realistic job behavior, are valid, unbiased selection tools.[56]

A study by Hinrichs illustrates the results in this area.[57] In this study, 47 assessment center participants were followed up eight years later to judge how accurately their assessment center evaluations predicted their future advancement; the overall assessment center rating *was* significantly related to position obtained after eight years for 30 individuals still with the company.

Yet the same study raises an important question regarding one of the assessment center's main disadvantages, its high cost.[58] The question, in other words, is whether a center can do its job less expensively than other selection techniques, and here the evidence is not clear. At least one study suggests that the assessment center approach is financially efficient.[59] In his study, however, Hinrichs concluded that a straightforward review of the participants' personnel files did as good a job of predicting which center participants would succeed in management as did their assessment center evaluations.

An Alternative

One alternative[60] has been aptly described as "assessment without a center"; it involves assessing job candidates on a series of carefully selected on-the-job activities. As the two writers point out:

> Why pull employees off the job for a week to put them through artificial experiences removed from what they normally do? We feel that the data already exist in most organizations that, if properly collected and interpreted, will allow for the process of internal selection and promotion, identification of potential managers, and employee development.

Basically, their approach consists of three steps. First, a *job analysis* is performed to determine the critical tasks and abilities required for each management position. Next, *assessor training* is carried out for the purpose of training selected managers to observe and assess managerial skills like decision making, communication, and technical competence. Next, the program is *implemented* with the specially trained assessors assessing managerial candidates *on the job,* in terms of the latter's motivation, technical competence, interpersonal skills, administrative abilities, decision-making abilities, and training and development skills.

♦ THE MINIATURE JOB TRAINING AND EVALUATION APPROACH

This approach is based on the assumption that a person who can demonstrate the ability to learn and perform a sample of a job will be able to learn and perform the job itself, given appropriate training. In this approach, therefore, the job seeker is trained to perform a sample of tasks involved on the job. Immediately following the training his or her ability to perform these tasks is measured. The approach can be at least a partial answer to the test relevance and test fairness issues, since it aims at selecting job applicants based on their *actual* performance on realistic samples of the jobs for which they will have to be trained rather than based on intermediate processes like paper-and-pencil tests.

The technique has been used successfully. One study involved a group of navy recruits who had been deemed unacceptable for various naval schools based on their performance on traditional test batteries. The recruits participated in several miniature job training and evaluation situations. In one (the "computation and projection miniature training and evaluation situation"), recruits were taught how to read a simplified plot diagram of the positions of two ships, their headings, and speed and how to extrapolate the new position of each ship and evaluate the danger of collision. Seamen who normally would have been barred from this type of training were actually found to be competent to pursue computation and projection schooling, based on the miniature training and evaluation approach.

Using the approach requires balancing its advantages and disadvantages. Advantages include the fact that it is "content relevant," which means that the recruit is tested with an *actual* sample of the job rather than just with a paper-and-pencil test which aims to predict performance on that job. This direct approach may also make it more acceptable (and fair) to disadvantaged persons than the usual paper-and-pencil test. On the other hand, with its emphasis on individual instruction during training, this approach is also relatively expensive as a screening device. This higher cost must be weighed against its advantages.[61]

OTHER SELECTION TECHNIQUES

♦ BACKGROUND INVESTIGATIONS AND REFERENCE CHECKS

Use

Almost all employers try to check and verify the background information and references of job applicants.[62] Estimates of the number of firms checking references range from 93% and up, with about 80% using telephone inquiries and the remainder using other background sources like commercial credit-checking companies and required reference letters.

The actual background investigation/reference check can take many forms. At a minimum, almost all employers try to verify an applicant's current position and salary with his or her current employer by telephone. Others call the applicant's current and previous supervisors to try to discover more about the person's motivation, technical competence, and ability to work with others. Some employers get background reports from commercial credit-rating companies; the latter can provide information on an applicant's credit standing, indebtedness, reputation, character, and life-style. Some employers ask for written references on their applicants. However, given the practical and legal ramifications of putting anything derogatory about an applicant in writing, the usefulness of such information is highly questionable.

Effectiveness

Handled correctly, the background check can be a useful source of information. It is an inexpensive and straightforward way of verifying factual information about the applicant, information regarding current and previous job title, current salary range, dates of employment, and educational background.

It is when more subjective information is requested (particularly in writing) that the validity of the reference check comes into question, and there are several reasons for this. The first reason is legal; laws like the Fair Credit Reporting Act of 1970 and Equal Employment Opportunity laws increase the likelihood that a rejected applicant will successfully demand access to the background information that was compiled and then bring suit against both the source of that information and the recruiting employer. (In one case, for instance, a man was awarded $56,000 after being turned down for a job because, among other things, he was called a "character" by a former employer.) From a practical point of view, it is not easy for a reference to prove that the bad appraisal he gave an applicant was warranted; the rejected applicant thus has various legal remedies, including suing the reference for defamation of character.[63]

But it is not just the fear of legal reprisal that can undermine the reference. Many supervisors simply don't feel good about diminishing a former employee's chances for a job, while others might prefer to give even an incompetent employee favorable reviews if it will help to get rid of him. Even when checking references via the phone, therefore, you have to be careful to ask the right questions and to try to judge if the reference is being evasive in his or her answers and, if so, why.

Judging from one recent study, human resource managers do not view reference letters as very useful. In this study, 12% replied that reference letters were "highly valuable," 43% call them "somewhat valuable," and 30% viewed them as having "little value," while 6% felt they had "no value." Asked whether they preferred written or telephone references, 72% favored the telephone reference, usually because it allows a more candid assessment and provides a greater interpersonal exchange. Not having a written record is also an appealing feature. In fact, reference letters ranked lowest—seventh out of seven—when rated by these human resource officers as selection tools. Ranked from top to bottom, these tools were, by the way, interview (the top-ranked selection tool), application blank, academic record, oral referral, aptitude and achievement tests, psychological tests, and finally, reference letters.[64]

Suggestions

There are several things you can do to make your reference checking more productive.[65] One is to use a structured form as in Figure 5.9. The form helps ensure that you do not overlook important questions, and the evidence shows that such forms can make the reference check more valid. Another suggestion is to use the references suggested by the applicant as merely a source for other references who may know of the applicant's performance. Thus, you might ask each of the applicant's references, "Could you please give me the name of another person who might be familiar with the applicant's performance?" In that way, you begin getting information from references who are assumedly more objective since they weren't referred directly by the applicant.

One suggestion along these lines is to conduct a reference audit rather than just a reference check.[66] The difference between a reference check and a reference audit is largely a matter of degree, but the comprehensiveness of the latter will probably produce more useful background information than the more usual perfunctory reference check.

A thorough reference audit requires contacting at least two superiors, two peers, and two subordinates from each position previously held by the candidate. In doing so, you should find that a reliable picture of the candidate is gradually formed and you will find that the red flags raised by one or two colleagues are in fact problems that can be traced back through several previous jobs and employers. Of course, some employers do have policies which preclude employees (outside the human resources department) from providing reference information, and you are always at risk when you ask candidates to self-select the references to whom you are to speak. However asking legitimate candidates to provide this kind of complete reference list for each job can and probably will lead to a more accurate picture of your candidate than will the usual poking around that reference checks often involve.

Such audits are not a waste of time. Consider the importance of management- and executive-level talent to your enterprise, and also consider the fact that in most human endeavors the person's past performance may well turn out to be the best predictor of his or her future performance at work. Particularly for key positions, in other words, the extra few hours digging is well worth the time.

Giving Employment References: Know the Law

You also must be acquainted with what you can and cannot say under the law when *supplying* employment references on former employees. The recent federal laws that affect references are the Privacy Act of 1974, the Fair Credit Reporting Act of 1970, the Family Education Rights and Privacy Act of 1974 (and Buckley Amendment of 1974), and the Freedom of Information Act of 1966. Among other things these laws give individuals and students

FIGURE 5.9
Telephone or Personal Interview Form
Source: Adapted by permission of the publisher from *Book of Employment Forms*, American Management Association. Copyright 1967 by the American Management Association.

TELEPHONE OR PERSONAL INTERVIEW

☐ FORMER EMPLOYER
☐ CHARACTER REFERENCE

COMPANY _____ ADDRESS _____ PHONE _____

NAME OF PERSON CONTACTED _____ POSITION OR TITLE _____

1. I WISH TO VERIFY SOME FACTS GIVEN BY (MISS, MRS.)
   MR.
   WHO IS APPLYING FOR EMPLOYMENT WITH OUR FIRM. WHAT WERE THE DATES OF HIS/HER EMPLOYMENT BY YOUR COMPANY?   FROM _____ 19 ___ TO _____ 19 ___

2. WHAT WAS THE NATURE OF HIS/HER JOB?   AT START _____

   AT LEAVING _____

3. HE/SHE STATES THAT HE/SHE WAS EARNING $ ____ PER ____ WHEN HE/SHE LEFT. IS THAT CORRECT?   YES   NO $ _____

4. WHAT DID HIS/HER SUPERIORS THINK OF HIM/HER? _____

   WHAT DID HIS/HER SUBORDINATES THINK OF HIM/HER? _____

5. DID HE/SHE HAVE SUPERVISORY RESPONSIBILITY?   YES   NO _____

   (IF YES) HOW DID HE/SHE CARRY IT OUT? _____

6. HOW HARD DID HE/SHE WORK? _____

7. HOW DID HE/SHE GET ALONG WITH OTHERS? _____

8. HOW WAS HIS/HER ATTENDANCE RECORD?   PUNCTUALITY? _____

9. WHAT WERE HIS/HER REASONS FOR LEAVING? _____

10. WOULD YOU REHIRE HIM/HER? (IF NO) WHY?   YES   NO _____

11. DID HE/SHE HAVE ANY DOMESTIC, FINANCIAL OR PERSONAL TROUBLE WHICH INTERFERED WITH HIS/HER WORK?   YES   NO _____

12. DID HE/SHE DRINK OR GAMBLE TO EXCESS?   YES   NO _____

13. WHAT ARE HIS/HER STRONG POINTS? _____

14. WHAT ARE HIS/HER WEAK POINTS? _____

REMARKS: _____

the right to know the nature and substance of information in their credit files and on file with government agencies and (under the Privacy Act) to review records pertaining to them on file with any private business that contracts with a federal agency. Therefore, when you receive a letter or telephone call asking for information on a former employee, student, or acquaintance, it is quite possible that your comments may eventually be shown to the man or woman you are describing. Also understand that "common law," and in particular the tort of defamation, applies to the information you supply. The communication is defamatory if it is false and tends to harm the reputation of another by lowering him or her in the estimation of the community or by deterring other persons from associating or dealing with him. You therefore stand a considerable risk of being sued for your comments.

Some suggested guidelines for defensible references are summarized in Figure 5.10. As you can see, guidelines include "don't volunteer information," "avoid vague statements," and "do not answer trap questions such as 'would you rehire this person?'" In practice many firms have a policy of not providing any information on former employees except for their dates of employment and position titles.[67]

In fact, being sued for defamation is increasingly a matter of concern for employers. In one California case, for instance, a jury awarded $60.3 million, including $53 million in punitive damages, to an independent sales representative whose contract had been terminated. In the case *Haun* v. *NEC Electronics,* an electronics industry newsletter published an article asserting that Haun had misused funds. NEC reprinted the article and sent it to its regional sales officers. Haun then sued NEC for breach of contract, fraudulent misrepresentation, and defamation even though NEC did not write the disparaging newsletter article. In another case, four employees were terminated for "gross insubordination" after disobeying a supervisor's order to review their expense account reports. In this Minnesota case (*Lewis* v. *Equitable Life Assurance*) the jury found that the employees' expense reports were actually honest. The employees argued for punitive damages under the Tort of Defamation. They argued that even though the employer did not publicize the defamatory matter to others, it should have known that the employees themselves, in having to defend themselves to future employers, would have to release the (slanderous) reason for their firing. The court agreed and upheld jury awards totaling more than a million dollars to these employees. In other words, the employer may get sued if the employee is terminated for potentially defamatory reasons, even if the employer doesn't publicize the reason for the termination.[68]

FIGURE 5.10
Guidelines for Defensible References
Source: Mary F. Cook, *Human Resources Director's Handbook* (Englewood Cliffs, N.J.: Prentice-Hall, 1984), p. 93.

1. Don't volunteer information. Respond only to specific company or institutional inquiries and requests. Before responding, telephone the inquirer to check on the validity of the request.

2. Direct all communication only to persons who have a specific interest in that information.

3. State in the message that the information you are providing is confidential and should be treated as such. Use qualifying statements such as "providing information that was requested"; "relating this information only because it was requested"; or "providing information that is to be used for professional purposes only." Sentences such as these imply that information was not presented for the purpose of hurting or damaging a person's reputation.

4. Obtain written consent from the employee or student, if possible.

5. Provide only reference data that relates and pertains to the job and job performance in question.

6. Avoid vague statements such as: "He was an average student"; "She was careless at times"; "He displayed an inability to work with others."

7. Document all released information. Use specific statements such as: "Mr. _____ received a grade of C — an average grade"; "Ms. _____ made an average of two bookkeeping errors each week"; or "This spring, four members of the work team wrote letters asking not to be placed on the shift with Mr. _____ ."

8. Clearly label all subjective statements based on personal opinions and feelings. Say "I believe . . ." whenever making a statement that is not fact.

9. When providing a negative or potentially negative statement, add the reason or reasons why, or specify the incidents that led you to this opinion.

10. Do not answer trap questions such as "Would you rehire this person?"

11. Avoid answering questions that are asked "off the record."

♦ THE POLYGRAPH AND HONESTY TESTING

The polygraph (or "lie detector") machine is a device that measures physiological changes, like increased perspiration, on the assumption that such changes reflect changes in the emotional stress that accompany lying. The usual procedure is for an applicant (or current employee) to be attached to the machine with painless electronic probes and to then be asked a series of obvious, neutral questions by the polygraph expert. These questions might, for instance, confirm that the person's name is John Smith and that he is currently residing in New York.

Once the person's emotional reactions to giving truthful answers to neutral questions like these have been ascertained, questions like "have you ever stolen anything without paying for it," "do you use drugs," or "have you ever committed a crime" can be asked. In theory, at least, the expert can then determine with some accuracy whether or not the applicant is lying.

Complaints about offensiveness plus grave doubts about the accuracy of the polygraph culminated in the Employee Polygraph Protection Act being signed into law by President Reagan on June 27, 1988. The law, which is now in effect, prohibits (with a few exceptions) employers from conducting polygraph examinations of all job applicants and most employees. Also prohibited under this law are other mechanical or electrical devices that attempt to measure honesty or dishonesty including psychological stress evaluators and voice stress analyzers. Paper-and-pencil tests and chemical testing (as for drugs) are not prohibited under federal laws.[69] Governmental (local, state, or federal) employers can continue to use polygraph exams under the law (but are restricted under a number of state laws), as can industries with national defense or security contracts; certain businesses with nuclear power-related contracts with the Department of Energy; businesses and consultants with access to highly classified information, as well as those with counter intelligence–related contracts with the FBI or Department of Justice; and private businesses that are (1) hiring private security personnel, or (2) hiring persons with access to drugs, or (3) doing ongoing investigations involving economic loss or injury to an employer's business (such as a theft).

Congress made it clear that even in the case of ongoing investigations, the employer's ability to use polygraphs will be limited and the testing procedures predetermined. Without going into all the details, the employer (to administer a polygraph during an ongoing investigation) must have a reasonable suspicion that the employee to be tested was involved in the incident under investigation. Furthermore, the employer must write and deliver to the employee tested a letter that, among other things, describes the specific incident and states that the employee has the right to consult with legal council. Furthermore, you have to provide your employees to be tested with all questions to be asked during the test in advance. And, you must provide a notice before testing begins that includes the fact that, among other things, the employee cannot be required to take the test. A form (Figure 5.11) must also be posted detailing polygraph protection, prohibitions, exemptions, and rights.

The virtual elimination of the polygraph as a screening device has triggered a burgeoning market for other types of honesty testing devices, and there are now a range of these from which to choose. Paper-and-pencil honesty tests are psychological tests designed to predict job applicants' proneness to dishonesty and other forms of counterproductivity.[70] Most of these tests measure attitudes regarding things like tolerance of others who steal, acceptance of rationalizations for theft, and admission of theft-related activities. Tests here include the Phase II profile, the marketing rights to which were recently purchased by Wackenhut Corporation of Coral Gables, Florida (which provides security services to employers), and similar tests published by London House, Incorporated, and Stanton Corporation.[71]

FIGURE 5.11
Employee Polygraph Notice

NOTICE

EMPLOYEE POLYGRAPH PROTECTION ACT

The Employee Polygraph Protection Act prohibits most private employers from using lie detector tests either for pre-employment screening or during the course of employment.

PROHIBITIONS

Employers are generally prohibited from requiring or requesting any employee or job applicant to take a lie detector test, and from discharging, disciplining, or discriminating against an employee or prospective employee for refusing to take a test or for exercising other rights under the Act.

EXEMPTIONS*

Federal, State and local governments are not affected by the law. Also, the law does not apply to tests given by the Federal Government to certain private individuals engaged in national security-related activities.

The Act permits *polygraph* (a kind of lie detector) tests to be administered in the private sector, subject to restrictions, to certain prospective employees of security service firms (armored car, alarm, and guard), and of pharmaceutical manufacturers, distributors and dispensers.

The Act also permits polygraph testing, subject to restrictions, of certain employees of private firms who are reasonably suspected of involvement in a workplace incident (theft, embezzlement, etc.) that resulted in economic loss to the employer.

EXAMINEE RIGHTS

Where polygraph tests are permitted, they are subject to numerous strict standards concerning the conduct and length of the test. Examinees have a number of specific rights, including the right to a written notice before testing, the right to refuse or discontinue a test, and the right not to have test results disclosed to unauthorized persons.

ENFORCEMENT

The Secretary of Labor may bring court actions to restrain violations and assess civil penalties up to $10,000 against violators. Employees or job applicants may also bring their own court actions.

ADDITIONAL INFORMATION

Additional information may be obtained, and complaints of violations may be filed, at local offices of the Wage and Hour Division, which are listed in the telephone directory under U.S. Government, Department of Labor, Employment Standards Administration.

THE LAW REQUIRES EMPLOYERS TO DISPLAY THIS POSTER WHERE EMPLOYEES AND JOB APPLICANTS CAN READILY SEE IT.

The law does not preempt any provision of any State or local law or any collective bargaining agreement which is more restrictive with respect to lie detector tests.

U.S. DEPARTMENT OF LABOR
EMPLOYMENT STANDARDS ADMINISTRATION
Wage and Hour Division
Washington, D.C. 20210

Notice must be posted

Several psychologists (including some speaking for the American Psychological Association) have expressed concerns about the proliferation of paper-and-pencil honesty tests.[72] Many of the supportive articles regarding these paper-and-pencil honesty tests have been written by the test publishers themselves, they say. And, they argue that additional independent peer review should be conducted before the validity of these devices is accepted.[73]

Given all this, what can an employer do to detect dishonesty? Several things. One expert suggests taking the following steps:

Ask blunt questions.[74] Within the bounds of legality, you can ask very direct questions in the face-to-face interview. For example, says this expert, there is nothing wrong with asking the applicant: "Have you ever stolen anything from an employer?" Other questions to ask include: "Have you recently held jobs other than those listed on your application?" "Have you ever been fired or asked to leave a job?" "What reasons would past supervisors give if they were asked why they let you go?" "Have past employers ever disciplined you or warned you about absences or lateness?" "Is any information on your application misrepresented or falsified?"

Listen, rather than talk. Specifically, allow the applicant to do the talking so you can learn as much as possible about the person.

Ask for a credit check. Include a clause in your application blank which gives you the right to conduct certain background checks on the applicant including credit checks and motor vehicle reports.

Check all references. Of course, rigorously pursue employment and personal references.

Consider a paper-and-pencil test. Consider utilizing paper-and-pencil honesty tests and psychological tests as a supplement to your honesty screening program.

Test for drugs. Devise a drug testing program and give each applicant a copy of the policy.

Conduct searches. Establish a search-and-seizure policy, giving each applicant a copy of the policy and requiring each to return a signed copy. Basically, the policy should state that all lockers, desks, and similar property remain the property of the company and may be inspected routinely.

An Example of an Honesty Screening Program

When the Adolf Coors company scrapped its polygraph testing requirement for job applicants, it substituted a three-step program that all new job applicants have to undergo. The steps include urinalysis, a paper-and-pencil honesty test, and a reference check. The company uses an outside lab to conduct the urinalysis test. Next, applicants take a Stanton Corporation paper-and-pencil survey of 83 questions on attitudes toward honesty and theft. The survey company provides Coors with a written report. This report categorizes applicants by levels of risk: For example, low-risk individuals are those who have never been involved in any extensive thefts, while marginal-risk applicants might be tempted to steal if they felt they wouldn't be caught. Finally, applicant references and background checks are performed by a company called Equifax Services. They involve contacting previous employers and educational institutions attended.[75]

A Caution

There are several reasons why great caution should be used in any honesty testing program. First, as noted earlier, considerable doubt has been expressed by many experts regarding just how valid many (or most) paper-and-pencil honesty testing instruments are. Their argument, basically, is that until more widespread peer evaluations are done, these tests should be used very cautiously, and certainly only as supplements to other techniques like reference checking. Second, on purely humanitarian grounds, one could argue that a rejection (let alone an incorrect rejection) for dishonesty carries with it some more stigma than does being rejected for, say, poor mechanical comprehension or even poor sociability. It's true that others may never know just why you rejected the candidate. However, he or she, having just taken and "failed" what may have been a fairly obvious "honesty test," may leave the premises feeling that his treatment was less than proper. Third, questions and tests in this area pose some serious invasion-of-privacy issues, delving as they do into some areas (such as how you feel about stealing, or whether you have ever stolen anything) that while perhaps legitimately asked are also very private matters. (This was, after all, one reason polygraphs were attacked in the first place.) And relatedly, there are more legal constraints that you must watch for: for instance, Massachusetts and Rhode Island both limit the use of paper-and-pencil honesty tests. In summary, use caution with these programs.

♦ GRAPHOLOGY

The use of graphology (handwriting analysis) is based on the assumption that the writer's basic personality traits will express themselves in his or her handwriting.[76] Handwriting analysis thus has some resemblance to projective personality tests.

In graphology, a complex technology and set of rules have evolved, through which the handwriting analyst studies an applicant's handwriting and signature in order to discover the person's needs, desires, and psychological makeup.[77] Figure 5.12, for instance, presents former President Richard Nixon's signature at several points in his career. According to one graphologist, the changes reflect an evolution from a confident, ambitious person to one less outgoing.

While many scientists doubt the validity of handwriting analysis, some writers estimate that over 1,000 U.S. companies use handwriting analysis to access applicants for certain strategic positions.[78] And the classified ads of some international newspapers like the *Economist* periodically run advertisements from graphologists offering to aid in an employer's selection process.

♦ PHYSICAL EXAMINATION

A medical examination is usually the next step in the selection process, although in some cases the examination takes place after the new employee starts work.[79]

FIGURE 5.12
Handwriting Exhibit Used by Graphologist
Source: Reproduced with permission from the *Telegraph Sunday Magazine* (London), January 23, 1977.

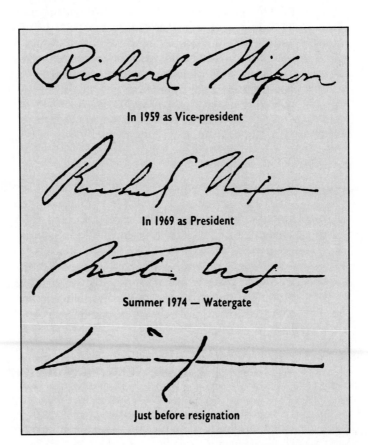

In 1959 as Vice-president

In 1969 as President

Summer 1974 — Watergate

Just before resignation

There are five main reasons for requiring preemployment medical exams. The exam can be used to determine that the applicant qualifies for the *physical requirements* of the position and to discover any *medical limitations* that should be taken into account in placing the applicant. The exam will also establish a *record and baseline* of the applicant's health for the purpose of future insurance or compensation claims. The examination can, by identifying health problems, also reduce *absenteeism and accidents* and, of course, detect *communicable diseases* that may be unknown to the applicant. The exam is usually performed by the employer's medical department (in the largest organizations), while smaller employers retain the services of consulting physicians to perform such exams, which are almost always paid for by the employer.

♦ DRUG SCREENING

Drug abuse is a serious problem at work. Counselors at the Cocaine National Help Line polled callers of the 800-Cocaine hot line and found that 75% admitted to occasional cocaine use at work, 69% said that they regularly worked under the influence of a drug, and 25% recorded daily use at work. The U.S. Chamber of Commerce estimates that employee drug and alcohol use costs American employers over $60 billion each year in reduced productivity, accidents, increased sick benefits, and higher worker's compensation claims.[80]

Because of the seriousness of this problem, more employers are including drug screening as part of their prehiring program. The most common practice is to test current employees when there is reason to believe the person has been using drugs and to also test new applicants just before they are formally hired. One recent American Management Association poll suggests that the upward trend in drug testing is dramatic: Testing rose from 21% of surveyed firms in 1986 to 37% in 1987 to 48% in December 1988. Virtually all (96%) of employers that conduct such tests use urine sampling.[81] The preferred initial drug-testing method is the immunoassay test. This test cannot differentiate between legal and illegal substances in the same chemical family so that, for instance popular over-the-counter pain killers like Advil and Nuprin can produce positive results for marijuana. Many companies upon receiving a positive initial test will then therefore conduct the more expensive thin-layer chromotography method test to validate the positve immunoassay test.

What should you do when a job candidate tests positive? Most companies will not hire such candidates (although most will not immediately fire current employees whose tests results are positive).[82] For example, 120 of the 123 companies responding to the question, "If test results are positive, what action do you take?" indicated that applicants checking positive are not hired. (The problem with firing current employees is more complicated since they have more legal recourse if dismissed. Current employees therefore must be told the reason for their dismissal if they are dismissed for a positive drug test.)

The evidence suggests that such preemployment drug screening is effective. One study concluded that for all drugs examined, the greater the frequency of drug use and the earlier the age at which the drug was first used, the greater the probability of a person being classified as unsuitable after hire.[83]

♦ VALIDITY OF VARIOUS SELECTION DEVICES

Table 5.1 summarizes the results of one study of the validity of various selection devices. Tests of actual performance—work samples, peer evaluations, and assessment centers—rate highest. Indirect evaluations, such as

TABLE 5.1   Validity of Certain Selection Devices

PREDICTOR	VALIDITY
Cognitive Ability and Special Aptitude	Moderate
Personality	Low
Interest	Low
Physical Ability	Moderate-High
Biographical Info.	Moderate
Interviews	Low
Work Samples	High
Seniority	Low
Peer Evaluations	High
Reference Checks	Low
Academic Performance	Low
Self Assessments	Moderate
Assessment Centers	High

Source: Neal Schmitt and Raymond Noe, "Personal Selection and Equal Employment Opportunity," in *International Review of Industrial and Organizational Psychology*, ed. Cary L. Cooper and Ivan T. Robertson. Copyright 1986 by John Wiley & Sons, Ltd. Reprinted by permission.

psychological tests or academic performance, rate lower. This suggests, again, that (1) predictors like these are best used in conjunction with other selection devices, like interviews and that (2) they must be employed properly to be of use. The following chapter explains how to use interviews effectively.

♦ COMPLYING WITH THE IMMIGRATION LAW

Under the Immigration Reform and Control Act of 1986, employees hired in the United States have to prove they are eligible to be employed in the United States. A person does not have to be a U.S. citizen to be employed under this act, but employers should ask a person who is about to be hired whether he or she is a U.S. citizen or if he or she is an alien lawfully authorized to work in the United States. To comply with this law, the employers should follow the following procedures:[84]

1. Hire only citizens and aliens lawfully authorized to work in the United States.

2. Continue to advise all new job applicants of your policy to such effect.

3. Require all new employees to complete and sign the verification form designated by the Immigration and Naturalization Service (INS) to certify that they are eligible for employment. This form is presented in Figure 5.13.

4. Examine documentation presented by new employees, record information about the documents on the verification form, and sign the form.

5. Retain the form for three years or for one year past the employment of the individual, whichever is longer.

6. If requested, present the form for inspection by INS or Department of Labor Officers. No reporting is required.

You will notice from the employment eligibility verification form in Figure 5.13 that there are two basic ways prospective employees can show their eligibility for employment. One is to show (from list A) a document such as a U.S. passport or alien registration card with photograph that proves both the person's identity and employment eligibility. However many prospective employees won't have one of these documents. Therefore the other way to verify employment eligibility is to provide one of the documents in list B

FIGURE 5.13
I–9 Employment Eligibility Verification

EMPLOYMENT ELIGIBILITY VERIFICATION

1 **EMPLOYEE INFORMATION AND VERIFICATION:** (To be completed and signed by employee.)

Name: (Print or Type) Last	First	Middle	Maiden
Address: Street Name and Number	City	State	ZIP Code
Date of Birth (Month/Day/Year)		Social Security Number	

I attest, under penalty of perjury, that I am (check a box):

☐ A citizen or national of the United States.

☐ An alien lawfully admitted for permanent residence (Alien Number A _____).

☐ An alien authorized by the Immigration and Naturalization Service to work in the United States (Alien Number A _____, or Admission Number _____, expiration of employment authorization, if any _____).

I attest, under penalty of perjury, the documents that I have presented as evidence of identity and employment eligibility are genuine and relate to me. I am aware that federal law provides for imprisonment and/or fine for any false statements or use of false documents in connection with this certificate.

Signature	Date (Month/Day/Year)

PREPARER/TRANSLATOR CERTIFICATION (If prepared by other than the individual.) I attest, under penalty of perjury, that the above was prepared by me at the request of the named individual and is based on all information of which I have any knowledge.

Signature	Name (Print or Type)		
Address (Street Name and Number)	City	State	Zip Code

2 **EMPLOYER REVIEW AND VERIFICATION:** (To be completed and signed by employer.)

Examine one document from those in List A and check the correct box, _or_ examine one document from List B _and_ one from List C and check the correct boxes. Provide the **Document Identification Number** and **Expiration Date**, for the document checked in that column.

List A Identity and Employment Eligibility	List B Identity	and	List C Employment Eligibility
☐ United States Passport	☐ A State issued driver's license or I.D. card with a photograph, or information, including name, sex, date of birth, height, weight, and color of eyes. (Specify State)_____		☐ Original Social Security Number Card (other than a card stating it is not valid for employment)
☐ Certificate of United States Citizenship	☐ U.S. Military Card		☐ A birth certificate issued by State, county, or municipal authority bearing a seal or other certification
☐ Certificate of Naturalization	☐ Other (Specify document and issuing authority)		
☐ Unexpired foreign passport with attached Employment Authorization	_____		☐ Unexpired INS Employment Authorization Specify form #
☐ Alien Registration Card with photograph			
Document Identification # _____	**Document Identification** # _____		**Document Identification** # _____
Expiration Date (if any) _____	**Expiration Date (if any)** _____		**Expiration Date (if any)** _____

CERTIFICATION: I attest, under penalty of perjury, that I have examined the documents presented by the above individual, that they appear to be genuine, relate to the individual named, and that the individual, to the best of my knowledge, is authorized to work in the United States.

Signature	Name (Print or Type)	Title
Employer Name	Address	Date

Form I-9 (03/20/87)
OMB No. 1115-0136

U.S. Department of Justice
Immigration and Naturalization Service

(which proves the person's identity), along with one of the documents in list C (showing the person's employment eligibility).

Note that employers cannot and should not use this new verification requirement or the so-called I–9 Employment Eligibility Verification form (Figure 5.13) to discriminate in any way based on the person's race or country of national origin. For example, the requirement that you verify employment does not give you any basis to reject an applicant just because he or she is a foreigner, or not a U.S. citizen, or an alien residing in the United

States, as long as that person can prove his or her identity and employment eligibility.

SMALL-BUSINESS APPLICATIONS: TESTING

Just because a company is small doesn't mean it shouldn't engage in personnel testing. Quite the opposite: Hiring one or two mistakes may not be a big problem for a very large firm, but could cause chaos in a very small operation. On the other hand the larger company by its nature will find it easier to finance and use tests because they have the money and personnel to finance testing programs and properly validate the tests they use.

There are a number of tests which (while used by big employers too) are so easy to administer they are particularly good for smaller firms. One that has been used for years is the Wonderlic Personnel Test. This deceptively easy-to-use test measures general mental ability. The test, in the form of a four-page booklet, takes under 15 minutes to administer. You first read the instructions on the front page and then time the candidate as he or she works the 50 problems on the two inside sheets. The person's test can then be easily scored with a scoring key: His or her score is comprised of the number of questions he or she answered right. You then compare the person's score to the minimum scores recommended for various occupations (see Figure 5.14), determining if the person achieved the minimally acceptable score for the type of job applied for.

A test like this can be useful for helping to identify people who are simply not up to the task of doing the job, but you have to be careful not to misuse it. In the past, for instance, unnecessarily high cut off scores were required by some employers for some jobs, a tactic which in effect unfairly discriminated against the members of some minority groups. Similarly, it would probably not be either fair or wise to choose between two candidates who both exceeded the minimum score for the job applied for by choosing the one with the higher score. Remember, also, that people of lower ability but higher motivation will often outperform those with higher ability but less motivation. Therefore tests like the Wonderlic are only useful supplements to a more comprehensive screening program. The Wonderlic is available to employers, business owners, and human resource directors with or without previous training in personnel testing.[85]

Another example of a test that is used by large companies but is equally valuable for small ones because of its ease of administration and interpretation is the Predictive Index. The index measures personality traits, drives, and behaviors that are work related—in particular, dominance (ranging from submissive to arrogant), extroversion (ranging from withdrawn to gregarious), patience (ranging from volatile to lethargic), and blame avoidance (ranging from sloppy to perfectionist). The Predictive Index test itself is a two-sided sheet in which candidates or current employees check off which words most describe them (such as "helpful" or "persistent"). The test is then easily scored at your office with the use of a scoring template.

The Predictive Index provides valuable information about the candidate. For example, for a job that you know involves painstaking attention to details, you'd want to think twice about a candidate who rates toward the careless end of the range; for an exceedingly boring job, you'd no doubt lean toward the more passive, patient of the candidates. While each candidate taking the Predictive Index will probably have his or her own unique pattern of responses, the Predictive Index program includes 15 standard patterns that are typical of many of the patterns you will see. For example, there is the "social interest" pattern, representing a person who is generally unselfish, congenial, persuasive, patient, and fairly unassuming; this is a

FIGURE 5.14

Minimum Scores on Wonderlic Personnel Test For Various Occupations

Source: Wonderlic Personnel Test Manual (Northfield, Ill.: E. F. Wonderlic & Associates, Inc., 1983), p. 6.

Position	No. of Questions Answered Correctly in 12 minutes
Administrator	30
Engineer	29
Accountant	28
Programmer	28
Supervisor/Manager	27
Management, Trainee	27
Field Repr. (Sales)	26
Salesman	26
Secretary	25
Accounting Clerk	25
Writer, News, etc.	25
Stenographer	24
Cashier	24
Bookkeeper	24
Foreman	24
Draftsman	23
Receptionist	23
Office, General	23
Lineman, Utility	22
Teller	22
Typist	21
Clerical	21
Key Punch Operator	20
Police, Patrolman	20
Skilled Trades	20
File Clerk	19
Maintenance	18
Telephone Operator	18
General Laborer	17
Factory, General	17
Labor, Skilled	17
Labor, Unskilled	16
Nurses Aide	15
Custodian	8

See the Tables presented in this Manual, "Test Scores by Position Applied For" and "Minimum Occupational Scores for The Wonderlic Personnel Test," for additional data on established scores.

person who'd be good with people and a good personnel interviewer, for instance. There's the "promotional," a person who is outgoing, gregarious, unconcerned about details, socially oriented, and (probably) a very good salesperson. As another example, there is the "operational" pattern, the pattern of, for instance, a good production worker who is concerned with doing his or her work by the book and being a good team worker while concerned with a sense of security and stability.[86]

Computerized testing programs like those described earlier in this chapter can also be especially useful for small employers. For example, when hiring office help smaller employers typically depend on informal tests of typing, and filing. A much better way to proceed is to use a program like the Minnesota Clerical Assessment Battery published by Assessment Systems Corp. This program runs on a personal computer and includes a typing test, proofreading test, filing test, business vocabulary test, business math test, and clerical knowledge test. It is therefore useful for evaluating the knowledge and skills of various office positions, including secretary, clerk-typist, bookkeeper, and filing clerk. And because it is computerized, administration and scoring is simplified and each test can be adapted to the particular position being applied for.[87]

SUMMARY

1. In this chapter we discussed several techniques for screening and selecting job candidates; the first was testing.

2. Test validity answers the question, "What does this test measure?" We discussed criterion validity and content validity.

3. As used by psychologists, the term reliability always means consistency. One way to measure this is to administer the same (or equivalent) test to the same people at two different points in time. Or you could focus on "internal consistency." Here, compare the responses to roughly equivalent items on the same test.

4. There are many types of personnel tests in use, including intelligence tests, tests of physical skills, tests of achievement, aptitude tests, interest inventories, and personality tests.

5. For a selection test to be useful, scores on the test should be related in a predictable way to performance on the job; you must *validate* the test. This involves five steps: (a) analyze the job, (b) choose your tests, (c) administer the test, (d) relate test scores and criteria, and (e) cross-validate and revalidate the test.

6. Under equal rights legislation, an employer may have to be able to prove that his or her tests are predictive of success or failure on the job. This usually involves a predictive validation study, although other means of validation are often acceptable.

7. Some basic testing guidelines include (a) use tests as supplements, (b) validate the tests for appropriate jobs, (c) analyze all current hiring and promotion standards, (d) beware of certain tests, (e) use a certified psychologist, and (f) maintain good test conditions.

8. The work sampling selection technique is based on the assumption that "the best indicator of future performance is past performance." Here you use the applicant's actual performance on the same (or very similar) job to predict his or her future job performance. The steps are (a) analyze applicant's previous work experience, (b) have experts list component tasks for jobs being recruited for, (c) select crucial tasks as work sample measures, (d) break down these tasks into steps, (e) test the applicant, and (f) relate the applicant's work sample score to his or her performance on the job.

9. Management assessment centers are a third screening device and involve exposing applicants to a series of real-life exercises. Performance is observed and assessed by experts, who then check on their assessments by watching the participants when they are back at their jobs. Examples of "real-life" exercises include a simulated business game, an in-basket exercise, and group discussions.

10. Even though most people prefer not to give bad references, most companies still carry out some sort of screening reference check on their candidates. These can be useful in raising red flags, and structured questionnaires can improve the usefulness of the responses you receive.

11. Other selection tools we discussed include the polygraph, honesty tests, graphology, and the physical examination.

12. Employee selection is directly related to employee motivation. Your aim is to select those who have the ability and potential to perform the job successfully. In this chapter we discuss a variety of tools—tests, previous experience, assessment centers—that can help an employer choose

the best qualified, most highly motivated candidates, those with the potential to do the job. The next step is to hire, orient, and train the new employees, to which we now turn.

KEY TERMS

testing	reliability	work sampling technique
validity	expectancy chart	
criterion validity	work samples	management assessment center
content validity		

DISCUSSION QUESTIONS

1. Explain what is meant by reliability and validity. What is the difference between them? In what respects are they similar?
2. Explain how you would go about validating a test. How can this information be useful to a manager?
3. Write a short essay discussing some of the ethical and legal considerations in testing.
4. Explain why you think a certified psychologist who is specially trained in test construction should (or should not) always be used by a company developing a personnel test battery.
5. Explain how you would use work sampling for employee selection.

◆ APPLICATION EXERCISES

◆ CASE INCIDENT

Use of References

The X-Press Company requires all applicants for employment to give the names of three former employers as references. In practice, in the selection procedure, one of the three is queried about the facts of earlier employment described on the application form.

Recently, the staff has speculated about the soundness of this practice. Some staff members have raised questions about the implications of the "sampling" procedure. They suggest that inquiries directed to one or the other of the two remaining names might produce quite different evidence. They argue that all three should be questioned if heavy reliance is to be placed on references as a basis for acceptance or rejection.

Another staff member has suggested that the entire procedure should be discarded. He argues that, in the first place, the statements made in reply to such inquiries are not reliable, that references do not disclose the most important facts. Second, he insists that staff members can and do place a wide range of interpretations on these statements.

The human resource manager has been concerned by these criticisms. She is particularly worried because of a recent experiment. In that test, all her staff members were asked to examine references for 50 recent applicants and to rank each for acceptance or rejection. Names of applicants were deleted. Staff members disagreed on more than 30 of the 50 references.

Questions

1. Do you agree that the firm should stop asking for references? Why? Why not?

2. What are they doing wrong now with respect to requesting and checking references?

3. What might the firm do to improve its reference procedures?

Source: Dale Yoder, *Personnel Management and Industrial Relations* (Englewood Cliffs, N.J.: Prentice-Hall, 1970), p. 480.

EXPERIENTIAL EXERCISE

Purpose: The purpose of this exercise is to give you practice in developing a test to measure *one specific ability* for the job of directory assistance operator in a telephone company. If time permits you will also be able to combine your tests into a test battery and validate it.

Required Understanding: You should be fully acquainted with the procedure for developing a personnel test and should read the following description of a directory assistance operator's duties:

> Customers contact directory assistance operators to obtain the telephone numbers of persons whose numbers are not yet listed, whose listings have changed, or whose numbers are unknown to the customer. The operators look up the requested number on computerized video displays and transmit numbers to the customers. A number must be found quickly so that the customer is not kept waiting. It is often necessary to look under various spellings of the same name since customers frequently give incorrect spellings.

You may assume that one-third of the applicants seen will become directory assistance operators. You wish for a test that will aid in selecting the best third of those available.

How to Set Up the Exercise: First, divide the class into teams of five or six.

> *Procedure:* Select an important ability (for a directory assistance operator) and develop a test to measure it. Only the materials available in the room are to be used. Telephone directories may not be furnished. The test should permit quantitative scoring and may be an individual or a group test.

Instructions for the Exercise. The students should go to their preassigned groups and (as per our discussion of test development in this chapter), each group should make a list of the abilities that seem relevant to success on the operators' job. Each group should then rate the importance of these abilities on a five-point scale. Then, develop a test.

Next, each team should be given a chance to demonstrate their tests on one of the other teams.

If time permits, the various tests (from each team) should be combined to form a test battery. (The instructor will want to provide some guidelines on which tests would make up the best battery.) Next, a group of eight to ten students take the test battery. Then, supply telephone directories to these students and have one person call out the names of persons whose numbers are to be accessed via computer. If you use a time limit, success could be measured by the number of correct responses each of the eight to ten students obtains. Finally, relate these scores to the students' test results. Did the test distinguish between high and low performers? What part of the job was not measured by the test?

Appendix

A Note on Test Unfairness:
The Problem of Test Unfairness

A test might be valid when all applicants are considered, but still discriminate unfairly against *subgroups* of applicants. Thus, suppose a test is administered to 100 applicants, 60 of whom are white and 40 black. You find that for the 100 applicants the test is valid. But on closer examination, it turns out that 80% of the whites are selected, while only 20% of the blacks are selected. The fact that a lower proportion of blacks are selected could put the burden of proof on the employer to prove that the blacks are not being unfairly discriminated against by the test. The employer could be required to validate the test separately for *both* blacks and whites.

Suppose the employer makes separate validation studies and finds the test is in fact valid for both blacks and whites. Then even though the test results in a larger proportion of rejects among blacks than whites, the test is, generally speaking, still legally acceptable. While it *does* "discriminate" between black and white candidates, it probably does not do so *unfairly* since it is valid (it predicts performance) for both groups.

It occasionally happens, however, that while a person's score on the test is a valid predictor of his or her performance on the job, members of one group consistently score better (or worse) than do members of another group and are therefore more likely to be hired. For example, assume an employer decides to hire applicants who will perform on the job in a "good" manner (equivalent to supervisor performance rating of 70–80). Further assume that the selection test is validated separately for whites and nonwhites and found to be valid for both. However, nonwhites who score 60 on the test tend to get "good" on-the-job performance ratings, while whites who score 80 on the test tend to get the "good" ratings.

If the employer decided to use the higher test score (80) as the cutoff score, then mostly whites would be hired, since relatively few nonwhites (for whom 60 was a high score) probably achieved scores as high as 80. (Perhaps nonwhites cannot read as well, for instance, and thus do more poorly, overall, than whites on the test, although once on the job the nonwhite who scores 60 will perform as well as the white who scores 80.)

Such a situation could be *unfairly discriminatory* to the nonwhites. Unfair discrimination exists when persons with equal probabilities of success on the job have unequal probabilities of being hired. In our case, a nonwhite who scores 60 and a white who scores 80 both have equal opportunities for being "good" performers. But since the employer chose to use the higher test score (80) as a cutoff, whites, primarily, were hired, thus unfairly discriminating against those nonwhites (who scored 60) *who had the same probability as the whites who scored 80 of performing in a "good" manner.*

There are two implications. First, employers should, whenever feasible, validate tests separately for both minorities and nonminorities, both to en-

FIGURE 5.15
Validation for Subgroups

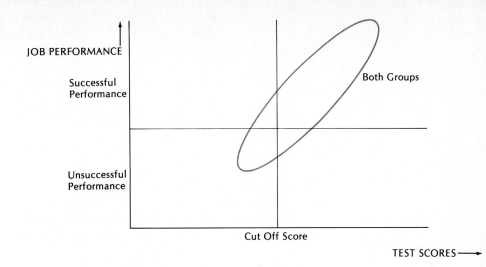

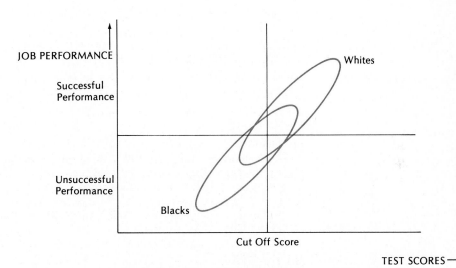

Once subgroups are analyzed it can be seen that the test is valid
for blacks and whites. Therefore, although there is adverse
impact, the test passes the standard for business necessity.

sure that the test is valid for both and to ascertain whether different cutoff
scores for each group might be appropriate.[88] Second, an employer can generally use different cut-off scores for each group (like 80 for whites and 60
for nonwhites) *as long as each cutoff score corresponds to the same level of
on-the-job performance* (in our case "good").[89]

On the other hand, your study might show that the test is valid for both
blacks and whites. Therefore, although there is adverse impact, the test
passes the standards for a business necessity (job relatedness) defense.

This is illustrated in Figure 5.15. Here, note that this test is valid for
both groups together and also for the subgroups, since (while most minority
candidates are rejected) they are "correctly" identified as probable unsuccessful performers.

Once subgroups are analyzed it can be seen that the test is valid for
blacks and whites. Therefore, although there is adverse impact, the test
passes the standard for business necessity.

NOTES

1. Frank Schmidt and others, "Impact of Valid Selection Procedures on Workforce
   Productivity," *Journal of Applied Psychology*, Vol. 64 (December 1979), pp. 609–

626. See also Robert M. Guion, "Changing Views for Personnel Selection Research," *Personnel Psychology*, Vol. 40, no. 2 (Summer 1987), pp. 199–213.

2. Robert E. Sibson, "The High Cost of Hiring," *Nation's Business*, February 1975, p. 85.

3. Commerce Clearing House, *Ideas and Trends*, November 16, 1988, p. 197.

4. Bureau of National Affairs, *Bulletin to Management*, September 10, 1987, p. 295.

5. Suzanne Cook, "How to Avoid Liability for Negligent Hiring," *Personnel* (November 1988), pp. 32–36.

6. Leona Tyler, *Tests and Measurements* (Englewood Cliffs, N.J.: Prentice-Hall, 1971), p. 24.

7. Bureau of National Affairs, Selection Procedure and Personnel Records, Personnel Policies Forum Survey, no. 114 (Washington, D.C.: BNA, 1976), p. 7. Some surveys, however, indicate that preemployment testing is losing favor. For example, see John Aberth, "Pre-employment Testing Is Losing Favor," *Personnel Journal*, Vol. 65, no. 9 (September 1986), pp. 96–99.

8. See Bureau of National Affairs, *Bulletin to Management*, May 26, 1988, p. 168; and Paul Blocklyn, "Pre-employment Testing," *Personnel* (February 1988), pp. 66–68.

9. Prentice-Hall, *Personnel Management: Policies and Practices Report*, no. 22, April 2, 1975 (Englewood Cliffs, N.J.).

10. For a discussion of this, see, for example, Joel Lefkowitz, "Pros and Cons of 'Trust in Testing' Legislation," *Personnel Psychology*, Vol. 33 (Spring 1980), pp. 17–24.

11. Barbara Lerner, *Personnel Psychology*, Vol. 33 (Spring 1980), pp. 11–16.

12. For several recent discussions of this, see Guion, "Changing Views for Personnel Selection Research," pp. 199–213; Karen Evans and Randall Brown, "Reducing Recruitment Risks Through Pre-Employment Testing," *Personnel* (September 1988), pp. 55–64; Edwin A. Fleishman, "Some New Frontiers in Personnel Selection Research," *Personnel Psychology*, Vol. 41, no. 4 (Winter 1988), pp. 679–701; Robin Inwald, "Five-Year Follow-up Study of Departmental Terminations as Predicted by Sixteen Pre-Employment Psychological Indicators," *Journal of Applied Psychology*, Vol. 73, no. 4 (November 1988), pp. 703–710.

13. Tyler, *Tests and Measurements*, p. 25. More technically, "validity refers to the degree of confidence one can have in inferences drawn from scores, considering the whole process by which the scores are obtained. Stated differently, validity refers to the confidence one has in the meaning attached to scores." (See Guion, "Changing Views for Personnel Selection Research," p. 208.)

14. Strictly speaking, a third way to demonstrate a test's validity is *construct validity*. A construct is a trait such as intelligence. Therefore, to take a simple example, if intelligence is important to the position of engineer, a test that measures intelligence would have construct validity for that position. To prove construct validity, an employer has to prove that the test actually measures the construct *and* that the construct is in turn required for the job. Federal agency guidelines make it difficult to prove construct validity, however, and as a result few employers use this approach as a means of satisfying the federal guidelines. See James Ledvinka, *Federal Regulation of Personnel and Human Resource Management* (Boston: Kent, 1982), p. 113.

15. Bureau of National Affairs, *Primer of Equal Employment Opportunity* (Washington, D.C.: BNA, 1978), p. 18. In practice, proving in court the criterion-related validity of paper-and-pencil tests has been difficult. In a review of the subject, for instance, two experts conclude that "in general, most judges very carefully scrutinized these validation studies and were often found to be quite critical in their evaluations. In fact, the criterion-related validity of the predictor was upheld in only 5 of the 12 cases reported." See Kleinman and Faley. See also Ronald Pannone, "Predicting Test Performance: A Content Valid Approach to Screening Applicants," *Personnel Psychology*, Vol. 37, no. 3 (Autumn 1984), pp. 507–514.

16. Ledvinka, *Federal Regulations*, p. 111.

17. Anne Anastasi, *Psychological Patterns* (New York: Macmillan, 1968), reprinted

in W. Clay Hamner and Frank Schmidt, *Contemporary Problems in Personnel* (Chicago: St. Claire Press, 1974), pp. 102–109. Discussion of reliability based on Marvin Dunnette, *Personnel Selection and Placement* (Belmont, Calif.: Wadsworth Publishing Company, Inc., 1966), pp. 29–30.

18. Based on J. Tiffin and E. J. McCormick, *Industrial Psychology* (Englewood Cliffs, N.J.: Prentice-Hall, 1965), pp. 104–105; C. H. Lawshe and M. J. Balma, *Principles of Personnel Testing*, 2nd ed. (New York: McGraw-Hill, 1966).

19. Experts sometimes have to develop separate expectancy charts and cutting points for minorities and nonminorities if the validation studies indicate that high performers from either group (minority or nonminority) score lower (or higher) on the test. See our discussion of differential validity in the appendix to this chapter. For a good discussion of how to evaluate a selection test, see Raymond Berger and Donna Tucker, "How to Evaluate a Selection Test," *Personnel Journal*, Vol. 66, no. 6 (February 1987), pp. 88–91.

20. Barry R. Nathan and Ralph A. Alexander, "A Comparison of Criteria for Test Validation: A Meta-analytic Investigation," *Personnel Psychology*, Vol. 41, no. 3 (Autumn 1988), pp. 517–535.

21. Guion, "Changing Views for Personnel Selection Research," pp. 207–208.

22. Ibid., p. 207.

23. For a discussion, see David A. Waldman and Bruce J. Avolio, "Homogeneity of Test Validity," *Journal of Applied Psychology*, Vol. 74, no. 2 (April 1989), pp. 371–374.

24. For a discussion of how to evaluate psychological tests, see, for example, Robin Inwald, "How to Evaluate Psychological/Honesty Tests," *Personnel Journal* (May 1988), pp. 40–46. Dr. Inwald suggests a number of pointers, including beware of tests for which little or no validation research exists; beware of studies that are not based on the prediction model of validation; beware of studies that do not tell you how many people were incorrectly predicted to have job problems; beware of studies (or tests) that claim to successfully predict dangerous, violent, or nonviolent behavior or tendencies because violent behavior "cannot be predicted"; beware of studies which report significant correlations as their evidence of validity (since unusually high correlations would be questionable); beware of studies that use small numbers of participants to predict important job performance outcomes; beware of studies that have not been cross-validated; beware of claims that tests are valid for use with occupational groups for whom validation studies have not yet been conducted; beware of studies based on individuals filling out questionnaires or tests anonymously; beware of studies that have not used real job candidates as subjects for their validation efforts; and beware of tests whose validation studies have been designed, conducted, and published only by the test developer or publishing company without replication by other independent psychological agencies.

25. See, for example, Floyd L. Ruch, "The Impact on Employment Procedures of the Supreme Court Decision in the Duke Power Case," *Personnel Journal*, Vol. 50, no. 4 (October 1971), pp. 777–783; Hubert Field, Gerald Bagley, and Susan Bagley, "Employment Test Validation for Minority and Non-minority Production Workers," *Personnel Psychology*, Vol. 30, no. 1 (Spring 1977), pp. 37–46; Ledvinka, *Federal Regulations*, p. 110.

26. See Ruch, "The Impact on Employment Procedures of the Supreme Court Decisions in the Duke Power Case," pp. 777–783, in Hamner and Schmidt, *Contemporary Problems in Personnel*, pp. 117–123; Dale Beach, *Personnel* (New York: Macmillan, 1970); Field, Bagley, and Bagley, "Employing Test Validation for Minority and Nonminority Production Workers," pp. 37–46; M. K. Distefano, Jr., Margaret Pryer, and Stella Craig, "Predictive Validity of General Ability Tests with Black and White Psychiatric Attendants," *Personnel Psychology*, Vol. 29, no. 2 (Summer 1976). Also, see the Winter 1976 issue of *Personnel Psychology*, Vol. 2, no. 4. See also James Norborg, "A Warning Regarding the Simplified Approach to the Evaluation of Test Fairness and Employee Selection Procedures," *Personnel Psychology*, Vol. 37, no. 3 (Autumn 1984), pp. 483–486; Charles Johnson, Lawrence Messe, and William Crano, "Predicting Job Performance of Low Income Workers: The Work Opinion Questionnaire," *Personnel Psychology*, Vol. 37, no. 2 (Summer 1984), pp. 291–299; Frank Schmidt, Benjamin Ocasio,

Joseph Hillery, and John Hunter, "Further Within-Setting Empirical Tests of the Situational Specificity Hypothesis in Personnel Selection," *Personnel Psychology*, Vol. 38, no. 3 (Autumn 1985), pp. 509–524.

27. Prentice-Hall, "PH/ASPA Survey: Employee Testing Procedures—Where Are They Headed?" *Personnel Management: Policies and Practices*, April 22, 1975, described in James Ledvinka and Lyle Schoenfeldt, "Legal Developments in Employment Testing: Albemarle," *Personnel Psychology*, Vol. 31, no. 1 (Spring 1978), p. 9.

28. Commerce Clearing House, *Ideas and Trends*, June 14, 1989, p. 108.

29. Ledvinka and Schoenfeldt, "Legal Developments," p. 9.

30. Ledvinka, *Federal Regulations*, p. 109.

31. Douglas Baker and David Terpstra, "Employee Selection: Must Every Job Test Be Validated?" *Personnel Journal*, Vol. 61 (August 1982), pp. 602–605.

32. Ledvinka, *Federal Regulations*, p. 110.

33. This is based on Marilyn Quaintance, "Test Security: Foundations of Public Merit Systems," *Personnel Psychology*, Vol. 33, no. 1 (Spring 1980), pp. 25–32.

34. William Roskind, "DECO Versus NLRB, and the Consequences of Open Testing in Industry," *Personnel Psychology*, Vol. 33, no. 1 (Spring 1980), pp. 3–9; and James Ledvinka, Val Markos, and Robert Ladd, "Long-Range Impact of 'Fair Selection' Standards on Minority Employment," *Journal of Applied Psychology*, Vol. 67, no. 1 (February 1982), pp. 18–36.

35. Susan Mendelsohn and Katheryn Morrison, "The Right to Privacy at the Work Place," Part 1: "Employee Searchers," *Personnel* (July 1988), p. 20.

36. Wayne Outten and Noah A. Kinigstein, *The Rights of Employees* (New York: Bantam Books, 1984), pp. 53–54.

37. Mendelsohn and Morrison, "The Right to Privacy in the Work Place," p. 22.

38. Outten and Kinigstein, *The Rights of Employees*, pp. 54–55.

39. Ibid., p. 55.

40. *Kehr* v. *Consolidated Freightways of Delaware*, Docket No. 86–2126, July 15, 1987, U.S. Seventh Circuit Court of Appeals. Discussed in Commerce Clearing House, *Ideas and Trends*, October 16, 1987, p. 165.

41. For a discussion of these see Commerce Clearing House, *Ideas and Trends*, October 16, 1987, pp. 165–166.

42. Except as noted, this is based largely on Laurence Siegel and Irving Lane, *Personnel and Organizational Psychology* (Homewood, Ill: Irwin, 1982), pp. 170–185. See also Tyler, *Tests and Measurements*, pp. 38–79, and Lawshe and Balma, *Principles of Personnel Testing*, pp. 83–160.

43. See, for example, Richard Reilly, Sheldon Zedeck, and Mary Tenopyr, "Validity and Fairness of Physical Ability Tests for Predicting Performance in Craft Jobs," *Journal of Applied Psychology*, Vol. 64, no. 3 (June 1970), pp. 262–274. See also Barten Daniel, "Strength and Endurance Testing," *Personnel Journal* (June 1987), pp. 112–122.

44. Siegel and Lane, *Personnel and Organizational Psychology*, p. 180. For an interesting example of use of the Minnesota Multiphasic Personality Inventory and other personality tests for detecting malingerers in the workplace, see Paul Lees-Haley, "How to Detect Malingerers in the Workplace," *Personnel Journal*, Vol. 65, no. 7 (July 1986).

45. If you read note 14, you will see that this approach calls for construct validation which, as was pointed out, is extremely difficult to demonstrate.

46. For a study describing how matching (1) task and working condition preferences of applicants with (2) actual job and working conditions can be achieved, see Ronald Ash, Edward Levine, and Steven Edgell, "Study of a Matching Approach: The Impact of Ethnicity," *Journal of Applied Psychology*, Vol. 64, no. 1 (February 1979), pp. 35–41. For a discussion of how a standard clerical test can be used to screen applicants who will have to use video displays, see Edward Silver and Corwin Bennett, "Modification of the Minnesota Clerical Test to Predict Performance on Video Display Terminals," *Journal of Applied Psychology*, Vol. 72, no. 1 (February 1987), pp. 153–155.

47. Emma D. Dunnette and W. D. Borman, "Personnel Selection and Classification Systems," *Annual Review of Psychology*, Vol. 30 (1979), pp. 477–525, quoted in Siegel and Lane, *Personnel and Organizational Psychology*, pp. 182–183.

48. Paul Wernamont and John T. Campbell, "Signs, Samples, and Criteria," *Journal of Applied Psychology*, Vol. 52 (1968), pp. 372–376; James Campion, "Work Sampling for Personnel Selection," *Journal of Applied Psychology*, Vol. 56 (1972), pp. 40–44, reprinted in Hamner and Schmidt, *Contemporary Problems in Personnel*, pp. 168–180; Sidney Gael, Donald Grant, and Richard Ritchie, "Employment Test Validation for Minority and Nonminority Clerks with Work Sample Criteria," *Journal of Applied Psychology*, Vol. 60, no. 4 (August 1974); Frank Schmidt and others, "Job Sample vs. Paper and Pencil Trades and Technical Test: Adverse Impact and Examinee Attitudes," *Personnel Psychology*, Vol. 30, no. 7 (Summer 1977), pp. 187–198.

49. See, for example, George Burgnoli, James Campion, and Jeffrey Bisen, "Racial Bias in the Use of Work Samples for Personnel Selection," *Journal of Applied Psychology*, Vol. 64, no. 2 (April 1979), pp. 119–123.

50. Siegel and Lane, *Personnel and Organizational Psychology*, pp. 182–183.

51. Ann Howard, "An Assessment of Assessment Centers," *Academy of Management Journal*, Vol. 17 (1974), pp. 115–134; see also Louis Olivas, "Using Assessment Centers for Individual and Organizational Development," *Personnel*, Vol. 57 (May–June 1980), pp. 63–67.

52. William Byham, "The Assessment Center as an Aid in Management Development," *Training and Development Journal*, Vol. 25 (December 1971). See also Richard Neidig and Pamela Neidig, "Multiple Assessment Center Exercises and Job Relatedness," *Journal of Applied Psychology*, Vol. 69, no. 1 (February 1984), pp. 182–186; Craig Russell, "Individual Decision Processes in an Assessment Center," *Journal of Applied Psychology*, Vol. 70, no. 4 (1985), pp. 737–746.

53. *Development Dimensions, Inc., 1977–1978 Catalog.* (Pittsburgh: Development Dimensions Press, 1977), discussed in Wayne F. Cascio and Val Silbey, "Utility of the Assessment Center as a Selection Device," *Journal of Applied Psychology*, Vol. 64, no. 4 (April 1979), pp. 107–118.

54. See, for example, Larry Alexander, "An Exploratory Study of the Utilization of Assessment Center Results," *Academy of Management Journal*, Vol. 22, no. 1 (March 1970), pp. 152–157.

55. Neal Schmitt, Raymond Noe, Roni Meritt, and Michael Fitzgerald, "Validity of Assessment Center Ratings for the Prediction of Performance Ratings and School Climate of School Administrators," *Journal of Applied Psychology*, Vol. 69, no. 2 (May 1984), pp. 207–213.

56. Steven Norton, "The Empirical and Content Validity of Assessment Centers Versus Traditional Methods of Predicting Management Success," *Academy of Management Review*, Vol. 20 (July 1977), pp. 442–453. Interestingly, a recent review concludes that assessment centers do predict managerial success, but after an extensive review, "we also assert that we do not know why they work." Richard Klimoski and Mary Brickner, "Why Do Assessment Centers Work? The Puzzle of Assessment Center Validity," *Personnel Psychology*, Vol. 40, no. 2 (Summer 1987), pp. 243–260.

57. John Hinrichs, "An Eight Year Follow-up of a Management Assessment Center," *Journal of Applied Psychology*, Vol. 63, no. 5 (October 1978), pp. 596–601.

58. Cascio and Silbey, "Utility of the Assessment Center as a Selection Device." See also Paul R. Sackett, "Assessment Centers and Content Validity: Some Neglected Issues," *Personnel Psychology*, Vol. 40 (Spring 1987), pp. 13–26.

59. David Groce, "A Behavioral Consistency Approach to Decision Making in Employment Selection," *Personnel Psychology*, Vol. 34, no. 1 (Spring 1981), pp. 55–64.

60. Donald Brush and Lyle Schoenfeldt, "Identifying Managerial Potential: An Alternative Assessment Center," *Personnel*, Vol. 57 (May–June 1980), pp. 72–73.

61. Arthur Cosiegel, "The Miniature Job Training and Evaluation Approach: Traditional Findings," *Personnel Psychology*, Vol. 36, no. 1 (Spring 1983), pp. 41–56.

62. See, for example, George Beason and John Belt, "Verifying the Job Applicant's

Background," *Personnel Administration* (November–December 1974), pp. 29–32; Bureau of National Affairs, "Selection Procedures and Personnel Records," *Personnel Policies Forum*, No. 114 (September 1976), p. 4. See also Paul Sackett and Michael M. Harris, "Honesty Testing for Personnel Selection: A Review and Critique," *Personnel Psychology*, Vol. 37, no. 2 (Summer 1985), pp. 221–245.

63. For additional information see Lawrence E. Dube, Jr., "Employment References and the Law," *Personnel Journal*, Vol. 65, no. 2 (February 1986), pp. 87–91.

64. Thomas von der Embse and Rodney Wyse, "Those Reference Letters: How Useful Are They?" *Personnel*, Vol. 62, no. 1 (January 1985), pp. 42–46.

65. Tiffin and McCormick, *Industrial Psychology*, pp. 78–79.

66. See Howard M. Fischer, "Select the Right Executive," *Personnel Journal* (April 1989), pp. 110–114.

67. James Bell, James Castagnera, and Jane Patterson Yong, "Employment References: Do you Know the Law?" *Personnel Journal*, Vol. 63, no. 2 (February 1984), pp. 32–36.

68. This is based on SKRSC Update, May–June 1985, Schachter, Kristoff, Ross, Sprague, and Curialle, California Street, San Francisco, Calif.

69. James Frierson, "New Polygraph Tests Limits," *Personnel Journal* (December 1988), pp. 84–89.

70. John Jones and William Terris, "Post-Polygraph Selection Techniques," *Recruitment Today* (May–June 1989), pp. 25–31.

71. Norma Fritz, "In Focus: Honest Answers-Post Polygraph," *Personnel* (April 1989), p. 8.

72. Bureau of National Affairs, *Bulletin to Management*, September 10, 1987, p. 296.

73. See, for example, Kevin Murphy, "Detecting Infrequent Deception," *Journal of Applied Psychology*, Vol. 72, no. 4 (November 1987), pp. 611–614, for a discussion of the difficulty of using such tests to provide convincing evidence of deception.

74. These are based on Commerce Clearing House, *Ideas and Trends*, December 29, 1988, pp. 222–223. See also Bureau of National Affairs, "Divining Integrity Through Interview," *Bulletin to Management*, June 4, 1987, p. 184.

75. This example is based on Bureau of National Affairs, *Bulletin to Management*, February 26, 1987, p. 65.

76. See, for example, "Corporate Lie Detectors Under Fire," *Business Week*, January 13, 1973. For a discussion of how to improve the validity of the polygraph test, see Robert Forman and Clark McCauley, "Validity of a Positive Control Polygraph Test Using the Field to Practice Model," *Journal of Applied Psychology*, Vol. 71, no. 4 (November 1986), pp. 691–698.

77. Ulrich Sonnemann, *Handwriting Analysis as a Psychodiagnostic Tool* (New York: Grune & Stratton, 1950), pp. 144–145.

78. Jitendra Sharma and Harsh Vardham, "Graphology: What Handwriting Can Tell You about an Applicant," *Personnel*, Vol. 52, no. 2 (March–April 1975), pp. 57–63. Note that one recent empirical study resulted in the conclusion that "we find ourselves compelled to conclude that it is graphology, rather than just our small sample of graphologists, that is invalid." These researchers conclude that when graphology does seem to "work," it does so because the graphologist is reading a spontaneously written autobiography of the candidate and is thereby obtaining biographical information about the candidate from that essay. See Gershon Ben-Shakhar, Maya Bar-Hillel, Yoram Bilu, Edor Ben-Abba, and Anat Flug, "Can Graphology Predict Occupational Success? Two Empirical Studies and Some Methodological Ruminations," *Journal of Applied Psychology*, Vol. 71, no. 4 (November 1986), pp. 645–653.

79. Joseph Famularo, *Handbook of Modern Personnel Administration* (New York: McGraw-Hill, 1972), pp. 12–17, 18.

80. Ian Miners, Nick Nykodym, and Diane Samerdyke-Traband, "Put Drug Detection to the Test," *Personnel Journal*, Vol. 66, no. 8 (August 1987), pp. 191–197.

81. This is based on Eric Rolfe Greenberg, "Workplace Testing: Who's Testing Whom?" *Personnel* (May 1989), pp. 39–45.

82. Eric Rolfe Greenberg, "Workplace Testing: Results of a New AMA Survey," *Personnel* (April 1988), p. 40.

83. Michael A. McDaniel, "Does Pre-Employment Drug Use Predict on the Job Suitability?" *Personnel Psychology*, Vol. 41, no. 4 (Winter 1988), pp. 717–729.

84. These are quoted from Commerce Clearing House, *Ideas and Trends*, May 1, 1987, pp. 70–71.

85. For information about ordering the Wonderlic contact E.F. Wonderlic and Associates, Inc., 820 Frontage Rd., Northfield, Ill. 60093. Their phone number is 312/446-8900.

86. Praendex, Inc., the publisher, can be contacted at 40 Washington Street, Wellesley Hills, Mass. 02181, 617/235-8872.

87. Reach Assessment Systems Corporation at 2233 University Ave., Suite 440, St. Paul, Minn. 55114, 612/647-9220.

88. David Robertson, "Update on Testing and Equal Opportunity," *Personnel Journal*, Vol. 56, no. 3 (March 1977), reprinted in Craig Schneier and Richard Beatty, *Personnel Administration Today* (Reading, Mass.: Addison-Wesley, 1978), p. 300.

89. Virginia R. Boehm, "Negro-White Differences in Validity of Employment and Training Selection Procedures: Summary of Research Evidence," *Journal of Applied Psychology*, Vol. 56 (1972), pp. 33–39, in Hamner and Schmidt, *Contemporary Problems in Personnel*, pp. 126–134. See also John Hunter and Frank Schmidt, "Differential and Single Group Validity of Employment Tests by Race: A Critical Analysis of Three Recent Studies," *Journal of Applied Psychology*, Vol. 63, no. 1 (1978), pp. 1–11. Note that the need for differential test scores is a separate problem from that of *differential validity*. Differential validity exists when the validity coefficients for two groups are significantly different in a statistical sense. Differential validity thus refers to the predictive capability of the test for each group. When a test is validated separately for two groups— say, white and nonwhite—it could thus turn out that (1) the test is *differentially valid*, in that the validity coefficients (the correlation between test score and job performance) are different for the two groups, and/or (2) different cutting scores are needed for each group, since using the same cutting score might be unfairly discriminatory to one group. In practice, *differential validity* is generally not a serious problem. Finally, also note that while the need for different cutting scores is an important source of test unfairness, there are other ways to use a test unfairly. One could, for instance (to use an extreme example), give nonminority candidates the test answers ahead of time.

Chapter 6

Interviewing Job Candidates

When you finish studying this chapter, you should be able to:

1. Discuss the findings regarding how useful most interviews are.
2. Explain at least 6 factors that affect the usefulness of interviews.
3. Explain each of our 9 guidelines for being a more effective interviewer.
4. Cite at least 15 questions you can ask interviewees.
5. List our 7 guidelines for interviewees.
6. Interview a job candidate effectively.

OVERVIEW

The purpose of this chapter is to give you the tools you will need to interview job candidates more effectively. We first discuss the pros and cons of interviewing and then turn to some of the factors we know affect the usefulness of interviews. We then present some specific guidelines for improving your "batting average" as an interviewer—and as an interviewee. Interviews are an important way to screen your candidates and to find those who are enthusiastic and who also have the skills and abilities to do the job (and therefore are motivated to do so). Selection interviews are thus the next personnel activity that has an influence on employee motivation.

Selection tools like applications and tests can be useful, but the screening tool that's used most often (and sometimes exclusively) is the *selection interview*, and there's good reason for this. Interviews give you a chance to size up the candidate personally, and to pursue questioning in a way that tests cannot. They give you an opportunity to make judgments on the candidate's enthusiasm and intelligence. And they give you an opportunity to assess subjective aspects of the candidate—facial expressions, appearance, nervousness, and so forth. Interviews can be, in other words, a *very* potent screening tool.

The trouble is that all too often interviews are not used to their best advantage. The interviewer himself or herself may be nervous, and pertinent questions aren't asked, for instance. The result is that the findings on the reliability and validity of interviews could lead one to believe that interviews are worthless, when in fact it's not the interview but the ineptness of the interviewer that creates the problem.

How useful *is* the interview? Not surprisingly, the evidence shows that an interview's usefulness depends on how it is carried out. Much of the earlier research gave selection interviews low marks in terms of reliability and validity.[1] However, recent studies show that an interview properly administered *is* a useful screening device.[2] We know, for example, that a *panel interview* (in which several interviewers share their perceptions of the candidate) can generate an accurate picture of the candidate.[3] And we know that interviews are more accurate predictors of performance when the interviewer does not telegraph or ask leading questions.[4] The key to an interview's usefulness, then, is the manner in which it is administered.[5] In this chapter we shall therefore focus on the problems that can undermine interviews, and how to avoid them. First, though, we review the basic types of interviews.

♦ TYPES OF INTERVIEWS

There are several basic types of interviews.

Nondirective

nondirective interview An unstructured conversational-style interview. The interviewer pursues points of interest as they come up in response to questions.

In a **nondirective interview,** you ask questions as they come to mind; here there is no special format to follow, and the conversation can wander off in various directions. As an interviewer you may have a job specification as a guide and you may or may not ask the same or similar questions of each applicant. Often, each applicant's interview starts off about the same, but the unstructured nature of the interview lets you wander far afield, asking questions based on the candidate's last statements. This allows you to pursue points of interest as they develop.

Patterned Interview

patterned interview An interview following a set sequence of questions. Printed forms with guidelines for evaluating the interview are commercially available.

In a **patterned interview** you follow a predetermined sequence of questions, perhaps using a patterned interview form as in Figure 6.1.

Perhaps the best known of these patterned interview forms was developed by Robert N. McMurry. Here you are provided with a special form as in Figure 6.1, with different forms available for different types of jobs—executive, sales, clerical, and technical, for instance. You are then directed to ask the questions printed in black ink on the form and write the answer in the appropriate place. In addition, though, are questions printed in *orange* ink (they are printed in very small type in Figure 6.1); these questions are guides to help you evaluate each of the interviewee's answers. Thus, in Figure 6.1 the question to be asked of the interviewee is, "Why are you

FIGURE 6.1
Patterned Interview Form—Executive Position
Source: Dartnell Corporation, Chicago.

PATTERNED INTERVIEW FORM—EXECUTIVE POSITION

Date_____ 19_____

SUMMARY

Rating: ☐1 ☐2 ☐3 ☐4 **Comments:** _____

In making final rating, be sure to consider not only what the applicant can do but also his/her stability, industry, perseverance, loyalty, ability to get along with others, self-reliance, leadership, maturity, motivation, and domestic situation and health.

_____

_____

_____

Interviewer:_____ Job Considered for:_____

Name_____ Date of birth_____ Phone No._____

Present address _____ City_____ State_____ How long there?_____
Is this a desirable neighborhood? Too high class? Too cheap?

Previous Address _____ City_____ State_____ How long there?_____
Is this a desirable neighborhood? Why did he/she move?

What kind of a car do you own? _____ Age_____ Condition of car _____
Will he be able to use his/her car if necessary?

Were you in the Armed Forces of the U.S.? Yes, branch _____

If not, why not? _____

Are you employed now? Yes ☐ No ☐ (If yes) How soon available? _____
What are his/her relationships with present employer?

Why are you applying for this position? _____
Is his/her underlying reason a desire for prestige, security, or earnings?

WORK EXPERIENCE. Cover all positions. This information is very important. Interviewer should record last position first. Every month since leaving school should be accounted for. Experience in Armed Forces should be covered as a job.

LAST OR PRESENT POSITION

Company _____ City _____ From _____19____ to _____19____
Do these dates check with his/her application?

How was job obtained _____ Whom did you know there? _____
Has he/she shown self-reliance in getting his/her jobs?

Nature of work at start _____ Starting salary_____
Will his/her previous experience be helpful on this job?

In what way did the job change? _____
Has he/she made good work progress?

Nature of work at leaving _____ Salary at leaving_____
How much responsibility has he/she had?   Any indication of ambition?

Superior_____ Title_____ What is he/she like? _____
Did he/she get along with superior?

How closely does (or did) he/she supervise you? _____ What authority do (or did) you have? _____

Number of people you supervised_____ What did they do? _____
Is he/she a leader?

Responsibility for policy formulation_____
Has he/she had management responsibility?

To what extent could you use initiative and judgment? _____
Did he/she actively seek responsibility?

Form No. EP-302-R   Copyright 1973 The Dartnell Corporation, Chicago, Ill. 60640. Printed in U.S.A.
                                      Developed by The McMurry Company

---

applying for this position?" In addition, though, you are directed to form an opinion of whether the applicant is applying for the position because of a "desire for prestige, security, or earnings."

The patterned interview is aimed at obtaining facts about the applicant's technical competence, as well as at uncovering personality patterns, attitudes, and motivation.[6] For example, you might ask the applicant,

"How old were you when you became fully self-supporting?" while deciding for yourself if "Someone always carried the applicant over the rough spots." Then, once the questionnaire is completed, you can review it carefully and make your recommendations based on what you learned about the applicant's technical competence, attitude, stability, perseverence, self-reliance, and motivation. Using a patterned interview form generally requires special training.

Structured Interview

A **structured** (or "situational") **interview**[7] is really a series of job-related questions with predetermined "preferred" answers that are consistently asked of all interviewees for a particular job. It is similar to the patterned interview in that you ask a predetermined, structured set of questions. But with the situational interview you can also ask job-related questions, questions that have been developed through job analysis. Acceptable answers are then chosen by a panel of supervisors who can then rate each applicant's answers to the job-related questions that are asked. The situational interview, as we will see later in this chapter, helps you to (1) *identify acceptable answers* ahead of time and (2) *get consensus among interviewers* regarding the acceptability of these answers. It thus results in more reliable interviews. This technique is described more fully later in this chapter.

Serialized or Sequential Interview

Most employers require that applicants be interviewed by several persons before reaching a decision, but this process is usually nondirective and informal: Each interviewer looks at the applicant from his or her own point of view, asks different questions, and forms an independent opinion of the candidate.

A more formal version of this is the **serialized interview**.[8] Here an applicant is interviewed by several people, only a few of whom will typically come from the department for which he or she is being considered. Each interviewer than rates the candidate on a standard structured evaluation form, and the ratings are compared before a hiring decision is made. Assuming that the structured form focuses on skills and traits that are required for satisfactory job performance, the serialized interview should result in more reliable and valid interviews than would a purely nondirective approach.

Panel Interview

The **panel interview** is widely used for officer training candidates in the Armed Forces and involves having the candidate interviewed by a group (or panel) of interviewers.

This approach has several advantages. The typical interview process often involves having the candidate cover basically the same ground over and over again with each interviewer. The panel interview, on the other hand, lets each interviewer pick up on the candidate's answers to questions posed by different interviewers, much as reporters do in press conferences. Since the panel brings more points of view to bear, it is more likely that new and incisive questions will be prompted by the panel arrangement. This approach can thus elicit deeper and more meaningful responses than are normally produced by a series of one-on-one interviews. However, this type of interview can also place extra stress on the candidate and may thus inhibit responses that would be elicited in a one-on-one interview. One variant is the *mass interview* in which several candidates are interviewed at once by a panel; the panel poses a problem to be solved, and then sits back and

---

structured interview A series of job-related questions with "preferred" answers that are asked of all job applicants. Unlike the preprinted patterned interviews, structured interviews can be adapted to ask questions about the specific job in question.

serialized interview An interview in which the applicant is interviewed sequentially by several supervisors and each rates the applicant on a standard form.

panel interview An interview in which a group of interviewers question the applicant, a method similar to a press conference.

COMPUTER APPLICATION IN INTERVIEWING:

THE COMPUTER-AIDED INTERVIEW

Computer-aided interviews are built on the principles of patterned and structured interviews. The basic idea is to present the applicant with a series of questions regarding his or her background, experience, education, skills, knowledge, and work attitudes, questions that relate to a specific job for which the person has applied.[1] The questions are presented in a multiple-choice format, one at a time, and the applicant is expected to respond to the questions on the computer screen by pressing a key corresponding to desired responses. Here are some sample interview questions for a person applying for a job in a retail store:[2]

Are you applying to work part time or full time?
   A. Part time (less than 40 hours per week).
   B. Full time (40 hours per week).
   C. Whatever is available.

The position for which you are applying may require you to lift boxes that weigh 25 to 30 pounds. Will this be a problem for you?
   A. It will definitely be a problem.
   B. It might be a problem.
   C. It will not be a problem.

Have you ever had a job where you worked directly with customers?
   A. Yes.
   B. No.
   C. If yes, ...

How would your supervisor rate your customer service skills?
   A. Outstanding.
   B. Above average.
   C. Average.
   D. Below average.
   E. Poor.

Note that the last question would be asked only if the applicant answered yes to the previous question.

Computer-aided interviews usually precede and supplement the face-to-face interview. At the end of the computer-aided interview a printed report is produced that lists all interview questions, applicants' responses, and follow-up comments and questions to be asked such as "give me some examples of why your supervisor would rate your customer service skills as outstanding" for the interviewer to ask. The typical computer-aided interview involves about 100 questions and is completed in under 20 minutes.

Computer-aided interviews can have some enormous benefits. Their ability to branch to follow-up questions allows topics to be pursued as they might be in a face-to-face interview; a lot of information can thus be obtained quickly without the interviewers' services. Several of the interpersonal interview problems we'll discuss later in this chapter (such as making a snap judgment about the interviewee based on his or her appearance) are also obviously avoided with this nonpersonal approach to interviewing. Particularly for larger companies with the resources to develop job-specific computer-aided interviews the savings in interviewer time and in avoiding hiring mistakes can be considerable.[3]

[1]This is based on Douglas D. Rodgers, "Computer-Aided Interviewing Overcomes First Impressions," *Personnel Journal* (April 1987), pp. 148–152.

[2]These are based on, and quoted from, Rodgers, "Computer-Aided Interviewing Overcomes First Impressions."

[3]For additional information on computer-aided interviewing's benefits, see, for example, Christopher Martin and Denise Nagao, "Some Effects of Computerized Interviewing on Job Applicant Responses," *Journal of Applied Psychology*, Vol. 74, no. 1 (February 1989), pp. 72–80.

watches which of the candidates takes the lead in formulating an answer, organizing the candidates, and so forth.

Stress Interview

The objective of the **stress interview** is to determine how an applicant will react to stress on the job; to use this approach, you should be skilled in its use and should be sure that stress is, in fact, an important characteristic of the job.

In the typical stress interview, the applicant is made uncomfortable by being put on the defensive by a series of frank (and often discourteous) questions from the interviewer. What the interviewer usually does is probe for weaknesses in the applicant's background. Having identified these, you then focus on them, hoping to get the candidate to lose his or her composure. Thus, a candidate for customer relations manager who obligingly mentions that she's had four jobs in the past two years might be told that frequent job changes reflect irresponsible and immature behavior, behavior that probably reflects the woman's upbringing. If the applicant then responds with a reasonable explanation of why the job changes were necessary, another topic might be pursued. On the other hand, if the person reacts with anger and disbelief, this might be taken as a symptom of low tolerance for stress.

This approach has its advantages and disadvantages. On the one hand, it can be a good way for identifying applicants who are hypersensitive and who might be expected to overreact to mild criticism with anger and abuse. On the other hand, the interviewer who uses this approach should be sure that a thick skin and an ability to handle stress are really required for the job, and that he or she has the skills to keep the interview (and hysterical interviewee) under control.

Appraisal Interview

While in this chapter we emphasize the selection interview, there are other circumstances that require interviews, most notably the formal interview that usually follows the performance appraisal. After the appraisal, the supervisor and subordinate will usually meet to discuss the latter's rating and the remedial action (if any) that's required. Many of the concepts and techniques explained in the present chapter are applicable to the **appraisal interview** as well, but a complete explanation of the appraisal interview will be postponed until Chapter 14.

COMMON INTERVIEWING MISTAKES

♦ INTRODUCTION

Earlier in this chapter we said the usefulness of interviews depends mostly on how they're carried out. Since there are several common interviewing mistakes that undermine the interview's usefulness, we should explain these first, since knowledge of the mistakes is the first step toward avoiding them.

♦ SNAP JUDGMENTS

First, we know that interviewers usually make up their minds about candidates during the first few minutes of the interview; prolonging the interview past this point usually adds little to change the decisions. One researcher even found that in 85% of the cases the interviewer had already made up his or her mind about the candidate *before* the interview even began, on the basis of the applicant's application form and personal appearance!

The problem is especially acute when you get negative feedback about the candidate before the interview. In one study, for instance, the researchers found that interviewers who received unfavorable reference letters about applicants were likely to give the applicant less credit for past successes and to hold the person more personally responsible for past failures. Furthermore, the final decision to accept or reject an applicant was always tied to what the interviewer *expected* of the person, based on the reference.[9]

◆ NEGATIVE EMPHASIS

Interviewers are also influenced more by unfavorable than favorable information about or from the candidate. Similarly, interviewers' impressions are much more likely to change from favorable to unfavorable than unfavorable to favorable; in fact, the interview itself is often mostly a search for negative information.

When you combine this negative emphasis with the fact that interviewers tend to make snap judgments early in the interview, you can see why most interviews tend to be loaded against the applicant. An applicant who is initially highly rated could easily end up with a low rating, given the fact that unfavorable information tends to carry more weight in the interview. And an interviewee who begins with a poor rating will find it very difficult to overcome that first bad impression during the interview.[10]

◆ NOT KNOWING THE JOB

We also know that interviewers who don't know precisely what the job entails and what sort of candidate is best suited for it usually develop incorrect stereotypes about what a good applicant is. They then erroneously match interviewees with their incorrect stereotypes. On the other hand, interviewers who have a clear understanding of what the job entails hold interviews that are more useful.

Take this example. In one study, 30 professional interviewers were used.[11] Half of them were just given a brief description of the jobs for which they were recruiting. Specifically, they were told "the eight applicants here represented by their application blanks are applying for the position of secretary." In contrast, the other 15 interviewers were given much more explicit job information:

> The eight applicants . . . are applying for the position of executive secretary. The requirements are typing speed of 60 words per minute, stenography speed of 100 words per minute, dictaphone use and bilingual ability in either French, German, or Spanish. . . .

The results were clear. The 15 interviewers who had more job information generally agreed among themselves about each candidate's potential, while those without complete job information did not. Interviewers who did not have full job information also did not discriminate very well among the applicants, and there was a tendency to give all applicants high ratings.

◆ PRESSURE TO HIRE

You are also going to do a worse job of interviewing if you are under pressure to hire more candidates. Here's an example. In one study a group of managers was told to assume that they were behind in their recruiting quota, while a second group was told that they were already ahead of their quota. Those who were told they were behind evaluated the same recruits much more highly than did the other group of managers.[12]

♦ CANDIDATE-ORDER ERROR

The order in which you see applicants can also affect how you rate them. In one study, managers were asked to evaluate a candidate who was "just average" after first evaluating several "unfavorable" candidates. The average candidate was evaluated much more favorably than he might otherwise have been, since in contrast to the unfavorable candidates the average one looked much better than he actually was.

This **candidate-order error** can be a major problem; in some studies, only a small part of the applicant's rating was based on his or her actual potential. Most of the applicant's rating was based on the effect of having followed very favorable or unfavorable candidates.[13]

♦ NONVERBAL BEHAVIOR

Another problem is that as an interviewer you may be unconsciously influenced by the applicant's nonverbal behavior. Often, in other words, it is not what the applicant says, *but how the person says it* that determines whether you rate the person high or low. For example, several studies have shown that applicants who demonstrate greater amounts of eye contact, head moving, smiling, and other similar nonverbal behaviors are rated higher, and that these nonverbal behaviors often account for more than 80% of the applicant's rating.[14] In one study, 52 human resource specialists reviewed videotaped job interviews in which what the applicants said—their verbal content—was identical; however, the interviewees' nonverbal behavior differed markedly. The interviewees in one group had been instructed to exhibit minimal eye contact, a low energy level, and low voice modulation. The interviewees in a second group demonstrated the opposite behavior. Of the 26 personnel specialists who saw the high-eye contact, high-energy-level candidate, 23 would have invited him or her for a second interview. On the other hand, all 26 of the personnel people who saw the low-eye-contact, low-energy-level candidate would not have recommended that person for a second interview.[15] One implication is that an otherwise inferior candidate who is trained to "act right" in an interview will often be appraised more highly than will a more competent applicant who has not developed the right nonverbal interviewing skills.

Another facet of this problem is the role played by the applicant's attractiveness, and whether the person is male or female.[16] In one study, researchers found that whether attractiveness was a help or a hindrance to job applicants depended on the sex of the applicant and the nature of the job he or she was seeking. Attractiveness was consistently an advantage for male applicants seeking white-collar jobs. Yet attractiveness was advantageous for female interviewees only when the job was *nonmanagerial*. When the position the woman was being interviewed for was *managerial*, there was, in fact, a tendency for the person's attractiveness to work against her—in terms of recommendation for hiring and suggested starting salary. One explanation may be that interviewers tend to equate attractiveness with femininity. Thus attractive ("more feminine") women are seen as less fit for "masculine-type" jobs like that of manager, quite aside from the women's actual qualifications or the talents actually needed for the job.

It will also not come as a surprise to many women that how they dress

candidate-order error An error of judgment on the part of the interviewer due to interviewing one or more very good or very bad candidates just before the interview in question.

will also affect the interviewer's selection decisions. In one study, 77 human resource administrators attending a conference evaluated videotapes of women interviewing for management positions. The women were dressed in one of four styles (as illustrated in Figure 6.2) ranging from a light beige dress in a soft fabric (style 1) to a bright aqua suit with a short belted jacket (style 2) to a beige tailored suit with a blazer jacket (style 3) to "the most masculine" outfit, a dark navy, tailored suit and a white blouse with an angular collar (style 4). A comparison of the hiring recommendations associated with each style suggests that, up to a point, the more masculine the style, the more favorable the hiring recommendations were. Specifically, applicants received more favorable hiring recommendations as style masculinity increased from style 1 to style 3. However, they then turned down for those "applicants" wearing style 4 (the most masculine style), which, one must surmise, was considered "too masculine" for the interviewers. The findings may not apply to every individual but suggest that it would be better for women to risk dressing "too masculine" rather than "too feminine" when applying for a management position.[17]

In summary, seven common interviewing mistakes are snap judgments, negative emphasis, not knowing the job, pressure to hire, candidate order, the effect of nonverbal factors, and emphasis on physical factors that are not job related. Understanding these common mistakes is the first step toward avoiding them. In addition, specific guidelines for the effective interview are presented next.

FIGURE 6.2
Four Specific Styles Used in Study
Source: Sandra Forsythe, Mary Frances Drake, and Charles Cox, "Influence of Applicants' Dress on Interviewers' Selection Decisions," *Journal of Applied Psychology,* Vol. 70, no. 2 (1985), p. 376. Copyright 1985 by the American Psychological Association. Reprinted by permission of the authors.

Costume 1- Least Masculine

Costume 2- Somewhat Masculine

Costume 3- Moderately Masculine

Costume 4- Most Masculine

♦ STEPS IN THE INTERVIEW

Regardless of whether your interview is nondirective, patterned, or some other it should ideally contain five steps: plan, establish rapport, question, close, and review.[18]

Planning the Interview

First, you should plan the interview in advance. Specifically, review the candidate's application and résumé, and note any areas that are vague or that may indicate strengths or weaknesses so that you can ask questions about them. You should review the job specification so that you'll go into the interview with a clear picture of the traits an ideal candidate should possess.

You should also plan the location in which the interview will take place. Ideally, it should be a private room. Telephone calls should not be put through, and other interruptions should be kept to a minimum.

Establishing Rapport

Next, greet the candidate and take steps to put the person at ease. The interviewing room itself should be conducive to reducing tensions and establishing rapport, and be private, quiet, and lacking in distractions. You might want to start the interview by asking noncontroversial questions—perhaps about the weather or the traffic conditions that day. A few minutes spent on questions like these can go far toward reducing the applicant's tension; this should in turn enable the person to respond more completely and intelligently to your questions.

In addition to reducing tensions, *establishing rapport* has another aim; it can help you make a friend of the applicant, whether the person is eventually offered a job or not. As a rule, all applicants—even unsolicited drop-ins at your office—should be given friendly, courteous treatment, not only on humanitarian grounds but because your reputation will be on the line.

Ask Questions

The interview next moves into the *asking questions* stage, and as explained previously there are several approaches you can use here: nondirective, for instance, or structured. Similarly, the questioning can be carried out on a one-to-one basis, by a panel, or by a series of interviewers.

In any event, there are several things to keep in mind when asking questions. First, avoid questions that can be answered "Yes" or "No"; instead, ask questions that require more elaborate answers. Don't put words in the applicant's mouth (for instance by asking, "You *have* called on discount stores, haven't you?"), nor should you telegraph the desired answer, for instance by nodding or smiling when the right answer is given. Don't interrogate the applicant as if the person is a prisoner, and don't be patronizing, sarcastic, or inattentive. Finally, don't monopolize the interview by rambling on yourself; similarly, don't let the applicant dominate the interview by rambling from point to point so you cannot ask all your questions. Instead, *do* ask open-ended questions, and *listen* to the candidate's answer to encourage him or her to express himself or herself fully.

Close the Interview

Toward the close of the interview, time should be set aside to answer any questions the candidate may have, and (if appropriate) to sell working at your firm to the candidate.

Try to end all interviews on a positive note. The applicant should be told if there is an interest in his or her background and, if so, what the next step will be. Similarly, rejections should be made diplomatically, for instance with a statement like, "Although your background is impressive, there are some other candidates whose experience is closer to our requirements." If the applicant is still being considered, but a decision can't be reached at once, the person should be told this. If your policy is instead to inform candidates of their status in writing, this should be done within a few days of the interview.

Review the Interview

After the candidate has left, you should review your notes of the interview, fill in the patterned interview form (if this was not done during the interview), and review the interview while it's still fresh in your mind. Remember that snap judgments and a negative emphasis are two common interviewing mistakes; carefully reviewing the interview after all the information is in and the candidate has left can help you to minimize these two problems.

♦ ADDITIONAL INTERVIEWING GUIDELINES

In addition to the do's and don'ts of questioning applicants, some additional guidelines to follow include:

1. *Use a structured form.* Interviews based on structured guides like that in Figure 6.3 usually result in the best interviews.[19] By forcing you to adhere to a preset sequence of questions, they help reduce your tendency to let unfavorable information bias your opinions. They also help you to more accurately recall the information produced in the interview and help to ensure that all interviewers ask all candidates the same questions. At a minimum, you should write out your questions before the interview.

2. *Delay your decision.* Interviewers often make their decisions before they ever see the candidate—on the basis of his or her application blank, for instance—or during the first few minutes of the interview. Another principle of good interviewing is thus to delay your decision as long into the interview as possible. Try to keep a record of the interview, and review this record after the interview; make your decision then.[20] We also know that the quality of the applicant will influence how long it takes you to make a decision, with the quickest decisions being made on the worst candidates—those that get off to the worst start, in terms of their answers to the interviewers' questions.[21] The time allotted for the interview is another important factor; allotting more time for an interview will make you less likely to make a premature decision.[22,23]

3. *Focus on traits that are more accurately assessed in the interview.* Some traits are more accurately assessed during interviews than others. These include the candidate's intelligence, ability to get along with others, and motivation to work. As two researchers conclude,

> the results rather consistently indicate two areas which both contribute heavily to interview decisions and show greatest evidence of validity . . . personal relations, and motivation to work. In other words, perhaps the interviewer should seek information on two questions: "What is the applicant's motivation to work?" and "Would he or she adjust to the social context of the job?" Such an approach would leave the assessment of abilities, aptitudes, and biographical data to other, and in all likelihood, more reliable and valid sources.[24]

4. *Get the interviewee to talk.* The main reason for the interview is to find out about the applicant and to do this you must get the person to talk.

FIGURE 6.3
Structured Interview Form

COOPERS & LYBRAND	CANDIDATE RECORD	NAP 100 (10/77)

CANDIDATE NUMBER　　NAME (LAST NAME FIRST)　　　　　　　　　　　COLLEGE NAME　　COLLEGE CODE

I [ ][ ] U 921 [ ]　　[ ][ ]　[ ][ ][ ]
　　(1-7)　　　　　　　　　　　　　　　　(8-27)　　　　　　　　　　　　(28-30)

INTERVIEWER NUMBER

[ ][ ][ ]O[ ][ ][ ]
(33-40)

INTERVIEWER NAME

SOURCE(41)
Campus ☐C
Walk-In ☐W
Intern ☐I
Agency ☐A

RACE (42)
White ☐W
Black ☐B
Asian ☐A
Hispanic ☐H
Am. Indian ☐I

SEX (43)
Male ☐M
Female ☐F
Init.
Cont.
Date [ ][ ][ ][ ][ ][ ]
(46-51)

DEGREE (53)
Bachelors ☐B
Masters ☐M
Law ☐L
Major:

AVERAGE (A = 4,0)
Overall [ ][ ] (54-55)
Acctg [ ][ ] (56-57)

CLASS STANDING (58-59)
Top 10% ☐10
Top 25% ☐25
Top Half ☐50
Bottom Half ☐75

CAMPUS INTERVIEW EVALUATIONS
ATTITUDE – MOTIVATION – GOALS

POOR ☐　　　　AVERAGE ☐　　　　GOOD ☐　　　　OUTSTANDING ☐
(POSITIVE, COOPERATIVE, ENERGETIC, MOTIVATED, SUCCESSFUL, GOAL-ORIENTED)
COMMENTS:

COMMUNICATIONS SKILLS – PERSONALITY – SALESMANSHIP

POOR ☐　　　　AVERAGE ☐　　　　GOOD ☐　　　　OUTSTANDING ☐
(ARTICULATE, LISTENS, ENTHUSIASTIC, LIKEABLE, POISED, TACTFUL, ACCEPTED, CONVINCING)
COMMENTS:

EXECUTIVE PRESENCE – DEAL WITH TOP PEOPLE

POOR ☐　　　　AVERAGE ☐　　　　GOOD ☐　　　　OUTSTANDING ☐
(IMPRESSIVE, STANDS OUT, A WINNER, REMEMBERED, LEVELHEADED, AT EASE, AWARE)
COMMENTS:

INTELLECTUAL ABILITIES

POOR ☐　　　　AVERAGE ☐　　　　GOOD ☐　　　　OUTSTANDING ☐
(INSIGHTFUL, CREATIVE, CURIOUS, IMAGINATIVE, UNDERSTANDS, REASONS, INTELLIGENT, SCHOLARLY)
COMMENTS:

JUDGMENT – DECISION MAKING ABILITY

POOR ☐　　　　AVERAGE ☐　　　　GOOD ☐　　　　OUTSTANDING ☐
(MATURE, SEASONED, INDEPENDENT, COMMON SENSE, CERTAIN, DETERMINED, LOGICAL)
COMMENTS:

LEADERSHIP

POOR ☐　　　　AVERAGE ☐　　　　GOOD ☐　　　　OUTSTANDING ☐
(SELF-CONFIDENT, TAKES CHARGE, EFFECTIVE, RESPECTED, MANAGEMENT MINDED, GRASPS AUTHORITY)
COMMENTS:

CAMPUS INTERVIEW SUMMARY

INVITE (Circle)	AREA OF INTEREST (Circle)	SEMESTER HRS.	OFFICES PREFERRED:	SUMMARY COMMENTS:
YES　NO	AUDIT　TAX	Acct'g. _____	No. 1 _____	
DATE AVAILABLE	MCS　ABC	Audit _____	No. 2 _____	
	Other _____	Tax _____	No. 3 _____	

To do this, make the applicant feel at ease early in the interview, perhaps with some general comment about the organization and the job; avoid asking too many direct questions; and draw out an applicant's opinions and feelings by repeating the person's last comment as a question (such as "You didn't like your last job?"). Some sample questions (such as "Why do you feel qualified for this job?" and "What attracted you to us?") are presented in Figure 6.4.

5. *Comply with equal employment requirements.* Remember that your employer may be called on to explain the selection procedures and questions used in the interview. You should therefore be alert to bias and make periodic checks on the number of minorities hired or recommended, along with the jobs they are recommended for. Using a structured interview form

FIGURE 6.4
Interview Questions from the Employer
Source: Adapted from Richard La-
throp, *Who's Hiring Who* (Reston,
Va.: Reston Publishing, 1976), pp.
169–171.

Openers

■ May I see your résumé?

■ What can I do for you?

■ Why are you interested in joining our company?

■ Why do you feel qualified for this job?

■ What do you think you can do for us?

■ What attracts you to us?

■ Tell me about your experience.

■ What pay do you have in mind? (Try tactfully to avoid answering this one early in the interview.)

Regarding motivation and interests

■ Is your present employer aware of your interest in a job change?

■ Why do you want to change jobs?

■ What caused you to enter your job field?

■ Why do you want to change your field of work?

■ Why are you leaving military service at this point?

■ What would you like to be doing five years from now? When you retire?

■ What is the ideal job for you?

■ If you had complete freedom of choice to be a great success in any job field, which would you choose? Why?

Regarding education and intellectual capacity

■ Describe your education for me.

■ Why did you pick your major?

■ What was your class standing?

■ What were your activities?

■ What honors did you earn?

■ What were your average grades?

■ Did your grades adequately reflect your full capability? Why not?

■ What courses did you like best/least and why?

■ Have you had any special training for this job?

is also advisable, since it can be standardized and validated as a selection tool for EEOC purposes.[25]

As explained in Chapter 2, *federal* Equal Employment laws generally do not prohibit interviewers from asking almost any questions, but the EEOC does look with suspicion on certain inquiries. As we explained, dubious questions include those concerning marital status, child care, availability for Saturday or Sunday work, arrest record, or any other questions that could have an adverse impact on women or minorities. Figures 6.1 and 6.3 present questions concerning, for instance, age, which may be illegal and should only be used with caution when it can be shown that they are clearly job related.[26]

FIGURE 6.4
(continued)

Regarding experience

- Why should I hire you?
- How do you fit the requirements for this job?
- What did you do in military service?
- What would you do to improve our operations?
- Who has exercised the greatest influence on you? How?
- What duties performed in the past have you liked best/least and why?
- What are your greatest strengths/limitations for this job?
- What are the strongest limitations you have found in past supervisors?
- Which supervisor did you like best and why?
- What kinds of people appeal most/least to you as work associates?
- How many people have you supervised? What types?
- What are your greatest accomplishments to date?
- What equipment can you work with?
- Why have you changed jobs so frequently?
- Have you ever been fired or asked to resign?
- Describe the biggest crisis in your career.
- What were you doing during the period not covered in your résumé?
- Why were you out of work so long?
- What was the specific nature of your illness during your extended hospitalization?
- Why did you leave your previous jobs?
- Could I see samples of your work?

Regarding pay

- What do you require?
- What is the *minimum* pay you will accept?
- What is your pay record for the last five years?
- Why do you believe you are qualified for so much more?
- We can't pay the salary you should have. Would you be willing to start lower and work up to that figure?
- What do you expect 'o be earning five years from now?

♦ THE STRUCTURED INTERVIEW

The *structured* or *situational* interview is a new approach to interviewing that we can define as *a series of job-related questions with predetermined answers that are consistently asked of all applicants for a particular job.*[27] The basic procedure involves having a committee of persons who are familiar with the job develop job-related interview questions, questions that are based on the actual duties of the job; these people then meet and reach consensus regarding what are and are not acceptable answers to these questions. The procedure consists of five steps as follows.

Step 1. Job Analysis

First, generate a description of the job in terms of job duties, required knowledge, skills, abilities and other worker qualifications.

Step 2. Evaluate the Job Duty Information

The job analysis should result in a list of job duties. The next step is to evaluate this job duty information. In particular, rate each job duty on its importance to job success and in terms of the amount of time required to perform it compared to other tasks. The aim here is to identify the main duties on the job.

Step 3. Develop Interview Questions

The employees who helped to develop and evaluate the job duties are then asked to develop the actual interview questions. The interview questions themselves are based on the listing of job duties, with more interview questions devoted to the more important job duties.

A situational interview contains several types of questions. *Situational questions* pose a hypothetical job situation to the applicant, such as "What would you do if the machine suddenly began heating up?" *Job knowledge questions* assess job knowledge that is both essential to job performance and must be known prior to entering the job; they often deal with the technical aspects of a job (such as "What is a ratchet wrench?"). *Worker requirements questions* usually take the form of "willingness questions," and include questions on the applicant's willingness and motivation to work, to do repetitive physical work, to travel, to relocate, and so forth.

The employees who develop the questions will also choose, for each question, *critical incidents* that reflect especially good or poor performance. For example, a critical incident-based situational question that could be asked of a supervisor is as follows:

> Your spouse and two teenage children are sick in bed with a cold. There are no relatives or friends available to look in on them. Your shift starts in three hours. What would you do in this situation?

Step 4. Develop Benchmark Answers to Interview Questions

Next, for each critical incident question, a five-point answer rating scale is constructed with specific answers developed for a good answer (a 5 rating), a marginal answer (a 3 rating), and a poor answer (a 1 rating).

For example, for the situational question earlier ("your spouse and two teenage children are sick in bed . . .") each member of the team that was developing the questions and answers was asked to come up with good, marginal, and poor answers based on "things you have actually heard said in an interview by people who subsequently were considered good, marginal, or poor as the case may be on the job." Each person then reads his or her answers to the other group members. After a group discussion, consensus is reached on the answers to use as 5, 3, and 1 benchmarks. The three benchmarks for the example question were "I'd stay home—my spouse and family come first" (1), "I'd phone my supervisor and explain my situation" (3), and "since they only have colds, I'd come to work" (5). Similarly, a set of questions and corresponding answers is developed for each of the other important job duties.

Step 5. Appoint Interview Committee and Implement

An interview committee should consist of three to six members, preferably the same employees who participated in the job analysis and the writing of the interviews and answers. Members of the committee may also come from supervisors above the job to be filled or include the job incumbent, peers, and human resource representatives who are familiar with the job. The same interview members should be used throughout the interviewing for a single job.[28]

Prior to the interview, the job duties and the questions and benchmark interview answers are distributed to the committee members and reviewed. Next, the interview itself is carried out by committee members, usually in a quiet, comfortable, nonstressful atmosphere. Ideally, one member of the panel is designated to introduce the applicant to the panel and to ask all questions of all applicants in this and succeeding interviews, so as to ensure consistency. However, all panel members record and rate the applicant's answers on the rating scale sheet, by indicating where the candidate's answer to each question falls relative to the ideal 1, 3, or 5 answers. At the conclusion of the interview, each applicant is directed to someone who explains the follow-up procedures and answers any questions that the applicant may have.[29]

SMALL BUSINESS APPLICATIONS: INTERVIEWING

Many of the points discussed in this chapter can be combined in a practical interview procedure for a small business. Such a procedure is especially useful when time and resources are scarce and when a quick way of assessing the demands of the job and the questions to ask is required. The procedure consists of four steps as follows:[30]

1. Develop behavioral specifications for the job.
2. Determine what basic factors to probe for.
3. Use an interview plan.
4. Match the candidate to the job.

♦ DEVELOP BEHAVIORAL SPECIFICATIONS

First, you want to specify the behaviors you will look for in candidates. Here, it is convenient to classify these behaviors or traits into four basic types: *intellectual capacity, motivation, personality strengths and limitations*, and *knowledge and experience. Intellectual capacity* refers to the person's intelligence and problem-solving capacity, as well as to specific intellectual aptitudes such as for mathematics or understanding mechanical activities. In assessing your candidate's intellectual capacity you'll be interested in not just the person's intellectual capacity or potential, but also the person's ability to apply that intellectual capacity since, for example, some very smart people may be superficial. Intellectual capacity is most accurately assessed through paper-and-pencil tests. However, we'll see that there are some areas you can probe to assess the person's capacities.

Motivation refers to the person's interests, aspirations, and energy level. *Personality strengths and limitations* refers to the candidate's psychological adjustment and to the nature and quality of the interpersonal relationships he or she has had. Here, you should be especially wary of self-defeating patterns of behavior, for example, extreme impatience or a desire to speak one's mind to a point where it impacts negatively on the person's ability to get along. Finally, with *knowledge and experience* you might want to focus on short verbal tests as well as on questions that probe what the candidate knows (or does not know) as it relates to the job at hand.

Developing Behavioral Specifications for the Job: What to Look for in the Candidate

Even a one-person business can take the time to develop a set of criteria regarding the kind of person that would be best for the job. A quick and efficient way of formulating such specifications is to ask the following questions:

Knowledge-Experience Factor: What must the candidate know about to perform the job? What experience is absolutely necessary to perform a job?

Motivation Factor: What should the person like doing to enjoy this job? Is there anything the person should not dislike? Are there any essential goals or aspirations the person should have? Are there any unusual energy demands on the job? How critical is the person's drive and motivation?

Intellectual Factor: Are there any specific intellectual aptitudes required (mathematics, mechanical, etc.)? How complex are the problems to be solved? What must a person be able to demonstrate he or she can do intellectually? How should the person problem solve (cautiously, deductively, etc.)?

Personality Factor: What are the critical personality qualities needed for success on the job (ability to withstand boredom, decisiveness, stability, etc.)? How must the job incumbent handle stress, pressure, and criticism? What kind of interpersonal behavior is required in the job up the line, at peer level, down the line, and outside the firm with customers?

♦ SPECIFIC FACTORS TO PROBE IN THE INTERVIEW

Next, use a combination of open-ended questions like those in Figure 6.4 to probe the candidate's suitableness for the job as follows:

Intellectual Factor: Here probe such things as complexity of tasks the person has performed, grades in school, tests (including scholastic aptitude tests, etc.), and how the person organizes his or her thoughts and communicates.

Motivation Factor: Probe such areas as the person's likes and dislikes (for each thing done, what he or she liked or disliked about it), the person's aspirations (including, importantly, the validity of each goal in terms of why he or she chose that goal), and the person's energy level, perhaps by asking them what they do on, say, a "typical Tuesday."

Personality Factor: Probe by looking for self-defeating patterns of behavior (aggressiveness, compulsive fidgeting, etc.) and by probing into the person's past interpersonal relations. Here, ask probing questions about all the person's past interactions that he or she brings up (working in a group at school, working with sorority sisters, leading the work team on the last job, etc.) and also try to judge the person's behavior in the interview itself—is the person personable? shy? outgoing?

♦ USING AN INTERVIEW PLAN

While you are going to be probing for four classes of information—intellectual, motivation, personality, and knowledge and experience—you should devise and use an interview plan to guide the interview. John Drake[31] suggests that significant topics you might want to cover include:

High school

College

Work experiences—summer, part time

Work experience—full time (one by one)

Goals and ambitions

Reactions to the job you are interviewing for

Self-assessments (by the candidate of his or her strengths and weaknesses)

Military experiences

Present outside activities

Your basic approach is to follow your plan, perhaps starting with an open-ended question for each topic such as "could you tell me about what you did when you were in high school?" Then (keeping in mind that you are trying to elicit information on four main traits—intellectual, motivation, personality, and knowledge and experience), you can accumulate information on each of those four traits as the person talks. Particular areas that you want to follow up on can usually be pursued by asking such questions as: "Could you elaborate on that please?", or by probing (as explained) such things as the complexity of tasks performed, test grades, what they like for each task, and dislike, and what their actual interactions were like.

♦ MATCH CANDIDATE TO THE JOB

If you followed your interview plan and probed for the four factors, you should now be able to summarize the candidate's general strengths and limitations and also draw some solid conclusions about the person's intellectual capacity, knowledge/experience, motivation, and personality. Your next step should be to compare your conclusions to both the job description (which should be prepared for each job) and to the list of behavioral specifications developed as explained. In that way you should have a rational basis for matching the candidate to the job, one based on an analysis of the traits and aptitudes actually required.

GUIDELINES FOR INTERVIEWEES

Before you get into a position where you have to do interviewing, you will probably have to navigate some interviews yourself. Here are some hints for excelling in your interview.

When being interviewed, the first thing to understand is that interviews are used primarily to help employers determine what you are like as a person.[32] In other words, information regarding how you get along with other people and your desire to work is of prime importance in the interview, since your skills and technical expertise are usually best determined through tests and a careful study of your educational and work history. Interviewers will look first for crisp, articulate answers. Specifically, whether you respond concisely, cooperate fully in answering questions, state personal opinions when relevant, and keep to the subject at hand are by far the most important elements in influencing the interviewer's decision.

There are seven things to do to get that extra edge in the interview.

First, *preparation is essential.* Before the interview, learn all you can about the employer, the job, and the people doing the recruiting. At the library, look through business periodicals to find out what is happening in the employer's field. Who is the competition? How are they doing? Try to unearth the employer's problems, and be ready to explain why you think you would be able to solve such problems, citing some of your *specific accomplishments* to make your case.

Second, *uncover the interviewer's real needs.* Spend as little time as possible answering your interviewer's first questions and as much time as possible getting him or her to describe his or her needs: what the person is looking to get accomplished, and the type of person he or she feels is needed. Use open-ended questions here such as: "Could you tell me more about that?"

PERSONNEL MANAGEMENT:

ON THE FRONT LINE

Like virtually all the other personnel management–related activities at Carter Cleaning Centers, the company currently has no organized approach to interviewing job candidates. Store managers, who do almost all the hiring, each have a few of their own favorite questions that they ask. But in the absence of any guidance from top management they all admit their interview performance leaves something to be desired. Similarly Jack Carter himself is admittedly most comfortable dealing with what he calls the "nuts and bolts" machinery aspect of his business and has never felt particularly comfortable having to interview management or other job interviewees. Jennifer is sure that lack of formal interviewing practices, procedures, and training account for some of the employee turnover and theft problems and she therefore wants to do something to improve her company's batting average in this important area.

The questions she has include these:

1. In general, what can I do to improve our employee interviewing practices here at Carter Cleaning Centers? Should we develop interview forms that list questions for management and nonmanagement jobs, and if so what form should these take and what questions should we include? I also wonder if we should implement a training program for our managers, and if so, what the content of such an interview-training program should be, specifically? In other words, if we did decide to start training our management people to be better interviewers, what should we tell them and how should we tell it to them?

Third, *relate yourself to the interviewer's needs.* Once you have a handle on the type of person your interviewer is looking for and the sorts of problems he or she wants solved, you are in a good position to describe your own accomplishments *in terms of the interviewer's needs.* Start by saying something like "one of the problem areas you've indicated is important to you is similar to a problem I once faced." Then, state the problem, describe your solution, and reveal the results.[33]

Fourth, *think before answering.*[34] Answering a question should be a three-step process: Pause—Think—Speak. *Pause* to make sure you under-

FIGURE 6.5
Interview Questions to Ask the Employer

Openers

- (After the usual cordialities:) Have you had a chance to review my qualifications brief?
- Did it raise any questions about my qualifications that I can answer?
- Did (the previous interviewer) give you the full story on my experience?

Regarding job content

- Would you mind describing the duties of the job for me, please?
- Could you show me where it fits in the organization?
- Is this a new position?
- What do you consider ideal experience for this job?
- Was the previous incumbent promoted?

FIGURE 6.5
(continued)

- Could you tell me about the people who would be reporting to me?
- How does their pay compare with that in other sections/companies?
- Are you happy with their performance?
- Have there been any outstanding cases of dissatisfaction among them?
- What is the largest single problem facing your staff now?
- Is there anything unusually demanding about the job I should know about?
- What have been some of the best results produced by people in this job?
- Could you tell me about the primary people I would be dealing with?
- What are their strengths and limitations as you see them?
- What are the primary results you would like to see me produce?
- May I talk with the person who last held this job? Other members of the staff?

Regarding your bid for the job, pay, and other closing questions

- Is there anything else I can tell you about my qualifications?
- I can be ready to go to work in —— days. Should I plan on that?
- Based on my qualifications, don't you think $——— a year would be appropriate for me in this job?
- Would you mind telling me the pay *range* the company has in mind for this job?
- Do you think more could be justified in light of my particular experience?
- Can you tell me the prospects for advancement beyond that level?
- I greatly appreciate your offer. How soon do you need a decision?
- Will it be all right if I let you know by (date)?

Regarding benefits
(Raise only after it looks like you will be offered the job—or separately with the personnel department)

- Could you tell me briefly about your benefits program? (Vacations, insurance, retirement, profit sharing, bonuses, hospitalization, etc.)

If the employer finally says "no"

- Do you know of others in the organization or elsewhere who would be interested in my experience?
- I very much like what you are doing. Could you keep my qualifications brief on hand for other openings in your office or referral to others?

stand what the interviewer is driving at, *think* about how to structure your answer, and then *speak*. In your answer, try to emphasize how hiring you will help the interviewer solve his or her problem.

Fifth, *appearance and enthusiasm are important*. Appropriate clothing, good grooming, a firm handshake, and the appearance of controlled energy are important.

Sixth, *make a good first impression*. Remember that studies of interviews show that in most cases interviewers make up their minds about the applicant during the first minutes of the interview. A good first impression may turn to bad during the interview, but it is unlikely. Bad first impressions are almost impossible to overcome. One expert suggests paying attention to the following "key interviewing considerations":

1. Appropriate clothing
2. Good grooming
3. A firm handshake
4. The appearance of controlled energy
5. Pertinent humor and readiness to smile
6. A genuine interest in the employer's operation and alert attention when the interviewer speaks
7. Pride in past performance
8. An understanding of the employer's needs and a desire to serve them
9. The display of sound ideas
10. Ability to take control when employers fall down on the interviewing job

Sample questions you can ask are presented in Figure 6.5 (see pages 236–37) and include "Would you mind describing the job for me?" and "Could you tell me about the people who would be reporting to me?"

Seventh, remember that your *nonverbal behavior* will often broadcast more about you than the actual verbal content of what you say. Here, maintaining *eye contact* is very important; in addition, speak with enthusiasm, nod agreement, and remember to take a moment to frame your answer so that it comes across as articulate and fluent.

SUMMARY

1. There are several basic types of interviews, including patterned, nondirective, structured, sequential, panel, stress, and appraisal interviews.
2. We discussed several factors and problems that can undermine the usefulness of an interview. These are making premature decisions, the fact that unfavorable information predominates, the extent to which the interviewer knows the requirements of the job, being under pressure to hire, the candidate-order effect, visual cues, and traits such as enthusiasm.
3. The five steps in the interview include: plan, establish rapport, question the candidate, close the interview, and review the data.
4. Guidelines for interviewers include: use a structured guide, know the requirements of the job, focus on traits you can more accurately evaluate (like motivation), let the interviewee do most of the talking, delay your decision, and remember the EEOC requirements.
5. The steps in a structured or situational interview include: job analysis, evaluate the job duty information, develop interview questions with critical incidents, develop benchmark answers, appoint interview committee, and implement.
6. As an interviewee, keep in mind that: interviewers tend to make premature decisions and let unfavorable information predominate; your appearance and enthusiasm are important; you should get the interviewer to talk; it is important to prepare before walking in—get to know the job and the problems the interviewer wants solved; and you should stress your enthusiasm and motivation to work, and how your accomplishments match your interviewer's need.
7. A quick procedure for conducting an interview involves: developing behavioral specifications; determining the basic intellectual, motivation,

personality, and experience factors to probe for; using an interview plan; and then matching the individual to the job.

8. Effective interviewing can contribute directly to increasing the performance in your organization. First, it helps you select the best qualified candidates—ones who have the ability and potential to do the job. Second, a candidate's motivation is one of the traits most accurately measured during an interview.

KEY TERMS

nondirective interview

patterned interview

structured interview

serialized interview

panel interview

stress interview

appraisal interview

candidate-order error

DISCUSSION QUESTIONS

1. Do interviews have to be a waste of time? Why? Why not?
2. Explain at least six factors that affect the usefulness of interviews.
3. Discuss our guidelines for being a more effective interviewer.
4. Write a short presentation entitled "How to Be Effective as an Interviewee."

♦ APPLICATION EXERCISES

♦ CASE INCIDENT

Vice-President for Discouragement

The selection program in a medium-sized manufacturing firm has, for several years, maintained a panel-type interviewing procedure, one interview following another, for all applicants who are believed likely to move into supervisory and managerial positions. After a preliminary screening interview by a recruiter, candidates meet with each of six company officers, including one representative of the industrial relations department.

One vice-president is insistent that he be included on all such panels. He is impressed with what he regards as a tendency of modern business to "coddle" and "baby" new recruits. He says they should know the basic "economic facts of life." He thinks they should be told to expect to work long hours and to encounter many frustrations and discouragements. Accordingly, in his visits with candidates, he "gets rough" and "gives them the works."

The effects of his interviewing are readily apparent. Several candidates regarded by other interviewers as most promising have decided against joining the firm. Some of them have said bluntly that they don't want to work with an outfit that has such a vice-president. One candidate advised two panel members that they ought to leave the firm on this account.

Questions
1. Do you think this firm has a good interviewing/screening procedure? Why? Why not?
2. Do you think these "realistic" job previews are a good idea? Why? Why not?

3. What should be done about this person someone has dubbed the "vice-president for discouragement"? He has several years to serve before retirement. Would it be fair, if it is possible, to keep him off the panels? Could he be encouraged to change his tactics? What approach would you suggest?

Source: Dale Yoder, *Personnel Management and Industrial Relations* (Englewood Cliffs, N.J.: Prentice-Hall, 1970), p. 324.

EXPERIENTIAL EXERCISE

Purpose. The purposes of this exercise are:
1. To give you practice in developing a structured interview form, and
2. To give you practice in using this form.

Required Understanding. The reader should be familiar with the interviewing problems we discussed, and with the example of the structured interview form presented in Figure 6.3.

How to Set Up the Exercise/Instructions:
1. Set up groups of four or five students. One student will be the "interviewee" while the other students in the group will develop the structured interview form and, as a group, interview the interviewee.
2. Instructions for the *interviewee:* Please do not read the exercise beyond this point (you can leave the room for a few minutes).
3. Instructions for the *interviewers.* You may be a plant manager or assistant plant manager but in any case you have to interview a candidate for programming supervisor in about an hour. Each of you knows you'd be best off using a structured interview form to guide the interview, so you're now meeting for about half an hour to *develop such a form,* based in part on the job description presented in Figure 3.10. (*Hint:* Start by listing the most relevant abilities and then rate these in importance on a 5-point scale. Then use the high-rated abilities on your interview form.)
4. As soon as you have completed your structured interview form, call in your interviewee and explain to him that he is a candidate for the job and that the plant manager, the assistant plant manager (whom the candidate will report to if hired), and perhaps one or more programmers will interview him as a group. You may tell the interviewee what his or her job summary calls for.

    Next, interview the candidate, with each interviewer separately keeping notes on his or her own copy of the group's structured interview form. Each interviewer can take turns asking questions.

    After the interview, discuss the following questions in the group: Based on each interviewer's notes, how similar were your perceptions of the candidate's responses? Did you all agree on the candidate's potential for the job? Did the candidate ask good questions of his or her interviewers? Did any of the interviewers find themselves jumping to conclusions about the candidate?

NOTES
1. Neal Schmitt, "Social and Situational Determinants of Interview Decisions: Implications for the Employment Interview," *Personnel Psychology,* Vol. 29 (Spring 1976), pp. 79–101; Lynn Ulrich and Don Trumbo, "The Selection Interview Since 1949," *Psychological Bulletin,* Vol. 63 (1965), pp. 100–116. See, however, Frank Landy, "The Validity of the Interview in Police Officer Selection," *Journal of*

Applied Psychology, Vol. 61 (1976), pp. 193–198. See also Vincent Loretto, "Effective Interviewing Is Based on More than Intuition," *Personnel Journal*, Vol. 65 (December 1986), pp. 101–107; and George Dreher et al., "The Role of the Traditional Research Design in Underestimating the Validity of the Employment Interview," *Personnel Psychology*, Vol. 41, no. 2 (Summer 1988), pp. 315–328.

2. Richard Arvey and James Campion, "The Employment Interview: A Summary and Review of Recent Research," *Personnel Psychology*, Vol. 35 (Summer 1982), pp. 281–322. See also Richard Arvey, Howard Miller, Richard Gould, and Philip Burch, "Interview Validity for Selecting Sales Clerks," *Personnel Psychology*, Vol. 40 (Spring 1987), pp. 1–12; and Amanda Phillips and Robert Dipboye, "Correctional Tests of Predictions from a Process Model of the Interview," *Journal of Applied Psychology*, Vol. 74, no. 1 (February 1989), pp. 41–52.

3. Landy, "The Validity"; M. Rothstein and D. Jackson, "Decision Making in the Employment Interview and Experimental Approach," *Journal of Applied Psychology*, Vol. 66 (1980), pp. 271–283.

4. Schmitt, "Social and Situational Determinants of Interview Decisions," pp. 79–101; G. Latham and others, "The Situational Interview," *Journal of Applied Psychology*, Vol. 65 (1980), pp. 422–427; A. Keenan, "Effects of the Non-Verbal Behavior of Interviewers on Candidates' Performance," *Journal of Occupational Psychology*, Vol. 49 (1976), pp. 170–176. See also Michael Campion and James Campion, "Evaluation of an Interviewee Skills Training Program in a Natural Field Experiment," *Personnel Psychology*, Vol. 40, no. 4 (Winter 1987), pp. 675–692.

5. Frank Landy and Don Trumbo, *Psychology of Work Behavior* (Homewood, Ill.: Dorsey Press, 1976), p. 185. See also Richard D. Arvey et al., "Interview Validity for Selecting Sales Clerks," *Personnel Psychology*, Vol. 40, no. 1 (Spring 1987), pp. 1–12.

6. Arthur Pell, *Recruiting and Selecting Personnel* (New York: Regents, 1969), pp. 120–121.

7. See Latham, "The Situational Interview"; Elliott Pursell, Michael Campion, and Sara Gaylord, "Structured Interviewing: Avoiding Selection Problems," *Personnel Journal*, Vol. 59 (November 1980), pp. 907–912. See also Jeff Weekley and Joseph Gier, "Reliability and Validity of the Situational Interview for a Sales Position," *Journal of Applied Psychology*, Vol. 72, no. 3 (August 1987), pp. 484–487. See also Michael A. Campion, Elliott Pursell, and Barbara Brown, "Structured Interviewing: Raising the Psychometric Properties of the Employment Interview," *Personnel Psychology*, Vol. 41, no. 1 (Spring 1988), pp. 25–42; and Steven Maurer and Charles Fay, "Effect of Situational Interviews, Conventional Structured Interviews, and Training on Interview Rating Agreement: An Experimental Analysis," *Personnel Psychology*, Vol. 41, no. 2 (Summer 1988), pp. 329–344.

8. Pell, *Recruiting and Selecting Personnel*, p. 119.

9. S. W. Constantin, "An Investigation of Information Favorability in the Employment Interview," *Journal of Applied Psychology*, Vol. 61 (1976), pp. 743–749. It should be noted that a number of the studies discussed in this chapter involve having interviewers evaluate interviews based on written transcripts (rather than face to face) and that a study suggests that this procedure may not be equivalent to having interviewers interview applicants directly. See Charles Gorman, William Grover, and Michael Doherty, "Can We Learn Anything About Interviewing Real People from 'Interviews' of Paper People? A Study of the External Validity Paradigm," *Organizational Behavior and Human Performance*, Vol. 22, no. 2 (October 1978), pp. 165–192. See also John Binning et al., "Effects of Pre-interview Impressions on Questioning Strategies in Same and Opposite Sex Employment Interviews," *Journal of Applied Psychology*, Vol. 73, no. 1 (February 1988), pp. 30–37; and Sebastiano Fisicaro, "A Reexamination of the Relation Between Halo Error and Accuracy," *Journal of Applied Psychology*, Vol. 73, no. 2 (May 1988), pp. 239–246.

10. David Tucker and Patricia Rowe, "Relationship Between Expectancy, Casual Attribution, and Final Hiring Decisions in the Employment Interview," *Journal of Applied Psychology*, Vol. 64, no. 1 (February 1979), pp. 27–34. See also Robert

Dipboye, Gail Fontenelle, and Kathleen Garner, "Effect of Previewing the Application on Interview Process and Outcomes," *Journal of Applied Psychology,* Vol. 69, no. 1 (February 1984), pp. 118–128.

11. Don Langdale and Joseph Weitz, "Estimating the Influence of Job Information on Interviewer Agreement," *Journal of Applied Psychology,* Vol. 57 (1973), pp. 23–27.

12. R. E. Carlson, "Selection Interview Decisions: The Effects of Interviewer Experience, Relative Quota Situation, and Applicant Sample on Interview Decisions," *Personnel Psychology,* Vol. 20 (1967), pp. 259–280.

13. R. E. Carlson, "Effects of Applicant Sample on Ratings of Valid Information in an Employment Setting," *Journal of Applied Psychology,* Vol. 54 (1970), pp. 217–222.

14. See Richard Arvey and James Campion, "The Employment Interview: A Summary and Review of Recent Research," *Personnel Psychology,* Vol. 35 (Summer 1982), p. 305.

15. T. V. McGovern and H. E. Tinsley, "Interviewer Evaluations of Interviewees' Nonverbal Behavior," *Journal of Vocational Behavior,* Vol. 13 (1978), pp. 163–171. See also Keith Rasmussen, Jr., "Nonverbal Behavior, Verbal Behavior, Resume Credentials, and Selection Interview Outcomes," *Journal of Applied Psychology,* Vol. 60, no. 4 (1984), pp. 551–556; Robert Gifford, Cheuk Fan Ng, and Margaret Wilkinson, "Nonverbal Cues in the Employment Interview: Links Between Applicant Qualities and Interviewer Judgments," *Journal of Applied Psychology,* Vol. 70, no. 4 (1985), pp. 729–736.

16. Madelaine Heilmann and Lewis Saruwatari, "When Beauty Is Beastly: The Effects of Appearance and Sex on Evaluation of Job Applicants for Managerial and Nonmanagerial Jobs," *Organizational Behavior and Human Performance,* Vol. 23 (June 1979), pp. 360–372. See also Tracy McDonald and Milton Hakel, "Effects of Applicant Race, Sex, Suitabilty, and Answers on Interviewers' Questioning Strategy and Ratings," *Personnel Psychology,* Vol. 38, no. 2 (Summer 1985), pp. 321–334. See also M. S. Singer and Christine Sewell, "Applicant Age and Selection Interview Decisions: Effect of Information Exposure on Age Discrimination in Personnel Selection," *Personnel Psychology,* Vol. 42, no. 1 (Spring 1989), pp. 135–154.

17. Sandra Forsythe, Mary Frances Drake, and Charles Cox, "Influence of Applicants' Dress on Interviewers' Selection Decisions," *Journal of Applied Psychology,* Vol. 70, no. 2 (1985), pp. 374–378.

18. Pell, *Recruiting and Selecting Personnel,* pp. 103–115.

19. Carlson, "Selection Interview Decisions," pp. 259–280.

20. William Tullar, Terry Mullins, and Sharon Caldwell, "Effects of Interview Length and Applicant Quality on Interview Decision Time," *Journal of Applied Psychology,* Vol. 64 (December 1979), pp. 669–674. See also Tracy McDonald and Milton Hakel, "Effects of Applicants' Race, Sex, Suitability, and Answers on Interviewers' Questioning Strategy and Ratings," *Personnel Psychology,* Vol. 38 (Summer 1985), pp. 321–334.

21. Tullar et al., "The Effects of Interview Lengths."

22. Ibid., p. 674.

23. See David Tucker and Patricia Rowe, "Consulting the Application Form Prior to the Interview: An Essential Step in the Selection Process," *Journal of Applied Psychology,* Vol. 63, no. 3 (1977), pp. 283–287.

24. Landy and Trumbo, *Psychology of Work Behavior.*

25. Robert Dipboye, Richard Arvey, and David Terpstra, "Equal Employment and the Interview," *Personnel Journal,* Vol. 55 (October 1976).

26. Frederic M. Jablin, "Use of Discrimination Questions in Screening Interviews," *Personnel Administrator,* Vol. 27, no. 3 (March 1982), pp. 41–44; also see Clifford M. Koen, Jr., "The Pre-employment Inquiry Guide," *Personnel Journal,* Vol. 59, no. 10 (October 1980), pp. 825–829.

27. This section based on Pursell, Campion, and Gaylord, "Structured Interviewing," and Latham et al., "The Situational Interview." See also Michael A. Campion, Elliott Pursell, and Barbara Brown, "Structured Interviewing:

Raising the Psychometric Properties of the Employment Interview," *Personnel Psychology*, Vol. 41, no. 1 (Spring 1988), pp. 25–42, and Jeff Weekley and Joseph Gier, "Reliability and Validity of the Situational Interview for a Sales Position," *Journal of Applied Psychology*, Vol. 72, no. 3 (August 1987), pp. 484–487.

28. Pursell et al., "Structured Interviewing," p. 910.

29. From a speech by industrial psychologist Paul Green and contained in BNA *Bulletin to Management*, June 20, 1985, pp. 2–3.

30. This is based on John Drake, *Interviewing for Managers: A Complete Guide to Employment Interviewing* (New York: AMACOM, 1982).

31. Ibid.

32. James Hollandsworth, Jr., and others, "Relative Contributions of Verbal, Articulative, and Nonverbal Communication to Employment Decisions in the Job Interview Setting," *Personnel Psychology*, Vol. 32 (Summer 1979), pp. 359–367. See also Sara Rynes and Howard Miller, "Recruiter and Job Influences on Candidates for Employment," *Journal of Applied Psychology*, Vol. 68, no. 1 (1983), pp. 147–154.

33. Richard Payne, *How to Get a Better Job Quickly* (New York: New American Library, 1979).

34. J. G. Hollandsworth, R. C. Ladinski, and J. H. Russel, "Use of Social Skills Training in the Treatment of Extreme Anxiety of Deficient Verbal Skills," *Journal of Applied Psychology*, Vol. 11 (1979), pp. 259–269.

PART TWO

TRAINING AND DEVELOPMENT

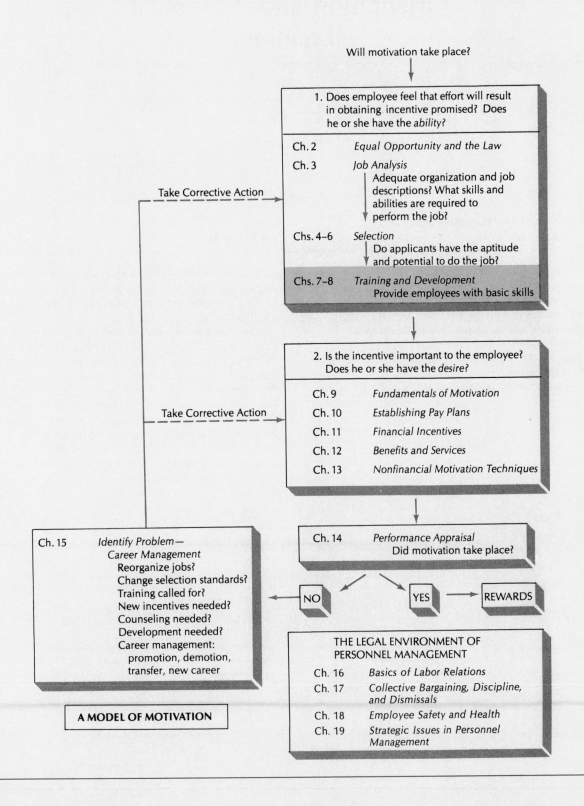

Will motivation take place?

1. Does employee feel that effort will result in obtaining incentive promised? Does he or she have the *ability*?

Ch. 2	*Equal Opportunity and the Law*
Ch. 3	*Job Analysis*
	Adequate organization and job descriptions? What skills and abilities are required to perform the job?
Chs. 4–6	*Selection*
	Do applicants have the aptitude and potential to do the job?
Chs. 7–8	*Training and Development*
	Provide employees with basic skills

Take Corrective Action

2. Is the incentive important to the employee? Does he or she have the *desire*?

Ch. 9	*Fundamentals of Motivation*
Ch. 10	*Establishing Pay Plans*
Ch. 11	*Financial Incentives*
Ch. 12	*Benefits and Services*
Ch. 13	*Nonfinancial Motivation Techniques*

Take Corrective Action

Ch. 15   *Identify Problem— Career Management*
Reorganize jobs?
Change selection standards?
Training called for?
New incentives needed?
Counseling needed?
Development needed?
Career management: promotion, demotion, transfer, new career

Ch. 14   *Performance Appraisal*
Did motivation take place?

NO   YES   REWARDS

THE LEGAL ENVIRONMENT OF PERSONNEL MANAGEMENT

Ch. 16	*Basics of Labor Relations*
Ch. 17	*Collective Bargaining, Discipline, and Dismissals*
Ch. 18	*Employee Safety and Health*
Ch. 19	*Strategic Issues in Personnel Management*

A MODEL OF MOTIVATION

Chapter 7

Orientation and Technical Training

When you finish studying this chapter, you should be able to:

1. List the important factors in an employee orientation and socialization program.
2. Develop and implement a training program.
3. Explain how to distinguish between training problems and those not amenable to training.
4. Discuss four training techniques.
5. Explain how you would go about identifying training requirements.
6. Prepare a job instruction training chart for a job.

OVERVIEW

As you can see from our motivation model, the next step in placing employees is to be sure they have the skills to do their jobs, and this often involves training. The main purpose of this chapter is thus to increase your effectiveness as a trainer. We first briefly explain orientation, which (with training) is used to assimilate the new employee into the organization. We then explain technical training, which involves determining what skills must be taught and teaching them. Then, in the next chapter, we turn to management development, which involves giving managers the leadership skills they need to do their present and future jobs. Training (and development) are thus the final steps in ensuring that your employees have the knowledge and skills they need to do their jobs.

Once you've successfully recruited and selected employees, your next stop is to orient and train them. Here is where you provide them with the information and skills they need to be successful on their new jobs.

As you can see from our model, orientation and training are important factors in motivation. For motivation to take place your employees must believe that effort will result in rewards. And it's through orientation and training that you provide them with the knowledge and skills they need to carry out their tasks successfully and earn those rewards.

ORIENTATION

♦ WHY USE ORIENTATION?

Think back for a moment about how you felt during your first day on a job. If you were like most people, you were a little tense and your anxiety level was probably higher than usual. Remember how relieved you were when some of the other people at work invited you to lunch! These kinds of "first-day jitters" are typical for new employees. Thus in one study at the Texas Instruments Company, researchers discovered the following about new employees:

The first days on the job were anxious and disturbing ones.

"New employee initiation" practices by peers intensified anxiety.

Anxiety interfered with the training process.

Turnover of newly hired employees was caused primarily by anxiety.

The new workers were reluctant to discuss problems with their supervisors.

employee orientation A procedure for introducing new employees to the organization and helping them adjust to the demands of the firm.

Employee orientation is aimed at minimizing such problems. Its purpose is to introduce the new employee and the organization to each other, to help them become acquainted, and to help them accommodate each other.[1]

♦ PROBLEMS OF ENTRY

There are three main reasons for such first-day jitters.[2] One is that any new situation involves *change*, and the more that things are different, the more change and uncertainty the person will have to cope with.

Unrealistic expectations are a second problem. New employees often have unrealistically high expectations about the advantages of their new jobs, and are often shocked at the reality of getting less than they bargained for.[3] Hall calls this **reality shock**, a condition caused by the incompatibility between what the employees expect in their new jobs (in terms of challenge, for instance) and the realities they are often confronted with (perhaps in terms of a boring first job).[4]

reality shock Employee disillusionment due to discrepancies between the recruiter's unrealistic description of a job and the actual duties required.

Finally, *surprise* can produce anxiety. The first surprise often comes when expectations about the job are not fulfilled, as when unrealistic expectations regarding job challenge collide with a job that is undemanding. Surprise may also occur when expectations about one's self are unmet, or when features of the job, such as the need to work late hours, are unanticipated.

♦ WHAT NEWCOMERS NEED

To minimize problems like these, new employees need two things. First, they need basic information about the employer. This basic information should include, for example, how to get on the payroll, how to obtain identification cards, what the working hours are, and who the new employee will be working with. The employer's new-employee **orientation program** is aimed at providing this type of data. New employees also need to be **socialized,** in other words to *learn the attitudes, standards, values, and patterns of behavior that are expected by the organization and its management;* the new employee, in other words, has to "learn the ropes."

Socialization serves several purposes. It reduces new-employee anxiety by familiarizing the person with what is expected in terms of attitudes, values, and behaviors. It helps ensure consistent and predictable behavior by molding the employee's attitudes and values to those of the employer. It reduces the need for policies, procedures, and rules, to the extent that employees know how to act—and do so. And by making the new employee feel like "one of the family" it can increase the person's commitment to the organization, and to that extent may boost morale, reduce turnover, and lead to higher performance than might occur in its absence. Socialization, therefore, is an important human resource process.

orientation program A training program for new employees in which the personnel department and supervisors outline policies, rules, regulations, and benefits of employment, usually provide an employee handbook, and provide introductions to fellow workers.

socialized Socialization programs teach new employees the attitudes, standards, values, and behaviors that are expected by the organization.

◆ ORIENTATION AND SOCIALIZATION TECHNIQUES

Orientation

Orientation means providing new employees with basic information about the employer, information that they need to perform their jobs satisfactorily. This basic information includes such facts as how to get on the payroll, how to obtain identification cards, what the working hours are, and who the new employee will be working with. Orientation is actually one component of the employer's new-employee socialization process, an ongoing process that involves instilling in all employees the prevailing attitudes, standards, values, and patterns of behavior that are expected by the organization and its departments. The employee's initial orientation, if handled correctly, can help reduce the new employee's first-day jitters as well as the reality shock the person might otherwise experience.

Orientation programs range from brief informal introductions to lengthy, formal programs. In the latter, the new employee is usually given a handbook or printed materials that cover matters like working hours, performance reviews, getting on the payroll, and vacations, as well as a tour of the facilities. As illustrated in the orientation handbook presented in Figure 7.1,[5] other information typically includes employee benefits, personnel policies, the employee's daily routine, company organization and operations, and safety measures and regulations.

Handbook Caveats

Given the real possibility that courts today will find that your employee handbook's contents represent a contract with the employee, disclaimers should be included that make it clear that statements of company policies, benefits, and regulations do not constitute the terms and conditions of an employment contract either express or implied. You should also stress that as the employer you have the right to change your policies and rules at any time without notice. Beyond that, common sense dictates that you document job performance problems and place a copy of that documentation in workers' files and train supervisors to conduct appraisals fairly and objectively.[6] Think twice before including statements in your handbook such as "no employee will be fired without just cause" or statements that imply or state that employees have tenure; they could be viewed as legal and binding commitments.

FIGURE 7.1
Contents of Orientation Handbook

Source: *Handbook of Modern Personnel Administration* by Joseph Famularo. Copyright 1972, McGraw-Hill Book Company. Used with permission.

Employee's Name:	Discussion Completed (please check each individual item)

I. Word of welcome

II. Explain overall departmental organization and its relationship to other activities of the company

III. Explain employee's individual contribution to the objectives of the department and his starting assignment in broad terms

IV. Discuss job content with employee and give him a copy of job description (if available)

V. Explain departmental training program(s) and salary increase practices and procedures

VI. Discuss where the employee lives and transportation facilities

VII. Explain working conditions:
    a. Hours of work, time sheets
    b. Use of employee entrance and elevators
    c. Lunch hours
    d. Coffee breaks, rest periods
    e. Personal telephone calls and mail
    f. Overtime policy and requirements
    g. Paydays and procedure for being paid
    h. Lockers
    i. Other _____

VIII. Requirements for continuance of employment—explain company standards as to:
    a. Performance of duties
    b. Attendance and punctuality
    c. Handling confidential information
    d. Behavior
    e. General appearance
    f. Wearing of uniform

IX. Introduce new staff member to manager(s) and other supervisors.
Special attention should be paid to the person to whom the new employee will be assigned.

X. Release employee to immediate supervisor who will:
    a. Introduce new staff member to fellow workers
    b. Familiarize the employee with his workplace
    c. Begin on-the-job training

If not applicable, insert N/A in space provided.

Employee's Signature	Supervisor's Signature
Date	Division

Form examined for filing:

Date	Personnel Department

Conducting the Orientation

The orientation activities themselves are usually split between the person's new supervisor and the human resource department. The supervisor often gets an orientation checklist similar to that in Figure 7.2. This helps to ensure that the supervisor has covered all the necessary orientation steps like "explain organization" and "introduce to fellow workers."

In most firms, though, the first part of the orientation is performed by the human resource specialist, who explains such matters as working hours and vacation. The employee is then introduced to his or her new supervisor, who continues the orientation by explaining the exact nature of the job, introducing the person to his or her new colleagues, and familiarizing the person with the workplace.

FIGURE 7.2

Supervisor's Orientation Checklist

Source: *Handbook of Modern Personnel Administration* by Joseph Famularo. Copyright 1972, McGraw-Hill Book Company. Used with permission.

ITEMS TO BE DISCUSSED BY DEPARTMENT HEAD OR SUPERVISOR WITH NEW EMPLOYEE:

FIRST DAY OF EMPLOYMENT
- ☐ 1. Introduction to Co-workers
- ☐ 2. Information on Location of Facilities
  - A. Coat Room
  - B. Cafeteria
  - C. Wash Room
  - D. Bulletin Board
  - E. Coffee Service
  - F. Provision for Lunch

RULES AND POLICIES
- ☐ 3. Hours: starting, lunch, dismissal time, hours per week
- ☐ 4. Pay: when, where, and how paid—overtime policy
     (Explain deductions when 1st check is received.)
- ☐ 5. Holidays and Vacations in Detail
- ☐ 6. Probationary Period
- ☐ 7. Absences: Pay Policies—before and after 5 months. When and whom to phone. Visit to Medical Dept. or Doctor's note before return to work after absence of 3 or more days.
- ☐ 8. Organization of Department
     Corporation—Division—Department—Section
- ☐ 9. Rules on:
     Tardiness, Telephone Coverage, Behavior, etc.

DURING FIRST TWO WEEKS OF EMPLOYMENT
- ☐ 10. Accident:
      Reporting accident or injury on job
- ☐ 11. Employee's Discount on XYZ Company products
- ☐ 12. Salary Checks—Explanation of Deductions
- ☐ 13. Salary Reviews
- ☐ 14. Employee Appraisal Plan
- ☐ 15. Suggestion System
- ☐ 16. Reporting Change in Address, Name, Phone, etc.
- ☐ 17. Invite Questions and Help on Problems

As indicated by check marks, all of the above items have been discussed with the employee.

The employee has been advised as to the time and extent of 1st vacation as shown by the Table on last page of this form.

Employee has been instructed to attend the second scheduled meeting and to bring this check list with him.

_____

DEPARTMENT HEAD OR SUPERVISOR

_____

DATE

A more detailed listing of what the human resource department and supervisor each might be expected to cover during orientation is summarized in Figure 7.3. The human resource department performs the general company orientation, including overview of the organization, policies and procedures, compensation, and the like. The person's new supervisor then does the specific departmental orientation, including department functions, and the employee's new job duties.

Even new executives can benefit from an orientation program. As one expert points out, "by the time a new executive has finished a year on the job, the company may have spent hundreds of thousands of dollars on him or her—including salary, bonus, and moving expenses. After committing that kind of money to finding and launching a new executive, it makes good business sense for human resources managers to make sure that everything possible is done to integrate the new man or woman into the company."

FIGURE 7.2
(continued)

```
NAME OF                                    STARTING
EMPLOYEE_____ DATE _____

DEPARTMENT _____ LOCATION_____
```

ITEMS COVERED BY PERSONNEL RELATIONS DEPARTMENT OR
BRANCH OFFICE ON FIRST DAY OF ORIENTATION: (45 minutes)

PART 1—Organization and Personnel Policies & Procedures

☐ 1. XYZ Company Organization
☐ 2. Basic Insurance Benefits *(Paid in full by the company)*
    ☐ A. Hospitalization
    ☐ B. Short-Term Disability
    ☐ C. Basic Life Insurance
    ☐ D. Travel Accident
☐ 3. Optional Insurance Benefits *(Paid for by you and the company)*
    ☐ A. Comprehensive Medical
    ☐ B. Contributory Life Insurance
    ☐ C. Long Term Disability

☐ 4. Vacations   ☐ 11. XYZ Company News
☐ 5. Holidays   ☐ 12. Tuition Refund Plan
☐ 6. Probationary Period   ☐ 13. Building Facilities
☐ 7. Compensation   ☐ 14. New Building
☐ 8. Job Evaluation   ☐ 15. XYZ Company and You
☐ 9. Medical Absence   ☐ 16. Equal Opportunity
☐ 10. Personal Status Change   Employment
      Notice

★ ★ ★ ★ ★

APPOINTMENT FOR SECOND MEETING: (45 minutes)

DATE _____ *TIME* _____

*IMPORTANT: BE SURE TO BRING THIS FORM BACK
WITH YOU, SIGNED BY YOUR MANAGER
WHEN YOU COME TO YOUR SCHEDULED
SECOND MEETING.*

PART II—Personnel Policies and Procedures

☐ 1. Review & Questions on   ☐ 7. XYZ Company Investment
    Part 1   Plan
☐ 2. Retirement Program   ☐ 8. U.S. Savings Bonds
☐ 3. College Gift Matching   ☐ 9. Employee Activities
    Plan
☐ 4. Time Off the Job   ☐ 10. Suggestion System
☐ 5. Award for Recruiting   ☐ 11. Personnel Inventory
☐ 6. Credit Union

```
_____
PERSONNEL RELATIONS STAFF REPRESENTATIVE

_____
DATE
```

One suggestion is to assign the new executive to a senior "sponsor," preferably the person to whom he or she will be reporting. The sponsor should make sure that the new executive gets up-to-date information about the firm's goals and strategy in written form and should discuss the material with him or her to answer any questions that may arise. There should also be a series of confidential briefings by the key department heads.[7]

Some companies also provide new employees with special anxiety-reduction seminars. For example, when the Texas Instruments Company found out how high the anxiety level of its new employees was, it initiated special full-day seminars. These focused on information about the company and the job and allowed many opportunities for questions and answers. The new employees were told what to expect in terms of rumors and hazing

FIGURE 7.3

Items Typically Covered by Employers During Orientation

Source: Reprinted from "Let's Not Forget about New Employee Orientation" by R. W. Hollman. Copyright 1976. Reprinted with permission from *Personnel Journal,* Costa Mesa, California. All rights reserved.

GENERAL COMPANY ORIENTATION	SPECIFIC DEPARTMENTAL ORIENTATION
The following items are among those typically included in this first phase: 1. Overview of the organization—brief history, what the organization does (products/services), where it does it (branches, etc.), how it does it (nature of operations), structure (organization chart), etc. 2. Policies and procedures—work schedules, vacations, holidays, grievances, identification badges, uniforms, leaves of absence (sickness, educational, military, maternity/paternity, personal), promotion, transfers, training, etc. 3. Compensation—pay scale, overtime, holiday pay, shift differentials, when and how paid, time clock, etc. 4. Benefits—insurance, retirement, tax sheltered annuities, credit union, employee discounts, suggestion system, recreational activities, etc. 5. Safety information—relevant policies and procedures, fire protection, first aid facilities, safety committee, etc. 6. Union—name, affiliation, officials, joining procedure, contract, etc. 7. Physical facilities—plant/office layout, employee entrance, parking, cafeteria, etc.	The following items are typically covered in this phase: 1. Department functions—explanation of the objectives, activities, and structure of the department, along with a description of how the department's activities relate to those of other departments and the overall company. 2. Job duties—a detailed explanation of the duties of the new employee's job (give him/her a copy of the job description) and how the job relates to the activities of the department. 3. Policies and procedures—those that are unique to the department, such as breaks, rest periods, lunch hour, use of time sheets, safety, etc. 4. Department tour—a complete familiarization with the departmental facilities, including lockers, equipment, emergency exits, supply room, etc. 5. Introduction to departmental employees.

from old employees. They were also told that it was very likely they would succeed on their jobs. These special seminars proved to be very useful. By the end of the first month, the new employees who had participated in the seminar were performing much better than were those who had not.[8] Orientation is one activity that contributes to the new employee's successful socialization into the firm; some other socialization activities are as follows.

Realistic Job Previews

realistic job previews Interviews aimed at showing job candidates the actual nature of their responsibilities and duties, as opposed to a glowing and unrealistic picture.

Realistic job previews are aimed at showing prospective employees what their jobs will actually entail (as opposed to the more traditional approach, where employers just try to make their firms look as attractive as possible).

Providing recruits with realistic previews of what to expect once they begin working in the organization is an effective way of minimizing reality shock. Schein points out that one of the biggest problems recruits and management encounter during the entry stage involves obtaining accurate information.[9] The recruiter, anxious to attract good candidates, and the candidate, anxious to present as favorable an impression as possible, often give and receive unrealistic information during the interview.[10] The result is that the interviewer may not be able to form a realistic picture of a candidate's career goals. At the same time, the candidate forms an unrealistically favorable image of the organization. Giving candidates realistic previews of what to expect once they begin working on the job can avert surprise and disappointment and improve the employee's performance.[11] Recently, several organizations including the Prudential Insurance Company, Texas Instruments, Southern New England Telephone, and the U.S. Military Academy have utilized this "realistic" approach, apparently with good results.[12]

Creating the Right Company Culture

culture An organization's culture is the prevailing attitudes and values that characterize its employees.

An organization's **culture** can be defined as the *prevailing attitudes and perceptions employees have of the sort of organization in which they are working.* In other words, employees pick up cues about their organizations—how fairly they are appraised or how friendly their leader is, for instance—and from these cues they form a composite picture concerning the sort of organization in which they are working.

Organizations use many techniques to create a prevailing culture and to socialize or absorb new employees into its tradition. At West Point, entering "plebes" are put under the command of upper classmen who help establish the Academy's values of "duty, honor, and country" in all new students. In their book *In Search of Excellence*, Peters and Waterman describe how at IBM numerous stories—almost legends—abound regarding how successful employees helped to operationalize the founder's motto that "IBM means service."

PepsiCo, Inc., is a good example of how employees can be socialized in practice. To top management of PepsiCo, creating an aggressive and competitive culture is an important part of achieving leadership in the soft drink industry.[13] In a multitude of ways, therefore, PepsiCo management endeavors to create this competitive culture. Severe pressure is put on managers to show continual improvement in market share, and careers often ride on tenths of a market share point, according to one source. A "creative tension" is nurtured at the company by constantly moving managers to new jobs. This tactic results in people working long hours and engaging in political maneuvering just to keep their jobs from being reorganized out from under them.

Like Marines, Pepsi executives are also expected to be physically fit. The company employs four physical fitness instructors at its headquarters, and one former executive claims that to get ahead in the company, a manager must stay in shape. The company also encourages one-on-one sports as well as interdepartmental games of soccer and basketball.

The pervasive culture of competition at Pepsi has the effect of screening out less competitive managers, of course. But the socialization process is very complete, and the ones that remain have the competitive values and attitudes that top management believes are required if their firm is to become number one.[14]

Foster Links

Another way to help socialize new employees is to foster links between them and their new coworkers or superiors, who act as mentors.[15] For example, some employers support formal programs such as buddy systems in which employee-mentors receive special training and serve as guides for newcomers.

Performance Feedback

Your employer's performance appraisal system also plays an important role in socialization.[16] Timely formal and informal feedback from superiors to newcomers about their performance may reduce the stress-producing uncertainty of "not knowing how you are doing, or where you stand." Similarly, they can help new employees to decide how to perform in the future. For example, an early appraisal can be used as a "sense-making" effort, in which any misperceptions can be corrected.[17]

Conclusion

In practice, though, "daily interactions with peers while working" seems to be the most important factor in helping newcomers to feel effective. While formal on-site orientation sessions and off-site residential training sessions were helpful for fostering loyalty to and identification with the company, job satisfaction and newcomer intentions to stay with the firm were not significantly correlated with programs like these.[18] The new employees' relationships with their peers were.

THE NATURE OF TECHNICAL TRAINING

♦ INTRODUCTION

technical training The process of teaching new employees the basic skills they need to perform their jobs.

Technical training involves giving new or present employees the basic skills they need to perform their jobs. Technical training might thus involve showing a machinist how to operate his new machine, a new salesperson how to sell her firm's product, or even a new supervisor how to interview and appraise employees. Whereas technical training is aimed at providing new employees with the skills they need to perform their current jobs, *management development* (explained in Chapter 8) is training of a more long-term nature: Its aim is to develop the employee for some future job with the organization or to solve some organizational problem concerning, for instance, poor interdepartmental communication. The techniques used in both training and development are often the same, however, so that distinguishing between the two is always somewhat arbitrary.

Whether called training or development, training today is big business. For example, one survey concluded that *Personnel Journal* subscriber companies spent over $5.3 billion on training and development in 1988: This represents a 38% increase in training and development expenditures from a similar 1986 12-month period.[19]

Among these companies, the 1988 average expenditure per company for a 12-month period was $218,200. Small organizations (those with fewer than 500 employees) spent an average of $92,400. Medium-sized organizations (500–4,999) spent an average of $234,000, while companies with more than 5,000 employees spent an average of $521,300 for training and development.

♦ THE BASIC TRAINING PROCESS

Any training program ideally consists of four steps, which are summarized in Figure 7.4. The purpose of the *assessment* step is to determine if there is a performance deficiency that can be rectified by training. Then, if one or more deficiencies that can be eliminated through training are identified, *training objectives* should be set; here you specify in observable, measurable

FIGURE 7.4
The Four Basic Steps in Training

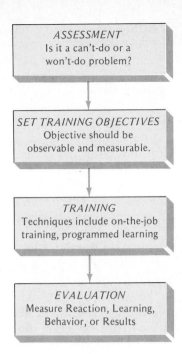

ASSESSMENT
Is it a can't-do or a
won't-do problem?

SET TRAINING OBJECTIVES
Objective should be
observable and measurable.

TRAINING
Techniques include on-the-job
training, programmed learning

EVALUATION
Measure Reaction, Learning,
Behavior, or Results

terms the performance you expect to obtain from the employees who are to be trained. In the *training* step the actual training techniques are chosen and the training takes place. Finally, there should be an *evaluation* step. Here the trainees' pre- and posttraining performances are compared, and the effectiveness of the training program is thus evaluated.

♦ LEGAL ASPECTS OF TRAINING

As explained in Chapter 2, equal employment legislation makes it illegal to discriminate unfairly against applicants or current employees on the basis of the person's age, race, sex, religion, or national origin. Several aspects of your training program must therefore be assessed with an eye toward the program's impact on women and minorities.[20] For example, the *admissions process* should be evaluated so that, where adverse impact exists and relatively few women or minorities are selected for the training program, you can show that the admissions procedures are valid—that they predict performance on the job for which the person is being trained.

Similarly, if you plan to use "completion of training" as a job prerequisite, you should attempt to show that the training program itself has no adverse impact on women or minorities. Specifically, these individuals should have as much chance of successfully completing the training as white males; if they do not, the validity of the training requirements should be demonstrated. For example, it could turn out that the reading level of your training manuals is too high for many minority trainees, and that they are thus doing poorly in the program *quite aside from their aptitude for the jobs for which they are being trained*. In such a case, your training program may be found to be unfairly discriminatory. As a rule, it appears that training success by itself is not a valid criterion for test selection and that actual on-the-job performance is preferred by most courts.[21]

♦ INTRODUCTION

The first step in training is to determine what training, if any, is required. Assessing the training needs of employees who are new to their jobs is a fairly straightforward matter. Your main task is to determine what the job entails and to break it down into subtasks, each of which is then taught to the new employee. But assessing the training needs of *present* employees can be more complex. Here the need for training is usually prompted by problems (like excess scrap), so you have the added task of deciding whether training is, in fact, the solution. Often, for instance, performance is down because the standards aren't clear or because the person is just not motivated.

The two main techniques for determining training requirements are *task analysis* and *performance analysis*. About 19% of employers reporting in one survey said they used **task analysis**—an analysis of the job's requirements—to determine the training required.[22] Task analysis is especially appropriate for determining the training needs of employees who are *new* to their jobs. About half the firms reporting said they used **performance analysis** to determine training requirements; this basically involves appraising the performance of *current* employees to determine if training could reduce performance problems like excess scrap or low output. Other techniques reportedly used to identify training needs included supervisor's reports, personnel records, management requests, observations, tests of job knowledge, and questionnaire surveys.[23]

To some extent your training program will also reflect your firm's overall human resource plans, plans that are themselves derived from the goals of the enterprise. Thus, a department store chain's goal to double their stores in the South means that plans must be made for staffing these new stores; these plans will in turn require that employees be selected and trained for the projected openings in the new stores.

task analysis A detailed study of a job to identify the skills required, so that an appropriate training program may be instituted.

performance analysis Careful study of performance to identify a deficiency and then correct it with new equipment, a new employee, or a training program, or some other adjustment.

♦ TASK ANALYSIS: ASSESSING THE TRAINING NEEDS OF NEW EMPLOYEES

Task analysis is especially appropriate for determining the training needs of employees who are new to their jobs. Particularly with lower-echelon workers, it is common to hire inexperienced personnel and train them—give them the necessary skills to perform the task. For such people the training needed is fairly obvious.[24] Here your aim is to develop the skills and knowledge required for effective performance, and so the training is usually based on task analysis—*a detailed study of the job itself to determine what specific skills*—like soldering (in the case of an assembly worker) or interviewing (in the case of a supervisor)—*are required*.

The *job description* and job specification are helpful in this regard. These list the specific duties and skills required on the job and become the basic reference point in determining the training required for performing the job.

Task Analysis Record Form

Some employers also use a *task analysis record form*. This consolidates information regarding the job's tasks and required skills in a form that's especially helpful for determining training requirements. As illustrated in Table 7.1, a task analysis record form contains six types of information:

Column 1. Here the job's main tasks and subtasks are listed. For example, if one major task is "Operate paper cutter," subtasks 1.1 through 1.5 might

TABLE 7.1   Tasks Analysis Record Form

TASK LIST	WHEN AND HOW OFTEN PERFORMED	QUANTITY AND QUALITY OF PERFORMANCE	CONDITIONS UNDER WHICH PERFORMED	SKILLS OR KNOWLEDGE REQUIRED	WHERE BEST LEARNED
1. Operate paper cutter	4 times per day		Noisy press-room: distractions		
1.1 Start motor					
1.2 Set cutting distance		±tolerance of 0.007 in.		Read gauge	On the job
1.3 Place paper on cutting table		Must be completely even to prevent uneven cut		Lift paper correctly	"
1.4 Push paper up to cutter				Must be even	"
1.5 Grasp safety release with left hand		100% of time, for safety		Essential for safety	On the job but practice first with no distractions
1.6 Grasp cutter release with right hand				Must keep both hands on releases	"
1.7 Simultaneously pull safety release with left hand and cutter release with right hand				"	"
1.8 Wait for cutter to retract		100% of time, for safety		"	"
1.9 Retract paper				Wait till cutter retracts	"
1.10 Shut off		100% of time, for safety			"
2. Operate printing press					
2.1 Start motor					
.					
.					
.					

Note: Task analysis record form showing some of tasks and subtasks performed by printing pressman.

include "Start motor," "Set cutting distance," "Place paper on cutting table," "Push paper up to cutter," and "Grasp safety release with left hand."

Column 2. Here you indicate the *frequency* with which the task and subtasks are performed. For example, is it performed only once at the beginning of the shift, or many times, hour after hour?

Column 3. Here indicate the *standards of performance* for each task and subtask. These show the level to be attained by the trainee and should be as specific as possible. They should be expressed in measurable terms like "± tolerance of 0.007 in.," "Twelve units per hour," or "Within two days of receiving the order," for instance.

Column 4. Here indicate the *conditions* under which the tasks and subtasks are to be performed. This is especially important if the conditions are crucial to the training—for example, where (as in the case of an air traffic controller) the person normally has to work under conditions of turmoil and stress.

Column 5. This is the heart of the task analysis form; here you list the *skills* or *knowledge* required for each of the tasks and subtasks. Here you specify exactly what knowledge or skills you must teach the trainee. Thus, for the subtask "Set cutting distance" the person must be taught how to read the gauge.

Column 6. Here you indicate whether the task is learned best *on* or *off the job.* Your decision here is based on several considerations. Safety is one: For example, prospective jet pilots must learn something about the plane off the job, in a simulator, before actually getting behind the controls.

Job Inventory

A more streamlined approach to task analysis is to develop a *job inventory.* Figure 7.5 presents a job inventory for identifying the training needs of new tire store managers. As illustrated, this job inventory lists each activity a tire store manager is expected to engage in, as well as its importance and the amount of time spent on it. Based on this inventory, you could prioritize the tasks involved in being a store manager, and from this determine which tasks—such as "assign and define duties to all new store employees"— you'll have to emphasize in training new tire store managers.

◆ PERFORMANCE ANALYSIS: DETERMINING THE TRAINING NEEDS OF CURRENT EMPLOYEES

Performance analysis basically involves verifying the fact that there is a significant performance deficiency, and then determining if that deficiency should be rectified through training or by some other means (such as changing the machinery or transferring the employee). The performance analysis procedure consists of ten steps, as summarized in Figure 7.6.[25]

Step 1. Performance Appraisal

The first step is to identify the performance discrepancy. This step involves appraising your employee's performance. In other words, if you want to improve your employee's performance, you must first determine what the person's performance is now and what you would like it to be. Examples of specific performance deficiencies are as follows:

I expect each salesperson to make ten new contracts per week, but John averages only six.

Other plants our size average no more than two serious accidents per month, and we're averaging five.

All sales reports are due at the end of the month, but by the middle of the following month we usually still have 20% of our reports outstanding.

Step 2. Cost/Value Analysis

Next determine whether rectifying the problem is worth the time and effort that you'll have to put into doing so. For example, ask "what is the cost of *not* solving the problem?" Sometimes not solving the problem is cheaper than setting up a training program to rectify it.

Step 3. Distinguish Between Can't Do and Won't Do Problems

This is the heart of your analysis. The crucial question here is: "Could the employee do the job if he or she wanted to?" To distinguish between can't

FIGURE 7.5
An Example of a Job Inventory Used with Tire Store Managers
Source: Kenneth Wexley and Gary Latham, *Developing and Training Human Resources* (Glenview, Ill.: Scott Foresman, 1981), p. 44.

	IMPORTANCE	AMOUNT OF TIME SPENT
INSTRUCTIONS: For each task activity, *circle* the number corresponding to its importance for *your* job and the amount of time you spend on it.	1 — *Not at all* important 2 — *Slightly* important 3 — *Moderately* important 4 — *Very* important 5 — *Extremely* important	0 — *Never* do this task 1 — *Very little time* compared to other tasks 2 — *Somewhat less time* compared to other tasks 3 — *Same amount of time* as other tasks 4 — *More time* compared to other tasks 5 — *A great deal more time* compared to other tasks
1. Assign and define duties to *all* new store employees.	1 2 3 4 5	0 1 2 3 4 5
2. Take a physical inventory monthly.	1 2 3 4 5	0 1 2 3 4 5
3. Assign accounts to salespeople for collection.	1 2 3 4 5	0 1 2 3 4 5
4. Monitor overtime payments to employees.	1 2 3 4 5	0 1 2 3 4 5
5. Make sure the inside and outside of building is maintained in a presentable condition.	1 2 3 4 5	0 1 2 3 4 5
6. Schedule and place advertisements in newspapers and radio.	1 2 3 4 5	0 1 2 3 4 5
7. Make certain customers are greeted when coming into store and properly handled upon leaving.	1 2 3 4 5	0 1 2 3 4 5
8. Establish a probationary period for new hires and review their performance periodically.	1 2 3 4 5	0 1 2 3 4 5
9. Advise staff accountant of store claims.	1 2 3 4 5	0 1 2 3 4 5
10. Arrange promissory notes payable at customer's bank if deemed necessary.	1 2 3 4 5	0 1 2 3 4 5
11. Ensure that trucks are routed profitably.	1 2 3 4 5	0 1 2 3 4 5
12. Hold safety meetings with store personnel.	1 2 3 4 5	0 1 2 3 4 5
13. Make telephone solicitations to customers.	1 2 3 4 5	0 1 2 3 4 5
14. Ensure that advertised products are available to customers.	1 2 3 4 5	0 1 2 3 4 5
15. Discuss career goals with employees.	1 2 3 4 5	0 1 2 3 4 5

do and won't do problems, ask three sets of questions: (1) *Does the person know what to do, and what you expect* in terms of performance? (2) Could the person do the job *if he or she wanted to?* and (3) *Does the person want to do the job,* and what are the consequences of performing well?

For example, assume the problem is that you have twice the scrap you should on the number 8 assembly line. You could proceed with our analysis as follows:

Do the assembly workers know what is expected of them? (If not, it is a *can't do* problem). After speaking with the assemblers, you find that while they know they should not have more than one reject per five assemblies, they did *not* know that their reject rate was twice as high. You therefore suggest

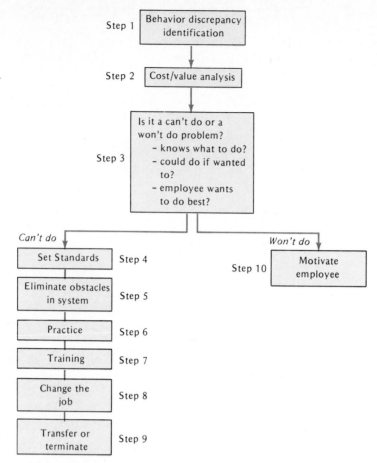

that a graph be placed at their work site indicating the hourly reject rate for the line.

Could they do the job if they wanted to? (If not, it's again a *can't do* prob-lem.) In other words, could the assemblers keep their rejects to one per five assemblies if they wanted to? Do they have the ability to do so? Are there any roadblocks or impediments preventing them from achieving this goal? Here you find some problems that seem amenable to training. For example, several of the assemblers need to be retrained regarding the proper way to solder a junction.

Do they want to do their jobs? (If not, it's a *won't do* problem.) What hap-pens when they achieve the desired reject rate? What happens when they do not attain the desired rate? Here you find that the assemblers are never praised for minimizing rejects, and in fact are never penalized for excessive rejects. You decide to solve this problem by having the supervisor on the line praise the assemblers each hour if the desired reject rate is attained and to express some displeasure when the rate is exceeded.

This analysis therefore identified several problems, only one of which required retraining. In this case it's possible that just the graph (which shows the assemblers how they are doing) and the supervisor's praise (which reinforces their good performance) may be sufficient to inexpen-sively rectify the problem, without the expense of retraining any assem-blers. These solutions could be tried first and, if they don't solve the prob-lem, resoldering training could be implemented. Once you identify the problem as either a *can't do* or a *won't do* problem, you can proceed as follows.

Step 4. Can't Do: Set Standards

Sometimes, as in our example, employees don't perform up to par because they don't know what par is, or because they think they are already performing up to standard. In this step, therefore, review your performance standards and your employees' understanding of what they are expected to do. Also determine if they know that they are not performing up to par.

Step 5. Can't Do: Eliminate Obstacles in the System; Use Job Aids

The next step is to identify and eliminate any obstacles to performance that are now present. Ask, for instance, "Does the material arrive at this person's work station on time?" Sometimes an easy solution is to use a *job aid*. For example, one firm found that its electronic assemblers were having trouble remembering which wire was to be soldered to which junction. The job aid in this case involved color coding all wires and junctions. The assemblers can now see at a glance which wire goes where.

Step 6. Can't Do: Practice

Sometimes employees lose a skill or knowledge they once had because of a lack of practice. Hotel fire drills are an example of practice being used to make sure employees maintain satisfactory skill and knowledge levels.

Step 7. Can't Do: Training

As we have seen, training is not always the best solution: in fact, it can sometimes be the most expensive one. But if it is a training problem, the rest of this chapter should enable you to do a better job of training.

Step 8. Can't Do: Change the Job

Sometimes the best way to handle can't do problems is to change the job. For example, most sales jobs consist of three parts: prospecting, demonstrating, and closing. Training someone who is good at prospecting and demonstrating to also close a deal is often difficult. On the other hand, some hotshot closers are best off not wasting their time prospecting and demonstrating. The solution here is to change the sales job by subdividing it and have one person prospect and demonstrate and another close.

Step 9. Can't Do: Transfer or Terminate

Finally, if after all your efforts the person obviously wants to do the job but can't, transfer or termination may be required.

Step 10. Won't Do: Reward or Punishment

Often, it's not a *can't do*, but a *won't do* problem; the employee *could* do the job if he or she *wanted* to. Here you have a motivation problem and must decide what rewards or punishments are appropriate. For our assemblers, for instance, the supervisor's praise may be enough of a reward to keep the assemblers' reject rates to a minimum. Other motivation techniques are explained in Chapters 9–12.

♦ SETTING TRAINING OBJECTIVES

Setting concrete, measurable training objectives is the bottom line that should result from determining training needs. For example, if you decide to proceed with the soldering retraining program for our assemblers, one training objective might be

Trainee will solder up to five wires to a junction within 30 seconds, in such a way that each wire can withstand a pull of up to 10 pounds.

Similarly, for a Xerox machine technician, a concrete training objective is as follows:

Given a tool kit and a service manual, the technical representative will be able to adjust the registration (black line along paper edges) on this Xerox duplicator within 20 minutes according to the specifications stated in the manual.[26]

Well-written behavioral objectives specify what the trainee will be able to accomplish after successfully completing the training program.[27] They thus provide a focus for the efforts of both the trainee and the trainer, as well as a benchmark for evaluating the success of the training program.

TRAINING AND TRAINING TECHNIQUES

After determining your employees' training needs—in particular the tasks and skills for which they need training and the knowledge they require—and setting training objectives, the actual training can take place. The actual training technique that is used—whether on-the-job training, programmed learning, or some other—will depend on several things, including the nature of the tasks and skills to be learned, the number of employees to be trained, and the employer's resources. The advantages and disadvantages of the most popular training techniques are explained shortly. First, however, because training is essentially a learning process, it would be useful to begin our discussion by briefly reviewing ten *principles of learning.*[28]

1. At the start of training, provide trainees with an *overview* of the material to be presented. Knowing the overall picture in advance helps the trainee to anticipate and understand each step in the training and to integrate the parts into a meaningful whole. One example of this approach is the overview that precedes each chapter in a textbook.

2. Make sure to use a variety of *familiar examples* when presenting materials to the trainees. Just as a picture is "worth a thousand words," often a familiar example that illustrates what the trainer is getting at can help crystalize the concept for the trainees.

3. Split the material into *meaningful chunks* rather than presenting it all at once. Trainees can only absorb a limited amount of information at a time; imagine how you'd like reading a textbook whose chapters were 80 pages each, for instance.

4. Try to use terms and concepts that are already *familiar* to trainees.

5. *Maximize the similarity* between the training situation and the work situation. Thus, if the person is being trained off the job and will eventually have to work in a noisy environment, make sure the person gets some practice under noisy conditions during training.

6. *Label or identify important features of the task.* Thus, if training a machine operator, give each important part of the machine a label (e.g., "starter switch"), and label each step of the procedure (e.g., "start machine," "place tube in press").

7. *Trainees learn best by doing.* Try to give them as much real-life practice as possible; practice and repetition are important for learning new skills. Skills that are practiced often are better learned and less easily forgotten.

8. *Provide reinforcement as quickly and frequently as possible.* Don't wait until the end of the day to tell trainees that they've done well. Instead, reinforce good performance often—whenever they do something right.

9. Trainees learn best when they *learn at their own pace.* No one likes having someone look over his or her shoulder as he or she tries to learn a new subject. Instead, people learn fastest when they are allowed to proceed at their own pace.

10. The trainees must be *motivated to learn.* This can be facilitated by explaining to trainees how training will affect their performance and rewards. Furthermore, other principles listed, such as break the material into meaningful chunks and provide quick reinforcement, will also motivate the trainees.

♦ ON-THE-JOB TRAINING

on-the-job training (OJT) Training a person to learn a job while working at it.

On-the-job training (OJT) involves having a person learn a job by actually performing it on the job. Virtually every employee, from mail-room clerk to company president, gets some on-the-job training when he or she joins a firm. This is why William Tracey calls it "the most common, the most widely accepted, and the most necessary method of training employees in the skills essential for acceptable job performance." In many companies, OJT is the *only* type of training available to employees and usually involves assigning new employees to experienced workers or supervisors who then do the actual training.[29]

There are several types of on-the-job training. Probably the most familiar is the *coaching or understudy method,* in which the employee is trained on the job by an experienced worker or the trainee's supervisor. At lower levels the coaching may just involve having trainees acquire the skills for running the machine by observing the supervisor. But this technique is also widely used at top-management levels. The position of *assistant to* is often used to train and develop the company's future top managers, for instance. *Job rotation* in which the employee (usually a management trainee) moves from job to job at planned intervals is another OJT technique. *Special assignments* similarly give lower-level executives firsthand experience in working on actual problems.

OJT has several advantages. It is relatively *inexpensive;* trainees learn while producing, and there is no need for expensive off-job facilities like classrooms or programmed learning devices. The method also *facilitates learning* since trainees learn by actually doing the job and get quick feedback about the correctness of their performance.

However there are several trainer-related factors to keep in mind when designing an OJT program.[30] The trainers themselves must be carefully trained and given the necessary training materials. (Often, instead, an experienced worker is simply told to "go train John.") Employees who will function as trainers should also be convinced that training new employees will not jeopardize their own job security and that their added training responsibility will be instrumental in obtaining rewards for them. Trainers and trainees should be paired so as to minimize differences in background, language, or age, and the choice of trainers should be based upon their ability and desire to teach. Experienced workers who are chosen as trainers should be thoroughly trained in the proper methods of instruction—in particular the principles of learning, explained previously, and perhaps the job instruction technique that we address next. Trainees should also be rotated to capitalize on the strengths of various trainers: John may be especially good at teaching new trainees how to solder, for instance, while Ruth is especially good at showing them how to paint the finished circuit board. Trainers should also understand the importance of close supervision in preventing training injuries. A useful step-by-step approach for giving a new employee on-the-job training can be summarized as follows:

STEP 1: PREPARATION OF THE LEARNER

1. Put the learner at ease—relieve the tension.
2. Explain why he or she is being taught.
3. Create interest, encourage questions, find out what the learner already knows about his or her job or other jobs.
4. Explain the why of the whole job and relate it to some job the worker already knows.
5. Place the learner as close to the normal working position as possible.
6. Familiarize the worker with the equipment, materials, tools, and trade terms.

STEP 2: PRESENTATION OF THE OPERATION

1. Explain quantity and quality requirements.
2. Go through the job at the normal work pace.
3. Go through the job at a slow pace several times, explaining each step. Between operations, explain the difficult parts, or those in which errors are likely to be made.
4. Again go through the job at a slow pace several times, explain the key points.
5. Have the learner explain the steps as you go through the job at a slow pace.

STEP 3: PERFORMANCE TRYOUT

1. Have the learner go through the job several times, slowly, explaining to you each step. Correct mistakes, and if necessary, do some of the complicated steps the first few times.
2. You, the trainer, run the job at the normal pace.
3. Have the learner do the job, gradually building up skill and speed.
4. As soon as the learner demonstrates ability to do the job, let the work begin, but don't abandon him or her.

STEP 4: FOLLOW-UP

1. Designate to whom the learner should go for help if he or she needs it.
2. Gradually decrease supervision, checking work from time to time against quality and quantity standards.
3. Correct faulty work patterns that begin to creep into the work, and do it before they become a habit. Show why the learned method is superior.
4. Compliment good work; encourage the worker until able to meet the quality/quantity standards.

♦ JOB INSTRUCTION TRAINING

job instruction training (JIT) Listing each of a job's basic tasks, along with a "key point" for each, in order to provide step-by-step training for employees.

Many jobs consist of a logical sequence of steps and are best taught in this manner—step by step. This step-by-step learning is called **job instruction training (JIT)**. It involves listing all necessary steps in the job, each in its proper sequence. Alongside each step you also list a corresponding "key point" (if any). The steps show *what* is to be done, while the key points show

how it's to be done—and *why*. Here is an example of a job instruction training sheet for teaching a trainee how to operate a large motorized paper cutter.

STEPS	KEY POINTS
1. Start motor	None
2. Set cutting distance	Carefully read scale—to prevent wrong-sized cut
3. Place paper on cutting table	Make sure paper is even—to prevent uneven cut
4. Push paper up to cutter	Make sure paper is tight—to prevent uneven cut
5. Grasp safety release with left hand	Do not release left hand—to prevent hand from being caught in cutter
6. Grasp cutter release with right hand	Do not release right hand—to prevent hand from being caught in cutter
7. Simultaneously pull cutter and safety releases	Keep both hands on corresponding releases—to avoid hands being on cutting table
8. Wait for cutter to retract	Keep both hands on releases—to avoid having hands on cutting table
9. Retract paper	Maker sure cutter is retracted; keep both hands away from releases
10. Shut off motor	None

♦ LECTURES

Just lecturing to new trainees can have several advantages. It is a quick and simple way of providing knowledge to large groups of trainees, as when the sales force must be taught the special features of some new product. While written material like books and manuals can also be used here, they may involve considerable printing expense, and don't permit the give and take of questioning that lectures do. You can therefore use a lecture as an integral part of your training program, with the actual practice required for learning the new skills provided by a training technique like on-the-job training.

How to Organize the Lecture

Many experienced lecturers use a technique called PREP when preparing their lectures. PREP stands for Point, Reason, Explanation, Point. For example, suppose you are trying to explain to some new lumber company salespeople why plywood companies make several types of plywood. Your PREP outline might be as follows:

Point	Plywood firms manufacture different types of plywood for different uses such as interior building, external applications, and boat building.
Reason	The plywood companies do this because each application—such as marine plywood or fire-retardant plywood—requires a unique and expensive manufacturing process, and it would

PERSONNEL MANAGEMENT:

ON THE FRONT LINE

At the present time the Carter Cleaning Centers have no formal orientation or training policies or procedures, and Jennifer believes this is one reason why the standards that she and her father would like employees to adhere to are generally not adhered to.

Several examples can illustrate this. In dealing with the customers at the front counters the Carters would prefer that certain practices and procedures be used. For example, all customers should be greeted with what Jack refers to as a "big hello." And any garments they drop off should immediately be inspected for any damage or unusual stains so these can be brought to the customer's attention, lest the customer later return to pick up the garment and erroneously blame the store for the damage or an unusual stain. The garments are then supposed to be immediately placed together in a nylon sack to separate them from other customers' garments. The ticket also has to be carefully written up with the customer's name, telephone number, and the date precisely and clearly noted on all copies. The counterperson is also supposed to take the opportunity to try to sell the customer some additional services, such as waterproofing, if a raincoat has been dropped off, or simply notifying the customer that "you know now that people are doing their spring cleaning, we're having a special on drapery cleaning all this month." Finally, as the customer leaves, the counterperson is supposed to make some courteous comment like "Have a nice day" or "Drive safely." Each of the other jobs in the stores—pressing, cleaning and spotting, periodically maintaining the coin laundry equipment, and so forth—similarly contain certain steps, procedures, and most important, standards which the Carters would prefer to see adhered to.

The company has also had other problems, Jennifer feels, because of a lack of adequate employee training and orientation. For example, two new employees became very upset last month when they discovered that they were not paid at the end of the week, on Friday, but instead were paid (as are all Carter employees) on the following Tuesday. The Carters use the extra two days in part to give them time to obtain everyone's hours and compute their pay. The other reason they do it, according to Jack, is that "frankly, when we stay a few days behind in paying employees it helps to ensure that they at least give us a few days notice before quitting on us. While we are certainly obligated to pay them anything they earn, we find that psychologically they seem to be less likely to just walk out on us Friday evening and not show up Monday morning if they still haven't gotten their pay from the previous week. This way they at least give us a few days' notice so we can find a replacement."

Other matters which could be covered during an orientation, says Jennifer, include company policy regarding paid holidays, lateness and absences, health and hospitalization benefits (there are none, other than workers' compensation) and general matters like maintaining a clean and safe work area, personal appearance and cleanliness, filling in time sheets, personal telephone calls and mail, company policies regarding matters like substance abuse, and eating or smoking on the job.

Jennifer believes that implementing orientation and training programs would help to ensure that employees know how to do their jobs the right way. And she and her father further believe that it is only when employees understand the right way to do their jobs that there is any hope that their jobs will in fact be accomplished the way the Carters want them to be accomplished. She therefore has the following questions:

1. Specifically what should we cover in our new employee orientation program and how should we cover this information?

2. In the personnel management course Jennifer took the book suggested using a task analysis record form to identify tasks performed by an em-

ployee. "Should we use a form like this for the counterperson's job and if so what, roughly speaking, would the completed, filled-in form look like?"

3. Having previously developed a job description for a store manager's job Jennifer would now like to develop a job inventory for store manager using an approach like that illustrated in Figure 7.5. How should she go about doing this?

4. Which specific training techniques should she use to train her pressers, her cleaner-spotters, her managers and her counterpeople, and why?

	not be advantageous or cost-effective to sell one grade of plywood for all applications.
Explanation	Here you might explain some of the specific requirements of marine plywood, fire-retardant plywood, exterior plywood, and so on, pointing out what sorts of manufacturing treatments are used to produce plywood appropriate for each of these applications.
Point	Repeat the point that plywood companies manufacture different grades of plywood for different applications.

Some useful guidelines for presenting your lecture can be summarized as follows:[31]

Give your listeners signals to help them follow your ideas. For instance, if you have a list of items, start by saying something like "There are four reasons why the sales reports are necessary. . . . The first . . . the second. . . ."

Don't start out on the wrong foot. For instance, don't start with any irrelevant joke or story or by saying something like "I really don't know why I was asked to speak here today."

Keep your conclusions short. Just summarize your main point or points in one or two succinct sentences.

Be alert to your audience. Watch body language for "closed" signals like fidgeting and arms crossed.

Maintain eye contact with the trainees in the program. At a minimum you should look at each section of trainees during your presentation.

Make sure that everyone in the room can hear. Talk loudly enough so that you can be heard by people in the last row and if necessary repeat questions that you get from trainees from the front of the room.

Control your hands. Get in the habit of leaving your hands hanging naturally at your sides rather than drifting to your face, and then your pocket, then your back, and so on.

Avoid putting your hands near your face. This can block your voice projection and also give the impression that you lack confidence in what you are saying.

Talk from notes rather than from a script. Write out clear, legible notes on large index cards and then use these as an outline, rather than memorizing the whole presentation.

Eliminate bad habits. Beware of distracting bad habits like jiggling coins in your pocket or pulling on an earlobe.

Practice. If you have the time, make sure to rehearse under conditions similar to those under which you will actually give your presentation.

♦ AUDIOVISUAL TECHNIQUES

Presenting information to trainees via audiovisual techniques like films, closed-circuit TV, audiotapes, or videotapes can be very effective, and today this technique is widely used.[32] At Weyerhaeuser Company, for instance, portions of entertainment films like *Bridge on the River Kwai* have been used as a basis for discussing interpersonal relationships in the company's management school. The Ford Motor Company uses films in its dealer training sessions to simulate problems and reactions to handling various customer complaints.

Audiovisuals are more expensive than are conventional lectures, but they offer some unique advantages. You should therefore consider using them in the following situations. First, *when there is a need to illustrate how a certain sequence should be followed over time,* such as when teaching wire soldering or telephone repair, the stop action, instant reply, and fast- or slow-motion capabilities of audiovisuals can be useful. Second, when there is a *need to expose trainees to events not easily demonstrable in live lectures,* such as a visual tour of a factory or open-heart surgery. Third, use it *when the training is going to be used organizationwide* and it is too costly to move the trainers from place to place.

There are three options when it comes to obtaining your company's video: You can buy a canned videotape or film, you can make your own, or you can have a production company produce the video for you. Dozens of businesses issue catalogs listing audiovisual programs on topics ranging from applicant interviewing to zoo management. If the training program is simple enough, you can use your own videotape equipment to produce the training program. Finally, many employers opt for bringing in a professional film production company to produce the training tape.

Teletraining

Companies today are also experimenting with *teletraining,* through which a trainer in a central location can train groups of employees at remote locations via television hookups.[33]

♦ PROGRAMMED LEARNING

programmed learning A systematic method for teaching job skills, involving presenting questions or facts, allowing the person to respond, and giving the learner immediate feedback on the accuracy of his or her answers.

Whether the programmed instruction device is a textbook, or machine, **programmed learning** always consists of three functions:

1. Presenting questions, facts, or problems to the learner.
2. Allowing the person to respond.
3. Providing feedback on the accuracy of his or her answers.

A page from a programmed instruction book for learning calculus is presented in Figure 7.7. Note how facts and questions are presented, that the learner can then respond, and that the book then provides feedback on the accuracy of his or her answers.

The main advantage of programmed learning is that it reduces training time by about one-third.[34] In terms of the principles of learning listed previously, programmed instruction can also facilitate learning since it lets trainees learn at their own pace, provides immediate feedback, and reduces the risk of error. On the other hand, trainees do *not* learn much more with programmed learning than they would with a conventional textbook approach. Therefore, the cost of developing the manuals, books, and machinery for programmed instruction (which can be quite high) has to be weighed against the accelerated but not better learning that should occur.

FIGURE 7.7

A Page from a Programmed Textbook

Source: Daniel Kleppner and Norman Ramsey, *Quick Calculus*. Copyright © 1965 by John Wiley & Sons, Inc. Reprinted by permission.

Sec. 2   Graphs

17   The most direct way to plot the graph of a function $y = f(x)$ is to make a table of reasonably spaced values of x and of the corresponding values of $y = f(x)$. Then each pair of values (x,y) can be represented by a point as in the previous frame. A graph of the function is obtained by connecting the points with a smooth curve. Of course, the points on the curve may be only approximate. If we want an accurate plot we just have to be very careful and use many points. (On the other hand, crude plots are pretty good for most purposes.)

Go to 18.

18   As an example, here is a plot of the function $y = 3x^2$. A table of values of x and y is shown and these points are indicated on the graph.

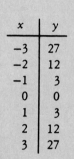

x	y
−3	27
−2	12
−1	3
0	0
1	3
2	12
3	27

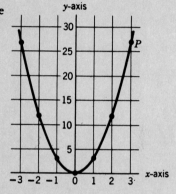

To test yourself, encircle below the pair of coordinates that corresponds to the point P indicated in the figure.

[(3,27) | (27,3) | none of these]

Check your answer. If correct, go on to 19. If incorrect study frame 16 once again and then go to 19.

♦ VESTIBULE OR SIMULATED TRAINING

vestibule or simulated training
Training employees on special off-the-job equipment, as in airplane pilot training, whereby training costs and hazards can be reduced.

Vestibule or **simulated training** is a technique in which trainees learn on the actual or simulated equipment they will use on the job, but are actually trained off the job. *Vestibule training* therefore aims to obtain the advantages of on-the-job training without actually putting the trainee on the job. Vestibule training is virtually a necessity on jobs where it is too costly or dangerous to train employees on the job. It is therefore useful for training new assembly-line workers where putting them right to work could slow production. Similarly, where safety is concerned—as with pilots—it may be the only practical alternative.

Vestibule training may just involve setting up in a separate room the equipment the trainees will actually be using on the job. However, it often

COMPUTER APPLICATION IN TECHNICAL
TRAINING: COMPUTER-ASSISTED INSTRUCTION

Many firms are now using computers to facilitate the training process. Computer-assisted instruction (CAI) systems like Control Data's Plato have several advantages. They provide *self-paced* individualized instruction that is one on one and easy to use, and trainees get *immediate feedback* to their input. CAI also provides *accountability* in that tests are taken on the computer so that management can monitor each trainee's progress and needs. A CAI training program can also be *easily modified* to reflect technological innovations in the equipment for which the employee is being trained. This training also tends to be more *flexible* in that trainees can usually use the computer almost any time they want, and thus get their training when they prefer. Computer-assisted instruction systems like Plato can also provide *simulation* capabilities. Specifically, the system can be designed to simulate complex or difficult tasks and to challenge trainees with "what if" questions like, "If wind velocity on the ground is 80 knots, then what will happen if you decrease your aircraft velocity below its stall speed?"

Some examples of how systems like Plato are being used can help to illustrate the usefulness of CAIs. In some schools, security analyst trainees are able to learn and manipulate various stock valuation models, by programming in various assumptions about economic growth rates and risks; they can thus assess how changes in these factors will influence the price of these stocks.

Plato is also being used to train airline pilots. Part of a pilot's training includes time in a cockpit trainer, in a flight simulator, and in an actual airplane—all expensive pieces of equipment. The Plato system minimizes the amount of time spent in the simulator and thus reduces training costs. By using this computerized system, pilots familiarize themselves with the complicated instrument panel before working with the actual equipment in a simulator or airplane. This is illustrated in the figure below.[1] While a textbook, film, or lecture could present photos of the same instruments, none could provide the almost realistic reactions and problems supplied by the CAI system.[2]

[1] *Plato: A New Way to Solve Training Problems*, Control Data Corporation, sales brochure.

[2] Ibid. See also Nancy Madlin, "Computer-Based Training Comes of Age," *Personnel*, Vol. 64, no. 11 (November 1987), pp. 64–65; Marilyn Gist et al., "The Influence of Training Method and Trainee Age on the Acquisition of Computer Skills," *Personnel Psychology*, Vol. 41, no. 2 (Summer 1988), pp. 255–266; and Ralph E. Ganger, "Computer-Based Training," *Personnel Journal*, Vol. 68, no. 6 (June 1989), pp. 116–123.

Pilot Training with Plato

Note: The Plato System (left) is used to train pilots in the use of complicated instrument panels. (Reprinted by permission of Control Data Corporation.)

involves the use of equipment simulators. In pilot training, for instance, the main advantages of flight simulators are as follows:[35]

Safety. Crews can practice hazardous flight maneuvers in a safe, controlled environment.

Learning efficiency. The absence of conflicting air traffic and radio chatter that exists in real flight situations enables total concentration on the business of learning how to fly the craft.

Money. The cost of flying a flight simulator is only a fraction of the cost of flying an aircraft. This includes savings on maintenance costs, pilot trainer cost, fuel cost, and the cost of not having the aircraft in regular service.

◆ LITERACY TRAINING TECHNIQUES

Functional illiteracy is an increasingly serious problem for many employers. By some estimates an estimated 25 million American adults 17 years old and older are "functional illiterates" either because they can't read at all or can only read up to a third- or fourth-grade level.[36] Yet as the U.S. economy shifts from goods to services, there is a corresponding need for workers who are more skilled and more literate.

Employers are responding to this problem in two main ways. More and more companies are, first, testing the basic skills of prospective employees. Of the 1,005 companies that responded to a 1989 American Management Association (AMA) survey on workplace testing, for instance, 345 companies (34.3%) indicated that they conduct basic skills testing.[37] In 89% of the responding companies job applicants who are deficient in basic skills are refused employment. At about 3% of the other companies current employees and candidates for promotion are similarly tested (and often rejected) based on their literacy scores.

The second response is to institute basic skills and literacy programs. Based on the AMA survey, the areas in which remedial training are needed tend to be fairly evenly split among mathematics, reading, and writing. The techniques used to do the required training range from lectures to sophisticated computer-assisted programs.

One simple approach is to have supervisors focus on basic skills by assigning employees writing and speaking exercises. After the exercise is completed, the supervisor can then provide personal feedback.[38] One way to do this is to turn materials routinely used in the employees' jobs into instructional tools. For example, if an employee needs to use a manual to find out how to replace a certain machine part, he or she should be taught how to use an index to locate the relevant section.[39] Another approach is to bring in outside professionals like teachers from a local high school or community college to institute, say, a remedial reading or writing program. The advantage here is that these teachers are already familiar with the special educational materials and programs required and so can easily institute the required training programs. Having employees attend, say, adult education or high school evening classes is another option.

Another approach gaining wider acceptance is based on a device called an interactive video disk (IVD). This technique combines the drama of video with the power of microcomputers.[40] One such program is Principles of Alphabet Literacy (PALS). It uses animated video and a computer-stored voice to enable nonreaders to associate sounds with letters and letters with words, and to use the words to create sentences.[41] A second IVD program is called SKILLPAC. This program, subtitled English for Industry, was designed primarily for nonnative English speakers and combines video, audio, and computer technologies to teach language skills in the context of the specific workplace situation in which those skills will be used.[42]

It does not pay to spend a lot of time hiring the best employees if the employees you hire aren't properly trained. In a recent book called *Made in America*, a group of MIT researchers concluded, for instance, that superior training is one reason why Japanese firms have often pulled ahead of American firms within the same industries. Japanese firms will spend weeks in meticulous training programs developing their workers' expertise, while comparable American firms will often almost ignore the training process, suggesting instead that new workers just "go follow Joe around" to learn what the job entails.

Again because so much is riding on such a relatively few employees, it is important that smaller firms, too, carefully train their employees. The concepts and techniques explained in this chapter should enable you to do so, but in addition here is a practical procedure you can use. It contains five steps:

Step 1. Set Training Objectives

First, write down your training objectives. For example, if your objective is to reduce an existing problem (such as too much scrap), or get new assemblers up to speed within two weeks, these objectives should be stated.

Step 2. Write a Detailed Job Description

As explained in Chapter 3, a detailed job description is, among other things, the heart of any good training program. A job description should list the daily and periodic tasks of each job, along with a summary of the steps in each task. Thus, for the job of printer presented in Table 7.1, a main task is "operate paper cutter." Below this, perhaps in paragraph form, the press operator's job description should then explain how the paper cutter should be operated, including steps such as start motor, set cutting distance, and place paper on cutting table. In other words, the job description should list, for each task, *what* is to be done, as well as *how* it is to be done. Care in developing the job description in the first place will thus be time well spent once the training program for printer must be developed.

Step 3. Task Analysis Record Form

Next, develop a task analysis record form as summarized in Table 7.1. However, for practical purposes, the small business owner might want to use an abbreviated task analysis record form containing only four columns. In the first, list *tasks* (including what is to be performed in terms of each of the main tasks, as well as the steps involved in each task). In column B, list *performance standards* (in terms of quantity, quality, accuracy, etc.). In column C, list *testable or trainable skills required.* Here list things the employee must know or do to perform the task. Distinguish between *testable* and *training* skills. For testable skills you will want to test the new employee beforehand to see if he or she is capable of performing the skill (such as whether the supposedly experienced mechanic knows how to read a micrometer). Other skills (like adjusting a particular machine) will have to be imparted to the employee via training. This column therefore provides you with specific skills (such as "Keep both hands on releases") that you'll want to make sure to stress in your training program. In the fourth column, column D, you may find it useful to list *aptitudes required.* These are the human aptitudes (such as mechanical comprehension, tolerance for boredom, and so on) that the employee should have to be trainable for the task and for which the employee can be screened ahead of time).

Step 4. Develop Training Sequence Form

Next, develop a training sequence form (also known as a job instruction sheet) for the job. As explained, the job instruction training sheet (also known as the job instruction "training sequence" for the job) should list the steps in each task (as listed on the job description, and task analysis record form), as well as key points for each.

Step 5. Prepare Training Program for the Job

Finally, you should now be ready to prepare all the final training documents and media for the job. Central to the training manual for the job should be the training sequence, listing steps in each job task, and key points. The person doing the actual training should also have (from a task analysis record form) a list of the testable or trainable skills required so that the trainer can concentrate on these skills (such as "lift paper correctly," or "regauge") in training and evaluating the trainee.

At a minimum, your training program should therefore include the job description, task analysis record form, training sequence form, and a separate trainer's manual. The latter contains a summary of the objectives of the training program, the three forms mentioned earlier, and a listing of the trainable skills required. For the trainee, the "training manual" might simply then consist of an introduction to the job and explanation of where the job fits in with the other jobs in the plant or office as well as a job description and training sequence form. At this point you also have to make a decision regarding what media to use in your training program. A simple but effective on-the-job training program using current employees or supervisors as trainers requires only the materials we just described. However, it could turn out that the nature of the job or the number of trainees demands producing or purchasing special audio or visual tapes or films, a slide presentation, or more extensive printed materials.

EVALUATING THE TRAINING EFFORT

After your trainees have completed their training programs (or perhaps at planned intervals during the training), the program should be evaluated to see how well its objectives have been met. Thus, if assemblers should be able to solder a junction in 30 seconds, or a Xerox technician repair a machine in 30 minutes, then the program's effectiveness should be measured based on whether these goals are met. It is unfortunate (but true) that most managers do not spend much time appraising the effects of their training programs. For example, are your trainees learning *as much* as they can? Are they learning *as fast* as they can? Is there a *better method* for training them? These are some of the questions you can answer by properly evaluating your training efforts.

There are two basic issues you'll have to address when evaluating a training program. The first is the design of the evaluation study and, in particular, whether *controlled experimentation* will be used. The second is *what training effect to measure*.

◆ CONTROLLED EXPERIMENTATION

experimentation Formal methods for testing the effectiveness of a training program, preferably with before and after tests.

Ideally, the best method to use in evaluating a training program involves controlled **experimentation**. In a control experiment, both a training group and a control (no training) group are used. Relevant data (for instance, on quantity of production or quality of soldered junctions) should be obtained both before and after the training effort in the group exposed to training and before and after a corresponding work period in the control group. In this way, it is possible to determine to what extent any change in performance in the training group resulted from the training itself, rather than from some organizationwide change like a raise in pay; the latter, one assumes, would have affected employees in both the training and control groups. In terms of current practices, however, one survey found that something less than half the companies responding attempted to obtain before and after measures from trainees; the number of organizations using control groups was negligible.[43] One expert suggests using an evaluation form like the one shown in Figure 7.8 to evaluate the development program.[44]

◆ WHAT TRAINING EFFECTS TO MEASURE

There are four basic categories of training outcomes or effects that can be measured:

1. *Reaction.* First, evaluate trainees' reactions to the program. Did they like the program? Did they think it worthwhile?

2. *Learning.* Second, you can test the trainees to determine if they learned the principles, skills, and facts they were to learn.

3. *Behavior.* Next ask whether the trainees' behavior on the job changed because of the training program. For example, are employees in the store's complaint department more courteous toward disgruntled customers than previously?

4. *Results.* Last, but probably most importantly, ask: "What final results were achieved in terms of the training objectives previously set? Did the number of customer complaints about employees drop? Did the reject rate improve? Did scrappage cost decrease? Was turnover reduced? Are production quotas now being met?" and so forth. Improved results are, of course, especially important. The training program may succeed in terms of the reactions from trainees, increased learning, and even

FIGURE 7.8

A Sample Outside-Training Evaluation Form

Source: Reprinted, by permission of the publisher, from "Effective Supervisory Training and Development, Part 3: Outside Programs," *Personnel* (February 1985), p. 42. © 1985, American Management Association, New York. All rights reserved.

EVALUATION OF OUTSIDE MANAGEMENT DEVELOPMENT PROGRAMS

Name_____ Title_____ Date_____
Program Attended:
Name of program_____ Dates_____
Location_____ Fee_____
Organization presenting program_____
1. How accurately did the program announcement describe what was covered at the program?
_____Very accurately _____Fairly accurately _____Inaccurately
2. To what extent did the subject content meet your needs and interests?
_____Very well _____To some extent _____Very little
3. How effective were the speakers and conference leaders?
_____Excellent _____Very good _____Good _____Fair _____Poor
4. How were the facilities, meals, etc?
_____Excellent _____Very good _____Good _____Fair _____Poor
5. What benefits do you feel you gained?
_____Knowledge of what other companies were doing.
_____New theory and principles that are pertinent.
_____Ideas and techniques that can be applied on the job.
_____Other (please explain).
6. How would you rate the entire program in relation to time and cost?
_____Excellent _____Very good _____Good _____Fair _____Poor
7. Would you like to attend a future program presented by the same organization?
_____Definitely _____Possibly _____No
8. Would you recommend that others from your company attend programs presented by the same organization?
_____Yes _____No _____Not sure
If yes, who should attend?_____
_____
_____
9. Other comments_____
_____
_____
_____

changes in behavior. But if the results are not achieved, then, in the final analysis, the training has not achieved its goals. If so, the problem may lie in the training program. Always remember, though, that the results may be inadequate because the problem was not amenable to training in the first place.

SUMMARY

1. In this chapter we focused on technical skills training for new employees and for present employees whose performance is deficient. For either, uncovering training requirements involves analyzing the cause of the problem and determining what (if any) training is needed. Remember to ask, "Is it a training problem?" Make sure the "problem" is not being caused by some more deep-rooted problem like poor selection or low wages.

2. We discussed some principles of learning that should be understood by all trainers. The guidelines include make the material meaningful (by providing a bird's-eye view, familiar examples, organizing the material, splitting it into meaningful chunks, and using familiar terms and visual aids); make provision for transfer of training; provide feedback; try to motivate your trainee; and provide for practice and repetition.

3. We discussed several training techniques. *Job instruction training* is useful for training on jobs that consist of a logical sequence of steps. *Vestibule* training combines the advantages of on- and off-the-job training.

4. On-the-job training is a third technical training technique. It might involve the understudy method, job rotation, or special assignments and committees. In any case, it should involve four steps: preparing the learner, presenting the operation (or nature of the job), performance tryouts, and a follow-up. Other training methods include audiovisual techniques, lectures, and computer-assisted instruction.

5. Most managers don't spend time evaluating the effects of their training program although they should. In measuring the effectiveness of a training program there are four categories of outcomes you can measure: reaction, learning, behavior, and results. In some cases where training seems to have failed, it may be because training was not the appropriate solution.

KEY TERMS

employee orientation	task analysis	programmed learning
reality shock	performance analysis	vestibule or simulated training
orientation program	on-the-job training (OJT)	experimentation
socialized	job instruction training (JIT)	
realistic job previews		
culture		
technical training		

DISCUSSION QUESTIONS

1. "A well-thought-out orientation program is especially important for employees (like recent graduates) who have had little or no work experience." Explain why you agree or disagree with this statement.

2. You're the supervisor of a group of employees whose task it is to assemble tuning devices that go into radios. You find that quality is not what it should be and that many of your group's tuning devices have to be brought back and reworked; your own boss says that "You'd better start doing a better job of training your workers."

    a. What are some of the "staffing" factors that could be contributing to this problem?

    b. Explain how you would go about assessing whether it is in fact a training problem.

3. Explain how you would apply our "principles of learning" in developing a lecture, say, on "orientation and training."

4. Pick out some task with which you are familiar—mowing the lawn, tuning a car—and develop a job instruction training sheet for it.

♦ APPLICATION EXERCISES

♦ CASE INCIDENT   **Charlie, The Railroad Agent**

Charlie Bagley was employed by a railroad in Farlin, Kansas, a city of about 30,000 people. As the railroad agent, Charlie was in charge of all the company's operations in the community. Before becoming an agent in Farlin, Charlie had been an agent in a small one-man agency for approximately 40 years. When the one-man agency was closed, Charlie asserted his seniority rights and became an agent in Farlin.

At the present location, Charlie had approximately 35 men for whom he was either directly or indirectly responsible. At age 72, Charlie was still working full time. He had maintained his present position for 12 years with no major difficulties.

One September evening, an unidentified automobile driver crossing the railroad tracks ran off the crossing, into a switch stand, back onto the road, and drove off. The accident was witnessed and reported by an employee of the company. The telegrapher on duty called the section supervisor directly responsible for the condition of the tracks.

The supervisor inspected the tracks and the switch stand and called Charlie. He told Charlie there was no damage to the tracks but there was about $5 damage to the switch stand. He also said that he could repair the stand the following day and that no report was necessary. Charlie did not make a report as was technically required by the rules and regulations and forgot about the incident. This was not an abnormal practice when everyone agreed to cover up an accident and save several hours required in filling out the long accident reports used by the company.

At the end of the month the section supervisor turned in a claim for overtime for making the inspection, thereby bringing to the attention of the division headquarters that an accident had not been reported. The section supervisor absolved himself of any responsibility by denying he had told Charlie that a report was unnecessary. Giving due consideration to the fact that Charlie had more than 50 years of service to the company and the fact that Charlie had two sons employed as agents, the superintendent asked Charlie to retire and take his pension. Charlie refused and replied that, after 50 years of service, working from eight to ten hours a day, six days a week, he had no other interests and that he was also financially committed to purchase a home, which would be impossible with only the income from a pension.

The incident prompted a formal investigation by the superintendent with union officials present; they decided that Charlie should be fired. Charlie was fired and signed up for his pension. Since Charlie had always maintained his membership in the telegraphers' union, the local chairperson for the union instigated a claim for Charlie's reinstatement. After two years, the full process of labor-management grievance procedures had been exhausted, and the case went to arbitration. The arbitrator's decision stated that an accident so trivial as this was insufficient cause to dismiss an employee of 50 years' service. The arbitrator ordered that Charlie be reinstated in his job as agent, that he receive full back pay from the date of his dismissal two years ago, and that a comparable place be found for the man who had been working Charlie's job.

Questions
1. Is there a need for training in this company? If so, who needs training? If needed, what should the nature of the training be?
2. Do you think the facts of this case support the need for a mandatory retirement age?
3. How would you go about convincing employees of the need to follow rules and regulations?
4. Is this an example of a "can't do" or a "won't do" problem? Why?

Source: Arno F. Knapper, *Cases in Personnel Management*, pp. 14–15. Copyright © 1977 John Wiley & Sons, Inc. Reprinted by permission of John Wiley & Sons, Inc.

EXPERIENTIAL EXERCISE

Purpose. The purpose of this exercise is to give you practice in developing a training program.

Required Understanding. You should be thoroughly familiar with the training methods we discussed in this chapter, including job instruction training; vestibule training; and on-the-job training. Since you'll be developing a training program for directory assistance operators you should read the following description of a directory assistance operator's duties:

> Customers contact directory assistance operators to obtain the telephone numbers of persons whose numbers are not yet listed, whose listings have changed, or whose numbers are unknown to the customer. These operators check the requested number via a computerized video display, which then transmits the numbers to the customers. If more than one number is requested, the operator reports the first number, and the system then transmits the second to the caller. A number must be found quickly so that the customer is not kept waiting. It is often necessary to check various spellings of the same name since customers frequently give incorrect spellings.

Next, read this: Imagine you are the supervisor of ten directory assistance operators in a small regional phone company that has no formal training program for new operators. Since you get one or two new operators every few months you think it would raise efficiency for you to develop a "new directory assistance operator's training program" for your own use in your department. Consider what such a program would consist of before proceeding to your assigned group.

How to Set Up the Exercise/Instructions: Divide the class into groups of four or five students. In keeping with the procedure we discussed for setting up a training program, your group should, at a minimum, go through the following steps:

1. List the duties and responsibilities of the job (of directory assistance operator) using the description provided.
2. List some assumed standards of work performance for the job.
3. Within your group, develop some assumptions about what parts of the job give new employees the most trouble (you would normally be able to do this based on your experience as the operators' supervisor).
4. Determine what kind of training is needed to overcome these difficulties.
5. Develop a "new directory assistance operator's training package." In this you will provide two things. First, you will provide a one-page outline showing the type(s) of training each new operator in your unit will go through. (For example, you might indicate that the first two hours on the job will involve the new operator observing existing operators; then four hours of lectures; and so on.) Second, in this package, if you are going to use job instruction training, show the steps to be included; if you're going to use lectures, provide an outline of what you'll discuss; and so on.

If time permits, a spokesperson from each group can put his or her group's training program outline on the board, and the class can discuss the relative merits of each group's proposal.

NOTES

1. Earl Gomerjail and M. Scott Meyers, "Breakthrough in on the Job Training," *Harvard Business Review*, Vol. 45 (July–August 1966). See also Commerce Clearing House, "Corning Glassworks Orientation System Reduces Turnover and Has Major Impact on the Bottom Line," *Ideas and Trends*, July 26, 1988, p. 126. Claudia Reinhardt, "Training Supervisors in First Day Orientation Techniques," *Personnel*, Vol. 65, no. 6 (June 1988), pp. 24–28.
2. Meryl Reis Louis, "Surprise and Sense Making: What Newcomers Experience in Entering Unfamiliar Organizational Settings," *Administrative Science Quarterly* (June 1980), pp. 226–251. See also Terry Newell et al., "After the Layoffs: Orienting New Employees," *Training and Development Journal*, Vol. 41, no. 9 (September 1987), pp. 34–36; and Joan Alevars and Arnold Frigeri, "Picking Up the Pieces After Downsizing," *Training and Development Journal*, Vol. 41, no. 9 (September 1987), pp. 29–31.
3. Kenneth Wexley and Gary Latham, *Developing and Training Human Resources in Organizations* (Glenview, Ill.: Scott, Foresman, 1981), p. 105.
4. Douglas Hall, *Careers in Organizations* (Pacific Palisades, Calif.: Goodyear, 1976).
5. Joseph Famularo, *Handbook of Modern Personnel Administration* (New York: McGraw-Hill, 1972), pp. 23.7–23.8. See also Ronald Smith, "Employee Orientation: Ten Steps to Success," *Personnel Journal*, Vol. 63, no. 12 (December 1984), pp. 46–49.
6. Bureau of National Affairs, *Bulletin to Management*, August 1, 1985, pp. 35–39.
7. Charles Durakis, "Making the New Executive a Team Member," *Personnel*, Vol. 62, no. 10 (1985), pp. 58–60.
8. See also Walter St. John, "The Complete Employee Orientation Program," *Personnel Journal*, Vol. 59 (May 1980), pp. 373–378.
9. Edgar H. Schein, *Career Dynamics* (Reading, Mass.: Addison-Wesley, 1978), p. 86.
10. D. W. Ilgen and W. Seely, "Realistic Expectations as an Aid in Reducing Voluntary Resignations," *Journal of Applied Psychology*, Vol. 59 (1974), pp. 452–455; Richard Reilly and others, "Effect of Realistic Previews: A Study and Discussion of the Literature," *Personnel Psychology*, Vol. 34 (Winter 1981), pp. 823–834; Bernard Dugoni and Daniel Ilgen, "Realistic Job Previews and the Adjustment of New Employees," *Academy of Management Journal*, Vol. 24 (September 1981), pp. 579–591. Roger Dean and John Wanous, "Effects of Realistic Job Previews

on Hiring Bank Tellers," *Journal of Applied Psychology*, Vol. 69, no. 1 (February 1984), pp. 61–68.

11. Ibid.

12. Wexley and Latham, *Developing and Training*, p. 105.

13. "Corporate Culture: The Hard to Change Values That Spell Success or Failure," *Business Week*, October 27, 1980, pp. 154–160; see also Thomas Peters and Robert Waterman, Jr., *In Search of Excellence* (New York: Harper & Row, 1982), p. 291.

14. For an interesting example of socialization in Japan, see Hiroshi Tanaka, "New Employee Education in Japan," *Personnel Journal*, Vol. 60 (January 1981), pp. 51–53. See also Joan Pearson, "The Transition into a New Job: Tasks, Problems, and Outcomes," *Personnel Journal*, Vol. 62 (April 1982), pp. 286–290.

15. Louis, "Surprise and Sense Making," p. 247.

16. Ibid.

17. Ibid.

18. Meryl Louis, Barry Posner, and Gary Powell, "The Availability and Helpfulness of Socialization," *Personnel Psychology*, Vol. 36, no. 4 (Winter 1983), pp. 857–866.

19. Morton E. Grossman, "The $5.3 Billion Bill for Training," *Personnel Journal* (July 1986), p. 54.

20. This is based on Wexley and Latham, *Developing and Training*, pp. 22–27. Note that these legal aspects apply equally to technical training and management development. See also Ron Zemke, "What Is Technical Training, Anyway?" *Training*, Vol. 23, no. 7 (July 1986), pp. 18–22. See also Bureau of National Affairs, "Sexual Harassment: Training Tips," *Fair Employment Practices*, June 25, 1987, p. 84.

21. James Russell, "A Review of Fair Employment Cases in the Field of Training," *Personnel Psychology*, Vol. 37, no. 2 (Summer 1984), pp. 261–276. See also Bureau of National Affairs, "Training to Accommodate the Needs of the Disabled," *Fair Employment Practices*, June 25, 1987, p. 80.

22. Bureau of National Affairs, *Training Employees*, Personnel Policies Forum, Survey 88 (Washington, D.C.: November 1965), p. 5.

23. B. M. Bass and J. A. Vaughan, "Assessing Training Needs," in Craig Schneier and Richard Beatty, *Personnel Administration Today* (Reading, Mass.: Addison-Wesley, 1978), p. 311. See also Ronald Ash and Edward Leving, "Job Applicant Training and Work Experience Evaluation: An Empirical Comparison of Four Methods," *Journal of Applied Psychology*, Vol. 70, no. 3 (1985), pp. 572–576. See also John Lawrie, "Break the Training Ritual," *Personnel Journal*, Vol. 67, no. 4 (April 1988), pp. 95–97.

24. E. J. McCormick and J. Tiffin, *Industrial Psychology* (Englewood Cliffs, N.J.: Prentice-Hall, 1974), p. 245. See also James C. Georges, "The Hard Realities of Soft Skills Training," *Personnel Journal*, Vol. 68, no. 4 (April 1989), pp. 40–45; Robert H. Buckham, "Applying Role Analysis in the Workplace," *Personnel*, Vol. 64, no. 2 (February 1987), pp. 63–65; and J. Kevin Ford and Raymond Noe, "Self-Assessed Training Needs: The Effects of Attitudes Towards Training, Managerial Level, and Function," *Personnel Psychology*, Vol. 40, no. 1 (Spring 1987), pp. 39–54.

25. These steps are adapted from Donald F. Michalak and Edwin G. Yager, *Making the Training Process Work* (New York: Harper & Row, 1979). Copyright 1979 by Donald F. Michalak and Edwin G. Yager. Reprinted by permission of Harper & Row, Publishers, Inc. See also Kenneth R. Kramm, "Productivity: A Training Issue?" *Personnel Journal*, Vol. 67, no. 11 (November 1988), pp. 117–121.

26. J. P. Cicero, "Behavioral Objectives for Technical Training Systems," *Training and Development Journal*, Vol. 28 (1973), pp. 14–17. See also Larry D. Hales, "Training: A Product of Business Planning," *Training and Development Journal*, Vol. 40, no. 7 (July 1986), pp. 87–92, and Arnold H. Wensky and Robert Legendre, "Training Incentives," *Personnel Journal*, Vol. 68, no. 4 (April 1989), pp. 102–108.

27. I. L. Goldstein, *Training: Program Development and Evaluation* (Monterey, Calif.: Wadsworth, 1974). See also Stephen B. Wehrenberg, "Learning Con-

tracts," *Personnel Journal*, Vol. 67, no. 9 (September 1988), pp. 100–103, and Murray B. Heibert and Norman Smallwood, "Now for a Completely Different Look at Needs Analysis," *Training and Development Journal*, Vol. 41, no. 5 (May 1987), pp. 75–79.

28. Kenneth Wexley and Gary Yukl, *Organizational Behavior and Personnel Psychology* (Homewood, Ill.: Irwin, 1977), pp. 289–295.

29. Wexley and Latham, *Developing and Training*, p. 107.

30. Ibid., pp. 107–112. Four steps in on-the-job training based on William Berliner and William McLarney, *Management Practice and Training* (Homewood, Ill.: Irwin, 1974), pp. 442–443. See also Robert Sullivan and Donald Miklas, "On-the-Job Training That Works," *Training and Development Journal*, Vol. 39, no. 5 (May 1985), pp. 118–120, and Stephen B. Wehrenberg, "Supervisors as Trainers: The Long-Term Gains of OJT," *Personnel Journal*, Vol. 66, no. 4 (April 1987), pp. 48–51.

31. Michalak and Yager, *Making the Training Process Work*, pp. 108–111. See also Richard Wiegand, "Can *All* Your Trainees Hear You?" *Training and Development Journal*, Vol. 41, no. 8 (August 1987), pp. 38–43.

32. Wexley and Latham, *Developing and Training*, pp. 131–133. See also Teri O. Grady and Mike Matthews, "Video . . . Through the Eyes of the Trainee," *Training*, Vol. 24, no. 7 (July 1987), pp. 57–62.

33. Mary Boone and Susan Schulman, "Teletraining: A High-tech Alternative," *Personnel*, Vol. 62, no. 5 (May 1985), pp. 4–9. See also Ron Zemke, "The Rediscovery of Video Teleconferencing," *Training*, Vol. 23, no. 9 (September 1986), pp. 28–36; and Carol Haig, "Clinics Fill Training Niche," *Personnel Journal*, Vol. 66, no. 9 (September 1987), pp. 134–140.

34. G. N. Nash, J. P. Muczyk, and F. L. Vettori, "The Role and Practical Effectiveness of Programmed Instruction," *Personnel Psychology*, Vol. 24 (1971), pp. 397–418.

35. Wexley and Latham, *Developing and Training*, p. 141. See also Raymond Wlozkowski, "Simulation," *Training and Development Journal*, Vol. 39, no. 6 (June 1985), pp. 38–43.

36. Harold W. McGraw, Jr., "Adult Functional Illiteracy: What to Do About It," *Personnel* (October 1987), p. 38.

37. This is based on Ellen Sherman, "Back to Basics to Improve Skills," *Personnel*, July 1989, pp. 22–26.

38. Ibid., p. 24.

39. Bureau of National Affairs, *Bulletin to Management*, December 17, 1987, p. 408.

40. Nancy Lynn Bernardon, "Let's Erase Illiteracy from the Workplace," *Personnel* (January 1989), pp. 29–32.

41. Ibid. The PALS course was developed by educator Dr. John Henry Martin.

42. Ibid., p. 32. SKILLPAC was created by the Center for Applied Linguistics and Dr. Arnold Packer, senior research fellow at the Hudson Institute in Indianapolis, Indiana.

43. R. E. Catalano and D. L. Kirkpatrick, "Evaluating Training Programs—The State of the Art," *Training and Development Journal*, Vol. 22, no. 5 (May 1968), pp. 2–9. See also J. Kevin Ford and Steven Wroten, "Introducing New Methods for Conducting Training Evaluation and for Linking Training Evaluation to Program Redesign," *Personnel Psychology*, Vol. 37, no. 4 (Winter 1984), pp. 651–666. See also Basil Paquet et al., "The Bottom Line," *Training and Development Journal*, Vol. 41, no. 5 (May 1987), pp. 27–33; Harold E. Fisher and Ronald Weinberg, "Make Training Accountable: Assess Its Impact," *Personnel Journal*, Vol. 67, no. 1 (January 1988), pp. 73–75; and Timothy Baldwin and J. Kevin Ford, "Transfer of Training: A Review and Directions for Future Research," *Personnel Psychology*, Vol. 41, no. 1 (Spring 1988), pp. 63–105.

44. Donald Kirkpatrick, "Effective Supervisory Training and Development." Part 3: "Outside Programs," *Personnel*, Vol. 62, no. 2 (February 1985), pp. 39–42. See also James Bell and Deborah Kerr, "Measuring Training Results: Key to Managerial Commitment," *Training and Development Journal*, Vol. 41, no. 1 (January

1987), pp. 70–73. Among the reasons training might not pay off on the job are a mismatching of courses and trainee's needs, supervisory slip ups (with supervisors signing up trainees and then forgetting to have them attend the sessions when the training session is actually given), and no help applying skills back on the job. For a discussion, see Ruth Colvin Clark, "Nine Ways to Make Training Pay Off on the Job," *Training*, Vol. 23, no. 11 (November 1986), pp. 83–87. See also Herman Birnbrauer, "Troubleshooting Your Training Program," *Training and Development Journal*, Vol. 41, no. 9 (September 1987), pp. 18–20.

Chapter 8

Management Development Today

When you finish studying this chapter, you should be able to:

1. Explain the most frequent management development needs.
2. Describe the pros and cons of five management development methods.
3. List the steps in a typical management development program.
4. Explain how to use the case study development approach.
5. Describe how you would use five management development methods.

OVERVIEW

Management development is similar to technical training and is, in a sense, "technical training for managers," since it is aimed at providing managers with the leadership skills they need to do their jobs. The purpose of this chapter is to explain the main management development methods, including job rotation, leadership training, and management games. Then, once you've ensured (through selection, training, and development) that your employees have the skills to do their jobs, your next "motivation" job is to reward them, as discussed in the five chapters that follow.

management development Any attempt to improve current or future management performance by imparting knowledge, changing attitudes, or increasing skills.

Management development is any attempt to improve current or future managerial performance by imparting knowledge, changing attitudes, or increasing skills. It thus includes in-house programs like courses, on-the-job coaching, and rotational assignments, professional programs like American Management Association Seminars, and university programs like executive MBA programs.[1]

An ultimate aim of such development programs is, of course, to enhance the future performance of the organization itself. As a result, the management development *process* seeks to (1) assess and satisfy the company's needs (for instance, to fill future executive openings, or to make the firm more responsive) by (2) appraising the manager's performance and needs and then (3) developing the managers themselves.

Management development is a very big business. It is estimated that over 1 million American managers participate in management development programs yearly,[2] for a cost to American industry alone of several billion dollars yearly.[3]

Management development is important for several reasons. The main reason is that promotion from within is a major source of management talent. One survey of 84 employers reported that about 90% of supervisors, 73% of middle-level managers, and 51% of executives were promoted from within; virtually all these managers, in turn, required some development to prepare them for their new or prospective jobs. Similarly, management development facilitates organizational continuity by preparing employees and current managers to smoothly assume higher-level positions. It also helps to socialize management trainees by developing in them the right values and attitudes for working in the firm.[4]

◆ THE MANAGEMENT DEVELOPMENT PROCESS

Given its aim (of balancing the company's needs with the developmental needs of its managers) the management development process consists of two basic sets of tasks: personnel (managerial) planning and forecasting, and (2) manager needs—analysis and development. As explained in Chapter 4 ("Personnel Planning and Recruiting"), the personnel planning process involves projecting personnel (in this case management) positions to be filled, and then comparing the projected openings with the inside and outside candidates who are available. Companywide and individualized management development programs are then laid out to ensure that properly trained and developed managers are available when they are needed.

A management development program may be companywide, and basically open to all or most new or potential management recruits. Thus, the new college graduate may join Enormous Corp. and become part of (with two dozen colleagues) the company's companywide management development program. Here, she may be rotated through a preprogrammed series of departmental assignments and educational experiences, all aimed at identifying (for both her and the company) her management potential, and at providing the breadth of experiences (in, say, production and finance) that will make her more valuable in her first "real" assignment as group product leader. Here, superior candidates may be slotted onto a "fast track," a development program which prepares them more quickly to assume senior-level commands.

On the other hand, the management development program may be even more individualized, in that it is aimed at filling a specific position, such as CEO, perhaps with one of two potential candidates. When it is an executive

succession planning A process through which senior-level openings are planned for and eventually filled.

position to be filled, the process is usually called **succession planning.** Succession planning refers to a process of (1) personal planning and forecasting and (2) management needs analysis and development through which senior-level openings are planned for and eventually filled.

Career interests and aspirations, as well as performance appraisal, play crucial roles in management development. People do best on jobs that they like and for which they are suited. Therefore the development program should give the person a chance to assess his or her interests, as well as include some more formal career interests testing. Performance appraisal, meanwhile, serves to monitor the person's progress and potential, and to highlight what sorts of development activities might be needed to correct or compensate for deficiencies.

A typical management development program involves several steps. First, an *organization projection* is made; here you project your department's management needs based on factors like planned expansion or contraction. Next the personnel department reviews its *management skills inventory* to determine the management talent now employed. These inventories, you may recall, contain data on things like educational and work experience, career preferences, and performance appraisals. Next management *replacement charts* are developed. These summarize potential candidates for each of your management slots, as well as each person's development needs. As shown in Figure 8.1, the development needs for a future division vice-president might include *job rotation* (to obtain more experience in the firm's finance and production divisions), *executive development programs* (to provide training in strategic planning), and assignment for two weeks to the employer's *in-house management development center.*

◆ THE MOST FREQUENT MANAGEMENT DEVELOPMENT NEEDS

As illustrated in Table 8.1, different levels of management have different development needs.[5] For example, 15 high-ranked needs as expressed by those at the supervisory and middle management levels stress technical

FIGURE 8.1
Manpower Replacement Chart Showing Development Needs of Future Divisional Vice-President

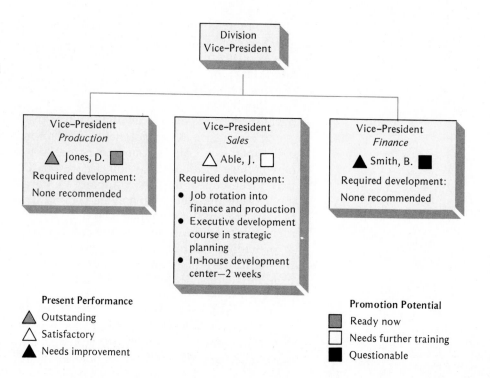

TABLE 8.1 Most Frequent Development Needs at Each Level of Management

EXECUTIVE LEVEL	MIDDLE LEVEL	SUPERVISORY LEVEL
1. Managing time Team building 3. Organizing and planning Evaluating and appraising employees 5. Coping with stress Understanding human behavior 7. Self-analysis Motivating others 9. Financial management Budgeting 11. Setting objectives and priorities Holding effective meetings 13. Oral communication 14. Labor/management relations 15. Decision making Developing strategies and policies	1. Evaluating and appraising employees 2. Motivating others 3. Setting objectives and priorities 4. Oral communication 5. Organizing and planning 6. Understanding human behavior 7. Written communication Managing time 9. Team building Leadership Decision making 10. Holding effective meetings Delegation Developing and training subordinates 15. Selecting employees	1. Motivating others 2. Evaluating and appraising others 3. Leadership 4. Oral communication 5. Understanding human behavior 6. Developing and training subordinates Role of the manager 7. Setting objectives and priorities Written communication 10. Discipline Organizing and planning 11. Managing time Counseling and coaching 14. Selecting employees 15. Decision making

skills like evaluating and appraising employees, setting objectives, communicating, and disciplining. At the executive level, on the other hand, the development needs stress general business skills like financial management, budgeting, and labor relations. You'll also note the increased need for team-building skills at higher management levels: "team building" was ranked eighteenth for supervisors, ninth for middle managers, and first for executives.

♦ POPULARITY OF VARIOUS DEVELOPMENT TECHNIQUES

On-the-job experiences (supplemented by coaching, rotational assignments, and other in-house training) are, by far, the most popular form of management development. This is illustrated by the following table, which shows the percentages for techniques reported by personnel managers as being the "most important means of development" in their firms:[6]

MEANS OF DEVELOPMENT	PERCENTAGE REPORTING MOST IMPORTANT (%)
On-the-job experience	68.2
Coaching by superiors	20.9
In-house classroom	4.7
Rotational assignment	2.4
University programs	2.3
Consultant programs	1.1
Other	1.1

Furthermore, different techniques are favored for different levels of management, as summarized in Table 8.2. In-house workshops (which teach, for instance, interviewing or leadership skills) and coaching plus on-the-job experience are most favored for supervisory employees. Coaching, in-house

TABLE 8.2   Type of Development Received

	PERCENT RECEIVING		
Type of Development	*Executive*	*Middle*	*Supervisory*
External conference/seminars	27.7%	26.1%	17.3%
In-house workshops	22.9	21.6	34.7
Coaching plus on-the-job experience	13.3	29.5	33.4
Participation in university programs	10.8	10.2	4.0
Association/professional conferences and workshops	16.8	4.5	0
Consultant programs	7.2	5.7	5.3
Self-study courses	1.2	2.3	5.3

Source: Reprinted, by permission of the publisher, from Lester Digman, "Management Development: Needs and Practices," *Personnel* (July–August 1980), p. 56. © 1980 American Management Association, New York. All rights reserved.

workshops, and external conferences and seminars are favored for middle managers. For executives, external conferences and seminars are the most important type of development.

MANAGERIAL ON-THE-JOB TRAINING

On-the-job training is one of the most popular development methods. Important techniques here include job rotation, coaching, junior boards, and understudy assignments.

♦ JOB ROTATION

job rotation A management training technique that involves moving a trainee from department to department to broaden his or her experience, and identify strong and weak points.

With **job rotation** you move management trainees from department to department to broaden their understanding of all phases of the business.[7] The trainee—often a recent college graduate—may spend several months in each department; this not only helps broaden his or her experience, but also helps the person discover the jobs he or she prefers. The person may just be an observer in each department, but more commonly gets fully involved in its operations; he or she thus learns the department's business by actually doing it, whether it involves sales, production, finance, or some other function.

Job rotation has several other advantages.[8] In addition to providing a well-rounded training experience for each person, it helps avoid stagnation through the constant introduction of new points of view in each department. And it tests the trainee and helps identify the person's strong and weak points. Periodic job changing can also improve interdepartmental cooperation; managers become more understanding of each other's problems, while rotation also widens the trainee's acquaintances among management.

Rotation does have disadvantages. It encourages "generalization" and tends to be more appropriate for developing general line managers than functional staff experts. You also have to be careful not to forget inadvertently a trainee at some deserted outpost.

There are several things you can do to improve a rotation program's success.[9] The program should be tailored to the needs and capabilities of the individual trainee, and not be a standard sequence of steps that all trainees take. The trainee's interests, aptitudes, and career preferences should be considered, along with the employer's needs; the length of time the trainee stays in a job should then be determined by how fast he or she is learning. Furthermore, the managers to whom these people are assigned should themselves be specially trained to provide feedback and to monitor performance in an interested and competent way.

The Goodyear Tire and Rubber Company's training program for college graduates is a good example of job rotation.[10] Each trainee's program is tailored to match his or her experience, education, and vocational preference. Programs vary from 6 to 15 months, beginning with 3 weeks in an orientation program becoming thoroughly acquainted with Goodyear. (Here they study the organization's structure, company objectives, and basic manufacturing processes, and participate in informal meetings with top company officials.) After an additional month of factory orientation, trainees discuss their career interests with top-level managers and select up to six assignments in special departments, each of which will last about one month. (For example, a chemical engineering graduate might rotate through departments for fabric development, chemical materials development research, central process engineering, process development, and chemical production.) Trainees then select specific job assignments as the starting point of their careers.

◆ COACHING/UNDERSTUDY APPROACH

In the coaching/understudy approach, the trainee works directly with the person he or she is to replace; the latter is in turn responsible for the trainee's coaching. Normally, the understudy relieves the executive of certain responsibilities, thereby giving the trainee a chance to learn the job.[11] This helps ensure that the employer will have trained managers to assume key positions when they're vacated due to retirement, promotions, transfers, or terminations. And it helps guarantee the long-run development of company-bred top managers.

To be effective, the executive has to be a good coach and mentor. Furthermore, this person's motivation to train the replacement will depend on the quality of the relationship between them. Some executives are also better at delegating responsibility, providing reinforcement, and communicating than are others, and this, too, will affect the results.

◆ JUNIOR BOARDS

junior board A method of providing middle-management trainees with experience in analyzing company problems by inviting them to sit on a junior board of directors and make recommendations on overall company policies.

Unlike job rotation (which aims to familiarize the trainees with the problems of each department), **junior boards** aim to give promising young middle managers experience in analyzing overall company problems. The idea of a junior board (also sometimes called *multiple management*) is to give trainees top-level analysis and policymaking experience by having 10 to 12 of them sit on a "junior" board of directors. The members of such committees come from various departments and make recommendations regarding top-level issues like organization structure, executive compensation, and interdepartmental conflict to the official board of directors. This technique has been used for years by a number of successful companies. It provides middle-management trainees with on-the-job training and experience in dealing with organization-wide problems.

◆ ACTION LEARNING

action learning A training technique by which management trainees are allowed to work full time analyzing and solving problems in other departments or government agencies.

Action learning[12] involves giving middle-management trainees released time to work full time on projects, analyzing and solving problems in departments other than their own. The trainees meet periodically with a four- or five-person project group, where their findings and progress are discussed and debated.

Action learning was first used in England, but it is similar to (and grounded in) other, earlier development techniques. It is similar to the *junior boards* discussed above, except that trainees generally work full time on their projects, rather than analyzing a problem as a committee as they would on junior boards. It is also similar to just giving a management trainee a special assignment or project; however, with action learning several trainees meet once a week as a project group to compare notes and discuss each other's projects. Action learning often involves cooperation among several employers. For example, an employee from General Electric might be assigned to a government agency for his research project, while the agency might assign one of its managers to GE for hers.

The idea of developing managers this way has pros and cons. It gives trainees real experience with actual problems, and to that extent can develop skills like problem analysis and planning. Furthermore, the trainees (working with the others in the group) can and do find solutions to major problems. The main drawback is that in releasing trainees to work on outside projects, the employer loses, in a sense, the full-time services of a competent manager, while the trainee often finds it hard to return to his or her old position (which is usually filled by a stand-in manager).

BASIC OFF-THE-JOB DEVELOPMENT TECHNIQUES

There are many techniques you can use to develop managers off the job, perhaps in a conference room at your headquarters or off the premises entirely at a university or special seminar. These techniques are addressed next.

◆ THE CASE STUDY METHOD

The case study method involves presenting a trainee with a written description of an organizational problem; the person then analyzes the case in private, diagnoses the problem, and presents his or her findings and solutions in a discussion with other trainees.[13] The case method approach is aimed at giving trainees realistic experience in identifying and analyzing complex problems in an environment in which their progress can be subtly guided by a trained discussion leader. Through the class discussion of the case, the trainee learns that there are usually many ways to approach and solve complex organizational problems and that the trainee's own solution is often influenced by his or her needs and values.

The case method has five main features:[14] (1) the use of actual organizational problems, (2) the maximum possible involvement of participants in stating their views, inquiring into others' views, confronting different views, and making decisions, resulting in (3) a minimal degree of dependence on the faculty members who, in turn (4) hold the position that there are rarely any right or wrong answers, that cases are incomplete and so is reality, and (5) who still strive to make the case method as engaging as possible through creation of appropriate levels of drama. As you can see, the instructor plays (or should play) a crucial role;[15] the person should be not a lecturer or expounder of principles lifted from textbooks, but rather a catalyst and coach. The instructor should also be a helpful source of information, while asking probing questions to elicit lively debate among trainees.

Problems to Avoid

Unfortunately, according to Argyris the case approach (as used in practice) often falls far short of this mark.[16] In practice, he says faculty often dominate classroom discussions by asking students questions that they then themselves proceed to answer, by answering specific questions asked by students, and by presenting statements of the facts about the case. Faculty, he found, also use "mystery to achieve mastery" by intentionally withholding information (for instance regarding what the company actually did and what its competitors were doing at the time when the case was written) with the aim of maintaining control of the classroom discussion. In his study of the case method, Argyris also found that there were inconsistencies between the approach that the faculty espoused and what they actually did. For example, (1) faculty say there are no right or wrong answers, yet some faculty members do take positions and give answers; (2) faculty say there are many different points of view possible, yet faculty members seem to select viewpoints and organize them in a way to suggest that they have a preferred route. Finally, few attempts were made by the faculty to relate the trainees' behavior in the classroom to their behavior back home. For example, faculty members missed several opportunities to relate the problems experienced by the company in the case to problems faced by the trainee's own employers.

There are several things you can do to make the case approach more effective. If possible, the cases should be actual cases from the trainee's own firm. This will help ensure that trainees understand the background of the case, as well as make it easier for trainees to transfer what is learned to their own jobs and situations. Argyris also contends that instructors have to guard against dominating the case analysis and make sure that they remain no more than a catalyst or coach. Finally, they must carefully prepare the case discussion, and let the students discuss the case in small groups before class.[17]

♦ MANAGEMENT GAMES

In a computerized management game, trainees are divided into five- or six-person companies, each of which has to compete with the other in a simulated marketplace. Each company sets a goal (such as "maximize sales") and is told it can make several decisions. For example, the group may be allowed to decide (1) how much to spend on advertising, (2) how much to produce, (3) how much inventory to maintain, and (4) how many of which product to produce. Usually the game itself compresses a two- or three-year period into days, weeks, or months. As in the real world, each company usually cannot see what decisions the other firms have made, although these decisions do affect their own sales. For example, if a competitor decides to increase its advertising expenditures, that firm may end up increasing its sales at the expense of yours.

Management games can be good development tools. People learn best by getting actively involved in the activity itself, and the games can be useful for gaining such involvement. Games are almost always interesting and exciting for the trainees because of their realism and competitiveness. They help trainees develop their problem-solving skills, as well as focus their attention on the need for planning, rather than on just putting out fires. The companies also usually elect their own officers and develop their own divisions of work; the games can thus be useful for developing leadership skills and for fostering cooperation and teamwork.

Management games also have their drawbacks. One problem is that the game can be expensive to develop and implement, particularly when (as is usually the case) it's computerized. Games also usually force the decision makers to choose alternatives from a closed list (for instance, they might have choices of only three levels of production); in real life managers are more often rewarded for creating new, innovative alternatives. On the whole, though, trainees almost always react favorably to a well-run game, and it is a good technique for developing problem-solving and leadership skills.

♦ OUTSIDE SEMINARS

Ealier in this chapter we listed the most important development needs at each level of management, including the need to develop specific skills like motivating others, appraising employees, leadership, communication, setting objectives, budgeting, and decision making.

Many organizations put on special seminars and conferences aimed at providing this sort of skill-building training for managers. The American Management Associations (AMA), for instance, provide thousands of courses in areas such as the following:

General management

Human resources

Sales and marketing

International management

Finance

Information systems and technology

Manufacturing and operations management

Purchasing, transportation, and physical distribution

Packaging

Research and technology management

General and administrative services

Insurance and employee benefits

The courses themselves range from "how to sharpen your business writing skills" to "strategic planning" and "assertiveness training for managers."[18] The outline of a typical course is presented in Figure 8.2; it is for a course in "advanced management techniques for experienced supervisors." As you can see, it is a two-and-a-half day advanced course for first-line manufacturing supervisors with three to five years of experience who want to enhance their management skills. Topics covered include review of management and organization concepts, developing effective interpersonal skills, communication, motivation, and developing leadership skills. As also illustrated, the course is offered in several cities; many of the AMA courses can also be presented on site at the employer's place of business if ten or more employees are enrolled. Other organizations offering management development services include AMR International, Inc., the Conference Board, and Xerox Educational Systems.

Many of these programs offer *continuing education units* (*CEUs*) for course completion. Earning CEUs for course completion provides, says the AMA, a recognized measure of educational accomplishment, one that is today used by more than 1,000 colleges to record successful program completions. CEUs generally can't be used to obtain degree-granting credit at most colleges or universities, but they do provide a record of the fact that the trainee participated in and completed a special conference or seminar.

♦ UNIVERSITY-RELATED PROGRAMS

Colleges and universities provide three types of management development activities. First, many schools provide *continuing education programs* in leadership, supervision, and the like. As with the AMA, these range from

FIGURE 8.2
Content for a Typical Middle-
Management American Management Association Training Program.
Source: American Management Association

4208Q/Advanced Management Techniques for Experienced Supervisors:
How to Work Effectively With People and Within the Organization

Who Should Attend:
An advanced course for First-Line Manufacturing Supervisors with 3–5 years' experience who want to enhance their management skills. Especially useful for supervisors who have completed course #4271—The Management Course For New Manufacturing Supervisors, or course #4202—Productivity Improvement Methods and Techniques.

Key Topics:
- Review of management and organization concepts and how they relate to today's employees: planning, organizing, coordinating, controlling; authority, responsibility, accountability, reportability; dollar relationship to human resources utilization and lost time

- How to develop effective interpersonal skills: understanding behavior and personality; relating to people as individuals; self-awareness and opportunities to develop; how to positively affect attitudes and working relationships; team development; how to develop a warmer, more relaxed climate in dealing with people; how to come across firmly but fairly.

- The communication workshop for supervisors: develop increased listening skills; writing and speaking clearly, concisely, and with more organization; how to use communication to reduce stress and fear; assertiveness in communication; how to sell your ideas to management

- The motivation workshop for supervisors: analyzing management style and its role in motivation; creating an environment where employees will work effectively; behavioral foundation for self-motivation; relating program content to actual problem situations.

- Developing your leadership skills: how you are perceived by others; habits that reduce your leadership potential; applying course content to leadership development

Special Feature:
Examination of the supervisor's role—defining responsibilities, duties, authority, and the restriction of authority. **Discussions** on worker psychology—how the supervisor can effectively motivate, and the importance of communications. **Discussion** of various discipline techniques—when and where to use them and their effects on performance and morale. **Presentation** on reviewing employee performance with emphasis on improving their production and morale.

one- to four-day programs to executive development programs lasting one to four months.

The Advanced Management Program of the Graduate School of Business Administration at Harvard University is an example of one of these longer programs. As can be seen in Figure 8.3 on page 292, each class in this program consists of a group of experienced managers from all regions of the world. The program uses cases and lectures to provide an employer's top-level management talent with the latest management skills, as well as with practice in analyzing complex organizational problems. Similar programs include the Executive Program of the Graduate School of Business Administration at the University of California at Berkeley, the Management Development Seminar at the University of Chicago, and the Executive in Business Administration Program of the Graduate School of Business at Columbia University. Most of these programs take the executives away from their jobs, putting them in university-run learning environments for their entire stay. The Columbia University program, for instance, is offered at Arden House in the Ramapo Mountains of New York.

Second, many colleges and universities also offer *individual courses* in areas like business, management, and health care administration that managers can take as matriculated or nonmatriculated students to fill gaps in their backgrounds. Thus, a prospective division manager with a gap in her experience with accounting controls might sign up for a two-course sequence in managerial accounting.

Finally, many schools also offer pertinent *degree programs* such as the MBA or Executive MBA. The latter is a Master of Business Administration

FIGURE 8.3

The experience called the Advanced Management Program:

A distinguished faculty

There are many things that make up the experience called the Advanced Management Program. And one of the more memorable is the case method of instruction, which uses real business situations requiring actual decisions, taught by a distinguished faculty experienced in the world of business. All classes are conducted by senior faculty members who have a full-time commitment to the unique needs of senior managers.

In addition, instruction is in facilities designed specifically for executive education and devoted exclusively to it. The innovative curriculum is a rigorous thirteen weeks. And during this time, peer interaction is the most intense and stimulating most executives will ever encounter.

These reasons, and more, explain why the Advanced Management Program numbers among its alumni more than eighteen hundred men and women with the title of chairman of the board, chief executive officer, chief operating officer, or vice chairman of the board.

1985 session dates are: **January 20 to April 18 and September 22 to December 19.**

Candidates are considered with twenty to twenty-five years experience who manage profit centers or head major functions in larger companies.

For specific information, call or write: Administrative Director Advanced Management Program Harvard Business School Boston, Massachusetts 02163 (617) 495-6163

degree program geared especially to middle managers and above, who generally take their courses on weekends, proceeding through the program with the same group of colleagues.

The Employer's Contribution

The employer usually plays a role in university-related programs like these.[19] First, many employers offer *tuition refunds* as an incentive for employees to develop job-related skills. Thus, engineers may be encouraged to enroll in technical courses aimed at keeping them abreast of changes in their field and supervisors may be encouraged to enroll in programs to develop them for higher-level management jobs.

Employers are also increasingly granting technical and professional employees extended *sabbaticals*—periods of time off—for attending a college or university to pursue a higher degree or to upgrade skills. For example, Bell Laboratories has a program that includes a tuition refund and released time for up to one year of on-campus study. In addition, the company has a doctoral support program that permits tuition refund and released time for studies one day a week (and, for some, a full year's study on campus to meet residence requirements).

Some companies have experimented with offering selected employees in-house degree programs in cooperation with colleges and universities. Many also offer a variety of in-house lectures and seminars by university staff.

For example, Technicon, a high-tech medical instruments company, asked Pace University to offer an executive education program for its key middle managers. The theme of the 14-month program was successful management of high-tech businesses. The coursework covered topics ranging from finance to executive communication.[20]

Universities and corporations are also experimenting with video-linked classroom education. For example, the School of Business and Public Administration at California State University, Sacramento, and a Hewlett-Packard facility in Roseville, California, are video-linked. A video-link allows for classroom learning on campuses with simultaneous broadcasting to other locations, including Roseville, via telephone communication lines.

◆ ROLE PLAYING

role playing A training technique in which trainees act out the parts of people in a realistic management situation.

Role playing had its origin in psychotherapy, but it has found wide use in industry for improving sales, leadership, and interviewing skills, as well as other skills. The aim of role playing is to create a realistic situation and then have the trainees assume the parts (or roles) of specific persons in that situation.[21]

One such role—that of Walt Marshal, supervisor—from a famous role-playing exercise called the New Truck Dilemma is presented in Figure 8.4. Roles like these for each of the participants (when combined with the general instructions for the role-playing exercise) can lead to a spirited discussion among the role players, particularly when each throws himself or herself into the role, rather than merely acting. The idea of the exercise is to solve the problem at hand and thereby develop trainees' skills in areas like leadership and delegating.

FIGURE 8.4
Typical Role in a Role-Playing Exercise
Source: Norman R. F. Maier and Gertrude Casselman Verser, *Psychology in Industrial Organizations*, 5th ed., p. 190. Copyright © 1982 by Houghton Mifflin Company. Used by permission of the publishers.

Walt Marshall — Supervisor of Repair Crew

You are the head of a crew of telephone maintenance workers, each of whom drives a small service truck to and from the various jobs. Every so often you get a new truck to exchange for an old one, and you have the problem of deciding to which of your crew members you should give the new truck. Often there are hard feelings, since each seems to feel entitled to the new truck, so you have a tough time being fair. As a matter of fact, it usually turns out that whatever you decide is considered wrong by most of the crew. You now have to face the issue again because a new truck, a Chevrolet, has just been allocated to you for assignment.

In order to handle this problem you have decided to put the decision up to the crew. You will tell them about the new truck and will put the problem in terms of what would be the fairest way to assign the truck. Do not take a position yourself, because you want to do what they think is most fair.

Role playing can be an enjoyable and inexpensive way to develop many new skills. With the New Truck Dilemma exercise, for instance, participants learn the importance of fairness in bringing about acceptance of resource allocation decisions. The role players can also give up their inhibitions and experiment with new ways of acting. For example, a supervisor could experiment with both a considerate and autocratic leadership style, whereas in the real world the person might not have this harmless way of experimenting. According to Maier, role playing also trains a person to be aware of and sensitive to the feelings of others.[22]

Role playing has some drawbacks. An exercise can take an hour or more to complete, only to be deemed a waste of time by participants if the instructor doesn't prepare a wrap-up explanation of what the participants were to learn. Some trainees also feel that role playing is childish, while others, having had a bad experience with the technique, are reluctant to participate at all.

♦ BEHAVIOR MODELING

behavior modeling A training technique in which trainees are first shown good management techniques (in a film), are then asked to play roles in a simulated situation, and are then given feedback and praise by their supervisor.

Behavior modeling is a relatively new development technique. It involves (1) showing trainees the right (or "model") way of doing something, (2) letting the person practice the right way to do it, and then (3) providing feedback regarding his or her performance.[23] It has been used, for example, to:

1. Train first-line supervisors to handle common supervisor-employee interactions better, including giving recognition, disciplining, introducing changes, and improving poor performance.

2. Train middle managers to better handle interpersonal situations involving, for example, giving directions, discussing performance problems, discussing undesirable work habits, reviewing performance, and discussing salary problems.

3. Train employees (and their supervisors) to take and give criticism, ask and give help, and establish mutual trust and respect.

The basic behavior modeling procedure can be outlined as follows:

1. *Modeling.* First, trainees watch films or videotapes that show model persons behaving effectively in a problem situation. In other words, trainees are shown the right way to behave in a simulated but realistic situation. The film might thus show a supervisor disciplining a subordinate, if teaching how to discipline is the aim of the training program.

2. *Role playing.* Next the trainees are given roles to play in a simulated situation; here they practice and rehearse the effective behaviors demonstrated by the models.

3. *Social reinforcement.* The trainer provides reinforcement in the form of praise and constructive feedback based on how the trainee performs in the role-playing situation.

4. *Transfer of training.* Finally, trainees are encouraged to apply their new skills when they are back on their jobs.

Example

An example can help illustrate the basic behavior modeling technique.[24] The training group (which consisted of first-line supervisors) was divided into two groups of ten, with each group meeting for 2 hours each week for 9 weeks. The sessions focused on management skills like orienting new employees, giving recognition, motivating poor performers, and correcting poor work habits.

COMPUTER APPLICATIONS IN MANAGEMENT

DEVELOPMENT: A COMPUTERIZED MANAGERIAL ASSESSMENT AND DEVELOPMENT PROGRAM

There are a number of Computerized Management Assessment and Development programs which can facilitate an employer's development process. One particularly useful example of such a management development tool is called ACUMEN.[1]

ACUMEN is a sophisticated managerial assessment and development program. The Education Version of ACUMEN consists of three elements: instructions, a self-assessment, and an assessment report. After spending approximately 20 minutes interacting with ACUMEN'S IBM-compatible program, you will receive a visual display or hard-output "management profile" that focuses on 12 basic management traits:

1. *Humanistic-helpful.* Measures your inclination to see the best in others, to encourage their growth and development, and to be supportive.
2. *Affiliation.* Measures the degree of friendliness, sociability, and outgoing tendencies you are likely to exhibit.
3. *Approval.* Measures your need to seek others' approval and support in order to feel secure and worthwhile as a person.
4. *Conventional.* Measures your need to conform, follow the rules, and meet the expectations of those in authority.
5. *Dependence.* Measures your tendency to be compliant, passive, and dependent on others.
6. *Apprehension.* Measures your tendency to experience anxiety and self-blame.
7. *Oppositional.* Measures your tendency to take a critical, questioning, and somewhat cynical attitude.
8. *Power.* Measures your tendency to be authoritarian and controlling.
9. *Competition.* Measures your need to be seen as the best and, to some extent, to maintain a self-centered attitude.
10. *Perfectionism.* Measures your need to seek perfection, and your tendency to base your self-worth on your own performance.
11. *Achievement.* Measures your need to achieve and have an impact on things.
12. *Self-actualization.* Measures your level of self-esteem, interest in self-development, and general drive to learn about and experience life to the fullest extent.

When you complete the self-assessment, ACUMEN analyzes your responses and generates scores on the twelve scales. Each scale represents a particular attitude, or thinking style. The way you think (your thinking style) affects:

- What you strive to achieve (your *goals*).
- Your effectiveness as a *leader.*
- How you relate to and *communicate* with other people.
- Whether you view *change* as positive or negative.
- How you respond to crises and *stress.*

The major aim of ACUMEN is to help you develop a fuller understanding and appreciation of how your own thinking styles and personal dispositions play a role in your productivity and management effectiveness. ACUMEN's

[1]ACUMEN is a Trademark of Human Factors Advanced Technology Group. This box from "What ACUMEN Is and How It Works," by HFATG.

analysis of your assessment responses, presented in graphic or textual form, provides this information.

When you view a graphic profile display, you will notice that each scale's extension is of varying length. On the circular graph, some scales extend a long way from the center of the circle while other segments are relatively short. Similarly, scales on the bar graph will vary in length. The longer extensions indicate styles that are more prominent in your profile. By comparing the extensions, you will be able to find the thinking styles that have the most impact on your own behavior.

The text printout on each scale provides you with detailed assessment and development information for each scale. For example, you might find you have a high score on the Humanistic Helpful Scale. You're told here that you are likely to enjoy developing, helping, and teaching others, like to motivate others and attempt to see the best in others. So far so good. However on the Oppositional Scale your low score indicates a fairly accepting, agreeable type of person. Up to a point, these may be laudable traits for managers. But in terms of development, you should (the printout says) "beware of being too reticent about making critical comments" (which you will have to do as a manager). In summary, a computerized management tool like ACUMEN can be very valuable, both for assessing management aptitudes (say, for future promotability) and for providing detailed development advice for the trainee.

Each training session followed the same format. First, the topic (such as handling a complaining employee) was introduced by two trainers. Next a film was presented that depicted a supervisor "model" effectively handling a complaining employee by following several guidelines that were shown in a film immediately before and after the "model film" was presented. (In the case of handling a complaining employee, these guidelines included avoid responding with hostility or defensiveness, ask for and listen openly to the employee's complaint, restate the complaint for thorough understanding, and recognize and acknowledge his or her viewpoint.) Next there was a group discussion of the model supervisor's effectiveness in demonstrating the desired behaviors, such as: "Did the person avoid responding with hostility or defensiveness?" Next the trainees practiced (via role playing) the desired behaviors in front of the class and then got feedback from the class on their effectiveness in demonstrating the desired behaviors. In each practice session, one trainee took the role of supervisor and another assumed the role of employee. No prepared scripts were used, and trainees were simply asked to recreate an incident that had occurred to one of them in the past 12 months.[25]

♦ IN-HOUSE DEVELOPMENT CENTERS

in-house development centers A company-based method for exposing prospective managers to realistic exercises to develop improved management skills.

Some employers have established **in-house development centers** in which prospective managers and executives are exposed to realistic problems and tasks, evaluated on their performance, and encouraged to develop improved management skills. These centers usually combine classroom learning (lectures and seminars, for instance) with other techniques like assessment centers, in-basket exercises, and role playing.

CBS, Inc., has used such a center since 1976.[26] The CBS School for Management, as it is called, is set in country club surroundings in Old Westbury, New York. Its basic aim is to give young managers firsthand experience at decision making.

To accomplish this, both their general management program (for upper-level managers) and professional management programs (for entry-level managers) stress the solution of concrete business problems through working with people. The programs use various teaching methods, but stress computerized case exercises. In one exercise, for instance, each student acts as a regional sales manager and has to make decisions regarding how to deal with a star saleswoman who wants to leave, and how to choose new salespeople. As trainees make decisions (like whether or not to boost the saleswoman's salary to entice her to stay), the computer indicates the implications of the decision; thus, if she is paid more, others may also want that increase in pay. Then, at the end of each day students get printouts indicating how their decisions reflected their ability to set goals, organize work, manage time, and supervise subordinates.

SPECIAL MANAGEMENT DEVELOPMENT TECHNIQUES

special management development techniques Special techniques (like leader match) to develop leadership ability, increase managers' sensitivity to others, and reduce interdepartmental conflicts.

There are also various **special management development techniques** that are aimed at developing leadership ability, increasing the manager's sensitivity to others, and reducing interdepartmental conflict.

◆ LEADER MATCH TRAINING

leader match training A program that identifies types of leaders and teaches them how to fit their leadership style to their situation.

Leader match training is aimed at teaching managers how to fit their leadership style to the situation, and is based on several assumptions. First, it assumes that whether a people-oriented or production-oriented style is appropriate depends on the degree of situational control the leader can exercise. This is summarized in Figure 8.5. Fred Fiedler, who developed this technique, contends that production-oriented leaders do best in situations where they can exercise either very high control or in situations where they have very little control over the situation. People-oriented leaders, on the other hand, do best in middle-of-the-road situations where they can exercise moderate amounts of control.

Fiedler explains his findings as follows. He says that in very-high-control situations—where the leader's word is "law" and the job is very routine—the group is ready to be directed and the subordinates expect to be told what to do. On the other hand, in the very-low-control situation—where the leader can't hire or fire, and the job to be done is nonroutine—the group will fall apart without the leader's active intervention and control. Thus, in both high- and low-control situations, a more no-nonsense, production- or task-oriented leadership style is called for. In the middle range, says Fiedler, the situation is not so clear cut, and the biggest problem is often that disagreements may break out and undermine the group's performance; here the leader must be supportive and people oriented, because it is important that he or she coax the subordinates to work together and with the leader.

The leader match program is in the form of a manual that contains questionnaires that enable the leader to assess his or her natural leadership style, as well as the degree of control inherent in his or her situation.[27] Fiedler contends that the problem for leaders consists of getting into and remaining in situations where they can perform well. He also argues that it is usually easier to change your situation (or to at least choose the right

FIGURE 8.5
Effects of People-Oriented and Task-Oriented Leaders in Various Situations
Source: Fred Fiedler, Martin Chemers, and Linda Mahar, *Improving Leadership Effectiveness: The Leader Match Concept* [New York: John Wiley, 1977].

Leader Type	SITUATIONAL CONTROL		
	High Control	Moderate Control	Low Control
People-oriented	*Performance:* Poor	*Performance:* Good	*Performance:* Poor
Task-oriented	*Performance:* Good.	*Performance:* Poor.	*Performance:* Relatively good.

situation) than it is to change your leadership style. He therefore presents several prescriptions aimed at enabling you to fit your style to the situation: for example, a task-oriented leader who finds herself misplaced in a situation of moderate control should take actions that give her more control of the situation, perhaps by having her boss give her the authority to hire and fire subordinates unilaterally.[28]

♦ VROOM-YETTON LEADERSHIP TRAINING

Vroom-Yetton leadership training A development program for management trainees that focuses on decision making with varying degrees of input from subordinates.

This method focuses on developing your ability to determine the degree to which your subordinates should be allowed to participate in the decision that must be made. First, Vroom and Yetton say there are several degrees of participation (as summarized in Figure 8.6), ranging from *no* participation to *minimum* participation, *more* participation, *still more* participation, and finally *consensus* management, or total participation. Next, Vroom and Yetton say that the right degree of participation depends on seven attributes of the situation, including the importance of the quality of the decision, the extent to which you possess sufficient information to make a high-quality decision by yourself, and the extent to which the problem is routine and structured or ambiguous and complicated. (These seven attributes are summarized in Table 8.3.) Finally, Vroom and Yetton present a chart for determining the appropriateness of employee participation in the form of a deci-

FIGURE 8.6
Five Degrees of Participative Leadership
Source: R. H. George Field, "A Test of Vroom-Yetton Normative Model of Leadership," *Journal of Applied Psychology,* vol. 67, no. 5 [October 1982], pp. 523–532. Copyright 1982 by the American Psychological Association. Reprinted by permission of the author.

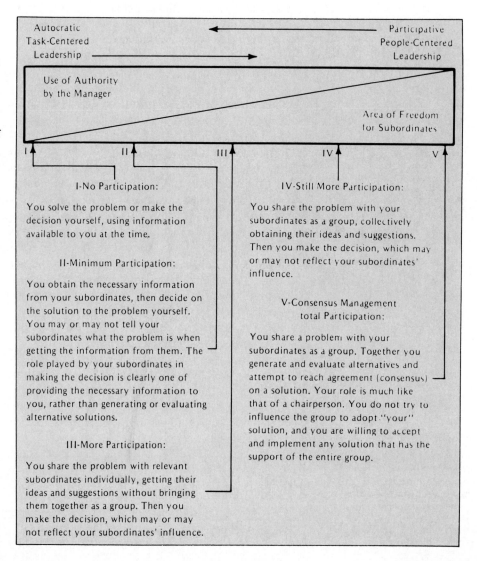

TABLE 8.3   Diagostic Questions Used in the Vroom-Yetton Model

PROBLEM ATTRIBUTES	DIAGNOSTIC QUESTIONS
(These determine the degree of participation that is appropriate.)	(These enable you to diagnose the presence or absence of each attribute.)
A. The importance of the quality of the decision	Is there a quality requirement such that one solution is likely to be more rational than another?
B. The extent to which the leader possesses sufficient information/expertise to make a high-quality decision by himself	Do I have sufficient information to make a high-quality decision?
C. The extent to which the problem is structured	Is the problem structured?
D. The extent to which acceptance or commitment on the part of subordinates is critical to the effective implementation of the decision	Is acceptance of decision by subordinates critical to effective implementation?
E. The prior probability that the leader's autocratic decision will receive acceptance by subordinates	If you were to make the decision by yourself, is it reasonably certain that it would be accepted by your subordinates?
F. The extent to which the subordinates are motivated to attain the organizational goals as represented in the objectives explicit in the statement of the problem	Do subordinates share the organizational goals to be obtained in solving this problem?
G. The extent to which subordinates are likely to be in conflict over preferred solutions	Is conflict among subordinates likely in preferred solutions?

sion tree, as presented in Figure 8.7. To use this exhibit, trainees are taught to work from left to right. First, determine whether the *quality of decision* is important, then determine if you have *sufficient information to make a high-quality decision*, and so forth. By starting on the left of the exhibit and answering each question "yes" or "no," the trainee can work his or her way across the decision tree and thereby determine the degree of participation that is best, given the nature of the decision that must be made.

In the development program based on this model, trainees are first taught the rudiments of the approach, such as the differences between the management styles, and the questions that must be asked to identify the nature of the problem (such as "How important is the quality of the decision?"). Next they are given a series of written case incident problems that briefly summarize the situation facing the trainees. For example, "Suppose you are the captain of a submarine that is being shelled by enemy torpedo boats. You must decide whether to sink to the bottom and wait for them to pass, or to surface and make a run for it in open waters. Which management style would you choose?" Trainees then use the decision tree to determine the best style, starting with the first column on the left. (This particular example is presented as a discussion question at the end of this chapter.) The results of training managers in the use of the Vroom-Yetton model indicate that the training is effective.[29]

♦ **DEVELOPING O.K. MANAGERS: TRANSACTIONAL ANALYSIS**

transactional analysis A method for helping two people communicate and behave on the job in an adult manner by understanding each other's motives.

Transactional analysis (TA) is aimed at analyzing the interpersonal "transactions" or communications between yourself and your subordinates. It can enable you to better analyze any interpersonal situation you find yourself

FIGURE 8.7
The Vroom-Yetton Model: Deciding How Much Employees Participate in the Decisions

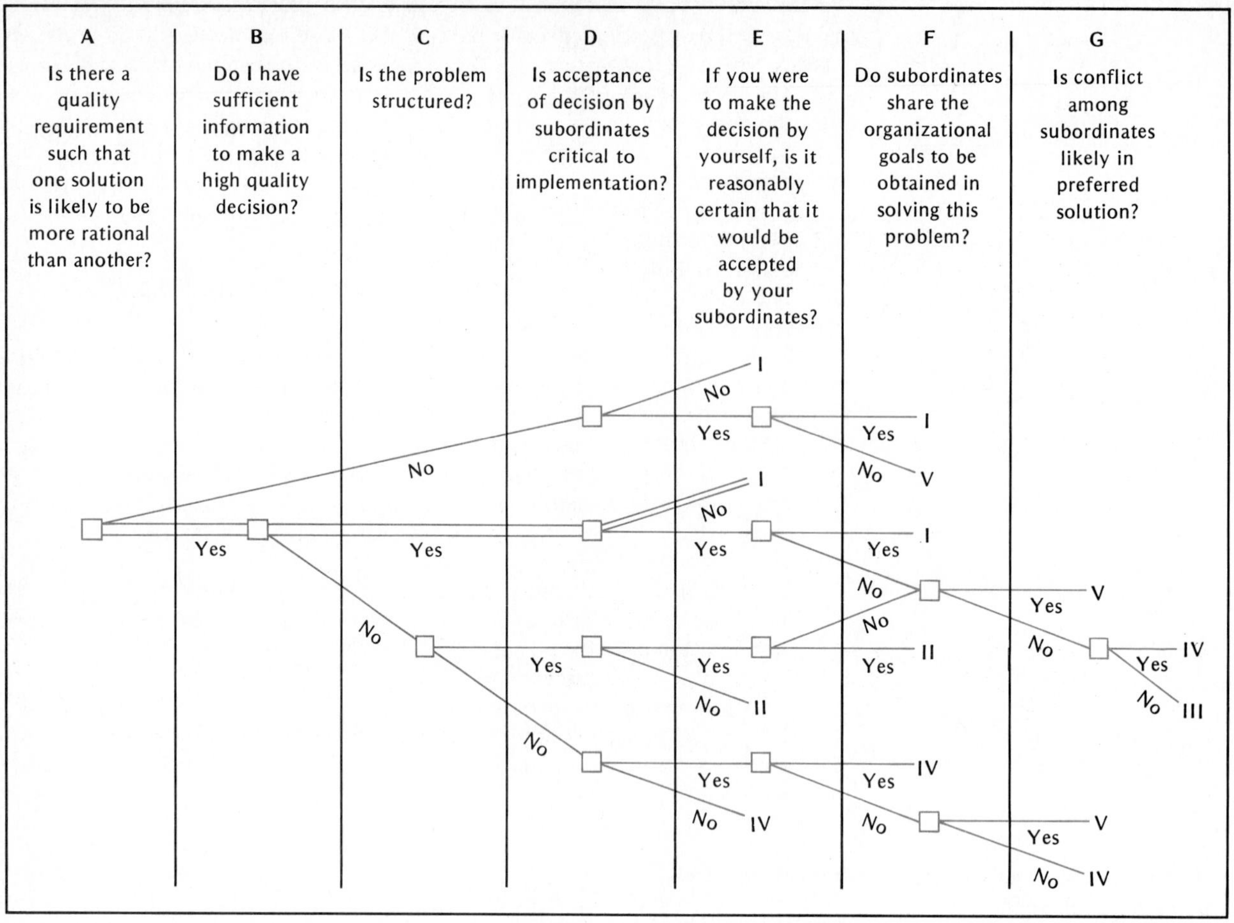

A	B	C	D	E	F	G
Is there a quality requirement such that one solution is likely to be more rational than another?	Do I have sufficient information to make a high quality decision?	Is the problem structured?	Is acceptance of decision by subordinates critical to implementation?	If you were to make the decision by yourself, is it reasonably certain that it would be accepted by your subordinates?	Do subordinates share the organizational goals to be obtained in solving this problem?	Is conflict among subordinates likely in preferred solution?

in by helping answer such questions as: "Why am I saying what I am saying to this subordinate?" and "Why is he saying what he is saying to me?"

To use transactional analysis, a person has to be able to analyze the particular *ego state* that he or she is in, and also that of the person being spoken to. There are three such ego states: *parent, adult,* and *child.*

When a person is in a particular ego state, he or she *behaves in characteristic ways.* Characteristics of a person acting in the *parent* state include being overprotective, distant, dogmatic, indispensable, and upright. A person in this state tends to argue not on the basis of logical facts, but on the basis of rules, or ways that were successful in the past. The person thus argues and explains much like his or her parent might have, all the while wagging a finger to show displeasure. A person operating in this mode is usually not an O.K. manager.

A person in the *child* ego state reflects all those behaviors that we normally attribute to childishness. For example, this person tends to take illogical, precipitous actions that provide him or her with immediate satisfaction. In an argument or discussion, this person's actions may include temper tantrums, silent compliance, coyness, and giggling.

A person in the *adult* state takes a rational, logical approach. He or she processes new data, carefully seeks out new information, thoughtfully considers these data, and then bases the argument on the facts. An adult manager is usually an O.K. manager: He or she is not out to "get" his subordinates, or to maneuver them into embarrassing positions. Instead, an adult manager is interested in confronting and solving problems in a straightforward, sensible manner by considering all points of view and arriving at a solution.

♦ ORGANIZATIONAL DEVELOPMENT

organizational development (OD) A program aimed at changing the attitudes, values, and beliefs of employees so that employees can improve the organization.

Today, new forms of organizations are emerging, ones that are more organic and adaptable. They are characterized by less adherence to the chain of command, more enlarged jobs, and a management culture that emphasizes openness, trust, and participative leadership.

As a manager, you may find it necessary to make your own organization more organic. Perhaps the organization suddenly has to adapt to a competitor's new and unique product. Or perhaps you're faced with emerging conflict between several of your department heads—conflict that is undermining the unit's creativity and flexibility. These are the kinds of situations that lead managers to turn to **organizational development (OD).** OD is defined as a program that is aimed at changing the attitudes, values, and beliefs of employees so that *the employees themselves* can identify and implement the sorts of technical changes (reorganizations, redesigned facilities, and the like) that are required, usually with the aid of an outside "change agent" or consultant.

The common denominator underlying most OD interventions is called *action research.* Specifically, most OD efforts involve (1) *gathering data about the organization* and its operations and attitudes, with an eye toward solving some particular problem (e.g., conflict between the sales and production departments); (2) *feeding back* these data to the parties (employees) involved; and then (3) having these parties *team-plan solutions* to the problems. In OD, the participants always get involved in gathering data about themselves and their organization, analyzing it, and planning solutions based on it.[30] Popular OD efforts include survey feedback, sensitivity training, and team building.

Survey Feedback

survey feedback A method of surveying employees' attitudes and providing feedback to department managers so that problems can be solved by managers and employees.

Attitude surveys like the one in Figure 8.8 can be a useful OD technique. They can be used to dramatically underscore the existence of some problem like low morale and as a basis for discussion among employees for developing alternative solutions. Finally, they can also be used to follow up on any change to see if it has been successful in terms of changing the participant's attitudes.

Scott Meyers has proposed an *involvement approach* to using attitude surveys.[31] At Texas Instruments, where this approach was developed, a questionnaire like that in Figure 8.9 is administered to a 10 to 20% sample of employees throughout the company. Profiles like the one in Figure 8.9 are then prepared from the results and delivered to each of the approximately 160 department managers. The heavy solid line shows the *company* average for this year and is the same on every department's profile. The thin solid line is this year's *department* results, while the dashed line is last year's results. As you can see, each department manager can thus compare his or her department's results for each item to both the total company results and to his or her last year's profile.

This feedback provides a useful basis upon which managers and employees can zero in on the problems and discuss and solve them. To avoid making department managers defensive, the process usually involves having survey results fed directly back to them rather than to top management. Then the department head presents and discusses these results in general terms in a group meeting of his or her department, before handing them to a committee of employees. These five or six people meet as often as necessary to analyze the results and make recommendations to the department manager. The latter, in turn, analyzes these recommendations with his or her boss, and the final recommendations are transmitted back to departmental employees. Problems and recommendations might include, for in-

FIGURE 8.8
Attitude Questionnaire of Texas
Instruments, Inc.

This questionnaire is designed to help you give us your opinions quickly and easily. There are no "right" or "wrong" answers—it is your own, honest opinion that we want. Please do not sign your name.

DIRECTIONS:
Check ( ) one box for each statement to indicate whether you agree or disagree with it. If you cannot decide, mark the middle box.

EXAMPLE:

I would rather work in a large city than in a small town .... Agree 2☐ ? 1☐ Disagree 0☐

	Agree	?	Disagree
1. The hours of work here are O.K.	2☐	1☐	0☐
2. I understand how my job relates to other jobs in my group	2☐	1☐	0☐
3. Working conditions in TI are better than in other companies	2☐	1☐	0☐
4. In my opinion, the pay here is lower than in other companies	2☐	1☐	0☐
5. I think TI is spending too much money in providing recreational programs	2☐	1☐	0☐
6. I understand what benefits are provided for TIers	2☐	1☐	0☐
7. The people I work with help each other when someone falls behind, or gets in a tight spot	2☐	1☐	0☐
8. My supervisor is too interested in his own success to care about the needs of other TIers	2☐	1☐	0☐
9. My supervisor is always breathing down our necks; he watches us too closely	2☐	1☐	0☐
10. My supervisor gives us credit and praise for work well done	2☐	1☐	0☐
11. I think badges should reflect rank as well as length of service	2☐	1☐	0☐
12. If I have a complaint to make, I feel free to talk to someone up-the-line	2☐	1☐	0☐
13. My supervisor sees that we are properly trained for our jobs	2☐	1☐	0☐
14. My supervisor sees that we have the things we need to do our jobs	2☐	1☐	0☐
15. Management is really trying to build the organization and make it successful	2☐	1☐	0☐
16. There is cooperation between my department and other departments we work with	2☐	1☐	0☐
17. I usually read most of Texins News	2☐	1☐	0☐
18. They encourage us to make suggestions for improvements here	2☐	1☐	0☐
19. I am often bothered by sudden speed-ups or unexpected slack periods in my work	2☐	1☐	0☐
20. Qualified TIers are usually overlooked when filling job openings	2☐	1☐	0☐
21. Compared with other TIers, we get very little attention from management	2☐	1☐	0☐
22. Sometimes I feel that my job counts for very little in TI	2☐	1☐	0☐
23. The longer you work for TI the more you feel you belong	2☐	1☐	0☐
24. I have a great deal of interest in TI and its future	2☐	1☐	0☐
25. I have little opportunity to use my abilities in TI	2☐	1☐	0☐

	Agree	?	Disagree
26. There are plenty of good jobs in TI for those who want to get ahead	2☐	1☐	0☐
27. I often feel worn out and tired on my job	2☐	1☐	0☐
28. They expect too much work from us around here	2☐	1☐	0☐
29. The company should provide more opportunities for employees to know each other	2☐	1☐	0☐
30. For my kind of job, working conditions are O.K.	2☐	1☐	0☐
31. I'm paid fairly compared with other TIers	2☐	1☐	0☐
32. Compared with other companies, TI benefits are good	2☐	1☐	0☐
33. A few people I work with think they run the place	2☐	1☐	0☐
34. The people I work with get along well together	2☐	1☐	0☐
35. My supervisor has always been fair in his dealings with me	2☐	1☐	0☐
36. My supervisor gets employees to work together as a team	2☐	1☐	0☐
37. I have confidence in the fairness and honesty of management	2☐	1☐	0☐
38. Management here is really interested in the welfare of TIers	2☐	1☐	0☐
39. Most of the higher-ups are friendly toward us	2☐	1☐	0☐
40. I work in a friendly environment	2☐	1☐	0☐
41. My supervisor lets us know what is expected of us	2☐	1☐	0☐
42. We don't receive enough information from top management	2☐	1☐	0☐
43. I know how my job fits in with other work in this organization	2☐	1☐	0☐
44. TI does a poor job of keeping us posted on the things we want to know about TI	2☐	1☐	0☐
45. I think TI informality is carried too far	2☐	1☐	0☐
46. You can get fired around here without much cause	2☐	1☐	0☐
47. I can be sure of my job as long as I do good work	2☐	1☐	0☐
48. I have plenty of freedom on the job to use my own judgment	2☐	1☐	0☐
49. My supervisor allows me reasonable leeway in making mistakes	2☐	1☐	0☐
50. I really feel part of this organization	2☐	1☐	0☐
51. The people who get promotions in TI usually deserve them	2☐	1☐	0☐
52. I can learn a great deal on my present job	2☐	1☐	0☐

(PLEASE CONTINUE ON REVERSE SIDE)

stance, "new employees are sometimes hired for good jobs that old employees could fill," so "post job openings on bulletin boards and explain procedure for bidding for these jobs."

Sensitivity Training

sensitivity training A method for increasing employees' insights into their own behavior by candid discussions in groups led by special trainers.

Sensitivity training aims to increase a participant's insights into his or her behavior and the behavior of others *by encouraging an open expression of feelings in the trainer-guided T-group "laboratory."*[32] (The "T" is for training.) The assumption is that newly sensitized employees will then find it easier to work together amicably as a team. Sensitivity training seeks to accomplish its aim (of increased interpersonal sensitivity) by requiring frank, can-

FIGURE 8.8
(continued)

	Agree	?	Disagree		Agree	?	Disagree
53. My job is often dull and monotonous	2☐	1☐	0☐	75. I'm really doing something worthwhile in my job	2☐	1☐	0☐
54. There is too much pressure on my job	2☐	1☐	0☐	76. I'm proud to work for TI	2☐	1☐	0☐
55. I am required to spend too much time on the job	2☐	1☐	0☐	77. Many TIers I know would like to see the union get in	2☐	1☐	0☐
56. I have the right equipment to do my work	2☐	1☐	0☐	78. I received fair treatment in my last performance review	2☐	1☐	0☐
57. My pay is enough to live on comfortably	2☐	1☐	0☐	79. During the past six months I have seriously considered getting a job elsewhere	2☐	1☐	0☐
58. I'm satisfied with the way employee benefits are handled here	2☐	1☐	0☐	80. TI's problem-solving procedure is adequate for handling our problems and complaints	2☐	1☐	0☐
59. I wish I had more opportunity to socialize with my associates	2☐	1☐	0☐	81. I would recommend employment at TI to my friends	2☐	1☐	0☐
60. The people I work with are very friendly	2☐	1☐	0☐	82. My supervisor did a good job in discussing my last performance review with me	2☐	1☐	0☐
61. My supervisor welcomes our ideas even when they differ from his own	2☐	1☐	0☐	83. My pay is the most important source of satisfaction from my job	2☐	1☐	0☐
62. My supervisor ought to be friendlier toward us	2☐	1☐	0☐	84. Favoritism is a problem in my area	2☐	1☐	0☐
63. My supervisor lives up to his promises	2☐	1☐	0☐	85. I have very few complaints about our lunch facilities	2☐	1☐	0☐
64. We are kept well informed about TI's business prospects and standing with competitors	2☐	1☐	0☐	86. Most people I know in this community have a good opinion of TI	2☐	1☐	0☐
65. Management ignores our suggestions and complaints	2☐	1☐	0☐	87. I usually read most of my division newspaper	2☐	1☐	0☐
66. My supervisor is not qualified for his job	2☐	1☐	0☐	88. I can usually get hold of my supervisor when I need him	2☐	1☐	0☐
67. My supervisor has the work well organized	2☐	1☐	0☐	89. Most TIers are placed in jobs that make good use of their abilities	2☐	1☐	0☐
68. I have ample opportunity to see the end results of my work	2☐	1☐	0☐	90. I receive adequate training for my needs	2☐	1☐	0☐
69. My supervisor has enough authority and backing to perform his job well	2☐	1☐	0☐	91. I've gone as far as I can in TI	2☐	1☐	0☐
70. I do not get enough instruction about how to do a job	2☐	1☐	0☐	92. My job seems to be leading to the kind of future I want	2☐	1☐	0☐
71. You can say what you think around here	2☐	1☐	0☐	93. There is too much personal friction among people at my level in the company	2☐	1☐	0☐
72. I know where I stand with my supervisor	2☐	1☐	0☐	94. The amount of effort a person puts into his job is appreciated at TI	2☐	1☐	0☐
73. When terminations are necessary, they are handled fairly	2☐	1☐	0☐	95. Filling in this questionnaire is a good way to let management know what employees think	2☐	1☐	0☐
74. I am very much underpaid for the work I do	2☐	1☐	0☐	96. I think some good will come out of filling in a questionnaire like this one	2☐	1☐	0☐

97. Please check on term which most nearly describes the kind of work you do: 1 ☐ Clerical or office   2 ☐ Production

3 ☐ Technical   4 ☐ Maintenance   5 ☐ Manufacturing   6 ☐ R & D   7 ☐ Engineering   8 ☐ Other

98. 1 ☐ Hourly   2 ☐ Salaried   99. 1 ☐ Male   2 ☐ Female   100. Do you supervise 3 or more TIers?   1 ☐ Yes   2 ☐ No

Name of your department:

Please write any comments or suggestions you care to make in the space below.

did discussions in the T-group, discussions of participant's personal feelings, attitudes, and behavior. Participants in such a group are encouraged to inform each other truthfully of how their behavior is being seen and to interpret the kind of feelings it produces.[33] As a result, it is a controversial method surrounded by heated debate, and is used much less today than in the past.[34]

Team Building

team building Improving the effectiveness of teams such as corporate officers and division directors through use of consultants, interviews, and team-building meetings.

Most OD efforts focus on improving the effectiveness of teams at work, teams such as a president and his or her vice-presidents, all members of the research department, or all division directors of a hospital.

FIGURE 8.9
Attitude Survey Profile

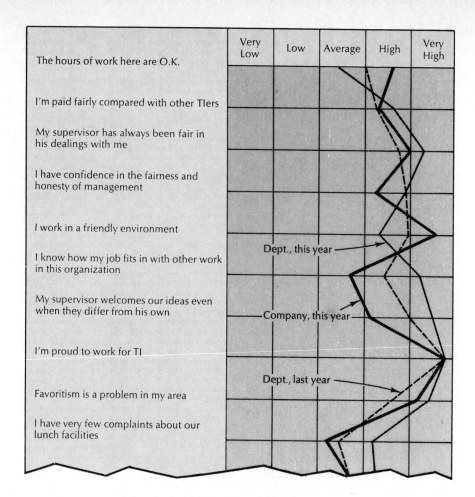

	Very Low	Low	Average	High	Very High
The hours of work here are O.K.					
I'm paid fairly compared with other TIers					
My supervisor has always been fair in his dealings with me					
I have confidence in the fairness and honesty of management					
I work in a friendly environment					
I know how my job fits in with other work in this organization					
My supervisor welcomes our ideas even when they differ from his own					
I'm proud to work for TI					
Favoritism is a problem in my area					
I have very few complaints about our lunch facilities					

Dept., this year
Company, this year
Dept., last year

In fact, the characteristic OD stress on action learning—letting the trainees solve the problem—is perhaps most evident when the OD program is aimed at improving a team's effectiveness. Data concerning the team's performance are collected and then fed back to the members of the group; the participants then examine, explain, and analyze the data and develop specific action plans or solutions for solving the team's problems.

According to French and Bell, the typical team-building program begins with the consultant interviewing each of the group members and the leader prior to the group meeting—asking them what their problems are, how they think the group functions, and what obstacles are in the way of the group performing better.[35] (Or the consultant may interview the entire group at once, using open-ended questions such as: "What things do you see getting in the way of this group being the better one?" Sometimes, an attitude survey is used to gather the basic background data for the meetings.) The consultant usually then categorizes the interview data into themes and presents themes to the group at the beginning of the meeting. Themes might include, for example, "Not enough time to get my job done," or "I can't get any cooperation around here." The themes are then ranked by the group in terms of their importance, and the most important ones form the agenda for the meeting. The group then examines and discusses the issues, examines the underlying causes of the problem, and begins work on some solution to the problems.

During one of these sessions it is likely that certain nonagenda items will emerge as a result of the participants' interaction. In discussing the theme "I can't get any cooperation around here," for instance, the group's discussion in the meeting might uncover the fact that the group's manager is not providing enough direction and is allowing vacuums to develop that are leading to conflict and a breakdown of cooperation. These new items or

PERSONNEL MANAGEMENT:

ON THE FRONT LINE

"Management development? Did you say management development? Jennifer, you're my daughter and I love you but I can't believe that with all the problems we're facing here—strong competition, softening economy, 400% turnover, employee theft, and supply and waste management cartage costs that are going through the roof—you actually want me to consider setting up some kind of a program that will turn that bunch of deadbeats that we have as managers into nice guys. I love you, Jenny, but please let's focus on the problems that we have to get solved today."

Actually, Jennifer was not altogether surprised with her father's reaction, but she did believe that her dad was being more than a little shortsighted. For example, she knew that some successful organizations, like Club Med, had a policy of rotating managers annually to help avoid their getting "stale," and she wondered whether such a program would make sense for Carter's. She also felt that some type of simulations might help managers do a better job of dealing with their customers and subordinates, and she further believed that periodic off-site meetings between her, her father, and the store managers might help to identify and solve problems with the stores. Outside seminars in areas like modern cleaning techniques might also help to boost the current store managers' interest and performance and, of course, there is also the possibility of scheduling potential managers (like a few of the current cleaner-spotters) for management development as well. The company really didn't have much money to spend on matters like this though, and Jennifer knew that to sell the idea to her father she would need a very concrete, tight set of recommendations. Questions she had included:

1. Given a budget of $750, what type of management development program can I formulate for my current store managers? The proposal must include the specific activities (like job rotation) in which my managers should engage over the next four months.

2. Would it be worthwhile for us to administer an attitude survey of all our employees? I know we don't have a big company, but I am curious as to whether employees would anonymously express to us their concerns and their likes and their dislikes and perhaps even help us identify problems like employee theft they are encountering on their job. If we do go ahead with the survey, what questions should we ask?

---

problems, as well as the agenda items (or themes), are generally pursued under the guidance of the consultant. Next, some action steps are formulated to bring about the changes deemed desirable. Then a follow-up meeting is often scheduled during which it is determined whether the action steps have been implemented and whether or not they were successful.

Again, notice how the typical team-building intervention relies on the participants themselves doing the research: Information about the group's problems are obtained from the group; members of the group then analyze and discuss the data in an atmosphere of cooperativeness; and, finally, the participants develop solutions or action steps for solving the problems that *they themselves* have identified.

Grid training is a formal approach to team building designed by Blake and Mouton.[36] As summarized in Table 8.4 Grid training is based on a device called the **managerial grid,** which represents different possible leadership styles (specifically whether the leader is more concerned with people or production).

The Grid program is aimed, first, at developing **"9,9" managers**—managers who are interested in getting results by being high on both their con-

grid training A formal approach to team building designed by Blake and Mouton.

managerial grid Numerical ratings for managers in a grid or matrix configuration based on their leadership style (whether people oriented or production oriented).

"9,9" managers Highest ranking on the grid program. A manager with this rating is highly concerned with people *and* with production.

TABLE 8.4 Managerial Grid Leadership Styles

TYPE OF LEADER AS RANKED ON GRID	TYPE OF CONCERN FOR PEOPLE	TYPE OF CONCERN FOR PRODUCTION
(1–1)	Low	Low
(1–9)	High	Low
(9–1)	Low	High
(9–9)	High	High

Source: Based on material in Robert R. Blake and Jane S. Mouton, *The Managerial Grid* (Houston: Gulf Publishing, 1964).

cern for production and for people; they want to get results through committed, cooperative subordinates, say Blake and Mouton. The Grid program assumes that possessing such a style makes it easier for you to work with your subordinates, superiors, and peers in analyzing group, intergroup, and organizational problems and developing action steps to solve these problems.

EXECUTIVE DEVELOPMENT: KEY FACTORS FOR SUCCESS

Ideally management/executive development is not just a menu of courses and programs from which managers partake, but is part of the employer's executive development process. As such it involves (as noted earlier) identifying likely management openings and then combining customized executive development courses and programs to fit the employer's succession-planning needs. As such it should be apparent that successful management development is multifaceted, involving factors like the chief executive's full commitment and a careful appraisal of the company's strategic plans.

The idea that there are several key factors for an executive development program's success is illustrated by the results of a survey of executive development practices in 12 leading corporations.[37] This study found a surprisingly high degree of consensus among the 12 corporations regarding the characteristics of ineffective and effective executive development process. In particular, five major success criteria were articulated by between 75% and 100% of the survey participants.

♦ FIVE KEY FACTORS FOR SUCCESS

These five key factors for success were as follows:

1. Extensive and visible involvement by the chief executive officer (CEO) is critical.

   In all but one of the companies, extensive and visible involvement by the CEO was described as "essential" and "the single most important determinant" of success for the executive development program. This extensive involvement not only helped guarantee that the company's executive development process was consistent with the direction in which the CEO wanted to see the company go; it also lent the process a credibility unachievable in any other way.

2. Corporations with a successful executive development process have a clearly articulated and understood executive development policy and philosophy.

In other words, the executive development process should ideally be built around a clearly articulated philosophy and purpose. For example, 10 of the 12 companies surveyed listed four common objectives of their executive development processes: ensuring that qualified executives would be available to fill current and future assignments; serving as a major vehicle to perpetuate the organization's heritage and shape its culture by communicating its mission, beliefs, values, and management practices; preparing executives to respond to the complex business issues of the changing environment by providing managers with the experience, knowledge, and skills they need in future assignments; and developing a cadre of individuals prepared to assume senior-level general management responsibilities.

3. Successful executive development policies and strategies are directly linked to the corporation's business strategies, objectives, and challenges.

Nine of the 12 companies participating in the study emphasized that their executive development policies and strategies were consciously linked to the company's business plans and objectives. For example, plans to expand overseas, diversify into new product lines, or consolidate manufacturing operations have implications for management/executive development activities. In the successful programs the development process was molded around the company's plans.

4. Successful executive development processes include three main elements: an annual succession planning process; planned on-the-job developmental assignments; and customized, internal, executive education programs supplemented by the selected use of university programs.

All the companies surveyed were emphatic in insisting that a development program could not be successful without all three ingredients. And they all emphasized that all three ingredients together—succession planning, developmental assignments, and customized programs—added up to a total executive development process.

As far as succession planning (planning which individuals would be available to fill which slots as they opened) was concerned all the companies engaged in several specific activities. In all 12 companies *replacement plans* were in place and were actively managed for key positions and individuals. Second, *development needs* are continually identified (based on these replacement plans) and plans are developed and implemented to address these development needs. Third, replacement and development plans are regularly monitored, and, fourth, a formal, annual planning and review cycle is in place to assess each *candidate's progress* and to review the company's replacement plans.

With respect to on-the-job development (the second ingredient), "all the study participants agreed that it was the single most effective developmental tool available to organizations." The four types of on-the-job experience used most often were: assignment of people to membership on task forces assembled to address specific issues, job rotation experiences lasting from one to two years, overseas assignments, and temporary assignments of relatively short duration.

With respect to the third ingredient, executive education, all the companies offered a mix of external university-type programs, and customized internal programs. Some of the companies expressed concern about the prohibitive costs of the external programs although virtually all sent selected employees to them.

5. Executive development is the responsibility of line management rather than of the human resources function.

In all but one of the companies in this survey the role of the human resource department was seen as crucial but supportive. Specifically, members of the personnel department or training staff served as facilitators of the executive development process and as a resource for line management regarding what development programs and activities to use and how to use them. However, the actual responsibility for achieving the goals of the executive development program—to fill future positions, or to eliminate current managerial shortcomings, for instance—is clearly the responsibility of line management in the more successful executive development programs.

◆ DEVELOPING THE INTERNATIONAL EXECUTIVE: GUIDELINES

Selecting and developing executives to run the employer's overseas operations presents management with a dilemma. On the one hand, there is what one expert calls "an alarmingly high failure rate when executives are relocated overseas." This failure rate is usually caused by poor or inappropriate selection and preplacement development.[38] On the other hand, in an increasingly globalized economy, employers will have to put emphasis on developing managers for overseas assignments despite these difficulties.

A number of companies, including Dow, Colgate-Palmolive, and Ciba-Geigy, have developed and implemented international executive relocation programs that are working successfully. In addition to the general requirements for successful executive development programs as outlined, preparing and training executives for overseas assignments include the following considerations as well:

1. Choose international transfer candidates whose educational backgrounds and experiences are appropriate for overseas assignments. As in most other endeavors, the best predictor of future performance is often a person's past performance. In this case the person who has already accumulated a track record of successfully adapting to foreign cultures (perhaps through college studies and overseas summer internships) will more likely succeed as an international transferee.

2. Choose those whose personalities and family situations can withstand the cultural changes they will encounter in their new environments. When many of these executives fail, it is not because they themselves couldn't adapt, but because their spouses or children were unhappy in their new foreign setting. Thus in the case of international assignments, the person's family situation probably should have more influence on the assignment than it would in a domestic assignment.

3. Brief candidates fully and clearly on all relocation policies. Here, it is extremely important that the transferee be given a realistic preview of what the assignment will entail, including the company's policies regarding matters such as moving expenses, salary differentials, and benefits (such as paid schooling for the employees' children). Given the expense of such a move—for both the employer and employee—surprises are best held to a minimum.

4. Give executives and their families comprehensive training in their new company's culture and language. At Dow Chemical, for instance, orientation begins with a briefing session, during which the transfer policy is explained in detail to the relocating executive. He or she is also given a briefing package compiled by the receiving area containing important information on a number of local matters (such as shopping and housing). In addition, an advisor—often the spouse of a recently returned expatriate—will visit the transferee and his or her spouse to explain what sort of emotional issues they are likely to face in the early stages

of the move—such as feeling remote from relatives, for instance. The option of attending a two-week language and cultural orientation program offered by a school like Berlitz is also extended. At Colgate-Palmolive a two-year orientation program prepares trainees for assignments in an international subsidiary.

5. Provide all relocating executives with a mentor to monitor their overseas careers and help them secure appropriate jobs with the company when they repatriate. At Dow, for instance, each expatriate is assigned a "godfather." This person is usually a high-level supervisor in the expatriate's particular function. The overseas assignee keeps his or her godfather up-to-date on his or her activities. For his part, the godfather keeps track of the expatriate's career while he or she is overseas. Specifically, all job changes and compensation actions involving the expatriate must be reviewed with and supported by the godfather. This helps to avoid the problem of having expatriates feel "lost" overseas, particularly in terms of the career progress they might have had by being headquartered closer to home.

6. Establish a repatriation program that will help returning executives and their families readjust to their professional and personal lives in their home country. At Dow, for instance, the head of the overseas assignee's department or division gives the transferee a letter stating that the foreign subsidiary guarantees that he will be able to return to a job at at least the same level as the one he is leaving. As much as a year in advance of the expatriate's scheduled return to headquarters, his or her new job is arranged for by the person's godfather who works in cooperation with the head of the returning executive's department.[39]

MANAGEMENT DEVELOPMENT IN THE SMALLER ORGANIZATION

The president of a smaller enterprise faces both unique advantages and disadvantages when it comes to developing employees for higher-level executive roles. On the negative side, this president does not have the resources or time to develop full-blown executive succession programs or to fund many outside programs like sending potential executives away to the Harvard Business School. Yet at the same time the president of a smaller firm has the advantage of working closer with and knowing more about each of his or her employees than does the CEO of a bigger, less personal firm.

A relative lack of resources notwithstanding, the small firm's president has few activities more important than that of developing senior managers. For most small companies with successful products, it is not a lack of financing that holds them back, but a lack of management talent. This is because all growing firms inevitably reach the point where the entrepreneur/owner can no longer solely make all the decisions. For the Dows and Colgate-Palmolives of the world, the question of succession planning and executive development is mostly a question of selecting the best of the lot and then developing them: There is usually an adequate supply of talent given these companies' enormous influx of new recruits. For the smaller company, the problem usually is not one of selecting the best of the lot, but merely making sure that key positions will be filled and that the president will have the foresight to know when to surrender one set of reins over some part of the company's operations.

As a result, there are four main steps in the smaller company's executive development process:

Step 1. Problem Assessment

Particularly in the smaller organization the executive development process has to begin with an assessment of the company's current problems and the owner's plans for the company's future. Obviously, if the owner/entrepreneur is satisfied with the current size of the firm and has no plans to retire in the near future, no additional management talent may be required.

On the other hand, if plans call for expansion, and/or current problems seem to be growing out of control, management development/succession planning might be the key. It often happens, for instance, that as the small company evolves from a mom and pop operation to a larger firm the management system that adequately served the owner in the past is no longer effective. Problems arise as manufacturing orders which were previously profitable now suddenly incur overtime costs and excessive waste, and the informal order-writing process that served the firm well in the past can no longer keep up with the volume of orders.

At this point the president has to assess the problems in his or her firm. Begin with an analysis of the company's financial statements. For example, what is the trend of key financial ratios, such as the ratio of manufacturing costs to sales, or of sales overhead to sales? Are your profit margins level, or heading up or down? Are fixed costs remaining about the same, or heading up as a percentage of sales? Next, analyze the organization function by function. In sales, is the backlog of orders growing? In manufacturing, are there inventory problems that require attention? In accounting, are you getting the accounting reports that you need and are the monthly and end-of-year reports produced in a timely fashion? Does the company have a personnel system in place such that as many personnel matters as possible—recruitment, testing, selection, training and so forth—are routinized and carried out in an effective manner? The point is that it is absolutely essential that the owner continually assess the problems in his or her firm with an eye toward determining when and if new management talent is needed.

Step 2. Management Audit

One reason management selection and development is so important in small firms is that the "problems" assessed in step 1 are often just symptoms of inadequate management talent in smaller firms. It's simply not possible for the owner/entrepreneur to run a $5 million company the way he or she did when the company was one-tenth the size and so the lack of adequate management is a depressingly familiar cause for many of the problems in the small growing firm.

As a result, your next step should be to use the problems found in step 1 as a starting point in conducting a management audit of the people you now have helping you manage your firm. One simple and effective way to do this is by evaluating them on the traditional management functions of planning, organizing, staffing, leading, and controlling. For example, within their own areas of responsibility have they instituted plans, and policies, and procedures that enable their activities to be carried out efficiently? Have they organized their activities in such a way that their subordinates have job descriptions and understand what their responsibilities are? In terms of staffing, have they selected competent employees, are their people adequately oriented and trained, and are the pay rates within their group viewed as fair and equitable? In terms of leadership, is the morale in their department satisfactory, and do their people seem to enjoy what they are doing? Is the person's interpersonal relations with other members of your team satisfactory? And in terms of control, has the person recommended and/or instituted a set of reports that provide him and you with the information you need to assess adequately how that department is doing?

Step 3. Analysis of Development Needs

Your next step is to determine whether any inadequacies uncovered in step 2 can be remedied via some type of development program. At one extreme, the person may not have the potential to grow beyond what he is now, and here development may serve no purpose. At the other extreme, the problems uncovered may just reflect a lack of knowledge. For example, sending your bookkeeper/accountant back to school for a course or two in management accounting could alleviate the problem. Another hard question to answer here is whether you (the owner/entrepreneur) may be responsible for some of the problems yourself, and whether you should direct yourself to some management development program (or out of the firm altogether).

Step 4. Identify Replacement Needs

Your assessment may lead to the need to recruit and select new management talent. Here, as explained in Chapter 3, you should determine ahead of time the intellectual, personality, interpersonal, and experience criteria to be used. And, of course, you should map out an on-the-job development program that gives the person the breadth of experience he or she needs to perform the job.

SUMMARY

1. Management development is aimed at preparing employees for some future jobs with the organization, or at solving organizationwide problems concerning, for instance, inadequate interdepartmental communication.

2. On-the-job experience is by far the most popular form of management development. However, the preferred techniques differ by organizational level, with in-house programs being preferred for first-line supervisors and external conferences and seminars more widely used for top executives.

3. Managerial on-the-job training includes job rotation, coaching, junior boards, and action learning. Basic off-the-job techniques include case studies, management games, outside seminars, university-related programs, role playing, behavior modeling, and in-house development centers. We also explained several special management development techniques, including leader match, Vroom-Yetton training, TA, and organizational development.

4. Organizational development (OD) is an approach to instituting change in which employees themselves play a major role in the change process by providing data, by obtaining feedback on problems, and by team planning solutions. We describe several OD methods including sensitivity training, Grid development, and survey feedback.

5. Grid programs (and other intergroup team-building efforts) aim at developing better problem solving and more cooperativeness at work through the "action research" process. Each work group analyzes work team problems and generates action plans for solving them. Then this same approach is used by special intergroup teams so that company-wide problems are solved.

6. Successful development programs include: CEO involvement; a clear development policy; linkage to plans; succession planning and development; and line responsibility.

management development	special management development techniques	survey feedback
succession planning	leader match training	sensitivity training
job rotation		team building
junior board	Vroom-Yetton leadership training	grid training
action learning		managerial grid
role playing	transactional analysis	"9,9" managers
behavior modeling		
in-house development centers	organizational development (OD)	

DISCUSSION QUESTIONS

1. How does the involvement approach to attitude surveys differ from simply administering surveys and returning the results to top management?

2. Compare and contrast three organizational development techniques.

3. Review the "submarine captain" example in our discussion of the Vroom-Yetton development method, and use their chart and technique to determine what approach the captain should use.

4. Describe the pros and cons of five management development methods.

5. List the key factors in a typical management development program.

♦ APPLICATION EXERCISES

♦ **CASE INCIDENT**   **What We Need Around Here Is Better Human Relations**

Hank called his three highest-ranking managers together for a surprise luncheon meeting. "Have lunch on United Mutual," said Hank, "I have an important topic I want to bring to your attention."

After Madeline, Raymond, and Allen ordered lunch, Hank launched into the agenda:

"As office manager, I think we have to move into a rigorous human relations training and development program for our front-line supervisors. It's no longer a question of whether we should have a program, it's now a question of what kind and when."

Allen spoke out, "Okay, Hank, don't keep us in suspense any longer. What makes you think we need a human relations training program?"

"Look at the problems we are facing. Twenty-five percent turnover among the clerical and secretarial staffs; productivity lower than the casualty insurance industry national standards. What better reasons could anybody have for properly training our supervisory staff?"

Madeline commented, "Hold on Hank. Training may not be the answer. I think our high turnover and low productivity are caused by reasons beyond the control of supervision. Our wages are low and we expect our people to work in cramped, rather dismal office space."

Hank retorted, "Nonsense. A good supervisor can get workers to accept almost any working conditions. Training will fix that."

"Hank, I see another problem," said Allen. "Our supervisors are so overworked already that they will balk at training. If you hold the training on company time, they will say that they are falling behind in their work. If the training takes place after hours or on weekends, our supervisors will say that they are being taken advantage of."

"Nonsense," replied Hank. "Every supervisor realizes the importance of good human relations. Besides that, they will see it as a form of job enrichment."

"So long as we're having an open meeting, let me have my input," volunteered Raymond. "We are starting from the wrong end by having our first-line supervisors go through human relations training. It's our top management who needs the training the most. Unless they practice better human relations, you can't expect such behavior from our supervisors. How can you have a top management that is insensitive to people and a bottom management that is sensitive? The system just won't work."

"What you say makes some sense," said Hank, "but I wouldn't go so far as to say top management is insensitive to people. Maybe we can talk some more about the human relations program after lunch."

Questions
1. What do you think Hank means by "human relations training?"
2. Should Hank go ahead with his plans for the human relations training and development program? Why or why not?
3. What do you think of Raymond's comment that top management should participate in human relations training first?
4. What is your opinion of Hank's statement that good leadership can compensate for poor working conditions?
5. If you were in Hank's situation, would you try to get top management to participate in a human relations training program?
6. What type of training and development activities would you recommend for first-line supervision at United Mutual? How would you analyze the need for such a program?
7. What other factors could be causing the problems Hank refers to?

Source: Andrew J. Dubrin, *Human Relations: A Job Oriented Approach*, pp. 242–243. © 1978. Reprinted by permission of Prentice-Hall, Englewood Cliffs, N.J.

EXPERIENTIAL EXERCISE

Purpose: The purpose of this exercise is to give you some experience in dealing with some problems encountered in implementing a change.

Required Understanding: You should be familiar with the contents of Chapter 8, although this exercise can precede reading of the chapter.

How to Set Up the Exercise: Divide the class into groups of four persons and assign a name to each person. The same four names will be used in each group. The instructor can assign extra persons to various groups as observers.

Once the class is divided into groups all students should read the "general instructions" and should assign roles to each group member. *Each person should read his or her instructions only.* (Roles are presented at the end of this exercise.)

It will help if, in each group, role players Jack, Walt, and Steve wear name tags so that Jane, the foreman, can call them by name. (It also helps to have all Janes stand up when they have finished reading their roles.) They may also continue to refer as needed to the data supplied with their instructions.

Instructions:

1. When all the Janes are standing, the instructor can remind the Jacks, Walts, and Steves that they were waiting for Jane in her office. When she sits down and greets them, this will indicate that she has entered her office, and each person should adopt his or her role.

2. At the instructor's signal, all Janes are seated. All groups should begin the role play simultaneously.

3. About 25 minutes should be required for the groups to reach a decision. If certain groups have trouble, the instructor may ask Jane, the foreman, to do the best she can in the next minute or two.

4. While groups are role playing, the instructor will write a table on the chalk board with the following column headings: (1) Group Number, (2) Solution, (3) Problem Employees, (4) Expected Production, (5) Method Used by Foreman, and (6) Sharing of Data.

5. Collecting results.
   a. Each group should report in turn, while remaining seated as a group. The instructor will enter in column 1 the number of the group called on to report.
   b. Each Jane reports the solution she intends to follow. The solutions may be of four types: (1) continuation of old method (i.e., rotation through all positions), (2) adoption of new method with each person working his best position, (3) a compromise (new method in the morning, old in the afternoon), or (4) integrative solution containing features of old and new solutions (e.g., each person spends more time on best position, two workers exchange positions and third works on his best position, all three exchange but confine changes to work their two best positions). The instructor will enter type of solution in column 2 and add notes to indicate whether a trial period is involved, a rest pause is added, and so on.
   c. Each Jane reports whether she had any special trouble with a particular employee. If so, the initial of the problem individual is entered in column 3.
   d. Jack, Walt, and Steve report whether production will stay the same, go up , or down, as a result of the conference. The estimates of Jack, Walt, and Steve should be recorded as "0," " +," and " −" signs in column 4.
   e. Group observers report on the way Jane handled the group and how the group responded. Enter a descriptive term in column 5 for Jane's method (e.g., tried to sell her plan, used group decision, blamed group, was participative, was arbitrary and somewhat abusive). If no observers were present in a group, data should be supplied by the group itself. For leading questions about method, see "Instructions for Observers."

6. Class discussion. Discuss differences obtained and see if they can be related to the attitude and the method of Jane. What kinds of resistance were encountered? Classify them into fear, hostility, and so on. What are the proper methods of dealing with each of these kinds of resistance? What study that we discussed is this situation similar to?

The instructions and roles follow. Please be sure to read only the general instructions and the roles which you have been assigned.

1. **General Instructions** You work in a plant that does a large number of subassembly jobs, such as assembling fuel pumps, carburetors, and starters. Jane Thompson is foreman of several groups, including the one

with which we are concerned today. Jack, Walt, and Steve make up your particular group, which assembles fuel pumps. The assembly operation is divided into three positions or jobs. Since the three jobs are simple and each of you is familiar with all of the operations, you find it desirable to exchange jobs or positions. You have worked together this way for a long time. Pay is based on a team piece-rate and has been satisfactory to all of you. Presently, each of you will be asked to be one of the following: Jane Thompson, Jack, Walt, or Steve. In some instances an observer will be present in your group. Today, Jane, the foreman, has asked Jack, Walt, and Steve to meet with her in her office. She said she wanted to talk about something.

2. **Instructions for Observers** *(May be omitted if desired)* Your job is to observe the method used by Jane in handling a problem with her workers. Pay special attention to the following:

   a. Method of presenting problem. Does she criticize, suggest a remedy, request their help on a problem, or use some other approach?

   b. Initial reaction of members. Do group members feel criticized or do they try to help Jane?

   c. Handling of discussion by Jane. Does she listen or argue? Does she try to persuade? Does she use threats? Or does she let the group decide?

   d. Forms of resistance expressed by the group. Did members express fear, hostility, satisfaction with present method, and so on?

   e. What does Jane do with the time-study data? (1) Lets group examine the table, (2) mentions some of the results, or (3) makes little or no reference to the data.

      Best results are obtained if Jane uses the data to pose the problem of how they might be used to increase production.

3. **Roles for Participants** *(Read only your own role, please.)*

   ROLE FOR JANE THOMPSON, FOREMAN You are the foreman in a shop and supervise the work of about 20 people. Most of the jobs are piece-rate jobs, and some of the employees work in teams and are paid on a team piece-rate basis. In one of the teams, Jack, Walt, and Steve work together. Each one of them does one of the operations for an hour and then they exchange, so that all employees perform each of the operations at different times. The workers themselves decided to operate that way and you have never given the plan any thought.

   Lately, Jim Clark, the methods expert, has been around and studied conditions in your shop. He timed Jack, Walt, and Steve on each the operations and came up with the following facts:

	TIME PER OPERATION (MIN.)			
	Position 1	*Position 2*	*Position 3*	*Total*
Jack	3	4	4½	11½
Walt	3½	3½	3	10
Steve	5	3½	4½	13
				34½

He observed that with the men rotating, the average time for all three operations would be one-third of the total time of 11½ minutes per complete unit. If, however, Jack worked in the No. 1 spot, Steve in the No. 2 spot, and Walt in the No. 3 spot, the time would be 9½ minutes, a reduction of over 17%. Such a reduction in time would amount to saving more than 80 minutes. In other words the lost production would be about the same as that which would occur if the men goofed off for 80 minutes in an eight-hour day. If the time were used for productive effort, production would be increased more than 20%.

This time study makes pretty good sense to you so you have decided to take up the problem with the team. You feel that they should go along with any change in operation that is made.

ROLE FOR JACK   You are one of three team members on an assembly operation. Walt and Steve are your teammates and you enjoy working with them. You get paid on a team basis and you are making wages that are entirely satisfactory. Steve isn't quite as fast as Walt and you, but when you feel he is holding things up too much each of you can help out.

The work is very monotonous. The saving thing about it is that every hour you all change positions. In this way you get to do three operations. You are best on the No. 1 position so when you get in that spot you turn out some extra work and so make the job easier for Steve who follows you in that position.

You have been on this job for two years and you have never run out of work. Apparently your group can make pretty good pay without running yourselves out of a job. Lately, however, the company has had some of its experts hanging around. It looks like the company is trying to work out some speedup methods. If they make these jobs any more simple you won't be able to stand the monotony. Jane Thompson, your foreman, is a decent gal and has never critiziced your team's work.

ROLE FOR STEVE   You work with Jack and Walt on an assembly job and get paid on a team piece-rate. The three of you work very well together and make a pretty good wage. Jack and Walt like to make a little more than you think is necessary, but you go along with them and work as hard as you can so as to keep the production up where they want it. They are good fellows, often help you out if you fall behind, and so you feel it is only fair to try and go along with the pace they set.

The three of you exchange positions every hour. In this way you get to work all positions. You like the No. 2 position the best because it is easiest. When you get in the No. 3 position you can't keep up and then you feel Jane Thompson, the foreman, watching you. Sometimes Walt and Jack slow down when you are on the No. 3 spot and then the foreman seems satisfied.

Lately the methods man has been hanging around watching the job. You wonder what he is up to. Can't they leave guys alone who are doing all right?

ROLE FOR WALT   You work with Jack and Steve on a job that requires three separate operations. Each of you works on each of the three operations by rotating positions once every hour. This makes the work more interesting and you can always help out the other fellow by running the job ahead in case one of you doesn't feel so good. It's all right to help out because you get paid on a team piece-rate basis. You could actually earn more if Steve were a faster worker, but he is a swell guy and you would rather have him in the group than someone else who might do a little bit more.

You find all three positions about equally desirable. They are all simple and purely routine. The monotony doesn't bother you much because you can talk, day dream, and change your pace. By working slow for a while and then fast you can sort of set your pace to music you hum to yourself. Jack and Steve like the idea of changing jobs, and even though Steve is slow on some positions, the changing around has its good points. You feel you get to a stopping place every time you change positions and this kind of takes the place of a rest pause.

Lately some kind of efficiency expert has been hanging around. He stands some distance away with a stopwatch in his hand. The company could get more for its money if it put some of those guys to work. You say to yourself, "I'd like to see one of these guys try and tell me how to do this job. I'd sure give him an earful."

If Jane Thompson, your foreman, doesn't get him out of the shop pretty soon, you're going to tell her what you think of her dragging in company spies.

Source: Norman R. F. Maier, *Psychology in Industrial Organizations,* 4th ed. (Boston: Houghton Mifflin, 1973), pp. 295–299.

NOTES

1. Lester A. Digman, "Management Development: Needs and Practices," *Personnel,* Vol. 57 (July–August 1980), pp. 45–57. See also James Cureton, Alfred Newton, and Dennis Tesolowski, "Finding Out What Managers Need," *Training and Development Journal,* Vol. 40, no. 5 (May 1986), pp. 106–107.

2. William Kearney, "Management Development Programs Can Pay Off," *Business Horizons,* Vol. 18 (April 1975), pp. 81–88.

3. According to a survey by Digman, the median percentage of executives receiving training during a typical year was 23%; middle managers, 38%; and first-line supervisors, 20%.

4. "Trends in Corporate Education and Training," Report no. 870 (1986), The Conference Board, 845 Third Avenue, New York, N.Y. 10022.

5. Digman, "Management Development," p. 56. See also James H. Cureton et al., "Finding Out What Managers Need," *Training and Development Journal,* Vol. 40, no. 5 (May 1986), pp. 106–107.

6. Lise Saari et al., "A Survey of Management Training and Education Practices in U.S. Companies," *Personnel Psychology* (Winter 1988), pp. 731–743.

7. Dale Yoder and others, *Handbook of Personnel Management and Labor Relations* (New York: McGraw-Hill, 1958), pp. 10–27.

8. Ibid. See also Jack Phillips, "Training Supervisors Outside the Classroom," *Training and Development Journal,* Vol. 40, no. 2 (February 1986), pp. 46–49.

9. Kenneth Wexley and Gary Latham, *Developing and Training Resources in Organizations* (Glenview, Ill.: Scott, Foresman, 1981), p. 118.

10. Ibid., pp. 118–119.

11. Ibid., p. 207.

12. This is based on Nancy Foy, "Action Learning Comes to Industry," *Harvard Business Review,* Vol. 56 (September–October, 1977), pp. 158–168.

13. Wexley and Latham, *Developing and Training,* p. 193.

14. Chris Argyris, "Some Limitations of the Case Method: Experiences in a Management Development Program," *Academy of Management Review,* Vol. 5, no. 2 (1980), pp. 291–298. For a discussion of the advantages of case studies over traditional methods, see, for example, Eugene Andrews and James Noel, "Adding Life to the Case Study," *Training and Development Journal,* Vol. 40, no. 2 (February 1986), pp. 28–33.

15. David Rogers, *Business Policy and Planning* (Englewood Cliffs, N.J.: Prentice-Hall, 1977), pp. 532–533.

16. Argyris, "Some Limitations of the Case Method," pp. 292–295.

17. Rogers, *Business Policy and Planning,* p. 533.

18. Mona Pintkowski, "Evaluating the Seminar Marketplace," *Training and Development Journal,* Vol. 40, no. 1 (January 1986), pp. 74–77.

19. Joseph Famularo, *Handbook of Modern Personnel Administration* (New York: McGraw-Hill, 1972), pp. 21.7–21.8. For an interesting discussion of how to design a management game that is both educational and stimulating, see Beverly Loy Taylor, "Around the World in 80 Questions," *Training and Development Journal,* Vol. 40, no. 3 (March 1986), pp. 67–70.

20. Lawrence G. Bridwell and Alvin B. Marcus, "Back to School—A High Tech Company Sent Its Managers to Business School—to Learn "People" Skills," *Personnel Administrator,* Vol. 32, no. 3 (March 1987), pp. 86–91.

21. John Hinrichs, "Personnel Testing," in Marvin Dunnette, ed., *Handbook of Industrial and Organizational Psychology* (Chicago: Rand McNally, 1976), p. 855.

22. Norman Maier, Allen Solem, and Ayesha Maier, *The Role Play Technique* (San Diego, Calif.: University Associates, 1975), pp. 2–3.

23. This section based on Allen Kraut, "Developing Managerial Skills via Modeling Techniques: Some Positive Research Findings—A Symposium," *Personnel Psychology*, Vol. 29, no. 3 (Autumn 1976), pp. 325–361.

24. Gary Latham and Lise Saari, "Application of Social-Learning Theory to Training Supervisors Through Behavior Modeling," *Journal of Applied Psychology*, Vol. 64, no. 3 (June 1979), pp. 239–246. Note that in one study in which managers were substituted for professional trainers, the researchers concluded that while behavior modeling resulted in favorable reactions and an increase in learning, it did not produce behavior change on the job or improved performance results. The researchers here conclude that behavior modeling could be improved by such techniques as persuading supervisors that the new behaviors that they are asked to learn are more effective than their current behaviors. See also James Russell, Kenneth Wexley, and John Hunter, "Questioning the Effectiveness of Behavior-Modeling Training in an Industrial Setting," *Personnel Psychology*, Vol. 37, no. 3 (Autumn 1984), pp. 465–481.

25. Herbert Meyer and Michael Raich, "An Objective Evaluation of Behavior-Modeling Training Program," *Personnel Psychology*, Vol. 36, no. 4 (Winter 1983), pp. 755–761.

26. "A Surprise CBS Morale Booster," *Business Week*, October 20, 1980, pp. 125–126.

27. Fred Fiedler, Martin Chemers, and Linda Mahar, *Improving Leadership Effectiveness: The Leader Match Concept* (New York: John Wiley, 1977).

28. Fred Fiedler and Linda Mahar, "The Effectiveness of Contingency Model Training: A Review of the Validation of Leader Match," *Personnel Psychology*, Vol. 32 (Spring 1979), pp. 45–62; Lewis Csoka and Paul Bons, "Manipulating the Situation to Fit the Leader Style: Two Validation Studies to Leader Match," *Journal of Applied Psychology*, Vol. 53 (June 1978), pp. 295–300; Boris Kabanoff, "A Critique of Leader Match and Its Implications for Leadership Research," *Personnel Psychology*, Vol. 34 (Winter 1981), pp. 749–764; Samuel Shiflett, "Is There a Problem with the LPC Score in Leader Match?" *Personnel Psychology*, Vol. 34 (Winter 1981), pp. 765–769; Arthur Jago and James Ragan, "The Trouble with Leader Match Is That It Doesn't Match Fiedler's Contingency Model," *Journal of Applied Psychology*, Vol. 71, no. 4 (November 1986), pp. 555–559; Martin Chemers and Fred E. Fiedler, "The Trouble with Assumptions: A Reply to Jago and Ragan," *Journal of Applied Psychology*, Vol. 71, no. 4 (November 1986), pp. 560–563.

29. See, for example, R. H. George Field, "A Test of the Vroom-Yetton Normative Model of Leadership," *Journal of Applied Psychology*, Vol. 67, no. 5 (October 1982), pp. 523–532.

30. Mark Frohman, Marshall Sashkin, and Michael Kavanagh, "Action Research as Applied to Organization Development," *Organization and Administrative Science*, Vol. 7 (Spring–Summer 1976), pp. 129–142; Paul Sheibar, "The Seven Deadly Sins of Employee Attitude Surveys," *Personnel*, Vol. 66, no. 6 (June 1989), pp. 66–71. See also George Gallup, "A Surge in Surveys," *Personnel Journal*, Vol. 67, no. 8 (August 1988), pp. 42–43.

31. M. Scott Meyers, "How Attitude Surveys Help You Manage," *Training and Development Journal*, Vol. 21 (October 1967), pp. 34–41. For a good explanation of how to conduct attitude surveys, see, for example, David York, "Attitude Surveying," *Personnel Journal*, Vol. 64, no. 5 (May 1985), pp. 70–73.

32. Based on J. P. Campbell and M. D. Dunnette, "Effectiveness of T-Group Experiences in Managerial Training and Development," *Psychological Bulletin*, Vol. 7 (1968), pp. 73–104.

33. Robert J. House, "T-Group Training: Good or Bad?" *Business Horizons*, Vol. 22 (December 1979), pp. 69–77.

34. John Kimberly and Warren Nielson, "Organization Development and Change in Organizational Performance," *Administrative Science Quarterly*, Vol. 20, no. 2

(June 1975); Peter Smith, "Controlled Studies of the Outcome of Sensitivity Training," *Psychological Bulletin*, Vol. 82 (1976), pp. 597–622. See also Rosemary Caffarella, "Managing Conflict: An Analytical Tool," *Training and Development Journal*, Vol. 38, no. 2 (February 1984), pp. 34–38.

35. Wendell French and Cecil Bell, Jr., *Organization Development* (Englewood Cliffs, N.J.: Prentice-Hall, 1978). See also David M. Zakeski, "Reliable Assessments of Organizations," *Personnel Journal*, Vol. 67, no. 12 (December 1988), pp. 42–44.

36. Robert Blake and Jane Mouton, *The Managerial Grid* (Houston, Tex.: Gulf, 1964). For an interesting description of the effectiveness of team building in solving a management problem, see, for example, Barry Miller and Ronald Phillips, "Team Building on a Deadline," *Training and Development Journal*, Vol. 40, no. 3 (March 1986), pp. 54–58.

37. Julie A. Fenwick-MacGrath, "Executive Development: Key Factors for Success," *Personnel* (July 1988), pp. 68–72.

38. Paul Blocklyn, "Developing the International Executive," *Personnel* (March 1989), pp. 44–47.

39. This section based on Ibid.

PART THREE

COMPENSATION AND MOTIVATION

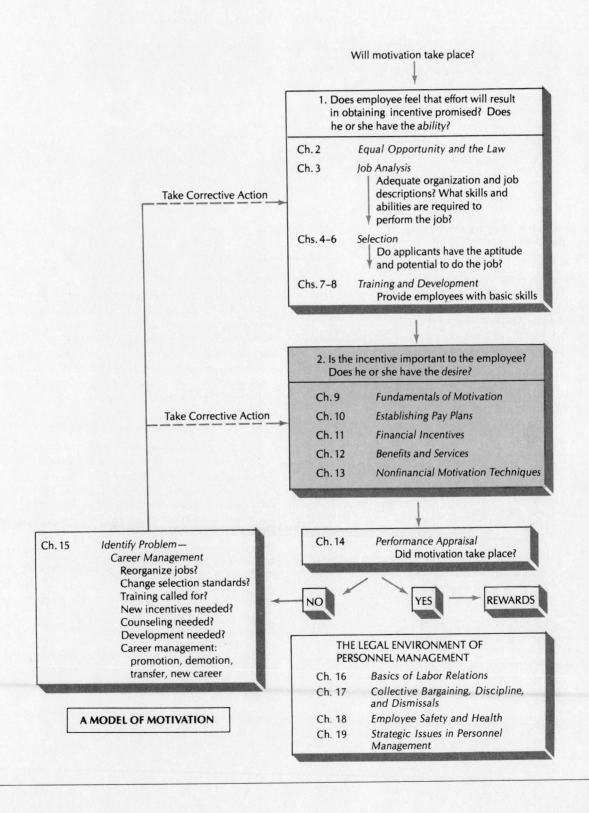

Will motivation take place?

1. Does employee feel that effort will result in obtaining incentive promised? Does he or she have the *ability*?

Ch. 2	*Equal Opportunity and the Law*
Ch. 3	*Job Analysis* Adequate organization and job descriptions? What skills and abilities are required to perform the job?
Chs. 4–6	*Selection* Do applicants have the aptitude and potential to do the job?
Chs. 7–8	*Training and Development* Provide employees with basic skills

Take Corrective Action

2. Is the incentive important to the employee? Does he or she have the *desire*?

Ch. 9	*Fundamentals of Motivation*
Ch. 10	*Establishing Pay Plans*
Ch. 11	*Financial Incentives*
Ch. 12	*Benefits and Services*
Ch. 13	*Nonfinancial Motivation Techniques*

Take Corrective Action

Ch. 15	*Identify Problem—* *Career Management* Reorganize jobs? Change selection standards? Training called for? New incentives needed? Counseling needed? Development needed? Career management: promotion, demotion, transfer, new career

Ch. 14	*Performance Appraisal* Did motivation take place?

NO — YES → REWARDS

A MODEL OF MOTIVATION

THE LEGAL ENVIRONMENT OF PERSONNEL MANAGEMENT

Ch. 16	*Basics of Labor Relations*
Ch. 17	*Collective Bargaining, Discipline, and Dismissals*
Ch. 18	*Employee Safety and Health*
Ch. 19	*Strategic Issues in Personnel Management*

Chapter 9

Fundamentals of Motivation

When you finish studying this chapter, you should be able to:

1. Explain what motivation is.
2. Develop an expectancy model diagram of motivation.
3. Discuss the Maslow needs hierarchy.
4. Compare and contrast the Maslow and the Herzberg motivation theories.
5. Summarize what we know about "What do people want?"
6. Explain how all your personnel management activities influence motivation.

OVERVIEW

This chapter starts a new part of this book, Part Three on motivating and compensating employees. In Chapter 1 we introduced our motivation model and said that people will be motivated if they think there's a good chance that (1) effort on their part will lead to (2) obtaining some desired reward. In Parts One and Two—Recruitment and Placement, and Training and Development—we discussed techniques aimed at ensuring that your employees have the skills and abilities to do their jobs, since it is only by being able to do their jobs that they will obtain their rewards and be motivated.

In Part Three, we turn to the second aspect of motivation—to the rewards themselves. (Recall that if your employees don't find the rewards—salary, promotion, etc.—attractive, they won't be motivated.) We devote four chapters (10–13) to the question of rewards, but before going on to these chapters we thought it important that we briefly review the fundamentals and mechanics of motivation—what it is, what rewards people find important, and how personnel management activities (like training) affect motivation.

The subject of motivation is central to everything you will study in personnel management. After all, the bottom line of recruiting, selecting, training, paying, and appraising workers is, largely, one of optimizing employee performance. And to do this you'll have to understand what motivates people—what makes them "tick"—as well as what the motivational implications are of HR processes like job analysis, selection, establishing pay plans, and performance appraisal. This is one reason why we've used the motivation model as a framework throughout this book: to underscore how each of the topics we explore contributes to ensuring a highly motivated employee. (Thus, recall that job analysis, selection, and training help ensure the person has the *ability*, while compensation helps ensure he or she has the *desire*, both of which are needed, we said, for motivated performance to occur.) This chapter briefly reviews some major theories of motivation, explains two applied motivation techniques (job enrichment and behavior modification) that HR managers often use, and, finally, summarizes how motivation affects and is affected by HR activities like job analysis, selection, and compensation management.

HUMAN NEEDS AND MOTIVATION

Most psychologists believe that all motivation is ultimately derived from a tension that results when one or more of our important needs are unsatisfied. Thus, a person who is hungry is motivated to find food; a person who needs security is motivated to find it; and a person with a compelling need to accomplish challenging tasks might try to conquer a mountain. The work of three psychologists—**Abraham Maslow, John Atkinson,** and **Frederick Herzberg**—is closely associated with human needs and motivation.

Abraham Maslow A distinguished psychologist who identified five basic categories of human needs: physiological, safety, social, ego, and self-actualization. Each need becomes active only after the need below it is satisfied.

John Atkinson A researcher who explained that everyone has a need for *achievement, power,* and *affiliation.*

Frederick Herzberg A theorist who believed that the best way to motivate someone is to satisfy higher ego needs, such as for recognition and sense of achievement.

needs hierarchy Maslow's view that human needs form a ladder, or hierarchy. When a person's most urgent need is satisfied, the next most urgent need becomes a prime motivating drive, etc.

◆ ABRAHAM MASLOW AND THE NEEDS HIERARCHY

Maslow says that man has five basic categories of needs: physiological, safety, social, ego, and self-actualization needs. He says these needs form a **hierarchy** or ladder (as in Figure 9.1) and that (generally speaking) each need becomes active or aroused only when the lower needs are reasonably satisfied.

Physiological Needs

The lowest level in Maslow's hierarchy contains the physiological needs. These are the most basic needs everyone has, for food, drink, shelter, and rest.

Safety Needs

When the physiological needs are reasonably satisfied—when one is no longer thirsty, has enough to eat, has a roof overhead, and so forth—then the safety needs become activated. They become the needs that the person tries to satisfy, the needs that motivate him. These are the needs for protection against danger or deprivation and the need for security.

FIGURE 9.1
Maslow's Needs Hierarchy

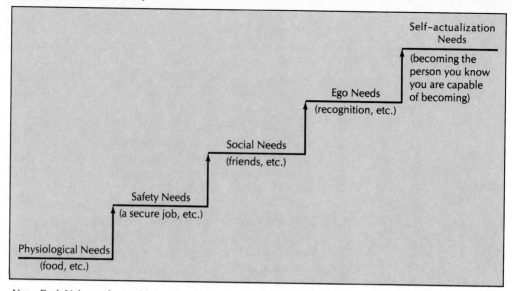

Note: Each higher-order need becomes active only when succeedingly lower-level needs are fairly well satisfied.

Social Needs

Once a person's physiological and safety needs are satisfied, according to Maslow, they no longer motivate behavior. Now the social needs become the active motivators of behavior—needs such as for affiliation, for giving and receiving affection, and for friendship.

Ego Needs

Next in the hierarchy are the ego needs, which McGregor has interpreted as:

1. Those needs that relate to one's self-esteem—needs for self confidence, for independence, for achievement, for confidence, for knowledge
2. Those needs that relate to one's reputation—needs for status, for recognition, for appreciation, for the deserved respect of one's fellows

One of the big differences between these ego needs and the physiological, safety, and social needs is that the ego needs (and the self-actualization needs discussed next) are rarely satisfied. Thus, according to Maslow, people have a constant, infinite need for more achievement, more knowledge, and more recognition. On the other hand, the physiological, safety, and social needs are finite; they can be and often are fairly well satisfied. As with all needs, ego needs motivate behavior, says Maslow, only when the lower-level needs are reasonably satisfied.

Self-Actualization

Finally, the highest-order need begins to dominate a person's behavior, once all lower-level needs are reasonably satisfied. This is the need for self-actualization or fulfillment, the need to become the person we feel we have the potential for becoming. This is the need that drives an artist to express herself on canvas, the need that motivates a student to work all day and then take a college degree in night school. This need, as with the ego needs, is rarely if ever satisfied.

◆ ATKINSON AND NEED ACHIEVEMENT THEORY

need achievement theory The theory that focuses on one of Maslow's "esteem" needs and aims at predicting the behavior of those ranking high or low in the need to achieve.

Need achievement theory focuses on one of Maslow's "esteem" needs—the need to achieve—and aims at predicting the behavior of those who rank high or low in the need to achieve. Atkinson says people who are high in achievement need have a predisposition to strive for success.[1] They are highly motivated to obtain the satisfaction that comes from accomplishing or achieving some challenging task or goal. They prefer tasks for which there is a reasonable chance for success and avoid those that are either too easy or too difficult. Relatedly, such people prefer getting specific, timely criticism and feedback about their performance. Studies show that people with a high need to achieve do perform better, especially on entrepreneurial tasks like starting a new business.[2] And one of the interesting aspects of achievement motivation is that people can apparently be trained to be more achievement-oriented.

◆ FREDERICK HERZBERG AND THE MOTIVATOR-HYGIENE THEORY

The Theory

motivator-hygiene theory of motivation Herzberg's theory that higher-level needs, such as the need for recognition, are insatiable, unlike physiological needs, or *hygienes*. Herzberg describes higher-level needs as *motivators*.

Herzberg says that man has a lower- and a higher-level set of needs, and that the best way to motivate someone is to offer to satisfy the higher-level needs. Offering a person a raise or better working conditions, says Herzberg, is no way to motivate someone, since lower-level needs are quickly satisfied. And once they are satisfied (once the person has enough income, for instance), the only way to motivate the person is by offering even more money, or even better working conditions, in an endlessly escalating process. The right way to motivate someone, says Herzberg, is to arrange the job in such a way that the person gets a "charge" out of doing it. Then, by performing the job, the person is motivated to keep trying to satisfy his or her *infinite craving* to satisfy higher-level needs for things like achievement and recognition.

Hygienes and Motivators

hygiene factors According to Herzberg, hygiene factors include not only physiological needs such as hunger and thirst but also salary, working conditions, and supervision. Offering more hygienes is not the best way to strengthen motivation, in Herzberg's view, since they just prevent dissatisfaction.

Based on his studies. Herzberg believes that the factors (which he calls *hygienes*) that can satisfy lower-level needs are different from those (which he calls *motivators*) that can satisfy (or partially satisfy) a person's higher-level needs. He says that if **hygiene factors** (like better working conditions, salary, and supervision) are inadequate, employees will become dissatisfied. But—and this is extremely important—adding more of these hygiene factors (like salary) to the job is not the way to try to motivate someone, since once the lower-level needs are satisfied, you will have to escalate your offer to further motivate the person. Hygienes like salary and working conditions, says Herzberg, will only prevent dissatisfaction (as when an employee thinks his or her salary is too low). Offering more hygienes is a very inefficient way to encourage motivation.

"motivator" factors Opportunities for achievement, recognition, responsibility, and more challenging jobs.

On the other hand, says Herzberg, "job content" or **"motivator" factors** (like opportunities for achievement, recognition, responsibility, and more challenging jobs) *can* motivate employees, because they appeal to employees' higher-level needs for achievement and self-esteem. These are *needs that are never completely satisfied* and for which most people have an infinite craving. Thus, according to Herzberg, the best way to motivate employees is to build challenge and opportunities for achievement into their jobs. The method Herzberg recommends for applying his theory is called *job enrichment*.

◆ JOB ENRICHMENT VERSUS JOB ENLARGEMENT AND JOB ROTATION

Though the terms are sometimes used interchangeably, job enlargement and job enrichment are not exactly the same thing. Job enlargement usually involves the *horizontal* expansion of the worker's job, by increasing the number of similar tasks he or she is assigned. For example, if the work involves assembling chairs, the worker who previously only bolted the seat to the legs might take on the additional tasks of assembling the legs and attaching the back as well. **Job enrichment** usually involves a *vertical* expansion of the worker's job, in that tasks formerly carried out by his or her supervisor are now assigned to the worker. It involves redesigning jobs, for example, by letting the person schedule his own work and check his own results. The purpose is to increase the opportunities for experiencing a feeling of responsibility, achievement, growth, and recognition by doing the job well.

job enrichment Herzberg's method for building "motivators" into the job by making work interesting and challenging. By carefully structuring the work situation, employees can be given a chance to experience a sense of achievement, as in assembling a product from start to finish.

Job rotation involves systematically moving workers from one job to another. Thus, on an assembly line, a worker might spend an hour fitting doors, the next hour installing headlamps, the next hour fitting bumpers, and so on.

Job enrichment is an important personnel management technique for several reasons. To a great extent *job design*—the determination of exactly which duties will together comprise one job—concerns the question of how specialized versus how broad the job will be. Thus in producing a job description for a job (as per Chapter 3), the degree to which the job involves (1) repetitively performing one or two duties or (2) performing (less frequently) a wider range of duties is or should be a basic concern. And making that determination requires knowing the pros and cons of job enrichment.

Aside from its basic use in job analysis, job enrichment is an important motivation technique. Personnel managers in particular are often called upon for advice on how to improve worker performance, attendance, and morale; job enrichment is one technique that may enable you to do so.

◆ PROS AND CONS OF JOB ENRICHMENT

Job enrichment can improve employee performance and attendance. Few rewards are as powerful as the sense of accomplishment and achievement that come from doing a job that you genuinely want to do, and doing it well. Thus, the person who collects stamps, builds a ham radio, or volunteers for time at the hospital generally doesn't have to be coerced or prodded into doing the job well since the job carries its own intrinsic rewards—in terms of challenge, achievement, and recognition. In other words, this sort of job—its contents, functions, and specific duties—is designed in such a way that performing it makes the person feel good. Needless to say, therefore, designing jobs to provide such intrinsic rewards *can* substantially increase employee morale and performance.

These advantages notwithstanding, job enrichment also has two big drawbacks. First, job enrichment can be expensive. Specifically, it increases costs for exactly those reasons that specialization reduces them: it requires more time for learning; there is more waste of material during the training period; there is more time lost in switching from task to task; employees are not quite as proficient at each task; and hiring is made less efficient.

The other drawback is that not all employees react well to job enrichment. Given a choice between working on a routine, "boring" job on an assembly line and working on a more enriched job, many employees choose the anonymity and simplicity of the assembly-line job.

So, how effective is job enrichment? It's really hard to say. Many programs have been successful while just as many have failed. Even where job enrichment programs have apparently been successful (at improving attendance or performance), it is impossible to say that it's the job enrichment that caused the improvement, since other changes are normally made as well. At the Volvo Auto Plant in Sweden, for instance, a job enrichment program seems to have caused improved attendance and performance. But while the jobs were being enriched, workers' wages were also being increased, better worker housing was being built near the plant by the company, and day care centers were established as well. It is therefore almost impossible to unscramble the effects of the job enrichment from the other changes that normally occur with the job enrichment. The bottom line seems to be that job enrichment can be effective. However, an employer has to diagnose the situation carefully to be sure that the benefits outweigh the costs and that the program is implemented properly.

◆ MEASURING HOW ENRICHED THE JOB IS NOW

According to Herzberg, the more of the characteristics on the following checklist that the job contains, the more enriched it is.[3]

	Yes	No
Direct feedback: Does the employee get timely, direct feedback concerning performance?		
Client relationships: Does the worker have a customer or client to serve, either external to the organization or inside it? For example, instead of typing memos for everyone on a first-come, first-served basis, each secretary in the typing pool is assigned to a specific department.		
New learning: Does the person's job entail new learning? In one case, for example, laboratory technicians were previously responsible only for setting up the laboratory equipment for the research scientists. After job enrichment, they were given additional responsibility for the research reports, which created the opportunity for them to analyze and evaluate data and to learn to write scientific reports.		
Scheduling: Can the person schedule his or her own work? Herzberg says that another ingredient is the opportunity to schedule one's own work. In one plant, for instance, workers previously were told when they could take coffee, rest, and lunch breaks. After enrichment, workers were held accountable for meeting quotas and could schedule their own breaks.		
Unique experience: Herzberg says that "in this day of mechanization and assembly intelligence when everyone is judged on sameness, there exists a countervailing need for some personal uniqueness at work—for providing aspects of jobs that the worker can consider as 'doing his own thing'." So, can the person "do his own thing"?		
Control over resources: Does the person have some control over resources? Herzberg recommends giving employees or groups of employees their own "minibudget," and pushing costs and profit centers down as low as is organizationally feasible.		
Direct communications with client: Does the worker have direct access to his or her customer or client?		
Personnel accountability: For example, inspectors should be eliminated and the employee allowed to both assemble and inspect his or her own product whenever possible. Is this the case on the job in question?		

◆ HOW TO ENRICH A SUBORDINATE'S JOB

There are at least five specific actions you can take to enrich a job.[4]

1. *Form natural work groups.* Change the job in such a way that each group is responsible for, or "owns," an identifiable body of work. For example, instead of having a typist in a typing pool do work for all departments, make the work of one or two departments the continuing responsibility of each group of typists.

2. *Combine tasks.* Let one person assemble a product from start to finish, instead of having it go through several separate operations that are performed by different people.

3. *Establish client relationships.* Let the worker have contact as often as possible with the client. For example, let your secretary research and respond to customers' requests, instead of automatically referring all problems to you.

4. *Vertical loading.* Let the worker plan and control his or her own job, instead of having it controlled by outsiders. For example, let the worker set his or her own schedule, do his or her own trouble-shooting, and decide when to start and stop work.

5. *Open feedback channels.* Finally, find more and better ways for the worker to get quick feedback on his or her performance.

◆ BASIC QUESTIONS TO ASK WHEN IMPLEMENTING A JOB ENRICHMENT PROGRAM

Job enrichment is not for everyone. Those thinking of implementing a job enrichment program should therefore first ask the following questions.[5]

1. *Is motivation central to the problem?* Ensure that the low performance is not a result of some other problem, like a poorly designed production system or inadequate training.

2. *Is there an easier way?* Related to the first point, ask, "Is there an easier way to improve the situation in question?" For example, sometimes improved personnel testing and training might eliminate the problem.

3. *Are salary and working conditions adequate?* Most job enrichment experts agree that enrichment will not reduce the problems caused by inadequate pay or working conditions. Employees usually have to be adequately satisfied with these for job enrichment to be effective. In other words, you can't use job enrichment to improve a subordinate's morale or performance when the person is dissatisfied with his or her salary or working conditions.

4. *Is the job low in providing intrinsic rewards?* It is not worthwhile trying to enrich a job that is already sufficiently interesting and challenging. (Remember to use the preceding checklist.)

5. *Is it technically and economically feasible to enrich the job?* In some cases there are simply too many costs involved in deautomating to make job enrichment pay for itself. Remember that the reason for having highly specialized, routine jobs in the first place was that manufacturers found them much more efficient.

6. *Is quality important?* It is usually the quality of the final product rather than its quantity that is the main beneficiary of job enrichment.

7. *Are workers ready for the change, and do they want it?* Some workers neither want nor need more challenging jobs. Not everyone is turned off by an apparently boring, routine job. Some people, in fact, seem to prefer the monotonous pace and derive their satisfaction from various non-work interests.

♦ EQUITY THEORY

equity theory of motivation A theory that assumes that people have a strong need to balance their inputs or labor and their rewards.

The **equity theory of motivation** assumes that people are strongly motivated to maintain a balance between what they perceive as their inputs, or contributions, and their rewards. Basically, equity theory states that if a person perceives an inequity, a tension or drive will develop in the person's mind, and the person will be motivated to reduce or eliminate the tension and perceived inequity.

Most human resource managers recognize that inequitable treatment does have profound effects on employee behavior. Mike might be happy with his $20,000 salary and work hard to earn it, until he learns that Jane down the hall earns $800 more for the same job. Mike's first reaction will very likely be to get a quick raise, but if that fails, his performance will probably diminish as he tries to reduce what he sees as an inequity, by reducing his contribution to the firm. The concept of equity thus plays a crucial role in salary management.

One of the tricky aspects of these inequities is that most people have an inflated view of their own performance and also tend to overestimate what other people are earning. Most people, in other words, have a sort of built-in predisposition toward viewing situations as inequitable.

Effect on Performance

According to equity theory, exactly *how* the person goes about reducing what is perceived as an inequity depends on whether he or she is paid on a piece-rate basis (by the piece) or on a straight salary basis (say, by the week):

1. If a person is paid on a *piece-rate* basis and thinks he or she is *overpaid*, the quantity the person produces should stay the same or may decrease, since producing *more* would simply increase the financial rewards to the person and therefore increase his perceived inequity even more. However, quality should increase, since this should allow an increase in the inputs a person sees himself as providing, thus reducing his perceived inequity.

2. On the other hand, if the person is paid per piece and views himself as *underpaid*, the quality of his work should go down, and the quantity he produces will probably increase, depending on how much the person is paid per piece he produces.

3. If the person is paid a *salary* (regardless of his output), and views himself as *overpaid*, then either the quantity or quality of his work should increase, since this will reduce the perceived inequity.

4. However, if the person is paid a salary and believes he is *underpaid*, then his quality and quantity should both decrease. This is summarized in Figure 9.2.

FIGURE 9.2
The Effects of a Perceived Inequity on Performance

	Employee thinks he is underpaid	Employee thinks he is overpaid
Piece-rate Basis	Quality down Quantity the same or up	Quantity the same or down Quality up
Salary Basis	Quantity or quality should go down	Quantity or quality should go up

behavior modification/operant conditioning A method of changing behavior through the use of rewards or punishment.

Behavior modification (a term that is often used synonymously with **operant conditioning**) involves changing (modifying) behavior through the use of rewards or punishment. Behavior modification is built on two principles: (1) Behavior that appears to lead to a positive consequence (reward) tends to be repeated, whereas behavior that appears to lead to a negative consequence tends not to be repeated[6] and (2) therefore, by providing the properly scheduled rewards, it is possible to change a person's motivation and behavior. The two important concepts in behavior modification are the *types of reinforcement* and the *schedules of reinforcement.*

♦ TYPES OF REINFORCEMENT

Assume you are a manager whose employees are chronically late for work. You want to use behavior modification to train them to come in on time. There are four types of reinforcement you could use: positive reinforcement, negative reinforcement, extinction, and punishment.

First, you could focus on reinforcing the *desired* behavior (which in this case is coming to work on time). To do this, you could use either positive or negative reinforcement. *Positive* reinforcement might involve giving rewards like praise or raises each time the person comes to work on time. *Negative* reinforcement also focuses on reinforcing the desired behavior—coming to work on time—but instead of providing a positive reward, the "reward" is that the employee avoids some negative consequence, such as being harassed or reprimanded for coming in late. The "reward" is thus a negative one: Employees come in on time to avoid some negative consequence like harassment or a reprimand.

Alternatively, you might focus on reducing the *un*desired behavior (coming in late) rather than on rewarding the desired behavior. With behavior modification, there are two types of reinforcement you can use to reduce undesired behavior: *extinction* and *punishment.* People tend to repeat behavior that they have learned leads to positive consequences; with *extinction*, reinforcement is withheld, so that over time, the undesired behavior (coming in late) disappears. For example, suppose an employee learns from experience that coming to work late invariably leads to a scolding by the supervisor, which in turns leads to much laughter and attention from the worker's peers. That laughter represents a positive reinforcement to the worker for coming in late. Extinction would involve the supervisor's ignoring the employee, thus removing the attention and laughter—the reinforcement—from the worker's friends as well.

Punishment is a second way to reduce undesired behavior. Here, for instance, you might reprimand or harass late employees. Punishment is the most controversial method of modifying behavior, and Skinner (who did much of the work in this area) recommends extinction rather than punishment for decreasing the frequency of undesired behavior at work.[7] In fact, whenever possible, managers are advised to use *positive reinforcement,* since this focuses on improving the *desired* behavior, rather than reducing the undesired behavior.

The four types of reinforcement—positive reinforcement, negative reinforcement, extinction, and punishment—are summarized in Figure 9.3.

♦ SCHEDULES OF POSITIVE REINFORCEMENT

The *schedule* with which positive reinforcement is applied is as important as the type of reinforcement used.[8] Basically, there are four schedules you could use:

FIGURE 9.3
Types of Reinforcement
Source: Adapted from John Ivancevich, Andrew Szilagyi, Jr., and Marc Wallace, Jr., *Organizational Behavior and Performance,* 1977, Scott, Foresman and Company. Reprinted by permission.

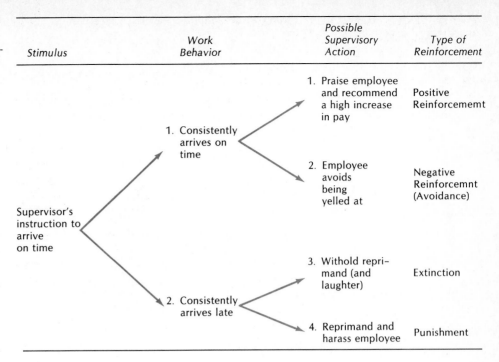

Stimulus	Work Behavior	Possible Supervisory Action	Type of Reinforcement
Supervisor's instruction to arrive on time	1. Consistently arrives on time	1. Praise employee and recommend a high increase in pay	Positive Reinforcememt
		2. Employee avoids being yelled at	Negative Reinforcemnt (Avoidance)
	2. Consistently arrives late	3. Withold reprimand (and laughter)	Extinction
		4. Reprimand and harass employee	Punishment

Fixed-Interval Schedule

A fixed-interval schedule is based on time. Here, the person gets reinforcement (a reward) only when the desired response occurs and *only after the passage of a specified fixed period of time* since the preceding reinforcement. For example, at the end of each week, you might go around and praise each employee who came to work on time every day that week.

Variable-Interval Schedule

Variable-interval schedules are also based on time. However, the person is reinforced at some *variable* interval around some average. For example, suppose you want to provide reinforcement on the average of once a day for all employees who come to work on time. You can visit them on average once a day—once on Tuesday, skip Wednesday, three times on Thursday, and so on—in such a way that the praise averages out to about once a day.

Fixed-Ratio Schedule

A fixed-ratio schedule is based on units of *output* rather than on time. With a fixed-ratio schedule, rewards are delivered only when a fixed number of desired responses occur. Most piece-rate incentive pay plans are on a fixed-ratio schedule. The worker is rewarded every time he or she produces a fixed number of pieces.

Variable-Ratio Schedule

Variable-ratio schedules are also based on units of output, but the number of desired outcomes necessary to elicit a reward changes around some average. The Las Vegas-type slot machines are good examples of rewards administered according to variable-ratio schedules. The number of times you can expect to hit a jackpot with such machines, *on the average* over the long term, is predictable. Yet the jackpots come randomly on a variable-interval schedule. Thus, you might get no jackpots for five times and then hit two in a row; you might go 50 times without a jackpot and then get one.

Which Ratio Schedule Is Most Effective?

Whether reinforcing an employee in a training program, disciplining an employee for ineffective behavior, or establishing a new incentive plan, there are three basic rules HR managers should keep in mind:

1. In general, the fastest way to get people to learn is to *not put them on schedule at all.* Instead, reinforce the desired outcome *continuously,* each and every time it occurs. The drawback is that the desired behavior also diminishes very rapidly once you stop reinforcing it. *Training* is accomplished fastest when you continuously reinforce the desired behavior.

2. Variable-ratio reinforcement (the Las Vegas type) is the most powerful at *sustaining* behavior. With this schedule, people will continue producing the desired response for a long time even without reinforcement, since they are always expecting to "hit the jackpot" on the next try. The example below illustrates how to put this idea into practice.

3. Fixed- and variable-ratio schedules are both better at sustaining behavior than are either of the interval schedules, which are based on time.

♦ EXAMPLE

An electronics manufacturer found that it had an acute absenteeism problem and that tardiness was a problem as well. Management concluded that a program should be initiated to reward the desired behavior (prompt and regular attendance) and a program was initiated. Under this program the employees could qualify for a monthly drawing of a prize only if they had perfect attendance and punctuality records for the period. This eligibility for the monthly drawing was contingent upon the desired behavior—good attendance. All absences of any kind precluded employee eligibility; the program was described in a company bulletin. A drawing was held on the last work day of each month in which a winner was selected at random from a basket containing the names of all employees who had maintained perfect attendance and punctuality records for that month. A small cash prize was awarded to the winner of each monthly lottery. In addition, to provide reinforcement to those not winning the lottery, the names of all employees who qualified were listed on the plant bulletin board and these people were praised by their supervisors.

The results of this program were fairly impressive: the average net monthly savings amounted to about $282 and the total yearly savings were in excess of $3,000 for a program that involved almost no cost to the company.

MOTIVATION: AN OVERVIEW

♦ AN EXPECTANCY APPROACH

Vroom's expectancy theory of motivation The theory that an employee's motivation increases when he or she values a particular outcome highly and when she or he feels a reasonably good chance of achieving the desired goal.

It would be useful to summarize and integrate these motivation theories, and to do so we can draw on what is called the **expectancy theory of motivation.** This theory assumes that a person's motivation to exert effort is based on his or her expectations of success.[9] Expectancy theory as formulated by psychologist Victor Vroom assumes that to motivate someone, it is not enough to offer the person something to satisfy his or her important needs. The reason for this, says Vroom, is that in order for the person to be motivated, he must also be reasonably sure that he has the *ability* to obtain the reward. For example, telling someone you will appoint her sales manager if she increases sales in her district will probably not motivate her if she knows the task is virtually impossible.

Basically, Vroom contends that for motivation to take place, two things must occur:

valence Vroom's term for the value of a goal to a person.

1. the **valence** or value of the particular outcome (such as becoming sales manager) must be high for the person.

2. the person must feel he or she has a reasonably good chance of accomplishing the task and obtaining the outcome. That is, the person must be convinced that effort will be *instrumental* in obtaining the reward.

A Model of Motivation

As illustrated in Figure 9.4, motivating someone can be thought of within an expectancy framework. Expectancy theory states that motivation will occur (1) if the incentive is of value to the person, and (2) if the person is reasonably sure that effort on his or her part will result in accomplishing the task and obtaining the incentive. This is the basis of motivation model we have used throughout this book.

As shown in the model, for motivation to take place, several things must occur. First, the incentive must be important to the person. (Theorists like Maslow, Herzberg, and Atkinson would suggest that certain needs—like those for recognition, esteem, and achievement—are the most important in our society.) Related to this, the incentive cannot just be important but must

FIGURE 9.4
A Model of Motivation

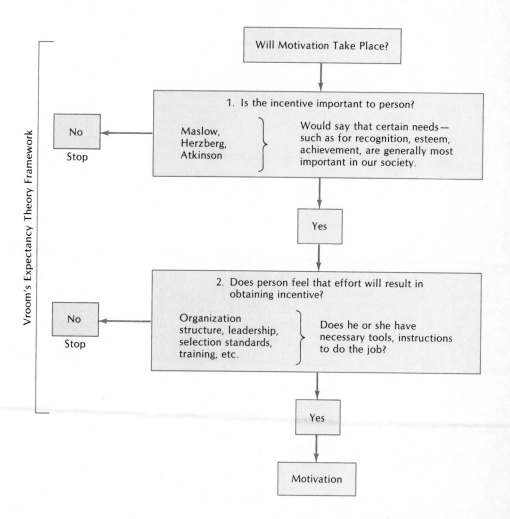

PERSONNEL MANAGEMENT:

ON THE FRONT LINE

As front-line managers Jennifer and her father know perhaps better than anyone the wide disparity there often is between the theory of motivation and its practical applications. In running her cleaning centers Jennifer finds she has many practical motivation problems that must be solved, but she's not sure that she sees the relevance of concepts like achievement-motivation or self-actualization.

This week, for instance, Jennifer had to come to grips with several of what she would consider to be "motivation problems." In this business, for one thing, productivity is always a problem. Each store's total labor bill should not exceed 28–30% of the store's revenues, but to maintain that ratio it is necessary for all employees to work industriously: Pressers have to produce about 30 pieces per hour, for instance, and the spotter-cleaner has to clean at least 85 pounds of garments per hour. Other jobs in the store—bagging the clothes, for instance, and "tagging them in"—marking each item with an identification number so the items can later be reassembled into a single order—have similar standards. Jennifer is also not sure that the problems she is having with employee theft, and with counterpersons who are not as friendly or professional as they should be are not at least partly motivation problems rather than lack of ability or training problems.

Jennifer knows that she will sooner or later have to come to grips with the "motivation" aspect of the problems her firm is encountering and that some of the most immediate problems to be solved involve employees' salaries, possible incentive pay plans, and in general doing something to overcome what Jennifer can only refer to as the lethargic attitude on the part of most of her employees. This lethargy, Jennifer believes, is a product of the highly routine and unattractive nature of most of the jobs in each store, since most of these jobs involve performing the same short-cycle jobs over and over and over again under hot conditions and for little pay. Jennifer therefore wonders:

1. To what extent are jobs like presser, cleaner-spotter, and counter person amenable to job enrichment? To the extent that any of these jobs are subject to improvement through job enrichment, what exactly should I do to enrich them?

2. What are the implications of equity theory for Jennifer and her first-line supervisors?

3. To what extent do you think people performing routine jobs like that of presser are able to satisfy their higher-level needs at work and what, if any, are the implications of this?

also be viewed as equitable if it is to elicit the desired motivation. (An *inequitable* reward can also elicit motivation if, for instance, a person paid a salary believes he or she is overpaid.) Second, the person must feel that effort *will in fact lead* to rewards. Here, other nonmotivational matters (including human factors like skills and work groups, and organizational factors like adequate plans, organization charts, and training) must be addressed, to ensure that there are no impediments to performing.

HOW ALL THE PERSONNEL MANAGEMENT
ACTIVITIES AFFECT MOTIVATION

People are motivated to accomplish those tasks which they feel will lead to rewards. This is the essence of motivation. And it's an idea that has important implications for all your "personnel management" activities. Specifically, here is how these activities directly affect employee motivation:

Chapter 3—Analyzing Jobs: Job analysis is in many ways the first personnel activity that affects motivation. Most people aren't too motivated to perform a job when they find they haven't the skills and abilities to do the job, and it's through job analysis that you determine what the job entails, and what skills and abilities you should look for in candidates for the job.

Chapter 4—Personnel Planning and Recruiting: Motivation depends on hiring employees who have the aptitude to do the job well, and the more qualified applicants you have, the higher your standards can be. Application blanks are the first step in screening out the best candidates for the job.

Chapter 5—Testing and Selection: In addition to application blanks and interviews, there are a variety of tools—test, previous experience, assessment centers, and so on—that can help you choose the best qualified, most highly motivated candidates: candidates with the ability to get the job done and get rewarded. Remember, it is this ability to do the job that is one prerequisite to motivation.

Chapter 6—Interviewing Job Candidates: Effective interviewing helps you select the best qualified, most highly motivated candidates—ones capable of doing the job and getting rewarded.

Chapter 7—Orientation and Training: How to ensure that your employees obtain the basic knowledge and skills necessary to perform their jobs—and therefore be motivated.

Chapter 8—Management Development: Here you provide your managers with the developmental activities they'll need to function more effectively.

Chapter 10—Establishing Pay Plans: Wages (or salaries) are the most widely used rewards for motivating performance, but to do so they must be adequate and equitable, and it is job evaluation (discussed in this chapter) that helps make them so.

Chapter 11—Financial Incentives: Financial incentives, which tie rewards to performance, are powerful motivation tools.

Chapter 12—Benefits and Services: Benefits and services are important rewards, and therefore influence employees' motivation. And (as we'll see in this chapter) employees' preferences for different benefits vary—with the employees' age, marital status, and so on—and so it is important to "customize" your benefits package to use them to your best advantage.

Chapter 13—Nonfinancial Motivation Techniques: To motivate employees you also want to tap their higher-level needs, and through quality circles, and so on, you build challenge—and thus rewards—into the job itself.

Chapter 14—Performance Appraisal: Here you appraise your employees' motivation and performance, and determine what rewards are appropriate.

Chapter 15—Career Management: Here you provide feedback to your employees, either to further increase their motivation, or, if necessary, to correct their mistakes, while providing them with career guidance.

SUMMARY

1. Basically, people are motivated or driven to behave in a way which they feel leads to rewards. Thus there are two basic requirements for motivating someone: (1) the incentive or reward must be important to the person; and (2) he or she must feel that effort on his or her part will probably lead to obtaining the reward. This is the essence of Vroom's expectancy theory of motivation.

2. Abraham Maslow says that people's needs can be envisioned in a hierarchy. Each succeedingly higher-level need does not become aroused un-

til the next lower-level need is fairly well satisfied. Working up the hierarchy, the five Maslow needs are: physiological, safety, social, ego, and self-actualization.

3. Herzberg says that the work factors involved in producing job satisfaction and motivation are separate and distinct from those which lead to job dissatisfaction. Those leading to job dissatisfaction (if they are absent) are the hygiene factors. These include "extrinsic" factors such as supervision, working conditions, and salary. The factors leading to satisfaction and motivation (if they are present) include intrinsic job factors such as achievement and challenge.

4. The equity theory of motivation assumes that people are strongly motivated to maintain a balance between what they perceive as their inputs or contributions and their rewards. The concept thus plays a crucial role in salary management.

5. Behavior modification is built on two principles: (1) behavior that appears to lead to a positive consequence (reward) tends to be repeated, whereas that which leads to a negative consequence tends not to be repeated; therefore, (2) you can change behavior by providing the properly scheduled rewards. By manipulating the types of reinforcement (positive, negative, extinction, and punishment), and the schedules of reinforcement (fixed and variable interval, and fixed and variable ratio) you can more effectively utilize discipline, incentives, and many other human resource management methods.

KEY TERMS

Abraham Maslow	motivator-hygiene theory of motivation	equity theory of motivation
John Atkinson		
Frederick Herzberg	hygiene factors	behavior modification
needs hierarchy	motivator factors	Vroom's expectancy theory of motivation
needs achievement theory	job enrichment	valence

DISCUSSION QUESTIONS

1. If you have not already done so, fill in the questionnaire in the experiential exercise to this chapter. What would you say this tells you about your important needs? About the tasks for which you would be best suited?

2. Explain what motivation is.

3. Develop an "expectancy model" diagram of motivation.

4. Discuss the Maslow needs hierarchy.

5. Compare and contrast the Maslow and Herzberg motivation theories.

6. Compare and contrast the Vroom and Herzberg theories of motivation. Are they compatible?

7. Summarize what we know about "What do people want?" How would you make use of this knowledge as a manager?

8. Explain how *all* the personnel management functions influence motivation.

9. "I don't need to know about any fancy motivation theories," your boss tells you, "what they all come down to is that you should practice the

Golden Rule—do unto others as you would have them do unto you." Explain whether you agree or disagree with this statement, and why.

♦ CASE INCIDENT

A Case of Motives and Behavior

Jack Dixon is the district sales manager for the eastern division of Colinary Stove, Inc., a medium-sized manufacturer of kitchen appliances, including electric and gas ranges, refrigerators, microwave ovens, dishwashers, trash compactors, and disposals. His district covers the New England states, New York, New Jersey, Pennsylvania, Ohio, Delaware, and Maryland. Job assignments of sales representatives reporting to him tend to fall into two district categories: (1) assignment to large metropolitan areas, where traveling is at a minimum and there are many established accounts that bring in a great deal of repeat orders, and (2) assignment to broad geographical areas outside of the metropolitan areas, where the company presently does not have many established accounts and desires to expand aggressively.

The company has established a policy to attract its sales representatives into the second type of job assignment. The policy essentially establishes a bonus commission for sales in the nonmetropolitan areas. All sales representatives are paid a straight 5% commission on sales credited to them. Sales in the expansion areas, however, will also receive an additional 3% commission. Thus, sales representatives will receive a total of an 8% commission on sales in the new areas. The company has estimated that, because of population growth and new industry moving into the area, an aggressive sales representative might be able to increase his or her annual income by as much as 30%.

Jack assumed that job assignments in the new areas would be extremely attractive to all the sales representatives. When a position became open last month, therefore, he presumed that he would have no trouble finding a person who wanted the job. He decided to offer the job first to the individual who had a combination of experience representing the firm and a high rate of performance measured by the annual sales he or she generated. Bob Jordan seemed to be a natural choice for the opening. He had 15 years of experience with the company and had recorded the highest level of sales in the district 3 out of the past 5 years.

Jack called Bob into his office in the morning and offered the position to him after explaining it and pointing out its advantages. He fully expected Bob to jump at the offer. Instead he was shocked by Bob's reply:

"I appreciate your offer, Jack, but I'm really going to have to think about it. My answer will probably be no. You know, the kids are in high school now and pretty used to their surroundings. Doris has a career here and she doesn't want to transfer. We like our house and would not like to leave our neighborhood. In addition, I've got a good shot at running for a position on our town council. I'd like to start devoting more of my time to township matters. I'm not sure what I'd do with the extra money. Sure, I can always use more money, but what the heck do I really need? Another car? A vacation? All in all, I'm pretty satisfied right where I am."

Questions
1. What kinds of needs would you attribute to Bob in his reaction to the job offer?
2. What kinds of needs do you think Jack Dixon *assumed* Bob would have in reacting to the offer?
3. What are the differences in these needs and how might such differences explain what happened?

4. Do you think Bob might have been operating under a different set of needs ten years ago, and would have reacted differently to such an offer?

5. How would you go about trying to get Bob to accept the job offer and make the change?

Source: John M. Ivancevich, Andrew D. Szilagyi, Jr., and Marc J. Wallace, Jr., *Organizational Behavior and Performance* (Santa Monica, Calif.: Goodyear, 1977), pp. 71–72.

EXPERIENTIAL EXERCISE

Purpose: The purposes of this exercise are:

1. To provide you with some information on what your needs are.
2. To give you information on what behaviors characterize people with different needs.

Required Understanding: This exercise can be used either prior to or after reading this chapter.

How to Set Up the Exercise: Readers should work on this exercise individually.

Instructions for the Exercise: First, fill in the following questionnaire:

	Yes	No
1. When you start a task, do you stick with it?	_____	_____
2. Do you try to find out how you are doing, and do you try to get as much feedback as possible?	_____	_____
3. Do you respond to difficult, challenging situations? Do you work better when there is a deadline or some other challenge involved?	_____	_____
4. Are you eager to accept responsibility? Do you set (and meet) measurable standards of high performance?	_____	_____
5. Do you seem to enjoy a good argument?	_____	_____
6. Do you seek positions of authority where you can give orders rather than take them? Do you try to take over?	_____	_____
7. Are status symbols especially important to you, and do you use them to gain influence over others?	_____	_____
8. Are you especially eager to be your own boss, even when you need assistance, or when joint effort is required?	_____	_____
9. Do you seem to be uncomfortable when you are forced to work alone?	_____	_____
10. Do you interact with other workers, and go out of your way to make friends with new workers?	_____	_____
11. Are you always getting involved in group projects, and are you sensitive to other people (especially when they are "mad" at you)?	_____	_____
12. Are you an "apple polisher," and do you try hard to get personally involved with your superiors?	_____	_____

Second, score your answers. According to George Litwin and Robert Stringer, "Yes" answers to questions 1–4 mean that you have a high need to achieve. You prefer situations which have moderate risks, in which you can identify your own contribution, and in which you receive concrete feedback concerning your performance.

"Yes" answers to questions 5–8 mean that you have a high need for power. You prefer situations in which you can get and maintain control of the means for influencing others.

Finally, "Yes" answers to questions 9–12 mean that you have a high need for affiliation. You have a strong desire to maintain close friendships and positive emotional relationships with others. (Keep in mind that a quick test like this can give you only the roughest guidelines about what your needs are.)

Next, if time permits, each student can write down on a sheet of paper the number of questions he or she answered "Yes" to for each of the three needs (achievement, power, affiliation). It's not necessary to sign your names. Pass these sheets on to your instructor.

Your instructor can then list respondents vertically on the board (#1, #2, etc.) and the number of "Yes" answers (for each respondent) in each of three columns headed achievement, power, and affiliation. (Student 1, for example, might show 2, 2, and 4 in the respective columns.) Did the test appear to distinguish between students on the basis of their needs? Do you think you could identify people in your class who have high needs to achieve? For power? For affiliation? What does this exercise tell you about the factors that characterize people who are high (or low) on each of these three needs?

Source: George Litwin and Robert Stringer, Jr., *Motivation and Organizational Climate* (Boston: Division of Research, Harvard Business School, 1968), pp. 173–174. Used with permission.

NOTES

1. John Campbell and Robert Pritchard, "Motivation Theory in Industrial and Organizational Psychology," in M. Dunnette, ed., *Handbook of Industrial and Organizational Psychology* (New York: Rand McNally, 1976), pp. 63–103.

2. David McClelland, *The Achieving Society* (New York: Van Nostrand Reinhold, 1961); Edwin Cornelius II and Frank Lane, "The Power Motive and Managerial Success in a Professionally Oriented Service Industry Organization," *Journal of Applied Psychology*, Vol. 69 (February 1984), pp. 32–39.

3. Based on Frederick Herzberg, "One More Time: How Do You Motivate Employees?," in *Harvard Business Review*, Human Relations Series, Part II (Boston: President and Fellows of Harvard College, 1969), pp. 115–124. Parts of this chapter are adapted from Gary Dessler, *Organization Theory* (Englewood Cliffs, N.J.: Prentice-Hall, 1986), pp. 332–341.

4. J. R. Hackman, Greg Oldham, Robert Johnson, and Kenneth Purdy, "A New Strategy for Job Enrichment," *California Management Review*, Vol. 17, no. 4, pp. 51–71.

5. For a discussion, see Ramon Aldag and Arthur Brief, *Task Design and Employee Motivation* (Glenview, Ill.: Scott, Foresman and Co., 1979), pp. 83–101.

6. W. Clay Hamner, "Reinforcement Theory and Motivation in Organizational Settings," in Henry Tosi and W. Clay Hamner, eds., *Organizational Behavior and Management: A Contingency Approach* (Chicago: St. Clair, 1974), pp. 86–112. This principle is also known as the *law of effect*.

7. Hamner, "Reinforcement Theory," p. 95.

8. Ibid., pp. 99–103.

9. David Nadler and Edward Lawler, III, "Motivation: A Diagnostic Approach," in J. Richard Hackman, Edward Lawler, III, and Lyman Porter, eds., *Perspectives on Behavior in Organizations* (New York: McGraw-Hill, 1977), pp. 26–38.

Chapter 10

Establishing Pay Plans

When you finish studying this chapter, you should be able to:

1. Describe the job evaluation process.
2. Discuss the legal considerations in compensation.
3. Explain what is meant by compensable factors.
4. Perform a job evaluation using the ranking method.
5. Price jobs using job evaluation results and a wage curve.

OVERVIEW

The main purpose of this chapter is to explain how to establish a pay plan. Developing a pay plan involves evaluating the relative worth of jobs (through the technique of job evaluation), and then pricing each job using wage curves and pay grades. In this chapter four evaluation methods (ranking, classification, point, and factor comparison) are explained, as is the process for developing wage curves and pay grades. Salaries or wages are the most widely used rewards for motivating performance, but to motivate they must be adequate and equitable—and job evaluation helps make them so.

◆ COMPENSATION AT WORK

employee compensation All forms of pay or rewards going to employees and arising from their employment.

Employee compensation means all forms of pay or rewards going to employees and arising from their employment.[1] Employee compensation has three components. It includes *direct financial payments* in the form of wages, salaries, incentives, commissions, and bonuses; *indirect payments* in the form of financial fringe benefits like employer-paid insurance and vacations; and *nonfinancial rewards* that are not easily quantifiable, rewards like more challenging jobs, flexible work hours, and a more prestigious office. In this chapter we explain how to formulate a plan for paying employees a fixed wage or salary; succeeding chapters cover financial incentives and bonuses, employee benefits, and nonmaterial rewards.

◆ THE ROLES OF MONEY IN WORK MOTIVATION

Psychologists know that people have many needs, only some of which can be satisfied directly with money. Other needs—for achievement, affiliation, power, or self-actualization, for instance—also motivate behavior but can only be satisfied indirectly (if at all) by money.

Yet even with all our more modern motivation techniques (like job enrichment), there's no doubt that money is still the most important motivator. As three researchers put it:

> Pay in one form or another is certainly one of the mainsprings of motivation in our society. . . . The most evangelical human relationist insists it is important, while protesting that other things are too (and are, perhaps in his view, nobler). It would be unnecessary to belabor the point if it were not for a tendency for money drives to slip out of focus in a miasma of other values and other practices. As it is, it must be repeated: Pay is the most important single motivator used in our organized society.[2]

◆ BASES FOR DETERMINING PAY

There are essentially two bases on which to pay employees: increments of time and volume of production.

Compensation Based on Time

Most employees are paid on the basis of the time they put in on the job. For example, blue-collar workers are usually paid hourly or daily *wages;* this is often called *day work.* Some employees—managerial, professional, and usually secretarial and clerical—are *salaried.* They are compensated on the basis of a set period of time (like a week, month, or year), rather than hourly or daily.

Piecework

The second basis on which employees are paid is called piecework. Piecework ties compensation directly to the amount of production (or number of "pieces") the worker produces. It is therefore most popular as an incentive pay system. In one simple version, for example, a worker's hourly wage is divided by the standard number of units he or she is expected to produce in one hour. Then for each unit he produces over and above this standard, he is paid an incentive rate (per piece). Salespeople's commissions are another example of compensation tied to "production" (in this case, sales).

◆ LINE, STAFF, AND COMPENSATION

The human resource department and supervisor both have important roles in the compensation process. The human resource director (and perhaps the compensation manager) administers your firm's compensation program. In conjunction with top management, personnel *formulates compensation policies* (regarding, for instance, whether to pay the same, or more or less than comparable firms), *conducts wage surveys* to find prevailing wage rates, *implements job evaluation programs* to determine the comparable worth of each job in the firm, and works with benefits consultants, insurance firms, and the like to *choose the benefit packages* for the firm's employees.

Yet line managers also play a major role in compensation management. Specifically, the line supervisor should:[3]

1. Review all job descriptions to make sure that they are accurate statements of duties actually assigned and performed, since compensation is typically tied to the job's duties and responsibilities.

2. Report all changes in assignments to make sure that descriptions are current.

3. Review all job evaluation results to ensure that decisions regarding the relative worth of each job are accurate.

4. Recommend pay increases on the basis of the facts and equities of each case and within the framework of existing policy.

5. Carefully review work methods and work standards.

6. Administer the incentive program, including effective performance appraisal.

7. Control overtime work and pay by determining the need for it, and assure its equitable distribution among employees.

8. Control abuses of benefit programs including unemployment compensation and sick leave.

9. Report compensation needs and problems to the appropriate managers.

10. Communicate all aspects of the compensation program to subordinates, including answering questions and handling complaints.

11. Understand and ensure compliance with applicable state and federal compensation laws including, for instance, the overtime provisions of the Fair Labor Standards Act.

12. Ensure compliance with the compensation provisions of the union contract.

BASIC CONSIDERATIONS IN DETERMINING PAY RATES

There are four basic factors you should consider before deciding how much to pay your employees: specifically, legal, union, policy, and equity factors should be considered.

◆ LEGAL CONSIDERATIONS IN COMPENSATION

There are, first, laws that affect the compensation you pay in terms of minimum wages, overtime rates, and benefits. The most important of these laws are as follows:[4]

1931 Davis-Bacon Act

Davis-Bacon Act A law passed in 1931 that sets wage rates for laborers employed by contractors working for the federal government.

This act provides for the secretary of labor to set wage rates for laborers and mechanics employed by contractors working for the federal government. Amendments to the act provide for employee benefits and require contractors or subcontractors to make necessary payment for these benefits.

1936 Walsh-Healey Public Contract Act

Walsh-Healey Public Contract Act A law from 1936 that requires minimum wage and working conditions for employees working on any government contract amounting to more than $10,000.

This act sets basic labor standards for employees working on any government contract that amounts to more than $10,000. The law contains minimum wages, maximum hours, and safety and health provisions. It requires that time and a half be paid for work over 8 hours a day and 40 hours a week.

1938 Fair Labor Standards Act

Fair Labor Standards Act Congress passed this act in 1936 to provide for minimum wages, maximum hours, overtime pay, and child labor protection. The law has been amended many times and covers most employees.

This act, originally passed in 1938 and since amended many times, contains minimum wage, maximum hours, overtime pay, equal pay, recordkeeping, and child labor provisions covering the majority of American workers—virtually all those engaged in the production and/or sales of goods for interstate and foreign commerce. In addition, agricultural workers and those employed by certain larger retail and service companies are included.

One important provision of the Fair Labor Standards Act governs overtime pay. It states that overtime must be paid at a rate at least one and a half times normal pay for any hours worked over 40 in a workweek. Thus, if a worker covered by the act works 44 hours one week, he or she must be paid for 4 of those hours at a rate equal to one and a half times the hourly or weekly base rate the person would have earned for 40 hours. For example, if the person earns $5 an hour (or $200 for a 40-hour week), he would be paid at the rate of $7.50 per hour (5 times 1.5) for each of the 4 overtime hours worked, or a total of $30 extra. If the employee instead receives time off for the overtime hours, the number of hours granted off must also be computed at the one and a half time rate so that, for example, a person working 4 hours overtime would be granted 6 hours off, in lieu of overtime pay.

The act also established a minimum wage for those covered by the act. This minimum wage not only sets a floor or base wage for employees covered by the act, but also serves as an index that usually leads to increased wages for practically all workers whenever the minimum wage is raised. (The minimum wage in 1990 was $3.80 per hour, and in 1991 $4.25 for the majority of those covered by the act. There is, until 1993, also a sub-minimum "training" wage, generally $3.61 per hour.) The act also contains Child Labor Provisions that prohibit employing minors between 16 and 18 years of age in hazardous occupations such as mining and carefully restricts employment of those under 16.

Certain categories of employees are exempt from the act or certain provisions of the act, and particularly from the act's overtime provisions. An employee's exemption depends on the responsibilities, duties, and salary of the job, but bona fide executives, administrative, and professional employees (like architects) are generally exempt from the minimum wage and overtime requirements of the act.[5]

1963 Equal Pay Act

Equal Pay Act An amendment to the Fair Labor Standards Act designed to require equal pay for women doing the same work as men.

This act is an amendment to the Fair Labor Standards Act and states that employees of one sex may not be paid wages at a rate lower than that paid to employees of the opposite sex for doing roughly equivalent work. Specifically, if the work requires equal skills, effort, and responsibility and is performed under similar working conditions, employees of both sexes must receive equal pay unless the differences in pay are based on a seniority system, a merit system, the quantity or quality of production, or "any factor other than sex." The act, in other words, takes into consideration that differences in pay may exist for men and women performing essentially the same jobs if those differences are based on such considerations as merit or the quality or quantity of the person's work. Unfortunately, even today, though, the average woman who works can still only expect to earn about 60 cents for each $1 earned by the average man who is working in the same occupation.[6]

1964 Civil Rights Act

Civil Rights Act This law makes it illegal to discriminate in employment because of race, color, religion, sex, or national origin.

Title VII of this act is known as the Equal Employment Opportunity Act of 1964. It established the Equal Opportunity Employment Commission (EEOC), and it makes it an unlawful employment practice for an employer to discriminate against any individual with respect to hiring, compensation, terms, conditions, or privileges of employment because of *race, color, religion, sex,* or *national origin.*

1974 Employee Retirement Income Security Act (ERISA)

Employee Retirement Income Security Act (ERISA) The law that provides government protection of pensions for all employees with company pension plans. It also regulates vesting rights (employees who leave before retirement may claim compensation from the pension plan).

This act, in effect, renegotiated every pension contract in the country. It provides for the creation of government-run employer-financed corporations that will protect employees against a failing pension plan. In addition, it set regulations regarding vesting rights. (Vesting refers to the equity the employees build up in their pension plan should their employment be terminated before retirement.) It also covers portability rights (the transfer of an employee's vested rights from one organization to another) and contains fiduciary standards to prevent dishonesty in the funding of pension plans.

The Tax Reform Act of 1986

The Tax Reform Act of 1986 was signed into law by President Reagan and represents the most extensive overhaul of the tax code in over 40 years.[7]

The new tax law affects employee compensation in two ways. The most familiar feature of the law is the reduction of the individual tax rates to just two brackets of 15% and 28%, which means employees take home more of their wages and salaries. In brief, the 15% tax bracket applies to taxable income up to $17,850 for singles, $25,288 for heads of households, and $29,750 for married couples filing joint returns. The 28% tax rate applies to income over those figures.

The second feature of the new law that affects compensation is the new treatment of employee benefits. The basic intent of this feature of the act seems to have been to increase benefits coverage for rank-and-file employees while reducing tax-favored benefits that can be provided to highly paid employees. We will discuss this benefits feature more fully in Chapter 11. However, suffice it to say that the new restrictions on benefits for higher-paid employees will probably shift their compensation from deferred benefits (such as retirement plans) to outright cash payments.

Other Legislation Affecting Compensation

Various other laws directly or indirectly impact your compensation decisions.[8] The *Age Discrimination in Employment Act of 1967* (ADEA) originally prohibited discrimination in hiring individuals between 40 and 65 years old and applied to employers with 25 or more employees (and labor organizations with 25 or more members). ADEA protected workers with respect to compensation, terms, conditions, or privileges of employment. In 1978 the law was amended to extend to age 70. It prohibited mandatory retirement of any employee under 70 years of age with a few exceptions, that is, college professors, top business executives, and employees with certain BFOQs.

ADEA was again amended in 1986 (effective January 1, 1987) prohibiting employers from requiring retirement at any age. The new law covers private employers with 20 or more employees, state and local governments, employment agencies that serve covered employers, and labor unions with 25 or more members. State and local governments have seven years before mandatory retirement is eliminated for police officers, prison guards, and firefighters. The seven-year exclusion also includes tenured university professors.[9]

The Rehabilitation Act of 1973 prohibits employers performing under federal contracts or subcontracts exceeding $25,000 from discriminating against handicapped persons. The *Vietnam Era Veterans' Readjustment Act of 1974* protects the rights of employees to return to their former jobs after engaging in military service.

Each of the 50 states currently has its own workers' compensation laws, which today cover over 85 million workers. Among other things, the aim of these laws is to provide a prompt, sure, and reasonable income to victims of work-related accidents. The *Social Security Act of 1935* has been amended several times and is aimed at protecting American workers from total economic destitution in the event of termination of employment beyond their control. Employers and employees contribute equally to the benefits provided by this act. *This act also provided for unemployment compensation—* jobless benefits—for workers unemployed through no fault of their own for up to 26 weeks in duration. The *federal wage garnishment law* limits the amount of an employee's earnings that can be garnished in any one week and protects the worker from discharge due to garnishment.

♦ **UNION INFLUENCES
ON COMPENSATION DECISIONS**

Labor relations laws and court decisions also impact compensation decisions. The National Labor Relations Act of 1935 (or Wagner Act) and associated legislation and court decisions legitimatized the labor movement. It gave it legal protection and gave employees the right to self-organization, to bargain collectively, and to engage in concerted activities for the purpose of collective bargaining or other mutual aid or protection. Historically, the wage rate has been the main issue in collective bargaining, although other issues including time off with pay, income security (for those in industries with periodic layoffs), cost-of-living adjustment, and various benefits—like health care—have also been important.[10]

In addition, the National Labor Relations Board (NLRB)—the group created by the National Labor Relations Act to oversee employer practices and to ensure that employees receive their rights—has made a series of rulings that underscore the need to involve union officials in developing the compensation package. For example, the employee's union must be provided with a written explanation of an employer's "wage curves"—the graph that relates jobs to pay rate—and is also entitled to know the salary of each employee in the bargaining unit.[11]

Union Attitudes Toward Compensation Decisions

Several studies shed some light on union attitudes toward compensation plans and underscore a number of commonly held union fears.[12] Many union leaders fear that any technical systems (like time and motion study) used to evaluate the worth of a job can quickly become a tool for management malpractice. They tend to feel that no one can judge the relative value of jobs better than the workers themselves. And, they feel that management's usual method of using several *compensable factors* (like "degree of responsibility") to evaluate and rank the worth of jobs can be a manipulative device for restricting or lowering the pay of workers. One implication seems to be that the best way to gain the cooperation of union members in evaluating the worth of jobs is to request and use their active involvement in the process of evaluating the relative worth of jobs and in assigning fair rates of pay to these jobs. On the other hand, management has to ensure that its prerogatives—such as to use the appropriate "job evaluation" technique to assess the relative worth of jobs—are not surrendered.

◆ COMPENSATION POLICIES

Your *compensation policies* will also influence the wages and benefits you pay, since these policies provide the basic compensation guidelines in several important areas. One is whether you want to be a leader or a follower regarding pay. For example, one hospital might have a policy of starting nurses at a wage at least 20% above the prevailing market wage and might pay even inexperienced nurses at least 10% more than for comparable work at other area hospitals.

Other important areas for which you'll need compensation policies are presented in Table 10.1.[13] As you can see important topics usually covered by compensation policies include basis for salary increases, promotion and demotion policies, overtime pay policy, and policies regarding probationary pay and leaves for military service, jury duty, and holidays. Compensation policies are usually written by the human resource or compensation director in conjunction with top management.[14]

TABLE 10.1 Topics Usually Covered by Compensation Policies

Hiring rates	Confidentiality
Levels compared with other employers	Relation to hourly rates
Breadth of salary ranges	Overtime
Basis for salary increases:	Vacations
Merit	Holidays
Tenure	Leave of absence
Age	Sick pay
Position in range	Exceptions
Period since last	Approval levels
Percent	Salary advances
Timing	Supervisory differentials
Market advances	Temporary assignments
Seniority	Separation pay, salary continuance, or
General versus individual	"notice pay"
Promotions	Probationary pay
Demotions	Learning pay
For cause	Military service
For company purposes	Jury duty
For personal reasons	Funeral leave
Transfers	Temporary hires
Red circles	Hours of work
Interruptions in service	School time off

Source: Stanley B. Henrici, *Salary Management for the Nonspecialist* (New York: AMACOM, 1980), p. 20.

♦ EQUITY AND ITS IMPACT ON PAY RATES

The *need for equity* is perhaps the most important factor in determining pay rates, and there are two types of equity you'll have to address: external equity and internal equity. Externally, pay must compare favorably with wages in other organizations or you'll find it hard to attract and retain qualified employees. Pay rates must also be equitable internally in that each employee should view his or her pay as equitable given other employees' pay rates in the organization.

In practice, the process of establishing pay rates while assuring external and internal equity involves five steps:

1. Conduct a *salary survey* of what other employers are paying for comparable jobs (to help ensure *external equity*).
2. Determine the worth of each job in your organization through *job evaluation* (to ensure *internal equity*).
3. Group similar jobs into *pay grades*.
4. Price each pay grade by using *wage curves*.
5. Fine tune pay rates.

Each of these steps is explained in the remainder of this chapter.

ESTABLISHING PAY RATES

♦ STEP 1. CONDUCT THE SALARY SURVEY

Introduction

salary survey A survey aimed at determining prevailing wage rates. A good salary survey provides specific wage rates for specific jobs. Formal written questionnaire surveys are the most comprehensive, but telephone surveys and newspaper ads are also sources of information.

benchmark job A job that is used to anchor the employer's pay scale and around which other jobs are arranged in order of relative worth.

Compensation or **salary surveys** play a central role in the pricing of jobs, and virtually every employer (regardless of size) therefore conducts such surveys for pricing one or more of their jobs.[15]

You'll use salary surveys in three ways. First, 20% or more of any employers' positions are usually *priced directly* in the marketplace, based on a formal or informal survey of what comparable firms are paying for comparable jobs. Second, survey data are used to price **benchmark jobs,** jobs that are used to anchor the employer's pay scale and around which other jobs are then slotted based on their relative worth to the firm. (*Job evaluation*, explained next, is the technique used to determine the relative worth of each job.) Finally, surveys also collect data on *benefits* like insurance, sick leave, and vacation time and so provide a basis on which to make decisions regarding employee benefits.

There are many ways you can conduct a salary survey. According to one British study, about 71% of the employers questioned rely to some extent on informal communication with other employers as a way of obtaining comparative salary information.[16] And 55% of the employers regularly review newspaper ads as a means of collecting comparative salary information, while 33% of the firms survey employment agencies to determine the wages to be paid for at least some of their jobs. About two-thirds of the firms also used commercial or professional surveys—surveys conducted by organizations like the American Management Association (or, in this case, their British counterparts) as an input into their own salary decisions. Finally, 22% of the firms also conducted formal surveys with other employers; these involved requesting formal responses to questionnaire-type surveys.

Formal and Informal Surveys by the Employer

Most employers rely heavily on formal or informal surveys of what other employers are doing.[17] Informal telephone surveys are good for collecting data on a relatively small number of easily identified and quickly recognized jobs, such as when a human resource director for a bank wants to determine quickly the salary at which a newly open cashier's job should be advertised. This informal phone technique is also good for checking discrepancies, such as when the human resource director wants to confirm if some area banks are really paying tellers 10% more than is his or her bank. Informal discussions among human resource specialists at professional conferences (like local meetings of the American Society of Personnel Administrators) are other occasions that typify these types of informal salary surveys.

Perhaps 20% to 25% of employers use formal questionnaire surveys to collect compensation information from other employers. One page from such a survey is presented in Figure 10.1 and is part of a questionnaire that inquires about things like number of employees, overtime policies, starting salaries, and paid vacations. Formal surveys like this let respondents answer at their leisure, and are quite comprehensive. On the other hand, they are also time consuming to complete, and some employers will object to completing them for competitive reasons.

For a salary survey to be useful, it must be sufficiently specific: 60% of the respondents in one study claimed that job categories were too broad or imprecise, as were industry categories, for instance. Therefore, make sure you construct your survey with enough detail to make it useful to you.[18]

Commercial, Professional, and Government Salary Surveys

Many employers also rely on surveys that are published by various commercial firms, professional associations, or government agencies.

For example, the *Bureau of Labor Statistics* annually conducts three types of surveys: (1) area wage surveys, (2) industry wage surveys, and (3) professional, administrative, technical, and clerical (PATC) surveys.

The BLS annually performs about 200 *area wage surveys,* including 81 in various areas of the country. (The remainder are for other government agencies.) These surveys focus on clerical and manual occupations in manufacturing and nonmanufacturing industries and provide pay data for jobs. This is illustrated in Table 10.2. As in the case of the data presented in this table, an employer in an area could use this information as an input into pricing various jobs. The area wage surveys also provide data on weekly work schedules, paid holidays and vacation practices, and health insurance pension plans, as well as on shift operations and differentials.

Industry wage surveys provide data similar to that in the area wage surveys, but by industry, rather than geographic area. They thus provide pay data for workers in selected jobs on a national basis for industries like building, trucking, and printing.

The *PATC surveys* provide pay data on 80 occupational levels in the fields of accounting, legal services, personnel management, engineering, chemistry, buying, clerical supervisory, drafting, and clerical. They provide information on straight-time earnings as well as production bonuses, commissions, and cost-of-living increases.

The American Management Association of New York is a professional association of managers that conduct and furnish executive, managerial, and professional compensation data as one of their services. For example, their *executive compensation service* provides about a dozen compensation reports on domestic executive positions as well as several foreign reports. The top-management report includes information from almost 4,000 firms covering about 31,000 executives in 75 top positions in 53 industries.[19] The

FIGURE 10.1
Portion of Compensation Survey
Source: Richard I. Henderson, *Compensation Management; Rewarding Performance*, 2nd ed., p. 269. © 1977. Reprinted by permission of Prentice-Hall, Englewood Cliffs, N.J.

Organizational Policy

Staff and Hours

Number of employees? _____

How many hours per week do your employees normally work? _____
    How much time allotted for lunch? _____
    How many breaks? _____ How much time allotted for them? _____

Do you have a 4-day workweek?   YES____ NO_____

Do any of your employees work on shifts?   YES ____ NO _____
If YES, answer below:

Shift	Shift Hours	% Premium Pay
Evening (2nd)	_____	_____
Late Night (3rd)	_____	_____
Other	_____	_____

Do you have any form of Flexitime (allowing employees to choose working hours)?
YES_____ NO _____

Salary Payment Policies

If your standard number of hours worked per week is less than 40, do you pay overtime for hours in excess of the normal workweek but less than 40? YES____NO____

If certain groups within the organization have less than a 40-hour workweek, please list them.

Group	Hours
_____	_____
_____	_____
_____	_____

What is overtime rate for individuals required to work on regularly scheduled holidays?
    1½ times normal pay_____ 2 times normal pay_____ Other_____

Have you paid a bonus or made a supplemental salary payment at any time within the past 12 months? YES_____NO_____ If YES: Date of last one _____
                                                    Approximate % of Salary_____

Have you granted any general across-the-board adjustments in salary within the past 24 months? YES _____ NO_____ If YES:

	Date	Approximate % Adjustment
1.	_____	_____
2.	_____	_____

Are they linked to the Bureau of Labor Statistics Consumer Price Index?
YES _____ NO_____If linked to any other price index, please indicate:

Starting Salaries — High School Graduates

What is your average starting salary for a high school graduate with *no* work experience who cannot type or take shorthand? $ _____

What is your average starting salary for a high school graduate with *no* work experience who can type 50–60 words per minute accurately? $ _____

What is your average starting salary for a high school graduate with *no* work experience who can type 50–60 words per minute and take shorthand 80–90 wpm? $_____

---

information covers both salaries and bonuses earned by these executives. The AMA also publishes a middle-management report providing similar compensation data on about 15,000 executives in 73 key jobs in about 650 firms. Their report on administrative and technical positions covers employee positions beneath middle management in about 600 companies, while their supervisory management compensation report surveys about 700 companies and 55 categories of first-line managers and staff supervisors; the data are reported both nationally and regionally.

The Administrative Management Society (AMS) conducts an annual survey of 13 clerical jobs, 7 data processing jobs, and a number of middle-management jobs in about 130 cities in the United States, Canada, and the West Indies (including many not covered by the BLS area wage surveys).

TABLE 10.2 Average Straight-time Weekly Earnings for Selected Office Occupations in 5 Areas, June-September 1986[1]

OCCUPATION AND LEVEL[2]	ALBANY-SCHENECTADY-TROY, NY	ANAHEIM-SANTA ANA-GARDEN GROVE, CA	BALTIMORE, MD	BILLINGS, MT	BOSTON, MA
	September	*September*	*August*	*July*	*August*
Secretaries	$385.50	$414.50	$377.50	$335.00	$385.00
Secretaries I	287.50	354.50	297.50	275.50	297.00
Secretaries II	310.50	347.00	336.50	—	350.50
Secretaries III	381.50	424.50	389.00	348.00	374.00
Secretaries IV	420.50	475.00	453.50	—	452.50
Secretaries V	450.50	558.50	519.50	—	498.00
Stenographers	—	—	451.00	—	352.50
Stenographers I	327.00	—	454.50	—	331.00
Stenographers II	369.00	—	—	—	—
Transcribing-machine typists	—	—	—	—	—
Typists	285.50	254.00	294.50	—	259.50
Typists I	234.00	242.00	238.00	—	239.00
Typists II	370.00	—	358.00	—	305.50
Word processors	—	354.50	309.50	278.50	330.00
Word processors I	—	318.50	291.50	268.50	288.00
Word processors II	—	390.00	337.50	—	366.00
File clerks	201.00	228.50	252.50	194.50	223.50
File clerks I	197.00	224.50	278.50	—	216.00
File clerks II	—	—	232.50	—	236.50
File clerks III	—	—	—	—	288.00
Messengers	—	271.50	247.50	—	221.50
Receptionists	—	246.00	240.50	—	296.00
Switchboard operators	296.50	265.00	272.00	240.00	277.50
Switchboard operator-receptionists	254.50	275.50	241.00	231.00	272.50
Order clerks	250.50	323.00	241.00	—	283.00
Order clerks I	—	281.50	233.00	—	256.50
Order clerks II	—	372.00	—	—	352.50
Accounting clerks	312.00	326.50	300.00	271.00	301.50
Accounting clerks I	—	275.00	235.00	253.50	221.00
Accounting clerks II	264.00	311.00	260.50	263.00	287.00
Accounting clerks III	322.00	367.50	308.50	306.00	325.00
Accounting clerks IV	398.00	417.00	481.00	—	394.50
Payroll clerks	377.50	329.50	331.50	297.50	334.00
Key entry operators	295.00	310.50	285.00	267.50	284.50
Key entry operators I	253.50	293.50	267.50	240.00	273.50
Key entry operators II	345.00	341.50	324.00	—	328.50

[1] Hourly earnings excluding premium pay for overtime and work on weekends, holidays, and late shifts.

[2] Percent increases have been adjusted to reflect a 12-month period even though the time span between annual surveys may have been other than 12 months.

Source: U.S. Department of Labor, Bureau of Labor Statistics, *Occupational Earnings and Wages, Trends in Metropolitan Areas, 1986 Summary 86–10.*

The AMS surveys report data on salaries, length of workweeks, overtime, paid holidays, and the extent of union membership among survey participants for over 600,000 employees. They can provide a useful reference for employers grappling with compensation decisions in the cities surveyed by the AMS.

Many other organizations also conduct periodic compensation surveys. Private consulting and/or executive recruiting companies like Hay Associates, Heidrick and Struggles, and Hewitt Associates annually publish data covering the compensation of top and middle management and members of boards of directors. Professional organizations like the American Society for Personnel Administrators, and the Financial Executives Institute publish surveys of compensation practices covering members of their associations. Published, packaged, or "canned" salary survey information is therefore widely available.

For many firms, jobs are simply priced competitively, based on their formal or informal salary surveys. In most cases, though, surveys are used to price benchmark jobs around which other jobs are then slotted based on their relative worth; determining the relative worth of a job is the purpose of *job evaluation*, to which we now turn.

♦ STEP 2. DETERMINE THE WORTH OF EACH JOB: JOB EVALUATION

Purpose of Job Evaluation

Job evaluation is aimed at determining the relative worth of a job. It involves a formal and systematic comparison of jobs in order to determine the worth of one job relative to another and eventually results in a wage or salary hierarchy. The basic procedure of job evaluation is to compare the *content of jobs* in relation to one another, for example, in terms of their effort, responsibility, and skills. If you know (based on your salary survey and compensation policies) how to price key benchmark jobs and can use job evaluation to determine the relative worth of all the other jobs in your firm relative to these key jobs, then you are well on your way to being able to equitably price all the jobs in your organization.

Compensable Factors

compensable factor A fundamental, compensable element of a job, such as skill, effort, responsibility, and working conditions.

Job evaluation involves comparing jobs to one another based on their content and it is the job's **compensable factors** that constitute what we mean by content.

There are two basic aproaches you could use for comparing several jobs. First, you could take a more intuitive approach. For example, you might decide that one job is "more important" than another, and not dig any deeper into why—in terms of specific job-related factors.

As a second alternative, you could compare your jobs to one another by focusing on certain basic factors each of the jobs have in common. In compensation management, these basic factors are called *compensable factors*. They are the factors that determine your definition of job content; they are the basic factors that determine how the jobs compare to each other; and they are the basic factors that help determine the compensation paid for each job.

Some employers develop their own compensable factors; most use factors that have been popularized by packaged job evaluation systems or by federal legislation. For example, the Equal Pay Act focuses on four compensable factors—*skills, effort, responsibility,* and *working conditions*—holding that women in jobs that are about the same as men's (in terms of these factors) should be paid the same. As another example, the job evaluation method popularized by the Hay consulting firm focuses on three compensable factors: *know-how, problem solving,* and *accountability.*

The compensable factors you focus on depend on the nature of the job and the method of job evaluation that is to be used. For example, you might choose to focus on the compensable factor *decision making* (among others) for a manager's job, while that factor might be inappropriate for the job of assembler.

Identifying compensable factors plays a pivotal role in job evaluation. In job evaluation each job is usually compared with all comparable jobs *using the same compensable factors.* You thus evaluate the same elemental components for each job and are then better able to compare jobs to each other—for example, in terms of the degree of skills, effort, responsibility, and working conditions present in each job.[20]

Planning and Preparation for the Job Evaluation

Job evaluation is mostly a judgmental process, one that demands close cooperation between supervisors, personnel specialists, and the employees and their union representatives. The main steps involved include identifying the need for the program, getting cooperation, and then choosing an evaluation committee; the latter then carries out the actual job evaluation.[21]

Identifying the need for job evaluation should not be a difficult task. For example, dissatisfaction reflected in high turnover, work stoppages, or arguments may result from the inequities of paying employees different rates for similar jobs.[22] Similarly, managers may express uneasiness with the current, informal way of assigning pay rates to jobs, accurately sensing that a more systematic means of assigning pay rates would be more equitable and manageable because rules, procedures, and an accepted method could be used for deciding how much to pay for each job.

Next, since employees may fear that a systematic evaluation of their jobs may actually reduce their wage rates, *getting employee cooperation* (for the evaluation) is a second important step. You can tell employees that, as a result of the impending job evaluation program, wage rate decisions will no longer be made just by management whim, that job evaluation will provide a mechanism for considering the complaints they have been expressing, and that no present employee's rate will be adversely affected as a result of the job evaluation.[23]

Next, you have to *choose a job evaluation committee,* and there are two reasons for doing so. First, the committee should bring to bear the points of view of several people who are familiar with the jobs in question, each of whom may have a different perspective regarding the nature of the jobs to be evaluated. Second (assuming the committee is composed at least partly of employees), the committee approach can help ensure greater acceptance by employees of the results of the job evaluations.

The committee itself usually consists of about five members, most of whom are employees. While management has the right to serve on such committees, their presence can be viewed with suspicion by employees and "it is probably best not to have managerial representatives involved in committee evaluation of nonmanagerial jobs...."[24] However, a personnel specialist can usually be justified on the grounds that he or she has a more impartial image than line managers and can provide expert assistance in the job evaluation. One method is to have this person serve in a nonvoting capacity. Union representation is possible. In most cases, though, the union's position is that it is only accepting job evaluation as an initial decision technique, and then reserving the right to appeal the actual job pricing decisions through grievance or bargaining channels.[25] Once constituted, each committee member then receives a manual explaining the job evaluation process and special instructions and training that explain how to conduct a job evaluation.

The evaluation committee serves three main functions. First, they usually identify 10 or 15 key benchmark jobs. These will be the first jobs to be evaluated and will serve as the anchors or benchmarks against which the relative importance or value of all other jobs can be compared and slotted into a hierarchy of jobs. Next, the committee may select compensable factors (although the human resource department will usually choose these themselves, as part of the process of determining the specific job evaluation technique to be used). Finally, the committee turns to its most important function, actually evaluating the worth of each job. For this, the committee will probably use one of the following job evaluation methods, such as the ranking method, the job classification method, the point method, or the factor comparison method.

Ranking Method of Job Evaluation

The simplest job evaluation method involves ranking each job relative to all other jobs, usually based on some overall factor like "job difficulty." There are several steps involved in ranking jobs.

1. *Obtain job information.* The first step is job analysis. Job descriptions for each job are prepared and these are (usually) the basis on which the rankings are made. (Sometimes job specifications also are prepared, but the job ranking method usually ranks jobs according to "the whole job" rather than a number of compensable factors. Therefore, job specifications—which provide an indication of the demands of the job in terms of problem solving, decision making, and skills, for instance—are not quite as necessary with this method as they are for other job evaluation methods.)

2. *Select raters and jobs to be rated.* It is often not practical to make a single ranking of all jobs in an organization. The more usual procedure involves ranking jobs by department or in "clusters" (i.e., factory workers, clerical workers). This eliminates the need for having to compare directly, say, factory jobs and clerical jobs.

3. *Select compensable factors.* In the ranking method, it is common to use just one factor (such as job difficulty) and to rank jobs on the basis of "the whole job." Regardless of the number of factors you choose, it's advisable to explain the definition of the factor(s) to the evaluators carefully so that they evaluate the jobs consistently.

4. *Rank jobs.* Next, the jobs are ranked. The simplest way to do this involves giving each rater a set of index cards, each of which contains a brief description of a job. These cards are then ranked from lowest to highest. Some managers use an "alternation ranking method" for making the procedure more accurate. Here you take the cards, first choosing the highest, and then the lowest, then the next highest and next lowest and so forth until all the cards have been ranked. Since it is usually easier to choose extremes, this approach facilitates the ranking procedure. A job ranking is illustrated in Table 10.3. Jobs in this small health facility are ranked from maid up to office manager. The corresponding pay scales are shown on the right.

5. *Combine ratings.* It's usual to have several raters rank the jobs independently. Then, once this is accomplished, the rating committee (or you) can simply average the rankings.

TABLE 10.3 Job Ranking by Olympia Health Care

RANKING ORDER	ANNUAL PAY SCALE
1. Office manager	$28,000
2. Chief nurse	27,500
3. Bookkeeper	19,000
4. Nurse	17,500
5. Cook	16,000
6. Nurse's aide	13,500
7. Maid	10,500

After ranking, it becomes possible to slot additional jobs between those already ranked and to assign an appropriate wage rate.

Pros and Cons. This is the simplest job evaluation method, as well as the easiest to explain. And it usually takes less time to accomplish than other methods.

Some of its drawbacks derive more from how it's used than the method itself. For example, there's a tendency to rely too heavily on "guesstimates." Similarly, ranking provides no yardstick for measuring the value of one job relative to another. For example, job No. 4 may in fact be five times "more valuable" than job No. 5, but with the ranking system all you know is that one job ranks higher than the other. Ranking is usually more appropriate for small organizations that can't afford the time or expense of developing a more elaborate system.

Job Classification (or Grading) Evaluation Method

classification (or grading) method A method for categorizing jobs.

classes Dividing jobs into classes based on a set of rules for each class, such as amount of independent judgment, skill, physical effort, etc., required for each class of jobs. Classes usually contain similar jobs—such as all secretaries.

grades A job classification system synonymous with class. Grade descriptions are written based on compensable factors listed in classification systems, such as the federal classification system. Grades often contain dissimilar jobs, such as secretaries, mechanics, and firefighters.

grade description Written descriptions of the level of, say, responsibility and knowledge required by jobs in each grade. Similar jobs can then be combined into grades or classes.

point method The job evaluation method in which a number of compensable factors are identified and then the degree to which each of these factors is present on the job is determined.

This is a simple, widely used method in which jobs are categorized into groups. The groups are called **classes** if they contain similar jobs (like all "fiscal assistant IVs"), or **grades** if they contain jobs that are similar in difficulty but are otherwise different (thus in the federal government's pay grade system a "press secretary" and a "fire chief" might both be graded ("GS–10"). (GS stands for General Schedule.)

There are several ways to categorize jobs. One is to draw up "class descriptions" (the analogs of job descriptions) and place jobs into classes based on their correspondence to these descriptions. Another is to draw up a set of classifying rules for each class (e.g., How much independent judgment, skill, physical effort, and so on, does the class of jobs require?) and then categorize the jobs according to these rules.

The usual procedure is to choose compensable factors and then develop class or grade descriptions that describe each class in terms of amount or level of compensable factor(s) in jobs. The federal classification system in the United States, for example, employs the following compensable factors: (1) difficulty and variety of work, (2) supervision received and exercised, (3) judgment exercised, (4) originality required, (5) nature and purpose of interpersonal work relationships, (6) responsibility, (7) experience, and (8) knowledge required. Based on these compensable factors, a **grade description** like that in Figure 10.2 is written. Then the evaluation committee reviews all job descriptions and slots each job into its appropriate class or grade; in the federal government system, for instance, the positions of automotive mechanic, welder, electrician, and machinist are classified as being in grade GS–10.

The job classification method has several advantages. Its main advantage is that most employers usually end up classifying jobs anyway, regardless of the job evaluation method that they use. They do this to avoid having to work with and price an unmanageable number of jobs; with the job classification method all your jobs, of course, are already grouped into several classes. The disadvantages are that it is difficult to write the class or grade descriptions, and considerable judgment is required in applying them. Yet many employers (including the U.S. government) use this method with success, and the government, in fact, has concluded that using a more quantitative method (like the two explained next) would cost much more than the additional accuracy warrants.[26]

Point Method of Job Evaluation

The **point method** is a more quantitative job evaluation technique. It involves identifying (1) several compensable factors, *each having several degrees,* as well as (2) the degree to which each of these factors is present in the job. Thus, assume that there are five degrees of *responsibility* your jobs

FIGURE 10.2
Examples of Grade-Level Definitions in the Federal Government
Source: Douglass Bartley, *Job Evaluation* (Reading, Mass.: Addison Wesley Publishing Company, Inc., 1981), p. 36.

GRADE	DEFINITION
GS-1	Includes those classes of positions the duties of which are to perform, under immediate supervision, with little or no latitude for the exercise of independent judgment—
	(A) the simplest routine work in office, business, or fiscal operations; or
	(B) elementary work of a subordinate technical character in a professional, scientific, or technical field.
GS-2	Includes those classes of positions the duties of which are—
	(A) to perform, under immediate supervision, with limited latitude for the exercise of independent judgment, routine work in office, business, or fiscal operations, or comparable subordinate technical work of limited scope in a professional, scientific, or technical field, requiring some training or experience; or
	(B) to perform other work of equal importance, difficulty, and responsibility, and requiring comparable qualifications.
GS-3	Includes those classes of positions the duties of which are—
	(A) to perform, under immediate or general supervision, somewhat difficult and responsible work in office, business or fiscal operations, or comparable subordinate technical work of limited scope in a professional, scientific, or technical field, requiring in either case—
	(i) some training or experience;
	(ii) working knowledge of a special subject matter; or
	(iii) to some extent the exercise of independent judgment in accordance with well-established policies, procedures, and techniques; or
	(B) top perform other work of equal importance, difficulty, and responsibility, and requiring comparable qualifications.
GS-4	Includes those classes of positions the duties of which are—
	(A) to perform, under immediate or general supervision, moderately difficult and responsible work in office, business, or fiscal operations, or comparable subordinate technical work in a professional, scientific, or technical field, requiring in either case—
	(i) a moderate amount of training and minor supervisory or other experience;

could contain. And assume a different number of *points* is assigned to each degree of each factor. Then, *once your evaluation committee determines the degree to which each compensable factor (like "responsibility") is present in the job,* you can add up the corresponding points for each factor and arrive at a total point value for the job. The result is thus a quantitative point rating for each job. The point method is apparently the most widely used job evaluation method and is explained in detail in the appendix to this chapter.

Factor Comparison Job Evaluation Method

The **factor comparison method** is also a quantitative technique and entails deciding which jobs have more of the chosen compensable factors than others. The method is actually a refinement of the ranking method. With the ranking method, you generally look at each job as an entity and rank the

factor comparison method A widely used method of ranking jobs according to a variety of skill and difficulty factors, then adding up these rankings to arrive at an overall numerical rating for each given job.

jobs on some overall factor like job difficulty. With the factor comparison method, you rank each job *several times—once for each compensable factor you choose.* For example, jobs might be ranked first in terms of the compensable factor "skill." Then they are ranked according to their "mental requirements," and so forth. Then these rankings are combined for each job into an overall numerical rating for the job. This is also a widely used method and is also explained in more detail in the appendix to this chapter.

♦ **STEP 3. GROUP SIMILAR JOBS INTO PAY GRADES**

pay grade A pay grade is comprised of jobs of approximately equal difficulty.

Once a job evaluation method has been used to determine the relative worth of each job, the committee can turn to the task of assigning pay rates to each job, but it will usually want to first group jobs into **pay grades.** If the committee used the ranking, point method, or factor comparison method it *could* assign pay rates to *each* individual job.[27] But for a larger employer such a pay plan would be difficult to administer, since there might be different pay rates for hundreds or even thousands of jobs. And even in smaller organizations there is a tendency to try to simplify wage and salary structures as much as possible. Therefore, the committee will probably want to group similar jobs (similar in terms of their ranking or number of points, for instance) into grades for pay purposes. Then, instead of having to deal with hundreds of pay rates, it might only have to focus on, say, 10 or 12 pay grades.[28]

A pay grade is comprised of jobs of approximately equal difficulty or importance as determined by job evaluation. If the point method was used, the pay grade consists of jobs falling within a range of points. If the ranking plan was used, the grade consists of all jobs that fall within two or three ranks. If the classification system was used, then the jobs are already categorized into classes or grades. (If the factor comparison method is used, the grade will consist of a specified range of pay rates, as explained in the appendix to this chapter.) Ten to 16 grades per "job cluster" (factory jobs, clerical jobs, etc.) is common.

♦ **STEP 4. PRICE EACH PAY GRADE—WAGE CURVES**

The next step is to assign pay rates to each of your pay grades. (Of course, if you chose *not* to slot jobs into pay grades, pay rates would instead have to be assigned to each individual job.) Assigning pay rates to each pay grade (or to each job) is usually accomplished with a **wage curve.**

wage curve Shows the relationship between the value of the job and the average wage paid for this job.

The wage curve depicts graphically the pay rates *currently* being paid for jobs in each pay grade relative to the points or rankings assigned to each job or grade, as determined by the job evaluation. An example of a wage curve is presented in Figure 10.3. Note that pay rates are shown on the vertical axis, while the pay grades (in terms of points) are shown along the horizontal axis. The purpose of the wage curve is to show the relationship between (1) the value of the job as determined by one of the job evaluation methods and (2) the current average pay rates for your grades.

The pay rates shown on the graph are traditionally those now paid by the organization; if there is reason to believe that the present pay rates are substantially out of step with the prevailing market pay rates for these jobs, benchmark jobs within each pay grade are chosen and priced via a compensation survey. These new market-based pay rates are then the wage rates plotted on the wage curve.

There are several steps in pricing jobs with a wage curve. First, *find the average pay for each pay grade,* since each of the pay grades consists of several jobs. Next, plot the pay rates for each pay grade as was done in Figure 10.3. Then fit a line (called a *wage line*) through the points just plotted. This

FIGURE 10.3
Plotting a Wage Curve

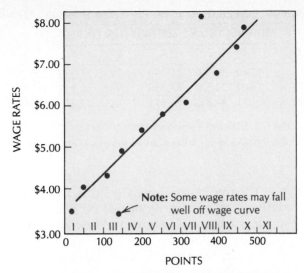

Note: The average pay rate for jobs in each grade (Grade I = 0–50 points, Grade II = 50–100 points, Grade III = 101–150 points, etc.) are plotted, and the wage curve fitted in.

can either be done freehand or by using a statistical method. Finally, *price jobs*. Wages along the wage line are the target wages or salary rates for the jobs in each pay grade. If the current rates being paid for any of your jobs or grades fall well above or below the wage line, that rate may be "out of line"; raises or a pay freeze for that job may be in order. Your next step, then, is to *fine tune* your pay rates.

♦ STEP 5. FINE TUNE PAY RATES

Finally, the pay rates for each pay grade are fine tuned. This will involve correcting out-of-line rates and (usually) developing rate ranges.

Developing Rate Ranges

rate ranges A series of steps or levels within a pay grade, usually based upon years of service.

Most employers do not just pay one rate for all jobs in a particular pay grade; instead, they develop **rate ranges** for each grade so that there might, for instance, be 10 levels or "steps" and 10 corresponding pay rates within each pay grade. This approach is illustrated in Table 10.4, which shows the pay rates and steps for some of the federal government pay grades. As of the time of this pay schedule, for instance, employees in positions that were classified in grade GS–10 could be paid annual salaries of between $24,011 and $31,211, depending on the level or step at which they were hired into the grade, the amount of time they were in the grade, and their merit increases (if any). Another way to depict the rate ranges for each grade is with a *wage structure*, as in Figure 10.4. The wage structure *graphically* depicts the range of pay rates (in this case, per hour) to be paid for each pay grade.

There are several benefits in using rate ranges for each pay grade. First, the employer can take a more flexible stance with respect to the labor market. For example, it makes it easier to attract experienced, higher-paid employees into a pay grade where the starting salary for the lowest step may be too low to attract such experienced personnel. Rate ranges also allow you to provide for performance differences between employees within the same grade or between those with differing seniorities. As in Figure 10.4, most employers structure their rate ranges to overlap a bit so that an employee with more experience or seniority may earn more than an entry-level person in the next higher pay grade.

TABLE 10.4   Federal Government Pay Schedule: Grades GS 8–GS 10

GRADE	RATES AND STEPS WITHIN GRADE									
	1	*2*	*3*	*4*	*5*	*6*	*7*	*8*	*9*	*10*
GS–8	19,740	20,398	21,056	21,714	22,372	23,030	23,688	24,346	25,004	25,662
GS–9	21,804	22,531	23,258	23,985	24,712	25,439	26,166	26,893	27,620	28,347
GS–10	24,011	24,811	25,611	26,411	27,211	28,011	28,811	29,611	30,411	31,211

Source: The U.S. Office of Personnel Management.

Note: Federal grades range from GS-1 to top grade of GS-18 (annual rate of $84,157).

The rate range is usually built around the wage line or curve. One alternative is to arbitrarily decide on a maximum and minimum rate for each grade, such as 15% above and below the wage line. As an alternative, some employers allow the rate range for each grade to become wider for the higher pay ranges, reflecting the greater demands and performance variability inherent in these more complex jobs.

Correcting Out-of-Line Rates

It is possible (as in Figure 10.3) that the wage rate for a job may fall well off the wage line (or well outside the rate range for its grade). *This means that the average pay for that job is currently too high or too low,* relative to other jobs in the firm. If a point falls well below the line, a pay raise for the job may be required. If the plot falls well above the wage line, pay cuts or a pay freeze may be required.

FIGURE 10.4
Wage Structure

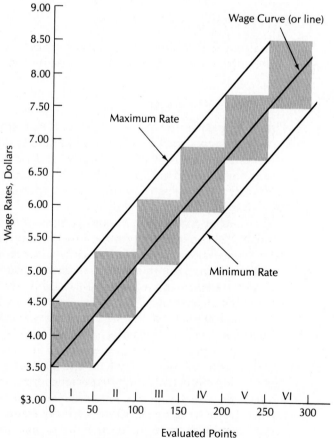

Note: This shows overlapping wage classes and maximum-minimum wage ranges.

For underpaid employees, the problem is easy to solve. Underpaid employees should have their wages raised to the minimum of the rate range for their pay grade, assuming you want to retain the employees and have the funds. This can be done either immediately or in one or two steps.

Rates being paid to overpaid employees are often called red circle, flagged, or overrates, and there are several ways to cope with this problem. One is to freeze the rate paid to employees in this grade until general salary increases bring the other jobs into line with it. A second alternative is to transfer or promote some or all of the employees involved to jobs where they can legitimately be paid their current pay rates. The third alternative is to freeze the rate for six months, during which time you try to transfer or promote the employees involved; if you cannot, then the rate at which these employees are paid is cut to the maximum in the pay range for their pay grade.

PRICING MANAGERIAL AND PROFESSIONAL JOBS

Developing a compensation plan to pay executive, managerial, and professional personnel is similar in many respects to developing a plan for any employees.[29] The basic aims of the plan are the same in that your goal is to attract good employees and maintain their commitment. Furthermore, the basic methods of job evaluation—classifying jobs, ranking them, or assigning points to them, for instance—are about as applicable to managerial and professional jobs as to production and clerical ones.

Yet for managerial and professional jobs, job evaluation only provides a partial answer to the question of how to pay these employees, because these jobs differ from production and clerical jobs in several respects. For one thing, managerial and professional jobs tend to emphasize nonquantifiable factors like judgment and problem solving more than do production and clerical jobs. Second, there is a tendency to pay managers and professionals based on ability—based on their performance or on what they can do—rather than on the basis of "static" job demands like working conditions. Developing compensation plans for managers and professionals therefore tends to be a relatively complex matter, one in which job evaluation, while still important, usually plays a secondary role to nonsalary issues like bonuses, incentives, and benefits.

◆ COMPENSATING MANAGERS

Basic Compensation Elements

There are five elements in a manager's compensation package: salary, benefits, short-term incentives, long-term incentives, and perquisites.[30]

The amount of salary managers are paid is usually a function of the value of the person's work to the organization and how well the person is discharging these responsibilities. As with other jobs, the value of the person's work is usually determined through job analysis and salary surveys and the resulting fine tuning of salary levels. Salary is the cornerstone of executive compensation, since it is on this element that the other four are layered, with benefits, incentives, and perquisites normally awarded in some proportion to the manager's base pay.

The other four elements include benefits, short- and long-term incentives, and perquisites. *Benefits* (including time off with pay, health care, employee services, survivors protection, and retirement coverage) are discussed in Chapter 12. *Short-term incentives* are designed to reward managers for attaining short-term (normally yearly) goals, while *long-term incentives* are aimed at rewarding the person for long-term performance (in terms of increased market share and the like). Incentives are discussed in Chapter 11. Perquisites (perks for short) begin where benefits leave off and are usually given to only a select few executives based on organizational level and (possibly) past performance. Perks include use of company planes, yachts, and executive dining rooms. These benefits are also covered in Chapter 12.

Executive compensation tends to emphasize performance incentives more than do other employees' pay plans, since organizational results are more likely to directly reflect the contributions of executives than those of lower-echelon employees. The heavy incentive component of executives' compensation can be illustrated with some examples of the highest-paid U.S. executives.[31] Recently, for instance, the president of United Technologies earned a salary of $545,000 and a bonus of $480,000 and exercised his long-term incentive stock option to earn an additonal $1,946,000; for the chairman of Rockwell International, his salary component was $460,000, the bonus was $655,000, and the long-term income was $1,055,000, for total compensation of $2,170,000. The president of Levi Strauss earned a salary of $276,000, a bonus of $125,000, and long-term income of $1,256,000. In general, bonuses today equal 25% or more of a typical executive's base salary in many countries, including the United States, the United Kingdom, France, and Germany.[32]

Determinants of Executive Pay

Compensation levels like these have prompted some writers to ask whether top managers are not overpaid. One even contends that the stockholders and public resent

> the prospect that key executives are becoming a privileged class, receiving special contracts or bonuses along with their extensive perquisites and often spectacular salaries—regardless of the performance of their companies. The rewards should not be, as a judge once said "a misuse or waste of corporate funds, or a gift to a favored few." Executive compensation practices that undermine public trust must be chained, or capitalists themselves will become a major force undermining capitalism.[33]

In point of fact, there *is* considerable disagreement regarding what determines executive pay and therefore whether top executives are worth what they are paid. At the lower levels of management (like first-line supervisor), there is no debate; supervisors' pay grades are usually set so that their median salaries are 10% to 25% above those of the highest-paid workers supervised. And many employers even pay supervisors for scheduled overtime, although the Fair Labor Standards Act does not require them to do so.[34]

It is at the topmost management levels that questions regarding pay abound. The traditional wisdom is that a top manager's salary is closely tied to the size of the firm.[35] Yet two experts who tested this idea by studying the relationship between pay and responsibility for the 148 highest-paid executives in the United States concluded that "the level of executive responsibility (as measured by total assets, total sales, total number of shares in the company, total value of the shares, and total corporate profits) is not an important variable in determining executive compensation."[36] Instead, say these experts, an executive's pay is mostly determined by the industry in which he or she works, and the "corporate power structure," since executives who also serve on their firms' boards of directors "are, to a large degree, dictators of their own destiny."

Yet there is conflicting evidence. In one study, for instance, the researcher found that a statistical analysis of the total cash compensation of the chief executive officers of 129 companies showed that they *were* paid for both responsibility and performance. This researcher found that four compensable factors—company size, profitability, number of employees, and experience) accounted for 83% of the differences in pay. Therefore, says this writer, it appears "that there are rational, acceptable, and abiding principles that govern the total cash compensation of top executives in manufacturing firms."[37]

Managerial Job Evaluation

Despite questions regarding the rationality of executive pay levels, job evaluation still plays an important role in pricing executive and managerial jobs, at least in most firms. According to one expert, "the basic approach used by most large companies to ensure some degree of equity among various divisions and departments is to classify all executive and management positions into a series of grades, to which a series of salary ranges is attached."[38]

As with nonmanagerial jobs, one alternative is to rank the executive and management positions in relation to each other, grouping those of equal value. However, the job classification and point evaluation methods are also used, with compensable factors like scope of the position, complexity, difficulty, and creative demands.

♦ COMPENSATING PROFESSIONAL EMPLOYEES

Compensating nonsupervisory professional employees like engineers and scientists presents some unique problems.[39] Investigative work like this puts a heavy premium on creativity and problem solving, compensable factors that are not easily compared or measured. Furthermore, the professional's economic impact on the firm is often related only indirectly to the person's actual effort; for example, the success of an engineer's invention depends on many factors, like how well it is produced and marketed.

The job evaluation methods we explained previously can be used for evaluating professional jobs.[40] The compensable factors here tend to focus on problem solving, creativity, job scope, and technical knowledge and expertise. Both the point method and factor comparison methods have been used, although the job classification method seems most popular. Here a series of grade descriptions are written, and then a position is slotted into the grade having the most appropriate definition.

Yet, in practice, traditional methods of job evaluation are rarely used for professional jobs since "it is simply not possible to identify factors and degrees of factors which meaningfully differentiate among the values of professional work."[41] "Knowledge and the skill of applying it," as one expert notes, "are extremely difficult to quantify and measure."[42]

As a result, most employers use a market-pricing approach in evaluating professional jobs. They price professional jobs in the marketplace to the best of their ability to establish the values for benchmark jobs; then these benchmark jobs and the employer's other professional jobs are slotted into a salary structure. Specifically, each professional discipline (like mechanical engineering or electrical engineering) usually ends up having four to six grade levels, each of which requires a fairly broad salary range. This somewhat more subjective approach to job evaluation helps ensure that the employer remains competitive when bidding for professionals whose attainments vary widely and whose potential employers are literally found worldwide.

COMPUTER APPLICATION IN COMPENSATION:

COMPUTERIZED REPORTS FOR SALARY ADMINISTRATION

Because of the routine nature of many salary administration decisions, the payroll department is usually one of the first to be computerized in any organization. In terms of decisions, for example, weekly or biweekly checks must be produced based on the number of hours (or salary) of each employee. From each person's gross pay, various deductions then must be routinely computed, deductions that include withholding taxes, Social Security taxes, and health insurance benefits payments. These are all routine decisions that lend themselves to computerization.

Computerization also facilitates producing salary administration reports, and there are several such reports that managers require.[1] The *Job Classification Listing Report* in Table 10.5 ranks all jobs in the supervisor's department, arranging them by base pay in descending order. (The "Value" column might reflect points in a Hay plan, for instance, while "base" indicates the person's base pay as compared with the midpoints and maximum pay in the person's rate range.) The *Manpower Control Report* indicates, for each position in the manager's department, the extent to which that position classification is fully staffed: In this case, for instance, the department is missing one part-time electrician and is budgeted for (and has) no part-time painters.

In addition to these periodic departmental reports, it is not uncommon for many other pay reports to be produced on an ad hoc basis. For example, the *Base Pay by Job Classification Report* lists the base pay of each employee in each job classification, along with their position effective date (the day they moved into that position), their employment date, and months of prior experience. This report can be valuable for comparing employees' pay within a job classification. The *Pay Increase Report* shows at a glance each employee's current pay, proposed increase, and new pay. A computerized report can be produced showing the total cost of all increases, by *job classification,* and in total for the organization.

Other computerized reports are produced as well. The *Pay Comparison Report* is useful because it shows (across departments) the salary ranges, position effective date, date employed, and months of prior experience (before joining the company) of each employee in a job classification. This can help to eliminate inequities that might otherwise occur, say, between electricians in different departments. The *Compa-Ratio Report* indicates how each employee in a job classification is being paid relative to the midpoint in his or her rate range. The *Average Salary Data Report* is produced for a single job classification and provides salary data. In Table 10.5, for instance, there are a total of four electricians in this job classification, their maximum base pay is $8.86 per hour, their minimum base pay is $8.45 per hour, and their average base pay is $8.67 per hour.

[1]Michael P. Jaquish, "Reports for Salary Administration," *Personnel Journal* (December 1988), pp. 79–83.

CURRENT ISSUES IN COMPENSATION MANAGEMENT

◆ THE ISSUE OF COMPARABLE WORTH

The Issue

Should women who are performing jobs *equal* to men or just *comparable* to men be paid the same as men? This is the basic issue in "comparable worth."

Equal pay legislation in the United States and other industrialized

TABLE 10.5 Job Classification Listing

Figure 1
JOB CLASSIFICATION LISTING

Dept	Job No	Title	Value	Base	Mid	Max
345	400	electrician	256	8.50	9.50	10.50
	350	painter	220	7.95	8.95	9.95
	326	secretary	197	7.50	8.50	9.50

Figure 2
MANPOWER CONTROL REPORT

Dept	Job No	Title	Budget/Actual FT	PT	Budget/Actual Full-Time Equiv
345	400	electrician	12/12	2/1	13/12.5
	350	painter	1/1	0/0	1/1

Figure 3
BASE PAY BY JOB CLASSIFICATION

Dept	Job No	Title	Employee	Base Pay	Posn Date	Emp Date	MPE*
345	400	electrician	Williams, Bill	8.86	2/22/86	2/22/86	46
235	400	electrician	Johnson, Joe	8.86	1/15/86	1/15/86	50
321	400	electrician	Jones, Henry	8.52	6/12/83	5/23/79	0
345	400	electrician	Glass, George	8.45	3/15/83	3/15/83	2

*months of prior experience

Figure 4
PAY INCREASE REPORT

Dept	Job No	Title	Employee	Curr Pay	Prop Inc	New Pay
345	400	electrician	Williams, Bill	8.86	.35	9.21
235	400	electrician	Johnson, Joe	8.86	.35	9.21
321	400	electrician	Jones, Henry	8.52	.35	8.87
345	400	electrician	Glass, George	8.45	.35	8.80

Figure 5
PAY INCREASE REPORT SHOWING TOTAL COST

Dept	Job No	Title	Employee	Prev Pay	Inc	New Pay
345	400	electrician	Williams, Bill	8.86	.35	9.21
235	400	electrician	Johnson, Joe	8.86	.35	9.21
321	400	electrician	Jones, Henry	8.52	.35	8.87
345	400	electrician	Glass, George	8.45	.35	8.80

Total cost 1.40

Figure 6
JOB CLASS INCREASE REPORT

Job No	Title	FT	PT	FTE	Indiv Incr	Total Cost
400	electrician	27	3	28.5	.35	9.98
326	secretary	11	1	11.5	.26	2.99
350	painter	3	0	3.0	.30	.90

Total cost per hour: $13.87
Annual cost: $28,849.60

Figure 7
PAY COMPARISON REPORT

Dept	Job No	Title	Employee	Base Pay	Posn Date	Emp Date	MPE*
345	400	electrician	Williams, Bill	8.86	2/22/86	2/22/86	46
235	400	electrician	Johnson, Joe	8.86	1/15/86	1/15/86	50
321	400	electrician	Jones, Henry	8.52	6/12/83	5/23/79	0
345	400	electrician	Glass, George	8.45	3/15/83	3/15/83	2

*months of prior experience

(continued)

TABLE 10.5 (continued)

Figure 8
COMPA-RATIO REPORT

Dept	Job No	Title	Employee	Base Pay	Posn Date	Emp Date	MPE*	Compa-ratio
345	400	electrician	Williams, Bill	8.86	2/22/86	2/22/86	46	93.26
235	400	electrician	Johnson, Joe	8.86	1/15/86	1/15/86	50	93.26
321	400	electrician	Jones, Henry	8.52	6/12/83	5/23/79	0	89.68
345	400	electrician	Glass, George	8.45	3/15/83	3/15/83	2	88.94

*months of prior experience

Figure 9
AVERAGE SALARY DATA REPORT

Dept	Job No	Title	Employee	Base Pay	Posn Date	Emp Date	MPE*	Compa-ratio
345	400	electrician	Williams, Bill	8.86	2/22/86	2/22/86	46	93.26
235	400	electrician	Johnson, Joe	8.86	1/15/86	1/15/86	50	93.26
321	400	electrician	Jones, Henry	8.52	6/12/83	5/23/79	0	89.68
345	400	electrician	Glass, George	8.45	3/15/83	3/15/83	2	88.94

total employees: 4   min base pay: 8.45   avg compa-ratio: 91.29
max base pay: 8.86   average base pay: 8.67

Source: Michael P. Jaquish, "Reports for Salary Administration," *Personnel Journal* (December 1988), pp. 80–81.

countries has a history of debate over whether "equal" or "comparable" should be the standard for comparison when comparing men's and women's jobs.[43] For years, "equal" was the standard in the United States, though "comparable" was and is used in Canada and many European countries.[44] In the United States, for instance, the 1963 Equal Pay Act prohibits sex-based pay discrimination, in that an "employer is prohibited from discriminating between employees on the basis of sex by paying wages to employees . . . at a rate less than the rate at which wages are paid to employees of the opposite sex . . . for equal work on jobs the performance of which requires equal skill, effort and responsibility, and which are performed under similar working conditions." For years, courts interpreted this to mean that an employee had to prove not only a disparity of wages between males and females, but also that the disparity exists in *substantially equal jobs* in order to show a case of sex discrimination exists against the employer.[45] As a result of recent court rulings, though, some experts now believe that *comparable worth* may become the standard in the United States.[46]

The issue of comparable worth refers to the requirement to pay equal wages for jobs of comparable (rather than strictly equal) value to the employer. In its more limited sense, this means jobs that (while not equal) *are at least quite similar,* jobs such as assemblers on one line versus assemblers on a different assembly line. In its broadest sense, though, *comparable worth includes comparing quite dissimilar jobs,* such as nurses to fire truck mechanics, nurses to public works mechanics, secretaries to parking lot attendants, nurses to tree trimmers, or secretaries to electricians.[47]

The Gunther Supreme Court Case

A pivotal case here was *Gunther* v. *County of Washington*. It involved Washington County, Oregon, prison matrons who claimed sex discrimination because male prison guards, whose jobs were somewhat different, received substantially higher pay.[48] In this case, the county had evaluated the men's jobs as having 5% more "job content" (based on a point evaluation system) than the female jobs and paid the males 35% more.

While the Supreme Court's decision for the female employee specifically stated that this was not a comparable worth case, many experts believe that the effect of their decision will be to make comparable worth the main consideration in future equal pay lawsuits. This is because prior to the *Gunther* case, wage discrimination claims based on sex had to be argued under the 1963 Equal Pay Act, so that the aggrieved employee had to show that the pay disparity existed in substantially equal jobs. In the *Gunther* case, however, the Supreme Court held that a sex-based pay discrimination case could be argued under Title VII of the 1964 Civil Rights Act. It was relatively difficult to prove pay discrimination under the Equal Pay Act, since the man and woman involved had to have the same or equal jobs; under Title VII of the 1964 Civil Rights Act, it appears that it will be easier to compare men's and women's wages in comparable, rather than just equal, jobs.

However, the concept of comparable worth was subsequently dealt a severe blow by the Ninth Circuit Court of Appeals, which ruled on the appeal of a State of Washington case that also first helped put comparable worth in the spotlight. Ruling in September 1985, the appeals court overturned a U.S. district court's ruling, rejecting the idea that the payment of wages based on the prevailing rates in the market can be in and of itself evidence of intentional discrimination. The court, in *AFSCME* v. *State of Washington,* also ruled that there was nothing in Title VII that was intended to "abrogate fundamental economic principles such as the laws of supply and demand or to prevent employers from competing in the labor market." However, as one law firm puts it, "until the U.S. Supreme Court rules on this issue, employers should continue to be cautious in initiating job evaluation studies and in perpetuating known wage disparities between male dominated and female dominated jobs, where the jobs are arguably of 'comparable value.'"[49] On December 31, 1985, an agreement was announced whereby the state of Washington agreed to pay 35,000 employees in female-dominated jobs almost $500 million in pay raises over seven years, in settlement of this suit.

Comparable Worth and Job Evaluation

comparable worth The concept by which women (who are usually paid less than men) can claim that men in *comparable* (rather than strictly equal) jobs are paid more.

The issue of *comparable worth* has important implications for an employer's job evaluation procedures. In virtually every comparable worth case that has reached a court, the claim revolved around the use of the point method of job evaluation in which each job is evaluated in terms of several factors (like effort, skill, and responsibility) and then assigned points based on the degree of each factor present in the job. The point method purports to be an objective, unbiased, quantitative method of arriving at equitable pay, and actually encourages assigning "comparable worth" ratings to different jobs. Thus, for an architectural firm, the position of Clerk-Typist IV might be evaluated as having the same number of points (and therefore comparable worth) as a junior engineer. This would seem to imply that both jobs should be paid the same, *although in practice market wage rates may be much higher for the (male-dominated) junior engineers than for the (female-dominated) clerk-typist.*[50]

Implications

The comparable worth issue has several implications for compensation management. Some argue that quantitative job evaluation methods like the point method need not be discarded, just used more wisely. For example, one approach is to stress prevailing market rates in pricing jobs, and then only use an evaluation method (like the point method) to slot in those jobs where a market price is not readily available.[51] Another practical solution (says one writer) is to allow employers to price their jobs as they see fit, but to ensure that women have equal access to all jobs, as do men; the idea here is to eliminate the wage discrimination issue by eliminating sex-segregated jobs.[52] To avoid "comparable worth" problems some questions to ask include the following:

Are your job duties and responsibilities clearly documented either by a job analysis questionnaire or a job description? Are they reviewed and updated annually?

When was your pay system last reviewed? If more than three years have passed, serious inequities could exist.

Do you have any circumstances where your system indicates that jobs are comparable, even in the marketplace, but you are paying those jobs occupied by females or minorities less than predominantly male and/or white jobs?

When was the last time you statistically checked the effect of your pay system on females and minorities? Could it be that you have discrimination in fact, though not in intent?

Is your pay system clearly documented in a salary administration manual? If not, the credibility and defensibility of your pay practices are ripe for challenge.[53]

♦ THE ISSUE OF PAY SECRECY

There are basically two opposing points of view with respect to the question "Should employees know what other employees in the organization are being paid?" The basic argument *for* "open pay" is that it improves employee motivation, and the basic thinking here is as follows. According to the expectancy theory of motivation (explained in Chapter 9) an employee's perception of how (and if) pay depends on effort has a direct bearing on the person's motivation. In other words, if employees believe that greater effort does not result in greater rewards then, generally speaking, greater effort (and therefore motivation) will not be forthcoming. On the other hand, if employees *do* believe that there is a direct relationship between effort and rewards then greater effort should result. Proponents of "open pay" contend that where workers do *not* know each other's pay they cannot easily (or at all) assess how effort and rewards are related, and as a result of this uncertainty motivation tends to suffer. (They cannot, for example, say "Smith doesn't work hard, so is paid less than Jones, who works hard.") A related argument is based on equity theory. Specifically, Lawler contends that pay secrecy can and does result in misperceptions of salary levels and, consequently, in feelings of inequity. Lawler believes that by following an "open pay" policy, organizations can reduce such misperceptions, by showing employees that they are in fact equitably paid. The opposing argument is that in practice there *are* usually real inequities in the pay scale, perhaps because of the need to hire someone "in a hurry," or because of the superior salesmanship of a particular applicant. And even if the employee in a similar job who is being paid more actually deserves the higher salary because of his effort, skill, or experience, it's possible that his lower-paid colleagues, viewing the world through their own point of view, may still convince themselves that they are underpaid relative to him.

The research findings to this point are sketchy. In one study a researcher found that managers' satisfaction with their pay increased following their firms' implementation of an open pay policy.[54] A survey conducted by the Bureau of National Affairs found that less than half the firms responding gave employees access to salary schedules. Those not providing such information indicated, among other things, that "secrecy prevents much quibbling . . . ," "salary is a delicate matter . . . ," open pay "could well lead to unnecessary strain and dissatisfaction among managers . . . ," and "open systems too often create misunderstandings and petty complaints." The author of this study notes that "whether the inequities result from a growth situation or some other factor, it is clear that some inequities and openness are incompatible."[55] The implication for compensation management seems to be that a policy of open pay can, under the best of conditions, improve employees' satisfaction with their pay and (possibly) their effort as well. On the other hand, if conditions are not right—and especially if there are any lingering inequities in the employer's pay structure—moving to an open pay policy is not advisable.

♦ THE ISSUE OF INFLATION AND COMPENSATION MANAGEMENT

Inflation and how to cope with it has been another important issue in compensation management. According to one estimate, a family of four earning $21,000 in 1975 would have to have earned just over $48,000 by 1990 to maintain the same purchasing power because of inflation, and because the family would move to higher income tax brackets as their income increased.[56]

A related problem—*salary compression*—was ranked as a major problem by 15% of the respondents in one study. Salary compression is a result of inflation. Its symptoms include (1) higher starting salaries, thereby compressing current employees' salaries; (2) unionized hourly pay increases that overtake supervisory and nonunion hourly rates, and (3) the recruitment of new college graduates at salaries above those of current job-holders.[57]

Dealing with salary compression is a tricky problem.[58] On the one hand, you do not want your long-termers to be treated unfairly or to become inordinately dissatisfied and possibly leave with their accumulated knowledge and expertise. On the other hand, the fact remains that mediocre performance or lack of assertiveness may in many cases explain the low salaries rather than salary compression.

In any case, there are several solutions to the pay compression problem.[59] As distasteful as it is to many employers to pay employees simply for seniority, you can institute a program of providing raises based on longevity. These raises could be distributed in flat dollar amounts, or as a percentage of base pay, or as a combination of the two. Second (as explained more fully in Chapter 11), a much more aggressive merit pay program can be installed. This may at least help reduce the morale problems associated with pay compression, since employees know they have the potential for earning higher raises. Third, supervisors can be authorized to recommend "equity" adjustments for selected incumbents who are both highly valued by the organization and also viewed as unfairly victimized by pay compression.

Inflation has also put some employers' pension plans in peril.[60] An executive who retired at the beginning of 1982 had lost about 45% of the purchasing power of a fixed-dollar company pension by 1990, for instance, a frightening state of affairs for retirees whose pensions are not indexed to inflation. While the rate of increase of consumer prices has recently slowed, some fear that inflation is only dormant and that rapid price increases will again be launched.

In the 1970s and early 1980s, employers tried to cope with inflation's impact in many ways. More employers granted across-the-board salary increases either in lieu of or in addition to performance-based merit increases. Others changed their pension plans to index them to inflation so that the value of the pension payments increases along with the rise in the price of goods.[61] Others changed the compensation mix to decrease the emphasis on taxable income like wages and salary and to substitute nontaxable benefits like flexible work hours, dental plans, daycare centers, and group legal and auto insurance plans.[62]

The cost-of-living adjustment (or COLA) clause is another way employers tried to cope with inflation.[63] The COLA clause was first adopted by the United Auto Workers and the General Motors Corporation in 1950; a study by the Bureau of Labor Statistics indicates that about 40% of the major union contracts negotiated for 1987 (covering 6.5 million workers) contained COLA provisions, down from 58% and 9.3 million workers in 1980.[64]

In fact, General Motors Corporation is eliminating COLAs for its 125,000 salaried employees. GM had previously instituted a pay-for-performance system and, pleased with the results, decided to expand it to all salaried workers. This move may signal the end of COLAs in the next UAW contract.[65]

In any event, the COLA or escalator clause is designed to maintain the purchasing power of the wage rate and operates as follows. Specified increases in the Consumer Price Index trigger increases in the wage rate, with the magnitude of the increase depending on the negotiated COLA formula.[66] The most common formula provides a 1 cent per hour wage adjustment for each 0.3% or 0.4% change in consumer prices.[67] Nonunion employees often then receive a similar adjustment. Periodically, the employer then takes a portion of the dollar COLA adjustment and builds it into the employee's base salary, a procedure known as "baking in."[68] Again, though, COLAs have become less of a concern to unions as inflation has moderated.

♦ THE ISSUE OF COST-OF-LIVING DIFFERENTIALS

Cost-of-living differences between localities have escalated from occasional inconveniences into serious compensation problems. For example, a family of four might live in Atlanta for just over $39,000 per year while the same family's annual expenditures in Chicago or Los Angeles would be over $46,000. Deciding whether and how to have differential pay rates for employees living in different locales and how to handle employees' moving from one area to another are thus important compensation issues today.

Employers are using several methods to handle cost-of-living differentials. The main approach is to give the transferred person a nonrecurring payment, usually in a lump sum, or perhaps spread over one to three years.[69] Other employers pay a differential for ongoing costs in addition to a one-time allocation; for example, one employer pays a differential of $6,000 per year to people earning $35,000 to $45,000 who are transferred from Atlanta to Minneapolis. The first $6,000 is a lump sum at the time of the move, and in the second year the employee gets another $6,000 in four quarterly increments. Employees already living in Minneapolis (or any other high-cost area) are not given any adjustment.[70] Other companies simply increase the employee's base salary rate. They give the person an automatic raise equal to the amount that living costs in the new locale exceed those in the old, in addition to any other promotion-based raise the employee may get.

SMALL-BUSINESS APPLICATIONS

♦ DEVELOPING A WORKABLE PAY PLAN

Developing a pay plan that is internally and externally equitable is no less important in a small firm than in a large one. Paying wage rates that are too high for the area may be unnecessarily expensive, and paying less may guarantee poor-quality help and rapid turnover. Similarly, wage rates that are internally inequitable will reduce morale and cause the president to be badgered mercilessly by employees demanding raises "The same as Joe down the hall." The president who wants to concentrate on major issues like sales would thus do well to institute a rational pay plan as soon as possible.

Your first step should be to conduct a wage survey. The basic methods for doing so were described earlier in this chapter, but in the smaller business you'll generally depend on less formal methods for collecting this information.

Three sources here can be especially useful. A careful perusal of the Sunday classified newspaper ads should yield useful information on wages offered for jobs similar to those you are trying to price. Second, your local Job Service office can be a wealth of information, compiling as it does extensive information on pay ranges and averages for many of the jobs listed in the *Dictionary of Occupational Titles.* (This is another reason for using job titles that are consistent with those in the *D.O.T.*) The Job Service office can provide information on wages within the local area served by that office, as well as on the geographic region served by the group of Job Service offices of which your office is one member. Finally, local employment agencies, always anxious to establish ties that could grow into business relationships, should be able to provide fairly good data regarding pay rates for different jobs.

Next, if you employ more than 20 employees or so, conduct at least a rudimentary job evaluation. For this, you will first require job descriptions, since these will be the source of data regarding the nature and worth of each job.

You will usually find it easier to split employees into three groups—managerial/professional, office/clerical, and plant personnel. For each of the three groups, determine the compensable factors to be evaluated and then rank or assign points to each job based on the job evaluation.

For each job or class of jobs (i.e., assemblers), you will want to create a pay range. The procedure for doing so was described earlier. However, in general, you should choose as the midpoint of your range the target salary as required by your job evaluation and then produce a range of about 30% around this average, broken into a total of five steps.

While it doesn't always work, you may find it useful to experiment with using the *Dictionary of Occupational Titles* data-people-things scores as a simple job evaluation method. As explained earlier (on page 95) the experts at the Department of Labor have gone to considerable trouble to produce data-people-things scores for each job in the *Dictionary of Occupational Titles*.

There are many situations in which these scores can be used for job evaluation purposes although they are not designed to be so used. Assigning job evaluation ratings to jobs based on the data-people-things scores seems to work best when you're dealing with jobs that are fairly similar in many respects. It often works well in evaluating all manufacturing jobs in a company's plant, for instance. Here you may have a range of jobs such as textile loom fixer, production supervisor, weaver, production crew member, and fabricator. Strictly speaking, the data-people-things scores for each job reflect the degree to which each of these three factors is present in each job (for instance, the degree to which the job requires manipulating data, dealing with people, or dealing with things). These scores are listed in the *Dictionary* for each job title. Therefore it is simple for you to, say, add up the D + P + T numerical score for each job to see if it produces for you what appears to be a logical hierarchy of jobs (in terms of their value to the company). Again, this approach is not for everyone, but it is so simple that it is worth a try. Of course, a weighting scheme could be included if you felt that one factor should be weighted more heavily than the others.

♦ COMPENSATION POLICIES

You must also have policies on compensation-related matters. For example, you have to have a policy on when and how raises are computed. Many small-business owners make the mistake of appraising employees on their anniversary date, a year after they are hired. The problem here is that the raise for one employee then becomes the standard for the next, and so on, for each of your employees. This produces a never-ending cycle of appraisals and posturing for ever higher raises.

The better alternative is to have a policy of once-a-year raises during a standard appraisal period, preferably about four weeks before the budget for next year must be produced. In this way, the administrative headache of conducting these appraisals and awarding raises is dealt with during a one- or two-week period. Furthermore, the total required raise money (which of course has to be outlined in advance by the company president) is then known more precisely when next year's budget is compiled. Other compensation policies include amount of holiday and vacation pay (as explained in the next chapter), overtime pay policy, method of pay (i.e., weekly, biweekly, monthly), garnishments, and time card or sign-on sheet procedures.

There are, as mentioned earlier in this chapter, a number of federal, state, and local laws to which small (and large) employers must adhere. Local and state laws will often cover companies not covered by the Fair Labor Standards Act, but the latter is actually quite comprehensive. It covers most employees of enterprises engaged in activities affecting interstate or foreign commerce. Retail and service companies are covered if their annual gross volume of business is not less than $362,500 a year and any other type of business is covered if its volume is not less than $250,000 a year.[71]

Misclassification of exempt employees is probably the biggest mistake made by smaller firms. As noted earlier, some employees are exempt from the overtime and/or minimum wage requirements of the FLSA. A common small-business mistake is to assume that putting someone on a yearly salary exempts them from the overtime provisions of the act. You cannot make someone exempt simply by paying them a yearly salary, nor can you make them exempt by claiming they are "managers" because they spend some of their time supervising other employees. Strictly speaking, the employee has to spend at least 50% of his or her time actually supervising other employees to be classified as an executive, managerial, or supervisory employee. It is not enough that they spend 80% of their time doing the same work as the people they supervise, and only 20% of their time actually supervising.[72]

There are other common wage-hour traps to avoid.[73] With respect to meal and break periods, an employee must generally be paid for meal periods unless the period is at least 20 minutes long, the employee is completely relieved of duties, and the employee can leave his or her work post. Also beware of how you handle compensatory time off. Many smaller employers believe they can have an employee work, say, 45 hours in one week, pay the person for 40 hours and give them compensatory time off of 5 hours in the following week. Under the law, this is not legal, for two reasons. First, if there is to be compensatory time off, the employer must provide $1\frac{1}{2}$ hours off for each overtime hour worked. Thus, if someone works 42 hours in one week, he or she should receive 3 hours of compensable time. Furthermore, the time off must be given in the same pay period—say, a one-week interval—that the overtime hours are worked. Furthermore, you cannot manipulate the pay period, for instance, by generally paying for a pay period that ranges from Monday morning through Sunday night but then temporarily changing the pay period to Saturday morning through Friday night in order to accommodate the need to work extra hours on a weekend because of a rush job. Great care also has to be taken when it comes to paying for time recorded. For example, suppose employees are required to clock in. They consistently clock in 15 minutes early or get into the habit of not clocking out for lunch. Here, it is possible that an inspector from the wage and hour division may conclude that the employees were improperly underpaid, since there is no record of them having clocked out for the period for which they were docked.

SUMMARY

1. There are two bases on which to pay employees compensation: increments of time and volume of production. The former includes hourly or daily wages and salaries. Basing pay on volume of production ties compensation directly to the amount of production (or number of "pieces" the worker produces).

2. Establishing pay rates involves five steps, each of which are explained in this chapter: conduct salary survey, evaluate jobs, develop pay grades, use wage curves, and fine-tune pay rates.

3. Job evaluation is aimed at determining the relative worth of a job. It involves comparing jobs to one another based on their content, which is usually defined in terms of compensable factors like skills, effort, responsibility, and working conditions.

4. The ranking method of job evaluation involves five steps: (a) obtain job information, (b) select clusters of jobs to be rated, (c) select compensable factors, (d) rank jobs, and (e) combine ratings (of several raters). This is a simple method to use, but there is a tendency to rely too heavily on guesstimates. The classification (or grading) method is a second qualitative approach that involves categorizing jobs based on a "class description" or "classification rules" for each class.

5. The point method of job evaluation requires identifying a number of compensable factors and then determining the degree to which each of these factors is present in the job. As explained in the appendix, it involves nine steps: (a) determine types of jobs to be evaluated, (b) collect job information, (c) select compensable factors, (d) define compensable factors, (e) define factor degree, (f) determine relative weights of factors, (g) assign point values to factors and degrees, (h) develop a job evaluation manual, and (i) rate the jobs. This is a quantitative technique, and many packaged plans are readily available.

6. The factor comparison method (as explained in the appendix) is a quantitative job evaluation technique that entails deciding which jobs have more of certain compensable factors than others. It is one of the most widely used job evaluation methods and entails eight steps: (a) obtain job information, (b) select key jobs, (c) rank key jobs by factors, (d) distribute wage rates by factors for each job, (e) rank jobs by wage rates, (f) compare the two sets of rankings to screen out unusable key jobs, (g) construct the job comparison scale, and (h) use the job comparison scale. This is a systematic, quantifiable method. However, it is also a difficult method to implement. Steps (e) and (f) can be skipped if you prefer.

7. Most managers group similar jobs into wage or pay grades for pay purposes. These are comprised of jobs of approximately equal difficulty or importance as determined by job evaluation.

8. The wage curve (or line) shows the average target wage for each pay grade (or job). It can help show you what the average wage for each grade *should be*, and whether any present wages (or salaries) are out of line. Developing a wage curve involves four steps: (a) find the average pay for each pay grade, (b) plot these wage rates for each pay grade, (c) draw the wage line, and (d) price jobs, after plotting present wage rates.

9. Developing a compensation plan for executive, managerial, and professional personnel is complicated by the fact that factors like performance and creativity must take precedence over "static" factors like working conditions. Market rates, performance, and incentives and benefits thus play a much greater role than does job evaluation for these employees.

10. Four main compensation issues we discussed were comparable worth, pay secrecy, inflation, and cost of living differentials.

11. In Chapters 4 through 8 we discussed recruitment and placement—finding and selecting employees who have the ability and potential to get the job done. In this chapter we focused on the second component of motivation—providing important rewards—in this case, wages and salaries. In the next three chapters we discuss other types of rewards, starting with financial incentives, to which we now turn.

KEY TERMS

employee compensation	salary surveys	grade description
Davis-Bacon Act	benchmark jobs	point method
Walsh-Healey Public Contract Act	compensable factors	factor comparison method
Fair Labor Standards Act	ranking method	pay grade
Equal Pay Act	classification (or grading) method	wage curve
Civil Rights Act	classes	rate ranges
Employee Retirement Income Security Act (ERISA)	grades	comparable worth

DISCUSSION QUESTIONS

1. What is the difference between exempt and nonexempt jobs?
2. Should the job evaluation depend on an appraisal of the job holder's performance? Why? Why not?
3. What is the relationship between compensable factors and job specifications?
4. What are the pros and cons of the following methods of job evaluation: ranking, classification, factor comparison, point method?
5. In what respect is the factor comparison method similar to the ranking method? How do they differ?
6. You will find five job descriptions presented in Figure 10.5. On the assumption that you will at some time want to evaluate these jobs using the point method, define compensable factors for these jobs, as well as factor degrees.

◆ APPLICATION EXERCISES

◆ CASE STUDY   **Job Evaluation for Bank Managers**

The chairman of the board of directors of the Second National Bank has proposed that all managerial positions be included in the bank's job evaluation plan. He has talked with executives in several large business organizations in which such a practice has been found entirely possible and helpful. He proposed this action to the board at its latest meeting. The president asked that no action be taken until he could discuss it with those who would be affected.

Most of the middle-management group appear to be opposed to such a procedure. The president, while trying to remain neutral, has expressed a fear that if salaries are fitted to job evaluation, he will lose his best people. Many department heads and assistants insist that their jobs simply can't be rated on the scale used for subordinate positions. Others argue that no individual or small group can possibly know what their jobs involve. It is also argued that the qualities for which managers are paid are so varied and intangible that no systematic comparison of jobs makes sense.

The personnel manager and his staff are united in favoring the idea.

FIGURE 10.5
Job Description A

DISTINQUISHING CHARACTERISTICS OF WORK

This is responsible supervisory and/or technically varied and complex typing and clerical work involving the exercise of independent judgment and initiative in the development of specialized work methods and procedures and their application to the solution of technical problems.

An employee in a position allocated to this class independently performs varied and complex clerical functions that require the use of initiative and judgment in carrying assignments to completion; performs specialized technical clerical work of a complex nature; types a variety of materials and reports which frequently include specialized scientific or legal terminology; supervises a small group of employees performing relatively complex clerical and related assignments; or supervises a larger group in the performance of more routinized or less difficult assignments.

Work is performed under the general supervision of a higher-level employee. Assignments are restricted only by their subject content and its relation to the activities or functional unit with which the incumbent is connected. Where the work situation involves the performance of individually difficult and varied clerical duties, the number of subordinate personnel for whom the Clerk Typist III is responsible is ordinarily small.

EXAMPLES OF WORK PERFORMED

(Note: These examples are intended only as illustrations of the various types of work performed in positions allocated to this class. The omission of specific statements of duties does not exclude them from the position if the work is similar, related, or a logical assignment to the position.)

Plans, assigns, corrects, and generally reviews the work of a large group of secretarial and clerical employees performing routine uncomplicated clerical activities or a smaller number of subordinate personnel performing individually difficult and varied tasks.

Performs independent clerical work of a technical nature requiring the exercise of independent and unreviewed judgment in making decisions concerning procedures to be followed in accomplishing the assigned tasks.

Compiles and edits information for special reports concerning the operation of the agency in which the employee gathers various information from the agency and other sources, and separates the data into pre-arranged categories.

Verifies, checks, and examines technical and complex surveys and other types of reports for accuracy, completeness, compliance with agency standards and policies, and adequacy.

Types, with speed and accuracy, involved correspondence, reports, records, orders, and other documents from rough drafts, transcribing machines, notes, and oral instructions in rough and/or finished form.

Composes important correspondence without review and/or specific instructions.

May perform all clerical work related to a particular phase of a program for which the supervisor is responsible.

Performs related work as required.

MINIMUM TRAINING AND EXPERIENCE

Graduation from a standard high school and two years of clerical and/or typing experience. Successful completion of post-high school training from an accredited college or university, or vocational or technical school may be substituted at the rate of 30 semester hours or 720 classroom hours on a year-for-year basis for the required experience.

An equivalency diploma issued by a state department of education or by the United States Armed Forces Institute, or a qualifying score on the Division of Personnel and Retirement Educational Attainment Comparison Test may be substituted for high school graduation.

NECESSARY SPECIAL REQUIREMENT

Ability to type at the rate of 35 correct words per minute.

The chairman of the board, through the president, has asked the human resource department to prepare a statement in favor of the development, explaining what it would do and how it would be done.

Problem:
You have been assigned the responsibility for a first draft of this statement, to be directed to the rest of the personnel staff for discussion.

Source: Dale Yoder and Paul D. Standohar, *Personnel Management & Industrial Relations* (Englewood Cliffs, N.J.: Prentice-Hall, 1982), p. 361.

FIGURE 10.5
Job Description B

DISTINGUISHING CHARACTERISTICS OF WORK

This is varied and highly responsible secretarial, clerical, and administrative work as the assistant to a high level administrator, an agency head, academic dean, major department head, or senior attorney.

An employee in a position allocated to this class performs a variety of secretarial, clerical and administrative duties requiring an extensive working knowledge of the organization and program under the supervisor's jurisdiction. Work involves performing functions that are varied in subject matter and level of difficulty and range from performance of standardized clerical assignments to performance of administrative duties which would otherwise require the administrator's personal attention. Work also includes relieving the supervisor of administrative detail and office management functions.

Work is performed under general supervision and only assigned projects which are highly technical or confidential are given close attention by the supervisor.

EXAMPLES OF WORK PERFORMED

(Note: These examples are intended only as illustrations of the various types of work performed in positions allocated to this class. The omission of specific statements of duties does not exclude them from the position if the work is similar, related, or a logical assignment to the position.)

Takes and transcribes dictation that may vary from simple correspondence to legal, medical, engineering, or other technical subject matter.

Serves as personal assistant to a high level administrative official by planning, initiating, and carrying to completion clerical, secretarial, and administrative activities.

Develops material for supervisor's use in public speaking engagements.

Attends conferences to take notes, or is briefed on meetings immediately after they take place in order to know what amendments were made and what developments have occurred in matters that concern the supervisor.

Makes arrangements for conferences including space, time, and place; and informs participants of topics to be discussed; and may provide them with background information.

Assists in and coordinates the preparation of operating and legislative budgets; examines budget documents to insure that they comply with state regulations.

Receives and routes telephone calls, answering questions which may involve the interpretation of policies and procedures.

Interviews and makes preliminary selection of clerical, stenographic, and secretarial employees, makes assignments, schedules hours of work, provides for office coverage, and reviews the work of subordinate employees.

Serves as office receptionist; greets, announces, and routes visitors.

Performs related work as required.

MINIMUM TRAINING AND EXPERIENCE

Graduation from a standard high school and four years of secretarial and/or clerical experience, two of which must have been at the Secretary II level or above.

Successfully completed classroom studies in secretarial science or commercial subjects beyond high school level may be substituted for the required non-specific experience at the rate of 710 classroom hours or 30 semester hours per year for up to a maximum of two years.

An equivalency diploma issued by a state department of education or by the United States Armed Forces Institute, or a qualifying score on the State Personnel Board Educational Attainment Comparison Test may be substituted for high school graduation.

NECESSARY SPECIAL REQUIREMENT

Ability to take and transcribe dictation at a rate of 80 words per minute and to type at a rate of 35 correct words per minute.

EXPERIENTIAL EXERCISE

Purpose: The purpose of this exercise is to give you experience in performing a job evaluation using either the ranking method or the point method.

Required Understanding: You should be thoroughly familiar with both the ranking and the point methods of job evaluation and with the five job descriptions presented at the end of this exercise. It would be helpful to have completed Discussion Question 6 on page 373.

FIGURE 10.5
Job Description C

DISTINGUISHING CHARACTERISTICS OF WORK

This is secretarial work of considerable variety and complexity.
An employee in a position allocated to this class performs duties which involve taking and transcribing dictation for a supervisor who is carrying out a moderately broad program; composing correspondence; and typing memoranda, reports and correspondence. Duties include making travel arrangements and keeping the supervisor's calendar. Assignments at this level involve relieving the supervisor of minor administrative and/or clerical functions and exercising considerable initiative in carrying out legal dictation of ordinary complexity and preparing and processing legal documents and records.
Work is performed under general or administrative supervision. Only projects which entail technical or confidential matters are given close attention by the immediate supervisor.

EXAMPLES OF WORK PERFORMED

(Note: These examples are intended only as illustrations of the various types of work performed in positions allocated to this class. The omission of specific statements of duties does not exclude them from the position if the work is similar, related, or a logical assignment to the position.)

Takes and transcribes dictation.
Receives and reads incoming mail. Screens items which she can handle herself, forwarding the rest to her supervisors or her subordinates, together with necessary background material.
Maintains alphabetical and chronological files and records of office correspondence, documents, reports, and other materials.
Acts as office receptionist; answers telephone, greets, announces and routes visitors.
Assists in expediting the work of the office including such matters as shifting clerical subordinates to take care of fluctuating work loads.
Assembles and summarizes information from files and documents in the office or other available sources for the supervisor's use on the basis of general instructions as to the nature of the information needed.
Performs all clerical work related to a particular phase of the supervisor's program, maintaining all records and composing correspondence relative to the project.
Composes and signs routine correspondence of a non-technical nature in her supervisor's name.
Keeps supervisor's calendar by scheduling appointments and conferences with or without prior clearance.
Performs related work as required.

MINIMUM TRAINING AND EXPERIENCE

Graduation from a standard high school and three years of secretarial and/or clerical experience.
Successfully completed classroom studies in secretarial science or commercial subjects beyond the high school level may be substituted at the rate of 720 classroom hours or 30 semester hours on a year-for-year basis.
An equivalency diploma issued by a state department of education or by the United States Armed Forces Institute, or a qualifying score on the Division of Personnel and Retirement Educational Attainment Comparison Test may be substituted for high school graduation.

NECESSARY SPECIAL REQUIREMENT

Ability to take and transcribe dictation at a rate of 80 words per minute and type at a rate of 35 correct words per minute.

How to Set Up the Exercise/Instructions

1. Divide the class into groups of four or five students. Half the groups will perform a job evaluation of the clerical positions described at the end of this exercise using the ranking method; the other half will do so using the point method (as described in the appendix to this chapter).

2. *Groups using the ranking method.* Perform a job evaluation by ranking the jobs described at the end of this exercise. You may use one or more compensable factors.

3. *Groups using the point method.* Perform a job evaluation on the jobs

FIGURE 10.5
Job Description D

DISTINGUISHING CHARACTERISTICS OF WORK

    This is varied and moderately complex typing and clerical work requiring the exercise of some independent judgment in the use of relatively involved work methods and procedures.
    An employee in a position allocated to this class is required to utilize the touch system in typing, from rough drafts and from transcription machine recordings, a variety of materials which may include specialized reports or tabular arrangements of numerical or statistical data. Work includes performing a variety of clerical duties which are individually of moderate complexity and difficulty, or where work is repetitive, there is some latitude for finality of decision or independence of action.
    Work is performed under general supervision with detailed instructions given in cases involving new or unusually difficult problems. Assignments may be made through the operation of established unit procedures, and work is reviewed by a higher level clerical or administrative supervisor while in progress or upon completion.

EXAMPLES OF WORK PERFORMED

    (Note: These examples are intended only as illustrations of the various types of work performed in positions allocated to this class. The omission of specific statements of duties does not exclude them from the position if the work is similar, related, or a logical assignment to the position.)

    Types correspondence, memoranda, reports, records, orders, stencils, and other office documents from rough drafts, transcribing machines, notes, and oral instructions for rough and finalized copy work which is general, complex, and often technical or scientific in nature.
    Verifies, codes, or classifies incoming materials and documents, and may be responsible for returning incorrect material to sender for correction and maintains follow-up procedures to be sure that corrected materials are returned; may make computations for reports and records or reduce information to a simple form for use by the agency.
    Gathers a variety of information from various sources for use by others in answering correspondence, preparing reports, conducting interviews, or writing speeches, articles, or news releases; may prepare simple reports or draft routine correspondence.
    Establishes and may be responsible for the complete maintenance of small files which would include responsibility for accurate filing and retrieval of materials.
    Answers telephone, screens and routes calls, takes messages, and may answer routine questions.
    May plan, assign, review, and correct work of lower level employees and train them in the performance of assigned duties.
    May operate a variety of general office machines with such accuracy as can be acquired from their use on the job and not from any skills possessed before appointment.
    Performs related work as required.

MINIMUM TRAINING AND EXPERIENCE

    Graduation from a standard high school and one year of clerical and/or typing experience.
    Successful completion of post-high school training from an accredited college or university, or vocational or technical school may be substituted at the rate of 30 semester hours or 720 classroom hours for the required experience.
    An equivalency diploma issued by a state department of education or by the United States Armed Forces Institute, or a qualifying score on the Division of Personnel and Retirement Educational Attainment Comparison Test may be substituted for high school graduation.

NECESSARY SPECIAL REQUIREMENT

    Ability to type at a rate of 35 correct words per minute.

described at the end of this exercise using the point method. This should include selecting compensable factors, defining these factors, defining factor degrees, determining the relative values of factors, assigning point values to factors and degrees, and rating the jobs. Since all the jobs you are evaluating are clerical they already comprise just one "cluster."

4. If time permits, a spokesperson from each point method group can put his or her group's factors, points, and ratings on the board. Did the "point method" groups end up with about the same results? How did

FIGURE 10.5
Job Description E

DISTINGUISHING CHARACTERISTICS OF WORK

This is secretarial and clerical work of moderate variety and complexity.
An employee in a position allocated to this class performs duties which involve taking and transcribing dictation for a supervisor; composing routine correspondence; typing memoranda, reports, and correspondence; and making travel arrangements and keeping supervisor's calendar. Heavy emphasis is placed on relieving the supervisor of as much clerical detail as possible, and work varies widely both in subject matter and level of difficulty.
Work is performed under general supervision and only projects which entail technical or confidential matters are given close attention by the immediate supervisor.

EXAMPLES OF WORK PERFORMED

(Note: These examples are intended only as illustrations of the various types of work performed in positions allocated to this class. The omission of specific statements of duties does not exclude them from the position if the work is similar, related, or a logical assignment to the position.)

Takes and transcribes dictation.
Types correspondence, articles, reports, manuals, and other materials on general or technical subjects; drafts routine acknowledgements in response to inquiries not requiring a supervisor's attention.
Examines, checks, and verifies complex statistical and other reports for completeness, propriety, adequacy, and accuracy of computations; determines conformity to established requirements; and personally follows up the more complicated discrepancies.
Keeps supervisor's calendar by clearing requests for and reminding him of appointments.
Makes travel arrangements and arranges travel itineraries.
Prepares special reports as required and maintains files and records.
Performs related work as required.

MINIMUM TRAINING AND EXPERIENCE

Graduation from a standard high school and one year of secretarial and/or clerical experience.
Successfully completed course work in secretarial science or commercial subjects beyond the high school level may be substituted at the rate of 720 classroom hours or 30 semester hours per year for one year of the required experience.
An equivalency diploma issued by a state department of education or by the United States Armed Forces Institute, or a qualifying score on the State Personnel Board Educational Attainment Comparison Test may be substituted for high school graduation.

NECESSARY SPECIAL REQUIREMENT

Ability to take and transcribe dictation at a rate of 80 words per minute and type at a rate of 35 correct words per minute.

they differ? Why do you think they differed? How did the point method groups' results differ from the ratings developed by the "ranking" groups?

5. The job descriptions for five secretarial jobs begin on page 374. They are *not* necessarily now in order of difficulty. The appropriate order of the jobs from lowest to highest is given below, but please do not read this until *after* you've completed this exercise.

(low) Job D; Job A; Job E; Job C; Job B

APPENDIX

Quantitative Job Evaluation Methods

THE FACTOR COMPARISON JOB EVALUATION METHOD

The factor comparison technique is a *quantitative* job evaluation method. It has many variations and appears to be one of the most widely used, the most accurate, and most complex job evaluation method.

It entails deciding which jobs have more of certain compensable factors than others and is actually a refinement of the ranking method. With the ranking method you generally look at each job as an entity and rank the jobs. With the factor comparison method you rank each job *several times— once for each compensable factor you choose.* For example, jobs might be ranked first in terms of the factor "skill." Then they are ranked according to their "mental requirements." Next, they are ranked according to their "responsibility," and so forth. Then these rankings are combined for each job into an overall numerical rating for the job. Here are the required steps:

Step 1. Obtain Job Information

This method requires a careful, complete job analysis. First, job descriptions are written. Then job specifications are developed, preferably in terms of the compensable factors the committee had decided to use. *For the factor comparison method, these compensable factors are usually* (1) *mental requirements*, (2) *physical requirements*, (3) *skill requirements*, (4) *responsibility*, and (5) *working conditions*. (Ideally, the people who wrote the job specifications are already written around them.) Typical definitions of each of these five factors are presented in Figure 10.6.

Step 2. Select Key "Benchmark" Jobs

Next, 15 to 25 key jobs are selected by the job evaluation committee. These jobs will have to be representative of the range of jobs under study. Thus, they have to select "benchmark jobs" that are acceptable reference points, ones that represent the full range of jobs to be evaluated.

Step 3. Rank Key Jobs by Factors

Here evaluators are asked to rank the key jobs on each of the five factors (mental requirements, physical requirements, skill requirements, responsibility, and working conditions). This ranking procedure is based on job descriptions and job specifications. Each committee member usually makes

FIGURE 10.6

Sample Definitions of Five Factors Typically Used in Factor Comparison Method

Source: Jay L. Otis and Richard H. Leukart, *Job Evaluation: A Basis for Sound Wage Administration,* p. 181. © 1954, renewed 1983. Reprinted by permission of Prentice-Hall, Englewood Cliffs, N.J.

1. Mental Requirements

Either the possession of and/or the active application of the following:
A. (inherent) Mental traits, such an intelligence, memory, reasoning, facility in verbal expression, ability to get along with people and imagination.
B. (acquired) General education, such as grammar and arithmetic; or general information as to sports, world events, etc.
C. (acquired) Specialized knowledge such as chemistry, engineering, accounting, advertising, etc.

2. Skill

A. (acquired) Facility in muscular coordination, as in operating machines, repetitive movements, careful coordinations, dexterity, assembling, sorting, etc.
B. (acquired) Specific job knowledge necessary to the muscular coordination only; acquired by performance of the work and not to be confused with general education or specialized knowledge. It is very largely training in the interpretation of sensory impressions.

Examples

(1) In operating an adding machine, the knowledge of *which key* to depress for a sub-total would be skill.
(2) In automobile repair, the ability to determine the significance of a certain knock in the motor would be skill.
(3) In hand-firing a boiler, the ability to determine from the appearance of the firebed how coal should be shoveled over the surface would be skill.

3. Physical Requirements

A. Physical effort, as sitting, standing, walking, climbing, pulling, lifting, etc.; both the amount exercised and the degree of the continuity should be taken into account.
B. Physical status, as age, height, weight, sex, strength and eyesight.

4. Responsibilities

A. For raw materials, processed materials, tools, equipment and property.
B. For money or negotiable securities.
C. For profits or loss, savings or methods' improvement.
D. For public contact.
E. For records.
F. For supervision.
　(1) Primarily the complexity of supervision *given* to subordinates; the number of subordinates is a secondary feature. Planning, direction, coordination, instruction, control and approval characterize this kind of supervision.
　(2) Also, the degree of supervision *received*. If Jobs A and B gave no supervision to subordinates, but A received much closer immediate supervision than B, then B would be entitled to a higher rating than A in the supervision factor.
　　To summarize the four degrees of supervision:
　　　Highest degree — gives much — gets little
　　　High degree　 — gives much — gets much
　　　Low degree　　— gives none — gets little
　　　Lowest degree — gives none — gets much

5. Working Conditions

A. Environmental influences such as atmosphere, ventilation, illumination, noise, congestion, fellow workers, etc.
B. Hazards—from the work or its surroundings.
C. Hours.

this ranking individually, and then a meeting is held to develop a consensus (among raters) on each job. The result of this process is a table, as in Table 10.6. This shows how each key job ranks on *each* of the five compensable factors.

Step 4. Distribute Wage Rates by Factors

This is where the factor comparison method gets a bit more complicated. In this step the committee members have to divide up the present wage now being paid for *each key job,* distributing it among the five compensable factors. They do this in accordance with their judgments about the importance to the job of each factor. For example, if the present wage for the job

TABLE 10.6 Ranking[1] Key Jobs by Factors

	MENTAL REQUIREMENTS	PHYSICAL REQUIREMENTS	SKILL REQUIREMENTS	RESPONSIBILITY	WORKING CONDITIONS
Welder	1	4	1	1	2
Crane operator	3	1	3	4	4
Punch press operator	2	3	2	2	3
Security guard	4	2	4	3	1

[1] 1 is high, 4 is low.

of common laborer is $4.26, our evaluators might distribute this wage as follows:

Mental requirements	$0.36
Physical requirements	2.20
Skill requirements	0.42
Responsibility	0.28
Working conditions	1.00
Total	$4.26

You make such a distribution for all key jobs.

Step 5. Rank Key Jobs According to Wages Assigned to Each Factor

Here you again rank each job, factor by factor. But here the ranking is based on the wages assigned to each factor. For example (see Table 10.7), for the "mental requirements" factor, the welder job ranks first, while the security guard job ranks last.

Each member of the committee first makes this distribution working independently. Then the committee meets and arrives at a consensus concerning the money to be assigned to each factor for each key job.

Step 6. Compare the Two Sets of Rankings to Screen Out Unusable Key Jobs

You now have two sets of rankings for each key job. One was your original ranking (from step 3). This shows how each job ranks on each of the five compensable factors. The second ranking reflects, for each job, the wages assigned to each factor. You can now draw up a table like the one in Table 10.8.

TABLE 10.7 Ranking[1] Key Jobs by Wage Rates

	HOURLY WAGE	MENTAL REQUIRE-MENTS	PHYSICAL REQUIRE-MENTS	SKILL REQUIRE-MENTS	RESPONSIBILITY	WORKING CONDITIONS
Welder	$9.80	4.00(1)	0.40(4)	3.00(1)	2.00(1)	0.40(2)
Crane operator	5.60	1.40(3)	2.00(1)	1.80(3)	0.20(4)	0.20(4)
Punch press operator	6.00	1.60(2)	1.30(3)	2.00(2)	0.80(2)	0.30(3)
Security guard	4.00	1.20(4)	1.40(2)	0.40(4)	0.40(3)	0.60(1)

[1] 1 is high, 4 is low.

TABLE 10.8 Comparison of Factor and Wage Rankings

	MENTAL REQUIRE- MENTS		PHYSICAL REQUIRE- MENTS		SKILL REQUIRE- MENTS		RESPONSIBILITY		WORKING CONDITIONS	
	A[1]	$[2]	A[1]	$[2]	A[1]	$[2]	A[1]	$[2]	A[1]	$[2]
Welder	1	1	4	4	1	1	1	1	2	2
Crane operator	3	3	1	1	3	3	4	4	4	4
Punch press operator	2	2	3	3	2	2	2	2	3	3
Security guard	4	4	2	2	4	4	3	3	1	1

[1] Amount of each factor based on step 3.
[2] Ratings based on distribution of wages to each factor from step 4.

For each factor, this shows *both* rankings for each key job. On the left is the ranking from step 3. On the right is the ranking based on wages paid. For each factor, the ranking based on the amount of the factor (from step 3) should be about the same as the ranking based on the wages assigned to the job (step 5). If there's much of a discrepancy, it suggests that the key job might be a "fluke," and from this point on, such jobs are no longer used as key jobs. (Many managers don't both to screen out "unusable" key jobs. To simplify things, they skip our steps 5 and 6, going instead from step 4 to step 7; this is an acceptable alternative.)

Step 7. Construct the Job-Comparison Scale

Once you've identified the usable, "true" key jobs, the next step is to set up the job-comparison scale (Table 10.9). (Note that there's a separate column for each of the five compensable factors.) To develop it, you'll need the assigned wage table from step 4.

For each of the factors (for all key jobs), you write the job next to the appropriate wage rate. Thus in the assigned wage table (Table 10.7) the welder job has $4.00 assigned to the factor "mental requirement." Therefore, on the job comparison scale (Table 10.9) write "welder" in the "mental requirements" factor column, next to the "$4.00" row. Do the same for all factors for all key jobs.

Step 8. Use the Job-Comparison Scale

Now, all the other jobs to be evaluated can be slotted, factor by factor, into the job-comparison scale. For example, suppose you have a job of plater that you want to slot in. You decide where the "mental requirements" of the plater job would fit as compared with the mental requirements of all the other jobs listed. It might, for example, fit between punch press operator and inspector. Similarly, you would ask where the "physical requirements" of the plater's job fit as compared with the other jobs listed. Here you might find that it fits just below crane operator. You would do the same for each of the remaining three factors.

An Example

Let us work through an example to clarify the factor comparison method. We'll just use four key jobs to simplify the presentation—you'd usually start with 15 to 25 key jobs.

Step 1. First, we do a job analysis.

Step 2. Here we select our four key jobs: welder, crane operator, punch press operator, and security guard.

TABLE 10.9 Job (Factor) Comparison Scale

	MENTAL REQUIREMENTS	PHYSICAL REQUIREMENTS	SKILL REQUIREMENTS	RESPONSIBILITY	WORKING CONDITIONS
.20	....	....	....	Crane Operator	Crane Operator
.30	....	....	....	....	Punch Press Operator
.40	....	Welder.............	Sec. Guard.........	Sec. Guard	Welder
.50					
.60	....	....	....	....	Sec. Guard
.70					
.80				Punch Press Operator	
.90					
1.00					
1.10				(Plater)	
1.20	Sec. Guard				
1.30	....	Punch Press Operator			
1.40	Crane Operator	Sec. Guard.........	(Inspector)..........	(Plater)	
1.50	....	(Inspector)..........		....	(Inspector)
1.60	Punch Press Operator				
1.70	(Plater)				
1.80	....	....	Crane Operator	(Inspector)	
1.90					
2.00	....	Crane Operator	Punch Press Operator	Welder	
2.20	....	(Plater)			
2.40	(Inspector)..........	....	....	....	(Plater)
2.60					
2.80					
3.00	....	....	Welder		
3.20					
3.40					
3.60					
3.80					
4.00	Welder				
4.20					
4.40					
4.60					
4.80					

Step 3. Here (based on the job descriptions and specifications) we rank key jobs by factor, as in Table 10.6.

Step 4. Here we distribute wage rates by factor, as in Table 10.7.

Step 5. Then we rank our key jobs according to wage rates assigned to each key factor. These rankings are shown in parentheses in Table 10.7.

Step 6. Next, compare your two sets of rankings. In each left-hand column (marked A) is the job's ranking from step 3 based on the *amount* of the compensable factor. In each right-hand column (marked $) is the job's ranking from step 5, based on the wage assigned to that factor, as in Table 10.8.

In this case, there are no differences between any of the pairs of A (amount) and $ (wage) rankings, so *all* our key jobs are usable. If there had been any differences (for example, between the A and $ rankings for the welder job's mental requirement factor) we would have dropped that job as a key job.

Step 7. Now we construct our job comparison scale as in Table 10.9. For this, we use the wage distributions from step 4. For example, let us say that in steps 4 and 5 we assigned $4.00 to the mental requirement factor of the welder's job. Therefore, we now write "welder" on the $4.00 row under the "mental requirements" column in the exhibit above.

Step 8. Now all our other jobs can be slotted, factor by factor, into our job-comparison scale. We do *not* distribute wages to each of the factors for our other jobs to do this. *We just decide where, factor by factor, each of our other jobs should be slotted.* We've done this for two other jobs in the factor comparison scale: They're shown in parentheses. Now we also know what the wages for these two jobs should be, and we can also do the same for *all* our jobs.

A Variation

There are several variations to this basic factor comparison method. One involves converting the dollar values on the factor comparison chart (Table 10.9) to points. (You can do this by multiplying each of the dollar values by 100, for example.) The main advantage in making this change is that your system would no longer be "locked in" to your present wage rates. Instead, each of your jobs would be compared with one another, factor by factor, in terms of a more "constant" point system.

Pros and Cons

We've presented the factor comparison method at some length because it is (in one form or another) a very widely used job evaluation method. Its wide use derives from several advantages. First, it is an accurate, systematic, quantifiable method for which detailed step by step instructions are available. Second, jobs are compared to other jobs to determine a *relative* value. Thus, in the job comparison scale you not only see that the welder requires *more* mental ability than a plater; you can also determine about *how much more* mental ability is required—apparently about twice as much ($4.00 versus $1.70). (This type of calibration is not possible with the ranking or classification methods.) Third, this is also a fairly easy job evaluation system to explain to employees.

Probably the most serious *disadvantage* of the factor comparison method is its complexity. While it is fairly easy to explain the factor comparison scale and its rationale to employees, it is difficult to show them how to *build* one. In addition, the use of the five factors is an outgrowth of the technique developed by its originators. Yet, using the same five factors for all organizations and for all jobs in an organization may not always be appropriate.

THE POINT METHOD OF JOB EVALUATION

The point method is widely used. Basically, it requires identifying several compensable factors (like skills and responsibility), each with several degrees, and also the *degree* to which each of these factors is present in the job. A different number of points is usually assigned for each degree of each factor. So once you determine the degree to which each factor is present in the job, you need only add up the corresponding number of points for each factor and arrive at an overall point value for the job.[74] Here are the steps:

Step 1. Determine Clusters of Jobs to Be Evaluated

Because jobs vary widely by department, you usually will not use one point rating plan for all jobs in the organization. Therefore, the first step is usually to *cluster* jobs, for example into shop jobs, clerical jobs, sales jobs, and so forth. Then the committee will generally develop a point plan for one group (or cluster) at a time.

Step 2. Collect Job Information

This involves job analysis and writing job descriptions and job specifications.

Step 3. Select Compensable Factors

Here select compensable factors, like education, physical requirements, or skills. (Often each cluster of jobs may require its own compensable factors.)

Step 4. Define Compensable Factors

Next, carefully define each compensable factor. This is to ensure that the evaluation committee members will each apply the factors with consistency. Some examples of definitions are presented in Figure 10.7. The definitions are often drawn up or obtained by the human resource specialist.

FIGURE 10.7
Two Factors and Their Degree Definitions (from a Five-Factor Point Plan)
Source: Joseph Famularo, *Handbook of Modern Personnel Administration*, pp. 28–29. Copyright © 1972 by McGraw-Hill Inc. Used with permission.

FACTOR 1: COMPLEXITY OF JOB

Refers to amount of judgment, planning, and initiative required. Consider the extent to which the job requires the exercise of discretion and the difficulty of the decisions that must be made. It is not necessary that all qualifications noted in a degree definition be present in order for a job to qualify for that degree. The best fit is used for assigning degrees.

1st Degree   35 points
Covers jobs that are so standardized as to require *little or no choice* of action including repetitive jobs that do not need close supervision.

2nd Degree   70 points
Follows detailed instructions and standard practices. Decisions are limited strictly to *indicated choices between prescribed alternatives* which *detail course of action.*

3rd Degree   105 points
Follows detailed instructions and standard practices, but, due to variety of factors to be considered, decisions require *some judgment, or planning to choose prescribed alternatives* which *detail course of action.*

4th Degree   140 points
General instructions and standard practices usually applicable. Due to variety and character of factors to be considered, decisions require some *initiative as well as judgment and planning to choose prescribed alternatives* which in turn require use of *resourcefulness or judgment to adapt to variations* in problems encountered.

FACTOR 2: RESPONSIBILITY FOR RELATIONSHIPS WITH OTHERS

This factor measures the degree to which the job requires the employee to get results by working with or through other people. Consider the extent to which the job involves responsibility for the work of others, and for contacts within and outside the company. The primary consideration is the nature of contact. Frequency of contact is contributory only.

1st Degree   15 points
Requires employee to get along harmoniously with fellow workers. Covers jobs with simple personal contacts within and outside own department involving little responsibility for working with or through other people, and simple telephone calls involving identification, referral of calls, taking or giving simple messages without discussion.

2nd Degree   30 points
Requires routine personal, telephone, or written contacts with others in or out of the company involving exchange and explanation of information calling for courtesy to avoid friction.

3rd Degree   45 points
Requires personal, telephone, or written contacts with others in or out of the company involving exchange and discussion of information calling for tact as well as courtesy to get cooperation or to create a favorable impression.

4th Degree   60 points
Requires personal, telephone, or written contacts with others in or out of the company involving the exercise of persuasion, discretion, and tact to get willing action or consent on a non-routine level.

Step 5. Define Factor Degrees

Next, define each of several degrees for each factor so that raters may judge the amount or "degree" of a factor existing in a job. Thus, for the factor "complexity" you might choose to have four degrees, ranging from "job is repetitive" through "requires initiative" (definitions for each degree are shown in Figure 10.7). The number of degrees usually does not exceed five or six, and the actual number depends mostly on judgment. Thus, if all employees either work in a quiet, air conditioned office, or in a noisy, hot factory, then two degrees would probably suffice for the factor "working conditions." One need not have the same number of degrees for each factor, and should limit degrees to the number necessary to distinguish among jobs.

Step 6. Determine Relative Values of Factors

The next step is to decide how much weight (or how many total points) to assign to each factor. This is important because for each cluster of jobs some factors are bound to be more important than others. Thus, for executives the "mental requirements" factor would carry far more weight than would "physical requirements." The opposite might be true of factory jobs.

So, the next step is to determine the relative values or "weights" that should be assigned to each of the factors. Assigning factor weights is generally done by the evaluation committee. The committee members carefully study factor and degree definitions, and then determine the relative value of the factors for the cluster of jobs under consideration. Here is one method for doing this:

First, assign a value of 100% to the highest-ranking factor. Then assign a value to the next highest factor *as a percentage of its importance to the first factor*, and so forth. For example,

Decision making   100%

Problem solving   85%

Knowledge   60%

Next, sum up the total percentage (in this case 100% + 85% + 60% = 245%). Then convert this 245% to a 100% system as follows:

Decision making: $100 \div 245 = 40.82 = 40.8\%$

Problem solving: $85 \div 245 = 34.69 = 34.7\%$

Knowledge: $60 \div 245 = 24.49 = 24.5\%$

Totals   100.0%

Step 7. Assign Point Values to Factors and Degrees

In step 6 total weights were developed for each factor, in percentage terms. Now assign points to each factor as in Table 10.10. For example, suppose it is decided to use a total number of 500 points in the point plan. Then since

TABLE 10.10   Evaluation Points Assigned to Factors and Degrees

	1ST DEGREE POINTS	2ND DEGREE POINTS	3RD DEGREE POINTS	4TH DEGREE POINTS	5TH DEGREE POINTS
Decision-making	41	82	123	164	204
Problem-solving	35	70	105	140	174
Knowledge	24	48	72	96	123

the factor "decision making" had a weight of 40.8%, it would be assigned a total of 40.8% × 500 = 204 points.

Thus it was decided to assign 204 points to the "decision-making" factor. *This automatically means that the highest degree for the decision-making factor would also carry 204 points.* Then assign points to the other degrees for this factor, usually in equal amounts from the lowest to the highest degree. For example, divide 204 by the number of degrees (say, 5); this equals 40.8. Then the lowest degree here would carry about 41 points. The second degree would carry 41 plus 41, or 82 points. The third degree would carry 123 points. The fourth degree would carry 164 points. Finally, the fifth and highest degree would carry 204 points. Do this for each factor (as in Table 10.10).

Step 8. Write the Job Evaluation Manual

Developing a point plan like this usually culminates in a "point manual" or "job evaluation manual." This simply consolidates the factor and degree definitions and point values into one convenient manual.

Step 9. Rate the Jobs

Once the manual is complete, the actual evaluations can begin. Raters (usually the committee) use the manual to evaluate jobs. Each job, based on its job description and job specification, is evaluated factor by factor to determine the number of points that should be assigned to it. First, committee members determine the *degree* (1st degree, 2nd degree, etc.) to which each factor (like decision making) is present in the job. Then they note the corresponding *points* (see Table 10.10) that were previously assigned to each of these degrees (in step 7). Finally, they add up the points for all factors, arriving at a *total point value* for the job. Raters generally start with rating key jobs, obtaining consensus on these. Then they rate the rest of the jobs in the cluster.

"Packaged" Point Plans

Developing a point plan of one's own can obviously be a time-consuming process. For this reason a number of groups (such as the National Electrical Manufacturer's Association and the National Trade Association) have developed standardized point plans. These have been used or adapted by thousands of organizations. They contain ready-made factor and degree definitions and point assignments for a wide range of jobs, and can often be used with little or no modification. One survey of U.S. companies found that 93% of those using a ready-made plan rated it successful.

Pros and Cons

Point systems have their advantages, as their wide use suggests. This is a quantitative technique that is easily explained to and used by employees. On the other hand, it can be difficult to develop a point plan, and this is one reason many organizations have opted for ready-made plans. In fact, the availability of a number of ready-made plans probably accounts in part for the wide use of point plans in job evaluation.

NOTES

1. Thomas Patten, Jr., *Pay: Employee Compensation and Incentive Plans* (New York: Free Press, 1977), p. 1. See also Jerry McAdams, "Why Reward Systems Fail," *Personnel Journal*, Vol. 67, no. 6 (June 1988), pp. 103–113; James Whitney, "Pay Concepts for the 1990s," Part I, *Compensation and Benefits Review,* Vol.

20, no. 2 (March–April 1988), pp. 33–44; and James Whitney, "Pay Concepts for the 1990s," Part II, *Compensation and Benefits Review*, Vol. 20, no. 3 (May–June 1988), pp. 45–50.

2. Orlando Behling and Chester Schriesheim, *Organizational Behavior* (Boston: Allyn & Bacon, 1976), p. 233.

3. Robert Sibson, *Compensation* (New York: AMACOM, 1981) pp. 284–286.

4. Based partly on Richard Henderson, *Compensation Management* (Reston, Va.: Reston, 1980).

5. A complete description of exemption requirements as found in U.S. Department of Labor, *Executive, Administrative, Professional & Outside Salesmen Exempted from the Fair Labor Standards Act* (Washington, D.C.: U.S. Government Printing Office, 1973).

6. Earl Mellor, "Weekly Earnings in 1985: A Look at More than 200 Occupations," *Monthly Labor Review*, Vol. 109, no. 9 (September 1986), pp. 27–34; BNA, *Fair Employment Practices*, 1988, p. 27. See also John R. Hellenbeck et al., "Sex Differences in Occupational Choice, Pay, and Worth: A Supply-Side Approach to Understanding the Male-Female Wage Gap," *Personnel Psychology*, Vol. 40, no. 4 (Winter 1987), pp. 715–744.

7. Commerce Clearing House, *Ideas and Trends in Personnel*, Ocober 31, 1986, pp. 169–171.

8. Henderson, *Compensation Management*, pp. 88–99.

9. Michael R. Carrell and Frank E. Kuzmits, "Amended ADEA's Effects on Human Resources Strategies Remain Dubious," *Personnel Journal*, Vol. 66, no. 5 (May 1987).

10. Henderson, *Compensation Management*, pp. 101–127.

11. Ibid., p. 115.

12. Edward Hay, "The Attitude of the American Federation of Labor on Job Evaluation," *Personnel Journal*, Vol. 26 (November 1947), pp. 163–169; Howard James, "Issues in Job Evaluation: The Union's View," *Personnel Journal*, Vol. 51 (September 1972), pp. 675–679; Henderson, *Compensation Management*, pp. 117–118; Harold Jones, "Union Views on Job Evaluations: 1971 vs. 1978," *Personnel Journal*, Vol. 58 (February 1979), pp. 80–85.

13. Stanley Henrici, *Salary Management for the Nonspecialist* (New York: AMACOM, 1980), p. 20.

14. Joseph Famularo, *Handbook of Modern Personnel Administration* (New York: McGraw-Hill, 1972), pp. 27–29. See also Bruce Ellig, "Strategic Pay Planning," *Compensation and Benefits Review*, Vol. 19, no. 4 (July–August 1987), pp. 28–43; Thomas Robertson, "Fundamental Strategies for Wage and Salary Administration," *Personnel Journal*, Vol. 65, no. 11 (November 1986), pp. 120–132.

15. "Use of Wage Surveys," *BNA Policy and Practice Series* (Washington, D.C.: Bureau of National Affairs, 1976), pp. 313–314. In a recent survey of compensation professionals, uses of salary survey data were reported. The surveys were used most often to adjust the salary structure and ranges. Other uses included determining the merit budget, adjusting individual job rates, and maintaining pay leaderships. D. W. Belcher, N. Bruce Ferris, and John O'Neill, "How Wage Surveys are Being Used," *Compensation and Benefits Review* (September–October 1985), pp. 34–51. For further discussion, see, for example, Kent Romanoff, Ken Boehm, and Edward Benson, "Pay Equity: Internal and External Considerations," *Compensation and Benefits Review*, Vol. 18, no. 3 (May–June 1986), pp. 17–25.

16. Helen Murlis, "Making Sense of Salary Surveys," *Personnel Management*, Vol. 17 (January 1981), pp. 30–33. For an explanation of how market analysis can be used to ensure fair and competitive pay for all jobs in the organization, see, for example, Peter Olney, Jr., "Meeting the Challenge of Comparable Worth," Part 2, *Compensation and Benefits Review*, Vol. 19, no. 3 (May–June 1987), pp. 45–53.

17. Henderson, *Compensation Management*, pp. 260–269.

18. Joan O'Brien and Robert Zawacki, "Salary Surveys: Are They Worth the Effort?" *Personnel*, Vol. 62, no. 10 (October 1985), pp. 70–74.

19. Patten, *Pay,* p. 177.

20. You may have noticed that job analysis as discussed in Chapter 3 can be a useful source of information on compensable factors, as well as on job descriptions and job specifications. For example, a quantitative job analysis technique like the position analysis questionnaire generates quantitative information on the degree to which the following five basic factors are present in each job: having decision-making/communication/social responsibilities, performing skilled activities, being physically active, operating vehicles or equipment, and processing information. As a result, a job analysis technique like the PAQ is actually as (or, some say, more) appropriate as a job evaluation technique in that jobs can be quantitatively compared to one another on those five dimensions and their relative worth thus ascertained. Another point worth noting is that you may find that a single set of compensable factors is not adequate for describing all your jobs. Many managers, therefore, divide their jobs into job clusters. For example, you might have a separate job cluster for factory workers, for clerical workers, and for managerial personnel. Similarly, you would then probably have a somewhat different set of compensable factors for each job cluster.

21. A. N. Nash and F. J. Carroll, Jr., "Installation of a Job Evaluation Program," from *Management of Compensation* (Monterey, Calif.: Brooks/Cole, 1975), reprinted in Craig Schneier and Richard Beatty, *Personnel Administration Today: Readings and Commentary* (Reading, Mass.: Addison-Wesley, 1978), pp. 417–425; and Henderson, *Compensation Management,* pp. 231–239. According to one survey, about equal percentages of employers use individual interviews, employee questionnaires, or observations by personnel representatives to obtain the actual job evaluation information. See Mary Ellen Lo Bosco, "Job Analysis, Job Evaluation, and Job Classification," *Personnel,* Vol. 62, no. 5 (May 1985), pp. 70–75. See also Howard Risher, "Job Evaluation: Validity and Reliability," *Compensation and Benefits Review,* Vol. 21, no. 1 (January–February 1989), pp. 22–36; and David Hahn and Robert Dipboye, "Effects of Training and Information on the Accuracy and Reliability of Job Evaluations," *Journal of Applied Psychology,* Vol. 73, no. 2 (May 1988), pp. 146–153.

22. See, for example, Donald Petri, "Talking Pay Policy Pays Off," *Supervisory Management,* May 1979, pp. 2–13.

23. As explained later, the practice of *red circling* is used to delay downward adjustments in pay rates that are presently too high given the newly evaluated jobs. See also E. James Brennan, "Everything You Need to Know About Salary Ranges," *Personnel Journal,* Vol. 63, no. 3 (March 1984), pp. 10–17.

24. Nash and Carroll, "Installation of a Job Evaluation," p. 419.

25. Ibid.

26. C. F. Lutz, "Quantitative Job Evaluation in Local Government in the United States," *International Labor Review,* June 1969, pp. 607–619.

27. If you used the job classification method, then of course the jobs are already classified.

28. David Belcher, *Compensation Administration* (Englewood Cliffs, N.J.: Prentice-Hall, 1973), pp. 257–276.

29. Dale Yoder, *Personnel Management and Industrial Relations* (Englewood Cliffs, N.J.: Prentice-Hall, 1970), pp. 643–645; Joseph Famularo, *Handbook of Modern Personnel Administration* (New York: McGraw-Hill, 1972), pp. 32.1–32.6 and 30.1–30.8.

30. Bruce Ellig, *Executive Compensation—A Total Pay Perspective* (New York: McGraw-Hill, 1982), pp. 9–10. See also Bryan J. Brooks, "Trends in International Executive Compensation," *Personnel,* Vol. 64, no. 5 (May 1987), pp. 67–71.

31. "No Sign of Recession in Pay at the Top," *Business Week,* May 10, 1982, pp. 76–80. See also Peter D. Sherer et al., "Managerial Salary-Raise Decisions: A Policy-Capturing Approach," *Personnel Psychology,* Vol. 40, no. 1 (Spring 1987), pp. 27–38.

32. Towers, Perrin, Forster & Crosby, *News Release,* June 1987, p. 3.

33. John Baker, "Are Corporate Executives Overpaid?" *Harvard Business Review,* Vol. 56 (July–August 1977), p. 52.

34. Ernest C. Miller, "Setting Supervisors' Pay at Pay Differentials," *Compensation Review*, Vol. 10 (Third Quarter 1978), pp. 13–16.

35. Nardash Agarwal, "Determinants of Executive Compensation," *Industrial Relations*, Vol. 20, no. 1 (Winter 1981), pp. 36–45. See also John A. Fossum and Mary Fitch, "The Effects of Individual and Contextual Attributes on the Sizes of Recommended Salary Increases," *Personnel Psychology*, Vol. 38, no. 3 (Autumn 1985), pp. 587–602.

36. Kenneth Foster, "Does Executive Pay Make Sense?" *Business Horizons*, September–October 1981, pp. 47–51; James Brinks, "Executive Compensation: Crossroads of the Eighties," *Personnel Administrator*, Vol. 26 (December 1981), pp. 23–26.

37. Foster, "Does Executive Pay Make Sense?" p. 50.

38. Famularo, *Handbook of Modern Personnel Administration*, pp. 32.1–32.6. See also Peter Sherer, Donald Schwab, and Herbert Henneman, "Managerial Salary-Raise Decisions: A Policy-Capturing Approach," *Personnel Psychology*, Vol. 40, no. 1 (Spring 1987), pp. 27–38.

39. Ibid., pp. 30.1–30.15.

40. Ibid., pp. 30.1–30.5. See also Patric Moran, "Equitable Salary Administration in High-Tech Companies," *Compensation and Benefits Review*, Vol. 18, no. 5 (September–October 1986), pp. 31–40.

41. Sibson, *Compensation*, p. 194.

42. Ibid.

43. Helen Remick, "The Comparable Worth Controversy," *Public Personnel Management Journal* (Winter 1981), pp. 371–383.

44. Ibid., p. 377.

45. James Brinks, "The Comparable Worth Issue: A Salary Administration Bomb Shell," *Personnel Administrator*, Vol. 26 (November 1981), pp. 37–40. See also Sarah L. Rynes et al., "Effects of Market Survey Rates, Job Evaluation, and Job Gender on Job Pay," *Journal of Applied Psychology*, Vol. 74, no. 1 (February 1989), pp. 114–123.

46. Ibid.

47. Ibid., p. 38; U.S. Department of Labor, *Perspectives on Working Women: A Data Book*, October 1980.

48. *County of Washington* v. *Gunther*; U.S. Supreme Court, No. 80–429 (June 8, 1981).

49. SKRSC Update, Schachter, Kristoff, Ross, Sprague, and Curiale, California Street, San Francisco, Calif., September–October 1985. For further information on comparable worth, see U.S. Commission of Civil Rights, *Comparable Worth: Issue for the 80's*, Vols. 1 and 2, June 6–7, 1984. See also Walter Fogel, "Intentional Sex-Based Pay Discrimination: Can It Be Proven?" *Labor Law Journal*, Vol. 27, no. 5 (May 1986), pp. 291–299.

50. See also David Thomsen, "Compensation and Benefits—More on Comparable Worth," *Personnel Journal*, Vol. 60 (May 1981), pp. 348–349. See also Marvin Levine, "Comparable Worth in the 1980s: Will Collective Bargaining Supplant Legislative and Judicial Interpretations?" *Labor Law Journal*, Vol. 38, no. 6 (June 1987), pp. 323–335; and Peter Olney, Jr., "Meeting the Challenge of Comparable Worth," Part II, *Compensation and Benefits Review*, Vol. 19, no. 3 (May–June 1987), pp. 45–53.

51. Brinks, "The Comparable Worth Issue," p. 40.

52. Michael Carter, "Comparable Worth: An Idea Whose Time Has Come?" *Personnel Journal*, Vol. 60 (October 1981), p. 794; and Peter Olney, Jr., "Meeting the Challenge of Comparable Worth," Part I, *Compensation and Benefits Review*, Vol. 19, no. 2 (March–April 1987), pp. 34–44.

53. Brinks, "The Comparable Worth Issue," p. 40.

54. Charles M. Futrell, "Effects of Pay Disclosure on Satisfaction for Sales Managers: A Longitudinal Study," *Academy of Management Journal*, Vol. 21, no. 1 (March 1978), pp. 140–144.

55. Mary G. Miner, "Pay Policies: Secret or Open? and Why?" *Personnel Journal,* Vol. 53 (February 1974), reprinted in Richard Peterson, Lane Tracy, and Alan Cabelly, *Readings in Systematic Management in Human Resources* (Reading, Mass.: Addison-Wesley, 1979), pp. 233–239.

56. Margaret Yao, "Inflation Outruns Pay of Middle Managers, Increasing Frustration," *The Wall Street Journal,* June 9, 1981, p. 1. See also, "The Impact of Inflation on Wage and Salary Administration," *Personnel,* Vol. 58 (November–December 1981), p. 55.

57. This section based on or quoted from "The Impact of Inflation on Wage and Salary Administration," p. 55.

58. Wendell C. Lawther, "Ways to Monitor (and Solve) the Pay Compression Problem," *Personnel* (March 1989), pp. 84–87.

59. Ibid., p. 87.

60. Robert Dockson and Jack Vance, "Retirement In Peril: Inflation and the Executive Compensation Program," *California Management Review,* Vol. 24 (Summer 1981), pp. 87–94.

61. Ibid.

62. Joan Lindroth, "Inflation, Taxes, and Perks: How Compensation Is Changing," *Personnel Journal,* Vol. 60 (December 1981), pp. 934–940.

63. Clarence Deitch and David Dilts, "The COLA Clause: An Employer Bargaining Weapon?" *Personnel Journal,* Vol. 61 (March 1982), pp. 220–223.

64. "Collective Bargaining in 1987," *Monthly Labor Review,* January 1987, p. 34.

65. "Dun's Business Monthly, Vol. 129, no. 1 (January 1987), p. 18. See, also, "End of an Era: COLA's on the Way Out," *Compensation and Benefits Review,* Vol. 18, no. 2 (March–April 1986), p. 4.

66. Patten, *Pay,* p. 181.

67. Deitch and Dilts, "The COLA Clause," p. 221.

68. Patten, *Pay,* p. 182.

69. Rugus Runzheimer, Jr., "How Corporations Are Handling Cost of Living Differentials," *Business Horizons,* Vol. 23 (August 1980), p. 39.

70. Ibid., p. 39.

71. Wayne Outten and Noah Kinigstein, *The Rights of Employees* (New York: Bantam Books, 1983), pp. 201–202.

72. "How to Avoid the Ten Most Common Wage-Hour Traps," Commerce Clearing House, *Ideas and Trends,* March 10, 1989, p. 43.

73. Ibid.

74. For a discussion, see, for example, Roger Plachy, "The Point Factor Job Evaluation System: A Step-by-Step Guide," Part I, *Compensation and Benefits Review,* Vol. 19, no. 4 (July–August 1987), pp. 12–27; Roger Plachy, "The Case for Effective Point-Factor Job Evaluation, Viewpoint I," *Compensation and Benefits Review,* Vol. 19, no. 2 (March–April 1987), pp. 45–48; Roger Plachy, "The Point-Factor Job Evaluation System: A Step-by-Step Guide," Part II, *Compensation and Benefits Review,* Vol. 19, no. 5 (September–October 1987), pp. 9–24; and Alfred Candrilli and Ronald Armagast, "The Case for Effective Point-Factor Job Evaluation, Viewpoint II," *Compensation and Benefits Review,* Vol. 19, no. 2 (March–April 1987), pp. 49–54. See also Robert J. Sahl, "How to Install a Point-Factor Job Evaluation System," *Personnel,* Vol. 66, no. 3 (March 1989), pp. 38–42.

Chapter 11

Financial Incentives

When you finish studying this chapter, you should be able to:

1. Compare and contrast at least six types of incentive plans.
2. Explain at least five reasons why incentive plans fail.
3. Discuss when to use—and when not to use—incentive plans.
4. Establish and administer an effective incentive plan.

OVERVIEW

The main purpose of this chapter is to explain how to use financial incentive plans—plans that tie pay to performance—to motivate employees. Several types of incentive plans, including piecework, the standard hour plan, commissions, and stock options are explained. Next we discuss why incentive plans fail, and when to use incentive plans.

Frederick Taylor Father of the scientific management movement, according to which a fair day's work should depend on a careful, formal process of inspection and observation.

fair day's work Frederick Taylor's observation that haphazard setting of piecework requirements and wages by supervisors was not sufficient, and that careful study was needed to define acceptable production quotas for each job.

scientific management Implies careful, "scientific" study of all the factors that go into work and includes workers' motivation and job satisfaction, as well as optimum production.

The use of financial incentives—financial rewards paid to workers whose production exceeds some predetermined standard—was popularized by **Frederick Taylor** in the late 1800s. As a supervisory employee of the Midvale Steel Company, he had become concerned with what he called "systematic soldiering"—the tendency of employees to work at the slowest pace possible and produce at the minimum acceptable level. What especially intrigued him was the fact that some of these same workers still had the energy to run home and work on their cabins, even after a hard 12-hour day. Taylor knew that if he could find some way to harness this energy during the workday, huge productivity gains would be achieved.

At this time, primitive piecework systems were already in use, but were generally ineffective. Workers were paid a piece rate based on informally arrived at quotas for each piece they produced. However, rate cutting on the part of employers was flagrant, and the workers knew that if their earnings became excessive, their pay per piece would be cut. As a result, most workers produced just enough to earn a decent wage, but little enough so that their rate per piece would not be cut. One of Taylor's great insights was in seeing the need for a standardized, acceptable view of a **fair day's work**. As he saw it, this fair day's work should depend not on the vague estimates of supervisors but on a careful, formal, scientific process of inspection and observation. It was this need to evaluate each job *scientifically* that led to what became known as the **scientific management** movement. In turn, scientific management gave way in the Depression–plagued 1930s to the human relations movement and its focus on satisfying workers' social needs. The strong interest today in quality-of-work-life programs is a continuation of that theme.

But with today's new interest in cutting costs, restructuring, and boosting performance, financial incentive or *pay for performance plans* are undergoing a major renaissance. Hewitt Associates found that 32% of the firms they surveyed recently offered some kind of incentive plan to their workers.[1] Kanter estimates that half a million companies offer company-wide profit sharing plans alone. In 1985 and 1986, General Motors moved 125,000 workers from a seniority-based pay plan to a merit pay plan. And at the new Saturn auto plant, workers will earn about 80% of the prevailing UAW standard wage, but get productivity bonuses, too. *Gainsharing plans* (like the Scanlon plan discussed shortly), in which groups of workers share in the fruits of their productivity improvements, are also increasingly popular. Pay for performance incentive plans like those explained in this chapter are thus sure to be of major importance throughout the 1990s.[2]

◆ **THE MANAGER'S ROLE IN ADMINISTERING INCENTIVES**

The human resource department plays a major role in developing and administering incentive plans. First, human resources works with industrial engineers in the area *of work measurement*. Work measurement is the technique used to study each job and determine a normal or baseline production rate; it is the base rate that the incentives will be based on.[3] Human resources also develops the details of the plans, including who will be eligible, what increases will be awarded for each level of performance, and how large a bonus can be awarded to persons in each grade level.[4]

Supervisors also play an important role in administering the incentive plan.[5] They help determine the proper work methods and help develop and monitor the work standards that are set by industrial engineers. They must also make sure that employees follow the methods that have been established, which itself involves both training and supervising the workers involved. Daily supervision is also required, in terms of monitoring employee performance, correcting improper procedures, and explaining to employees how they are doing.

Last (but not least) supervisors affect incentives through their effects on appraising performance. The basic aim of an incentive should be to encourage good performance by linking performance and rewards, and this in turn requires valid, accurate performance appraisals. When, as is sometimes the case, the supervisor undermines the appraisal system (for instance by indiscriminately scoring everyone high so they can all get a raise or by treating some employees unfairly), the result is to undermine the incentive plan as well. Line managers, too, therefore play a crucial role in administering the incentive system.

♦ TYPES OF INCENTIVE PLANS

There are many incentive plans in use and a number of ways to categorize them. For simplicity we will discuss the following types of incentives: incentives for production employees, incentives for managers and executives, incentives for salespeople, merit pay as an incentive (primarily for white-collar and professional employees), and organizationwide incentives.

INCENTIVES FOR PRODUCTION EMPLOYEES

♦ PIECEWORK PLANS

piecework A system of pay based on the number of items processed by each individual worker in a unit of time, such as items per hour or items per day.

Piecework is the oldest type of incentive plan, as well as the most commonly used. Earnings are tied directly to what the worker produces by paying the person a "piece rate" for each unit he or she produces. Thus, if Tom Smith gets 40 cents apiece for stamping out door jambs, then he would make $40 for stamping out 100 a day and $80 for stamping out 200.

Developing a workable piece-rate plan requires both job evaluation and (usually) industrial engineering. Job evaluation enables you to assign an hourly wage rate to the job in question. But the crucial issue in piece-rate planning is the production standard, and these standards are usually developed by industrial engineers. The standards are usually stated in terms of a standard number of minutes per unit or a standard number of units per hour. In Tom Smith's case, the job evaluation indicated that his door-jamb stamping job was worth $8 an hour. The industrial engineer determined that 20 jambs per hour was the standard production rate. Therefore, the piece rate (for each door jamb) was $8.00 divided by 20 = $0.40 per door jamb.

straight piecework plan Under this pay system each worker receives a set payment for each piece produced or processed in a factory or shop.

With a **straight piecework plan**, Tom Smith would simply be paid on the basis of the number of door jambs he produced; there would be no guaranteed minimum wage. However, after passage of the Fair Labor Standards Act it became necessary for most employers to guarantee their workers a minimum wage. With a **guaranteed piecework plan**, Tom Smith would be paid $4.25 per hour (the minimum wage) whether or not he stamped out 10.6 door jambs per hour (at $0.40 each). But as an incentive he would also be paid at the piece rate of $0.40 for each unit he produced over 10.6.

guaranteed piecework plan The minimum hourly wage plus an incentive for each piece produced above a set number of pieces per hour.

Piecework (to most people) implies *straight piecework*, a strict proportionality between results and rewards regardless of the level of output. Thus, in Smith's case, he continues to get 40 cents apiece for stamping out door jambs, even if he stamps out many more than planned, say, 500 per day. On the other hand, certain types of piecework incentive plans call for a sharing of productivity gains between worker and employer such that the worker does not receive full credit for all production above normal.[6]

Advantages and Disadvantages

Piecework incentive plans have several advantages. They are simple to calculate and easily understood by employees. Piece-rate plans appear equitable in principle, and their incentive value can be powerful since rewards are directly tied to performance.

Piecework also has some disadvantages. The main disadvantage is its somewhat unsavory reputation among many employees, a reputation based on some employer's habit of arbitrarily raising production standards whenever they found their workers earning "excessive" wages. In addition, piece rates are stated in monetary terms (like 40 cents per piece), so when a new job evaluation results in a new hourly wage rate the piece rate must also be revised; this can be a big clerical chore. The other disadvantage is more subtle; since the piece rate is quoted on a per piece basis, in workers' minds production standards become tied inseparably to the amount of money earned. When an attempt is then made to revise production standards, it meets considerable worker resistance, even if the revision is fully justified.[7]

♦ STANDARD HOUR PLAN

standard hour plan A plan by which a worker is paid a basic hourly rate but is paid an extra percentage of his or her base rate for production exceeding the standard per hour or per day. Similar to piecework payment but based on a percent premium.

The **standard hour plan** is very similar to the piece-rate plan, with one major difference. With a piece-rate plan the worker is paid a particular *rate per piece* that he or she produces. With the standard hour plan the worker is rewarded by a *percent premium that equals the percent by which his or her performance is above standard*. The plan assumes that the worker has a guaranteed base rate.

As an example, suppose the base rate for Smith's job is $8 per hour. (The base rate may, but need not, equal the hourly rate determined by the job evaluation.) And again assume that the production standard for Smith's job is 20 units per hour, or 3 minutes per unit. Suppose that in one day (8 hours) Smith produces 200 door jambs. According to the production standard, this *should have taken Smith 10 hours* (200 divided by 20 per hour); instead it took him 8 hours. He produced at a rate that is 25% (40 divided by 160) higher than the standard rate. The standard rate would be 8 hours times 20 (units per hour) = 160: Smith *actually* produced 40 more, or 200. He will therefore be paid at a rate that is 25% above his base rate for the day. His base rate was $8 per hour times 8 hours equals $64. So he'll be paid 1.25 times 64 or $80.00 for the day.

The standard hour plan has most of the advantages of the piecework plan and is fairly simple to compute and easy to understand. But the incentive is expressed in units of times instead of in monetary terms (as it is with the piece-rate system). Therefore, there is less tendency on the part of workers to link their production standard with their pay. Furthermore, the clerical job of recomputing piece rates whenever hourly wage rates are reevaluated is avoided.[8]

♦ GROUP INCENTIVE PLANS

group incentive plan A plan in which a production standard is set for a specific work group, and its members are paid incentives if the group exceeds the production standard.

Some employers use **group incentive plans**, and there are several ways to do this.[9] One approach is to set work standards for each member of the group and maintain a count of the output of each member. Members are then paid based on one of three formulas: (1) all members receive the pay earned by the highest producer, (2) all members receive the pay earned by the lowest producer, or (3) all members receive payment equal to the average pay earned by the group. The second approach is to set a production standard based on the final output of the group as a whole; all members then receive the same pay, based on the piece rate that exists for the group's job. The group incentive can be based on either the piece rate or standard hour plan, but the latter is somewhat more prevalent.

There are several reasons to use a group plan. Sometimes several jobs are interrelated, as they are on assembly lines. Here one worker's performance reflects not only his or her own effort but that of coworkers as well, so here group incentives make sense. One writer points out that in Japan "the first rule is never reward only one individual"; instead, employees are rewarded as a group in order to reduce jealously, make group members indebted to one another (as they would be to the group), and encourage a sense of cooperation.[10] There tends to be less bickering among group members as to who has "tight" production standards and who has loose ones. We also know that groups can bring pressure to bear on their members and keep shirkers in line, assuming the group as a whole agrees with the standards that are set. This in turn can help reduce the need for supervision. Group incentive plans also facilitate on-the-job training, since each member of the group has an interest in getting new members trained as quickly as possible.[11]

The chief disadvantage of group plans is that each worker's rewards are no longer based just on his or her own efforts. To the extent that the person does not see his or her effort leading to the desired reward, a group plan is usually not as effective as an individual plan. In one study, however (where the researchers arranged to pay the group based on the performance of its best member), the group incentive plan proved as effective as an individual incentive plan in improving performance.[12]

attendance incentive plan A plan for reducing employee absence, for instance, by allowing unused sick leave to be converted into additional pay or vacation at the end of each year.

♦ **ATTENDANCE INCENTIVE PLANS**

Another example of the use of incentives is to reduce employee absence. A typical incentive program was implemented in a nonprofit hospital with about 3,000 employees. At the end of the year eligible employees could convert up to 24 hours of unused sick leave into additional pay or vacation. To determine the size of the incentive, the number of hours absent was subtracted from 24. The surplus, if any, could either be added to the next year's vacation allowance or converted to additional pay at the employee's wage rate. In this case, absenteeism declined an average of 11.5 hours (32%) during the incentive period.[13]

However, incentive plans like this have to be used with caution. In one case, for instance, the so-called attendance bonus plan instituted by a small manufacturer actually backfired. Here the rules for the plan were simple. Each employee with no more than three hours of lost time per quarter, excluding time off for jury duty and funerals, received a $25 bonus. An additional $25 bonus was paid to any employee who earned all four quarterly bonuses in a calendar year. The plan actually resulted in the company paying about $7,500 in bonuses but getting an *increase* in hours absent of about 12.3%. The number of employees with perfect attendance did increase but this improvement was offset by reduced attendance of the remaining employees.[14]

INCENTIVES FOR MANAGERS AND EXECUTIVES

Because of the role that managers play in determining divisional and corporate profitability, most employers pay their managers and executives some type of bonus or incentive.[15] A recent survey found, for instance, that about 90% of large companies pay managers and executives annual ("short-term") bonuses,[16] while another found that about 70% of small firms have such plans.[17] Similarly, long-term incentive plans (like stock options), which are intended to motivate and reward management for the corporation's long-term growth and prosperity, are used by over 50% of U.S. firms.[18] The widespread use of managerial and executive bonuses reflects the fact that these incentive plans can and do pay for themselves by improving management and thus organizational performance.[19] We can conveniently distinguish between short-term incentives and long-term incentives for managers and executives.

♦ SHORT-TERM INCENTIVES: THE ANNUAL BONUS

annual bonus Plans that are designed to motivate short-term performance of managers and are tied to company profitability.

Most firms have **annual bonus** plans that are aimed at motivating the short-term performance of their managers and executives. Unlike salaries (which are rarely reduced to reflect a falloff in performance), short-term incentive bonuses can easily result in plus or minus adjustments of 25% or more in total pay.

There are three basic issues to be considered in awarding short-term incentives: eligibility, fund-size determination, and individual awards. *Eligibility* is usually decided in one of three ways. The first criterion is *key position*, in which a job-by-job review is conducted to identify the key jobs (typically only line jobs) that have a measurable impact on profitability. The second approach to determining eligibility involves setting a *salary level* cutoff point; here all employees earning over a threshold amount are automatically eligible for consideration for short-term incentives. Finally, eligibility can be determined by *salary grade*. This is a refinement of the salary cutoff approach and assumes that all employees at a certain grade or above should be eligible for the short-term incentive program.[20] The simplest approach is just to use *salary level* as a cutoff.[21] As a rule, bonus eligibility begins somewhere around $40,000 to $50,000.[22]

In general, the size of the bonus is usually greater for top-level executives. Thus, an executive with a $150,000 salary may be able to earn another 80% of his or her salary as a bonus, while a manager in the same firm earning $80,000 can only earn another 30%. Similarly, a supervisor might be able to earn up to 15% of his or her base salary in bonuses. Average bonuses range from a low of 10% to a high of 80% or more: A typical company might establish a plan whereby executives could earn 45% of base salary, managers 25%, and supervisory personnel 12%.

How Much to Pay Out (Fund Size)

Next, a determination must be made regarding *fund determination*—the amount of bonus money that will be available—and there are several formulas used to do this. For example, some companies use a *nondeductible formula*. Here a straight percentage (usually of the company's net income) is used to create the short-term incentive fund. Others use a *deductible formula* on the assumption that the short-term incentive fund should begin to accumulate only after the firm has met a specified level of earnings threshold.

In practice, what proportion of profits is usually paid out as bonuses? Here there are no hard and fast rules, and some firms do not even have a formula for developing the bonus fund.[23] One alternative is to reserve a minimum amount of the profits, say, 10% for safeguarding stockholders' investment, and then to establish a fund for bonuses equal to, say, 20% of the corporate operating profit before taxes in excess of this base amount. Thus, if the operating profits were $100,000, then the management bonus fund might be 20% of $90,000 or $18,000.[24] Some other illustrative formulas used for determining the executive bonus fund are as follows:

Ten percent of net income after deducting 5% of average capital invested in business.

Twelve and one-half percent of the amount by which net income exceeds 6% of stockholders' equity.

Twelve percent of net earnings after deducting 6% of net capital.[25]

Deciding Individual Awards

The third issue is deciding the *individual awards* to be paid and here the main task is determining the amounts. Typically a target bonus is set for each eligible position and adjustments are then made for greater or less than targeted performance. A maximum amount, perhaps double the target bonus, may be set. Performance ratings are obtained for each manager and preliminary bonus estimates are computed. Estimates for the total amount of money to be spent on short-term incentives are thereby made and compared with the bonus fund available. If necessary, the individual estimates are then adjusted. A related question concerns whether managers will receive bonuses based on individual performance, corporate performance, or both.

The important thing to keep in mind here is that there is a difference between a profit-sharing plan and a true, individual incentive bonus. In a profit-sharing plan, each person gets a bonus based on the company's results, regardless of the person's actual effort. With a true individual incentive, though, it is the manager's individual effort and performance that is rewarded with a bonus.

Here, again, there are no hard and fast rules. Top-level executive bonuses are generally tied to overall corporate results (or divisional results if the executive is, say, the vice-president of a major division). The assumption here is that corporate results reflect the person's individual performance. But as one moves farther down the chain of command, corporate profits become a less accurate gauge of a manager's contribution; here (say with supervisory personnel or with the heads of functional departments) the person's individual performance is a more logical determinant of his or her bonus.

Many experts argue that in most organizations managerial and executive-level bonuses should be tied to *both* organizational and individual performance, and there are several ways to do this.[26] Perhaps the simplest is the *split award method*, which breaks the bonus into two parts. Here the manager actually gets two separate bonuses, one based on his or her individual effort and one based on the organization's overall performance. Thus a manager might be *eligible* for an "individual performance" bonus of *up to* $10,000 but receive an individual performance bonus of only $8,000 at the end of the year, based on his or her individual performance evaluation. In addition, though, the person might also receive a second bonus of $8,000 based on the *company's* profits for the year. Thus, even if there are no company profits, the high-performing manager would still get an individual-performance bonus.

One drawback to this approach is that it pays too much to the marginal performer, even if his or her own performance is mediocre, since he or she at least gets that second, company-based bonus. One way to get around this is by using the *multiplier method*. For example, a manager whose individual performance was "poor" might not even receive a company-performance-based bonus, on the assumption that the bonus should be a *product* of individual and corporate performance; when either is very poor, the product is zero.

Whichever approach is used, the basic point to keep in mind is that:

Truly outstanding performers should never be paid less than their normal reward, regardless of organizational performance, and should get substantially larger awards than do other managers. They are people the company cannot afford to lose, and their performance should always be adequately rewarded by the organization's incentive system . . . marginal or below average performers should never receive awards that are normal or average, and poor performers should be awarded nothing. The money saved on these people should be given to above average performers.[27]

◆ LONG-TERM INCENTIVES

Long-term incentives are intended to motivate and reward management for the corporation's long-term growth and prosperity and to inject a long-term perspective into the executive's decisions. If only short-term criteria were used, a manager could, for instance, increase profitability by reducing plant maintenance, a tactic that might, of course, catch up with the company over two or three years. Another purpose of these plans is to encourage executives to stay with the company by providing them with the opportunity to accumulate capital (like company stock) based on the firm's long-term success. Long-term incentives or **capital accumulation programs** are most often reserved for senior executives.[28] There are six popular long-term incentive (or capital accumulation) plans: stock options, stock appreciation rights, performance achievement plans, restricted stock plans, phantom stock plans, and book value plans.[29] The popularity of these plans changes over time due to economic conditions and trends, internal company financial pressures, changing attitudes toward long-term incentives and changes in tax law as well as other factors. A current example is the impact of the 1986 Tax Reform Act, which affects taxation rates and establishes a new set of rules on benefit plans.[30] Among other things, the act created a two-tier federal personal income tax beginning in 1988, basically with one lower tax rate of 15% and a higher income tax rate of 28%. It also eliminated the favorable capital gains tax of only 40% of one's regular federal income rate.[31] A basic purpose of long-term incentives like incentive stock options, stock appreciation rights, and book value plans was to reduce the after-tax bite of taxes on the executive's incentive pay. The reduction in maximum tax rates and the elimination of favorable treatment for capital gains has thus increased the value of cash as a substitute for these long-term incentives.[32]

capital accumulation programs
Long-term incentives most often reserved for senior executives. Six popular plans include stock options, stock appreciation rights, performance achievement plans, restricted stock plans, phantom stock plans, and book value plans.

Stock Options

stock option The right to purchase a stated number of shares of a company stock at a stated price during a stated period of time. An executive is given the right to purchase shares in the future at today's price. If the company grows, share prices may rise and the executive may benefit, assuming the economy is stable.

A **stock option** is the right to purchase a stated number of shares of company stock at a stated price during a stated period of time; the executive thus hopes to profit by exercising his or her option in the future, *but at today's price*. The assumption is that the price of the stock will go up, rather than down or stay the same. Unfortunately, this depends partly on considerations outside the executive control, such as general economic conditions. Stock price *is*, of course, affected by the firm's profitability and growth, and to the extent that the executive can affect these factors the stock option can be an incentive. However, in one survey it was found that over half the executives saw little or no relation between their performance and the value of their stock options.[33] During the 1970s, stock options fell into disfavor, partly because of their weak incentive value and partly because stock market prices had generally retreated. But the bull market of the 1980s again placed stock options in a favorable light, although the crash of 1987 did change that. And here again, the new tax law impacts incentive stock options (ISOs); for example, ISOs are now taxed as ordinary income when the securities are sold.[34]

One alternative to stock options is a *book value plan*. Here managers are permitted to purchase stock at current book value, a value anchored in the value of the company's assets. Executives here can earn dividends on the stock they own, and as the company grows the book value of their shares may grow too. When these employees leave the company, they can then sell the shares back to the company at the new higher book value.[35] The book value approach avoids the uncertainties of the stock market, emphasizing instead reasonable growth.

Other Plans

There are several other types of popular long-term incentive plans. Stock appreciation rights (SARs) are usually combined with stock options; they permit the recipient to either exercise the option (by buying the stock) or instead simply take an appreciation in the stock price in either cash, stock, or some combination of these. A *performance achievement plan* awards shares of stock that are earned for the achievement of predetermined financial targets, such as profit or growth in earnings per share. With *restricted stock plans*, shares are usually awarded without cost to the executive but with certain restrictions that are specified in the Internal Revenue Code; for example, there is risk of forfeiture if an executive leaves the company before the specified time limit elapses. Finally, under *phantom stock plans* executives receive not shares but "units" that are similar to shares of company stock. Then at some future time they receive value (usually in cash) equal to the appreciation of the "phantom" stock that they own.[36]

Implementing Long-Term Incentives

The results of one study by consultants McKinsey and Company, Inc., indicate that the simple expedient of giving managers stock options may be the simplest and wisest route as far as providing long-term incentives for top executives. In the McKinsey study about one-half the companies surveyed had stock options only and about one-half had performance-based plans in which managers were given cash bonuses for long-term performance.

The results indicated that in most cases the return to shareholders of companies with long-term cash performance incentives did not differ significantly from those companies which had only stock-based incentive plans (like stock options). This was so even though companies that paid cash bonuses had spent more to fund their incentive plans. Their most serious problem in awarding cash bonuses lay in identifying the proper performance measures. The survey concludes that successful long-term incentive plans should (1) use measures of performance that correlate with shareholder wealth creation (that is, return on equity and growth), not earnings per share growth, (2) establish valid target levels and communicate them clearly to participants, and (3) provide for target adjustment under certain well-defined circumstances (in other words, the performance standards can be modified if market conditions warrant it).[37]

INCENTIVES FOR SALESPEOPLE

Compensation plans for salespeople have typically relied heavily on incentives in the form of sales commissions, although the use of commissions varies by industry. In the tobacco industry, for instance, salespeople are usually paid entirely via commissions, while in the transportation equipment industry salespeople tend to be paid by salary. However, the most prevalent approach is to use a combination of salary and commissions to compensate salespeople.[38]

The widespread use of incentives for salespeople is due to three things: tradition, the unsupervised nature of most sales work, and the assumption that incentives are needed to motivate salespeople. And, unlike most other employees, salespeople do seem clearly to prefer being paid on an incentive basis; over 95% of the respondents in one study said they preferred to be paid on an incentive basis, for instance.[39] The pros and cons of salary, commission, and combination plans are as follows:

◆ SALARY PLAN

In this kind of plan the salespeople are paid a fixed salary, although there may be occasional incentives in the form of bonuses, sales contest prizes, and the like.[40]

There are several reasons you might want to use straight salary. The plan works well when your main objective is prospecting work (in terms of finding new clients) or where the salesperson is primarily involved in account servicing. For example, a field sales engineer who is paid on a salary basis might have the following duties:

Developing and executing sales and product training programs for distributor's sales force.

Doing missionary work with selected manufacturers and major oil companies to encourage them to recommend his or her products to their dealers.

Participating in national and local trades shows.

Suggesting ideas for new products and promotional programs.[41]

Jobs like these are often found in industries that sell technical products; this is one reason why both the aerospace and transportation equipment industries have a relatively heavy emphasis on salary plans for their salespeople.

There are several advantages to paying salespeople on a straight salary basis. Salespeople know in advance what their income will be, and the employer also has fixed, predictable sales force expenses. It makes it simple to switch territories or quotas or to reassign salespeople, and it can develop a high degree of loyalty among the sales staff. Commissions tend to shift the sales person's emphasis to "making the sale" rather than prospecting and cultivating long-term customers; this long-term perspective *is encouraged* by straight salary compensation.

However, the salary plan does have disadvantages. The main disadvantage is that it does not depend on results.[42] In fact, salaries are often tied to seniority (rather than to performance), and this can be demotivating to potentially high performing salespeople, who see seniority—not performance—being rewarded.

◆ COMMISSION PLAN

Here salespeople are paid in direct proportion to their sales—for results, and only for results.

The commission plan has several advantages. Salespeople have the greatest possible incentive, and there is a tendency to attract high-performing salespeople who see that effort will clearly lead to rewards. Sales costs are proportional to sales (rather than fixed), and the company's selling investment is reduced. The commission basis is also easy to understand and compute.

But the commission plan also has drawbacks. Salespeople focus on making a sale and on high-volume items; cultivating dedicated customers and working to push hard-to-sell items may be neglected. Wide variances in income between salespeople may occur; this can lead to a feeling that the plan is inequitable. More serious is the fact that salespeople are encouraged to neglect nonselling duties like servicing small accounts. In addition, pay is often excessive in boom times and very low in recessions.

◆ COMBINATION PLAN

Most companies pay their salespeople a combination of salary and commissions, and there is a sizable salary component in most such plans. The most frequent percentage split reported in one study was 80% base salary and 20% incentives. A close second was a 70/30 split, with a 60/40 split being the third most frequent reported arrangement.[43]

Combination plans provide not only some of the advantages of both straight salary and straight commission plans, but also some of the disadvantages of each. Salespeople have a floor to their earnings so their families' security is ensured. Furthermore, the company can direct its salespeople's activities by detailing what services the salary component is being paid for, while the commission component provides a built-in incentive for superior performance.

However, the salary component is not tied to performance, and the employer is therefore trading away some of the incentive value of what the person is paid. Combination plans also tend to become complicated, and misunderstandings can result. This might not be a problem with a simple "salary plus commission" plan, but most plans are not so simple. For example, there is a "commission plus drawing account" plan where a salesperson is paid basically on commissions but can *draw on future earnings* to get through low sales periods. Similarly, in the "commission plus bonus" plan, salespeople are again paid primarily on the basis of commissions. However, they are also given a small bonus for directed activities like selling slow-moving items.

An example can help illustrate the complexities of the typical combination plan. In one company, for instance, the following three-step formula is applied:

Step 1: Sales volume up to $18,000 a month. Base salary plus 7% of gross profits plus 1/2% of gross sales.

Step 2: Sales volume from $18,000 to $25,000 a month. Base salary plus 9% of gross profits plus 1/2% of gross sales.

Step 3: Over $25,000 a month. Base salary plus 10% of gross profits plus 1/2% of gross sales.

In all cases, base salary is paid every two weeks, while the earned percentage of gross profits and gross sales is paid monthly.[44]

◆ SPECIAL AWARDS

special awards Individual bonuses, such as TVs, paid on the basis of performance ratings.

The sales force also may get various **special awards**.[45] At Oakite Company, for instance, several recognition-type awards are used to boost sales. For example, there are four or five honorable mention awards, as well as a President's Cup for the Top Division Manager and a VIP Club for the top 10% of the sales force in total dollars sales. The VIP Club is well publicized within the firm and has a lot of prestige attached to it. Part of the Consumer Products Division of Ciba-Geigy's Airwick Industries sells Bianca breath fresheners. To boost their sales, the sales vice-president offered the salesperson who sold the most products over quota a $10,000 "picnic basket" that included such things as a Panasonic television, Lenox china, and gourmet delicacies. At Homelite Company, a sales manager is measured partly on the basis of whether he or she achieved 100% performance in each of the company's product categories based on historical trends and planned sales levels. If so, the manager achieves 1,000 points, while 120% means 1,200 points, and so forth. Sales managers who then finish in the top 25% in points are eligible for a trip in addition to their usual commissions.

INCENTIVES FOR OTHER PROFESSIONALS AND WHITE-COLLAR EMPLOYEES: MERIT PAY

♦ MERIT PAY AS AN INCENTIVE

merit pay Any salary increase awarded to an employee on his or her individual performance.

merit raise Merit raise is another term for merit pay.

Merit pay or **merit raise** is any salary increase that is awarded to an employee based on his or her individual performance. It is different from a bonus in that it represents a continuing increment, whereas the bonus represents a one-time payment. Although the term *merit pay* can apply to the incentive raises given to any employees—exempt or nonexempt, office or factory, management or non-management—the term is more often used with respect to white-collar employees and particularly professional, office, and clerical employees. In one survey, for instance, more than 80% of the responding companies with office/clerical, professional/technical, sales, and managerial employees said they provided for individual pay adjustments under a merit plan. By contrast, plant/service workers were included in merit plans in only 44% of the companies; instead, automatic seniority increases were provided to this latter group.[46]

Merit pay has both its advocates and detractors and is the subject of much debate.[47] Advocates of merit pay argue that only pay (or other rewards) that is tied directly to performance can motivate improved performance. They contend that the effect of awarding pay raises across the board (without regard to individual performance) may actually detract from performance by showing employees that they will be rewarded the same regardless of how they perform.

On the other hand, detractors of merit pay present some good reasons why merit pay plans can backfire. One is that the usefulness of the merit pay plan depends on the validity of the performance appraisal system, and if performance appraisals are viewed as unfair, so, too, will the merit pay that is based on them.[48] Similarly, supervisors often tend to minimize differences in employee performance when computing merit raises; they instead give most employees about the same raise, either because of a reluctance to alienate some employees or because of a desire to give everyone a raise that will at least help them stay even with the cost of living. A third problem is that almost every employee thinks he or she is an above-average performer; being paid a below-average merit increase can thus be demoralizing.[49] However, while problems like these can undermine a merit pay plan, there seems little doubt that merit pay can and does improve performance. But you must make sure that the performance appraisals are carried out effectively.[50]

In general, many companies today are moving away from traditional pay practices based on seniority and toward pay practices based on employee performance. Among these new practices are the wide use of merit pay. Others include pegging pay to specific results and a pay-for-skill system, specifically, one that provides individual incentive for upgrading skills.[51]

Merit Pay: Two New Options

Traditional merit pay plans have two basic characteristics: (1) merit increases are usually granted to employees at a designated time of the year in the form of a higher base salary (or "raise") which is then distributed in equal payments, during the next 12 months, and (2) the merit raise is usually based exclusively on individual performance (although the overall level of company profits may affect the total sum available for merit raises).[52] Two adaptations of merit pay plans are becoming more popular today: One awards merit raises in one lump sum once a year, while the other ties awards to both individual and organizational performance.

Lump-sum merit raises are attractive for several reasons. Since the employee's merit raise (of, say, 5% of his or her base salary) is awarded in one lump sum, the rise in payroll expenses can be significantly reduced each year. (Traditionally, someone with a salary of $20,000 per year might get a 5% increase. This moves her to a new base salary of $21,000, and if she gets another 5% increase next year then the new merit increase of 5% is tacked on not just to the $20,000 base salary but to the extra $1,000 she received last year. Traditional merit increases are thus cumulative, while some lump-sum merit raises are not.) Another advantage is that lump-sum merit raises can help contain benefit costs, since the level of benefit coverage is often tied to a person's current base pay. Lump-sum merit increases can also be more dramatic as motivators than traditional merit pay raises. For example, a 5% lump-sum merit increase to our $20,000 employee is $1,000, as opposed to a traditional weekly increment of $19.25 for 52 weeks. Furthermore, knowing that base salary levels are not being permanently impacted by merit pay decisions can give management more flexibility (say, in a particularly good year) to award somewhat higher lump-sum merit pay.

Moving to a lump-sum merit pay plan like this requires consideration of several points. Perhaps most important, if you are going to surrender the merit pay tool for raising base salaries, any substantial base salary inequities should first be eliminated. That way, weaker performers' salaries are not permanently frozen in above higher-performers' salaries. The timing of the merit increases may also become more important, since you must now consider the impact of the lump-sum payments on your company's cash flow.

Another merit pay alternative is to award lump-sum merit pay based on both individual and organizational performance. A sample matrix for doing so is presented in Table 11.1. In this example the company's performance might be measured by rate of return or sales divided by payroll costs. Company performance is then weighted equally with the employee's performance as measured by his or her performance appraisal. Thus, an outstanding performer would still receive a lump-sum award even if the organization's performance was marginal, while employees with unacceptable performance would receive no lump-sum awards even for a year in which the organization's performance was outstanding. The advantage of this multiple-measures approach is that it forces employees to focus on organizational goals like profitability and improved productivity. The drawback is that it can reduce the motivational value of the reward by reducing the impact of the employee's own performance on the reward.[53]

♦ **INCENTIVES FOR PROFESSIONAL EMPLOYEES**

Professional employees are those whose work involves the *application of learned knowledge to the solution of the employer's problems*, including lawyers, doctors, economists, and engineers. Professionals almost always reach their positions through prolonged periods of formal study.[54]

Pay decisions regarding professional employees involve unique prob-

TABLE 11.1 Lump-Sum Award Determination Matrix (an example)

THE EMPLOYEE'S PERFORMANCE (WEIGHT = .50)	THE ORGANIZATION'S PERFORMANCE (WEIGHT = 0.50)				
	Outstanding *(1.00)*	*Excellent* *(0.80)*	*Commendable* *(0.60)*	*Acceptable* *(0.40)*	*Marginal or Unacceptable* *(0)*
Outstanding (1.00)	1.00	0.90	0.80	0.70	0.50
Excellent (0.80)	0.90	0.80	0.70	0.60	0.40
Commendable (0.60)	0.80	0.70	0.60	0.50	0.30
Acceptable (0.00)	—	—	—	—	—
Unacceptable (0.00)	—	—	—	—	—

Source: John F. Sullivan, "The Future of Merit Pay Programs," *Compensation and Benefits Review,* May–June 1989, p. 29.
Instructions. To determine the dollar value of each employee's incentive award, (1) multiply the employee's annual, straight time wage or salary as of June 30 times his or her maximum incentive award and (2) multiply the resultant product times the appropriate percentage figure from this table. For example, if an employee had an annual salary of $20,000 on June 30 and a maximum incentive award of 7% and if her performance and the organization's performance were both "excellent," the employee's award would be $1,120 ($20,000 × 0.07 × 0.80 = $1,120).

lems. One is that for most professionals money has historically been less important than it has been for other groups of employees. This is partly because professionals tend to be paid well anyway, and partly because they tend to be more driven by the desire to produce high-caliber work and receive recognition from colleagues in their profession. As a result (and as just a rule of thumb), professionals who go to work for employers do not do so with high-income expectations unless their plan is to move into management. What they do expect is reasonable pay progress and equitable treatment, and without these they will quickly become dissatisfied.

However, that's not to say that professionals don't like to receive financial incentives (and, in fact, the use of such plans are gaining popularity, especially among high-tech firms, as explained shortly). For example, studies in science-based industries like pharmaceuticals and aerospace consistently show that firms with the most productive research and development groups have incentive pay plans for their professionals, usually in the form of bonuses. Here there is usually a conservative relationship between bonus and salary, in other words, a tendency to award smaller portions of total pay in the form of a bonus. The time cycle of these incentive plans also tends to be longer than one year, reflecting the years of development that often go into designing, developing, and marketing a new product.

While not strictly incentives, there *are* many nonsalary items professionals must have to do their best work. These range from better equipment and facilities and a supportive management style to support for professional journal publications, special bonuses for inventions, company-paid memberships in professional organizations and attendance at meetings, and support for additional education.

◆ REWARDING KEY CONTRIBUTORS

Today, as never before, you have to single out and reward key contributors—mostly selected managers, and professionals—for their roles in making your firm successful. Among the factors fueling this trend are the demand for innovation in firms doing business in a competitive world market, deregulation (which has firms in many industries battling for a foothold in a newly competitive environment), and a flood of venture capital that has created a multitude of small start-ups all battling for market position.

How do organizations typically reward their key contributors? Accord-

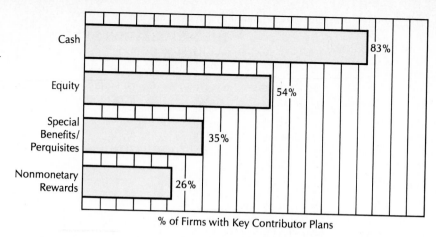

FIGURE 11.1
Vehicles Used to Reward Key Contributors
Source: Michael F. Spratt and Bernadette Steele, "Rewarding Key Contributors," *Compensation and Benefits Review*, July–August 1985, p. 30.)

ing to a recent *Hay Executive and Key Contributor Compensation Survey* of high-technology firms about 76% of the participants reported having some type of formal or informal key contributor plan. (This makes them about six times more likely to have such a plan than U.S. industry in general, according to another Hay survey.)

In the high-tech survey, cash was the most common reward and was typically a one-time award in a lump sum. As you can see in Figure 11.1, 83% of the firms with key contributor programs used cash in a lump-sum payment to pay key contributors. About half of these firms used some type of stock payment plan (stock options or stock grants) similarly to reward key contributors. With respect to cash payments, maximum opportunities for individuals ranged from $5,000 to $30,000 (typically $5,000) for key personnel. Other rewards used included nonmonetary rewards like automobiles, trips, and research funding, as well as sabbaticals, public recognition, freedom-to-choose projects, and "general work-life improvements."[55]

ORGANIZATIONWIDE INCENTIVE PLANS

Many employers have installed incentive plans in which virtually all employees can participate, namely, profit sharing, employee stock ownership plans, and Scanlon plans.

◆ PROFIT-SHARING PLANS

profit-sharing plan A plan whereby most employees share in the company's profits.

In a **profit-sharing plan**, most employees receive a share of the company's profits. The number of companies with profit-sharing plans has doubled every five years since 1951, and there are now a multitude of such plans in existence.[56] For example, such plans are in place at General Motors, Pan Am, and Uniroyal.

Research on the effectiveness of profit-sharing plans is sketchy. In one survey, about half the companies contacted felt their profit-sharing plans had been beneficial,[57] but these benefits are not necessarily in terms of increased performance and motivation. Instead, the organizational benefits are probably more subtle. For example, these plans may increase each worker's sense of commitment to the organization, as well as the person's sense of participation and partnership. They may also reduce turnover and encourage employee thrift.

There are several types of profit-sharing plans, but the most popular are cash plans. Here a percentage of profits (usually 15% to 20%) is distributed as profit shares at regular intervals. One example of this is the *Lincoln Incentive System*, which was first instituted at the Lincoln Electric Com-

PERSONNEL MANAGEMENT:

ON THE FRONT LINE

The question of whether to pay Carter Cleaning Center employees an hourly wage or an incentive of some kind has always intrigued Jack Carter.

His basic policy has always been to pay employees an hourly wage, except that his managers do receive an end-of-year bonus depending, as Jack puts it, "on whether their stores do well or not that year."

He has, however, experimented in one store with incentive plans, with mixed results. Jack knows that a presser should press about 25 "tops" (jackets, dresses, blouses) per hour. Most of his pressers do not attain this ideal standard, though. In one, for instance, a presser named Walt was paid $6 per hour, and Jack noticed that regardless of the amount of work he had to do, Walt always ended up making about $180 at the end of the week. If it was a holiday week, for instance, and there were a lot of clothes to press he might average 22 to 23 tops per hour (someone else did pants) and so he'd earn perhaps $190 to $200 and still finish up each day in time to leave by 3:00 P.M. so he could pick up his children at school. But when things were very slow in the store his productivity would drop to perhaps 12 to 15 pieces an hour, so that at the end of the week he'd still end up earning close to $180, and in fact not go home much earlier than he did when it was busy.

Jack spoke with Walt several times and while Walt always promised to try to do better, it gradually became apparent to Jack that Walt was simply going to earn his $180 per week no matter what. While Walt never told him so directly it dawned on Jack that Walt had a family to support and was not about to earn less than his "target" wage regardless of how busy or slow the store was. The problem was the longer Walt kept pressing each day the longer the steam boilers and compressors had to be kept on to power his machines and the fuel charges alone ran close to $5 per hour. Jack clearly needed some way short of firing Walt to solve the problem, since the fuel bills were eating up his profits.

His solution was to tell Walt that instead of an hourly $6 wage he would henceforth pay him 25 cents per item pressed. That way, said Jack to himself, if he presses 25 items per hour at 25 cents each he will in effect get a small raise and will get more items pressed per hour and will therefore be able to shut the machines down earlier.

On the whole, the experiment worked well. Walt generally presses 25 to 35 pieces per hour now. He gets to leave earlier, and with the small increase in pay he generally earns his target wage. Two problems have arisen though. The quality of Walt's work dipped a bit, and his manager has to spend a minute or two each hour counting the number of pieces Walt pressed that hour. Otherwise Jack is fairly pleased with the results of his incentive plan and he's wondering whether to extend it to other employees and other stores.

Jennifer's questions are:

1. Should this plan in its present form be extended to pressers in the other stores?

2. Should other employees be put on a similar plan? Why? Why not?

3. Is there another incentive plan you think would work better for the pressers?

4. A store manager's basic job is to keep total wages to no more than 30% of sales and to maintain both the fuel bill, and the supply bill at about 9% of sales. Managers can also directly affect sales by ensuring courteous customer service and by ensuring that the work is done properly. What suggestions would you make to Jennifer for an incentive plan for store managers?

pany of Ohio. In one version of the Lincoln plan, most employees work on a guaranteed piecework basis, and total annual profits (less taxes, 6% dividends to stockholders, and a reserve for investment) are distributed each year among employees based on their merit rating.[58] Versions of the Lincoln plan also include a suggestion system that pays individual workers rewards for savings resulting from suggestions. The Lincoln plan has been quite successful.

Profit sharing has perhaps reached its logical conclusion in Japan, where for many employees there is a semiannual bonus that reflects both the national economic level and the performance of the enterprise; the amount of this semi-annual profit-sharing bonus is usually the equivalent of 5 to 6 months' salary for each employee.[59]

There are also *deferred profit-sharing plans*. Here a predetermined portion of profits is placed in each employee's account under the supervision of a trustee. There is a tax advantage to such plans, since income taxes are deferred, often until the employee retires and is thus taxed at a lower tax rate.

Employee Stock Ownership Plan (ESOP) This plan usually involves having a corporation contribute shares of its own stock to a trust in which additional contributions are made annually. The trust distributes the stock to employees on retirement or separation from service.

◆ EMPLOYEE STOCK OWNERSHIP PLAN (ESOP)

Under the most basic form of ESOP, a corporation contributes shares of its own stock—or cash to be used to purchase such stock—to a trust that is established for the purpose of purchasing shares of the company's stock for employees.[60] These contributions are generally made annually in proportion to total employee compensation, with a limit of 15% of compensation. The trust holds the stock in individual employee accounts and distributes the stock to employees upon retirement or other separation from service (assuming the employee has worked at the employer long enough to earn ownership of the stock).

An employee stock ownership plan has several advantages. The corporation receives a tax deduction when it makes its contribution; the deduction is equal to the fair market value of the shares that are transferred to the trustee. The employee is not taxed until he or she receives a distribution from the trust, usually at retirement when the person's tax rate is reduced. Furthermore, the Employee Retirement Income Security Act (ERISA) allows a firm to borrow against employee stock held in trust and then repay the loan in pretax rather than after tax dollars, another tax incentive for using such plans.[61] Research here is again sketchy, but it seems likely that these plans do encourage employees to develop a sense of ownership in and commitment to the firm.[62]

Scanlon plan An incentive plan developed in 1937 by Joseph Scanlon and designed to encourage cooperation, involvement, and sharing of benefits. Plan involves attitudes, suggestions by workers, and benefits formulas.

◆ SCANLON PLAN

Few would argue with the fact that the most powerful way of ensuring high performance is to synchronize the organization's goals with those of its employees: to ensure, in other words, that the two sets of goals overlap, and that by pursuing his or her goals, the worker pursues the employer's goals as well. Many techniques have been proposed for obtaining this idyllic state, but few have been implemented as widely or successfully as the **Scanlon plan**, an incentive plan developed in 1937 by Joseph Scanlon, a United Steel Worker's Union official.[63]

The Scanlon plan has three basic features. The first is the *philosophy of cooperation* on which it is based. It assumes that managers and workers have to rid themselves of the "us" and "them" attitudes that normally inhibit employees from developing a sense of ownership in the company, substituting instead a climate in which everyone cooperates because he or she understands that economic rewards are contingent on honest cooperation.

A pervasive philosophy of cooperation must therefore exist in the firm for the plan to succeed.[64]

The second feature of the plan is the *involvement system*.[65] This takes the form of two levels of committees—the departmental level and the executive level. Productivity-improving suggestions are presented by employees to the appropriate departmental-level committees, which then selectively transmit valuable suggestions to the executive-level committee. The latter then decides whether to implement the suggestion.

The third element of the plan is the *sharing of benefits formula*. Basically, the Scanlon plan assumes that employees should share directly in any extra profits resulting from their cost-cutting suggestions. If a suggestion is implemented and successful, all employees usually share in 75% of the savings. For example, assume that the normal monthly ratio of payroll costs to sales is 50%. (Thus, if sales are $600,000, payroll costs should be $300,000.) Assume suggestions are implemented and result in payroll costs of $250,000 in a month where sales were $550,000, and payroll costs therefore *should have been* $275,000 (50% of sales). The saving attributable to these suggestions is $25,000 ($275,000 minus $250,000). Workers would typically share in 75% of this ($18,750) while $6,250 would go to the firm. In practice, a portion, usually one quarter of the $18,750, is set aside for the months in which labor costs exceed the standard.

The Scanlon plan has been very successful in terms of reducing costs and increasing a sense of sharing and cooperation among employees. In one recent study, labor costs were cut by 10%, and grievances were cut in half after implementation of such a plan.[66]

Yet a number of Scanlon plans have failed, and we know there are certain conditions required for their success. They are usually more effective where there is a relatively small number of participants, generally less than 1,000. They are more successful where there are stable product lines and costs, since it is important that the labor costs/sales ratio remain fairly stable. Good supervision and healthy labor relations seem essential. And, of course, it is crucial that there be strong commitment to the plan on the part of management, particularly during the confusing phase-in period.[67]

♦ **GAINSHARING PLANS**

Gainsharing An incentive plan that engages many or all employees in a common effort to achieve a company's productivity objectives; resulting cost savings are shared among employees at the company.

The Scanlon plan is actually an early version of what today is known as a **gainsharing plan**, an incentive plan that engages many or all employees in a common effort to achieve a company's productivity objectives; resulting incremental cost savings gains are shared among employees and the company.[68] In addition to the Scanlon plan, other popular types of gainsharing plans include the Rucker and Improshare plans.

The basic difference in these plans is in the formula used to determine employee bonuses.[69] The Scanlon formula divides payroll expenses by total sales. The Rucker plan uses sales value minus materials and supplies all divided into payroll expenses as the formula's ratio. The Improshare plan is different, in that it creates production standards for each department. The Scanlon and Rucker plans include participative management systems using committees. Improshare does not include a participative management component but instead considers participation an outcome of the bonus plan. In a survey of 223 companies with gainsharing plans, 95 of the responding firms had custom-designed plans, while the rest used standardized plans like Scanlon, Rucker, or Improshare.[70]

Steps in Gainsharing Plan

The employer wishing to implement its own gainsharing plan should address eight basic steps.[71] First, establish general plan objectives. These might include the company's need to improve productivity, or reinforce teamwork, for instance. Second, define specific performance measures. These usually include productivity measures such as labor or hours or cost per unit produced, loans processed per hour, or total cost per full-time employee. Possible financial measures usable here include profits before interest and taxes, and return on net assets. The third step is the funding formula, such as "payroll expenses divided by total sales." This creates the pot of dollars that is shared among participants. (In one study, by the way, an average of 46.7% of incremental gains were provided to employees with the remainder staying with the company.)[72] Fourth, determine a method for dividing and distributing the employees' share of the gains among the employees themselves. Typical methods here include equal percentage of pay or equal shares, although some plans also try to modify awards to a limited degree based on individual performance. Fifth, the size of the payment must be meaningful enough to get participants' attention and motivate their behavior. One expert suggests a potential of 4–5% of pay and a 70–80% chance of achieving such an objective as an effective combination. The sixth component is the payment form, which is usually in cash but occasionally in common stock or deferred cash. Seventh, you must decide how frequently bonuses are to be paid. This in turn depends on the performance measures used: Most financial performance measures tend to be computed annually, while labor productivity measures tend to be computed quarterly or monthly.

Finally, the eighth component is the support or participative system to be used to involve the employees. Here the systems most commonly used include steering committees, update meetings, suggestion systems, coordinators, problem-solving teams, department committees, training programs, newsletters, inside auditors, and outside auditors.

Making the Plan Work

The gainsharing approach to incentives is simple in concept, but several issues must be addressed to ensure that your plan works in practice.[73] First, in most gainsharing plans, employee involvement is the single most crucial factor to its success. Obviously if your employees mistrust your motives for installing the plan, or do not believe their suggestions will be listened to, or believe that for some reason the plan will boomerang against them, the plan will not likely succeed. In general, therefore, top management and supervisory personnel have to support participatory management actively and willingly to make these plans work. Furthermore, they generally work better with a work force that is technically knowledgeable, motivated by higher compensation and more involvement, and interested in learning more about the financial ramifications of their work. Employee opinion surveys are often used to gather information to predict how a workforce will react to a gainsharing plan. Topics to touch on in such a survey include employee satisfaction, degree of confidence and trust in supervisor, perceived supervisory competence, level of interdepartmental cooperation, willingness to make suggestions, current level of job performance, and willingness to participate in job-related decision making.[74,75,76]

DEVELOPING EFFECTIVE INCENTIVE PLANS

♦ INCENTIVE PLAN PROBLEMS

There are a number of reasons why incentive plans fail, most of which can be explained in terms of what we know about human motivation. For motivation to take place, the worker must believe that effort on his or her part will lead to rewards, *and* he or she must want that reward. In most cases where incentive plans fail, it is because one or both of these conditions are not met.[77] *Unfair standards*—standards that are too high or unattainable—are thus one cause for incentive plan failure. A second is the real or imagined fear that *rates will be cut or standards raised* if performance exceeds the standard for too long a time. Rate cuts have long been the nemesis of incentive plans, and the problem persists to this day, for instance, among manufacturers who reduce a salesperson's territory as soon as his or her commissions become "excessive." *Group restrictions* and peer pressure can work both for and against the plan; if a group views the plan as fair, it can keep loafers in line and maintain high production. But the opposite is also true, and if for any reason the group views the plan as unfair it will—through education, ostracism, or punishment—see that the production levels of group members are held down. Other plans fail because employees *do not understand them* either because the plan is too complex or because it is not communicated to employees in an understandable way.

In summary, incentive plans can motivate employees. For example, two experts conclude that:

> There is considerable evidence that installation of such plans usually results in greater output per man hour, lower unit cost, and higher wages in comparison with outcomes associated with the straight payment system.[78]

But we also know that incentive plans can fail. So far we have discussed some of the causes of such failures. Now let us turn to some specific guidelines for developing effective incentive plans.[79]

1. *Ensure that effort and rewards are directly related.* Our motivation model shows that for an incentive to motivate employees, they must see that effort will lead to their obtaining the reward. Your incentive plan should therefore reward employees in *direct proportion* to their increased productivity. Employees must also perceive that they can *actually do the tasks* required. Thus, the standard has to be attainable, and you have to provide the necessary tools, equipment, and training.[80]

2. *The plan must be understandable and easily calculable by the employees.* Employees should be able to calculate easily the rewards they will receive for various levels of effort (remember it's important for them to see the effort–reward link). Therefore, your plan should be understandable and easily calculable.

3. *Set effective standards.* Standards on which your incentive plan is built should be effective, which requires several things. The standards should be viewed as *fair* by your subordinates. They should be set high, but *reasonable*—there should be about a 50:50 chance of success at reaching it. And the goal should be *specific*—this is much more effective than telling someone to "do your best."

4. *Guarantee your standards.* Around the turn of the century employers often raised production standards (or cut the piecerate) whenever employees' pay became "excessive." Today, employees remain suspicious that *exceeding* the standard will result in *raising* the standards, and to protect their own long-term interests they do not produce above standard, and the incentive plan fails. Therefore, it's important that you view the standard as a *contract* with your employees. Once the plan is operational, you should use great caution before decreasing the size of the incentive in any way.[81]

5. *Guarantee an hourly base rate.* Particularly for plant personnel it's usually advisable to guarantee employees' base rate.[82] They'll therefore know that no matter what happens they can at least earn a minimum guaranteed base rate.

COMPUTER APPLICATION IN FINANCIAL INCENTIVES: APPRAISAL STATISTICS

Remember that effective merit pay plans are always built on a foundation of fair and accurate appraisals. Some supervisors "grade" more stringently than others; some truly have mostly stars; and others are subject to the traditional rating errors. Comparing the results of various departments or divisions may flag certain problems for closer examination.

After accumulating appraisal data from various departments and/or supervisors, extract the particular area(s) you would like to review. You may extract more than one area at a time by sorting the data first by department (in ascending alphabetical order) and then by supervisor's last name (again in ascending alphabetical order).

Then, examine statistical averages and variances. Too little variance indicates a central tendency—a supervisor who does not want to distinguish between employees, so all are rated average. Looking at the minimum and maximum scores actually awarded will tell whether or not there is a restricted range; in other words, another indication of little differentiation between employees. Of course, the range may be restricted on the high side (an "easy grader") or the low side. If there is very little difference in ratings, then superior performers are not getting reinforcement and poor performers are not being given clear expectations of what they must do to improve. Penley and Penley point out that small variance indicates ". . . undifferentiated feedback to the employees."[1]

You may also wish to examine the timeliness of appraisals. If your company policy is to appraise the employee on or before the anniversary of hiring date, then that month and day are entered. In another column, enter the date the appraisal was actually done. By subtracting the appraisal date from the hire date, you are able to quickly view the timeliness of appraisals. This is possible because packages such as Lotus 1–2–3 store Gregorian dates based on the number of days since December 31, 1899.[2]

By analyzing the results of the appraisal process, it is possible to see problem areas which demand further training. Cleaning up these problems may well be a prerequisite to installing an effective incentive plan.

[1]Larry E. Penley and Yolanda E. Penley, *Human Resources Simulation: Using Lotus 1–2–3* (South-Western Publishing Co., Carrollton, Texas), 1988, p. 121.

[2]Gregory T. LeBlond and Douglas Ford Cobb, *Using Lotus 1–2–3* (Que Corporation, Indianapolis), 1983, p. 169.

♦ IN SUMMARY: WHEN TO USE INCENTIVE PLANS

There are two bases on which you can compensate employees: time and output. Straight salary or wages involve compensating employees based on increments of time (such as hourly, daily, or weekly). Incentive plans (calling for piecework or commissions) involve compensating employees based on their output.[83] Under what conditions should you pay employees on a time basis? On an output (incentive) basis? Here are some guidelines (as summarized in Table 11.2).

♦ WHEN TO PAY ON A TIME BASIS

1. *When units of output are difficult to distinguish and measure.* You have to be able to distinguish and identify clearly each worker's output to pay them on an incentive basis. Where you can't, then straight salary or wages (or perhaps a group incentive plan) is more appropriate.

TABLE 11.2   When to Base Pay on Incentives Instead of Time

	BASE PAY ON INCENTIVES	BASE PAY ON TIME
Units of output	Easy to measure	Hard to measure
Employee's control of output	They can control it	They can't
Effort/reward relationship	Clear	Not clear
Work delays	Under employee's control	Beyond employee's control
Quality	Not too important	Paramount
Good supervision and agreement on what is a "fair day's work"	No	Yes
Must know precise labor costs to stay competitive	Yes	No

2. *When employees are unable to control quantity of output.* Where employees have little control over the quantity of output (such as on machine-paced assembly lines) pay based on time is more appropriate.

3. *When there is not a clear relationship between effort and output.* Similarly, if there is no clear, direct relationship between the worker's effort and his or her output—as when jobs are highly interrelated—pay based on time is more appropriate.

4. *When delays in the work are frequent and beyond employees' control.* It is clearly impractical to tie workers' pay to their output if production delays are beyond workers' control.

5. *When quality considerations are especially important.* Virtually all incentive plans tie pay to the quantity, rather than the quality of output. When quality is a primary consideration (as with engineering and other professional personnel) pay based on time is more appropriate.

6. *When precise advance knowledge of unit labor costs is not required by competitive conditions.* Installing an incentive plan requires a substantial investment in industrial engineering, methods analysis, and computation of unit labor costs. If this type of precise cost control is not required by competitive conditions, it is probably not worthwhile to develop them just to install an incentive plan.

◆ WHEN PAYMENT SHOULD BE BASED ON OUTPUT (INCENTIVE PLANS)

Similarly, pay based on *output* would be preferable if:

1. Units of output can be measured.

2. There is a clear relationship between employee effort and quantity of output.

3. The job is standardized, the work flow is regular, and delays are few or consistent.

4. Quality is less important than quantity or, if quality is important, it is easily measured and controlled.

5. Competitive conditions require that unit labor costs be definitely known and fixed in advance of production.[84]

In addition to the incentives-implementation methods discussed to this point, there are several other hints that will improve incentive-planned effectiveness. These include the following:

◆ ADAPT INCENTIVES FOR NONEXEMPTS TO THE FAIR LABOR STANDARDS ACT

Particularly for smaller companies that may not be familiar with this problem, it is important to keep in mind that under the FLSA, only certain kinds of bonuses are excludable from overtime pay calculations.[85] The basic problem is that overtime rates must be paid to nonexempt employees based on their previous week's earnings, and unless the incentive bonuses are structured properly the amount of the bonuses themselves become part of the week's wages. They must then be included in base pay when computing any overtime that week.

Certain kinds of bonuses are excludable from overtime pay calculations. For example, Christmas and gift bonuses which are not based on employees' hours worked, or paid pursuant to a contract, or so substantial that employees consider it a part of their wages do not have to be included in overtime pay calculations. Similarly, purely discretionary bonuses in which the employer retains discretion over whether the bonus will be paid and the amount of the bonus are also excludable.

The problem is that many other types of incentive pay definitely must be included in your calculations. Under the FLSA, bonuses to be included in overtime pay computations include those promised to newly hired employees, those provided in union contracts or other agreements, and those announced to induce employees to work more productively, steadily, rapidly, or efficiently or to induce them to remain with the company. Such bonuses would include individual and group production bonuses, bonuses for quality and accuracy of work, efficiency bonuses, attendance bonuses, length-of-service bonuses, and sales commissions.[86]

To see how incentive bonuses can impact overtime pay, consider the following example. Alison works 45 hours in a particular week at a straight time rate of $5.00 an hour. In that week she also earns a production bonus of $18.00. Her new regular rate for that week becomes $45 \times \$5.00 = \$225.00 + \$18.00 = \$243.00$, and $243.00 divided by 45 equals $5.40 per hour. Her new hourly rate is therefore $5.40 per hour for that week. Additional half-time pay is due her for the 5 hours overtime she worked. Her total weekly pay for that week is therefore $\$243.00 + 5 \ (1/2 \ \text{times} \ \$5.40) = \$256.50$.

The problem can be even more complicated with gainsharing and other productivity-related bonuses since these are usually paid over intervals longer than a single pay period. Here, determining the new regular rate for overtime pay calculations can be deferred until after the bonus is determined. However, at that point the bonus must be apportioned over the workweeks in which it was earned. This actually requires employers to go back and recalculate overtime rates for all of those weeks, retroactively. This can be very time consuming, as you can imagine.

According to one expert, an expeditious way of getting around this problem is to design your incentive bonuses as a percentage-of-wage bonus.[87] Basing the bonus awarded on a percentage of each employee's total pay—straight time and overtime for the period involved—protects the company from liability for any additional overtime pay under the FLSA. One way to do it is to design the incentive plan so that it generates a percentage that is applied to all wages. For example, each employee is paid a bonus equal to a predetermined percentage of his or her salary. This percentage can be based on the number of weeks he or she is in the plan, or the person's level of participation, or some other criteria.

♦ CONSIDER THE CURRENT BUSINESS STAGE OF THE COMPANY[88]

In designing your incentive plan, you should also consider your firm's life-cycle stage. For example, small companies experiencing rapid growth usually prefer a broader-based profit sharing plan to the more complicated individual incentive- or gainsharing-type plans. For one thing, profit-sharing plans tend to be simpler and less expensive to implement and require much less planning and administrative paperwork. Furthermore, small firms' employees tend to feel a more direct effect on the company's profitability than do those embedded in much larger firms. Similarly, companies in a survival or turnaround situation or ones threatened by takeover may also opt for less complicated profit-sharing plans. That way top and middle managers can focus all their energies on the crisis rather than on the administrative effort required to implement gainsharing or individualized incentive plans.

♦ STRESS PRODUCTIVITY AND QUALITY MEASURES IF POSSIBLE

Remember that profitability is not always the same as productivity and that it is usually productivity and quality for which employees should be held accountable, not profitability. The reason is that productivity and quality are controllable, whereas profitability may be influenced by factors like competition and government regulations. As a result, unless it is a more simple overall profit-sharing plan that you are opting for, be careful to formulate your productivity and/or quality standards carefully, focusing on measures that employees can actually control.

♦ GET EMPLOYEE INPUT IN SYSTEM DESIGN

It is usually a mistake to implement an incentive plan by Fiat without input from your employees. Therefore, many employers use a program design team made up of selected employees and supervisors. They work with the compensation specialist in the development of the plan, perhaps by explaining idiosyncracies that need to be taken into consideration or by helping them understand the culture and attitudes in the plant.

SUMMARY

1. The scientific use of financial incentives can be traced back to Frederick Taylor. While such incentives became somewhat less popular during the human relations era, most writers today agree that they can be quite effective.

2. Piecework is the oldest type of incentive plan. Here a worker is paid a piece rate for each unit he produces. With a *straight* piecework plan, workers are paid on the basis of the number of units produced. With a *guaranteed* piecework plan each worker receives his or her base rate (such as the minimum wage) regardless of how many units he or she produces.

3. Other useful incentive plans for plant personnel include the standard hour plan and group incentive plans. The former rewards workers by a percent premium that equals the percent by which their performance is above standard. Group incentive plans are useful where the workers' jobs are highly interrelated.

4 Several incentive plans are discussed for white-collar personnel. Most sales personnel are paid on some type of salary plus commission (incentive) basis. The trouble with straight commission is that there is a tendency to focus on "big-ticket" or "quick-sell" items and to disregard long-term customer building. Management employees are often paid according to some bonus formula that ties the bonus to, for example, increased sales. Stock options are one of the most popular executive incentive plans.

5. Profit sharing and the Scanlon plan are examples of organizationwide incentive plans. The problem with such plans is that the link between a person's efforts and rewards is sometimes unclear. On the other hand, such plans may contribute to developing a sense of commitment among employees. Gainsharing and merit plans are two other popular plans.

6. When incentive plans fail it is usually because (a) the worker does not believe that effort on his or her part will lead to obtaining the reward, or (b) the reward is not important to the person. Specific incentive plan problems therefore include unfair standards, fear of a rate cut, group restrictions, lack of understanding, and lack of required tools, or training.

7. We suggested using incentive plans when units of output are easily measured, employees can control output, the effort-reward relationship is clear, work delays are under employee's control, quality is not paramount, and the organization must know precise labor costs anyway (to stay competitive).

KEY TERMS

Frederick Taylor	group incentive plan	merit raise
fair day's work	attendance incentive plan	profit-sharing plan
scientific management	annual bonus	Employee Stock Ownership Plan (ESOP)
piecework	capital accumulation programs	Scanlon plan
straight piecework	stock option	gainsharing
guarantee piecework plan	special awards	
standard hour plan	merit pay	

DISCUSSION QUESTIONS

1. Compare and contrast six types of incentive plans.
2. Explain five reasons why incentive plans fail.
3. How would you apply the Expectancy Model of motivation we presented in Chapter 9 to the question of incentives?
4. Describe the nature of some important management incentives.
5. When and why would you pay a salesperson a salary? A commission? Salary and commission combined?

♦ CASE INCIDENT

Sales Quotas

The Superior Floor Covering Company has an incentive program for its salespeople. Incentive earnings are based on the amount of sales in relation to an assigned quota.

The quota is computed each year by management, taking into account the number and type of customers in each salesperson's territory and the previous year's sales records for the company and for its competitors. In the administration of this incentive program, the following problems have arisen. Suggest the solutions you would consider in eliminating these difficulties. Note also the parallels between the problems here and those involving blue-collar, manufacturing incentive plans.

1. Some of the best salespeople now have too many accounts in the area assigned to them. From the company's point of view, it would be advantageous to reduce the size of the districts covered by each of these representatives and to add several new salespeople who could give more thorough coverage. The outstanding salespeople resent this proposal, however, claiming that it would penalize them for their success.

2. The top-earning salespeople also complain that their base quotas increase each year, reflecting their previous success. This, too, they feel is discrimination against success.

3. Management believes that the company is not acquiring as many new accounts as it should. So-called missionary work, trying to induce a store that has not previously purchased Superior products to become a customer, takes more time and energy than selling old customers. Also, the results of this missionary work may not show up for several years. The present incentive plan gives no credit for this type of work.

4. When business is booming within a salesperson's territory, he may receive high bonus earnings even without great effort on his part. When there is a great deal of unemployment in his territory or when competition decides to lower prices to penetrate this new market, his bonus earnings may decline even though his sales efforts are at a maximum.

Source: George Strauss and Leonard R. Sayles, *Personnel: The Human Problems of Management*, 4th ed. (Englewood Cliffs, N.J.: Prentice-Hall, 1980), p. 636. Reprinted by permission.

EXPERIENTIAL EXERCISE

Purpose: The purpose of this exercise is to give you practice in reviewing:

1. The conditions under which time versus performance-based incentives are appropriate.

2. The advantages of companywide versus individual incentives.

3. The standards (sales, productivity, etc.) to which incentives can be tied.

Required Understanding: You should be thoroughly familiar with our discussion of financial incentives and come to class prepared to discuss the following case incident:

A Case of Incentives: The Bonus Policy of Ezell Musical Instrument Company [89]
Ezell Musical Instrument Company (EMI) is located in Frederick, Maryland. It is a medium-sized operation that has grown out of a family-owned company. Like many companies, it has to face tough competition at home and abroad. M. G. Ezell III is now the president of the firm.

Several years ago, when Ezell first took over, he thought about how he might build morale in the company. He felt that the company had good workers and that he would like to reward them for past services to encourage them to be more productive. EMI was not unionized. He hesitated about raising base wages because it might make the firm uncompetitive if foreign competition increased.

EMI was having an exceptionally good year, both for sales and profits. As a result, Ezell thought that the best way to reward the employees was to give them a Christmas–New Year's bonus. As he said to Abe Stick, his human resource manager, "Nothing like the old buck to make a man work harder." His bonus system was as follows:

WAGES OR SALARY	BONUS
<$16,500	$500
$16,501–17,500	$600
$17,501–18,500	$700
$18,501–20,000	$800
>$20,000	8% of salary or wage

The bonuses were well received. Many people thanked the president, and Stick heard lots of good comments from the supervisors in January about how much harder the employees were working.

The next year, more foreign competitors entered the market. Materials were harder to get and more expensive. Sales were down 5% and profits were down 15%. Ezell did not feel he could afford the same bonuses as last year. As a result, the bonuses were decreased as follows:

WAGES OR SALARY	BONUS
<$16,500	$250
$16,501–17,500	$300
$17,501–18,500	$350
$18,501–20,000	$400
>$20,000	4% of salary or wage

This time Stick heard little from the supervisors about increased productivity. He asked Harry Bell, one of the supervisors, what the reaction was to the bonuses.

Bell: To tell you the truth, Abe, I have morale problems. My people worked hard this year. It wasn't their fault sales or profits were down. Many expected last year's bonus or better. So they spent most of the old figure for Christmas gifts. When they got that letter from M. G. telling them they were getting only half of last year's on December 27, there was gloom and doom and some mumblings. Some of my people seem to be working less hard than at any time I can remember.

Stick: But that's not fair, Harry. They never received any bonuses before. Now they should be glad they received anything.

Bell: That's not the way they see it!

Stick decided not to discuss the matter with Ezell. Stick figured the problem would blow over. But this year was even worse. Sales held but were not up to the prior year's levels. But profits were almost nonexistent. The board of directors decided to omit the dividend.

Now, Ezell has come to Stick. Ezell says: "Abe, I don't see how we can pay any bonus this year. Do you think we can get by without causing a big drop in morale?"

How to Set Up the Exercise: Divide the class into groups of four or five students. Everyone should briefly review "A Case of Incentives."

Instructions for the Exercise: After discussing the case each group should develop answers to the following questions:

1. What does this case illustrate about the motivational impact of bonuses and incentives?

2. What could Ezell have done to prevent this problem in the first place?

3. Why should Bell expect that the employees would react negatively to the reduction in bonuses when they are not guaranteed as part of an employee's compensation?

4. Have rewards been accurately tied to performance by the Ezell compensation policy? If not, how might this failure be the cause of their problems?

5. What alternative formula or policy for discussing extra income to employees would you suggest?

6. What would you do now if you were Ezell? Stick?

If time permits, the class should discuss their recommendations.

NOTES

1. For example, see "Sharing the Wealth: HROs Role in Making Incentive Plans Work," *Training* (January 1979), pp. 30–31; Hewitt Associates, *News and Information*, October 7, 1986. See also Robert D. Pritchard et al., "Incentive Systems: Success by Design," *Personnel*, Vol. 66, no. 5 (May 1989), pp. 63–68.

2. Orlando Behling and Chester Schriesheim, *Organizational Behavior* (Boston: Allyn & Bacon, 1976), p. 250. See also, for example, Robert Opshal and Marvin Dunnette, "The Role of Financial Compensation in Industrial Motivation," *Psychological Bulletin*, Vol. 66 (1966), pp. 94–118. For a good example of how to implement a performance-based pay plan, see Stuart Freedman, "Performance-Based Pay: A Convenience Store Case Study," *Personnel Journal*, Vol. 64 (July 1985), pp. 30–34; Rosabeth Moss Kanter, "The Attack on Pay," *Harvard Business Review*, Vol. 66 (March–April 1987), pp. 60–67; Michael Smith, Edward O. Dowd, and George Christ, "Pay for Performance—One Company's Experience," *Compensation and Benefits Review* (May–June 1987), pp. 19–27; and Robert L. Heneman et al., "The Relationship Between Pay for Performance Perceptions and Pay Satisfaction," *Personnel Psychology*, Vol. 41, no. 4 (Winter 1988), pp. 745–760.

3. Robert Rice, "Survey of Work Measurement and Wage Incentives in the USA," *Management Services* (January 1978), p. 10.

4. Don Marshall, "Merit Pay Without Headaches: How to Design a Plan for Nonexempt," *Compensation Review*, Vol. 7, no. 2 (Second Quarter 1975), pp. 32–41.

5. Robert Sibson, *Compensation* (New York: AMACOM, 1982), pp. 166–167.

6. Richard Henderson, *Compensation Management* (Reston, Va.: Reston, 1979), p. 363. For a discussion of the increasing use of incentives for blue-collar employees, see, for example, Richard Henderson, "Contract Concessions: Is the Past Prologue?" *Compensation and Benefits Review*, Vol. 18, no. 5 (September–October 1986), pp. 17–30.

7. David Belcher, *Compensation Administration* (Englewood Cliffs, N.J.: Prentice-Hall, 1973), p. 314.

8. *Measured day work* is a third type of individual incentive plan for production workers. See, for example, Mitchell Fein, "Let's Return to MDW for Incentives," *Industrial Engineering* (January 1979), pp. 34–37.

9. Henderson, *Compensation Management*, pp. 367–368. See also David Swinehart, "A Guide for More Productive Team Incentive Programs," *Personnel Journal*, Vol. 65, no. 7 (July 1986).

10. Jon P. Alston, "Awarding Bonuses the Japanese Way," *Business Horizons*, Vol. 25 (September–October 1982), pp. 6–8.

11. See, for example, Peter Daly, "Selecting and Assigning a Group Incentive Plan," *Management Review* (December 1975), pp. 33–45. For an explanation of how to develop a successful group incentive program, see K. Dow Scott and Timothy Cotter, "The Team That Works Together Earns Together," *Personnel Journal*, Vol. 63 (March 1984), pp. 59–67.

12. Manuel London and Greg Oldham, "A Comparison of Group and Individual Incentive Plans," *Academy of Management Journal*, Vol. 20, no. 1 (1977), pp. 34–41. Note that the study was carried out under controlled conditions in a laboratory setting. See also Thomas Rollins, "Productivity-Based Group Incentive Plans: Powerful, But Use with Caution," *Compensation and Benefits Review*, Vol. 21, no. 3 (May–June 1989), pp. 39–50; discusses several popular group incentive plans, including gainsharing, and lists dos and don'ts for using them.

13. Dale Schlotzhauer and Joseph Rosse, "A Five-Year of a Positive Incentive Absence Control Program," *Personnel Psychology*, Vol. 38, no. 3 (Autumn 1985), pp. 575–585.

14. George Schneller IV and Richard Kopelman, "Using Incentives to Increase Absenteeism: A Plan That Backfired," *Compensation Review* (Second Quarter 1983), pp. 40–45.

15. W. E. Reum and Sherry Reum, "Employee Stock Ownership Plans: Pluses and Minuses," *Harvard Business Review*, Vol. 55 (July–August 1976), pp. 133–143; Ralph Bavier, "Managerial Bonuses," *Industrial Management*, March–April 1978, pp. 1–5. See also James Thompson, L. Murphy Smith, and Alicia Murray, "Management Performance Incentives: Three Critical Issues," *Compensation and Benefits Review*, Vol. 18, no. 5 (September–October 1986), pp. 41–47.

16. Bureau of National Affairs, *Bulletin to Management*, January 6, 1983, p. 1.

17. James Brinks, "Executive Compensation: Crossroads of the 80s," *Personnel Administrator*, Vol. 26 (December 1981), p. 24.

18. "Long-Term Incentives: Trends and Approaches," *Personnel*, Vol. 57 (July–August 1982), pp. 60–61.

19. S. B. Prasod, "Top Management Compensation and Corporate Performance," *Academy of Management Journal* (September 1974), pp. 554–558; John Bouike, "Performance Bonus Plans: Boom for Managers and Stockholders," *Management Review* (November 1975), pp. 13, 18; "How Pay and Save Grows and Grows," *Forbes*, April 16, 1979, p. 113.

20. Bruce R. Ellig, "Incentive Plans: Short-Term Design Issues," *Compensation Review*, Vol. 16, no. 3 (Third Quarter 1984), pp. 26–36.

21. Bruce Ellig, *Executive Compensation—A Total Pay Perspective* (New York: McGraw-Hill, 1982), p. 187.

22. Ibid., p. 187.

23. Ibid., p. 188.

24. See, for example, Bavier, "Managerial Bonuses," pp. 1–5. See also Charles Tharp, "Linking Annual Incentive Awards to Individual Performance," *Compensation and Benefits Review*, Vol. 17 (November–December 1985), pp. 38–43.

25. Ellig, *Executive Compensation*, p. 189.

26. F. Dean Hildebrand, Jr., "Individual Performance Incentives," *Compensation Review*, Vol. 10 (Third Quarter 1978), p. 32.

27. Ibid., pp. 28–33.

28. Edward Redling, "The 1981 Tax Act: Boom to Managerial Compensation," *Personnel*, Vol. 57 (March–April 1982), pp. 26–35.

29. The following based on Redling, "The 1981 Tax Act," pp. 26–35.

30. See both William M. Mercer-Meidinger, Inc., "How Will Reform Tax Your Benefits?" *Personnel Journal*, Vol. 65, no. 12 (December 1986), pp. 49–63, and Jack H. Schechter, "The Tax Reform Act of 1986: Its Impact on Compensation and Benefits," *Compensation and Benefits Review*, Vol. 18, no. 6 (November–December 1986), pp. 11–24.

31. Paul Greenlaw, "Cash Emerges as Compensation Hero," *Personnel Journal* (July 1988), pp. 96–105.

32. See also Paul Bradley, "Justify Executive Bonuses to the Board," *Personnel Journal* (September 1988), pp. 116–125, and his "Long Term Incentives: International Executives Need Them Too," *Personnel* (August 1988), pp. 40–42.

33. Belcher, *Compensation Administration*, p. 548.

34. Schechter, "The Tax Reform Act of 1986," p. 23. See also Rein Linney and Charles Marshall, "ISOs vs. NQSOs: The Choice Still Exists," *Compensation and Benefits Review*, Vol. 19, no. 1 (January–February 1987), pp. 13–25.

35. Basically, book value per share equals the firm's assets minus its prior (basically debt) liabilities, divided by the number of shares. See, for example, John Annas, "Facing Today's Compensation Uncertainties," *Personnel*, Vol. 33, no. 1 (January–February 1976).

36. Ray Stata and Modesto Maidique, "Bonus System for Balanced Strategy," *Harvard Business Review*, Vol. 59 (November–December 1980), pp. 156–163; Alfred Rappaport, "Executive Incentives Versus Corporate Growth," *Harvard Business Review*, Vol. 57 (July–August 1978), pp. 81–88. See also Crystal Graef, "Rendering Long-Term Incentives Less Risky for Executives," *Personnel*, Vol. 65, no. 9 (September 1988), pp. 80–84.

37. Jude Rich and John Larson, "Why Some Long-Term Incentives Fail," *Compensation Review*, Vol. 16 (First Quarter 1984), pp. 26–37. See also Eric Marquardt, "Stock Option Grants: Is Timing Everything?" *Compensation and Benefits Review*, Vol. 20, no. 5 (September–October 1988), pp. 18–22.

38. This section based primarily on John Steinbrink, "How to Pay Your Sales Force," *Harvard Business Review*, Vol. 57 (July–August 1978), pp. 111–122.

39. Belcher, *Compensation Administration*, pp. 505–507.

40. Straight salary by itself is not, of course, an incentive compensation plan as we use the term in this chapter.

41. Steinbrink, "How to Pay," p. 112.

42. T. H. Patten, "Trends in Pay Practices for Salesmen," *Personnel*, Vol. 43 (January–February 1968), pp. 54–63.

43. Steinbrink, "How to Pay," p. 115.

44. In the salary plus bonus plan, salespeople are paid a basic salary and are then paid a bonus for carrying out specified activities.

45. This is based on "Sales Incentives Get the Job Done," *Sales and Marketing Management*, September 14, 1981, pp. 67–120.

46. "Adjusting Salaries for Inflation," *Personnel*, Vol. 56 (November–December 1981), p. 54. See also James W. Hathaway, "How Do Merit Bonuses Fare?" *Compensation and Benefits Review*, Vol. 18, no. 5 (September–October 1986), pp. 50–57, for a discussion of replacing merit increases with merit bonuses.

47. See, for example, Herbert Meyer, "The Pay for Performance Dilemma," *Organizational Dynamics* (Winter 1975), pp. 39–50; Thomas Patten, Jr., "Pay for Performance or Placation?" *Personnel Administrator*, Vol. 24 (September 1977), pp. 26–29; William Kearney, "Pay for Performance? Not Always," *MSU Business Topics* (Spring 1979), pp. 5–16. See also Hoyt Doyel and Janet Johnson, "Pay Increase Guidelines with Merit," *Personnel Journal*, Vol. 64 (June 1985), pp. 46–50.

48. Nathan Winstanley, "Are Merit Increases Really Effective?" *Personnel Administrator*, Vol. 27 (April 1982), pp. 37–41. See also William Seithel and Jeff Emans, "Calculating Merit Increases: A Structured Approach," *Personnel*, Vol. 60, no. 5 (June 1985), pp. 56–68.

49. James T. Brinks, "Is There Merit in Merit Increases?" *Personnel Administrator*, Vol. 25 (May 1980), p. 60.

50. *Merit Pay: Fitting the Pieces Together* (Chicago: Commerce Clearing House, 1982).

51. Rosabeth Moss Kanter, "From Status to Contribution: Some Organizational Implications of Changing Basis for Pay," *Personnel*, Vol. 64, no. 1 (January 1987), pp. 12–37.

52. Suzanne Minken, "Does Lump Sum Pay Merit Attention?" *Personnel Journal* (June 1988), pp. 77–83.

53. John F. Sullivan, "The Future of Merit Pay Programs," *Compensation and Benefits Review* (May–June 1988), pp. 22–30.

54. This section based primarily on Robert Sibson, *Compensation* (New York: AMACOM, 1981), pp. 189–207.

55. Michael Sprat and Bernadette Steele, "Rewarding Key Contributors," *Compensation and Benefits Review*, Vol. 17 (July–August 1985), pp. 24–37.

56. John Hoerr, "Why Labor and Management Are Both Buying Profit-Sharing," *Business Week*, January 10, 1983, p. 84.

57. Bert Metzger and Jerome Colletti, "Does Profit Sharing Pay?" (Evanston, Ill.: Profit Sharing Research Foundation, 1971), quoted in Belcher, *Compensation Administration*, p. 353. See also D. Keith Denton, "An Employee Ownership Program That Rebuilt Success," *Personnel Journal*, Vol. 66, no. 3 (March 1987), pp. 114–118.

58. Belcher, *Compensation Administration*, p. 351.

59. Mary O'Connor, "Employee Profit Sharing in Japan," *Personnel Journal*, Vol. 60 (August 1981), p. 614.

60. Based on Randy Swad, "Stock Ownership Plans: A New Employee Benefit," *Personnel Journal*, Vol. 60 (June 1981), pp. 453–455.

61. Donald Sullivan, "ESOPs," *California Management Review*, Vol. 20, no. 1 (Fall 1977), pp. 55–56. For a discussion of the effects of employee-stock ownership on employee attitudes, see Katherine Klein, "Employee-Stock Ownership and Employee Attitudes: A Test of Three Models," *Journal of Applied Psychology*, Vol. 72, no. 2 (May 1987), pp. 319–331.

62. Everett Allen, Jr., Joseph Melone, and Jerry Rosenbloom, *Pension Planning* (Homewood, Ill.: Irwin, 1981), p. 316. Note that the Tax Reduction Act of 1975 has also led to the creation of the so-called TRAFOP. This is basically a regular employee stock ownership plan, except that a portion of the investment tax credit that employers receive for investing in capital equipment can be invested in the employee stock ownership plan.

63. Brian Moore and Timothy Ross, *The Scanlon Way to Improved Productivity: A Practical Guide* (New York: Wiley, 1978), p. 2.

64. J. Kenneth White, "The Scanlon Plan: Causes and Correlates of Success," *Academy of Management Journal*, Vol. 22 (June 1979), pp. 292–312.

65. Moore and Ross, *The Scanlon Way*, pp. 1–2.

66. George Sherman, "The Scanlon Plan: Its Capabilities for Productive Improvement," *Personnel Administrator* (July 1976).

67. White, "The Scanlon Plan," pp. 292–312.

68. Barry W. Thomas and Madeline Hess Olson, "Gainsharing: The Design Guarantees Success," *Personnel Journal* (May 1988), pp. 73–79.

69. See Theresa A. Welbourne and Louis Gomez-Mejia, "Gainsharing Revisited," *Compensation and Benefits Review* (July–August 1988), pp. 19–28.

70. Carla O'Dell and Jerry McAdams, *People, Performance and Pay* (American Productivity Center and Carla O'Dell, 1987), p. 34.

71. Thomas and Olson, "Gainsharing," pp. 75–76.

72. O'Dell and McAdams, *People, Performance, and Pay*, p. 42.

73. Jeffrey Ewing, "Gainsharing Plans: Two Key Factors," *Compensation and Benefits Review* (January–February 1989), pp. 49–53.

74. See, for example, Brian Moore and Timothy Ross, *The Scanlon Way to Improved Productivity: A Practical Guide* (New York: Wiley, 1978), pp. 157–164.

75. Ewing, "Gainsharing Plans: Two Key Factors," pp. 51–52.

76. Ibid., p. 52.

77. See Ronald Goettinger, "Why Isn't Your Incentive Compensation Working?" *Personnel Journal*, Vol. 60 (November 1981), pp. 840–841.

78. Robert Opsahl and Marvin Dunnette, "The Role of Financial Compensation in Industrial Motivation," *Psychological Bulletin*, Vol. 66 (1966), pp. 94–118, in Larry Cummings and William Scott, *Readings in Organizational Behavior and*

Human Performance (Homewood, Ill.: Irwin/Dorsey, 1969). See also Behling and Schriesheim, *Organizational Behavior*. Both sets of authors point out, though, that the installation of an incentive plan is not (and can't be) an isolated event. Improved work methods and clearer policies always accompany incentive plans, and it is often hard to determine whether it is the incentive plan or these other improvements that led to the improved performance.

79. Based on R. D. Pritchard, C. W. VonBergan, Jr., and P. J. DeLeo, "An Evaluation of Incentive Motivation Techniques in Air Force Technical Training," Air Force Human Resources Laboratory Technical Report (1974); Robert Pritchard, Philip DeLeo, and Clarence W. VonBergan, Jr., "A Field Experiment Test of Expectancy–Valence Incentive Motivation Techniques," *Organizational Behavior and Human Performance*, Vol. 15 (1976), pp. 355–406; J. K. Louden and Jay Wayne Deagan, *Wage Incentives* (New York: Wiley, 1959), pp. 25–28; Opsahl and Dunnette, *The Role of Financial Compensation in Industrial Motivation*, pp. 350–368. See also Thomas Rollins, "Pay for Performance: The Pros and Cons," *Personnel Journal*, Vol. 66, no. 6 (June 1987), pp. 104–111.

80. Opsahl and Dunnette, *The Role of Financial Compensation in Industrial Motivation*.

81. Gary Yukl and Gary Latham, "Consequences of Reinforcement Schedules and Incentives Magnitudes for Employee Performance: Problems Encountered in an Industrial Setting," *Journal of Applied Psychology*, Vol. 60 (June 1975).

82. Louden and Deagan, *Wage Incentives*, p. 26.

83. Based on Belcher, *Compensation Administration*, pp. 309–311. See also Edward Lawler III, "Reward Systems," in J. R. Hackman and J. L. Suttle, *Improving Life at Work* (Santa Monica, Calif.: Goodyear, 1977), pp. 191–219. See also Kent E. Romanoff, "The Ten Commandments of Performance Management," *Personnel*, Vol. 66, no. 1 (January 1989), pp. 24–28.

84. Belcher, *Compensation Administration*, pp. 309–310.

85. This is based on William E. Buhl, "Keeping Incentives Simple for Nonexempt Employees," *Compensation and Benefits Review* (March–April 1989), pp. 14–19.

86. Ibid., pp. 15–16.

87. Ibid., pp. 17–18.

88. The following are based on Michael J. Cissell, "Designing Effective Reward Systems," *Compensation and Benefits Review* (November–December 1987), pp. 49–56.

89. John Ivancevich, Andrew Szilagyi, Jr., and Marc Wallace, *Organizational Behavior and Performance* (Santa Monica, Calif.: Goodyear, 1977), pp. 470–471.

Chapter 12

Benefits and Services

When you finish studying this chapter, you should be able to:

1. Explain the main features of at least ten employee benefit plans.
2. Cite the eight policy areas that must be considered in regard to vacations and holidays.
3. Cite the four key policy areas involved in pension plans.
4. Define vesting.
5. Discuss how employees' ages affect their choice of benefits.
6. Explain the cafeteria approach.

OVERVIEW

The main purpose of this chapter is to explain the pros and cons of various employee benefit plans. We discuss four types of plans: supplemental pay benefits (such as unemployment insurance), insurance benefits (such as workers' compensation), retirement benefits (such as pensions), and employee services (such as dining facilities). We explain that employees' preferences for various benefit plans differ, and that it is therefore useful to individualize an organization's benefits package. We therefore present a technique for building flexibility into benefit plans (or "customizing them"): the cafeteria approach. Benefits and services are important rewards and therefore influence employee's motivation. And (as we discuss in this chapter) employees' preferences for different benefits vary—with the employee's age, marital status, and so on—therefore it's important to customize the benefits package to ensure that it contributes to improving performance at work.

benefits Any supplements to wages given to employees. They may include health and life insurance, vacation, pension, profit sharing, education plans, discounts on company products.

The financial incentives we have discussed are paid to *specific* employees whose work is above standard. Employee **benefits**, on the other hand, are available to *all employees* based on their membership in the organization (although the amount of the benefit may be in proportion to the importance of the job).

Administering benefits today represents an increasingly specialized and expensive task. It demands specialized expertise because workers are becoming more sophisticated in financial matters and are therefore demanding new types of benefits, and because federal legislation—concerning pregnancy benefits, for instance—requires that benefit plans comply with new laws. Furthermore, benefit plans became increasingly expensive to administer during the 1970s and early 1980s, although they have recently begun to moderate. For example, benefit costs as a percentage of payroll rose from 25.5% in 1961 to 41.2% in 1981 but fell to about 36% in 1985 before rising slightly, to about 39% today. But at that rate they were still averaging about $10,700 per year per full-time employee. Roughly speaking, legally required benefits like Social Security make up about 30% of the total benefit cost to employers. Paid leave (vacations, holidays) constitutes 25%, insurance 20%, pension and savings plans 13%, and supplemental pay (including nonproduction bonuses) 8%.[1]

One big problem with benefits is that employees often don't know the market value and high cost (to the employer) of their benefits; they significantly undervalue them. The results of one study indicate that this problem can be overcome with what the researchers call an information-enhancement approach. This involves, for instance, indicating the benefits' true cost on each employee's pay stub.[2]

There are many benefit plans, and to simplify our discussion, they are classified as (1) pay supplements (for time not worked), (2) insurance benefits, (3) retirement benefits, and (4) services.

SUPPLEMENTAL PAY BENEFITS (PAY FOR TIME NOT WORKED)

supplemental pay benefits Benefits for time not worked. They include unemployment insurance, vacation and holiday pay, sick pay, severance pay, and supplemental unemployment benefits.

All firms provide **supplemental pay benefits**—benefits, in other words, for time not worked. These include unemployment insurance (if the person is laid off), vacation and holiday pay, sick pay, severance pay (if the person is terminated), and supplemental unemployment benefits (which guarantee income if the plant is closed down for a period). We'll discuss each benefit in turn.

◆ UNEMPLOYMENT INSURANCE

unemployment insurance Provides weekly benefits if a person is unable to work through some fault other than his or her own.

All states have **unemployment insurance** or compensation acts. These provide for weekly benefits if a person is unable to work through some fault other than his or her own. The benefits derive from an *unemployment tax* on employers that can range from 0.1% to 5% of taxable payroll in most states. States (to repeat) each have their own unemployment laws; however, these all follow federal guidelines. Your organization's unemployment tax reflects its experience with personnel terminations.

Unemployment benefits are meant for workers who are terminated through no fault of their own. Thus (strictly speaking), a worker who is fired for chronic lateness does not have a legitimate claim to benefits. But in practice many managers take a lackadaisical attitude toward protecting their employers against unwarranted claims. Employers therefore end up spending thousands of dollars more per year on unemployment taxes than would be necessary if they protected themselves against such claims.

One way to protect your employer is by carefully reviewing the personnel procedures itemized in Table 12.1. Determine whether you could answer yes to questions such as "Do you tell employees whom to call when they're late?" or "Do you have a rule that three days absence without calling in is reason for automatic discharge?" By establishing policies and rules in these

TABLE 12.1 An Unemployment Insurance Cost Control Survey

CAUSE—DO YOU . . .	YES	NO	SOME-TIMES	CAUSE—DO YOU . . .	YES	NO	SOME-TIMES
Lateness				3. Mail job abandonment letter	___	___	___
1. Tell employees whom to call when late	___	___	___	4. Mail job review questionnaire three to six months after separation	___	___	___
2. Keep documented history of lateness and warning notices	___	___	___	**Layoff**			
3. Suspend chronically late employees before discharging them	___	___	___	1. Hire employees with established "benefit year" if you anticipate layoffs	___	___	___
Absenteeism				2. Keep employees on when the cost to replace them would more than offset paying their salary	___	___	___
1. Tell employees whom to call when absent	___	___	___	3. Transfer employees to different departments	___	___	___
2. Rule that three days absence without calling in is reason for automatic discharge	___	___	___	4. Have a flexible work week that reflects high and low periods of productivity	___	___	___
3. Keep documented history of absence and warning notices	___	___	___	5. Temporarily lay off employees for one week during slack periods	___	___	___
4. Request doctor's note on return to work	___	___	___	6. Attempt to find temporary or part-time jobs for laid-off employees	___	___	___
Illness				**Job Refusal**			
1. Keep job open, if possible	___	___	___	1. Issue a formal notice to employees collecting benefits to return to work	___	___	___
2. Offer leave of absence	___	___	___				
3. Request doctor's note on return to work	___	___	___	2. Require new employees to stipulate in writing their availability to work overtime, night shifts, etc.	___	___	___
Pregnancy				**Not Qualified**			
1. Follow EEOC ruling, "no discharge"	___	___	___	1. Set probationary periods to evaluate new employees	___	___	___
2. Request doctor's note indicating how long employee may work	___	___	___	2. Conduct follow-up interviews one to two months after hire	___	___	___
3. Change jobs within company when practical	___	___	___	**Deliberate Unsatisfactory Performance**			
4. Offer maternity leave	___	___	___				
Leave of Absence				1. Document all instances, recording when and how employees did not meet job requirements	___	___	___
1. Make written approval mandatory	___	___	___				
2. Stipulate date for return to work	___	___	___				
3. Offer position at end of leave	___	___	___				
Leave Job Voluntarily							
1. Conduct exit interview	___	___	___				
2. Obtain a signed resignation statement	___	___	___				

TABLE 12.1 (continued)

CAUSE—DO YOU . . .	YES	NO	SOME-TIMES	CAUSE—DO YOU . . .	YES	NO	SOME-TIMES
2. Require supervisors to document the steps taken to remedy the situation	___	___	___	(b) anticipates and reports costly turnover trends	___	___	___
3. Require supervisors to document employee's refusal of advice and direction	___	___	___	(c) successfully protests unwarranted claims and charges for unemployment benefits	___	___	___
Violation of Company Rule				(d) recommends appropriate tax remedies:			
1. Make sure all policies and rules of conduct are understood by all employees	___	___	___	1. Verify the contribution rate assigned by the state	___	___	___
2. Require all employees to sign a statement acknowledging acceptance of these rules	___	___	___	2. Test for Rate Modification	___	___	___
3. Meet with employee and fill out documented warning notice	___	___	___	3. Test for Voluntary Contribution and advisability of a joint account	___	___	___
4. Discharge at the time violation occurs, or suspend	___	___	___	4. Determine advantage of transfer of experience resulting from mergers, acquisition, or other corporate changes	___	___	___
Wrong Benefit Charges				**Communication**			
1. Check state charge statement for				1. Hold periodic workshops with key personnel to review procedures and support effort to reduce turnover costs	___	___	___
(a) correct employee	___	___	___				
(b) correct benefit amount	___	___	___	2. Immediately investigate who or what is responsible for costly errors and why	___	___	___
(c) correct period of liability	___	___	___	**Management Reports**			
Claim Handling				1. Point to turnover problems as they occur by			
1. Assign a claims supervisor or central office to process all separation information	___	___	___	(a) location	___	___	___
				(b) department	___	___	___
2. Respond to state claim forms on time	___	___	___	(c) classification of employee	___	___	___
3. Use proper terminology on claim form and attach documented evidence regarding separation	___	___	___	(d) job position	___	___	___
				2. Evaluate the effectiveness of current policies and procedures used to			
4. Attend hearings and appeal unwarranted claims	___	___	___	(a) recruit	___	___	___
5. Conduct availability checks and rehire employees collecting benefits	___	___	___	(b) select	___	___	___
				(c) train	___	___	___
				(d) supervise	___	___	___
Administration				(e) separate	___	___	___
1. Have a staff member who knows unemployment insurance laws and who				3. Help create policies and procedures for			
(a) works with the personnel department to establish proper use of policies and procedures	___	___	___	(a) less costly layoffs	___	___	___
				(b) increased survival rate	___	___	___
				(c) retention of employees	___	___	___

Explanation: Each "no" or "sometimes" answer represents an area where you lack control; each "yes" is a strong point that acts to save you money.

Source: Reprinted from the January 1976 issue of *Personnel Administrator.* Copyright 1976, the American Society for Personnel Administration.

PERSONNEL MANAGEMENT:

ON THE FRONT LINE

Carter Cleaning Centers has traditionally provided only legislatively required benefits for its employees. These include participation in their state's unemployment compensation program, Social Security, and workers' compensation (which is provided through the same insurance carrier that insures the stores for such hazards as theft and fire). The principals of the firm—Jack, Jennifer, and their families—have individual family-supplied health and life insurance.

At the present time, Jennifer can see several things wrong with the company's policies regarding benefits and services. First, she wants to do a study to determine whether similar companies' experiences with providing health and life insurance benefits suggests they enable these firms to reduce employee turnover and perhaps pay lower wages. Jennifer is also concerned with the fact that at the present time the company has no formal policy regarding vacations or paid days off or sick leave. Informally, at least, it is understood that employees get one week vacation after one year's work, but in the past the policy regarding paid vacations for days such as New Year's and Thanksgiving has been very inconsistent: Sometimes employees who have been on the job only two or three weeks are paid fully for one of these holidays while at other times employees who have been with the firm for six months or more have been paid for only half a day. Jennifer knows that this policy must be made more consistent.

She also wonders whether it would be advisable to establish some type of day care center for the employees' children. She knows that for many of the employees, including Walt, the children either have no place to go during the day (they are preschoolers) or have no place to go after school, and she wonders if a benefit such as day care would be in the best interests of the company.

1. Draw up a policy statement regarding vacations, sick leave, and paid days off for Carter Cleaning Centers.

2. What are the advantages and disadvantages to Carter Cleaning Centers of providing its employees with health, hospitalization, and life insurance programs?

3. How should Jennifer go about determining whether a day care center would be advisable for the company?

---

areas you will be able to show that an employee's termination was a result of the person's inadequate performance (rather than lack of work or some other cause beyond his control). Some additional guidelines for cutting unemployment insurance costs include:

Understand the unemployment insurance code. Many states publish an updated employer's guide annually with names such as "Twenty-seven Ways to Avoid Losing Your Unemployment Appeal." You or someone on your staff should become an expert in understanding the unemployment insurance code in your state and how the system works.

Train managers and supervisors. The real key to success is properly training your manager and supervisors so that they avoid the sorts of mistakes that can contribute to terminated employees who might otherwise not be eligible to successfully apply for unemployment compensation.

Conduct exit interviews. If you conduct exit interviews with everyone who leaves your organization, you can use the information in protesting unemployment claims.

Verify unemployment claims. Remember to check every unemployment claim against the individual's personnel file. Make sure to double-check the reasons the employee gives for why he or she left your employ.

File on a timely basis. Make sure to file your protest (against a former employee's claim) on a timely basis. In most states you have ten days in which to protest a claim.

Know your local unemployment insurance official. Most unemployment officers appreciate cooperative employers and are historically understaffed and overworked. Taking a hostile, adversarial position may undermine your ability to get the benefit of their doubt on a claim you might otherwise have won.

Audit the annual benefit charges statement. Once a year you will receive a benefit charges statement regarding the status of your unemployment compensation account. Thoroughly audit this since errors (such as inaccurate charges against your account) may be included in it.[3]

In summary, persons in most states are eligible for unemployment benefits if they were terminated through no fault of their own. If they quit without good cause or if they refuse a suitable position or if they are discharged through misconduct of some type, they are *not* eligible. Your unemployment tax is based on the number of former employees who are eligible for (and receive) unemployment benefits. It is therefore to the employer's advantage to set clear policies and procedures concerning matters such as lateness, absenteeism, and job refusal.

♦ **VACATIONS AND HOLIDAYS**

Specific policies concerning holidays and vacations vary from employer to employer. Paid vacations may vary from 1 week per year to 4 weeks or more. Paid holidays may range from a minimum of 4 or 5 to as many as 13 or more. But regardless of the organization, there are certain key personnel policy areas that must be addressed.[4]

Eligibility requirements. Your plan should specify the length of service required in order to earn vacations and the length of vacation time. Some plans call for the employee gradually to accumulate vacation time, for example, one hour of vacation time for each week of service.

Vacation pay. Some plans give the employee his or her regular base rate of pay while on vacation; others provide for vacation pay based on average earnings.

Earned right. Some organizations provide for accrued vacation time that is paid if an employee leaves before taking his vacation.

With respect to *holidays*, key personnel policy areas include:

Number of paid holidays. This varies from a minimum of about 5 to 13 or more. Some common holidays:

New Year's Day	Veterans' Day
Memorial Day	Thanksgiving Day
Independence Day	Martin Luther King's Birthday
Labor Day	President's Day
	Christmas Day

Provision for holidays on a Saturday or Sunday. Employees are often given the following Monday off when the holiday falls on a Sunday and Friday off when a holiday falls on a Saturday.

Premium pay for work on a regular holiday. Most organizations provide for some premium—such as time-and-a-half—to employees who work on a holiday.

◆ SICK LEAVE

Sick leave provides pay to an employee when he or she is out of work because of illness. Most sick leave policies grant full pay for a specified number of "permissible" sick days—usually up to about 12 per year. The so-called sick days are usually accumulated at the rate of, say, one day per month of service.

In the past, most organizations haven't rewarded employees who didn't take their sick days. (Thus, if the worker wasn't "out sick" for his or her permissible seven or eight days per year, he or she simply lost the time off.) Since this acted as a somewhat illogical negative incentive system, there's been a tendency for organizations to buy back unused sick leave time. They do this by paying their employees a daily equivalent pay for each sick leave day not used. One drawback to this is that it can encourage sick employees to come to work regardless of their illness.[5]

◆ SEVERANCE PAY

Some employers provide **severance pay**—a one-time payment—when terminating an employee. The payment may range from three or four days' wages to as much as one year's salary. Others today provide "bridge" severance pay by keeping employees (especially managers) on the payroll for several months till they've found a new job.

Such payments make sense on several grounds. It is a humanitarian gesture as well as good public relations. In addition, most managers expect employees to give them at least one or two weeks notice if they plan to quit; it therefore seems appropriate to provide at least one or two weeks severance pay if an employee is being terminated.

Plant closings around the country have put thousands of employees out of work, often with little or no notice and no severance pay. Many states have been attempting to fight such closings, and a recent Supreme Court ruling (*Fort Halifax Packing Co.* v. *Coyne*, 1987) paves the way for states to cushion the economic impact of such closings. The Court has ruled that states may force employers to provide severance pay to workers who lose their jobs because of plant closings. In the *Fort Halifax* case, laid-off packing company workers will be paid amounts ranging from $490 to $8,680.[6] The Worker Adjustment and Retraining Notification ("plant closing") Act of 1989 requires covered employers to give employees 60 days written notice of plant closures or mass layoffs.

◆ SUPPLEMENTAL UNEMPLOYMENT BENEFITS

These benefits provide, in effect, for a "guaranteed annual income." In some industries (such as auto making), shutdowns to reduce inventories or change machinery are common, and in the past employees were laid off or furloughed and had to depend on unemployment insurance. **Supplemental unemployment benefits** are paid by the company and *supplement* unemployment benefits, thus enabling the workers to better maintain their standards of living. Supplemental benefits are becoming more prevalent in collective bargaining agreements and provide supplemental unemployment benefits (over and above state employment compensation) for three contingencies: layoffs, reduced workweeks, and relocation. These plans are normally found in heavy manufacturing operations such as in the auto and steel industries. Here, weekly or monthly plant shutdowns are typical, and some plan for guaranteeing minimum annual income is more appropriate.

INSURANCE BENEFITS

♦ WORKERS' COMPENSATION

Workers' compensation laws[7] are aimed at providing sure, prompt income and medical benefits to work-related accident victims or their dependents, regardless of fault.[8] Every state has its own workers' compensation law. However, there has been continuing congressional interest in the past few years in establishing minimum national standards for state compensation laws, and this has provided an impetus for improving employer's job-related accident and illness benefits. Improvements have included expanded medical coverage, increased weekly benefits, and rehabilitation provisions.[9] Some states have their own insurance programs, but most require employers to carry workers' compensation insurance with private state-approved insurance companies.

Workers' compensation benefits can be either monetary or medical. In the event of a worker's death or disablement, the person's dependents are paid a cash benefit based on prior earnings—usually one-half to two-thirds of the worker's average weekly wage, per week of employment. In most states there is a set time limit—such as 500 weeks—for which benefits can be paid. If the injury causes a specific loss (such as an arm), the employee may receive additional benefits based on a statutory list of losses, even though he or she may return to work. In addition to these cash benefits, employers must furnish medical, surgical, and hospital services needed by the employee.

For an injury or illness to be covered by workers' compensation, it is only necessary to prove that it arose while the employee was on the job. It does not matter that the employee may have been at fault; if he or she was on the job when the injury occurred, he or she is entitled to workers' compensation. For example, suppose all employees are instructed to wear safety goggles when working at their machines. One worker does not and is injured while on the job. The company must still provide workers' compensation benefits; the fact that he was at fault in no way waives his claim to benefits.

Workers' compensation is usually handled by state administrative commissions. However, neither the state nor the federal government contributes any funds for workers' compensation. *Employers* are responsible for insuring themselves or for arranging for the appropriate coverage through an insurance company.

Controlling Workers' Compensation Costs

Minimizing the number of workers' compensation claims is an important goal for all employers. While the claims themselves will generally be paid by the employer's insurance company, the costs of the premiums are a function of the number and amounts of claims that are paid. Minimizing such claims is thus important.

In practice, there are four main ways you can reduce such claims. First, screen out before hiring applicants who have an unusually high incidence of filing such claims. The insurance company providing your firm with workers' compensation insurance will generally have access to such data. Second (as explained in more detail in Chapter 19, Employee Safety and

Health), you can screen out accident-prone workers and also reduce accident-causing conditions in your facilities. Third, you can reduce the accidents and health problems that trigger these claims, for instance, by instituting effective safety and health programs and by complying with government standards on these matters.

Finally, you can institute rehabilitation programs for injured employees, since workers' compensation costs increase the longer an employee is unable to return to work. The object here, therefore, is to institute corrective physical therapy programs (including exercise equipment, career counseling to guide injured employees into new, less strenuous jobs, and nursing assistance, for instance) so as to reintegrate workers compensation recipients back into your work force.[10]

◆ LIFE INSURANCE

group life insurance Provides for lower rates for the employer or employee and includes all employees, including new employees, regardless of health or physical condition.

Most employers provide **group life insurance** plans for their employees. Because it is a group plan, it contains several important advantages for employers and employees. As a group, employees can obtain lower rates than if they bought such insurance as individuals. And group plans usually contain a provision for including all employees—including new ones—regardless of health or physical condition.

In most cases the employer pays 100% of the base premium, which usually provides life insurance equal to about two years' salary. Additional life insurance coverage is then paid for by the employee. In some cases the cost of even the base premium is split 50:50 or 80:20 between the employer and employee, respectively. In general, there are three key personnel policy areas to be addressed: the benefits-paid schedule (benefits are usually tied to the annual earnings of the employee), supplemental benefits (continued life insurance coverage after retirement, double indemnity, and so on), and financing (the amount and percent that the employee contributes).[11]

◆ HOSPITALIZATION, MEDICAL, AND DISABILITY INSURANCE

Most employers make available to their employees some type of hospitalization, medical, and disability insurance; along with life insurance, these benefits form the cornerstone of almost all benefit programs.[12] Hospitalization, health, and disability insurance is aimed at providing protection against hospitalization costs and loss of income arising from accidents or illness occurring from off-the-job causes. Most employers purchase such insurance from life insurance companies, casualty insurance companies, or Blue Cross (for hospital expenses) and Blue Shield (for physician expenses) organizations.

Most health insurance plans provide, at a minimum, *basic hospitalization, surgical*, and *medical insurance* for all eligible employees as a group. As with life insurance, group rates are usually lower than individual rates and are generally available to all employees—including new ones—regardless of health or physical condition. Most basic plans pay for hospital room and board, surgery charges, and medical expenses (such as doctors' visits to the hospital). Some group plans also provide *major medical* coverage to meet high medical expenses that result from long-term or serious illnesses; with hospitalization costs rapidly rising this is an increasingly popular option.

Many employers are also sponsoring health-related insurance plans covering things like eye care and dental services. In fact, dental insurance plans have been one of the fastest-growing items over the past few years, with the number of persons in the United States with dental coverage growing from 4.6 million in 1967 to about 100 million today.[13] In most employer-sponsored dental plans, participants must pay a specified amount of deductible dental expenses (typically $25 or $50 each year) before the plan kicks in with benefits. In a majority of the cases the participants in such plans have premiums paid for entirely by their employers, though.[14]

Accidental death and dismemberment coverage is another option. It provides a fixed lump-sum benefit in addition to life insurance benefits when death is accidental and also provides a range of benefits in case of accidental loss of limbs or sight. Other options provide payments for diagnostic visits to the doctor's office, vision care, hearing aid plans, payment for prescription drugs, and dental care plans. Employers must provide the same health care benefits to employees over the age of 65 that are provided to younger workers, even though the older workers are eligible for the federally funded *Medicare* health insurance plan. Prior to that time, many older employees had no choice but to take the (often inferior) Medicare option.[15]

Disability insurance is aimed at providing income protection or compensation for loss of salary due to illness or accident. The disability payments usually begin when normal sick leave is used up and may continue to provide income to age 65 or beyond.[16] The disability benefits usually range from 50 to 75% of the employee's base pay if he or she is disabled.

The **Health Maintenance Organization (HMO)** Act of 1973 was aimed at stimulating a nationwide prepaid health care system, *requiring* employers to offer an HMO as an alternative to conventional group health plans. Many employers therefore offer membership in an HMO as a hospital/medical option. The HMO itself is a medical organization consisting of several specialists (surgeons, psychiatrists, and so on). The HMO generally provides routine round-the-clock medical services at a specific site and usually stresses preventive medicine in a clinic-type arrangement to employees who pay a nominal fee. The HMO also receives a fixed annual fee per employee from the employer (or employer and employee), regardless of whether any service actually is provided.[17]

health maintenance organization (HMO) A prepaid health care system that generally provides routine round-the-clock medical services as well as preventive medicine in a clinic-type arrangement for employees, who pay a nominal fee in addition to the fixed annual fee the employer pays.

Reducing Health Benefits' Costs

The average cost per employee of health benefits has risen from about $300 in 1980 to over $1,800 today in some firms; giant firms like General Motors spend hundreds of millions of dollars per year just on health care benefits. As a result, human resources executives listed "health care cost containment" as the issue that most concerns personnel and human resources executives in both 1988 and 1989, far ahead of concerns such as downsizing and delayering, AIDS in the workplace, EEO/AA, and occupational safety and health.[18] Caught between rising benefits costs and the belt tightening occurring in firms today, managing and reducing health care costs now therefore tops many manager's to-do lists. As a result, beginning in the early 1980s, many employers have been changing their medical plans to do the following:

1. Move away from "first-dollar" medical benefits. In 1982, only about 30% of the surveyed companies required employees to pay a front-end deductible on hospital expenses. By 1990, the percentage had more than doubled, with 70% using a deductible.

2. Increase annual deductibles. In 1982, the average deductible was $100. Today, almost 40% use a deductible of $150 or more.

3. Reimburse less than 100% of hospital costs. In 1982, 67% of companies provided full reimbursement for hospital costs versus only 42% of companies in 1990.

4. Limit the annual out-of-pocket medical expenses an employee pays. Interestingly, the number of plans with a "stop-loss" amount, which limits the out-of-pocket expense an employee would have to pay during a year, has increased from 80% to 89% recently. In other words, while employers are asking employees to pay higher deductibles, the companies are giving employees more protection against catastrophic medical expenses.

5. Require medical contributions. Whereas only 31% of employers required employee contributions to their medical premiums in 1982, about 46% of plans required them by 1990.[19]

In addition, more and more firms are focusing on health promotion and preventive health care as a way of reducing their health care program costs. For example, according to one survey, 56% of the firms were sponsoring drug and alcohol abuse programs, 31% were offering stop-smoking sessions, 45% were providing physical fitness classes, 18% have exercise facilities on company premises, 36% were offering stress management seminars and hypertension screening, and 29% were providing education on nutrition and helping employees lose weight. Most employers—70%—were training employees in first aid and CPR. Most of the employers were also increasing their communication efforts: 69% explain the problem of rising health care costs to employees and 54% offer tips about how to use company health benefits wisely.[20]

Figures 12.1, 12.2, and 12.3 illustrate how one firm—Ryder System, Inc.—is implementing health care plan cost-control programs. The first figure (12.1) is a memo to employees from M. A. Burns, Ryder's president, introducing the firm's benefit improvement and cost-control program. The second, a brochure entitled "Benefit Improvements and Cost Control Program" (Figure 12.2) summarizes the cost-control measures the firm's "Take Care" program now includes. As you can see, second surgical opinions, encouraging employees to be "amateur auditors" in reviewing their hospital bills, encouraging outpatient survey, and other modifications including raising the deductible amount aim at reducing the employer's health care plan costs or at least stemming the increase in these costs. Employees are encouraged to talk to their doctor to get information about their conditions and any treatment or medication prescribed, and to be educated consumers of health care services. The third figure (12.3) presents a brochure called "Get a Second Opinion," which lists the procedure to be used in getting a second surgical opinion. For example, the employee should tell the doctor that he or she wants a second surgical opinion, and then get the name of a specialist or consulting surgeon. Questions to be asked include "What are the reasons for my surgery?" "What are the benefits of this surgery?" and "How will it improve my health?" As indicated in the third figure, the Ryder medical plan now requires a second surgical opinion for certain elective, nonemergency surgeries such as a back surgery, cataract removal, and coronary bypass surgery. During the period the Ryder Take Care program was put into effect, the number of confinements fell from 2,819 to 1,843 and the number of days confinement dropped from 13,607 and 9,493. In other words, both number of confinements and number of days confined dropped by about one-third, probably as a result of the new program.

Managing Health Care Costs: AIDS

By now, the fatal nature of AIDS—Acquired Immune Deficiency Syndrome—is unfortunately well known to everyone.[21] Between the discovery of the illness in 1981 and 1987, 50,000 Americans were diagnosed as having AIDS. Recently, 400 new cases were being reported to the Centers for Disease Control (CDC) each week, with about 300 dying each week from AIDS-related

FIGURE 12.1
Cost Control Program Cover Letter

RYDER SYSTEM INC.
3600 NW 82nd Avenue PO Box 520816
Miami Florida 33152

August 15, 1983

TO: Ryder Medical Plan Participants

FROM: M. A. Burns, President

SUBJECT: **BENEFIT IMPROVEMENTS AND COST CONTROL PROGRAM**

The Ryder Medical Plan provides benefits to protect employees from the financial burden which can accompany medical problems. We want to continue to provide this protection and to keep quality health care affordable for our employees, their dependents, and the company. However, we can no longer do this alone; we need your help.

It is no secret that health care costs are increasing at alarming rates. In the past ten years Ryder's costs for medical and dental benefits have risen from less than $300 to over $1800 per employee per year. As individuals and as a corporation, it becomes imperative that we take steps to control this excessive medical inflation.

There are a number of approaches to controlling medical costs. Many companies have transferred the burden to their employees by slashing benefits or by increasing employee contributions. Ryder management has reviewed our Medical Plan and feels that such drastic measures are not necessary at this time. However, September 1 we will implement some modifications to the Ryder Medical Plan to control these medical costs. This program involves improvements in coverage as well as changes which are designed to make us more concerned health care consumers.

As a company, we intend to do our part as well. Where the volume of employee usage warrants it, we will contact hospitals and seek discounts for timely payments. We will monitor surgical bills and apply "Reasonable and Customary" checks to eliminate the payment of excessive charges.

We have initiated a TAKE CARE program to help our employees become educated consumers. A series of pamphlets will explain the modifications to the Ryder Medical Plan and encourage you to seek the most benefit from your health care dollar.

In short, we intend to encourage good health care habits and the prudent use of our nation's health care system so our employees can continue to enjoy quality health care.

TAKE CARE: TAKE CARE of yourself – TAKE CARE of your family – TAKE CARE of how you use your health benefits – and they will be there to TAKE CARE of you.

Tony

MAB:jmf

FIGURE 12.2
Ryder Cost Control Program

1985
BENEFIT
IMPROVEMENTS
AND COST
CONTROL
PROGRAM

TAKE CARE

TAKE CARE

Ryder Financial and Communication Services
5042 Linbar Drive Nashville, TN 37211

93120 Printed in U.S.A. 12/84 1M

Do Your Part to Help Control Soaring Medical Costs

Talk to Your Doctor. Ask questions. You have the right to information about your condition and any treatment or medication your doctor recommends. If your physician is using medical terms, ask for an explanation in words that are familiar to you. If medication is prescribed, ask what it will do, what effects you should expect.

Become an Educated Consumer of Health Care Services. Read about what's new in alternative health care. Newspapers, radio and television have frequent news items and in-depth programming concerning this very important issue.

Consider Alternatives to Hospital Stays. Many procedures today can be done easily and safely in your physician's office, in an ambulatory care center, or in a hospital's outpatient facilities. Continuing improvements in equipment and techniques make this alternative more and more viable. Ask your doctor if it's appropriate for your surgery—most will be happy to accommodate you. It saves them time and often difficult hospital scheduling as well. After surgery and the acute care following it, recuperation at home is usually more agreeable, comfortable and convenient.

Take a Look at Your Lifestyle. You've been talking about it —now do it—stop smoking, lose weight, exercise, learn to handle stress. There are many services available for little or no cost which will help you achieve your personal improvement goals. Your health is your responsibility; it depends on your decisions. You have to decide how to live, whether to see a doctor, which doctor to see, how soon to go, and whether to take the advice offered. To be healthy, you have to be in charge.

Send for Your Free Copy of "TAKE CARE OF YOURSELF." To help you get started on your way to becoming a better informed health care consumer and improving your lifestyle, we are offering you a free copy of "TAKE CARE OF YOURSELF," a consumer's guide to medical care written by Donald M. Vickery, M.D. and James F. Fries, M.D. To get your free copy, just complete the order form on the enclosed brochure, or write to M. A. Burns, President, Ryder System, Inc., P.O. Box 661218, Miami Springs, Florida 33266

FIGURE 12.2
(continued)

1985 Benefit Improvements & Cost Control Program

This brochure was developed to summarize the 1985 FCS Comprehensive Plan improvements, modifications and cost control measures. Read it carefully. You'll find increased coverage in several areas, and you'll find changes in the way some benefits are administered. Over the coming months you will be receiving additional brochures that further explain the details of this program.

We are asking you to **TAKE CARE**—Your decision to use your benefits wisely can result in medical services which are more convenient and less costly for you and your family.

Effective January 1, 1985

Second Surgical Opinion
You will be encouraged to seek a second opinion from a medical doctor (M.D.) for a specified list of elective surgeries. You will be reimbursed 100% of the reasonable and customary charges for this consultation.

TAKE CARE If a second opinion is not obtained for these designated procedures, doctor and hospital charges related to that surgery will be reimbursed at 64% of Plan coverage.

Amateur Auditors
If you find that your hospital bill includes charges for services that you did not receive and you have the hospital adjust the bill, 25% of the savings realized will be passed on to you. This provision applies to all hospital invoices totaling less than $10,000 (hospital invoices which exceed $10,000 are professionally audited).

Outpatient Surgery
The FCS Plan has been improved to cover all hospital charges for any out-patient surgery at 100% up to $1,000.

All related charges, such as surgeon, radiologist, anesthesiologist and pathologist fees will be reimbursed at 80% of the reasonable and customary charges after satisfaction of the calendar year deductible.

Chiropractic
A maximum of 25 visits will be considered in any 12-month period. Chiropractic benefits are limited to the lesser of $25 or 50% of the actual charge, excluding initial X-rays, after satisfaction of the calendar year deductible.

Other Modifications
• An employee will only be considered an employee under the Plan, that is, he or she cannot also be considered as a dependent of another employee. Dependent children will be eligible for benefits under only one employee's (or parent's) coverage.

• All hospital emergency room charges are considered under the comprehensive provisions, at 80% after satisfaction of the deductible, with the exception of charges resulting from an accident.

• The employee contribution for optional medical coverage of dependents has been increased by 10%, and will now be $46.48 per month.

Medicare Coverage
Employees age 65 through 69 and their eligible dependents are eligible for participation in the FCS Comprehensive Medical Plan and Medicare. Each employee will have the opportunity to elect which Plan is primary in accordance with governmental regulations. The FCS Comprehensive Medical Plan will be primary and Medicare secondary unless the employee elects otherwise. Benefits payable under this Plan and Medicare will be coordinated.

Comprehensive Deductible
The Comprehensive deductible amount will be increased to $200 per family per calendar year.

Life Insurance
Basic Life Insurance has been increased to 1 x annual base pay.

Supplemental Life Insurance has two improvements:

A. Rate has been reduced from $.40/$1000 to $.35/$1000

B. An employee can elect supplemental insurance equal to 1, 2 or 3 x annual pay.

Example:
An employee earning $6.25 per hour—equals $13,000 per year—can purchase:

	Monthly Payroll Deduction
1 x earnings $13,000	$ 4.55
2 x earnings $26,000	$ 9.10
3 x earnings $39,000	$13.65

These changes apply to all employees covered by the FCS Comprehensive Plan. This summary provides only a brief description of the improvements and changes. The provisions of the FCS Comprehensive Plan are the determining authority in the event of any conflict between the information presented here and that specified by the Plan document.

Your benefit plan's booklet is being revised to reflect these changes. You should review it carefully when you receive it.

If you have questions regarding any of the revisions, call the **TAKE CARE** Hot Line: **(305) 593-3537**

FIGURE 12.3
Ryder "Get a Second Opinion" Pamphlet

TAKE CARE...

GET A SECOND OPINION

ASK YOUR DOCTOR
OR CALL TOLL-FREE
(800) 638-6833

TAKE CARE

Know the advantages

Consider the following reasons why you should take advantage of this program. A second surgical opinion may:

☐ Prevent an unnecessary operation.

☐ Relieve your doubts about the need for an operation.

☐ Recommend an alternative form of treatment.

☐ Save you money that might have been spent on unnecessary surgical or medical bills.

The final decision is yours

The final decision to have the operation rests with you and your family. After discussing your condition with two physicians, you'll be more likely to have the information you need to make an informed choice.

TAKE CARE . . . Get a Second Surgical Opinion.

TAKE CARE

Call the **TAKE CARE** Hot Line (305) 593-3537 for more information regarding the Second Surgical Opinion Provision of the Ryder Medical Plan.

Ryder System, Inc. 3600 N.W. 82nd Ave. Miami, FL 33166 Printed in U.S.A. 98315M

**Ryder Medical Plan
—Second Surgical Opinion Provision**

Effective September 1, 1983, the Ryder Medical Plan requires a Second Surgical Opinion for certain elective, non-emergency surgeries for full coverage under the Plan. The second surgical opinion must be sought from a Medical Doctor (M.D.). The cost of the second opinion is covered by the Plan.

If you are advised by your doctor to have one of the surgeries listed below and you consult another doctor for a second opinion, you will be eligible for full benefits coverage under the Ryder Medical Plan if you decide to have the surgery. This coverage applies regardless of the outcome of the second opinion.

If the second doctor disagrees with the first, and you wish a third opinion, the cost of the third consultation is covered under the Major Medical Provisions of the Plan.

If you do not consult a second doctor to obtain a second opinion concerning recommended surgery, payment of eligible hospital and doctor charges relating to that surgery will be reduced to 80% of Plan coverage.

The following non-emergency surgeries require a second surgical opinion under the Ryder Medical Plan.

☐ Adenoidectomy
☐ Back Surgery
☐ Breast Surgery
☐ Cataract Removal
☐ Coronary Bypass
☐ D&C (Dilation and Currettage)
☐ Deviated Septum Repair
☐ Foot Surgery including Bunionectomy
☐ Gall Bladder Removal
☐ Hemorrhoidectomy
☐ Hernia Repair
☐ Hysterectomy
☐ Knee Surgery
☐ Prostate Removal
☐ Tonsillectomy
☐ Varicose Vein Surgery

The Second Surgical Opinion Provision does not apply in the case of emergency, nor does it apply to any surgical procedure not listed above. If you obtain a second opinion for a surgical procedure not listed above, the fee for that consultation will be covered under Major Medical Provisions of the Plan.

FIGURE 12.3
(continued)

TAKE CARE . . . Get a Second Surgical Opinion

Your doctor has recommended that you have surgery. There are risks and benefits associated with any surgery and you should know the risks and benefits of the operation your doctor is recommending. And, since doctors do not always agree on the best method of treatment, it is in your best interest to get a Second Surgical Opinion.

One doctor may recommend surgery; another may tell you to wait a while; another may suggest a more conservative type of treatment. When you ask the right questions, receive thorough information, and have the opinions of two doctors, you increase your chances of making the decision that is right for you.

Getting a second surgical opinion may delay your decision regarding surgery. This normally isn't a problem, because elective, non-emergency surgery usually doesn't need to be performed immediately—but be sure to check with your doctor to be certain that a short delay will not be harmful.

A second surgical opinion *should not* be used to delay or avoid having an emergency operation. When there is time, a second opinion should give you additional information to help you decide if surgery is the best alternative for you.

If surgery is needed on an emergency basis, it must be done right away or within a few days, as in the case of acute appendicitis or injuries from an accident. *Because any delay could be life-threatening, second opinions are seldom possible for this kind of surgery.*

How to get a Second Surgical Opinion

Getting a second surgical opinion is simple. Follow these steps:

1. **Tell your doctor that you want a Second Surgical Opinion.**

   Since consultations are a normal part of medical practice, most physicians will encourage you to seek a second opinion.

2. **Get the name of a specialist or consulting surgeon.**

   Don't hesitate to ask your doctor to give you the names of two or more doctors to see. If your doctor makes a referral and he or she is in a group practice, the consultant should not belong to the same group practice.

   The U. S. Government provides a toll-free number which you can call for the names of specialists in your local area:

   (800) 638-6833

   In Maryland, the number to call is (800) 492-6603.

   Other sources for names of consultants are a teaching hospital or medical school in your area, the local medical society, the local Professional Standards Review Organization, or you can call the **TAKE CARE** Hot Line (305) 593-3537.

3. **Make an appointment with the consultant of your choice.**

   Tell this physician you have had surgery recommended, the type of surgery, and that you would like a second opinion.

4. **Have your medical records sent to the consultant.**

   Although this is not required, it is helpful for the consulting physician to see the results of previous tests and examinations. If the specialist performs tests, they also will be covered by the Ryder Medical Plan.

Ask questions

You have the right to ask questions about your condition and the operation. You also have the right to be given answers which are easy to understand. If a physician is using medical terms, ask for an explanation in words that are familiar to you.

When surgery is recommended, you should ask your physician the following questions. The answers will help you decide what to do.

- [ ] What are the reasons for my surgery?
- [ ] What are the benefits of this surgery? How will it improve my health?
- [ ] What are the risks of this surgery?
- [ ] Will there be after or continuing effects from this surgery?
- [ ] How long will my recovery take?
- [ ] What will happen if I do not have the operation?
- [ ] Are there other ways of treating my condition?

Ask any other questions you might have. Weigh the benefits and risks of having the operation against the benefits and risks of *not* having it.

If the second doctor agrees that surgery is the best way to treat your problems, he or she will usually refer you back to the first doctor for the surgery.

If the second doctor disagrees with the first, you'll probably find that you have the facts you need to make your decision. If you are confused by different opinions, you may wish to go back to the first doctor to further discuss your case. Or you may wish to talk to a third physician.

conditions. The CDC estimates that over 1.5 million Americans are infected with the AIDS virus.

In addition to the human suffering caused by AIDS, its potential impact on insurance companies and employers plans must be considered. At the present time anticipated costs approach $150,000 per claimant, a number with the potential for undermining many benefits plans, if left unchecked.

The problem is that reining in these costs is hampered by several unique aspects of the AIDS disease. While the disease at the present time is always terminal, intensive medical intervention is usually only necessary for short periods of time: For most of the time, the need is more custodial than anything else, and can often be as well administered at home or in nonhospital facilities as inside hospitals themselves. Yet while reduced costs are therefore possible with alternative treatment facilities, most employers' medical plans generally don't cover such alternative treatment facilities. Such plans are thus self-defeating in requiring more expensive care where such care is not needed. There is also a constellation of psychological barriers that inhibit early diagnosis and more cost-effective treatment. Many AIDS sufferers are reluctant to discuss their illness with their employers for fear of losing their job and/or their insurance benefits. At the same time, the reactions of fearful coworkers to AIDS sufferers often further impedes an open discussion of the problem. The very nature of the disease also makes traditional cost-containment efforts virtually useless: obtaining second surgical opinions, outpatient surgery, or mandating psychiatric restrictions have little or no bearing in the treatment of AIDS, for instance.

Several insurance companies have concluded that the best way to control the cost of AIDS is to rethink the benefits plans themselves, with an eye toward providing required care in the least costly way. This often means treating the AIDS sufferer in his or her home and allowing this cost to be paid under the benefits plan (as is usually not allowed now). The emphasis increasingly will thus be on *individual case management (ICM)*. Here a special ICM nurse will be assigned to the patient and an alternative treatment plan will be designed. The plan itself will be individualized, taking into consideration the patient's ability to care for himself or herself, the availability of others who are able to help in the person's treatment, and the age and condition of the patient. A case history can illustrate this:

> When the patient was admitted to the hospital, the insurance carrier's precertification office questioned him at length and determined that he was suffering from a late stage of mylobacterium intracellular, an opportunistic disease most commonly found among AIDS patients. After six weeks in the hospital, the patient was discharged to an intensive home care routine costing $390 per day. If he had remained in the hospital, the cost would have been $1,100 per day. The attempt at home care lasted only 12 days, at which time the patient's condition degenerated to a point where permanent hospitalization was necessary. Even this modest success with home care resulted in a savings to the plan of $8,520.[22]

In summary, several steps recommended by one expert to help contain the health care benefits costs associated with AIDS are as follows:

Medical plans should be expanded to provide coverage for outpatient services and alternate treatment facilities.

Hospitalization precertification programs should be expanded to provide early warning of AIDS patients.

Individual care management should be used to find the most appropriate type of care for each individual.

Employers should not penalize or stigmatize those employees who admit they have AIDS.[23]

Mental Health Benefits

The mental health component of their health plans is the fastest-rising benefits cost for many employers. It's estimated that employers spend just over 8% of their health plan dollars on mental health treatment.[24] These costs are rising quickly, because of widespread drug and alcohol problems in society, an increase in the number of states (to 29 today) that require employers to offer a minimum package of mental health benefits, and because other health care claims are also higher for employees with high mental health claims.

For the employer, the bottom line is that the cost of mental health care benefits is substantial. In one financial services firm in New York City, the company found it paid $1.5 million on mental health benefits in 1987, a 61% increase over 1986 costs. The $1.5 million represented over 37% of the company's total major medical costs.

The first step in slowing rising mental health benefits like these is for employers to identify whether and to what extent a problem exists. Thus, after assessing the size of the problem, this financial services firm rejected the idea of placing across-the-board limits on mental health coverage. Instead, they redesigned the mental health portion of their health benefits plan. The new plan emphasizes a utilization review to certify treatment, increased outpatient benefits, and a selected network of cost-efficient providers along with the provision of customized treatment plans in a negotiated provider network. The new program cut mental health benefit plans significantly while still providing needed benefits for company employees.[25]

The Pregnancy Discrimination Act

Pregnancy Discrimination Act (PDA) An amendment to Title VII of the Civil Rights Act that prohibits sex discrimination based on "pregnancy, childbirth, or related medical conditions." It requires employers to provide benefits—including sick leave and disability benefits and health and medical insurance—the same as for any employee not able to work because of disability.

The **Pregnancy Discrimination Act (PDA)**, technically an amendment to Title VII of the Civil Rights Act, became a law in 1978. It aimed at prohibiting sex discrimination based on "pregnancy, childbirth, or related medical conditions."[26] Before enactment of this law, temporary disability benefits for pregnancies were generally paid in the form of either sick leave or disability insurance, if at all. However, while most employers provide temporary disability income to their employees for up to 26 weeks for most illnesses, those that provided benefits for pregnancy usually limited benefits to only 6 weeks for normal pregnancies. Many believed that the shorter duration of pregnancy benefits constituted discrimination based on sex, and it was this issue that the Pregnancy Discrimination Act was aimed at settling.

Specifically, the act requires employers to treat women affected by pregnancy, childbirth, or related medical conditions the same as any employees not able to work, with respect to all benefits, including sick leave and disability benefits, and health and medical insurance. Thus, it is now illegal for most employers to discriminate against women, by providing benefits of lower amount or duration for pregnancy, childbirth, or related medical conditions. For example, if an employer had provided up to 26 weeks of temporary disability income to employees for all illnesses, it is now required to provide up to 26 weeks for pregnancy and childbirth also, rather than the more typical 6 weeks that prevailed before the act.

While the Pregnancy Discrimination Act requires that for purposes of benefits pregnancy be treated as any other disability, it does not address the more basic issue of whether women who take pregnancy disability leave have a right to return to their old jobs after having a baby. In January 1987 the U.S. Supreme Court decided that a California law granting leave and reinstatement rights to pregnant women was valid. Furthermore, HR770, the Family and Medical Leave Act, was introduced into Congress in 1989. If eventually passed, such a law will allow employees to take up to 10 weeks of disability leave in any one year of parental leave. Workers taking such leave would be entitled to be restored by their employer to the position they held when the leave commenced or to an equivalent position, and the provisions would apply to both men and women.

Interestingly, even some feminist groups have come out against granting special pregnancy benefits to women. They say it mediates against equality in the workplace by seeking special treatment with regard to select issues. Furthermore, they argue that special benefits for pregnancy make women of childbearing age potentially more expensive employees and thereby increases the likelihood they will be discriminated against, for instance, in hiring. It remains to be seen what the final disposition of this matter will be.

In the meantime, though, states and companies are moving ahead on their own. For example, 6 states have recently passed parental leave laws, bringing the total with such laws to 15. And many firms, including Campbell Soup and American Express, have policies allowing up to three months' unpaid leaves for all employees—male or female—with a newborn at home. We'll return to a discussion of parental leave shortly.

Cobra Requirements

The ominously titled COBRA—the Comprehensive Omnibus Budget Reconciliation Act—was passed by Congress in 1985 and signed into law April 27, 1986. Among other things, it requires most private employers to make available to terminated or retired employees and their families continued health benefits for a period of time, generally 18 months. The former employee must pay for this coverage, as well as a small fee for administrative costs.

You need to take care in administering COBRA, especially when it comes to informing employees of their COBRA rights. For one thing, you don't want a terminated or retired employee to get injured and then come back and claim that he or she didn't know he could have continued his insurance coverage. Also, you want to comply with the law. Therefore, when a new employee first becomes eligible for your company's insurance plan, an explanation of COBRA rights should be received and acknowledged. More important, any employees who are separated from the company for any reason should have to sign a form acknowledging that they have received and understand their COBRA rights.

RETIREMENT BENEFITS

♦ SOCIAL SECURITY

Social Security Provides three types of benefits: retirement income at the age of 62 and thereafter; survivor's or death benefits payable to the employee's dependents, regardless of age at time of death; and disability benefits payable to disabled employees and their dependents. These benefits are payable only if the employee is insured under the Social Security Act.

retirement benefits Provide the employee with an income when he or she retires.

Many people assume that **Social Security** is something they collect only when they are old, but it actually provides three types of benefits. First are the familiar **retirement benefits**. These provide you with an income if you retire at age 62 or thereafter *and* are insured under the Social Security Act. Second, there are *survivor's* or death benefits. These provide monthly payments to your dependents regardless of your age at death, again assuming you were insured under the Social Security Act. Finally, there are *disability payments*. These provide monthly payments to you and your dependents if you become totally disabled for work and meet certain specified work requirements.[27] The Medicare program (which provides a wide range of health services to people 65 or over) is also administered through the Social Security system.

Social Security (technically, federal old age and survivor's insurance) is paid for by a tax (of a total of 15.02% of pay as of 1989) on the employee's wages; employees and their employer share equally in this tax. If you are self-employed, you pay the entire sum, less 2% of your self-employment income, or $5,859 at most.

♦ **PENSION PLANS**

pension plans Plans that provide a fixed sum when employees reach a predetermined retirement age or when they can no longer work due to disability.

group pension plan A plan in which the employer and/or employee makes a set contribution to a pension fund.

deferred profit-sharing plan A plan in which a certain amount of profits is credited to each employee's account, payable at retirement, termination, or death.

savings plan A plan in which employees contribute for their retirement a fixed percentage of their weekly wage, usually matched by a certain percentage by the employer.

defined benefit A plan that contains a formula for determining retirement benefits.

defined contribution A plan in which the employer's contribution to employees' retirement or savings funds are specified.

There are three basic types of **pension plans**.[28] In the **group pension plan**, the employer (and possibly the employee) makes a set contribution to a pension fund. A second type of pension plan is actually a **deferred profit-sharing plan**. Here, a certain amount of profits is credited to each employee's account. These benefits are then distributed to the employee (or his dependents) upon his retirement or death. Finally, under **savings plans** employees set aside a fixed percentage of their weekly wages for their retirement; the company usually matches from 50% to 100% of the employee's contribution.[29]

The basic types of pension plans can be further subdivided. For example, we can distinguish between defined benefit pension plans and defined contribution benefit plans.[30] A **defined benefit** pension plan contains a formula for determining retirement benefits so that the actual benefits to be received are defined ahead of time. For example, the plan might include a formula that designates a dollar amount or a percentage of annual salary for computing the individual's eventual pension. On the other hand, a **defined contribution** plan specifies what contribution the employer will make to a retirement or savings fund set up for the employee. The defined contribution plan does not define the eventual benefit amount, only the periodic contribution to the plan. In a defined benefit plan, the employee knows ahead of time what his or her retirement benefits will be upon retirement. With a defined contribution plan, the employee cannot be sure of his or her retirement benefits; those benefits depend on both the amounts contributed to the fund plus the retirement fund's investment earnings.

There are two major types of defined contribution plans.[31] In *savings and thrift plans*, employees contribute a portion of their earnings to a fund and this contribution is usually matched in whole or in part by the employer. In *deferred profit sharing plans* employers typically contribute a portion of their profits to the pension fund, regardless of the level of employee contribution.

The entire area of pension planning is an extremely complicated one, partly because of the many federal laws governing pensions. For example, companies want to ensure that their pension contributions are tax deductible and it's therefore necessary to adhere to the pertinent income tax codes. We've also seen (in Chapter 10) that the Employee Retirement Income Security Act of 1974 (ERISA) restricts what companies can, cannot, and must do in regard to pension plans (more on this in a moment). In unionized companies, the union must be allowed to participate in the administration of the pension plan (under the Taft-Hartley Act).

While an employer usually has to develop a pension plan to meet its own unique needs, there are several key policy issues to consider:[32]

Membership requirements. For example, what is the minimum age or minimum service at which employees become eligible for a pension?

Benefit formula. This usually ties the pension to the employee's final earnings, or an average of his or her last three of four years' earnings.

Retirement requirements. Although 65 is often considered a "standard" retirement age, federal law prohibits forced retirement of any competent employee. Yet most people opt for early retirement.[33] In companies such as General Motors, for example, only a small proportion of production and office workers retire as late as 65.[34] Partly due to union pressure and partly because early retirement helps open up jobs for younger employees, many employers now encourage early retirement. For example, some plans call for "30 and out." This permits an employee to retire after 30 years of continuous service, regardless of the person's age. In some cases—such as in the U.S. Army and among New York City employees—employees can retire with reduced pensions after 20 years of continuous service, regardless of the employee's age.[35]

Funding. The question of how the plan is to be funded is another key issue. One aspect of this is whether the plan will be contributory or noncontributory. In the former, contributions to the pension funds are made by both employees and the employer. In a noncontributory fund—the prevailing type, by the way—only the employer contributes. Another aspect of this is that many pension plans are underfunded. Although under the Employee Retirement Income Security Act most pension plans are now "guaranteed" (as explained following), the fact of the matter is that in an alarming number of cases many employers' pension funds do not have adequate funds to cover expected pension benefits.[36]

vesting Provision that money placed in a pension fund cannot be forfeited for any reason.

Vesting. **Vesting** is another critical issue in pension planning. It refers to the money that the employer and employee have placed in the latter's pension fund *which cannot be forfeited for any reason.* Naturally, the employees' contributions are always theirs and cannot be forfeited. However, until the passage of ERISA—the Employee Retirement Income Security Act—in 1974, the employer's contribution was not necessarily vested. Thus, suppose a person worked for a company for 30 years and the company then went out of business one year before he or she was to retire at age 65. Unless that employee's rights to the company's pension contributions were *vested*—due to a union agreement or company policy, for instance—he or she might well find himself with no pension.[37]

◆ ERISA AND THE TAX REFORM ACT OF 1986

Employee Retirement Income Security Act (ERISA) Signed into law by President Ford in 1974 to require that pension rights be vested, and protected by a government agency, the PBGC.

As a reaction to problems such as these, the **Employee Retirement Income Security Act (ERISA)** was signed into law by President Ford in 1974.[38]

Debate regarding regulation of pension funds had actually begun in 1965, at which time private retirement plans covered some 25 million workers. At that time plans were paying nearly $2.75 billion annually in benefits to almost 2.5 million beneficiaries and had accumulated reserves in excess of $75 billion. By the end of 1974 (when ERISA was enacted), the assets of all private pension plans were close to $200 billion, and today more than 35 million workers are covered by employer pension plans. ERISA was aimed at protecting the interests of these workers and in stimulating the growth of pension plans.

Before enactment of ERISA, pension plans often failed to deliver expected benefits to employees. For example, when the Studebaker Auto Company went out of business in 1964, it terminated its pension plan; this left nearly 8,500 participants with either sharply reduced benefits or none at all. Any number of reasons—business failure, inadequate funding—could result in employees losing their expected pensions.

Under ERISA, pension rights had to be vested under one of three formulas.[39]

100% vesting after 10 years of service (often referred to as *cliff vesting*).

25% vesting after 5 years, increasing 5% a year to 50% vesting after 10 years, and by 10% a year to 100% vesting after 15 years.

50% vesting after 5 years of service if the employee's age and years of service total 45 (or after 10 years of service if less), and increasing by 10% a year thereafter.

COMPUTER APPLICATIONS IN BENEFITS:

BENEFITS SPREADSHEET

In the 1990s, companies will continue to be concerned about controlling benefits costs. One prerequisite to this is to be fully aware of how much the benefits offered are actually costing the company, on an ongoing basis. A benefits spreadsheet will provide this information.

The spreadsheet should list: each employee (by name or number); the job code (so you can compare benefits by job category in response to ERISA requirements); pay rate (annual, monthly, or hourly, since subsequent spreadsheet formulas will then calculate the appropriate rate for the benefit being considered); department (if you wish to compare departments or divisions); and each benefit listed, all in separate columns. In order to accurately track your current liabilities for benefits accrued but not used, list separate columns for liability and use of these benefits.

For example, suppose you want a report on accrued vacations. In the liability column, calculate the accumulation minus use, times current hourly rate of pay. It is this column which will highlight how costly it is to allow employees to accumulate vacation or sick leave from year to year. If an employee accrues at a $10 an hour rate now but does not use the vacation time until retirement, the cost of those hours could easily double or treble, as his or her pay rises.

In the use columns, first record the number of vacation hours used. Then, in a separate column, calculate the cost of the use (hours times hourly rate) so that you can compare months, quarters, and/or annual vacation cost to the company. In some instances, it may also be appropriate to add to this calculation the cost of paying someone else to fill in while the employee is gone. (This may be due to the hiring of a temporary employee or having to pay another regular employee time-and-a-half for extra hours.)

In order to prepare reports tied to specific benefits without affecting the overall spreadsheet, simply adjust the column-width of those columns you do not want to appear to zero. The columns will still be in the spreadsheet but will not appear in the printed report. You may thus use the benefits spreadsheet to help you comply with COBRA, or to calculate possible profit sharing formulas, stock options, and 401K contributions.

Once you have established a spreadsheet, you may also print individual employee reports from the overall spreadsheet. Periodic reports to employees help to keep the value of the benefit package meaningful. On this report, you can show how much vacation and sick leave have accrued, how much was used in a given period, which health plan has been chosen, who the beneficiary of the life plan is, as well as what options the employee has not selected. You can show not only what the employee is paying for the benefits, but (perhaps more importantly) also the company's contribution. With these reports, you not only keep the employee informed, you also give the employee accurate and complete information.

However, the Tax Reform Act of 1986 further tightened up these vesting rules and is now the law of the land. As of today, participants in a pension plan must have a nonforfeitable right to 100% of their accrued benefits after five years of service. Or, as an alternative, the employer may choose to phase in vesting over a period of from three to seven years. Under the Tax Reform Act of 1986 an employer can require that an employee complete a period of no more than two years service to the company before becoming eligible to participate in the plan. However, if you require more than one year of service the plan must grant employees full and immediate vesting rights at the end of their required service.[40]

Among other things, the **Pension Benefits Guarantee Corporation (PBGC)** was established under ERISA to assure that pensions meet vesting

Pension Benefits Guarantee Corporation (PBGC) Established under ERISA to assure that pensions meet vesting obligations; also insures pensions should a plan terminate without sufficient funds to meet its vested obligations.

obligations; the PBGC also insures pensions should a plan terminate without sufficient funds to meet its vested obligations.[41]

♦ FASB 87 AND THE OMNIBUS BUDGET RECONCILIATION ACT OF 1987

The problem of underfunded or unfunded pension plans also helped prompt the Financial Accounting Standards Board to introduce "Employers Accounting for Pensions," commonly known as FASB 87. This rule (which is one of a multitude of rules to which Certified Public Accountants in the United States must adhere) mandates that:[42]

1. For both reported earnings and balance sheet calculations, accounting for defined benefits plans (those in which participating employees receive previously agreed upon *defined* benefits when they retire) must estimate the size of the liability the employer is accumulating by using market interest rates. Since the cost of funding specific, defined benefits (of, say, $1,000 per month) 20 years from now will rise with a rise in market interest rates, this means that the reported liability to the employer will reflect more closely the plan's actual cost than it did previously. (Previously, the firm's auditors could choose an interest rate and remain with that rate from year to year.)

2. The corporate balance sheet must include the unfunded liability of an underfunded pension plan.

3. If changes in the surplus of the plan (should the plan have a surplus) exceed 10% of its assets or liabilities, such changes must be reflected in the earnings statement in the form of operating earnings.

Note that Statement No. 87 does not apply to defined *contribution* plans. Unlike defined benefits plans, defined contribution plans do not guarantee how much money an employee will receive on retirement, but only what each party's contribution to the plan will be.

The Omnibus Budget Reconciliation Act of 1987, passed by Congress and signed by the president on December 22, 1987, further lays out rules regarding the funding of pension liabilities.[43]

♦ WORKING WOMEN AND RETIREMENT BENEFITS

Between 1960 and today, the number of working women more than doubled to about 49 million. This increase has created pressure on the part of women and many women's groups to change three particular aspects of pension laws that they believe are discriminatory on the basis of sex:

The traditional rules regarding the accumulation of pension credits

The limited right of a homemaker to her spouse's workplace pension

The gender-based actuarial tables used to calculate the rate at which accrued pensions are paid

As a result of this pressure, changes have already been made. The Retirement Equity Act seeks to increase women's share of private sector retirement benefits by changing some of ERISA's rules. For example, prior to the Retirement Equity Act, a woman who left her job to have a child before she was vested and remained at home until the child reached school age was likely to lose what credits she had previously amassed and would have to start over again when she returned to work. Now, a nonvested employee who leaves the employer's service and then comes back within five years can get credit for that earlier service, and employees who are absent from work because of pregnancy, childbirth, adoption, or infant care are protected against break-in-service penalties for a year. The act also lowers the maximum age from 25 to 21 that a private pension plan can require an employee to attain before he or she can participate in the plan and allows women on maternity leave for up to five years to retain certain pension benefits and to require a spouse's written permission before a pension plan participant can waive survivor benefits. In a divorce settlement, the act also authorizes the court to award a person the right to part of the former spouse's pension as part of the benefit.[44]

Furthermore, on July 16, 1983, the U.S. Supreme Court decided that sex-based longevity tables which distinguish between men and women can no longer be used and that if employees contribute toward their benefits, men and women must be charged the same and paid the same. Previously, separate tables were used to account for the fact that women have a longer life expectancy than men and therefore are likely to receive their pension payments for a longer period of time.

♦ INDIVIDUAL RETIREMENT ACCOUNTS

individual retirement accounts (IRA) Pension plans qualified under tax laws to receive favorable tax treatment and that are established individually by employees.

Despite the rapid growth of private pensions, more than 40 million American workers were not covered in 1974 by "qualified" pension plans (plans that are qualified under the tax laws to receive favorable tax treatment, such as deferral of taxes on investment income). Congress, therefore, included provisions in ERISA that would let employees establish their own qualified pension plans; the result was the **individual retirement account**, or **IRA**.

An IRA pension plan has the following basic features. Under the Economic Recovery Tax Act of 1981 (ERTA), anyone who earned an income—even if he or she was already enrolled in a company pension plan—could invest in an IRA.[45] The person could make a tax-deductible investment of up to $2,000 in his or her IRA; if the person also contributed to a separate IRA for his or her nonworking spouse, they could make an overall contribution of $2,250. Employers (or individual workers) who wanted to establish such plans found a multitude of financial institutions that had established IRA-investment vehicles. For example, money could be invested through savings banks, insurance companies, brokerage houses, and mutual funds. In addition to the fact that the annual investments are tax deductible, the income earned on the investment (the financial institution might invest the funds in stocks or bonds, for instance) is *tax deferred*, in that you don't pay taxes on the income until you cash in your accounts.[46] This usually occurs after you retire, when your tax bracket is probably lower than it is while you're working.

The 1986 Tax Reform Act has had a major effect on IRAs, changing many of the previous provisions. The new law states that no deductible IRA contribution can be made by active participants in an employer-sponsored retirement plan, or their spouses, if their income is above $50,000 (adjusted gross income) on joint returns or $35,000 on single returns. If income falls between $40,000 and $50,000 on joint returns or $25,000–$35,000 on single returns, the amount that can be deducted is cut back. The new law will discourage many from saving for retirement through IRAs.[47]

♦ RECENT TRENDS

In periods of high inflation, the purchasing power of retirees' pensions declines rapidly. This is unfortunate both for retirees (who see their purchasing power dwindling) and for employers (who find inflation destroying the effectiveness of their pension plans). According to one survey of 577 companies, close to one-half of the firms surveyed (48%) had provided at least one postretirement pension increase during the period 1980–1984. The primary reason cited by 76% of the firms was to respond to the cumulative effect of inflation. The recent low levels of inflation may, therefore, explain why relatively few companies—only 13%—have made similar increases in one recent year.

Retirement benefits are also getting a new twist with the so-called **golden offerings**—early retirement windows and other voluntary separation arrangements. These so-called golden offerings appear to correlate with the state of the economy and are usually aimed at avoiding mandatory layoffs by offering special retirement packages to long-term employees. According to one survey of a cross section of industries and locations across the United States, about one-third of companies offered such voluntary separation plans in the past few years, while another 9% are considering an offering for this year.

Most of the plans take the form of **early retirement window** arrangements. Here, only older employees (often age 50+) are eligible to participate. Here the "window" represents the fact that the company opens up (for a limited time only) the chance for an employee to retire earlier than usual. The financial incentive is usually a combination of improved or liberalized pension benefits plus a cash payment.

The other voluntary separation plans operate more like "bonuses" for leaving and may apply even to recent hires. The offerings are usually made regardless of age and the financial incentive is typically a cash payment which varies substantially by company but often is in the range of one week's pay per year of service. About one-third of those employees eligible to walk through the early retirement windows accept the offer, while about one-fourth of those offered other separation plans do likewise.[48]

Early Retirement Windows

Early retirement windows like these must be used with caution if you are to avoid charges of age discrimination. The problem is that age discrimination is the fastest-growing type of discrimination claim today, and unless structured properly, early retirement programs can be challenged as de facto programs for forcing the discharge of older employees against their will.[49] While it is generally legal to use incentives like early retirement benefits to encourage individuals to choose early retirement, the employee's decision must be voluntary. In fact, in several cases individuals who were eligible for and elected early retirement later challenged their early retirement by claiming that their decision was not voluntary. In one case, for instance (*Paolillo* v. *Dresser Industries, Inc.*), employees were told on October 12 that they were eligible to retire under a "totally voluntary" early retirement program and that they must inform the company by October 18 to take advantage of this benefit. However, they were not informed of the details of the program (such as the amount of medical insurance and pension benefits for each individual employee) until October 15. This did not leave much time, so that employees who had at first elected early retirement were able to subsequently sue, claiming coercion. The U.S. Court of Appeals for the Second Circuit (New York) agreed with their claim, arguing that an employee's decision to retire must be voluntary and without undue strain.[50]

As an employer you must therefore exercise great caution in encouraging employees to take early retirement. The decision must be voluntary and "without undue strain," and the waivers that they sign should meet certain EEOC guidelines. In particular, in agreeing to accept early retirement and waive future Age Discrimination in Employment Act claims, the waiver itself must be knowing and voluntary, not provide for the release of prospective rights or claims, and not be an exchange for consideration that included

golden offerings Offers to current employees aimed at encouraging them to retire early—perhaps even with the same pensions they would expect if they retired at, say, age 65.

early retirement window A type of "golden offering" by which employees are encouraged to retire early, the incentive being liberal pension benefits plus, perhaps, a cash payment.

benefits to which the employee was already entitled. It should give the employee ample opportunity to think over the agreement and seek advice by legal counsel.[51]

EMPLOYEE SERVICES BENEFITS

While an employer's insurance and retirement benefits account for the main part of its benefits costs, most also provide a range of services including personal services (such as counseling), job-related services (such as child care facilities), and executive perquisites (such as company cars and plans for its executives).

◆ PERSONAL SERVICES BENEFITS

First, many companies provide service benefits in the form of personal services that most employees need at one time or another; these include credit unions, legal services, counseling, and social and recreational opportunities.

Credit Unions

Credit unions are usually separate businesses that are established with the assistance of the employer. Employees usually become members of a credit union by purchasing a share of the credit union's stock for $5 or $10. Members can then deposit savings that accrue interest at a rate determined by the credit union's board of directors. And perhaps more important to most employees, loan eligibility and the rate of interest paid on the loan are usually much more favorable than are those found in financial institutions such as banks and finance companies.

Counseling Services

Employers are also providing a wider range of counseling services to employees. These include financial counseling (for example, in terms of how to overcome existing indebtedness problems), family counseling (covering marital problems, and so on), career counseling (in terms of analyzing one's aptitudes and deciding on a career), job placement counseling (for helping terminated or disenchanted employees find new jobs), and preretirement counseling (aimed at preparing retiring employees for what many find is the trauma of retiring). Many employers also make available to employees a full range of legal counseling through legal insurance plans.[52] In the *open panel* legal plan, employees can choose their own attorney and then be reimbursed according to the fee schedule in the policy. In the *closed panel* legal plan, employees are required to use one of a number of specified attorneys, who are paid directly by the insurance plan.

Employee Assistance Programs (EAPs)

Originally established to deal with industrial alcoholism in the 1940s, EAPs have today been expanded to help all employees deal with problems arising from drug and alcohol abuse, marital and family problems, financial problems, gambling, stress, mental health, and a host of other issues and problems. The EAP helps not only the individual but also the organization by eliciting management support, helping to control health costs, and promoting better employee relations and productivity. EAPs offer a variety of services, including assessment programs and treatment programs: Each offers counseling.

It is estimated that 50–75% of all employers with 3,000 or more employees now offer EAPs,[53] and there are four basic employee assistance program models in use today.[54] In the *in-house model* the entire assistance staff is employed by the company. In the *out-of-house model* the company contracts a vendor to provide employee assistance staff and services either in its own offices, the company's offices, or a combination of both. In the *consortium model* several companies pool their resources to develop a collaborative EAP program. Finally, in the *affiliate model*, a vendor already under contract to an employer subcontracts a local professional rather than use its own salaried staff. This is usually to service employees in a client company location in which the EAP vendors do not have an office. Key ingredients for ensuring a successful EAP program include:[55]

Specify goals and philosophy. The short- and long-term goals expected to be achieved for both the employee and employer should be specified and the values and assumptions underlying the plan should be enumerated.

Develop a policy statement. Next, a comprehensive EAP policy statement should be prepared. This should define the purpose of the program, employee eligibility, the roles and responsibility of various personnel in the organization, and procedures for taking advantage of the plan.

Ensure professional staffing. At a minimum, staff members should have at least two years' experience working with the problem to be dealt with by the EAP, such as alcoholism and addiction. Give careful consideration to the professional and state licensing requirements as they apply to the people staffing these facilities and, if necessary, retain the services of an experienced person to consult with you in drawing up job specifications for the required staff.

Maintain confidential recordkeeping systems. Everyone involved with the EAP—including secretaries and support staff—must understand the importance of confidentiality. Furthermore, make sure files are locked, access is limited and monitored, and identifying information (which might otherwise find itself in an employee's computerized records) is kept to a minimum.

Provide supervisory training. While this needn't involve extensive training, supervisors should certainly understand the program's policies, procedures, and services as well as the company's policies regarding confidentiality. And perhaps more important, all supervisors should get some training regarding the outward symptoms of problems like alcoholism as well as how to encourage employees to use the services of the EAP.

Be aware of legal issues. For example, in most states counselors must disclose suspicions of child abuse to an appropriate state agency: Your in-house counselors thus put your company in the legal position of having to comply in such an instance. Three ways to safeguard your interests here include retaining legal advice on establishing your EAP, carefully screening the credentials of the staff you hire, and obtaining professional liability insurance for the EAP.

Other Personal Services

Finally, some employers also provide a wide range of social and recreational opportunities for its employees, including company-sponsored athletic events, dance clubs, annual summer picnics, craft activities, and parties.[56] Other companies—such as IBM, Xerox, and Hallmark—are paying *adoption benefits*, roughly equivalent to the pregnancy benefits they give new mothers.[57] Company-paid auto insurance plans[58] and new health care benefits such as dental coverage (provided by about 60% of employers) and vision care (provided by about 15% of employers) are other examples of increasingly popular benefits.[59] Corporate-run treatment programs for alcoholics, blood pressure testing programs, employer-sponsored exercise programs, and even programs to help employees stop smoking through hypnosis are other examples of personal benefits.[60] In practice, the benefits you can offer are limited only by your creativity in thinking up new benefits. One study of innovative benefits, for instance, found Canadian companies offering the following employee benefits, among others:

Lakefront vacations—the company owns lakeshore property and rents cottages and campsites to employees at low rates.

Weight loss program—several companies subsidize costs of weight loss workshops.

Adoption benefit—companies pay amounts of $500 to $1,500 per child for adoption costs.

Company country club—the company maintains a golf course, tennis courts, and football and baseball fields.

Cultural subsidy—the company will pay 33% of the cost of tickets to cultural activities such as theater, ballet, museum, and so on up to $100 per year per employee.

Lunch-and-learn program—interested employees can attend lunchtime talks on a variety of subjects, including stress management, weight control, computer literacy, fashion, and travel.

Home assistance—employees may use up to $1,500 of their annual profit-sharing award to save for a down payment on a house or to reduce their down payment, up to a maximum of $15,000.[61]

♦ JOB-RELATED SERVICE BENEFITS

Job-related services such as assistance in moving and day care centers (that are aimed directly at helping employees perform their jobs) constitute a second group of services.

Parental Leave

Parental leave is increasingly a benefit whose time has come. It's estimated that over 44% of the workers today are women and that 80% of them are expected to become pregnant at some time during their work lives.[62] Furthermore, one recent survey concluded that 52% of mothers with children below the age of 1 were already back at work, up from 32% in 1977. This makes it more important for companies to make provision for parental leaves.

Partly as a response to this, there is pending federal and state legislation to require mandatory parental leave upon the birth of a child, and many employers are already voluntarily instituting such plans. For example, in a survey of 384 of the nation's largest 1,500 companies, it was found that 95% of employers provided disability leave to pregnant women under their health insurance benefit plans. Fifty-two percent of employers provided job-protected, unpaid leave to women (for one to three months), and 37% provided a similar job-protected, unpaid leave to men when a child was born. Many other employers are reevaluating their parental leave policies. The range of possibilities might include:[63]

Disability leave with full or partial salary reimbursement
Additional unpaid leave of one to three months

A transition period of part-time work for one month to one year

Reinstatement to the same or a comparable job at all stages of the leave.

The features of one such piece of parental leave legislation—the Family and Medical Leave Act, which was recently considered by Congress—help illustrate the thrust of such legislation. As mentioned above, private sector workers would be eligible for up to 10 weeks of parental leave every 2 years and up to 15 weeks per year of medical leave. It would apply (if passed) to employers with 50 or more employees and would cover employees who have been with the firm for at least 1 year and worked at least 20 hours per week.

Subsidized Child Care

Today, over 50% of all American women with children under 6 years old are in the work force, up from 32% of 1970, and 19% in 1960.[64] One increasingly popular benefit stemming directly from that trend is *subsidized day care*.[65] Many employers simply investigate the day care facilities in their communities and recommend certain ones to interested employees. But more employers are setting up company-sponsored day care facilities themselves, both to attract young mothers to the payroll and to reduce absenteeism. Often (as at the Wang Laboratories day care facility in Lowell, Massachusetts), the center is a private tax-exempt venture run separately from but subsidized by the company. Employees are charged $30 a week for a child's care, and about 75 children from 2 to 4 years old are now enrolled. Where successful, the day care facility is usually close to the workplace (often in the same building), and the employer provides 50% to 75% of the operating costs. To date, however, the publicity these programs have received exceeds their actual use, with most surveys showing fewer than 5% of employers providing subsidized day care.

A survey found that employers can gain considerably by instituting subsidized day care centers; increased ability to attract employees, lower absenteeism, improved employee attitudes toward the employer, favorable publicity to the employer, and lower turnover rates are some of the benefits attributable to day care programs.[66] To make sure that the program is worthwhile and that its costs do not get out of hand, however, good planning is essential. This often starts with a questionnaire such as that in Figure 12.4. It is used to survey employees in order to answer such questions as: "What would you be willing to pay for care for one child in a child care center near work?" and "Have you missed work during the past six months because you needed to find new care arrangements?" To date, however, the evidence regarding the actual effects of employer-sponsored child care on employee absenteeism, turnover, productivity, recruitment, or job satisfaction is contradictory, and no firm conclusions can be drawn.[67]

Elder Care

With the average age of the U.S. population rising, elder care is increasingly a concern for many employers and individuals. Similar in some respects to child care, an elder care program is designed to help employees who must, in turn, help elderly parents or relatives who are not fully able to care for themselves.[68]

From the point of view of the employer, elder care benefits are important for much the same reason as are child care benefits: the responsibility for caring for an aging relative can and will impact the employee's performance at work. A number of employers are therefore instituting elder care benefits, including flexible hours, long-term care insurance coverage, and company-sponsored day care centers.

The elder care program instituted by Aerospace Company helps to illustrate what a typical program involves. Utilizing a program kit made available by the American Association of Retired Persons, the company program involved:

1. A lunchtime elder care fair. Here 31 community organizations involved with providing services to older people came to explain to employees the services that were available.

2. Next, there were ten lunchtime information sessions for employees aimed at explaining various aspects of elder care, such as independent versus dependent living and housing, the aging process, and legal concerns of elder care.

3. Finally, the company also distributed AARP's publication entitled "Care Management Guide." This lists potential problems associated with elder care in a question and answer format.

Subsidized Employee Transportation

As gasoline prices fluctuate, some employers are providing some type of subsidized employee transportation.[69]

Such transportation can take several forms. In one large program the Seattle First National Bank negotiated separate contracts with a transit system to provide free year-round transportation to more than 3,000 of the bank's employees. At the other extreme, some employers just facilitate employee car pooling, perhaps by acting as the central clearing house to identify employees from the same geographic areas that work the same hours.

Food Services

Food services are provided in some form by most employers; they let employees purchase meals, snacks, or coffee, usually at relatively low prices. Most food operations are nonprofit, and, in fact, some firms provide food services below cost. The advantages to the employee are clear, and for the employer it can mean ensuring that employees do not drift away for long lunch hours. Even employers that do not provide full dining facilities generally make available food services such as coffee wagons or vending machines for the convenience of their employees.

Educational Subsidies

Educational subsidies such as tuition refunds have long been a popular benefit for employees seeking to complete their high school, college, or university programs or for those interested in some other type of continuing education program. Educational subsidies may range from total payment of all tuition and expenses to some percentage of expenses to a flat fee per year of, say, $250 to $300. Some employers have experimented with providing in-house college programs such as Master of Business Administration programs, in which college faculty teach courses on the employer's premises. Other in-house educational programs include remedial work in basic literacy and training for improved supervisory skills. As far as tuition reimbursement programs are concerned, one survey found that nearly all companies (of 619 companies surveyed) pay for courses directly related to an employee's present job. Most companies also reimburse nonjob-related courses (such as a secretary taking an accounting class) that pertain to the company business (79%) and those that are part of a degree program (66%). Furthermore, about 14% of the employers pay for self-improvement classes

Those planning a child-care program may want to survey employees and/or non-employees who live within recruiting range. The new edition of Employers and Child Care *suggests these "frequently asked" questions.*

Questionnaire

1. Would you be willing to give some time and your expertise to help organize (identify the program being proposed)?
   Many people, including some with no children, might volunteer to help organize or manage a program that is parent controlled.

2. Do you have dependent children under 6 years old living at home? If so, how are they cared for while you work?

3. How much do you pay for child care services for each child using services?
   $ _____ for _____ hours per week for child _____ years old.
   The amount an employee presently pays may indicate what parents are willing to pay.

4. Would you be interested in enrolling a dependent child in a child care center located close to where you work?
   The answer to this question, of course, does not constitute a commitment to enroll a child, but asking the question may avoid surprise that so many (or so few) are interested.

5. What is the age of the child (children) that you would be interested in enrolling in the child care center?
   List ages, using age brackets that determine teacher-child ratios for state licensing laws. Some centers have reported more demand for infant care (seldom available in the community) rather than preschool care.

6. What hours and days would you need child care?

7. Do any of the children that you're interested in enrolling have a handicap? If so, what is the child's condition?
   Planners may or may not be able to accommodate handicapped children, depending on the kind of handicap and the number of children affected.

8. What would you be willing to pay for care for one child in a child care center near work?
   List alternative ranges of fees. Answers may be lower than parents are willing to pay once the center has opened. A better indicator of what employees will pay may be a comparison of family income with fees currently being paid at other centers.

9. What is your total gross family income?
   A rule of thumb often used is that a family can spend 10 percent of its gross income for child care. If planners are considering a sliding scale that will charge high-income families more, will there be enough high-income interest to balance enrollment by low-income families?

such as a foreign language, even though they are unrelated to company business or the employee's job.[70]

♦ EXECUTIVE PERQUISITES

Perquisites (perks, for short) are usually given to only a select few executives, usually based on organizational level.

Perks can range from the substantial to the (almost) insignificant. In

FIGURE 12.4
(continued)

10. If all the following forms of child care service were available to you, which would be your first choice?

11. Do you believe a service at the company (or nonprofit organization) that supplied you with names of child care providers in your community would help you in making your own child care arrangements?

12. How would you describe your present child care arrangements.
   - Cost of care—
     _____ too expensive
     _____ moderate
     _____ inexpensive
   - Location of care
     _____ close to home
     _____ close to work
     _____ inconvenient distance to travel
     _____ other: _____
   - Hours of care
     _____ available during times needed
     _____ not available as early as needed
     _____ not available as late as needed

   Other items could include evaluation of activities for children in present program, adequacy of staff, etc.

13. Have you missed work during the past 6 months because (give number of days)
    _____ child was ill
    _____ sitter was ill
    _____ needed to find new care arrangements
    _____ other

14. Were you late for work during the past 6 months because of child care problems?
    _____ No
    _____ Yes
    How many times? Describe problems: _____

15. Have you left work early during past 6 months because of child care problems?
    _____ No
    _____ Yes
    How many times? Describe problems: _____

16. Do you ever waste time or make mistakes because you are worried about your child care problems?
    _____ No
    _____ Some
    _____ A lot
    What problems bother you most? _____

addition to his $200,000 annual salary, for instance, the president of the United States has an expense account of $50,000 for household expenses and entertainment, $100,000 for travel, and pays no rent for using the White House or Camp David (not to mention a fleet of limousines, *Air Force One*, and various helicopters!).[71] At the other extreme, perks may entail little more than the right to use the executive washroom.

In between these extremes, there are a multitude of popular perks. These include *management loans* (which typically enable senior officers to exercise their stock options); *salary guarantees* (also known as "golden parachutes"), to protect executives even if their firms are the targets of acquisitions or mergers; *financial counseling* (to handle top executive's investment programs); and *relocation benefits*, often including subsidizing mortgages, buying back the executives current house, and paying for the actual move.[72] A potpourri of other executive perks would include time off with pay (including work at home, sabbaticals, and severance pay), outplacement assistance, company cars, chauffeured limousines, security systems, company planes and yachts, executive dining rooms, physical fitness programs, legal services, tax assistance, liberal expense accounts, club membership, season tickets, credit cards, and children's education. As you can see, employers have many ways of making their hard-working executives' lives as pleasant as possible!

Companies offer perquisites for many reasons. These range from prestige and tax deductibility to protection (in the case of those managers who require armored limousines).

A study by the Wyatt Company illustrates the pervasiveness of executive perquisites. This study involved 50 major employers in California and concluded that on average, the value of executive perquisites was equivalent to 10 to 12 percent of the annual cash compensation (salary and annual incentive bonus) for these companies.[73]

FLEXIBLE BENEFITS PROGRAMS

flexible benefits program Individualized benefits plans allowed by some employers to accommodate employee preferences for benefits, subject to certain constraints.

"Variety is the spice of life," the saying goes; this applies very well to company benefits, since the benefits that one worker finds attractive may be unattractive to another. As a result, there is a trend toward individualizing benefits plans today.

♦ EMPLOYEE'S PREFERENCES FOR VARIOUS BENEFITS

Two researchers carried out a study that provides some insight into employees' preferences for various benefits.[74] They mailed questionnaires covering seven possible benefit options to 400 employees of a Midwest public utility company. Properly completed questionnaires were received from 149 employees (about 38% of those surveyed). The seven benefit options were as follows:

1. A five-day workweek with shorter working days of 7 hours and 35 minutes.
2. A four-day workweek consisting of 9 hours and 30 minutes each day.
3. Ten Fridays off each year with full pay. This includes ten three-day weekends per year, in addition to any three-day weekends previously scheduled.
4. Early retirement through accumulating ten days per year until retirement age. The retirement age will be 65 minus the number of accumulated days. Full pay will continue until age 65 is reached.
5. Additional vacation of two weeks per year with full pay. The additional vacation will be added to the present vacation.
6. A pension increase of $75 per month.
7. Family dental insurance. The company will pay the entire cost of family dental insurance.

Finally, employees were also asked to show their relative preference for a *pay increase of 5%*, in addition to any general wage increase negotiated.

FIGURE 12.5

Preference for Various Benefits
Source: Reprinted from the November 1975 issue of *Personnel Administrator*, copyright 1975, The American Society for Personnel Administration.

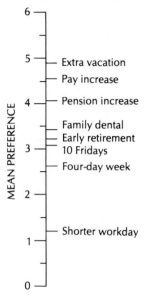

Results

Overall results are shown in Figure 12.5. Note that two extra weeks of vacation was clearly the most preferred benefit, while the pay increase was second in preference. Overall, the shorter workday was by far the least preferred benefit option.

But this is not the full story; as you can see in Table 12.2, the employee's age, marital status, and sex influenced his or her choice of benefits. For example, younger employees were significantly more in favor of the *family dental plan* than were older employees. Younger employees also showed a greater preference for the *four-day workweek*. As might be expected, preference for the *pension* option increased significantly with employee age. Married workers showed more preference for the *pension* increase and for the family dental plan than did single workers. The preference for the family dental plan increased sharply as the number of dependents increased.

Because employees do have different preferences for benefits, some employers have attempted to individualize their benefits plans.[75]

◆ THE "CAFETERIA" APPROACH

The *cafeteria benefit plan* enables employees to pick and choose from available options and, literally, to develop their own benefit plan.

The basic idea of such plans is to allow the employee to put together his or her own benefit plan, subject to two constraints. First, the organization has to set total cost limits carefully. (This limits what it will spend for each total benefits package.) Second, each benefit plan must include certain *non*optional items. These include, for example, Social Security, workers' compensation, and unemployment insurance.

Subject to these two constraints, employees can pick and choose from the available options. Thus, a young married employee might opt for the company's life and dental insurance plans, while an older employee opts for an approved pension plan. The list of possible options can be quite long and would probably include many of the benefits discussed in this chapter: vacations, insurance benefits, pension plans, educational services, and so on.

An example of a flexible compensation plan was instituted at IDS Financial Services, a Minneapolis-based American Express subsidiary. The 2,500 IDS employees covered by the plan automatically got core benefits that included a minimal level of life insurance, a number of vacation days based upon years of service, short-term disability that pays 100% of salary and

TABLE 12.2   How Different Employees Ranked Seven Benefits[1]

RANKING OF EMPLOYEE PREFERENCE BY AGE, MARITAL STATUS, SEX, AND NUMBER OF DEPENDENTS

Option	Age in Years			Marital Status		Sex		Dependents		
	18–35	36–49	50–65	Single	Married	Males	Females	0	1–3	4 or more
Extra vacation	1	2	2	1	1	1	1	2	1	1
Pay increase	2	1	3	2	2	2	3	1	3	3
Pension increase	6	3	1	3	3	3	2	3	2	4
Dental plan	3	4	7	7	4	4	7	8	5	7
Early retirement	7	5	4	4	5	5	5	4	4	6
10 Fridays	5	6	5	5	6	6	4	5	6	7
Four-day week	4	7	6	6	7	7	6	6	7	5
Shorter Workday	8	8	8	8	8	8	8	7	8	8

[1] 1 is low, 8 is high

Source: Reprinted from the November 1975 issue of *Personnel Administrator*, copyright 1975, The American Society for Personnel Administration.

gradually drops to 70% over time, long-term disability that begins after a 150-day absence, and an attendance bonus that is earned when no health-related time off is taken during the year. However, the company also contributed 5% of salary that the employee can use toward any one or a combination of three options. As this writer puts it, "one choice is to put all or part of the 5% in a tax-deferred savings plan. For the first 3% the employee puts in, the company will add another 2½%; . . . a second option is to take all or part of the 5% as cash. Option 3 is to put a portion of the entire credit toward extra benefits including medical coverage, life insurance, long-term disability, and vacation (employees can buy up to 5 days)."[76]

Building this type of individual choice into a benefit plan can obviously be advantageous, but there are also disadvantages. The main problem is that the implementation of a cafeteria plan can involve substantial clerical and administrative costs. Each employee's benefits have to be carefully priced out and updated periodically, and even a medium-sized company would undoubtedly have to use a computer to administer such a plan.[77] Although most employees favor flexible benefits, many don't like to spend the time involved in choosing among available benefit options. Various consulting firms have therefore development computerized games such as one called "FlexSelect," a user-friendly interactive program for personal computers that helps employees make choices under a flexible benefits program.[78]

Current Use

Cafeteria-type, flexible benefits plans are spreading fast, with many new employers adding these plans every year. By today it is estimated that well over 1000 companies were on-line with some form of choice making among employee benefits. As you can see from Figure 12.6, the number of flexible compensation programs soared from a handful prior to 1980 to more than 1000 in 1989.

FIGURE 12.6
Flexible Compensation Programs
Source: Hewitt Associates, *On Flexible Compensation;* (January 1986), p. 1; 1989 Survey of Flexible Compensation Programs and Practices, (April 1990), p. 1.

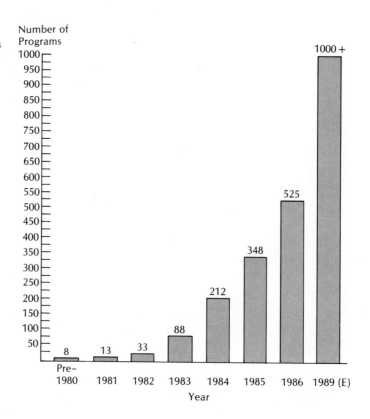

◆ COMPUTERS AND BENEFITS ADMINISTRATION

Whether it is a flexible benefits plan or some other, computers play an important role in benefits administration. For even a smaller company with 40 to 50 employees, the administrative problems of keeping track of the benefits status of each employee can be a time-consuming task as employees are hired and separated, and as they utilize or want to change their benefits. Even a fairly straightforward problem like keeping track of who is eligible for vacations, and when, becomes a chore when a lot of employees are involved. As a result, most companies at least make use of some sort of benefits spreadsheet (see the box) to facilitate tracking benefits. Others use packaged software to update things like vacation eligibility and to trigger, say, a memo to a supervisor when one of his or her subordinates is overdue for some time off.

Keeping Employees Informed

Computers are also being used to inform employees about their benefits and to answer routine questions that might otherwise go unasked or absorb a human resource manager's time.[79] Such questions include: "In which option of the medical plan am I enrolled?" "Who are my designated beneficiaries for the life insurance plan?" "If I retire in two years, what will be my monthly retirement income?" and "What is my current balance in the company savings plan?"

At General Foods Corporation, for instance, employees use a computer system called "Benefits Window." The Benefits Window project provides employees with the capability of easily looking up information regarding their benefits programs at centrally located interactive Kiosks conveniently situated around the facilities. As illustrated in Figure 12.7, employees can punch in their Social Security numbers and then easily identify such basic plan status items as their beneficiaries, the value of their Thrift Investment Plan (TIP) accounts, the value of their contributory retirement accounts, and the value of their ESOP accounts. Furthermore, a "what if" feature allows employees to determine the impact on take-home pay of various levels of pretax savings plan contributions.

FIGURE 12.7
Employee Benefits Menu
Source: Anthony J. Barra, "Employees Keep Informed with Interactive KIOSKs," *Personnel Journal* (October 1988), p. 46.

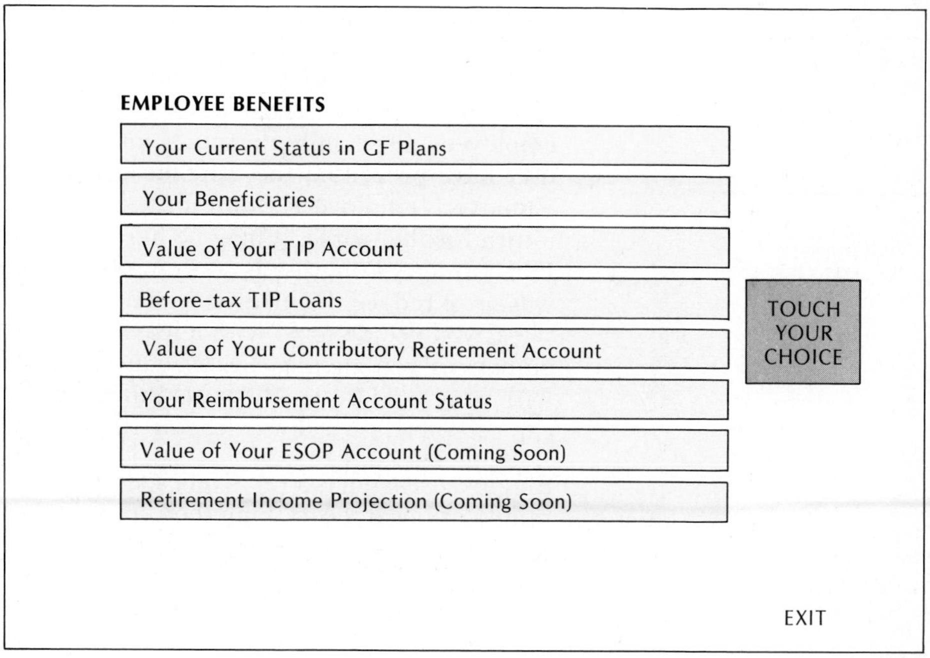

EMPLOYEE BENEFITS

- Your Current Status in GF Plans
- Your Beneficiaries
- Value of Your TIP Account
- Before-tax TIP Loans
- Value of Your Contributory Retirement Account
- Your Reimbursement Account Status
- Value of Your ESOP Account (Coming Soon)
- Retirement Income Projection (Coming Soon)

TOUCH YOUR CHOICE

EXIT

Employee leasing is an HRM approach that has several uses. As explained in Chapter 4 (Personnel Planning and Recruiting), some employers use employee leasing firms to reduce or eliminate the need for recruiting and screening employees with their own in-house staff. Recall that such leasing firms usually arrange to have all the employer's employees transferred to the employee leasing firm. The employee leasing firm thus becomes the legal employer and handles all employee-related paperwork. This usually includes recruiting, hiring, tax liabilities (Social Security payments, unemployment insurance, and so on), as well as, often, day-to-day details like performance appraisals (with the assistance of the on-site supervisor).

While the idea of having a leasing company take over the time-consuming job of managing personnel can be attractive, it is with respect to benefits management that employee leasing is often most advantageous. For many smaller employers the most serious personnel problem they face is getting insurance: even group rates for things like life or health insurance can still be quite high when only 20 or 30 employees are involved.

This is where employee leasing comes in. Remember that the leasing firm is the legal employer of your employees. Therefore, your employees are absorbed into a much larger insurable group, along with other employers' former employees. The bottom line is that the employee leasing company can thus often provide benefits that much smaller companies cannot obtain or cannot obtain at anywhere near as favorable a cost. As a small-business owner, you may thereby be able to get insurance for your people that you couldn't otherwise obtain. Furthermore, there will be some instances in which an employee leasing company arrangement actually costs an employer virtually nothing, even with the leasing firm's fee. This is because the fee may be more than outweighed by the reduced benefits cost to the employer, plus the savings in in-house labor costs gained by letting the leasing company handle HRM.[80]

Employee leasing may sound too good to be true, and it often is. Many employers are understandably uncomfortable allowing a third party to become the legal employer of their employees (who literally have to be terminated by the employer and rehired by the leasing firm). There is also the matter of the somewhat erratic history of some employee leasing firms, a number of which have gone out of business after apparently growing successfully for several years. Such a business failure leaves the original employer with the need to hire back all its employees, and with the problem of finding new insurance carriers to take on the job of insuring these "new" employees. Especially for much smaller firms, the original insurance plan may have prevented the original insurer from cutting off services to the employer's employees. But if the health history of your employees has taken a turn for the worse, it may be hard to repurchase insurance at any price. Furthermore, Congress is continually tinkering with the tax code in such a way as to reduce the insurance benefits attractiveness of employee leasing.

If you decide to go with a leasing firm there are several commonsense guidelines you should use. Of course, check the prospective leasing firm with your local Better Business Bureau. Get a full list of local clients so you can completely check the leasing firm's references. Furthermore:[81]

Employee leasing is a relatively specialized field given the legal and tax code ramifications of everything they do. You should therefore work with a leasing firm that specialize in the business rather than one that offers leasing as only part of its services.

Choose a financially stable and well-managed leasing firm. You should attempt to check the firm's capitalization and credit rating and look carefully at the number of years it has been in business.

Look for a firm that provides benefits that are at least as good or better than those you now offer. Make sure the firm pays its bills. If the leasing firm does not pay its insurance premiums on time it could be a catastrophe for your firm. While the leasing firm may be the legal entity responsible for the payments, remember that from a practical point of view, it is your employees that are left without insurance, and this will turn into a problem for your firm.

Review their policies. Finally, remember that most leasing firms do not just administer your own firm's personnel policies; instead, they will institute their own personnel policies (regarding, for instance, performance appraisals, periodic review for raises, and so on). It is therefore important to ensure their personnel policies are consistent with yours and that any inconsistencies are worked out before the transition.

BENEFITS TODAY AND TOMORROW

♦ THE BENEFITS PICTURE TODAY

There are few companies in the United States today that don't offer at least some fringe benefits to their employees.[82] For example, almost every responding company to a *Personnel Journal* survey (98.8%) provides group health insurance, regardless of company size. Of these, about 60% provide an HMO option, 25% provide a PPO option, and 90% on average provide some type of group dental plan benefits. The use of supplemental health benefits is extensive too: Between 25% and 45% of responding companies (depending on size) provide vision care plan benefits, about 50% of responding companies have a prescription drug plan, about 55% have some type of employee assistance programs, and about 40% of the responding companies provide health education/promotion/wellness programs.

Most respondents even provide retirement/pension benefits. For example, 88% of large companies (those with 5,000 or more employees), 78% of medium-sized companies (500–4,999), and 73% of smaller companies (fewer than 500 employees) provide defined contribution plans, while about 67% of all the firms have defined benefit plans.

In addition, most employers also offer death and disability benefits. For example, about 76% of all companies regardless of size provide group life insurance benefits, about 85% of the firms provide accidental death and disability insurance, and 85% provide long-term disability insurance on average, regardless of size.

♦ THE BENEFITS SCENE TOMORROW

Benefits directors from 100 major U.S. industrial companies recently offered their predictions regarding employee benefits in the 1990s in a survey conducted by Hewitt Associates, a large consulting and actuarial firm.[83] Against a backdrop of changing demographics—in particular an increase in the average age of employees and the proportion of women in their work force—it is not surprising that about half the respondents expect the average benefit cost to increase.

However, benefit costs are not projected to increase across the board. For example, these experts expect little change in the areas of life insurance, disability, and time off. But with regard to retirement benefits, almost half predict that costs will rise. On the other hand, the trend toward early retirement appears to have bottomed out, and as a result, many of the experts expect less use in the future of special early retirement windows.

From a list of possible emerging benefits practices, the respondents chose several as being the most likely to become more popular. Eighty percent said there will be more use of flexible benefits plans as a way to maintain benefits during the period of cost squeeze. Furthermore, 82% expect an increase in long-term care coverage such as that provided by nursing homes (not currently covered adequately under Medicare or most private plans). Between 70 and 80% of the respondents also expect more use of flextime and an increase in elder care benefits. Most also expect much wider use of employer-sponsored day care. Almost all the respondents (92%) expected computerization to be used widely by the early 1990s to facilitate benefits administration and particularly the administration of flexible benefits plans.

SUMMARY

1. The financial *incentives* we discussed are usually paid to specific employees whose work is above standard. Employee *benefits*, on the other hand, are available to *all* employees based on their membership in the organization. We discussed four types of benefit plans: pay supplements, insurance, retirement benefits, and services.

2. Supplemental pay benefits provide pay for time not worked. They include unemployment insurance, vacation and holiday pay, severance pay, and supplemental unemployment benefits.

3. Insurance benefits are another type of employee benefit. Workers' compensation, for example, is aimed at ensuring prompt income and medical benefits to work accident victims or their dependents regardless of fault. Most employers also provide group life insurance and group hospitalization, accident, and disability insurance.

4. Two types of retirement benefits were discussed: Social Security and pensions. Social Security does not just cover retirement benefits but survivors and disability benefits as well. There are three basic types of pension plans: group, deferred profit sharing, and savings plans. One of the critical issues in pension planning involves *vesting*—the money that employer and employee have placed in the latter's pension fund, which cannot be forfeited for any reason. ERISA basically ensures that pension rights become vested and protected after a reasonable amount of time.

5. Most employers also provide benefits in the form of employee services. These include food services, recreational opportunities, legal advice, credit unions, and counseling.

6. Surveys suggest two conclusions regarding employee's preferences for benefits. First, *overall*, time off (such as two extra weeks vacation) seems to be the most preferred benefit. Second, the employee's age, marital status, and sex clearly influence his or her choice of benefits. (For example, younger employees were significantly more in favor of the family dental plan than were older employees.) This suggests the need for individualizing the organization's benefit plans.

7. The *cafeteria approach* allows the employee to put together his or her own benefit plan, subject to total cost limits and the inclusion of certain nonoptional items. Several firms have installed cafeteria plans; they require considerable planning and computer assistance.

KEY TERMS

benefits

supplemental pay benefits

unemployment insurance

sick leave

severance pay

supplemental unemployment benefits

insurance benefits

workers' compensation

group life insurance

Health Maintenance Organization (HMO)

Pregnancy Discrimination Act

Social Security

retirement benefits

pension plans

group pension plan

deferred profit-sharing plan

savings plan

defined benefit

defined contribution

vesting

Employee Retirement Income Security Act (ERISA)

Pension Benefits Guarantee Corporation (PBGC)

Individual Retirement Account (IRA)

golden offerings

early retirement window

employee services benefits

flexible benefits programs

DISCUSSION QUESTIONS

1. You are applying for a job as a manager and are at the point of negotiating salary and benefits. What questions would you ask your prospective employer concerning benefits? Describe the benefit package you would try to negotiate for yourself.

2. Explain how you would go about minimizing your organization's unemployment insurance tax.

3. Explain how ERISA protects employees' pension rights.

4. In this chapter we presented findings concerning the preferences by age, marital status, and sex for various benefits. Basically, what were these findings and how would you make use of them if you were a human resource manager?

◆ APPLICATION EXERCISES

◆ CASE INCIDENT   **Sick Leave in Spring Valley**

Slashes in federal aid programs to cities, a decline in revenue from a 2 percent sales tax, and higher costs in everything from cleaning supplies to wages had brought hard times to the elected officials of Spring Valley. The combination of these factors made it seem impossible for Robert Donizetti—the city manager—and the budget committee of the City Council to provide a balanced budget for the city.

Situated in a northeastern state, Spring Valley had a population of twelve thousand, a declining one that matched its declining revenue. In casting about for means to finance the small city's operations, Donizetti saw few opportunities for increasing the revenue. In the past year one of its chief employers, the Acme Manufacturing Company, had been forced to close its local factory, and all parts of the local economy had been affected by the national business recession. Hence, Donizetti went carefully over departmental budgets seeking ways to cut costs and eliminate waste.

One area in which Donizetti decided savings could be effected was through changes in policy concerning sick leave. The city's work force consisted of only about 150 full-time employees, and figures in Donizetti's office showed that sick leave in the past six years averaged 7.34 days per year per employee. This was not only costly in dollars in terms of Spring Valley's budget but it meant a loss of labor efficiency and productivity. His statistics showed that female and older employees used more sick leave than males and younger workers. Donizetti prepared the following tables of sick leave averages by age and sex for the budget committee:

SICK LEAVE IN SPRING VALLEY BY SEX, 1978–83		
Year	Male	Female
1978	6.1	7.9
1979	5.9	7.7
1980	6.4	8.4
1981	6.3	8.7
1982	6.5	8.5
1983	6.8	8.9

SICK LEAVE IN SPRING VALLEY BY AGE, 1978–83		
Year	Under 30	Over 30
1978	5.1	6.8
1979	5.3	8.4
1980	5.7	8.1
1981	5.5	7.7
1982	5.8	8.3
1983	5.6	8.6

Spring Valley had not had many labor conflicts. Employee relations were handled through the human resource director, William Danforth, and the City Employees' Association, whose president was Jessica Blum. In respect to sick leave, the city had in recent years agreed to include in it family care, doctor appointments, and emergency time off for such events as funerals.

After study of the problem, Donizetti recommended that the City Employees' Association and the human resource department together devise a sick leave incentive program. It would serve as an incentive to save sick leave, as a deterrent to sick-leave abuse, and as an equitable plan for the different uses of sick leave.

On June 6 the human resource department presented its proposal. Under its plan, employees would be reimbursed on February 1 of each year for 20 percent of the sick leave credits accumulated during the past year. An employee would have to have built up 45 sick leave days in order to draw cash payments, a move intended to reduce turnover in employment in the city.

The City Employees' Association made a counterproposal that included a choice by the employee to consider sick leave as vacation time or else to triple it and add it to retirement service. Unused credits diverted to retirement were to be made at a rate of 100 percent.

The main point of contention at this stage concerned the percentage of sick leave credit for which an employee might be reimbursed. The city offered no alternative to minimum yearly reimbursement while the employees demanded that some sort of retirement-related incentive be adopted. After several fruitless negotiations, the two parties agreed to present the problem to a fact finder. His or her findings and suggestions for resolution of the issues would be used as a basis for further negotiations. The fact finder chosen, Alfred Cartaret, conducted private hearings with both parties and submitted his report on July 15.

Questions

1. Assume that you are the fact finder in the case. Analyze the sick leave problem in Spring Valley and propose a plan equitable to both parties.

2. If you were the city manager, entrusted with pursuing the best interests of the city, which provisions in the proposal would you accept and which would you attempt to change?

3. Assume that you are the union negotiator. Which provisions would you accept and which would you attempt to change?

Source: From *Practicing Public Management: A Casebook* by C. Kenneth Meyer et al. Copyright © 1983 by St. Martin's Press, Inc., and used with permission of the publisher.

NOTES

1. Bradley Braden, "Increases in Employer Costs for Employee Benefits Dampen Dramatically," *Monthly Labor Review* (July 1988), pp. 3–7.

2. Marie Wilson, Gregory Northcraft, and Margaret Neale, "The Perceived Value of Fringe Benefits," *Personnel Psychology*, Vol. 38, no. 2 (Summer 1985), pp. 309–320.

3. This is based on Bonnie De Clark, "Cutting Unemployment Insurance Costs," *Personnel Journal*, Vol. 62 (November 1983), pp. 868–870.

4. Robert E. Sibson, *Wages and Salaries: A Handbook for Line Managers* (New York: American Management Association, 1967), pp. 236–237. See also Richard L. Bunning, "A Prescription for Sick Leave," *Personnel Journal*, Vol. 67, no. 8 (August 1988), pp. 44–49. Explains how one company set up an effective sick leave policy based on positive reinforcement rather than discipline.

5. Miriam Rothman, "Can Alternatives to Sick Pay Plans Reduce Absenteeism?" *Personnel Journal*, Vol. 60 (October 1981), pp. 788–791.

6. *San Francisco Chronicle*, June 2, 1987, p. 10.

7. Joseph Famularo, *Handbook of Modern Personnel Administration* (New York: McGraw-Hill, 1972), pp. 51–62.

8. Richard Henderson, *Compensation Management* (Reston, Va.: Reston, 1979), p. 250. For an explanation of how to reduce workers' compensation costs, see Betty Strigel Bialk, "Cutting Workers' Compensation Costs," *Personnel Journal*, Vol. 66, no. 7 (July 1987), pp. 95–97.

9. Henderson, p. 90. Also see Bureau of National Affairs, "Workers' Compensation Total Disability Benefits by State," 1989, pp. 172–173, for a list showing workers' compensation by state.

10. See, for example, Betty Strigel Bialk, "Cutting Workers' Compensation Costs," *Personnel Journal* (July 1987), pp. 95–97.

11. Sibson, *Wages and Salaries*, p. 235.

12. "Survey of Salaries Employees Benefits Plans," *CPA Journal* (July 1981), p. 7.

13. Rita Jain, "Employer-Sponsored Dental Insurance Eases the Pain," *Monthly Labor Review* (October 1988), p. 18.

14. Ibid., p. 23.

15. Bureau of National Affairs, *Bulletin to Management*, December 23, 1982, p. 1; "TEFRA—The Tax Equity and Fiscal Responsibility Act of 1982," *Personnel*, Vol. 59 (November–December 1982), p. 43.

16. A. N. Nash and S. J. Carroll, Jr., "Supplemental Compensation," in *Perspectives on Personnel: Human Resource Management*, Herbert Heneman III and Donald Schwab, eds. (Homewood, Ill.: Irwin, 1978), p. 223.

17. Thomas Snodeker and Michael Kuhns, "HMO's: Regulations, Problems, and Outlook," *Personnel Journal*, Vol. 60 (August 1981), pp. 629–631.

18. Bureau of National Affairs, "Employee Benefit Costs," *Bulletin to Management*, February 2, 1989, pp. 36–37; Commerce Clearing House, "Benefit Costs Remain the Number One Issue for HR Executives, The Human Resource Institute Says," *Ideas and Trends*, September 7, 1989, p. 166.

19. Hewitt Associates, "Health Care Costs Becoming Shared Responsibility," *News and Information*, June 21, 1984. See also, *Health Care Cost Containment* (New York: William Mercer-Meidinger, 1984), as discussed in *Compensation Review* (Fourth Quarter 1984), pp. 8–9; and Thomas Paine, "Outlook for Compensation and Benefits: 1986 and Beyond," Hewitt Associates, October 30, 1985. See also John Parkington, "The Trade-off Approach to Benefits Cost Containment: A Strategy to Increase Employee Satisfaction," *Compensation and Benefits Review*, Vol. 19, no. 1 (January–February 1987), pp. 26–35; Hewitt Associates, "Employer-Sponsored Medical Plans Designed to Make Employees Better Health Care Consumers, Study Says," *News and Information*, July 28, 1989 (100 Half Day Road, Lincolnshire, Ill.: 60015); Janet Norwood, "Measuring the Cost and Incidence of Employee Benefits," *Monthly Labor Review*, Vol. 111, no. 8 (August 1988), pp. 3–8; Robert C. Penzkover, "Health Incentives at Quaker Oats," *Personnel Journal*, Vol. 68, no. 3 (March 1989), pp. 114–118; and Anne Skagen, "Managing Health Care Costs," Part III, "Focus on Case Management," *Compensation and Benefits Review*, Vol. 20, no. 6 (November–December 1988), pp. 56–63; Hewitt Associates, "News and Information," February 6, 1990.

20. Hewitt Associates, "Employers Trim Future Health Care Costs by Keeping Employees 'Well,'" *News and Information*, June 7, 1984; and Morton Grossman and Margaret Magnus, "The Boom in Benefits," *Personnel Journal* (November 1988), pp. 51–55. See also "Could Wellness Programs Thrive?" *Personnel*, Vol. 65, no. 3 (March 1988), pp. 6–7, lists specific examples of wellness programs now in place. See also Marjorie Blanchard, "Wellness Programs," *Personnel Journal*, Vol. 68, no. 5 (May 1989), pp. 30–31, for examples of wellness program benefits, and BNA, "Benefit Cost Containment Trend Continues," 1989, p. 2, for examples of how companies are proceeding.

21. The following is based on Michael Gomez, "Managing Health Care Costs," Part I, "The Dilemma of AIDS," *Compensation and Benefits Review* (September–October 1988), pp. 23–31.

22. Quoted from ibid., p. 28.

23. Ibid., p. 31.

24. This is based on Thomas C. Billet, "Managing Health Care Costs," Part II, "Coping with Mental Health," *Compensation and Benefits Review* (September–October 1988), pp. 32–36.

25. Ibid., pp. 35–36.

26. This is based on Paul Greenlaw and Diana Foderaro, "Some Practical Implications of the Pregnancy Discrimination Act," *Personnel Journal*, Vol. 58 (October 1979), pp. 677–681. See also Commerce Clearing House "Supreme Court Says Giving Women Pregnancy Leave Is Lawful Even in the Case Where Men Receive No Disability Leave Whatever," *Ideas and Trends in Personnel*, January 23, 1987, pp. 9–10.

27. Jerome B. Cohen and Arthur Hanson, *Personnel Finance* (Homewood, Ill.: Irwin, 1964), pp. 312–320. See also BNA, January 14, 1988, pp. 12–13. This article explains changes in the Social Security law and presents an exhibit showing how to estimate your Social Security benefits.

28. See Henderson, *Compensation Management*, pp. 289–290; Famularo, *Handbook*, pp. 37.1–37.9; Edward Katz, "The Unsung Benefits of Employee Savings Plans," *Personnel Journal*, Vol. 58 (January 1979), pp. 30–31; Edward Redling, "Voluntary Deferred Compensation—Off Again, On Again," *Personnel*, Vol. 56 (1979), pp. 64–67.

29. See Evert Allen, Jr., Joseph Melone, and Jerry Rosenbloom, *Pension Planning* (Homewood, Ill.: Irwin, 1981).

30. Avy Graham, "How Has Vesting Changed Since Passage of Employee Retirement Income Security Act?" *Monthly Labor Review* (August 1988), pp. 20–25.

31. Ibid., p. 20.

32. Sibson, *Wages and Salaries*, p. 234.

33. For a discussion of demographic trends with specific reference to average age of employers, see, for example, D. Quinn Mills, "Human Resources in the 1980's," *Harvard Business Review*, Vol. 58 (July–August 1979), pp. 154–163.

34. *The Economist*, August 5, 1978, p. 57.

35. For a discussion of the pros and cons of early retirement, see, for example, Jeffrey Sonnenfelt, "Dealing with the Aging Workforce," *Harvard Business Review*, Vol. 57 (November–December 1978), pp. 81–92.

36. A. F. Ehrbar, "Those Pension Plans Are Even Weaker than You Think," *Fortune*, Vol. 94, no. 5 (November 1977), pp. 104–107, discussed in H. Chruden and A. Sherman, Jr., *Personnel Management* (Cincinnati: South-Western 1980), pp. 500–501. See also Carroll Roarty, "How Merabank Lowered Pension Costs Without Lowering Morale," *Personnel Journal*, Vol. 66, no. 11 (November 1987), pp. 64–71, which relates how this bank changed its profit sharing and pension plans and saved money without sacrificing morale.

37. See Irwin Tepper, "Risk vs. Return in Pension Fund Investment," *Harvard Business Review*, Vol. 56 (March–April 1977), pp. 100–107, and William Rupert, "ERISA: Compliance May Be Easier than You Expect and Pay Unexpected Dividends," *Personnel Journal*, Vol. 55 (April 1976).

38. Robert Paul, "The Impact of Pension Reform on American Business," *Sloan Management Review*, Vol. 18 (Fall 1976), pp. 59–71. See also John M. Walbridge, Jr., "The Next Hurdle for Benefits Manager: Section 89," *Compensation and Benefits Review*, Vol. 20, no. 6 (November–December 1988), pp. 22–35.

39. Henderson, *Compensation Management*, p. 292.

40. Bureau of National Affairs, "Tax Reform Act: Major Changes in Store for Compensation Programs," *Bulletin to Management*, October 9, 1986, p. 1.

41. In fact, unfunded pension liabilities of American firms have continued to grow. "Pension Survey: Unfunded Liabilities Continue to Grow," *Business Week*, August 25, 1980, pp. 94–97. See also James Benson and Barbara Suzaki, "After Tax Reform," Part III, "Planning Executive Benefits," *Compensation and Benefits Review*, Vol. 20, no. 2 (March–April 1988), pp. 45–57; and BNA, February 23, 1989, p. 57. "Post-Retirement Benefits Impact of FASB New Accounting Rule."

42. Robert Arnott and Peter Bernstein, "The Right Way to Manage Your Pension Fund," *Harvard Business Review* (January–February 1988), pp. 95–102.

43. A task force of consultants from William A. Mercer Meidinger Hansen, Inc., "The Omnibus Budget Reconciliation Act of 1987: What It Means to Pensions and Employee Benefits," *Compensation and Benefits Review* (March–April 1988), pp. 14–32.

44. Judith Mazo, "Another Compliance Challenge for Employers: The Retirement Equity Act," *Personnel*, Vol. 62, no. 2 (February 1985), pp. 43–49. See also Deborah Nikkel, "HIRS Implementation: A Systematic Approach," *Personnel*, Vol. 62, no. 2 (February 1985), pp. 66–69. See also Jack Schechter, "The Impact of Tax Reform on Employee Benefits: A Half Time Report," *Personnel*, Vol. 65, no. 1 (January 1988), pp. 46–51.

45. Randy Cepuch, "Should You Put IRA on the Payroll?" *Personnel Journal*, Vol. 61 (November 1982), p. 812.

46. Allen et al., *Pension Planning*, pp. 406–410. Note that self-employed individuals can establish Keogh (for H.R. 10) pension plans. Basically, 15% of earned income (or up to $7,500) can be invested in such a plan; if the person is not only self-employed but also the owner of the business, then all his or her full-time employees must also be covered by the plan.

47. William M. Mercer-Meidinger, Inc., "How Will Reform Tax Your Benefits?" *Personnel Journal*, Vol. 65, no. 12 (1986), pp. 52–53. See also Steven Baderian and Ivy Stempel, "Coping with COBRA," *Compensation and Benefits Review*, Vol. 19, no. 3 (May–June 1987), pp. 28–36.

48. "Plan Design and Experience in Early Retirement Windows and in Other Voluntary Separation Plans," prepared by the staff of Hewitt Associates, 1986. See also Eugene Seibert and Joanne Seibert, "Retirement Windows," *Personnel*

Journal, Vol. 68, no. 5 (May 1989), pp. 30–31, examples of wellness program benefits.

49. Marco Colosi, Philip Rosen, and Sara Herrin, "Is Your Early Retirement Package Courting Disaster?" *Personnel Journal* (August 1988), pp. 59–67.

50. *Paolillo* v. *Dresser Industries*, 821F.2d81 (2d cir. 1987).

51. See also Eugene Seibert and Jo Anne Seibert, "Look into Window Alternatives," *Personnel Journal* (May 1989), pp. 80–87.

52. See Henderson, *Compensation Management*, pp. 336–339. See also Lewis Burger, "Group Legal Service Plans: A Benefit Whose Time Has Come," *Compensation and Benefits Review*, Vol. 18, no. 4 (July–August 1986), pp. 28–34.

53. Richard T. Hellan, "Employee Assistance: An EAP Update: A Perspective for the '80s," *Personnel Journal*, Vol. 65, no. 6 (1986), p. 51.

54. See Dale Masi and Seymour Friedland, "EAP Actions & Options," *Personnel Journal* (June 1988), pp. 61–67.

55. These are based on Masi and Friedland, "EAP Actions & Options."

56. For a discussion of group legal and auto insurance plans, see Joan Lindroth, "Inflation, Taxes, and Perks: How Compensation Is Changing," *Personnel Journal*, Vol. 60 (December 1981), p. 938.

57. "Goodies," *Dun's Review*, July 1981, pp. 49–50.

58. Lindroth, "Inflation, Taxes, and Perks," p. 938.

59. Mary Zippo, "Employee Benefits Update," *Personnel*, Vol. 57 (May–June 1980), pp. 39–40.

60. *Dun's Review*, July 1981, p. 50.

61. The Research Staff of Hewitt Associates, *Innovative Benefits*, Hewitt Associates, 160 Bloor Street East, Toronto, Ontario.

62. This is based on Margaret Meiers, "Parental Leave and the Bottom Line," *Personnel Journal* (September 1988), pp. 108–115.

63. Ibid., pp. 110–112.

64. Jennifer S. MacLeod, "Meeting the Needs of Today's Working Parents," *Employment Relations Today*, Vol. 13, no. 2 (Summer 1986), p. 127. See also Susan Velleman, "A Benefit to Meet Changing Needs: Child-Care Assistance," *Compensation and Benefits Review*, Vol. 19, no. 3 (May–June 1987), pp. 54–58.

65. *Dun's Review*, July 1981, p. 49. See also Velleman, "A Benefit to Meet Changing Needs," pp. 54–62. See also BNA, "Child Care Benefits Offered by Employers," March 17, 1988, pp. 84–85.

66. "Employers and Child Care: Establishing Services Through the Workplace," Women's Bureau, U.S. Department of Labor, Washington, D.C., 1982. See also BNA, "Special Survey on Child Care Assistance Programs," *Bulletin to Management*, March 26, 1987. Donald J. Petersen and Douglas Massengill, "Child Care Programs Benefit Employers, Too," *Personnel*, Vol. 65, no. 5 (May 1988), pp. 58–62, and Toni A. Campbell and David E. Campbell, "Employers and Child Care," *Personnel Journal*, Vol. 67, no. 4 (April 1988), pp. 84–87.

67. Thomas Miller, "The Effects of Employer-Sponsored Child Care on Employee Absenteeism, Turnover, Productivity, Recruitment or Job Satisfaction: What Is Claimed and What Is Known," *Personnel Psychology*, Vol. 37, no. 2 (Summer 1984), pp. 277–289.

68. Commerce Clearing House, "As the Population Ages, There is Growing Interest in Adding Elder Care to the Benefits Package," *Ideas and Trends*, August 21, 1987, pp. 129–131.

69. Mary Zippo, "Subsidized Employee Transportation: A Three Way Benefit," *Personnel*, Vol. 57 (May–June 1980), pp. 40–41.

70. Hewitt Associates, "Survey of Educational Reimbursement Programs," 1984.

71. Bruce Ellig, *Executive Compensation—A Total Pay Perspective* (New York: McGraw-Hill, 1982), p. 141.

72. Lindroth, "Inflation, Taxes, and Perks," p. 939.

73. A. W. Smith, Jr., "Will Perquisites Survive?" *Compensation and Benefits Review*, Vol. 17 (November–December 1985), pp. 44–52.

74. J. Brad Chapman and Robert Ottemann, "Employee Preference for Various Compensation and Fringe Benefit Options" (Berea, Ohio: ASPA Foundation, 1975). See also, William White and James Becker, "Increasing the Motivational Impact of Employee Benefits," *Personnel* (January–February 1980), pp. 32–37, and Barney Olmsted and Suzanne Smith, "Flex for Success!" *Personnel*, Vol. 66, no. 6 (June 1989), pp. 50–55.

75. Ibid.; Albert Cole, "Flexible Benefits Are a Key to Better Employee Relations," *Personnel Journal* (January 1983), pp. 49–53. See also, Lance Tane, "Guidelines to Successful Flex Plans: Four Companies' Experiences," *Compensation and Benefits Review*, Vol. 17 (July–August 1985), pp. 38–45; Peter Stonebraker, "A Three-Tier Plan for Cafeteria Benefits," *Personnel Journal*, Vol. 63, no. 12 (December 1984), pp. 50–53; and Commerce Clearing House, "Flexible Benefits: Will They Work for You?" Chicago, 1983; and George F. Dreher, Ronald A. Ash, and Robert D. Bretz, "Benefit Coverage and Employee Cost: Critical Factors in Explaining Compensation Satisfaction," *Personnel Psychology*, Vol. 41, no. 2 (Summer 1988), pp. 237–254.

76. Barbara Anne Soloman, "The Change to 'Flexible': No Easy Task," *Personnel*, Vol. 62, no. 5 (May 1985), pp. 10–12.

77. Henderson, *Compensation Management*, p. 312; "Flexible Benefits Are Spreading Fast," *Dun's Business Month*, September 1981, pp. 82–84. See Caroline A. Baker, "Flex Your Benefits," *Personnel Journal*, Vol. 67, no. 5 (May 1988), pp. 54–58, for discussion of the pros and cons of three basic approaches to flexible benefits.

78. For information about this program, contact Towers, Perrin, Forster, and Crosby, 245 Park Avenue, New York, NY 10167. Hewitt Associates similarly has a program called FlexSystem (Hewitt Associates, New York, N.Y.). See also John Parkington, "The 'Trade-off' Approach to Benefits Cost Containment: A Strategy to Increase Employee Satisfaction," *Compensation and Benefits Review*, Vol. 19, no. 1 (January–February 1987), pp. 35–36, which explains a simple way of determining what your employees prefer in benefits.

79. This is based on Anthony Barra, "Employees Keep Informed with Interactive KIOSKs," *Personnel Journal* (October 1988), pp 43–51.

80. For a discussion see, for example, Marvin Selter, "On the Plus Side of Employee Leasing," *Personnel Journal* (April 1986), pp. 87–91; David Altaner, "Employees for Lease," *Weekly Business News/Sun Sentinel*, November 9, 1987, pp. 8–9.

81. John Naisbitt, "Employee Leasing Takes Off," *Success!* April 1986, p. 12.

82. Morton Grossman and Margaret Magnus, "The Boom in Benefits," *Personnel Journal* (November 1988), pp. 51–59.

83. Thomas Paine, "Benefits in the 1990s," *Personnel Journal* (March 1988), pp. 82–92.

Chapter 13

Nonfinancial Motivation Techniques

When you finish studying this chapter, you should be able to:

1. Define quality of work life.
2. Explain the pros and cons of flextime.
3. Explain how to set up a quality circle program.
4. Discuss the guidelines to follow in ensuring an effective quality improvement program.

Overview

The main purpose of this chapter is to explain how to use several nonfinancial "motivation" techniques and programs to improve the company culture, quality of work life and performance of your enterprise. After explaining what is meant by "quality of work life" programs, we focus in on three important programs—alternative work arrangements, quality circle programs, and companywide quality improvement programs. Each of these programs contributes to the quality of work life in the enterprise by providing employees with more opportunities for flexibility, creativity, and responsibility than they might have otherwise. And, in so doing each program contributes to intrinsic motivators (recall Chapter 9) like the needs for achievement and to self-actualize, and thereby, hopefully, to improved performance at work.

Many changes are occurring in the environment of personnel management. Information technology (PCs, etc.) increasingly demands a more sophisticated, better-trained work force. Of the sixteen million or so jobs added by the U.S. economy in the 1990s, virtually all are in service jobs, jobs (like consultants, salespeople, food service workers, and nurses) that don't readily lend themselves to highly restrictive work rules or supervisory practices. At the same time the supply of available labor is growing more slowly than in the past, and the average age of that work force is rising—two more factors which are putting a premium on using new methods for getting the best out of your work force. And superimposed over all this is the change in work itself (and in how modern businesses are managed), changes which reflect the increasing globalization and need for responsiveness that corporate success today requires.

These changes are naturally influencing the personnel management methods employers use, and no where is this more apparent than in their worker reward and involvement systems. In particular, employers are increasingly utilizing nonfinancial motivation techniques like quality improvement programs and flexible work arrangements. Programs like these, as we will see in this chapter, aim at eliciting the best that workers can offer, by treating them responsibly, by giving them more discretion over their jobs, and in general by providing them with the opportunity to use their problem-solving skills to accomplish difficult jobs and thereby satisfy their needs to achieve and to self-actualize. Some of the most important of these nonfinancial personnel motivation/involvement methods are discussed in this chapter, and include such closely-related programs as:

Alternative Work Arrangements. These generally involve allowing employees to design relatively flexible work days and/or work weeks for themselves so as to better accommodate the employees' personal needs and preferences.

Quality Circle Programs. These include the establishment of specially-trained work teams which meet periodically (usually weekly) to analyze and solve problems in their work areas.

Companywide Quality Improvement (QI) Programs. These programs are instituted to improve the quality of the employer's product or services; the basic approach involves a coordinated, companywide effort built around monitoring customer satisfaction and using employee teams and involvement to continually improve quality.

♦ QUALITY OF WORK LIFE POLICIES

To many employers and experts the underlying aim of programs like these is the **quality of work life** of employees. In practice, quality of work life (QWL) may be defined as the degree to which employees are able to satisfy their important personal needs by working in the firm. In this view programs like flexible work hours, quality circles and QI programs (discussed below) all contribute to the quality of work life by contributing to:

1. Fair, equitable, and supportive treatment of employees.
2. An opportunity for all employees to use their skills to the utmost and to self-actualize—to become all that they are capable of becoming.
3. Open, trusting communications between all employees.
4. An opportunity for all employees to take an active role in making important decisions that involve their own jobs.

5. Adequate and fair compensation.
6. A safe and healthy environment.

While the phrase *quality of work life* is quite new, its conceptual foundations were actually laid some years ago, with the work of behavioral scientists such as Chris Argyris. At the time, Argyris was mostly concerned with the emotional health of workers. Basically, he argued that as people mature into adults they develop needs for independence, broader interests, and superordinate positions—an overall need, in other words, to control their own destinies. And, says Argyris, the typical company, with its rigid rules (such as having the boss determine the exact hours that employees must work), actually stifles employees' needs to control their lives and grow. Employees must be given more freedom, said Argyris, and his position helped set the stage for today's QWL movement.

Some employers, like IBM, have made coordinated efforts aimed at improving employees' involvement and overall quality of work life. In addition to using flexible hours and quality circles, many other personnel policies regarding, for instance, pay (all IBM employees are salaried), line managers (who are encouraged to maintain supportive relationships with subordinates), and opinion surveys (aimed at monitoring employees concerns) are aimed at ensuring that employees' needs are being satisfied and that the quality of work life in the firm is high.

ALTERNATIVE WORK ARRANGEMENTS

◆ FLEXTIME

Flextime is a plan whereby employees' flexible workdays are built around a core of midday hours, such as 11 to 2. It is called flextime because workers determine their own starting and stopping hours. For example, they may opt to work from 7 to 3 or 11 to 7. According to one study, the number of companies using flextime has increased from 15% in 1978 to over 30% today. Well over 10% of the U.S. work force is on a flextime schedule, not counting professionals, managers, salespeople, and self-employed persons who customarily set their own work hours anyway.[1]

Flextime in Practice

In practice, most employers who use flextime allow employees only limited freedom regarding the hours they work. This is summarized in Table 13.1, which shows the earliest starting time, latest starting time, and core periods that are most popular. As you can see, employers still try to hold fairly close to the traditional 9 to 5 day. For example, in 67% of the companies' employees can't start work before 7 A.M., and in almost all firms employees must not clock in before 6 A.M. Similarly, in about half the firms, employees can't start work later than 9 A.M., and employees in about 40% of the firms must be in by 10 A.M. Therefore, the effect of flextime for most employees is to give them about 1 hour leeway in terms of starting before 9 or leaving after 5. Similarly, about 15% of the employers made 9 A.M.– 3 P.M. their core period, while another 28% made their core period 9 A.M.– 4 P.M.

The Pros and Cons of Flextime

Some flextime programs have been quite successful.[2] Because less time is lost due to tardiness, the ratio of worker-hours worked to worker-hours

TABLE 13.1   Typical Flextime Schedules

FLEXTIME STARTING TIMES			
Earliest Starting Time	*Percent of Respondents*	*Latest Starting Time*	*Percent of Respondents*
Before 6 A.M.	10%	8–9 A.M.	55%
6–7 A.M.	21%	9–10 A.M.	31%
7–8 A.M.	67%	10–11 A.M.	9%
8–9 A.M.	2%	11–12 Noon	0%
After 9 A.M.	0%	After 12 Noon	5%

FLEXTIME CORE HOURS		WORK WEEK SCHEDULING	
Time	*Percent of Respondents*	*Scheduling Plan*	*Percent of Respondents*
8 A.M.–3 P.M.	5%	5 days, 40 hours	64%
8 A.M.–4 P.M.	19%	5 days, 37½ hours	18%
8 A.M.–5 P.M.	10%	5 days, 35 hours	8%
9 A.M.–3 P.M.	15%	5 days, 38¾ hours	3%
9 A.M.–4 P.M.	28%	5 days, 36¼ hours	2%
9 A.M.–5 P.M.	6%	4 days, 40 hours	1%
10 A.M.–2 P.M.	4%	All others	4%
10 A.M.–3 P.M.	3%		
10 A.M.–4 P.M.	5%		
11 A.M.–3 P.M.	3%		
Noon–6 P.M.	1%		

Note: Types of industries represented are business and human services (including government agencies, medical institutions, educational institutions, nonprofit organizations, employment agencies, consulting firms, and publishing firms), 39%; banking/financial/insurance, 28%; manufacturing/processing, 21%; retail/wholesale sales and distribution, 7%. Number of employees in represented companies: very small companies (1–100), 24%; small companies (101–1,000), 37%; medium-sized companies (1,000–10,000), 24%; large companies (over 10,000), 10%.

Source: *1986 AMS Flexible Work Survey* (Willow Grove, Pa.: Administrative Management Society, 1986), pp. 3, 4, 9.

paid (a measure of productivity) increases. It has also been shown to reduce absenteeism and to cut down on "sick" leave being used for personal matters. The hours actually worked seem to be more productive, and there is less slowing down toward the end of the workday. Workers tend to leave early when work is slack and work later when it is heavy. The use of flextime also seems to be related to an increased receptiveness on the part of employees to changes in other procedures.

Flextime is also advantageous from the workers' point of view. It may reduce the tedium associated with the timing of their work and democratize their work. It also tends to reduce the distinction between managers and workers and requires more delegation of authority by supervisors.

There are also disadvantages. Flextime is complicated to administer and may be impossible to implement where large groups of workers must work interdependently.[3] It also requires the use of time clocks or other time records, and this can be disadvantageous from the point of view of workers.

Surveys covering some 445 employees (including drug companies, banks, electronics firms, and government agencies) indicate that the percentage of employees reporting productivity increases as a result of flextime programs range from a low of 5% or 10% in some firms to about 95% in one airline. On the whole, about 45% of employees involved in flextime programs report that the program has resulted in improved productivity.[4] The failure rate of flextime is also remarkably low, reportedly 8%, according to one study.[5]

Conditions for Success

There are several things you can do to make your flextime program more successful.[6] *Management resistance*—particularly at the supervisory level and particularly before the program is actually tried—has torpedoed several programs before they became operational, so supervisory indoctrination programs are important prerequisites to success. Second, flextime is usually more successful with clerical, professional, and managerial jobs, and less so with factory jobs (the nature of which tend to demand interdependence among workers). Third, experience indicates that the greater the flexibility of a flextime program, the greater the benefits the program can produce (although the disadvantages, of course, multiply as well). Fourth, how the program is installed is important; a flextime project director to oversee all aspects of the program should be appointed, and frequent meetings should take place between supervisors and employees to allay their fears and clear up misunderstanding. A pilot study, say, in one department, is advisable.[7]

Also, flextime may be especially valuable for the employer when the group must share limited resources. For example, computer programmers often spend as much as two-thirds of their time waiting to make computer runs. In situations like these flextime may be especially beneficial. As one researcher concludes, "because flextime expands the amount of time that the computer is available to the programmer, this allows its usage to be spread over more hours, and the time in queues to make runs and get output back is reduced."[8]

◆ THREE- AND FOUR-DAY WORKWEEKS

four-day workweek An arrangement that allows employees to work four ten-hour days instead of the more usual five eight-hour days.

A number of employers have also switched to a **four-day workweek**. Here employees work four 10-hour days instead of the more usual five 8-hour days.[9]

Advantages

Compressed workweek plans have been fairly successful since they have several advantages (see Table 13.2). Productivity seems to increase since there are fewer start-ups and shutdowns. Workers are more willing to work some evenings and Saturdays as part of these plans. According to a study by the American Management Association, 80% of the firms on such plans reported that the plan "improves business results"; three-fifths said that production was up and almost two-fifths said that costs were down. Half the firms also reported higher profits. Even the four-day firms *not* reporting positive results reported that cost and profit factors at least remained the same. A study by the Bureau of Labor Statistics suggests that the four-day workweek is generally effective (in terms of reducing paid overtime, reducing absenteeism, and improving efficiency). Furthermore, workers also gain; there is a 20% reduction in commuter trips and an additional day off per week. Additional savings (for example, in child care expenses) may also occur.

Keep in mind, though, that there has not been a lot of experience with shortened workweeks, and it is possible that the improvements are short-lived. In one study, for instance, 4-day weeks resulted in greater employee satisfaction and productivity and less absenteeism when evaluated after 13 months, but these improvements were not found after 25 months.[10] A recent review of 3-day, 38-hour workweeks concluded that compressed workweek schedules have significant positive and long-lasting effects on the organization if handled properly. Regardless of individual differences, those employees who have experienced the 3/38 schedule reacted favorably to it, particu-

TABLE 13.2 Advantages and Disadvantages of Flextime (in rank order)

RANK ORDER	ADVANTAGES
1	Improves employee attitude and morale
2	Accommodates working parents
3	Results in fewer traffic problems—workers can avoid congested streets and highways
4	Increases production
5	Decreases tardiness
6	Accommodates those who wish to arrive at work before interruptions begin
7	Facilitates employee scheduling of medical, dental, and other types of appointments
8	Decreases absenteeism
9	Accommodates the leisure-time activities of employees
10	Decreases turnover
	DISADVANTAGES
1	Lack of supervision during all hours of work
2	Finding key people unavailable at certain times
3	Causes understaffing at times
4	Accommodating employees whose output is the input for other employees is a problem
5	Inability to schedule meetings at convenient times
6	Employee abuse of flextime program
7	Keeping track of hours worked or accumulated is a problem
8	Planning work schedules is difficult
9	Inability to coordinate projects

Source: *1986 AMS Flexible Work Survey* (Willow Grove, Pa.: Administrative Management Society, 1986), p. 4.

larly if they had participated in the decision to implement the new program and if their jobs have been enriched by the schedule change. Fatigue did not appear to be a problem in this survey.[11]

Disadvantages

There are also some disadvantages, some of them potentially quite severe (see Table 13.2). Tardiness, for example, may become a problem. Of more concern is the fact that fatigue was cited by a number of firms as a principal drawback of the four-day workweek (note that fatigue was a main reason for adopting 8-hour days in the first place).

◆ OTHER FLEXIBLE WORK ARRANGEMENTS

job sharing A concept that allows two or more people to share a single full-time job.

work sharing A temporary reduction in work hours by a group of employees during economic difficulties to prevent layoffs.

flexiplace A flexible work arrangement in which employees are allowed or encouraged to work at home or in a satellite office closer to home.

Employers are also taking other steps to accommodate the needs of their employees. **Job sharing** is a concept that allows two or more people to share a single full-time job; for example, two people may share a 40-hour-per-week job, with one working mornings and the other working afternoons. About 10% of the firms questioned in one survey indicated that they allow for job sharing.[12] **Work sharing** refers to a temporary reduction in work hours by a group of employees during economic hard times as a way of preventing layoffs; thus 400 employees may all agree to work (and get paid for) only 35 hours per week in order to avoid having the firm lay off 30 workers. **Flexiplace**, in which employees are allowed or encouraged to work at home or in a satellite office closer to home, is another example of flexible work arrangement that is becoming more popular today.

Telecommuting is another option. Here employees work at home, usually with video displays, and use telephone lines to transmit letters, data, and completed work back to the home office. For example, Best Western Hotels in Phoenix is using the residents of the Arizona Center for Women, a minimum-security prison, as an office staff. It is estimated that some 7 million Americans are telecommuting today, in various jobs from lawyer to clerk to computer expert.[13]

Still other employers, especially in Europe, are switching to a plan they call *flexyears*. Under this plan, employees can choose (at six-month intervals) the number of hours they want to work each month over the next year. A full-timer, for instance, might be able to work up to 173 hours a month. In a typical flexyear arrangement, an employee who wants to average 110 hours a month might work 150 hours in January (when the children are at school and when the company needs extra help to cope with the January sales). In February, she may work only 70 hours because she wants to, say, go skiing. In March, she may then work the full 173 hours to build up her credit, which will enable her to accompany her husband on a business trip abroad in the following month.[14]

USING QUALITY CIRCLE PROGRAMS

quality circle A group of five to ten specially trained employees who meet on a regular basis to identify and solve problems in their work area.

A **quality circle** is a group of five to ten specially trained employees who meet for an hour once a week for the purpose of spotting and solving problems in their work area.[15] The circle is usually composed of a normal work group—a group of people who work together to produce a specific component or service.

♦ STEPS IN ESTABLISHING A QUALITY CIRCLE

The four steps in establishing and leading a quality circle include *planning, training, initiation,* and *operating.*

Planning the Circle

The planning phase usually takes about one month and typically begins with a top-level executive making the decision to implement the quality circle (QC) technique. This usually leads to identifying and selecting a consultant who will assist top management in implementing the quality circles in the firm, although in some cases an in-house *facilitator* will be identified and sent out for special circle methods training. The facilitator then returns to the firm and handles the tasks the consultant would otherwise have been responsible for.

One of the most important steps in this first phase involves selecting the quality circle *steering committee*. The steering committee becomes the group that directs quality circle activities in the organization. The committee is usually multidisciplinary in that it draws on employees from functions such as production, human resource, quality control, training, marketing, engineering, finance, and the union. Committees usually contain up to 15 members, and the chief executive is often a member. (The success of the quality circle concept often hinges on how committed to the technique workers feel top management is; therefore, the steering committee almost always has at least one or two top managers as members.)

The steering committee has several responsibilities. Perhaps most important, it should establish circle objectives in terms of the kinds of *bottom-line improvements* they would like to see. Yardsticks include reduced errors and enhanced quality, more effective teamwork, increased job involvement, increased motivation, and an increased attitude of problem prevention. At the same time, the steering committee determines actions that are considered outside the charter of the circles—for instance, benefits and salaries, employment practices, policies on discharging employees, personalities, and grievances.

The steering committee also chooses the in-house facilitator, the person who will be responsible for daily coordination of the firm's quality circle activities. In most cases the facilitator devotes full time to the quality circle tasks and is responsible for such specific quality circle duties as coordinating the activities of the circles, training leaders for each circle, attending circle meetings and providing expert advice and backup coordination, and maintaining records to reflect circle achievements.

During this first phase, the steering committee, working with the facilitator, selects leaders for the pilot program. (Two or three work areas are usually chosen as pilot areas for the QC program.) Although the steering committee is responsible for choosing these leaders, in practice the supervisor/leaders are usually selected by the managers of the departments where the pilot programs will operate; they are then confirmed by the steering committee.

Initial Training

In the second phase, the facilitator and pilot project leaders meet (usually with the consultant) and are trained in basic QC philosophy, implementation, and operation. This training course typically takes four days and includes various activities. On the first day, the consultant meets with the trainees to discuss the nature and objectives of quality circles. On the remaining days, trainees use case studies to learn quality circle leadership techniques.

Initiating the Circles

The third phase involves initiating the pilot program's circles. This usually begins with department managers conducting quality circle familiarization meetings with employees, with the facilitator, circle leaders, and (ideally) an executive participating as speakers. Employees are told they will be contacted later for their decisions regarding whether or not they want to join a circle. Then, circle leaders contact each employee to determine circle membership, and the circles are constituted. The facilitator distributes member manuals for circle leaders at this point; the manuals contain an overview of the QC idea, as well as an explanation of data collection and problem-solving techniques. The basic techniques are usually learned by each circle in about eight weeks.

The Circle in Operation

Next, each circle can turn to its real job: problem solving and analysis. In practice, this involves five steps: problem identification, problem selection, problem analysis, solution recommendations, and solution review by management. Each step is explained next.

Problem Identification. The problems identified by circle members are usually mundane and may not be especially interesting to anyone outside the circle's work area. These problems might include how to keep the area cleaner, how to improve the work group's product quality, or how to speed up the packing of the work group's crates. Problems such as these may seem uninteresting to those outside the work group, but to the group they represent small impediments that, taken as a whole, reduce the group's performance. And, they are exactly the sort of problems for which the work group members are, in a very real sense, the resident experts at solving.

Notice that circle members generally do *not* spend their time identifying big interdepartmental organizational problems. These problems are more appropriately within the purview of management.

Problem Selection. Next, members select the number one problem they wish to focus on. Circle members usually know better than anyone else what impediments are making it difficult for them to do their jobs and are thus in the best position to prioritize problems.

Problem Analysis. In this next step, circle members collect and collate data relating to the problem and analyze them using data collection, analysis, and problem-solving techniques for which they are especially trained.

It is important to stress that it is the group members, rather than outside experts or the group leader/supervisor, who solve the problem. A big benefit—perhaps the biggest benefit—derived from quality circles is the sense of satisfaction that members get from being involved in the actual problem analysis process. If they are prohibited from analyzing the problem by an inept leader, they will not only miss this sense of satisfaction but may actually resent (rather than be committed to) implementing the solution. Quality circles are as much a people-building opportunity as a quality-improving one, and to derive all the benefits from a circle the members themselves must be involved in the problem selection, analysis, and implementation. Workers generally derive a great sense of satisfaction and commitment from this sort of challenge, and solving the problem without the worker's involvement is really missing the point of the quality circle idea.

Solution Recommendations. The group's solution is then presented to management orally by group members, with the aid of charts and graphs they prepare themselves. The presentation is usually oral rather than written and more often than not is prepared by employees on their own time at break, lunch, and after work. Most group members derive a great sense of excitement and challenge out of being able to prepare this presentation and sell their ideas.

Solution Review and Decision by Management. Quality circles operate through the normal management chain of command. The presentation is made to the individual to whom the supervisor (frequently the circle leader) reports, not to the steering committee or to somebody on the executive level. Top managers may be present as observers, but the rule is to adhere to the chain of command for any approvals required.

According to one source, from 85% to 100% of circle suggestions are approved by the manager, often in the presentation meeting itself. Occasionally the manager will need some verification of studies done and may even ask a staff person to assist in the verification. In those unusual instances in which a manager must decline a recommendation, he or she is trained to explain why it was turned down, so as not to dampen the enthusiasm of the circle members.

♦ **PROBLEMS THAT QUALITY CIRCLES ENCOUNTER**

Quality circle expert Donald Dewar says that circles typically encounter certain problems. And he says that if these problems can be anticipated, recognized, and dealt with by a firm's managers, then the effectiveness of their quality circle program will be enhanced. Some important recurring problems follow.

"This Is Just 'Another' Program"

One problem is that employees are often skeptical of the quality circle program, assuming either that it is just another participation program (such as a suggestion program) or a device for tricking the workers into producing more.

PERSONNEL MANAGEMENT:

ON THE FRONT LINE

As a recent graduate and a person who keeps up the business press, Jennifer is not unfamiliar with the benefits of nonfinancial motivation such as quality circle programs.

Jack has actually installed a quality-of-work-life program of sorts at Carter, and it has been in place for about five years. He holds employee meetings periodically but particularly when there is a serious problem in a store—such as very-poor-quality work or too many breakdowns—he schedules a meeting with all the employees in that store and meets with them as soon as the store closes. Hourly employees get extra pay for these meetings, and they actually have been fairly useful in helping Jack to identify several problems. Jennifer is now curious as to whether these employee meetings should be formalized and perhaps a formal quality circle program initiated.

1. Would you recommend a quality circle program to Jennifer? Why? Why not?

2. Given what you know about the supervision of these stores, would you recommend a management by objectives program for store managers? Why or why not?

3. Are new work arrangements such as flextime or four-day workweeks practical at Carter? Why?

The solution here is to confront this issue head on, before the subject is brought up. The worst thing to do is not mention it at all and let the workers' resentment and skepticism grow. If there is one factor that separates successful from unsuccessful quality circle programs, it is a top management which is clearly committed to the program.

"Management Pays No Attention to Our Ideas"

Sometimes employees complain that management pays no attention to their ideas, either because management does, in fact, ignore the quality circle's suggestions or because previous participation programs (such as a suggestion program) resulted in little or no feedback from management.

Part of the solution here is to emphasize that circle members are *not* being asked to generate a list of problems to be turned over to management. Instead, they are being asked to identify problems and their causes and then to solve these problems, *largely on their own*.

Selecting Problems Outside the Circle's Areas of Expertise

Dewar says that "perhaps the number one pitfall to successful quality circle operation is the selection of problems outside the members' areas of expertise." Sometimes, for instance, a new circle completes its training and proceeds to pick a problem in someone else's area—as when a production group tries to solve a shipping problem or when a circle tries to grapple with a more complex interdepartmental problem.

As the leader of a circle, you can avoid this problem by keeping the circle's members on the track. Thus, when the circle is about to begin generating a list of problems to consider, you should caution them to focus on problems within their own areas—where they are the experts. And then when the circle is selecting a high-priority problem from the list of problems, you have to repeat this advice.

"We Can't Start Circles Now— Meetings Will Hurt the Schedule"

Coming from managers and supervisors, this is exactly the sort of statement that will undermine the circle program, in that it seems to reflect management's less than wholehearted support for the program. From the supervisors' points of view, of course, their concerns seem well founded, since the prospect of eight to ten people sitting around for an hour talking every week can easily be translated into an extra several hundred dollars in costs and missed schedules.

Solving (or avoiding) this problem involves, first, showing managers and supervisors data regarding the past successes of quality circles. Many circle programs have, in fact, been responsible for some huge successes, and even when the successes have been more minor, management has generally concluded that the benefits have far exceeded the costs.

Fear of Interference from the Union

According to Dewar, unions are rarely an obstacle. When they have expressed concern, he says, it is usually because they think quality circles might take up such issues of wage levels, personnel matters, or grievances. These are normally the prerogatives of the union and are not, as we pointed out earlier, within the purview of the quality circle.

Therefore, the union president, says Dewar, should be invited to take a seat on the steering committee. Also, point out that union stewards will be members of circles and that the circles themselves will make for a more competitive organization that will provide greater job security for all.

Dewar suggests informing union officials of circle activities prior to initiation of those activities in an organization. This gets them involved at the start, avoids putting them in the position of not being able to answer members' questions about the circles, and also gives management an opportunity to assure them that the circle program is not a speed-up technique.

◆ QUALITY CIRCLES TODAY

By the mid–1980s, the original wave of employer enthusiasm and support for quality circle programs had begun to wane for several reasons. Perhaps the biggest reason was that many QCs failed to produce measurable cost savings for the sponsoring employer, in part because their bottom-line aims were too vague. And in many other firms, the participative QCs simply proved incompatible with the management styles and cultures existing in those firms.

Rather than throw out the baby with the bath water, though, many firms today are taking steps to make their QCs more workable. Some firms are turning to what are in essence second-generation QCs, ones that are geared more specifically to preventing problems through a companywide quality management approach. To distinguish them from traditional quality circles, these new work groups are often referred to by other names such as employee participation teams (EPTs) or employee performance and recognition groups.

Some of the differences between traditional quality circles and these "second generation" employee participation teams can be illustrated by the new programs now in place at Northrop Corporation and at Honeywell Corporation. At Northrop the groups are no longer voluntary and now involve all workers on the shop floor. The groups are responsible for setting improvement targets and keeping reports on their progress, and compete with other groups to achieve goals. At Honeywell Corporation (one of the the pioneer users of QCs), the company has replaced about 700 of their traditional quality circles with about 1,000 work groups. As is characteristic of the second generation of quality circles, these Honeywell groups are generally not voluntary and involve instead most shop-floor employees. And, in contrast to the bottom-up approach of quality circles, problems are often assigned to work groups by management.

Beyond tightening up the running of the teams themselves, other firms have found that instituting quality circles without corresponding changes in management styles and company culture is futile.

One major banking company ran into problems with their quality circle program: their experience is illustrative of these problems, and how they were solved by one service company.[16] The bank instituted quality circle teams to improve efficiency, communications, and team spirit. However, when asked how they liked their quality circle program, participants reportedly used words such as "nuisance," "a joke," and "very unproductive" to describe circle meetings. Participants claimed there were no ideas generated during the sessions, that the sessions themselves were dull and boring, and that most felt a lack of emotional involvement. Most also claimed they really didn't understand what they were to do or accomplish with the quality circles. An investigation led to the conclusion that it was widespread apprehension among employees that was undermining the program: The underlying culture at the bank was just not conducive to a participative quality circle program.

Several changes were implemented to change this culture. In a program like this, the bottom-up participation which management wants to encourage has to be fostered by a fundamental change in philosophy from top management on down. In other words, managers must make it clear to everyone that they will listen to and act on employees' input, they must create trust and confidence by example, and they must take other steps to show in concrete terms that they mean what they say about wanting employee input. This firm began by changing some policies that contradicted this sort of approach. For example, the annual polygraph examinations (which were legal at the time) and the time clock were eliminated. An interdepartmental employee quality circle committee was instituted. This committee in turn established a two-way dialogue between management and workers through regularly scheduled meetings. The basic theme of these meetings was company profitability for survival; it was explained repeatedly that such profitability was the surest route to job security.

As a result of their experience, the consultants to this project suggest the following guidelines for introducing a QC program:

1. Level with the chief executive officer about the organization's current state of management and employee thinking.
2. The CEO and senior officials must be models for change in implementing constructive ideas.
3. Make the program voluntary.
4. In the beginning, provide group members with solvable problems. Be prepared to change structures, policies, and procedures. Keep objectives simple.
5. Emphasize that these are not complaint sessions.
6. Communicate and educate every person in the organization about the program. Emphasize that group members need support.
7. Establish a climate of care and feedback.
8. Involve line managers and make them leaders of the groups whenever possible.

COMPUTER APPLICATIONS IN INCENTIVES:

ATTITUDE SURVEYS

According to a Louis Harris survey reported by *Industry Week*,[1] in 1989 fewer employees were satisfied with their jobs than in 1988. The reasons given were based on a dissonance between expectations and experiences in ethical management behavior, concern for employees, and communication. Mergers and acquisitions have only exacerbated the feelings of mistrust of management. Companies that value their workers apparently get input from them on company policies, perceptions of management, work or company restructuring, benefit packages (current and proposed changes), or reasons for turnover.

The use of employee attitude surveys has grown since 1944 when the National Industrial Conference Board "had difficulty finding fifty companies that had conducted opinion surveys."[2] Today most companies are aware of the need for employee anonymity, the impact of both the design of the questions and also their sequence, and the importance of effective communication, including the purpose of the survey before it's taken and feedback to the employees after it's completed. Computerization of surveys can provide anonymity, if there is no audit trail to the user, especially for short answers that are entered rather than written or typed on a distinguishable machine.

Survey software packages are available that generate questions on a number of standard topics and can be customized by modifying existing questions or by adding questions. If the survey is computerized, then reports can be generated with ease to provide snapshots of a given period of time, trend analyses, and breakdowns according to various demographics. You may be interested in responses by age, sex, job categories, departments, divisions, functions, or geography.

The survey may be conducted by placing microcomputers in several locations convenient for employee use. Employees are advised where the computers will be, for how long, and when the data will be collected (e.g., daily at 5 P.M. for a week). The screen should not be viewable by supervisors or passersby. While there may be some risk that employees will take the survey more than once, there are comparable risks with other methods. (For example, who completes the survey mailed to the employee's home?)

In addition to the survey topics listed above, managers may be interested in knowing how they are perceived by their peers and subordinates. Packages that may be customized are available which allow the manager to complete a self-assessment tool used to compare self-perceptions to the opinions of others. This comparison may assist in the development of a more effective manager. The same protection for anonymous participation is required, as is the necessity for communicating the purpose of the assessment, and feedback to participants.

Employees who are leaving the company are often asked their opinions during a formal or informal exit interview. Concerned about future references, employees often state innocuous reasons for leaving; reasons known to be acceptable to the company. However, if the exiting employees could respond to computer questions (such as, If you could change some aspect of supervision, what would it be? If you could change some aspect of our benefits, what would it be?) and be assured that answers would not be looked at until several people had responded, more helpful information might be learned

[1]Stanley J. Modio, "Whatever It Is, It's Not Working," *Industry Week*, Vol. 238, no. 14 (July 17, 1989), p. 27.

[2]Martin Wright, "Helping Employees Speak Out About Their Jobs and the Workplace, *Personnel*, vol. 63 (September 1986), p. 56.

9. Provide additional training to complement quality circle training. Introduce the circles as an ongoing process of good supervision to the supervisors themselves.[17]

COMPREHENSIVE QUALITY-IMPROVEMENT PROGRAMS

◆ INTRODUCTION

As the experience of the banking company suggests, there is a lot more to implementing successful quality circle programs than organizing several groups and telling them to "go at it." At the bank, for instance, management philosophies and styles had to be changed, and a new company culture (complete with no more polygraphs, and so on) had to be molded.

In fact, we now know that the most successful QC programs aren't run in vacuums, but are often part of comprehensive companywide quality improvement programs: the teams' quality improvement projects are conducted within company-wide plans and quality targets and goals; efforts are made to ensure the full support of middle managers; extensive training opportunities are provided; and the culture and reward systems are geared to encouraging employee involvement. The experience of the following company illustrates what such comprehensive programs involve, and the impact HR management can have.

◆ BACKGROUND

In 1989, Miami-based Florida Power & Light Company (FPL), Florida's largest utility, became the first company outside of Japan to win the Deming Prize. Awarded annually (and since 1986 outside of Japan) by the Union of Japanese Scientists and Engineers, the prize recognizes outstanding achievement in quality control management. The steps taken by the company to achieve this difficult task help to illustrate the activities involved in implementing comprehensive companywide quality improvement programs and the role of HR management in doing so.

◆ THREE BASIC FEATURES OF THE PROGRAM

FPL's quality improvement program contains three basic components or phases: policy deployment, quality in daily work, and quality improvement teams. Policy deployment "is the process through which company management works together to focus resources on achieving customer satisfaction"; quality in daily work means "that each employee applies quality improvement practices to all his or her activities to improve the quality of products and services"; and quality improvement teams mean that employees working in teams engage in selected problem solving.

Policy Deployment

One problem traditional quality circle programs run into is a lack of direction of the circles themselves. In many applications, in other words, the circles themselves generate problems to study without any coherent direction from top management regarding what the high-priority problems should be.

Policy deployment provides such direction. At FPL the policy deployment process begins by finding out what FPL customers actually want and then compiling these needs in a customer needs table. In other words, annual surveys are made of customer needs and these are then summarized and prioritized into five or six main categories of needs. These needs then drive the "corporate agenda"—the plans regarding where the company and the team should focus their efforts.

The point of the policy deployment process, according to the company, is to concentrate company resources on a few priority issues. Recently, for instance, the objectives emerging from the customer needs assessment included:

- Improve public confidence in safety programs.
- Reduce the number of complaints to the Florida Public Service Commission.
- Improve the reliability of electric service.
- Continue to emphasize safe, reliable, and efficient operation of nuclear plants.
- Strengthen fossil unit reliability, and availability.

These objectives are then translated into more measurable terms, such as "increase fossil plant availability to about 95% of total time by 1992." Measurable objectives like these, which FPL refers to as *policies*, are then distributed to all FPL employees via what they call their *Annual Guide to Corporate Excellence*. This publication folds out into a wall chart and, as the company puts it, "Hung in offices throughout FPL, it reminds one and all to check whether their QI teams and daily work are contributing to the corporate vision."[18] It is thus through this process that the measurable quality objectives (or "policies") of FPL are deployed throughout the company, thus giving this process its name.

In summary, the entire thrust of quality improvement at FPL is to identify customer needs and then satisfy them. Company plans, objectives, and measurable policies are formulated based on the annual survey of customer needs. These policies (and top management's corresponding plans for FPL) then become the guidelines within which the quality improvement teams do their work.

Quality Improvement Teams

FPL uses four kinds of quality improvement teams or circles: functional teams, cross-functional teams, task teams, and lead teams. (In total, about 1,700 quality improvement teams operate at FPL.) *Functional teams* are comprised of volunteers who typically work together as natural work units on a daily basis. These teams generally choose their own problems and meet one hour each week. The basic aim here is to involve first-line employees in improving their daily work activities so as to enhance the quality of their work life and to develop their skills. *Cross-functional teams* are ongoing teams that are formed to address problems that cut across organizational boundaries. *Task teams* are comprised of members who are appointed from one or more departments to work on specific problems. Task teams spend various amounts of time in meetings, depending upon the urgency of the problem. They are usually constituted specifically to support policy deployment or locally identified high priority issues. When the problem of a task team is solved, the team is disbanded.

Finally, *lead teams* are headed by a vice president or other manager and serve as steering committees for the activities of the teams that operate in their areas. It is the lead team, for instance, that determines how and which team members are selected to serve on which teams, and which establish guidelines regarding frequency and duration of team meetings.

The basic customer-oriented policies (such as "improve reliability of service") emerging from the policy deployment process forms the framework within which quality improvement teams focus their efforts. While the teams then generally select their own problem topics (called "themes"), certain topics are off limits. These include the company's union agreement, absenteeism, pay, salaries, promotions, the apprenticeship program, and in general safety rules produced by a joint safety committee.

Four Main Features of FPL QI Teams

It is informative to review four main features of FPL's quality improvement teams: training, facilitators, computerization, and "quality improvement stories."

Team members undergo extensive training and this is one area in which the company's human resource management system has a major impact on its quality circle and quality improvement programs. One training program is called "Team member training." This is open to all employees who are in the process of becoming team members. In this two-day program employees receive training in special techniques such as statistical quality control and in group decision making techniques such as brainstorming. Workbooks, case studies, and video presentations are used.

Other training programs include the "team member training course," for "team members who are ready to move on to more advanced statistical quality control," the "team leader training course" (in which individuals about to assume team leadership learn about such things as how to identify, prioritize, analyze, and solve quality-related problems), and the "project team training course" for individuals forming project teams.

Three other features of FPL quality improvement teams are pertinent. *Facilitators*—employees who have completed team leader training and want to move on to provide assistance to other teams—coach team leaders and help coordinate quality improvement efforts between teams and functional units. The company also uses a *management information system* called "Information Central." This keeps the files on team membership and on the projects each team is working on. Finally, teams present their proposals regarding problems and solutions to management via *quality improvement stories*. This is basically a seven-step structured set of instructions as follows:

Step 1. The team must provide an overall reason for solving the targeted problem, based on FPL's stated high priority needs.

Step 2. Here, they must describe the current situation. To do this, tools such as histograms, Pareto diagrams, control charts, graphs, and check sheets are used to collect data on all aspects of the theme or problem area and to study the theme from various viewpoints.

Step 3. In this third *analysis step*, the cause of the problem is identified using techniques such as cause-and-effect diagrams and Pareto diagrams.

Step 4. Countermeasures are presented based on tools and techniques such as cost-benefit analysis and an analysis of countermeasure barriers and potential aids. In this step, the structured instructions for the FPL story format calls for the team to develop and evaluate potential countermeasures, develop an action plan, and obtain cooperation and approvals for their proposed plan.

Step 5. Results are reported to confirm that the problem and its root causes have been decreased and that the target for improvement has been met. Here (as is stressed throughout the company's quality improvement program) results are reported in concrete terms, for instance using histograms and Pareto diagrams.

Step 6. Next, the team must explain how it has *standardized* the countermeasures it presented. They must explain how the work process has been changed, how employees have been trained on the revised process and countermeasures, and how the team suggests replicating the countermeasures in other company departments.

Step 7. Finally, *future plans* are summarized, usually with respect to moving the team on to its next problem or theme.

With about a thousand stories presented per year there is no shortage of examples of quality improvement team efforts. For example, one team discovered that it was bird droppings, not inclement weather that caused some of FPL's high-voltage lines to short out fairly often. As another example, FPL put many of its teams to work analyzing the company's trucks, equipment, and processes, with the aim of improving safety. One quality improvement team decided to focus on a safety problem faced by meter readers (who are the company's most injured employees): frequent dog bites. A team decided that if they could find a way to warn the meter readers that a dog was normally around the house, the employee would be better prepared. Furthermore, if necessary, a call could be made to the home just prior to the meter reader's visit, so that the dog could be locked up. Their recommendation was that a postcard should be placed into bills periodically asking if the homeowner has a dog. They got 20,000 cards back. Meter reading at FPL is done with an electronic reading machine. This electronic reader is now programmed to beep when a meter reader gets to a home where there is a dog. Calls are also made to the homes of dog owners on the morning of the visit. This has resulted in a huge increase in safety company-wide.

Quality in Daily Work

In addition to using quality improvement teams, FPL uses "quality in daily work" (QIDW) to spread the gospel of satisfying customer needs throughout the company. Here, individual employees are urged to identify their "customers" and their needs, keeping in mind that the customer may be external or internal (i.e., within the company). It is also stressed that employees should understand the objectives of their jobs, and the quality standards to be met. The basic thrust of QIDW is to encourage individual employees to take a quality improvement-perspective approach to their work, on an individual basis.

♦ HUMAN RESOURCE MANAGEMENT AND THE QUALITY IMPROVEMENT EFFORT

FPL managers and employees learned a lot about how to build an effective QI program over the years. For example, FPL's initial approach to quality improvement was to institute just a quality circle program. These circles were generally not operating within the context of quality improvement objectives and policies like those now produced by the company's policy deployment process. Furthermore, the original circle program was erroneously designed around a separate, parallel "organization within an organization." Each of these original teams had facilitators appointed to them and the regular departmental supervisors were told in no uncertain terms "don't mess with them." Based on FPL's experience, there are many personnel-related steps to take that can help to ensure a more effective quality improvement program. Some HR guidelines based on FPL's experience are as follows:

- Recognize that instituting quality improvement teams and a quality improvement program means doing so *within the context of a policy deployment-type process* so that the program has direction.

- *Do not institute quality circles as separate, parallel organization structures.* Instead, institute the teams in layers from top to bottom using the natural organization structure to form the teams. Simply trying to superimpose quality circles outside of the normal chain of command elicited resistance from the supervisors, many of whom made comments like "I don't know what these people are doing—they're not helping me do my job."[19] The teams should, to the greatest extent possible, be composed of natural work units. Employ existing reporting systems and remain compatible with existing organization structure as much as possible.

- *Do not treat the quality improvement program as if it has an end.* It is important to emphasize that a quality improvement program that is successful is really a systematic way of doing business, one that has no end.

- *Training is essential.* In Japan (and in a successful program like that at FPL) quality improvement is successful largely because training continually upgrades the problem analysis and statistics skills of even first-line employees. This training is crucial both to provide the required analytical skills, and also to emphasize the firm's commitment to the program.

- Whether or not the company achieves its quality goals is, while very important, almost secondary. The important thing is creating an organization of *self-directed quality seekers* within the framework of customer-oriented quality objectives and policies. Give employees the skills they need to analyze and solve problems; then get them to analyze and solve the problem, and follow up on their suggestions. The new culture that emerges is at the heart of the program.

- FPL found that a *management by objectives program is not enough* to accomplish these sorts of aims, by the way. MBO did not provide for the kind of analysis and follow-up demanded by a quality improvement program.

- Do not focus exclusively on "boosting productivity," or assume that emphasizing quality means that productivity will necessarily fall. In fact (and this is very important) FPL and other companies instituting these kinds of programs find that *as quality increases so does productivity*—and costs will actually go down. However, some quality improvements will be more cost effective than others, so it is still important to keep quality improvements cost effective.

- As explained above, assessing customer needs as a first step in policy deployment should result in a corporate agenda of prioritized needs to be met. It is important here to *work on only a few needs* at once: Do not dilute your resources.

- *Employee recognition and employee satisfaction are essential.* Personal satisfaction and intrinsic rewards come from the responsibility of seeing that "quality begins with me." It also comes from encouraging employees to identify and devise countermeasures against problems, and from giving them the tools and leeway necessary to get this job done. This attitude, found FPL, develops over time from confidence that "my ideas count, they will be given an audience, and they can affect change." In fact, when FPL asked their employees early in the program what they wanted most they didn't say "more money." They said they wanted their suggestions implemented and wanted recognition from their supervisors; these are two important things that the quality improvement teams provided for. (Recall our discussions of achievement and self-actualization needs, and job enrichment in Chapter 9.)

- Also reward *individual and team efforts in a more concrete manner*, not generally with money but with rewards like merchandise or pins. These, the company found, "stay with the employee-suggester for years, and serve as continual recognition/reinforcers of a job well done." Furthermore, it is essential that individual and team suggestions be implemented.

- Quality circle programs are generally best implemented within the context of more comprehensive quality improvement programs. Related to this, remember that a quality improvement program is more than the sum of its parts: it is not just an incentive program, or a quality circle program or a training program, for instance. Most importantly, *quality improvement requires instituting a new culture in the firm*, one that values (and focuses all employees' thoughts on) the central issue of continually seeking out and instituting incremental quality improvements to meet customer needs. Individually (through QIDW) and collectively (through quality improvement teams), employees thus must be given the skills to identify, analyze, and solve quality problems, as well as the motivation to do so. Producing a new company culture that encourages this kind of behavior may be the biggest challenge that a quality-seeking company (and its HR unit) has to face; the task of molding a company like this can take years. In any case the first steps need to be taken by top management: "From the board of directors to every supervisor, management must adopt the principles and language of quality, follow the processes, set examples and guide others. A substantial commitment is necessary for employee education, and for awareness and recognition programs. These programs require reallocation of budgets and personnel, and will take time to produce results but will be worth it."[20]

- In carrying out changes like these, one of the most remarkable aspects of the quality improvement program effort is that *both the company and the employee gain*. Satisfying customer needs is the *raison d'être* of any company: An effective quality improvement program will help to ensure that customer needs are met, and that the company is successful. But at the same time (as this is occurring), comprehensive companywide quality improvement programs like FPL's also help ensure that in many ways employees' most important personal needs—not just for money, but to achieve difficult goals, and to grow and to self-actualize—are met. In doing so, QI programs boost (or should boost) the quality of work life in the firm, and to that extent the employees' personal growth, satisfaction, and sense of accomplishment.

SUMMARY

1. *Quality of work life* refers to the degree to which employees are able to satisfy their important personal needs by working in the organization. It reflects such things as fair, equitable treatment; an opportunity for each worker to use his or her skills to the utmost; and an opportunity for all employees to take an active role in making important job-related decisions.

2. *Flextime* is a plan whereby employees' flexible workdays are built around a core of midday hours, such as 11 to 2. It seems to improve employee attitudes and morale, increases production, and decreases tardiness; however, unavailability of key people at certain times and, generally, scheduling activities like meetings can be problems. Flextime and other flexible work arrangements are aimed in part at tapping employees' needs to be treated as responsible human beings, and to that extent they boost quality of work life.

3. A *quality circle* is a group of five to ten specially trained employees who meet for an hour once a week for the purpose of spotting and solving problems in their work area.

4. Steps in establishing a *quality circle* program include planning, training, initiating, and operating. Problems to be aware of include: attitudes such as, "This is just another program," and "Management pays no attention to our ideas"; selecting problems outside the circle's expertise; problems that are too difficult to handle; scheduling problems; and fear of interference from the union.

5. Comprehensive companywide quality improvement programs like that at FPL basically aim at improving the customer-orientation of a firm by appealing to employees' higher-order needs. A framework of objectives or policies is first laid out based on satisfying customers' needs. Then a comprehensive program of training, incentives, quality circles, and (in general) culture-modification is carried out to appeal to employees' sense of responsibility. As at FPL, it's not just the specific techniques (like selection, or training, or incentives) that ensure high performance; the culture of the firm—its basic shared values and attitudes—is important, too.

6. By this point you should understand how personnel management concepts and techniques can be used to (a) ensure the person has the skills and aptitudes for the job, and is (b) motivated to perform it. In the next part of the book—Part Four—we turn to the problem of appraising the employee's performance and taking corrective action as needed.

KEY TERMS

quality of work life	job sharing	quality circle
flextime	work sharing	quality improvement program
four-day workweek	flexiplace	

DISCUSSION QUESTIONS

1. Define what is meant by a quality circle.
2. Explain the steps involved in operating a circle (including problem identification and problem selection).
3. Explain how you would set up a companywide quality improvement program.
4. Explain the pros and cons of flextime and the four-day workweek.

◆ APPLICATION EXERCISES

◆ CASE INCIDENT   Hawkins's Nob Hill Plant

Mr. Kiplinger is plant manager of the Nob City division of the Hawkins Company. He was originally transferred to Nob City in 1980 from the home office in Altoona (Pennsylvania). He, his wife, and their four children reside in Nob City. Reporting directly to Mr. Kiplinger are his key staff officers, the office manager, the human resource and safety manager, and the production manager. The line command includes supervisors who report directly to the production manager.

The workers have a certain set of expectations concerning their own rights and privileges. Some of these "privileges" are obvious, while others are rather subtle. One of the more widely held values on the part of the workers is what they call "leniency." The workers know they have a job to do and expect that in the process of doing it, management will leave them alone. The main obligation they feel to the company is that of producing. Obedience to supervisors is displayed so long as it is directly related to a job to be done. Hostility is directed toward management when discipline or forced obedience is exerted as a means of asserting the will of management. Conversely, the workers commend management when given certain privileges or when flexibility is shown in discipline.

"Job shifting" provides another route for circumventing formal supervisory authority and is a type of vertical and horizontal mobility in the plant. Job shifting is done by "bidding" for a vacancy in the plant, prompted either by desire for a job with higher status or as a means to escape an unpleasant supervisor. The supervisors resent this practice, since they feel that they should have the prerogative of choosing their own subordinates—and not the other way around.

A third right includes the use of company material for home repairs. The workers expect that they should have access to the company's finished product, either without charge or at a very large discount, and that company equipment should be made available for use in repairing broken down machinery or household furnishings.

One day Skip Kiplinger received a call from the home office notifying him that he could expect about $2 million worth of new equipment to be added to his plant's equipment. Along with the equipment addition, the home office notified Skip that it was transferring Ann Hirtmann from the plastics division in Pottstown to replace the retiring Ed Patterson as production manager. Hirtmann was a former Army officer and had an outstanding industrial record, too. It was hoped by the board of directors that the change of leadership and the addition of equipment would add considerably to Hawkins's profit margin.

One of Hirtmann's first moves was to stop the practice of allowing workers to have access to company equipment and to reduce the discount given on the purchase of company-made equipment. She was able to do this after showing Kiplinger that several thousands of dollars in sales had been lost from abuse of this particular privilege in the last year alone; some workers had resold company equipment at considerable profits. Another move was to eliminate the job-shifting policy and to replace it with a new seniority system. The new system was roundly applauded by supervisors and other supervisory personnel, but workers became noticeably irritable and frustrated. Hirtmann believed that once an order was given, it was to be followed without question. Generally, she paid attention to employee grievances only when they reached critical proportions.

Hirtmann made rounds every hour to check on the progress of the work flow. In the course of six months she instituted many technical changes designed to speed up production and reduce labor costs. These improvements were reflected in the profit margin, but during this six-month period, dissension had been building up, almost unnoticed tensions in the plant ran high, and employees were becoming very defensive. Dissatisfaction over the installment of new machinery became a focal point of the disruption. If the company could afford $2 million for machinery, workers grumbled, it could afford higher wages.

About the eighth month, Hirtmann was notified by the home office that she would attend a month-long managerial seminar in Chicago. Mr. Kiplinger decided to leave Hirtmann's post vacant in her absence and to have each shift supervisor be responsible for his or her particular shift with no further supervision.

Kiplinger learned through the supervisors that the people on the first shift wanted their restrooms painted and, because the rooms were exposed to the afternoon sun, they also asked for some shades and a fan. Without hesitation, Kiplinger told the maintenance crew to go to work on the job. In addition, he told the supervisors to feel free to handle such minor grievances and requests on their own authority until Hirtmann returned.

Within the next week, another request was presented. This time the workers complained about working a 5½-day week. Kiplinger considered the point and proposed that if production reached 20,000 pounds per day (a 5,000-pound increase) he could then institute a five-day schedule. Within a few days, production reached the level indicated. Unfortunately, Kiplinger was in a difficult position because the Altoona office demanded even more production to meet their orders. Kiplinger then had to go back to the workers and ask them to continue on the 5½-day schedule for another few days until the orders were filled. Although there was some grumbling, most of the workers continued to perform effectively. Within a week, the press for more production was reduced so that it was possible to institute the promised five-day schedule.

It had been the practice to blow a steam whistle in the plant at the beginning and end of the shift, as well as at five-minute rest periods and at lunch. One of the workers suggested that the company use the public address system instead. At first, employees ridiculed the new system, but in a few days they took announcements as a matter of course; in one instance when the announcement was not made, the employees returned from lunch just the same. Later on in the month, the announcements were dropped, yet the employees started and stopped work promptly.

Between the first and the last of the month, the daily output of the plant had increased steadily from 25,000 pounds to about 33,000 pounds.

Kiplinger was puzzled. He could not understand why production was up 32 percent with no production manager present.

Questions

1. Why do you think production was up by 32 percent with no production manager present?

2. How, specifically, do you think Hirtmann's actions influenced plant workers' "higher-order needs"?

3. Do you think Hirtmann's leadership style was appropriate for this situation?

4. What would you do now if you were Kiplinger?

Source: Based on "Kiplinger's Question" in Theodore Herbert, *Organizational Behavior: Readings and Cases* (New York: Macmillan, 1976), pp. 360–361.

EXPERIMENTAL EXERCISE

Purpose: The purpose of this exercise is to give you an opportunity to develop a quality improvement program.

Required Understanding: You should understand the quality improvement techniques explained in this chapter.

How to Set Up the Exercise: Break the class into groups of four or five students.

Instructions for the Exercise:

1. Each group should read the Hawkins case in this chapter.

2. Next, each group should develop a quality improvement program they believe will help provide a long-term solution to the situation at Hawkins.

3. If time permits, a spokesperson from each group should present the group's solution to the class for class discussion.

NOTES

1. Donald Peterson, "Flexitime in the United States: The Lessons of Experience," *Personnel*, Vol. 57 (January–February 1980), pp. 21–37; *1987 AMS Flexible Work Survey* (Willow Grove, Pa: Administrative Management Society, 1987); Commerce Clearing House, "ASPA/CCH Survey on Alternative Work Schedules," June 26, 1987.

2. Peterson, "Flexitime in the United States," p. 22.

3. Stanley Nollen, "Does Flexitime Improve Productivity?" *Harvard Business Review*, Vol. 56 (September–October 1977), pp. 12–22.

4. Ibid.

5. Stanley Nollen and Virginia Martin, *Alternative Work Schedules Part One: Flextime* (New York: AMACOM, 1978), p. 44.

6. Peterson, "Flextime in the U.S.," pp. 29–31.

7. Another problem is that some employers let workers "bank" extra hours by working, say, 45 hours one week so they need work only 35 hours the next week. The problem is that in the 45-hour week the employees should, strictly speaking, be paid an overtime rate for the extra 5 hours worked. Some employers handle this problem by letting hours worked vary from day to day but requiring each week to be a 40-hour week. Others are experimenting with letting workers accumulate hours and be paid overtime if necessary. See J. C. Swart, "Flexitime's Debit and Credit Option," *Personnel Journal*, Vol. 58 (January–February 1979), pp. 10–12.

8. David Ralston, David Gustafson, and William Anthony, "Employees May Love Flextime, but What Does It Do to the Organization's Productivity?" *Journal of Applied Psychology*, Vol. 70, no. 2 (1985), pp. 272–279.

9. Janis Hedges, "New Patterns for Working Time," *Monthly Labor Review*, February 1973, pp. 3–8.

10. John Ivancevich and Herbert Lyon, "The Shortened Work Week: A Field Experiment," *Journal of Applied Psychology*, Vol. 62, no. 1 (1977), pp. 34–37.

11. Janina Latack and Lawrence Foster, "Implementation of Compressed Work Schedules: Participation and Job Redesign as Critical Factors for Employee Acceptance," *Personnel Psychology*, Vol. 38, no. 1 (Spring 1985), pp. 75–92. Interestingly, one way to determine how your employees will react to a 4/40 or flextime work schedule apparently is to ask them ahead of time. One study suggests that these will be the reactions that emerge three to six months after commencement of the program. See Randall B. Dunham, Jon L. Pierce, and Maria B. Castaneda, "Alternative Work Schedules: Two Field Quasi-Experiments," *Personnel Psychology*, Vol. 40, no. 2 (Summer 1987), pp. 215–242.

12. Commerce Clearing House, *Ideas and Trends*, February 26, 1982, p. 61.

13. "These Top Executives Work Where They Play," *Business Week*, October 27, 1986, p. 132.

14. "After Flexible Hours, Now It's Flexiyear," *International Management* (March 1982), pp. 31–32.

15. This section based on Donald Dewar, *The Quality Circle Guide to Participation Management* (Englewood Cliffs, N.J.: Prentice-Hall, 1980). See also James Thacker and Mitchel Fields, "Union Involvement in Quality-of-Work Life Efforts: A Longitudinal Investigation," *Personnel Psychology*, Vol. 40, no. 1 (Spring 1987), pp. 97–112. They conclude that unions' fears of QCs may be misplaced and that after quality-of-work-life involvement, "A majority of the rank and file members who perceived QWL as successful gave equal credit for the success to

both union and management. The rank and file members who perceived QWL as unsuccessful tended to blame management for the lack of success." See also Anat Rafaeli, "Quality Circles and Employee Attitudes," *Personnel Psychology*, Vol. 38 (Fall 1985), pp. 603–615; Mitchell Lee Marks, Edward Hackett, Philip Mirvis, and James Grady, Jr., "Employee Participation in a Quality Circle Program: Impact on Quality of Work Life, Productivity, and Absenteeism, "*Journal of Applied Psychology*, Vol. 71, no. 1 (February 1986), pp. 61–69, and "Quality Circles: A New Generation," *BNA Bulletin to Management*, Vol. 38, no. 2 (January 1987), pp. 10–15. See also Preston C. Bottger and Phillip Yetton, "Improving Group Performance by Training in Individual Problem Solving," *Journal of Applied Psychology*, Vol. 72, no. 4, (November 1987), pp. 651–657, and Murray R. Barrick and Ralph Alexander, "A Review of Quality Circle Efficacy and the Existence of Positive-Finding Bias," *Personnel Psychology*, Vol. 40, no. 3 (Autumn 1987), pp. 579–592.

16. Gopal Pati, Robert Salitore, and Saundra Brady, "What Went Wrong with Quality Circles?" *Personnel Journal* (December 1987), pp. 83–89.

17. Ibid., p. 86.

18. "Building a Quality Improvement Program at Florida Power & Light," *Target* (Fall 1988), p. 6.

19. Private conversation with Wayne Brunetti, Executive Vice President, Florida Power & Light Company.

20. "Building a Quality Improvement Program at Florida Power & Light," *Target* (Fall 1988), p. 8.

PART FOUR

APPRAISAL AND CAREER MANAGEMENT

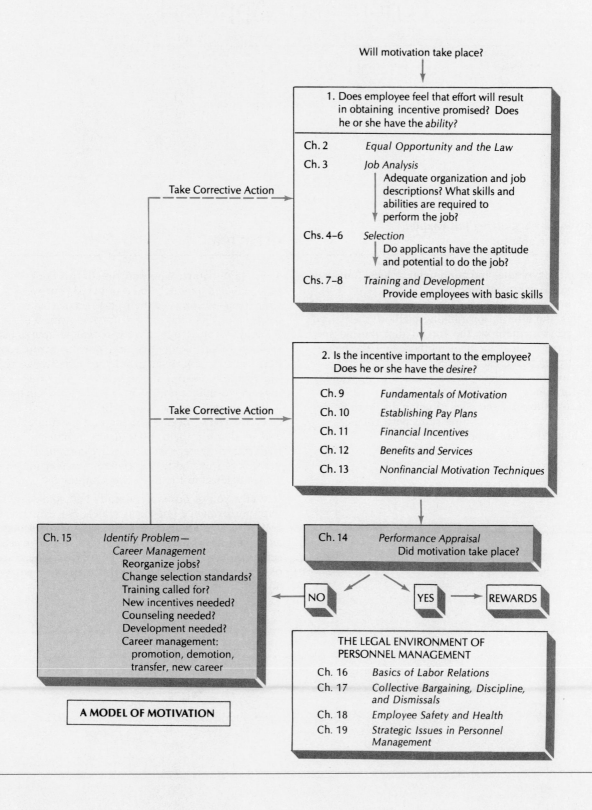

Will motivation take place?

1. Does employee feel that effort will result in obtaining incentive promised? Does he or she have the *ability?*

Ch. 2	*Equal Opportunity and the Law*
Ch. 3	*Job Analysis*
	Adequate organization and job descriptions? What skills and abilities are required to perform the job?
Chs. 4–6	*Selection*
	Do applicants have the aptitude and potential to do the job?
Chs. 7–8	*Training and Development*
	Provide employees with basic skills

Take Corrective Action

2. Is the incentive important to the employee? Does he or she have the *desire?*

Ch. 9	*Fundamentals of Motivation*
Ch. 10	*Establishing Pay Plans*
Ch. 11	*Financial Incentives*
Ch. 12	*Benefits and Services*
Ch. 13	*Nonfinancial Motivation Techniques*

Take Corrective Action

Ch. 14	*Performance Appraisal*
	Did motivation take place?

Ch. 15 *Identify Problem—*
Career Management
Reorganize jobs?
Change selection standards?
Training called for?
New incentives needed?
Counseling needed?
Development needed?
Career management:
 promotion, demotion,
 transfer, new career

NO   YES   REWARDS

A MODEL OF MOTIVATION

THE LEGAL ENVIRONMENT OF PERSONNEL MANAGEMENT

Ch. 16	*Basics of Labor Relations*
Ch. 17	*Collective Bargaining, Discipline, and Dismissals*
Ch. 18	*Employee Safety and Health*
Ch. 19	*Strategic Issues in Personnel Management*

Chapter 14

Performance Appraisal

When you finish studying this chapter, you should be able to:

1. Develop, evaluate, and administer at least four performance appraisal tools.
2. List and discuss the pros and cons of graphic rating scales, the alternation ranking method, the paired comparison method, the forced distribution method, the critical incident method, and the behaviorally anchored rating scale.
3. Explain the problems to be avoided in appraising performance.
4. Discuss the pros and cons of using different potential raters to appraise a person's performance.
5. Hold an effective appraisal interview.

OVERVIEW

This chapter starts a new section of this book. Once you have selected, trained, and motivated your workers, the next step is to appraise their performance, and the main purpose of this chapter is to provide you with several techniques for doing so. We will explain how to use several appraisal techniques and how to avoid common performance appraisal problems. Finally, we will explain how to review the appraisal with your subordinate. Performance appraisal (as you can see in our motivation model) is the step where you find out how effective you've been at hiring and placing employees, and motivating them. Should any problems be identified, your next steps would involve communicating with your employee and taking remedial career action—topics we discuss in the following chapter.

Actually, you've probably already had some experience with performance appraisal scales. For example, some colleges ask students to rank instructors on scales such as the one in Table 14.1. Do you think this is an effective scale? Do you see any ways to improve it? These are two of the questions you should be in a better position to answer by the end of this chapter.

There are actually several reasons to appraise performance.[1] First, performance appraisals provide information upon which *promotion* and *salary* decisions can be made. These are the most frequent uses of performance appraisals.

Second, performance appraisals provide an opportunity for you and your subordinate to sit down and *review* the subordinate's work-related behavior. Most people need and want some feedback concerning their performance (especially when it is favorable!) and the appraisal provides this feedback. Finally, it also allows you and your subordinate to map out a *plan* for rectifying any performance deficiencies that might be identified.

♦ THE SUPERVISOR'S ROLE IN APPRAISAL

Both line managers and human resource specialists play important roles in the appraisal process. Line managers play a central role because the supervisor usually does the actual appraising. As a result, supervisors have a responsibility to see to it that they are completely familiar with the appraisal techniques to be used, that they understand (and can avoid) the problems that can cripple an appraisal system, and that they do the appraisal fairly and objectively.

The human resource department, on the other hand, serves as a policy-making and advisory function with respect to performance appraisals. In one survey, for example, about 80% of the companies responding said that the human resource department provides *advice and assistance* regarding

TABLE 14.1   A Scale of Appraising Instructors

INSTRUCTOR
DEPARTMENT
COURSE NUMBER OR TITLE

I. The following items reflect some of the ways teachers can be described in and out of the classroom. For the instructor named above, please circle the number that indicates the degree to which you feel each item is descriptive of him or her. In some cases, the statement may not apply to this individual. In these cases, check *Does not apply or don't know* for that item.

	NOT AT ALL DESCRIPTIVE	VERY DESCRIPTIVE	DOESN'T APPLY OR DON'T KNOW
1. Has command of the subject, presents material in an analytic way, contrasts various points of view, discusses current developments, and relates topics to other areas of knowledge.	1 2 3 4 5 6 7		( )
2. Makes himself clear, states objectives, summarizes major points, presents material in an organized manner, and provides emphasis.			
3. Is sensitive to the response of the class, encourages student participation, and welcomes questions and discussion.			
4. Is available to and friendly toward students, is interested in students as individuals, is himself respected as a person, and is valued for advice not directly related to the course.			
5. Enjoys teaching, is enthusiastic about his subject, makes the course exciting, and has self-confidence.			

Note: Additional items may be presented by instructor and/or department.

Source: Richard Miller, *Developing Programs for Faculty Evaluation* (San Francisco: Jossey-Bass Publishers, 1974), p. 43.

which appraisal tool to use but leaves final decisions on appraisal procedures to operating division heads; in the rest of the firms the personnel office prepares detailed forms and procedures and insists that all departments use them.[2] Personnel is also responsible for training supervisors to improve their appraisal skills. Finally, personnel is responsible for monitoring the use of the appraisal system, particularly in regard to ensuring that the format and criteria being measured don't become outdated. In one survey, for example, half the employers were in the process of revising their appraisal programs, while several others were conducting reviews to see how well their programs were working.[3]

♦ STEPS IN APPRAISING PERFORMANCE

Performance appraisal involves three steps: define the job, appraise performance, and provide feedback. *Defining the job* means making sure that you and your subordinate agree on what you expect him or her to accomplish and on what standards the person's performance will be appraised. *Appraising performance* means comparing your subordinate's actual performance to the standards set in step one; this usually involves some type of rating form. Third, performance appraisal usually requires one or more *feedback sessions* during which the subordinate's performance and progress are discussed and during which plans are laid out for any development that is required.

♦ PROBLEMS TO AVOID
IN PERFORMANCE APPRAISAL

Problems may arise in each of the three steps. Some appraisals fail because subordinates are not informed ahead of time exactly what you expect of them in terms of good performance. Other appraisals fail because of the problems built into the forms or procedures used to actually appraise the performance; a lenient supervisor might rate all subordinates "high," for instance, although many are actually unsatisfactory. Still other problems arise during the interview-feedback session, problems that include arguing and poor communications. Figure 14.1 summarizes these common evaluation problems. We address these problems and how to avoid them on the following pages.

HOW TO DEFINE THE JOB

♦ CLARIFY WHAT PERFORMANCE YOU EXPECT

The job description usually isn't sufficient to clarify what you want your subordinate to do because most job descriptions are written not for specific jobs but for groups of jobs. All sales managers in the firm might have the same job description, for instance, although as the boss of a sales manager you may have some very specific ideas regarding what you expect *your* sales manager to do. For instance, his or her job description may list duties such as "supervise sales force" and "is responsible for all phases of marketing the division's products." However, you may expect your sales manager to do the following: personally sell at least $600,000 worth of products per year by handling the division's two largest accounts, keep the sales force happy, and keep customers away from the executives (including you).

To operationalize this you should set measurable standards for each of these activities. The "personal selling" activity can be measured in terms of how many dollars of sales he or she generates personally. "Keeping the sales

FIGURE 14.1
Common Performance Evaluation Problems
Source: John E. Oliver, "Performance Appraisals That Fit," *Personnel Journal*, Vol. 64, no. 6 (June 1985), p. 69.

Problems can occur at any stage in the evaluation process. Some of the pitfalls to avoid in performance appraisals are:

1) Lack of standards. Without standards, there can be no objective evaluation of results, only a subjective guess or feeling about performance.

2) Irrelevant or subjective standards. Standards should be established by analyzing the job output to ensure that standards are job related.

3) Unrealistic standards. Standards are goals with motivating potential. Those that are reasonable but challenging have the most potential to motivate.

4) Poor measures of performance. Objectivity and comparison require that progress toward standards or accomplishment of standards be measurable. Examples of measurable standards include quantifiable measures such as 10 rejects per 1,000 units or 10 sales per 100 calls, as well as qualitative measures, such as projects completed or not completed.

5) Rater errors. Rater errors include rater bias or prejudice, halo effect, constant error, central tendency, and fear of confrontation.

6) Poor feedback to employee. Standards and/or ratings must be communicated to the employee in order for the performance evaluation to be effective.

7) Negative communications. The evaluation process is hindered by communication of negative attitudes, such as inflexibility, defensiveness, and a non-developmental approach.

8) Failure to apply evaluation data. Failure to use evaluations in personnel decision making and personnel development negates the primary purpose of performance evaluations. The use and weighting of multiple criteria as well as the frequency of evaluation also present problems.

force happy" might be measured in terms of turnover (on the assumption that less than 10% of the sales force will quit in any given year if morale is high). "Keeping customers away from executives" can be measured in terms of "customer complaints reaching top management," with a standard of "no more than ten customer complaints per year" being the target the sales manager is to shoot for.

In summary, the first step in performance appraisal is to ask, "What do I really expect this person to do?"

♦ AN EXAMPLE

For an example of how to link job descriptions with the performance appraisal, review Figure 14.2.[4] The approach illustrated will not work for all employees (for instance, you may want to use just one appraisal form for all jobs in your firm), but it can be used when separate appraisal forms are practical for each job. The figure shows an appraisal form for the position of administrative secretary. In this case the job's five main sets of duties have been taken from the job description and prioritized; importance ratings are indicated as percentages at the top of each of the five categories (typing and stenography, reception, and so on). Notice that these job description statements each contain an indication of the level of performance the administrative secretary should shoot for, and the appraisal form lets five levels of performance be rated from "fails to meet job requirements" to "exceeds job requirements." There is also a place on the form for comments, and for evaluation of "general performance" attributes like reporting for work on time and observing work rules.

FIGURE 14.2
Sample Performance Appraisal Form
Source: James Buford, Jr., Bettye Burkhalter, and Grover Jacobs, ''Link Job Descriptions to Performance Appraisals,'' *Personnel Journal* (June 1988), pp. 135–136.

PERFORMANCE APPRAISAL FORM

PART I Identification

| Name _____ |
| Position _____ |
| Rating period from _____ to _____ |
| Rater name _____ |
| Rater title _____ |
| Department _____ |

Rating Scale Key

1	Fails to meet job requirements
2	Essentially meets job requirements
3	Fully meets job requirements
4	Meets job requirements with distinction
5	Exceeds job requirements

Figure 1

PART II Rating Scales for Task Areas

Position: Administrative Secretary
Duties and Responsibilities

A. Typing and stenography   PCT. (30%)   RATING: 1 2 3 4 5

Comments

Producing accurate typewritten documents in the proper format at 60wpm from a variety of sources, including oral dictation: From oral dictation, dictating machine, shorthand notes or standard formats, transcribes correspondence for general manager; transcribes minutes of meetings; types notices, agendas, schedules, and other internal material; types surveys for trade associations; compiles and types operating reports and other reports, including text and tables; types copy for trade magazines and newspapers; composes and types letters, memoranda, copy and other documents as needed or on request.

B. Reception   PCT. (25%)   RATING: 1 2 3 4 5

Comments

Receiving and recording initial contacts in person or on the telephone and courteously assisting callers or visitors: Answers incoming telephone calls, takes message, provides information or routes call to appropriate individual; greets visitors, provides information or directs to appropriate office or individual; acts as hostess and provides incidental services to visitors in waiting status; operates automatic answering service; maintains log of callers and visitors to cooperative.

C. Scheduling   PCT. (20%)   RATING: 1 2 3 4 5

Comments

Managing calendar efficiently including arranging appointments, meetings, travel and similar activities; maintains calendar and makes appointments for general manager, board members and other staff; prepares requests for reimbursement for official travel; assists with arrangements of annual meeting; makes arrangements for in-service training meetings, including rooms, coffee breaks and food service when necessary; schedules use of organizational facilities; arranges lodging, travel and fees for outside speakers and consultants.

D. Filing and records management   PCT. (15%)   RATING: 1 2 3 4 5

Comments

Creating and maintaining appropriate filing systems and promptly locating and retrieving needed material upon request: Develops space allocation plan and filing system for correspondence, minutes, reports, regulations and related material; places material into proper location in file; searches for and retrieves material from files; culls, files and removes material to central location or destroys as needed; maintains and preserves vital records; organizes data from file search into usable format.

E. General office service   PCT. (10%)   RATING: 1 2 3 4 5

Comments

Performing related office duties in accordance with acceptable practice and prescribed procedures; processes mail through postage meter, records readings and posts; opens and distributes incoming mail; makes copies of documents; maintains petty cash fund; clips articles from papers and magazines related to the organization; maintains bulletin board; performs other job duties as assigned.

THE APPRAISAL ITSELF: HOW
TO APPRAISE PERFORMANCE

♦ GRAPHIC RATING SCALE TECHNIQUE

graphic rating scale A scale that lists a number of traits and a range of performance for each. The employee is then rated by identifying the score that best describes his or her level of performance for each trait.

The simplest and most popular technique for appraising performance is called a **graphic rating scale**. A typical rating scale is shown in Figure 14.3. Note that the scale lists a number of traits (such as quality and quantity) as well as a range of performance (from unsatisfactory to exceptional) for each. Each subordinate is rated by circling or checking the score that best

FIGURE 14.2
(continued)

PART III: Performance Appraisal Form

Does the employee report for and remain at work as required? ☐ yes ☐ no   If no, please explain.

Does the employee follow instructions and observe work rules? ☐ yes ☐ no   If no, please explain.

Does the employee get along and cooperate with co-workers on the job? ☐ yes ☐ no   If no, please explain.

Does the employee have the knowleges, skills, abilities and other qualifications needed for successful job performance? ☐ yes ☐ no   If no, please explain.

Describe any specific actions employee needs to take to improve job performance.

Summarize this employee's overall job performance as determined in your joint discussion.

PART IV: Signatures

This report is based on my observation and
knowledge of both the employee and the job.

My signature indicates that I have reviewed this appraisal. It
does not mean that I agree with the results.

_____   _____
Supervisor   Date

_____   _____
Reviewer   Date

_____   _____
Employee   Date

describes his or her level of performance for each trait. The assigned values for each trait are then added up and totaled.

♦ **ALTERNATION RANKING METHOD**

Another popular simple method for evaluating employees is to rank them from best to worst on some trait. Since it is usually easier to distinguish between the worst and best employees than to simply rank them, an **alternation ranking method** is most popular. First, list all subordinates to be rated, and then cross out the names of any not known well enough to rank. Then, on a form such as that in Figure 14.4, indicate the employee who is the highest on the characteristic being measured and also the one who is the lowest.

alternation ranking method Ranking employees from best to worst on a particular trait.

FIGURE 14.3
Example of a Graphic Rating Scale
Source: Dale Yoder, *Personnel Management,* 6th ed. (Englewood Cliffs, N.J.: Prentice-Hall, 1970), p. 240. Reprinted by permission.

Employee: _____ Job title: _____ Date: _____

Department: _____ Job number: _____ Rater: _____

FACTOR	SCORE – RATING				
	UNSATIS-FACTORY — So definitely inadequate that it justifies release	FAIR — Minimal; barely adequate to justify retention	GOOD — Meets basic requirement for retention	SUPERIOR — Definitely above norm and basic requirements	EXCEP-TIONAL — Distinctly and consistently outstanding
QUALITY — Accuracy, thoroughness, appearance and acceptance of output					
QUANTITY — Volume of output and contribution					
REQUIRED SUPERVISION — Need for advice, direction or correction					
ATTENDANCE — Regularity, dependability and promptness					
CONSERVATION — Prevention of waste, spoilage; protection of equipment					

Reviewed by: _____ (Reviewer comments on reverse)

Employee comment: _____

Date: _____ Signature or initial: _____

Then choose the next highest and the next lowest, *alternating* between highest and lowest until all the employees to be rated have been ranked.

♦ **PAIRED COMPARISON METHOD**

paired comparison method Ranking employees by making a chart of all possible pairs of the employees for each trait and indicating which is the better employee of the pair.

The **paired comparison method** helps to make the ranking method more effective. For every trait (quantity of work, quality of work, and so on), every subordinate is compared to every other subordinate in pairs.

Suppose there are five employees to be rated. In the paired comparison method you make a chart, as in Figure 14.5, of all possible pairs of employees *for each trait.* Then for each trait indicate (with a + or −) who is the better employee of the pair. Next, the number of times an employee is rated better is added up. In Figure 14.5, employee Bob ranked highest for quality of work, while Art was ranked highest for creativity.

FIGURE 14.4
Rating-Ranking Scale Using Alternation Ranking Technique
Source: Dale Yoder, *Personnel Management*, 6th ed. (Englewood Cliffs, N.J.: Prentice-Hall, 1970), p. 237. Reprinted by permission.

RATING-RANKING SCALE

Consider all those on your list in terms of their (quality). Cross out the names of any you cannot rate on this quality. Then select the one you would regard as having most of the quality. Put his name in Column I, below, on the first line, numbered 1. Cross out his name on your list. Consult the list again and pick out the person having least of this quality. Put his name at the bottom of Column II, on the line numbered 20. Cross out his name. Now, from the remaining names on your list, select the one having most of the quality. Put his name in the first column on line 2. Keep up this process until all names have been placed in the scale.

COLUMN I (MOST)	COLUMN II (LEAST)
1. _____	11. _____
2. _____	12. _____
3. _____	13. _____
4. _____	14. _____
5. _____	15. _____
6. _____	16. _____
7. _____	17. _____
8. _____	18. _____
9. _____	19. _____
10. _____	20. _____

◆ FORCED DISTRIBUTION METHOD

forced distribution method Similar to grading on a curve; predetermined percentages of ratees are placed in various performance categories.

The **forced distribution method** is similar to "grading on a curve." With this method, predetermined percentages of ratees are placed in various performance categories. For example, you may decide to distribute employees as follows:

15% high performers

20% high-average performers

30% average performers

20% low-average performers

15% low performers

One practical way to do this is to write each employee's name on a separate index card. Then, for each trait being appraised (quality of work, creativity, and so on), simply place the employee's card in one of the appropriate categories.

An Example

Merck and Company, with about 31,000 employees, has used a forced distribution appraisal method for the past few years with some success. It ties in with their merit pay system and is used for all exempt employees, who receive merit pay increases based on their performance ratings.

Merck's reason for instituting a forced distribution system says a lot about the method's advantages.[5] They instituted it when they found that

FIGURE 14.5
Ranking Employees by the Paired Comparison Method

FOR THE TRAIT "QUALITY OF WORK"					
	Men Rated:				
As Compared to:	A Art	B Bob	C Chuck	D Diane	E Ed
A Art		+	+	−	−
B Bob	−		−	−	−
C Chuck	−	+		+	−
D Diane	+	+	−		+
E Ed	+	+	+	−	

↑ Bob Ranks Highest Here

FOR THE TRAIT "CREATIVITY"					
	Men Rated:				
As Compared to:	A Art	B Bob	C Chuck	D Diane	E Ed
A Art		−	−	−	−
B Bob	+		−	+	+
C Chuck	+	+		−	+
D Diane	+	−	+		−
E Ed	+	−	−	+	

↑ Art Ranks Highest Here

Note: + means "better than," − means "worse than." For each chart, add up the number of +'s in each column to get the highest-ranked employee.

80% of their exempt employees were receiving ratings of 4 and above on their 5-point scale. In other words, there was little differentiation between employees for purposes of salary administration: Even employees who had significant accomplishments throughout the year were getting only slightly higher ratings than were employees who routinely did a good but not extraordinary job. As a result, neither the performance appraisal system nor merit pay plan had the effects on motivation that Merck wanted; a new forced distribution method was thus put in place. Its main purpose was to provide for greater differentiation among employees so that outstanding employees could be identified and rewarded.

At Merck, all exempt employees now receive an annual performance appraisal in December. They meet with their supervisors to review their accomplishments for the year (compared with previously established goals) and receive one of five ratings: EX (exceptional), WD (with distinction), HS (high Merck standard), RI (room for improvement), and NA (not acceptable)

The key to the new appraisal system is that only limited percentages of a manager's subordinates can fall in each of the five categories. For example (see Figure 14.6), 5% of the department's employees can receive EX ratings, 15% can receive WD ratings, and the vast majority—70%—should fall in the "high Merck standard" middle level of the range. In other words, this system forces the supervisor to identify no more than 20% of his or her exempt employees who are doing above average in attaining their planned objectives, when compared with their Merck peers.

The program is working well, largely because the company has worked hard to overcome forced distribution's inherent problems. Merck knew, for example, that it's not realistic to force a manager with only four or five employees to distribute them into five classes. They therefore use a "role-up" system. Here several departments in the same division are reviewed together for the purpose of meeting the percentage distribution requirements of the rating system. (At each "role-up" meeting, the supervisor can argue for two out of five employees receiving an EX rating.) The big problem, though, was getting employees who viewed themselves as high achievers to understand that getting an HS (high Merck standard) does not equate to getting a C on a report card.

Still, at Merck (or at other companies, or when rating college students, for that matter), there is always the question of whether the person's absolute or relative performance should be rated. On balance, however, the pro-

FIGURE 14.6
Merck's Distribution System for Performance Appraisals and Pay Increases

MERCK'S DISTRIBUTION SYSTEM FOR PERFORMANCE APPRAISALS AND PAY INCREASES				
EXEMPT PERFORMANCE RATING DEFINITIONS				
PERFORMANCE RATINGS		**PERFORMANCE DEFINITIONS**		
RATING	DISTRIBUTION TARGET	SPECIFIC JOB MEASURES/ ONGOING DUTIES	PLANNED OBJECTIVES	MANAGEMENT OF PEOPLE
EX Exceptional Within Merck	5%	Far above Merck peers Capitalized on un-expected events to gain superior results	Made significant breakthroughs or exceptional achievements	Outstanding leader Exceptional development/ recruitment of people Superior communications
WD Merck Standard with distinction	15%	Clearly superior to Merck peers in most respects Took advantage of unexpected events to achieve unusually good results	Objectives met and many exceeded	A clear leader among Merck peers Top-quality people recruited/developed Excellent communications
HS High Merck Standard	70%	Comparable to Merck peers Made use of unexpected events to achieve very good results	Objectives met	A very good leader. Hires very good people/develops people as well as peers Very good communications
RI Merck Standard with Room for Improvement	8%	Work is not quite as good as Merck peers Contended with unexpected events	Most objectives met. Some shortfalls	Adequate leader Hires good people Satisfactory communications
NA Not Adequate for Merck	2%	Work is not up to that of Merck peers Did not fully cope with unexpected events	Missed significant objectives	Poor leader Communications could be better
PR Progressing	Not applicable	Typically this employee is new to the company or in a significantly different assignment. Normally this rating would apply only during the first year in the new job.		

gram at Merck has been successful, particularly insofar as it enables the employer to identify high achievers and reward them.

♦ CRITICAL INCIDENT METHOD

With the **critical incident method**, the supervisor keeps for each subordinate a record of uncommonly good or undesirable examples (or "incidents") of that person's work-related behavior. Then every six months or so, the supervisor and subordinate meet and discuss the latter's performance using the specific incidents as examples.

This method can always be used to supplement the primary appraisal technique and as such has several advantages. For one thing, it provides you with some specific hard facts for explaining the appraisal. It ensures that you think about the subordinate's appraisal all during the year (because the incidents must be accumulated) and that the rating therefore does not just reflect the employee's most recent performance. Ideally keeping a running list of critical incidents also provides some concrete examples of what specifically your subordinate can do to eliminate any performance deficiencies.

You can gear the critical incident method directly to the specific job expectations you laid out for your subordinate at the beginning of the appraisal. Thus, in the example presented in Table 14.2, one of the assistant plant manager's continuing duties was to supervise procurement and to minimize inventory costs. The critical incident shows that he let inventory storage costs rise 15%, and this would provide a specific example of what performance he must improve in the future.

A subjective approach like the critical incident method may not be too good for comparing employees and making salary or promotion decisions, so it is often used together with a rating-ranking technique. However, it is useful for identifying specific examples of good and poor performance in terms of the specific activities you expect your subordinate to perform and planning how deficiencies can be corrected.

♦ NARRATIVE FORMS

Some firms use narrative forms to evaluate personnel. For example, the form used in Figure 14.7 presents the "progress development summary"

TABLE 14.2 Examples of Critical Incidents for an Assistant Plant Manager

CONTINUING DUTIES	TARGETS	CRITICAL INCIDENTS
Schedule production for plant	Full utilization of personnel and machinery in plant; orders delivered on time	Instituted new production scheduling system; decreased late orders by 10% last month; increased machine utilization in plant by 20% last month
Supervise procurement of raw materials and inventory control	Minimize inventory costs while keeping adequate supplies on hand	Let inventory storage costs rise 15% last month; overordered parts "A" and "B" by 20%, underordered part "C" by 30%
Supervise machinery maintenance	No shutdowns due to faulty machinery	Instituted new preventive maintenance system for plant; prevented a machine breakdown by discovering faulty part

used by the Allstate Insurance Company to evaluate the progress and the development of its exempt employees. As you can see, the person's supervisor is asked to describe the employee's performance for the period covered in terms of position standards and to outline goals, action plans, and development activities designed to aid the employee in meeting or exceeding these position standards. A summary performance rating for supervision, experience, and overall performance is also provided for in the form.[6]

♦ BEHAVIORALLY ANCHORED RATING SCALES

behaviorally anchored rating scale (BARS) An appraisal method that aims at combining the benefits of narrative critical incidents and quantified ratings by anchoring a quantified scale with specific narrative examples of good or poor performance.

A **behaviorally anchored rating scale (BARS)** aims at combining the benefits of narrative critical incidents and quantified ratings by anchoring a quantified scale with specific narrative examples of good or poor performance, as in Figure 14.8. Its proponents claim that it provides better, more equitable appraisal than do the other tools we have discussed.[7]

Developing a BARS typically requires five steps:[8]

1. *Generate critical incidents.* Persons who know the job being appraised (jobholders and/or supervisors) are asked to describe specific illustrations (critical incidents) of effective and ineffective performance.

2. *Develop performance dimensions.* These people then cluster these incidents into a smaller set (say, five or ten) of performance dimensions. Each cluster (dimension) is then defined.

3. *Reallocate incidents.* Another group of people who also know the job then reallocate the original critical incidents. They are given the clusters' definitions and the critical incidents and asked to reassign each incident to the cluster they think fits best. Typically, a critical incident is retained if some percentage (usually 50% to 80%) of this second group assigns it to the same cluster as did the group in step 2.

4. *Scale the incidents.* This second group is generally asked to rate (7- or 9-point scales are typical) the behavior described in the incident as to how effectively or ineffectively it represents performance on the appropriate cluster's dimension.

5. *Develop final instrument.* A subset of the incidents (usually six or seven per cluster) are used as "behavioral anchors" for each dimension.

Example

Here is an example of how this works in practice. Three researchers developed a BARS for grocery checkout clerks who were working in a large western grocery chain.[9] They collected a number of critical incidents and then clustered them into eight performance dimensions:

KNOWLEDGE AND JUDGMENT
CONSCIENTIOUSNESS
SKILL IN HUMAN RELATIONS
SKILL IN OPERATION OF REGISTER
SKILL IN BAGGING
ORGANIZATIONAL ABILITY OF CHECKSTAND WORK
SKILL IN MONETARY TRANSACTIONS
OBSERVATIONAL ABILITY

In Figure 14.8 you will find the behaviorally anchored rating scale for one of these dimensions, "knowledge and judgment." Notice how there is a scale (ranging from 1 to 7) for rating performance from "extremely poor" to "extremely good." Notice also how the BARS is *behaviorally anchored*

FIGURE 14.7
Allstate's Progress Development
Summary

Allstate's Progress Development Summary

Allstate·

PROGRESS/DEVELOPMENT SUMMARY
EXEMPT EMPLOYES

Employe's Name _____ Office _____ Dept. Code _____

Job Title _____ Period of Report: From _____ To _____

Service Date _____ Time on Present Job _____

NARRATIVE: Describe employe's performance for the period covered in terms of position standards, i.e., compare performance to each of the established accountabilities listed in the Position Analysis. Comment on such things as quantity and quality of work, planning ability, leadership, judgement, dependability, and learning ability if these characteristics contribute to or detract from work performance.

(OVER)

J756-4 PRINTED IN U.S.A.

with specific critical incidents. For example, there is a specific critical incident ("by knowing the price of items, this checker would be expected to look for mismarked and unmarked items") that helps anchor or specify what is meant by "extremely good" performance. Similarly, there are other critical incident anchors all along the scale.

Advantages

Developing a BARS can be more time consuming than developing other appraisal tools, such as graphic rating scales. But BARS are also said to have some important advantages:[10]

FIGURE 14.7
(continued)

Allstate's Progress Development Summary

NARRATIVE: Discuss and outline goals, action plans, and innovative development activities designed to aid the employe in meeting or exceeding position standards.

Check one box in each of the sections below.

SUPERVISION:
Is able to meet or (exceed) position standards with minimum of extra supervision.

☐ No   ☐ Yes

EXPERIENCE:
Has experience normally required to meet the expected level of performance for the position.

☐ No   ☐ Yes

OVERALL PERFORMANCE RATING:

☐ Performance is unacceptable.

☐ Performance is acceptable but needs improvement to meet expected level for the position.

☐ Performance meets expected level for the position.

☐ Performance consistently and significantly exceeds expected level for the position.

NOTE: It is the manager's or immediate supervisor's responsibility to review the entire contents of this Summary with the employe.

EMPLOYE COMMENTS: (Comment on overall evaluation, career goals, and if next promotional position may require it, availability for relocation.)

Employe Signature _____

Evaluated By _____ Date _____

Manager's Signature _____ Date _____

Approved By _____ Date _____

Personnel Dept By _____ Date _____

1. *A more accurate gauge.* People who know the job and its requirements better than anyone else develop BARS. The resulting BARS should therefore be a very good gauge of performance on that job.

2. *Clearer standards.* The critical incidents along the scale help to clarify what is meant by "extremely good" performance, "average" performance, and so forth.

3. *Feedback.* The use of the critical incidents may be more useful in providing feedback to the people being appraised.

4. *Independent dimensions.* Systematically clustering the critical incidents into five or six performance dimensions (such as "knowledge and

FIGURE 14.8

A Behaviorally Anchored Rating Scale for the Performance Dimension "Knowledge and Judgment" for Grocery Checkout Clerks

Source: Lawrence Fogli, Charles Hulin, and Milton Blood, "Development of First Level Behavioral Job Criteria," *Journal of Applied Psychology*, Vol. 55 (1971), p. 6. Copyright 1971 by the American Psychological Association. Reprinted by permission of the authors.

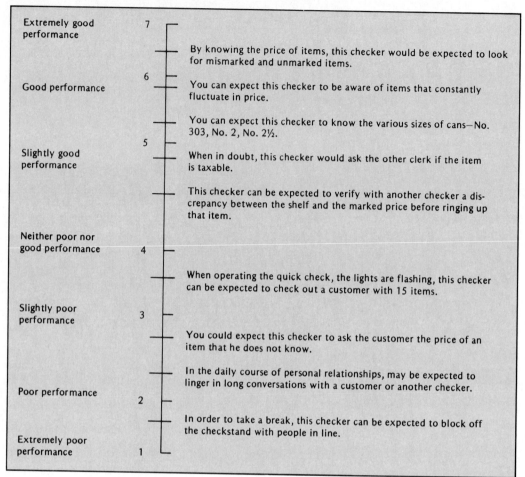

judgment") should help to make the dimensions more independent of one another. For example, a rater should be less likely to rate an employee high on *all* dimensions simply because he or she was rated high in "conscientiousness."

5. *Consistent.*[11] BARS evaluations also seem to be relatively consistent and reliable, in that different raters' appraisals of a person tend to be similar.

◆ THE MANAGEMENT BY OBJECTIVES (MBO) METHOD

management by objectives (MBO) Involves setting specific measurable goals with each employee and then periodically reviewing the progress made.

Stripped to its essentials, **MBO** involves setting specific measurable goals with each employee and then periodically discussing his or her progress toward these goals. While you could engage in a modest MBO program with subordinates by participatively setting goals and periodically providing feedback, the term MBO almost always refers to a comprehensive *organization-wide, goal-setting and appraisal program* that consists of six main steps:

1. *Set the organization's goals.* Establish an organizationwide plan for next year and set goals.

2. *Set departmental goals.* Here, department heads and their superiors jointly set goals for their departments.

3. *Discuss departmental goals*. Department heads discuss the department's goals with all subordinates in the department (often at a department-wide meeting) and ask them to develop their own individual goals; in other words, how can each employee contribute to the department's attaining its goals?

4. *Define expected results* (set individual goals). Here, department heads and their subordinates set short-term performance targets.

5. *Performance reviews: measure the results*. Here, department heads compare actual performance for each employee with expected results.

6. *Provide feedback*. Department heads hold periodic performance review meetings with subordinates to discuss and evaluate the latters' progress in achieving expected results.

Problems to Avoid

There are three problems in using MBO. Setting *unclear, unmeasurable objectives* is the main problem. Setting an objective such as "will do a better job of training" is useless. "Will have four subordinates promoted during the year," on the other hand, is a clear, measurable objective.

Second, MBO is *time consuming*. Taking the time to set objectives, to measure progress, and to provide feedback can take several hours per employee per year over and above the time you already spend doing each person's appraisal. Many managers believe the extra time is worth it; you will have to judge for yourself.

Third, setting objectives with the subordinate sometimes turns into a *tug of war*, with you pushing for higher quotas and the subordinate pushing for lower ones. That is why knowing the job and the person's ability is so important. To motivate performance the objectives must be fair and attainable. The more you know about the job, its problems, how other workers are performing on the job, and this person's ability, the more confident you can be about the standards you set.

In summary, here are some *Do's* and *Don'ts* of MBO:

Do define the person's job responsibilities and duties.

Do learn as much as possible about what reasonable challenging objectives would be for the job.

Do set specific measurable output objectives.

Do make sure the objective is viewed as *fair and attainable*.

Don't let MBO be too *time consuming*.

Don't get into a *tug of war* in setting the subordinate's goals.

◆ MIXING THE METHODS

In practice, most firms combine several appraisal tools. An example of one such mixed method is illustrated in Figure 14.9. This presents a rating form used to appraise the performance of managers in a large airline. Notice that it is basically a graphic rating scale, with descriptive phrases included to define the traits being measured. But, in addition, there is a "comments" section below each trait. This allows the rater to jot down several relevant critical incidents.

The practice of using both narrative and rating-ranking tools to appraise performance mostly results from the fact that each serves a different purpose. Quantifiable rating-ranking methods permit comparisons of employees and are therefore useful for making salary, transfer, and promotion decisions. Narratives, on the other hand, are useful for providing specific examples of good or poor performance.[12]

FIGURE 14.9
One Page from a Typical Management Appraisal Form

MAJOR PERFORMANCE STRENGTHS/WEAKNESSES

Read the definitions of each management factor below and choose the ranking which most accurately describes the employee. If, after reading the definition, it is determined that the skill area was not
demonstrated because of the nature of the employee's position, indicate as Non-Applicable (N/A).
Your evaluation on each of the management factors below should relate directly to the employee's
actual performance on the job.

PLANNING SKILL — Degree to which incumbent:

- Assessed and established priorities of result area.
- Designed realistic short and long range plans.
- Formulated feasible timetables.
- Anticipated possible problems and obstacles toward reaching required results.

Ranking Code	(CHECK ONE)	
1	Far exceeds requirements	
4	Usually meets requirements	
3	Fully meets requirements	
2	Usually exceeds requirements	
5	Fails to meet requirements	

Comments:

ORGANIZING SKILL — Degree to which incumbent:

- Grouped activities for optimal use of personnel and material resources in order to achieve goals.
- Clearly defined responsibilities and authority limits of subordinates.
- Minimized confusion and inefficiencies in work operations.

Ranking Code	(CHECK ONE)	
3	Fully meets requirements	
2	Usually exceeds requirements	
5	Fails to meet requirements	
1	Far exceeds requirements	
4	Usually meets requirements	

Comments:

CONTROLLING SKILL — Degree to which incumbent:
- Established appropriate procedures to be kept informed of subordinate's work progress.
- Identified deviations in work goal progress.
- Adjusted to deviations in work to ensure that established goals were met.

Ranking Code	(CHECK ONE)	
5	Fails to meet requirements	
4	Usually meets requirements	
3	Fully meets requirements	
2	Usually exceeds requirements	
1	Far exceeds requirements	

Comments:

Note: This is one page from a multipage form used to appraise managers.

APPRAISING PERFORMANCE: PROBLEMS AND ISSUES

♦ DEALING WITH THE FIVE MAIN RATING SCALE APPRAISAL PROBLEMS

There are five main problems that can undermine appraisal tools such as graphic rating scales: unclear standards, halo effect, central tendency, leniency or strictness, and bias.

Unclear Standards

unclear performance standards An appraisal scale that is too open to interpretation; instead, include descriptive phrases that define each trait and what is meant by standards like "good" or "unsatisfactory."

Unclear performance standards are one problem. For example, look at the graphic rating scale in Table 14.3. Although the chart seems objective enough, it would probably result in unfair appraisals. This is because the traits and degrees of merit are open to interpretation. For example, different supervisors would probably define "good" performance, "fair" performance, and so on differently. The same is true of traits such as "quality of work" or "creativity."

There are several ways to rectify this problem. The best way is for you to develop and include descriptive phrases that define each trait, such as was the case in Figure 14.3. There, we defined on the scale what was meant by "exceptional," "superior," and "good" quality of work. If your employer has not done this, you should draw up your own guidelines. You will then be more apt to appraise each of your subordinates consistently, and you will be on more solid ground when it comes to explaining your ratings to the subordinates or to others.

Halo Effect

halo effect In performance appraisal, the problem that occurs when a supervisor's rating of a subordinate on one trait biases the rating of that person on other traits.

The **halo effect** means that your rating of a subordinate on one trait ("gets along with others") biases how you rate that person on other traits (such as "quantity of work"). This problem often occurs with employees who are especially friendly (or unfriendly) toward the supervisor since an unfriendly employee will often be rated unsatisfactory for all traits rather than just for the trait "gets along well with others." Being aware of this problem is a major step toward avoiding it. Supervisory training can also alleviate the problem.[13]

Central Tendency

central tendency A tendency to rate all employees the same way, such as rating them all average.

Many supervisors have a **central tendency** when filling in rating scales. For example, if the rating scale ranges from 1 to 7, they will tend to avoid the highs (6 and 7) and lows (1 and 2) and put most of their checks between 3 and 5. If you use a graphic rating scale, this central tendency could mean that all employees are simply rated "average." Naturally, this restriction can distort the evaluations seriously, making them almost useless for promotion, salary, or counseling purposes. *Ranking* employees (instead of using a graphic rating scale) can avoid this central tendency problem because all employees must be ranked and thus can't all be rated average. In fact, this is one of the main advantages of the ranking approach.

Leniency or Strictness

strictness/leniency The problem that occurs when a supervisor has a tendency to rate all subordinates either high or low.

Some supervisors tend to rate all their subordinates consistently high (or low), just as some instructors are notoriously high graders and others are not. This **strictness/leniency** problem is especially serious with graphic rat-

TABLE 14.3 A Graphic Rating Scale with Unclear Standards

	EXCELLENT	GOOD	FAIR	POOR
Quality of work				
Quantity of work				
Creativity				
Integrity				

Note: For example, what exactly is meant by "good," "quantity of work," and so forth?

ing scales because the supervisor can conceivably rate *all* subordinates either high or low. When you must *rank* subordinates, you are forced to distinguish between high and low performers. Strictness/leniency is thus not a problem with the ranking or forced distribution approach.

In fact, if you have to use a graphic rating scale, it is a good idea to *assume* a distribution of performances—that, say, only about 10% of your people should be rated "excellent," 20% "good," and so forth. In other words, try to get a spread (unless, of course, you are sure all your people really do fall into just one or two categories). The easiest way to do this is to use the forced distribution approached: Put each subordinate's name on a separate index card and then *for each trait to be appraised* put about 10% of your subordinates into the top category, about 20% into the next highest category, and so on. Then fill in the graphic rating scale for each person.

Bias

bias The tendency to allow individual differences such as age, race, and sex affect the appraisal rates these employees receive.

Individual differences among ratees in terms of characteristics like age, race, and sex affect the ratings they get, often quite apart from the employee's actual performance.[14] In one study, for instance, researchers found a systematic tendency to evaluate ratees over 60 years of age lower on "performance capacity" and "potential for development" than younger employees.[15] The ratee's race and sex may also affect the person's rating, although here the **bias** is not necessarily consistently against the minority or women, as it seems to be in the case of older workers. In one study in which objective performance measures (such as graphic rating scales) were used, high-performing females were often rated significantly higher than were high-performing males. Similarly, low-performing blacks were often rated significantly higher than were low-performing whites.[16]

An interesting picture of how the employee's age can distort his or her evaluation emerges from a study of registered nurses. Where the nurses were 30–39 years old, supervisors and nurses exhibited perfect average agreement in performance ratings, indicating that the nurses and their supervisors each rated the nurses' performance virtually the same. In the 21–29 category, on the other hand, supervisors actually rated subordinates higher than they rated themselves. However, for the 40–61 subordinate age category, the supervisors rated subordinates' performance lower than subordinates rated their own performance. The conclusion here may be that supervisors are tougher in appraising older subordinates: They don't give them as much credit for their success, while attributing any low performance to their lack of ability.[17]

The employee's previous performance can also affect the supervisor's evaluation of his or her current performance. In one study, for instance, the researchers concluded that "raters who develop systematic expectations regarding the performance of a specific ratee may find it difficult to accurately evaluate that ratee's performance if he or she departs from a previous pattern of performance."[18] The actual misevaluation can take several forms in practice. Sometimes the rater may systematically overestimate improvement on the part of a poor worker or may overestimate declines on the part of a good worker, for instance. In some situations—especially when the change in behavior is more gradual—the rater may simply be insensitive to changes in the ratee's behavior. In any case, it is important when rating performance to do so objectively and to try to block from your mind the effects of things such as the person's earlier performance.

♦ HOW TO AVOID APPRAISAL PROBLEMS

First, be sure you are thoroughly familiar with the problems as just discussed. Understanding the problem is a big step toward avoiding it.

Second, choose the right appraisal technique. Each of the techniques, such as the graphic rating scale or critical incident method, has its own advantages and disadvantages. For example, as summarized in Table 14.4, the ranking method avoids central tendency but can cause ill feelings among employees whose performance is in fact very similar—as when all are actually "high." Similarly, both graphic ratings and ranking methods are good for comparing employees for salary and promotion decisions.

How to Be Sure the Subordinate Views the Appraisal as a Fair One[19]

There are five things you can do here. First, be sure to evaluate your subordinate's performance *frequently*, even if the formal appraisal takes place only once a year. If the person is doing well, this feedback will provide reinforcement. If he or she is not doing well, the feedback gives him or her an opportunity to improve and means there won't be any surprises when the formal appraisal rolls around.

Four other things: First, make sure it is clear that you are *familiar with the performance* of the person being appraised—this is when critical incidents can be useful. Second, make sure there is *agreement* between you and your subordinate concerning his or her job duties. Third, *solicit the subordinate's help* when you formulate the plans for eliminating performance weaknesses. (These plans are usually developed as part of the appraisal interview, which we explain in the following section.) Finally, keep in mind that *subordinates who participate in developing the appraisal tool* also react more favorably to the resulting appraisal interview.[20]

♦ TRAINING OF RATERS

Training supervisors to eliminate rating errors such as halo, leniency, and central tendency can improve their effectiveness as appraisers.[21] In the tra-

TABLE 14.4 **Important Advantages and Disadvantages of Appraisal Tools**

	ADVANTAGES	DISADVANTAGES
Graphic rating scales	Simple to use; provides a quantitative rating for each employee.	Standards may be unclear; halo effect, central tendency, leniency, bias can also be problems.
Alternation ranking	Simple to use (but not as simple as graphic rating scales). Avoids central tendency and other problems of rating scales.	Can cause disagreements among employees and may be unfair if all employees *are*, say, excellent.
Forced distribution method	End up with a predetermined number of people in each group.	Appraisal results depend on the adequacy of your original choice of cutoff points.
Critical incident method	Helps specify what is "right" and "wrong" about the employee's performance; forces supervisor to evaluate subordinates on an ongoing basis.	Difficult to rate or rank employees relative to one another.
Behaviorally anchored rating scale	Provides behavioral "anchors." BARS is very accurate.	Difficult to develop.
MBO	Tied to jointly agreed upon performance objectives.	Time consuming.

ditional method, raters are shown a videotape of jobs being performed and are asked to rate the worker. Ratings made by each participant are then placed on a flip chart and the various errors (such as leniency and halo) are explained. For example, if a trainee rated all criteria (such as quality, quantity, etc.) about the same, the trainer might explain that halo error had occurred; if a trainee rated all videotaped workers very high, this might be explained as leniency error. Typically, the trainer gives the correct rating and then illustrates the rating errors the participants made.[22] According to one study, computer-assisted instruction training improved managers' ability to conduct performance appraisal discussions with their subordinates.[23]

Rater training is also no panacea for reducing rating errors or improving the accuracy of appraisals. From a practical point of view, several factors, including the extent to which pay is tied to performance ratings, union pressure, turnover rates, time constraints, and the need to justify ratings may be more important than training in influencing the ratings they actually give. This means that improving an appraisal procedure's accuracy involves not only training but also remedying outside factors such as union pressure. And it means that rater training to be effective should also address real-life problems such as the fact that union representatives will try to pressure supervisors to rate everyone high.[24]

◆ PERFORMANCE APPRAISAL AND FAIR-EMPLOYMENT PRACTICE

Performance appraisal can have a big impact on a firm's equal employment compliance efforts.[25] Since the passage of Title VII the courts have addressed various issues (including promotion, layoff, and compensation decisions) in which performance appraisals have played a significant role. And, in their decisions, they have often found that the inadequacies of the employer's appraisal system lay at the root of some discriminatory action concerning promotion, layoff, or compensation. Court cases and significant rulings affecting performance appraisals are summarized in Table 14.5.[26]

One case involved layoff decisions. Here the court held that the firm had violated Title VII when on the basis of poor performance ratings it laid off several Spanish-surnamed employees.[27] The court concluded that the practice was illegal because:

1. The appraisals were based on subjective supervisory observations.
2. The appraisals were not administered and scored in a standardized fashion.
3. Two of the three supervisory evaluators did not have daily contact with the employees being evaluated.

TABLE 14.5   Appraisal: A Summary of Court Cases and Significant Rulings

CASE	YEAR	COURT	PREVAILING PARTY	SIGNIFICANT RULING(S)
Griggs v. *Duke Power Company*	1971	Supreme	Employee	EEOC guidelines first endorsed. Adverse impact requires demonstration of job-relatedness. Employer intent to discriminate irrelevant.
Marquez v. *Omaha District Sales Office, Ford Division of the Ford Motor Company*	1971	Appeals, 8th Circuit	Employee	Documentation necessary. Misuse of legal appraisal system may violate Title VII.
Rowe v. *General Motors*	1972	Appeals, 5th Circuit	Employee	Lack of appraiser training condemned. Subjective performance standards condemned.

TABLE 14.5 (continued)

CASE	YEAR	COURT	PREVAILING PARTY	SIGNIFICANT RULING(S)
				Communication of performance standards required.
Harper v. *Mayor and City Council of Baltimore*	1972	District	Employee	Neutral results may indicate discrimination. Consistent evaluation dimensions required.
Brito v. *Zia Company*	1973	Appeals, 10th Circuit	Employee	Performance appraisals are "employment tests." Adverse impact requires demonstration of validity of appraisal system. Objective performance standards should supplement subjective standards. Standardized administration and scoring of appraisals required.
Wade v. *Mississippi Cooperative Extension Service*	1974	District	Employee	Job analysis required. Appraisal on general traits condemned.
Albemarle Paper Company v. *Moody*	1975	Supreme	Employee	Appraisals as criteria must be job-related. Endorsement of EEOC guidelines regarding criterion development.
Patterson v. *American Tobacco Company*	1978	Appeals, 4th Circuit	Employee	Job analysis necessary. Objective performance standards required.
Zell v. *United States*	1979	District	Organization	Regular evaluations supported. Job-related standards demonstrated. Performance standards properly communicated.
Ramirez v. *Hofheinz*	1980	Appeals, 5th Circuit	Organization	Subjective performance standards supported. Past record of employer important.
Turner v. *State Highway Commission of Missouri*	1982	District	Organization	Documentation complete.
Carpenter v. *Stephen F. Austin State University*	1983	Appeals, 5th Circuit	Employee	Updated analysis. Performance standards required to be demonstrably job-related. Appraiser training required.
Chamberlain v. *Bissel, Inc.*	1982	District	Employee	Failure to warn of declining performance in evaluations
Kresyman v. *Bolger*	1984	Kansas District	Organization	Testimony at trial indicated incidents leading to unfavorable evaluations were very minor. However, court noted that the question at hand was whether racial discrimination had taken place, and court's answer was no.
Grant v. *C&P Telephone Co.*	1984	District Court of D.C.	Organization	The plaintiff's work records were not only reviewed by upper level personnel, he was warned repeatedly that termination was imminent if his work did not improve.
Nord v. *U.S. Steel*	1985	11th Circuit	Employee	The plaintiff successfully demonstrated that she had good performance appraisals before requesting a promotion. After request, her appraisals became negative, leading to her eventual termination.

Source: Based on Sami M. Abbasi, Kenneth W. Hollman and Joe H. Murrey, Jr., "Employment at Will: An Eroding Concept in Employment Relationships," *Labor Law Journal*, Vol. 38, no. 1 (January 1987), pp. 26–27, and Gerald Barrett and Mary Kernan, "Performance Appraisal and Terminations: a Review of Court Decisions Since *Brito* v. *Zia* with Implications for Personnel Practices," *Personnel Psychology*, Vol. 40, no. 3 (Autumn 1987), pp 489–501.

An important aspect of this case was that the court in effect accepted performance appraisals as tests. In other words, they concluded that the performance appraisal procedure used by the company had to comply with EEOC employee selection guidelines and that in this case it did not. While the appraisals *were* based on the "best judgments and opinions" of the appraisers, they were *not* based on any objective criteria that were supported by some kind of record of validity.

Based on this, some experts have contended that the performance appraisal development process should comply with the strict guidelines for developing any test; however today it's generally assumed that this is not required.[28] For example, two writers recently concluded that conducting testlike validation procedures when developing performance appraisals is not required for the firm's appraisal process to be legally defensible. They further contend that insisting on such validation can be "potentially damaging as it could eventually place the profession in a position it cannot satisfactorily defend."[29] And they conclude:

> Organizations should be concerned about the integrity and fairness of their performance appraisal procedures. But, efforts designed to improve and validate performance appraisal instruments do not necessarily have the legal value that some commentators in the field believe.[30]

This being the case, a checklist for developing a defensible appraisal process includes the following:[31]

1. Conduct a job analysis to ascertain characteristics (such as "timely project completion") required for successful job performance. Graphically:

   Job Analysis ——————→ Performance Standards ——————→ Performance Appraisal

2. Incorporate these characteristics into a rating instrument. (Note that while the professional literature recommends rating instruments that are tied to specific job behaviors, i.e., BARS, the courts routinely accept less sophisticated approaches such as graphic rating scales).

3. Make sure that definitive performance standards are provided to all raters and ratees.

4. Use clearly defined individual dimensions of job performance (like quantity or quality) rather than undefined, global measures of job performance (like "overall performance").

5. Because they provide objective, observable evidence, recognize that behaviorally based performance dimensions are highly advisable but not mandatory in a defensible appraisal program.

6. When using graphic rating scales, avoid abstract trait names (for example, loyalty, honesty) unless they can be defined in terms of observable behaviors.

7. While they can be useful, employ subjective supervisory ratings (in terms of essays, for instance) only as one component of the overall appraisal process.

8. Train supervisors to use the rating instrument properly. This includes instructions on how to apply performance appraisal standards ("outstanding," etc.) when making judgments. Make sure supervisors are trained to apply standards uniformly: In six of ten cases decided against the employer, the plaintiffs were able to show that subjective standards had been applied unevenly to minority and majority employees.[32]

9. Allow appraisers substantial daily contact with the employee being evaluated.

10. Whenever possible, have more than one appraiser conduct the appraisal and conduct all such appraisals independently. As explained shortly,

this process can help to "cancel out" individual errors and biases on the part of individual appraisers.

11. Based on court cases, utilize formal appeal mechanisms and a review of ratings by upper-level personnel.

12. Document evaluations and reasons for the termination decision (if any). Credibility is enhanced when appraisals and instances of poor performance are documented.

13. Where appropriate, provide some form of performance counseling or corrective guidance to assist poor performers in improving their performance. Courts look favorably on this practice.

♦ WHO SHOULD DO THE APPRAISING?

An important question concerns who should actually rate an employee's performance. While rating by the person's supervisor is still the prevailing approach, several options are actually possible.

Appraisal by the Immediate Supervisor

Supervisors' ratings are the heart of most appraisal systems. This is because getting a supervisor's appraisal is relatively easy and also makes a great deal of sense. The supervisor should be—and usually is—in the best position to observe and evaluate his or her subordinate's performance. Therefore, most appraisal systems rely heavily on the supervisor's evaluation.

Using Peer Appraisals

The appraisal of an employee by his or her peers has proven to be effective in predicting future management success. From a study of military officers, for example, we know that peer ratings were quite accurate in predicting which officers would be promoted and which would not.[33] And in another study that involved more than 200 industrial managers, peer ratings were similarly useful in predicting who would be promoted.[34] One potential problem here is "logrolling," in which all the peers simply get together to rate each other high.

Using Rating Committees

Many employers use rating committees to evaluate employees. These committees are often composed of the employee's immediate supervisor and three or four other supervisors; everyone on the committee should be able to intelligently evaluate the employee's performance.

There are several advantages to using multiple raters. First, while there may be a discrepancy in the ratings made by the different supervisors, the composite ratings tend to be more valid than those of individual raters[35] since the combined use of several raters can help cancel out problems like bias and halo effect on the part of individual raters. (Fair employment practice thus makes using multiple raters advisable.) Furthermore, where there *are* differences in raters' ratings, they usually stem from the fact that raters at different levels in the organization often observe different facets of an employee's performance; the appraisal ought to reflect these differences.[36] Even where a committee is not used, it is common to at least have the appraisal reviewed by the manager immediately above the one who makes the appraisal. This was found to be standard practice in 16 of 18 companies surveyed in one study.[37]

Self-ratings

Some employers have experimented with using employees' self-ratings of performance (usually in conjunction with supervisors' ratings), but this is generally not a recommended option. The basic problem is that most studies show that employees consistently rate themselves higher than they are rated by supervisors or peers.[38] In one study, for example, it was found that when asked to rate their own job performances, 40% of the employees in jobs of all types placed themselves in the top 10% ("one of the best"), while virtually all remaining employees rated themselves either in the top 25% ("well above average"), or at least in the top 50% ("above average"). Usually, no more than 1% or 2% will place themselves in a below-average category, and then those are almost invariably in the top below-average category.

Thus, self-appraisals should be used quite carefully. Supervisors requesting self-appraisals (say, for work-planning and review purposes) should be forewarned that their appraisals and the self-appraisals may tend to accentuate differences and rigidify positions.[39] And, of course, even if self-appraisals are not formally requested, each employee will undoubtedly enter the performance-reviewing meeting with his own self-appraisal in mind, and this self-rating will almost invariably be higher than the supervisor's rating.

THE APPRAISAL INTERVIEW

♦ MAIN TYPES OF INTERVIEWS

appraisal interviews Interviews with an employee to make development plans, to maintain satisfactory performance if promotion is not indicated, or to correct unsatisfactory performance.

There are really three types of **appraisal interviews**, each with its own objectives. This is summarized next:[40]

SUMMARY-OF-PERFORMANCE APPRAISAL	APPRAISAL INTERVIEW OBJECTIVE
(1) Satisfactory–Promotable	(1) Make development plans
(2) Satisfactory–Not promotable	(2) Maintain performance
(3) Unsatisfactory–Correctable	(3) Plan correction
Unsatisfactory–Uncorrectable	Fire or tolerate (no interview needed)

In the last situation (unsatisfactory–uncorrectable), there is usually no need for any appraisal interview because the person's performance is not correctable anyway.

Satisfactory–Promotable

In this type of interview the person's performance is satisfactory and there is a promotion ahead. This is the easiest of the three appraisal interviews. Your objective is to discuss the person's career plans and to develop a specific action plan for the educational and professional development the person needs to move on to his or her next job.

Satisfactory–Not Promotable

This interview is for employees whose performance is satisfactory but for whom promotion is not possible. There may be no promotion ahead because the person has reached his level of competence or because there is no more room in the company or because of some educational barrier. Furthermore, some employees are happy where they are and don't want a promotion.[41] Your objective here is not to improve or develop the person but to maintain satisfactory performance.

Maintaining satisfactory performance under these conditions is not easy. You will have to find a few motivators that are important to the person and that are enough to maintain satisfactory performance. These motivators might include some extra time off, a small bonus, some extra authority to handle a somewhat enlarged job, and feedback regarding performance in the form of an occasional "well done!"

Unsatisfactory–Correctable

When the person's performance is deemed unsatisfactory but correctable, the objective of the interview is to lay out an action plan (as explained later) for correcting the unsatisfactory performance. It is never easy to tell someone that his performance is unsatisfactory, and this is usually the most difficult of appraisal interviews.

◆ HOW TO PREPARE FOR THE APPRAISAL INTERVIEW

There are three things to do.[42] First, *assemble the data*. Study the person's job description, compare the employee's performance to the standards, and review the files of the employee's previous performance appraisals. Next, *prepare the employee*. Give your employees at least a week's notice to review their work, read over their job descriptions, analyze problems, and gather their questions and comments. Stress that the appraisal review is mainly to help them know where they stand. Finally, *choose the time and place*. Find a mutually agreeable time for the interview and allow enough time in your schedule for the entire interview. Interviews with lower-level personnel like clerical workers and maintenance staff will probably take no more than an hour. Appraising management employees often takes two or three hours. Be sure the interview is done in a private place where you won't be bothered by phone calls or visitors.

◆ HOW TO CONDUCT THE INTERVIEW

There are four things to keep in mind here.[43] First, *set the tone at the start of the interview*. Explain how the interview will proceed and emphasize that you are having a two-way conversation. Make it clear that your employee has your undivided attention and that you have blocked out enough time for the interview. Second, *be as positive as you can as you assess your employee's strong and weak points*. Don't talk about past mistakes or faults: Rehashing past events and becoming mired in trivial examples of what the person has done wrong will get you nowhere. Instead, stress solving problems. If you must criticize, criticize the *act* rather than the subordinate. (For example, emphasize that "sales are down" rather than "you aren't selling enough.") Third, *summarize your own and your employee's views*. Clarify areas in which you and your employee differ and try to resolve the differences by emphasizing why you think the employee should improve. Your employee may disagree; the important point is that you both understand each other's reasons and points of view.

Finally, make sure that you and your employee *develop an action plan*. Work with the person to set improvement goals that are specific and practical, along with a timetable for achieving them. Here, it's usually best to focus on the two or three most important areas in which you want improvement rather than on all the areas identified in the appraisal.

The action plan might look like this:

```
┌─────────────────────────────────────────────────────────────────────┐
│                         ACTION PLAN                                    │
│                                                                        │
│                                          Date: May 18                  │
│                                                                        │
│                                                                        │
│  For: John, Assistant Plant Manager                                    │
│  Problem: Parts inventory too high                                     │
│  Objective: Reduce plant parts inventory by 10% in June                │
│                                                                        │
│                                                                        │
│  Action Steps              When      Expected Results                  │
│  Determine average         6/2       Establish a base from which to    │
│    monthly parts inventory              measure progress               │
│  Review ordering quantities 6/15     Identify overstock items          │
│    and parts usage                                                     │
│  Ship excess parts to      6/20      Clear stock space                 │
│    regional warehouse and                                              │
│    scrap obsolete parts                                                │
│  Set new ordering quanti-  6/25      Avoid future overstocking         │
│    ties for all parts                                                  │
│  Check records to measure  7/1       See how close we are to objective │
│    where we are now                                                    │
└─────────────────────────────────────────────────────────────────────┘
```

Then, conclude the interview, thanking the employee for his or her time and effort and summarize the main points once more.[44]

How to Encourage Your Subordinate to Talk in the Interview

Getting your subordinates to talk is probably the single biggest factor in bringing about some constructive change in their behavior.[45] You are not going to change someone's behavior or develop an action plan by arguing, cajoling, or monopolizing the interview. The only way to bring about positive change is to get the person talking so he or she can recognize the deficiency and accept the need for change. The do's and don'ts of getting your subordinate to talk can be summarized as follows:

DO

1. *Try silence.* When your subordinate says something, don't rush in with a comment; silence (plus an occasional nod or "uh-huh") will often be enough to get the person to elaborate on what he or she means.

2. *Use open-ended questions,* such as: "What do you think we could do to improve sales in your region?"

3. *State questions in terms of a problem,* such as: "Suppose you were production manager and you thought there was too much waste?"

4. *Use a command,*[46] such as: "go on," "tell me more," and "keep talking."

5. *Use choice questions,* such as: "What are some things you don't like about working for the company?"

6. *Restate the person's last point as a question.* For instance, if he says, "I

PERSONNEL MANAGEMENT:

ON THE FRONT LINE

After spending several weeks on the job, Jennifer was surprised to discover that her father had not formally evaluated any employee's performance for all the years that he had owned the business. Jack's position was that he had "a hundred higher priority things to attend to," such as boosting sales and lowering costs, and, in any case, many employees didn't stick around long enough to be appraisable anyway. Furthermore, contended Jack, manual workers such as those doing the pressing and the cleaning did periodically get positive feedback in terms of praise from Jack for a job well done or criticism, also from Jack, if things did not look right during one of his swings through the stores. Similarly, Jack was never shy about telling his managers about store problems so that they, too, got some feedback on where they stood.

This informal feedback notwithstanding, Jennifer believes that a more formal appraisal approach is needed. She believes that there are criteria such as quality, quantity, attendance, and punctuality that should be evaluated periodically even if a worker is paid on piece rate. Furthermore, she feels quite strongly that the managers need to have a list of quality standards for matters such as store cleanliness, efficiency, safety, and adherence to budget on which they know they are to be formally evaluated.

1. Is Jennifer right about the need formally to evaluate the workers? The managers? Why or why not?

2. Develop a performance appraisal method for the workers and managers in each store.

---

just don't think I can get the job done," try to draw him out by restating his point as a question, "You don't think you can get the job done?"

7. Try to get at the feelings underlying what the person is saying. Is the person frustrated by a lack of promotion possibilities? Does he or she think the treatment is unfair?

On the other hand,

DON'T

1. Do all the talking.
2. Use restrictive questions (like "would you" or "did you") that can be answered in one or two words.
3. Be judgmental by saying things such as "you shouldn't have."
4. Give free advice, such as "If I were you . . ."
5. Get involved with name calling (such as "Boy, that was stupid!")
6. Ridicule (for instance, by saying, "How did you manage that?")
7. Digress (for instance, by saying, "That reminds me of a funny story . . .").
8. Use sarcasm (for instance, by saying, "I'd hoped for more but I should have known better knowing you").

How to Handle a Defensive Subordinate

Defensiveness is more of a problem than you might imagine. Most employees rate their performance higher than it actually is: 70% of your employees might rank themselves in the top 20%, for instance. Therefore resistance, protest, and defensiveness should be expected.

Defenses are a very important and familiar aspect of our lives. When a person is accused of poor performance, the first reaction will often be *de-*

nial. By denying the fault, the person avoids having to question his or her competence. Others react to criticism with *anger and aggression.* This helps them let off steam and postpones confronting the immediate problem until they are able to cope with it. Still others react to criticism by *retreating* into a shell.

In any event, understanding and dealing with defensiveness is an important appraisal skill. Psychologist Mortimer Feinberg suggests the following:

1. *Recognize that defensive behavior is normal.*
2. *Never attack a person's defenses.* Don't try to "explain someone to themselves" by saying things like "you know the real reason you're using that excuse is because you can't bear to be blamed for anything." Instead, try to concentrate on the act itself ("sales are down") rather than on the person ("you're not selling enough").
3. *Postpone action.* Sometimes the best thing to do is to do nothing at all. People frequently react to sudden threats by instinctively hiding behind their "masks." But, given sufficient time, a more rational reaction takes over.
4. *Recognize your own limitations.* Don't expect to be able to solve every problem that comes up, especially the human ones. More important, remember that a supervisor should not try to be a psychologist. Offering your people understanding is one thing; trying to deal with deep psychological problems is another matter entirely.

How to Criticize a Subordinate

When some criticism is required, it should be done in a manner that helps the person maintain his or her dignity and sense of worth. Specifically, criticism should be done in private and should be done constructively, with you providing examples of critical incidents and specific suggestions of what could be done and why. Avoid once-a-year "critical broadsides" by appraising subordinates often, on a daily basis, so that at the formal review there are no surprises. Never say the person is "always" wrong (since no one is ever "always" wrong or right) and don't make a joke of the incident (your joking may seem sarcastic). Again, criticize the act ("sales are down") rather than the person ("you're not selling enough"). Finally, criticism should be objective and free from any personal feelings on your part.

How to Ensure That the Appraisal Interview Leads to Improved Performance[47]

You should clear up job-related problems and set improvement goals and a schedule for achieving them. In one study the researchers found that whether or not subordinates expressed *satisfaction* with their appraisal interview depended mostly on three things: not feeling threatened during the interview; having an opportunity to present their ideas and feelings and to influence the course of the interview; and having a helpful and constructive supervisor conduct the interview. But you don't just want your subordinates to be satisfied with their performance interview. Your main aim should be to get them to improve their subsequent performance. And here the researchers found that *clearing up job-related problems with the appraisee* and *setting measurable performance targets and a schedule for achieving them*—an action plan—were the two actions that consistently led to improved employee performance.

How to Handle a Formal Written Warning

There will be times when your employee's performance is so poor that a formal written warning is required. Such written warnings serve two pur-

COMPUTER APPLICATION IN PERFORMANCE APPRAISAL:

PERFORMANCE ANALYSIS

One measure of the performance of HRM interviewers is how long the people they place stay with the company. This retention measure can be quantified, which makes it suitable for computerization. Personnel/HRM professionals often begin their careers interviewing applicants, sometimes without adequate training in interviewing techniques. And one purpose of an effective performance appraisal system is to pinpoint areas in which an employee needs further training.

If company research shows a high turnover rate of employees within the first six months of employment, for example, this implies mismatches between the employee and the position. The problem may be an inadequate job analysis (or its outcome, a poor job description), inaccurate job specifications, or a poorly trained interviewer. The first step is to establish what the retention rates are, both for interviewer and for the supervisor. (The supervisors are recorded because of their significant impact on retention, regardless of the input of HRM in the hiring process).

Retention rates can be calculated by capturing the names, race, sex, position code of job applied for, department code where referred, and supervisor's code (a unique number or letters assigned to each supervisor who has hiring responsibilities). By linking this spreadsheet to one which lists new hires and one which lists terminations, retention rates can be calculated regularly. A macro (which combines several keystrokes into one set of directions taking two keystrokes) can link the spreadsheets, complete the calculations, and print the report.

A table can be constructed in which supervisors who have hired someone in the specified time frame are identified by a unique number or a two- or three-letter abbreviation. Each time a new employee is hired, one column of data would include the supervisor's identification. Through a database count or extraction, you can total the number of employees hired by each supervisor in that time period. You can count only those supervisors to whom a given interviewer referred applicants by adjusting the formula to perform that discrimination of data. This is particularly helpful if the interviewer feels that one supervisor significantly impacted the retention rate negatively. This is an example of "What if . . . ?" which allows managers to see how a change in facts affects the outcome—and possibly the manager's decision.

While retention rates should not be used as the sole measure of the effectiveness of an interviewer, it offers one objective performance measure on which to base decisions about future goals and/or training.

poses: (1) They may serve to shake your employee out of his or her bad habits and cause improvement, and (2) they can help you defend your decision both to your own boss, and (if needed) to the courts.

In brief, such written warnings should identify the standard of behavior under which the employee is judged, make it clear that the employee was aware of the standard, specify any violation of the standard, and afford the employee an opportunity to correct his or her behavior.

PERFORMANCE APPRAISAL TODAY

We should briefly review how employers use performance appraisals today since such information can help you formulate your own performance appraisal process. A summary of one survey of current practice suggests the following:[48]

Almost all companies responding do have formal appraisal programs. About 93% of smaller organizations (those with fewer than 500 employees) have such programs, while about 97% of large organizations have them.

In general, rating scales are by far the most widely used appraisal technique. About 62% of small organizations use rating scales, 20% use essays, and about 19% use MBO. Among large organizations, 51% use rating scales, just over 23% use essays, and about 17% use MBO.

However, a closer reading of the actual appraisal forms shows that about 87% of the responding employers actually use some combination of rating and narrative appraisals. Specifically, those using ratings as the main appraisal technique typically ask appraisers for narrative comments to justify ratings and to describe employee strengths and weaknesses and document development plans.[49] Those using essays as the main appraisal technique usually require an overall performance rating to facilitate employee comparisons for compensation decisions and other competitive actions like promotion.

Ninety-two percent of appraisals are made by the employee's immediate supervisor. These appraisals are in turn reviewed by the appraiser's supervisor in 74% of the responding organizations.

Only about 7% of the organizations use self-appraisal in any part of the overall appraisal process.

Virtually all (99%) of employees are informed of the results of their appraisals. Overall, about 77% are given a chance to respond with written comments on their appraisals.

In most companies (69%) appraisals are done annually.

Instructions are important: 82% of employers provide written instructions for appraisers, and 60% provide training.

SUMMARY

1. Appraising performance plays a crucial role in improving motivation at work. People want and need feedback regarding how they are doing, and appraisal provides an opportunity for you to give them that feedback. And if performance is not up to par, the appraisal conference provides an opportunity to review your subordinate's progress and map out a plan for rectifying any performance deficiencies that might be identified.

2. Before the appraisal, make sure to clarify what performance you expect so that the employee knows what he or she should be shooting for. Ask, in other words, "What do I really expect this person to do?"

3. We described several performance appraisal tools, including the graphic rating scale, alternation ranking method, forced distribution method, BARS, MOB, and critical incident method.

4. Each of these techniques has its own advantages and disadvantages. Appraisal problems to beware of include unclear standards, the halo effect, the central tendency, the leniency or strictness problem, and bias.

5. Most subordinates probably want some specific explanation or examples regarding why they were appraised high or low and, for this, compiling *critical incidents* can be useful. Here, a running record of uncommonly good or undesirable examples of each person's work-related behavior should be maintained. This approach can be useful for identifying specific examples of good and poor performance in terms of the specific activities you expect your subordinates to perform. Even if your

firm requires that you summarize the appraisal in a form like a graphic rating scale, maintaining a list of critical incidents can be useful when the time comes to discuss the appraisal with your subordinate.

6. It is important that your subordinate view the appraisal as a fair one, and in this regard there are four things you can do: Evaluate his or her performance frequently; make sure you are familiar with the person's performance; make sure there is an agreement between you and your subordinate concerning his or her job duties; and finally, solicit the person's help when you formulate plans for eliminating performance weaknesses.

7. There are three types of appraisal interviews, each with its own objectives. The first is for performance that is unsatisfactory but correctable. Here, the objective of the interview is to lay out an action plan for correcting the unsatisfactory performance. The second type of interview is for employees whose performance is satisfactory but for whom promotion is not possible. Your objective here is not to improve or develop the person but to maintain satisfactory performance. Finally, there is the satisfactory–promotable interview in which the main objective is to discuss the person's career plans and to develop a specific action plan for the educational and professional development the person needs to move on to the next job.

8. To prepare for the appraisal interview there are three things to do: Assemble the data, prepare the employee, and choose the time and place.

9. In actually conducting the interview, the main things to keep in mind are to set the tone at the start of the interview, be as positive as you can, summarize your own and your employee's views, and then develop an action plan like the one presented in this chapter.

10. To bring about some constructive change in your subordinate's behavior it is important to get the person to talk in the interview. Do's for encouraging the person to talk include: Try silence, use open-ended questions, state questions in terms of a problem, use a command question, use choice questions to try to understand the *feelings* underlying what the person is saying, and restate the person's last point as a question. On the other hand, *don't* do all the talking, use restrictive questions, be judgmental, give free advice, get involved with name calling, ridicule, digress, or use sarcasm.

11. The best way to handle a defensive subordinate is to proceed very carefully. Specifically, recognize that defensive behavior is normal, never attack a person's defenses, postpone actions, and recognize your own limitations.

12. If you are genuinely interested in using the appraisal interview to improve your subordinate's subsequent performance, the most important thing you should aim to accomplish is to clear up job-related problems and set improvement goals and a schedule for achieving them.

KEY TERMS

graphic rating scale	critical incident method	unclear performance standards
alternation ranking method	behaviorally anchored rating scale (BARS)	halo effect
paired comparison method		central tendency
forced distribution method	management by objectives (MBO)	strictness/leniency
		bias
		appraisal interviews

DISCUSSION QUESTIONS

1. Discuss the pros and cons of at least four performance appraisal tools.
2. Develop a graphic rating scale for the following jobs: secretary, engineer, directory assistance operator.
3. Evaluate the rating scale in Table 14.1. Discuss ways to improve it.
4. Explain how you would use the alternation ranking method, the paired comparison method, and the forced distribution method.
5. Over the period of a week, develop a set of critical incidents covering the classroom performance of one of your instructors.
6. Explain in your own words how you would go about developing a behaviorally anchored rating scale.
7. Explain the problems to be avoided in appraising performance.
8. Discuss the pros and cons of using different potential raters to appraise a person's performance.
9. Explain the four types of appraisal interview objectives and how they affect how you manage the interview.
10. Explain how to conduct an appraisal interview.
11. Answer the question: "How would you get the interviewee to talk during an appraisal interview?"

♦ APPLICATION EXERCISES

♦ **CASE INCIDENT**   **Appraising the Secretaries at Sweetwater U**

Rob Winchester, newly appointed vice-president for administrative affairs at Sweetwater State University, faced a tough problem shortly after his university career began. Three weeks after he came on board in September Sweetwater's president, Rob's boss, told him that one of his first problems would involve ways to improve the appraisal system used to evaluate secretarial and clerical performance at Sweetwater U. Apparently, the main difficulty was that the performance appraisal was traditionally tied directly to salary increases given at the end of the year. So most administrators were less than accurate when they used the graphic rating forms that were the basis of the clerical staff evaluation. In fact, what usually happened was that each administrator simply rated his or her clerk or secretary as "excellent." This cleared the way for all support staff to receive a maximum pay increase every year.

But the current university budget simply did not have funds enough to fund another "maximum" annual increase for every staffer. Furthermore, Sweetwater's president felt that the custom of providing invalid feedback to each secretary on his or her year's performance was not a healthy situation, so he had asked the new vice-president to revise the system. In October, the vice-president sent a memo to all administrators telling them that in the future no more than half of the secretaries reporting to any particular administrator could be appraised as "excellent." This move, in effect, forced each supervisor to begin ranking his or her secretaries for quality of performance. The vice-president's memo met widespread resistance immediately—from administrators, who were afraid that many of their secretaries would begin leaving for more lucrative jobs in private industry, and from secretaries, who felt that the new system was unfair and reduced each secretary's chance of receiving a maximum salary. A handful of secretaries began quietly picketing outside the president's home on the university campus. The picketing, caustic remarks by disgruntled administrators, and rumors of an impending "slowdown" by the secretaries (there were about 250 on the campus) made Rob Winchester wonder whether he had made the right decision by setting up forced ranking. He knew, however, that there were a few performance appraisal experts in the School of Business, so he decided to set up an appointment with them to discuss the matter.

He met with them the next morning. He explained the situation as he had found it: the present appraisal system had been set up when the university first opened ten years earlier, and the appraisal form had been developed primarily by a committee of secretaries. Under that system, Sweetwater's administrators fill out forms similar to the one shown in Table 14.3. This once-a-year appraisal (in March) had run into problems almost immediately since it was apparent from the start that administrators vary widely in their interpretations of job standards, as well as in how conscientiously they filled out the forms and supervised their secretaries. Moreover, the defects of this procedure had become conspicuous at the end of the first year when it became obvious to everyone that each secretary's salary increase was tied directly to the March appraisal. For example, those rated "excellent" received the maximum increases, those rated "good" received smaller increases, and those given neither rating received only the standard across-the-board cost-of-living increase. Since universities in general—and Sweetwater U in particular—have paid secretaries somewhat lower salaries than those prevailing in private industry, some secretaries left in a huff that first year. From that time on most administrators simply rated all secretaries as excellent in order to save themselves staff turnover, thus ensuring each a maximum increase. In the process, they also avoided the hard feelings aroused by the significant performance differences otherwise highlighted by administrators.

Two of the Sweetwater experts agreed to consider the problem, and in two weeks they came back to the vice-president with the following recommendations. First, the form used to rate the secretaries was grossly insufficient. As written, it was unclear what "excellent" or "quality of work" meant, for example. As a result, most of the administrators they had spoken to were unclear as to the meaning of each item in the rating. They recommended instead a form like that in Figure 14.3. In addition, they recommended that the vice-president rescind his earlier memo and no longer attempt to force university administrators arbitrarily to rate at least half their secretaries as something less than excellent. The two consultants pointed out that this was, in fact, an unfair procedure since it was quite possible that any particular administrator might have staffers who were all or virtually all excellent—or conceivably, although less likely, all below standard. The experts said that the way to get all the administrators to take the appraisal process more seriously was to stop tying it to salary increases. In other words, they recommended that every administrator fill out a form like that in Figure 14.3 for each of his or her secretaries at least once a year and then use this form for the basis of a counseling session. Salary increases, however, would have to be made on some basis other than the performance appraisal so that administrators would no longer hesitate to fill out the rating forms honestly.

The vice-president thanked the two experts and went back to his office to ponder their recommendations. Some of the recommendations (such as substituting the new rating form for the old) seemed to make sense. Nevertheless, he still had serious doubts as to the efficacy of any graphic rating form, particularly if he were to decide in favor of his original forced-ranking approach. The experts' second recommendation—to stop tying the appraisals to automatic salary increases—made sense but raised at least one very practical problem: If salary increases were not to be based on performance appraisals, on what were they to be based? He began wondering whether the experts' recommendations weren't simply based on ivory tower theorizing.

Questions

1. Do you think that the experts' recommendations will be sufficient to get most of the administrators to fill out the rating forms properly? Why? Why not? What additional actions (if any) do you think will be necessary?

2. Do you think that Vice-President Winchester would be better off dropping the use of graphic rating forms, substituting instead one of the other techniques we discussed in this chapter, such as a ranking method?

3. What performance appraisal system would you develop for the secretaries if you were Rob Winchester? Defend your answer.

EXPERIENTIAL EXERCISE

Purpose: The purpose of this exercise is to give you practice in developing and using a performance appraisal form.

Required Understanding: You are going to develop a performance appraisal form for an instructor and should therefore be thoroughly familiar with the discussion of performance appraisal in this chapter.

How to Set Up the Exercise: Divide the class into groups of four or five students.

Instructions for the Exercise

1. First, based upon what you now know about performance appraisal, do you think Table 14.1 is an effective scale for appraising instructors? Why? Why not?

2. Next, your group should develop its own tool for appraising the performance of an instructor. Decide which of the six appraisal tools (graphic rating scales, alternation ranking, and so on) you are going to use and then design the instrument itself.

3. Next, have a spokesperson from each group put his or her group's appraisal tool on the board. How similar are the tools? Do they all measure about the same factors? Which factor appears most often? Which do you think is the most effective tool on the board? Can you think of any way of combining the best points of several of the tools into a resulting performance appraisal tool?

NOTES

1. Kenneth Teel, "Performance Appraisal: Current Trends, Persistent Progress," *Personnel Journal* (April 1980), pp. 296–301. See also Christina Banks and Kevin Murphy, "Toward Narrowing the Research-Practice Gap in Performance Appraisals," *Personnel Psychology*, Vol. 38, no. 2 (Summer 1985), pp. 335–346. For a description of how to implement an improved performance appraisal system, see, for example, Ted Cocheu, "Performance Appraisal: A Case in Point," *Personnel Journal*, Vol. 65, no. 9 (September 1986), pp. 48–53; Weitzel, "How to Improve Performance Through Successful Appraisals," *Personnel*, Vol. 64, no. 10 (October 1987), pp. 18–23; William H. Wagel, "Performance Appraisal with a Difference," *Personnel*, Vol. 64, no. 2 (February 1987), pp. 4–6; and Jeanette Cleveland et al., "Multiple Uses of Performance Appraisal: Prevalence and Correlates," *Journal of Applied Psychology*, Vol. 74, no. 1 (February 1989), pp. 130–135.

2. Teel, "Performance Appraisal," p. 301.

3. Ibid. See also Martin Friedman, "Ten Steps to Objective Appraisals," *Personnel Journal*, Vol. 65, no. 6 (June 1986).

4. This is based on James Buford, Jr., Bettye Burkhalter, and Grover Jacobs, "Link Job Descriptions to Performance Appraisals," *Personnel Journal* (June 1988), pp. 132–140.

5. This is based on Commerce Clearing House, "Merck's New Performance Appraisal/Merit Pay System Is Based on Bell-Shaped Distribution," *Ideas and Trends*, May 17, 1989, pp. 88–90.

6. Commerce Clearing House Editorial Staff, "Performance Appraisal: What Three Companies Are Doing," Chicago, 1985. See also Richard Girard, "Are Performance Appraisals Passe?" *Personnel Journal*, Vol. 67, no. 8 (August 1988), pp. 89–90, which explains how companies can appraise performance using incidents instead of formal performance appraisals.

7. See, for example, Timothy Keaveny and Anthony McGann, "A Comparison of Behavioral Expectation Scales and Graphic Rating Scales," *Journal of Applied Psychology*, Vol. 60 (1975), pp. 695–703. See, also, John Ivancevich, "A Longitudinal Study of Behavioral Expectation Scales: Attitudes and Performance," *Journal of Applied Psychology* (April 1980), pp. 139–146.

8. Based on Donald Schwab, Herbert Heneman III, and Thomas DeCotiis, "Behaviorally Anchored Scales: A Review of the Literature," *Personnel Psychology*, Vol. 28 (1975), pp. 549–562. For a discussion, see also Uco Wiersma and Gary Latham, "The Practicality of Behavioral Observation Scales, Behavioral Expectations Scales, and Trait Scales," *Personnel Psychology*, Vol. 30, no. 3 (Autumn 1986), pp. 619–628.

9. Lawrence Fogli, Charles Hulin, and Milton Blood, "Development of First Level Behavioral Job Criteria," *Journal of Applied Psychology*, Vol. 55 (1971), pp. 3–8. See also Terry Dickenson and Peter Fellinger, "A Comparison of the Behaviorally Anchored Rating and Fixed Standard Scale Formats," *Journal of Applied Psychology* (April 1980), pp. 147–154.

10. Keaveny and McGann, "A Comparison of Behavioral Expectation Scales," pp. 695–703; Schwab, Heneman, and DeCotiis, "Behaviorally Anchored Rating Scales"; and James Goodale and Ronald Burke, "Behaviorally Based Rating Scales Need Not Be Job Specific," *Journal of Applied Psychology*, Vol. 60 (June 1975).

11. Wayne Cascio and Enzo Valenzi, "Behaviorally Anchored Rating Scales: Effects of Education and Job Experience of Raters and Ratees," *Journal of Applied Psychology*, Vol. 62, no. 3 (1977), pp. 278–282. See also Gary P. Latham and Kenneth N. Wexley, "Behavioral Observation Scales for Performance Appraisal Purposes," *Personnel Psychology*, Vol. 30, no. 2 (Summer 1977), pp. 255–268; H. John Bernardin, Kenneth M. Alvares, and C. J. Cranny, "A Recomparison of Behavioral Expectation Scales to Summated Scales," *Journal of Applied Psychology*, Vol. 61, no. 5 (October 1976), p. 564; Frank E. Saal and Frank J. Landy, "The Mixed Standard Rating Scale: An Evaluation," *Organizational Behavior and Human Performance*, Vol. 18, no. 1 (February 1977), pp. 19–35; Frank J. Landy and others, "Behaviorally Anchored Scales for Rating the Performance of Police Officers," *Journal of Applied Psychology*, Vol. 61, no. 6 (December 1976), pp. 750–758; and Kevin R. Murphy and Joseph Constans, "Behavioral Anchors as a Source of Bias in Rating," *Journal of Applied Psychology*, Vol. 72, no. 4 (November 1987), pp. 573–577.

12. See Martin Levy, "Almost-Perfect Performance Appraisals," *Personnel Journal*, Vol. 68, no. 4 (April 1989), pp. 76–83, for a good example of how one company fine tuned its form for individual performance.

13. Teel, "Performance Appraisal," pp. 297–298.

14. For a discussion of this see, for example, Wayne Cascio, *Applied Psychology in Personnel Management* (Reston, Va.: Reston, 1978), pp. 337–341.

15. B. Rosen and T. H. Gerdee, "The Nature of Job Related Age Stereotypes," *Journal of Applied Psychology*, Vol. 61 (1976), pp. 180–183.

16. William J. Bigoness, "Effect of Applicant's Sex, Race and Performance on Em-

ployer's Performance Ratings: Some Additional Findings," *Journal of Applied Psychology*, Vol. 61 (February 1976). See also Duane Thompson and Toni Thompson, "Task-Based Performance Appraisal for Blue Collar Jobs: Evaluation of Race and Sex Effects," *Journal of Applied Psychology*, Vol. 70, no. 4 (1985), pp. 747–753.

17. Gerald Ferris, Valerie Yates, David Gilmore, and Kendrith Rowland, "The Influence of Subordinate Age on Performance Ratings and Casual Attributions," *Personnel Psychology*, Vol. 38, no. 3 (Autumn 1985), pp. 545–557. As another example, see Gregory Dobbins and Jeanne Russell, "The Biasing Effects of Subordinate Likeableness on Leader's Responses to Poor Performers: A Laboratory and Field Study," *Personnel Psychology*, Vol. 39, no. 4 (Winter 1986), pp. 759–778. See also Michael E. Benedict and Edward Levine, "Delay and Distortion: Passive Influences on Performance Appraisal Effectiveness," *Journal of Applied Psychology*, Vol. 73, no. 3 (August 1988), pp. 507–514, and James Smither et al., "Effect of Prior Performance Information on Ratings of Present Performance: Contrast Versus Assimilation Revisited," *Journal of Applied Psychology*, Vol. 73, no. 3 (August 1988), pp. 487–496.

18. Kevin Murphy, William Balzer, Maura Lockhart, and Elaine Eisenman, "Effects of Previous Performance on Evaluations of Present Performance," *Journal of Applied Psychology*, Vol. 70, no. 1 (1985), pp. 72–84. See also Kevin Williams, Angelo DeNisi, Bruce Meglino, and Thomas Cafferty, "Initial Decisions and Subsequent Performance Ratings," *Journal of Applied Psychology*, Vol. 71, no. 2 (May 1986), pp. 189–195.

19. Frank Landy, Janet Barnes, and Kevin Murphy, "Correlates of Perceived Fairness and Accuracy of Performance Evaluation," *Journal of Applied Psychology*, Vol. 63 (December 1978), pp. 751–754; Frank Landy, Janet Barnes-Farrell, and Jeanette Cleveland, "Perceived Fairness and Accuracy of Performance Evaluation: A Follow-Up," *Journal of Applied Psychology*, Vol. 65 (June 1980), pp. 355–356; Jerald Greenberg, "Determinants of Perceived Fairness of Performance Evaluations," *Journal of Applied Psychology*, Vol. 71, no. 2 (May 1986), pp. 340–342.

20. Stanley Silverman and Kenneth Wexley, "Reaction of Employees to Performance Appraisal Interviews as a Function of Their Participation in Rating Scale Development," *Personnel Psychology*, Vol. 37, no. 4 (Winter 1984). For a discussion of the use of participative management for developing a more effective performance appraisal system, see David Cowfer and Joanne Sujansky, "Appraisal Development at Westinghouse," *Training and Development Journal*, Vol. 41, no. 7 (July 1987), pp. 40–45.

21. W. C. Borman, "Effects of Instruction to Avoid Halo Error in Reliability and Validity of Performance Evaluation Ratings," *Journal of Applied Psychology*, Vol. 65 (1975), pp. 556–560; Borman points out that since no control group (a group of managers who did not undergo training) was available, it is possible that the observed effects were not due to the short five-minute training experience. G. P. Latham, K. N. Wexley, and E. D. Pursell, "Training Managers to Minimize Rating Errors in the Observation of Behavior," *Journal of Applied Psychology*, Vol. 60 (1975), pp. 550–555; John Ivancevich, "Longitudinal Study of the Effects of Rater Training on Psychometric Error in Ratings," *Journal of Applied Psychology*, Vol. 64 (1979), pp. 502–508. For a related discussion, see, for example Bryan Davis and Michael Mount, "Effectiveness of Performance Appraisal Training Using Computer Assistance Instruction and Behavior Modeling," *Personnel Psychology*, Vol. 37 (Fall 1984), pp 439–452.

22. Walter Borman, "Format and Training Effects on Rating Accuracy and Rater Errors," *Journal of Applied Psychology*, Vol. 64 (August 1979), pp. 410–412, and Jerry Hedge and Michael Cavanagh, "Improving the Accuracy of Performance Evaluations: Comparison of Three Methods of Performance Appraiser Training," *Journal of Applied Psychology*, Vol. 73, no. 1 (February 1988), pp. 68–73.

23. Ryan Davis and Michael Mount, "The Effectiveness of Performance Appraisal Training Using Computer-Assisted Instruction and Behavior Modeling," *Personnel Psychology*, Vol. 37, no. 3 (Autumn 1984), pp. 439–452.

24. Dennis Warnke and Robert Billings, "Comparison of Training Methods for Improving the Psychometric Quality of Experimental and Administrative Perform-

ance Ratings," *Journal of Applied Psychology*, Vol. 64 (April 1979), pp. 124–131. See also Timothy Athey and Robert McIntyre, "Effect of Rater Training on Rater Accuracy: Levels of Processing Theory and Social Facilitation Theory Perspectives," *Journal of Applied Psychology*, Vol. 72, no. 4 (November 1987), pp. 567–572.

25. This is based primarily on Gary Lubben, Duane Tompason, and Charles Klasson, "Performance Appraisal: The Legal Implications of Title VII," *Personnel* (May–June 1980), pp. 11–21.

26. Shelley Burchett and Kenneth DeMeuse, "Performance Appraisal and the Law," *Personnel*, Vol. 62, no. 7 (July 1985), pp. 34–35.

27. *Brito* v. *Zia Company*, 478 F.2d 1200 10th Cir. (1973).

28. For example of those arguing for making performance appraisals like tests, see, for example, C. G. Banks and L. Roberson, *Academy of Management Review*, Vol. 10 (1985), pp. 128–142.

29. Gerald Barrett and Mary Kernan, "Performance Appraisal and Terminations: A Review of Court Decisions Since *Brito* v. *Zia* with Implications for Personnel Practices," *Personnel Psychology*, Vol. 40, no. 3 (Autumn 1987), p. 499.

30. Ibid., p. 501.

31. Wayne Cascio and H. John Bernardin, "Implications of Performance Appraisal Litigation for Personnel Decisions," *Personnel Psychology* (Summer 1981), pp. 211–212, and Barrett and Kernan, "Performance Appraisal and Terminations," pp. 489–504.

32. Barrett and Kernan, "Performance Appraisal and Terminations," p. 501.

33. R. G. Downey, F. F. Medland, and L. G. Yates, "Evaluation of a Peer Rating System for Predicting Subsequent Promotion of Senior Military Officers," *Journal of Applied Psychology*, Vol. 61 (April 1976), and Glenn McEvoy and Paul Buller, "User Acceptance of Peer Appraisals in an Industrial Setting," *Personnel Psychology*, Vol. 40, no. 4 (Winter 1987), pp. 785–798.

34. Allan Kraut, "Prediction of Managerial Success by Peer and Training Staff Ratings," *Journal of Applied Psychology*, Vol. 60 (February 1975). See also Michael Mount, "Psychometric Properties of Subordinate Ratings of Managerial Performance," *Personnel Psychology*, Vol. 37, no. 4 (Winter 1984), pp. 687–702.

35. Robert Libby and Robert Blashfield, "Performance of a Composite as a Function of the Number of Judges," *Organizational Behavior and Human Performance*, Vol. 21 (April 1978), pp. 121–129; Walter Borman, "Exploring Upper Limits of Reliability and Validity in Job Performance Ratings," *Journal of Applied Psychology*, Vol. 63 (April 1978), pp. 135–144.

36. Walter C. Borman, "The Rating of Individuals in Organizations: An Alternate Approach," *Organizational Behavior and Human Performance*, Vol. 12 (1974), pp. 105–124.

37. Teel, "Performance Appraisal," p. 301.

38. George Thornton III, "Psychometric Properties of Self-appraisal of Job Performance," *Personnel Psychology*, Vol. 33 (Summer 1980), p. 265; Cathy Anderson, Jack Warner, and Cassie Spencer, "Inflation Bias in Self-assessment Evaluations: Implications for Valid Employee Selection," *Journal of Applied Psychology*, Vol. 69, no. 4 (November 1984), pp. 574–580. See also Shaul Fox and Yossi Dinur, "Validity of Self-assessment: A Field Evaluation," *Personnel Psychology*, Vol. 41, no. 3 (Autumn 1988), pp. 581–592; and John W. Lawrie, "Your Performance: Appraise It Yourself!" *Personnel*, Vol. 66, no. 1 (January 1989), pp. 21–33, a good explanation of how self-appraisals can be used at work.

39. Herbert Myer, "Self-appraisal of Job Performance," *Personnel Psychology*, Vol. 33 (Summer 1980), pp. 291–293; Robert Holzbach, "Rater Bias in Performance Ratings: Superior, Self, and Peer Ratings," *Journal of Applied Psychology*, Vol. 63, no. 5 (October 1978), pp. 579–588. Herbert G. Heneman III, "Comparison of Self and Superior Ratings of Managerial Performance," *Journal of Applied Psychology*, Vol. 59 (1974), pp. 638–642; Richard J. Klimoski and Manuel London, "Role of the Rater in Performance Appraisal," *Journal of Applied Psychology*, Vol. 59 (1974), pp. 445–451; Hubert S. Field and William H. Holley, "Subordinates' Characteristics, Supervisors' Ratings, and Decisions to Discuss Appraisal

Results," *Academy of Management Journal*, Vol. 20, no. 2 (1977), pp. 215–221. See also Robert Steel and Nestor Ovalle II, "Self-appraisal Based Upon Supervisory Feedback," *Personnel Psychology*, Vol. 37, no. 4 (Winter 1984), pp. 667–685. See also Gloria Shapiro and Gary Dessler, "Are Self-appraisals More Realistic Among Professionals or Nonprofessionals in Health Care?" *Public Personnel Management*, Vol. 14 (Fall 1985), pp. 285–291; James Russell and Dorothy Goode, "An Analysis of Managers' Reactions to Their Own Performance Appraisal Feedback," *Journal of Applied Psychology*, Vol. 73, no. 1 (February 1988), pp. 63–67; and Michael M. Harris and John Shaubroeck, "A Meta-Analysis of Self-Supervisor, Self-Peer, and Peer-Supervisor Ratings," *Personnel Psychology*, Vol. 41, no. 1 (Spring 1988), pp. 43–62.

40. This is based on Robert Johnson, *The Appraisal Interview Guide* (New York: AMACOM, 1979), pp. 45–50. See also Michael E. Cavanagh, "Employee Problems: Prevention and Intervention," *Personnel Journal*, Vol. 66, no. 9 (September 1987), pp. 35–38. Includes a manager's problem counseling checklist for how to address employee problems.

41. Johnson, *The Appraisal Interview Guide*, Chapter 9.

42. Judy Block, *Performance Appraisal on the Job: Making It Work* (New York: Executive Enterprises Publications, 1981), pp. 58–62. See also Terry Lowe, "Eight Ways to Ruin a Performance Review," *Personnel Journal*, Vol. 65, no. 1 (January 1986).

43. Block, *Performance Appraisal on the Job*.

44. Johnson, *The Appraisal Interview*, p. 45. See also Paul Reed and Mark Kroll, "A Two-Perspective Approach to Performance Appraisal," *Personnel*, Vol. 62, no. 10 (October 1985), pp. 51–57.

45. George Thornton III, "Psychometric Properties of Self-appraisals of Job Performance," *Personnel Psychology*, Vol. 33 (Summer 1980), p. 265.

46. These are based on Johnson, *Appraisal Interview Guide*, Chapter 14.

47. Ronald Burke, William Weitzel, and Tamara Weis, "Characteristics of Effective Employee Performance Review and Development Interviews: Replication and Extension," *Personnel Psychology*, Vol. 31 (Winter 1978), pp. 903–919. See also Joane Pearce and Lyman Porter, "Employee Response to Formal Performance Appraisal Feedback," *Journal of Applied Psychology*, Vol. 71, no. 2 (May 1986), pp. 211–218.

48. Allan Locher and Kenneth Teel, "Appraisal Trends," *Personnel Journal* (September 1988), pp. 139–145. This paper describes a survey sent to 1,459 organizations belonging to the Personnel and Industrial Relations Association of Southern California; 324 companies responded.

49. Ibid., p. 140.

Chapter 15

Career Management: From First Assignment to Retirement

When you finish studying this chapter, you should be able to:

1. Discuss some factors which influence career decisions.
2. Explain career-management considerations in making initial job assignments.
3. Explain how to better manage promotions and transfers.
4. Discuss how to manage non-disciplinary layoffs, and retirement.

OVERVIEW

There are several times during one's employment when career-related decisions must be made, and this chapter discusses how such decisions are best carried out. We first explain career planning and assessment basics, and in particular the factors (like interests) that affect career choices. We then discuss the three major times when career-related decisions must be made, (1) at the employee's first assignment with your firm, (2) when promotions and transfers are being considered, and (3) when non-disciplinary separations like layoffs and retirement must occur. As you can see from our model, effective performance (as appraised using the methods in Chapter 14) is usually rewarded—perhaps with a promotion. Ineffective performance, however, may require transfer to a more suitable job, or (as explained in Chapter 17, which covers discipline and dismissals) termination.

INTRODUCTION: PERSONNEL MANAGEMENT AND CAREER DEVELOPMENT

Personnel activities like screening, training, and appraising serve two basic roles in organizations. First, their traditional role has been to staff the organization—to fill its positions with employees who have the requisite interests, abilities, and skills. Increasingly, however, these activities are taking on a second role—that of ensuring that the long-run interests of the employees are protected by the organization and that, in particular, the employee is encouraged to grow and realize his or her full potential. Referring to *staffing* or *personnel management* as *human resource management* reflects this second role. A basic assumption underlying the focus on human resource management is that the organization has an obligation to utilize its employees' abilities to the fullest and to give each employee a chance to grow and to realize his or her full potential, and to develop a successful career.[1] One way this trend is manifesting itself is in the increased emphasis many managers are placing on **career planning and development,** an emphasis, in other words, on giving employees the assistance and opportunities that will enable them to form realistic career goals and realize them.

career planning and development Giving employees the assistance to form realistic career goals and the opportunities to realize them.

Activities like personnel planning, screening, and training play a big role in the career development process. Personnel planning, for example, can be used not just to forecast open jobs but to identify potential internal candidates and the training they would need to fill these jobs. Similarly, an organization can use its periodic employee appraisals not just for salary decisions but for identifying the development needs of individual employees and for ensuring that these needs are met. All the staffing activities, in other words, can be used to satisfy the needs of both the organization and the individual in such a way that they both gain: the organization from improved performance from a more dedicated work force and the individual from a richer, more challenging and appropriate career.[2]

FACTORS THAT AFFECT CAREER CHOICES

The first step in planning a career (your own or someone else's) is to learn as much as you can about the person's interests, aptitudes, and skills.

♦ IDENTIFY THE PERSON'S CAREER STAGE

career cycle The stages through which a person's career evolves.

Each person's career goes through stages, and it is important that you understand the nature of this **career cycle.** It is important, first, because the stage you are in will influence (as explained below) your knowledge of and preference for various occupations. Second (and related to this) such knowledge can improve your own performance as a supervisor by giving you a better insight into your employee's behavior. (For example, many employees undergo a "midlife crisis" at age 40 or so, during which they agonize over the fact that their accomplishments have not kept pace with their expectations: The result of this introspection can be a period of prolonged disappointment for employees, during which their performance can be adversely affected.) The main stages one's career goes through can be summarized as follows:[3]

growth stage Period from birth to age 14 during which the person develops a self-concept by identifying with and interacting with other people such as family, friends, and teachers.

Growth Stage

The **growth stage** lasts roughly from birth to age 14 and is a period during which the person develops a self-concept by identifying with and interacting with other people such as family, friends, and teachers. Toward the beginning of this period, role playing is important, and children experiment with different ways of acting; this helps them to form impressions of how other people react to different behaviors and contributes to their developing a unique self-concept, or identity. Toward the end of this stage, the adolescent (who by this time has developed some preliminary ideas of what his or her interests and abilities are) begins some realistic thinking about alternative occupations.

Exploration Stage

exploration stage The period from around ages 15 to 24 during which a person seriously explores various occupational alternatives, attempting to match these alternatives with his or her interests and abilities.

The **exploration stage** is the period, roughly from ages 15 to 24, during which a person seriously explores various occupational alternatives, attempting to match these alternatives with what he or she has learned about them (and about his or her own interests and abilities from school, leisure activities, and part-time work). Some tentative broad occupational choices are usually made during the beginning of this period. This choice is refined as the person learns more about the choice and about himself until, toward the end of this period, a seemingly appropriate choice is made and the person tries out for a beginning job.

Probably the most important task the person has in this and the preceding stage is that of developing a realistic understanding of his or her abilities and talents. Similarly, the person must discover and develop his or her values, motives, and ambitions and make sound educational decisions based on reliable sources of information about occupational alternatives.

Establishment Stage

establishment stage The period, roughly from ages 24 to 44, that is the heart of most people's work lives.

The **establishment stage** spans roughly ages 24 to 44 and is the heart of most people's work lives. Sometime during this period (toward the beginning, it is hoped), a suitable occupation is found and the person engages in those activities that help him or her earn a permanent place in it. Often (and particularly in the professions) the person locks on to a chosen occupation early. But in most cases, this is a period during which the person is continually testing his or her capabilities and ambitions against those of the initial occupational choice.

trial substage The period from about age 25 to 30 during which the person determines whether or not the chosen field is suitable and if it is not, attempts to change it.

The establishment stage is itself comprised of three substages. The **trial substage** lasts from about ages 25 to 30: During this period the person determines whether or not the chosen field is suitable; if it is not, several changes might be attempted. (Jane Smith might have her heart set on a career in retailing, for example, but after several months of constant travel as a newly hired assistant buyer for a department store, she might decide that a less travel-oriented career such as that in market research is more in tune with her needs.) Roughly between the ages of 30 and 40, the person goes through a **stabilization substage** during which firm occupational goals are set and the person does more explicit career planning to determine the sequence of promotions, job changes, and/or any educational activities that seem necessary for accomplishing these goals. Finally, somewhere between the mid-thirties and midforties, the person may enter the **midcareer crisis substage.** During this period people often make a major reassessment of their progress relative to original ambitions and goals. They may find that they are not going to realize their dreams (such as being company president) or that, having accomplished what they set out to do, their dreams are not all they were cut out to be. Also during this period, people have to decide how important work and career are to be in their total life. It is often during this midcareer crisis substage that the person is, for the first time, faced with the difficult decisions of what he or she really wants, what really can be accomplished, and how much must be sacrificed to achieve this. It is usually during this crisis stage that some people first realize they have what Schein

stabilization substage The period, roughly from age 30 to 40, during which firm occupational goals are set and more explicit career planning is made to determine the sequence for accomplishing these goals.

midcareer crisis substage The period occurring between the mid-thirties and mid-forties during which people often make a major reassessment of their progress relative to their original career ambitions and goals.

calls *career anchors*—basic concerns for security or for independence and freedom, for instance—which they will not give up if a choice has to be made.

Maintenance Stage

Between the ages of 45 and 65, many people simply slide from the stabilization substage into this **maintenance stage.** During this latter period the person has typically created for himself or herself a place in the world of work and most efforts are now directed to securing that place.

Decline Stage

As retirement age approaches, there is often a deceleration period during which many people are faced with the prospect of having to accept reduced levels of power and responsibility and have to learn to accept and develop new roles as mentor and confidante for those who are younger. There is then the more or less inevitable retirement, after which the person is faced with the prospect of finding alternative use for the time and effort formerly expended on his or her occupation.

♦ IDENTIFY OCCUPATIONAL ORIENTATION

Career-counseling expert **John Holland** says that a person's personality (including values, motives, and needs) is another important determinant of career choices, and that there are six basic "personal orientations" that determine the sorts of careers to which people are drawn. For example, says Holland, a person with a strong *social orientation* might be attracted to careers that entail interpersonal rather than intellectual or physical activities and to occupations such as social work. Based on research with his *Vocational Preference Test* (*VPT*), Holland says there are six basic personality types or orientations.[4]

1. *Realistic orientation.* These people are attracted to occupations that involve physical activities requiring skill, strength, and coordination. Some examples include forestry, farming, and agriculture.

2. *Investigative orientation.* These people are attracted to careers that involve cognitive (thinking, organizing, understanding) rather than affective (feeling, acting, or interpersonal and emotional) activities. Examples include biologist, chemist, and college professor.

3. *Social orientation.* These people are attracted to careers that involve interpersonal rather than intellectual or physical activities. Examples include clinical psychology, foreign service, and social work.

4. *Conventional orientation.* These people prefer careers that involve structured, rule-regulated activities, as well as careers where it is expected that the employee subordinate his or her personal needs to those of the organization. Examples include accountants and bankers.

5. *Enterprising orientation.* These people are attracted to careers that involve verbal activities aimed at influencing others. Examples include managers, lawyers, and public relations executives.

6. *Artistic orientation.* People here are attracted to careers that involve self-expression, artistic creation, expression of emotions, and individualistic activities. Examples include artists, advertising executives, and musicians.

Most people have more than one orientation (they might be social, realistic, and investigative, for example), and Holland believes that the more similar or comparable these orientations are, the less internal conflict or indecision a person will face in making a career choice. To help illustrate this, Holland suggests placing each orientation in one corner of a hexagon, as in Figure 15.1. As you can see, the model has six corners, each of which represents one personal orientation (for example, enterprising). According to Holland's research, the closer two orientations are in this figure, the more compatible they are. Thus, adjacent categories (realistic-investigative, enterprising-social) are quite similar, while those diagonally opposite (enterprising-investigative, artistic-conventional) are quite dissimilar. Holland believes that if your number one and number two orientations fall side by side, you will have a relatively easy time in choosing a career. However, if your orientations turn out to be opposite (such as realistic and social), you may experience a great deal of indecision in making a career choice because your interests are driving you toward very different types of careers.

In Table 15.1, we have summarized some of the occupations that have been found to be the best match for each of these six personal **occupational orientations.** For example, researchers have found that people with realistic orientations often gravitate toward occupations such as carpentry, engineering, farming, forestry, highway patrol, and machinist. Similarly, those with investigative orientations gravitate toward astronomy, biology, and chemistry.

occupational orientation The theory developed by John Holland that says there are six basic personnel orientations that determine the sorts of careers to which people are drawn.

◆ IDENTIFYING SKILLS

Successful performance depends not just on motivation but on ability as well; even the most highly motivated golfer is not about to play like Jack Nicklaus, for instance, nor will the most highly motivated singer sing like Barbra Streisand. The same applies to your interests and occupational orientations; you may (for example) have a conventional orientation, but whether you have the *skills* to be an accountant, banker, credit manager, or police officer will largely determine *which specific occupation* you choose in the end. Therefore, you have to identify your skills—or those of your employee.

occupational skills The skills needed to be successful in a particular occupation. According to the *Dictionary of Occupational Titles*, occupational skills break down into three groups depending on whether they emphasize data, people, or things.

An Exercise

One useful exercise for identifying occupational skills is as follows: Take a blank piece of paper and write in the heading "The Most Enjoyable Occupational Tasks I Have Had." Then write a short essay that describes the tasks. Make sure to go into as much detail as you can about what your duties and

FIGURE 15.1
Choosing an Occupational Orientation

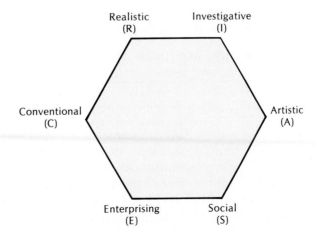

TABLE 15.1 Occupations Scoring High on Each Occupational Orientation Theme

REALISTIC	INVESTIGATIVE	ARTISTIC	SOCIAL	ENTERPRISING	CONVENTIONAL
Consider these occupations if you score *high* here:					
Agribusiness managers	Biologists	Advertising executives	Auto sales dealers	Agribusiness managers	Accountants
Carpenters	Chemists	Art teachers	Guidance counselors	Auto sales dealers	Auto sales dealers
Electricians	Engineers	Artists	Home economics teachers	Business education teachers	Bankers
Engineers	Geologists	Broadcasters	Mental health workers	Buyers	Bookkeepers
Farmers	Mathematicians	English teachers	Ministers	Chamber of Commerce executives	Business education teachers
Foresters	Medical technologists	Interior decorators	Physical education teachers	Funeral directors	Credit managers
Highway patrol officers	Physicians	Medical illustrators	Recreation leaders	Life insurance agents	Executive housekeepers
Horticultural workers	Physicists	Ministers	School administrators	Purchasing agents	Food service managers
Industrial arts teachers	Psychologists	Musicians	Social science teachers	Realtors	IRS agents
Military enlisted personnel	Research and development managers	Photographers	Social workers	Restaurant managers	Mathematics teachers
Military officers	Science teachers	Public relations directors	Special education teachers	Retail clerks	Military enlisted personnel
Vocational agricultural teachers	Sociologists	Reporters	YMCA/YWCA directors	Store managers	Secretaries

Note: For example, if you score high on "realistic," consider a career as a carpenter, engineer, farmer, and so on.

Source: Reproduced by special permission of the publisher, Consulting Psychologists Press, Inc., Palo Alto, CA 94306, from *Manual for the SVIV-SCII*, Fourth Edition, by Jo-Ida C. Hansen and David P. Campbell. © 1985 by the Board of Trustees of Leland Stanford Junior University.

responsibilities were and (especially) what it was about each task that you found enjoyable. (In writing your essay, by the way, notice that it's not necessarily the most enjoyable *job* you've had but the most enjoyable *task* you've had to perform; after all, you may have had jobs that you really didn't like except for one of the specific duties or tasks in the job, which you really got a kick out of.) Next, on other sheets of paper, do the same thing for two other tasks you have had. Now, go through your three essays and *underline the skills that you mentioned the most often.* For example, did you get a big kick out of putting together and *coordinating* the school play when you worked in the principal's office one year? Did you especially enjoy the hours you spent in the library *doing research* for your boss when you worked one summer as an office clerk?[5]

Aptitudes and Special Talents

aptitudes and special talents These include intelligence, numerical aptitude, mechanical comprehension, and manual dexterity, as well as talents such as artistic, theatrical, or musical ability that play an important role in career decisions.

Your **aptitudes and special talents** also play an important role in career decisions and have long been used by career counselors to help guide their clients. Aptitudes include intelligence, numerical aptitude, mechanical comprehension, and manual dexterity. For career planning purposes, a person's aptitudes are usually measured with a test battery such as the general aptitude test battery (GATB), an instrument that measures a variety of aptitudes including intelligence and mathematical ability. Considerable work has been done to relate aptitudes, such as those measured by the GATB, to specific occupations. For example, the U.S. Department of Labor's *Dictionary of Occupational Titles* lists the nature and titles of hundreds of occupations, along with the aptitudes required for success in these occupations, as measured by the GATB.[6]

♦ IDENTIFYING CAREER ANCHORS

Edgar Schein Based on his research at the Massachusetts Institute of Technology, he identified five career anchors.

career anchors A concern or value that you will not give up if a choice has to be made.

Edgar Schein says that career planning is a continuing process of discovery—one in which a person slowly develops a clearer occupational self-concept in terms of what his or her talents, abilities, motives, needs attitudes, and values are. Schein also says that as you learn more about yourself, it becomes apparent that you have a dominant **career anchor,** a *concern or value that you will not give up if a choice has to be made.* These career anchors, as their name implies, are the pivots around which a person's career swings; a person becomes conscious of them as a result of learning about his or her talents and abilities, motives and needs, and attitudes and values. Based on his research at the Massachusetts Institute of Technology, Schein believes that these career anchors, while crucial in career decisions, are difficult to predict ahead of time because they are evolutionary and a product of a process of discovery. Some people, in fact, may never really find out what their career anchors are until they have to make a major choice—such as whether to take the promotion to the headquarters staff or strike out on their own by starting a business. And it is at this point that all the person's past work experiences, interests, aptitudes, and orientations converge into a meaningful pattern (or career anchor) that helps show what is personally the most important. Based on his study of MIT graduates, Schein identified five career anchors.[7]

Technical/Functional Career Anchor

People who have a strong technical/functional career anchor seem to make career choices based on the technical or functional content of the work, such as engineering or financial analysis. They tend to avoid decisions that would drive them toward general management. Instead, they make decisions that will enable them to remain and grow in their chosen technical or functional fields.

Managerial Competence as a Career Anchor

Other people showed a strong motivation to become managers, "and their career experience enables them to believe that they have the skills and values necessary to rise to such general management positions." A management position of high responsibility is the ultimate goal of these people. When pressed to explain why they believed they had the skills necessary to gain such positions, many answered that they were qualified for these jobs because of what they saw as their *competencies* in a combination of three areas: (1) analytical competence (ability to identify, analyze, and solve problems under conditions of incomplete information and uncertainty); (2) interpersonal competence (ability to influence, supervise, lead, manipulate, and control people at all levels); and (3) emotional competence (the capacity to be stimulated by emotional and interpersonal crises rather than exhausted or debilitated by them, and the capacity to bear high levels of responsibility without becoming paralyzed). Therefore, Schein concludes that "the person who wants to rise to higher levels of management and be given higher levels of responsibility must be *simultaneously* good at analyzing problems, handling people, and handling his or her own emotions in order to withstand the pressures and tensions of the executive suite."

Creativity as a Career Anchor

Some of the graduates had gone on to become successful entrepreneurs, and to Schein these people seemed to have an enveloping need "to build or to create something that was entirely their own product—a product or process that bears their name, a company of their own, or a personal fortune that reflects their accomplishments." For example, one graduate had become a successful purchaser, restorer, and renter of townhouses in a large city; another had built a successful consulting firm; another formed a new computer-based financial service organization.

Autonomy and Independence as Career Anchors

Some seemed driven by the need to be on their own, free from the kind of dependence that can arise when a person elects to work in a large organization where promotions, transfers, and salary decisions make them dependent on others. Many of these graduates also had a strong technical/functional orientation, but instead of pursuing this orientation in an organization, they had decided instead to become consultants, working either alone or as part of a relatively small firm. Other members of this group had become a professor of business, a free-lance writer, and a proprietor of a small retail business.

Security as a Career Anchor

A few of the graduates seemed to be mostly concerned with long-run career stability and job security. They seemed willing to do what was required to maintain job security, a decent income, and a stable future in the form of a good retirement program and benefits. They were therefore much more willing to let the organization they were working for decide what their careers should be.

For those interested in *geographical security*, maintaining a stable, secure career in familiar surroundings was generally more important to these people than was pursuing superior career choices, if choosing the latter meant injecting instability or insecurity into their lives—by forcing them to pull up roots and move to another city. For others, security meant *organizational security*, and they might today opt for government jobs, where tenure still tends to be a way of life.

Assessing Career Anchors

To help you identify career anchors, take a few sheets of blank paper and write out your answers to the following questions.[8]

1. What was your major area of concentration (if any) in high school? Why did you choose that area? How did you feel about it?
2. What is (or was) your major area of concentration in college? Why did you choose that area? How did you feel about it?
3. What was your first job after school (include military if relevant)? What were you looking for in your first job?
4. What were your ambitions or long-range goals when you started your career? Have they changed? When? Why?
5. What was your first major change of job or company? What were you looking for in your next job?
6. What was your next major change of job, company, or career? Why did you initiate or accept it? What were you looking for? (Do this for each of your major changes of job, company, or career.)
7. As you look back over your career, identify some times you have especially enjoyed. What was it about those times that you enjoyed?
8. As you look back, identify some times you have not especially enjoyed. What was it about those times you did not enjoy?
9. Have you ever refused a job move or promotion? Why?

10. Now review all your answers carefully, as well as the descriptions for the five career anchors (managerial competence, technical/functional, security, creativity, autonomy). Based on your answers to the questions, rate each of the anchors below from 1 to 5; 1 equals low importance, 5 equals high importance:

Managerial competence _____

Technical/functional competence _____

Security _____   Creativity _____   Autonomy _____

♦ WHAT DO YOU WANT TO DO?

We have explained occupational orientations, skills, and career anchors and the role these play in choosing a career. But there is (at least) one more exercise you should try that can prove enlightening, and that is to answer the question, "If you could have any kind of job, what would it be?" Invent your own job if need be, and don't worry about what you *can* do—just what you *want to do*.[9]

♦ IDENTIFYING HIGH-POTENTIAL OCCUPATIONS

Learning about yourself is only half the job of picking an occupation; you also now have to identify those occupations that are just right (given your occupational orientations, skills, career anchors, and occupational preferences) as well as those which will be in high demand in the years to come.

Finding Out About Occupations and Careers

You will need as much information as you can get about the nature of various occupations, since (remember) your aim is to match (1) your or your employee's skills and preferences with (2) an occupation that just fits skills and preferences.

Investigating occupations is going to take hours (or perhaps days or weeks) of library research. The *Dictionary of Occupational Titles* is the bible of the vocational field and lists detailed job descriptions for more than 20,000 occupations. The *Dictionary of Occupational Titles* provides, for each title, a listing of the responsibilities, duties, and procedures for each job in the manual. Also listed for each job are the physical demands of the job, as well as individual working conditions, and (based on the judgment of experts) the interests, aptitudes, educational requirements, and vocational preparation required of those seeking each job. (In Canada, try the *Canadian Classification and Dictionary of Occupations*, published by Manpower and Immigration.) The *Occupational Outlook Handbook* gives an outline for about 700 occupations, including the prospects for the occupation and the major work, required training, earnings, and working conditions. There is also an *Occupational Outlook Handbook for College Graduates*, and the U.S. Employment Service publishes *Occupations in Demand*, a comprehensive listing of jobs most frequently requested of 2,500 job service offices around the country. *Occupations in Demand* provides for each occupation information on local areas having large numbers of openings, industries requesting workers, pay ranges, and average number of openings available. It also lists jobs not requiring previous work experience.

Occupational Outlook Quarterly is published every three months and provides information on (among other things) occupations that are most in demand. Another source is the *Encyclopedia of Careers and Vocational Guidance*, which provides descriptions of over 650 occupations. For information on federal jobs and filling out applications, try the U.S. Office of Personnel Management's *Handbook X118*, which gives detailed job descriptions for hundreds of government positions. The U.S. Office of Education, in conjunction with Harvard University, has developed a computerized career information system called the *Guidance Information System* (GIS). Using this computerized system, you provide input on your occupational preferences and skills and the system suggests one or more feasible matching occupations.

CAREER MANAGEMENT AND THE FIRST ASSIGNMENT

♦ CAREER-MANAGEMENT GUIDELINES

Understanding your employee's occupational interests, anchors, and skills and then placing him or her onto a career track that's most fitting is one way to use "personnel" to help optimize personal growth and development. Factors to keep in mind here include:

reality shock A period that may occur at the initial career entry when the new employee's high job expectations confront the reality of a boring, unchallenging job.

Avoid Reality Shock

Perhaps at no other stage in the person's career is it more important for the organization to take career development issues into account than at the initial entry stage during which the person is recruited, hired, and given a first assignment and boss. For the employee this is a critical period, a period during which he or she has to develop a sense of confidence, learn to get along with the first boss and with coworkers, learn how to accept responsibility, and, most important, quickly gain an insight into his or her talents, needs, and values as they relate to initial career goals. For the new employee, in other words this is (or should be) a period of *reality testing* during which his or her initial hopes and goals first confront the reality of organizational life and of the person's talents and needs.

For many first-time workers, this turns out to be a disastrous period, one in which their often naive expectations first confront the realities of organizational life. The young MBA or CPA graduate, for example, might come to the first job seeking a challenging, exciting assignment in which to apply the new techniques learned in school and to prove his or her abilities and gain a promotion. In reality, however, the trainee is often turned off by being relegated to an unimportant low-risk job where he or she "can't cause any trouble while we're trying him out," or by the harsh realities of interdepartmental conflict and politicking, or by a boss who is neither rewarded for nor trained in the unique mentoring tasks needed to properly supervise new employees.[10]

Provide Challenging Initial Jobs

Most experts therefore agree that one of the most important things you can do is to provide new employees with challenging first jobs. In one study of young managers at AT&T, for example, the researchers found that the more challenging a person's job was in his or her first year with the company, the more effective and successful the person was even five or six years later.[11] Based on his own research, Hall contends that challenging initial jobs provide "one of the most powerful yet uncomplicated means of aiding the career development of new employees. . . ."[12] In most organizations, however, providing such jobs seems more the exception than the rule. In one survey of research and development organizations, for example, only 1 out of 22 companies had a formal policy of giving challenging first assignments.[13] And this, as one expert has pointed out, is an example of "glaring misman-

PERSONNEL MANAGEMENT:
ON THE FRONT LINE

Career planning has always been a pretty low priority item for Carter Cleaning, since "just getting workers to come to work and then keeping them honest is enough of a problem," as Jack likes to say. Yet, Jennifer thought it might not be a bad idea to give some thought to what a career planning program might involve for Carter. A lot of their employees had been with them for years in dead-end jobs, and she frankly felt a little bad for them: "Perhaps we could help them gain a better perspective on what they want to do," she thought. And she definitely believed that the store management group needed some better career direction if Carter Cleaning was to develop and grow. Her questions:

1. What would be the advantages to Carter Cleaning of setting up such a career planning program?
2. Who should participate in the program? All employees? Selected employees?
3. Describe the program you would propose for injecting a career planning and development perspective into the Carter Cleaning Centers.

agement" when one considers the effort and money invested in recruiting, hiring, and training new employees.[14]

Provide Realistic Job Previews in Recruiting

Providing recruits with realistic previews of what to expect once they begin working in the organization can be an effective way of minimizing reality shock and improving their long-term performance. Schein points out that one of the biggest problems recruits (and management) encounter during the crucial entry stage involves obtaining accurate information in a "climate of mutual selling."[15] The recruiter (anxious to hook good candidates) and the candidate (anxious to present as favorable an impression as possible) often give and receive unrealistic information during the interview. The result is that the interviewer may not be able to form a realistic picture of the candidate's career goals, while at the same time the candidate forms an unrealistically favorable image of the organization.[16]

Realistic job previews can, we know, significantly improve the survival rate among employees who are being hired for relatively complex jobs like those of management trainee, salesperson, or life insurance agent,[17] although such realistic previews do not seem to make much difference in the survival rates of those (such as telephone operators or sewing machine operators) who have less complex jobs.[18,19]

Be Demanding

Management experts[20] know that there is a "Pygmalion effect"[21] in the relationship between a new employee and his or her boss.[22] In other words, the more you expect and the more confident and supportive you are of your new employees, the better they will perform. Therefore, as two experts put it, "Don't assign a new employee to a 'dead wood,' undemanding, or unsupportive supervisor."[23] Instead, choose specially trained, high-performing, supportive supervisors who can set high standards for new employees during their critical exploratory first year.

Provide Periodic Job Rotation and Job Pathing

The best way new employees can test themselves and crystallize their career anchors is by trying out a variety of challenging jobs. By rotating the person to jobs in various specializations—from financial analysis to production to human resource, for example—the employee gets an opportunity to assess his or her aptitudes and preferences. At the same time, the organization obtains a manager with a broader multifunctional view of the organization.[24] One extension of this is called *job pathing*,[25] which assumes that carefully sequenced job assignments can have a big impact on personal development.

Improved Career-Oriented Performance Appraisals

Edgar Schein contends that supervisors must understand that valid performance appraisal information is in the long run more important than protecting the short-term interests of one's immediate subordinates.[26] Therefore, he says, supervisors need concrete information regarding the appraisee's potential career path; information, in other words, about the nature of the future work for which he or she is appraising the subordinate, or which the subordinate desires.[27]

Encourage Career-Planning Activities

Employers also have to take steps to increase employees' involvement in their own career planning and development. For example, some employers are experimenting with activities designed specifically to make employees aware of the need for career planning and of improving career decisions. Here, for example, employees might learn about the rudiments of career planning and the stages in one's career and engage in various activities aimed at crystallizing career anchors and formulating more realistic career goals.[28] Similarly, employers are increasingly engaging in career-counseling meetings (perhaps as part of the performance appraisal meeting) during which the employee and his or her supervisor (or perhaps a human resource director) assess the employee's progress in light of his or her career goals and identify development needs.[29]

◆ WHAT THE INDIVIDUAL CAN DO

There are two basic things you or your employee can and should do to improve the career decisions you make.[30] First, you have to *take charge* of your own career by understanding that there are major decisions to be made and that making them requires considerable personal planning and effort. In other words, you cannot leave your choices in the hands of others but must decide where you want to go in terms of a career and what job moves and education are required to get there. Related to this, you have to become an effective *diagnostician*. You have to determine (through career counseling, testing, self-diagnostic books, and so on) what your talents or values are and how these fit with the sorts of careers you are considering.[31] In summary, therefore, the key to career planning is self-insight—into what you want out of a career, into your talents and limitations, and into your values and how they will fit in with the alternatives being considered. As Schein points out: "too many people never ask, much less attempt to answer, these kinds of questions. It was shocking to me when I conducted the interviews for the MIT panel study and discovered how many respondents said that they had never in 10 years of their careers asked themselves the kind f questions which I was asking just to fill in the details of their job history."[32]

COMPUTER APPLICATIONS IN CAREER MANAGEMENT:

COMPUTERIZED CAREER AND JOB SEARCH COUNSELING

One of the thorniest problems a job-hunter faces is the relative dearth of qualified advisors out there to help you in your job search. As explained elsewhere, some employers have a policy of retaining outplacement specialists for the purpose of providing career counseling and job search help to the employees they lay off. However, such qualified outplacement specialists generally (though not always) deal exclusively with employer-paid assignments: you can't just walk into one and have them help you, in other words. Beyond this, the field of job search help runs the gamut from the generally qualified college career counseling centers (which can help you with your career choice) to (at the other extreme) the sometimes less-than-reputable "job search experts" who may charge an up-front fee of $2,000 or more and give you very little in return.

Some personnel managers, realizing the shortage of qualified help but not being able to commit to the substantial fees that outplacement specialists often charge, provide computer-assisted programs to help discharged employees with their career and job search decisions. These computerized programs are generally also available to anyone who asks. They cost from $100 to $300.

One good example of such a computerized program is Career Navigator, published by outplacement specialist Drake Bean Morin, Inc., 100 Park Avenue, New York, New York 10017. The program contains both a comprehensive manual and a set of computer disks. It covers all the steps a job searcher would normally go through, from identifying career interests through sending thank you letters after a job is obtained.

For example, section 2 ("Know Yourself") takes you step by step through a program in which you identify your interests, define your values, identify your accomplishments, and identify your skills. Here, you'll not only be able to zero in on several ideal job preferences; you will also generate a list of accomplishment statements that will be useful for building your resume and conducting interviews later in your job search.

Succeeding sections of the program take you step by step through the job search itself. By interacting with the computer you will learn how to use the telephone effectively, to write effective letters (the program will actually print these out for you, in the proper format), and how to interview effectively. The computerized program will help you create your resume and will print it for you (again in the proper format). And, it will help you organize a job research campaign plan and give you a computerized printout of weekly action plans. It will even assess your weekly progress. It then gives you help in negotiating your offers, evaluating them, and even in assessing the first three months on the new job.

MANAGING PROMOTIONS AND TRANSFERS

Performance appraisal and career management often lead to concrete personnel actions such as promotion and transfer: These matters are addressed next.

♦ MAKING PROMOTION DECISIONS

There are three main promotion-related decisions you have to make, and how these decisions are made will affect your employees' motivation, performance, and morale.

Decision 1: Seniority or Competence?

Probably the most important decision concerns whether promotion will be based on seniority or competence, or some combination of the two. From the point of view of motivation, promotion based on competence is best. However, your ability to use competence as a sole criterion depends on several things, most notably whether or not your firm is unionized or governed by civil service requirements. Union agreements often contain a clause such as the following that emphasizes seniority in promotions: "In the advancement of employees to higher paid jobs when ability, merit, and capacity are equal, employees with the highest seniority will be given preference."[33] Although this might seem to leave the door open for giving a person with less seniority (but slightly better ability) the inside track for a job, labor arbitrators have generally held that where clauses such as these are binding only *substantial differences in abilities can be taken into account.* In one case, for example, the arbitrator ruled that seniority should be disregarded only when an employee with less seniority stood "head and shoulders" above the employees with greater seniority.[34] Similarly, many organizations in the public sector are governed by civil service regulations that emphasize seniority rather than competence as the basis for promotion.[35]

Decision 2: How Is Competence Measured?

Where promotion *is* to be based on competence, you'll have to decide how competence will be defined and measured. As we explained in the previous chapter, defining and measuring *past* performance is a fairly straightforward matter: The job is defined, standards are set, and one or more appraisal tools are used to record the employee's performance. But promotion also requires predicting the person's *potential;* thus, you must have some valid procedure for predicting a candidate's future performance.

Many employers simply use prior performance as a guide and extrapolate, or assume, that (based on the person's prior performance) he or she will perform well on the new job. This is the simplest procedure to use.

On the other hand, some employers use tests to evaluate promotable employees[36] and to identify those employees with executive potential.[37] Others use assessment centers to assess management potential.

Decision 3: Formal or Informal?

Next (particularly if you decide to promote based on competence), you have to decide if the process will be a formal or informal one. Many employers still depend on an informal system. Here, the availability and requirements of open positions are kept secret, and the promotion decisions are made by key managers from among employees they know personally and also from among those who, for one reason or another, have impressed them with their activities or presence.[38] The problem is that when you don't make employees aware of what jobs are available, what the criteria are for promotion, and how promotion decisions are made, the link between performance and promotion is cut and the effectiveness of promotion as a reward is diminished.

Many employers therefore do establish formal, published promotion policies and procedures. Here, employees are generally provided with a formal promotion policy statement that describes the criteria by which promotions are awarded. Formal systems often include a policy of open posting of jobs, which states that open positions and their requirements will be posted and circulated to all employees. As explained in Chapter 4, many employers also compile detailed information on the qualifications of employees, while others use manpower replacement charts. Computerized information systems can be especially useful for maintaining qualifications inventories on hundreds or thousands of employees. The net effect of such actions is twofold: (1) an employer can ensure that all qualified employees are considered for openings and (2) promotion becomes more closely linked with performance in the minds of employees and as a result its effectiveness as a reward increases.

♦ HANDLING TRANSFERS

Reasons for Transfers

A transfer involves a movement from one job to another, usually with no change in salary or grade. There are several reasons why such changes take place. *Employees* may seek transfers for personal enrichment, for more interesting jobs, for greater convenience—better hours, location of work, and so on—or for jobs offering greater possibilities for advancement.[39] *Employers* may transfer a worker from a position where he or she is no longer needed to one where he or she is needed, or to retain a senior employee (bumping where necessary a less senior person in another department), or (more generally) to find a better fit for the employee within the firm. Many employers choose to consider *demotions* as transfers, specifically transfers into a lower employment classification.

Effect on Family Life

Many firms have had policies of routinely transferring employees from locale to locale, either to give their employees more exposure to a wide range of jobs or to fill open positions with trained employees. Such easy-transfer policies have fallen into disfavor, though, partly because of the cost of relocating employees (paying moving expenses, buying back the employee's current home, and perhaps financing his or her next home, for instance) and partly because it was assumed that frequent transfers had a bad effect on an employee's family life.

But one study seems to indicate that the latter argument, at least, is without merit.[40] The study compared the experiences of "mobile" families who had moved on the average of once every two years with "stable" families who had lived in their communities for more than eight years.

In general, the stable families were no more satisfied with their marriages and family life or children's well-being than were the mobile families. In fact, mobile men and women believed their lives to be more interesting and their capabilities greater than did stable men and women. Likewise, they were more satisfied with their family lives and marriage than were stable men and women.

However, mobility *was* associated with dissatisfaction with social relationships among men and women (for instance, in terms of "opportunities to make friends at work and in the community"). Developing new social relationships was cited as a problem for children of mobile parents, with "missing old friends and making new friends" a bigger problem for teenagers than for younger children.

The major finding of this study, though, is that for these people there were few differences between mobile and stable families. Few families in the mobile group believed moving was easy. However, despite their mobility, these families were as satisfied with all aspects of their lives (except social relationships) as were stable families. Yet—this study notwithstanding—there is no doubt that employees do resist geographical transfers more today than they did even a few years ago. In one study, for instance, "the proportion of top executives who are 'eager' or 'willing' to make a geographic move has dropped ten percentage points to 51.5% since 1979, while 45% described themselves as reluctant."[41]

◆ INTRODUCTION

Employee separations are a fact of life in organizations and can be initiated by either employer or employee. For the employer, reduced sales or profits may require *layoffs,* for instance, while employees, on the other hand, may terminate their employment so as to *retire* or to seek better jobs.

The "Plant Closing" Law

Until recently there were no federal laws requiring notification of employees in the event an employer decided to close its facility. However, on February 4, 1989, the Worker Adjustment and Retraining Notification Act (popularly known as the "Plant Closing" law) became effective. Basically, the law requires employers of 100 or more employees to give 60 days notice before closing a facility or starting a layoff *of 50 people or more.* The law does not prevent the employer from closing down, nor does it require the saving of jobs. The Worker Adjustment and Retraining Notification Act simply seeks to give employees time to seek other work or retraining by giving them advance notice of the close down.

Not all plant closings and layoffs are covered by the law, although many are. As an employer you are responsible for giving notice to employees who will or "reasonably may be expected to" experience a covered "employment loss." Employment losses include terminations (other than discharges for cause, voluntary departures, or retirement), layoffs exceeding six months, or reductions of more than 50% in employees' work hours during each month of any six month period. Generally speaking, workers who are reassigned or transferred to certain employer-sponsored programs, or who are given an opportunity to transfer or relocate to another employer location within a reasonable commuting distance need not be notified. While there are exceptions to the law, the penalty for failing to give notice is fairly severe: one day's pay and benefits to each employee for each day notice that should have been given, up to 60 days.

The law is not entirely clear about how the notice to employees must be worded. However, if you write a letter to individual employees to be laid off, a paragraph toward the end of the letter that might suit the purpose would be as follows:

> Please consider this letter to be your official notice, as required by the federal Plant Closing law, that your current position with the company will end 60 days from today because of a (layoff or closing) that is now projected to take place (on October 9). After that day your employment with the company will be terminated, and you will no longer be carried on our payroll records or be covered by any company benefit programs. Any questions concerning the plant closing law or this notice will be answered in the personnel office.[42]

◆ MANAGING LAYOFFS

Layoff Defined

layoff A term that refers to a situation in which there is no work available for the employee who is being sent home, but management expects the situation to be temporary and intends to recall the employee when work is again available.

The term **layoff** refers to a situation in which three conditions are present: (1) there is no work available for the employee who is being sent home, (2) management expects the no-work situation to be temporary and probably short term, and (3) management intends to recall the employee when work is again available.[43] (A layoff is therefore not a *termination,* which is a permanent severing of the employment relationship, although some employers do use "layoff" as a euphemism for discharge or termination. The subjects of discipline, discharge, and dismissal are discussed in Chapter 17.)

Bumping/Layoff Procedures

Employers who encounter frequent business slowdowns and layoffs usually draw up detailed procedures that allow employees to use their seniority to remain on the job. Most layoff procedures have these features in common:[44]

1. For the most part, seniority is the ultimate determiner of who will work.

2. Seniority can give way to merit or ability but usually only when none of the senior employees is qualified for a particular job.

3. Seniority is usually based on the date the employee joined the organization, not the date he or she took a particular job.

4. Because seniority is usually companywide, an employee in one job is usually allowed to bump or displace an employee in another job provided a more senior employee is able to do the job in question without further training.

Alternatives to Layoffs

Many employers today recognize the enormous investments they have in their "human resources," investments they made in recruiting, screening, and training their employees and in developing their commitment and loyalty. As a result, many employers are more hesitant to lay off employees at the first signs of business decline; instead, they are using new approaches to either blunt the effects of the layoff or eliminate the layoffs entirely.

There are several alternatives to layoff. With the **voluntary reduction in pay plan,** all employees agree to reductions in pay in order to keep everyone working. Other employers arrange to have all or most of their employees accumulate their *vacation time* and to concentrate their vacations during slow periods; temporary help thus does not have to be hired for vacationing employees during peak periods, and employment automatically falls off when business declines. Other employees agree to take **voluntary time off,** which again has the effect of reducing the employer's payroll and avoiding the need for a layoff. Control Data Corporation avoids layoff with what they call their **rings of defense** approach. In their plan, temporary supplemental employees are hired with the specific understanding that their work is of a temporary nature and they may be laid off at any time or fired. Then when layoffs come, the first "ring of defense" is the cadre of supplemental workers. Control Data contends that because of their understood temporary nature, hard feelings are avoided when these people are laid off, while permanent Control Data employees can be secure in the knowledge that they probably will never be laid off.[45]

Outplacement Counseling[46]

This is a systematic process by which a terminated person is trained and counseled in the techniques of (1) self-appraisal and (2) securing a new job that is appropriate to his or her needs and talents.[47] As the term is generally used, outplacement does not mean the employer takes responsibility for placing the terminated person in a new job. Instead, it is a counseling service whose purpose is to provide the person with advice, instructions, and a sounding board to help formulate career goals and successfully execute a job search. **Outplacement counseling** thus might more accurately (but more ponderously) be called "career counseling and job search skills for terminated employees." The counseling itself is done either by the employer's in-

voluntary reduction in pay plan An alternative to layoffs in which all employees agree to reductions in pay to keep everyone working.

voluntary time off An alternative to layoffs in which some employees agree to take time off to reduce the employer's payroll and avoid the need for a layoff.

rings of defense An alternative layoff plan in which temporary supplemental employees are hired with the understanding that they may be laid off at any time.

outplacement counseling A systematic process by which a terminated person is counseled in the techniques of career self-appraisal and in securing a new job that is appropriate to his or her needs and talents.

house specialist or by outside consultants. The outplacement counseling is considered part of the terminated employee's support or severance package.

In practice, outplacement counseling is aimed at providing a terminated employee with much the same knowledge and skills as contained in this chapter (and its appendix). As summarized in Figure 15.2, the first part of the counseling includes a *personal debriefing* aimed at reducing the trauma of the termination, and then *vocational testing* to identify the person's occupational orientations, skills, and aptitudes. The next step is to define the person's *prior work accomplishments* in order to identify not only the person's salable skills but the key accomplishments, or "worthpoints," he or she can use to sell himself or herself for potential jobs. Specific *job objectives* (in terms of where the person would like to be five years hence, for instance) are then determined. Next, outplacement moves in to its *job search skills* phase, in which the person is trained in basic job search skills like résumé preparation, writing direct-mail letters, and being interviewed. In one survey 14 of the 41 respondents offered terminated employees both severance pay and other outplacement services, while 17 of the 41 had severance pay plans alone.[48]

Outplacement counseling is usually conducted by special firms set up for this purpose, firms such as Drake Bean Morin Inc., and Right Associates Inc. Middle- and upper-level managers who are let go will typically have office space and secretarial services they can use at local offices of such firms.

FIGURE 15.2
Outplacement Counseling: Steps in the Job Search
Source: F. Leigh Branham, "How to Evaluate Executive Outplacement Services," *Personnel Journal,* April 1983, p. 325.

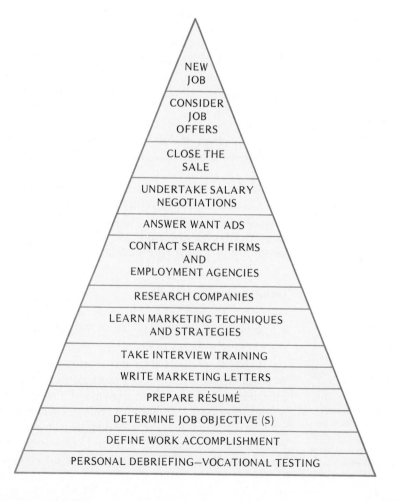

NEW JOB

CONSIDER JOB OFFERS

CLOSE THE SALE

UNDERTAKE SALARY NEGOTIATIONS

ANSWER WANT ADS

CONTACT SEARCH FIRMS AND EMPLOYMENT AGENCIES

RESEARCH COMPANIES

LEARN MARKETING TECHNIQUES AND STRATEGIES

TAKE INTERVIEW TRAINING

WRITE MARKETING LETTERS

PREPARE RÉSUMÉ

DETERMINE JOB OBJECTIVE (S)

DEFINE WORK ACCOMPLISHMENT

PERSONAL DEBRIEFING—VOCATIONAL TESTING

Exit Interviews

Many employers conduct final *exit interviews* with employees who are leaving the firm for any reason. The interviews are usually conducted by the human resource department and are aimed at eliciting information about the job or related matters that might give the employer a better insight into what is right—or what is wrong—about the company. The assumption, of course, is that since the employee is leaving, he or she will be candid.

That the person will be candid is questionable. The person might have his own ax to grind, for instance, and could use the exit interview to try to retaliate against former foes. Or the person might simply not want to cause trouble that might come back to haunt him when he needs references for a new job.

In fact, based on the results of one survey, the kind of information you can expect to obtain from exit interviews is questionable. The researchers found that at the time of separation, 38% of those leaving blamed "salary and benefits," while only 4% blamed "supervision." Followed up 18 months later, though, 24% blamed supervision and only 12% blamed salary and benefits. Getting to the real problem during the exit interview may thus require some heavy digging.[49]

♦ ADJUSTING TO DOWNSIZINGS AND MERGERS

When a downsizing or merger requires a reduction in force attention must also be given to the employees left behind. Certainly those dismissed should be treated fairly. But it is often those "left behind" that you'll need to build your future business around. Adjusting to the needs of these people is thus important.

Three Basic Elements

There are at least three main elements to consider in dealing with the downsizings' survivors: information, recommitment, and ongoing support.[50] First, the remaining employees require *information*—about the changes, the reasons behind them, and about their future status with the company. Second, you want the active *recommitment* of survivors, a recommitment that will let them give their best effort to and remain with your firm. Finally, during and for several months after the transition, the survivors will need your organization's *ongoing support* in terms of assistance, feedback, and opportunities to express concerns and receive reassurances.

Dealing with the Survivors Immediately After the Downsizing

In terms of your survivors, you will face one of two situations immediately following the downsizing.[51] In the first case you may anticipate no further reductions and here you can assure your people that no further reductions are planned. However, remember not to promise that no further reductions will occur unless that is really what you mean. Do not make any statements orally or in writing that could be construed as a binding contract in the future.

The second situation is more difficult because here you know that future reductions will probably take place. Here the best you can do is to be honest with those remaining, explaining that while future downsizings will probably occur they will be informed of these reductions as soon as possible. Here you may well experience a transitory drop in productivity and an increased attrition, but the alternative is being dishonest with all the people involved.

Specific Steps to Take

A postdownsizing program instituted at Duracell, Inc., illustrates the steps involved in a well-conceived program. In this case, Duracell managers worked with consultants from an outplacement firm to develop a three-phase program for dealing with the employees who survived: It involved announcement activities, immediate follow-up, and long-term support.[52]

After several months of planning, the program began with a series of *announcement activities*. These included a full staff meeting at the facility, followed by a program in which every employee was informed individually of his or her status with the firm. In addition, each survivor received a description of the support services and assistance being made available to those leaving Duracell. This served two purposes: It helped reduce the survivors' concern about their friends and former colleagues, and it helped make sure the survivors had the information they needed (for instance, regarding severance pay packages) that would enable them to make an active choice to stay with the firm.

Next, there was an *immediate follow-up* phase during the first few days after the announcement. Here survivors were split into interdepartmental groups that included the senior management of the facility. At these sessions, employees wre encouraged to discuss how they felt about the layoffs and to express their concerns and feelings about their future with the company and the future of the facility as a team. Based on some of the concerns raised at these first meetings, follow-up meetings were held soon after. These allowed members of each department to discuss specific work-related issues and problems and gave management an opportunity to discuss the new organization structure and work assignments. Here productivity goals were also discussed, so that employees' concerns regarding postreduction work loads could be confronted head on.

A mechanism for providing *long-term support* was also built into the program. Here, key management was encouraged to meet with the remaining staff frequently and informally in order to provide ongoing support to these people in an "open-door" atmosphere. The meetings were held frequently and informally, often over lunch or coffee. Finally, there was a follow-up meeting with the survivors about two months after the downsizing to make sure all concerns had been aired and addressed.[53]

Handling the Merger/Acquisition

In terms of dismissals and downsizings, mergers or acquisitions are usually one sided: In many mergers, in other words, one company essentially acquires the other, and it is often the employees of the latter that find themselves out looking for new jobs.

In terms of dismissal procedures and survivor adjustments, layoffs after mergers can be handled like any others, with one big difference. In an acquirer-acquiree situation the employees in the acquired firm will be hypersensitive to mistreatment of their colleagues. It thus behooves you to take care that those let go are treated with kid gloves. Seeing your former colleagues fired is bad enough for morale. Seeing them fired under conditions which might be misperceived as bullying by the representatives of the acquiring firm rubs salt in the wound and poisons the relationship for years to come. As a rule, therefore,[54]

Avoid the appearance of power and domination.

Avoid win/lose behavior.

Remain businesslike and professional in all dealings.

Maintain as positive a feeling about the acquired company as possible.

Remember that the degree to which your organization treats the acquired group with care and dignity will impact the confidence, productivity, and commitment of those remaining for years to come.

♦ RETIREMENT

Retirement for most employees is a bittersweet experience. For some it is the culmination of their careers, a time when they can relax and enjoy the fruits of their labor without worrying about the problems of work. For others, it is the retirement itself that is the trauma, as the once busy employee tries to cope with being suddenly "nonproductive" and with the strange (and not entirely pleasant) experience of being home every day with nothing to do. For many retirees, in fact, maintaining a sense of identity and self-worth without a full-time job is the single most important task they'll face. And it's one that employers are increasingly trying to help their retirees cope with, as a logical last step in the career management process.[55]

Preretirement Counseling

About 30% of the employers in one recent survey said they had formal pre-retirement programs aimed at easing the passage of their employees into retirement.[56] The most common preretirement practices were

Explanation of Social Security benefits (reported by 97% of those with pre-retirement education programs)

Leisure-time counseling (86%)

Financial and investment counseling (84%)

Health counseling (82%)

Living arrangements (59%)

Psychological counseling (35%)

Counseling for second careers outside the company (31%)

Counseling for second careers inside the company (4%)

Among employers that did *not* have preretirement education programs, 64% believed that such programs were needed, and most of these said their firms had plans to develop them within two or three years.

Another important trend here is that of granting part-time employment to employees as an alternative to outright retirement. Several recent surveys of blue- and white-collar employees showed that about half of all employees over age 55 would like to continue working part-time after they retire, and employers can probably be expected to build such alternatives into their career-management processes.

SUMMARY

1. The key to managing your career is insight into what you want out of a career, into your talents and limitations, and into your values and how they fit with the alternatives you are considering.

2. The main stages in a person's career include: growth stage (roughly birth to age 14), exploration stage (roughly 15 to 24), establishment stage (roughly ages 24 to 44, the heart of most people's work lives), maintenance stage (45 to 65), and decline stage (preretirement). The establishment stage itself may consist of a trial substage, a stabilization substage, and a midcareer crisis substage.

3. The first step in planning your career is to learn as much as you can about your own interests, aptitudes, and skills. Start by identifying your

occupational orientation: realistic, investigative, social, conventional, enterprising, and artistic. Next, identify your skills and rank them from high to low.

4. Next, identify your career anchors: technical/functional, managerial, creativity, autonomy, and security. Then ask yourself what you want to do.

5. There are many sources you can turn to for learning about occupations and careers. These include the *Dictionary of Occupational Titles*, the *Occupational Outlook Handbook*, *Occupational Outlook Quarterly*, the *Encyclopedia of Careers and Vocational Guidance*, and the office of personnel management's *Handbook X118*.

6. The supervisor plays an important role in the career management process. Some important guidelines include: avoid reality shock, be demanding, provide realistic job previews, conduct career-oriented performance appraisals, and encourage job rotation.

7. In making promotion decisions, you have to decide between *seniority and competence*, a *formal or informal system*, and how to *measure competence*.

8. Transfers today are reportedly not as traumatic as they are popularly thought to be, but the proportion of top executives willing to transfer is still falling.

9. A layoff is a situation in which there is no work available for the employee being sent home, but management expects the situation to be temporary and the employee to be recalled. In most cases, formal bumping/layoff procedures are developed; these generally tie layoffs to seniority. Alternatives to layoffs include voluntary pay reductions, voluntary time off, and specially scheduled vacation time. The "plant closing law" rules should be adhered to.

KEY TERMS

career planning and development	maintenance stage	career anchors
career cycle	decline stage	reality shock
growth stage	John Holland	layoff
exploration stage	occupational orientations	voluntary reduction in pay plan
establishment stage	occupational skills	voluntary time off
trial substage	aptitudes and special talents	ring of defense
stabilization substage	Edgar Schein	outplacement counseling
midcareer crisis substage		

DISCUSSION QUESTIONS

1. Briefly describe each of the stages in a typical career.

2. What is a career anchor? What are the main types of career anchors discussed in this chapter?

3. What are the main types of occupational orientations discussed in this chapter?

4. Describe some important sources of information you could use to learn about careers of interest to you.

5. Develop a résumé for yourself, using the guidelines presented in this chapter. (See the appendix.)

6. Write a one-page essay stating "Where I would like to be career-wise ten years from today."

7. Explain career-related factors to keep in mind when making the employee's first assignments.

8. What are some of the important factors to consider when making promotion and transfer decisions?

9. Discuss a program you would set up to help your employer adjust to a mandatory downsizing.

♦ APPLICATION EXERCISES

♦ CASE INCIDENT   The Wrong Job

Jill Allen accepted a new promotion with mixed feelings. She was proud of having her work recognized, but she had some doubts about how she would like the new work. Her former job had involved regular contacts with sales people—troubleshooting, helping them with special customer problems, and so on. Her new job in market research was essentially a research job, working with population data, industry marketing reports, and the like.

Jill missed the routine of her old office and the people she had worked with. She had a private office now, but she felt she really did not have the educational background for the job. When she submitted her first report, the division head was nice enough—suggesting some changes that in fact meant that Jill had really used the wrong approach. Her boss said not to worry, "We all have to learn a new job." The more Jill thought about it, the more she wanted to go back to the old job. But she hesitated for fear that she would be considered a failure by management and thus disqualified for any future promotions.

1. If you were Jill's boss, what could you do to correct this situation?

2. Could this situation have been avoided all together?

Source: George Strauss and Leonard R. Sayles, *Personnel; The Human Problems of Management* (Englewood Cliffs, N.J.: Prentice Hall, 1972), p. 408.

EXPERIENTIAL EXERCISE

♦ CAREER CHOICE: A COUNSELING INTERVIEW

Because you are reading this book you are probably at a point in your career where you have already made some important choices, such as choice of an occupation or general field of work or choice of a degree program. However, there are always other issues to be resolved and decisions to be made throughout a career.

It sometimes aids the decision process to talk it over with someone else. In this exercise, you will be working in groups of three. Each person will have the opportunity to be interviewed about his or her career choices, to be a career interviewer (or counselor), and to be an observer. Try to learn from each role—how to be a better career decision maker, how to be a better career counselor, and how to be a more sensitive observer of interviewing and helping processes.

Instructions for the Exercise: The class should split into groups of three. There will be three rounds to the exercise. In each round, there will be three roles: interviewer, interviewee, and observer. At the end of each round, you will switch roles and assume a role you haven't played yet. Therefore, at the end of the third round, each person in the trio should have had a chance to try every role.

Step 1. Round 1. Pick one person to act as interviewer, one as interviewee, and one as observer. For 15 minutes, the interviewer will conduct a counseling interview with the interviewee on the topic of career choice. Interview questions are provided as a guide; questions may be selected or the interviewer may make them up.

During the interview, the observer should be silent and should take notes on the process of the interview. The observer should also act as *timekeeper*, stopping the interview after 15 minutes.

For the next 5 minutes, the observer will feed back his or her observations and all three members will discuss the interview. Focus on the following two issues:

a. What did the interviewee learn?

b. What did the interviewer or interviewee do that helped or hindered the interview?

Step 2. Round 2. Switch roles (for example, interviewer becomes interviewee, interviewee becomes observer, observer becomes interviewer). Follow the same procedure as in Round 1.

Step 3. Round 3. Switch roles again, as in Round 2. Be sure that no one plays the same role twice. Follow the same procedure as in Round 1.

Step 4. Class Discussion. Meet again as a class. Discuss what the interviewees seemed to be learning. What career choice issues were discussed most frequently? What choices or solutions were considered?

Also discuss what people learned about the process of interviewing and helping. What did the interviewer do that helped or hindered the decision-making process? What did the interviewee do to help or hinder his or her own progress?

Interview Questions

1. How would you describe yourself as a person?
2. What are you best at doing? Worst?
3. What do you really enjoy doing most? Least?
4. What have been one or two of your best successes—times when you felt especially productive and proud of your capabilities and potential?
5. What would you stop doing if you could?
6. What would you like to do more?
7. What would you like to learn more about?
8. What aspects of yourself do you like most? Least?
9. Could you describe your ideal self?
10. Who are your heroes? What do you like about them?
11. If you could have any job at all, what would you do? What would be an ideal job for you?
12. What do you plan to do during the next five years? (If you haven't yet decided, pretend you had to decide *right now*. What would you choose to do?)

13. What are the pros and cons of the different career options you are considering right now?

14. What way are you leaning?

15. Pretend a person amazingly similar to you (background, interests, plans, and so on) came to you for advice on the same issue you're wrestling with now. What advice would you give this person?

Source: Douglas Hall, *Careers in Organizations* (Pacific Palisades, Calif.: Goodyear, 1976), pp. 127–128.

Appendix

Finding the Right Job

HELPING YOU GET THE RIGHT JOB

You have identified your occupational orientation, skills, and career anchors and have picked out the occupation you want and laid plans for a career. And (if necessary) you have embarked on the required training. Your next step is to find a job that you want in the company and locale you want to work in. The following are some techniques for doing so.

♦ JOB SEARCH TECHNIQUES

Do Your Own Research

Perhaps the most direct way of unearthing the job you want where you want it is to pick out the geographic area in which you want to work and find out all you can about the companies in that area that appeal to you and the people you have to contact in those companies to get the job you want. Most public libraries have local directories. For example, the reference librarian in one Fairfax County, Virginia, library made the following suggestions for patrons seeking information on local businesses:

Industrial Directory of Virginia
Industrial Directory of Fairfax County
Principal Employers of the Washington Metro Area
The Business Review of Washington

Some other general reference material you can use include *Who's Who in Commerce and Industry, Who's Who in America, Who's Who in the East,* and *Poor's Register.* Using these guides, you can find the person in each organization who is ultimately responsible for hiring people in the position you seek.

Personal Contacts

According to one survey, the most popular way to seek job interviews, especially for jobs paying $30,000 or more, is to rely on personal contacts such as friends and relatives.[57] For example, one Department of Labor study indicates that about 19% of managers get their jobs through friends and about 6% got them through relatives. The way to proceed is to let as many *responsible* people as you can know that you are in the market for a job and, specifically, what kind of job you want. (Beware, though, if you are currently employed and don't want your job search getting back to your current boss; if that is the case, better just pick out two or three *very* close friends and tell them that it is absolutely essential that they be discreet in poking around and looking for a job for you.)

No matter how close your friends or relatives are to you, by the way, you don't want to impose too much on them by shifting the burden of your job search to them. Therefore, it is sometimes best to ask them just for the name of someone they think you should talk to in the kind of firm in which you'd like to work, and then do the digging yourself.

Answering Advertisements

Most experts agree that this is a low-probability way to get a job, and it becomes increasingly less likely that you will get a job this way as the level of a job increases. Answering ads, in other words, is fine for jobs that pay under $20,000 per year, but its highly unlikely that as you move up in management you are going to get your job by simply answering classified ads. Low probability though it be, good sources of classified ads for professionals and managers include *The New York Times, The Wall Street Journal,* and a separate *Wall Street Journal* listing of job openings.

Be very careful in replying to blind ads, however. Some executive search firms and companies will run ads even when no position exists just to gauge the market, and there is always the chance that you can be trapped into responding to your own firm. In responding to these ads, also be sure to create the right impression with the materials you submit; check the typing, style, grammar, neatness, and so forth, and check your résumé to make sure it is geared to the job for which you are applying. In your cover letter, be sure to have a paragraph or so in which you specifically address why your background and accomplishments are appropriate to the job being advertised; you must respond clearly to the company's identified needs.

Employment Agencies

Agencies are especially good at placing people in jobs up to about $30,000 but can be useful for higher paying jobs as well. Their fees for professional and management jobs are usually paid by the employer. Assuming you know the job you want, review eight or so back issues of the Sunday classified ads (in your library) to identify the agencies that consistently handle the positions you want. Approach three or four initially, preferably in response to specific ads, and avoid signing any contract that gives an agency exclusive rights to place you.

Executive Recruiters

These firms are retained by employers to seek out top talent for their clients, and their fees are always paid by the employer. They fill positions in the $40,000 and up category, although $50,000 is often the lower limit. They do not do career counseling, but if you know the job you want, it pays to contact a few. Send your résumé and a cover letter summarizing your job objective in precise terms (including job title and size company you want), work-related accomplishments, current salary, and salary requirements. They are listed in the Yellow Pages under "Executive Search Consultants," but beware, since some *non*search firms now also use the "Executive Search" label. Remember that with a search firm you never pay a fee. A list of executive recruiters is also available for $3.00 from the Management Information Service of the American Management Association, 135 West 50th Street, New York, NY 11020.

Career Counselors

These people will not help you find a job per se; rather, they specialize in aptitude testing and career counseling. They are listed in the Yellow Pages under "Career Counseling" or "Vocational Guidance." Their services usually cost $200 or $300 and include psychological testing and interviews with an experienced career counselor. Check the firm's services, prices, and history as well as the credentials of the person you will be dealing with.

Executive Marketing Consultants

These firms manage your job-hunting campaign. They are generally not recruiters and *do not have jobs to fill.* Depending on the services you choose, your cost will range from $300 to $4,000 or more. The process may involve months of weekly meetings. Services include résumé and letter writing, interview skill building, and developing a full job-hunting campaign. Before approaching one, though, you should *definitely* do some in-depth self-appraisal (as explained in this chapter) and read books like Richard Bolles's *The Quick Job Hunting Map* and *What Color Is Your Parachute?*

Then check out three or four of these firms (they are listed in the Yellow Pages under "Executive Search Consultants") by visiting each and asking: What exactly is their program? How much does each service cost? Are there any extra costs, such as charges for printing and mailing résumés? What does the contract say? After what point will you get no rebate if you're unhappy with the services? Then, review your notes, check the Better Business Bureau, and decide which of these firms (if any) is for you.

♦ WRITING YOUR RÉSUMÉ

Your résumé is probably your most important selling document, one that can determine if you "make the cut" and get offered a job interview. Here are some résumé pointers, as offered by employment counselor Richard Payne and other experts.[58] An example of a good résumé is presented in Figure 15.3.

Your Address, etc.

Start your résumé with your name, address, and telephone number. Using your office phone number, by the way, can indicate either that (1) your employer knows you are leaving or (2) that you don't care if he finds out. You're usually therefore best off using your home phone number.

Job Objective

State your job objective next. This should summarize in one sentence the specific position you want, where you want to do it (type and size of company), and a special reason an employer might have for wanting you to fill the job. For example, "Production manager in a medium-size manufacturing company in a situation in which strong production scheduling and control experience would be valuable." Always try to put down the most senior title you know you can expect to secure, keeping in mind the specific job for which you are applying.

Job Scope

Indicate the scope of your responsibility in each of your previous jobs, starting with your most recent position. For each of your previous jobs, write a paragraph that shows job title, who you reported to directly and indirectly, who reported to you, how many people reported to you, the operational and human resource budgets you controlled, and what (in one sentence) your job entailed.

Your Accomplishments

Next (and this is *very important*) indicate your "worth" in each of the positions you held. This is the heart of your résumé. It shows, for each of your previous jobs, (1) the concrete action you took and why you took it and (2) the specific result of your action—the "payoff." For example, "As production supervisor, I introduced a new process to replace costly hand soldering

FIGURE 15.3
Example of a Good Résumé
Source: Richard Payne, *How to Get a Better Job Quicker* (New York: Signet, 1979), pp. 80–81.

CONRAD D. STAPLETON
77 Pleasantapple Way
Coltsville, NY 10176   *CONFIDENTIAL*
(914) 747-1012

JOB OBJECTIVE	*Senior Product Manager* in a situation requiring extensive advertising and promotion experience.
PRESENT POSITION	VALUE-PLUS DIVISION, INTERCONTINENTAL CORPORATION
1986-Present	*Product Manager,* NEW PRODUCTS, LAUNDRYON SOAP and CARBOLENE CLEANER, reporting to Group Product Manager.
	Recommended and obtained test market authorization, then managed all phases of development of THREE test brands, scheduled for introduction during Fall/Winter 1986. Combined first year national volume projects to $20 million, with advertising budget of $6 million. Concurrently developing several new products for 1987 test marketing.
	Also responsible for two established brands: LAUNDRYON SOAP, a $7 million brand, and CARBOLENE CLEANER, a $4 million regional brand. Currently work with three advertising agencies on test and established brands.
1983-1985	*Product Manager,* WEEKENDER PAINTS, a $6 million brand.
	Developed and implemented a repositioning of this brand (including new copy and new package graphics) to counter a 10-year sales downtrend averaging 10% a year. Repositioning increased test market volume 16%, and national volume 8% the following year.
	Later initiated development of new, more competitive copy than advertising used during repositioning. Test area sales increased 35%. National airing is scheduled for Fall 1986.
	Developed plastic packaging that increased test market volume 10%.
	Also developed and implemented profit improvement projects which increased net profit 33%.
1982	*Product Manager,* SHINEZY CAR WASH, a $4 million brand.
	Initiated and test marketed an improved aerosol formula and a liquid refill. Both were subsequently expanded nationally and increased brand volume 26%.
	RICHARDS-DONALDS COMPANY
1981-1982	*Assistant Product Manager,* reporting to Product Manager.
	Concurrent responsibility on PAR and SHIPSHAPE detergents. Developed locally tailored annual promotion plans. These resulted in 30% sales increase on PAR and stabilization of SHIPSHAPE volume.
1980-1981	*Product Merchandising Assistant*
	Developed and implemented SUNSHINE SUDS annual promotion plan.

FIGURE 15.3
(continued)

CONRAD D. STAPLETON . . . page 2

1979-1980	Academic Leave of Absence to obtain MBA. See EDUCATION.
1977-1979	*Account Manager*, Field Sales.
	Account Manager for Shopper's Pal, the most difficult chain in Metropolitan Westchester. Achieved sales increase of 10% and distribution of all Lever products, introduced while I was on territory. Based on this performance was awarded Food'N Things Cooperatives, the second most difficult account, and achieved similar results.
EDUCATION	READING SCHOOL, University of Maryland
	MBA in Marketing Management. Average grade 3.5 out of 4.0. Thesis: "The Distribution of Pet Supplies through Supermarkets," graded 4.0 out of 4.0. Courses included quantitative methods, finance, accounting and international business.
	ELTON COLLEGE, Kansas City, Missouri
	BA in Liberal Arts. Was one of 33, out of freshman class of 110, who completed four years of this academically rigorous program. Theses required each year. Judge in Student Court during senior year.
PERSONAL	Single, U.S. Citizen.

of component parts. The new process reduced assembly time per unit from 30 to 10 minutes and reduced labor costs by over 60 percent." Use several of these worth statements for each job.

Length

Keep your résumé to two pages or less and list education, military service (if any), and personal background (hobbies, interests, associations) on the last page.

Personal Data

Do not put personal data regarding age, marital status, or dependents on top of page one. If you must include it, do so at the end of the résumé, where it will be read after the employer has already formed an opinion of you.

Finally, two last points. First, do not produce a slipshod résumé: Avoid overcrowded pages, difficult-to-read copies, typographical errors, and other problems of this sort. Second, do not use a make-do résumé—one from ten years ago. Produce a new résumé for each job you are applying for, gearing your job objective and worth statements to the job you want.

♦ HANDLING THE INTERVIEW

You have done all your homework and now the big day is almost here; you have an interview next week with the person who is responsible for hiring for the job you want. What do you have to do to excel in the interview? Here are some suggestions. (Also review interviewing in Chapter 6 at this point.)

Prepare, Prepare, Prepare

First, remember that preparation is essential. Before the interview, learn all you can about the employer, the job, and the people doing the recruiting. At the library, look through business periodicals to find out what is happening in the employer's field. Who is his competition? How are they doing?

Uncover the Interviewer's Needs

Spend as little time as possible answering your interviewer's first questions and as much time as possible getting the person to describe the needs: What the person is looking to get accomplished and the type of person needed. Use open-ended questions, such as "Could you tell me more about that?"

Relate Yourself to the Person's Needs

Once you have a handle on the type of person your interviewer is looking for and the sorts of problems he or she wants solved, you are in a good position to describe your own accomplishments *in terms of the interviewer's needs*. Start by saying something like, "One of the problem areas you've indicated is important to you is similar to a problem I once faced." Then, state the problem, describe your solution, and reveal the results.

Think Before Answering

Recall (from Chapter 6) that answering a question should be a three-step process: pause, think, speak. Pause to make sure you understand what the interviewer is driving at, think about how to structure your answer, and then speak. In your answer, try to emphasize how hiring you will help the interviewer solve his or her problem.

Appearance and Enthusiasm are Important

Appropriate clothing, good grooming, a firm handshake, and the appearance of controlled energy are important.

First Impressions Count

Studies of interviews show that in almost 80% of the cases, interviewers make up their minds about the applicant during the first few minutes of the interview. A good first impression may turn to bad during the interview, but it is unlikely. Bad first impressions are almost impossible to overcome.

NOTES

1. Except as noted, this section is based on J. Richard Hackman and J. Lloyd Suttle, *Improving Life at Work* (Santa Monica, Calif.: Goodyear, 1977); see also William Steiges, "Can We Legislate the Humanization of Work?" in W. Clay Hamner and Frank Schmidt, *Contemporary Problems in Personnel* (Chicago: St. Clair Press, 1974).
2. J. Lloyd Suttle, *Improving Life at Work*, p. 4.
3. Donald Super and others, *Vocational Development: A Framework for Research* (New York: Teachers College Press, 1957), and Edgar Schein, *Career Dynamics: Matching Individual and Organizational Needs* (Reading, Mass.: Addison-Wesley, 1978).
4. John Holland, *Making Vocational Choices: A Theory of Careers* (Englewood Cliffs, N.J.: Prentice-Hall, 1973).
5. Richard Bolles, *The Quick Job Hunting Map* (Berkeley, Calif.: Ten Speed Press, 1979), pp. 5–6.
6. Ibid., p. 5.
7. Schein, *Career Dynamics*, pp. 128–129.
8. Ibid., pp. 257–262.
9. This example is based on Richard Bolles, *The Three Boxes of Life* (Berkeley, Calif.: Ten Speed Press, 1976).
10. Bolles, *What Color Is Your Parachute?* (Berkeley, Calif.: Ten Speed Press, 1976), p. 86.

11. *The Guidance Information System*, Time Share Corporation, 630 Oakwood Avenue, West Hartford, Conn. 06110, described in Andrew Dubrin, *Human Relations: A Job-Oriented Approach* (Reston, Va.: Reston, 1982), p. 358.

12. Gail Martin, "The Job Hunters Guide to the Library," *Occupational Outlook Quarterly* (Fall 1980), p. 10.

13. Robert Jameson, *The Professional Job Changing System* (Verona, N.J.: Performance Dynamics, 1975).

14. Richard Payne, *How to Get a Better Job Quicker* (New York: New American Library, 1987).

15. Ibid.

16. Richard Reilly, Mary Tenopyr, and Steven Sperling, "The Effects of Job Previews on Job Acceptance and Survival Rates of Telephone Operator Candidates," *Journal of Applied Psychology*, Vol. 64 (1979).

17. Schein, *Career Dynamics*, p. 19.

18. As opposed to more routine jobs, for example, as telephone operators or sewing machine operators.

19. D. W. Ilgen and W. Seely, "Realistic Expectations as an Aid in Reducing Voluntary Resignations," *Journal of Applied Psychology*, Vol. 59 (1974), pp. 452–455.

20. Douglas Bray, Richard Campbell, and Donald Grant, *Formative Years in Business* (New York: Wiley, 1974).

21. J. Sterling Livingston, "Pygmalion in Management," *Harvard Business Review*, Vol. 48 (July–August 1969), pp. 81–89.

22. Joel Ross, *Managing Productivity* (Reston, Va.: Reston, 1979).

23. Douglas Hall and Francine Hall, "What's New in Career Management?" *Organizational Dynamics*, Vol. 4 (Summer 1976).

24. H. G. Kaufman, *Obsolescence and Professional Career Development* (New York: AMACOM, 1974).

25. Hall and Hall, "What's New in Career Management?" p. 350.

26. For a discussion of the role played by the supervisor in appraisals, see Donald Hall, "Career Planning for Employee Development: A Primer for Managers," *California Management Review*, Vol. 20 (1977), pp. 23–25.

27. Schein, *Career Dynamics*, p. 19.

28. See, for example, D. B. Miller, *Personal Vitality* (Reading, Mass.: Addison-Wesley, 1977), and *Personal Vitality Workbook* (Reading, Mass.: Addison-Wesley, 1977).

29. Albert Griffith, "Career Development: What Organizations Are Doing About It," *Personnel*, Vol. 57 (1980), pp. 63–69; see also Richard Vosburgh, "The Annual Human Resource Review (A Career Planning System), *Personnel Journal*, Vol. 59 (October 1980), pp. 830–837.

30. Schein, *Career Dynamics*, pp. 252–253, and Bowen and Hall, "Career Planning and Employee Development," p. 279.

31. For self-diagnosis books, see, for example, G. A. Ford and G. L. Lippitt, *A Life Planning Workbook* (Fairfax, Va.: NTL Learning Resources, 1972).

32. Schein, *Career Dynamics*, p. 253.

33. Pigors and Meyers, *Personnel Administration*, p. 283.

34. James Healy, "The Factor of Ability in Labor Relations," in *Arbitration Today*, Proceedings of the Eighth Annual Meeting of the National Academy of Arbitrators, 1955, pp. 45–54, quoted in Pigors and Meyers, *Personnel Administration*, p. 283.

35. Charles Halaby, "Bureaucratic Promotion Criteria," *Administrative Science Quarterly*, Vol. 23 (September 1978), pp. 466–484.

36. National Industrial Conference Board, *Personnel Practices in Factory and Office*, Studies in Personnel Policy No. 145 (1954), pp. 12–69.

37. Bureau of National Affairs, *Finding and Training Potential Executives*, Personnel Policies Form, Survey No. 58, September 1960, p. 4.

38. See, for example, Joseph Famularo, *Handbook of Modern Personnel Administration* (New York: McGraw-Hill, 1972), p. 17.

39. Commerce Clearing House, *Personnel Practices/Communications*, p. 1351.

40. Ibid.

41. Commerce Clearing House, "Top Executives Are Growing Reluctant to Relocate," *Ideas and Trends*, December 10, 1982, p. 218.

42. Quoted from Commerce Clearing House, *Ideas and Trends*, August 9, 1988, p. 133; see also Bureau of National Affairs, "Plant Closing Notification Rules: A Compliance Guide," *Bulletin to Management*, May 18, 1989.

43. Commerce Clearing House, *Personnel Practices/Communications*, p. 1402.

44. Ibid., p. 1410.

45. Commerce Clearing House, "Ideas and Trends in Personnel," July 9, 1982, p. 131.

46. Ibid., pp. 132–146.

47. Ibid., p. 132.

48. Hermine Zagat Levine, "Outplacement and Severance Pay Practices," *Personnel*, Vol. 62, no. 9 (September 1985), pp. 13–21.

49. Joseph Zarandona and Michael Camuso, "A Study of Exit Interviews: Does the Last Word Count?" *Personnel*, Vol. 62, no. 3 (March 1985), pp. 47–48.

50. These are based on Lee Feldman, "Duracell's First Aid for Downsizing Survivors," *Personnel Journal* (August 1989), pp. 91–94.

51. This is based on Steven Jesseph, "Employee Termination, II: Some Do's and Don'ts," Personnel, February 1989, pp. 36–38.

52. Feldman, "Duracell's First Aid for Downsizing Survivors," p. 94.

53. Ibid.

54. These are based on Dan Kleinman, "Witness to a Merger," *Personnel Journal* (November 1988), pp. 64–67.

55. Remember that certain highly paid executives and employees who will receive pensions of at least $25,000 a year at retirement can be forced to retire at 65, under federal law.

56. "Preretirement Education Programs," *Personnel*, Vol. 59 (May–June 1982), p. 47. For a discussion of why it is important for retiring employees to promote aspects of their lives aside from their careers, see Daniel Halloran, "The Retirement Identity Crisis—and How to Beat It," *Personnel Journal*, Vol. 64 (May 1985), pp. 38–40. For an example of a program aimed at training pre-retirees to prepare for the financial aspects of their retirement, see, for example, Silvia Odenwald, "Pre-Retirement Training Gathers Steam," *Training and Development Journal*, Vol. 40, no. 2 (February 1986), pp. 62–63.

57. Robert Jameson, *The Professional Job Changing System* (Verona, N.J.: Performance Dynamics, 1975). See also Kenneth McRae, "Career-Management Planning: A Boon to Managers and Employees," *Personnel*, Vol. 62, no. 5 (May 1985), pp. 56–60.

58. Richard Payne, *How to Get a Better Job Quicker* (New York: Signet, 1979).

PART FIVE

THE LEGAL ENVIRONMENT
OF PERSONNEL MANAGEMENT

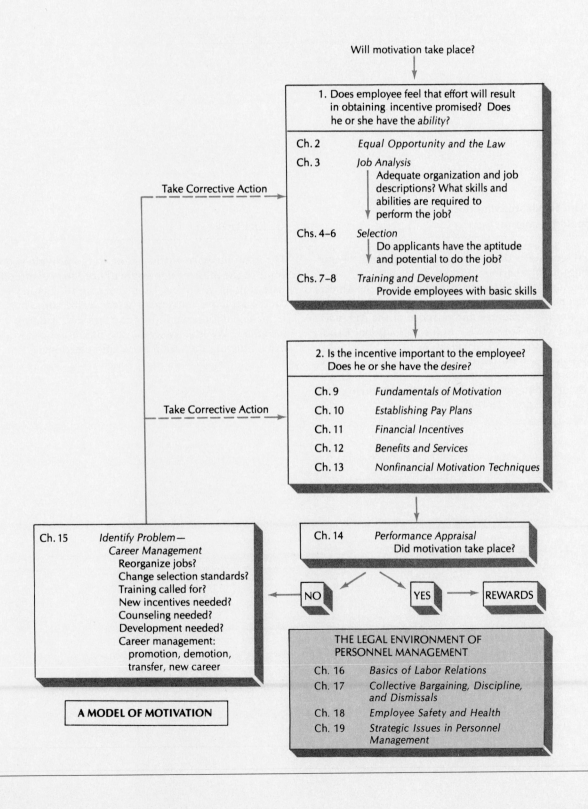

Will motivation take place?

1. Does employee feel that effort will result in obtaining incentive promised? Does he or she have the *ability*?

Ch. 2	*Equal Opportunity and the Law*
Ch. 3	*Job Analysis* Adequate organization and job descriptions? What skills and abilities are required to perform the job?
Chs. 4–6	*Selection* Do applicants have the aptitude and potential to do the job?
Chs. 7–8	*Training and Development* Provide employees with basic skills

Take Corrective Action

2. Is the incentive important to the employee? Does he or she have the *desire*?

Ch. 9	*Fundamentals of Motivation*
Ch. 10	*Establishing Pay Plans*
Ch. 11	*Financial Incentives*
Ch. 12	*Benefits and Services*
Ch. 13	*Nonfinancial Motivation Techniques*

Take Corrective Action

Ch. 15	*Identify Problem— Career Management* Reorganize jobs? Change selection standards? Training called for? New incentives needed? Counseling needed? Development needed? Career management: promotion, demotion, transfer, new career

Ch. 14	*Performance Appraisal* Did motivation take place?

NO   YES → REWARDS

THE LEGAL ENVIRONMENT OF PERSONNEL MANAGEMENT

Ch. 16	*Basics of Labor Relations*
Ch. 17	*Collective Bargaining, Discipline, and Dismissals*
Ch. 18	*Employee Safety and Health*
Ch. 19	*Strategic Issues in Personnel Management*

A MODEL OF MOTIVATION

Chapter 16

Basics of Labor Relations

When you finish studying this chapter, you should be able to:

1. Deal more effectively with a unionization drive and a bargaining session.
2. Cite important incidents in the history of the American labor movement.
3. Explain the structure and purpose of the AFL-CIO.
4. Discuss "five sure ways" to lose a National Labor Relations Board (NLRB) election.
5. Discuss the main features of at least three major pieces of labor legislation.
6. Present examples of what to expect during the union drive and election.

OVERVIEW

The main purpose of this chapter is to provide you with some of the information you will need to deal effectively with unions. After briefly discussing the history of the American labor movement we describe some basics of labor legislation, including the subject of unfair labor practices. We also describe the union actions you can expect during the union drive and election.

Today over 17 million American workers belong to unions—a number that amounts to around 17% of the total number of men and women working in America today. In some industries—mining, construction, transportation—it is impossible to get a job without joining a union. And unions do not just appeal to private sector blue-collar workers; more and more white-collar workers and public employees are turning to unions as well.

Why are unions important? How did they get that way? What do unions want of their members? Why do workers join unions? These are some of the questions addressed in this chapter.[1]

♦ A BRIEF HISTORY OF THE AMERICAN UNION MOVEMENT

To understand what unions are and what they want, it is useful to understand "where they've been." The first thing to notice in Table 16.1—a summary of the important incidents in the American union movement—is that unions have been around for quite some time. As early as 1790, for example, skilled craftsmen (shoemakers, tailors, printers, and so on) organized themselves into trade unions. They posted their "minimum wage" demands and had "tramping committees" go from shop to shop to ensure that no member accepted a lesser wage.

From these earliest unions to the present time, the history of the union movement has been one of alternate expansion and contraction. Union membership grew until a major depression around 1837 resulted in a decline in membership. Membership then began increasing as America entered its Industrial Revolution. In 1869 a group of tailors met and formed the Knights of Labor; the "Knights" were interested in political reform and agitation and often sought political changes. By 1885 it had 100,000 members and (as a result of winning a major strike against a railroad) exploded to 700,000 members the following year. Partially because of their focus on social reform (and partly due to a series of unsuccessful strikes), the Knights' membership dwindled rapidly thereafter, and by 1893 (when they were dissolved) they had virtually no members.

In 1886 Samuel Gompers formed the American Federation of Labor. It consisted primarily of skilled workers and (unlike the Knights) eschewed social reform for practical "bread and butter" gains for its members. The Knights of Labor had engaged in a "class struggle" to alter the form of society and *thereby* get a bigger chunk of benefits for its members. Gompers, on the other hand, aimed at raising the day-to-day wages and improving the

TABLE 16.1 Some Important Milestones in American Labor Movement

1790	Earliest unions formed	1947	Taft-Hartley Act passed
1850	National Union of Typographers formed	1955	AFL and CIO merge
		1959	Landrum-Griffin Act passed
1869	Knights of Labor formed	1963	Executive Order 10988
1886	American Federation of Labor (AFL) formed	1964	The Civil Rights Act
		1969	Executive Order 11491
1893	Knights of Labor dissolved	1975	Executive Order 11838
1929	Start of Great Depression	1978	Civil Service Reform Act
1932	Norris-LaGuardia Act passed	1989	*TWA* v. *Independent Federation of Flight Attendants*
1935	Wagner Act passed		
1938	Congress of Industrial Organizations (CIO) formed		

working conditions of his constituents. The AFL grew rapidly until after World War I, at which point its membership exceeded 5½ million people.

As you can see from Figure 16.1, the 1920s was a period of stagnation for the American union movement, and by 1923 AFL membership had declined to about 3½ million members. This decline and stagnation was a result of several things, including a postwar depression, manufacturers' renewed resistance to unions, the death of Samuel Gompers, and the blossoming (if misleading) prosperity of the 1920s. By 1929 (as a result of the Great Depression) millions of workers lost their jobs, and by 1933 union membership was down to less than 3 million workers.

About midway through the 1930s membership began to increase. As part of his New Deal programs, President Roosevelt passed the National Industrial Recovery Act which, among other things, made it easier for labor to organize. Other federal laws (as well as prosperity and World War II) were also contributing factors to the rapid increase in membership from 1935 through the late 1950s. Then membership again began to decline, from about 34% of the labor force in 1955 to about 20% in 1980.[2]

Today, the labor movement is undergoing dramatic changes and has been for more than ten years. At the present time, organized labor's share of the work force in the United States is down to 17% and is still dropping; if this trend persists, by the year 2000 unions will represent only 13% of all nonfarm workers, down from a peak of about 34% in 1955. The union membership proportion is dropping because the number of union members is falling even though total employment is rising.[3]

FIGURE 16.1
Union Membership in the United States

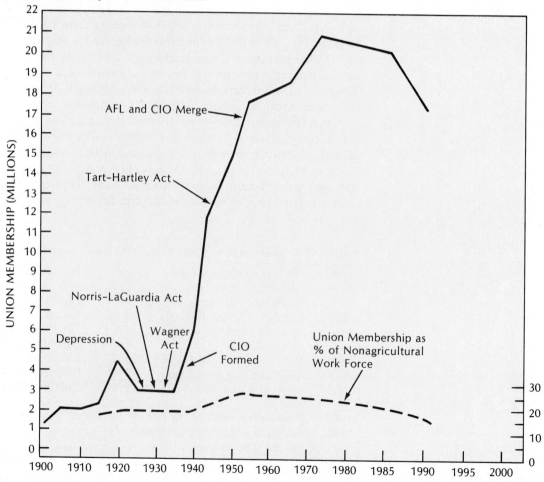

Several things have contributed to this decline. Traditionally, unions have appealed mostly to blue-collar workers, and the proportion of blue-collar jobs has been decreasing as service sector and white-collar service jobs have increased. Furthermore, by 1950 most "easily organized" blue-collar workers in industries such as mining, transportation, and manufacturing had already been unionized. An economic slowdown in the late 1950s further hampered union membership drives.[4]

Several economic factors, including intense international competition, outdated equipment and factories, mismanagement, new technology, and government regulation, have hit those industries that have traditionally been unionized. Other changes, including the deregulation of trucking, airlines, and communications, have helped to erode union membership as well.[5] The effect of all this has been the permanent layoff of hundreds of thousands of union members, the permanent closing of company plants, the relocation of companies to nonunion settings (either in the United States or overseas), and mergers and acquisitions that have eliminated union jobs and impacted collective bargaining agreements (as when former Frank Lorenzo, chairman of Texas Air, took Eastern Airlines into bankruptcy to void its union agreements).

Furthermore, there now exists what *Business Week* refers to as a "growing web of laws and court rulings" that provides the sorts of protection that up to a few years ago only unions could provide.

This web of laws and court rulings is substantial. Foremost on the list are those court decisions (discussed elsewhere in this book) that erode the employment-at-will doctrine and make it more difficult for employers in many states to fire employees without just cause. Increasingly, for instance, courts are deciding that employers can be held to job security assurances that are implied in their employee manuals and that employees can't be fired for disobeying an order that violates public policy (for instance, firing an employee who refuses to commit perjury to protect the employer). On this and many other fronts, employee rights regarding job security, privacy, occupational safety and health, equal employment opportunities, pension vesting, and pay policies are now provided by law. To that extent, the role formerly played by unions has been reduced. Federal and local governments taking on the responsibility for these formerly union roles, the shift from a manufacturing to a service economy, and the increased sophistication of both employers and employees suggest that a fundamental shift will be taking place in the role traditionally played by the labor movement—one that may lead to a reduction in the role unions have traditionally played in influencing the work life of their members.[6]

Unions Reassert Themselves

Needless to say, unions are aware of these trends and are acting to reassert their dominance as employees' representatives. The AFL-CIO has released a study by its Committee on the Evolution of Work titled "The Changing Situation of Workers and Their Unions." The main conclusion of this study was that the country's unions have "fallen behind the pace of change." As a result, the AFL-CIO is undertaking new activities. One is a program to train 1,000 unionists in the fundamentals of how to react (and not react) to the TV camera and how to better explain themselves and the aspirations of the union movement to the general public. Another is a new organizing drive for service workers beginning with the health care industry. At Blue Cross/Blue Shield for instance seven unions are currently working together to organize the separate Blue Cross/Blue Shield companies across the nation.[7] In 1988 the AFL-CIO began its first major TV ad campaign, under the slogan

"America works best when we say union, yes." The ads address such topics as job security, fair treatment, juggling work with family responsibilities, and overcoming favoritism.[8]

During the last ten years or so, the major union effort has been aimed at organizing white-collar workers (service-oriented industries—insurance, banking, retail trade, government—are now being organized by unions, for example). More than 10% of white-collar workers have already become unionized and the number is increasing rapidly, particularly among professionals (many of whom work in the public sector).[9]

Similarly, there has been a trend toward unionization and collective bargaining in the public sector. A major impetus to this was President Kennedy's executive order (E.O.) 10988. This, according to Davey, "gave positive encouragement to collective bargaining as a process" (for federal employees). Before this there had been no bargaining "in the proper sense" by unionized federal employees, who worked instead through devices such as lobbying. E.O. 10988 also stimulated the drive for unionization among employees of state, municipal, and county agencies, and "union growth has been nothing short of spectacular in the period since 1962."[10]

In summary, unions are beginning to regain some lost ground. They are becoming more activist today, for instance in terms of advertising for workers and aggressively pursuing white-collar workers. And beyond that (as we'll see in this and Chapter 17), they are taking other activist steps, including sophisticated "corporate campaigns" aimed at winning over reluctant corporate boards of directors, and using their pension-plan clout to win control of several firms.[11]

◆ WHY DO WORKERS ORGANIZE?

A tremendous amont of time and money has been spent trying to analyze "why workers unionize," and many theories have been proposed. Yet there is no simple answer to the question, partly because each worker probably joins for his or her own unique reasons.

Yet it does seem clear that workers do not unionize just to get more pay or better working conditions. While these *are* important factors, the urge to unionize seems to boil down to the belief on the part of workers that it's only through unity that they can get their fair share of the "pie" and also protect themselves from the arbitrary whims of management. In practice, this usually means that low morale is a main determinant of unionization.

In turn, nonexistent or ineffective two-way communications between management and employees is a major cause of organizing activity and low morale. Fear of job loss is another important concern that can lead to organizing activity. (Yet in reality unions have not been able to protect such job security as evidenced by the huge loss of union jobs in manufacturing industries and airlines).

Research Findings

Several recent studies confirm the fact that low morale is a major reason why workers turn to unions. In one study, the researchers conducted an attitude survey to determine how satisfied employees were with various aspects of their jobs, including supervision, kind of work, and pay. By coincidence, attempts were made several months later to unionize employees in various units of this company. The results of this study showed that employees who were more dissatisfied were more prone to subsequently engage in unionization activity and to unionize. For example, in all cases employees in the units where *no* unionization activity took place were more satisfied than those in the units with unionization activity. An interesting aspect of this study was that (in retrospect) the company found that it had enough information from the attitude survey to have predicted the degree of future union activity in its organization.[12]

Generally, it is often dissatisfaction with basic bread and butter issues that lead to pro union voting, rather than noneconomic issues such as opportunities for achievement on the job (although noneconomic issues are often important as well). The importance of bread and butter issues in union voting is illustrated in Table 16.2, which summarizes the correlation between *job satisfaction* and voting for *union representation* in one study. Notice that dissatisfaction with basic issues such as job security and wages was most strongly correlated with a vote for the union, while the employees' satisfaction with things such as supervisor and type of work were less so.[13] The author of this study contends, by the way, that dissatisfaction alone will not automatically lead to unionization. First, she says *dissatisfied employees must first believe they are without the ability to influence a change in the conditions causing the dissatisfaction.* Then, she adds, a large enough group of employees would have to believe it could improve things through collective action. Dissatisfied employees who believe the union will be instrumental in achieving their goals thus presents a very potent combination.[14]

The bottom line (to repeat) is that the urge to unionize often boils down to the belief on the workers' part that it is only through unity that they can get their fair share of the pie and also protect themselves from the arbitrary whims of management. Here is how one writer describes the reasons behind the early unionization of automobile workers:

> In the years to come, economic issues would make the headlines when union and management met in negotiations. But in the early years the rate of pay was not the major complaint of the autoworker. . . . Specifically, the principal grievances of the autoworkers were the speed-up of production and the lack of any kind of job security. As production tapered off, the order in which workers were laid off was determined largely by the whim of foremen and other supervisors. The system encouraged workers to curry favor by doing personal chores for supervisory employees—by bringing them gifts or outright bribes. The same applied to recalls as production was resumed. The worker had no way of knowing when he would be laid off, and had no assurance when, or whether, he would be recalled. . . . Generally, what the workers revolted against was the lack of human dignity and individuality, and a working relationship that was massively impersonal, cold, and nonhuman. They

TABLE 16.2 Correlation Between Job Satisfaction and Voting for Union Representation

ISSUE	CORRELATION WITH VOTE FOR UNION
Are you satisfied with the job security at this company?	−.42
Are you satisfied with your wages?	−.40
Taking everything into consideration, are you satisfied with this company as a place to work?	−.36
Do supervisors in this company treat all employees alike?	−.34
Are you satisfied with your fringe benefits?	−.31
Do your supervisors show appreciation when you do a good job?	−.30
Do you think there is a good chance for you to get promoted in this company?	−.30
Are you satisfied with the type of work you are doing?	−.14

Source: Adapted from Jeanne M. Brett, "Why Employees Want Unions," *Organizational Dynamics,* Spring 1980, p. 51. © 1980 by AMACOM a division of American Management Associations.

wanted to be treated like human beings—not like faceless clockcard numbers.[15] [See Figure 16.2 for a picture of early auto plant working conditions.][16]

♦ WHAT DO UNIONS WANT?
WHAT ARE THEIR AIMS?

We can generalize by saying that unions have two sets of aims, one for *union security* and one for *improved wages, hours, working conditions,* and *beliefs* for their members.

FIGURE 16.2
Early Auto Plant Working Conditions
Source: Warner Pflug, *The UAW in Pictures* (Detroit: Wayne State University Press, 1971), p. 14.

Note: In addition to the back-breaking work required in the early auto plants, health hazards were an ever-present danger. Lighting was often poor, dust filled the air, and unguarded moving belts led to many injuries.

Union Security

union security A primary aim of unions, union security reflects their desire to establish security for themselves by gaining the right to represent a firm's workers and, where possible, be the exclusive bargaining agent for all employees in the unit. Five types of union security are possible: closed shop, union shop, agency shop, open shop, maintenance of membership arrangement.

First (and probably foremost), unions seek to establish **security** for themselves. They fight hard for the right to represent a firm's workers and to be the *exclusive* bargaining agent for all employees in the unit. (Here, they negotiate contracts for all employees *including* those not members of the union.) In the early days of the union movement, getting such recognition was a difficult task; employers used lawsuits, blacklists, lockouts, armed guards, and spies to fight unionization. Today, federal legislation and a new business environment usually combine to make the union drive less traumatic for all concerned. Five types of union security are possible.

closed shop A form of union security in which the company can hire only union members. This was outlawed in 1947 but still exists in some industries (such as printing).

1. **Closed Shop.**[17] The company can hire only union members. This was outlawed in 1947 but still exists in some industries (such as printing).

2. **Union Shop.** The company *can* hire nonunion people but they must join the union after a prescribed period of time and pay dues. (If not, they can be fired.)

union shop A form of union security in which the company can hire nonunion people but they must join the union after a prescribed period of time and pay dues. (If they do not, they can be fired.)

3. **Agency Shop.** Employees who do not belong to the union still must pay union dues (on the assumption that the union's efforts benefit *all* the workers).

4. **Open Shop.** It is up to the workers whether or not they join the union—those who do not also do not pay dues.

agency shop A form of union security in which employees who do not belong to the union must still pay union dues (on the assumption that union efforts benefit all workers).

5. **Maintenance of Membership Arrangement.** Employees do not have to belong to the union. However, *union members* employed by the firm *must* "maintain membership" in the union for the contract period.

open shop Perhaps the least attractive type of union security from the union's point of view, the workers decide whether or not to join the union, and those who do not do not pay dues.

Improved Wages, Hours, and so on for Members

Once their security is assured, unions fight to better the lot of their members—to improve their wages, hours, and working conditions, for example. And the typical labor agreement still gives the union a role in personnel management activities, including recruiting, selecting, compensating, promoting, training, and discharging employees. The assumption is that this involvement will facilitate the union's attempts to improve their members' job security, pay, and benefits.

maintenance of membership arrangement A form of union security in which employees do not have to belong to the union; however, union members employed by the firm must maintain membership in the union for the contract period.

♦ THE AFL-CIO

What It Is

American Federation of Labor and Congress of Industrial Organizations (AFL-CIO) A voluntary federation of 109 national and international labor unions in the United States formed by the merger of the AFL and CIO in 1955.

The **American Federation of Labor and Congress of Industrial Organizations (AFL-CIO)** is a voluntary federation of about 100 national and international labor unions in the United States. It was formed by the merger of the AFL and CIO in 1955, with AFL's George Meany as its first president, and, for many people, it has become synonymous with the word "union" in America.

There are about 2½ million workers who belong to unions that are not affiliated with the AFL-CIO. Of these workers, about one-half belong to the largest "independent" union, the United Auto Workers (about 1 million members).[18] The formerly independent Teamsters union, with about 2 million members, rejoined the AFL-CIO in October 1987.

The Structure of the AFL-CIO

The organization chart of the AFL-CIO is shown in Figure 16.3. As you can see, it is a federation made up mostly of national unions and members.

As you may also surmise from this figure, there are three layers in the structure of the AFL-CIO (and other American unions). First, there is the

FIGURE 16.3
Organization Chart of AFL-CIO

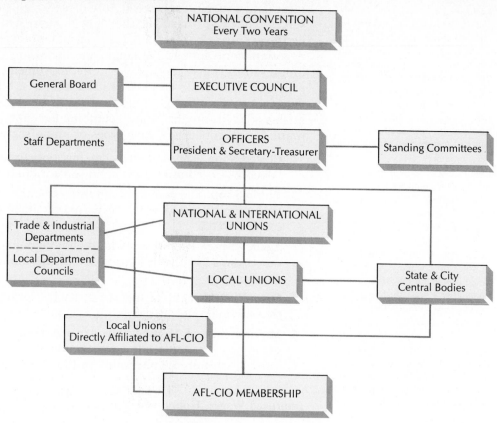

local union. This is the union the worker joins and to which he or she pays dues. And it is usually the local union that signs the collective bargaining agreement determining the wages and working conditions. The local is in turn a single chapter in the *national* union. For example, if you were a type-setter in Detroit, you would belong to the local union there, but the local union is one of hundreds of local chapters of the International Typographical Union, whose headquarters is in Colorado Springs.

Now (getting back to Figure 16.3), the third layer in the structure of unions is the *national federation,* in this case, the AFL-CIO. This federation is comprised of about 100 national (and international) unions, which in turn comprise more than 60,000 local unions.

Once again, most people tend to think of the ALF-CIO as the most important part of the labor movement, but it is not. In fact, the AFL-CIO itself really has little power, except what it is allowed to exercise by its constituent national unions. Thus, the president of the teachers' union wields more power in that capacity than in his capacity as a vice-president of the AFL-CIO. Yet as a practical matter the AFL-CIO does act as a spokesman for labor, and its president, Lane Kirkland, has accumulated a political clout far in excess of some "figurehead" president.

UNIONS AND THE LAW

♦ BACKGROUND

Today, it is almost impossible to read a newspaper and not find some reference to labor law: items referring to the Taft-Hartley Act, the NLRB (National Labor Relations Board), and "unfair labor practices" abound, for instance. And as a manager, you are going to find that a working knowledge of these laws may be a prerequisite to success. Labor laws specify what you can (and cannot) do if your place of work is being unionized, what "unfair labor practices" are, and a multitude of other important points. We will therefore discuss some important labor laws in this section.

Until about 1930 there were no special labor laws. Employers were not required to engage in collective bargaining with employees, and they were virtually unrestrained in their behavior toward unions: The use of spies, blacklists, and the firing of "agitators" were normally condoned (or at least left undisturbed) by judges. "Yellow dog" contracts (whereby management could require *non*union membership as a condition for employment) were widely enforced. And most union weapons—even strikes—were held illegal.

This one-sided situation lasted in America from the Revolution to the Great Depression (around 1930). Since then (in response to changing public attitudes, values, and economic conditions) labor law has gone through three clear changes: from "strong encouragement" of unions, to "modified encouragement coupled with regulation," and finally to "detailed regulation of internal union affairs."[19]

◆ PERIOD OF STRONG ENCOURAGEMENT: THE NORRIS-LAGUARDIA ACT (1932) AND THE WAGNER ACT (1935)

The Norris-LaGuardia and Wagner acts marked a shift in labor law from repression to strong encouragement of union activity.[20] The first of these acts was passed during the Depression. During this time unemployment was rampant, and many policymakers felt that only through bargaining collectively could employees influence their work situations.

Norris-LaGuardia Act This law marked the beginning of the era of strong encouragement of unions and guaranteed to each employee the right to bargain collectively "free from interference, restraint, or coercion."

The **Norris-LaGuardia Act** set the stage for a new era in which union activity was *encouraged*. It guaranteed to each employee the right to bargain collectively "free from interference, restraint, or coercion." It declared yellow dog contracts unenforceable. And it limited the courts' abilities to issue injunctions for activities such as peaceful picketing and payment of strike benefits.

Yet as a practical matter this act did little to restrain employers from fighting labor organizations by whatever means they could muster. Therefore, in 1935 the National Labor Relations (or Wagner) Act was passed; this added "teeth" to the Norris-LaGuardia Act. It did this by (1) banning certain types of *unfair labor practices*, (2) providing for secret ballot elections and majority rule (for determining whether a firm's employees were to unionize), and (3) creating the **National Labor Relations Board (NLRB)** for enforcing these two provisions.

National Labor Relations Board (NLRB) The agency created by the Wagner Act to investigate unfair labor practice charges and provide for secret ballot elections and majority rule in determining whether or not a firm's employees wanted a union.

Wagner Act This law banned certain types of unfair labor practices and provided for secret ballot elections and majority rule for determining whether or not a firm's employees want to unionize.

unfair labor practices Under the Wagner Act, it is unfair for management to "interfere with, restrain, or coerce employees" in exercising their legally sanctioned right of self-organization.

Employer Unfair Labor Practices

The **Wagner Act** deemed "statutory wrongs" (but not crimes) these five employer **unfair labor practices:**

1. It is unfair for managements to "interfere with, restrain, or coerce employees" in exercising their legally sanctioned right of self-organization.

2. It is an unfair practice for company representatives to dominate or interfere with either the formation or the administration of labor unions. Among other management actions found to be unfair under stipulations 1 and 2 are bribery of employees, company spy systems, moving a business to avoid unionization, and blacklisting union sympathizers.

3. Companies are prohibited from discriminating in any way against employees for their legal union activities.

4. Employers are forbidden from discharging or discriminating against employees simply because the latter had filed "unfair practice" charges against the company.

5. Finally, it made it an unfair labor practice for employers to refuse to bargain collectively with their employees' duly chosen representatives.

An unfair labor practice charge is filed (see Figure 16.4) with the National Labor Relations Board. The board then investigates the charge and determines if formal action should be taken. Possible actions (as summarized in Figure 16.5) include dismissal of the complaint, request for an in-

FIGURE 16.4
NLRB Form 501: Filing an Unfair Labor Practice Charge

FORM EXEMPT UNDER
44 U.S.C. 3512

FORM NLRB 501
(2 81)

UNITED STATES OF AMERICA
NATIONAL LABOR RELATIONS BOARD
CHARGE AGAINST EMPLOYER

INSTRUCTIONS: File an original and 4 copies of this charge with NLRB Regional Director for the region in which the alleged unfair labor practice occurred or is occurring.

DO NOT WRITE IN THIS SPACE

CASE NO.   DATE FILED

1. EMPLOYER AGAINST WHOM CHARGE IS BROUGHT

a. NAME OF EMPLOYER

b. NUMBER OF WORKERS EMPLOYED

c. ADDRESS OF ESTABLISHMENT (street and number, city, State, and ZIP code)

d. EMPLOYER REPRESENTATIVE TO CONTACT

e. PHONE NO.

f. TYPE OF ESTABLISHMENT (factory, mine, wholesaler, etc.)

g. IDENTIFY PRINCIPAL PRODUCT OR SERVICE

h. THE ABOVE-NAMED EMPLOYER HAS ENGAGED IN AND IS ENGAGING IN UNFAIR LABOR PRACTICES WITHIN THE MEANING OF SECTION 8(a), SUBSECTIONS (1) AND _____ OF THE NATIONAL LABOR RELATIONS ACT,
(list subsections)
AND THESE UNFAIR LABOR PRACTICES ARE UNFAIR LABOR PRACTICES AFFECTING COMMERCE WITHIN THE MEANING OF THE ACT.

2. BASIS OF THE CHARGE (be specific as to facts, names, addresses, plants involved, dates, places, etc.)

BY THE ABOVE AND OTHER ACTS, THE ABOVE-NAMED EMPLOYER HAS INTERFERED WITH, RESTRAINED, AND COERCED EMPLOYEES IN THE EXERCISE OF THE RIGHTS GUARANTEED IN SECTION 7 OF THE ACT.

3. FULL NAME OF PARTY FILING CHARGE (if labor organization, give full name, including local name and number)

4a. ADDRESS (street and number, city, State, and ZIP code)

4b. TELEPHONE NO.

5. FULL NAME OF NATIONAL OR INTERNATIONAL LABOR ORGANIZATION OF WHICH IT IS AN AFFILIATE OR CONSTITUENT UNIT (to be filled in when charge is filed by a labor organization)

6. DECLARATION

I declare that I have read the above charge and that the statements therein are true to the best of my knowledge and belief.

By _____   _____
(signature of representative or person filing charge)   (title, if any)

Address _____
(telephone number)   (date)

WILLFULLY FALSE STATEMENTS ON THIS CHARGE CAN BE PUNISHED BY FINE AND IMPRISONMENT
(U.S. CODE, TITLE 18, SECTION 1001)

FIGURE 16.5
Possible Actions NLRB Can Take When It Receives Unfair Labor Practice Charge
Source: Bruce Feldacker, *Labor Guide to Labor Law* (Reston, VA.: Reston, 1980).

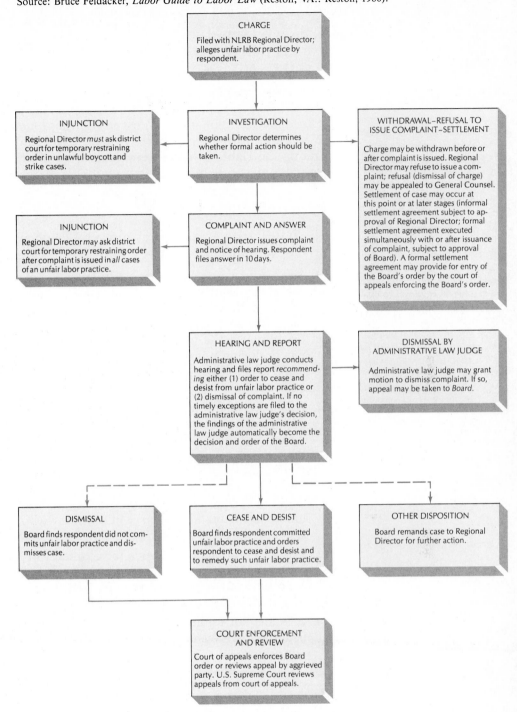

junction against the employer, and an order that the employer cease and desist.

From 1935 to 1947

Union membership increased rapidly after passage of the Wagner Act in 1935. Other factors (such as an improving economy and aggressive union leadership) contributed to this as well. But by the mid-1940s the tide had begun to turn. Largely because of a series of massive postwar strikes, public policy began to shift against what many viewed as the union excesses of the times; the stage was set for passage of the Taft-Hartley Act of 1947.

♦ PERIOD OF MODIFIED ENCOURAGEMENT COUPLED WITH REGULATION: THE TAFT-HARTLEY ACT (1947)

Taft-Hartley Act Also known as the Labor-Management Relations Act, this law prohibited union unfair labor practices and enumerated the rights of employees as union members. It also enumerated the rights of employers and allowed the president of the United States to temporarily bar national emergency strikes.

union unfair labor practices The Taft-Hartley Act banned unions from restraining or coercing employees from exercising their guaranteed bargaining rights; prohibited unions from causing an employer to discriminate in any way against an employee in order to encourage or discourage membership in a union; prohibited a union to refuse to bargain "in good faith" with the employer about wages, hours, and other employment conditions; and prohibited a union from engaging in "feather-bedding."

The **Taft-Hartley** (or Labor-Management Relations) **Act** reflected the public's less enthusiastic attitudes toward unions. Its provisions were aimed at limiting unions in four ways: (1) by prohibiting *union* unfair labor practices, (2) by enumerating the rights of employees as union members, (3) by enumerating the rights of employers, and (4) by allowing the president of the United States to temporarily bar *national emergency* strikes.

Union Unfair Labor Practices

The Taft-Hartley Act enumerated several labor practices that unions were prohibited from engaging in:

1. First, unions were banned from restraining or coercing employees from exercising their guaranteed bargaining rights. For example, some specific actions on the part of unions that the courts have held illegal under this provision include stating to an antiunion employee that he will lose his job once the union gains recognition; issuing patently false statements during union organizing campaigns; making threats of reprisal against employees subpoenaed to testify against the union at NLRB hearings.

2. It is also an unfair labor practice for a union to cause an employer to discriminate in any way against an employee in order to encourage or discourage his membership in a union. In other words, the union cannot try to force an employer to fire a worker because he or she doesn't attend union meetings, opposes union policies, or refuses to join a union. There is one exception to this. Where a closed or union shop prevails (and union membership is therefore a prerequisite to employment), the union may demand discharge of a worker who fails to pay his initiation fees and dues.

3. It is an unfair labor practice for a union to refuse to bargain "in good faith" with the employer about wages, hours, and other employment conditions. Also, certain types of strikes and boycotts are considered union unfair labor practices.

4. It is also an unfair labor practice for a union to engage in "feather-bedding." (Here an employer is required to pay an employee for services not performed.)

Rights of Employees

right-to-work laws Legislation that outlawed labor contracts that made union membership a condition for retaining employment.

The Taft-Hartley Act also protected the rights of *employees* against their unions. For example, many people felt that compulsory unionism violated the basic American right of freedom of association. New **right to work laws** sprang up in 19 states (mainly in the South and Southwest) and outlawed labor contracts that made union membership a condition for retaining employment. In New York, for example, many printing firms have union shops. There, you can't work as a pressman unless you belong to a printers' union. In Florida such union shops—except those covered by the Railway Labor Act—are illegal. There, printing shops typically employ both union and non-union pressmen. This provision also allowed an employee to present grievances directly to the employer (without going through the union) and required the employee's authorization before union dues could be subtracted from his or her paycheck.

Rights of Employers

The Taft-Hartley Act also explicitly gave *employers* certain collective bargaining rights. First, it gave them full freedom to express their views concerning union organization. For example, you can as a manager tell your employees that in your opinion unions are worthless, dangerous to the economy, and immoral. You can even, generally speaking, hint that unionization (and subsequent high-wage demands) might result in the permanent closing of the plant (but not its relocation). Employers can set forth the union's record in regard to violence and corruption (if appropriate) and can play upon the racial prejudices of workers (by describing the union's philosophy toward integration). In fact, your only major restraint is that you must avoid threats, promises, coercion, and direct interference with workers who are trying to reach a decision. There can be no threat of reprisal or force or promise of benefit.[21]

In addition, the employer (1) cannot meet with his or her employees on company time within 24 hours of an election and (2) cannot suggest to employees that they vote against the union *while they are at home or in your office,* although you *can* while they are in their work area or where they normally gather.

National Emergency Strikes

national emergency strikes Strikes that might "imperil the national health and safety."

The Taft-Hartley Act also allows the president of the United States to intervene in the case of **national emergency strikes.** These are strikes (for example, on the part of steel firm employees) that might "imperil the national health and safety." The president may appoint a board of inquiry and, based on their report, apply for an injunction restraining the strike for 60 days. If no settlement is reached during that time, the injunction can be extended for another 20 days. During this last period, employees are polled (in a secret ballot) to ascertain their willingness to accept the employer's last offer.

◆ PERIOD OF DETAILED REGULATION OF INTERNAL UNION AFFAIRS: THE LANDRUM-GRIFFIN ACT (1959)

Landrum-Griffin Act The law aimed at protecting union members from possible wrongdoing on the part of their unions.

In the 1950s, Senate investigations revealed a number of unsavory practices on the part of some unions, and the result was the **Landrum-Griffin Act** (officially, the Labor-Management Reporting and Disclosure Act). An overriding aim of this act was to protect union members from possible wrongdoing on the part of their unions.

Bill of Rights

First, this law contained a "bill of rights" for union members. Among other things, this provided for certain rights in the nomination of candidates for union office. It also affirms a member's right to sue his or her union and ensures that no member can be fined or suspended without due process—which includes a list of specific charges, time to prepare defense, and a fair hearing. It also requires that officers provide copies of the collective bargaining agreement to all union members.

Union Elections

This act also laid out ground rules covering union elections. For example, national (and international) unions must elect officers at least once every five years, using some type of secret ballot mechanism. Also, local unions must elect officers at least every three years, again by secret ballot. The elections must adhere to the union's constitution and bylaws, and every member in good standing is entitled to one vote.

Union Officers

The act also regulates the kind of person who can serve as a union officer. For example, persons convicted of felonies (bribery, murder, grand larceny, and so on) are barred from holding a union position as officer for a period of five years after conviction.

Employer Wrongdoing

The Senate investigating team also discovered some flagrant examples of employer wrongdoing. Union agents had been bribed, and so-called "labor relations consultants" had been used to buy off union officers, for example.

Such bribery had been a federal crime starting with the passage of the Taft-Hartley Act. But the Landrum-Griffin Act greatly expanded the list of unlawful employer actions. For example, companies can no longer make payments to their own employees for the purpose of enticing them into not joining the union. It also requires an extensive list of reports from both unions and employers, covering things such as use of labor relations consultants.

♦ LABOR LAW TODAY

The Labor Law Reform Bill was debated by the Senate of the United States in June 1978, and although it did not pass (and is therefore not law), its proposals help to illustrate some of the ways in which the union movement hopes to bolster its sagging numbers.[22]

From the lobbying that surrounded the debate, it seems apparent that one of organized labor's aims in regard to this bill was to make it more difficult for "antiunion" companies to continue to resist being organized. For example, some companies—such as J. P. Stevens, a textile firm headquartered in the Southeast—had a long history of engaging in protracted litigation in order to resist union organizing efforts. The purpose of this bill, then, was to close some of the loopholes of previous labor laws and to make it more difficult for confrontation-oriented employers to maneuver around existing laws—for example, by making it more difficult for employers to fire workers for union activities and by denying federal contracts to "willful violators of NLRB rulings."

Recent NLRB and Court Decisions

Against the backdrop of such efforts, the question of whether the courts and the NLRB are contributing to a more encouraging or discouraging climate for unions today is not entirely clear cut, although the 1980s on balance were not encouraging years in the courts for unions. On the one hand, some NLRB decisions will probably have the effect of favoring unionization. In one case (known as the *Jean Country* case), a union and a shopping center took their case to the NLRB. The basic question here was whether the union could picket a store (Jean Country) on private property in a shopping mall. Under the old rule (which dated back to 1986), the NLRB would balance the union's right to engage in labor activity with the property owner's right to decide how its property should be used. It would then decide whose rights prevailed in that instance. Technicalities aside, in this case the NLRB basically modified its rule, thus making it easier for unions to show why their rights should prevail.[23]

On the other hand, many important recent court decisions have gone against unions, and these decisions could have the effect of weakening workers' union rights. One problem involves the Taft Act's prohibitions against inhibiting organizing activity. Recall that when originally enacted in 1935, the act was aimed at encouraging collective bargaining and protecting workers' rights to organize. Until recently, workers' rights under Taft have been expanded in many ways. For example, courts found that union employees had the right to have a representative present at disciplinary interviews.[24]

However these Taft Act protections were eroded by court decisions throughout the 1980s. For example, in one decision[25] the NLRB in effect made it more difficult for workers adversely affected by outrageous Taft Act violations to take legal action. It required that they seek administrative redress instead. In another decision,[26] the NLRB held it would no longer evaluate the impact of misleading employer campaign statements upon worker free choice in a representation election.[27]

The Supreme Court's decision on February 28, 1989 in *TWA* v. *Independent Federation of Flight Attendants* is another recent instance of the court's strengthening management's hand. The question here basically involved this: Can lower-seniority current employees who transferred into the jobs of higher-seniority employees who are out on strike keep their new jobs even after the strike ends and the strikers want their jobs back? As early as 1938 the Supreme Court had held that permanent replacements brought in from *outside* the company did not have to give up their jobs when a strike ends. The new TWA ruling extends that principle to workers from *inside* the company as well, since the Court held that these lower-seniority employees did not have to surrender their jobs to the returning strikers. Instead, said the Court, management could leave these lower-seniority employees in their new jobs, as promised. The TWA case arose under the Railway Labor Act, although it is probably applicable to Taft-Hartley cases as well.

This last point is an important one: For the first time, the Supreme Court held that management can announce that it will continue to operate during a strike, "and that employees *in the bargaining unit* who wish to work during the strike will be considered the new permanent holders of any jobs they fill, assuming they want to stay in those jobs."[28] Strikers who want to return to work must wait for an opening to occur, said the Court. This may prove discouraging to union members considering a walkout, given the employer's right to also bring in outside replacements. In summary, the pendulum today seems to have swung a bit more toward "discouragement of union activities."

THE UNION DRIVE AND ELECTION

It is through the union drive and election[29] that a union tries to be recognized to represent employees. This process involves five basic steps: (1) initial contact, (2) authorization cards, (3) hearing, (4) campaign, and (5) the election.

◆ STEP 1. INITIAL CONTACT

During the *initial contact* stage, the union determines the employees' interest in organizing, and an organizing committee is established.

COMPUTER APPLICATIONS IN LABOR RELATIONS:

COMPUTERS ASSIST BOTH LABOR AND MANAGEMENT

Both sides of labor-management relations may benefit from the use of computers. Management may track grievances to see where and on what subjects training is needed. Labor may find that computers provide new ways to assist members.

Management is able to track trends in grievances within any given time period for the whole company, a division or department, or a particular supervisor or group of supervisors. For example, the researcher might hypothesize that supervisors with less than one year of experience in their positions might generate more grievances than experienced supervisors. If this proves to be true, then either new supervisors should be trained before starting in the position or should be offered frequent training sessions during their first year. However, research might prove that in some departments, this hypothesis is not true. Thus, if there are a number of grievances from a large department, an investigation might reveal the need for (1) managerial training, probably defined by the subject of the grievances, (2) better communication on a topic (such as the importance of following safety rules), or (3) the development of a process which allows more input from employees before instituting new policies. Grievance topics may be coded for easy computer tracking. Grievances may incorporate more than one code.

Labor, too, can benefit from computerization. With the demographic changes in the workplace, labor is searching for new ways to meet the needs of its members and potential members. One area of concern which has continued for many years is a concern for job security due to mergers and acquisitions that have cost many employees their jobs. Another is the trend toward service industries and away from manufacturing that has led to a need for knowledgeable workers who are more highly educated. A third is the many low-paying jobs that have been generated by the service industry. When closed shops were legal, the union hall was the place to find a job. This function has now generally been replaced by temporary employment agencies. However, unions could still fulfill this function for the benefit of their members. Not only are there many craft and skill workers who need the kind of expertise offered by unions to adequately find placement, there are many technical and knowledge-based workers who need to keep up to date on skills, equipment, and procedures through both information sharing and hands-on training. Computer-based networks nationwide would help to adjust the unemployment caused by having skills in one location and jobs in another. As Hallett suggests, unions could become "the single best source of information, training, standards, and individuals [with] specific skills and talents."[1] With the support of international unions, locals could be linked effectively and relatively inexpensively (using telephone lines) to provide this source of information, thus assuring their members a degree of job security.

[1]Geffrey J. Hallet, "Unions in Our Future?" *Personnel Administration*, Vol. 31, no. 4 (April 1986), pp. 40–94.

The initiative for the first contact between the employees and the union may come from the employees, from a union already representing other of the firm's employees, or from a union representing workers elsewhere. Sometimes a union effort starts with a disgruntled employee contacting the local union office to learn how to organize his or her place of work. Sometimes, though, the campaign starts when a union decides it wants to expand to representing other employees in the firm or when the company looks like an important or easy target. In either case, there is an initial contact between a union representative and a few employees at their workplace.

Once an employer becomes a target, a union official usually assigns a representative to determine employee interest. The representative visits the firm to find out if enough employees are interested in the union to make a campaign worthwhile. He or she also identifies employees who would make good leaders in an organizing campaign and calls these people together to establish them as an **organizing committee.** The objective here is to "educate the committee about the benefits of forming a union, the law and procedures involved in forming a local union, and the issues management is likely to raise during a campaign."[30]

The union must follow certain guidelines when it begins contacting employees. The law allows union organizers to solicit employees for membership as long as it does not endanger the performance or safety of the employees. Therefore, much of the contact often takes place off the job, for example, at home or at eating places near work. Organizers can also safely contact employees on company grounds during off hours (such as lunch or break time). Under some conditions, union representatives may solicit employees at their work stations, but this is rare. Yet, in practice, there will be much informal organizing going on at the workplace as employees debate the merits of organizing. In any case, this *initial contact* stage may be deceptively quiet. In some instances the first inkling management has of a union campaign is the distribution or posting of a handbill soliciting union membership.

Labor Relations Consultants

Labor relations consultants are increasingly having an impact on the bargaining process, with both management and unions now being supplemented by trained outside advisors. These advisors may be public relations firms, law firms, researchers, psychologists, labor relations specialists, or public relations firms. In any case, their role is to provide advice and related services to both management and unions, not only when a certification vote is anticipated (although this is when most of them are used) but at other times as well. For the employer, the consultant's services may range from ensuring that the firm properly fills out routine forms to managing the whole union campaign. Unions, on the other hand, may use public relations firms to improve their image or specialists to manage corporate campaigns aimed at pressuring corporate shareholders and creditors into influencing top management to agree to a union's demands.

The use by management of consultants who are often referred to disparagingly by unions as "union busters" has apparently grown tremendously over the past 25 years. A study by the AFL-CIO's Department of Organization and Field Services concluded, for example, that management consultants were involved in 85% of the elections they surveyed between July 1982 and March 1983, and that the consultant "ran the show" for the employers 72% of the time.[31] The widespread use of such consultants—only some of whom are actually lawyers—has raised the question of whether these consultants have advised their clients to engage in activities that are illegal under the various labor laws or that at least violate the spirit of these laws. One tactic, for instance, is to delay the union vote with lengthy hearings at the NLRB. The longer the delay in the vote, it is argued, the more time the employer has to drill antiunion propaganda into the employees. During these delays employees who are not antiunion can be eliminated and the bargaining unit can be packed with promanagement employees.[32] Other consultants are accused of advising employers to lie to the NLRB, for example, by backdating memoranda in order to convince the board that the wage increase being offered was decided months before the campaign ever began.[33]

The ethics of the matter aside, any employers using such consultants

organizing committee Employees of a firm, identified by union officials as good prospects, who are established as a committee to be educated about the benefits of forming a union.

PERSONNEL MANAGEMENT:

ON THE FRONT LINE

Last week something happened at one of the Carter stores that upset Jack and Jennifer. As is often the case, one of the workers involved with cleaning and spotting had to be fired because of poor-quality work. The nature of the business is such that employees are continually quitting, being fired, and being rehired somewhere else, and the fact is it is not unusual for a worker in the industry to have worked in all or most of the stores in a geographic area during the period of five or so years. Because job switching is so much a part of the industry, Jack and Jennifer were therefore taken aback when Bob, the man who was fired, reacted almost violently. He threw a bottle of chemicals to the floor, began shouting that Jack was "incompetent, unfair, and unfit to be an employer" and proceeded to warn that he was forthwith driving to the local headquarters of the textile workers union to get them to begin organizing the Carter's firm. Subsequently, several of Carter's store managers reported that employees were talking among themselves much more animatedly during lunch than they usually do and that a man who one manager believes is a local union representative has been meeting with the employees after work as well. Jennifer has several questions:

1. Is it possible that her firm is in the first stages of an organizing campaign? How could she find out for sure?

2. What steps should she take now to determine if such organizing activity is going on?

3. If this firm is being organized, what steps should she take next?

are generally required to report their use. For example, under the Labor-Management Reporting and Disclosure Act of 1959, employers must report "any agreement or arrangement with a labor relations consultant or other independent contractor or organization pursuant to which such person undertakes activities where an object thereof, directly or indirectly, is to persuade employees to exercise or not to exercise, or persuade employees as to the manner of exercising, the right to organize and bargain collectively. . . ."[34] Unions, for their part, may be expected to file complaints such as that presented in Figure 16.6 informing the Labor Department of unreported consultant activities.

◆ STEP 2. OBTAINING AUTHORIZATION CARDS

In order to petition the NLRB for the right to hold an election, the union must show that a sizable number of employees *may* be interested in being organized. The next step is thus for union organizers to try to get the employees to sign **authorization cards;** 30% of the eligible employees in an appropriate bargaining unit must sign before an election can be petitioned.

During this stage, both union and management typically make use of various forms of propaganda. The union claims it can improve working conditions, raise wages, increase benefits, and generally get the workers better deals. Management need not be silent; it can attack the union on ethical and moral grounds and could cite the cost of union membership, for example. Management can also explain its track record, express facts and opinions, and explain the law applicable to organizing campaigns and the meaning of the duty to bargain in good faith (if the union should win the election) to its employees. However, neither side can threaten, bribe, or coerce employees, and an employer may not make promises of benefit to employees or make

authorization cards In order to petition for a union election, the union must show that at least 30% of employees may be interested in being unionized. Employees indicate this interest by signing authorization cards.

FIGURE 16.6
Labor Relations Consultant
Complaint Form
Source: Reproduced in *Labor Relations Consultants: Issues, Trends, and Controversies—A BNA Special Report,* Bureau of National Affairs, 1985, pp. 68–69.

COMPLAINT OF EMPLOYER NON-COMPLIANCE WITH THE REPORTING REQUIREMENTS OF THE LABOR-MANAGEMENT REPORTING AND DISCLOSURE ACT OF 1959*

(See accompanying instructions)

TO: The Honorable Secretary of Labor of the United States:

The undersigned wishes to advise you of the existence of facts indicating that the employer named below has engaged in reportable conduct under Section 203(a) of the Labor Management Reporting and Disclosure Act of 1959 (LMRDA). Accordingly, this will request that you advise the undersigned promptly of whether the named employer has filed the appropriate reports with the United States Department of Labor concerning such activity. If so, please provide a copy of such report(s) to the undersigned with an appropriate billing, if any.**

If no report has been filed by the named employer, the undersigned hereby requests that you conduct an investigation in accordance with your authority under Section 601 of the LMRDA If you determine that a violation exists, or that reporting by the employer will be required in the future, the undersigned requests that you obtain compliance from the employer now or at the appropriate time and that you advise the undersigned accordingly.

A. Employer concerning whom Complaint is being filed:
  1. Name:_____
  2. Street Address:_____
  3. City, State and Zip Code:_____
  4. Type of establishment (factory, hospital, retail store, office, etc.):_____
  5. Principal product or service:_____

B. Consultant, if any, which the employer has engaged to perform reportable conduct:
  1. Name:_____
  2. Street Address:_____
  3. City, State and Zip Code:_____
  4. Type of consultant (individual, attorney, consulting firm, trade association, psychologist, public official, etc.):_____

C. 1. The named employer is required to report under Section 203(a) of the Act because: [Place an "X" in those boxes which apply]

  a. It made an agreement or arrangement with, or a payment to, a "labor relations consultant" or other person or organization for that party to undertake any activity intended to persuade employees about whether or how to exercise their rights to join, form or assist a union and/or to bargain collectively. Specifically, the employer:

  ☐ Hired a labor relations consultant to handle his labor relations, which included activities intended to persuade employees either directly or indirectly about how to exercise their organizing or bargaining rights.

(CONTINUED ON OTHER SIDE)

*ᶜ 1981, Connerton & Bernstein, 1899 L Street, N.W., Suite 800, Washington, D.C. 20036. May be reproduced by any labor organization without permission of the copyright holder.
**I understand that the first 9 reports are free and that the charge thereafter is 10 cents per page. I also understand that most reports do not exceed two or three pages.

unilateral changes in terms and conditions of employment that were not planned to be implemented prior to the onset of union organizing activity.

What Management Can Do

There are also several steps management can take with respect to the authorization cards themselves. The NLRB has ruled that "an employer may lawfully inform employees of their right to revoke their authorization cards, even where employees have not solicited such information," for instance, and the employer can distribute pamphlets such as the one in Figure 16.7, which explains just *how* employees can revoke their cards.[35] However, management can go no further than explaining to employees the procedure for card revocation and furnishing resignation language such as that in Figure 16.7. Any type of *material* assistance—postage and stationery, for example—

FIGURE 16.6
(continued)

☐ Paid a consultant to make a speech or write an advertisement or other material to convince employees not to unionize or to seek decertification.
☐ Paid a consultant to organize anti-union activities or committees among employees.
☐ Other (describe below).

b. It made an agreement or arrangement with, or a payment to, any such party to supply the employer with information about the activities of employees or a union in connection with a labor relations matter involving the employer (other than information for use solely in connection with a legal proceeding, such as an arbitration case, administrative hearing, or court proceeding). Specifically, the employer:

☐ Hired a labor relations consultant to research the union's history or organizational structure and activities for use as propaganda during a union election campaign.
☐ Paid a consultant to obtain copies of other contracts the union has with other companies in order to prepare for collective bargaining.
☐ Other (describe below).

c. It made any expenditure to obtain the type of information referred to in (b) above. Specifically, the employer:

☐ Paid for copies of reports filed with the government by a union which is trying to organize the employer's employees.
☐ Other (described below).

d. It made a payment to an employee (including a supervisor) to persuade other employees about how to exercise their legal rights to organize and bargain collectively without informing all employees about the payments beforehand or at the time they were made. Specifically, the employer:

☐ Secretly paid an employee to convince other employees not to unionize.
☐ Paid a supervisor to convince employees that the union they were joining would do them more harm than good.
☐ Other (describe below).

e. It made an expenditure in connection with the commission of an unfair labor practice. Specifically, the employer:

☐ Paid a supervisor to threaten employees with punishment for their attempts to join a union.
☐ Hired a lawyer or consultant to engage in "surface bargaining," that is, going through the motions of bargaining without really trying to come to an agreement.
☐ Paid for the printing and distribution of any letter or other written matter which makes promises of benefit or threats of reprisal regarding union activities or sympathies.
☐ Other (describe below):

2. Set forth the activities, arrangements and/or expenditures you have marked above. Be specific as to names, dates and places (use additional sheets if needed):

D. Individual or organization submitting complaint:
 1. Name:_____
 2. Street Address:_____
 3. City, State and Zip Code:_____
 4. Telephone Number:_____
 5. If organization, individual to contact:_____

_____
SIGNATURE   **DATE**

is prohibited. The employer also cannot follow up to determine which employees have actually revoked their authorization cards.

What can you do about educating employees who have not yet decided whether to sign their cards? Above all, it is an unfair labor practice to tell employees that they cannot sign a card or to give them the impression that it is against their best interests to do so. What you *can* do, though, is explain the legal and practical consequences of signing or not signing. For example, management *can* prepare its supervisors to be able to explain what the card authorizes the union to do. This is important, because most authorization cards do more than just authorize the union to petition an election. For example, an authorization card such as that in Figure 16.8 actually does three things: It allows the union to seek a representation election (in other words, it can be used as evidence that 30% of your employees have an interest in

In its *White* decision, the NLRB found the following question and answer, included in a pamphlet distributed to employees, to be unobjectionable —

Question: How do I go about getting my union card back from the union?

Answer: Some unions will not return signed authorization cards once they have them. I don't know what Local [name] would do. If an employee wants the card back, a certified letter can be sent to the union and a copy to the NLRB. Whether or not an employee chooses to try to get an authorization card returned is solely that employee's decision. Here are the addresses [of the union and the NLRB] for your information.

In another decision, the Board found no objection to a sample letter management distributed to its employees —

To: Local 294, Hotel, Motel & Restaurant Workers
         [address]

         I hereby request a withdrawal from [the union]. If this request is not granted, I am terminating my union membership, effective immediately.

         Name _____ Membership No._____
         Date _____

Morco, Inc. dba Towne Plaza Hotel, 1981, 258 NLRB No. 16, 1981-82 CCH NLRB ¶ 18, 47B

Note: Sample of acceptable information an employer can give employees to facilitate the latter withdrawing their authorization cards.

organizing), it designates the union as a bargaining representative in all employment matters, and it means the employee has applied for membership in the union and that he or she will be subject to union rules and bylaws. The latter is especially important; the union, for instance, may force the employee to picket and fine any member who does not comply with union instructions. Explaining the serious legal and practical implications of signing the card can thus be an effective management weapon. Finally, do not look through signed authorization cards if confronted with them by union representatives; doing so could be construed as an unfair labor practice by the NLRB, which could view it as spying on those who signed. It could also later form the basis of a charge alleging discrimination due to union activity if someone who signed a card is subsequently disciplined. Examining signed cards could also give rise to a claim that the union should be recognized as the employees' bargaining representative without an election: The union could claim the employer no longer has a good faith doubt that a majority of the employees signed cards authorizing the union to represent them, since it saw the cards.

UNITED GLASS AND CERAMIC WORKERS OF NORTH AMERICA, AFL-CIO, CLC

OFFICIAL MEMBERSHIP APPLICATION AND AUTHORIZATION

I, hereby apply for membership in the United Glass and Ceramic Workers of North America, AFL-CIO, CLC. I hereby designate and authorize the United Glass and Ceramic Workers of North America, AFL-CIO, CLC, as my collective bargaining representative in all matters pertaining to wages, rates of pay and other conditions of employment. I also authorize the United Glass and Ceramic Workers of North America, AFL-CIO, CLC, to request recognition from my employer as my bargaining agent.

SIGNATURE OF APPLICANT _____

EMPLOYED BY _____

APPLICATION RECEIVED BY _____

DATE _____

During this stage, unions can picket the company, subject to three constraints: (1) they must file a petition for an election within 30 days after the start of picketing, (2) the firm cannot already be lawfully recognizing another union, and (3) there cannot already have been a valid NLRB election during the past 12 months.

♦ **STEP 3. HOLD A HEARING**

At this point, one of two things can occur. If the employer chooses *not* to contest union recognition, no hearing is needed and a "consent election" is held immediately. Or your firm could contest the union's right to an election. If the employer chooses not to contest the union's right to an election and/or the scope of the bargaining unit and/or which employees are eligible to vote in the election, no hearing is needed and the parties can stipulate an election. If an employer does wish to contest the union's right, it can insist on a hearing to determine those issues. Thus, an employer's decision about whether to insist on a hearing is a strategic one based upon the facts of each case and whether it feels it needs additional time to develop a campaign to try to persuade a majority of its employees not to elect a union to represent them.

Most companies do contest the union's right to represent their employees, and decline to voluntarily recognize the union, claiming that a significant number of their employees do not really want the union. It is at this point that the National Labor Relations Board gets involved. The NLRB is usually contacted by the union, which submits NLRB Form 502 (Figure 16.9). Based on this, the regional director of the NLRB sends a hearing officer to investigate. The examiner sends both management and union a notice of representation hearing (NLRB Form 852, Figure 16.10). This states the time and place of the hearing.

There are usually two main issues to be investigated in a hearing. First, does the record indicate that there is enough evidence to hold an election? (For example, did 30% or more of the employees in an appropriate bargaining unit sign the authorization cards?) Second, the examiner also must decide what the bargaining unit will be. The latter is an especially crucial matter for the union, for employees, and for the employer. The **bargaining unit** is the group of employees that the union will be authorized to represent and bargain collectively for. If the entire organization is viewed as a bargaining unit, the union will represent all employees. (For example, they might end up representing all professional white-collar and blue-collar employees, although the union is oriented mostly toward blue-collar workers. However, only nonsupervisory, nonmanagerial, and nonconfidential employees may be represented by a union; professional and nonprofessional employees may be included in the same bargaining unit only if the professionals agree to it.) If your firm disagrees with the examiner's decision regarding the bargaining unit, you can challenge the decision; this will require a separate step and NLRB ruling.

There are also other questions to be addressed in the NLRB hearing. These include: "Does the employer qualify for coverage by the NLRB?" "Is the union a labor organization within the meaning of the National Labor Relations Act?" "Do any existing collective bargaining agreements or prior elections bar the union from holding a representation election?"

Finally, if the results of the hearing are favorable for the union, the NLRB will direct that an election be held and will issue a Decision and Direction of Election notice to that effect, and NLRB Form 666 (Figure 16.11) will be sent to the employer to be posted.

bargaining unit The group of employees the union will be authorized to represent.

FIGURE 16.9

NLRB Form 502: Request from Union for Holding an NLRB Hearing

FORM EXEMPT UNDER 44 U S C 3512

UNITED STATES GOVERNMENT
NATIONAL LABOR RELATIONS BOARD
PETITION

DO NOT WRITE IN THIS SPACE	
Case No.	Date Filed

INSTRUCTIONS: Submit an original and 4 copies of this Petition to the NLRB Regional Office in the Region in which the employer concerned is located. If more space is required for any one item, attach additional sheets, numbering item accordingly.

The Petitioner alleges that the following circumstances exist and requests that the National Labor Relations Board proceed under its proper authority pursuant to Section 9 of the National Labor Relations Act.

1. PURPOSE OF THIS PETITION *(If box RC, RM, or RD is checked and a charge under Section 8(b)(7) of the Act has been filed involving the Employer named herein, the statement following the description of the type of petition shall not be deemed made.)* **(Check One)**

☐ **RC-CERTIFICATION OF REPRESENTATIVE** - A substantial number of employees wish to be represented for purposes of collective bargaining by Petitioner and Petitioner desires to be certified as representative of the employees.

☐ **RM-REPRESENTATION (EMPLOYER PETITION)** - One or more individuals or labor organizations have presented a claim to Petitioner to be recognized as the representative of employees of Petitioner.

☐ **RD-DECERTIFICATION** - A substantial number of employees assert that the certified or currently recognized bargaining representative is no longer their representative.

☐ **UD-WITHDRAWAL OF UNION SHOP AUTHORITY** - Thirty percent (30%) or more of employees in a bargaining unit covered by an agreement between their employer and a labor organization desire that such authority be rescinded.

☐ **UC-UNIT CLARIFICATION** - A labor organization is currently recognized by Employer, but Petitioner seeks clarification of placement of certain employees: *(Check one)* ☐ In unit not previously certified.   ☐ In unit previously certified in Case No. _____.

☐ **AC-AMENDMENT OF CERTIFICATION** - Petitioner seeks amendment of certification issued in Case No. _____ *Attach statement describing the specific amendment sought.*

2. Name of Employer	Employer Representative to contact	Telephone Number

3. Address(es) of Establishment(s) involved *(Street and number, city, State, ZIP code)*

4a. Type of Establishment *(Factory, mine, wholesaler, etc.)*	4b. Identify principal product or service

5. Unit Involved *(In UC petition, describe **present** bargaining unit and attach description of proposed clarification.)*	6a. Number of Employees in Unit:
Included	Present
	Proposed *(By UC/AC)*
Excluded	6b. Is this petition supported by 30% or more of the employees in the unit? * ____ Yes ____No *Not applicable in RM, UC, and AC

(If you have checked box RC in 1 above, check and complete EITHER item 7a or 7b, whichever is applicable)

7a. ☐ Request for recognition as Bargaining Representative was made on *(Date)* _____ and Employer declined recognition on or about *(Date)* _____ *(If no reply received, so state).*

7b. ☐ Petitioner is currently recognized as Bargaining Representative and desires certification under the Act.

8. Name of Recognized or Certified Bargaining Agent *(If none, so state)*	Affiliation
Address and Telephone Number	Date of Recognition or Certification

9. Expiration Date of Current Contract, If any *(Month, Day, Year)*	10. If you have checked box UD in 1 above, show here the date of execution of agreement granting union shop *(Month, Day, and Year)*

11a. Is there now a strike or picketing at the Employer's establishment(s) Involved? Yes ____ No ____	11b. If so, approximately how many employees are participating?

11c. The Employer has been picketed by or on behalf of *(Insert Name)* _____, a labor organization, of *(Insert Address)* _____ Since *(Month, Day, Year)* _____

12. Organizations or individuals other than Petitioner *(and other than those named in items 8 and 11c)*, which have claimed recognition as representatives and other organizations and individuals known to have a representative interest in any employees in unit described in item 5 above. *(If none, so state)*

Name	Affilation	Address	Date of Claim *(Required only if Petition is filed by Employer)*

I declare that I have read the above petition and that the statements are true to the best of my knowledge and belief.

_____
(Name of Petitioner and Affilation, if any)

By _____   _____
(Signature of Representative or person filing petition)   *(Title, if any)*

Address _____   _____
(Street and number, city, State, and ZIP Code)   *(Telephone Number)*

WILLFUL FALSE STATEMENTS ON THIS PETITION CAN BE PUNISHED BY FINE AND IMPRISONMENT (U. S. CODE, TITLE 18, SECTION 1001)

◆ STEP 4. THE CAMPAIGN

During the campaign that precedes the election, both the union and the employer make appeals to employees for their votes; the most prevalent union and management campaign issues are summarized in Tables 16.3 and 16.4. The union emphasizes that it will prevent unfairness, set up a grievance/

FIGURE 16.10
NLRB Form 852: Notice of Representation Hearing

FORM NLRB-852
(6-61)

UNITED STATES OF AMERICA

BEFORE THE NATIONAL LABOR RELATIONS BOARD

Case No.

NOTICE OF REPRESENTATION HEARING

The Petitioner, above named, having heretofore filed a Petition pursuant to Section 9 (c) of the National Labor Relations Act, as amended, 29 U.S.C. Sec 151 et seq., copy of which Petition is hereto attached, and it appearing that a question affecting commerce has arisen concerning the representation of employees described by such Petition,

YOU ARE HEREBY NOTIFIED that, pursuant to Section 3(b) and 9(c) of the Act, on the day of   , 19   , at

a hearing will be conducted before a hearing officer of the National Labor Relations Board upon the question of representation affecting commerce which has arisen, at which time and place the parties will have the right to appear in person or otherwise, and give testimony.

Signed at   on the   day of   , 19

Regional Director, Region
National Labor Relations Board

seniority system, and improve unsatisfactory wages. Union strength, they emphasize, will provide employees with a voice in determining wages and working conditions, as well as with other benefits. For its part, management will emphasize that improvements such as those the union promises are not dependent on unionization, and that wages are good or equal to or better than they would be under a union contract. Management will also emphasize the financial cost of union dues; the fact that the union is an "outsider" and that if the union wins, a strike may follow;[36] and can even attack the union on ethical and moral grounds, while insisting that employees will not be as well off and may lose freedom. But neither side can threaten, bribe, or coerce employees.

FIGURE 16.11
NLRB Form 666: Notice to Employees

Form NLRB 666
(7-72)

★NOTICE TO EMPLOYEES

FROM THE

National Labor Relations Board

A PETITION has been filed with this Federal agency seeking an election to determine whether certain employees want to be represented by a union.

The case is being investigated and NO DETERMINATION HAS BEEN MADE AT THIS TIME by the National Labor Relations Board. IF an election is held Notices of Election will be posted giving complete details for voting.

It was suggested that your employer post this notice so the National Labor Relations Board could inform you of your basic rights under the National Labor Relations Act.

YOU HAVE THE RIGHT under Federal Law

- To self-organization
- To form, join, or assist labor organizations
- To bargain collectively through representatives of your own choosing
- To act together for the purposes of collective bargaining or other mutual aid or protection
- To refuse to do any or all of these things unless the union and employer, in a state where such agreements are permitted, enter into a lawful union security clause requiring employees to join the union.

It is possible that some of you will be voting in an employee representation election as a result of the request for an election having been filed. While NO DETERMINATION HAS BEEN MADE AT THIS TIME, in the event an election is held, the NATIONAL LABOR RELATIONS BOARD wants all eligible voters to be familiar with their rights under the law IF it holds an election.

The Board applies rules which are intended to keep its elections fair and honest and which result in a free choice. If agents of either Unions or Employers act in such a way as to interfere with your right to a free election, the election can be set aside by the Board. Where appropriate the Board provides other remedies, such as reinstatement for employees fired for exercising their rights, including backpay from the party responsible for their discharge.

♦ STEP 5. THE ELECTION

Finally the election can be held within 30 to 60 days after the NLRB issues its Decision and Direction of Election. The election is by secret ballot and the NLRB provides the ballots (see Figure 16.12), voting booth and ballot box, and counts the votes and certifies the results of the election.

The union becomes the employees' representative if they win the election, and winning means getting a majority of the votes *cast, not* a majority of the workers in the bargaining unit. (It is also important to keep in mind that where an employer commits an unfair labor practice, a "no union"

FIGURE 16.11
(continued)

NOTE:

The following are examples of conduct which interfere with the rights of employees and may result in the setting aside of the election.

- Threatening loss of jobs or benefits by an Employer or a Union
- Misstating important facts by a Union or an Employer where the other party does not have a fair chance to reply
- Promising or granting promotions, pay raises, or other benefits, to influence an employee's vote by a party capable of carrying out such promises
- An Employer firing employees to discourage or encourage union activity or a Union causing them to be fired to encourage union activity
- Making campaign speeches to assembled groups of employées on company time within the 24-hour period before the election
- Incitement by either an Employer or a Union of racial or religious prejudice by inflammatory appeals
- Threatening physical force or violence to employees by a Union or an Employer to influence their votes

Please be assured that IF AN ELECTION IS HELD every effort will be made to protect your right to a free choice under the law. Improper conduct will not be permitted. All parties are expected to cooperate fully with this agency in maintaining basic principles of a fair election as required by law. The National Labor Relations Board as an agency of the United States Government does not endorse any choice in the election.

NATIONAL LABOR RELATIONS BOARD
an agency of the
UNITED STATES GOVERNMENT

THIS IS AN OFFICIAL GOVERNMENT NOTICE AND MUST NOT BE DEFACED BY ANYONE

TABLE 16.3 Prevalent Union Campaign Issues

ISSUE	PERCENT OF CAMPAIGNS
Union will prevent unfairness, set up grievance procedure/seniority system	82%
Union will improve unsatisfactory wages	79
Union strength will provide employees with voice in wages, working conditions	79
Union, not outsider, bargains for what employees want	73
Union has obtained gains elsewhere	70
Union will improve unsatisfactory sick leave/insurance	64
Dues/initiation fees are reasonable	64
Union will improve unsatisfactory vacations/holidays	61
Union will improve unsatisfactory pensions	61
Employer promises/good treatment may not continue without union	61
Employees choose union leaders	55
Employer will seek to persuade/frighten employees to vote against union	55
No strike without vote	55
Union will improve unsatisfactory working conditions	52
Employees have legal right to engage in union activity	52

Source: Adapted from *Union Representation Elections: Law and Reality,* by Julius G. Getman, Stephen B. Goldberg, and Jeanne B. Herman. Copyright 1976 by Russell Sage Foundation. Reprinted by permission of Basic Books, Inc., Publishers.

TABLE 16.4 Prevalent Management Campaign Issues

ISSUES	PERCENT OF CAMPAIGNS
Improvements not dependent on unionization	85%
Wages good/equal to/better than under union contract	82
Financial costs of union dues outweigh gains	79
Union is outsider	79
Get facts before deciding; employer will provide facts and accept employee decision	76
If union wins, strike may follow	70
Loss of benefits may follow union win	67
Strikers will lose wages; lose more than gain	67
Unions not concerned with employee welfare	67
Strike may lead to loss of jobs	64
Employer has treated employees fairly/well	60
Employees should be certain to vote	54

Source: Adapted from *Union Representation Elections: Law and Reality*, by Julius G. Getman, Stephen B. Goldberg, and Jeanne B. Herman. Copyright 1976 by Russell Sage Foundation. Reprinted by permission of Basic Books, Inc., Publishers.

election may be reversed. As representatives of their employer, supervisors must therefore be very careful not to commit such "unfair" practices.)

♦ HOW TO LOSE AN NLRB ELECTION

Of the 3,600 or so collective bargaining elections held recently, about half were lost by companies.[37] Yet according to a study by the University Research Center many of these elections should probably *not* have been lost. According to expert Matthew Goodfellow, there is no sure way an employer can win an election; however, there are five sure ways an employer could *lose* one.

FIGURE 16.12
Sample NLRB Ballot

UNITED STATES OF AMERICA
National Labor Relations Board
OFFICIAL SECRET BALLOT
FOR CERTAIN EMPLOYEES OF

Do you wish to be represented for purposes of collective bargaining by —

MARK AN "S" IN THE SQUARE OF YOUR CHOICE

YES ☐   NO ☐

DO NOT SIGN THIS BALLOT. Fold and drop in ballot box.
If you spoil this ballot return it to the Board Agent for a new one.

Reason 1. Asleep at the Switch

In 68% of the companies studied (of those that lost to the union) executives were caught unaware, having not paid attention to symptoms of low employee morale. In these companies turnover and absenteeism had increased, productivity was erratic, and safety was poor. Grievance procedures were rarely used. When the first reports of authorization cards being distributed began trickling back to top managers, they usually responded with a knee-jerk reflex action. A barrage of one-way communications ensued in which top management bombarded workers with letters describing how the company was "one big family" and calling for a "team effort."

It is interesting that even once union efforts had begun, management often made no serious effort to ascertain *from the employees themselves* what it was that troubled them enough to force them into the arms of the union. As the researcher points out, "what must be done—even at the last minute—is to uncover the issues that vex employees." Keep in mind, though, that this can be a ticklish business. Knowing *what* questions to ask and *how* (without committing unfair labor practices) and knowing how to work within NLRB rules that inhibit "corrective actions" (such as giving everyone a raise) in the preelection period usually requires specialized training.[38]

Yet the best strategy is to not be caught asleep in the first place:

> Overall, prudence dictates that management spend time and effort even when the atmosphere is calm testing the temperature of employee sentiments and finding ways to remove irritants. Doing that cuts down on the possibility that an election will ever take place, while trying to dissipate discontent during a short campaign is difficult.

In practice, nonunionized employers usually have human resource policies that reduce the sort of dissatisfaction that often precedes a unionization effort. At Diamond Shamrock Corporation, for instance, job security, competitive wages, and a corporate benefits plan that is the same for both white-collar and blue-collar workers have helped make this a large nonunionized firm.[39]

Reason 2. Appointing a Committee

Of the losing companies 36% formed a committee to manage the campaign. According to the expert, there are three fallacies in this:

1. *Promptness* is the essence of the election situation, and committees are notorious for deliberation.
2. Most of the members of such a committee are *neophytes* so far as an NLRB situation is concerned, and their views therefore are mostly reflections of wishful thinking rather than experience.
3. A committee's decision is usually a homogenized decision, with everyone seeking to *compromise* differences. The result is often close to the most conservative opinion—but not necessarily the most knowledgeable or most effective.

This expert suggests, instead, giving full responsibility to a single decisive executive. This person should in turn be assisted by a human resource director and a consultant/advisor with broad experience in labor relations.

Reason 3. Concentrating on Money and Benefits

In 54% of the elections studied the company lost the election because top management concentrated on the "wrong" issues: money and benefits. As this expert puts it:

Employees may want more money, but quite often if they feel the company treats them fairly, decently, and honestly, they are satisfied with reasonable, competitive rates and benefits. It is only when they feel ignored, uncared for, and disregarded that money becomes a major issue to express their dissatisfaction.

Reason 4. Industry Blind Spots

The researcher found that in some industries employees felt more ignored and disregarded than in others. For example, in industries that are highly automated (such as paper manufacturing and automotive), there was some tendency for executives to regard hourly employees as "just cogs in the machinery." This also seemed to be the case among white-collar workers in the insurance industry and in most public utilities. Here (as in reason 3) a solution is to begin paying more serious attention to the needs and attitudes of employees.

Reason 5. Delegating Too Much to Divisions or Branches

For companies with plants scattered around the country, unionization of one or more plants tends to lead to unionization of others. Organizing several of the plants gives the union a "wedge" in the form of a contract that can be used to tempt workers at other plants.

Part of the solution here is to keep our first four "reasons" in mind and thereby keep those first few plants from being organized. Beyond that, firms with multiplant operations should not blindly relegate all decisions concerning personnel and industrial relations to the plant managers. Effectively dealing with unionization—taking the "pulse" of the workers' attitudes, knowing what is bothering them, reacting appropriately when the union first appears, and so on—generally requires strong centralized guidance from the head office and its human resource staff.

♦ THE SUPERVISOR'S ROLE

The extent to which you as a supervisor can help or hinder your employers' attempts to limit union organizing activity depends largely on your knowledge of and training in the rules regarding union organizing. Where you are not thoroughly familiar with what you can and cannot do to legally hamper organizing activities, your effect may be to commit an unfair labor practice and thereby (1) cause a new election to be held after your company has won a previous election or (2) cause your employer to have to forfeit a second election and go directly to contract negotiation. In one case, for example, a plant superintendent reacted to a union's initial organizing attempt by prohibiting distribution of union literature in the plant's lunchroom. Since solicitation of off-duty workers in nonwork areas is generally legal, the company subsequently allowed the union to post union literature on the company's bulletin board and to distribute union literature in nonworking areas inside the plant. However, the NLRB still ruled that the initial act of prohibiting distribution of the literature in the lunchroom was an unfair labor practice, one that was not "made right" by the company's subsequent efforts. In this case, the NLRB used the action of the plant superintendent as one reason for invalidating an election that the company had won.[40] To avoid such problems, employers should do two things: First, they should develop clear rules governing distribution of literature and solicitation of workers. Second, they should train supervisors in how to administer these rules.[41]

Rules Regarding Literature and Solicitation

There are a number of steps an employer can take to legally restrict union organizing activity.[42]

*Non*employees can always be barred from soliciting employees during their work time—that is, when the employee is on duty and not on a break. Thus, if the company cafeteria is open to whomever is on the premises, union organizers *can* solicit off-duty employees who are in the cafeteria but cannot solicit the cafeteria workers (such as cooks) who are not on a break.

Employers can usually stop employees from soliciting other employees for any purpose if one or both employees is on paid-duty time and not on a break.

Most employers (not including retail stores, shopping centers, and certain other employers) can bar nonemployees from the building's interiors and work areas as a right of private property owners. In certain cases, nonemployees can also be barred from exterior private property areas such as parking lots—if there is a business reason (such as safety) and the reason is not just to interfere with union organizers.

Employees can be denied access to interior or exterior areas only if the employer can show that the rule is required for reasons of production, safety, or discipline.

In general, off-duty employees cannot be considered to have the same status as nonemployees and therefore cannot be prohibited from remaining on the premises or returning to the premises unless this prohibition is also required for reasons of production, safety, or discipline.

Finally, note that the above restrictions are only valid provided they are not imposed in a discriminatory manner with respect to union activity while other types of solicitation or distribution of literature *are* permitted at times and places the union activity is prohibited. For example, if employees are permitted to collect money for wedding, shower, and baby gifts; or sell Avon products or Tupperware; or engage in other solicitation during their working time, that employer will not be able to lawfully prohibit them from soliciting for a union during working time because it would discriminate on the basis of union activity, which is an unfair labor practice. The same is true with respect to permitting other kinds of nonwork related literature to be distributed in working areas or during working time.

In summary, two examples of specific rules aimed at limiting union organizing activity are as follows:

Solicitation of employees on company property during working time interferes with the efficient operation of our business. Nonemployees are not permitted to solicit employees on company property for any purpose. Except in break areas where both employees are on break or off the clock, no employee may solicit another employee during working time for any purpose.

Distribution of literature on company property not only creates a litter problem but also distracts us from our work. Nonemployees are not allowed to distribute literature on company property. Except in the performance of his or her job, an employee may not distribute literature unless both the distributor and the recipient are off the clock or on authorized break in a break area or off company premises. Special exceptions to these rules may be made by the company for especially worthwhile causes such as United Way, but written permission must first be obtained and the solicitation will be permitted only during break periods.[43]

The Need for Training

In addition to instituting rules, supervisors should be trained in their enforcement. As one expert puts it:

> Supervisors have a right to prohibit interference with their employer's business activity and to restrict interference with the performance of an employee's job. Employers who have successfully maintained their nonunion status have supervisors who exercise these rights. But to legally dissuade employees from unionizing and to control union activity, supervisors must be trained; they must know the pitfalls and the methods of legitimately implementing their rights.[44]

There are several things to keep in mind when implementing such a training program. First, the overall aim of the program should be to familiarize supervisors with the rules governing organizing activity (as discussed) and, if possible, there should be an emphasis on what the supervisors *can* do, rather than on what they can't do. (Typically in these training sessions, the don'ts far outnumber the do's, and the effect is to inhibit supervisory action.) Training should also be given in advance of a union organizing attempt; once the union has begun its efforts, training is often too late, in that some supervisors have already inadvertently committed unfair labor practices. The training should also provide a practice session in which supervisors can apply the do's and don'ts. For example, they should be exposed to simulations of the kinds of situations they may encounter and be given an opportunity to apply what they have learned; case studies can be useful here. In summary, first-line supervisors can play an important role in limiting union organizing activities. However, to avoid their creating costly legal headaches, they should be properly trained in "preventive labor relations."[45]

♦ **ADDITIONAL GUIDELINES FOR EMPLOYERS WISHING TO STAY UNION FREE**

Several additional guidelines for preserving a union-free workplace include:

1. *Practice preventive employee relations.* Sound discipline policies, open worker-management communications, and fair salaries, wages, and benefits can contribute to preserving a union-free workplace.

2. *Recognize the importance of location.* Unions have traditionally been weaker in the South and Southwest than in the North, Northeast, or Far West, for instance.

3. *Seek early detection.* Again, you should detect union-organizing activity as early as possible, and your best source here is probably your first-line supervisors. These people should be trained to look for changes in employee behavior. In addition, you and your people should also look for direct signs of union activity such as posters, buttons, and authorization cards.

4. *Do not volunteer.* Obviously, never voluntarily recognize a union without a secret election supervised by the NLRB.

5. *Beware the authorization cards.* As explained above, authorization cards must be handled correctly. When confronted by the union submitting authorization cards get another manager in as a witness and do not touch (or, worse, count or examine in any way) the cards. When the organizer leaves, call your lawyer.

6. *Present your case.* Again, present your case to your employees forcefully and relentlessly. Executives' speeches to employees during working hours, informal meetings in the dining areas, and informational letters are all tools you can use.

7. *Postpone the election.* There may be an advantage to you in postponing the election as late as possible. This will give you more time to prepare and communicate your case, and could well wear down the union's resolve and majority.

8. *Pick your time carefully.* Within the guidelines set by the NLRB you should carefully choose the time and date of the election. For example, you may find that employees are in a better frame of mind on Friday than on Monday and that payday affords you an opportunity to get in the final word by stuffing some information in their pay envelopes.[46]

9. *Consider your options.* Finally, consider the option of *not* staying union free. While we have emphasized staying union free, some employers do opt to let the union in. Union membership may make health benefits at group rates available that many employers could not afford; and industry- or association-wide wage agreements can remove the burden of having to negotiate salaries and raises with each of your employees. Too, some unions may be easier to get along with than others, if you have a choice. Therefore, consider your options.

◆ DECERTIFICATION ELECTIONS: WHEN EMPLOYEES WANT TO OUST THEIR UNION

Winning an election and signing an agreement do not necessarily mean that the union is in the company to stay—quite the opposite. The same law that grants employees the right to unionize also provides a way for them to legally terminate their union's right to represent them. The process is known as *decertification*, and it has been exercised increasingly in recent years. From 1973 to 1982 the number of decertification elections increased from 453 to 892, and has since exceeded 600 each year. In 75% of these elections, the employees voted for decertification.[47]

Decertification campaigns do not differ much from certification campaigns (those leading up to the initial election).[48] For its part, the union organizes membership meetings, house-to-house visits, mails literature into the homes, and uses phone calls, NLRB appeals, and, sometimes, threats and harassment to win the election.[49] For its part, managers use meetings—including one-on-one meetings, small-group meetings, and meetings with entire units—as well as legal or expert assistance, letters, and improved working conditions in its attempts to obtain a decertification vote.

Employers are also increasingly turning to what unions refer to as "union-busting" consultants. These consultants (who claim they act as "marriage brokers" between workers and management)[50] provide, among other things, managers and supervisors with detailed advice concerning how to behave during the preelection period.[51] According to at least one account, some of these consultants may even explain how to pay an illegal pay raise in the middle of a union organizing campaign on the assumption that "the probability is that you will never get caught. If you do get caught the worst that can happen is a second election and the union loses 96% of these elections."[52]

On the whole, however, these consultants' strategies seem to be to assist management in improving their communications with the shop floor and in identifying and eliminating the basic pressures that led to the pro-union vote in the first place. Ideally, therefore, this is usually not a last-minute effort. Instead, a promanagement vote on either a certification or decertification election tends to be the result of long-term sensible actions on the part of management, actions which have as their goal winning the trust and confidence of employees:

Decertification cannot be accomplished just at election time. You must earn the confidence of employees over at least a year's period of time, through effective performance evaluation programs, personnel development programs, and overall good communication between employees and management during the contract. Also, through examples at other nonunion operations within the company, employees come to realize they would be better off without a union.[53]

SUMMARY

1. Union membership has been alternately growing and shrinking since as early as 1790. A major milestone was the creation, in 1886, of the American Federation of Labor by Samuel Gompers. Most recently the trend in unionization has been toward organizing white-collar workers, particularly since the proportion of blue-collar workers has been declining. In any case, we saw that while wages and benefits are important factors in unionization, workers are also seeking fair, humane, and equitable treatment.

2. In addition to improved wages and working conditions, unions seek security when organizing. We discussed five possible arrangements, including the closed shop, the union shop, the agency shop, the open shop, and maintenance of membership.

3. The AFL-CIO is a national federation comprised of 109 national (and international) unions. It can exercise only that power it is allowed to exercise by its constituent national unions.

4. During the period of strong encouragement of unions, the Norris-LaGuardia and Wagner acts were passed; these marked a shift in labor law from repression to strong encouragement of union activity. They did this by banning certain types of unfair labor practices, by providing for secret ballot elections, and by creating the National Labor Relations Board.

5. The Taft-Hartley Act reflected the period of modified encouragement coupled with regulation. It enumerated the rights of employees with respect to their unions, enumerated the rights of employers, and allowed the president to temporarily bar national emergency strikes. Among other things, it also enumerated certain union unfair labor practices. For example, it banned unions from restraining or coercing employees from exercising their guaranteed bargaining rights. And employers were explicitly given the right to express their views concerning union organization.

6. The Landrum-Griffin Act reflected the period of detailed regulation of internal union affairs. It grew out of discoveries of wrongdoing on the part of both management and union leadership and contained a "bill of rights" for union members. (For example, it affirms a member's right to sue his or her union.)

7. There are four steps in a union drive and election: the initial contact, obtaining authorization cards, holding a hearing with the NLRB, and the election itself. Remember that the union need only win a majority of the votes *cast*, *not* a majority of the workers in the bargaining unit.

8. There are five surefire ways to lose an NLRB election: Be caught sleeping at the switch, form a committee, emphasize money and benefits, have an industry blind spot, and delegate too much to divisions. Supervisors should be trained regarding how to administer the employer's union literature and solicitation rules.

union security
closed shop
union shop
agency shop
open shop
maintenance of membership arrangement
American Federation of Labor and Congress of Industrial Organizations (AFL-CIO)

Norris-LaGuardia Act
National Labor Relations Board (NLRB)
Wagner Act
unfair labor practices
Taft-Hartley Act
union unfair labor practices

right-to-work laws
national emergency strikes
Landrum-Griffin Act
organizing committee
authorization cards
bargaining unit

DISCUSSION QUESTIONS

1. Explain the structure and purpose of the AFL-CIO.
2. Discuss five sure ways to lose an NLRB election.
3. Describe some important tactics you would expect the union to use during the union drive and election.
4. Briefly explain why "labor law has gone through a cycle of repression and encouragement."
5. Explain in detail each step in a union drive and election.

♦ APPLICATION EXERCISES

♦ CASE INCIDENT 1 · France Rivet Company

The France Rivet Company has no union. Many efforts have been made to organize employees, but no union has asked for recognition as bargaining agent. Whether any or a large proportion of employees may be union members is not known by the employer.

During the past two days, however, pickets representing an international industrial union have appeared before the plant. They carry banners describing the employer as "unfair." The industrial relations director has talked to a half-dozen employees. He asked them if they belonged to a union or if they knew why the plant is being picketed. All answers were negative.

Up to this time, the pickets have been rather ineffective. Few, if any, employees have been prevented from working. Trucks have continued deliveries. Some feeling of tension, however, is apparent; employees obviously dislike crossing the picket line. Customers may also object, although none is known to have avoided the plant on that account.

The industrial relations director, however, is under pressure to get rid of the pickets. Plant officials and managers are afraid they may shut out customers or interfere with both receiving and shipping of materials. Sev-

---

Source: Dale Yoder, *Personnel Management and Industrial Relations,* 6th ed., pp. 480–481. © 1970. Reprinted by permission of Prentice-Hall, Englewood Cliffs, N.J.

eral managers have suggested that the whole procedure is a shakedown—that some union official is getting set to ask for a payoff. Other members of the managerial group think legal action should be taken; they want the industrial relations director to get an injunction. The firm's business is nationwide.

Questions
1. What, in your opinion, should the industrial relations director say or do?
2. Has he handled the matter properly to this point?
3. Prepare a memorandum he might hand to his firm's top managers in which he predicts what are likely to be the significant developments and suggests what action, if any, will be appropriate.

NOTES

1. Parts of this section are based on Paul A. Samuelson, *Economics* (New York: McGraw-Hill, 1967), Chapter 7; Dale Yoder, *Personnel Management and Industrial Relations* (Englewood Cliffs, N.J.: Prentice-Hall, 1970), Chapter 16; Arthur Sloane and Fred Witney, *Labor Relations* (Englewood Cliffs, N.J.: Prentice-Hall, 1977); Leonard Sayles and George Strauss, *Managing Human Resources* (Englewood Cliffs, N.J.: Prentice-Hall, 1977), Chapter 7; Edwin Beal, Edward Wickersham, and Philip Kienast, *The Practice of Collective Bargaining* (Homewood, Ill.: Irwin, 1976), Chapter 2; Gordon Bloom and Herbert Northrup, *Economics of Labor Relations* (Homewood, Ill.: Irwin, 1977), Chapter 2; and Dennis Chamot, "Professional Employees Turn to Unions," *Harvard Business Review*, Vol. 54, no. 3 (May–June 1976). Also see Bernard Bass and Charles Mitchell, "Influences on the Felt Need for Collective Bargaining in Business and Science Professionals," *Journal of Applied Psychology*, Vol. 61, no. 6 (December 1976), pp. 770–772; Harold W. Davey, *Contemporary Collective Bargaining* (Englewood Cliffs, N.J.: Prentice-Hall, 1972), pp. 342–360. In 1988 total union membership (including only dues-paying members) was 17,002,000. Note that in addition to the 17 million, however, an additional 2.2 million employees are represented by unions. The latter work in unionized organizations but do not pay dues although represented by the union: Commerce Clearing House, "Union Membership: 16.8 Percent of the Workforce Belong to Unions in 1988," *Ideas and Trends in Personnel*, February 23, 1989, p. 81.
2. "American Union Busting," *The Economist*, November 19, 1979, pp. 39–50.
3. "Beyond Unions: A Revolution in Employee Rights Is in the Making," *Business Week*, July 8, 1985, p. 72; Bureau of National Affairs, "Union Membership in 1988," *Bulletin to Management*, April 13, 1989.
4. See Robert Schrank, "Are Unions an Anachronism?" *Harvard Business Review*, Vol. 57 (September–October 1979), pp. 107–115.
5. "AFL-CIO Launching New Strategy to Win Over Nonunion Workers," *Compensation and Benefit Review*, Vol. 18, no. 5 (September–October 1986), p. 8; Shane R. Premeaux, R. Wayne Moody, and Art Bethke, "Decertification: Fulfilling Unions' 'Destiny'?" *Personnel Journal*, Vol. 66, no. 6 (June 1987), p. 144; and Peter A. Susser, "The Labor Impact of Deregulation," *Employment Relations Today*, Vol. 13, no. 2 (Summer 1986), pp. 117–123.
6. "Beyond Unions," pp. 72–77.
7. Commerce Clearing House, *Ideas and Trends*, January 10, 1986, p. 7.
8. Commerce Clearing House, "Union Organizing: AFL-CIO Begins Major TV Ad Campaign, Its First Ever," *Ideas and Trends*, June 1, 1988, p. 81.
9. Sar Levitan and Frank Gallo, "Collective Bargaining and Private Sector Employment," *Monthly Labor Review* (September 1989), pp. 24–33.
10. For an excellent overview of current labor-management relations, see the August 1986 issue of *Labor Law Journal*, Vol. 37, no. 8.
11. Dennis Chamot, "Unions Need to Confront the Results of New Technology," *Monthly Labor Review* (August 1987), p. 45. Closely related to unions, *employee associations* of government employees have grown steadily over the past few

years. For a discussion, see Sar Levitan and Frank Gallo, "Can Employee Associations Negotiate New Growth?" *Monthly Labor Review* (July 1989), pp. 5–13.

12. W. Clay Hamner and Frank Schmidt, "Work Attitude as Predictors of Unionization Activity," *Journal of Applied Psychology*, Vol. 63, no. 4 (1978), pp. 415–521. See also Amos Okafor, "White Collar Unionization: Why and What to Do," *Personnel*, Vol. 62, no. 8 (August 1985), pp. 17–20.

13. Jeanne Brett, "Why Employees Want Unions," *Organizational Dynamics* (Spring 1980), and John Fossum, *Labor Relations* (Dallas, Tex.: Business Publications, 1982), p. 4.

14. Clive Fullager and Julian Barling, "A Longitudinal Test of a Model of the Antecedents and Consequences of Union Loyalty," *Journal of Applied Psychology*, Vol. 74, no. 2 (April 1989), pp. 213–227.

15. Warner Pflug, *The UAW in Pictures* (Detroit: Wayne State University Press, 1971), pp. 11–12.

16. See also M. Gordon and others, "Commitment to the Union: Development of a Measure and an Examination of Its Correlates," *Journal of Applied Psychology* (August 1980), pp. 474–499. For an interesting discussion of this see Bert Klandermans, "Perceived Cost and Benefits of Participation in Union Action," *Personnel Psychology*, Vol. 39, no. 2 (Summer 1986), pp. 379–398.

17. These are based on Richard Hodgetts, *Introduction to Business* (Reading, Mass.: Addison-Wesley, 1977), pp. 213–214.

18. "Boardroom Reports," The Conference Board, New York, December 15, 1976, p. 6. See also "Perspectives on Employment," *Research Bulletin #194*, 1986, The Conference Board, 845 Third Avenue, New York, N.Y. 10020.

19. The following material is based on Sloane and Witney, *Labor Relations*, p. 137.

20. Ibid., p. 106.

21. Ibid., p. 121.

22. Quoted from D. Quinn Mills, "Flawed Victory in Labor Law Reform," *Harvard Business Review*, Vol. 57 (May–June 1979), pp. 92–102. The law also proposed to increase the size of the NLRB from five to seven members and to permit the board to speed its process of review of decisions by administrative law judges. See also "Labor's Long Winter May Be Coming to an End," *Business Week*, February 23, 1987, p. 140.

23. Commerce Clearing House. This is based on "NLRB Announces New Rule on When Unions Can Picket Stores in Malls," *Ideas and Trends*, November 2, 1988, pp. 181–184. Jean Country and Brook Shopping Centers, Inc., as nominee for Dollar Land Syndicate (Retail and Wholesale Employees Union, Local 305, AFL-CIO), 291 NLRB No. 4, Sept. 27, 1988. It should be noted that the NLRB held that in balancing the interests involved, it was essential to consider whether those seeking to exercise the right to organize on private property had reasonable alternative means of doing so without trespassing on the owner's property. Previously, the NLRB had held it must sometimes refrain from considering that issue in determining whether such organizational rights could be exercised under a balancing test.

24. This is based on "Taft Act Losing Teeth," a summary of a speech by Professor Charles Craver of the George Washington University National Law Center, in Bureau of National Affairs, *Bulletin to Management*, March 16, 1989, p. 88.

25. Clear Pine Moldings.

26. Midland National Life Insurance Company.

27. Craver, "Taft Losing Teeth," p. 88.

28. Commerce Clearing House, "Supreme Court Ruling Gives Management Greater Power to Fill Jobs During a Strike," *Ideas and Trends*, March 23, 1989, p. 46.

29. See William J. Glueck, "Labor Relations and the Supervisor," in M. Jean Newport, *Supervisory Management: Tools and Techniques* (St. Paul, Minn.: West, 1976), pp. 207–234. See also "Big Labor Tries the Soft Sell," *Business Week*, October 13, 1986, p. 126.

30. William Fulmer, "Step by Step Through a Union Election," *Harvard Business Review*, Vol. 60 (July–August 1981), pp. 94–102.

31. *Labor Relations Consultants: Issues, Trends, Controversies* (Rockville, Md.: Bureau of National Affairs, 1985), p. 7.

32. Ibid., p. 71.

33. Ibid., p. 72.

34. Ibid., p. 62.

35. Commerce Clearing House, "More on Management's Pre-election Campaign Strategy," *Ideas and Trends in Personnel*, August 20, 1982, pp. 158–159.

36. Fulmer, "Step by Step," p. 94. See also "An Employer May Rebut Union Misrepresentations," Bureau of National Affairs, *Bulletin to Management*, January 16, 1986, p. 17.

37. Based on Matthew Goodfellow, "How to Lose an NLRB Election," *Personnel Administrator*, Vol. 23 (September 1976), pp. 40–44. Union win–loss ratio based on "Union Win–Loss Ratio Stable in '88," Bureau of National Affairs, *Bulletin to Management*, April 20, 1989, p. 121.

38. This is one reason why the use of consultants in this area is increasing. See, for example, "American Union Busting," *The Economist*, November 17, 1979, pp. 39–50.

39. Stuart Dien and Kenneth Rose, "Formal Policies and Procedures Can Forestall Unionization," *Personnel Journal*, Vol. 61 (April 1982), pp. 275–277.

40. Frederick Sullivan, "Limiting Union Organizing Activity Through Supervisors," *Personnel*, Vol. 55 (July–August 1978), pp. 55–65.

41. Ibid., p. 60.

42. Ibid., pp. 62–65.

43. Ibid., pp. 64–65. The appropriateness of these sample rules may be affected by factors unique to an employer's operation, and they should therefore be reviewed by the employer's attorney before implementation.

44. Ibid., p. 60.

45. For a discussion, see James Rand, "Preventive-Maintenance Techniques for Staying Union-Free," *Personnel Journal*, Vol. 59 (June 1980), pp. 497–508.

46. Charles Wentz, Jr., "Preserving a Union-Free Workplace," *Personnel* (October 1987), pp. 68–72.

47. Francis T. Coleman, "Once a Union, Not Always a Union," *Personnel Journal*, Vol. 64, no. 3 (March 1985), p. 42. See total article, pp. 42–45, for an excellent discussion of the benefits of decertification for both employers and workers. See also "Decertification: Fulfilling Unions' Destiny?" *Personnel Journal*, Vol. 66 (June 1987), pp. 144–148.

48. William Fulmer, "When Employees Want to Oust Their Union," *Harvard Business Review*, Vol. 56 (March–April 1978), pp. 163–170; Coleman, "Once a Union, Not Always a Union," pp. 42–45. See also "Decertification: Fulfilling Unions' Destiny?" pp. 144–148.

49. Ibid., p. 167.

50. *The Economist*, November 17, 1979, p. 50.

51. See also William Fulmer and Tamara Gilman, "Why Do Workers Vote for Union Decertification?" *Personnel*, Vol. 58 (March–April 1981), pp. 28–35, and Shane Premeaux et al., "Managing Tomorrow's Unionized Workers," *Personnel* (July 1989), pp. 61–64, for a discussion of some important differences (in preferred management styles) between unionized and nonunionized employees.

52. Ibid.

53. Fulmer, "When Employees Want," p. 168. See also "Decertification: Fulfilling Unions' Destiny?" p. 148; and James Thacker et al., "The Factor Structure of Union Commitment: An Application of Confirmatory Factor Analysis," *Journal of Applied Psychology*, Vol. 74, no. 2 (April 1989), pp. 228–232.

Chapter 17

Collective Bargaining, Discipline, and Dismissals

When you finish studying this chapter, you should be able to:

1. Explain how to prepare for union contract negotiations.
2. List at least ten hints on collective bargaining.
3. Define impasse, mediation, and strike.
4. Establish a grievance procedure.
5. Explain how to discipline an employee.
6. Discuss the steps in dismissing an employee.

OVERVIEW

The union drive and election is just the first phase of the union's interaction with your firm. Collective bargaining and contract administration come next. These other two phases—discussed in this chapter—include preparing for negotiations, actually bargaining, and handling grievances. Discipline, a main source of grievances, is also explained in this chapter, as are procedures for dismissing employees.

collective bargaining The process through which representatives of management and the union meet to negotiate a labor agreement.

When (and if) the union is recognized as your employees' representative, a day is set for meeting at the bargaining table. Here representatives of management and the union meet to negotiate a labor agreement. This will contain agreements on specific provisions covering wages, hours, and working conditions.

What exactly is **collective bargaining?** According to the National Labor Relations Act:

> For the purpose of (this act) to *bargain collectively* is the performance of the mutual obligation of the employer and the representative of the employees to meet at reasonable times and confer in good faith with respect to wages, hours, and terms and conditions of employment, or the negotiation of an agreement, or any question arising thereunder, and the execution of a written contract incorporating any agreement reached if requested by either party, but such obligation does not compel either party to agree to a proposal or require the making of a concession.

In plain language, this means that both management and labor are required, under law, to negotiate wages, hours, and terms and conditions of employment "in good faith." In a moment we will see that the *specific* terms that are negotiable (since "wages," "hours," and "conditions of employment" are too broad to be useful in practice) have been clarified by a series of court decisions.

♦ **WHAT IS "GOOD FAITH"?**

good faith bargaining A term that means both parties are communicating and negotiating. Also, that proposals are being matched with counterproposals and that both parties are making every reasonable effort to arrive at agreements. It does not mean that either party is compelled to agree to a proposal.

Bargaining in **good faith** is the cornerstone of effective labor-management relations. It means that both parties communicate and negotiate. It means that proposals are matched with counterproposals and that both parties make every reasonable effort to arrive at an agreement.[1] It does *not* mean that either party is compelled to agree to a proposal. Nor does it *require* that either party make any specific concessions (although as a practical matter, some may be necessary).

When is Bargaining Not "in Good Faith"?

As interpreted by the NLRB and the courts, a violation of the requirement for good faith bargaining may include the following:

1. *Surface bargaining.* This involves merely going through the motions of bargaining, without any real intention of completing a formal agreement.

2. *Concession.* Although not required to make a concession, the courts' and Board's definitions of good faith suggest that a willingness to compromise is an essential ingredient in good faith bargaining.

3. *Proposals and demands.* The NLRB considers the advancement of proposals as a factor in determining overall good faith.

4. *Dilatory tactics.* The law requires that the parties meet and "confer at reasonable times and intervals." Obviously, refusal to meet at all with the union does not satisfy the positive duty imposed on the employer.

5. *Imposing conditions.* Attempts to impose conditions that are so onerous or unreasonable as to indicate bad faith will be scrutinized by the Board.

6. *Unilateral changes in conditions.* This is viewed as a strong indication

that the employer is not bargaining with the required intent of reaching an agreement.

7. *Bypassing the representative.* An employer violates its duty to bargain when it refuses to negotiate with the union representative. The duty of management to bargain in good faith involves, at a minimum, recognition that this *statutory representative* is the one with whom the employer must deal in conducting bargaining negotiations.

8. *Commission of unfair labor practices during negotiations.* Such action may reflect upon the good faith of the guilty party.

9. *Providing information.* Information must be supplied to the union, upon request, to enable it to understand and intelligently discuss the issues raised in bargaining.

10. *Bargaining items.* Refusal to bargain on a "mandatory" item (one *must* bargain over these) or insistence on a "permissive" item (one *may* bargain over these) is usually viewed as bad faith bargaining.[2] (We will present these items following.)

♦ **THE NEGOTIATING TEAM**

Both union and management send a negotiating team to the bargaining table. The management team is usually smaller, consisting of perhaps three or four persons. If the employer is large enough to have a vice-president or director of industrial relations, that person would undoubtedly be on the team. In addition, there might be a line manager and perhaps one or two attorneys from a law firm that specializes in labor law. On the union side will be the local's business agent, as well as several of its officers. Your shop's union steward (local union representative) might attend, as well as a representative of the national union. The latter might be the chief spokesperson for the union; more typically, though, he or she provides expert advice and helps maintain consistency among the local agreements that are reached across the country.

Preparations

Both teams usually go into the bargaining sessions having "done their homework." Union representatives have sounded out union members on their desires and conferred with union representatives of related unions. In large industrial unions (such as the Auto Workers), negotiation objectives are usually set by top national officers.

Management uses a number of techniques and procedures to prepare for bargaining. First, it prepares the data on which to build its bargaining position.[3] Pay and benefit data are compiled and include comparisons to local pay rates and rates paid for similar jobs within the industry. Data on the distribution of your work force (in terms of age, sex, and seniority, for instance) are also important, since these factors determine what you will actually pay out in benefits. Internal economic data regarding cost of benefits, overall earnings levels, and the amount and cost of overtime are important as well. Management will also "cost" the current labor contract and determine the increased cost—total, per employee, and per hour—of the union's demands. Another important step here is to *identify probable union demands.* Here you will use information from grievances and feedback from supervisors to determine ahead of time what the union's demands might be (and thus prepare counteroffers and arguments ahead of time).[4] Attitude surveys (to test the reactions of employees to various sections of the contract that management may feel require change or modification) and informal conferences with local union leaders (to discuss the operational effectiveness of the contract and to send up trial balloons on management ideas for change) are other popular tactics.

THE ACTUAL BARGAINING SESSIONS

◆ BARGAINING ITEMS

voluntary bargaining items Items in collective bargaining, over which bargaining is neither illegal nor mandatory—neither party can be compelled against its wishes to negotiate over these items.

illegal bargaining items Items in collective bargaining that are forbidden by law; for example, the clause agreeing to hire "union members exclusively" would be illegal in a right-to-work state.

mandatory bargaining items Items in collective bargaining that a party must bargain over if they are introduced by the other party—for example, pay.

Labor law sets out categories of items that are subject to bargaining: These are *mandatory, voluntary,* and *illegal* bargaining items.

Voluntary (or permissible) **bargaining items** are neither mandatory nor illegal; they become a part of negotiations only through the joint agreement of both management and union. Neither party can be compelled against its wishes to negotiate over voluntary items. And you cannot hold up signing your contract because the other party refuses to bargain on a voluntary item.

Illegal bargaining items are, of course, forbidden by law. The clause agreeing to hire "union members exclusively" would be illegal in a right-to-work state, for example.

There are about 70 basic items over which bargaining is **mandatory** under the law, and these are presented in Figure 17.1. They include wages, hours, rest periods, layoffs, transfers, benefits, and severance pay. Others are added as the law evolves. For instance, drug testing evolved into a mandatory item as a result of court decisions in the 1980s.[5]

FIGURE 17.1
Mandatory Bargaining Items
Source: Reed C. Richardson, *Collective Bargaining by Objectives: A Positive Approach,* pp. 113–115. © 1977. Reprinted by permission of Prentice-Hall, Inc., Englewood Cliffs, N.J.

Wages
Hours
Discharge
Arbitration
Holidays—paid
Vacations—paid
Duration of agreement
Grievance procedure
Layoff plan
Reinstatement of economic strikers
Change of payment from hourly base to salary base
Union security and checkoff
Work rules
Merit wage increase
Work schedule
Lunch periods
Rest periods
Pension plan
Retirement plan
Bonus payments
Price of meals provided by company
Group insurance—health, accident, life
Promotions
Seniority
Layoffs
Transfers
Work assignments and transfers
No-strike clause
Piece rates
Stock-purchase plan
Workloads
Change of employee status to independent contractor
Management-rights clause
Cancellation of seniority upon relocation of plant
Discounts on company products
Shift differentials
Contract clause providing for supervisors' keeping seniority in unit
Procedures for incoming tax withholding

Severance pay
Nondiscriminatory hiring hall
Plant rules
Safety
Prohibition against supervisor's doing unit work
Superseniority for union stewards
Checkoff
Partial plant closing
Hunting on employer forest reserve where previously granted
Plant closedown and relocation
Change in operations resulting in reclassifying workers from incentive to straight time, or cut work force, or installation of cost-saving machine
Plant closing
Job-posting procedures
Plant reopening
Employee physical examination
Union security
Bargaining over "Bar List"
Truck rentals—minimum rental to be paid by carriers to employee-owned vehicles
Musician price list
Arrangement for negotiation
Change in insurance carrier and benefits
Profit-sharing plan
Motor-carrier—union agreement providing that carriers use own equipment before leasing outside equipment
Overtime pay
Agency shop
Sick leave
Employer's insistence on clause giving arbitrator right to enforce award
Company houses
Subcontracting
Discriminatory racial policies
Production ceiling imposed by union
Most-favored-nation clause
Drug testing

♦ BARGAINING STAGES[6]

Bargaining typically follows several stages of development.[7] *First*, each side presents its demands. (At this stage both parties are usually quite far apart on some issues.) *Second*, there is a reduction of demands. (At this stage each side trades off some of its demands to gain others.) *Third* comes the subcommittee studies: The parties form joint subcommittees to try to work out reasonable alternatives. *Fourth*, an informal settlement is reached and each group goes back to its sponsor: Union representatives check informally with their superiors and the union members; management representatives check with top management. *Finally*, once everything is in order, a formal agreement is fine-tuned and signed.

Some Hints on Bargaining

Reed Richardson has the following advice for bargainers:[8]

1. Be sure you have set *clear objectives* for every bargaining item and you understand on what grounds the objectives are established.
2. *Do not hurry.*
3. When in doubt, *caucus* with your associates.
4. Be *well prepared* with firm data supporting your position.
5. Always strive to keep some *flexibility* in your position. Don't get yourself out on a limb.
6. Don't just concern yourself with what the other party says and does; *find out why.* Remember that economic motivation is not the only explanation for the other party's conduct and actions.
7. Respect the importance of *face saving* for the other party.
8. Constantly be alert to the *real intentions* of the other party with respect not only to goals but also priorities.
9. Be a good *listener.*
10. Build a reputation for being *fair but firm.*
11. Learn to *control your emotions;* don't panic. Use emotions as a tool, not an obstacle.
12. Be sure as you make each bargaining move that you know its *relationship* to all other moves.
13. Measure each move against your *objectives.*
14. Pay close attention to the *wording* of every clause negotiated; words and phrases are often a source of grievances.
15. Remember that collective bargaining negotiations are, by their nature, part of a *compromise* process. There is no such thing as having all the pie.
16. Learn to *understand* people and their personalities.
17. Consider the impact of present negotiations on those in *future years.*

♦ IMPASSES, MEDIATION, AND STRIKES[9]

Impasse Defined

impasse A situation that occurs when the parties aren't able to move further toward settlement, usually because one party is demanding more than the other will offer.

In collective bargaining, an **impasse** occurs when the parties are not able to move further toward settlement. An impasse usually occurs because one party is demanding more than the other will offer; for example, the most the employer will offer is still less than the least the union will accept. Sometimes an impasse can be resolved through a "third party," a disinter-

612   THE LEGAL ENVIRONMENT OF PERSONNEL MANAGEMENT

ested person such as a mediator or arbitrator. If the impasse is not resolved in this way, a work stoppage, or *strike*, may be called by the union to bring pressure to bear on management.

Third-Party Involvement

third-party involvement Interventions by a third party used to overcome an impasse, such as mediation, fact-finding, and arbitration.

mediation Intervention in which a neutral third party tries to assist the principals toward reaching agreement.

Three types of third-party interventions are used to overcome an impasse: mediation, fact-finding, and arbitration. With **mediation** a neutral third party tries to assist the principals toward reaching agreement. The mediator usually holds meetings with each party to determine where each stands regarding their position, and then this information is used to find some common ground for further bargaining. The mediator is always a go-between and as such communicates assessments of the likelihood of a strike, the possible settlement packages available, and the like; he or she does not have the authority to fix a position or make a concession.

fact-finder A neutral party who studies the issues in a dispute and makes a public recommendation of what a reasonable settlement ought to be.

In certain situations (as in cases of a national emergency dispute where the president of the United States determines that it would be a national emergency for a strike to occur), a *fact-finder* may be appointed. A **fact-finder** is a neutral party who studies the issues in a dispute and makes a public recommendation of what a reasonable settlement ought to be.[10] For example, presidential emergency fact-finding boards have successfully resolved impasses in certain critical transportation disputes.

arbitration The most definitive type of third-party intervention, in which the arbitrator usually has the power to determine and dictate the settlement terms.

Arbitration is the most definitive type of third-party intervention, in that the arbitrator often has the power to determine and dictate the settlement terms. Unlike mediation and fact-finding, arbitration can thus guarantee a solution to an impasse. With binding arbitration, both parties are committed to accepting the arbitrator's award. With nonbinding, they are not. Arbitration may also be voluntary or compulsory (in other words, imposed by a government agency). In the United States, voluntary binding arbitration is the most prevalent.

Strikes

strike Refusal by employees to work until their demands are met by the employer.

economic strike A strike that results from a failure to agree on the terms of a contract.

unfair labor practice strike A strike aimed at protesting illegal conduct by the employer.

wildcat strike An unauthorized strike occurring during the term of a contract.

sympathy strike A strike that takes place when one union strikes in support of the strike of another.

There are four main types of **strikes.** An **economic strike** results from a failure to agree on the terms of a contract—from an impasse, in other words. **Unfair labor practice strikes,** on the other hand, are aimed at protesting illegal conduct by the employer. A **wildcat strike** is an unauthorized strike occurring during the term of a contract. A **sympathy strike** occurs when one union strikes in support of the strike of another.[11] Picketing is one of the first activities occurring during a strike. The purpose of picketing is to inform the public about the existence of the labor dispute and (often) to encourage others to refrain from doing business with the struck employer.

Employers can make several responses when they become the object of a strike. One is to *shut down* the affected area and thus halt their operations until the strike is over. A second alternative is to *contract out* work during the duration of the strike in order to blunt the effects of the strike on the employer. A third alternative is for the employer to *continue operations*, perhaps using supervisors and other nonstriking workers to fill in for the striking workers. (FAA administrators and supervisors were brought in to replace striking air controllers several years ago, for instance.) A fourth alternative is the hiring of replacements for the strikers. In an economic strike, such replacements can be deemed "permanent" and would not have to be let go to make room for strikers who decided to return to work. If the strike was an unfair labor practice strike, the strikers would be entitled to return to their jobs upon making an unconditional offer to do so.

Preparing for the Strike

When a strike is imminent, you'll have to make plans to deal with it. For example, two experts say that when a strike is imminent or already under way, following these guidelines can minimize confusion.[12]

- Pay all striking employees what they are owed on the first day of the strike.
- Secure the facility. Supervisors should be on the alert for strangers on the property and access should be controlled. The company should consider hiring guards to protect replacements coming to and from work, and to watch and control the picketers, if necessary.
- Notify all customers. You may decide not to notify customers but to respond to inquiries only. A standard official response to all customers should be prepared and should be merely informative.
- Contact all suppliers and other persons with whom you do business who will have to cross the picket line. Establish alternative methods of obtaining supplies.
- Make arrangements for overnight stays in the facility and for delivered meals, in case the occasion warrants such action.
- Notify the local unemployment office of your need for replacement workers.
- Photograph the facility before, during, and after picketing. If necessary, install videotape equipment and a long-distance microphone to monitor picket line misconduct.
- Record any and all facts concerning strikers' demeanor and activities and such incidents as violence, threats, mass pickets, property damage, or problems. Record police response to request for assistance.
- Gather the following evidence: number of pickets and their names; time, date, and location of picketing; wording on every sign carried by pickets; and descriptions of picket cars and license numbers.

Other Alternatives

boycotts The combined refusal by employees and other interested parties to buy or use the employer's products.

Management and labor each have one other weapon in their arsenal to try to break an impasse and achieve their aims. Unions sometimes try to organize **boycotts,** with the aim of pressuring the employer into making concessions. In fact, some unions are now hiring "boycott consultants" to organize the "corporate campaigns" that put pressure on related firms—such as banks that hold the employer's main loans. In this way the union hopes to pressure the employer and its owners into agreeing to its terms.

lockout A refusal by the employer to provide opportunities to work.

For its part, employers can try to break an impasse with the use of a *lockout.* A **lockout** is a refusal by the employer to provide opportunities to work; in other words, the employees are (sometimes literally) locked out and prohibited from doing their jobs (and thus getting paid).

A lockout is not generally viewed as an unfair labor practice by the NLRB. For example, if your product is a perishable one (such as vegetables), then a lockout may be a legitimate tactic to neutralize or decrease union power. A lockout is only viewed as an unfair labor practice by the NLRB when the employer acts for a prohibited purpose. It is not a prohibited purpose to try to bring about a settlement of negotiations on favorable terms to the employer. Lockouts today are not generally used, though; employers are usually reluctant to cease operations when employees are willing to continue working (even though there may be an impasse at the bargaining table).[13] However, in 1989, baseball players went on strike, and the owners threatened a lockout; the players then returned to work.

♦ THE AGREEMENT ITSELF

The actual agreement may be 20 or 30 pages, or more than 100. It may contain just general declarations of policy or a detailed specification of rules and procedures. The tendency today is toward the longer, more detailed contract. This is largely a result of the increased number of items the agreements have been covering.

The main sections of a typical contract cover subjects such as these:

1. Management rights
2. Union security and dues checkoff
3. Grievance procedures
4. Arbitration of grievances
5. Disciplinary procedures
6. Compensation rates
7. Hours of work and overtime
8. Benefits: vacations, holidays, insurance, pensions
9. Health and safety provisions
10. Employee security-seniority provisions
11. Contract expiration date

But this list just shows the main categories of subjects. The Bureau of National Affairs in Washington has published a "contract clause finder" which you can use as a checklist to guide your discussions during bargaining.

♦ CHANGES TO EXPECT AFTER BEING UNIONIZED

It goes without saying that unionization of your employees will have profound effects on you and your organization. Professor Dale Beach says there are five basic areas in which the union's impact will be felt:[14] It will restrict management's freedom of action, it will result in union pressure for uniformity of treatment of all employees, it will require improved human resources policies and practices, it will require one spokesperson to be used for the employees, and it will lead to centralization of labor relations decision making.

Perhaps the most obvious impact of the union is that it restricts management's freedom of action. Decisions such as who gets laid off when business is slow, who gets to work overtime, and who gets a raise will now be subject to challenge by the union, for example.

Partly because of the prospect of such challenges (and partly because the union contract contains written provisions regarding pay, benefits, promotion, and the like), unionization also leads to a systematizing, centralizing, and sophistication of the employer's human resources policies, procedures, and rules. With unionization, for instance, your employer might take steps to (1) advise all plant managers that union-related questions should be referred to the headquarters' labor relations specialist; (2) formulate a compensation plan and particularly a system of wage classes; and (3) develop an improved, more objective procedure for appraising employee performance, so that union challenges are more easily defended against.

♦ THE IMPORTANT ROLE
OF CONTRACT ADMINISTRATION

Hammering out a labor agreement is not the last step in collective bargaining; in some respects, it is just the beginning. No labor contract can ever be so complete that it covers all contingencies and answers all questions. For example, suppose the contract says you can only discharge an employee for "just cause." You subsequently discharge someone for speaking back to you in harsh terms. Was it within your rights to discharge this person? Was speaking back to you harshly "just cause"?

Problems like this are usually handled and settled through the **grievance procedure** of the labor contract. This procedure provides an orderly system whereby employer and union determine whether or not the contract has been violated:[15] it is the vehicle for administering the contract on a day-to-day basis. Through this grievance process various clauses are interpreted and given meaning and the contract is transformed into a "living organism." (Remember, though, that this **day-to-day collective bargaining** involves *interpretation* only; it usually does *not* involve negotiating new terms or altering existing ones.)[16]

grievance Any factor involving wages, hours, or conditions of employment that is used as a complaint against the employer.

grievance procedure An orderly system whereby employer and union determine whether or not the contract has been violated.

day-to-day collective bargaining The process of grievance resolution through which the collective bargaining agreement's clauses are interpreted (but *not* renegotiated).

♦ WHAT ARE THE SOURCES OF GRIEVANCES?

From a practical point of view it is probably easier to list those items that *don't* precipitate grievances than to list the ones that do. Just about any factor involving wages, hours, or conditions of employment has and will be used as the basis of a grievance.

However, some grievances are more serious than others since they are usually more difficult to settle. Discipline cases (discussed below) and seniority problems (including promotions, transfers, and layoffs) would top this list. Others would include grievances growing out of job evaluation and work assignments, overtime, vacations, incentive plans, and holidays.[17] Here are five actual examples of grievances as presented by Reed Richardson:[18]

Absenteeism. An employer fired an employee for excessive absences. The employee filed a grievance stating that there had been no previous warnings or discipline related to excessive absences.

Insubordination. An employee on two occasions refused to obey a supervisor's order to meet with him unless a union representative was present at the meeting. As a result, the employee was discharged and subsequently filed a grievance protesting discharge.

Overtime. Sunday overtime work was discontinued after a department was split. Employees affected filed a grievance protesting loss of the overtime work.

Plant rules. The plant had a posted rule barring employees from eating or drinking during unscheduled breaks. The employees filed a grievance claiming the rule was arbitrary.

Seniority. A junior employee was hired to fill the position of a laid-off senior employee. The senior employee filed a grievance protesting the action.

Always Ask: What Is the Real Problem?

It is important to remember that a grievance is often just a symptom of an underlying problem. For example, an employee's concern for his or her security may prompt a grievance over a transfer, work assignment, or promotion. Sometimes bad relations between supervisors and subordinates are to blame: This is often the cause of grievances over "fair treatment," for example. Organizational factors such as automated jobs or ambiguous job descriptions that frustrate or aggravate employees are other potential causes of grievances. Union activism is another cause; for example, the union may solicit grievances from workers to underscore ineffective supervision. Problem employees are yet another cause of grievances. These are individuals, who, by their nature, are negative, dissatisfied, and grievance prone.[19] *Disciplinary measures*—a major source of grievances—and *dismissal*—a frequent result of disciplinary measures—are explained later in this chapter.

♦ **THE GRIEVANCE PROCEDURE**

Most collective bargaining contracts contain a carefully worded grievance procedure. This specifies the various steps in the procedure, time limits associated with each step, and specific rules such as "all charges of contract violation must be reduced to writing."

Grievance procedures differ from company to company. Some contain simple two-step procedures. Here the grievant, union representative, and company representative first meet to discuss the grievance. If a satisfactory solution is not found, the grievance is then brought before an independent "third-person" arbitrator, who hears the case, writes it up, and makes a decision.

At the other extreme, the grievance procedure may contain six or more steps. The first step might be for the grievant and shop steward to meet informally with the grievant's supervisor and try to find a solution. If one is not found, a formal grievance is filed and a meeting scheduled among the employee, shop steward, and the supervisor's boss. The next steps involve meetings between higher and higher echelon managers. Finally, if top management and the union cannot reach agreement, the grievance may have to go to arbitration.

An Example of What to Expect

Professors Arthur Sloane and Fred Witney say that the best way to demonstrate the working of a grievance procedure is through an example. They present the following as an actual situation that typifies the grievance process in industry.[20]

Background

Tom Swift, a rank and file member of Local 1000, was employed by the XYZ Manufacturing Company for a period of five years. His production record was excellent, he caused management no trouble, and during his fourth year of employment received a promotion. One day Swift began preparations to leave the plant 20 minutes before quitting time. He put away his tools, washed up, got out of his overalls, and put on his street clothes. Jackson, an assistant supervisor in his department, observed Swift's actions. He immediately informed Swift that he was going to the "front office" to recommend his discharge. The next morning Swift reported for work, but Jackson handed Swift a pay envelope. In addition to wages, it included a discharge notice. The notice declared that the company discharged Swift because he had made ready to leave the plant 20 minutes before quitting time. Swift immediately contacted his union steward, Sue Thomas. Swift told Thomas the circumstances, and the steward believed that the discharge constituted a violation of the collective bargaining contract. A clause in the agreement provided that an employee could be discharged only for "just cause." Disagreeing with the assistant foreman and the "front office," shop steward Thomas felt that the discharge was *not* for just cause.

Step 1: The steps in processing the complaint through the grievance procedure were clearly outlined in the collective bargaining agreement. First, it was necessary to present the grievance to the supervisor of the department in which Swift worked. Both Thomas and Swift approached the supervisor, and the written grievance was presented to him. The supervisor was required to give his answer on the grievance within 48 hours after receiving it. He complied with the time requirements, but his answer did not please Swift or Thomas. The supervisor supported the action of the assistant supervisor and refused to recommend the reinstatement of Swift.

Step 2: Not satisfied with the action of the foreman, the labor union (through Thomas the steward) initiated the second step of the grievance procedure. This step required the appeal of the complaint to the superintendent of the department in which Swift worked. The superintendent supported the decisions of his supervisor and assistant supervisor. Despite the efforts of the steward (who vigorously argued the merits of Swift's case), the department superintendent refused to reinstate the worker. Hence the second step of the grievance procedure was exhausted, and the union and the employee were still not satisfied with the results. (Keep in mind that the vast majority of grievances *are* usually settled in these first two steps of the grievance procedure.)

Step 3: Accordingly, the union went to the third step of the grievance procedure. Grievance personnel for the third step included the general superintendent and his representative from the company, and the labor union was represented by the organization's plantwide grievance committee. The results of the negotiation at this third step proved satisfactory to Swift, the union, and the company. After 45 minutes of spirited discussion, the management group agreed with the union that discharge was not warranted in this particular case. (Management's committee, by the way, was persuaded by the following set of circumstances. Everyone conceded that Swift had an outstanding record before the dismissal occurred. In addition, the discussion revealed that Swift had asked the department supervisor whether there was any more work to be done before he left his bench to prepare to leave for home. The supervisor had replied in the negative. Finally, it was brought out that Swift had had a pressing problem at home which he claimed was the motivating factor in his desire to prepare to leave early.) It was concluded that Swift would be reinstated in his job but would be penalized by a three-day suspension without pay.

Step 4: What would have occurred if the company and the labor union had *not* reached a satisfactory agreement at the third step of the grievance procedure? In this particular contract, the grievance procedure provided for a fourth step. Grievance procedure personnel at the fourth step included (for the company) the vice-president in charge of industrial relations or his representative and (for the union) an officer of the international union or his representative.[21] In most agreements, a final step would require taking the grievance outside the company to arbitration (the arbitrators' decision generally cannot be appealed to the courts except in discrimination cases).

♦ **GRIEVANCE HANDLING IN NONUNION ORGANIZATIONS**

Virtually every labor agreement signed today contains a grievance procedure clause, but the fact is that *non*unionized employers need such procedures as well. As you can see from the preceding example, a grievance procedure helps to ensure that every employee is treated fairly and equitably, and unionized firms should not hold a monopoly in fair treatment.[22] So even where a firm has *not* been unionized, adhering to a formal grievance procedure can help ensure that morale and productivity remain high and that labor-management peace prevails.[23]

Many nonunionized companies do offer grievance procedures.[24] In one study, 24 out of 41 companies responding reported they had grievance procedures for nonunionized employees. In 10 of these firms the grievance procedure covers all employees (including executives), while in most of the others the procedures were reserved for rank and file workers and (in some firms) first-line supervisors. Another survey indicated that two-thirds of the 62 nonunion respondents had grievance policies. Several of these use either an open-door policy or a step procedure with arbitration, while most use both an open-door policy and a step procedure with arbitration.[25] Using juries of peers, ombudsmen, and outside arbitrators are other alternatives that have been used successfully.[26] An example of a typical grievance procedure, one developed for a nonunionized hospital in Maryland, can be summarized as follows:

Step 1.

Discuss the problem or dissatisfaction with your supervisor who will attempt to resolve it in accordance with established hospital human resources policies within two working days, unless there are extenuating circumstances.

Step 2.

Should the problem remain unsolved, your supervisor will endeavor to make an appointment for you to discuss the matter with your department head within the next three working days.

Step 3.

Should the problem continue to remain unsolved, the employee should present the problem or dissatisfaction in writing (a form is available) and forward it to the director of employee relations, who will either schedule a meeting with all interested parties or will present a recommendation within five working days for a resolution of the problem based on hospital personnel policies and practices.

Step 4.

Most matters of employee concern should be resolved at the conclusion of step 3. However, for that unusual problem that may not have been resolved to the employee's satisfaction, the employee may request that the matter be brought to the attention of administration for consideration and decision. An administrative decision will be rendered and communicated in writing to all interested parties within ten working days. This decision will be final and binding.[27]

In most nonunion firms' grievance procedures, the employers' top executives were the "court of last resort," although occasionally the last person a grievant could appeal to was the personnel or industrial relations manager. At least one expert has suggested, though, that legislation be passed that gives even nonunionized workers the right to an appeals process and, if necessary, to binding arbitration by an outside arbitrator.[28]

PERSONNEL MANAGEMENT:

ON THE FRONT LINE

Being in the laundry and cleaning business, the Carters have always felt strongly about not allowing employees to smoke, eat, or drink in their stores. Jennifer was therefore surprised to walk into a store and find two employees eating lunch at the front counter. There was a large pizza in its box, and the two of them were sipping colas and eating slices of pizza and submarine sandwiches off paper plates. Not only did it look messy, but there were also grease and soda spills on the counter and the store smelled from onions and pepperoni, even with the four-foot-wide exhaust fan pulling air out through the roof. In addition to being a turnoff to customers, the mess on the counter increased the possibility that a customer's order might actually become soiled in the store.

While this was a serious matter, neither Jennifer nor her father felt that what the counter people were doing was grounds for immediate dismissal, partly because the store manager had apparently condoned their actions. The problem was they didn't know what to do. It seemed to them that the matter called for more than just a warning, but less than dismissal. Jennifer had these questions:

1. Should a disciplinary system be established at Carter's Cleaning Centers?

2. If so, what should it cover, and how would you suggest they deal with the errant counter people?

◆ GUIDELINES FOR HANDLING GRIEVANCES

Developing the Proper Environment

The best way to "handle" a grievance is to develop a work environment in which grievances don't occur in the first place.[29] Because of this, *constructive grievance handling* depends first on your ability to recognize, diagnose, and correct the causes of potential employee dissatisfaction (causes such as unfair appraisals, inequitable wages, or poor communications) *before* they become formal grievances.

Some Guidelines: Do's and Don'ts[30]

As a manager, your behavior in handling grievances is very important. You are on the "firing line" and must therefore steer a course between fair treatment of employees and maintaining the rights and prerogatives of management. As you might imagine, this is often not an easy course to steer. Walter Baer has developed a list of do's and don'ts that you will find useful guides in handling grievances.[31] Some of the most critical ones are presented next:

DO

Investigate and handle each and every case as though it may eventually result in an arbitration hearing.

Talk with the employee about his or her grievance; give the person a good and full hearing.

Require the union to identify specific contractual provisions allegedly violated.

Comply with the contractual time limits of the company for handling the grievance.

Visit the work area of the grievance.

Determine if there were any witnesses.

Examine the grievant's personnel record.

Fully examine prior grievance records.

Treat the union representative as your equal.

Hold your grievance discussions privately.

Fully inform your own supervisor of grievance matters.

DON'T

Discuss the case with the union steward alone—the grievant should definitely be there.

Make arrangements with individuals that are inconsistent with the labor agreement.

Hold back the remedy if the company is wrong.

Admit to the binding effect of a past practice.

Relinquish your rights as a manager to the union.

Settle grievances on the basis of what is "fair." Instead, stick to the labor agreement, which after all should be your standard.

Bargain over items not covered by the contract.

Treat as arbitrable claims demanding the discipline or discharge of managers.

Give long written grievance answers.

Trade a grievance settlement for a grievance withdrawal (or try to make up for a bad decision in one grievance by bending over backward in another).

Deny grievances on the premise that "your hands have been tied by management."

Agree to informal amendments in the contract.

♦ GRIEVANTS' LEGAL RECOURSE

One effect of the Labor Management Relations Act of 1947 (the Taft-Hartley Act) was to bring under a single body of federal law most matters concerning union contracts and related industrial disputes.[32] One implication was that unionized employees generally (but not always) had to take their grievance complaint through their union contract's grievance and arbitration procedure rather than sue their employer. The only gray area involved the question of "preemption." Specifically, did federal or state law apply if, for example, an employee was fired in violation of state law? For example, if an employee is fired for reporting illegal activities and the law in his state protects whistle blowers, must he adhere to his contract's grievance procedures in protesting his firing, or can he simply sue in state court? (*Non-unionized* employees' rights to sue under such conditions were never in doubt.)

In 1988, the U.S. Supreme Court in *Lingle* v. *Norge Division of Magic Chef, Inc.* unanimously ruled that union members with grievances can sue their employers if certain conditions are met. The suit must concern a violation of state law. And resolving the case must be "independent" of the union contract: "Resolution of the state law claim (must) not require construing the collective bargaining agreement" the court wrote. In the *Lingle* case, for example, the employee was allegedly terminated for lying on her workers' compensation claim. Her position was that her claim was consistent with her doctor's diagnosis and that her firing violated state workers' compensation laws. The details of resolving this dispute did not require looking at and interpreting the union contract, the Court said.

Implications for Management

The main implication of *Lingle* is that unionized employers must now be more wary about violating state law with respect to their employees. For example, if you fire a union member for reporting occupational safety hazards in a state where such terminations are illegal, there is a good chance you'll now have more than a grievance to contend with. In all likelihood, the union (being relatively sophisticated in these matters) may well refer the facts to its attorneys, who may opt to file a lawsuit rather than recommend a grievance be filed. (It is possible, but not as likely, that a *non*union employee would have the information and resources to undertake such a lawsuit.)

DISCIPLINE AND DISMISSAL IN UNION AND NONUNION ORGANIZATIONS

♦ INTRODUCTION: WHY DISCIPLINE

Few actions an employer takes are as sure to trigger grievances as are disciplining an employee or (if the misbehavior continues) *dismissing* him (or her). And yet, there will undoubtedly be times when you have to discipline a subordinate, usually because a rule or procedure was violated. The basic purpose of **discipline** is to encourage employees to behave sensibly at work, where "sensible behavior" is defined as adhering to rules and regulations. In an organization, rules and regulations serve about the same purpose that laws do in society, and discipline is called for when one of these rules or regulations is violated.[33] Discipline is an important source of grievances in unionized firms and in nonunionized firms that have grievance procedures.[34]

discipline A procedure that corrects or punishes a subordinate because a rule or procedure has been violated.

♦ FAIRNESS IN DISCIPLINING

While you obviously want your discipline process to be effective (in terms of reducing the incidence of undesirable employee behavior), most employers should also aim to make their discipline process fair and just. This is partly because meting out discipline fairly is the right thing to do and partly because it will help ensure that any disciplinary actions survive the scrutiny of third parties like NLRB investigators.

Prerequisites to Disciplining

A fair and just discipline process is based on three prerequisites: *rules and regulations*, a *system of progressive penalties*, and an *appeals process*.

The first prerequisite is a set of clear *rules and regulations*. These rules address things like theft, destruction of company property, drinking on the job, and insubordination.[35] Examples of rules used by employers include:

Poor workmanship is not acceptable. Each employee is expected to perform his work properly and efficiently and to meet established standards of quality.

Liquor and drugs do not mix with work. The use of either during working hours or reporting for work under the influence of either is strictly prohibited.

The vending of anything in the plant without authorization is not allowed, nor is gambling in any form permitted.

Certain shop areas are designated as "no-smoking" areas because of potential fire hazards. These signs must be observed at all times.

Acts of physical violence, including horseplay, are not permitted.

The purpose of these rules is to inform employees ahead of time as to what is and is not acceptable behavior. Employees have to be told, preferably in writing, what is not permitted. This is usually done during the employee's orientation, and the rules and regulations are usually listed in the employee orientation handbook.

A *system of progressive penalties* is a second prerequisite to effective disciplining. Penalties may range from oral warnings to written warnings to suspension from the job to discharge. The severity of the penalty is usually a function of the type of offense and the number of times the offense has occurred. For example, about 90% of the companies responding to one survey issue warnings for the first unexcused lateness. However, for a fourth offense, discharge is the more usual disciplinary action.

Finally, you should have an *appeals process* as part of your disciplinary process; this helps to ensure that discipline is meted out fairly and equitably.

Most unionized (and many nonunionized) firms have appeals processes that include arbitration as a last step. It is therefore important that you do all you can to ensure that your disciplinary actions will be viewed as fair and thus worthy of being upheld by an impartial arbitrator. Based on past disciplinary cases, here are important guidelines that arbitrators may look for when deciding whether there was "just cause" for your disciplinary action:

The discipline should be in line with the way management usually responds to similar incidents. In one case the employer's rule stated that "leaving the plant without permission during working hours" made the worker subject to immediate discharge. A worker did leave the plant and was thus discharged. The arbitrator later found that employees frequently left the plant while they were clocked in and went openly into town for personal matters. Since the rule was not consistently applied in the past, the arbitrator ruled that the worker was wrongfully discharged.[36]

The employee should be adequately warned of the consequences of his or her alleged misconduct. The person should be told of any undesirable behavior that is noted and the consequences that may result if the employee chooses not to change that behavior.

The rule that allegedly was violated should be "reasonably related" to the efficient and safe operation of the particular work environment. Employees, in other words, are usually allowed by arbitrators to question the reason behind any rule or order.

Management must adequately investigate the matter before administering discipline. Furthermore, the investigation must be fair and objective.

The investigation should produce substantial evidence of misconduct.

Applicable rules, orders, or penalties should be applied evenhandedly and without discrimination.

The penalty should be reasonably related to the misconduct and to the employee's past history. In other words, each employee should be judged on the basis of his or her personal record; only then should the appropriate discipline be imposed.[37]

♦ **OTHER IMPORTANT GUIDELINES FOR EFFECTIVE DISCIPLINING**

Other important disciplining guidelines include the following:

Right to "Counsel"

All union employees have the right to bring help when they are called in for an interview that they reasonably believe might result in disciplinary action. Typically, unionized employees may bring a union representative and nonunion employees—if they are aware of their rights—may bring a co-worker. Note that this is a legal right that employees have according to the National Labor Relations Board.[38] The employee and representative also have a right to information on the nature of the interview before they meet to discuss the disciplinary meeting with the employer.

Don't Rob Your Subordinate of His or Her Dignity[39]

Things to keep in mind here include:

1. Discipline your subordinate in *private* (unless he or she requests counsel).
2. Avoid entrapment. Don't deliberately rig a situation that causes him or her to require disciplining.
3. Don't use an otherwise innocent and one-time offender as an example.
4. Don't suddenly tighten your enforcement where enforcement has previously been lax.

Remember That the Burden of Proof Is on You

In our society, a person is always considered innocent until proved guilty. This is also the case with disciplinary matters; the burden of proof is always on you to prove that a rule or regulation was violated and that the penalty was necessary.

Don't Fail to Get the Facts

Any good law enforcement officer will tell you it is important to "get all the facts." Don't base your decision on hearsay evidence. Don't base it just on your "general impression." Instead, get the facts.

Don't Act While Angry

Very few people can be objective and sensible when they are angry. It is therefore a good idea to cool off a bit before disciplining your subordinates.

Make the Offense Clear

In the case of discipline, you want to bring your subordinate's behavior into line with your employer's rules and regulations. To do this, you have to make it clear exactly what rule or regulation was broken, how it was broken, and what the correct behavior is.

Provide Adequate Warning

There are few offenses that require immediate suspension or discharge. In most cases (particularly for a first or second offense), an oral or written warning is adequate.

Make Sure the Discipline Is Equitable

No one likes to be treated in a manner that is not just. That's why overly severe penalties, inconsistently applied rules, favoritism, and other discriminatory actions breed dissatisfaction. Make sure that rules and penalties are applied equitably.

Get the Other Side of the Story

Things are not always what they seem. Don't just accept what you see or what someone tells you at face value. Instead, get the other side of the story by letting your subordinate fully explain what happened and why it happened. You may find that there were mitigating circumstances or that the person wasn't aware of the rule.

♦ DISCIPLINE WITHOUT PUNISHMENT

The traditional discipline process described above has two major potential shortcomings. First (though fairness guidelines like those above can take the edge off this) no one ever feels good about being punished—and yet that is exactly what discipline is: an employee does something wrong, and he or she is punished. Here, as with any incidence of punishment, there may be a residual of bad feelings among all involved. A second shortcoming is that, as the saying goes, "a person convinced against his or her will is of the same opinion still." In other words, forcing your rules on employees may gain short-term compliance, but not their active cooperation when you are not on hand to enforce the rules.

"Discipline without punishment" (or "nonpunitive discipline") is aimed at avoiding these disciplinary problems. This is accomplished by gaining the active acceptance of your rules by the employee and by reducing as much as possible the punitive nature of the discipline itself.

How exactly is this achieved? Assume that there has been a breach of discipline (such as disregarding safety rules) or unsatisfactory work performance (such as carelessness in handling materials). In such an event, the following steps would constitute a typical nonpunitve approach to discipline:[40]

Step 1: The first step is to issue an "oral reminder." As a supervisor, your goal here is to get the employee to agree to solve the problem. You will meet privately with the employee and (instead of warning him or her of possible disciplinary sanctions) remind the person of (1) the reason for the rule and of (2) the fact that he or she has a responsibility to meet performance standards. You will keep a written record of the incident in a separate working file in your desk rather than in the employee's personnel file.

Step 2: Should another incident arise within four to six weeks, issue the employee a formal "written reminder," a copy of which is placed in the personnel file. In addition, a second discussion is held privately with the employee, again without any threats. As in step 1, the aim is to discuss the need for the rule and to obtain the employee's acceptance of the need to act responsibly at work. Make sure the person understands the rule and your explanation for why improvement is required, and express your confidence in the person's ability to act responsibly at work. Should another such incident occur in the next six weeks or so, a follow-up meeting might be held to reiterate the need to act responsibly and to investigate the possibility that the person is ill-suited to or bored with the job. Usually, though, the next step (after the written reminder, step 2) would be step 3, a paid one-day leave.

Step 3: A paid one-day "decision-making leave" is the next step. If another incident occurs in the next six weeks or so, the employee is told to take a one-day leave with pay to stay home and consider whether or not the job is right for him or her and whether or not the person wants to abide by the company's rules. The fact that the person is paid for the day is a final expression of the company's hope that the employee can and will act responsibly with respect to following the rules. When the employee returns to work, he or she meets with you, and gives you a decision regarding whether or not the rules will be followed. At that point (assuming a positive response), you again explain your confidence in the employee and, if necessary, work out a brief action plan to help the person change his or her behavior.

Step 4: If no further incidents occur in the next year or so, the one-day suspension would be purged from the person's file; if the behavior repeats itself, dismissal (discussed below) would be required.

The process must of course be fine-tuned to take care of exceptional circumstances. Criminal behavior or in-plant fighting might be grounds for immediate dismissal, for instance. And if several incidents occurred at very close intervals, step 2—the written warning—might be skipped.

Does the nonpunitive approach to discipline work? Preliminary evidence suggests that it does. Employees seem to welcome the less punitive aspects of these kinds of programs, and employees don't seem to abuse the system by misbehaving to get a free day off with pay. Grievances, sick leave usage, and disciplinary incidents all seem to drop in firms using these new procedures. However, there will still be times when dismissals—discussed next—will be required.

♦ MANAGING DISMISSALS

Dismissal is the most drastic disciplinary step you can take toward an employee,[41] and it is thus a step that must be taken with deliberate care. Specifically, the dismissal should be *just*, in that *sufficient cause* exists for the dismissal. Furthermore, the dismissal should occur only after *all reasonable steps* have been taken to rehabilitate or salvage the employee have failed. However, there are undoubtedly times when dismissal is required, and in these instances it should be carried out forthrightly.[42]

Reasons for Dismissal

Reasons for dismissal can be classified as either unsatisfactory performance, misconduct, lack of qualifications for the job, or changed requirements of the job. *Unsatisfactory performance* may be defined as a persistent failure to perform assigned duties or to meet prescribed standards on the job.[43] Specific reasons here include excess absenteeism, tardiness, a persistent failure to meet normal job requirements, or an adverse attitude toward the company, supervisor, or fellow employees. *Misconduct* may be defined as deliberate and willful violation of the employer's rules and may include stealing, rowdyism, and insubordination. *Lack of qualifications* for the job is defined as an employee's incapability of doing the assigned work although the person is diligent. Since the employee in this case may be trying to do the job, it is especially important that every effort be made to salvage this person. *Changed requirements of the job* may be defined as an employee's incapability of doing the work assigned after the nature of the job has been changed. Similarly, an employee may have to be dismissed when his or her job is eliminated, perhaps as a result of the sorts of consolidations that swept through American firms in the mid- and late 1980s. Here again, the employee may be truly industrious, so every effort should be made to retrain or transfer this person, if possible.

Insubordination, as mentioned, is sometimes the grounds for dismissal although it may be harder to prove than are other reasons for dismissal. Stealing, chronic tardiness, and poor quality work are fairly concrete

COMPUTER APPLICATION IN COLLECTIVE BARGAINING: ESTIMATING OFFERS.

COSTS WITH COMPUTERS

Management students, whether they ultimately work for management or labor, are usually introduced to gaming—computer simulations that answer "what-if . . ." questions. Sometimes the simulations are complex strategies; sometimes they are as basic as looking at cash-flow projections. These same concepts may be applied to labor-management negotiations. When labor suggests a 5% wage increase the first year, followed by 3% each of the next two years, management counters with 3, 3, 5, understanding that their proposal will cost less over the course of the three years. However, costing out other benefits may not be as easily understood. Therefore, programs which rapidly calculate the dollar cost of benefits (both direct and indirect costs) offer the opportunity for more knowledgeable bargaining.[1]

To quickly calculate the costs of offers or counteroffers, a simple table based on the percent of (1) each step in salary ranges, or (2) each employee's annual pay, or (3) a particular benefit can be altered. For example, if each wage step is 4% higher than the one below, and the first step of each grade equals the middle step of the previous grade, simply changing the first grade's first step in the table of the wage plan will update it. Then, by linking this table to the rate each employee is paid (keyed to that table), the new total cost is available. If an employee is paid at the rate of step 4, grade 3, a cell address next to that employee's name tells the company what is budgeted for that employee. If that employee has worked an average of 100 hours overtime each of the last three years, a formula would be placed next to the employee's name which includes the cell address plus the hourly rate (if the wage plan is not in hourly figures) times 100 (to represent the 100 hours).

If one side suggests that the benefits package should be raised by 7% to include so many dollars for child care, the negotiator should have available the number of employees who have expressed an interest in this benefit and how many children are involved as well as a range of possible costs of child care in the area. By combining this information with the current percentage of payroll assigned to benefit costs, it will be clear whether or not the 7% is a realistic figure of probable costs. The negotiator might be willing to give 5% and, with data of probable use and cost figured in, be able to negotiate a wording of the benefit which will better control costs, keeping them within the intended range.

Computers, then, help to prepare the negotiator for the bargaining sessions, and could possibly shorten the time spent bargaining. If bargaining is done off-site, portable or laptop computers with 30 or 40 megabyte memories provide support.

[1]M. Steven Potash, "A Scientific Approach to Bargaining," *ABA Journal* (January, 1986), p. 58.

grounds for dismissal, while insubordination is sometimes harder to translate into words. To that end it may be useful to remember that some acts are or should be considered insubordinate whenever and wherever they occur. These include:

1. Direct disregard of the boss's authority. At sea, this is called mutiny.

2. Flat out disobedience of, or refusal to obey, the boss's orders—particularly in front of others.

3. Deliberate defiance of clearly stated company policies, rules, regulations, and procedures.

4. Criticizing the boss in public. Contradicting or arguing with him or her is also negative and inappropriate.

5. Blatantly ignoring the boss's reasonable instructions.

6. Contemptuous display of disrespect; making insolent comments, for example; and, more important, portraying these feelings in the attitude shown while on the job.

7. Showing disregard for the chain of command by going around the immediate supervisor or manager with a complaint, suggestion, or political maneuver. Although the employee may be right, that may not be enough to save him or her from the charges of insubordination.

8. Leading or participating in an effort to undermine and remove the boss from power. If the effort doesn't work (and it seldom does), those involved will be "dead in the water."[44]

Of course, as in most other human endeavors, it is dangerous to take the position that any of these acts should "always" lead to dismissal. Even at sea (as the movie *The Caine Mutiny* illustrates), there may be extenuating circumstances for the apparent insubordination. Cases like these should therefore be reviewed by the supervisor's boss.

Termination at Will

termination at will Termination of employment by either the employer or employee for any reason.

For more than 100 years the prevailing rule in the United States has been that without an employment contract, the employment relationship can be terminated "at will" by either the employer or the employee. In other words, the employee could resign for any reason, at will, and the employer could similarly dismiss an employee for any reason, at will. Today, however, dismissed employees are increasingly taking their cases to court, and in many states employers are finding that they no longer have a blanket right to fire. Instead, federal laws and various state court rulings increasingly limit management's right to dismiss employees at will.

Consider an example. You're fired for no apparent reason and given two weeks' pay and two hours to leave the firm. You've worked for this company for almost three years with consistently good reviews. Your job, you know, was not dissolved; instead, you were replaced by someone with less seniority and experience—and at lower pay. You ask your supervisor why you were fired, and he says he just can't tell you. What legal recourse do you have?

Increasingly, today, the answer to this question depends on the state where you work.[45] The United States today is one of the few remaining industrialized countries without federal legislation addressing management's right to dismiss employees at will. And in only three states—Michigan, Pennsylvania, and Wisconsin—has legislation been introduced that would erode the "at-will" rule. Yet, today, despite this dearth of laws, discharged employees are turning to their state courts for relief—and winning their cases.

In 20 states—California, Connecticut, Idaho, Illinois, Indiana, Kansas, Maryland, Massachusetts, Michigan, Missouri, Montana, New Hampshire, New Jersey, New York, Oregon, Pennsylvania, Texas, Virginia, Washington, and West Virginia—courts have ruled that there are "public policy exceptions" to the common law doctrine that employees may be discharged for whatever reason an employer chooses. They have held, for instance, that it is against "public policy" for an employer to fire an employee because the person refused to give false testimony in court to protect the employer, or refused to sell a drug that the employee knew was tainted.

In 13 states—California, Connecticut, Idaho, Louisiana, Maine, Massachusetts, Michigan, Montana, Nebraska, New Hampshire, North Carolina, Oklahoma, and Washington—courts have taken the position that company manuals or handbooks (or even employment interviews) may constitute "implied contracts" to which an employer is legally bound to adhere. In Idaho, for instance, the state Supreme Court ruled in *Jackson* v. *Minidoka Irrigation* that the employee handbook was an enforceable employment contract with respect to discharge hearings, retirement benefits, and vacation pay.

Courts in 7 states—Florida, Illinois, Minnesota, Missouri, North Dakota, South Carolina, and Washington—have granted limited exceptions to the at-will doctrine for other reasons, usually when an employee provides some "additional consideration for his employment" in addition to performing his or her services. In Florida, for instance (where the employment at will rule is still strictly adhered to) a court in *Chatelier* v. *Robertson* found for the employee, who had transferred his business to his employer in exchange for lifetime employment but was subsequently fired.

Finally, remember that employees may also be protected by existing federal laws. The Civil Rights Act (and state fair employment laws) prohibit employers from discharging employees because of their age, race, sex, religion, or national origin. Under federal law, for instance, if the employee is over 40 and is replaced by someone younger—even if that person is also over 40—the dismissed employee may have a basis for an age discrimination charge. As another example, employees who report safety violations at their place of work are generally protected from discharge by the Occupational Safety and Health Act.

Avoiding Wrongful Discharge Suits

With the increased likelihood that terminated employees can and will sue for wrongful discharge, it behooves you as an employer to protect yourself against wrongful-discharge suits. The time to do that is now, rather than after mistakes have been made and suits have been filed. Here is what one expert recommends to avoid wrongful discharge suits:

- Have applicants sign the *employment application* and make sure it contains a clearly worded statement that employment is for no fixed term and that the employer can terminate at any time. In addition, the statement should include a written statement informing the job candidate that "nothing on this application can be changed."

- You should also review your *employee manual* to look for and delete statements that could prejudice your defense in a wrongful-discharge case. For example, delete any reference to the fact that "employees can be terminated only for just cause" (unless you really mean that) and consider *not* outlining progressive discipline procedures in the manual since you may be obligated to stick with the rules and follow the steps exactly or be sued for failing to do so. Similarly, references to probationary periods or permanent employment may be unwise since they imply a permanence you may not really mean to imply.

- Make sure that no one in a position of authority makes *promises* you do not intend to keep, such as by saying that "if you do your job here, you can't get fired."

- You should have clear written work rules listing infractions that may require *discipline* and *discharge*, and then make sure to adhere to the rules. Generally, employees must be given an opportunity to correct unacceptable behavior, and you should deal with your worst offenders first and be careful not to single out any one person.

- If a rule is broken, you should get the worker's side of the story in front of witnesses, preferably in writing. Then make sure to *check out* the story, getting both sides of the issue.

- Before taking any irreversible steps, *review* the person's personnel file. For example, long-seniority employees may merit more opportunities to correct their actions than newly hired workers.

- Finally, consider *"buying out"* a wrongful discharge claim with settlement pay, and do not stand in the way of a terminated employee's future employment since a person with a new job is less likely to bring a lawsuit against the former employer than someone who remains unemployed.[46]
- Other mistakes to avoid include:
  Don't discharge anyone who is about to vest in employee benefits.
  Don't discharge a female employee just before her maternity leave.
  Don't "constructively discharge" employees by placing them in a lower paying job in hopes of a resignation.
  Don't try to induce employees to waive existing rights in exchange for gaining other rights.
  Don't deviate from internal complaint resolution guidelines and procedures.
  Don't oversell promises of job security in handbooks or oral discussions.[47]

Dismissal Procedures: Summary Do's and Don'ts

In summary, the following do's and don'ts should be followed in developing your dismissal procedures:

DO'S

Hold warning discussions before any final action. An employee must be made aware that he or she is not performing satisfactorily.

Provide extremely explicit final warnings before dismissals. It should be made clear that the employee was made to realize that his or her job was in jeopardy. It should also be clear where and how the person's performance is not meeting the standards for the job, the length of time that the person has to meet these standards, and that termination will result if he or she is unsuccessful.

Make sure you have written confirmation of the final warning.

Give the employee adequate notice in addition to the final warning. This should state a specific date by which the employee will be terminated if his or her performance is not satisfactory.

Provide pay in lieu of notice in cases where, for example, a disgruntled employee might adversely affect the morale of his or her fellow workers. One week of severance pay for each year of service, up to a prescribed maximum, is the most common rule.[48]

Reassure individuals and customers who will be affected by the termination that the company will continue to serve them.

Prepare a checklist of all property that should be accounted for, including computer disks and manuals.

Change security codes and locks previously used by discharged individuals.

If the dismissal involves large numbers of employees (say, 25 or more), prepare and secure approval for a news release.

Always prepare for the possibility that the discharged individual may act irrationally or even violently either immediately or in weeks to come.

Decide beforehand how you are going to handle telling other employees about this person's dismissal. An informal departmental meeting of those directly involved with this person is usually sufficient. Whether the termination is the result of poor performance or some other factor, it is usually best just to say that the company and the individual, based on a variety of circumstances, have agreed to part company. Be very careful not to make any defamatory statements.

DON'TS

Deliver the bad news yourself. If you can, have someone else present, preferably a human resources manager.

Get into personalities. You can state the business reasons for the decisions, but avoid humiliating the individual by getting into personal attacks.

Get your stories mixed up by giving the dismissed employee one reason, and his or her colleagues another set of reasons for the dismissal.

Let the person find out about his or her dismissal through the grapevine because you inadvertently let it slip to someone who shouldn't have known. Make sure to maintain confidentiality until you deliver the message yourself.

Ask the employee, except in cases of fraud and theft, to clean out his or her desk or locker immediately and leave the office, and don't have a security guard escort the person out of the building.[49]

The Termination Interview

Dismissing an employee is one of the most difficult tasks you'll face at work.[50] The dismissed employee—even though warned many times in the past—will often still react with total disbelief or even violence. Guidelines for the termination interview itself are as follows:

Step 1. Plan the interview carefully. According to experts at Hay Associates, this means:

Schedule the meeting on a day early in the week.

Make sure the employee keeps the appointment time.

Never inform an employee over the phone.

Ten minutes should be sufficient for notification.

Avoid Fridays, preholidays, and vacation times when possible.

Use a neutral site, never your own office.

Have employee agreements, human resources file, release announcement (internal and external) prepared in advance.

Be available at a time after notification.

Have phone numbers ready for medical or security emergencies.

Step 2. Get to the point. Do not beat around the bush by talking about the weather or by making other small talk. As soon as the employee enters your office, give the person a moment to get comfortable, and then inform the person of your decision.

Step 3. Describe the situation. Briefly, in three or four sentences, explain why the person is being let go. For instance, "Production in your area is down four percent, and we are continuing to have quality problems. We have talked about these problems several times in the past three months and the solutions are not being followed through. We have a make a change."[51] Remember to describe the situation, rather than attacking the employee personally by saying things like "your production is just not up to par." Also emphasize that the decision is final and irrevocable; other in-house positions were explored, management at all levels concurs, and all relevant factors—performance, workload, and so on—were considered. Don't take more than 10–15 minutes for the interview.

Step 4. Listen. It is important to continue the interview until the person appears to be talking freely and reasonably calmly about the reasons for his or her termination and the support package (including severance pay) he or she is to receive. Do not get into arguments; instead, *actively listen*

FIGURE 17.2

Behavioral Reaction Chart: Reaction to Termination and Suggested Response
Source: Hay Associates, Philadelphia, Pa. 19103.

If the employee is	Hostile and angry	Defensive and bargaining	Formal and procedural (lawsuit?)	Stoic	Crying/ sobbing
The underlying feelings and motivations may be	Hurt Anger Disappointment Relief	Guilt Fear Uncertainty Disbelief	Vengeful Suppressed Controlled	Shock Disbelief Numbness	Sadness Grief Worry
The manager, in turn, might handle the employee's reaction with these responses	•Summarize what you have heard in a tentative style: "It sounds as if you are pretty angry about this." •Avoid confronting the anger or becoming defensive. •Remain objective; stick to the facts and give the employee helpful information.	•Let the employee know you realize this is a difficult time for him or her as well as for yourself. •Don't get involved in any bargaining discussions. •Offer reassurance about the future and connect this to the counseling process.	•Allow the employee freedom to ask any questions as long as they pertain to his or her own case. •Try to avoid side issues and discussion of "political" motivations. •Keep the tone formal. This is a good way to lead into the role the career counselor will play.	•Communicate to the employee that you recognize his or her shock and say the details can be handled later if the employee prefers. •Ask if there are any specific questions for the moment. If not, tell the employee about the career counselor and make the introduction.	•Allow the person an opportunity to cry if that occurs. Just offer some tissues. •Avoid inane comments such as "What are you crying about, it's not that important." •When the person regains composure, press on with the facts and explain the counseling process.

and get the person to talk by using open-ended questions, restating his or her last comment, and using silence and a nod of your head. Use the Behavioral Reaction Chart (Figure 17.2) to gauge the person's reaction and to decide how best to proceed.

Step 5. Discuss the severance package. Next, carefully review all elements of the severance package. Describe severance payments, benefits, access to office support people, and how recommendations will be handled. However, under no conditions should any promises or benefits beyond those already in the support package be implied. Do not promise to "look into" something and get back to the subordinate at a later date. This will simply complicate the termination process. The termination should be complete when the person leaves your office.

Step 6. Identify the next step. The terminated employee may be disoriented and unsure of what to do next. You should explain where the employee should go upon leaving your office and remind the person who to contact at the company regarding questions about the support package or references.

CONCLUSION: THE FUTURE OF UNIONISM

◆ THE UNIONS FALL ON HARD TIMES

We have seen that the ten years from 1975 to 1985 were hard times for unions, and that during those years their rolls dropped steeply. In 1975, about 29% of the nonfarm U.S. work force belonged to unions. By 1989, that figure had dropped to about 17%. This slide actually began in the early 1950s. By then, most easily organized workers in industries like mining, transportation, and manufacturing had already been unionized. And an economic slowdown in the late 1950s further hampered union membership drives.

By the 1970s and 1980s, other changes were occurring. Most of the new jobs being created in our economy are in the service sector, and today roughly 66% are employed in service firms. These workers have never been highly unionized. Many work part time, and the typical firm is small. This makes it harder and more costly for unions to organize them, in part because it requires dealing with many more employers.[52]

The last ten years have also been an era of restructuring for American industry. Faced with intense international competition, outdated equipment, and corporate raiders, hundreds of thousands of union members have been laid off as firms tried to consolidate and boost their profits.

Deregulation in industries like trucking, airlines, and communications have helped to erode union membership as well.[53] When Frank Lorenzo, former chairman of Texas Air, took over Continental Airlines, he demanded that the airline's unions renegotiate their wage agreements. When they refused, he took the airline into bankruptcy. This gave him an opportunity to void existing union agreements and negotiate new deals with all concerned.

Changes like these are taking their toll on unions. For one thing, union membership has fallen off dramatically. For another, unions are not only negotiating lower wage increases for their workers, but in many cases they are giving back previously won raises for union members who remain.

In a major test for unions, workers at Nissan Motor Manufacturing Corp. U.S.A. in Smyrna, Tennessee, rejected the United Auto Workers in the first union vote at a wholly owned U.S. Japanese auto plant.[54] After a bitter, 18-month union organizing campaign workers voted more than 2 to 1 against UAW representation in 1989, apparently because pay, job security, and management practices were already so favorable at the plant. At the same time, entering 1990 strike activity had declined, partly because court decisions (like TWA, discussed in Chapter 16) made it easier for employers to replace strikers, and partly because there is today "less of the old-fashioned posturing, chest beating, and table pounding" during negotiations.[55]

Doublebreasting is another way that companies are putting unions under more pressure. It refers to a tactic whereby employers avoid their obligations under union contracts by establishing and running nonunion companies to which they may transfer union work. This is permitted by the NLRB under certain circumstances and is, for instance, a common practice in the construction industry.

Also, as explained in Chapter 16, the labor laws and court rulings for which unions fought so long are now in place. And ironically they provide just the sorts of protection (of occupational health, for instance) that up to a few years ago only unions could provide.[56]

Beyond this technology will have an impact on unionization. Computer systems and other modern technologies which allow "the elimination of workers by design" may serve to reduce labor demand, for instance. For one thing, electronic work (as in the processing of credit card claims) is highly portable compared with the factories of old. Modern office work can thus be shifted almost literally at the touch of a button from a facility in one state to another, even overseas.[57] And while creating new-skill jobs, office automation also leads to the deskilling of old jobs, such as the elimination of many tasks from the typical secretary's job of coordinating, typing, transcribing, and filing.[58]

What's Next for Unions?

Does this all mean that we no longer need unions? Probably not. But what it does mean is a change in the way that unions do business and also in the way they see their role. As a result, the AFL-CIO is embarking on new activities. One is a program to train a thousand unionists in the fundamentals of how to react to the TV camera. They want to better explain themselves and the union movement to the general public. During the last ten years or so, unions have also made a major effort to organize white-collar workers. More than 10% of white-collar workers have already been unionized. *Worker ownership of firms* and new approaches to *worker-management cooperation* are two other big ways in which the role of the union movement is changing.

Worker Ownership and Control

Today, unions are no longer satisfied to get the best deal they can for their members and leave management to run the firm. Increasingly they are going after ownership and control. As Lynn R. Williams, president of the United Steel Workers Union, puts it, "We're not going to sit around and allow management to louse things up like they did in the past."[59]

And it's not just by promising to "give back" wage concessions and other benefits that unions win all or partial control of the board. Today, some 8 million workers belong to employee stock ownership plans. Recall that these "ESOPs" are basically pension plans through which a company's employees accumulate shares of the company's stock. As a result, nonmanagement employees now sit on boards of directors at more than 300 firms in their role as representatives of the firm's employee stock ownership plans.

Union-Management Cooperation

When the Japanese began manufacturing their Toyotas, Hondas, and Nissans in America, they brought over a lot more than their technological expertise. They brought over a cooperative, team-based management style that, as we've seen, is now operating successfully at scores of plants around the United States.

For example, when GM decided to build its all-new Saturn car, its planning included the United Auto Workers Union. Joint GM/UAW study groups were organized. To reach a consensus between management and labor, "agreement teams" were formed. Six people—three union and three management—along with an advisor met to rough out an outline for a bargaining contract. Each team listed about 16 items that were necessary for an agreement, and the teams then broke up to hammer out more detailed agreements.

The agreement is indicative of the agreements of the future. There are no hourly employees at the Saturn corporation. All are on salary, and there is heavy emphasis on tying rewards to performance. There is a grievance procedure that calls for final and binding arbitration. And the contract has no termination date nor is there a "no-strike" clause in the agreement.

Yet, many union leaders remain skeptical of the new cooperation. Many feel it smacks of collaboration—irresponsibly cooperating with an enemy. Other union officials fear that the new harmony could undermine the union's attraction for its members, by making management seem less an adversary. But on the whole, labor-management cooperation seems to be off on a sure footing. We may indeed be witnessing the dawning of a new age in union-management cooperation.

Is There Such a Thing as Good Union-Management Relations?

It's often easy to get the impression that labor-management bargaining tends to be violent and abusive. This is because it is the handful of failures—strikes, pickets, and so on—that make news, not the tens of thousands of amicably hammered out agreements.[60]

Success stories such as these do not have to mean that managements were "soft" or unions corrupt—just the opposite. Hard bargaining and effective contract administration on both sides is likely to lead to a healthy union agreement, while apathy or one-sided dominance leads to agreements that are doomed to failure. As Samuelson says, "in healthy cases, each side has a respect for the rights of the other. The two sides are not in love, but they are compatible."

SUMMARY

1. Bargaining collectively "in good faith" is the next step if and when the union wins the election. Good faith means that both parties communicate and negotiate, and that proposals are matched with counterproposals. We discussed the structure of the negotiating teams and their preparations. We also discussed the actual bargaining sessions and the distinction between mandatory, voluntary, and illegal bargaining items. We also listed some hints on bargaining, including do not hurry, be prepared, find out why, and be a good listener.

2. An impasse occurs when the parties aren't able to move further toward settlement. *Third-party involvement*—namely, arbitration, fact-finding, or mediation—is one alternative. Sometimes, though, a *strike* occurs. Preparing for the strike involves such steps as secure the facility, notify all customers, and photograph the facility. Boycotts and lockouts are two other "anti-impasse" weapons sometimes used by labor and management.

3. Grievance handling has been called "day-to-day collective bargaining." It involves the continuing interpretation of the collective-bargaining agreement (but usually not its renegotiations).

4. Just about any management action might lead to a grievance, but the most serious actions involve discipline cases, seniority problems, actions growing out of a job evaluation and work assignments, and overtime and benefits. But remember that a grievance is often just a symptom; always try to find the underlying problem.

5. Most agreements contain a carefully worded grievance procedure. It may be a two-step procedure or (at the other extreme) involve six or more steps. In any case, the steps usually involve meetings between higher and higher echelon managers until (if agreement isn't reached) the grievance goes to arbitration. Grievance handling is as important in nonunion organizations as in those that are unionized.

6. Disciplinary actions are one big source of grievances. Discipline should be based on rules, adhere to a system of progressive penalties, and permit an appeals process. Other "fairness" guidelines include the fact that the discipline should be in line with the way management usually responds to similar incidents. Other important guidelines include emphasize rules, remember that the burden of proof is on you, and don't fail to get the facts.

7. A dismissal is a drastic step, one for which there are several possible reasons: unsatisfactory performance, misconduct, lack of qualifications, and changed requirements for the job. Guidelines to follow include: hold warning discussions, provide written confirmation along with adequate notice, and provide pay in lieu of notice, if necessary. Remember that courts are increasingly limiting your right to fire an employee at will.

8. In the termination interview, do the required planning, get to the point, describe the situation, listen, discuss the severance package, and identify the next step. Anticipating and preparing for various behavioral reactions—like shock—can be facilitated by following the chart in Figure 17.2.

KEY TERMS

collective bargaining

good faith

voluntary bargaining items

illegal bargaining items

mandatory bargaining items

impasse

third-party involvement

mediation

fact-finder

arbitration

strikes

economic strike

unfair labor practice strike

wildcat strike

sympathy strike

boycotts

lockout

grievance

grievance procedure

day-to-day collective bargaining

discipline

termination at will

DISCUSSION QUESTIONS

1. Discuss what you, as a supervisor, should keep in mind about how to prepare for union contract negotiations.

2. What is meant by good faith bargaining? When is bargaining not in good faith?

3. You are the president of a small (30 employees) firm. While you are not unionized, you would like to have an appeals process that would serve a purpose similar to that of a grievance procedure. Discuss what this appeals process might entail.

4. Define *impasse, mediation,* and *strike,* and explain the techniques that are used to overcome an impasse.

5. Assume you have been asked by your boss to give a lecture to new supervisors on how to discipline subordinates. Explain what you would say to them.

6. Explain the reasons for a dismissal and how you would handle a termination interview.

7. What are the primary issues concerning a wrongful discharge policy?

8. Analyze and critique the eroding "employment at will" concept. How does this change affect human resource management within the organization?

Botched Batch

"All right, I admit I made an error in preparing those data processing cards, but I told the operations manager about it right away, and he could have stopped the computer run," protested Bonnie Flint. "Seeing as how I've always been one of your best workers, how can you justify suspending me and rescinding my promotion, and not doing anything to him?"

"The simple fact is that if you hadn't been negligent, we wouldn't have had to deal with a whole string of problems that cost us several thousand dollars to correct," replied human resources manager Judy Martin. "Since you were primarily responsible for the foul-up, you deserve the discipline."

Was the disciplinary decision proper?

FACTS

A computer department employee made an entry error that botched up an entire run of computer reports. Efforts to rectify the situation produced a second set of improperly run reports. As a result of the series of errors, the employer incurred extra costs of $2,400, plus a weekend of overtime work by other computer department staffers. Management suspended the employee for three days for negligence, and also revoked a promotion for which she previously had been approved.

Protesting the discipline, the employee stressed that she had attempted to correct her error in the early stages of the run by notifying the manager of computer operations of her mistake. Maintaining that the resulting string of errors could have been avoided if the manager had followed up on her report and stopped the initial run, the employee argued that she had been treated unfairly because the manager had not been disciplined even though he compounded the problem, while she was severely punished. Moreover, citing her "impeccable" work record and management's acknowledgment that she had always been a "model employee," the worker insisted that the denial of her previously-approved promotion was "unconscionable."

Questions
1. Do you believe the disciplinary decision was proper?
2. What changes, if any, would you make in this firm's disciplinary process?

AWARD

(Please do *not* read beyond here until after you have completed the Experiential Exercise.) The arbitrator upholds the three-day suspension, but decides that the promotion should be restored.

DISCUSSION

"There is no question," the arbiter notes, that the employee's negligent act "set in motion the train of events which resulted in running two complete sets of cards reflecting improper information." Stressing that the employer incurred substantial cost because of the error, the arbiter cites "unchallenged" testimony that management had commonly issued three-day suspensions for similar infractions in the past. Thus, the arbiter decides, the employer acted with just cause in meeting out an "even-handed" punishment for the negligence.

Turning to the denial of the already approved promotion, the arbitrator says that this action should be viewed "in the same light as a demotion for disciplinary reasons." In such cases, the arbiter notes, management's decision normally is based on a pattern of unsatisfactory behavior, an employee's inability to perform, or similar grounds. Observing that management had never before reversed a promotion as part of a disciplinary action, the arbiter says that by tacking on the denial of the promotion in this case, the employer substantially varied its disciplinary policy from its past practice. Since this action on management's part was not "evenhanded," the arbiter rules, the promotion should be restored.

POINTERS

Arbiters tend to frown on management decisions to demote an employee for temporary performance problems on the grounds that such a penalty constitutes a "permanent punishment." For example, in one case, an arbitrator emphasized that "permanent demotion is not a proper form of discipline where an employee's capabilities are conceded and his performance generally is satisfactory, but where his attitudes of the moment are improper." Stressing that undesirable behavior, such as occasional carelessness or a failure to obey instructions, usually can be corrected by suspending the employee for a reasonable period, the arbiter noted that such discipline does not "offend the basic seniority rights of the employee and does not inflict upon the employee an indeterminate sentence."

Source: Bureau of National Affairs, *Bulletin to Managers*, September 13, 1985, p. 3.

EXPERIENTIAL EXERCISE

Purpose: The purpose of this exercise is to provide you with some experience in analyzing and handling an actual grievance.

Required Understanding: Students should be thoroughly familiar with the case at the end of this chapter entitled "Botched Batch". However, *do not read the "Award" or "Discussion" sections until after the groups have completed their deliberations.*

How to Set Up the Exercise/Instructions: Divide the class into groups of four or five students. The group should take the arbitrator's point of view and assume that they are to analyze the case and make the arbitrator's decision. Review the case again at this point but please do not read the answer.

Each group should answer the following questions:

1. What would your decision be if you were the arbitrator? Why?
2. Do you think that following their experience in this arbitration the parties will be more or less inclined to settle grievances by themselves without resorting to arbitration?

NOTES

1. Dale Yoder, *Personnel Management* (Englewood Cliffs, N.J.: Prentice-Hall, 1972), p. 486.
2. Quoted in Reed Richardson, *Collective Bargaining by Objectives* (Englewood Cliffs, N.J.: Prentice-Hall, 1977), p. 150; adapted from Charles Morris, ed., *The Developing Labor Law* (Washington, D.C.: Bureau of National Affairs, 1971), pp. 271–310.
3. John Fossum, *Labor Relations* (Dallas, Tex.: Business Publications, 1982), pp. 246–250.
4. *Boulwareism* is the name given to a strategy, now generally held in disfavor, by which the company, based on an exhaustive study of what it thought its employees wanted, made but one offer at the bargaining table and then refused to bar-

gain any further unless convinced by the union on the basis of new facts that its original position was wrong. The NLRB subsequently found that the practice of offering the same settlement to all units, insisting that certain parts of the package could not differ among agreements and communicating to the employees about how negotiations were going, amounted to an illegal pattern. Fossum, *Labor Relations*, p. 267.

5. Commerce Clearing House, "Drug Testing/Court Rulings," *Ideas and Trends*, January 25, 1988, p. 16.

6. Bargaining items based on Richardson, *Collective Bargaining*, pp. 113–115; bargaining stages based on William Glueck, "Labor Relations and the Supervisor," in M. Gene Newport, *Supervisory Management* (St. Paul, Minn.: West, 1976), pp. 207–234.

7. See also Yoder, *Personnel Management*, pp. 517–518.

8. Richardson, *Collective Bargaining*, p. 150.

9. Fossum, *Labor Relations*, pp. 298–322.

10. Ibid., p. 312.

11. Ibid., p. 317.

12. Stephen Cabot and Gerald Cureton, "Labor Disputes and Strikes: Be Prepared," *Personnel Journal*, Vol. 60 (February 1981), pp. 121–126.

13. For a discussion of the cost of a strike see Woodruff Imberman, "Strikes Cost More than You Think," *Harvard Business Review*, Vol. 57 (May–June 1979), pp. 133–138. The NLRB held in 1986 in *Harter Equipment, Inc.*, 280 NLRB No. 71, that an employer could lawfully hire temporary replacements during the course of a lockout, in the absence of proof of specific antiunion motivation, in order to bring economic pressure to bear upon a union to support a legitimate bargaining position.

14. Dale Beach, *Personnel* (New York: Macmillan, 1975), pp. 117–119.

15. Arthur A. Sloane and Fred Witney, *Labor Relations*, 5th ed. (Englewood Cliffs, N.J.: Prentice-Hall, 1977), pp. 229–231. Copyright 1985. Reprinted by permission of Prentice-Hall, Englewood Cliffs, N.J.

16. Richardson, *Collective Bargaining*, p. 184.

17. Lester Bittel, *What Every Supervisor Should Know* (New York: McGraw-Hill, 1974), p. 308, based on a study of 1,000 grievances made by the American Arbitration Association.

18. Richardson, *Collective Bargaining*.

19. J. Brad Chapman, "Constructive Grievance Handling," in Newport, *Supervisory Management*, pp. 253–274.

20. Quoted from Sloane and Witney, *Labor Relations*, pp. 219–221.

21. Ibid., p. 221.

22. See, for example, Clyde Summers, "Protecting All Employees Against Unjust Dismissal," *Harvard Business Review*, Vol. 58 (January–February 1980), pp. 132–139, and George Bohlander and Harold White, "Building Bridges: Non-Union Employee Grievance Systems," *Personnel*, July 1988, pp. 62–66.

23. Chapman, "Constructive Grievance Handling," p. 253.

24. Thomasine Rendero, "Grievance Procedures for Nonunionized Employees," *Personnel* (January–February 1980), pp. 4–10.

25. Maryellen Lo Bosco, "Non-Union Grievance Procedures," *Personnel*, Vol. 62, no. 1 (January 1985), pp. 61–64.

26. Alan Balfour, "Five Types of Non-Union Grievance Systems," *Personnel*, Vol. 61, no. 3 (March–April 1984), p. 69–76. Note, by the way, that according to one study, the results of the grievance rather than its quick resolution in step 1 is most important to employees. See Michael Gordon and Roger Bowlby, "Propositions About Grievance Settlements: Finally, Consultation with Grievants," *Personnel Psychology* (Spring 1988), pp. 107–124.

27. Balfour, "Five Types of Non-Union Grievance Procedures," p. 7. Take note that in one study, the grievant's work history—even if irrelevant to the grievance—influenced how management decided on the grievance. See Brian Klaas, "Mana-

gerial Decision-Making About Employee Grievances," *Personnel Psychology*, Spring 1989, pp. 53–68.

28. Summers, "Protecting All Employees."

29. Ibid., pp. 264–266.

30. See ibid., p. 273, for an excellent checklist.

31. For a full discussion of these and others, see Walter Baer, *Grievance Handling: 101 Guides for Supervisors* (New York: American Management Association, 1970). For an interesting discussion of major league baseball's grievance arbitration system, see Glenn Wong, "Major League Baseball's Grievance Arbitration System: A Comparison with Nonsport Industry," *Labor Law Journal*, Vol. 38, no. 2 (February 1987), pp. 84–99.

32. The following is based on Commerce Clearing House, "Unionized Employee Claiming a Violation of State Law Can Sue Employer, Supreme Court Rules," *Ideas and Trends*, June 15, 1988, pp. 89–91.

33. Bittel, *What Every Supervisor Should Know.*

34. Brian Heshizer and Harry Graham, "Discipline in the Non-Union Company," *Personnel*, Vol. 59 (March–April 1982), pp. 71–78.

35. Commerce Clearing House, *Personnel Practices/Communications* (Chicago: CCH, 1982), pp. 2351–2352.

36. Commerce Clearing House, *Ideas and Trends in Personnel* (Chicago: CCH, April 8, 1982), p. 88.

37. Commerce Clearing House, "One Thing Unions Offer Is 'Fair Discipline'—But Management Can Offer That Too," *Ideas and Trends in Personnel*, September 3, 1982, p. 168.

38. Commerce Clearing House, "Non-union Employees, NLRB Rules, Have the Right to Help During Questioning by Management," *Ideas and Trends in Personnel*, August 6, 1982, p. 151.

39. These are based on George Odiorne, *How Managers Make Things Happen* (Englewood Cliffs, N.J.: Prentice-Hall, 1961), pp. 132–143; see also Bittel, *What Every Supervisor Should Know*, pp. 285–298.

40. Non-punitive discipline discussions based on David Campbell, et al., "Discipline Without Punishment—At Last," *Harvard Business Review* (July–August 1985), pp. 162–178; and Gene Milbourn, Jr., "The Case Against Employee Punishment," *Management Solutions* (November 1986), pp. 40–45.

41. Joseph Famularo, *Handbook of Modern Personnel Administration* (New York, McGraw-Hill, 1972), pp. 65.3–65.5.

42. Ibid.

43. Ibid., pp. 65.4–65.5.

44. From a press release dated August 6, 1987. The Goodrich & Sherwood Company, 521 Fifth Avenue, New York, N.Y. 10017. Reprinted in Commerce Clearing House, *Ideas and Trends*, October 2, 1987, p. 157.

45. Bureau of National Affairs, *The Employment-at-Will Issue* (Washington, D.C.: BNA, 1982). See also Emily Joiner, "Erosion of the Employment at Will Doctrine," *Personnel*, Vol. 61, no. 5 (September–October 1984), pp. 12–18; Harvey Steinberg, "Where Law and Personnel Practice Collide: The At Will Employment Crossroad," *Personnel*, Vol. 62, no. 6 (June 1985), pp. 37–43.

46. Based on a speech by Peter Panken and presented in BNA, *Bulletin to Management*, June 20, 1985, pp. 11–12.

47. Based on comments by attorney Richard Curiale in BNA, *Bulletin to Management*, November 17, 1983, p. 8. See also BNA, *Bulletin to Management*, May 18, 1989, p. 154; averting wrongful discharge litigation, specific guidelines.

48. Bureau of National Affairs, "Severance Pay Perusal," *Fair Employment Practices* (Washington, D.C.: BNA, January 13, 1983), p. 7.

49. Commerce Clearing House, "How to Discharge: Some Guidelines," *Ideas and Trends in Personnel*, January 11, 1988, p. 4. Except as noted, this section was based on Miriam Rothman, "Employee Termination, I: A Four-Step Procedure," *Personnel* (February 1989), pp. 31–35; and Steven Jesseph, "Employee Termination, II: Some Do's and Don'ts," *Personnel* (February 1989), pp. 36–38.

50. William J. Morin and Lyle York, *Outplacement Techniques* (New York: AMA-COM, 1982), pp. 101–131, and F. Leigh Branham, "How to Evaluate Executive Outplacement Services," *Personnel Journal*, Vol. 62 (April 1983), pp. 323–326.

51. Morin and York, *Outplacement Techniques*, p. 117.

52. "Perspectives on Employment," *Research Bulletin #194* (1986), The Conference Board, 845 Third Avenue, New York, N.Y. 10020.

53. "AFL-CIO Launching New Strategy to Win Over Nonunion Workers," *Compensation and Benefits Review*, Vol. 18, no. 15 (September–October 1986), p. 8. See also Shane Permeaux, R. Wayne Mondy, and Art Bethke, "Decertification: Fulfilling Unions' Destiny?" *Personnel Journal*, Vol. 66, no. 6 (June 1987), p. 144, and Peter A. Susser, "The Labor Impact of Deregulation," *Employment Relations Today*, Vol. 13, no. 2 (Summer 1986), pp. 117–123.

54. Bureau of National Affairs, "Union 'No' at Nissan," *Bulletin to Management*, August 10, 1989, pp. 249–250.

55. Bureau of National Affairs, "Strike Decline: Positive, Negative Factors," *Bulletin to Management*, April 13, 1989, p. 113.

56. "Beyond Unions: A Revolution in Employee Rights Is in the Making," *Business Week*, July 8, 1985, pp. 72–77.

57. Dennis Chamot, "Unions Need to Confront the Results of New Technology," *Monthly Labor Review* (August 1987), p. 45.

58. Cynthia Costello, "Technological Change and Unionization in the Service Sector," *Monthly Labor Review* (August 1987), pp. 45–46. See also Audrey Freedman, "How the 1980s Have Changed Industrial Relations," *Monthly Labor Review* (May 1988), p. 36; for a contrary view see John T. Dunlop, "Have the 1980s Changed U.S. Industrial Relations?" *Monthly Labor Review* (May 1988), pp. 29–34.

59. "The Battle for Corporate Control," *Business Week*, May 18, 1987, p. 107.

60. See Samuelson, *Economics*, pp. 132–133.

Chapter 18

Employee Safety and Health

When you finish studying this chapter, you should be able to:

1. Provide a safer environment for your employees to work in.
2. Reduce the occurrence of unsafe acts on the part of your employees.
3. Explain the basic facts about OSHA—its purpose, standards, inspection, and rights and responsibilities.
4. Explain the supervisor's role in safety.
5. Compare and contrast unsafe acts and unsafe conditions.
6. Explain what causes unsafe acts.
7. Answer the question, Is there such a thing as "accident-prone" people?
8. Describe at least five techniques for reducing accidents.
9. Discuss four important occupational health problems and how they are dealt with.

OVERVIEW

The main purpose of this chapter is to provide you with the basic knowledge you will need to deal effectively with employee safety and health problems at work. Today, every manager needs a working knowledge of OSHA—the Occupational Safety and Health Act—and so we discuss it at some length. Specifically, we review its purpose, standards, and inspection procedures, as well as the rights and responsibilities of employees and employers under OSHA. Early in the chapter we also stress the importance of the supervisor in safety and stress the importance of obtaining top management's commitment to organizationwide safety.

There are three basic causes of accidents—chance occurrences, unsafe conditions, and unsafe acts—and we explain the latter two in some detail, as well as how to deal with them. We'll see that unsafe acts are caused by people, and that certain personality traits may underlie the "accident-prone" employee. We discuss several specific techniques for preventing accidents and four important employee health problems: alcoholism, drug addiction, emotional illness, and stress.

The subject of safety and accident prevention is of tremendous concern to managers for several reasons. For one thing, the figures concerning work-related accidents are staggering. The National Safety Council reports, for example, that for a recent year there were more than 11,000 deaths and almost 2 million injuries resulting from accidents at work. And many safety experts feel that such figures seriously underestimate the actual number of injuries.[1]

But figures like these don't tell the full story. They don't reflect the human suffering incurred by the injured workers and their families. They don't reflect the economic costs incurred by these people's employers—costs for things such as time off, insurance, and medical payments. Nor do they reflect the legal implications of the problem—such as the managers who were sued or imprisoned for failing to ensure safe workplaces.

♦ THREE REASONS FOR SAFETY PROGRAMS

Safety expert Willie Hammer says that safety programs are undertaken for three fundamental reasons: moral, legal, and economic.[2]

Moral

First, managers undertake accident prevention on purely humane grounds. They do so to minimize the pain and suffering the injured worker and his family are often exposed to as the result of an accident.

Legal

There are also legal reasons for undertaking a safety program. Today, there are federal, state, and municipal laws covering occupational safety and health, and penalties for noncompliance have become quite severe. Organizations are subject to fines, and supervisors can (and have) received jail sentences if found responsible for fatal accidents. In 1971, for example, there was a tunnel disaster outside Los Angeles, California. The company building the tunnel was found guilty of 16 counts of gross negligence and fined $205,000. The project manager on the job was found guilty of 16 counts of gross negligence and was sentenced to five years in jail and ten years probation.[3] In 1989, an employer and five of its officers were charged with aggravated battery by the state of Illinois, which said the company permitted employees to be exposed to toxic substances.[4]

Economic

Finally, there are economic reasons for being safety conscious, since the cost to the company of even a small accident can be quite high. Workers' compensation insurance simply compensates the injured worker for his or her injury. It does *not* cover the other direct and indirect costs associated with that injury. Among these are payments for settlements of injury or death claims, legal fees for defense against claims, costs of rescue operations, loss of function and of operations income, training costs for replacements, and increased insurance costs.[5] For example, Lester Bittell estimates that for an accident that comes to $600 for compensation, a company pays another $2,000 for related expenses. These related expenses cover things such as lost time for employees who stop to watch or assist, supervisor's lost time, and changing production schedules. Here is an example he presents to illustrate his point.[6]

A chemical worker was scalded when a kettle of hot dye slipped from a sling while it was being poured into a vat. Here are what the costs came to:

Compensation paid for burns	400
Medical expense, including first aid	180
Total "compensation" costs	580
Time lost away from job:	
Injured worker's makeup pay while home 3½ days	90
Follow-up medical visits	210
Fellow workers standing by watching at time of accident	220
Supervisor's time recording, and so on	120
Total cost of time lost	640
Production loss:	
Downtime on dye operation	160
Slowed-up production rate of other workers	80
Materials spoiled and labor for cleaning it up	140
Damage to equipment	290
Total production and related costs	670
Total cost of accident (not including overhead which could raise total as much as 50%)	1,890

BASIC FACTS ABOUT THE OCCUPATIONAL SAFETY AND HEALTH ACT

♦ PURPOSE

Occupational Safety and Health Act The law passed by Congress in 1970 "to assure so far as possible every working man and woman in the nation safe and healthful working conditions and to preserve our human resources."

The **Occupational Safety and Health Act**[7] was passed by Congress in 1970; its purpose, as stated by Congress, was "to assure so far as possible every working man and woman in the nation safe and healthful working conditions and to preserve our human resources." The only employers not covered under the act are self-employed persons, farms in which only immediate members of the farm employer's family are employed, and certain workplaces that are already protected by other federal agencies or under other statutes. Federal agencies are covered by the act, although provisions of the act usually don't apply to state and local governments in their role as employers.

Occupational Safety and Health Administration (OSHA) The agency created within the Department of Labor to set safety and health standards for almost all workers in the United States.

Under the provisions of the act, the **Occupational Safety and Health Administration (OSHA)** was created within the Department of Labor. The basic purpose of OSHA is to set safety and health standards, standards that apply to almost all workers in the United States. The standards are enforced through the Department of Labor, and to ensure compliance, OSHA has inspectors working out of branch offices throughout the country. The act also created the National Institute for Occupational Safety and Health (NIOSH), which was established to conduct scientific research on health hazards and job safety and suggest ways to remove or diminish them.

♦ OSHA STANDARDS

The basic "general" standard under which OSHA operates states that each employer shall furnish to each of his employees employment and a place of employment which are free from recognized hazards that are causing or are likely to cause death or serious physical harm to his employees.

In carrying out this basic mission, OSHA is responsible for promulgating legally enforceable standards. The standards themselves are contained in five volumes, covering general industry standards, maritime standards, construction standards, other regulations and procedures, and a field operations manual.

The standards are very complete and seem to cover just about any hazard one could think of, doing so in great detail. The volume containing general industry standards, for example, sets detailed standards for 17 separate areas, as follows:

Walking and working surfaces	Fire protection
Means of egress	Compressed gas and compressed air equipment
Powered platforms, man lifts, and vehicle-mounted work platforms	Materials handling and storage
Occupational health and environmental control (ventilation, etc.)	Machinery and machine guarding
Hazardous materials	Hand and portable powered tools and other hand-held equipment
Personal protective equipment	Welding, cutting, and braising
General environmental controls (sanitation, etc.)	Special industries (textiles, etc)
	Electrical
Medical and first aid	Toxic and hazardous substances

The standards themselves, as mentioned, are presented in great detail. For example, a small part of the standard governing scaffolds is presented in Figure 18.1. Note also that OSHA regulations don't just enumerate recommended standards (like the one describing what guard rails should look like, in Figure 18.1). For example, as of March 17, 1989, all provisions of OSHA's Hazard Communication Standard were in effect. These require employers to establish hazard communication programs for the purpose of informing employees about chemical hazards. These hazards have to be communicated through training programs, container labels, and particularly materials safety data sheets (known as MSDS), which list the nature of a treatment for hazardous substances. Employers were cited for over 18,000 violations of the Hazard Communication Standard in 1988.[8]

◆ OSHA RECORDKEEPING PROCEDURES

Under OSHA, employers with 11 or more employees must maintain records of occupational injuries and illnesses as they occur. (Employers having 10 or fewer employees are now exempt from recordkeeping unless they are selected to participate in the annual statistical survey carried out by the Bureau of Labor Statistics, a move aimed at simplifying OSHA compliance for small businesses.)

Both occupational injuries and occupational illnesses must be reported. An occupational illness is any abnormal condition or disorder caused by exposure to environmental factors associated with employment. Included

FIGURE 18.1
OSHA Standards Example
Source: *General Industries Standards*, U.S. Department of Labor, OSHA (Revised November 7, 1978), p. 36.

Guardrails not less than 2″ × 4″ or the equivalent and not less than 36″ or more than 42″ high, with a midrail, when required, of a 1″ × 4″ lumber or equivalent, and tow boards, shall be installed at all open sides on all scaffolds more than 10 feet above the ground floor. Tow boards shall be a minimum of 4″ in height. Wire mesh shall be installed in accordance with (a) (17) of this section.

here are acute and chronic illnesses that may be caused by inhalation, absorption, ingestion, or direct contact with toxic substances or harmful agents. As summarized in Figure 18.2, *all* occupational illnesses must be reported.[9] Similarly, *most* occupational injuries also must be reported. Specifically, occupational injuries must be recorded if they result in medical treatment (other than first aid), loss of consciousness, restriction of work (one or more lost workdays), restriction of motion, or transfer to another job.[10] If an on-the-job accident occurs that results in the death of an employee or in the hospitalization of five or more employees, all employers, regardless of size, are required to report the accident, in detail, to the nearest OSHA office. The form often used to report occupational injuries or illness is shown in Figure 18.3.

♦ INSPECTIONS AND CITATIONS

OSHA standards are enforced through a series of inspections and (if necessary) citations. Originally every employer covered by the act was subject to inspection by OSHA compliance officers who were authorized to "enter without delay and at reasonable times any factory, plant, establishment . . . where work was performed . . . ," and to "inspect and investigate during regular working hours, and at other reasonable times, . . . any such place of employment and all pertinent conditions, structures, machines, . . . and to question privately any such employer, owner, operator, agent or employee."[11] However, based on a 1978 Supreme Court ruling (*Marshall v. Bar-*

FIGURE 18.2
What Accidents Must Be Reported under the Occupational Safety and Health Act (OSHA)
Source: *What Every Employer Needs to Know about OSHA Recordkeeping* (Washington, D.C.: U.S. Department of Labor, 1978), p. 3.

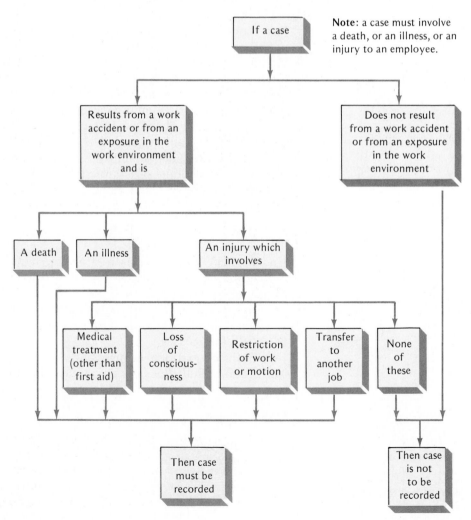

FIGURE 18.3
Form Used to Record Occupational Injuries and Illnesses

OSHA No. 101
Case or File No. _____

Form approved
OMB No. 44R 1453

Supplementary Record of Occupational Injuries and Illnesses

EMPLOYER
  1. Name _____

  2. Mail address _____
               (No. and street)   (City or town)   (State)

  3. Location, if different from mail address _____

INJURED OR ILL EMPLOYEE
  4. Name _____ Social Security No. _____
        (First name)   (Middle name)   (Last name)

  5. Home address _____
         (No. and street)   (City or town)   (State)

  6. Age _____   7. Sex: Male_____ Female_____ (Check one)

  8. Occupation _____
           (Enter regular job title, *not* the specific activity he was performing at time of injury.)

  9. Department _____
           (Enter name of department or division in which the injured person is regularly employed, even
           though he may have been temporarily working in another department at the time of injury.)

THE ACCIDENT OR EXPOSURE TO OCCUPATIONAL ILLNESS
  10. Place of accident or exposure _____
             (No. and street)   (City or town)   (State)
      If accident or exposure occurred on employer's premises, give address of plant or establishment in which
      it occurred. Do not indicate department or division within the plant or establishment. If accident oc-
      curred outside employer's premises at an identifiable address, give that address. If it occurred on a pub-
      lic highway or at any other place which cannot be identified by number and street, please provide place
      references locating the place of injury as accurately as possible.

  11. Was place of accident or exposure on employer's premises? _____ (Yes or No)

  12. What was the employee doing when injured? _____
             (Be specific. If he was using tools or equipment or handling material,
_____
           name them and tell what he was doing with them.)

  13. How did the accident occur? _____
          (Describe fully the events which resulted in the injury or occupational illness. Tell what
_____
happened and how it happened. Name any objects or substances involved and tell how they were involved. Give
_____
full details on all factors which led or contributed to the accident. Use separate sheet for additional space.)

OCCUPATIONAL INJURY OR OCCUPATIONAL ILLNESS
  14. Describe the injury or illness in detail and indicate the part of body affected. _____
          (e.g.: amputation of right index finger
_____
at second joint; fracture of ribs; lead poisoning; dermatitis of left hand, etc.)

  15. Name the object or substance which directly injured the employee. (For example, the machine or thing
      he struck against or which struck him; the vapor or poison he inhaled or swallowed; the chemical or ra-
      diation which irritated his skin; or in cases of strains, hernias, etc., the thing he was lifting, pulling, etc.)
_____

  16. Date of injury or initial diagnosis of occupational illness _____
          (Date)

  17. Did employee die? _____ (Yes or No)

OTHER
  18. Name and address of physician _____

  19. If hospitalized, name and address of hospital _____
_____
    Date of report _____ Prepared by _____
    Official position _____

low's, Inc.), OSHA may no longer conduct warrantless inspections without an employer's consent. It may, however, inspect after acquiring a judicially authorized search warrant or its equivalent.[12]

Inspection Priorities

OSHA has established a list of inspection priorities ranging from "imminent danger" to "random inspections." Imminent danger situations are given top priority. This is a condition where it is likely a danger exists that can cause death or serious physical harm immediately. Second priority is given to investigation of catastrophies, fatalities, and accidents that have already occurred. (Such situations must be reported to OSHA within 48 hours.) Third priority is given to valid employee complaints of alleged violation of standards. Next in priority are periodic "high-hazard" inspections; these are aimed at high-hazard industries, occupations, or health substances. Finally, random inspections (and reinspections) generally have last priority.

Under an inspection policy instituted in 1979, OSHA no longer follows up on *every* employee complaint with an inspection, as it previously did. The thrust now is to focus on priority problems.[13] Under the new priority system, OSHA conducts an inspection within 24 hours when a complaint indicates an immediate danger, and within 3 working days when a serious hazard exists. For a "nonserious" complaint filed in writing by a worker or a union OSHA will respond within 20 working days. Otherwise, "nonserious" complaints are handled by writing to the employer and requesting corrective action. This shift to "high priority" inspections is partly a result of restrictions placed on OSHA inspections by Congress and the courts. The need to obtain warrants and to exempt firms having 10 or fewer employees and good safety records from safety inspections are some examples of these restrictions.

OSHA today is increasingly focusing its efforts on the highest hazard worksites. Of the 71,303 OSHA inspections made recently, more than 72% were concentrated on high-hazard worksites. The agency cited 119,706 alleged violations and assessed penalties totaling $9,190,039.[14] In 1989, Lockheed Aeronautical was hit with nearly $1.5 million in proposed penalties, for instance. Of these establishment inspections, most were restricted to high-hazard industries with a likelihood of serious problems.[15]

The Inspection Itself

Before an inspection, the OSHA inspector becomes familiar with as many relevant facts as possible about the workplace.[16] The inspection itself begins when the OSHA officer arrives at the place of work. He or she displays official credentials and asks to meet an appropriate employer representative. (You should always insist on seeing the officer's credentials, which include photograph and serial number.) The officer explains the purpose of the visit, the scope of the inspection, and the standards that apply. An authorized *employee* representative is also given an opportunity to accompany the officer during the inspection. Other employees will also be consulted during the inspection tour, and the inspector can stop and question workers (in private if necessary) about safety and health conditions. Each employee is protected under the act from discrimination for exercising his or her disclosure rights.

Finally (after checking the premises and employer's records), a closing conference is held between the inspector and the employer (or his representative). Here the inspector discusses with the employer what has been found in terms of all apparent violations for which a citation may be issued or recommended. Note that the inspector does *not* indicate any proposed penalties; only the OSHA area director has that authority. At this point the employer can produce records to show compliance efforts.

Citations and Penalties

citations Summons informing employers and employees of the regulations and standards that have been violated in the workplace.

After the inspection report is submitted to the OSHA office, the area director determines what citations, if any, will be issued. The **citations** inform the employer and employees of the regulations and standards that have been violated and of the time set for rectifying the problem. These citations must be posted at or near the place the violation occurred. Under some circumstances the inspector can post a citation immediately (to ensure that employees receive protection in the shortest possible time).

The area director can also propose penalties. These range up to $1,000 for serious violations and up to $10,000 and six months in jail for falsifying records or reports. Any employer who willfully or repeatedly violates the act can be fined up to $10,000 for each such violation.

Although such penalties may seem substantial, many believe the penalty is not effective for two reasons. First, in large companies penalties of even $10,000 "are a joke" according to one OSHA representative.[17] The second problem is the built-in appeals approach. Under the act, an employer can appeal the penalty to the independent Occupational Safety and Health Review Commission and thus gain an extension. The review process normally lasts about 3 years, and during this period the employer is not required to correct a violation and OSHA cannot enforce the standard unless there is some imminent danger: "As a result, more than 40% of the serious-hazard citations OSHA issues are challenged."[18]

Yet, appeals or not, OSHA is not without teeth. For example, a $2.6 million penalty was recently levied against IBP, Inc., for more than 1,000 alleged violations of OSHA recordkeeping requirements. The meat packer was brought to OSHA's attention by the union there, which charged IBP with keeping fraudulent records to mask high injury rates.[19]

◆ THE RESPONSIBILITIES AND RIGHTS OF EMPLOYERS AND EMPLOYEES

As summarized in Figure 18.4, both employers and employees have certain responsibilities and rights under the Occupational Safety and Health Act. Employers, for example, are responsible for meeting their duty to provide "a workplace free from recognized hazards," for being familiar with mandatory OSHA standards, for informing all employees about OSHA, and for examining workplace conditions to make sure they conform to applicable standards. Employers have the right to seek advice and off-site consultation from OSHA, to request and to receive proper identification of the OSHA compliance officer before inspection, and to be advised by the compliance officer of the reason for an inspection.

Employees also have certain rights and responsibilities, although they *cannot* be cited for violations of their responsibilities. They are responsible, for example, for complying with all applicable OSHA standards, for following all employer safety and health rules and regulations, and for reporting hazardous conditions to the supervisor.

Employees have a right to demand safety and health on the job without fear of punishment, and employers are specifically forbidden to punish or discriminate against workers for exercising rights such as complaining to an employer, union, or OSHA about job safety and health hazards.

Dealing with Employee Resistance

While employees have a responsibility to comply with OSHA standards, the fact is they often resist complying, and in most such cases the *employer* remains liable for any penalties.[20] The problem of employee resistance is typified by the refusal of longshoremen to wear hard hats as mandated by the OSHA requirements. Historically, longshoremen have resisted wearing hard hats, and their resistance did not cease with the advent of OSHA. Employers have attempted to defend themselves against penalties for such noncompliance by citing worker intransigence and fear of wildcat strikes and walkouts. Yet in most cases courts have held that employers were liable for safety violations at the workplace regardless of the fact that the violations were due to employee resistance.[21] The result is that as an employer you are often in a difficult position; on the one hand, the courts and the occupa-

FIGURE 18.4

Employer/Employee Rights and Responsibilities Under OSHA

Source: U. S. Department of Labor, *All About OSHA* (Washington, D.C.: U.S. Government Printing Office, April 1976).

Responsibilities

As an employer, you must:

- Meet your general duty responsibility to provide a hazard-free workplace and comply with the occupational safety and health standards, rules, and regulations issued under the Act.

- Be familiar with mandatory OSHA standards and make copies available to employees for review upon request.

- Inform all employees about OSHA.

- Examine workplace conditions to make sure they conform to applicable safety and health standards.

- Remove or guard hazards.

- Make sure employees have and use safe tools and equipment (including personal protective equipment) and that such equipment is properly maintained.

- Use color codes, posters, labels, or signs to warn employees of potential hazards.

- Establish or update operating procedures and communicate them so that employees follow safety and health requirements for their own protection.

- Provide medical examinations when required by OSHA standards.

- Report to the nearest OSHA office, **within 48 hours**, the occurrence of any employment accident which is fatal to one or more employees or which results in the hospitalization of five or more employees.

- Keep OSHA-required records of work-related injuries and illnesses, and post the annual summary during the entire month of February each year. (This applies to employers with eight or more employees.)

- Post, at a prominent location within the workplace, the OSHA poster (OSHA 2203) informing employees of their rights and responsibilities. (In States operating OSHA-approved job safety and health programs, the State's equivalent poster and/or OSHA 2203 may be required.)

- Cooperate with the OSHA compliance officer by furnishing names of authorized employee representatives who may be asked to accompany the compliance officer during the inspection. (If none, the compliance officer will consult with a reasonable number of employees concerning safety and health in the workplace.)

- Not discriminate against employees who properly exercise their rights under the Act.

- Post OSHA citations of apparent violations of standards or of the general duty clause at or near the worksite involved. Each citation, or copy thereof, shall remain posted until the violation has been abated, or for 3 working days, whichever is longer.

- Abate cited violations within the prescribed period.

Rights

As an employer, you have the right to:

- Seek advice and off-site consultation as needed by writing, calling, or visiting the nearest OSHA office. (OSHA will not inspect merely because an employer requests assistance.)

- Be active in your industry association's involvement in job safety and health.

- Request and receive proper identification of the OSHA compliance officer prior to inspection of the workplace.

- Be advised by the compliance officer of the reason for an inspection.

- Have an opening and closing conference with the compliance officer.

- File a Notice of Contest with the nearest OSHA area director within 15 working days of receipt of a notice of citation and proposed penalty.

- Apply to OSHA for a temporary variance from a standard if unable to comply because of the unavailability of materials, equipment, or personnel to make necessary changes within the required time.

- Apply to OSHA for a permanent variance from a standard if you can furnish proof that your facilities or method of operation provide employee protection that is at least as effective as that required by the standard.

- Take an active role in developing job safety and health standards through participation in OSHA Standards Advisory Committees, through nationally recognized standards setting organizations, and through evidence and views presented in writing or at hearings.

- Avail yourself, if you are a small business employer, of long-term loans through the Small Business Administration

---

tional safety and health review commission claim that employers must vigorously seek employee compliance; yet on the other hand doing so is often all but impossible.

There are several tactics you can use to overcome this problem.[22] First, the courts have held that an employer can bargain in good faith with representatives of its employees for the right to discharge or discipline any employee who disobeys an OSHA standard. Yet most unions have thus far refused to bargain over hard hats (and many other OSHA issues) because they oppose having penalties assessed against their members. As a second alternative, one expert suggests greater use of arbitration in safety disputes. Arbitration is already widely used to resolve employee grievances, and the use of a formal arbitration process by aggrieved employers could provide a relatively quick and inexpensive method for resolving an OSHA-related complaint. Other employers have turned to positive reinforcement and training for the purpose of gaining employee compliance; more on this shortly.

◆ THE CHANGING NATURE OF OSHA

The Occupational Safety and Health Act and Administration both have been criticized on many grounds, and it is not unusual for the U.S. Congress to

FIGURE 18.4
(continued)

(SBA) to help bring your establishment into compliance, either before or after an OSHA inspection.

- Be assured of the confidentiality of any trade secrets observed by an OSHA compliance officer during an inspection.

Responsibilities

As an employee, you should:

- Read the OSHA poster at the jobsite.
- Comply with all applicable OSHA standards.
- Follow all employer safety and health rules and regulations, and wear or use prescribed protective equipment while engaged in work.
- Report hazardous conditions to the supervisor.
- Report any job-related injury or illness to the employer, and seek treatment promptly.
- Cooperate with the OSHA compliance officer conducting an inspection if he or she inquires about safety and health conditions in your workplace.
- Exercise your rights under the Act in a responsible manner.

Rights

As an employee, you have the right to:

- Review copies of any of the OSHA standards, rules, regulations, and requirements that the employer should have available at the workplace.
- Request information from your employer on safety and health hazards in the area, on precautions that may be taken, and on procedures to be followed if an employee is involved in an accident or exposed to toxic substances.

- Request (in writing) the OSHA area director to conduct an inspection if you believe hazardous conditions or violation of standards exist in your workplace.
- Have your name withheld from your employer, upon request to OSHA, if you file a written and signed complaint.
- Be advised of OSHA actions regarding your complaint and have an informal review, if requested, of any decision not to make an inspection or not to issue a citation.
- File a complaint to OSHA within 30 days if you believe you have been discriminated against, discharged, demoted, or otherwise penalized because of asserting an employee right under the Act, and be notified by OSHA of its determination within 90 days of filing.
- Have the authorized employee representative where you work accompany the OSHA compliance officer during the inspection tour.
- Respond to questions from the OSHA compliance officer, particularly if there is no authorized employee representative accompanying the compliance officer.
- Observe any monitoring or measuring of hazardous materials and have the right of access to records on those materials, as specified under the Act.
- Request a closing discussion with the compliance officer following an inspection.
- Submit a written request to the National Institute for Occupational Safety and Health (NIOSH) for information on whether any substance in your workplace has potential toxic effects in the concentrations being used, and have your name withheld from your employer if you so request.
- Object to the abatement period set in the citation issued to your employer by writing to the OSHA area director within 15 working days of the issuance of the citation.
- Be notified by your employer if he or she applies for a variance from an OSHA standard, testify at a variance hearing, and appeal the final decision if you disagree with it.
- Submit information or comment to OSHA on the issuance, modification, or revocation of OSHA standards, and request a public hearing.

have more than 100 OSHA reform bills on its agenda.[23] Critics have argued, for example, that too many of OSHA's rules are nit-picking, that OSHA has had an overly adverse affect on small businesses (for whom the penalties are, relatively, more difficult to bear), and that its emphasis on complying with standards has been ineffective (instead, one critic argues, the emphasis should be on performance—on number of accidents and illnesses reduced—rather than on dictating the specific means for doing so).[24]

In response to these sorts of criticisms (and in response to various court decisions), OSHA has made several changes in its policies and procedures over the last few years. Small businesses with ten or fewer employees no longer have to file accident reports or undergo routine inspections, and the accident report itself has been simplified and condensed.[25] As mentioned, OSHA inspectors must also now obtain warrants before entering an employer's premises.

Other changes have taken place as well. Starting in 1981, the funding of OSHA was severely reduced by the Reagan administration. In addition, the Reagan administration issued an executive order requiring no regulatory action be "undertaken unless potential benefits to society from the regulation outweigh the potential costs to society." This action has done much to stop the initiation of further OSHA health and safety standards.[26] Generally, businesspeople seem to feel that OSHA has become less "heavy handed" than it has been in the past and better trained and more professional.

And a new emphasis on health (on occupation-related illnesses) has done much to raise OSHA's credibility.[27]

THE SUPERVISOR'S ROLE IN SAFETY

As a safety-minded manager, your basic aim must be *to instill in your workers the desire to work safely.* Minimizing hazards (by ensuring that spills are wiped up, machine guards are adequate, and so forth) is important, but no matter how safe the workplace is, there will be accidents unless workers *want* to act safely and do. Of course, you could try closely watching each subordinate, but most managers know this won't work. In the final analysis, your best (and perhaps only) alternative is to instill in workers the desire to work safely. Then, where needed, enforce your safety rules.[28]

♦ TOP MANAGEMENT COMMITMENT

Most safety experts agree that this "worker commitment" to safety has to begin with top management. And the fact is that companies that do have this safety commitment have much better safety records than those who don't. Historically, for example, DuPont's accident rate has been much lower than that of the chemical industry as a whole. (In its U.S. plants, DuPont had an annual rate of 0.12 accidents per 100 workers, which was one-twenty-third of the national Safety Council's average rate for all manufacturers in that year. If DuPont's record had been average, it would have spent more than $26 million in additional compensation and other costs, or 3.6 percent of its profits. To recover the difference, DuPont would have had to increase sales by about $500 million, given the company's 5.5% net return on sales at that time).[29] And it seems likely that this good safety record is at least partly due to an organizational commitment to safety, a commitment that is evident in the following description:[30]

> One of the best examples I know of in setting the highest possible priority for safety takes place at a DuPont Plant in Germany. Each morning at the DuPont Polyester and Nylon Plant the director and his assistants meet at 8:45 to review the past 24 hours. The first matter they discuss is not production, but safety. Only after they have examined reports of accidents and near misses and satisfied themselves that corrective action has been taken do they move on to look at output, quality, and cost matters.

In summary, it is probably safe to say that without the full commitment of all levels of management, any attempts to reduce unsafe acts on the part of workers will meet with little success. And, related to this, keep in mind that the first-line supervisor is a critical link in the chain of management. As safety expert Willie Hammer states:

> A prime requisite for any successful accident prevention program is to leave no doubt in the mind of any employee that managers are concerned about accident prevention. The most effective means by which this can be done is for the manager at the highest level possible to issue a directive indicating his accident prevention policies and then to insure that lower level managers, supervisors, and other employees carry them out. . . . For the workers the supervisor represents management. He has to see that the intention and orders of management are carried out by exerting personal authority and influence. If the supervisor does not take safety seriously, those under him or her will not either. . . .

♦ WHAT YOU AS A SUPERVISOR CAN DO TO PREVENT ACCIDENTS

Some specific actions you can take to prevent accidents are presented in Table 18.1. They include training the worker in the proper procedures, checking safety equipment such as machinery guards, and making periodic inspections to monitor hazardous locations and worker behavior.

WHAT CAUSES ACCIDENTS?

♦ THE THREE BASIC CAUSES OF ACCIDENTS

Safety experts know that there are three basic factors that contribute to accidents in organizations: chance occurrences, unsafe conditions, and unsafe acts on the part of employees. Chance occurrences (such as walking past a plate-glass window just as someone hits a ball through it) contribute to accidents but are more or less beyond management's control; we will therefore focus on *unsafe conditions* and *unsafe acts.*

♦ UNSAFE CONDITIONS (WORK-RELATED ACCIDENT-CAUSING FACTORS)

unsafe conditions The mechanical and physical conditions that cause accidents.

Unsafe conditions (of one sort or another) are one main cause of accidents. They include such things as:

Improperly guarded equipment

Defective equipment

Hazardous arrangement or procedure in, on, or around machines or equipment

Unsafe storage: congestion, overloading

Improper illumination—glare, insufficient light

Improper ventilation—insufficient air change, impure air source[31]

The OSHA standards are aimed at eliminating or minimizing these kinds of unsafe conditions. These standards address in detail the mechanical and physical conditions that cause accidents. But on a day-to-day basis many supervisors find that a brief checklist of "unsafe conditions" can be very useful for spotting problems. One such checklist is presented in Figure 18.5.

While accidents can happen anywhere, there are some "high danger" zones. About one-third of industrial accidents occur around forklift trucks, wheelbarrows, and other handling and lifting areas, for example. The most serious accidents usually occur near metal and woodworking machines and saws or around transmission machinery like gears, pulleys, and flywheels. Falls on stairs, ladders, walkways, and scaffolds are the third most common cause of industrial accidents. Hand tools (like chisels and screwdrivers) and electrical equipment (extension cords, electric drop lights, and so on) are other big accident causers.[32]

Three Other Work-Related Accident Factors

In addition to the unsafe conditions we just discussed, safety experts know that three more work-related factors contribute to accidents: *the job itself, the work schedule,* and the *psychological climate* of the workplace.

For example, we know that some *jobs* are inherently more dangerous than others. According to one study, for example, the job of crane operator

TABLE 18.1   Error Prevention

CAUSES OF PRIMARY ERRORS	PREVENTIVE MEASURES TO BE TAKEN BY DESIGNER OR METHODS ENGINEER
1. Improvising procedures that are lacking in the field	1. Provide adequate instructions.
2. Following prescribed but incorrect procedures	2. Ensure that procedures are correct.
3. Failure to follow prescribed procedures	3. Ensure that procedures are not too lengthy, too fast, or too slow for good performance, and are not hazardous or awkward.
4. Lack of adequate planning for error or unusual conditions	4. Provide backout or emergency procedures in instructions.
5. Lack of understanding of procedures	5. Ensure that instructions are easy to understand.
6. Lack of awareness of hazards	6. Provide warnings, cautions, or explanations in instructions.
7. Untimely activation of equipment	7. Provide interlocks or timer lockouts. Provide warning or caution notes against activating equipment unless disconnected or disengaged from load, or other damaging conditions.
8. Errors of judgment, especially during periods of stress	8. Minimize requirements for making hurried judgments, especially at critical times, through programmed contingency measures.
9. Critical components installed incorrectly	9. Provide designs permitting such components to be installed only in the proper ways. Use asymmetric configurations on mechanical equipment or electrical connectors; use female or male threads or different-sized connections on critical valves, filters, or other components in which direction of flow is important.
10. Exceeding prescribed limitations on load, speed, or other parameter	10. Provide governors and other parameter limiters. Provide warnings on exceeding limitations, inadequate strength of stressed parts, use of excessive mechanical leverage.
11. Lack of suitable tools or equipment	11. Ensure that need for special tools or equipment is minimized; develop and provide those that are necessary; stress their need in instructions.
12. Interference with normal habits	12. Ensure that recognition and activation patterns are in accordance with usual practices and expectancies.
13. Lack of data on which to make correct or timely decisions	13. Ensure that response time is adequate for corrective action; if not, provide automatic corrective devices.
14. Hampered activities because of interference between personnel	14. Ensure that space is adequate to perform required activities simultaneously.
15. Inability to concentrate because of unsafe conditions or equipment	15. Ensure that personnel must not work close to unguarded moving parts, hot surfaces, sharp edges, or other dangers.
16. Error or delay in use of controls	16. Avoid proximity, interference, awkward location, or similarity of critical controls. Locate control close to readout. Locate readout above control so hand or arm making adjustment does not block out readout instrument. Ensure that controls are labeled prominently for easy understanding.

TABLE 18.1   (continued)

CAUSES OF PRIMARY ERRORS	PREVENTIVE MEASURES TO BE TAKEN BY DESIGNER OR METHODS ENGINEER
17. Error or delay in reading instruments	17. Ensure that instruments are labeled and designed for easy understanding; do not require reader to turn head or move body; and that visibility problems due to glare or lack of light, legibility, viewing angle, contrast, or reflections are avoided. Provide direct readings of specific parameters so operator does not have to interpret.
18. Inadvertent activation of controls	18. For critical functions provide controls that cannot be activated inadvertently; use torque types instead of push buttons. Provide guards over critical switches.
19. Controls activated in wrong order	19. Place functional controls in sequence in which they are to be used. Provide interlocks where sequences are critical.
20. Control settings by operator not precise enough	20. Provide controls that permit making settings or adjustments without need for extremely fine movements. Use click-type controls.
21. Controls broken by excessive force	21. Ensure that controls are adequate to withstand maximum stress an operator could apply. Provide warning and caution notes for those devices that could be overstressed.
22. Failure to take action at proper time because of faulty instruments	22. Provide procedures to calibrate instruments periodically, or provide the means to ensure during operation that they are working correctly.
23. Confusion in reading critical instruments because of instrument clutter	23. Make critical instruments most prominent or locate in easiest-to-read area.
24. Failure to note critical indication	24. Provide suitable auditory or visual warning device that will attract operator's attention to problem.
25. Involuntary reaction or inability to perform properly because of pain due to burns, electrical shock, puncture wound, or impact.	25. Insulate or guard against hot surfaces, "live" electrical conductors, sharp objects, and hard surfaces.
26. Fatigue	26. Avoid placing on operator severe and tiring physical and mental requirements such as loads, concentration times, vibration, personal stress, awkward positions.
27. Vibration and noise cause irritation and inability to read meters and settings or to operate controls	27. Provide vibration isolators or noise-elimination devices.
28. Irritation and loss of effectiveness due to high temperature and humidity	28. Provide environmental control. Prevent entrance or generation of heat or moisture from external sources or from internal equipment or processes.
29. Loss of effectiveness due to lack of oxygen, or to presence of toxic gas, airborne particulate matter, or odors	29. Prevent generation or entrance of contaminants into the occupied space. Provide suitable life support equipment. Avoid presence near occupied areas of lines or equipment containing hazardous gases or liquids.
30. Degradation of capabilities due to extremely low temperatures	30. Ensure that design provides for adequate heating or insulation protective shelter, equipment, or clothing.
31. Fixation or hypnosis	31. Avoid procedures or designs that require visual concentrations for long periods of time.

TABLE 18.1 (continued)

CAUSES OF PRIMARY ERRORS	PREVENTIVE MEASURES TO BE TAKEN BY DESIGNER OR METHODS ENGINEER
	Avoid humming equipment. Provide alternative reference points. Provide procedures to relieve monotony.
32. Disorientation of vertigo	32. Provide adequate reference points or means to maintain orientation.
33. Slipping and falling	33. Incorporate friction surfaces or devices, guard rails, access hole covers on floor openings, or protective harness in designs.
34. Inattention	34. Avoid long intervals between procedural steps. Provide female voice on audio devices to attract attention. Provide bright, colorful, and pleasant work areas.

Source: Willie Hammer, *Occupational Safety Management and Engineering*, 3d ed. (Englewood Cliffs, N.J.: Prentice-Hall, 1985), pp. 114–115. © 1985. Reprinted by permission of Prentice-Hall, Englewood Cliffs, N.J.

results in about three times more accident-related hospital visits than does the job of supervisor. Similarly, the work in some departments is inherently safer than the work in others. For example, the bookkeeping or human resources departments usually have fewer accidents on the whole than do shipping or production departments.

Work schedules also affect accident rates, since accidents increase late in the day. Accident rates usually don't increase too noticeably during the first five or six hours of the workday. But beyond that, the accident rate increases faster than the increase in the number of hours worked. This is due partly to fatigue and partly to the fact that accidents occur more often during night shifts.

Finally, many experts believe that the *psychological climate* of the workplace also affects the accident rate. For example, accidents occur more frequently in plants with a high seasonal layoff rate and where there is hostility among employees, many garnisheed wages, and blighted living conditions. Temporary stress factors such as high workplace temperature, poor illumination, and a congested workplace are also related to high accident rates. One writer says that these findings mean that psychological climate affects accident rates.[33] He says that workers who work under stress, or who feel that their jobs are threatened or insecure, seem to have more accidents than those who do not.[34]

◆ WHAT CAUSES UNSAFE ACTS (A SECOND BASIC CAUSE OF ACCIDENTS)

unsafe acts Behavior tendencies and undesirable attitudes that cause accidents.

There is little double that **unsafe acts** (not unsafe conditions) are the main cause of accidents, and that *people* cause these unsafe acts.

Most safety experts and managers long ago discovered that it is impossible to eliminate accidents simply by reducing unsafe conditions. This is because *people* cause accidents, and to date no one has found a sure-fire way to make employees work safely. The result is a number of unsafe acts such as:

Failing to secure equipment

Failing to use safe attire or personal protective equipment

Throwing materials

FIGURE 18.5
Checklist of Mechanical or Physical Accident-Causing Conditions
Source: Courtesy of the American Insurance Association. From "A Safety Committee Man's Guide," I-64.

I. General Housekeeping

Adequate and wide aisles—no materials protruding into aisles

Parts and tools stored safely after use—not left in hazardous positions that could cause them to fall

Even and solid flooring—no defective floors or ramps that could cause falling or tripping accidents

Waste cans and sand pails—safely located and properly used

Material piled in safe manner- not too high or too close to sprinkler heads

Floors—clean and dry

Firefighting equipment - unobstructed

Work benches orderly

Stockcarts and skids safely located, not left in aisles or passageways

Aisles kept clear and properly marked no air lines or electric cords across aisles

II. Material Handling Equipment and Conveyances

On all conveyances, electric or hand, check to see that the following items are all in sound working conditions:

Brakes—properly adjusted
Not too much play in steering wheel
Warning device—in place and working
Wheels—securely in place; properly inflated
Fuel and oil—enough and right kind
No loose parts

Cables, hooks or chains- not worn or otherwise defective
Suspended chains or hooks conspicuous
Safely loaded
Properly stored

III. Ladders, Scaffold, Benches, Stairways, etc.

The following items of major interest to be checked:

Safety feet on straight ladders
Guard rails or hand rails
Treads, not slippery
Not splintered, cracked, or rickety

Properly stored
Extension ladder ropes in good condition
Toe boards

IV. Power Tools (stationary)

Point of operation guarded
Guards in proper adjustment
Gears, belts, shafting, counterweights guarded
Foot pedals guarded
Brushes provided for cleaning machines
Adequate lighting
Properly grounded
Tool or material rests properly adjusted

Adequate work space around machines
Control switch easily accessible
Safety glasses worn
Gloves worn by persons handling rough or sharp materials
No gloves or loose clothing worn by persons operating machines

V. Hand Tools and Miscellaneous

In good condition—not cracked, worn, or otherwise defective
Properly stored

Correct for job
Goggles, respirators, and other personal protective equipment worn where necessary

VI. Welding

Arc shielded
Fire hazards controlled
Operator using suitable protective equipment

Adequate ventilation
Cylinder secured
Valves closed when not in use

VII. Spray Painting

Explosion-proof electrical equipment
Proper storage of paints and thinners in approved metal cabinets

Fire extinguishers adequate and suitable; readily accessible
Minimum storage in work area

VIII. Fire Extinguishers

Properly serviced and tagged
Readily accessible

Adequate and suitable for operations involved

Operating or working at unsafe speeds—either too fast or too slow

Making safety devices inoperative by removing, adjusting, disconnecting them

Using unsafe equipment or using equipment unsafely

Using unsafe procedures in loading, placing, mixing, combining

Taking unsafe positions under suspended loads

Lifting improperly

Distracting, teasing, abusing, startling, quarreling, horseplay

Unsafe acts such as these can short-circuit even the best attempts on your part to minimize unsafe conditions. It is therefore important that we discuss what we know about what causes such unsafe acts.[35]

Personal Characteristics and Accidents

Ernest McCormick and Joseph Tiffin have developed a model that summarizes how personal characteristics (such as personality) are linked to accidents; it is presented in Figure 18.6. They say that personal characteristics (personality, motivation, and so on) serve as the basis for certain "behavior tendencies"—such as the tendency to take risks—and undesirable attitudes. These behavior tendencies in turn result in unsafe acts—such as failure to follow procedures and inattention. In turn, such unsafe acts drastically increase the probability of a person's incurring an accident.

Are There "Accident-Prone" People?

You have probably come across people whom you would consider "accident prone." (Perhaps it is the person who is always dropping things or bumping into doors or falling, for instance.) But to a psychologist, the phrase "accident prone" means something quite specific. It implies the possession of those *qualities* or *traits* that have been found from research to lead to an undue number of accidents.[36] Thus, to most psychologists, accident proneness is a *personality type,* and a person who is accident prone can be identified by a number of specific and measurable personality traits.

There is considerable doubt as to whether such a personality type exists. Most experts doubt that accident proneness is universal—that there are some people who will have many accidents no matter what situation they are put in. Instead, the consensus seems to be that the person who is accident prone on one job may not be on a different job—that accident proneness is "situational." We will discuss some of the relevant findings.

What Traits Characterize Accident-Prone People?

For years psychologists have tried to determine what package of traits distinguishes those who are accident prone from those who are not. The original interest in this was based on the discovery that a small percentage of workers (say, 20%) were responsible for a large percentage (say, 70%) of the accidents. Researchers assumed that the workers having more accidents were accident prone and set about trying to find a bundle of traits that made them so.

Today, it is generally recognized that these original findings were somewhat inaccurate and misleading; they were more a result of the statistical analysis than the accident proneness of the workers. (One problem was the small number of accidents per worker the researchers had to deal with. For example, suppose you flip a coin many, many times. Over the long run you

FIGURE 18.6
How Personal Factors May Influence Employee Accident Behavior

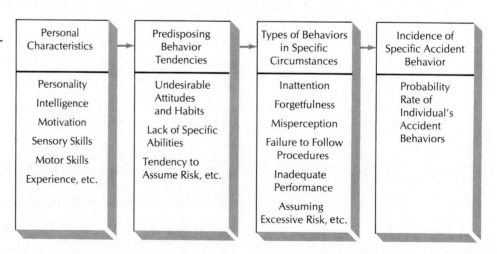

would expect to get one-half heads and one-half tails. But suppose you just flipped the coin several times—say, three or four. Here you might well get three tails in a row or four heads. In that case you obviously would not consider yourself "head prone" or "tail prone," yet that is about what early researchers concluded from the accident-proneness experiments.)

In any case, years of research failed to unearth any set of traits that accident repeaters seemed to have in common. Today, we believe that the personal traits that contribute to accidents probably differ from situation to situation. For example, *personality traits* (such as emotional stability) may distinguish accident-prone workers on jobs involving risk; and *motor skills* may distinguish accident-prone workers on jobs involving coordination. In fact, many human traits *have* been found to be related in accident repetition *in specific situations.*[37]

Vision

Vision is related to accident frequency for many jobs. For example, passenger car drivers, intercity bus drivers, and machine operators who have high visual skills have fewer injuries than those who do not.[38]

Age and Length of Service

We also know that accidents are generally most frequent between the ages of 17 and 28, declining thereafter to reach a low in the late fifties and sixties.[39] While different patterns might be found with different jobs, this age factor seems to be a fairly general one.

Perceptual Versus Motor Skills

One researcher concludes that "where [a worker's] perceptual [visual inspection] skill is equal to, or higher than, his motor skill, the employee is a relatively safe worker. But where the perception level is *lower* than the motor level, the employee is accident prone and his accident proneness becomes greater as this difference increases.[40] This theory seems to be a twist on the "look before you leap" theme; a worker who reacts quicker than he can perceive is more likely to have accidents.

Vocational Interests

In the Strong-Campbell Vocational Interest Test (discussed in Chapter 5), there are scales for, among other things, aviator and banker. One researcher equated "adventuresomeness" with the aviator scale and "cautiousness" with the banker scale. He then developed an "accident-proneness" index by subtracting the second from the first. Then, in a study of both hazardous and nonhazardous jobs in a food-processing plant, he found that employees with high accident-proneness scores had higher accident rates (see Figure 18.7) on *both* the hazardous and nonhazardous jobs.

In summary, these findings are not a complete picture of the personal traits that have been found to be related to higher accident rates. Some researchers, for example, believe that accident proneness is a type of deviant behavior that is characterized by impulsiveness and is found in *all* accident-prone people.[41] What they *do* suggest is that *for specific jobs* it seems to be possible to identify accident-prone individuals and to screen them out.

FIGURE 18.7
Accident-Proneness Index and Its Relationship to Frequency of Accidents
Source: J. T. Kunce, "Vocational Interest and Accident Proneness," *Journal of Applied Psychology*, Vol. 51 (1967), pp. 223–225. Copyright 1967 by the American Psychological Association. Reprinted by permission of the author.

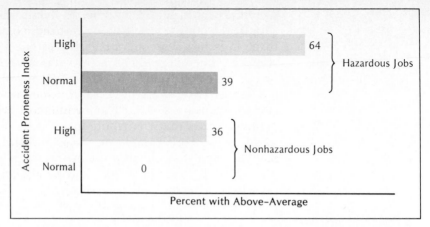

Note: Relationship between an "accident-proneness" index (based on the Strong Vocational Interest Blank) and accident rates of 62 male employees on jobs rated hazardous and nonhazardous in a food-processing plant.

HOW TO PREVENT ACCIDENTS

♦ BASIC APPROACHES TO PREVENTING ACCIDENTS

There are several ways to go about preventing accidents. The National Safety Council, for example, says that accident prevention depends on the three E's—engineering, education, and enforcement: the job should be *engineered* for safety, employees should be *educated* in safe procedures, and safety rules should be *enforced*.[42]

But, in practice, accident prevention boils down to two basic activities: reducing unsafe conditions and reducing unsafe acts.

♦ REDUCING UNSAFE CONDITIONS

Reducing unsafe conditions is primarily in the domain of safety engineers: their task is to remove or reduce physical hazards. However, all supervisors and managers do play a role in reducing unsafe conditions. Some use a brief checklist like the one in Figure 18.5. Other guidelines for reducing unsafe conditions were presented in Table 18.1. The Self-inspection Checklist in the appendix to this chapter can also be useful here.

♦ REDUCING UNSAFE ACTS THROUGH SELECTION AND PLACEMENT

One way to reduce accidents is to screen out accident-prone persons before they are hired. Accidents are similar to other types of poor performance, and you should therefore be interested in screening out these people, just as you might be interested in screening out applicants who are potentially "short tenure," "theft prone," or "low performers." We discussed the techniques for doing so in Chapters 4 to 6.

Psychologists have in fact had some success in screening out individuals who might be accident prone for some specific job. The basic technique involves identifying the human trait (such as visual skill) that might be related to accidents on the job. Then determine whether scores (on this trait) are indeed related to accidents on the job. Biographical (application blank) data, tests, and interview questions are some of the tools that you can use. For example:[43]

Emotional stability and personality tests. Psychological tests—especially tests of emotional stability—have been used to screen out accident-prone taxicab drivers. Here (as you might imagine) the test was an especially effective screening device when administered to the applicant under disturbing and distracting conditions (as he might encounter on the road). In this case, researchers found that taxi drivers who made five or more errors on such tests averaged three accidents, while those who made fewer than five averaged only 1.3 accidents.[44]

Measures of muscular coordination. We also know that *coordination* is a predictor of safety for certain jobs. In one study, more than 600 employees were divided into two groups according to test scores on coordination tests. Here it was found that the poorest quarter had 51% more accidents than those in the better three quarters.[45]

Tests of visual skills. We have already seen that good vision plays an important part in preventing accidents in many occupations, including driving and operating machines. In another study (made in a paper mill) 52 accident-free employees were compared with 52 accident-prone employees. Here the researcher found that 63% of the no-accident group passed a vision test, while only 33% of the accident group passed it.[46]

In summary, Professor Norman Maier concludes that:

> Of great practical importance is the fact that there is a definite relationship between these accident-proneness tests and proficiency on the job. By selecting employees who do well—that is, score low—on accident-proneness tests, managers can reduce accidents and improve the caliber of the employees at the same time.[47]

Genetic Screening for Employment Purposes

Some have proposed the possibility of genetic screening as a technique for reducing injuries and disease at work. This approach, which uses genetic tests, is based on the belief that individual differences in susceptibility to toxic exposure exist—that, in other words, some people are just genetically more susceptible to, say, chemical pollutants than are others. Genetic tests would provide information that is theoretically predictive of an individual's health status on the job. However, it is expected that genetic screening on the job will be slow to evolve for two reasons. First, there is strong evidence that genetic differences are distributed unequally across different ethnic populations so that genetic screening would elicit charges of employment discrimination. Second, genetic screening may run afoul of other legal roadblocks, including employee privacy rights and state workers' compensation laws (since, for example, genetic monitoring of employees for changes in genetic material as a result of repeated work exposure may jeopardize an employer's defense by showing a consistent, incremental pattern of genetic impairment over years of exposure to a toxic agent). In summary, as one expert concludes, "the foreseeable future promises far-reaching scientific advances that will permit the employment applications of G.S. practices." However, whether such applications will ever become widespread, considering the legal and ethical ramifications of genetic screening, remains a matter of conjecture.[48]

◆ REDUCING UNSAFE ACTS THROUGH PROPAGANDA

Many organizations use propaganda of one sort or another—such as safety posters—as part (or all) of their safety programs. Such posters (and other propaganda) can be useful; in one study, for example, their use apparently increased safe behavior by more than 20%.[49]

On the other hand, it is also true that you can't substitute posters for a comprehensive safety program; instead, they should be used in conjunction with other attempts to reduce unsafe conditions and acts. For example, it helps to key posters to your own safety program. Thus, if you are emphasizing protective gloves this month, the "poster of the month" should underscore this emphasis. It is also important to change posters frequently.[50]

♦ **REDUCING UNSAFE ACTS THROUGH TRAINING**

We also know that experience greatly reduces accidents. Since training can provide a substitute for experience, it follows that safety training can also significantly reduce accidents. Such training is especially appropriate with new employees. You should instruct them in safe practices and procedures, warn them of potential hazards, and work on developing their predisposition toward safety. OSHA has published two booklets, "Training Requirements Under OSHA" and "Teaching Safety and Health in the Workplace," that you may find useful here.

♦ **REDUCING UNSAFE ACTS THROUGH POSITIVE REINFORCEMENT**

Introduction

Safety programs based on positive reinforcement have been used successfully to improve safety at work.[51] One such program was instituted in a wholesale bakery that bakes, wraps, and transports pastry products to retail outlets nationwide.[52] An analysis of the safety-related conditions existing in the plant before the study suggested a number of areas that needed improvement. For example, new hires received no formal safety training and safety was rarely mentioned on a day-to-day basis. Commercial safety posters were placed at the entrance to the work area and on a bulletin board in the dining room but were often not updated for up to six months. No single person was responsible for safety. Similarly, an *analysis* revealed that safe practices were probably not being maintained by employees because they received little or no positive reinforcement for performing safely. Managers said little or nothing to employees who took the time to act safely. Although the accident rate had been climbing, many employees had yet to experience an injury because of performing unsafely, so this "negative reinforcement" also was missing.

The Safety Program

The safety program stressed positive reinforcement and training. A reasonable "safety goal" (in terms of observed incidents performed safely) was set and communicated to workers to ensure that they knew what was expected of them in terms of good performance. Next came a training phase in which employees were presented with safety information during a 30-minute training session. Here employees were shown pairs of slides (35mm transparencies) which depicted scenes that were staged in the plant. In one transparency, for example, the wrapping supervisor was shown climbing over a conveyor; the parallel slide illustrated the supervisor walking around the conveyor. After viewing an unsafe act, employees were asked to describe verbally what was wrong ("what's unsafe here?"). Then, once the problem had been aired, the same incident was again shown performed in a safe manner and the safe-conduct rule was explicitly stated ("go around, not over or under conveyors").

At the conclusion of the training phase the employees were shown a graph with their pretraining safety record (in terms of observed incidents performed safely) plotted and were encouraged to consider increasing their performance to the new safety goal for the following reasons: for their own protection; to decrease costs for the company; and, last, to help the plant get out of last place in the safety ranking of the parent company. Then the graph and a list of safety rules (do's and don'ts) were posted in a conspicuous place in the employees' work area.

Reinforcement and Safety

The graph then played an important role in the final positive reinforcement phase of the study. First, whenever observers walked through the plant collecting safety data, they posted on the graph the percentage of incidents they had seen performed safely by the group as a whole, thus providing the workers with feedback on their safety performance. Workers could therefore compare their current safety performance with their previous performance and with their assigned goal. In addition, supervisors praised workers when they performed selected incidents safely. Safety in the plant subsequently improved markedly.[53]

◆ REDUCING UNSAFE ACTS THROUGH TOP MANAGEMENT COMMITMENT

Reducing accidents is largely a result of developing a *safety-conscious attitude* on the part of employees. And it is apparent that without the full commitment of top management these attitudes will probably not materialize. According to one researcher, in fact, "one of the most consistent findings in the literature is that in factories having successful safety programs, there was a strong management commitment to safety.[54] In practice, this commitment manifests itself in top management's being personally involved in safety activities on a routine basis, in top management's giving safety matters high priority in company meetings and production scheduling, in top management's giving the company safety officer high rank and status, and by building safety training into new workers' training. A safety "self-inspection checklist" for top management is presented in the appendix to this chapter.

◆ SUMMARY: HOW TO REDUCE ACCIDENTS

1. Check for *unsafe conditions;* use a checklist like the one in Figure 18.5.
2. Thorough *selection;* try to screen out employees who might be accident prone for the job in question.
3. *Encourage and train* your employees to be safety conscious: show them you are serious about safety.
4. *Enforce safety rules.*
5. Regularly conduct *safety and health inspections,* and all accidents should be investigated along with "near misses." You should also have a reliable system for letting employees notify management about hazardous conditions.[55]

EMPLOYEE HEALTH: PROBLEMS AND REMEDIES[56]

◆ ALCOHOLISM AND SUBSTANCE ABUSE

Managers today deal with a complex set of problems, and among the most frustrating are the problems of worker alcoholism, drug addiction, and substance abuse—all of which seem to be increasing.[57]

For example, alcoholism is a serious and widespread disease, one not confined to "skid row" individuals. In fact, 50% of alcoholics are women, 25% are white-collar workers, 45% are professional/managerial personnel, 37% are high school graduates, and 50% have completed or attended college. Most are members of households. Some experts estimate that as many as 50% of all "problem employees" in industry are actually alcoholics. In one auto assembly plant, 48.6% of the grievances filed over the course of one year were alcohol related.[58] In the United States alone substance abusers cost employers about $30 billion in lost production alone and account for 40% of all industrial fatalities.

The effects of alcoholism on the worker and the work are severe.[59] Both the quality and quantity of the work decline sharply. A form of "on-the-job absenteeism" occurs as efficiency declines. The alcoholic's on-the-job accidents do *not* appear to increase significantly, apparently because he or she becomes much more cautious (but his effectiveness suffers as well). However, the *off*-the-job accident rate is three to four times higher than for nonalcoholics. Contrary to popular opinion, turnover among alcoholics is not unusually high. The morale of other workers is affected as they have to do the work of their alcoholic peer.

Recognizing the alcoholic on the job is also a major problem. The early symptoms are often similar to those of other problems and are thus hard to classify. The supervisor is not a professional psychiatrist, and without specialized training, identifying—and dealing with—the alcoholic is a difficult task.

A chart showing observable behavior patterns that indicate alcohol-related problems is presented in Table 18.2. As you can see, alcohol-related problems range from tardiness (in the earliest stages of alcohol abuse) to prolonged unpredictable absences in its later stages.[60]

Traditional Techniques Used to Deal with These Problems

Four traditional techniques for dealing with these problems include disciplining, discharge, in-house counseling, and referral to an outside agency. Discipline short of discharge is used more often with alcoholics; this technique is used infrequently for dealing with drug problems or emotional illness. Discharge is frequently used to deal with alcoholism and drug problems; it is almost never used in the case of serious emotional illness.

In-house counseling, one example of an *employee assistance program*, is used often in dealing with alcoholics and those with emotional disorders. In most cases the counseling is offered by the personnel department or the company's medical staff. Immediate supervisors who have received special training also provide counseling in many instances.

Many companies use outside agencies such as Alcoholics Anonymous, psychiatrists, and clinics to deal with the problems of alcoholism and emotional illness. Outside agencies are used less often in the case of drug problems.

In summary, discipline (short of discharge), in-house counseling, and referral to an outside agency are the techniques used most often to cope with alcoholism and emotional illness. There seems to be a tendency to discharge employees with drug problems; however, many respondents in this survey "did not indicate how they cope with drug problems."[61]

Trice[62] suggests a number of specific actions managers can take to deal with employee alcoholism—actions which all involve supervisory training or company policy. He says supervisors should be trained to identify the alcoholic and the problem he or she creates. Employers should also establish a company policy that recognizes alcoholism as a health problem and places it within the firm's health plan.

TABLE 18.2 Observable Behavior Patterns

STAGE	ABSENTEEISM	GENERAL BEHAVIOR	JOB PERFORMANCE
I Early	Tardiness Quits early Absence from work situations ("I drink to relieve tension")	Complaints from fellow employees for not doing his or her share Overreaction Complaints of not "feeling well" Makes untrue statements	Misses deadlines Commits errors (frequently) Lower job efficiency Criticism from the boss
II Middle	Frequent days off for vague or implausible reasons ("I feel guilty about sneaking drinks"; "I have tremors")	Marked changes Undependable statements Avoids fellow employees Borrows money from fellow employees Exaggerates work accomplishments Frequent hospitalization Minor injuries on the job (repeatedly)	General deterioration Cannot concentrate Occasional lapse of memory Warning from boss
III Late Middle	Frequent days off; several days at a time Does not return from lunch ("I don't feel like eating"; "I don't want to talk about it"; "I like to drink alone")	Aggressive and belligerent behavior Domestic problems interfere with work Financial difficulties (garnishments, and so on) More frequent hospitalization Resignation: does not want to discuss problems Problems with the laws in the community	Far below expectation Punitive disciplinary action
IV Approaching Terminal Stage	Prolonged unpredictable absences ("My job interferes with my drinking")	Drinking on the job (probably) Completely undependable Repeated hospitalization Serious financial problems Serious family problems: divorce	Uneven Generally incompetent Faces termination or hospitalization

Note: Based on content analysis of files of recovered alcoholics in five organizations. From *Managing and Employing the Handicapped: The Untapped Potential,* by Gopal C. Pati and John I. Adkins, Jr., with Glenn Morrison (Lake Forest, Ill.: Brace-Park, Human Resource Press, 1981).

Source: Gopal C. Pati and John I. Adkins, Jr., "The Employer's Role in Alcoholism Assistance," *Personnel Journal,* Vol. 62, no. 7 (July 1983), p. 570.

The Drug-Free Workplace Act of 1988

Today, because of the seriousness of the problem and the passage of a new federal law, most employers are taking additional steps to deal with alcohol and substance abuse on the job. The federal Drug-Free Workplace Act of 1988 became effective on March 18, 1989: It requires employers with federal government contracts or grants to ensure a drug-free workplace by taking (and certifying that they have taken) a number of steps. Specifically, to be eligible for contract awards or grants, employers must agree to:

Publish a policy prohibiting the unlawful manufacture, distribution, dispensing, possession, or use of controlled substances in the workplace.

Establish a drug-free awareness program that informs employees about the dangers of workplace drug abuse.

Inform employees that they are required, as a condition of employment, not only to abide by the employer's policy, but also to report any criminal convictions for drug-related activities in the workplace.

Notify the federal contracting or granting agency of any criminal convictions of employees for illegal drug activity in the workplace.

Take appropriate personnel action against any employee convicted of a criminal drug offense.

Make a "good faith" effort to maintain a drug-free workplace by complying with the law's requirements.[63]

♦ GUIDELINES FOR DEALING WITH SUBSTANCE ABUSE

Beyond this, there are a number of guidelines to follow. To repeat, experts recommend that management develop a *formal written policy* on substance abuse on the job. This should clearly state management's philosophy and position on drug abuse and on the use and possession of illegal drugs on company premises, and set standards for appropriate conduct both on and off the job. The policy should also list the methods (such as urinalysis) that might be used to determine the causes of poor performance and state the company's views on rehabilitation, including workplace counseling. Specific penalties for policy violation should be noted. This policy should then be communicated to all employees.

Supervisors, says this expert, should be the company's first line of defense in combating drug abuse in the workplace but should not try to become company detectives or medical diagnosticians. Guidelines that supervisors should follow include:

If an employee appears to be under the influence of drugs or alcohol, ask how the employee feels and look for signs of impairment such as slurred speech. An employee judged to be unfit for duty may be sent home, but under no circumstances should the person be fired on the spot.

Make a written record of your observations and follow up each incident. In addition to issuing a written reprimand, managers should inform workers of the number of warnings the company will tolerate before requiring termination.

Troubled employees should be referred to the company's employee assistance program.

Additional steps the employer can take to combat substance abuse on the job include *administering urine tests, conducting workplace inspections* (searching employees for illegal substances), and *using undercover agents* (which should be used only as a last resort, according to this expert).[64]

Remember, though, that techniques such as these entail legal risks, and employees have sued successfully over invasion of privacy rights, wrongful discharge, defamation, and illegal searches. Therefore, before implementing any drug control program:

Ask: *How would you inform workers about your substance abuse policy?* Providing employees with adequate notice of rules and procedures for handling drug-related problems is "critical to avoiding wrongful discharge allegations." Here you can use employee handbooks, bulletin board postings, pay inserts, and the like to publicize your substance abuse plans.

Ask: *What testing, such as urinalysis, will be required of prospective and current employees?* If you decide to implement drug-screening programs, you have to be careful to choose appropriate tests that include reliable procedures for analysis, verification, and retesting. The conditions under which testing may occur and the procedures for handling employees who refuse to be tested should be explained.

Ask: *What accommodations would you make for employees who voluntarily seek treatment for drug or alcohol problems?* Since substance abuse is considered a physical handicap under federal and some state laws, you may be required to make "reasonable accommodations" for employees who enter alcohol or drug treatment programs.

Ask: *Is supervisory training provided?* Since managers are often the first to observe signs of trouble on the job they should be taught how to recognize and document possible substance abuse-related performance problems.

Others factors must be considered. For example, searches on company property even without prior notice may be legal so long as they are conducted in a reasonable manner and avoid violating employees' privacy expectations. Similarly, conducting internal undercover investigations may be legal and even advised if there are repeated reports of employees using or selling drugs on the job. However, any such activities may trigger employee lawsuits and should be conducted only after a thorough review of their legal implications.[65]

♦ THE PROBLEMS OF JOB STRESS AND BURNOUT

To some extent, problems such as alcoholism and drug abuse are often a consequence of stress, especially *job stress.* Here job-related factors such as overwork, relocation, and problems with customers eventually put the person under so much stress that the result is some pathological reaction such as drug abuse.

There are two main sources of job stress: environmental and personal.[66] First, a variety of external, *environmental factors* can lead to job stress. These include your work schedule, pace of work, job security, route to and from work, and the number and nature of customers or clients. Yet no two people will react to the same job in the very same way, since *personal factors* also influence your stress. For example, type A personalities—people who are workaholics and who feel driven to always be on time and meet deadlines—normally place themselves under greater stress than do others. Similarly, your tolerance for ambiguity, patience, self-esteem, health and exercise, work, and sleep patterns can also affect how you react to stress. Add to job stress the stress caused by nonjob problems like divorce, and, as you might imagine, many workers are "accidents waiting to happen."

Regardless of its source, however, job stress has serious consequences for both the employee and the organization. The human consequences of job stress include anxiety, depression, anger, and various physical consequences, such as cardiovascular disease, headaches, and accidents. In some cases it can lead to other human consequences, including drug abuse, over and under eating, and poor interpersonal relations. Stress also has serious

PERSONNEL MANAGEMENT:

ON THE FRONT LINE

Employees' safety and health are very important matters in the laundry and cleaning business. Each facility is a small production plant in which machines, powered by high-pressure steam and compressed air, work at high temperatures washing, cleaning, and pressing garments often under very hot, slippery conditions. Chemical vapors are continually produced, and caustic chemicals are used in the cleaning process. High temperature stills are almost continually "cooking down" cleaning solvents in order to remove impurities so that the solvents can be reused. If a mistake is made in this process—like injecting too much steam into the still—a "boilover" occurs, in which boiling chemical solvent erupts out of the still and over the floor and anyone who happens to be standing in its way.

As a result of these hazards and the fact that chemically hazardous waste is continually produced in these stores, several government agencies (including OSHA and the EPA) have instituted strict guidelines regarding the management of these plants. For example, posters have to be placed in each store notifying employees of their right to be told what hazardous chemicals they are dealing with and what the proper method for handling each chemical is. Special waste-management firms must be used to pick up and properly dispose of the hazardous waste.

A chronic problem the Carters (and most other laundry owners) have is the unwillingness of the part of the cleaning-spotting workers to wear safety goggles. Not all the chemicals they use require safety goggles, but some—like the hydrofluorous acid used to remove rust stains from garments—are very dangerous. The latter is kept in special plastic containers, since it dissolves glass. The problem is that wearing safety goggles can be troublesome. They are somewhat uncomfortable. They also become smudged easily and thus cut down on visibility. As a result, Jack has always found it almost impossible to get these employees to wear their goggles. Jennifer has several questions:

1. How should her firm go about identifying hazardous conditions that should be rectified?

2. Would it be advisable for her firm to set up a procedure for screening out accident-prone individuals?

3. How would you suggest she get all employees to behave more safely at work? Also, how would you advise her to get those who should be wearing goggles to wear the goggles?

---

consequences for the organization, including reductions in the quantity and quality of job performance, increased absenteeism and turnover, and increased grievances.

Yet stress is not necessarily dysfunctional. Andrew DuBrin makes the point that some stress can actually have positive consequences for the person and the organization. Some people, for example, only work well under at least modest stress and find they are more productive as a deadline approaches. Others find that stress may result in a search that leads to a better job or to a career that makes more sense, given the person's aptitudes. A modest level of stress may even lead to more creativity if a competitive situation results in new ideas being generated.[67] As a rule, however, employers don't worry about the sorts of modest stress that lead to such positive consequences. Instead, and for obvious reasons, they focus on dysfunctional stress and its negative consequences.

There are a number of things you can do to alleviate stress, ranging from common sense remedies such as getting more sleep and eating better (so as to build your resistance to stress) to more exotic remedies such as biofeedback and meditation. Finding a more suitable job, getting counseling, and planning and organizing each day's activities are other sensible responses.[68] In his book *Stress and the Manager*, Dr. Karl Albrecht suggests the following to reduce stress on the job:[69]

Build rewarding, pleasant, cooperative relationships with as many of your colleagues and employees as you can.

Don't bite off more than you can chew.

Build an especially effective and supportive relationship with your boss.

Understand his or her problems and help the boss to understand yours.

Negotiate realistic deadlines on important projects with your boss. Be prepared to propose deadlines yourself, instead of having them imposed on you.

Study the future. Learn as much as you can about likely coming events and get as much lead time as you can to prepare for them.

Find time every day for detachments and relaxation.

Take a walk now and then to keep your body refreshed and alert.

Make a noise survey of your office area and find ways to reduce unnecessary racket.

Get away from your office from time to time for a change of scene and a change of mind.

Reduce the amount of trivia to which you give your attention. Delegate routine paperwork to others whenever possible.

Limit interruptions. Try to schedule certain periods of "uninterruptibility" each day and conserve other periods for your own purposes.

Make sure you know how to delegate effectively.

Don't put off dealing with distasteful problems such as counseling a problem employee.

Make a constructive "worry list." Write down the problems that concern you and beside each write down what you're going to do about it, so that none of the problems will be hovering around the edges of your consciousness.

The organization and its human resources specialists and supervisors also play a big role in identifying and remedying job stress. For the supervisor, this typically involves monitoring each subordinate's performance in order to identify the symptoms of stress and then informing the person of the organizational remedies that may be available, such as job transfers or counseling. The personnel specialist's role includes using attitude surveys to identify organizational sources of stress (such as high-pressure jobs), refining selection and placement procedures to ensure the most effective person-job match, and making available career planning aimed at ensuring that the employee moves toward a job that makes sense in terms of his or her aptitudes and aspirations.

Burnout

Dr. Herbert Freudenberger, an expert on the overachiever, says that today many people may be falling victim to **burnout**—the total depletion of your physical and mental resources caused by excessive striving to reach some unrealistic work-related goal. Burnout, he contends, is often the end result of too much job stress, especially when that stress is combined with the fact that you become preoccupied with attaining unattainable work-related goals. In his book, *Burnout: How to Beat the High Cost of Success*, Freudenberger lists some of these other signs of possible impending burnout:[70]

burnout The total depletion of physical and mental resources caused by excessive striving to reach some unrealistic work-related goal.

You are unable to relax.

You identify so closely with your activities that when they fall apart you do too.

The positions you worked so hard to attain often seem meaningless now.

You are working more now but enjoying it less.

Your need for a particular crutch such as smoking, liquor, or tranquilizers is increasing.

You are constantly irritable, and family and friends are often commenting that you don't look well.

You would describe yourself as a workaholic and constantly strive to obtain your work-related goals to the exclusion of almost all outside interest.

Who Suffers from Burnout?

Burnout, Freudenberger says, is mostly limited to dynamic goal-oriented individuals or idealists who are overdedicated to whatever they undertake. The potential burnout victim thrives on intensity, often setting up his life to lurch from crisis to crisis, deadline to deadline. Burnout victims usually don't lead well-balanced lives, in that virtually all their energies are focused on achieving their work-related goals. The burnout victim is usually a workaholic for whom the constant stress of seeking an unattainable goal to the exclusion of other activities can lead to physical and perhaps mental collapse.

What, then, can you do if you think you might be a candidate for burnout? Here are some suggestions:

Break your patterns. First, survey how you spend your time. For example, are you doing a variety of things or the same one over and over? The more well rounded your life is, the more protected you are against burnout. If you've stopped trying new activities, start them again—for instance, travel or new hobbies.

Get away from it all periodically. Schedule occasional periods of introspection into your life, during which you can get away from your usual routine, perhaps alone, to get a perspective on where you are and where you are going.

Reassess your goals in terms of their intrinsic worth. Are the goals you've set for yourself obtainable? Are they really worth the sacrifices you'll have to make?

Think about your work. Could you do as good a job without being so intense or by also pursuing some outside interests?

Reduce stress. Organize your time more effectively, build a better relationship with your boss, negotiate realistic deadlines, find time during the day for detachment and relaxation, reduce unnecessary noise around your office, and limit interruptions.

Avoiding Stress-Related Disability Claims

In addition to the obvious humanitarian reasons for reducing work stress, keep in mind that there are good economic and legal reasons for doing so, too. It has been estimated that stress-related disability claims account for 11% of all occupational disease claims and, in addition, courts are increasingly giving stress-related claims a sympathetic ear. As of now, only Florida, Georgia, and Kansas do not compensate employees disabled by stress.[71] Most other states do compensate workers for stress-related claims as long as the source of the stress is at least unusual (such as inconsistent supervision). But in some states "unusual circumstances" are not even required, as in one case where the individual received workers' compensation for suffering a mental breakdown after assuming new duties.[72]

In fact, various jurisdictions around the country have awarded workers' compensation for stress resulting from a wide range of conditions. These include inconsistent job performance evaluations, criticism of job performance by supervisors, and lack of adequate communication. As a result, minimizing such claims usually begins with good supervision and includes, at a minimum, the following steps:

Adequately train supervisors. Make sure they are aware of the possible legal/disability implications of creating stressful situations for their subordinates. Make sure they are skilled in interpersonal skills, performance evaluation, communication, discipline and discharge, and other matters like conflict management.

Adequate communications. Make sure your employees know that channels of communication are open and functioning and that if they have a problem it can be brought to the attention of top management.

Use attitude surveys. Where practical, use a survey of employee attitudes to monitor attitudes and particular supervisor-caused stress.

Good hiring. Make sure you do your best to hire the right people for the right job and to make sure they have realistic previews of what the job entails. Check references carefully, and watch how your applicant acts in the interview, since the interview itself is a stressful situation.

♦ ASBESTOS EXPOSURE AT WORK

There are four major occupational respiratory diseases at work, caused by asbestos, silica, lead, and carbon dioxide. Of these, asbestos has become a major concern, in part because of publicity surrounding asbestos in buildings such as schools constructed before the mid–1970s. Major efforts are now under way to rid these buildings of the cancer-causing asbestos.

As with other respiratory diseases at work, the problem with asbestos derives from its presence in the workplace air. The heaviest exposures are linked to the tens of thousands of workers engaged in general building renovation; other at-risk workers include those involved with automatic brake and clutch repair and those in the tire industry, which uses talc, a product that contains asbestos-like minerals.

Sensing a serious problem, the U.S. Labor Department issued new rules to sharply lower worker exposure to asbestos. They dropped the allowable level of asbestos in the workplace air from 2 fibers a cubic centimeter to 0.2 fibers, averaged over an eight hour day. The new standard is expected to reduce the risk of worker cancer from 64 per 1000 workers to about 6.7 per 1000; the risk of asbestosis is expected to fall from 50 per 1000 workers to 5 per 1000. Unions are pushing for further reductions to 0.1 fibers per cubic centimeter.

OSHA standards require several actions with respect to preventing asbestos—related workplace disease. The new standards require that companies monitor the air whenever an employer expects the level of asbestos to rise to one half the allowable limit. You would therefore have to monitor if you expected asbestos levels of 0.1 fibers per cubic centimeters in this case. Second, engineering controls—walls, special filters, and so forth—are then required to maintain a level of asbestos that complies with OSHA standards. Respirators can only be used if additional efforts are still required to achieve compliance.

Unlike obvious workplace hazards such as broken guardrails, the effects of respiratory hazards like asbestos are insidious. In the case of asbestosis or asbestos-related cancer, the effects may not show up for years, if ever. The insidious nature of these health hazards is thus one reason to be extra careful in reducing their occurrence in your firm; the practical need to comply with OSHA standards is, of course, another. A major lawsuit—the National Tire Workers Litigation Project—aimed at testing and suing on behalf of tire workers with asbestosis provides another incentive for reducing this occupational health hazard.

◆ VIDEO DISPLAY HEALTH PROBLEMS AND HOW TO AVOID THEM

Many workers today—from stockbrokers and newspaper editors to accountants and clerks—must spend hours each day working with video display terminals (VDTs), and this is creating a new set of health problems at work. According to a recent study by the National Institute for Occupational Safety and Health, short-term eye problems like burning, itching, and tearing as well as eye strain and eye soreness are common complaints of video display operators. Surveys have found that 47% to 76% of operators complain of such problems, and while no permanent vision problems have surfaced yet, long-term studies are under way. The institute's studies have also addressed the possible radiation, muscular, and stress problems of working at a video display terminal. With respect to radiation, researchers conclude that "the VDT does not present a radiation hazard to the employees working at or near a terminal."[73] (However, that point today remains a matter of heated debate.)

But backaches and neckaches *are* widespread among those using displays. This is often because employees try to compensate for display problems like glare and immovable keyboards by maneuvering into awkward body positions. Researchers also found that employees who were tied to VDTs and had heavy work loads were prone to psychological distress like anxiety, irritability, and fatigue.

The institute has therefore provided general recommendations regarding the use of VDTs; these can be summarized as follows:

1. Give employees rest breaks. The institute recommends a 15-minute rest break after 2 hours of continuous VDT work for operators under moderate work loads and 15-minute breaks every hour for those with heavy work loads.

2. Design the maximum flexibility into the work station so that it can be adapted to the individual operator. For example, use movable keyboards, adjustable chairs with midback supports, and a video display in which screen height and position are independently adjustable.

3. Reduce glare with things such as shades over windows, proper positioning of terminal screen hoods, antiglare filters on the VDT screen, and recessed or indirect lighting.

4. VDT workers should have a complete preplacement vision exam to ensure properly corrected vision for adequate performance and reduced visual strain.

Generally speaking, VDT vision problems can be reduced by using the right equipment and a little common sense. Some simple techniques are summarized in Figure 18.8. As you can see, the basic worker-task relationship is fairly straightforward when traditional paperwork tasks are involved, since the light just bounces from the ceiling to the paper and then to the worker's eyes. But once a VDT is involved, your employee may find himself or herself dealing with direct glare as well as reflected glare in addition to the visual demands of watching the little screen. Therefore, as the figure illustrates, adjustable stands, partitions, venetian blind–type window

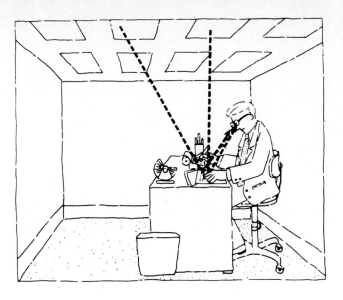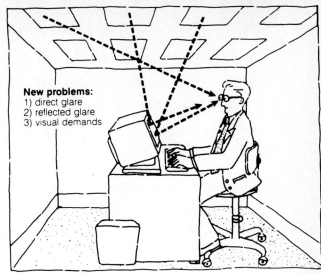

New problems:
1) direct glare
2) reflected glare
3) visual demands

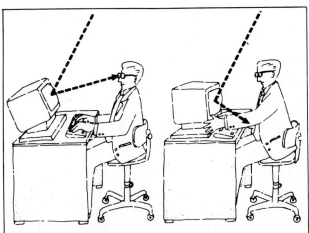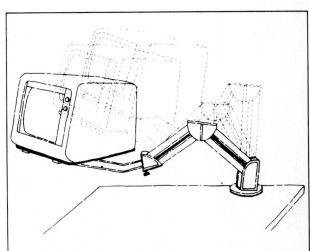

Figure 3: The fixed position of the VDT on the left causes light from an overhead light source to reflect off the task surface and into the operator's eyes. By installing an adjustable stand, as shown on the right, the VDT can be repositioned so reflected light misses the operator's eyes.

Figure 4: The most effective VDT stands permit almost unlimited adjustment of task position.

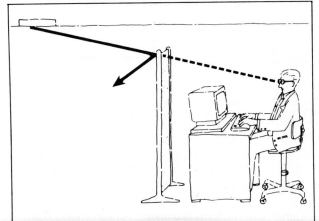

Figure 5: Floor-mounted partitions can be used to block light from light sources, but other corrective measures usually produce more effective results.

FIGURE 18.8
Simple Techniques for Reducing VDT Vision Problems
Source: Bureau of National Affairs, "Solutions to VDT Viewing Problems," *Datagraph,* November 5, 1987, pp. 356, 357.

controls, screen filters, and fully adjustable VDT stands can go far toward minimizing VDT-caused visual problems.[74]

♦ AIDS AND THE WORKPLACE

As everyone knows by now, AIDS—Acquired Immune Deficiency Syndrome—is a disease that undermines the body's immune system, leaving the person susceptible to a wide range of serious and usually fatal diseases.

Some of the most crucial AIDS-related questions employers must deal with concern their legal responsibilities in dealing with AIDS sufferers. While case law is only now evolving on this issue, several tentative conclusions are warranted. First, it appears that an employer cannot single out an employee to be tested for AIDS because to do so would be to subject the person to discriminatory treatment. Similarly, you can probably require a physical exam that included an AIDS test as a condition of employment but refusing to hire the person because of positive test results could put you at risk of a handicap discrimination suit. It also appears that AIDS will be considered a protected handicap under the federal 1973 Vocational Rehabilitation Act and also under most state handicap laws. Mandatory leave cannot be required of a person with AIDS unless work performance has deteriorated, and preemployment inquiries about AIDS (such as inquiries about any other illnesses or disabilities) would not be advisable. At the present time, providing sympathy and support and making reasonable accommodations to persons with AIDS and using education and counseling to deal with the fears of the person's coworkers seem to be the only concrete prescriptions for dealing with the concerns this disease will elicit at work.[75]

Developing an AIDS Policy

From a practical point of view your procedure for dealing with AIDS will usually begin with a statement of your firm's AIDS policy.

The purpose of the AIDS policy is twofold: to reassure employees regarding the impossibility of spreading AIDS through casual contact and to lay out the legal rights of employees to work who are diagnosed with an AIDS-related condition. The policy therefore usually contains a medical overview of what we know about AIDS and lists a number of supervisors' responsibilities such as maintain confidentiality of all medical conditions and medical records, contact the employee assistance services department, and obtain written medical opinions.[76]

♦ WORKPLACE SMOKING

The Nature of the Problem

Smoking is a serious problem for employees and employers. The congressional Office of Technology Assessment estimates that each employee smoker costs an employer between $2,000 and $5,000 yearly, for instance.[77] These costs derive from higher health and fire insurance, as well as increased absenteeism and reduced productivity (which occurs when, for instance, a smoker takes a ten-minute break to finish a cigarette down the hall). Employers today are also being hit with lawsuits brought by nonsmoking employees who are (perhaps rightfully) concerned with inhaling secondhand smoke. And for the smoking employees, of course, smoking is known to be associated with numerous health problems. Smoking at work is therefore a serious problem.

COMPUTER APPLICATIONS IN OCCUPATIONAL SAFETY:

USING COMPUTERS TO MONITOR SAFETY

Companies that must comply with state and federal laws (OSHA,[1] RCRA,[2] OSHA Hazard Communication Law,[3] and SARA[4]) are obligated to file federal reports, monitor employee exposure to various hazards to note trends, and provide employees with information on hazards in their workplaces. Computers can assist in all three areas.

Reporting
Most federal forms can be formatted and formulated on a company's computer so that only the raw data needs to be entered. The computer will perform the instructed calculations and print out the results in an acceptable format. If a piece of information has been input in error, only that figure needs to be changed. Recalculations are automatic. With some forms, the typing of results takes several hours. This task is completed in minutes with a computer. One of several programs available for providing the correct information in proper sequence is PRO-AM, by Safety, Inc.

Monitoring
Computers can track personal exposure level (PEL) for noise, particulates, vapors, or other contaminates for a given location, giving timely warnings of trigger points. A dosimeter sensor can be plugged directly into a personal computer to translate readings on an hourly basis. Not only does this protect, say, the hearing of workers, it can also spot equipment that needs servicing if, for example, a given decibel level indicates increased friction. Trends of various hazards can also be plotted for work redesign to make the workplace safer.

Communicating
The effectiveness of training in any area depends in part on the Hawthorne Effect: the degree to which the student feels that the training is important and accurate. In communicating the hazards of a workplace, employees might not listen because they feel that *they* will not be exposed to those particular hazards, or that they are already careful, or that their work situation does not support those safeguards. If the supervisors push for results to the point of ignoring torn gloves, holes in respirators, inadequate ventilation, or workers who are not wearing safety glasses, then employees will ignore the training. Also, employees may not understand key parts of the training.

Interactive computers can help with some of these problems. If an employee is assigned to work with a hazardous substance that was discussed with her a few weeks before, the knowledge may have become hazy. Access to a personal computer can allow the employee to refresh her memory on how to handle the substance and what to avoid doing. If there are words within the explanation that are not clear, an interactive program will allow the employee to question that word (and any words in the subsequent definition) until she is ready to return to the original explanation. How recently an employee has reviewed the information correlates with the degree of retention, and computer-assisted instruction provides training any time the employee needs help.

[1]Occupational Safety and Health Act, 1970.

[2]Resource Conservation and Recovery Act, 1980.

[3]1986.

[4]Superfund Amendments Reauthorization Act, 1986, which requires Material Safety Data Sheets.

What You Can and Cannot Do

Suppose you want to institute a smoking ban, or a policy against hiring any smokers in the future: What are your legal rights? The answer depends on several things, including the state in which you are located, whether or not your firm is unionized, and the details of the situation. This is thus a matter about which we can't be very specific. Currently, 14 states regulate smoking in the private sector workplace, and here your position would be stronger if you decided to impose a smoking ban. (States restricting private worksite smoking are Arkansas, Connecticut, Florida, Missouri, Minnesota, Montana, Nebraska, Nevada, New Jersey, New York, Utah, Vermont, Washington, and West Virginia.)[78] There are no hard and fast rules, though. For example, in states in which the termination-at-will doctrine has been modified by the courts, firing an employee who is forced to quit smoking could present legal problems. And the presence of a union contract generally means that instituting a ban on smoking for unionized employees who formerly were allowed to smoke means altering "conditions of work." It is therefore subject to collective bargaining. You therefore have to proceed cautiously.

FIGURE 18.9
Degrees of Restrictions on Employee Smoking—A Scale
Source: J. Carroll Swart, "Corporate Smoking Policies: Today and Tomorrow," *Personnel,* August 1988, p. 62.

Policy A
It is the policy of the company to hire nonsmokers only. Smoking is prohibited off the job, and smoking is prohibited on the job.

Policy B
Smoking is prohibited in all areas on company premises.

Policy C
Smoking is prohibited in all areas in company buildings.

Policy D
Smoking is prohibited in all areas in company buildings, with few exceptions. Smoking is permitted in the smoking section of the cafeteria (or room with a similar function in your company, if there is no cafeteria); in specially designated smoking rooms (smoking lounges); and in private offices, which may be designated "smoking permitted" or "no smoking" by the occupant.

Policy E
Smoking is prohibited in all common areas except those designated "smoking permitted." Smoking is permitted in specially designated smoking rooms (smoking lounges).
In open offices and in shared workspace areas where smokers and nonsmokers work together, where smokers' and nonsmokers' preferences are in conflict, employees and management will endeavor to find a satisfactory compromise. On failure to find a compromise, the preferences of the nonsmoker will prevail.
Private offices may be designated "smoking permitted" or "no smoking" by the occupant.

Policy F
It is the policy of the company to respect the preferences of both smokers and nonsmokers in company buildings. Where smokers' and nonsmokers' preferences are in conflict, employees and management will endeavor to find a satisfactory compromise. On failure to reach a compromise, the preferences of the nonsmoker will prevail.

Policy G
The company places no restrictions on employee smoking (the company does not have a smoking policy).

"Smoking Permitted" is synonymous with "Designated Smoking Area." The latter term is increasing in usage.

A basic assumption is that all companies have policies prohibiting smoking in areas where there are safety and fire hazards and where sensitive equipment may be damaged. In reference to the scale above, the term "smoking policy" refers to a written statement or statements that place restrictions on smoking and intend to accommodate health concerns.

In general, though, you do not have to hire smokers. Specifically, you can deny a job to a smoker as long as you do not use "smoking" as a surrogate for some other kind of discrimination. The EEOC, in other words, says that a policy of not hiring smokers is legal as long as the rules apply to all applicants and employees.[79] You therefore can institute a policy now against hiring people who smoke.

The problem arises, of course, when you try to implement smoking restrictions in a facility where you already have smokers or people who were hired thinking they could smoke. Here the best advice seems to be to proceed with the aid of counsel or to proceed very cautiously one step at a time, starting with restrictions that are not overly confining.

Smoking Policies

This notwithstanding, it is clear that employer smoking bans are on the rise. Either because of health concerns, economic concerns, or the fear that nonsmoking employees will themselves sue for a workplace free of second-hand smoke, more and more employers are instituting smoking bans. In one survey of 283 employers conducted in 1988, for instance, one quarter of the organizations polled prohibited smoking anywhere on company premises—up from 14% in 1987. (More than four out of five insurance companies and utilities banned smoking in the workplace.) Beyond that, the number of companies with some type of smoking policies has also shot up, from 16% in 1980 to 60% in 1988. Smoking is most likely to be banned in public areas such as reception areas, hallways and aisles, meeting rooms, and storage rooms.[80]

The bottom line is that from a practical point of view most employers probably should be considering some smoking restrictions. To that end a range of policies can be considered. As summarized in Figure 18.9, policies can range from strict total prohibitions down to "smokers and nonsmokers should courteously work out a compromise among themselves." Again, what you decide to do depends on your own philosophy regarding this matter as well as the particular attributes of your case.

SUMMARY

1. The area of safety and accident prevention is of concern to managers at least partly because of the staggering number of deaths and accidents occurring at work. We said there are three reasons for safety programs: moral, legal, and economic.

2. The purpose of OSHA is to ensure every working person a safe and healthful workplace. OSHA standards are very complete and detailed, and are enforced through a system of inspections in which inspectors, following a list of inspection priorities, visit workplaces. These inspectors can issue citations and recommend penalties to their area directors.

3. Supervisors play a key role in safety to monitor workers. Workers have a responsibility to act safely. A commitment to safety on the part of top management that is filtered down through the management ranks is an important aspect of any safety program.

4. There are three basic causes of accidents: chance occurrences, unsafe conditions, and unsafe acts on the part of employees. Unsafe *conditions* (such as defective equipment) are one big cause of accidents. In addition, three other work-related factors (the job itself, the work schedule, and the psychological climate) also contribute to accidents.

5. Unsafe *acts* on the part of employees are a second basic cause of acci-

dents. Such acts are to some extent the result of certain behavior tendencies on the part of employees, and these tendencies are possibly the result of certain personal characteristics.

6. Most experts doubt that there are accident-prone people who have accidents regardless of the job. Instead, the consensus seems to be that the person who is accident prone in one job may not be on a different job. For example, vision is related to accident frequency for drivers and machine operators but might not be for other jobs, such as accountants.

7. There are several approaches you could use to prevent accidents. One is to reduce unsafe *conditions* (although this is somewhat more in the domain of safety engineers). The other approach is to reduce unsafe *acts*— for example, through selection and placement, training, positive reinforcement, propaganda, and top management commitment.

8. Alcoholism, drug addiction, stress, and emotional illness are four important and growing health problems among employees. Alcoholism is a particularly serious problem and one that can drastically lower the effectiveness of your organization. Techniques including disciplining, discharge, in-house counseling, and referrals to an outside agency are used to deal with these problems.

9. Stress and burnout are other potential health problems at work. Reducing job stress involves such things as getting away from work for a while each day, delegating, and developing a "worry list."

10. Asbestosis, video display health problems, AIDs, and workplace smoking are other employee health problems discussed in this chapter.

KEY TERMS

Occupational Safety and Health Act

Occupational Safety and Health Administration (OSHA)

citations

unsafe conditions

unsafe acts

burnout

DISCUSSION QUESTIONS

1. How would you go about providing a safer environment for your employees to work in?
2. Discuss how you would go about minimizing the occurrence of unsafe acts on the part of your employees.
3. Discuss the basic facts about OSHA—its purpose, standards, inspection, and rights and responsibilities.
4. Explain the supervisor's role in safety.
5. Explain what causes unsafe acts.
6. Answer the question, "Is there such a thing as an accident-prone person?"
7. Describe at least five techniques for reducing accidents.
8. Analyze the legal and safety issues concerning AIDS.
9. Explain how you would reduce stress at work.

CASE INCIDENT   **Hartley Corporation**

The Hartley Corporation is composed of ten autonomous divisions and corporate headquarters. The case focuses on the Bien Works. Its organization is given in Figure 18.10.

Bien Works is housed in a building erected in 1904. The building is five stories high. The top two are not used, since the floors are too dangerous. The second and third floors have holes and rotted places in them.

The third floor holds the rack shop, lab, and marketing departments. The second floor contains the office, some warehousing, and some buffing compound production lines. The first floor contains the warehousing for heavier materials and the rest of the manufacturing lines. The main operation is manufacturing. The rack shop is a support unit to make racks for drying chemicals. The works is nonunion.

Jesse Fuller has been with Hartley for 20 years, all of it in conjunction with the Bien Works. He holds a B.S. in chemistry from City University of New York. He worked his way through college. He's done almost everything at Bien. He started as a supervisor in the manufacturing unit. He's run the rack shop, supervised the warehouse for two years, sold the compounds. The office and lab are white-collar or technical jobs, so he's not worked there. His employees like him, although they are a bit afraid of him, too. He has a terrible temper, which he loses about once a month. When this happens, everyone tries to get out of his way.

Jesse is now 53 years old. He's happy with the Bien Works. He likes the town and wouldn't move. Bien is like his own firm, since he's isolated geographically from Hartley.

Since Bien makes more money for Hartley than his budget calls for, it lets Jesse alone. He has lower turnover than expected. Absenteeism is also low. His safety and health record is about average. All in all, Hartley and Jesse are happy with the Bien Works.

Except for OSHA. For some reason, the OSHA inspector came around Bien often. The local inspector was James Munsey. In April, he came to Bien when Jesse was at a meeting at Hartley. He determined that the buffing manufacturing was producing unsafe gases. As is his right, he shut the plant down that day. Jesse flew back and modified the gas filters. James passed the filters, and Bien started production again.

In May, James came back and shut the plant again when Jesse was at a Rotary meeting. Again, the filters were cleaned and modified. This time Jesse was really angry. After the plant was reopened and James gone, Jesse held a meeting of all employees. At the meeting, he said:

FIGURE 18.10
Organization Chart: Bien Works

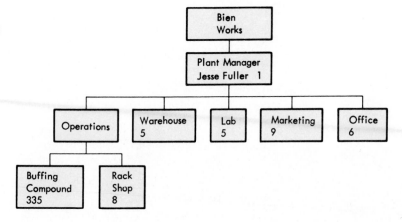

Look, this OSHA guy is killing us. This is an old works. We can't afford to be shut down. At my recent meeting at corporate headquarters, I tried to make the case that we needed a new building here. The sharp pencil boys pointed out that we are profitable now, but not if we have to build a new plant. The industry is overcrowded, and Hartley will close this plant rather than spend money on it. If we get shut down or have to buy a lot of antipollution garbage, they could shut us down. That OSHA guy is the enemy—just like a traffic cop. We've got to pull together, or we could all sink together.

The employees had never seen Jesse so angry before, and they feared for their jobs now more than ever. There was a lot of unemployment in the area.

Questions
1. What do you think of Jesse's approach to safety?
2. What changes, if any, would you recommend? Explain why.

Source: William F. Glueck and George Stevens, *Cases and Exercises in Personnel/Human Resources Management*, 3d ed. (Plano, Tex.: Business Publications, 1983), pp. 145–146. Copyright 1983, Business Publications, Inc. Reprinted by permission.

EXPERIENTIAL EXERCISE

Purpose: The purpose of this exercise is to give you practice in identifying unsafe conditions.

Required Understanding: You should be familiar with material covered in this chapter, particularly that on unsafe conditions and that in Figure 18.5 and the appendix.

How to Set Up the Exercise/Instructions: Divide the class into groups of four or five students.

Assume that you are a safety committee retained by the school to identify and report on any possible unsafe conditions in and around the school building.

Each group will spend about 45 minutes in and around the building you are now in for the purpose of identifying and listing possible unsafe conditions. (*Hint:* Make use of Figure 18.5.)

Return to the class in about 45 minutes, and a spokesperson from each group should list on the board the unsafe conditions you think you have identified. How many were there? Do you think these also violate OSHA standards? How would you go about checking?

Appendix

Self-inspection Checklists

General

		OK	ACTION NEEDED
1.	Is the required OSHA workplace poster displayed in your place of business as required where all employees are likely to see it?	☐	☐
2.	Are you aware of the requirement to report all workplace fatalities and any serious accidents (where 5 or more are hospitalized) to a federal or state OSHA office within 48 hours?	☐	☐
3.	Are workplace injury and illness records being kept as required by OSHA?	☐	☐
4.	Are you aware that the OSHA annual summary of workplace injuries and illnesses must be posted by February 1 and must remain posted until March 1?	☐	☐
5.	Are you aware that employers with 10 or fewer employees are exempt from the OSHA recordkeeping requirements, unless they are part of an official BLS or state survey and have received specific instructions to keep records?	☐	☐
6.	Have you demonstrated an active interest in safety and health matters by defining a policy for your business and communicating it to all employees?	☐	☐
7.	Do you have a safety committee or group that allows participation of employees in safety and health activities?	☐	☐
8.	Does the safety committee or group meet regularly and report, in writing, its activities?	☐	☐
9.	Do you provide safety and health training for all employees requiring such training, and is it documented?	☐	☐
10.	Is one person clearly in charge of safety and health activities?	☐	☐

Develop Your Own Checklist.

These Are Only Sample Questions.

Source: OSHA Handbook for Small Business.

	OK	ACTION NEEDED
11. Do all employees know what to do in emergencies?	☐	☐
12. Are emergency telephone numbers posted?	☐	☐
13. Do you have a procedure for handling employee complaints regarding safety and health?	☐	☐

Workplace

ELECTRICAL WIRING, FIXTURES AND CONTROLS

	OK	ACTION NEEDED
1. Are your workplace electricians familiar with the requirements of the National Electrical Code (NEC)?	☐	☐
2. Do you specify compliance with the NEC for all contract electrical work?	☐	☐
3. If you have electrical installations in hazardous dust or vapor areas, do they meet the NEC for hazardous locations?	☐	☐
4. Are all electrical cords strung so they do not hang on pipes, nails, hooks, etc?	☐	☐
5. Is all conduit, BX cable, etc., properly attached to all supports and tightly connected to junction and outlet boxes?	☐	☐
6. Is there no evidence of fraying on any electrical cords?	☐	☐
7. Are rubber cords kept free of grease, oil and chemicals?	☐	☐
8. Are metallic cable and conduit systems properly grounded?	☐	☐
9. Are portable electric tools and appliances grounded or double insulated?	☐	☐
10. Are all ground connections clean and tight?	☐	☐
11. Are fuses and circuit breakers the right type and size for the load on each circuit?	☐	☐
12. Are all fuses free of "jumping" with pennies or metal strips?	☐	☐
13. Do switches show evidence of overheating?	☐	☐
14. Are switches mounted in clean, tightly closed metal boxes?	☐	☐

Develop Your Own Checklist.

These Are Only Sample Questions.

	OK	ACTION NEEDED
15. Are all electrical switches marked to show their purpose?	☐	☐
16. Are motors clean and kept free of excessive grease and oil?	☐	☐
17. Are motors properly maintained and provided with adequate overcurrent protection?	☐	☐
18. Are bearings in good condition?	☐	☐
19. Are portable lights equipped with proper guards?	☐	☐
20. Are all lamps kept free of combustible material?	☐	☐
21. Is your electrical system checked periodically by someone competent in the NEC?	☐	☐

EXITS AND ACCESS

	OK	ACTION NEEDED
1. Are all exits visible and unobstructed?	☐	☐
2. Are all exits marked with a readily visible sign that is properly illuminated?	☐	☐
3. Are there sufficient exits to ensure prompt escape in case of emergency?	☐	☐
4. Are areas with limited occupancy posted and is access/egress controlled to persons specifically authorized to be in those areas?	☐	☐
5. Do you take special precautions to protect employees during construction and repair operations?	☐	☐

FIRE PROTECTION

	OK	ACTION NEEDED
1. Are portable fire extinguishers provided in adequate number and type?	☐	☐
2. Are fire extinguishers inspected monthly for general condition and operability and noted on the inspection tag?	☐	☐
3. Are fire extinguishers recharged regularly and properly noted on the inspection tag?	☐	☐
4. Are fire extinguishers mounted in readily accessible locations?	☐	☐

Develop Your Own Checklist.

These Are Only Sample Questions.

		OK	ACTION NEEDED
5.	If you have interior standpipes and valves, are these inspected regularly?	☐	☐
6.	If you have a fire alarm system, is it tested at least annually?	☐	☐
7.	Are plant employees periodically instructed in the use of extinguishers and fire protection procedures?	☐	☐
8.	If you have outside private fire hydrants, were they flushed within the last year and placed on a regular maintenance schedule?	☐	☐
9.	Are fire doors and shutters in good operating condition?	☐	☐
	Are they unobstructed and protected against obstruction?	☐	☐
10.	Are fusible links in place?	☐	☐
11.	Is your local fire department well acquainted with your plant, location and specific hazards?	☐	☐
12.	Automatic Sprinklers:		
	Are water control valves, air and water pressures checked weekly?	☐	☐
	Are control valves locked open?	☐	☐
	Is maintenance of the system assigned to responsible persons or a sprinkler contractor?	☐	☐
	Are sprinkler heads protected by metal guards where exposed to mechanical damage?	☐	☐
	Is proper minimum clearance maintained around sprinkler heads?	☐	☐

HOUSEKEEPING AND GENERAL WORK ENVIRONMENT

		OK	ACTION NEEDED
1.	Is smoking permitted in designated "safe areas" only?	☐	☐
2.	Are NO SMOKING signs prominently posted in areas containing combustibles and flammables?	☐	☐
3.	Are covered metal waste cans used for oily and paint soaked waste?	☐	☐
	Are they emptied at least daily?	☐	☐
4.	Are paint spray booths, dip tanks, etc., and their exhaust ducts cleaned regularly?	☐	☐

	OK	ACTION NEEDED

5. Are stand mats, platforms or similar protection provided to protect employees from wet floors in wet processes? ☐ ☐

6. Are waste receptacles provided, and are they emptied regularly? ☐ ☐

7. Do your toilet facilities meet the requirements of applicable sanitary codes? ☐ ☐

8. Are washing facilities provided? ☐ ☐

9. Are all areas of your business adequately illuminated? ☐ ☐

10. Are floor load capacities posted in second floors, lofts, storage areas, etc.? ☐ ☐

11. Are floor openings provided with toe boards and railings or a floor hole cover? ☐ ☐

12. Are stairways in good condition with standard railings provided for every flight having four or more risers? ☐ ☐

13. Are portable wood ladders and metal ladders adequate for their purpose, in good condition and provided with secure footing? ☐ ☐

14. If you have fixed ladders, are they adequate, and are they in good condition and equipped with side rails or cages or special safety climbing devices, if required? ☐ ☐

15. For Loading Docks:

Are dockplates kept in serviceable condition and secured to prevent slipping? ☐ ☐

Do you have means to prevent car or truck movement when dockplates are in place? ☐ ☐

MACHINES AND EQUIPMENT

	OK	ACTION NEEDED

1. Are all machines or operations that expose operators or other employees to rotating parts, pinch points, flying chips, particles or sparks adequately guarded? ☐ ☐

2. Are mechanical power transmission belts and pinch points guarded? ☐ ☐

3. Is exposed power shafting less than 7 feet from the floor guarded? ☐ ☐

4. Are hand tools and other equipment regularly inspected for safe condition? ☐ ☐

Develop Your Own Checklist.

These Are Only Sample Questions.

EMPLOYEE SAFETY AND HEALTH 685

	OK	ACTION NEEDED	
5. Is compressed air used for cleaning reduced to less than 30 psi?	☐	☐	**Develop Your Own Checklist.**
6. Are power saws and similar equipment provided with safety guards?	☐	☐	
7. Are grinding wheel tool rests set to within 1/8 inch or less of the wheel?	☐	☐	**These Are Only Sample Questions.**
8. Is there any system for inspecting small hand tools for burred ends, cracked handles, etc.?	☐	☐	
9. Are compressed gas cylinders examined regularly for obvious signs of defects, deep rusting or leakage?	☐	☐	
10. Is care used in handling and storing cylinders and valves to prevent damage?	☐	☐	
11. Are all air receivers periodically examined, including the safety valves?	☐	☐	
12. Are safety valves tested regularly and frequently?	☐	☐	
13. Is there sufficient clearance from stoves, furnaces, etc., for stock, woodwork, or other combustible materials?	☐	☐	
14. Is there clearance of at least 4 feet in front of heating equipment involving open flames, such as gas radiant heaters, and fronts of firing doors of stoves, furnaces, etc.?	☐	☐	
15. Are all oil and gas fired devices equipped with flame failure controls that will prevent flow of fuel if pilots or main burners are not working?	☐	☐	
16. Is there at least a 2-inch clearance between chimney brickwork and all woodwork or other combustible materials?	☐	☐	
17. For Welding or Flame Cutting Operations: Are only authorized, trained personnel permitted to use such equipment?	☐	☐	
Have operators been given a copy of operating instructions and asked to follow them?	☐	☐	
Are welding gas cylinders stored so they are not subjected to damage?	☐	☐	
Are valve protection caps in place on all cylinders not connected for use?	☐	☐	
Are all combustible materials near the operator covered with protective shields or otherwise protected?	☐	☐	
Is a fire extinguisher provided at the welding site?	☐	☐	
Do operators have the proper protective clothing and equipment?	☐	☐	

Materials

OK   ACTION NEEDED

1. Are approved safety cans or other acceptable containers used for handling and dispensing flammable liquids? ☐ ☐

2. Are all flammable liquids that are kept inside buildings stored in proper storage containers or cabinets? ☐ ☐

3. Do you meet OSHA standards for all spray painting or dip tank operations using combustible liquids? ☐ ☐

4. Are oxidizing chemicals stored in areas separate from all organic material except shipping bags? ☐ ☐

5. Do you have an enforced NO SMOKING rule in areas for storage and use of hazardous materials? ☐ ☐

6. Are NO SMOKING signs posted where needed? ☐ ☐

7. Is ventilation equipment provided for removal of air contaminants from operations such as production grinding, buffing, spray painting and/or vapor degreasing, and is it operating properly? ☐ ☐

8. Are protective measures in effect for operations involved with X-rays or other radiation? ☐ ☐

9. For Lift Truck Operations:
   Are only trained personnel allowed to operate forklift trucks? ☐ ☐

   Is overhead protection provided on high lift rider trucks? ☐ ☐

10. For Toxic Materials:
    Are all materials used in your plant checked for toxic qualities? ☐ ☐

    Have appropriate control procedures such as ventilation systems, enclosed operations, safe handling practices, proper personal protective equipment (e.g., respirators, glasses or goggles, gloves, etc.) been instituted for toxic materials. ☐ ☐

Develop Your Own Checklist.

These Are Only Sample Questions.

Employee Protection

Develop
Your Own
Checklist.

These
Are Only
Sample
Questions.

	OK	ACTION NEEDED

1. Is there a hospital, clinic or infirmary for medical care near your business? ☐ ☐

2. If medical and first-aid facilities are not near-by, do you have one or more employees trained in first aid? ☐ ☐

3. Are your first-aid supplies adequate for the type of potential injuries in your workplace? ☐ ☐

4. Are there quick water flush facilities available where employees are exposed to corrosive materials? ☐ ☐

5. Are hard hats provided and worn where any danger of falling objects exists? ☐ ☐

6. Are protective goggles or glasses provided and worn where there is any danger of flying particles or splashing of corrosive materials? ☐ ☐

7. Are protective gloves, aprons, shields or other means provided for protection from sharp, hot or corrosive materials? ☐ ☐

8. Are approved respirators provided for regular or emergency use where needed? ☐ ☐

9. Is all protective equipment maintained in a sanitary condition and readily available for use? ☐ ☐

10. Where special equipment is needed for electrical workers, is it available? ☐ ☐

11. When lunches are eaten on the premises, are they eaten in areas where there is no exposure to toxic materials, and not in toilet facility areas? ☐ ☐

12. Is protection against the effects of occupational noise exposure provided when the sound levels exceed those shown in Table G-16 of the OSHA noise standard? ☐ ☐

NOTES

1. Bureau of National Affairs, *Bulletin to Management*, January 16, 1986, pp. 20–21.

2. Willie Hammer, *Occupational Safety Management and Engineering* (Englewood Cliffs, N.J.: Prentice-Hall, 1985), p. 6. For a description of the standards to apply when hiring safety specialists, see, for example, Ted Ferry, "Guidelines for Hiring Safety Personnel," *Personnel Journal*, Vol. 65, no. 9 (September 1986), pp. 40–45.

3. Hammer, *Occupational Safety Management and Engineering*, p. 7. For further discussion, see, for example, Gregory Pokrass, "Civil and Criminal Law Liability Exposure of the Safety Professional," *Professional Safety*, Vol. 32, no. 4 (April 1987), pp. 10–13.

4. *Illinois* v. *Chicago Magnet Wire Corp.*, Illinois Supreme Court, No. 65588, 2/2/89; discussed in Bureau of National Affairs, "OSHA Act not Preempted: Criminal Prosecution in Illinois," *Bulletin to Management*, February 9, 1989, p. 41.

5. Willie Hammer, *Occupational Safety Management and Engineering*, 3rd ed. (Englewood Cliffs, N.J.: Prentice-Hall, 1985), pp. 4–5.

6. Lester Bittel, *What Every Supervisor Should Know* (New York: McGraw-Hill, 1974), copyright 1974. Reproduced with the permission of the Gregg/McGraw-Hill Book Company. See also John J. Coleman III, "When Injured Workers Return," *Personnel Journal*, Vol. 68, no. 2 (February 1989), pp. 54–63, for a chart showing how employers should handle the return of an injured worker.

7. Much of this is based on "All About OSHA" (revised), U.S. Department of Labor, Occupational Safety and Health Administration (Washington, D.C., 1980).

8. Bureau of National Affairs, "OSHA Hazard Communication Standard Enforcement," *Bulletin to Management*, February 23, 1989, p. 58.

9. Ibid., p. 13.

10. "What Every Employer Needs to Know About OSHA Record Keeping," U.S. Department of Labor, Bureau of Labor Statistics (Washington, D.C., 1978), report 412–3, p. 3.

11. "All About OSHA," p. 18.

12. "Supreme Court Says OSHA Inspectors Need Warrants," *Engineering News Record*, June 1, 1978, pp. 9–10.

13. Michael Verespej, "OSHA Revamps Its Inspection Policies," *Industry Week*, September 17, 1979, pp. 19–20. See also Horace E. Johns, "OSHA's Impact," *Personnel Journal*, Vol. 67, no. 11 (November 1988), pp. 102–107.

14. Bureau of National Affairs, *Bulletin to Management*, January 16, 1986, p. 23; see also Bureau of National Affairs, *Bulletin to Management*, March 30, 1989, p. 103.

15. Commerce Clearing House, *Ideas and Trends*, April 8, 1982, p. 87.

16. This section is based on "All About OSHA," pp. 23–25.

17. Michael Verespej, "Has OSHA Improved?" *Industry Week*, August 4, 1980, pp. 48–56.

18. Ibid., p. 55.

19. Bureau of National Affairs, "OSHA Action: AIDS, Health Care, and Record Fine," *Bulletin to Management*, July 30, 1989, p. 241.

20. Roger Jacobs, "Employee Resistance to OSHA Standards: Toward a More Reasonable Approach," *Labor Law Journal* (April 1979), pp. 219–230.

21. Ibid., p. 220.

22. These are based on ibid., pp. 227–230.

23. Verespej, "Has OSHA Improved?" p. 50.

24. Murray Weidenbaum, "Four Questions for OSHA," *Labor Law Journal* (August 1979), pp. 528–531; Barry Crickmer, "Regulation: How Much Is Enough?" *Nation's Business* (March 1980), pp. 26–33.

25. "What Every Employer Needs to Know About OSHA Record Keeping."

26. Hammer, *Occupational Safety Management and Engineering*, pp. 62–63.

27. Verespej, "Has OSHA Improved?" pp. 50–51; "New Ways to Short Cut Costly Rules," *Dun's Review* (February 1980), pp. 62–69.

28. Bittel, *What Every Supervisor Should Know,* p. 25. For an example of an effective safety training program, see, for example, Michael Pennacchia, "Interactive Training Sets the Pace," *Safety and Health*, Vol. 135, no. 1 (January 1987), pp. 24–27, and Philip Poynter and David Stevens, "How to Secure an Effective Health and Safety Program at Work," *Professional Safety*, Vol. 32, no. 1 (January 1987), pp. 32–41.

29. David S. Thelan, Donna Ledgerwood, and Charles F. Walters, "Health and Safety in the Workplace: A New Challenge for Business Schools," *Personnel Administrator*, Vol. 30, no. 10 (October 1985), p. 44.

30. Hammer, *Occupational Safety Management and Engineering.*

31. "A Safety Committee Man's Guide," Aetna Life and Casualty Insurance Company, Catalog 872684.

32. Ibid., pp. 17–21. See also "Safety Program: High Priority," Bureau of National Affairs, *Bulletin to Management*, May 4, 1989, p. 144, for safety programs with regard to office design and work station safety.

33. Willard Kerr, "Complementary Theories of Safety Psychology," in Edwin Fleishman and Alan Bass, *Industrial Psychology* (Homewood, Ill.: Dorsey Press, 1974), pp. 493–500.

34. See also Dove Zohar, "Safety Climate in Industrial Organization: Theoretical and Applied Implications," *Journal of Applied Psychology*, Vol. 65 (February 1980), pp. 96–102. See also Paul Goodman and Steven Garber, "Absenteeism and Accidents in a Dangerous Environment: Empirical Analysis of Underground Coal Mines," *Journal of Applied Psychology*, Vol. 73, no. 1 (February 1988), pp. 81–86.

35. List of unsafe acts from "A Safety Committee Man's Guide," Aetna Life and Casualty Insurance Company.

36. A. G. Arbous and J. E. Kerrich, "The Phenomenon of Accident Proneness," *Industrial Medicine and Surgery*, Vol. 22 (1953), pp. 141–148, reprinted in Fleishman and Bass, Industrial Psychology, p. 485.

37. Ernest McCormick and Joseph Tiffin, *Industrial Psychology* (Englewood Cliffs, N.J.: Prentice-Hall, 1974), pp. 522–523; Norman Maier, *Psychology and Industrial Organization* (Boston: Houghton-Mifflin, 1965), pp. 458–462; Milton Blum and James Nayler, *Industrial Psychology* (New York: Harper & Row, 1968), pp. 519–531. For example, David DeJoy, "Attributional Processes and Hazard Control Management in Industry," *Journal of Safety Research*, Vol. 16 (Summer 1985), pp. 61–71.

38. McCormick and Tiffin, *Industrial Psychology,* p. 523.

39. John Miner and J. Frank Brewer, "Management of Ineffective Performance," in Marvin Dunnette, ed., *Handbook of Industrial and Organizational Psychology* (Chicago: Rand McNally, 1976), pp. 995–1031; McCormick and Tiffin, *Industrial Psychology*, pp. 524–525. Younger employees probably have more accidents also, at least in part because they fail to perceive specific situations as being as risky as do older employees. See, for example, Peter Finn and Barry Bragg, "Perception of the Risk of an Accident by Young and Older Drivers," *Accident Analysis and Prevention*, Vol. 18, no. 4 (August 1986). See also Olivia Mitchell, "The Relation of Age to Workplace Injuries," *Monthly Labor Review*, Vol. 111, no. 7 (July 1988), pp. 8–13.

40. Blum and Nayler, *Industrial Psychology,* p. 522.

41. Miner and Brewer, "Management of Ineffective Performance," in Dunnette, ed., *Handbook of Industrial and Organizational Psychology*, pp. 1004–1005.

42. Bittel, *What Every Supervisor Should Know,* p. 249.

43. Maier, *Psychology and Industrial Organization*, pp. 463–467; McCormick and Tiffin, *Industrial Psychology*, pp. 533–536; and Blum and Nayler, *Industrial Psychology*, pp. 525–527.

44. D. Wechsler, "Test for Taxicab Drivers," *Journal of Personnel Research*, Vol. 5 (1926), pp. 24–30, quoted in Maier, *Psychology and Industrial Organization*, p. 64. See also Leo DeBobes, "Psychological Factors in Accident Prevention," *Per-*

sonnel Journal, Vol. 65 (January 1986). See also Curtiss Hansen, "A Causal Model of the Relationship Among Accidents, Biodata Personality, and Cognitive Factors," *Journal of Applied Psychology,* Vol. 74, no. 1 (February 1989), pp. 81–90.

45. Maier, *Psychology and Industrial Organization,* p. 463.

46. S. E. Wirt and H. E. Leedkee, "Skillful Eyes Prevent Accidents," Annual Newsletter, National Safety Council, Industrial Nursing Section, November 1945, pp. 10–12, quoted in Maier, *Psychology and Industrial Organization,* p. 466.

47. Maier, *Psychology and Industrial Organization,* p. 464.

48. Judy D. Olian, "Genetic Screening for Employment Purposes," *Personnel Psychology,* Vol. 37, no. 3 (Autumn 1984), pp. 423–438.

49. S. Laner and R. J. Sell, "An Experiment on the Effect of Specially Designed Safety Posters," *Occupational Psychology,* Vol. 34 (1960), pp. 153–169, in McCormick and Tiffin, *Industrial Psychology,* p. 536.

50. McCormick and Tiffin, *Industrial Psychology,* p. 537. A group of international experts met in Belgium in 1986 and concluded that a successful safety poster must be simple and specific and reinforce safe behavior rather than negative behavior. See "What Makes an Effective Safety Poster," *National Safety and Health News,* Vol. 134, no. 6 (December 1986), pp. 32–34.

51. OSHA has published two useful training manuals: *Training Requirements of OSHA Standards* (February 1976) and *Teaching Safety and Health in the Work Place,* U.S. Department of Labor, Occupational Safety and Health Administration (1976); J. Surry, "Industrial Accident Research: Human Engineering Approach" (Toronto: University of Toronto, Department of Industrial Engineering, June 1968), Chapter 4, quoted in McCormick and Tiffin, *Industrial Psychology,* p. 534. For an example of a very successful incentive program aimed at boosting safety at Campbell Soup Company, see Frederick Wahl, Jr., "Soups on for Safety," *National Safety and Health News,* Vol. 134, no. 6 (December 1986), pp. 49–53.

52. Judi Komaki, Kenneth Barwick, and Lawrence Scott, "A Behavioral Approach to Occupational Safety: Pinpointing and Reinforcing Safe Performance in a Food Manufacturing Plant," *Journal of Applied Psychology,* Vol. 63 (August 1978), pp. 434–445.

53. Judi Komaki, Arlene Heinzmann, and Lorealie Lawson, "Effect of Training and Feedback: Component Analysis of a Behavioral Safety Program," *Journal of Applied Psychology,* Vol. 65 (June 1980), pp. 261–270.

54. Zohar, "Safety Climate," p. 97. For a discussion of the importance of getting employees involved in managing their own safety program, see John Lutness, "Self-managed Safety Program Gets Workers Involved," *Safety and Health,* Vol. 135, no. 4 (April 1987), pp. 42–45.

55. Bureau of National Affairs, "Workplace Safety: Improving Management Practices," *Bulletin to Management,* February 9, 1989, pp. 42 and 47.

56. This section based largely on Miner and Brewer, "The Management of Ineffective Performance," pp. 1005–1023.

57. James Schreir, "Survey Supports Perceptions: Work-Site Drug Use is on the Rise," *Personnel Journal* (October 1987), pp. 114–118.

58. Gopal Pati and John Adkins, Jr., "The Employer's Role in Alcoholism Assistance," *Personnel Journal,* Vol. 62, no. 7 (July 1983), pp. 568–572. For a discussion of how the work environment can encourage drug dealing, see Richard Lyles, "Should the Next Drug Bust Be in Your Company?" *Personnel Journal,* Vol. 63 (October 1984), pp. 46–49.

59. Harrison Trice, "Alcoholism and the Work World," *Sloan Management Review,* no. 2 (Fall 1970), pp. 67–75, reprinted in Hammer and Schmidt, *Contemporary Problems in Personnel,* rev. ed., pp. 496–502. Note also that dependence on ordinary substances can be as devastating as hard drug problems. See, for example, Peter Minetos, "Are You Addicted to Legal Drugs?" *Safety and Health,* Vol. 136, no. 2 (August 1987), pp. 46–49.

60. Pati and Adkins, "The Employer's Role in Alcoholism Assistance." See, also, Commerce Clearing House, "How Should Employers Respond to Indications an

Employee May Have an Alcohol or Drug Problem?" *Ideas and Trends*, April 6, 1989, pp. 53–57.

61. Based on Miner and Brewer, "Management of Ineffective Performance." The survey was conducted jointly by the American Society for Personnel Administration and the Bureau of National Affairs. The results were based on an analysis of the questionnaire data made by Professors Miner and Brewer, who acknowledge the assistance of John B. Schappi, associate editor of the Bureau of National Affairs, and Mary Green Miner, director of BNA Surveys, in making this information available.

62. Trice, "Alcoholism and the Work World." See also Larry A. Pace and Stanley J. Smits, "Substance Abuse: A Proactive Approach," *Personnel Journal*, Vol. 68, no. 4 (April 1989), pp. 84–90, and Commerce Clearing House, "Typical Behavior Changes in an Employee with a Drinking Problem," *Ideas and Trends*, April 6, 1989, p. 56.

63. This is quoted from Bureau of National Affairs, "Drug-Free Workplace: New Federal Requirements," *Bulletin to Management*, February 9, 1989, pp. 1–4. Note that the Drug-Free Workplace Act does not mandate or mention testing employees for illegal drug use.

64. From Henry Balevic, "Drug Abuse in the Workplace" (Personnel Services, Inc., 2303 W. Meadowview Road, Greensboro, N.C. 27407), Reprinted in *Bureau of National Affairs, Bulletin to Management*, August 29, 1985, p. 72. Stanley Smits and Larry Pace, "Workplace Substance Abuse: Establish Policies," *Personnel Journal* (May 1989), pp. 88–93.

65. *Bureau of National Affairs, Bulletin to Management*, December 19, 1985, p. 200. Based on a speech by San Francisco attorneys Victor Schachter and Robert Kristoff. See also Alfred Klein, "Employees Under the Influence—Outside the Law?" *Personnel Journal*, Vol. 65, no. 9 (September 1986), pp. 56–58; Martin Aron, "Drug Testing: The Employer's Dilemma," *Labor Law Journal*, Vol. 38, no. 3 (March 1987), pp. 157–165; "Drug Testing 'To Do' List," Bureau of National Affairs, *Bulletin to Management*, August 10, 1989, p. 250.

66. This is based on Terry Beehr and John Newman, "Organizational Stress, Employer Health, and Organizational Effectiveness: A Factor Analysis, Model, and Literature Review," *Personnel Psychology*, Vol. 31 (Winter 1978), pp. 665–699. See also Stephan Motowizlo, John Packard, and Michael Manning, "Occupational Stress: Its Causes and Consequences for Job Performance," *Journal of Applied Psychology*, Vol. 71, no. 4 (November 1986), pp. 618–629.

67. Andrew DuBrin, *Human Relations: A Job Oriented Approach* (Reston, Va.: Reston, 1978), pp. 66–67.

68. John Newman and Terry Beehr, "Personal and Organizational Strategies for Handling Job Stress: A Review of Research and Opinion," *Personnel Psychology* (Spring 1979), pp. 1–43. See also Bureau of National Affairs, "Work Place Stress: How to Curb Claims," *Bulletin to Management*, April 14, 1988, p. 120.

69. Karl Albrecht, *Stress and the Manager* (Englewood Cliffs, N.J.: Spectrum, 1979).

70. Herbert Freudenberger, *Burn-Out* (Toronto: Bantam Books, 1980). See also Susan Jackson, Richard Schwab, and Randall Schuler, "Toward an Understanding of the Burnout Phenomenon," *Journal of Applied Psychology*, Vol. 71, no. 4 (November 1986), pp. 630–640, and James R. Redeker and Johnathan Seagal, "Profits Low? Your Employees May Be High!" *Personnel*, Vol. 66, no. 6 (June 1989), pp. 72–76.

71. This is based on Philip Voluck and Herbert Abramson, "How to Avoid Stress-Related Disability Claims," *Personnel Journal* (May 1987), pp. 95–98.

72. For a discussion, see ibid., p. 96.

73. See, for example, Michael Smith and others, "An Investigation of Health Complaints and Job Stress in Video Display Operations," *Human Factors* (August 1981), pp. 387–400; see also Bureau of National Affairs, "How to Protect Workers from Reproductive Hazards," *Fair Employment Practices*, July 23, 1987, pp. 89–90. See also Commerce Clearing House, "Suffolk County New York Passes Law Covering Employers with Twenty Terminals or More Regarding VDT Regulation," *Ideas and Trends*, 1988, p. 48.

74. Bureau of National Affairs, "Solutions to VDT Viewing Problems," *Bulletin to Management,* November 5, 1987, pp. 356–357.

75. Bureau of National Affairs, "AIDS and the Workplace: Issues, Advice, and Answers," *Bulletin to Management,* November 14, 1985, pp. 1–6. See also David Ritter and Ronald Turner, "AIDS: Employer Concerns and Options," *Labor Law Journal,* Vol. 38, no. 2 (February 1987), pp. 67–83, and Bureau of National Affairs, "How Employers Are Responding to AIDS in the Workplace," *Fair Employment Practices,* February 18, 1988, pp. 21–22. For a complete guide to services and information regarding "The Work Place and AIDS," see *Personnel Journal,* Vol. 66, no. 10 (October 1987), pp. 65–80. See also William H. Wager, "AIDS: Setting Policy, Educating Employees at Bank of America," *Personnel,* Vol. 65, no. 8 (August 1988), pp. 4–10. See also Margaret Magnus, "AIDS: Fear and Ignorance," *Personnel Journal,* Vol. 67, no. 2 (February 1988), pp. 28–32, for poll regarding major workplace comments associated with AIDS.

76. Commerce Clearing House, "The Wells Fargo AIDS Policy," *Ideas and Trends,* April 5, 1988, pp. 52–53.

77. Marco Colossi, "Do Employees Have the Right to Smoke?" *Personnel Journal* (April 1988), pp. 72–79.

78. Commerce Clearing House, "State Laws Regulating Smoking," *Ideas and Trends,* January 9, 1987, pp. 4–5.

79. Jim Collison, "Workplace Smoking Policies: Sixteen Questions and Answers," *Personnel Journal* (April 1988), p. 81.

80. Bureau of National Affairs, "Smoking Bans on the Rise," *Bulletin to Management,* March 16, 1989, p. 82.

Chapter 19

Strategic Issues in Personnel Management

When you finish studying this chapter, you should be able to:

1. Discuss the trends influencing the nature of work and the work force in the 1990s.
2. Explain the impact these trends will have on the personnel management (HRM) function.
3. Discuss HRM's role in strategic planning.
4. Develop personnel policies and a personnel policy manual.
5. Conduct an HRM audit.
6. Better understand what your philosophy of personnel management is and might be.

OVERVIEW

The purpose of this chapter is to discuss strategic issues in personnel management and in particular personnel's role in creating and implementing your company's strategic plan. We explain how various trends such as demographic trends will influence human resource management and the evolving role of human resource management in response to these trends—in terms of dealing with an aging work force, for instance. We'll see that personnel's role is therefore changing in many ways today, and in particular in the degree to which the human resource manager must be involved with strategic planning. Personnel's role in strategic planning is then discussed as are the methods to be used in developing the personnel policies and policy manual used to help implement personnel's role in the strategic plan. At the end of this chapter we tie together what we have said to this point. This should help you to develop a unifying philosophy of personnel management and to understand how each chapter fits in our model and affects employee motivation.

We are speeding through a period of change for HRM, a period of change that reflects inescapable demographic, social, economic, and technological trends. These trends will dramatically influence the nature of work and the work force in the years ahead and will shape the evolving role of human resource management. We have to understand these trends to understand their impact on HRM.

♦ DEMOGRAPHIC TRENDS

There are, first, dramatic demographic shifts taking place in North America.[1] The first thing to understand is that the rate of growth of the work force is projected to decline swiftly over the next few years. According to projections by the U.S. Labor Department, the labor force is expected to expand by about 21 million people (or 18%) between now and the year 2000. This marks a dramatic slowdown in the labor force's growth, which between 1972 and 1986 grew by almost 31 million people, or 35%. This means that in the years immediately ahead of you, there will be as many as 500,000 fewer new entrants into the labor market; as you can imagine, this will make the HRM manager's task more difficult in terms of recruiting, screening, and training employees.

The rapid growth of the labor force's size in the 1970s reflected the so-called "baby boom" generation, those people born between 1946 and 1964. These baby boomers began crowding into the labor market around 1966. Their numbers helped to expand the economy and also made it easier for HR managers to focus on issues like cost containment, since recruitment and screening (while important) were not the most critical problems. This buyers' market has now ended, however, and it is the (relatively few) sellers who now have the upper hand in selecting the firms they will work for.

Furthermore, the *nature* of the work force will change dramatically too, and become increasingly composed of Hispanics, minorities, and women. For example, between now and the year 2000, the white labor force is projected to increase less than 15%, while the black labor force will grow by nearly 29%, and the Hispanic labor force will grow by more than 74%. During the period 1986–2000, Hispanics will account for nearly 29% of labor force growth, Asian and "other races" (including Alaskan natives) will account for over 11% of labor force growth, and (in total) blacks, Hispanics, and "Asians and other races" should account for 57% of labor force growth. If you include non-Hispanic white women, then the combined share of future growth for these minority-and-women groups reaches more than 90%. Women alone are projected to account for 64% of the net increase in the labor force over this period.[2] Many of these individuals are less likely to have the skills needed by business and much of the resulting training job will therefore shift to HRM.

♦ FAMILY TRENDS

The American family is also changing. For example, the wife remained home to raise the children in roughly 70% of all U.S. families in 1955. Today, that arrangement exists in less than half of American households and other changes are taking place too. For one thing, about two-thirds of all single mothers (separated, divorced, widowed, or never married) are in the labor force today, as are almost 45% of mothers with children under three. In most families, therefore, both parents (not to mention single parents) are increasingly forced to work to make ends meet today. This in turn is creating pressures on HRM in areas such as benefits (child care, parental leave, and so on), flexible work hours, and flexible career ladders.

◆ TRENDS IN THE NATURE OF WORK

The nature of the work that employees will have to do is changing too. Perhaps the biggest change involves the shift from manufacturing to services. Today, for example, nearly two-thirds of the work force is employed in producing and delivering services; in fact, the blue-collar industrial work force declined over 12% during the 1980s. While about 21 million new jobs are projected for the 1986–2000 period the goods-producing industries are projected to have almost no growth in employment during these years. Service-producing industries, therefore, will account for nearly all of the projected growth in new jobs. Although output is expected to continue to increase at over 2% per year, manufacturing employment is actually projected to decline by more than 800,000 jobs between now and the year 2000, thanks to increasing technological innovation and automation and rising productivity.

Along with this shift from manufacturing to services, five occupational groups are projected to expand faster than average over the next ten years. Technicians, service workers, professional workers, sales workers, and executive and management employees will all experience faster than average employment growth between now and the year 2000. Increasingly, jobs will require at least one year of college, while the share of jobs requiring high school completion as the predominant educational level will decline slightly. There will be a sharp decline in the share of jobs where less than a high school education is sufficient to perform the job. New jobs will thus increasingly require a higher level of education, while at the same time the workers available for these jobs will increasingly come from minority groups who are less likely to have the requisite skills and education. Basic skills training, selection on the basis of training potential, and programs to encourage continuing education will thus take on added importance over the next few years.

◆ TECHNOLOGICAL TRENDS

At the same time technological advances will continue to shift employment from some occupations to others while contributing to gradual increases in productivity. For example, telecommunication already makes it relatively easy for many workers to work at home. Computer-aided design/computer-aided manufacturing systems plus robotics will also increase rapidly. By 1990, for instance, General Motors had about 14,000 robots building automobiles (compared to about 1,000 in 1984); researchers at Carnegie Mellon University estimate that there are between 100,000 and 200,000 robots in the United States as of 1990. Manufacturing advances like these will obviously eliminate many blue-collar jobs, replacing them with fewer but more highly skilled jobs.

Similar changes are taking place in office automation, where personal computers, word processing, and management information systems continue to change the face of office work.

The skills required to operate these new technologies will obviously have major effects on all levels of organizational functioning. Labor-intensive blue-collar and clerical functions will decrease while technical, managerial, and professional functions will increase. Here, again, therefore, the nature of work will change and with it the nature of the work force with which HRM must cope.

♦ POLITICAL/LEGAL TRENDS

Personnel managers will also have to continue to cope with changing political and legal trends, most of which will be aimed at further solidifying workers' rights. One of the most important trends here is the evolving case-work regarding the employment-at-will concept. As explained earlier in this book, the employment-at-will concept is based on the assumption that both employer and employee can discontinue the employment relationship at any time. Today, however, this nonbinding concept of employment is increasingly under attack in the United States, where it is contributing to more lawsuits being filed by former employees challenging the fairness of employment termination. As explained, various bases have been used for filing these suits, including "breach of implied covenant of good faith and fair dealing" and "constructive discharge." While several states still effectively prohibit virtually any challenges to the employment-at-will concept within their borders, the number of such states is diminishing and the trend in this area is definitely toward solidifying workers' rights.

Mandated health benefits represent another example of political/legal changes with which HRM will have to cope. Senator Ted Kennedy has said that mandated health benefit legislation is inevitable. He said employers must decide whether they will oppose such legislation or work with Congress to make sure it takes a form they can live with.

♦ COMPETITIVE AND MANAGERIAL TRENDS

Increasing international and domestic pressures will also continue to shape organizations. Competition is already international and this trend can only intensify in the years ahead. In America many Japanese cars are already American made, while in Europe the Ford Taurus (known there as Granada) is ubiquitous. Long–gone American TV shows like "Mannix" and "Kojak" now play on French TV (with French translations), while driving in from De Gaulle airport half the billboards today advertise Japanese, or American, or German products. Sorbonne students fight to buy a pair of Levis jeans. The point is that competition today is not just intense, it is intense across national borders, and there is no doubt that every company will have to seek performance improvements in the years ahead.

At the same time, several factors are boosting the intensity of domestic competition as well. The international nature of competition is itself one factor, injecting as it does new competitors onto the American scene (as between General Motors and Toyota's American plants). The wave of mergers (prompted, in part, by deregulation, junk bonds, and increasingly aggressive raiders) will continue to create the need for more cost-effective performance on the part of companies.

One result is that downsizing today has become a continuing corporate activity. Fewer than half the employers that downsized in 1988–89 cited a "business downturn"—actual or forecast—as the reason. About 57% of the human resources managers in one survey listed "improved staff utilization," mergers and acquisitions, and other reasons (such as budget cuts) for their staff cuts. Only about 43% of the 1,084 employers responding were forced to make reductions due to economic slowdowns.[3] Of the 424 companies that downsized, 30% planned to do so again in the next 12 months. And companies are not just getting leaner: Increased competition and shorter product life cycles are creating ever-more need for more flexible, adaptable companies as well, companies that are more decentralized and participative and that increasingly rely on cooperative project teams to "intrapreneur" new products and ensure the customers' needs are fulfilled, and HRM must be in the vanguard helping companies make the required changes.

Trends like these will demand a change in the traditional role of the "personnel" department, one that shifts it more from "staff" to "line," and from being a reactor to top management's plans to a partner in developing and implementing strategy.

◆ THE EVOLUTION
OF PERSONNEL MANAGEMENT

By way of background, personnel management has evolved in three main stages.[4] In the early 1900s personnel people first took over hiring and firing from foremen, ran the payroll department, and administered benefit plans. It was a job consisting largely of ensuring that procedures were followed. As technology in such areas as testing and interviewing began to emerge, the personnel department began to play an expanded role in employee selection, training, and promotion.

The emergence of a strong union movement in the 1930s drove the second expansion of personnel's role. The rise of unions substantially increased the status and power of the personnel function. Companies now needed the personnel department to counter the union's efforts to organize the company or (failing that) to deal effectively with the union.

The third major change in personnel resulted from the discrimination legislation of the 1960s and 1970s. Because of the large penalties that lawsuits could bring to a company, effective employment practices became more important. In this phase (as in phase 2), personnel continued to make a positive contribution by providing expertise in areas like recruitment, screening, and training. Thus the personnel department could perform these staff activities for the company, freeing line managers to concentrate on primary responsibilities like production and sales. Notice, though, that whether dealing with unions (phase 2) or equal employment (phase 3), personnel gained status in these two stages as much for what they could do to protect the organization from problems as for the positive contribution they made to the firm's effectiveness. Personnel's role, in other words, was largely reactive.

Today, though, "personnel" is speeding through phase 4, and its role is shifting and must continue to shift from protector and screener to planner and change agent. The metamorphosis of personnel into human resource management reflects this, and in fact today's and tomorrow's human resources department will be a very different one from that in the past.

◆ SPECIFIC CHANGES

There are, first, some specific ways in which the human resources function will change.[5]

Employee Benefits

Changing demographics and a changing work force will demand changes in employee benefits. For instance, elder care—direct or indirect care provided to aging relatives—will become more popular as employees and their relatives get older.

Furthermore, the tendency toward earlier retirement seems to have bottomed out. The expectation for the next decade is for a very gradual increase in the retirement age: For example, the average retirement age is expected to increase for salaried employees in 40% of the companies recently surveyed and for union employees in about one-third of them. Less than 20% of the respondents expect a decrease in this average age.[6] The United States has already adopted a gradual increase in the normal retirement age for Social Security purposes.

Consistent with the gradually rising retirement age, about one-third of the organizations surveyed expected early retirement windows to be used less frequently than in the past. In turn, the firm's gradually aging work force will trigger other personnel management changes, as employers have to cope with elder care, motivating plateaued workers, upgrading employees' skills, and instituting more flexible work hours.

Designing New Organizations

Peter Drucker contends that automation will require changes in job design, in the flow of work, and in organizational relationships.[7] Automation on the factory floor requires, for instance, that first-line supervisors change into genuine managers. The traditional functions of first-line supervision are being eroded by automation and either transferred to the work force or built into the process. And, of course, implementing "people" changes like these is traditionally the responsibility of the human resource management function.

Adjusting to Knowledge Workers

Even in the smokestack industries the manual labor component of the work force now accounts for no more than 25%. In most other industries, it is down to one-sixth or less. Productivity of white-collar workers and especially of the rapidly growing groups of knowledge workers is thus the big productivity challenge in developed countries. And the critical factors in knowledge work productivity are things like attitudes, work flow, job relationships, and the designs of jobs and teams. Above all, knowledge work productivity depends on placing the right person on the job. And, again, says Drucker, these are all jobs for the human resources manager.

Restructuring Career Ladders and Compensation

The shift to knowledge work and knowledge workers also creates a need to rethink and to restructure career ladders, compensation, and recognition.[8] The traditional career ladder in most businesses has only managerial rungs. But for most knowledge workers, a promotion to a management job is a wrong reward, says Drucker. The good ones often prefer to keep on doing professional or technical work. This, says Drucker, is not a new problem. Thirty years ago General Electric Company established "parallel ladders" of advancement and rewards for "individual professional contributors." The shift to knowledge work will also force us to rethink the traditional organizational structure. The existing structure—derived from the nineteenth-century military—sees the manager as the boss, with everybody else as the subordinate. In the knowledge-based organization, knowledge workers are the "bosses," and the "manager" is in a supporting role as their planner and coordinator. But this means that jobs—their responsibilities, relationships, and rewards—have to be thought through and redesigned, again, probably, by the human resource management group.

Recruitment

As discussed, the number of new workers available to the labor force is expected to grow much more slowly over the next ten years than it has in the past. This will make recruitment more difficult. As one expert puts it: "In a scarce labor market, the human resource department needs to differentiate itself and the company from the competition so that they can attract the desirable, highly qualified job seekers who are in demand."[9] Recruiting top-notch candidates during the next ten years will therefore be a very challenging task.

Training

The training function will take on added importance in the next ten years as increasingly complex knowledge jobs must be filled in part by a work force that is often ill prepared educationally to meet the new challenges.[10] Increasingly, human resource management will be called upon to implement a growing range of training programs, from basic skills and literacy training up through computer skills training and training in interpersonal communications and leadership. Thus in this area, too, the role of personnel will have to expand in the next few years.

♦ THE CHANGING ROLE OF PERSONNEL/ HUMAN RESOURCE MANAGEMENT

The role of personnel will change in three other major ways as well. There will be an expansion of its consultative role, a new emphasis on its line function, and its role in developing and implementing corporate strategy will be expanded.

First, personnel's traditional role as consultant to the company should increase in the years ahead; in fact, top HRM jobs are increasingly demanding a proven track record in providing top-notch consulting services on previous jobs. As firms must cope with shorter product life cycles, increased competition, and a more sophisticated work force, HRM's expert advice in areas like redesigning organizations, monitoring attitudes, instituting quality improvement teams, and molding company culture will be in high demand.

Paradoxically, while personnel's consultative/staff role will expand, its line role will expand as well. Drucker points out, in fact, that there are already quite a few precedents for "personnel" being a line function. He notes that it has always been so in the largest Japanese firms and in the military, where "personnel" might make, say, staffing decisions more or less unilaterally. And the Vatican's "personnel department," which picks and appoints the bishops of the Catholic church, is strictly a "line department." Today, even the most prestigious and influential American human resources department generally only advises and assists line managers. To make the jump to a more line-oriented role, the way these departments are staffed will probably change, too. For example, the vice-president for human resource management may increasingly have a top-level operating background and come up through the ranks before assuming the personnel role.

But perhaps the most striking change in Personnel will be its evolving role in developing and implementing corporate strategy. Traditionally corporate strategy—the company's plan for how it will balance its internal strengths and weaknesses with external opportunities and threats in order to maintain a competitive advantage—was a job primarily for the company's operating (line) managers. Thus Company X's president might decide to enter new markets, drop product lines, or embark on a five-year cost-cutting plan. He or she would then more or less leave the personnel implications of that plan (hiring or firing new workers, hiring outplacement firms for those fired, and so on) to be carried out by personnel. But today things are different. Strategies increasingly involve merging employees from different firms, and companies face the demographic and work force changes described above. It is now increasingly necessary to involve personnel in the earliest stages of developing the firm's strategic plan. Human resource management will move from "reactor" to "developer and implementer" of strategy.

STRATEGIC PLANNING AND HUMAN RESOURCE MANAGEMENT

♦ STRATEGIC PLANNING DEFINED

strategic plan Course of action the firm plans to pursue in becoming the sort of enterprise it wants to be, given the firm's external opportunities and threats and its internal strengths and weaknesses.

To understand the human resources manager's role in strategic planning, we should begin by explaining what "strategic planning" means.

A company's **strategic plan** outlines the course of action the firm plans to pursue in becoming the sort of enterprise that it wants to be, given the firm's external opportunities and threats and its internal strengths and weaknesses. Deciding whether Mom and Pop's Supermarket will compete with Enormous Markets head to head by building similar superstores or deciding what sorts of competitive advantage Burger King should use to compete with McDonald's both involve strategic planning.

An organization's strategic plan always seeks to balance two sets of forces: the company's external opportunities and threats, on the one hand, and its internal strengths and weaknesses, on the other. Companies that successfully balance these external and internal forces succeed, as McDonald's has by diversifying its product line beyond Big Macs, by extending store hours, and by expanding overseas. Those that don't, fail, as happened to the original Braniff Airlines several years ago. Their plan to pursue external opportunities and expand worldwide was inconsistent with their limited "internal" financial and managerial resources.

To illustrate more clearly what strategic planning is all about and how such plans fail, consider several more examples. Starting in the early 1900s, W. T. Grant's grew to a nationwide chain, competing with Woolworth's and Kresge's in the "5&10" category. Around 1970 Grant's management decided to change strategy and to convert their stores to "Grant's City" stores. They were to be large, K-mart–type stores, selling a wide range of clothing, home furnishings, and appliances at discount prices—a great strategy for the external market, perhaps, but the wrong one for Grant's. Grant's was unprepared internally to execute the new strategy effectively—its people couldn't properly handle big-ticket credit sales, for instance—and the firm was out of business within three years.

Delta Airlines' successful strategy is another good example. Delta's strategy has always been based on several basic components. It organized its flights around a hub-and-spoke system with flights from, say, Miami connecting with flights to New York in the Atlanta hub. It kept its fleet new by cycling out older planes early, before maintenance costs grew too high. And it maintained a nonunion high-morale work force with intelligent and progressive human resource management. This helped to ensure that customers got superior service. It also ensured that employees would willingly shift from job to job as the need arose with, say, a reservations clerk filling in for a baggage handler when the going got rough. As a result, while Delta workers are individually very well paid, Delta's total labor bill is proportionately less than many of its competitors, since the staff is used more efficiently.

In practice, strategies like Delta's succeed or fail for one of two reasons (and this is where the human resource manager comes in, by the way). A strategy may fail because it is simply a *poor strategy*, in that it doesn't fit the market or the company's strengths and weaknesses—that's a big part of why Braniff didn't make it, for example. Second, a firm's strategy can fail because of poor *execution*. In part, that's probably why Grant's went down in failure following a strategy essentially the same as that of K–Mart. On the other hand, Delta Airlines' strategy (and that of companies like McDonald's and Domino's Pizza, to name a few) generally succeeded because (1) they were good strategies (balancing the firms' external threats and opportunities, and internal strengths and weaknesses) which were also (2) perfectly executed. And today, because of the trends discussed earlier, the HR manager must increasingly play a pivotal role in strategic planning to ensure the plan is a good one that succeeds.

◆ HMR'S ROLE IN STRATEGIC PLANNING

There are three ways the human resource department helps top management formulate and execute the company's strategic plans: first, by helping supply intelligence regarding the company's external opportunities and threats; second, by supplying intelligence about the company's internal strengths and weaknesses; and third, by helping execute the plan, for instance, by eliminating a weakness that could be an impediment to the plan.

External Opportunities and Threats

Let's look at a few examples. The HR manager can, first, help the CEO formulate the strategic plan by supplying intelligence about the company's external opportunities and threats. For example, labor power projections regarding labor availability must be crucial to firms like Burger King (and others) who depend so heavily on entry-level labor. For a company like Burger King, the strategic implications of a diminishing entry-level labor pool include the need for increased automation of facilities and just possibly the need to reduce the growing dependence on company-owned stores and thus shift the recruiting burden to local franchisees. Installing smaller, less labor-intensive drivethrough locations is another strategic possibility that could emerge from such strategic input.

HRM is in a unique position to supply other data on external opportunities and threats as well. Details regarding advanced incentive plans being used by competitors, opinion survey data from your employees that elicit suggestions about customer complaints, and information about pending legislation like labor laws or mandatory health insurance are some other examples.

Internal Strengths and Weaknesses

Second, personnel can also help top management formulate strategy by supplying information regarding the company's internal strengths and weaknesses.

For example, many plans fail because they are not compatible with the company's current human resources. At W. T. Grant's, the lack of trained personnel to manage the firm's new credit system helped cripple the company's plan. Twenty-five years ago or so the downfall of Ford's Edsel car was in part preordained by the unavailability at Ford of enough accountants and other middle managers to implement Ford's new Edsel Division.

The whole area of mergers and acquisitions is another area that's ripe for HRM's input. While financial and business considerations will usually prevail here, it is usually useful (and often essential) for the CEO to also know about matters like morale problems in the acquired firm, incompatibility of corporate cultures, and potential problems in merging compensation, seniority, and benefit plans. For example, just two months after it officially acquired Crocker National Corporation, Wells Fargo surveyed 1,500 Crocker employees, to make sure that if there was a problem, they knew about it as quickly as possible.

HRM, therefore, should be a source of strategic input regarding the company's strengths and weaknesses. This certainly applies to obvious areas like management talent and competitiveness of the firm's compensation plan. But increasingly it must include less obvious matters such as the attractiveness of a merger candidate in human resource terms, the potential people problems likely to occur as a result of introducing a new technology, and the human resource benefits and drawbacks of pursuing one strategic plan or another.

Successful Execution

Finally, HRM should be heavily involved in the successful *execution* of the company's strategic plan, for instance, by helping to eliminate weaknesses that could inhibit the plan. Today Personnel is already heavily involved in the execution of most firm's downsizing and restructuring strategies, in terms of outplacing employees, instituting pay for performance plans, reducing health care costs, and retraining employees. However, these activities are probably just the tip of the iceberg, considering the trends evolving today. Intensifying domestic and international competition, the changing nature of the work force, jobs that are increasingly complex and based on information technology, and continuing merger and divestiture activities mean that management will have to base strategic decisions more than ever on personnel considerations. Creating the right company culture, keeping key personnel after a merger, matching training needs and people with jobs, and solving the human problems (stress and low morale, for example) that can arise when employees' jobs are put in jeopardy are a few examples of the sorts of activities the human resource manager will play in helping execute the strategic plan.[11] But perhaps more to the point is this: In an increasingly service and high-tech based economy, committed employees (rather than just "manufacturing efficiency" or "low overall costs" or some other) will increasingly be the competitive advantage of choice. And this will thrust HRM into the central and strategic role of implementing the methods and procedures that will be necessary to help elicit that sort of commitment.

◆ STRATEGIC HUMAN RESOURCE MANAGEMENT: EXAMPLES

The programs carried out by the human resource department at Colgate-Palmolive provide an example of HRM's role in strategy development and implementation.

Colgate-Palmolive Company is a global manufacturing company with sales of over $5 billion that recently received new "marching orders." After assuming the presidency several years ago, the new CEO developed and communicated a new strategic direction for the company based on what he called his "corporate initiatives."[12] Among other things, the new strategy emphasized concentrating on new products, being the low-cost producer, simplifying businesses and structures, pushing decision making down, promoting entrepreneurial action, and improving morale and motivation. The new strategy was aimed at making Colgate a leaner, more responsive competitor in its global markets and in focusing the company more clearly on health-related products.

Consistent with this new strategy, several major steps were made almost at once. Four major businesses were divested, including two sports and recreation companies. A major reorganization took place that eliminated one level of senior management. Additional resources were diverted to new product development and research and development. And the human resource programs at Colgate-Palmolive got a new mandate to help Colgate achieve its new goals.

The programs laid out for Colgate HRM provide a glimpse of how HRM today is being pressed to get involved in strategic management. At Colgate-Palmolive, HRM was directed by the president to develop and execute programs designed to create a company culture that would achieve the following:

Encourage a spirit of teamwork and cooperation within and among business units in working toward common objectives, with an emphasis on identifying, acknowledging, and rewarding personal and unit excellence.

Foster entrepreneurial attitudes among the managers and innovative thinking among all employees.

Emphasize the commonality of interest between the employees and shareholders.[13]

To that end, numerous HRM programs had to be designed. For example, the company's executive incentive compensation plan was redesigned to place more emphasis on individual performance and achieving operating targets. Employee benefits were redesigned to make them more flexible and responsive to employees' needs. At the same time, cost controls and employee sharing of costs were instituted, two changes that were accomplished by effectively communicating both the changes and the reasons for them. The bottom line was that by implementing a number of programs (including those aimed at redesigning compensation and benefits), HRM was able to contribute to a refocusing of Colgate employees' efforts in a manner that contributed to the execution of Colgate's strategic plan.

DEVELOPING PERSONNEL POLICIES

♦ PERSONNEL POLICIES AND STRATEGY IMPLEMENTATION

policies Guides to action that assure consistency under a particular set of circumstances and within the framework of the company's plan.

As at Colgate, the implementation of a strategic plan generally involves formulating more specific departmental **policies**, "guides to action that assure consistency under a particular set of circumstances and within the framework of the company's plan."[14] These in turn guide the activities of the departments in question. Thus suppose your strategy is to maximize unit sales while reducing costs. This leads to a *production* policy to stress mass–produced items (rather than hand–built ones) and to a *distribution* policy to stress franchised sales (since this might create more sales quicker than would slowly building a company–owned set of dealers).

Much the same applies to *personnel* policies. Personnel policies regarding such matters as how much to pay, how to screen candidates, how disciplinary matters are dealt with, how incentives are earned, or how aggressively affirmative action will be pursued don't (or shouldn't) just emerge spontaneously. Instead, *personnel policies should follow from and be consistent with the company's basic mission and plan*. And, as in Colgate's case, they should enable the company and its managers to better implement that plan.

Some examples help illustrate how.[15] At Vulcan Materials Company in Birmingham, Alabama, maintaining its number one position in construction products means being a low-cost leader. This means personnel policies that stress encouraging productivity, absenteeism control, and high worker safety. Burlington Industries is embarked on a different strategic plan. Facing highly competitive pressures in the textile industry, it had to sell off some businesses, reduce the number of employees, and work hard to consolidate plants and decentralize. Here personnel policies had to help the company get more responsive to customers' needs, since these needs (for different textiles) change so rapidly. Here, therefore, training policies emphasize how to improve employee decision making and team effort and emphasize understanding the customer's needs, developing customer linkages, and improving delegation and decision making (to help make the firm more responsive).

Tandy Corporation is another example of how personnel policies are formulated to support company strategy. In the case of this electronics/computer firm, success depends largely on the profitability of its retail sales. In turn, these sales are based on the sales ability of retail sales employees, most of whom are selling items (like computers and electronic instruments) that require solid product knowledge and an intelligent sales effort.

At Tandy, therefore, personnel policies (regarding selection, and compensation, for instance) are aimed at attracting, hiring, and motivating the kinds of people required for Tandy's success. For example, Tandy's selection policy must emphasize identifying candidates who will be successful selling Tandy's products, since 80% of the company's employees are in direct sales. To this end, Tandy developed a computerized program to administer a skill assessment profile. This is aimed at determining a candidate's aptitude for activities like qualifying customers, making sales presentations, closing sales, and providing after-sales customer service. Similarly, its training policies emphasize effective sales training, and its compensation policy puts a heavy premium on sales performance: In fact, 75% of the management compensation plans at Tandy, including that of the vice-president of human resources, is tied to the company's profits.[16]

Personnel Policies and Company Productivity

One recent study at Columbia University suggests there is also a link between personnel policies and company productivity.[17] The results suggest three conclusions: (1) There are strong correlations among individual personnel policies such that they "cluster" into identifiable types of HRM systems; (2) different sets of personnel policies (or HRM systems) occur in different environments; and (3) certain types of HRM systems are more often associated with high productivity than are others.

The study focused on six personnel policy areas:

1. *Job design,* and in particular whether jobs were designed flexibly and broadly or rigidly and narrowly;
2. *Promotions,* and in particular whether promotions in the firm were based on merit or on seniority;
3. *Recruiting,* and in particular whether promotion from within or external recruiting was stressed;
4. *Training,* and in particular, whether a formal training program was available;
5. *Grievance procedures,* and in particular, whether a formal grievance procedure ending in third party arbitration was available; and
6. *Communication,* and in particular, whether communication and information mechanisms other than formal grievance procedures ending in arbitration were used.

The author of the study found, first, that the policies tended to be correlated, and that they clustered into identifiable types of HRM systems. For example, System 1-type companies tended to rely on inflexible job design, seniority-based promotion, restrictive promotion from within policies, and grievance procedures ending in third-party arbitration. System 9-type companies tended to rely on flexible job design, formal training programs, formal communications systems other than grievance procedures, and a high level of promotions from within.

In turn, different types of environments, industries, and companies tended to have characteristic types of HRM systems. Thus the more rigid and formalized System 1-type systems tended to predominate in older, larger, capital-intensive companies with unionized work forces. Many large nonunion firms, on the other hand, had more flexible System 9-type HRM systems. As another example, what the researcher dubs "System 4-Do Nothing, Find a Body" HRM systems were often found among young, high growth, small, nonunion R&D capital-intensive firms: Here, the cost of doing so may have precluded setting up a comprehensive formal set of HRM policies and procedures.

An interesting conclusion of this study—one to consider as you turn to actually developing personnel policies, below—is that more often than not "high commitment" HRM systems were associated with the highest productivity firms. In other words, clusters or sets of personnel policies like System 9 (flexible job design, employee training, merit-based rewards, and so on) were found in firms with the highest levels of observed productivity. In fact, the study concluded that many businesses would experience a significant increase in labor productivity if they adopted System 9, and no business would experience a loss in productivity. The results are only preliminary and don't necessarily imply a cause-effect relationship between HRM policy and productivity. However, given the growing emphasis on a more sophisticated work force, on globalization, on competition, and on the need for responsiveness, they are well worth keeping in mind as your Personnel Policies Manual is put together.

♦ PROS AND CONS OF POLICIES

Policies (and particularly written policies) are important for three reasons. They standardize decisions (for instance, regarding sick leave) which therefore needn't be remade time and again. They ensure consistent and therefore fair treatment of employees, all of whom should be governed by the same set of, say, disciplinary policies and rules. And policies as explained should be extensions of the company's strategic plan: They should thus breathe life into general aims like "let's maximize units sold and minimize costs" by providing specific guidelines for each department such as "select only the most productive workers."

Yet policies for all their value can have their drawbacks, particularly when they get too restrictive. In his book *Up the Organization*, Robert Townsend claimed that "the only people who read policy manuals are goldbricks and martinets."[18] Several years ago the chairman of Dana Corporation was reported to have publicly burned a 22-inch stack of policy manuals for much the same reason.[19] The point is that the policy manual should be in a sense a living document, evolving and changing as management's plans and philosophy evolves. Furthermore, never forget that any policy is exactly that, a guide. Policies are not immutable laws, and in our society even laws tend to be applied by judges who remember the mitigating circumstances of the situation. It is important, therefore, not to poison the enormous usefulness of policies and policy manuals with the overly restrictive application of an unmanageable network of policy guidelines.

COMPUTER APPLICATION IN STRATEGIC HRM:

EXPERT SYSTEMS IN HRM

An Expert System is a program that attempts to simulate how human experts solve problems. This is done by entering knowledge from one or more "expert" sources into what is known as a "knowledge base." This knowledge base includes the rules for solving a specific type of problem. When a user queries the expert system, the rules are evaluated, and the user is presented with an "expert" answer.[1]

Users of electronic spreadsheets (like Lotus 1-2-3 and VP Planner Plus) are already building knowledge systems to handle complex problems. Current uses include producing sales reports quickly when products, data, or rules change frequently. One-time reports using relatively small data bases can be combined with macros to use the time of the manager or professional more efficiently. This type of system is called a *performance aid*. The user sets the rules (*if* this is the situation, *do* that, *otherwise* do this), which can be combined (AND) or contrasted (OR) with other rules.

In HRM, knowledge systems are useful in several areas. For example, as cafeteria benefit plans proliferate, the interaction of decisions made by employees may violate a rule that requires that at least 60% of the employees must choose term life insurance in order for that benefit to be offered at a group rate. The computerized HRM aid could signal management of that fact, as well as allow employees to ask "what-if" questions to see the impact of various decisions on outcomes such as income tax rate, total retirement income, early retirement, or net pay after deferring income.

Knowledge systems are also valuable in reviewing the impact of changes in career ladders, in the weighting of elements in job analysis, and in the effect of recruitment on such outcomes as total wage and benefits costs, EEO categories, and promotional opportunities. Risk managers can more accurately assess the cost of various combinations of benefit packages and differing experience ratings of health plans. Supervisors can more clearly evaluate the impact of merit pay with computer systems which establish percentage increases based on performance ratings. The company can also judge the bottom line impact of various percentage raises for various levels of demonstrated accomplishment based on performance appraisal. While small knowledge systems are useful in contract negotiations, large expert systems will give more accurate estimates of strategic decisions on HRM without bias or emotion and without overlooking significant details.

With the demographic shifts in the United States and the increasing rate of change in the external environment, HR managers must be able to offer ways for companies to remain competitive domestically and internationally. Knowledge–based expert systems will become a part of the arsenal.

[1]Mary Lynn Manns, unpublished manuscript, February 19, 1990.

Legal Aspects

Also remember that your policy manual should not be a formal contract with your employees.[20] In both your policy manual and employee handbook, you should prominently display a disclaimer pointing out that the manual or handbook is not a contract and that employees may be terminated by the employer at any time for any reason. Also note that the manual or handbook may be revised, supplemented, or deleted at any time by the employer. In general you should also avoid any terminology that might be construed as limiting your rights as an employer, for instance, terms such as "permanent employee" or "termination for cause." Legal pitfalls like these, too, will obviously detract from the long-term usefulness of your policy book.

♦ THE POLICY DEVELOPMENT PROCESS

We'll discuss the specific steps in developing personnel policies next, but first there are two basic things about this process that you should know. First, most policies arise out of management's past practices.[21] The managers of any firm naturally have to make decisions and take actions as situations arise. As time goes by these tend to be codified either formally or informally in a network of policies for the firm. Even if the owner of a five-person store doesn't believe in written policies, her company will have policies nevertheless. These will emerge as decisions must be made in response to questions employees ask, such as: how long must they work to take their first vacation, and how long can that vacation be. Management's past practices are thus the place to start when formulating a set of written policies for the firm.

The second point is that good policies always flow from the basic strategic plan and philosophy of the owners and top management of the firm. Thus the firm that decides to stress cost reduction, efficiency, and specialized jobs should produce a very different set of personnel policies than will the firm in which creativity and entrepreneurial spirit are the guiding goals.

Developing a set of personnel policies involves the following steps:[22]

Step 1. Define Your Audience

First, decide on the purpose of the manual and on who the policies and the policy manual are aimed at. In general, personnel policy manuals are aimed at those supervisory employees who are charged with implementing the policies, including the human resources manager, department heads, and supervisors. In general, the policy manual contains the basic policies (regarding attendance, compensation, and so forth) that managers and supervisors need to administer the company's personnel policies.

Step 2. Form a Policy Committee

The actual work of formulating, codifying, producing, and communicating the policies and policy manual is usually assigned to a policy committee. The membership of such committees vary, but it is customary to appoint a high-ranking personnel officer to chair the committee and to have representation from all the organization's key functional areas.

Step 3. Select Sources of Information

There are several sources of information you can use in developing your company's policies and policy manual. *Existing policy statements* and policy manuals are a useful starting point. *Other manuals* and handbooks (such as employee handbooks from various departments or divisions, training manuals, and any other written rules or procedures that various departments or divisions use) are valuable too. *Other employer's policy manuals* are another good source, one that can sometimes be tapped by offering to trade or compare policy manuals between the two firms. On delving through your organization's file cabinets, you will also find various *memos and other similar records* under file headings such as human resources, employee benefits, wage and salary, and EEO. Review these memos and records carefully, making sure to seek out memos to and from individuals (like wage and salary administrators) whose paperwork may contain embryonic policies.

Several other sources can be tapped. *In-house experts*, including people like company attorneys, benefits administrators, and accountants, can provide useful information in their areas of expertise. *"Packaged" written and computerized personnel policy manuals* complete with numerous sample policies (such as the excellent *Encyclopedia of Personnel Policies*) are also available.[23]

Step 4. Determine Length and Writing Style

Next, some basic decisions must be made regarding the length of each policy and the writing style to be used. A personnel policy on a matter like performance appraisals may range from a single paragraph to two pages or more, depending upon the amount of detailed information to be included. Here a decision needs to be made regarding how much detail there should be. The decision on detail, in turn, will hinge on the question of just how specific (and, therefore, restrictive) you want the policy to be and/or on the extent to which you want your manual to be an education/training document that supervisors can use to bone up on how to perform some activity like appraising performance.

Step 5. Organization and Format

You also have to decide on the organization and format of the manual and on the format of each policy statement as well.

There are several specific issues to be addressed. In general, you will want a foreword, table of contents, and an index to make the job of looking up the policy easier for all involved. Another important question here involves deciding which specific policies are to be covered. (We shall address this point below.) The policy committee will also have to decide what sort of numbering system to use for each policy area (for example, "attendance and time off" policies might be numbered 100 through 199, while "compensation" policies are numbered 300 through 399). In any event, you'll want to devise a logical numbering system, one in which decimal points are used to facilitate grouping major policy areas (such as 1.0—Employment), and subsidiary areas (such as 1.2—Equal Employment Opportunity), and even more specific areas (such as 1.21—Employment Advertising). Also be careful here to allow within your numbering system for future expansion in areas where policies may be formulated in the future.

A number of things should not be included in the manual. Policies that do not apply to most of your readers (such as special benefit plans for top executives), policies that are in the planning stages, and, of course, confidential information should be left out. Also leave out information that changes often, such as names and titles of individuals and telephone extension numbers.

A decision must also be made on the format of each policy itself. As in Figure 19.1 it is common to specify on top of the page the subject and to present a rationale (often called "authorization") for the policy, followed by the policy itself. However, depending upon the use to which the policy is put, many organizations also include, as in Figure 19.1, a detailed procedure for the supervisor to follow in implementing the policy.

Step 6. Design Factors

Several practical considerations enter into the design of any manual. You want it to be easy to use, so a heavy-grade paper, well-marked and reinforced tabs, and a sufficiently wide three-ring binder are important to make sure the manuals don't start falling apart.

FIGURE 19.1
Leave Authorization Sample Policy Form
Source: Sue Ellen Thompson, *The Personnel Manager's Encyclopedia of Personnel Policies,* Business & Legal Reports, 1983, p. 130.06.

Subject: Maternity Leave

Organization: Anonymous

Example of: Policy Confined to Maternity Leave

EFFECTIVE: _____ (Revised)

RATIONALE: Section 701 of the Civil Rights Act of 1964 was amended effective October 1, 1978: "(K) The terms 'because of sex' or 'on the basis of sex' include but are not limited to, because of or on the basis of pregnancy, childbirth, or related medical conditions; and women affected by pregnancy, childbirth, or related medical conditions shall be treated the same for all employment–related purposes, including receipt of benefits under fringe benefit programs, as other persons not so affected but similar in ability or inability to work . . ."
In a word, pregnancy will be treated as any other disability and will be eligible for Temporary Disability Benefits (TDB) in the same amount and degree as any other eligible circumstance.

PROCEDURE: 1. All female employees should be made aware that it is in their long–term interest to advise the Employee Relations Department of their pregnancy as soon as it is confirmed by their physician.
2. Upon receipt of this notification, the individual should be encouraged to attend a counseling appointment with the Employee Relations Manager or his/her assigned agent for the purpose of explaining:
   (a) that it may be necessary during the course of her condition to change her work assignment for the health and safety of herself and the child as advice and consultation with the physician may dictate.
   (b) that, at the discretion of the Com-

Step 7. Approval Procedures

Particularly in smaller companies the company president and even his or her board may want to make the final approval of all policies in the manual. After all, this may be the first time that these policies have been codified, and policies regarding matters like vacation, compensation, and discipline can have a big impact on the health and welfare of the firm. In larger organizations the president might want to review the manual, and certainly the head of human resource management. It is also wise to have copies of the preliminary manual distributed to department heads for their input and advice before anything is finalized.

Step 8. Distribution and Copy Control

While it shouldn't contain anything confidential, neither do you want copies of the personnel manual floating uncontrolled throughout or beyond your firm. It is therefore advisable to number each manual and maintain in HRM a master list showing each manual's location and to whom it is signed out.

Step 9. Introducing the Manual to Supervisors

You want to avoid the impression that there is some subterranean process going on aimed at changing all the personnel policies in the firm. Be up front with everyone immediately, and have the new policy committee issue a written announcement that the policy manual project is underway. In addition to heading off unneeded speculation, such an announcement can also elicit recommendations from the management and supervisory staff about the policies that exist now and any policies they feel should be added.

From a practical point of view do not simply foist a brand new set-in-stone manual on your managers and supervisors unannounced. Not only can this trigger unnecessary resistance from those who feel they were not consulted; it may also put you in the position of overlooking an important point that a more participatory approach would have uncovered. Therefore as the manual moves forward toward completion, hold small-group meetings within each department among members of the policy committee and supervisors.

The manual itself will lose some of its effectiveness unless instructions and training are provided to explain its use. An orientation/training program explaining the manual to all managers and supervisors (either together or in groups) can thus ensure that the manual is used, and used properly.

♦ POLICY MANUAL TABLE OF CONTENTS EXAMPLES

An example of a table of contents for a personnel policies manual is presented in Figure 19.2. It contains a relatively detailed breakdown of virtually all the policy areas an employer might want to address. These include Absenteeism, Holidays, Interviewing and Selection, Promotion from Within, and Safety Programs. Again, though, the policies to be addressed and the format of the table of contents should be individualized to your own firm.

♦ AUDITING THE HRM FUNCTION

While the firm's personnel policies and focus should be consistent with the company's strategic plan, the bottom line should always be: "To what extent is HRM effectively carrying out its function?" In other words designing a set of policies and an HRM philosophy that is consistent with where the company wants to go is only part of the job. Effectively carrying out those functions is another.

Several suggestions have been made for how to assess how HRM in a firm is actually doing. One approach is to use accounting and statistical techniques to calculate the cost of human resources, for instance the dollar investment in human assets that good training provides. In this way the bottom-line contribution of HRM can be concretely assessed.[24] For an employer with the wherewithal to conduct such a program, it may well be worth considering. A second, less rigorous, but still effective approach follows.

The HR Review

At a minimum, an "HR review" should be conducted, one aimed at tapping top managers' opinions regarding how effective HRM has been. Former New York Mayor Ed Koch used to ask New Yorkers "How am I doing?" While an "HR review" is more comprehensive than that, its value lies in its similar simplicity. Such a review should contain two parts: what should be and what is.[25]

The question "what should be" refers to the broad aims of the HRM department and involves two things. It should start, first, with a very broad philosophy or *vision statement*. This might envision HRM as being "recognized as an excellent resource rather than a bureaucratic entity, a business-oriented function, and the conscience of the company," and so forth. This vision might also enumerate the characteristics of the HRM staff, for in-

FIGURE 19.2
Sample Table of Contents for a Personnel Policy Manual
Source: Sue Ellen Thompson, *The Personnel Manager's Encyclopedia of Personnel Policies,* Business
& Legal Reports, 1983, Table of Contents.

Contents

Part II: Encyclopedia of Policies

stance, as "experts in their areas of responsibility, demonstrating a commitment to excellence, and being creative, analytical problem solvers." The vision statement should thus set the tone for HRM.

Second, this broad vision gets more focus with an HRM *mission statement.* This describes what the mission of the department should be, for instance "to contribute to the achievement of the company's business objectives by assisting the organization in making effective and efficient use of employee resources and, at the same time, assisting employees at all levels in creating for themselves satisfying and rewarding work lives."[26]

Next, the focus of the HR review then shifts to an evaluation of "what is?" This part of the evaluation consists of six steps and involves input from the corporate HRM staff, division heads, divisional HRM heads, and those other experts (like the benefits administrator) that report directly to the head of corporate HRM. The issues to be addressed are as follows:

1. *What are the HRM functions?* Here the participants listed above (division heads and so forth) provide their opinions about what they think

HRM's functions should be. As you might imagine the list can be extensive, ranging from EEO enforcement and managing health benefits, to employee relations management, recruitment and selection, training, and even community relations management. The important point here is to crystallize what HRM and its main "clients" believe are HRM's functions.

2. *How important are these functions?* The participants then rate each of these functions on a 10-point scale of importance, ranging from low (1–3) to medium (4–7) to high (8–10). This provides an estimate of how important each of the 15 or 20 identified HRM functions are in the views of HRM executives and their clients (like division managers).

3. *How well is each of the functions performed?* Next, have the same participants evaluate how well each of these HRM functions are actually being performed. Here, for example, you may find that four functions—say, employee benefits, compensation, employee relations, and recruiting—receive "high" ratings from more than half of the raters. Other functions may get "medium" or "low" ratings.

4. *What needs improvement?* The next step is to determine which of the functions rated most important rate as high, or medium, or low in terms of "how well is each of the functions performed?" Functions (like "labor relations") that are assessed as highly important but evaluated as low in terms of performance will require the quickest attention. To formalize the comparison of importance and performance ratings, have the participants compare the median importance and performance ratings for each of the 15 to 20 functions identified in step 1.

   More important, the discussions at this stage will help identify the HRM functions in which the department has to improve its performance. The discussions arising at this point should help to pinpoint specific problems that contributed to the "low performance" ratings and help provide recommendations for improving HRM's performance on low-rated functions (say, selection, or training).

5. *How effectively does the corporate HR function use resources?* This next step consists of checks to determine if the HRM budget is being allocated and spent in a way that's consistent with the functions HRM should be stressing. First, make an estimate of where the HRM dollars are being spent—for instance, on recruiting, EEO compliance, compensation management, and so on. Also try to distinguish between ongoing work and new programs (such as a quality improvement program that may be installed two years hence). Questions to ask here are: "Is expense allocation consistent with the perceived importance and performance of each of the HRM functions?" and "Should any dollars be diverted to low performing functions to improve their effectiveness?"

6. *How can HR become optimally effective?* This final step is aimed at allowing you one last, broader view of the areas that need improvement and how they should be improved. For example, at this step it may be apparent that a large divisionally organized company needs to strengthen divisional and on-site HRM staffs so that responsibilities for certain HRM functions can be moved closer to the user.

TOWARD A PHILOSOPHY OF PERSONNEL MANAGEMENT

♦ THE NEED FOR A PHILOSOPHY

In Chapter 1 we said that people's actions are always based in part on the assumptions they make and that this was especially true in regard to human resource management. The basic assumptions you make about people—Can they be trusted? Do they dislike work? Can they be creative? Why do they act as they do?—together comprise your philosophy of personnel management. And the people you hire, the training you provide, your leadership style all reflect (for better or worse) this basic philosophy.

In Chapter 1 we also discussed some factors that will mold and influence your own philosophy, including the philosophy of your employer's top management, you own basic assumptions about people, and your background and experiences. In addition, we have seen that *motivation* is an essential issue, one that should be a cornerstone of your personnel management philosophy.

Yet throughout this book we have emphasized the "nuts and bolts" of personnel management by focusing mainly on the concepts and techniques all managers need to carry out their personnel–related tasks. It is therefore easy to lose sight of the fact that these techniques, while important, cannot be administered effectively without some unifying philosophy. For, to repeat, it is this philosophy or *vision* that helps guide you in deciding *what people to hire, what training to provide*, and *how to motivate employees*.

♦ A MOTIVATION MODEL

Because motivating employees is so important, we have used our Motivation Model to introduce and tie together the chapters in this book. Motivating employees, we said, requires three things:

First, ensure that your subordinate feels that effort on his or her part will probably lead to obtaining a coveted reward (make sure he or she has the *ability* to do the job). For this, you have to provide an adequate organization structure and clear job descriptions. You have to determine the human requirements of the job (in terms of knowledge and skills, for instance) and recruit and select people who meet these requirements; finally, you have to provide the necessary training and development. We covered these topics in Chapters 2 to 8: *recruitment and selection* and *training and development*.

Second, find out what the person wants, holding it out as a possible reward (make sure the person has the *desire* to do the job). For this, you will need an understanding of what motivates people. And, you will need a sound understanding of the financial and nonfinancial rewards you can use; we covered these topics in Chapters 9 to 13: *compensation and motivation*.

Finally, you have to check on the *results* of your efforts to motivate your employees and take the necessary corrective action. This involves appraisal and career development; we discussed this in Chapters 14 and 15: *appraisal and development*.

♦ A BROADER VIEW OF THE ROLE OF PERSONNEL MANAGEMENT: THE QUALITY OF WORK LIFE

We also saw that managers are increasingly measuring their actions in terms of *quality of work life*, which means the degree to which employees are able to satisfy their important personal needs by working in the organization. In practice, this means providing employees with fair, equitable treatment; an opportunity for each employee to use his or her skills to the utmost and to self-actualize; open, trusting communications; providing all employees with an opportunity to take an active role in making important job-related decisions; adequate and fair compensation; and a safe and healthy environment. We explained several techniques, including quality improvement programs and flexible hours that are aimed at improving the employee's quality of work life. Keep in mind, though, that quality of work life goes beyond mere techniques, in that the quality of work life that prevails in your unit will reflect not just techniques but your basic attitudes and assumptions about people. Thus a *Theory Y* leader who believes the best about his or her subordinates will probably treat these people in a way that enhances their QWL. In an organization with the opposite assumptions, you can be sure that a lower quality of work life will prevail as the manager tries to closely monitor and control each worker's actions. Related to this, remember that virtually every personnel-related action you take affects the quality of work life in some way. Thus *selection* should emphasize placing the right person on the right job, where that person can have a more satisfying, rewarding (and motivating) experience. Similarly, an equitable *grievance procedure* will help protect employee rights and dignity and therefore contribute to the quality of work life. Every personnel action you take, in other words, affects your employee's quality of work life, and your actions will in turn reflect your basic assumptions about people. It is when your personnel actions should be geared not just to satisfying your organization's staffing needs but also to satisfying your employees' needs to grow and to self-actualize that your *personnel management system* can be properly referred to as a *human resource management* system.

SUMMARY

1. Demographic, social, economic, and technological trends are forcing changes on organizations and on personnel. These trends include, for instance, a dramatic slowdown in the growth of the labor force, the growth of Hispanics, minorities, and women as members of the work force, more two-worker families, an increasing emphasis on knowledge-based work, and an increasingly internationalized competition.

2. In the face of trends like these, the role of human resource management is evolving. Specific ways in which the personnel function will change include changes in employee benefits, new organization structures, restructuring career ladders, dealing with an aging work force, experimenting with new recruitment methods, and doing more training of workers to help them cope with the new knowledge-based jobs.

3. Perhaps the most striking change in personnel will be its evolving role in developing and implementing corporate strategy. A company's strategic plan outlines the course of action the firm plans to pursue in becoming the sort of enterprise that it wants to be given its external opportunities and threats and its internal strengths and weaknesses. To this end, personnel helps top management to formulate and execute the company's strategic plan by helping to supply intelligence regarding the company's external opportunities and threats, by supplying intelligence about the company's internal strengths and weaknesses, and by helping execute the plan, for instance, by eliminating a weakness that could be an impediment to the plan.

4. A policy is a guide to action that ensures consistency under a particular set of circumstances and within the framework of the company's strategic plan. Developing a set of policies involves the following steps: Define your audience, form a policy committee, select source of information, determine length and writing style, organization and format, design factors, approval procedures, distribution and copy control, and introduce the manual to supervisors.

KEY TERMS

strategic plan   policies

1. Write an essay titled "My Philosophy of Personnel Management."
2. Explain how each chapter in this book affects motivation and the quality of work life.
3. Write an essay in which you summarize how you would use specific personnel management techniques to select, train, motivate, and appraise employees.
4. Explain the impact of workforce trends on personnel management.
5. Discuss HRM's role in strategic planning.
6. Explain how you would develop a personnel policies manual.

NOTES

1. Unless otherwise noted, this section is based on Eric Framholtz et al., "The Tenor of Today," *Personnel Journal* (June 1987), pp. 61–70; Ronald Kutcher, "Overview and Implications of the Projections to 2000," *Monthly Labor Review* (September 1987), pp. 3–9; Laura Herren, "The New Game of HR: Playing to Win," *Personnel* (June 1989), pp. 19–22.
2. Ronald Kutcher, "Overview and Implications of the Projections to 2000," pp. 3–4.
3. American Management Association Survey, *Personnel* (New York: AMA, October 1989).
4. This is based on Edward E. Lawler III, "Human Resources Management: Meeting the New Challenges," *Personnel* (January 1988), pp. 24–25.
5. This section is based on ibid., pp. 24–27; Michael Driver, Robert Coffey, and David Bowen, "Where Is HR Management Going?" *Personnel* (January 1988), pp. 28–31; Eric G. Flamholtz et al., "Personnel Management: The Tone of Tomorrow," *Personnel Journal* (July 1987), pp. 43–48; and Laura Herren, "The New Game of HR: Playing to Win," *Personnel* (June 1989), pp. 19–22.
6. *Personnel Journal*, March 1988.
7. Peter Drucker, *The Wall Street Journal*, January 20, 1988.
8. See ibid.
9. Herren, "The New Game of HR," p. 20.
10. See ibid., p. 22.
11. Two writers point out that it is important not to fall in the trap of assuming that HRM is involved only in strategic planning to the extent of matching personnel activities with strategies, forecasting labor power requirements and supplies, and presenting means for integrating HRM into the overall effort to match corporate strategy. Instead, they say, there is a "reciprocal interdependence between a firm's business strategy and its human resources strategy." In other words, the company's human resources (and therefore human resource management department) can be among other things a way to gain an improved competitive position. See Cynthia Lengnick-Hall and Mark Lengnick-Hall, "Strategic Human Resources Management: A Review of the Literature and a Proposed Typology," *Academy of Management Review* (July 1988), pp. 454–470.
12. This is based on Robert Burg and Brian Smith, "Restructuring Compensation and Benefits to Support Strategy," Part I, "Executive Compensation," *Compensation and Benefits Review*, (November–December 1987), pp. 15–22.
13. Ibid., p. 17.
14. Sue Ellen Thompson, *Encyclopedia of Personnel Policies*, Business and Legal Reports, 1983, p. 1.02.
15. These are based on Margaret Magnus, "Personnel Policies in Partnership with Profit," *Personnel Journal* (September 1987), pp. 102–109.
16. Ibid.
17. This section is based on personal correspondence with Professor Casey Ichni-

owski, Graduate School of Business Administration, Columbia University, Uris 713, New York, New York 10027, April 1990.

18. Robert Townsend, *Up the Organization* (New York: Knopf, 1970), p. 47.

19. Thomas Hestwood, "Make Policy Manuals Useful and Relevant," *Personnel Journal* (April 1988), p. 43.

20. For discussion, see Thomas Hestwood, "Make Policy Manuals Useful and Relevant," *Personnel Journal* (April 1988), pp. 43–46.

21. Unless otherwise noted, this section is based on Thompson, *Encyclopedia of Personnel Policies*, pp. 1.07–1.40.

22. These are based on ibid., pp. 1.12–1.40.

23. See ibid.

24. For a recent discussion along these lines, see Joel Lapointe and Jo Ann Verdin, "How to Calculate the Cost of Human Resources," *Personnel Journal* (January 1988), pp. 34–45.

25. This is based on Bruce R. Ellig, "Improving Effectiveness Through an HR Review," *Personnel* (June 1989), pp. 56–64.

26. Ellig, "Improving Effectiveness Through an HR Renew," p. 57.

Appendix:

International Issues in Human Resource Management

INTRODUCTION

You don't have to look very far to see how important international business has become to companies here and abroad. In the United States, exports are expected to increase by over 74% in the next ten years, a rate of growth that's over twice that of any other component of the Gross National Product.[1]

This rapid growth of exports reflects the fact that many more U.S.-based companies are focusing their marketing efforts not only here, but abroad. Huge "global" companies like Proctor & Gamble, IBM, and Citibank have long had extensive overseas operations, of course. However, with the European market unification of 1992, the opening up of Eastern Europe, and the rapid development of demand in other areas of the world, more and more companies are going to find that their success (and perhaps their survival), depends on their ability to market and manage overseas. And, of course, to foreign companies the United States is "overseas" and tens of thousands of foreign firms already have thriving operations on (and beyond) our U.S. shores.

As a result of this internationalization, companies must increasingly be managed globally, even though such globalization confronts managers with some herculean challenges. Market, product, and production plans must often now be coordinated on a worldwide basis, for instance, and organization structures capable of balancing centralized home-office control with adequate local autonomy must be created.

Some of the most pressing challenges facing employers concern the impact of globalization on a company's human resource management system. These challenges range from (1) general issues like how to select, train, and compensate managers who must be sent to foreign posts, to (2) dealing with country-specific differences which demand corresponding country-specific fine tuning of a firm's human resource management policies. These two sets of challenges are addressed next.

As we have already touched on at several points in this book, there are at least three major general HRM issues a global company has to address: selecting managers for overseas assignments, orienting and training these people, and then compensating them.

♦ SELECTION FOR MULTINATIONAL MANAGEMENT

The thing you have to remember about selecting multinational managers is that you must be as careful to define the job demands and human requirements as you would for any domestic job. Many companies make the mistake of evaluating only the technical (such as manufacturing knowledge) demands of the overseas job, while ignoring the cultural demands and need for adaptability that characterize such overseas jobs. Thus, as one vice president for international human resources puts it: "There is too much emphasis on executives' technical abilities and too little on their cultural skills and family situation . . . when international executive relocations fail, they generally fail either because expatriates can't fathom the customs of the new country or because their families can't deal with the emotional stress that a company's relocation entails."[2] In the same vein, one expert on Japanese multinational enterprises argues that Japanese multinationals have had better success rates with the employees they send overseas than do U.S. firms; she argues that this is largely a product of superior selection and training.[3]

As is often the case with employee selection, the best rule is often that past experience is the best predictor of future success. Companies like Colgate-Palmolive therefore look for overseas candidates whose work and nonwork experience, education, and language skills already demonstrate a commitment to and facility in living and working with different cultures.[4] Even several successful summers spent traveling overseas or participating in foreign student programs would seem to provide some concrete basis for believing that the potential transferee can accomplish the required adaptation when he or she arrives overseas.

Realistic previews at this point are also crucial. Both the potential transferee and his or her family need to have all the information you can provide on the problems to expect in the new job (such as mandatory private schooling for the children) as well as any information obtainable on the cultural benefits, problems, and idiosyncracies of the country in question. International human resource managers speak about avoiding "culture shock" in much the same way as we discussed using realistic previews to avoid "reality shock" amongst new employees in Chapter 6. In any case, the golden rule here is to "spell it out ahead of time" as Ciba-Geigy does for its international transferees.[5]

The question arises as to whether there are paper-and-pencil tests that can be used to more effectively select employees for overseas assignments and here the answer seems to be "yes." Generally speaking, of course, the development and use of any such test should ideally be company-specific and validated as a tool for placing candidates overseas. However, companies have developed and validated general-purpose tests that focus on the aptitudes and personality characteristics of successful overseas candidates. One such assessment tool is called the Overseas Assignment Inventory. Based on 12 years of research involving more than 7,000 cases the test's publisher indicates that it is useful in identifying characteristics and attitudes such candidates should have.[6]

◆ ORIENTING AND TRAINING EMPLOYEES FOR INTERNATIONAL ASSIGNMENTS

When it comes to providing the orientation and training required for success overseas, the practices of most U.S. firms reflect more form than substance. One consultant (who admittedly is in the business of providing training for overseas assignments) says that (despite many companies' claims) there is generally little or no systematic selection and training for assignments overseas. One relevant survey concluded that a sample of company presidents and chairpersons agreed that international business was growing in importance and required employees firmly grounded in the economics and practices of foreign countries. However, few of their companies actually provided such overseas-oriented training to their employees.[7]

What sort of special training do overseas candidates need? One firm specializing in such programs prescribes a four-step approach.[8] Level 1 training focuses on the impact of cultural differences, and on raising trainees' awareness of such differences and the impact on business outcomes of these cultural differences. Level 2 focuses on attitudes and aims at getting participants to understand how attitudes (both negative and positive) are formed and how they influence behavior. (For example, unfavorable stereotypes may subconsciously influence how a new manager responds to and treats his new foreign subordinates.) Finally, Level 3 training provides factual knowledge about the target country, while Level 4 provides skill building in areas like language and adjustment and adaptation skills. (Additional guidelines for developing international executives—such as "brief candidates fully and clearly on all relocation policies," and "provide all relocating executives with a mentor to monitor their overseas careers and help them secure appropriate jobs with the company when they repatriate"— were discussed in Chapter 8.)

Beyond these special training practices there is also the need for more traditional training and development of your overseas employees. At IBM, for instance, such development involves using a series of rotating assignments that will permit overseas IBM managers to grow professionally. At the same time, IBM and a number of other major firms have established management development centers around the world where executives can come to hone their skills. Beyond that, classroom programs (such as those at the London Business School, or at INSEAD in Fountainebleu, France) provide overseas executives the sorts of opportunities to hone their functional skills that similar programs stateside do for their U.S.-based colleagues.

◆ INTERNATIONAL ISSUES IN COMPENSATION MANAGEMENT

Generally speaking, the whole area of international compensation management presents some tricky problems. On the one hand, there is a certain logic in maintaining companywide pay scales and policies so that, for instance, divisional marketing directors throughout the world are all paid within the same narrow range. This reduces the risk of perceived inequities and dramatically simplifies the job of keeping track of disparate country-by-country wage rates.

And yet not adapting pay scales to local markets can present an HR manager with more problems than it solves. The fact is that it can be enormously more expensive to live in some countries (like Japan) than others (like Greece), and if these cost of living differences aren't considered it may be almost impossible to get managers to take "high cost" assignments.

Yet even here the answer is usually not just to pay, say, marketing directors more in one country than in another. For example, you could thereby elicit resistance when telling a marketing director in Japan who's earning $2,000 per week to move to your division in Spain, where her pay for the same job (cost of living notwithstanding) will drop by half. One way to handle this problem is to pay a similar base salary companywide and then add on various allowances according to individual market conditions.[9]

The problem here is that determining what equitable wage rates should be in many countries is no simple matter. As we explained in Chapter 10, there is a wealth of "packaged" compensation survey data already available in the United States, but such data is not so easy to come by overseas. As one expert on the matter has said, "Unfortunately, local sources of compensation information in foreign countries are hard to find, and often only compound the problem rather than help to bridge the gap."[10] As a result, he says that "one of the greatest difficulties in managing total compensation on a multinational level is establishing a consistent compensation measure between countries that builds credibility both at home and abroad."

Some multinational companies deal with this problem by conducting their own annual compensation surveys. For example, Kraft conducts an annual study of total compensation in Belgium, Germany, Italy, Spain, and the United Kingdom. Kraft tries to maintain a fairly constant sample group of study participants (companies) in their survey. It then focuses on the total compensation paid to each of ten senior management positions held by local nationals in these firms. The survey covers all forms of compensation including cash, short- and long-term incentives, retirement plans, medical benefits, and perquisites.[11] The company then uses this data to establish a competitive value for each element of pay. This information in turn becomes the input used for annual salary increases and proposed changes in the benefit package.

One international compensation trend of growing importance concerns the awarding of long-term incentive pay to overseas managers. While it may not seem particularly logical, many U.S. multinationals only permit the top managers at corporate headquarters to participate in long-term incentive programs like stock option plans.[12] Equally problematical is the fact that many of the multinationals that do offer overseas managers long-term incentives (32 out of 40 doing so in one survey) only use overall corporate performance criteria when awarding incentive pay. Since the performance of the company's stock on a U.S. stock market may have little relevance to, say, a West Berlin manager in your German subsidiary, the incentive value of such a reward is highly suspect. This is particularly so in that, as one expert writes, "Regardless of size, a foreign subsidiary's influence on its parent company's stock price (U.S. dollars) is more likely to result from exchange rate movements than from management action."[13]

The answer here, more multinationals are finding, is to formulate new long-term incentives specifically for overseas executives. More and more U.S. multinationals are thus devising performance-based long-term incentive plans that are tied more closely to performance at the subsidiary level. These can help build a sense of ownership among key local managers while providing the financial incentives needed to attract and keep the people you need overseas.

MANAGING INTER-COUNTRY DIFFERENCES IN HUMAN RESOURCE MANAGEMENT

♦ INTRODUCTION

There are two basic sets of issues in international HRM management. One, as explained above, is the more general set of issues regarding how to select, train, and compensate managers, given the unique demands that dealing with new and different cultures places on international transferees. The second set of thorny international HRM issues derives from the fact that there are wide ranging differences in legal systems, labor availability, and so on amongst countries. As a result, multinationals must, to some extent, fine tune their HRM policies to the unique needs of each country in which they do business. We turn now to a closer examination of these sorts of intercountry differences and their impact on HRM.

◆ INTER-COUNTRY DIFFERENCES IMPACTING HRM

To a large extent companies operating only within the borders of the United States enjoy the luxury of dealing with a relatively limited set of economic, cultural, and legal variables. Notwithstanding the range from liberal to conservative, for instance, America's is basically a capitalist competitive society. And, while a multitude of cultural and ethnic backgrounds are represented in America's workforce, various shared values (such as an appreciation for democracy) help to blur the otherwise sharp cultural differences. And while the different states and municipalities (as explained in Chapter 2) certainly have their own laws affecting HRM, a basic legal framework as laid down by federal law helps to produce a fairly predictable set of legal guidelines regarding matters such as employment discrimination, labor relations, and safety and health.

A company operating multiple units abroad is generally not blessed with such relative homogeneity. For example, minimum legally mandated holidays may range from none in the United Kingdom to five weeks per year in Luxembourg. And, while there are no formal requirements for employee participation in Italy, employee representatives on boards of directors are required in companies with more than 30 employees in Denmark. The point is that the management of the human resource function in multinational companies is complicated enormously by the need to adapt personnel policies and procedures to the unique differences amongst countries in which each subsidiary is based. Here are some inter-country differences which demand such adaptation.[14]

Cultural Factors

There are wide-ranging cultural and ethnic differences from country to country which demand corresponding differences in personnel practices among a company's foreign subsidiaries. We might generalize, for instance, that given the cultural background of the Far East and the importance there of the patriarchical system the typical Japanese worker's view of his or her relationship to his employer has an important impact on how that person works. Human resource incentive plans in Japan therefore tend to focus on the work group while in the West the more usual prescription is to focus on individual worker incentives.[15]

In addition to mediating for differences in HR practices these sorts of cultural differences also suggest that HR staff in a foreign subsidiary is best comprised of citizens of the subsidiary's host country. A high degree of sensitivity and empathy for cultural and attitudinal demands of coworkers is always important when selecting employees to staff overseas operations, as we explained above. However, such sensitivity is especially important when the job is HRM and the work involves all those "human" jobs like job interviewing, testing, orienting, training, counseling, and (if need be) terminating. As one expert puts it, "An HR staff that shares the employee's cultural background is more likely to be sensitive to the employee's needs and expectations in the work place—and is thus more likely to manage the company successfully."[16]

Economic Factors

Differences in economic systems among countries also influence the role played by HRM. In free enterprise systems, for instance, need for efficiency tends to favor HR policies that value high productivity, efficient workers, and staff cutting where market forces dictate it. Moving along the scale toward more socialist systems, on the other hand, HR practices tend to shift more toward preventing unemployment, even at the expense of sacrificing efficiency.

Labor Cost Factors

Differences in labor costs may also produce corresponding differences in HR practices. High labor costs can require a focus on efficiency, for instance, and on all those HR practices aimed at improving employee performance. On the other hand, the lower labor costs associated with some less developed countries may make it cost effective to spend less on employee productivity-boosting activities.

Industrial Relations Factors

Industrial relations (and particularly the relationship between the worker, the union, and the employer) varies dramatically from country to country and has an enormous impact on human resource management practices. In the Federal Republic of Germany, for instance, "co-determination" is the rule. Here employees have the legal right to have a voice in setting company policies. In this and several other countries workers elect their own representatives to the supervisory board of the employer, and there is also a vice president for labor at the top management level.[17] On the other hand, in many other countries the state interferes very little in the relations between employers and unions. In the United States, for instance, HR policies on most matters such as wages and benefits are set not by the state but by the employer or by the employer in negotiations with its labor unions. In Germany, on the other hand, the various laws on co-determination including the Works Constitution Act (1972), the Co-Determination Act (1976), and the ECSC Co-Determination Act (1951) largely determine what HR policies will be in many German firms.

Europe 1992[18]

As of 1992 the twelve separate countries of the European community are unified into a common market for goods, services, capital, and even labor. Generally speaking, tariffs for goods moving across borders from one EC country to another disappeared, and employees (with some exceptions) found it easier to move relatively freely between jobs in various EC countries.

Figure A.1 summarizes current employment practices and policies among EC countries. The figure underscores two things. First (in line with our discussion of inter-country differences, above), you can see that there are some wide-ranging differences in HR practices among EC countries. Thus as you can see in Figure A.1 many countries have minimum wages while others do not, and maximum hours permitted in the work day and work week vary from no maximum in the United Kingdom to 48 per week in Greece and Italy. Similar differences are apparent in matters like minimum annual holidays, minimum notice to be given by employer, termination formalities, and employee participation.

Second, the impact of "1992" will be to gradually reduce these sorts of differences among member countries. However, these changes will be

FIGURE A.1 Current Employment Practices and Policies Among EC Countries

Country	Employment Formalities	Minimum Pay	Max. Hours (Including overtime)	Minimum Annual Holiday	Minimum Notice to Be Given by Employer	Termination Formalities	Employee Participation
Belgium	Certain terms must be in writing.	Yes	8 per day; 40 per week	4 weeks.	Workers: 14–28 days. Others: 3 months for up to 5 years' service + 3 mos. for every 5 years' service. Higher paid employees notice period agreed on when notice given or decided by Court.	Can terminate without notice for gross misconduct (but this does not include all instances of incompetence). Redundancy payments.	Work councils.
Denmark	Contracts usually oral.	No, but must conform to one of 2 compulsory wage systems.	Depends on collective agreement.	2½ days per month.	Workers depends on collective agreement. Others: 1–6 months.	Can terminate without notice for gross misconduct; unfair dismissal and redundancy payments.	Employee representatives on board of directors where there are more than 30 employees.
France	Contracts in writing. Collective agreements may be generally binding.	Yes	10 per day. 39 per week.	2½ days per month (includes 5 Saturdays).	1 month after 6 months' service; 2 months after 2 years' service.	Unfair dismissal. Redundancy payments. Authorization of redundancies required.	Employee and union representatives. Works councils.
Germany	Fixed-term agreements restricted; collective agreements may be generally binding.	No, but if a collective agreement, this must make provision.	8 per day. 48 per week.	18 days.	Workers: 2 weeks to 3 months. Others: 6 weeks to 6 months from end of calendar-year quarter.	Unfair dismissal. Prior consultation on redundancies or dismissals with works council and in some cases the labor authorities.	Works councils.
Greece	No substantial formalities.	Yes	48 per week.	4 weeks (after 1 year's employment).	Workers: none. Others: 1 month to 2 years.	Severance payments of 5–52 days' pay for workers or 1–24 months' pay for other employees. If notice given, only ½ payable.	Employee committees.

Country	Contract requirements	Collective agreement	Working hours	Holiday	Notice	Dismissal	Employee representation
Ireland	Employees may require employers to supply written statements of employment.	No	No generally applicable statutory maximum.	3 weeks.	1–8 weeks.	Unfair dismissal. Redundancy payments.	No formal requirements.
Italy	Contracts in writing. National collective agreements.	Collective agreement.	48 per week. 8 per day.	Collective agreement.	Collective agreement.	Severance payments. Can dismiss only for redundancy or good cause.	No formal requirements.
Luxembourg	Written contracts must be provided. Agreements may be binding on a sector.	Yes	40 per week, 8 per day.	25 working days (5 days' holiday equals one week).	4 weeks to 6 months, depending on category of worker and length of service.	Severance payments, 1–12 months. Prior notification of redundancy and redundancy payments.	Employees' representatives. Joint works councils. Employee directors.
The Netherlands	No substantial formalities.	Yes	48 per week. 8½ per day. 5½ days per week.	4 weeks.	Interval of payment (usually 2 weeks or 1 month) or a period of up to 13 weeks (26 weeks for older employees) based on length of service, whichever is longer.	Authorization of labor office usually required to dismiss with notice. May need to go to the Court; either procedure can take several months.	Works council in undertakings with 35 or more employees.
Portugal	Fixed-term contracts must be in writing.	Yes	Office workers: 42 hours per week. Others: 48 per week; 8 per day.	Not less than 21 days nor more than 30 days.	Redundancy-notice period fixed when conditions of redundancy established.	Can dismiss only for "just cause" or redundancy. Prior notification of redundancies.	Workers' commissions and registered trade unions.
Spain	No substantial formalities.	Yes	40 per week. 9 per day	2½ days per month.	1 month after 1 year's service, 3 months after 2 years.	Only for specified causes. Dismissal for other causes: compensation to 45 days pay per year of service.	Employee delegates and committees, employee directors.
United Kingdom	Written statement of terms of employment.	No	No	No	1–13 weeks.	Unfair dismissal. Redundancy payments. Prior notification of redundancies.	No formal requirements.

Source: Sedel, Rae, "Europe 1992: HR Implications of the European Unification," *Personnel*, October 1989, p. 22 (reprinted with permission of the publisher from *Personnel Today*, April 4, 1989).

gradual, not all-at-once. Social legislation and examinations by the European Commission are at the present time slowly harmonizing some of these differences. However, even if all of these differences summarized in the figure are eventually eliminated, HR practices will still differ from country to country; cultural differences will require that, no doubt. Even into the far-distant future, in other words, managing human resources multinationally will present some tricky problems for HR managers.

NOTES

1. "The Gross National Product," *Occupational Outlook Quarterly* (Fall 1989), U.S. Department of Labor.

2. Paul Blocklyn, "Developing the International Executive," *Personnel* (March 1989), p. 44.

3. Rosalie L. Tung, "Human Resource Planning in Japanese Multinationals: A Model for U.S. Firms?" *Journal of International Business Studies*, Vol. 15, no. 2 (Fall 1984), pp. 139–149.

4. See, for example, Blocklyn, "Developing the International Executive," p. 45.

5. Ibid., p. 45.

6. Discussed in Madelyn Callahan, "Preparing the New Global Manager," *Training and Development Journal* (March 1989), p. 30. The publisher of the inventory is the New York consulting firm Moran, Stahl & Boyer.

7. Ibid., pp. 29–30.

8. This is based on Callahan, "Preparing the New Global Manager," p. 30.

9. James Stoner and R. Edward Freeman, *Management*, 4th ed. (Englewood Cliffs, N.J.: Prentice-Hall, 1989), p. 783.

10. Hewitt Associates, "On Compensation," (May 1989), p. 1 (Hewitt Associates, 86–87 East Via De Ventura, Scottsdale, Arizona 85258).

11. Hewitt Associates, "On Compensation," p. 2.

12. This is based on Brian Brooks, "Long-Term Incentives: International Executives Need Them, Too," *Personnel* (August 1988), pp. 40–42.

13. Brooks, "Long-Term Incentives: International Executives Need Them, Too," p. 41.

14. These are based on Eduard Gaugler, "HR Management: An International Comparison," *Personnel* (August 1988), pp. 24–30.

15. For a discussion of this see Gaugler, "HR Management," p. 26.

16. Gaugler, "HR Management," p. 27. See also Simcha Ronen and Oded Shenkar, "Using Employee Attitudes to Establish MNC Regional Divisions," *Personnel* (August 1988), pp. 32–39.

17. This is discussed in Gaugler, "HR Management," p. 28.

18. This is based on Rae Sedel, "Europe 1992: HR Implications of the European Unification," *Personnel* (October 1989), pp. 19–24.

Glossary

Achievement People motivated by high needs to achieve want situations with moderate risk and quick, concrete feedback concerning their performance.

Action learning A training technique by which management trainees are allowed to work full time analyzing and solving problems in other departments or government agencies.

Adverse impact The overall impact of employer practices that result in significantly higher percentages of members of minorities and other protected groups being rejected for employment, placement, or promotion.

Affiliation People who have a need for close friendship and for maintaining friendly relations with others are affiliation oriented.

Affirmative action Steps in recruitment, hiring, upgrading jobs, and so on that are designed and taken for the purpose of eliminating the present effects of past discrimination.

Age Discrimination in Employment Act of 1967 The act prohibiting arbitrary age discrimination and specifically protecting individuals over 40 years old.

Agency shop A form of union security in which employees who do not belong to the union must still pay union dues (on the assumption that union efforts benefit all workers).

Albermarle Paper Company v. Moody Supreme Court case in which it was ruled that the validity of job tests must be documented and that employee performance standards must be unambiguous.

Alternation ranking method Ranking employees from best to worst on a particular trait. First the highest, and then the lowest is chosen, continuing until all employees are ranked.

American Federation of Labor and Congress of Industrial Organization (AFL-CIO) A voluntary federation of 109 national and international labor unions in the United States formed by the merger of the AFL and CIO in 1955.

Americans with Disabilities Act The act requiring employers to make reasonable accommodations for disabled employees, it prohibits discrimination against disabled persons.

Annual bonus Plans that are designed to motivate short-term performance of managers and are tied to company profitability.

Application blank Usually, the first step in the screening process for job applicants. The application provides information on education, prior work record, strong and weak points.

Appraisal interview A discussion following a performance appraisal in which supervisor and employee discuss the employee's rating and possible remedial actions.

Aptitudes and special talents These include intelligence, numerical aptitude, mechanical comprehension, and manual dexterity, as well as talents such as artistic, theatrical, or musical ability that play an important role in career decisions.

Arbitration The most definitive type of third-party intervention, in which the arbitrator usually has the power to determine and dictate the settlement terms.

Arline v. School Board of Nassau County U.S. Supreme Court ruling that persons with contagious diseases are covered by the Vocational Rehabilitation Act of 1973.

John Atkinson A researcher who explained that everyone has a need for *achievement*, *power*, and *affiliation*.

Attendance incentive plan A plan for reducing employee absence, for instance, by allowing unused sick leave to be converted into additional pay or vacation at the end of each year.

Authority The right to make decisions, direct others' work, and give orders.

Authorization cards In order to petition for a union election, the union must show that at least 30% of employees may be interested in being unionized. Employees indicate this interest by signing authorization cards.

Background investigations Procedures for checking histories of job candidates that may involve contacting previous employers, verifying dates of employment, salary, job title, and requesting reports from credit agencies, requiring letters of reference, and so forth.

Bargaining unit The group of employees the union will be authorized to represent.

Behaviorally anchored rating scale (BARS) An appraisal method that aims at combining the benefits of narrative critical incidents and quantified ratings by anchoring a quantified scale with specific narrative examples of good or poor performance.

Behavior modeling A training technique in which trainees are first shown good management techniques (in a film), are then asked to play roles in a simulated situation, and are then given feedback and praise by their supervisor.

Behavior modification/operant conditioning A method of changing behavior through the use of rewards or punishment.

Benchmark job A job that is used to anchor the employer's pay scale and around which other jobs are arranged in order of relative worth.

Benefits Any supplements to wages given to employees. They may include health and life insurance, vacation, pension, profit sharing, education plans, discounts on company products.

Bias The tendency to allow individual differences such as age, race, and sex affect personnel decisions regarding employees.

Bona fide occupational qualification (BFOQ) Requirement that an employee be of a certain religion, sex, or national origin where that is reasonably necessary to the organization's normal operation. Specified by the 1964 Civil Rights Act.

Boycott The combined refusal by employees and other interested parties to buy or use the employer's products.

Burnout The total depletion of physical and mental resources caused by excessive striving to reach some unrealistic work-related goal.

Business necessity Justification for an otherwise discriminatory employment practice, provided there is an overriding legitimate business purpose.

California Federal Savings and Loan Association v. *Guerra* U.S. Supreme Court ruling that employers must provide pregnant employees unpaid pregnancy leave for the period during which the employee is disabled because of the pregnancy, childbirth, or related medical conditions.

Candidate-order error An error of judgment on the part of the interviewer due to interviewing one or more very good or very bad candidates just before the interview in question.

Capital accumulation programs Long-term incentives most often reserved for senior executives. Six popular plans include stock options, stock appreciation rights, performance achievement plans, restricted stock plans, phantom stock plans, and book value plans.

Career anchors A concern or value that you will not give up if a choice has to be made.

Career cycle The stages through which a person's career evolves.

Career planning and development Giving employees the assistance to form realistic career goals and the opportunities to realize them.

Central tendency A tendency to rate all employees the same way, such as rating them all average.

Citations Summons informing employers and employees of the regulations and standards that have been violated in the workplace.

Civil Rights Act Federal law that makes it illegal to discriminate in employment because of race, color, religion, sex, or national origin.

Classes Dividing jobs into classes based on a set of rules for each class, such as amount of independent judgment, skill, physical effort, and so forth, required for each class of jobs. Classes usually contain similar jobs—such as all secretaries.

Classification (or grading) method A method for categorizing jobs into groups.

Class or grade description Written descriptions of job duties, with similar jobs combined into groups or classes.

Closed shop A form of union security in which the company can hire only union members. This was outlawed in 1947 but still exists in some industries (such as printing).

Collective bargaining The process through which representatives of management and the union meet to negotiate a labor agreement.

College recruiting Company recruiters travel to college campuses to interview students.

Comparable worth The concept by which women (who are usually paid less than men) can claim that men in *comparable* (rather than strictly equal) jobs are paid more.

Compensable factors Fundamental, compensable elements of a job, such as skill, effort, responsiblity, and working conditions.

Computerized forecasting Determining future staff needs by projecting a firm's sales, volume of production, and personnel required to maintain this volume of output, with computers and software packages.

Content validity A test that is "content valid" is one in which the test contains a fair sample of the tasks and skills actually needed for the job in question.

Correlation analysis Determination of statistical relationships between two variables, for example, staff levels and a measure of business activity.

Criterion validity A type of validity based on showing that scores on the test ("predictors") are related to job performance ("criterion").

Critical incident method Keeping a record of uncommonly good or undesirable examples of an employee's work-related behavior and reviewing it with the employee at predetermined times.

Culture An organization's culture is the prevailing attitudes and values that characterize its employees.

ger and thirst but also salary, working conditions, and supervision. Offering more hygienes is not the best way to strengthen motivation, in Herzberg's view, since they just prevent dissatisfaction.

Illegal bargaining items Items in collective bargaining that are forbidden by law; for example, the clause agreeing to hire "union members exclusively" would be illegal in a right-to-work state.

Impasse A situation that occurs when the parties are not able to move further toward settlement, usually because one party is demanding more than the other will offer.

Implied authority The authority exerted by a personnel manager by virtue of others' knowledge that he or she has access to top management (in areas like testing and affirmative action).

Individual retirement accounts (IRAs) Pension plans qualified under tax laws to receive favorable tax treatment that are established individually by employees.

In-house development centers A company-based method for exposing prospective managers to realistic exercises to develop improved management skills.

Insurance benefits Include workers' compensation benefits, life insurance plans, and hospitalization, medical, and disability insurance.

Job analysis The procedure for determining the duties and skill requirements of a job and the kind of person who should be hired for it.

Job description A list of a job's duties, responsibilities, reporting relationships, working conditions, and supervisory responsibilities—one product of a job analysis.

Job enrichment Herzberg's method for building "motivators" into the job by making work interesting and challenging. By carefully structuring the work situation, employees can be given a chance to experience a sense of achievement, as in assembling a product from start to finish.

Job instruction training (JIT) Listing each of a job's basic tasks, along with a "key point" for each, in order to provide step-by-step training for employees.

Job posting Posting notices of job openings on company bulletin boards is an effective recruiting method.

Job rotation A management training technique that involves moving a trainee from department to department to broaden his or her experience, and identify strong and weak points.

Job sharing A concept that allows two or more people to share a single full-time job.

Job specification A list of a job's "human requirements," that is, the requisite education, skills, personality, and so on—another product of a job analysis.

Johnson* v. *Transportation Agency, Santa Clara County U.S. Supreme Court ruling that public and private employers may voluntarily adopt hiring and promotion goals to benefit minorities and women.

Junior board A method of providing middle-management trainees with experience in analyzing company problems by inviting them to sit on a junior board of directors and make recommendations on overall company policies.

Landrum-Griffin Act The law aimed at protecting union members from possible wrongdoing on the part of their unions.

Layoff A term that refers to a situation in which there is no work available for the employee who is being sent home, but management expects the situation to be temporary and intends to recall the employee when work is again available.

Leader match training A program that identifies types of leaders and teaches them how to fit their leadership style to their situation.

Line manager A manager who is authorized to direct the work of subordinates and responsible for accomplishing the organization's goals.

Local market conditions Employment may go up or down in a specific city or region, for instance, as a result of factory closing or new industry.

Lockout A refusal by the employer to provide opportunities to work.

Maintenance of membership arrangement A form of union security in which employees do not have to belong to the union; however, union members employed by the firm must maintain membership in the union for the contract period.

Maintenance stage The period from about ages 45 to 65 during which the person secures his or her place in the world of work.

Management assessment centers A situation in which management candidates are asked to make decisions in hypothetical situations and are scored on their performance. It usually also involves testing and the use of management games.

Management by objectives (MBO) Involves setting specific measurable goals with each employee and then periodically reviewing the progress made.

Management development Any attempt to improve current or future management performance by imparting knowledge, changing attitudes, or increasing skills.

Management process The five basic functions of planning, organizing, staffing, leading, and controlling.

Managerial grid Numerical ratings for managers in a grid or matrix configuration based on their leadership style (whether people oriented or production oriented).

Mandatory bargaining items Items in collective bargaining that a party must bargain over if they are introduced by the other party—for example, pay.

Abraham Maslow A distinguished psychologist who identified five basic categories of human needs: physiological, safety, social, ego, and self-actualization. Each need becomes active only after the need below it is satisfied.

David McClelland A theorist who agrees with Atkinson on the universal need for achievement, power, and affiliation. These needs can be used to motivate employees on the job.

Mediation Intervention in which a neutral third party tries to assist the principals toward reaching agreement.

Meritor Savings Bank, FSB* v. *Vinson U.S. Supreme Court's first decision on sexual harassment. Held that existence of a hostile environment even without economic hardship is sufficient to prove harassment, even if participation was voluntary.

Merit pay Any salary increase awarded to an employee on his or her individual performance.

Merit raise Merit raise is another term for merit pay.

Midcareer crisis substage The period occurring between the midthirties and midforties during which people often make a major reassessment of their progress relative to their original career ambitions and goals.

Motivation model The model of human behavior emphasizing that people are motivated to accomplish those tasks that they feel (1) will lead to (2) rewards. It stresses that both ability and desire are required for motivation.

"Motivator" factors Opportunities for achievement, recognition, responsibility, and more challenging jobs.

Motivator-hygiene theory of motivation Herzberg's theory that higher-level needs, such as the need for recognition, are insatiable, unlike physiological needs, or *hygienes*. Herzberg describes higher-level needs as *motivators*.

National emergency strikes Strikes that might "imperil the national health and safety."

National Labor Relations Board (NLRB) The agency created by the Wagner Act to investigate unfair labor practice charges and provide for secret ballot elections and majority rule in determining whether or not a firm's employees wanted a union.

Need achievement theory The theory that focuses on one of Maslow's "esteem" needs and aims at predicting the behavior of those ranking high or low in the need to achieve.

Needs hierarchy Maslow's view that human needs form a ladder, or hierarchy. When a person's most urgent need is satisfied, the next most urgent need becomes a prime motivating drive, and so forth.

9, 9 managers Highest ranking on the grid program. A manager with this rating is highly concerned with people *and* with production.

Nondirective interview An unstructured conversational-style interview. The interviewer pursues points of interest as they come up in response to questions.

Norris-LaGuardia Act This law marked the beginning of the era of strong encouragement of unions and guaranteed to each employee the right to bargain collectively "free from interference, restraint, or coercion."

Occupational market conditions The Bureau of Labor

Statistics of the U.S. Department of Labor publishes projections of labor supply and demand for various occupations, as do other agencies.

Occupational orientation The theory developed by John Holland that says there are six basic personal orientations that determine the sorts of careers to which people are drawn.

Occupational Safety and Health Act The law passed by Congress in 1970 "to assure so far as possible every working man and woman in the nation safe and healthful working conditions and to preserve our human resources."

Occupational Safety and Health Administration (OSHA) The agency created within the Department of Labor to set safety and health standards for almost all workers in the United States.

Occupational skills The skills needed to be successful in a particular occupation. According to the *Dictionary of Occupational Titles*, occupational skills break down into three groups, depending on whether they emphasize data, people, or things.

On-the-job training (OJT) Training a person to learn a job while working at it.

Open shop Perhaps the least attractive type of union security from the union's point of view: the workers decide whether or not to join the union, and those who do not do not pay dues.

Organizational development (OD) A program aimed at changing the attitudes, values, and beliefs of employees so that employees can improve the organization.

Organization chart A chart showing the titles of managers' positions and connecting them by lines indicating accountability and responsibility.

Organizing committee Employees of a firm, identified by union officials as good prospects, who are established as a committee to be educated about the benefits of forming a union.

Orientation program A training program for new employees in which the personnel department and supervisors outline policies, rules, regulations, and benefits of employment; usually provide an employee handbook; and provide introductions to fellow workers.

Outplacement counseling A systematic process by which a terminated person is counseled in the techniques of career self-appraisal and in securing a new job that is appropriate to his or her needs and talents.

Paired comparison method Ranking employees by making a chart of all possible pairs of the employees for each trait and indicating which is the better employee of the pair.

Panel interview An interview in which a group of interviewers question the applicant, a method similar to a press conference.

Participant diary/logs Daily listings, made by workers, of every activity in which they engage, along with times—to provide comprehensive pictures of various jobs.

Patterned interview An interview following a set sequence of questions. Printed forms with guidelines for evaluating the interview are commercially available.

Pay grade A pay grade is comprised of jobs of approximately equal difficulty.

Pension Benefits Guarantee Corporation (PBGC) Established under ERISA to assure that pensions meet vesting obligations; also insures pensions should a plan terminate without sufficient funds to meet its vested obligations.

Pension plans Plans that provide a fixed sum when employees reach a predetermined retirement age or when they can no longer work due to disability.

Performance analysis Careful study of performance to identify a deficiency and correct it with new equipment, a new employee, a training program, or some other adjustment.

Personnel management (personnel management or staffing function) The concepts and techniques one needs to carry out the "people" or personnel aspects of a management position, including recruiting, screening, training, rewarding, and appraising.

Personnel replacement charts Company records showing present performance and promotability of inside candidates for the most important positions.

Piecework A system of pay based on the number of items processed by each individual worker in a unit of time, such as items per hour or items per day.

Point method The job evaluation method in which a number of compensable factors are identified and then the degree to which each of these factors is present on the job is determined.

Policies Guides to action that assure consistency under a particular set of circumstances and within the framework of the company's plan.

Position analysis questionnaire (PAQ) A questionnaire used to collect quantifiable data concerning the duties and responsibilities of various jobs.

Position replacement card A card prepared for each position in a company to show possible replacement candidates and their qualifications.

Power People motivated by power seek situations in which they can make suggestions, offer opinions, and talk others into things.

Pregnancy Discrimination Act (PDA) An amendment to Title VII of the Civil Rights Act that prohibits sex discrimination based on "pregnancy, childbirth, or related medical conditions." It requires employers to provide benefits—including sick leave and disability benefits and health and medical insurance—the same as for any employee not able to work because of disability.

Process of establishing pay rates Salary surveys play a central role in pricing of jobs. Salary surveys may be formal or informal and may rely upon commercial firms, professional associations, and government agencies.

Profit-sharing plan A plan whereby most employees share in the company's profits.

Programmed learning A systematic method for teaching job skills, involving presenting questions or facts, allowing the person to respond, and giving the learner immediate feedback on the accuracy of his or her answers.

Qualifications inventories Systematic records, either manual or computerized, listing employees' education, career and development interests, languages, special skills, and so forth, to be used in forecasting inside candidates for promotion.

Quality circle A group of five to ten specially trained employees who meet on a regular basis to identify and solve problems in their work area.

Quality of work life This has been defined as "the degree to which employees are able to satisfy their important personal needs by working in the organization."

Quality-of-work-life programs Techniques—such as flexible work hours, managment by objectives, employee participation programs, quality circle programs, new work arrangements, job enrichment—as well as a sense of trust and commitment that pervade all levels of the organization.

Quota strategy Employment strategy aimed at mandating the same results as the good faith effort strategy through specific hiring and promotion restrictions.

Ranking method The simplest method of job evaluation that involves ranking each job relative to all other jobs, usually based on overall difficulty.

Rate ranges A series of steps or levels within a pay grade, usually based on years of service.

Ratio analysis A forecasting technique for determining future staff needs by using ratios between sales volume and number of employees needed.

Realistic job previews Interviews aimed at showing job candidates the actual nature of their responsibilities and duties, as opposed to a glowing and unrealistic picture.

Reality shock A period that may occur at the initial career entry when the new employee's high job expectations confront the reality of a boring, unchallenging job.

Recruitment sources Recruitment may involve many media, including newspapers, magazines, directories, radio, TV, posters, direct mail, agencies, college recruiting, job posting, and so forth.

Reliability If a test is reliable, those who take it will tend to score about the same when retested later or when given an equivalent test.

Restricted policy Another test for adverse impact, involving demonstration that an employer's hiring practices exclude a protected group, whether intentionally or not.

Retirement benefits Provide the employee with an income when he or she retires.

Reverse discrimination Claim that due to affirmative action quota systems, white males are discriminated against.

Right-to-work laws Legislation that outlawed labor contracts which made union membership a condition for retaining employment.

Role playing A training technique in which trainees act out the parts of people in a realistic management situation.

Salary survey A survey aimed at determining prevailing wage rates. A good salary survey provides specific wage rates for specific jobs. Formal written questionnaire surveys are the most comprehensive, but telephone surveys and newspaper ads are also sources of information.

Savings plan A plan in which employees contribute for their retirement a fixed percentage of their weekly wage, usually matched by a certain percentage by the employer.

Scanlon Plan An incentive plan developed in 1937 by Joseph Scanlon and designed to encourage cooperation, involvement, and sharing of benefits. Plan involves attitudes, suggestions by workers, and benefits formulas.

Edgar Schein Based on his research at the Massachusetts Institute of Technology, he identified five career anchors: creativity, managerial, security, technical, autonomy/independence.

Scientific management Implies careful, "scientific," study of all the factors that go into work and includes workers' motivation and job satisfaction, as well as optimum production.

Sensitivity training A method for increasing employees' insights into their own behavior by candid discussions in groups led by special trainers.

Serialized interview An interview in which the applicant is interviewed sequentially by several supervisors and each rates the applicant on a standard form.

Severance pay A one-time payment some employers provide when terminating an employee.

Sexual harassment Harassment, on the basis of sex, that has the purpose or effect of substantially interfering with a person's work performance or creating an intimidating, hostile, or offensive work environment.

Sick leave Provides pay for an employee when he or she is out of work because of illness.

Socialized Socialization programs teach new employees the attitudes, standards, values, and behaviors that are expected by the organization.

Social Security Provides three types of benefits: retirement income at the age of 62 and thereafter; survivor's or death benefits payable to the employee's dependents, regardless of age at time of death; and disability benefits payable to disabled employees and their dependents. These benefits are payable only if the employee is insured under the Social Security Act.

Special awards Individual bonuses, such as TVs, paid on the basis of performance ratings.

Special management development techniques Special techniques (like leader match) to develop leadership ability, increase managers' sensitivity to others, and reduce interdepartmental conflicts.

Stabilization substage The period, roughly from age 30 to 40, during which firm occupational goals are set and more explicit career planning is made to determine the sequence for accomplishing these goals.

Staff manager A manager who assists and advises line managers in accomplishing the organization's goals.

Staff (service) function The function of a personnel manager in assisting and advising line management.

Standard hour plan A plan by which a worker is paid a basic hourly rate but is paid an extra percentage of his or her base rate for production exceeding the standard per hour or per day. Similar to piecework payment but based on a percent premium.

Stock option The right to purchase a stated number of shares of a company stock at a stated price during a stated period of time. An executive is given the right to purchase shares in the future at today's price. If the company grows, share prices may rise and the executive may benefit, assuming the economy is stable.

Straight piecework plan Under this pay system, each worker receives a set payment for each piece produced or processed in a factory or shop.

Stress interview An interview in which the applicant is made uncomfortable by a series of often rude questions. This technique helps identify hypersensitive applicants and those with low or high stress tolerance.

Strictness/leniency The problem that occurs when a supervisor has a tendency to rate all subordinates either high or low.

Strike Refusal by employees to work until their demands are met by the employer.

Structured interview A series of job-related questions with "preferred" answers that are asked of all job applicants. Unlike the preprinted patterned interviews, structured interviews can be adapted to ask questions about the specific job in question.

Succession planning A process through which senior-level openings are planned for and eventually filled.

Supplemental pay benefits Benefits for time not worked. They include unemployment insurance, vacation and holiday pay, sick pay, severance pay, and supplemental unemployment benefits.

Supplemental unemployment benefits Provide for a "guaranteed annual income" in certain industries where employers must shut down to change machinery or due to reduced work. These benefits are paid by the company and supplement unemployment benefits.

Survey feedback A method of surveying employees' attitudes and providing feedback to department managers so that problems can be solved by managers and employees.

Sympathy strike Takes place when one union strikes in support of the strike of another.

System I The organizational system, described by Rensis Likert, in which managers mistrust subordinates and thus feel compelled to coerce them to work. (Corresponds to Theory X.)

System IV Likert's alternative system in which managers have confidence in workers and purposely involve them in decision-making processes. (Corresponds to Theory Y.)

Taft-Hartley Act Also known as the Labor Management Relations Act, this law prohibited union unfair labor practices and enumerated the rights of employees as union members. It also enumerated the rights of employers and allowed the president of the United States to temporarily bar national emergency strikes.

Task analysis A detailed study of a job to identify the skills required, so that an appropriate training program may be instituted.

Frederick Taylor Father of the scientific management movement, according to which a fair day's work should depend on a careful, formal process of inspection and observation.

Team building Improving the effectiveness of teams such as corporate officers and division directors through use of consultants, interviews, and team-building meetings.

Technical training The process of teaching new employees the basic skills they need to perform their jobs.

Termination at will Termination of employment by either the employer or employee for any reason.

Testing Testing techniques provide efficient, standardized procedures for screening large numbers of applicants for employment and promotion.

Theory X McGregor's set of assumptions which holds that workers cannot be trusted and must be coerced into doing their jobs.

Theory Y McGregor's alternative theory that people do *not* have an aversion to work and are capable of self-control in the work situation.

Third-party involvement Interventions by a third party used to overcome an impasse, such as mediation, fact-finding, and arbitration.

Title VII of the 1964 Civil Rights Act The section of the act that says you cannot discriminate on the basis of race, color, religion, sex, or national origin with respect to employment.

Transactional analysis A method for helping two people communicate and behave on the job in an adult manner by understanding each other's motives.

Trend analysis Study of a firm's past employment needs over a period of years to predict future needs.

Trial substage The period from about age 25 to 30 during which the person determines whether or not the chosen field is suitable and if it is not, attempts to change it.

Unclear performance standards An appraisal scale that is too open to interpretation; instead, include descriptive phrases that define each trait and what is meant by standards like "good" or "unsatisfactory."

Unemployment insurance Provides weekly benefits if a person is unable to work through some fault other than his or her own.

Unfair labor practices Under the Wagner Act, it is unfair for management to "interfere with, restrain, or coerce employees" in exercising their legally sanctioned right of self-organization.

Unfair labor practice strike A strike aimed at protesting illegal conduct by the employer.

Union security A primary aim of unions, by which unions reflect their desire to establish security for themselves by gaining the right to represent a firm's workers and, where possible, be the exclusive bargaining agent for all employees in the unit. Five types of union security are possible: closed shop, union shop, agency shop, open shop, maintenance of membership arrangement.

Union shop A form of union security in which the company can hire nonunion people but they must join the union after a prescribed period of time and pay dues. (If they do not, they can be fired.)

Union unfair labor practices The Taft-Hartley Act banned unions from restraining or coercing employees from exercising their guaranteed bargaining rights; prohibited unions from causing an employer to discriminate in any way against an employee in order to encourage or discourage membership in a union; prohibited a union from refusing to bargain "in good faith" with the employer about wages, hours, and other employment conditions; and prohibited a union from engaging in "feather-bedding."

United Steelworkers of America* v. *Weber U.S. Supreme Court ruling of a reverse discrimination case in which the Court found for the company.

Unsafe acts Behavior tendencies and undesirable attitudes that cause accidents.

Unsafe conditions The mechanical and physical conditions that cause accidents.

U.S.* v. *Paradise U.S. Supreme Court ruling that the courts can impose racial quotas to address the most serious cases of racial discrimination.

Valence Vroom's term for the value of a goal to a person.

Validity A test's validity is the accuracy with which the test measures what it is supposed to measure.

Vestibule or simulated training Training employees on special off-the-job equipment, as in airplane pilot training, whereby training costs and hazards can be reduced.

Vesting Provision that money placed in a pension fund cannot be forfeited for any reason.

Vietnam Era Veterans' Readjustment Assistance Act of 1974 Requires that employers with government contracts of $10,000 or more take affirmative action to employ and advance disabled veterans and qualified veterans of the Vietnam era.

Vocational Rehabilitation Act of 1973 The act requiring certain federal contractors to take affirmative action for disabled persons.

Voluntary bargaining items Items in collective bargaining over which bargaining is neither illegal nor mandatory—neither party can be compelled against its wishes to negotiate over these items.

Voluntary reduction in pay plan An alternative to layoffs in which all employees agree to reductions in pay to keep everyone working.

Voluntary time off An alternative to layoffs in which some employees agree to take time off to reduce the employer's payroll and avoid the need for a layoff.

Vroom's expectancy theory of motivation The theory that an employee's motivation increases when he or she values a particular outcome highly and when she or he feels a reasonably good chance of achieving the desired goal.

Vroom-Yetton leadership training A development program for management trainees that focuses on decision making with varying degrees of input from subordinates.

Wage curve Shows the relationship between the value of the job and the average wage paid for this job.

Wagner Act This law banned certain types of unfair labor practices and provided for secret ballot elections and majority rule to determine whether or not a firm's employees want to unionize.

Walsh-Healey Public Contract Act A law from 1936 that requires minimum wage and working conditions for employees working on any government contract amounting to more than $10,000.

Wards Cove* v. *Atonio U.S. Supreme Court decision that makes it difficult to prove a case of unlawful discrimination against an employer.

Wildcat strike An unauthorized strike occurring during the term of a contract.

Workers' compensation Provides employer-funded income and medical benefits to work-related accident victims or their dependents, regardless of fault.

Work samples Choosing several tasks necessary to a job and then testing applicants' performance on these actual tests.

Work sampling technique A testing method based on measuring performance on actual, basic job tasks.

Work sharing A temporary reduction in work hours by a group of employees during economic difficulties to prevent layoffs.

Name and Organization Index

Subject Index

Labor needs, planning, 2
Labor relations
    See also Unions
    computer applications in, 586
    consultants on, 587–88
    international differences in, 723
    laws on, 6
    line vs. staff responsibilities in, 14
    specialists on, 12
Labor Relations Consultant Complaint
    Form, 589–90
Lakefront vacations, 451
Landrum-Griffin Act (1959), 583–84, 588
Law(s), 6
    See also Equal employment opportu-
        nity legislation; Legal issues; Su-
        preme Court; *specific laws*
    common, 196–97
    decline of unions and, 573
    immigration, 203–5
    labor, 578–85
    on parental leave, 451–52
    wage garnishment, 345
    workers' compensation, 345
Layoffs, 8, 53–54, 516, 550–53
Lead (element), 671
Leaderless group discussion, 189
Leader match training, 297–98
Leadership
    as managerial function, 2
    managerial grid, 306
    participative, 298
    people-oriented, 297
    task-oriented, 297
    Vroom-Yetton training model, 298–99
Lead teams, 484
Learning
    action, 287–88
    principles of, 262–63
    programmed, 268–69
Leasing, employee, 460–61
Leave
    decision-making, 625–26
    parental, 442, 451–52
    sick, 430
Lectures, training, 265–67
Legal issues
    AIDS at work, 33–34
    in background investigations and ref-
        erence checks, 194
    in compensation, 342–45
    in employment references, 195–97
    in grievances, 621–22
    in pay rates, 371
    of personnel policy, 707
    safety programs, 643
    in selection, 172
    in testing, 180–83
    in training, 255
    in weighted applications, 166–67
Legal trends, 697
Legislation. *See* Law(s)
Leniency in performance appraisals,
    513–14
Letters of reference, 194–95
Lewis v. *Equitable Life Assurance*, 197
Liability for negligent hiring, 172–73
Life insurance, 432
Life-style, 6
Lincoln Incentive System, 406–8
Line function of personnel manager, 10
Line management, 8–10, 12–16, 129,
    307–8, 342, 394
Lingle v. *Norge Division of Magic Chef,
    Inc.*, 621
Literacy training, 271
Literature, union, 600

Loans, management, 455
Local 28 Sheet Metal Workers v. *EEOC*,
    63
Local employment agencies, 369
Local equal employment opportunity
    legislation, 43, 44
Local labor conditions, 127
Local market conditions, 127
Lockouts, 614–15
Logs, job analysis and, 87–88
Longevity tables, sex-based, 447
Longshoremen, 649
Lump-sum merit raises, 404, 405
Lunch-and-learn program, 451
Lunch rooms, temporary employees
    and, 141

M

McDonnell-Douglas Test, 46
Machines, information on, 80
Made in America, 272
Magazine advertisement, 134
Maintenance stage of career cycle, 538
Major medical coverage, 432
Management, 2, 696
    See also Career management; Execu-
        tives; Management development;
        Managers; Personnel manage-
        ment
    audit, 310
    authorization cards and, 588–92
    bargaining preparation, 610
    computer applications in, 295
    cooperation with union, 634
    individual care (ICM), 440
    loans, 455
    multinational, 719
    multiple, 287
    participative, 409
    quality circle and, 478
    resistance to flextime, 474
    scientific, 393
    traits, 295
    trends in, 6, 697
Management assessment centers,
    189–93
Management by objectives (MBO), 487,
    510–11, 515
Management development, 2, 282–319
    computerized, 295–96
    defined, 283
    executive development, 284, 306–11
    motivation and, 335
    nature and purpose of, 283–86
    off-the-job techniques, 288–97
    on-the-job training, 285, 286–88
    in smaller organization, 309–11
    special techniques, 297–306
    training contrasted with, 254
Management Development Seminar
    (University of Chicago), 291
Management games, 191
Management information system, 485
Management skills inventory, 284
Managerial competence as career an-
    chor, 541
Managerial grid, 305–6
Managerial job evaluation, 361
Managerial judgment, 121
Managers
    See also Management development;
        Supervisor(s); *specific types of
        managers*
    administration of financial incen-
        tives, 393–94
    compensation of, 359–61

financial incentives for, 396–400
functions performed by, 2
unemployment insurance cost-cutting
    through and, 428
Mandatory bargaining items, 611
Mandatory retirement, 33
Manpower Report, 127–28
Manual, employee, 629
Manual of Guidelines, 35
Marital status, 153, 154
Market conditions, 127
Marketing consultants, executive, 562
Market-pricing approach to profes-
    sional compensation, 361
Marquez v. *Omaha District Sales Office,
    Ford Division of the Ford Motor
    Company*, 516
Marshall v. *Barlow's, Inc.*, 646–47
Martin v. *Wilks*, 42–43, 63
Masculine style, hiring recommenda-
    tions and, 226
Mass interview, 221–23
Master of Business Administration pro-
    grams, 291–92
Materials safety data sheets (MSDS),
    645
Matrices, access, 125–26
Measurement of work, 393
Mechanical reasoning test, 184
Media, advertising, 131–34, 148–49, 150
Mediation in collective bargaining, 613
Medical benefits, controlling costs of, 8
Medical examination, 53, 201–2
Medical insurance, 432–42
Medicare, 433, 442
Membership arrangement, union, 577
Membership in organizations, discrimi-
    natory questions about, 153
Mental age, 184
Mental health benefits, 441
Mentors, 309
Mergers, 554–55, 697
Meritor Savings Bank, FSB v. *Vinson*, 36
Merit pay, 403–4, 405, 412
Merit raise, 403–4, 405
Methods-improvement training, 8
Midcareer crisis substage of career
    cycle, 537–38
Middle managers, behavior modeling
    for, 294
Military background, discriminatory
    questions about, 153
Miniature job training and evaluation
    approach, 193–94
Minimum wage, 343, 571
Minnesota Clerical Assessment Battery,
    206
Minnesota Multiphasic Personality In-
    ventory, 186
Minnesota Rate of Manipulation Test,
    185, 186
Minority labor force, 5, 695
    See also Equal employment opportu-
        nity
Misconduct, 626
Mission statement, 712
Modeling, behavior, 294–96
Money, motivation and, 341, 393–94
    See also Incentives, financial
Morale, 10
Moral reasons for safety programs, 643
Motivation, 19–22, 233, 234, 322–39
    See also Incentives, financial; Incen-
        tives, nonfinancial
    ability and, 19–21
    behavior modification and reinforce-
        ment, 330–32

Shut down, 613
Sick leave, 430
Silica, 671
Simulated training, 269–71
Simulations, 189–93
Situational questions, 232
Situational (structured) interview, 221, 222, 231–33
Skill banks, 130
SKILLPAC, 271
Skills, 351, 539–40
Skills inventory, 93, 123–24
Small business(es)
  benefits in, 460–61
  financial incentives in, 414–15
  interviews in, 233–35
  job analysis and descriptions in, 102–6
  management development in, 309–11
  pay plans in, 369–71
  recruiting by, 150–51
  testing in, 205–7
  training in, 272–73
Smoking, 141, 674–77
Snap judgments in interviews, 223–24, 228
Socialization, 248–54
Social needs, 324
Social orientation, 538
Social orientation, 538
Social reinforcement, 294
Social relationships, 549
Social Security Act (1935), 345
Social Security benefits, 442–43
Solicitation, union, 600
Special assignments, 263
Special awards, 402–3
Special talents, 540
Split award method, 398
Spreadsheets, 57, 445, 707
Spurlock v. *United Airlines*, 49
SRA Test of Mechanical Aptitude, 184
Stability, emotional, 661
Stabilization substage of career cycle, 537
Staffing, 2, 93, 141
Staff management, 8–16, 129, 342
Staff (service) functions of personnel manager, 10
Standard hour plan, 395
Standards, 163
  hiring, 179
  incentive plan, 411
  OSHA, 644–45
  of performance, 80, 101, 179, 411, 513
  promotion, 179
  setting, 261
Standards for Educational Psychological Testing, 35
Stanford-Binet Test, 184
State equal employment opportunity legislation, 43, 44
State fair employment laws, 629
State job service agencies, 151
Statistical analysis, job specifications based on, 107
Steering committee, quality circle, 476–77
Stock appreciation rights (SARs), 400
Stock options, 399–400
Stock ownership plan, employee (ESOP), 408
Straight piecework plan, 394
Strategic human resource management, 707, 716n11
Strategic planning, 701–4
Strategy, corporate, 700–701

Stress, job, 667–69, 670–71
Stress and the Manager (Albrecht), 669
Stress interview, 223
Strictness in performance appraisals, 513–14
Strike(s), 582, 583, 585, 613–14
Stromberg Dexterity Test, 185, 186
Strong-Campbell Inventory, 186
Strong-Campbell Vocational Interest Test, 659
Structured ("situational") interview, 221, 222, 228, 229, 231–33
Subordinates
  See also Employees
  in appraisal interview, 522–23
  criticizing, 524
  defensive, 523–24
  job enrichment for, 328
  maintaining dignity of, 624
Substance abuse, 663–67
Succession planning, 284, 307
Suits, invasion-of-privacy, 182–83
Superfund Amendments Reauthorization Act (1986), 675
Supervisor(s)
  administration of incentive plans, 393–94
  behavior modeling for, 294
  coaching by, 263, 285, 287
  combatting drug abuse and, 666
  interviews, 84
  introducing manual to, 710–11
  job information collection and, 84
  orientation checklist of, 249, 250
  role in performance appraisal, 497–98, 518, 519
  role in safety, 652–53
  training, 183, 428, 450, 518, 671
  unionization and, 599–601
Supplemental pay benefits, 425–31
  severance pay, 430
  sick leave, 430
  supplemental unemployment benefits, 430–31
  unemployment insurance, 425–29
  vacations and holidays, 429–30
Supply Report, 127
Support, ongoing, 553
Supreme Court
  See also specific decisions rendered
  on business necessity, 48
  equal employment opportunity decisions, 31, 33, 39–43, 44, 49
  labor law decisions, 585
  Title VII interpretations of, 62–63
Surface bargaining, 609
Survey(s)
  attitude, 301–3, 482, 671
  of benefits, 347
  feedback, 301–3
  salary, 347–51, 369
  unemployment insurance cost control, 426–27
  wage, 342
Survivor's benefits, 442
Sympathy strike, 613
System I & IV, 18–19

T

Tactics, dilatory, 609
Taft-Hartley Act (Labor Management Relations Act of 1947), 443, 582–83, 585, 621
Talents, special, 540
Task analysis, 256–58, 272
Task-oriented leaders, 297

Tasks, combining, 328
Task teams, 484
Tax
  capital gains, 399
  deferred, 447
  unemployment, 425
Tax Reduction Act (1975), 422n62
Tax Reform Act (1986), 344, 399–400, 444–46, 447
Team building, 303–6
Teamwork, 704
Technical/functional career anchor, 541
Technical societies, 138–39
Technical training. *See* Training
Technicians, 696
Technological trends, 5–6, 633, 696
Telecommuting, 475–76
Telephone reference, 195
Teletraining, 268
Television advertisement, 134
Temporary employees, recruitment of and benefits for, 141
Temporary help agencies, 139, 140–41
Temp-to-perm policy, 141
Tenure, job, 154
Termination, 261
  COBRA rights and, 442
  discharge, 53, 629–30, 664
  interview, 631–32
  layoffs vs., 550–51
  outplacement counseling, 551–52
  severance pay, 430
  unemployment benefits after, 425–29
  at will, 628
Testing, 173–87
  computer applications in, 188, 206
  conditions for, 176, 180
  defined, 173
  discriminatory, 52
  for drugs, 200
  ethical and legal issues in, 180–83
  guidelines for, 179–80
  intelligence, 179–80
  motivation and, 335
  objective, 191
  personality, 185–86, 661
  physical examination, 201–2
  polygraph, 53
  for promotion, 173
  reality, 544
  relevance and fairness issues, 193, 210–11
  reliability of, 175–79
  security of, 182
  small business application, 205–7
  thematic apperception, 174
  types of, 183–87
  use of, 173–74
  validity of, 49, 174–75, 177–78, 181, 202, 203
  visual, 661
T-group laboratory, 302–3
Theft, employee, 154–59, 190–91
Thematic Apperception Test, 174, 186
Theory X, 18
Theory Y, 18, 715
Thin-layer chromatography, 202
Third-party involvement (collective bargaining), 613
"30 and out," 444
Three-day workweeks, 474–75
Time basis of payment, 341–42, 412–13
Time off, voluntary, 551
Time sheets, 140
Title VII of 1964 Civil Rights Act, 31–32, 41, 42, 44, 47, 50, 365
  compensation and, 53